Victoria Crosses on the Western Front
Third Ypres 1917

Victoria Crosses on the Western Front
Third Ypres 1917

31st July 1917 to 6th November 1917

Paul Oldfield

Pen & Sword
MILITARY

First published in Great Britain in 2017 by
Pen & Sword Military
an imprint of
Pen & Sword Books Ltd
47 Church Street
Barnsley
South Yorkshire
S70 2AS

ISBN 978 1 47382 708 0

The right of Paul Oldfield to be identified as the Author of this Work
has been asserted by him in accordance with the Copyright, Designs and
Patents Act 1988.

A CIP catalogue record for this book is available from the British Library

Typeset in Ehrhardt by
Mac Style Ltd, Bridlington, East Yorkshire
Printed and bound in the UK by CPI Group (UK) Ltd, Croydon,
CRO 4YY

Pen & Sword Books Limited incorporates the imprints of Atlas,
Archaeology, Aviation, Discovery, Family History, Fiction, History,
Maritime, Military, Military Classics, Politics, Select, Transport,
True Crime, Air World, Frontline Publishing, Leo Cooper,
Remember When, Seaforth Publishing, The Praetorian Press, Wharncliffe
Local History, Wharncliffe Transport, Wharncliffe True Crime
and White Owl.

For a complete list of Pen & Sword titles please contact
PEN & SWORD BOOKS LIMITED
47 Church Street, Barnsley, South Yorkshire, S70 2AS, England
E-mail: enquiries@pen-and-sword.co.uk
Website: www.pen-and-sword.co.uk

Contents

Chapter 3: Battle of Langemarck (Master Map 6)

Chapter 4: Local Operations September 1917 (Master Maps 4 and 6)

Chapter 5: Battle of the Menin Road (Master Maps 4 and 5)

Chapter 6: Battle of Polygon Wood (Master Map 5)   142

Chapter 7: Battle of Broodseinde (Master Maps 4, 5 and 6)   154

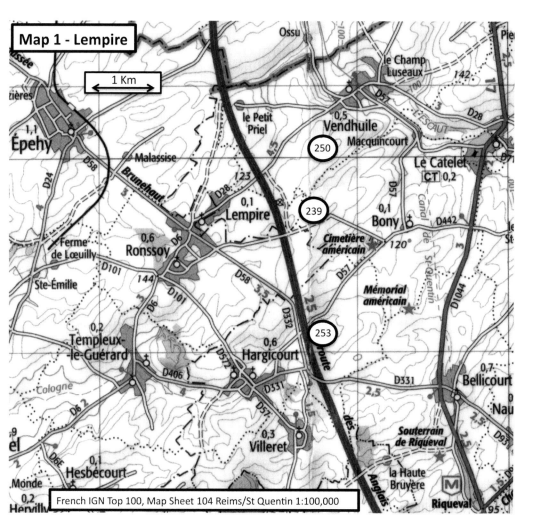

Map 1 - Lempire

1 Km

French IGN Top 100, Map Sheet 104 Reims/St Quentin 1:100,000

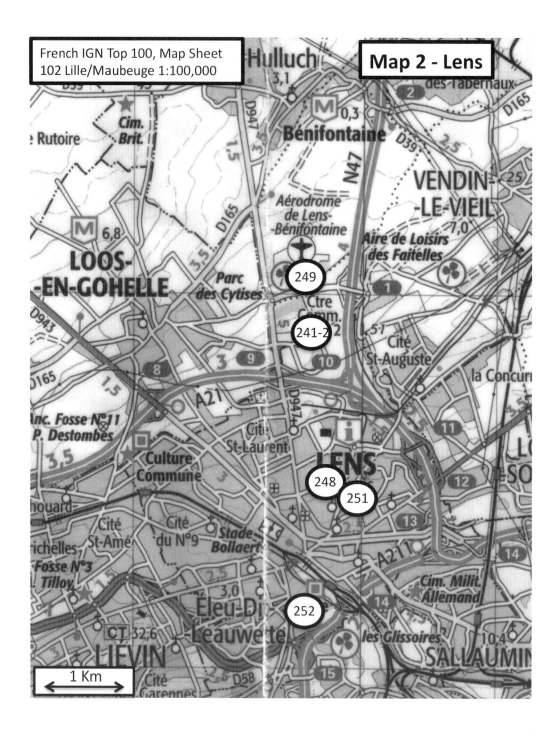

French IGN Top 100, Map Sheet
102 Lille/Maubeuge 1:100,000

Map 2 - Lens

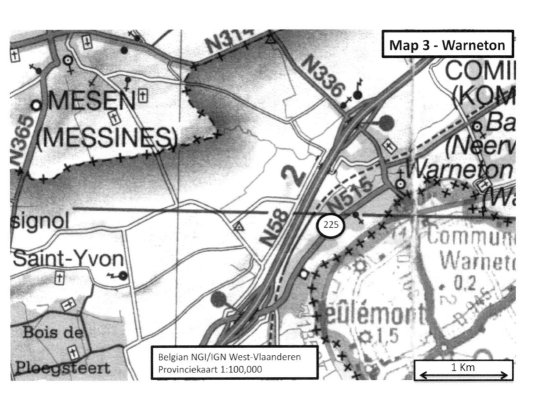

Map 3 - Warneton

Belgian NGI/IGN West-Vlaanderen
Provinciekaart 1:100,000

1 Km

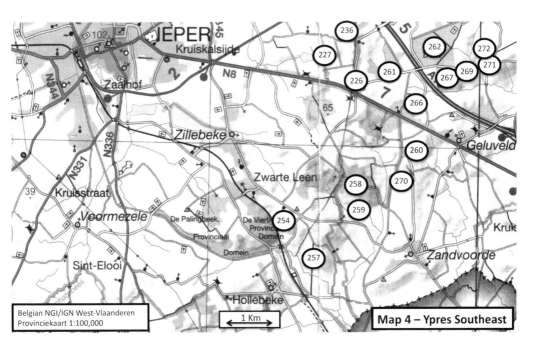

Belgian NGI/IGN West-Vlaanderen
Provinciekaart 1:100,000

1 Km

Map 4 – Ypres Southeast

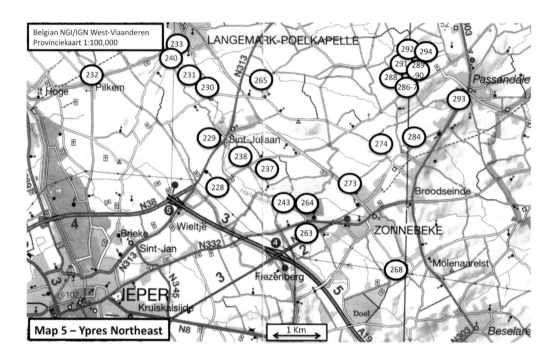

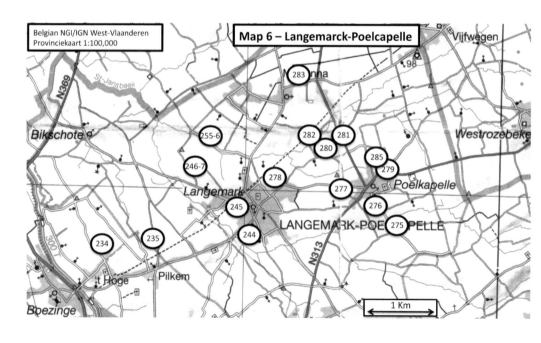

Abbreviations

AA	Anti-Aircraft
AASC	Australian Army Service Corps
ACT	Australian Capital Territory
ADC	Aide-de-Camp
ADS	Advanced Dressing Station
AFC	Australian Flying Corps
AIF	Australian Imperial Force
ASC	Army Service Corps
ATS	Auxiliary Territorial Service
AWOL	Absent without leave
Att'd	Attached
BA	Batchelor of Arts
BCh or ChB	Bachelor of Surgery
BEF	British Expeditionary Force
BMA	British Medical Association
Brig-Gen	Brigadier-General
BS	Bachelor of Surgery
BSM	Battery Sergeant Major
BSc	Batchelor of Science
Bty	Battery (artillery unit of 4–8 guns)
CAMC	Canadian Army Medical Corps
Capt	Captain
CB	Companion of the Order of the Bath
CB	Confined to Barracks
CBE	Commander of the Order of the British Empire
CCF	Combined Cadet Force
CCGS	Canadian Coast Guard Service
CCS	Casualty Clearing Station
CEF	Canadian Expeditionary Force
CFA	Canadian Field Artillery
CFC	Canadian Forestry Corps
CGA	Canadian Garrison Artillery
Ch.B	Bachelor of Surgery
Ch.M	Master of Surgery

CIE	Companion of the Order of the Indian Empire
C-in-C	Commander-in-Chief
CM	Master of Surgery
CMG	Companion of the Order of St Michael & St George
CO	Commanding Officer
Col	Colonel
Cpl	Corporal
CQMS	Company Quartermaster Sergeant
CRA	Commander Royal Artillery
CRE	Commander Royal Engineers
CSgt	Colour Sergeant
CSEF	Canadian Siberian Expeditionary Force
CSI	Companion of the Order of the Star of India
CSM	Company Sergeant Major
CStJ	Commander of the Most Venerable Order of the Hospital of Saint John of Jerusalem
Cty	Cemetery
CVO	Commander of the Royal Victorian Order
CWGC	Commonwealth War Graves Commission
DAAG	Deputy Assistant Adjutant General
DBE	Dame Commander of the Order of the British Empire
DCL	Doctor of Civil Law
DCM	Distinguished Conduct Medal
DJStJ	Dame of Justice of the Most Venerable Order of the Hospital of Saint John of Jerusalem
DL	Deputy Lieutenant
DLI	Durham Light Infantry
DSC	Distinguished Service Cross
DSO	Distinguished Service Order
Dvr	Driver
ED	Efficiency Decoration
EEC	European Economic Community
FM	Field Marshal
FRCS	Fellow of the Royal College of Surgeons
FRS	Fellow of the Royal Society
GC	George Cross
GCB	Knight Grand Cross of the Order of the Bath
GCMG	Knight Grand Cross of the Order of St Michael & St George
Gen	General
GOC	General Officer Commanding
GOC-in-C	General Officer Commanding in Chief
GSO1, 2 or 3	General Staff Officer Grade 1 (Lt Col), 2 (Maj) or 3 (Capt)

HE	High Explosive
HMAT	Her/His Majesty's Australian Transport/Troopship
HMHS	Her/His Majesty's Hospital Ship
HMP	Her/His Majesty's Prison
HMS	Her/His Majesty's Ship
HMT	Her/His Majesty's Transport/Troopship/Hired Military Transport
HMNZT	Her/His Majesty's New Zealand Transport/Troopship
HRH	His/Her Royal Highness
JP	Justice of the Peace
KBE	Knight Commander of the Most Excellent Order of the British
KC	King's Counsel
KCB	Knight Commander of the Order of the Bath
KCIE	Knight Commander of the Order of the Indian Empire
KCMG	Knight Commander of St Michael and St George
KCVO	Knight Commander of the Royal Victorian Order
KGStJ	Knight of Grace of the Most Venerable Order of the Hospital of Saint John of Jerusalem
Kia	Killed in action
KJStJ	Knight of Justice of the Most Venerable Order of the Hospital of Saint John of Jerusalem
Kms	Kilometres
KOSB	King's Own Scottish Borderers
KOYLI	King's Own Yorkshire Light Infantry
KRRC	King's Royal Rifle Corps
LCpl	Lance Corporal
LG	London Gazette
LLD	Legum Doctor (Doctor of Law)
LOL	Loyal Orange Lodge
LRCP&S	Licentiate, Royal College of Physicians & Surgeons
Lt	Lieutenant
Lt Col	Lieutenant Colonel
Lt Gen	Lieutenant General
LTh	Licentiate in Theology
Maj	Major
Maj Gen	Major General
MA	Master of Arts
MB	Bachelor of Medicine
MB BCh	Bachelor of Medicine, Bachelor of Surgery
MB BChir	Bachelor of Medicine & Bachelor of Surgery
MBE	Member of the Order of the British Empire
MC	Military Cross
MCC	Marylebone Cricket Club

MD	Medical Doctor
MDS	Main Dressing Station
MGC	Machine Gun Corps
MGRA	Major General Royal Artillery
MID	Mentioned in Despatches
M.Inst.CE	Member of the institute of Civil Engineers
MM	Military Medal
MO	Medical Officer
MP	Member of Parliament
MRCP	Member of the Royal College of Physicians
MRCS	Member of the Royal College of Surgeons
MSM	Meritorious Service Medal
MT	Motor Transport
MVO	Member of the Royal Victorian Order
NSW	New South Wales
NZEF	New Zealand Expeditionary Force
NZHS	New Zealand Hospital Ship
OBE	Officer of the Order of the British Empire
OC	Officer Commanding
OP	Observation Post
OStJ	Officer of the Most Venerable Order of the Hospital of Saint John of Jerusalem
OTC	Officers' Training Corps
P&O	Pacific & Orient
PC	Police Constable
PM	Prime Minister
PoW	Prisoner of War
PPCLI	Princess Patricia's Canadian Light Infantry
Pte	Private
QC	Queen's Counsel
RA	Royal Artillery
RAC	Royal Agricultural College
RAC	Royal Armoured Corps
RAF	Royal Air Force
RAFVR	Royal Air Force Volunteer Reserve
RAAF	Royal Auxiliary Air Force/ Royal Australian Air Force
RAC	Royal Armoured Corps
RAMC	Royal Army Medical Corps
RAN	Royal Australian Navy
RASC	Royal Army Service Corps
RCMP	Royal Canadian Mounted Police
RCN	Royal Canadian Navy
RE	Royal Engineers

RFA	Royal Field Artillery
RFC	Royal Flying Corps
RGA	Royal Garrison Artillery
RHA	Royal Horse Artillery
RMC	Royal Military College
RMO	Regimental Medical Officer
RMS	Royal Mail Ship/Steamer
RN	Royal Navy
RNR	Royal Naval Reserve
RNVR	Royal Naval Volunteer Reserve
RSA	Returned Services Association
RSL	Returned and Services League
RSM	Regimental Sergeant Major
RTO	Railway Transport Officer
SAI	South African Infantry
Sgt	Sergeant
SMLE	Short Magazine Lee Enfield
SNCO	Senior non-commissioned officers
SOE	Special Operations Executive
Spr	Sapper
SS	Steam Ship
TA	Territorial Army
TD	Territorial Decoration
TF	Territorial Force
TMB	Trench Mortar Battery
Tr	Trench
UN	United Nations
UNICEF	United Nations Children's Fund
UOTC	University Officers' Training Corps
USAAF	United States Army Air Force
USS	United States Ship
VAD	Voluntary Aid Detachment
VD	Volunteer Decoration
VDC	Volunteer Defence Corps
VC	Victoria Cross
VIP	Very Important Person
WA	Western Australia
WAAF	Women's Auxiliary Air Force
WAAC	Women's Auxiliary Army Corps
WG	Welsh Guards
WO1 or 2	Warrant Officer Class 1 or 2
YMCA	Young Men's Christian Association

Introduction

The fifth book in this series covers the Third Battle of Ypres and a few minor actions elsewhere on the Western Front between late July and early November 1917. Seventy VC recipients are included. In common with previous books in the series, it is written for the battlefield visitor as well as the armchair reader. Each account provides background information to explain the broad strategic and tactical situation, before focusing on the VC action in detail. Each is supported by a map to allow a visitor to stand on, or close to, the spot and at least one photograph of the site. Detailed biographies help to understand the man behind the Cross.

As far as possible chapters and sections within them follow the titles of battles, actions and affairs as decided by the post-war Battle Nomenclature Committee. VCs are numbered chronologically 225, 226, 227 etc from 31st July to 6th November 1917. As far as possible they are described in the same order; but when a number of actions were fought simultaneously the VCs are covered out of sequence on a geographical basis in accordance with the official battle nomenclature.

Refer to the master maps to find the general area for each VC. If visiting the battlefields it is advisable to purchase maps from the respective French and Belgian 'Institut Géographique National'. The French IGN Top 100 and Belgian IGN Provinciekaart at 1:100,000 scale are ideal for motoring, but 1:50,000, 1:25,000 or 1:20,000 scale maps are necessary for more detailed work, e.g. French IGN Serie Bleue and Belgian IGN Topografische Kaart. They are obtainable from the respective IGN or through reputable map suppliers on-line.

Ranks are as used on the day. Grave references have been shortened, e.g. 'Plot II, Row A, Grave 10' will appear as 'II A 10'. There are some abbreviations, many in common usage, but if unsure refer to the list provided.

I endeavour to include memorials to each VC in their biographies. However, two groups have been omitted because they apply to them all and to include them in each biography would be unnecessarily repetitive. First, every VC is commemorated in the VC Diary and on memorial panels at the Union Jack Club, Sandell Street, Waterloo, London. Second, commemorative paving stones are being laid in every VC's birthplace in the British Isles on, or close to, the 100th anniversary of their VC action. In many cases the location of the paving stones and the dates of their dedication ceremonies are unknown at the time of going to print.

Thanks are due to too many people and organisations to mention here. They are acknowledged in 'Sources' and any omissions are my fault and not intentional. However, I would like to single out fellow members of the 'Victoria Cross Database Users Group' without whom I could not complete these books – Doug and Richard Arman, Vic Tambling and Alan Jordan. Vic Tambling died during the final stages of writing and will be greatly missed not only for his tireless and meticulous research but also for his companionship and wonderful humour.

Paul Oldfield
Wiltshire
May 2017

Chapter One

Battle of Pilkem Ridge

31st July 1917

225 Cpl Leslie Andrew, 2nd Wellington (2nd New Zealand Brigade, New Zealand Division), La Basse Ville, Belgium

226 Capt Harold Ackroyd, RAMC att'd 6th Royal Berkshire (53rd Brigade, 18th Division), South of Westhoek, Belgium

227 Capt Thomas Colyer-Fergusson, 2nd Northamptonshire (24th Brigade, 8th Division), Bellewaarde, Belgium

228 Capt Noel Chavasse, RAMC att'd 1/10th King's (166th Brigade, 55th Division), East of Wieltje, Belgium

229 2Lt Denis Hewitt, 2nd att'd 14th Hampshire (116th Brigade, 39th Division), St Julien, Belgium

230 Pte George McIntosh, 1/6th Gordon Highlanders (152nd Brigade, 51st Division), North of St Julien, Belgium

231 Sgt Alexander Edwards, 1/6th Seaforth Highlanders (152nd Brigade, 51st Division), North of St Julien, Belgium

232 Cpl James Davies, 13th Royal Welsh Fusiliers (113th Brigade, 38th Division), Pilkem, Belgium

233 Sgt Ivor Rees, 11th South Wales Borderers (115th Brigade, 38th Division), Langemarck, Belgium

234 Sgt Robert Bye, 1st Welsh Guards (3rd Guards Brigade, Guards Division), Northwest of Pilkem, Belgium

235 Pte Thomas Whitham, 1st Coldstream Guards (2nd Guards Brigade, Guards Division), Pilkem, Belgium

236 Brig Gen Clifford Coffin, Royal Engineers commanding 25th Brigade (8th Division), Westhoek, Belgium

237 LSgt Tom Mayson, 1/4th King's Own (Royal Lancaster) (164th Brigade, 55th Division), East of Wieltje, Belgium

238 Lt Col Bertram Best-Dunkley, 2/5th Lancashire Fusiliers (164th Brigade, 55th Division), East of Wieltje, Belgium

Despite the problems dogging the French in the summer of 1917, Haig was determined to press on with an offensive in Flanders. Using overly optimistic intelligence reports, he argued that clearing the Belgian coast could precipitate a German collapse, and urged the government to send all available reinforcements. He feared that the French could collapse themselves in 1918 unless

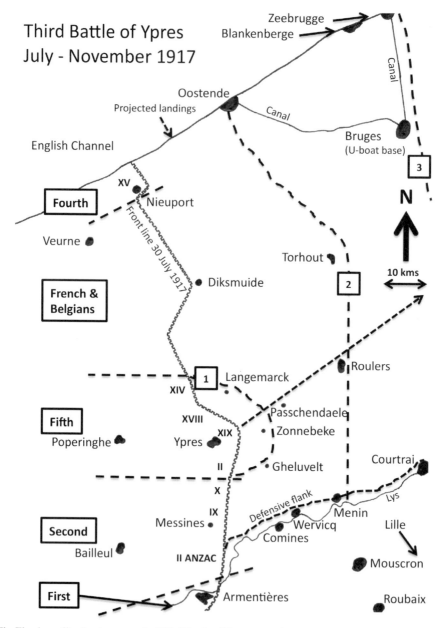

**Third Battle of Ypres
July - November 1917**

Zeebrugge
Blankenberge

Canal

Oostende
Projected landings
Canal

Bruges
(U-boat base)

3

English Channel

N

XV

Fourth

Nieuport

Front line 30 July 1917

Veurne

Torhout

2

10 kms

French &
Belgians

Diksmuide

Roulers

1 Langemarck

XIV

Fifth

XVIII

Passchendaele

Poperinghe

XIX

Zonnebeke

Ypres

Courtrai

II

Gheluvelt

X

Lys

IX

Defensive flank

Menin

Messines

Wervicq

Lille

Second

Comines

Bailleul

II ANZAC

Mouscron

First

Armentières

Roubaix

The Flanders offensive, known as the Third Battle of Ypres, opened on 31st July 1917. Its ultimate objective was to clear the Belgian coast to deny the Germans use of the U-boat base at Bruges. Haig also hoped to precipitate a German collapse in Belgium. The map shows the front just before the offensive on 30th July and the formations engaged on 31st July. A number of objectives were set. The first (1) was to be reached by the end on the first day. The second (2) was to cut the strategically vital railway running behind the German lines and the third (3) was to include the capture of the U-boat base at Bruges. Subsequent objectives (not shown) were to clear the rest of the Belgian coast up to the border with the Netherlands and to penetrate eastwards almost to Ghent. The general thrust of the intended advance is shown by the dashed arrow pointing northeast, using the River Lys as a defensive right flank. The arrow on the coast marks the intended amphibious landing (Operation Hush) that never occurred. The strategy was overly optimistic and by the end of 1917 little more than the first day's objective had been seized.

the war was concluded in 1917. The War Cabinet was sceptical about further operations in Flanders, despite the success at Messines in June, even though the clearance of the Belgian coast was a high priority. Approval to proceed was finally given on 21st July, five days after the preparatory bombardment commenced. However, the War Cabinet wanted results commensurate with the effort and losses incurred, or it would consider transferring support to the Italian Front.

On the extreme left, Fourth Army took over the coastal sector with a single corps (XV). To its south were the French and the Belgians. Gough's Fifth Army HQ handed over to Third Army and moved north to command the main effort of the Flanders offensive. It had four corps (from south to north – II, XIX, XVIII and XIV) for the main attack, each consisting of four divisions, of which two were to make the initial assault (three in II Corps). On the right, Plumer's Second Army had three Corps (II ANZAC, IX and X). In outline, the plan was for Second Army to hold the enemy reserves and protect Fifth Army's right flank while it advanced northeast towards Bruges. Haig hoped that progress would allow Fourth Army to launch a coastal attack to coincide with the high tides of 7th/8th August.

The intricate Flanders drainage system had been destroyed by years of shelling, but veterans testified that it was not the wettest sector on the Western Front. Much was done to improve drainage and it was expected that the worst areas would be passed over quickly. The British were supported by a huge number of guns; 752 'heavies' and 1,422 field pieces, which between 15th July and 2nd August expended almost 4,300,000 shells. In addition to the infantry there were three tank brigades each of seventy-two tanks and the RFC had 406 aircraft and eighteen balloon sections.

On the first day, four successive objectives were to be seized, the Blue, Black, Green and Red Lines, involving an average advance of 4,600m. The offensive was due to open on 25th July, but Gough wanted a delay to allow the enemy batteries to be mastered and the French requested a further delay to compensate for artillery preparations lost to bad weather. Haig realised there would be insufficient time to coincide with the high tides, but agreed reluctantly; the attack was set for 31st July. Meanwhile the best of the summer weather slipped away.

The German positions were almost everywhere on the reverse slope and the success of the bombardment was reliant on aerial observation. The battle for air superiority began on 11th July. During the preparatory period there were many raids and gas shelling and discharges were common. The Germans moved their batteries to avoid counter-battery fire and also disrupted the British preparations with gas barrages. From 28th July the British employed the full force of the artillery while moving forward to their attack positions.

Although the enemy overlooked the whole of the salient, the assault troops were largely unmolested. By 3 a.m. on 31st July all were in position and waiting for zero hour at sunrise (3.50 a.m.). Just before the attack, gas shells were fired into known enemy battery positions to prevent interference during the initial assault. The

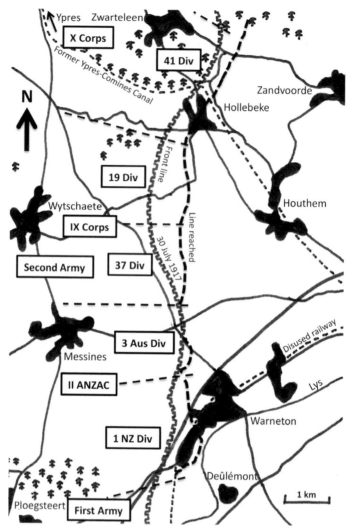

The Second Army area on 31st July 1917 showing the modest gains made in support of the main Fifth Army attack to the north.

morning was misty with low cloud curtailing air operations and hampering artillery observers. The troops were initially guided by thermite flares and oil bombs fired by trench mortars, which created a great deal of smoke and unnerved the enemy. Within an hour the Blue Line had fallen except on the Gheluvelt plateau. At 5.05 a.m. fresh troops continued the advance and ran into the numerous strongpoints and pillboxes with which the Germans had fortified the area.

On the right of Second Army in II ANZAC Corps, 3rd Australian Division on the left took part in the general advance, while the New Zealand Division on the right demonstrated towards Warneton in conjunction with a converging attack in the south. The intention was to divert German attention and resources away from the main offensive to the north by appearing to threaten Lille.

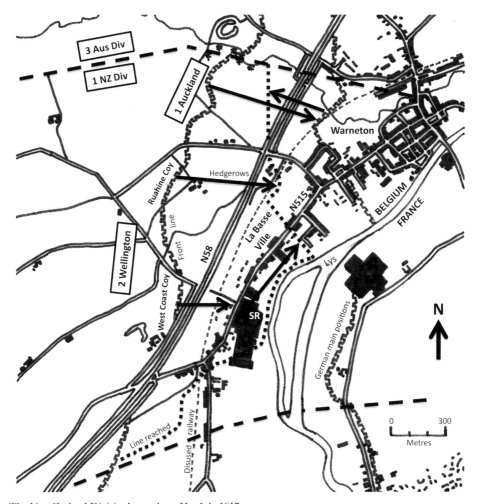

The following labels appear on the map:

3 Aus Div

1 NZ Div

1 Auckland

Warneton

Ruahine Coy

Hedgerows

2 Wellington

Front line

N515

La Basse Ville

BELGIUM

FRANCE

N58

West Coast Coy

Lys

SR

German main positions

N

Line reached

Disused railway

0   300
Metres

The New Zealand Division's attack on 31st July 1917.

The New Zealand Division had three tasks that were to be completed a few days prior to the offensive. First, it was to make a feint by establishing posts commanding the River Lys on the right, not for occupation, but to give the impression they were to cover the construction of bridges. Second it was to capture La Basse Ville and third to advance the line northeast of the village among the hedgerows. After dark on 26th July, dummy trenches were dug and tapes laid to the river, simulating preparations for a night attack. Some forward posts were also established to cover the right flank of 1st New Zealand Brigade after the capture of La Basse Ville.

The Hawkes Bay Company was selected for the attack on La Basse Ville by 2nd Wellington. It left its trenches at 1.30 a.m. on 27th July and under cover of the barrage, which fell at 2 a.m., stormed the village. The right captured the ruined sugar refinery at the southern edge of the village, the centre captured the village and the left cleared the hedgerows. Posts were established around the captured village, which were held by an officer and forty-four men. To avoid hostile shelling in

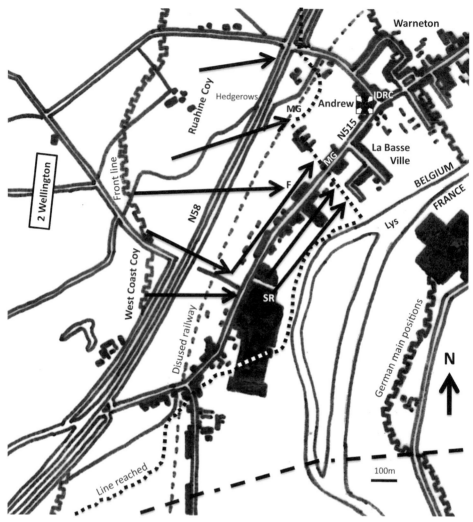

La Basse Ville is much more built-up than in 1917, but the road layout remains largely the same. The Ruahine Company on the left set off from positions forward of the front line. The precise start points for the various elements of the West Coast Company are not known. The site of the sugar refinery (SR) is now covered by an enormous factory. The other factory (F) site is also marked, as are the two significant machine-gun (MG) positions. The one on the former railway pinned down the right of Ruahine Company. The one in the estaminet on the N515, was captured by Leslie Andrew before he and Private Ritchie continued along the road to In den Rooster Cabaret (IDRC).

Travel along the N515 from Ploegsteert eastwards towards Warneton. Go under the N58 and after travelling 1,450m along Faubourg de Lille park on the right side of the road. The machine-gun position silenced by Andrew and Ritchie was on the other side of the road. Continue 300m until there is a turning on the left (Gravier du Rooster/Roostergraveel); the road sign has been painted over in white and is difficult to read until close up. This is the site of In den Rooster Cabaret. Another seventy metres along the N515 towards Warneton on the right is a memorial to Andrew. Turn into Gravier du Rooster and park to see the memorial and consider the action fought here. Walk northwest along Gravier du Rooster for 300m to the former railway line, now a foot/cycle path. Turn left (south) along it for 230m. This is the position of the other machine-gun that held up Ruahine Company.

daylight, the rest of the Company was withdrawn to the original front line. However, at 4.45 a.m. a German box barrage fell around La Basse Ville, cutting off the posts; and by 6 a.m. the village was back in German hands. The Company suffered fifty-five casualties amongst the 139 men who went into the attack.

It was clear that the Germans would resist strongly any renewed attempt to advance in the Lys valley. Accordingly the Second Army commander, General Plumer, decided that the next attack would not be in isolation and would coincide with the main offensive. In addition to capturing La Basse Ville and clearing the hedge system to the north, the enemy positions between the front line and the railway on the left were to be raided. The attack area was held on the right by 1st Wellington and on the left by 2nd Auckland, but it was decided to attack through them with the original units (2nd Wellington and 1st Auckland) as their preparations were well advanced and they knew the ground.

The raid to the north was allotted to 1st Auckland, while 2nd Wellington would be the right battalion of the whole offensive. Its West Coast Company (Captain H McKinnon – MC Bar for this action), assisted by 10 and 11 Platoons of the Taranaki Company and nine Hawkes Bay Company men as guides, a total force of 224 men, were to capture La Basse Ville. Two platoons of the Ruahine Company (Captain M Urquhart) were responsible for the hedgerows (ninety-four men).

Along the western edge of the village a series of fortified shell-holes put up stubborn resistance. However, the leading Wellington platoon seized the sugar refinery and two platoons worked up the village street, one on each side, while the fourth platoon made for the northern factory. The southern part of the village and the two factories fell in half an hour, the houses on the main street being cleared by bombs and bayonets. Dugouts were found full of dead and a few snipers beyond the village were killed or forced to flee along the riverbank towards Warneton, where

Looking north along the railway to show the relationship between the two machine-gun positions. There was much less vegetation in 1917.

many fell victim to rifle and Lewis gun fire. Within an hour the whole area had been cleared and consolidation was in progress.

Corporal Leslie Andrew was detailed to deal with the estaminet on the Warneton road and his team pushed forward close behind the barrage. A machine gun post on the railway line to the north was holding up Ruahine Company and they diverted towards it. Several Germans were killed, allowing Ruahine Company to continue its advance. Andrew's team dashed after the barrage and continued towards its objective at the estaminet, from where a machine gun fired continuously. The attackers moved round one side and crawled through a patch of thistles to close the distance. A shower of bombs was followed by a charge. Some of the garrison fled towards the river, while others were killed and the machine gun was captured. Andrew and Private LR Ritchie continued about 300m along the road towards Warneton behind the standing barrage. On the edge of the village was an inn, In den Rooster Cabaret. Some German survivors sought refuge in the cellar and there was a machine gun post in an open trench beside it. They rushed the post and bombed the cellars and adjoining dugouts, before returning to their own lines.

In the centre, the Ruahine Company's right platoon was to establish posts on the railway line, but it came under heavy fire from two machine guns in the embankment. Several men fell and the rest were forced into cover in shell-holes. No further progress was possible until Corporal Andrew approached. While Andrew's men dealt with one gun, the pinned down platoon captured the other. The platoon on the left had the task of clearing the hedgerows. Two of its three parties were wiped out. The third party, under Sergeant SC Foot (DCM for this action), reached its objective, but was forced back by fire from the railway. Foot sent Private A Stumbles

The estaminet machine-gun position was on the other side of the road here. In the distance the cluster of buildings and vehicles is at In den Rooster Cabaret.

In den Rooster Cabaret and Gravier du Rooster leading to the railway line.

round the north flank while he worked round the other. Both were marksmen and in a few seconds eight Germans had been shot dead, resulting in another twenty-four surrendering. The rest of the hedge system was cleared without difficulty and advanced posts were established and consolidated with the help of the support company.

At 5 a.m., an enemy counterattack between the river and the road (N515) was caught in the SOS barrage and heavy small arms fire. During the day, La Basse Ville was subjected to a severe bombardment and at 3.15 p.m. another counterattack by fifty Germans on the right was held off by a post of an officer and ten men, who inflicted thirty casualties on the enemy party. At 7.30 p.m. the Germans were seen massing near In den Rooster. They attacked through the SOS barrage, but were once again forced back with heavy losses. That night, 1st Wellington relieved 2nd Wellington. 2nd Wellington's casualties in this operation were thirty-seven killed or died of wounds and ninety-seven wounded out of 328 who took part. The Battalion captured five machine guns, two mortars, and took forty-two prisoners. In addition to Andrew's VC, the Battalion received twenty other gallantry awards.

To the north 1st Auckland encountered well constructed German shell-hole positions, but the right reached its objective after a brief encounter. The left was hit by intense machine gun and mortar fire and was unable to make much progress. However, the raid achieved its purpose, with eighty Germans being killed and twelve taken prisoner. Under cover of the raid, a series of posts 450m in front of the front line were consolidated by 2nd Auckland in line with the new 2nd Wellington posts on the right. 1st Auckland's losses were only two killed and twenty wounded.

On the left of II ANZAC Corps, 3rd Australian Division captured a line of posts along the Warneton – Gapaard road. IX Corps advanced about 500m and X Corps, astride the Comines Canal, took Hollebeke and advanced 500–900m east of Battle Wood.

On Fifth Army's right, II Corps attacked with three divisions (from right to left – 24th, 30th and 8th) against the strongly defended Gheluvelt plateau. Here the

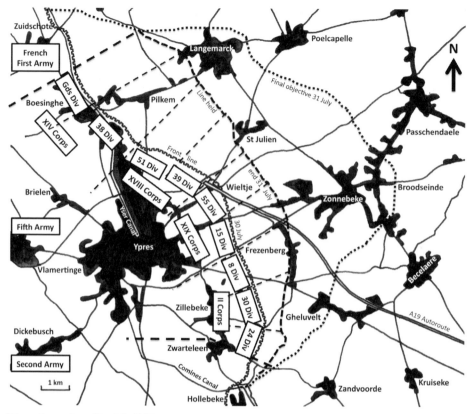

The main attack on 31st July 1917.

outpost sector comprised three wooded features – Shrewsbury Forest, Sanctuary Wood and Chateau Wood. 24th Division's advance on the right was held up by pillboxes around Shrewsbury Forest and enfilade fire from Dumbarton Wood and fell short of its objective.

30th Division in the centre had the most difficult task and was reinforced by 53rd Brigade (18th Division). The advance through the Blue Line up to the Black Line was entrusted to 21st Brigade on the right and 90th Brigade on the left. Thereafter 89th Brigade would pass through on the right and 53rd Brigade on the left to the Green Line. If conditions allowed, 53rd Brigade was to press on to the Red Line.

On the right, 21st Brigade was caught by enemy artillery while struggling through Sanctuary Wood and lost touch with the barrage. Stirling Castle Ridge was not secured until 6 a.m. and attempts to press on were beaten back with heavy losses. On the left, 90th Brigade's left mistakenly attacked Chateau Wood in 8th Division's area instead of Glencorse Wood and fell short of the Black Line.

On their way forward to their start positions, the leading battalions of 53rd Brigade (6th Royal Berkshire and 8th Suffolk) suffered casualties. 6th Royal Berkshire had the most, losing nineteen men while crossing the Canal. At 7.15 a.m., 53rd Brigade moved forward from the Ritz Street area behind 90th Brigade. 8th Suffolk was on the right and 6th Royal Berkshire on the left, with a company of 10th Essex as

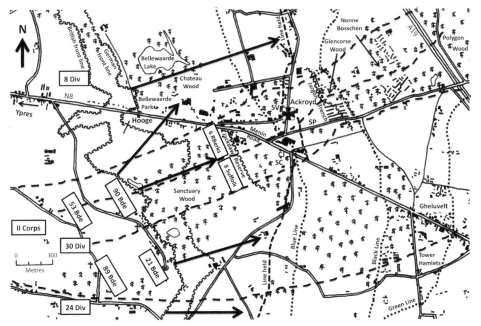

Drive east along the Menin Road from Ypres. Pass Hooge Crater Cemetery on the right (there is a café in the Museum opposite) and Bellewaerde Park on the left. The road bends to the right and 400m beyond is the 18th Division memorial on the right. This is Clapham Junction (CJ), one of the places where Harold Ackroyd was particularly active in attending to the wounded. Turn back and after 200m turn right into Oude Kortrijksstraat towards Polygon Wood. Turn left into Frezenbergstraat after just under 200m and park on the roadside on the right. In front the road continues through Surbiton Villas (SV), where Ackroyd was also very active. On the right is the western edge of Glencorse Wood. Harold was killed somewhere in the fields in front of the Wood. Two other abbreviations are used on the map: SC = Stirling Castle and SP = Strongpoint.

moppers-up. Following were 8th Norfolk, to consolidate and garrison strongpoints, and 11th Royal Fusiliers to form a defensive right flank.

The leading battalions suffered casualties in Sanctuary Wood from enemy artillery and machine gun fire. They were to form up behind the Black Line in Jargon Trench on the western side of Glencorse Wood for the advance to the Green Line. As they passed the eastern edge of Sanctuary Wood, it was reported that Glencorse Wood had been taken; but it was apparent from the hostile fire from the Menin Road and Stirling Castle that all was not well.

They pressed on to Jackdaw Reserve, forward of which were very few men of 90th Brigade (30th Division) and it was clear that the Black Line had not been taken. Heavy fire was being received from Surbiton Villas and Clapham Junction. 8th Suffolk advanced rapidly up to the Menin Road, which was secured by 9 a.m. Beyond there was stiff resistance and progress was only possible by short rushes. A strongpoint where Jargon Drive crossed the road towards Polygon Wood caused the main problem. Fifteen rounds of Stokes mortar and sixty from a captured German anti-tank gun were fired into the strongpoint. A footing was gained, during which a large number of defenders were killed and a machine gun and twenty prisoners were

Looking along the Menin Road towards Ypres at Clapham Junction with the 18th Division memorial on the left.

taken, but the rest of the line was unable to keep up. The Germans counterattacked along Jargon Trench and forced them back. The left company was held up by a machine gun until it was destroyed. The Ridge was then gained, but further advance resulted in heavy casualties and the company was forced back. A support company went forward and the line advanced 200m east of Surbiton Villas, but heavy fire forced it back to the Surbiton Villas Ridge.

6th Royal Berkshire made its way up the slope towards the Menin Road and reached Jackdaw Reserve, but the supporting tanks bogged down south of the Road. The advance continued at 8.50 a.m. and was met by heavy machine gun fire from around Clapham Junction and Glencorse Wood, confirming that the Black Line had not been taken by 30th Division. The mortar and machine gun sections attached to 6th Royal Berkshire were well behind, but some support was obtained from the mortar attached to 8th Suffolk. Slow progress was made, covered by Lewis guns, and a line was reached running north from Surbiton Villas. British troops could be seen on the left around Westhoek. A determined effort was made to continue on this flank and two platoons of D Company were pushed into the line north of the road running east from Chateau Wood to gain touch with 8th Division. By 9.50 a.m. Jargon Switch, the crossroads northwest of Glencorse Wood and Surbiton Villas

Glencorse Wood on the left, with Surbiton Villas just right of centre and one of the car parks for Bellewaerde Park on the far right. Harold tended the wounded all over this area.

had been taken, but with heavy losses. The Battalion was scheduled to depart from Jargon Trench at 10.10 a.m., but it was still well short and the barrage had already moved on. Orders were issued that when the next phase of the barrage resumed the Battalion was to attempt to take Jargon Trench. The barrage fell behind the Germans who were holding up 6th Royal Berkshire and little was achieved. A small party of bombers managed to get into a strongpoint at the southwest corner of Glencorse Wood before being driven back.

The advance was halted 750m short of the Green Line and consolidation began along the line of the road running north from Surbiton Villas, with Battalion HQ in the Menin Road tunnel. On the left, a company of 8th Norfolk came forward and took the remnants of D Company, 6th Royal Berkshire (twenty-one men), under command. It also gained touch with 2nd Lincolnshire (8th Division).

At midday three German aircraft flew overhead and directed artillery fire onto the broken down tanks and the new line, but a threatened counterattack did not materialise. 6th Royal Berkshire's front from right to left was held by A, B and D Companies, with a company each of 10th Essex and 8th Norfolk on the left. About 4 p.m. a party of 17th Manchester (90th Brigade) completed the line connecting with 8th Division. C Company, 6th Royal Berkshire was in support about 100m behind. 53rd Brigade was relieved overnight by 89th Brigade. 6th Royal Berkshire had suffered 254 casualties (forty-four killed and died of wounds, 182 wounded and twenty-eight missing).

Throughout the operations, 6th Royal Berkshire's MO, **Captain Harold Ackroyd**, calmly went about his duties, tending the wounded under heavy machine gun and shellfire. Rather than waiting in his aid station for casualties to be brought to him, he went out looking for the wounded. He was particularly active around Clapham Junction and towards Hooge, where the casualties lay thickest, and he personally saved many lives. On one occasion he carried a wounded officer into cover under heavy fire. He also went forward of Jargon Switch to bring in a wounded man under constant machine gun and sniper fire. No fewer than twenty-three separate recommendations for the VC were made. On 11th August, while tending a wounded man in a shell-hole near Jargon Trench, he got up to fetch the stretcher-bearers and was shot dead by a sniper.

Surbiton Villas

Bellewaerde Park

From Oude Kortrijksstraat looking north towards Westhoek, with Glencorse Wood on the right. Harold Ackroyd was killed somewhere in this field.

8th Division's advance on the left of II Corps was led by 23rd (left) and 24th Brigades (right). Two battalions in each brigade were to seize the Blue Line, each supported by four tanks. The other two battalions were then to pass through and take the Black Line. Finally 25th Brigade, supported by twelve tanks, was to take the Green Line.

In 24th Brigade, 1st Worcestershire was on the right and 2nd Northamptonshire was on the left for the attack on the Blue Line. They were followed by 2nd East

Wide angled view from the PPCLI Memorial in the foreground looking south towards Bellewaerde Park behind the trees in the centre. Colyer-Fergusson emerged from the trees on the right and stormed Jacob Trench at the top of the rise left of centre where there is a definite crop boundary.

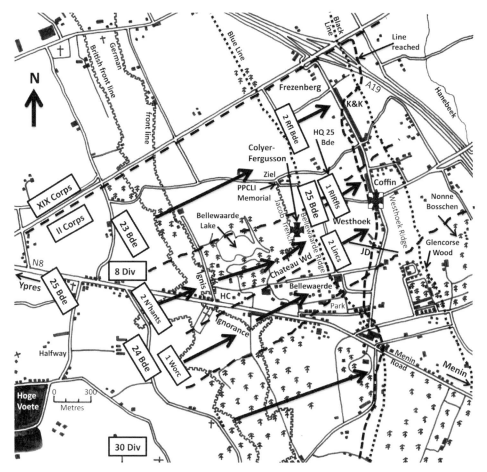

Drive east along the Menin Road (N8) from Ypres. Pass Hooge Crater (HC) Cemetery on the right and Bellewaerde Park on the left. The road bends to the right and after 200m turn left into Oude Kortrijkstraat. Turn left into Frezenbergstraat after just under 200m. Drive north crossing the line of Jabber Drive (JD). After just under 1,100m turn left into Grote Molenstraat. This road twists and turns through fields and farms for just over a kilometre to the junction with Oude Kortrijkstraat. On the right is Ziel House, HQ 23rd Brigade on 31st July 1917. On the left is the PPCLI memorial. Park here and look south. Colyer-Fergusson rushed Jacob Trench in the area of the knoll about 400m from the PPCLI memorial.

Return along Oude Kortrijkstraat to Westhoek crossroads. Go over and continue for 500m. Turn right into Nonnebossenstraat and park. Walk on for 200m to the bridge over the A19. Look back for a good view of Westhoek Ridge. Clifford Coffin moved all over this area in full view of the enemy.

Lancashire and 1st Sherwood Foresters respectively. 2nd Northamptonshire's advance was led by A and D Companies in two waves from Kingsway and Kingsway Support. **Captain Thomas Colyer-Fergusson**, commanding B Company, moved his men 100m forward prior to zero hour to avoid the enemy counter-barrage he knew would fall when the attack commenced. The leading companies took sixty prisoners in Ignis and Ignorance Trenches close to the Hooge craters. The support companies took up the advance, following the barrage closely. The left of the Battalion skirted the southern and eastern edges of Bellewaerde Lake prior to assaulting Bellewaarde Ridge. The right negotiated the chaos of fallen trees, wire obstacles and a muddy ravine in Chateau Wood.

Emerging from the Wood, Colyer-Fergusson realised the Battalion was in danger of losing the barrage. He detected a well-wired and protected machine gun post in Jacob Trench, just short of the Blue Line, that had escaped the barrage. If left it would have halted the advance so, without waiting for his Company, he collected six men, including his orderly, 7756 Private Basil Ellis, and 7929 Sergeant (Acting CQMS) WG Boulding, and rushed Jacob Trench, taking it at about 5.30 a.m. Soon after a counterattack came in from the left front, which Colyer-Fergusson's party met with rifle fire, killing twenty to thirty of the enemy and the remainder surrendered.

The rest of B Company was arriving when a machine gun opened fire nearby. Taking Ellis with him, Colyer-Fergusson attacked and captured the gun, which he turned on another group of Germans, killing about thirty-five of them. The rest were forced into a neighbouring unit's area, where they surrendered. B and C Companies were ordered to press on for 100–200m to establish posts on the Blue Line. While organising this a sniper or stray round hit Colyer-Fergusson in the head and he died soon afterwards. Boulding and Ellis received the DCM for this action. Ellis was killed on 24th March 1918 and is buried in Fouquescourt British Cemetery (III A 2).

The support battalions reached the Black Line at about 6 a.m., where they came under heavy fire from across the Hanebeek and from Glencorse Wood, which had not been taken by 30th Division. As a result, 24th Brigade and the right of 23rd Brigade had to pull back 450m behind Westhoek ridge.

XIX Corps in the right centre advanced to plan. On the right, 15th Division reached the Black Line with only a few delays. On the left, 55th Division attacked

A closer view of the Jacob Trench area, with the rise captured by Colyer-Fergusson on the left, beyond which can be seen the top of one of the rides in Bellewaerde Park. Bellewaerde Lake is behind the trees on the right.

with 165th Brigade on the right and 166th Brigade on the left. It gained the Black Line by 6.05 a.m., although at Spree and Pond Farms the enemy held out for another three hours.

1/10th King's (166th Brigade) was in support during the assault on the Blue Line by 1/5th Loyal North Lancashire. 1/10th King's met little resistance until reaching the Steenbeek, where it encountered uncut wire and was hit by small arms fire from Capricorn Trench. A tank forced a way through and the advance resumed, although the tank was destroyed by three direct hits. By 7.45 a.m. the Battalion was on its objective but continued to suffer casualties from snipers while it consolidated its gains. **Captain Noel Chavasse**, the MO, who had been awarded the VC for his actions at Guillemont in August 1916, set up his Regimental Aid Post in a dugout at Setques Farm. Battalion HQ moved away from the area due to the intensity of the shelling, but Chavasse remained. He spent the day assisting the wounded and waving to men to direct them to the Aid Post. While helping to carry a badly wounded man he was hit by a shell splinter in the right side of his head and his skull may have been fractured. Having walked back to Wieltje to have the wound dressed, he refused further aid and walked back to his Aid Post, where he continued to deal with the wounded.

The two northern Corps advanced to form the defensive flank on the left in conjunction with the French. XVIII Corps, in the left centre, established a line along the Steenbeek on a frontage of 2,700m from St Julien northwards almost to the Pilkem-Langemarck road.

39th Division's advance was led by 117th Brigade on the left and 116th Brigade on the right. They were to take the Blue, Black and Green Lines, whereupon 118th Brigade was to pass through and take the Green Dotted Line. When the Blue Line fell in 116th Brigade's area, 14th Royal Hampshire passed through 11th Royal Sussex and headed for the Black Line, with 13th Royal Sussex on the right and 17th Sherwood Foresters (117th Brigade) on the left. Numerous pillboxes and fortified

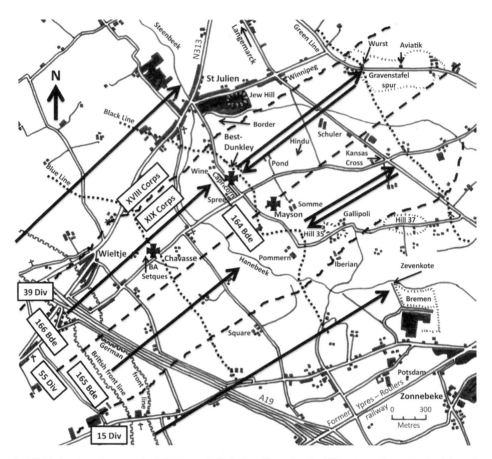

In Wieltje head northeast on the N313 towards St Julien. Go under the A19 and turn immediately right and follow the road round to the left. Continue for 700m and park at the Birrell Anthony (BA) memorial on the right. Look northeast along the road. Setques Farm, where Noel Chavasse established his aid post, was just beyond the line of trees on the left. Nothing remains of it except the pond within the tree line.

From the site of Setques Farm continue for one kilometre to Spree Farm on the left. There is space to park in front of it. Capricorn Trench and Capricorn Support ran either side of the Farm in a roughly northwest-southeast direction. The farm was HQ to 2/5th Lancashire Fusiliers and it and Capricorn Support were retaken by an ad hoc force led by Bertram Best-Dunkley following the German counterattacks on the afternoon of 31st July 1917. Immediately after Spree Farm is a left turn at Fortuinhoek, which leads into St Julien, where there is a café and a few shops.

From Spree Farm continue east to Fortuinhoek and turn immediately right into Hazeweidestraat. Continue along it for 900m to the top of Hill 35. On the way you pass Pommern on the right. There is space to park for a short while in the entrance track leading south to Iberian Farm. Look north of the road over Somme and Pond Farms, the site of Hindu Cott and the Wieltje road. Tom Mayson was active all over this area. Also look west towards Wieltje and the site of Setques Farm. The whole area between it and Hill 35 is open and exposed to fire. Noel Chavasse moved freely all over this area to bring in the wounded. If the view northwards is obscured, on the opposite side of the road from the Iberian Farm turning is a track leading north. Follow it until you can see more clearly.

farms were encountered but, with the assistance of a tank, Hampshire, Mousetrap and Juliet Farms were taken and the objective was secured.

On the Black Line **2nd Lieutenant Denis Hewitt** reorganised his company while awaiting the resumption of the barrage. He was hit by a shell fragment, which set light to his clothing and some signal cartridges in his haversack. He calmly pulled out the cartridges and put out the fire, despite being wounded and badly burned. He then led his men forward in the face of heavy machine gun fire. Having played a major part in the capture of the Black Dotted Line, an intermediate objective between the Black Line and the Steenbeek, he was killed by a sniper during consolidation. At 7.10 a.m. groups of soldiers pressed on down the slope, overcoming opposition at Alberta to reach the Green Dotted Line on the far side of the Steenbeek. However, later in the day they were forced back to the Black Dotted Line. On the left, 117th

Drive northeast from Wieltje on the N313 into St Julien. In the village turn left into Peperstraat. Continue for 450m to some large factory buildings on the right. Park on the grass verge and look left (southwest) across the road. The Black Dotted Line, which Denis Hewitt played such a prominent role in securing, ran across these fields about 100–150m from the road, gradually converged with it at the crossroads in St Julien where you turned off the N313. Juliet Farm stands on a slight rise 700m to the southwest. The Black Line, where he was hit by a shell fragment, was about 100m in front of the Farm.

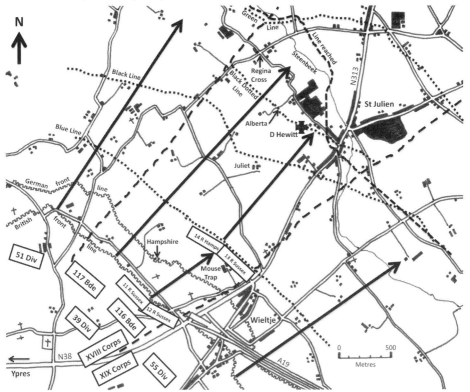

Looking northeast from the Birrell Anthony memorial. Setques Farm was just beyond the line of trees on the left.

Brigade took three pillboxes at Regina Cross, while two tanks dealt with the Alberta strongpoint. By 8 a.m. the whole of 39th Division was across the Steenbeek and on its objectives.

51st Division's supporting barrage was, … *that fine ye could have lighted your pipe at it!* The two assault brigades (152nd right and 153rd left) were to go right through to the Green Line. Eight tanks were allocated to help mop up on the Blue and Black

From Peperstraat, looking southwest towards Juliet Farm on the skyline in the centre. Alberta was on the right behind the current farm buildings and in line with the three poplar trees.

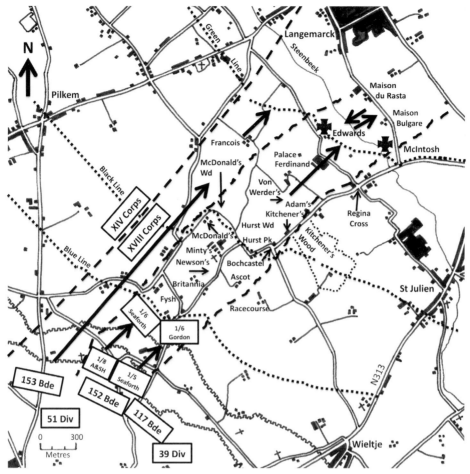

Drive northeast from Wieltje on the N313 into St Julien. In the village turn left into Peperstraat. Continue for 1,250m to the crossroads (Regina Cross) and turn right into Bruine-Broekstraat. After 250m pull in on the grass verge on the left. The Steenbeek is fifty metres in front. From the bridge look north. George McIntosh crossed the stream about here. Continue driving along the road, cross the bridge and turn immediately left into Cayennestraat. Drive for 500m, passing Maison Bulgare (closer to the road than in 1917) and stop just before Maison du Rasta (slightly north of its position in 1917). Look southwest over the Steenbeek towards Ferdinand Farm, site of part of Alexander Edwards' VC action.

Lines and also to cross the Steenbeek to cover the consolidation of the bridgeheads. 152nd Brigade's attack on the Blue Line was led by 1/5th Seaforth Highlanders on the right and 1/8th Argyll and Sutherland Highlanders on the left. The Black Line was then to be taken by the support battalions, 1/6th Gordon Highlanders on the right and 1/6th Seaforth Highlanders on the left.

Assembly went ahead smoothly despite some crowding in the forward trenches. Thirty-seven platoons squeezed into 650m of the front line, with another twenty-two platoons behind in Hardy's Trench (long disused and overgrown with grass) and four carrying platoons, one per battalion, in X Trench to the rear. The bombardment was effective against the enemy trenches and wire, but less so against buildings and pillboxes. Strong concrete emplacements were encountered at Fysh, Britannia, McDonald, Ferdinand and Minty Farms and also at Newson and Von Werder House. The barrage was also effective and each line was assaulted close behind it, although some of the farm complexes resisted strongly.

As the leading battalions attacked the Blue Line, 1/6th Gordons lay in no man's land to avoid the enemy barrage. The Battalion resumed the advance from the Blue Line at 5.13 a.m., led by D and A Companies and two platoons of B Company. Strong opposition was encountered from machine gun posts, but by 5.30 a.m. Ascot Cottage, Newson House, Minty Farm and other strongpoints had been taken and the Black Line secured. The exception was on the left, where a D Company platoon was pushed out to gain touch with 1/6th Seaforth Highlanders. This platoon captured a machine gun in the Black Line and neutralised other machine guns in MacDonald's Wood until they were destroyed by a tank. Two platoons of A Company passed through the Black Line as soon as it was captured and seized objectives in Hurst Wood, Bochcastel and Kitchener's House. Half a platoon of B Company pushed beyond Kitcheners' Wood and reached Adam's House. One and a half platoons reached Hurst Wood and dealt with two machine guns on its northern edge; thirty-two prisoners were taken there. A section pushed on to Von Werder's House, but the rest lost direction. Another section pushed out to the left and reached the neighbourhood of Francois Farm where two machine guns were dealt with and fifty-one prisoners taken. The loss of direction was discovered and they proceeded to Von Werder House to consolidate there.

While all this activity was going on, C Company left Hardy's Trench and filed up Boar Lane to assemble in the front line. At 6.30 a.m. it advanced to a point between the Blue and Black Lines. No touch was made here with 16th Rifle Brigade (117th Brigade, 39th Division) on the right, so that flank was pushed out to Racecourse Farm. Machine guns between that point and Kitcheners' Wood were dealt with and the advance continued to 450m in front of the Black Line, where the Company reorganised in preparation to move on the Green Line. At 7.30 a.m. the advance continued and the Green Line was reached at 7.50 a.m., having encountered little resistance. A German airplane flew over and disappeared over its own lines. The company commander wisely ordered the front line to advance 100m and the support

Langemarck church   Maison du Rasta   Maison Bulgare

The Steenbeek from the bridge on Bruine-Broekstraat. From right to left in the distance are Maison Bulgare, Maison du Rasta and the church in Langemarck. George McIntosh crossed the stream in this vicinity.

line to fall back 100m, as a few minutes later a barrage fell harmlessly on the old positions. By 8.30 a.m. the Battalion was establishing itself in these two lines about 250m southwest of the Steenbeek.

While C Company was consolidating the Green Line in front of the Steenbeek, two machine guns opened fire from a concrete emplacement on the far bank. **Private George McIntosh** headed for a bridge over the stream. His pack and kilt were hit, but, undeterred, he waded across the stream on his own, armed only with a revolver and a grenade. Working his way around the flank using shell-holes for cover, he closed with the emplacement and twenty Germans surrendered immediately. He threw the grenade into the emplacement anyway and rushed in. Two of the crew were killed, a third was wounded and the remainder fled. He then waved 16th Rifle Brigade forward to secure the position and returned in triumph with two light machine guns.

On the left of 152nd Brigade, 1/6th Seaforths took the Black Line without delay, except at MacDonald's Farm and Wood. They were secured eventually, assisted by flanking fire from 1/6th Gordons and Tank C50. C Company was to capture the Green Line but became embroiled in the fighting around MacDonald's Farm and the company commander was knocked out. **Sergeant Alexander Edwards** led his platoon on and located a machine gun. Armed with two revolvers, he made his way behind it, then charged the position and dealt with the crew of ten. On

Maison du Rasta

Maison Bulgare

Pillbox

Looking across the Steenbeek, which runs across the centre of the picture, although not visible, from the southwest. This is where Alexander Edwards led his men to seize the Green Line. On the far side of the stream are Maison du Rasta on the left and Maison Bulgare on the right. Between them is a surviving pillbox from the battle.

his way back a sniper shot him in the right arm but, rather than make good his escape, Edwards stalked the offending German and shot him. Despite the wound he insisted on carrying on the advance. Progress towards the Green Line was made against steadily increasing resistance. As the objective came into sight machine guns opened fire from across the Steenbeek. Edwards realised that the success of the operation depended upon capturing this objective. Disregarding his wound, he spurred on his men until the Green Line was taken. Covered by the Company Lewis guns, he crawled forward with his platoon to within 100m of the stream and, protected by a tank, began to dig a shallow trench. It had been planned to cross the Steenbeek to establish an outpost at Maison du Rasta, but it was impossible to pass the fire swept banks. Edwards bided his time, demonstrating great skill in consolidating this position and was very daring in conducting a reconnaissance to see how the advance could be continued.

The reverse view of the previous picture. Maison Bulgare is on the left and Maison du Rasta is on the right with the pillbox between them and the Steenbeek beyond. Ferdinand Farm is on the far side of the Steenbeek beyond the pillbox surrounded by poplar trees.

Drive north out of Ypres along Pilkemseweg and at the crossroads in Pilkem turn left towards Boesinghe. After 175m turn left into Bikschotestraat and park immediately on the left. Corner House, stormed by James Davies, is on the opposite side of the Boesinghe road.

From the crossroads in Pilkem head northeast towards Langemarck, through Iron Cross crossroads (ICC) passing the magnificent Welsh memorial and Cement House Cemetery on the right. Cross the Steenbeek and park at the 20th Light Division memorial on the left. Au Bon Gite, captured by Ivor Rees, was on the other side (south) of the road, a few metres closer to the Steenbeek.

A little later a squadron of 1st King Edward's Horse (XVIII Corps) deployed in front of Palace Farm. It had moved forward in response to a call from 6th Black Watch for reinforcements. As it reached a line about 130m west of the Steenbeek, it came under heavy fire and a number of men and horses were lost. The squadron dismounted around Ferdinand Farm, where at 12.30 p.m. it was ordered by the CO 1/6th Seaforth Highlanders to take up a defensive position covering posts that he had established east of the Steenbeek.

XIV Corps had extra ground to cover and the assault divisions (38th and Guards) had to use their reserve brigades for the final advance to the Green Dotted Line. On 27th July the Germans withdrew slightly in this area. Most of A Company, 15th Royal Welsh Fusiliers, was lost in follow up reconnaissance patrols and the line had to be adjusted to comply with the Guards Division advance on the left.

On the right of 38th Division, 114th Brigade sustained heavy losses before capturing the pillboxes at Iron Cross road junction. On the left, 113th Brigade was led by 13th Royal Welsh Fusiliers on the right and 16th Royal Welsh Fusiliers on the left, with 15th Royal Welsh Fusiliers in support and 14th Royal Welsh Fusiliers on carrying duties. Each leading battalion allocated two companies to take the Blue Line and the other two were to pass through to carry the Black Line. Finally, 15th Royal Welsh Fusiliers was to pass through to take the Green Line. 115th Brigade would then take up the lead to seize the Green Dotted Line beyond the Steenbeek.

There was a little opposition to the advance on the Blue Line, particularly on the left from snipers and machine guns. On the right the Blue Line fell easily to A and B Companies, 13th Royal Welsh Fusiliers, by 4.55 a.m., but as C and D Companies took up the lead towards the Black Line resistance increased. The Battalion was involved in a sharp fight for Pilkem, where it came upon pillboxes for the first time (there were 280 of them on 38th Division's front alone). In front

The crossroads in Pilkem looking west towards Boesinghe. The road on the left, Pilkemseweg, leads to Ypres. Corner House is the first building on the right side of the Boesinghe road after the 70 kph speed limit sign.

of Pilkem village, Corner House had been converted into a strongpoint, supported by a nearby pillbox. Several efforts to outflank the pillbox failed with numerous casualties, and the assault line disappeared into the cover of shell-holes. **Corporal James Davies** in C Company rushed forward and, although he was hit, reached the pillbox, where he bayoneted one man and the second wisely surrendered. The Battalion then continued as far as Corner House. Davies took charge of some bombers and overcame the strongpoint. He was wounded again in this action, but a little later crawled forward to deal with a sniper. His gallantry ensured the fall of the Black Line by 6 a.m. Records show that he died of his wounds on 31st July, but his platoon commander in a letter stated that he died at Canada Farm (where he is buried) at 6.30 p.m. next day.

On the left, 16th Royal Welsh Fusiliers had some trouble with snipers because the Guards Division on its left was held up for half an hour. 15th Royal Welsh Fusiliers set off from the Blue Line at 5 a.m. and met with considerable opposition at Battery Copse. Few officers remained uninjured and the Battalion was left behind by the barrage. Fire was received from enemy occupied houses along Brierley Road and the smoke barrage confused the men as they tried to get forward. The CO was wounded and ordered the survivors to consolidate on Iron Cross Ridge, some distance short of the intended objective on the Green Line. By the time 113th Brigade was relieved, on 4th August, it had suffered 808 casualties.

Meanwhile 115th Brigade had moved up for the attack on the Steenbeek, which was made more difficult by 113th Brigade halting short of the Green Line. The

The site of Corner House.

Looking across the Steenbeek towards Langemarck. Au Bon Gite was in the centre amongst the buildings on the right hand side of the road.

attack was launched from Iron Cross Ridge by 11th South Wales Borderers on the right and 17th Royal Welsh Fusiliers on the left. 11th South Wales Borderers approached the Ridge at 8.50 a.m. Resistance was fierce and a number of pillboxes and converted farms had to be dealt with, but the attack was successful. By 12.30 p.m. a line had been established west of the Steenbeek and 400 prisoners had been taken by 115th Brigade.

At about 12.30 p.m. parties from A, C and D Companies 11th South Wales Borderers crossed the stream and established posts on the far bank. Losses had been heavy and each leading battalion in the Brigade had to be reinforced from the support battalions; a company of 16th Welsh was allocated to 17th Royal Welsh Fusiliers and a company of 10th South Wales Borderers to 11th South Wales Borderers. Light trench mortar sections that went forward with the assault battalions dealt with machine guns firing from wooden huts by the railway.

The 20th (Light) Division memorial is on the left of the road. Au Bon Gite was in the vicinity of the hedge on the other side.

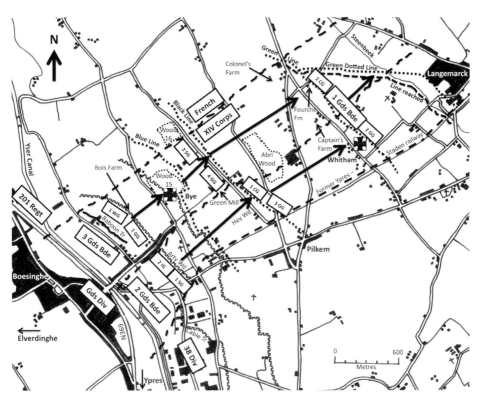

Drive north out of Ypres along Pilkemseweg. At the crossroads in Pilkem turn right towards Langemarck. After 950m turn left into Groenestraat and continue 550m to where the road crosses the line of the railway (now a cycle path). Park here and walk 100m northeast along the cycle path towards Langemarck to the Thomas Whitham memorial. The machine-gun holding up 3rd Grenadier Guards was on the higher ground to your front.

Return to the crossroads in Pilkem, continue westwards for just over a kilometre and turn right signed for Artillery Wood Cemetery. Pass the Cemetery on the left and continue through a right and left dogleg. Park at the farm 200m further on. This was the southern edge of Wood 15 in 1917. Robert Bye's first action was behind the farm buildings. Continue 1,350m and turn right and right again after 300m. Follow this road southeast until you see a large concrete bunker in a field on the right. Just before it is the entrance to a grassy lane with just enough space to pull over for a few minutes. This is the northeast corner of Wood 16, the site of Robert Bye's second action.

During 115th Brigade's advance, **Sergeant Ivor Rees** of 11th South Wales Borderers led his platoon in outflanking a machine gun. He rushed the first post from twenty metres away, shooting one of the gun team, bayoneting another and capturing the machine gun. Without pausing he bombed the large concrete shelter at Au Bon Gite (a former roadside inn) that was holding up progress, killing five of the enemy and capturing thirty prisoners and a machine gun. 17th Royal Welsh Fusiliers was also delayed by machine gun fire from its left flank and lost the barrage, but it reached the Steenbeek at 12.30 a.m., although only 200 men remained. As a result of Rees' gallantry both battalions were able to establish bridgeheads over the stream.

At 3.10 p.m. counterattacks began. Telephone communications had been maintained to two forward artillery observer posts and these proved invaluable in breaking up the attacks. Although the German counterattacks were not universally effective, one did reach Au Bon Gite. 11th South Wales Borderers was forced back and at 4.30 p.m. Au Bon Gite had to be given up.

North of the railway the Guards Division had avoided an opposed crossing of the Canal by following up the German withdrawal on 27th July. 1st Guards Brigade pushed forward patrols and by next day had advanced the line to the southern end of Artillery Wood and Bois Farm, in contact with 38th Division on the right in Cable Trench and with the French on the left. The shrapnel barrage and machine gun support in this area were perfect and the troops advanced fifty metres behind. 2nd and 3rd Guards Brigades led on the right and left respectively, followed by 1st Guards Brigade, which was to make the final push over the Steenbeek.

2nd Guards Brigade advanced from Baboon Trench at zero (4.28 a.m. in this area), led by 1st Scots Guards on the right and 2nd Irish Guards on the left. 1st Scots Guards was held up by pillboxes in Artillery Wood. The flanks crept around the opposition, but began to lose the barrage. However, 2nd Guards Brigade was able to take the Blue Line shortly after 4.30 a.m. At 5.20 a.m. the third and fourth waves passed through and met considerable opposition from machine guns in concrete positions in Hey Wood. Despite suffering some casualties, the Black Line had fallen by 6 a.m. and a number of prisoners were taken, as well as twelve machine guns and a trench mortar.

The support battalions of 2nd Guards Brigade took up the advance to the Green Line; 3rd Grenadier Guards on the right and 1st Coldstream Guards on the left. By the time these battalions crossed the Canal, soon after 5.30 a.m., most of the bridges had been destroyed by German artillery fire and the troops had to improvise crossings with whatever material was to hand. Having passed through the Black Line, 3rd Grenadier Guards on the right encountered considerable opposition from machine guns in concrete emplacements along the railway and a support company had to come forward to reinforce the leading waves.

Nos 3 and 4 Companies, 1st Coldstream Guards, were held up by fire from emplacements on the north side of the Ypres-Staden railway embankment and the support companies had to be brought up. Meanwhile 3rd Guards Brigade had been held up by pillboxes in Abri Wood and 1st Coldstream Guards extended its front to the left to assist in clearing the position. On the right 3rd Grenadier Guards was held up by the enfilade fire of a machine gun in front of 1st Coldstream Guards. Using his own initiative, **Private Thomas Whitham** in the leading 1st Coldstream Guards wave worked his way from shell-hole to shell-hole behind the enemy machine gun post to capture the gun, an officer and two other ranks.

Thomas Whitham's memorial on the railway line: looking up the slope to where he captured the machine gun that was holding up 3rd Grenadier Guards.

From the junction of Groenestraat with the former railway looking north. The former railway line is the track on the right leading to Langemarck in the distance. Thomas Whitham's VC action was in the field in front of the house on the far left.

The Green Line was reached near Captain's Farm, in contact with the flanking brigades. Many prisoners and a 4.2″ gun in a concrete emplacement were taken. During the afternoon, 1st Scots Guards was withdrawn into reserve and later that evening 2nd Irish Guards was also withdrawn. There were no strong counterattacks in this area although enemy shelling, mainly on the Green Line, went on into the following morning. The other two battalions were relieved by 1st Guards Brigade the following night.

3rd Guards Brigade was led by 1st Grenadier Guards on the right and 1st Welsh Guards on the left. They were to capture the Blue and Black Lines, whereupon 4th Grenadier Guards and 2nd Scots Guards, right and left respectively, would pass through to seize the Green Line. As two platoons of No.2 Company, 1st Welsh Guards, approached Wood 15 they were halted by heavy fire from a large pillbox in the midst of the tangled stumps and broken branches. The barrage moved on leaving them without support. Advancing in the second wave,

The site of Wood 15. The pillbox attacked by Robert Bye was to the right of the trees behind the farm.

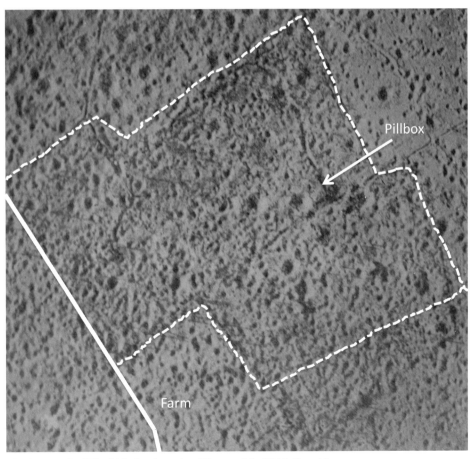

Air photograph of Wood 15 after the action (History of the Welsh Guards).

Sergeant Robert Bye crawled close to the pillbox and managed to get behind it, where he bombed the defenders until they gave up the fight. Forty Germans were killed in this area.

During the advance on the Black Line by 3rd Guards Brigade, machine guns fired into the left flank of both 1st Welsh Guards and 2nd Guards Brigade from Wood 16. Bye volunteered to take a party and clear the remaining opposition. He dashed forward, stumbling over the broken ground so many times that observers were sure he had been killed, but he managed to get behind one of the pillboxes and bombed the machine gunners into submission. 1st Grenadier Guards came under heavy machine gun fire from Green Mill, but five rounds from a Stokes trench mortar assisted in capturing this post and the advance swept on to the Black Line. Bye joined the advance to the Green Line, taking a number of prisoners and rendering assistance to the assault companies. He killed, wounded or captured over seventy enemy during the course of the day.

3rd Guards Brigade's support battalions, 4th Grenadier Guards and 2nd Scots Guards, formed up either side of Wood 15 and advanced to the Black Line behind the leading battalions. 4th Grenadier Guards was held up for a while by a machine gun in Abri Wood, but otherwise the advance to the Green Line was achieved without difficulty. The French 201st Regiment on the left was held up at Colonel's Farm and 2nd Scots Guards had to throw back a defensive flank, assisted by a company of 1st Welsh Guards. At 2.45 p.m. the French captured Colonel's Farm and consolidation of the Green Line commenced. Later in the day 1st Welsh Guards and then 2nd Scots Guards were ordered back into reserve at Elverdinghe. HQ 3rd Guards Brigade was pleased with the results it had achieved for the relatively low cost of 400 casualties. Medical arrangements worked so well that all the wounded had been cleared from the battlefield by 10 a.m.

The Guards Division was just about everywhere on the Green Line by 8 a.m. as planned. At 8.50 a.m. two battalions of 1st Guards Brigade, 2nd Grenadier Guards on the right and 2nd Coldstream Guards on the left, passed through on the way to the Steenbeek 725m away. The right was checked within eighty metres of the

From the northeast corner of Wood 16 looking south. Wood 15 was to the left of the eight prominent poplars on the skyline in the centre. One of the few surviving German concrete shelters is in the foreground.

stream by machine guns left untouched by delays to 38th Division on the right, while the left established outposts on the east bank by 9.30 a.m.

In summary, the initial advance in Fifth Army had been successful except on the Gheluvelt plateau, where II Corps had made only limited gains. Except for a few places, enemy observation over the Ypres salient had been eliminated. At 10.10 a.m. the barrage began to creep forward again to support the continuation of the advance by II and XIX Corps.

In II Corps, 8th Division's reserve, 25th Brigade, had moved up from Halfway House, passing either side of Bellewaarde Lake. Those passing north of it were largely unscathed, but to the south there were losses to machine gun fire from the direction of Glencorse Wood. The advance to the Green Line was to be made by three battalions – 2nd Lincolnshire on the right, 1st Royal Irish Rifles in the centre and 2nd Rifle Brigade on the left, with 2nd Royal Berkshire in support. A section of tanks was allocated to each battalion. Battalions were to announce their arrival on the Green Line by buglers sounding the respective regimental call. If the Green Line was taken and enemy resistance was weak, a further advance to the Red Line was to be made by 2nd Royal Berkshire, supported by a section of tanks and B Squadron, 1/1st Yorkshire Dragoons. As 25th Brigade advanced, 24th Brigade was to take over the whole of the Black Line and 23rd Brigade was to follow up and relieve 2nd Royal Berkshire on the Red Line. See map on p. 15.

As soon as it was known that the Black Line had been taken, commander 25th Brigade, **Brigadier General Clifford Coffin**, went forward with his battalion COs to reconnoitre. It was apparent from the outset that the situation on Westhoek Ridge was worse than anticipated. Heavy enemy fire was being received from Glencorse Wood, Kit and Kat and Westhoek crossroads. In addition many houses along the road through Westhoek were held by machine gun teams and snipers. A message was sent back to HQ 8th Division to arrange a fresh attack and reschedule the artillery programme. In the meantime the assault battalions moved up as close as possible to the planned forming up line. HQ 25th Brigade was established at Jaffa Avenue about 8.45 a.m.

Coffin visited HQ 23rd Brigade at Ziel House. More time was needed to clear up the situation, but it was realised that the message to HQ 8th Division was unlikely

Looking along the length of Westhoek Ridge from the south with the western edge of Glencorse Wood on the right. 25th Brigade advanced from the low ground on the left over the ridge and attempted to continue down the slope to the right towards the Hanebeek.

to get through in time. 23rd Brigade was optimistic that an immediate attack would work. Coffin was not convinced, but acknowledged the danger of delaying and decided to carry out the attack to the original timetable. Coffin sent a company of 2nd Royal Berkshire to protect the right flank, with the rest of the Battalion following to form a defensive flank as the advance progressed. Orders did not reach 2nd Rifle Brigade on the left until the start time of 10.10 a.m. and consequently it was late in setting off.

Elsewhere the advance began well, but after a few hundred metres the leading battalions were checked by machine gun fire, particularly on the right from across

From the bridge over the A19 looking west to Westhoek Ridge, which runs across the picture. Glencorse Wood is on the far left. The Hanebeek is behind the camera position.

the Hanebeek and from Glencorse Wood and Nonne Bosschen. Coffin went forward and found 2nd Lincolnshire halted on the Ridge and he could see no movement in the centre or on the left. The 2nd Royal Berkshire company formed a flank in Jabber Drive as 30th Division to the south was held up in front of Glencorse Wood. It redirected two 2nd Lincolnshire companies that had drifted too far to the right.

The centre company (B) of 1st Royal Irish Rifles reached the Hanebeek, but it was forced back by intense fire from the right almost to its start line by midday. A gap developed between the right of 2nd Rifle Brigade and the left of 1st Royal Irish Rifles. The right of 1st Royal Irish Rifles managed to get well forward but, being isolated, it was forced to fall back. A line was established along the Ridge.

The enemy was seen massing to counterattack in the Hanebeek valley. 1st Royal Irish Rifles had suffered severe casualties, so 2nd Royal Berkshire sent a company to a position 360m east of Ziel House to strengthen the centre and prepare to counterattack if necessary. The German attacks made good use of the ground to get forward, but were fairly disjointed and lacked commitment. However, at 1.30 p.m., 2nd Lincolnshire reported fresh enemy troops massing for another attack, which was launched against 2nd Lincolnshire and 1st Royal Irish Rifles at 2 p.m. This was more determined than previous efforts. 2nd Lincolnshire had to give some ground, but it was regained. The trenches held by the centre company of 1st Royal Irish Rifles were reached, but the Germans were driven back.

Throughout these attacks Coffin was with his troops where they had established themselves in shell-holes. Holding on was essential if the gains made to the north were to be held. In full view of the enemy, he moved casually from hole to hole disregarding the heavy fire. He issued orders and advice and generally inspired confidence and cheerfulness in everyone he met. At one time in the afternoon he even brought up ammunition himself.

At 2.40 p.m. orders were issued to consolidate, as it was clear there would be no further advance that day. Coffin visited 2nd Rifle Brigade on the left and found the Battalion very exposed. As a result he arranged for 2nd Middlesex (23rd Brigade)

to move forward to fill the gap. The Germans did not attack again, but from 5 p.m. onwards threatened 2nd Rifle Brigade's position. The artillery drew back the barrage 300m and 2nd Royal Berkshire sent its reserve company to support 2nd Rifle Brigade. Enemy losses due to artillery and small arms fire were heavy.

It was largely due to Coffin's gallant conduct that the line was held until relief came. Although not mentioned in his citation, the battle fought in almost the same location on 16th August certainly added weight to the award of the VC. The forward positions were taken over by 23rd and 24th Brigades and 25th Brigade left 2nd Royal Berkshire under HQ 24th Brigade to strengthen the right flank when it pulled back into reserve. 30th and 24th Divisions were also unable to make any progress and the whole of II Corps' front was deadlocked.

XIX Corps made better progress. The reserve brigades of 15th and 55th Divisions had about 1,600m to cover to reach the Green Line, which here included the German Third Line on the reverse slope of the Zonnebeke–St Julien Spur. Each brigade advanced with two battalions leading. 45th Brigade (15th Division) on the right was exposed to fire from its right where 8th Division (II Corps) had been checked. The right was forced to halt at Potsdam House, but the left reached Bremen Redoubt near Zevenkote at about 11.30 a.m. The left battalion gained the objective about Hill 37 at 11.45 a.m. Simultaneously with the resumption of the II and XIX Corps attacks, 39th Division (XVIII Corps) sent its reserve (118th Brigade) to connect the defensive left flank with the main attack to the south in the XIX and II Corps areas. Despite heavy casualties, it reached its objectives.

55th Division's initial advance by 165th and 166th Brigades went just about to plan, seizing the first two enemy defence lines up to the Black Line. After heavy fighting, a foothold was established east of the Steenbeek from Pommern Redoubt to within 550m of St Julien, but some key strongpoints on the Black Line continued to hold out. See map on p. 18.

At 8.30 a.m., 164th Brigade advanced from Congreve Walk, a kilometre southwest of Wieltje. At 10.10 a.m. it was scheduled to pass through the leading brigades on the Black line and continue the advance up to the Green line. Its objective was the third enemy line (Gheluvelt–Langemarck Line), with advanced posts on the line Toronto–Aviatik Farm. The Brigade was led by 1/4th Loyal North Lancashire on the right and 2/5th Lancashire Fusiliers on the left, each with a trench mortar and machine gun section attached. 1/4th Royal Lancaster and 1/8th King's were in support respectively for mopping up. During consolidation 1/8th King's was to be in support to the two forward battalions, while 1/4th Royal Lancaster was to fall back into reserve, digging in on the line Gallipoli–Somme–Hindu Cott.

However, before this could take place the eastern portion of Pommern Redoubt and trenches around Spree Farm had be to be taken. Heavy fire was received from the high ground east of Pommern Redoubt, Capricorn Keep and Pond Farm in addition to flanking fire from Square Farm, which 15th Division on the right had not taken. Despite these problems, 164th Brigade's advance began well. The barrage was easy to follow, but not sufficiently intense to prevent enemy machine guns firing through it. Strong resistance was encountered at Somme, Gallipoli, Pond and Schuler Farms and Hindu Cott, in addition to some dugouts along the Wieltje road southeast of Hindu Cott and the track running west of north between Hindu Cott and Schuler Farm.

The right encountered six 77mm batteries firing point blank at Kansas Cross. These were taken, each by an individual platoon. A Company, 1/4th Royal Lancaster was sent back as planned to dig in as a reserve about Gallipoli Farm. The forward elements of the Battalion were in contact with 45th Brigade on the right, but not with 2/5th Lancashire Fusiliers on the left.

During the advance on the right, **Lance Sergeant Tom Mayson**'s 10 Platoon, C Company, 1/4th King's Own Royal Lancaster, was to mop up Somme Farm and any remaining strongpoints between Hill 35 and Pond Farm. He followed 4 Platoon, 1/4th Loyal North Lancashire and reached the Black Line according to plan, but then ran into heavy opposition. A machine gun on the left was dealt with by other troops, but Mayson's platoon had to engage another to their front before they could move on. Tank F19 knocked out an anti-tank gun before being knocked out itself. The advance resumed, but another machine gun opened fire from the left. Without waiting for orders, Mayson crawled towards the gun 130m away, making best use of the cover of a mound and a ditch. Twenty metres away he threw a grenade which put the machine gun and four of the crew out of action. The remaining three crewmen ran into the cover of a dugout. Mayson gave chase and killed them all with his bayonet. His action restored the momentum of the advance and allowed it to keep up with the barrage.

During mopping-up Mayson knocked out another machine gun team singlehandedly, killing six of the enemy. His platoon mopped up dugouts on the Wieltje road assisted by Tank F16, taking sixteen prisoners in the process. A great deal of machine gun fire was coming from Pond Farm on the left and no one seemed to be doing anything about it. The Germans here gave in without much of a fight and Mayson's men found themselves surrounded by 100–150 prisoners. The Battalion second in command, Captain Gardner, ordered Mayson to dig in in front of Pond Farm. By then Mayson's party was only twelve strong, including three stragglers from 1/4th Loyal North Lancashire and 1/8th King's. He checked Somme Farm, where he found the Brigade Forward Station already in situ and at 11.15 a.m. began to dig in near the Wieltje road.

On the left, 2/5th Lancashire Fusiliers advanced with C and D Companies leading from Liverpool Trench and A and B in support from Congreve Walk. Similar to the right of the Brigade, good progress was made behind the leading brigades until reaching the Hanebeek, where heavy small arms fire was encountered which steadily increased in intensity. When 200–300m short of the Black Line, fire was being received from strongpoints at Wine House, Spree Farm, Pond Farm and Hindu Cott; the former two locations should have been taken already. The companies

From the site of Hindu Cott looking southwest. The prominent poplar tree on the left skyline is on top of Hill 35. Somme Farm is the large complex of buildings left of centre and Pond Farm is on the far right.

tried to shake out into extended order, but in the confusion this was not achieved properly all day. All the officers in C Company were casualties and **Lieutenant Colonel Bertram Best-Dunkley** personally took command of the leading wave of two platoons, leading them through intense fire to take the remaining positions in the Black Line at Wine House, Spree Farm, Capricorn Support and Capricorn Keep.

The Battalion lost almost half its strength in reaching its start line, but it was imperative to keep going to keep up with the barrage. The advance went on, mixed up with 1/8th King's. The Battalion was held up early in the advance by a gun battery and machine guns at Pond Farm and lost the barrage. Opposite Wine House about 275m of uncut wire was encountered and had to be cut through under fire. The left company lost heavily and veered left while attempting to take Canvas and Capital Trenches. After bitter fighting, Pond Farm and Hindu Cott were taken. Heavy machine gun fire was also received from Schuler Farm, a strongpoint with a supporting battery near the Langemarck–Zonnebeke road, and the advance began to break down. Best-Dunkley intervened and rallied the forward companies in an enveloping movement, saving the left of the Battalion from failure. At noon a line of trenches covering battery positions west of the road was reached and mistaken for the German Third Line, which was still some 550m away. Both left battalions were very weak by this time. Wurst Farm was reached by an officer and forty men and a patrol went as far as Aviatik Farm, while a small force dug in west of Schuler Farm. 2/5th Lancashire Fusiliers was in contact with 1/6th Cheshire (39th Division) on the left, but that Battalion was not in touch with the battalions on its left. As a result, the troops in this area came under heavy machine gun fire from their left rear.

The difficulties encountered by 164th Brigade were overcome with great determination and the advance halted a little short of the Green Line about 11.30 a.m. Large numbers of prisoners were taken. Specially assigned parties calmly went about their task of collecting enemy maps and documents and bagging them for immediate carriage to the rear for examination. Consolidation commenced just southwest of the Zonnebeke–Winnipeg road, but by then the support battalions were intermingled with the leading battalions. 1/8th King's passed into support

across the whole front of 164th Brigade and 1/4th Royal Lancaster went into Brigade reserve.

The situation soon after noon was that the Green Line had been reached in many places; but the troops were stretched out and weak and the protective barrage had ended. Air patrols failed to notice a massive enemy build up along the Passchendaele Ridge and it was not until after 1 p.m. that ground observer reports began to come through. At 2 p.m. it began to rain and an intense German artillery barrage fell on the Green Line between the Ypres–Roulers railway and east of St Julien, i.e. mainly on the XIX Corps front. A few minutes later masses of Germans advanced against the front and flanks.

The left and centre of 118th Brigade (39th Division) was pushed back east of the Steenbeek and in front of St Julien. The right, on the extremity of the Gravenstafel spur, was exposed, swung back its left flank and gradually fell back towards St Julien and Border House. 118th Brigade's withdrawal exposed 164th Brigade's (55th Division) left flank around Wurst Farm, where a defensive flank was established. The enemy tried to overrun the post at Winnipeg, which resisted until 2.30 p.m. 2/5th Lancashire Fusiliers was in danger of being cut off and a withdrawal of 650m was ordered through Winnipeg. A new line was formed between Hill 35, Somme Farm and Border House. While a defensive flank was being organised on Jew Hill, six waves of German infantry appeared over the crest of the Zonnebeke spur, supported by heavy artillery fire and low-flying strafing aircraft. This counterattack also affected 15th Division on the right. A fighting withdrawal took place, while the Black Line was hurriedly prepared for defence. A party of 130 men from the Brigade staff, 2/5th Lancashire Fusiliers and 1/8th King's just south of Schuler Farm beat off repeated attacks, until they had lost eighty men. They were forced to fight their way back to the Black Line; only twenty-five made it, but the resistance there did much to stem the enemy advance.

As the rear guard reached the Black Line the enemy tried to rush in. Best-Dunkley had already established his Battalion HQ at Spree Farm but was forced out. Collecting every available man, he led them in retaking Capricorn Support. At 4.30 p.m. the artillery joined in and the enemy was driven back. About 8 p.m., Best-Dunkley was wounded. No other officers could be found (eighteen out of nineteen were casualties), and 200160 Orderly Room Sergeant Fred Haworth

Spree Farm from the south with the outskirts of St Julien peering over the rise on the far left. Bertram Best-Dunkley established his Battalion HQ here and had to recover it later in the day in a desperate counterattack.

assumed command of the Battalion for a period, holding off attacks until relieved the next morning. He was awarded the DCM for this splendid performance. As he was carried back, Best-Dunkley sent a message to the divisional commander saying he hoped he was not disappointed with the result. Apparently he was not, since the loss of ground later in the day was not the fault of 164th Brigade. Best-Dunkley died of wounds on 5th August.

At 2.30 p.m. the Germans attacked 15th Division on the right and were heavily enfiladed by 1/4th Royal Lancaster on the Green Line. However, due to shortage of ammunition this effective fire had to be curtailed. By 3 p.m. the left of the Battalion was under severe pressure due to the withdrawal of 2/5th Lancashire Fusiliers to the north and reinforcements from the Brigade reserve were rushed up to extend the line. At the same time the attack to the south broke into 15th Division and swung north into 1/4th Royal Lancaster's right flank. Under attack from left and right the Battalion had to conform to the retirement elsewhere. Abandoning Kansas Cross, it fought its way back to the Black Line. Mayson hung on to his post near

From the top of Hill 35 looking northwest over most of 55th Division's area.

the Wieltje road, but was forced to pull back when his men ran out of ammunition. In his statement after the action, Mayson believed he could have held on longer, despite both flanks being open, if he had had more ammunition. He took command of an isolated post in the Black Line with a Lewis gun and four men and fought off repeated attacks. Despite the wound to his knee, Mayson ignored the doctors and returned to his company, where he remained until it was relieved.

A company was rushed to Hill 37 and ordered to hold there while the whole of 164th Brigade fell back to the Black line with both its flanks in the air. At 4.30 p.m. the British barrage fell on the line Hill 37 – Border House and remained there until it was confirmed that the Black Line had been reoccupied. On the right Pommern Redoubt was occupied and a line was dug to Iberian Farm, in contact with 45th Brigade (15th Division). Patrols were maintained on the slopes towards Hill 35. On the left 2/5th Lancashire Fusiliers and 1/8th King's were established in Capricorn Support and around Spree Farm with elements of 166th Brigade. At 6 p.m. a protective barrage 360m in front of the Black Line was very effective in halting further counterattacks. This fire was maintained for four hours and harassing fire continued all night. After dark 164th Brigade fell back to the old British front line, while 165th and 166th Brigades held the Black Line.

When 164th Brigade fell back the Germans infiltrated behind the left of 45th Brigade (15th Division). After a short stand, the left of the Brigade was pushed off Hill 37 and at 4.15 p.m. it was back on the Black Line, with an advanced post at Iberian Farm. The right of the Brigade withdrew to a line 350m in advance of the Black Line, with its right in touch with 8th Division south of the railway.

Soon after 4 p.m. the drizzle turned into a downpour. Although it hampered the artillery observers it also slowed down the enemy advance and it was not until 6 p.m. that the leading Germans approached the Black Line, where the artillery drove them back. The protective barrage and harassing fire was kept up all night. In the withdrawal from the Green Line the three reserve brigades had lost about seventy percent of their strength; in the late evening relief by the initial assault brigades began.

The Germans also counterattacked on the flanks. At about 2.30 p.m. waves of Germans advanced down the slopes either side of Langemarck towards the northern defensive flank along the Steenbeek. 51st Division's front had been stable for a few hours and an intense barrage and small arms fire drove the attackers back. Once the German counterattacks had been defeated, parties in 152nd Brigade took advantage of the German disorder and rushed over two rickety footbridges or waded across the Steenbeek. Edwards led a party of 1/6th Seaforth Highlanders to seize Maison du Rasta, while another party 200m to the south captured Maison Bulgare. However, the two bridgeheads were dangerously isolated and the stream behind continued to swell, threatening to cut them off. Reluctantly, they were withdrawn to the west bank, much to the disgust of those who had captured them. See map on p. 21.

At about 6 p.m., Major Humphrey Swann (formerly Schwann), commanding the King Edward's Horse squadron around Ferdinand Farm, was shot in the leg by a German sniper as he went to meet CO 1/6th Seaforth Highlanders to discuss arrangements for the night. Edwards went out under heavy fire to dress the officer's wounds and helped him into the cover of a trench. Next day Edwards was wounded in the leg but while having it dressed only complained about the awful weather. The doctor told him to go to hospital forthwith, but when he left the aid post, Edwards rejoined his platoon.

152nd Brigade took 500 prisoners and captured a field gun, two anti-tanks guns, two heavy trench mortars and nineteen machine guns. The Brigade suffered 728 casualties, including 250 in 1/6th Seaforth Highlanders and 180 in 1/6th Gordon Highlanders. In its post-operational report, HQ 152nd Brigade commented on the value of the training carried out ahead of the attack, enabling pillboxes and other machine gun strongpoints to be engaged and overcome without losing the barrage. It also mentioned that, despite the change in weather and appalling ground conditions, the men had retained their sense of humour. As one platoon pulled back into reserve after the battle, a man fell into a shell-hole with water over his head. He came up quacking like a duck and his comrades took up the cry and quacked all the way back to camp. Later in the campaign the novelty wore off.

The view southwest from Hill 35 over the exposed ground towards Setques Farm.

After dark Chavasse went into the old no man's land with a torch and searched for more wounded. He also assisted in carrying some of them back. It rained all night, but without resting he was back at the Aid Post at dawn to receive a surge of walking cases. One of his assistants was a captured German MO. Having dealt with the casualties, he directed them to the Dressing Station at Wieltje. During a lull he was standing in the doorway of the dugout when a shell passed him and exploded at the bottom of the stairs. Being German built, the entrance of the dugout faced the incoming shellfire. A man who was about to be evacuated was killed. Chavasse was probably slightly wounded and was already in intense pain from his earlier wound, but still refused to leave his post. Stretcher-bearers offered to take him back, but he gave the place to another man. See map on p. 18.

At 3 a.m. on 2nd August another shell entered the dugout while Chavasse was asleep on the table. The explosion killed or seriously wounded everyone in the

Setques Farm was in the foreground, with Hill 35 in the right distance. The Wieltje road along which Noel Chavasse dragged himself runs off to the right rear.

dugout. Chavasse received four or five wounds, including a gaping hole in the abdomen that bled heavily. Dragging himself up the steps and along the trench, he reached the road and staggered and crawled towards Wieltje, eventually stumbling into a 1/4th Loyal North Lancashire dugout. Men were sent to check the other occupants of the Aid Post and while they were away Chavasse found strength to look at another officer's wounds. The only survivor was 356629 Private CA Rudd, Chavasse's orderly, who succumbed to his wounds on 10th August. Chavasse was taken to No.32 Casualty Clearing Station at Brandhoek where the only double VC at that time, Arthur Martin-Leake, was the CO. Chavasse underwent an operation to remove the splinters, but died on 4th August. Such was this man's standing that the whole Battalion attended his funeral next day. Rudd is buried close to him in Brandhoek New Military Cemetery at Vlamertinghe.

Heavy rain set in during the night of 31st July/1st August. Enemy attacks on 1st and 2nd August gained ground but were later driven back. On 2nd August, 116th Brigade occupied the ruins of St Julien without opposition and later in the day a series of posts was established along the Steenbeek north of the village. The weather remained wet for a few more days, adding to the problems of resupply and clearing the wounded. Although the objectives of the attack on 31st July were not achieved in full, the elimination of enemy observation over the Ypres Salient was a major success in itself.

Chapter Two

Local Operations in France August 1917

6th August 1917

239 Pte William Butler, 17th West Yorkshire att'd 106th Trench Mortar Battery (106th Brigade, 35th Division), East of Lempire, France

While the Third Battle of Ypres raged in Flanders, 35th Division held a relatively quiet part of the line in France. At 3.30 a.m. on 6th August the Germans launched a silent raid on Gillemont Farm, which was held by 17th Royal Scots. About 150 enemy in three parties poured into the trenches. One

From the centre of Ronssoy drive southeast along the D58. Pass a sports pitch on the right and 150m after it turn left at a minor crossroads. Go over the A26 and continue for 650m. This is where the British front line crossed the road in front of Gillemont Farm. The eight Stokes trench mortars of 106th Trench Mortar Battery were sited four either side of the road in the front line. This is where William Butler disposed of the live mortar bomb.

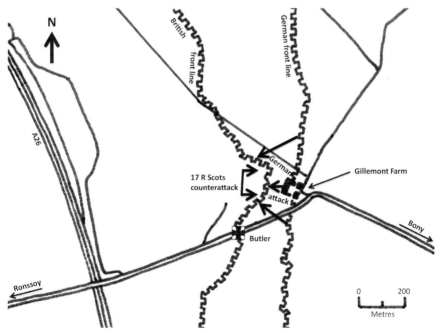

sergeant held a Lewis gun post in the forward area, known as the island. He sent his men back for more ammunition and was last seen firing at point blank range. The Royal Scots were forced back 100m, but then rallied and counterattacked to throw the raiders out of the trenches and restore the situation. Casualties amounted to two men killed (21633 Sergeant J Lennon, commemorated on the Thiepval Memorial, and Lance Sergeant J Wishart buried in Villers-Faucon Communal Cemetery), one missing and fifteen wounded. Enemy losses were unknown, but at least seven were hit.

Private William Butler was in charge of a Stokes mortar and when the trenches were shelled, he opened fire. Shortly afterwards the fly-off lever of a Stokes bomb fuse came off before it was dropped down the tube. The time fuse was ignited and would explode within seconds. Picking it up Butler rushed to the emplacement entrance and was about to dispose of it when he noticed a party of infantrymen passing. He shouted to them to hurry past and turned to shield them from the bomb with his own body. When they had passed he threw the bomb onto the parados and it exploded the second it left his hand, causing great damage to the trench. Fortunately he was not badly injured, but his quick thinking and disregard for his own safety saved many lives in the emplacement and amongst the passing soldiers in the trench.

Unlike modern mortar bomb fuses that explode on impact, the early Stokes mortar had a time fuse that could be set for up to eleven seconds delay. Two safety pins were removed before firing. The first to be removed allowed the striker to move down and hit the detonator. The second, taken out just before the bomb went into the tube, held back a fly-off lever, which was prevented from springing off by the mortar tube until in flight. The No.2 of the mortar crew was responsible for inserting the bombs into the tube. His hand must have slipped, allowing the fly-off lever to come away before it was confined in the mortar tube.

Gillemont Farm from the southwest. William Butler's mortar was in the front line trench, which crossed the road just beyond the tall weeds on the left side.

Lens and Hill 70

15th–24th August 1917

241 Pte Michael O'Rourke, 7th Battalion CEF (2nd Canadian Brigade, 1st Canadian Division), Hill 70, near Lens, France

242 Pte Harry Brown, 10th Battalion CEF (2nd Canadian Brigade, 1st Canadian Division), Hill 70, near Lens, France

248 Sgt Frederick Hobson, 20th Battalion CEF (4th Canadian Brigade, 2nd Canadian Division), Lens, France

249 Maj Okill Learmonth, 2nd Battalion CEF (1st Canadian Brigade, 1st Canadian Division), Loos, France

251 CSM Robert Hanna, 29th Battalion CEF (6th Canadian Brigade, 2nd Canadian Division), Hill 70, near Lens, France

252 Cpl Filip Konowal, 47th Battalion CEF (10th Canadian Brigade, 4th Canadian Division), Lens, France

Haig had foreseen that the War Cabinet might stop his offensive in Flanders and had made arrangements for less ambitious operations elsewhere in case of this eventuality. One such area was the partially ruined coal mining town of Lens. It was on the front of First Army, which had conducted attacks in this area in June. Haig encouraged General Sir Henry Horne to continue in an effort to envelop the town, with a view to then threatening Lille from the south.

On 10th July the Canadian Corps was ordered to take over three miles of front from I Corps from the Souchez river northwards to Bois Hugo, including opposite Hill 70. It was to prepare to capture Lens on or before 30th July in order to draw enemy reserves away from Flanders and from the French offensive on the Aisne. Lieutenant General Sir Arthur Currie, newly appointed commander of the Canadian Corps, was not happy about the objectives, as Lens was dominated from the north by Hill 70 and from the southeast by Sallaumines Hill. Without taking these two features it would be all but impossible to hold Lens. Hill 70 afforded excellent observation, particularly over the Douai Plain to the east, into the German rear areas. Horne was persuaded to make it the main objective, as its seizure would precipitate a major reaction from the Germans. While the main attack was being prepared, minor operations would be launched to make the Germans believe it would fall along the entire First Army front south of the La Bassée Canal.

Destruction of the enemy wire was incomplete on 30th July and the attack was delayed to 3rd August and then due to the weather to the 6th and later 15th August. Hill 70 lies to the north of Lens and its capture had been a major preoccupation since the failure to hold it after it was taken on 25th September 1915 in the Battle of Loos. The objective on 15th August was a two-mile arc on its eastern slopes from

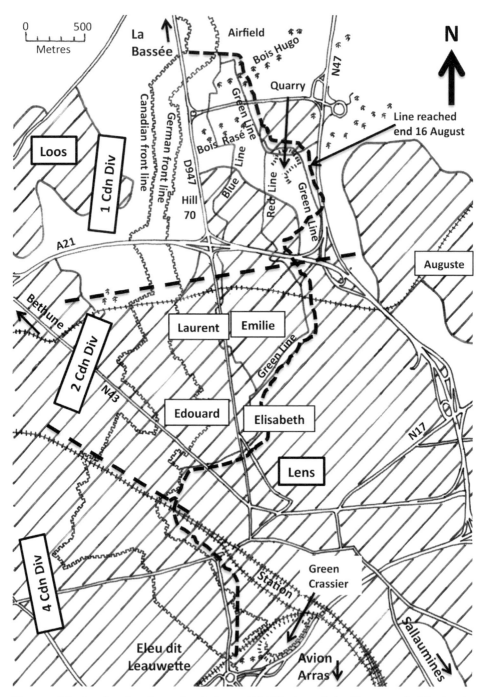

The area of the Canadian Corps' operations in August 1917. The heavy dashed line, generally following the Green Line, is the extent of the advance by 22nd August. Diagonal lines denote heavily built up areas today, some of which were undeveloped in 1917.

Cité St Elisabeth to Bois Hugo. Every aspect of the operation was rehearsed on taped ground near Aix Noulette.

It was known that the Germans would launch immediate counterattacks with fresh troops from behind the thinly held forward areas. The artillery was ready for this, covering the likely concentration areas and routes forward. Three two-seater Sopwiths of 43 Squadron RFC were to be overhead throughout to spot these moves. They were also to detect active enemy batteries and direct the artillery onto them. When the position had been seized, it was to be held by platoon strongpoints, supported by forty-eight machine guns. Each strongpoint was allocated a party of engineers.

The delays in launching the attack had the positive effect of allowing the artillery more preparation time. The Canadian Corps artillery under Brigadier General EWB Morrison was very thorough. Morrison's staff officer was Major HA Brooke (later Field Marshal Lord Alanbrooke). Part of the artillery programme was to deceive the Germans into thinking the main attack on Lens would come from the west rather than the northwest. This included firing more than 3,500 drums and 900 gas shells into Lens. Before the attack the artillery managed to neutralise forty of 102 enemy batteries in the area. On 14th August, I Corps to the north carried out assault demonstrations with dummy tanks to distract German attention.

15th August 1917

The barrage crashed down at 4.25 a.m., just as dawn was breaking. The creeping barrage was fired by nine field artillery brigades, with 160 machine guns also contributing. On the right flank, Special Companies RE fired burning oil drums into Cité St Elisabeth and the smoke drifted up Hill 70 on the southwesterly wind. The left flank was masked by 4″ Stokes mortar smoke bombs.

The attack was launched by two brigades each of 1st and 2nd Canadian Divisions. 1st Canadian Division on the left attacked with 3rd (left) and 2nd (right) Canadian Brigades. 2nd Canadian Division, on a frontage of 1,550m on the right, attacked with 5th (left) and 4th (right) Canadian Brigades. The German second position was the Blue Line and the final objective, the German third line, was the Green Line on the lower reverse slope. 2nd Canadian Brigade had the longest distance to advance and had an intermediate Red Line objective, forming a chord curving to the final objective.

The German artillery came down three minutes after zero, but counter-battery fire quickly neutralised much of it. The Canadian infantry broke through all resistance in a swift onslaught. Within twenty minutes the first objective beyond the Lens–La Bassée road (Blue Line) had been reached by both divisions, an average advance of 550m.

2nd Canadian Division fought through the ruins of Cité St Edouard and Cité St Laurent. As the advance progressed on the right, a defensive flank was formed

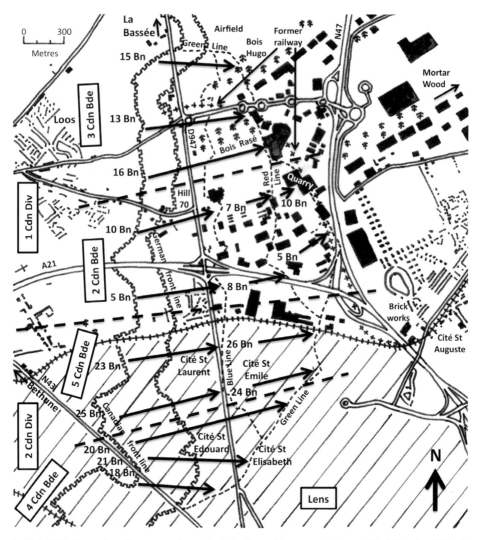

On 15th/16th August battalions generally reached the Green Line except in front of 2nd Canadian Brigade, where the Red Line was the limit. The advances by 5th and 10th Battalions next day are shown below the Chalk Quarry, much of which has been built over in recent years.

facing the northern edge of Lens. After a pause of thirty minutes, the leading battalions (18th, 21st and 20th) of 4th Canadian Brigade pressed on behind the barrage through Cité St Elisabeth and the remainder of Commotion Trench was seized.

5th Canadian Brigade had further to travel and replaced 25th and 22nd Battalions with 24th and 26th Battalions. They pressed on through Cité St Emile to the final objective, which was reached at about 6 a.m. despite heavy machine gun fire from Cité St Auguste and the adjacent brickworks.

On the left, in 1st Canadian Division, 2nd Canadian Brigade was led by 5th and 10th Battalions on the right and left respectively, with 8th and 7th Battalions

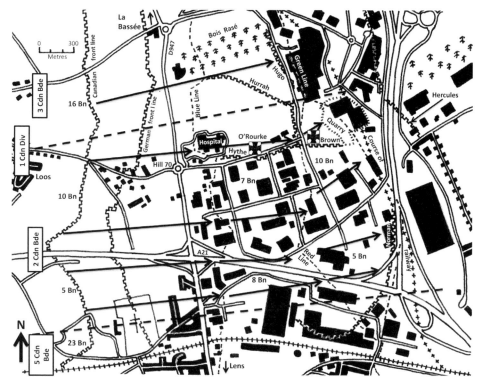

Drive north on the D947 from Lens towards La Bassée. Cross over the A21, continue north for 750m to the roundabout on top of Hill 70 and turn right into Rue Leon Droux. Immediately on the left, behind the thick hedge and trees, is a hospital. Continue for 250m to where the Blue Line crossed the road. Michael O'Rourke was active in bringing in the wounded to the east of the Blue Line. Continue 750m to the T-junction, turn left into Rue des Poissonniers and park in a disused gateway on the left after fifty metres. Cross the road and look east into the former chalk quarry, the scene of Harry Brown's VC action.

in support. 10th Battalion had A Company on the right and D Company on the left, supported by C and B Companies respectively. The Battalion went over 715 strong. The German SOS barrage fell four minutes after zero and there was some hard fighting, particularly on the left, but the front line was taken quickly and the support companies of both battalions passed through. Casualties increased as German resistance stiffened, but the advance was unstoppable and they seized the Blue Line on top of Hill 70. 8th (right) and 7th (left) Battalions passed through to an intermediate position on the German second position (Red Line), which was taken by 6.20 a.m. after some sharp actions against machine gun posts. A final advance of 450m down the eastern slope to Norman Trench and Chalk Quarry (Chalk Pit in some accounts) on the Green Line, commenced after a planned pause of twenty minutes.

The smoke was clearing and the pause gave the Germans time to steady themselves along the front of Cité St Auguste and prepare to meet the next attack. The support companies of 8th and 7th Battalions were met by intense machine gun and rifle fire as they continued the advance. Forward movement was limited to individual short rushes between shell holes and the barrage was lost. 8th Battalion on the right made some progress on its right before the momentum petered out and the men took cover in shell holes.

B Company on the left of 7th Battalion was the only one to reach its objective in the strongly defended Chalk Quarry. A small party of rifle grenadiers and riflemen wiped out a machine gun strongpoint at the junction of Hugo Trench and Hurrah Alley. On the extreme left bombers made contact with 16th Battalion to the north. Then, with more men from B Company, they bombed along Hurrah Alley towards the northern flank of the Chalk Quarry. Meanwhile the remainder of the Company advanced under cover of Lewis guns. Three scouts knocked out a machine gun post manned by a crew of five, but another strongpoint at the junction of Hythe Alley with the Chalk Quarry continued to hold up the advance. Although the strongpoint was manned by thirty Germans, the rifle grenadiers soon got the range and the garrison was destroyed.

C Company on the right was hit by very destructive machine gun and rifle fire. In addition the effectiveness of the barrage was reduced on the reverse slope of the Hill 70 feature. Dashing between shell holes, the Company reached the wire in front of the Chalk Quarry, where it used its Lewis guns and snipers to good effect against the enemy moving between Hercules Trench and the railway. It was agreed between the two company commanders that B Company would complete the attack on the left.

On entering the Quarry, B Company came under fire from a machine gun in a dugout, which was neutralised by a Lewis gun while riflemen closed in and killed the crew. B Company was then able to work through the Quarry, capturing fifty Germans. About fifty men rushed to the far side of the Quarry to set up a series of posts about sixty-five metres in front of the Green Line. However, the situation was far from secure. C Company was held up in front of the wire and B Company was under heavy enfilade fire from the right, where 8th Battalion was also held up in front of the wire before the Green Line. B Company was in danger of being outflanked and overwhelmed when the Battalion second in command arrived to assess the situation. He decided the position was untenable and ordered a withdrawal to the Red Line, to which 8th Battalion conformed. However, about forty men of B Company held on northeast of the Quarry. Casualties had been very heavy. 7th Battalion on the Red Line was reduced to just over 120 men and a platoon of C Company, 10th Battalion, was attached as reinforcements.

3rd Canadian Brigade, led by 16th, 13th and 15th Battalions, occupied the western edge of Bois Rasé and Bois Hugo, before continuing another 350m to the final objective. There were some casualties from machine guns in Bois Hugo before they were cleared up by bombers. A medium trench mortar hit 15th Battalion, but it was captured and its remaining 500 rounds were fired into the northeast end of Bois Hugo.

In anticipation of the attack, the previous night the Germans had moved up their reserve battalions to Mortar Wood, 550m northeast of Cité St Auguste and to the brickworks at the southwest corner of the Cité. While the gains were being consolidated between 7 a.m. and 9 a.m., local counterattacks were delivered by German reserves from Bois Hugo, the wood near Chalk Quarry, the brickworks and from Lens against four points on the Green Line. The smoke cleared, allowing forward artillery observers to see over the Douai Plain. Together with air observers, they identified German movements quickly and broke them up with the artillery as planned. Any survivors were checked by small arms fire.

Meanwhile, at zero hour, 4th Canadian Division launched diversionary attacks to the south opposite Lens and gas projectors were fired opposite Avion two miles south of Lens. The divisional artillery fired the same barrage as the divisions to the north. A simulated assault by 12th Canadian Brigade drew a great deal of German fire away from Hill 70. At 8.25 a.m., 11th Canadian Brigade advanced, pushing strong patrols forward between the Souchez River and Lens railway towards the centre of town. These patrols were subjected to strong counterattacks, resulting in over 400 casualties and were driven back. Nevertheless the aim had been achieved; strong enemy forces and artillery had been diverted against 11th Canadian Brigade that would otherwise have been free to attack the right flank of 2nd Canadian Division.

At 12.45 p.m., German counterattacks developed along the whole Canadian front. Four waves advancing against 3rd Canadian Brigade in Bois Rasé and Bois Hugo were all but wiped out by the artillery and machine guns. Another attack against 2nd Canadian Brigade from Cité St Auguste was stopped and a small loss of ground about Cité St Elisabeth was regained later in the afternoon. In all eighteen counterattacks were defeated, with huge losses being inflicted. The Germans did succeed in entering Chicory Trench, but by 6.40 p.m. they had been evicted again.

At 6 p.m., 2nd Canadian Brigade's advance was planned to resume to seize the final objective from the morning. Although the barrage crept forward, there was no infantry attack. 7th and 8th Battalions had suffered heavy losses and were exhausted; they had less than 200 men to go forward between them. The COs had seen strong German reinforcements reach the objective trench and cancelled the attack. If they had gone forward they risked being wiped out, exposing that section of the line to counterattack and the loss of the top of Hill 70. The barrage was fired as planned and broke up another threatened German counterattack. Lewis guns and rifle fire caused many casualties to the enemy as they fell back. Counterattacks persisted throughout the evening and at one time all the guns of the three Canadian divisions and I Corps were employed in firing defensive tasks.

Casualties had been heavy on both sides. Canadian losses were 1,056 killed and 2,432 wounded. German losses are difficult to estimate; but by 9 p.m. 350 had been taken prisoner and a day later this had grown to 970. Many men were saved by the tireless efforts of the stretcher-bearers, including **Private Michael O'Rourke**

The Blue Line crossed Rue Léon Droux just here. The area from which Michael O'Rourke rescued the wounded is in the hospital grounds beyond the hedge on the left of the road.

in 7th Battalion. He worked unceasingly throughout the action for three days and nights despite being exhausted. He brought wounded men into safety, dressed them and found them food or water. Throughout he was subjected to very heavy fire of all types. Several times he was knocked down and partially buried by exploding shells. On one occasion he saw a comrade who had been blinded stumbling around in front of the trench. In full view of the enemy, who were sniping at him, O'Rourke jumped out of the trench and brought the man back. On another occasion he went forward about fifty metres in front of the barrage under very heavy and accurate fire from enemy machine guns and snipers to bring in another man. When the line of advanced posts was retired to the line to be consolidated, he went forward again under very heavy fire and brought back a wounded man who had been left behind. He displayed an absolute disregard for his own safety, going wherever the wounded were and undoubtedly saved many lives.

16th August 1917

During the night, 5th and 10th Battalions took over 2nd Canadian Brigade's front from 8th and 7th Battalions. Orders were issued to take the objective at 4 p.m. on 16th August. The attack was launched after a short bombardment behind a rolling barrage. 10th Battalion was on the left and 5th Battalion on the right. The infantry attacked down the 350m slope to the objective. In 10th Battalion (by then reduced to 333 effectives), A Company on the right was about 200m from the Chalk Quarry when it was hit by very heavy machine gun fire from the right flank where 5th Battalion made slower progress. Despite this, advancing by short rushes, the southern end of the Quarry was reached at 4.15 p.m., albeit with heavy losses. The Quarry was cleared three times and a strongpoint was established on the right. B Company on the left and C Company in the centre also came under heavy fire and established a line in front of the objective in shell holes. They too worked forward slowly, engaging strongpoints with Lewis gun and rifle fire before assaulting. Large numbers of Germans were bayoneted in the trench and more were shot down as they attempted to escape to the east.

It was found that the Germans were massing for a counterattack at that time. Fierce close quarter fighting followed around Chalk Quarry where a hundred German dead were counted, plus another 130 prisoners, of whom a hundred were wounded. A block was established to the front along a communication trench. The Germans blew up two dugouts, but there were no casualties to Canadian troops. Lewis gun and bombing posts were pushed forward about seventy metres beyond the Quarry. A German doctor and seven stretcher-bearers were found in another dugout and helped to clear the wounded. The right post had to be reinforced by C Company, as 5th Battalion was not as advanced on that flank. Consolidation continued under heavy machine gun and field gun fire. At 5.15 p.m. the Germans were seen massing for a counterattack on the right, but it was dispersed by artillery and Lewis and machine gun fire. Snipers remained very active. A German aircraft flew over and shortly afterwards heavy artillery fire landed in the area of the Chalk Quarry.

B Company, 5th Battalion, on the right drove home its attack, but the left of A Company on the left flank was all but wiped out and contact with 10th Battalion was lost. The Germans attacked simultaneously. Although the artillery dealt with most of the attacking force, some Germans got through and a bitter fight followed. The Canadians prevailed and took fifty prisoners and eight machine guns in Norman Trench. In an hour the objectives had been secured; but counterattacks followed. By 5.30 p.m., 5th Battalion's two assault companies were down to about ten men each and had used all their ammunition. They were forced to fall back fifty metres, but at 6.30 p.m. reinforcements arrived with more bombs and the line went forward again to reoccupy the Green Line. The Germans continued to harass the survivors, ammunition ran low again and the only machine gun was put out of action. More supplies were sent forward, but another withdrawal of fifty metres was made.

Five enemy aircraft were overhead for some time, firing their machine guns while the men tried to dig in. They returned at 7 p.m. coinciding with a heavy enemy bombardment, during which A Company, 10th Battalion, suffered many casualties.

At 7.15 p.m. a series of counterattacks were launched over the following ninety minutes, but they were mainly broken up by effective SOS artillery fire. In 10th

Looking east over the former Chalk Quarry/Pit.

Battalion all communications from the companies back to Battalion HQ were cut and messages had to be sent by runner. An urgent message needed to be delivered to Battalion HQ from the front line and two runners were sent. One of them was killed. Despite a shattered arm and numerous shrapnel fragments in his right thigh, **Private Harry Brown** kept going, passed through an intense barrage and managed to reach the support line held by D Company. He searched out an officer at Company HQ even though the position was under heavy shellfire. He fell down the dugout steps, but remained conscious long enough to deliver the message before collapsing. He died a few hours later in a dressing station. As a result of the message getting through the forward position was saved, at least temporarily, and many casualties were averted.

All the counterattacks failed in the face of well directed artillery and machine gun fire. However, 5th Battalion to the south was forced back to a line of shell holes about 200m short of the objective. 2nd Canadian Brigade went into action 3,370 strong. It lost 249 killed, 1,177 wounded and 225 missing up to 19th August. It captured 489 Germans and seized thirty-eight machine guns and eighteen assorted mortars. That night 1st Canadian Brigade relieved 3rd Canadian Brigade and next night relieved 2nd Canadian Brigade as well. 10th Battalion had suffered 429 casualties, including forty-three killed and fifty-six missing. It took 225 prisoners over the two days. In addition to Brown's VC, the Battalion was awarded three DSOs, nine DCMs, seven MCs and sixty MMs, including a second bar.

Unfortunately 10th Battalion also had a deserter during this action. 20726 CQMS William Alexander deserted his post as 14 Platoon's sergeant on 16th August and was found in Les Brebis two days later, where the Battalion had been billeted before the battle. He claimed to have been knocked down by a shell, but he was unmarked. A field general court martial found him guilty of desertion on 26th September and he was sentenced to death. The sentence was confirmed all the way up the chain of command and he was shot on 18th October (Barlin Communal Cemetery Extension – II D 43).

17th/18th August 1917

A few minor actions took place on 17th August, resulting in a section of Norman Trench being occupied to join up the flanks of 1st and 2nd Canadian Divisions. Late on the 17th the Germans attempted again to regain Hill 70. They tried to wear down the Canadian artillery by firing false SOS signals and provoking the forward troops to call for unnecessary fire support. There was a concentrated mustard gas bombardment on 1st Canadian Division's batteries and then attacks were delivered across 1st Canadian Division's front, particularly against the Quarry. An attack launched at 11.30 p.m. was stopped 100m short of the Quarry by the small arms fire of 4th Battalion. Other attacks three hours later met the same fate. Throughout the night there were heavy artillery exchanges.

The artillery reverted to normal rates of fire until 4.12 a.m. on the 18th, when the German artillery began searching the rear areas and communication trenches with heavy guns and gas shells. At the same time a bombardment was opened across the whole front of 2nd Canadian Division, but it was strongest on the right. The Canadian machine guns responded and at 4.15 a.m. the artillery opened fire on the SOS lines in response to red flares put up by the forward troops. In 4th Canadian Brigade (2nd Canadian Division), HQ 20th Battalion was hit by a heavy shell at 4.32 a.m. and all telephone lines back and forward were cut. The line to Brigade HQ was repaired quickly, but communications forward to companies were limited to runners and occasionally by power buzzer once the earths had been repaired.

At 4.15 a.m. the Germans attacked 4th Canadian Brigade's 21st Battalion on the right and the right of 20th Battalion up to Nabob Alley. The Germans attempted to seize Chicory Trench on 2nd Canadian Division's right flank, but were driven off. However, they got into Commotion Trench between the Lens–La Bassée road (D947) and Nabob Alley. In 20th Battalion, A Company's Lewis guns and a Brigade machine gun were brought into action from some houses and parties of A and B Companies engaged the enemy with their rifles. The Germans were pushed out of Commotion and part of Conductor Trenches into no man's land and were

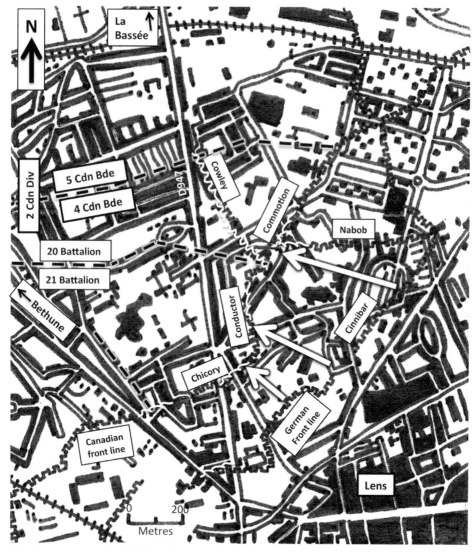

The German attack against 4th Canadian Brigade on 18th August.

followed by the A and B Company parties in hand-to-hand combat. Two platoons of B Company counterattacked into the northern flank of the German attack, while a third platoon held the trench. The Germans tried to get round the flank of the two attacking platoons, but they were beaten back by the third platoon.

In A Company, **Sergeant Frederick Hobson** saved a serious situation. The crew of a Lewis gun was wiped out, so he dashed forward and dug out the gun and the surviving crewman, Private AG Fuller. Hobson took control of the gun and engaged the enemy at close range. When the gun jammed, he ordered the wounded Fuller to clear it while he, although wounded, single-handedly attacked the enemy with a bayonet and used his rifle as a club. He was killed by a rifle shot, but by then the

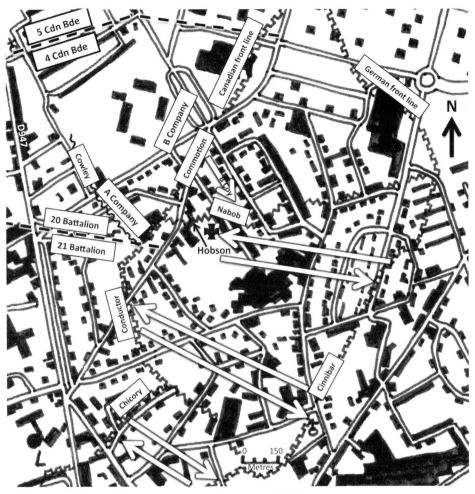

Frederick Hobson's VC action took place in open country in 1917, but the area has been completely built over since. Drive north on the D947 Lens – La Bassée road. Turn right into Chemin Chevalier and keep going northeastwards. After 750m the road bears left and shortly after there is a left turn into Rue Joseph Louis de Lagrange. Park on the roadside and look back the way you came. On the left is a fitness centre and Nabob Trench crossed the road through it.

Lewis gun was back in action and reinforcements came up to push the Germans back into no man's land. B Company's Lewis guns caused heavy enemy casualties by enfilade fire. There were an estimated 250 German bodies in no man's land on 20th Battalion's front alone. The Battalion suffered only thirty-three casualties in this action, but had a total of 180 between 14th and 20th August, including twenty-nine killed or died of wounds.

To the north, in 1st Canadian Division's area, the front of 1st Canadian Brigade was bombarded at 11.35 p.m. on 17th August and at 1.53 a.m. and 4.00 a.m. on the 18th. At 4.45 a.m. an attack north of the Quarry fell on the two companies of 2nd Battalion astride Bois Hugo. German bombers with a flamethrower penetrated the northern position held by 4 Company, but were driven out again by a bombing

Looking southwest along Chemin Chevalier. Nabob crossed the road here and through the fitness centre on the left. The VC action was behind the building, but the land is private and the best view is down the driveway.

party led by Lieutenant Gilbert Edwards and Private Lapointe, who used captured German stick grenades when their own supplies ran out. The flamethrower operator was shot in the side by Acting CSM RC Allday and taken prisoner, but died later at Noeux les Mines. Five dead Germans were left in the trench.

Elsewhere the enemy was raked by artillery and small arms fire and was halted, in some cases on the parapet. **Major Okill Learmonth** MC, commanding 3 Company south of the wood, was wounded twice, but continued to direct the defence, standing on the parapet, hurling grenades at the Germans and several times catching enemy bombs and throwing them back. He was wounded a third time and his leg was broken. Although too weak to carry on fighting, he continued to direct his junior officers in the conduct of the defence and as a result the position was held. A bombing party of 3 Company pushed into the woods and drove back many of the raiders who were then engaged by snipers.

Looking north in Parc des Cytises from the rear of the security building (on the left) along the path in the centre through Bois Hugo. The front line trench defended by Okill Learmonth and 3 Company ran parallel with the path and to the right of it.

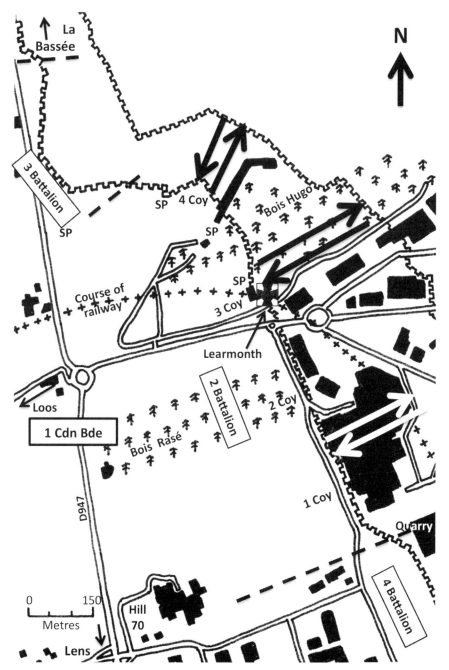

Drive north on the D947 from Lens towards La Bassée. Cross over the A21 and continue north for 750m to the roundabout on top of Hill 70. Go straight on for another 650m to the next roundabout and turn right. A central concrete barrier along the road prevents you turning left into the car park, so continue to the next roundabout and come back the way you came in and turn right into the parking area for Parc des Cytises. Enter the park and walk east for about 150m along the central path to the security building. Learmonth's VC action was just behind it. Face east at the building and look left along the path through Bois Hugo. Walk along the path a little way and look right into the undergrowth to see the remains of the front line trench defended by Learmonth and 3 Company.

The shallow remains of the trench in Bois Hugo.

At 7.30 a.m. and 7.53 a.m. SOS flares were sent up, but there was no increase in artillery fire. Messages were also sent back at 7.57 a.m. and 8.15 a.m., but it was not until 8.20 a.m. that the artillery opened fire and dispersed the enemy massing for another attack. The gunners later explained that they had not fired earlier as their observers were in very good positions and could see as much as the infantry. German aircraft flew low and fired into the trenches, particularly in the morning, but the rest of the day was relatively quiet. 2nd Battalion was relieved by 3rd Battalion that night. Two company commanders (Majors Learmonth and FR Spence) and twenty other ranks were killed and 118 were wounded in this action.

21st August 1917

It was then decided to abandon Norman Trench and pull back to Noggin Trench midway between the Red and Green Lines. 4th Canadian Division advanced its posts slightly on the outskirts of Lens and extended its front northwards to include the Béthune road. Lieutenant General Currie decided to clear Lens and the lower slopes of Hill 70, using a brigade each of 2nd and 4th Canadian Divisions. 4th Canadian Division had suffered considerable casualties during its advance from the west on 15th August, so the intention this time was to close in from the west and north simultaneously. The objective was to occupy the German front line on a frontage of 2,750m from Eleu dit Leauwette on the Arras road to east of Cité St Emile.

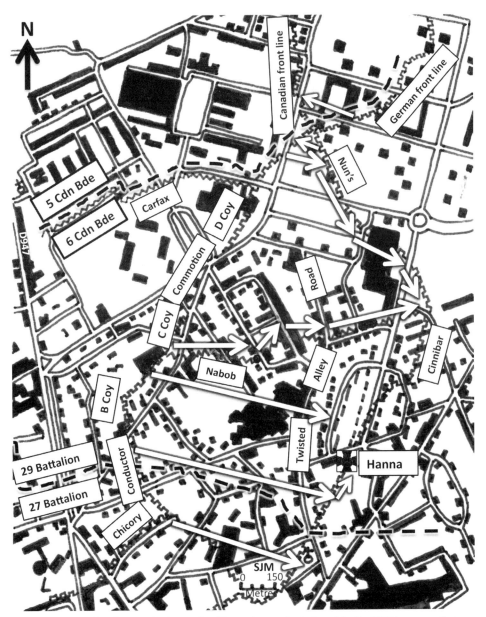

N

Robert Hanna's VC action was in the north of Lens close to Stade Jean Moulin (SJM), an area that was undeveloped in 1917 but is now completely built over. Drive north along Rue Jean Moulin (Twisted Alley Road) and turn left signed for Stade Jean Moulin. Park in front of the church on the left. Walk north along Rue Jean Moulin for thirty metres. Cinnabar Trench crossed the road here to the northeast. This is the section of trench cleared by B Company and Hanna.

The attack was launched at 4.35 a.m. on 21st August by 10th Canadian Brigade (4th Canadian Division) on the right and 6th Canadian Brigade (2nd Canadian Division) on the left. The full weight of the artillery was in support, including 1st Canadian Division's guns and four British batteries. Before the attack, heavy and medium guns bombarded Lens. They continued during the operation, inflicting heavy casualties on the Germans sheltering in cellars. In addition a British heavy artillery group fired a diversionary barrage to the north of the intended objective.

6th Canadian Brigade's objectives were Nun's Alley and Cinnabar (Cinnibar on trench maps) and Combat Trenches. 27th Battalion was on the right and 29th Battalion on the left, with 28th Battalion in support and 31st Battalion in reserve. Each assault battalion had a company of 28th Battalion attached to it as well as a Stokes mortar section. Two machine guns per battalion were allocated to help hold the objective after capture. The start of the Canadian attack was launched in the dark and coincided with an enemy counterattack. On 6th Canadian Brigade's left flank the advancing troops met the Germans attacking in the opposite direction; a desperate bayonet fight followed.

27th Battalion on the right faced the strongly defended triangle between the Lens–Béthune and Lens–La Bassée roads. It had 450m of open ground to cross on the northwest edge of Lens. The enemy positions were well defended and had the advantages of deep cellars and concealed communications trenches to move reinforcements and supplies. The advance was delayed by machine guns, but the objectives were eventually taken. However, 50th Battalion on the right (10th Canadian Brigade) was unable to keep up and provide flank protection. The right company therefore consolidated a flank slightly in rear of the objective to take account of the ground and the failure of 50th Battalion. The centre ran into strong opposition, uncut wire and machine guns, but managed to gain a footing on the objective, occupying a position in Combat Trench with a block in Cinnabar Trench. However, it was unable to take a 450m section of Cinnabar Trench southwest of its junction with Combat and Conductor Trenches. The left gained the objective and made contact with 29th Battalion.

Prior to the attack, on the night of 18th/19th August, 29th Battalion had relieved 20th Battalion and elements of 21st and 25th Battalions in Commotion Trench. During the next night, scouts and reconnaissance parties pushed forward, set up a post 175m along Nabob Alley and established mastery over no man's land.

In the attack, 29th Battalion was to advance with B Company on the right, C Company in the centre and D Company (less one platoon) on the left, which was to establish contact with 5th Canadian Brigade on the left flank. A Company took over the front line the previous night and was to hold it while the other three companies went forward. It was then to establish a series of posts in rear of the objective as the nucleus of a new support line.

Assembly went smoothly, but at 4.12 a.m. the Germans began shelling, resulting in the first casualties. The Canadian artillery was also falling short around the junction of Carfax and Commotion Trenches. At 4.30 a.m. the Germans bombarded the left of Commotion Trench occupied by two platoons of D Company and a platoon of A Company. One of the D Company platoons was to attack Nun's Alley while the other protected the left flank. Casualties were heavy, including both D Company platoon commanders The Germans got into Commotion Trench on the right of 5th Canadian Brigade and the left of 29th Battalion, but they were held by a party of a sergeant and five men with a Lewis gun until a platoon of B Company, 28th Battalion arrived and drove the Germans back. Contact with 25th Battalion on the flank was re-established.

When the advance commenced five minutes later, the troops in this area were badly disorganized. Only part of D Company was able to go forward. The left platoon was destroyed by machine guns and in close quarter fighting with Germans in no man's land, but despite this a small party rushed the German block in Nun's Alley. Another platoon was all but wiped out by machine gun fire and a platoon of A Company was sent forward to support D Company. The combined party got into Nun's Alley to establish a block near the corner of Nun's Alley and Cinnabar Trench. A platoon of 28th Battalion also assisted. A bombing party then moved along Nabob Alley towards Cinnabar Trench. As it progressed, it collected a few survivors of C Company and almost all of Nabob Alley was captured, despite the Germans getting behind the party periodically by emerging from side trenches. A point where Nabob Alley and Nun's Alley met Cinnabar Trench was reached and held.

The left of C Company in the centre also ran into Germans in the middle of no man's land on the line of Twisted Alley Road. A desperate struggle at bayonet point followed, but after fifteen minutes the Germans were forced back to their trenches.

The point where Cinnabar Trench crossed Twisted Alley Road. Robert Hanna's VC action was beyond the house on the other side of the road.

Uncut wire was encountered around Nabob Alley and most of the left platoon was destroyed by machine guns. The centre platoon suffered heavy casualties and was held up by wire. The right platoon almost reached the objective until running into machine guns in a strongpoint surrounded by wire. The whole centre of 29th Battalion's attack therefore failed, except on the extreme right, where some of C Company got into Cinnabar Trench. At the same time the Germans were reinforcing their lines from houses in front. The remaining C Company officer and sergeant were both killed, but the survivors opened rapid fire and inflicted heavy losses on the Germans. However, the Germans still came on overland or from dugouts or through a tunnel.

On the right, B Company reached the objective with comparatively fewer casualties. A threat from the right was halted by a bombing party and contact was made with 27th Battalion. Learning that C Company was in trouble, the acting company commander sent a bombing party towards the water tower. The officer was killed and the company commander took up the lead himself, deploying snipers outside the trench to cover the bombers. They made progress along the trench for a short distance until the supply of bombs ran out. The company commander was severely wounded in the arm and a platoon commander was killed by a sniper. **CSM Robert Hanna** took command of B Company and led a small party in a successful assault on a strongpoint, personally bayoneting three Germans, clubbing another to death and capturing a machine gun. This was after three attacks on the strongpoint had failed and all the officers in his company had become casualties. He was unable to make further headway in the face of strengthening opposition and a shortage of bombs. Germans also appeared to the front, so he established a block in a portion of Cinnabar Trench and held it against repeated counterattacks throughout the morning.

At 10.30 a.m. a German aircraft was shot down by a Lewis gunner. By noon, with the support of 28th Battalion, 29th Battalion had taken most of Nun's Alley and the northeast end of Cinnabar Trench, but the Germans hung on to 450m of it, together with several small trenches off Nabob Alley. The Battalion's position was precarious. Carrying parties of 31st and 28th Battalions brought up fresh supplies of bombs and the intention was to launch a simultaneous attack by the three forward parties to drive the Germans out of the remainder of Cinnabar Trench. This never happened. Instead the Germans launched repeated counterattacks.

After repelling the counterattacks for some time, the men were exhausted and ammunition began to run low. The positions gained by 6th Canadian Brigade had to be evacuated. The parties in Nabob and Nun's Alleys withdrew to establish blocks in front of Commotion Trench, which was secured to meet further counterattacks. The artillery was also brought back to the first barrage line. Sixty-two prisoners were brought back by 6th Canadian Brigade and the withdrawal to the original positions was completed by 7 p.m. Additional posts were retained in Nabob Alley and Conductor and Combat Trenches.

At 9 p.m. the Germans opened another bombardment ahead of an attack on the left around Nun's Alley and also on the right. The attack was forced back with some difficulty. When 6th Canadian Brigade was relieved on 23rd August, it had suffered 825 casualties, including 116 killed and seventy-two missing.

Ahead of the main attack on 20th August, 10th Canadian Brigade attempted to establish forward posts in School House and Aloof Trench with 46th and 50th Battalions. Although the positions were reached, the troops were forced out again and nothing was achieved except to put the enemy on alert. Early on 21st August, 10th Canadian Brigade suffered the same enemy artillery fire as 6th Canadian Brigade, particularly on the left. The attack was launched by 50th Battalion on the left, 46th Battalion in the centre and 47th Battalion on the right.

50th Battalion on the left suffered over one hundred casualties from shellfire as it waited for the attack to commence. A last minute change of assault companies had to be made. As the leading companies neared the German lines they were met with intense artillery and small arms fire from Aloof Trench. Only three parties, the largest only twenty strong, reached the objective, the junction of the Béthune and La Bassée roads. The rest of 50th Battalion was back in its start positions within ninety minutes. The three parties were unable to link up with other troops and were forced to pull back; very few made it.

46th Battalion in the centre met strong resistance to its left company, but the right and centre companies were on the objective quickly and at 6 a.m. reported contact with 47th Battalion. The left took much longer to reach the objective. By 9 a.m. the junction of Amalgam and Great Peter Street had been secured and a post was established at the junction of Amalgam and the second railway crossing. A post was also established at the junction of Aloof and Great Peter Street, but contact with 50th Battalion was lost. A German raid at 3 a.m. on the 22nd was held and some prisoners were taken. From information secured from them, the Battalion raided a number of cellars and took fourteen more prisoners.

47th Battalion on the right escaped most of the overnight shelling but as the attack set off, the early morning mist and drizzle lifted and the Battalion suffered many casualties from the German barrage and heavy small arms fire. Many of the officers and senior NCOs were casualties and an ill-timed smoke barrage added to the confusion. A Company and a platoon of D Company on the left met comparatively little resistance and were soon consolidating the objective. B Company and a platoon of C Company on the right gained all their objectives except for two strongpoints in ruined houses along the Lens–Arras road, where heavy wire and steel knife rests were encountered. There was also heavy enfilade fire from a large mine dump, the Green Crassier, on the right. The Germans launched six counterattacks during the day.

In a smaller attack supported by trench mortars at 5.30 p.m., two parties under Captains CE Bailey MC and DB Weldon on the right of 47th Battalion gained the strongpoints on the west side of the Lens–Arras road. They accounted for over a hundred enemy. Rather chillingly, sixteen prisoners had to be disposed of

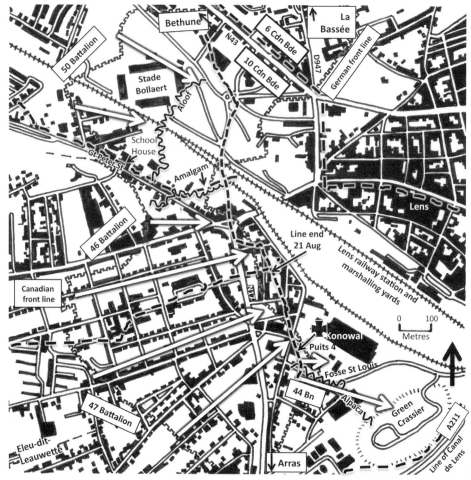

Approach Lens and Eleu–dit–Leauwette from the south on the N17. On reaching a large roundabout go straight on signed for Lens Centre along Rue d'Arras. Go under a bridge and after 350m turn right opposite a service station and immediately left into Rue Arthur Fauqueur. This is the original Lens – Arras road. Continue north for 150m to the junction with Rue Saint Louis on the right signed for Parc de la Glissoire (Green Crassier). This junction was where Puits 4 ended in 1917 and the scene of Filip Konowal's VC action.

immediately and this was achieved with a ten pound ammonal charge. Smoke and burning oil on the Green Crassier helped to conceal from the Germans what was happening and caused confusion. However, further advance was blocked by machine gun fire from a cluster of ruined buildings. **Corporal Filip Konowal** and his men were stuck in a water filled trench with a wounded captain.

10th Canadian Brigade held on to its gains, but north of the Lens–Béthune road, as the day wore on, 6th Canadian Brigade's situation worsened and communications between battalions and Brigade HQ broke down. The battalions were all but cut off by a zone of shell swept ground behind them and it was not possible to coordinate further action.

The German retention of Aloof Trench caused a nasty salient in 10th Canadian Brigade's line. On the morning of 22nd August, 50th Battalion attacked again with three bombing parties. Only the one to the south had any success, bombing along Aloof Trench to establish a post. Another attempt at 4 a.m. next morning was hit by heavy German artillery fire before the attack commenced. One platoon reached Fosse 1, but because of strong resistance the Battalion was forced to retire to its original positions. It did, however, retain the southern end of Aloof Trench.

On the 23rd, 44th Battalion attempted to seize the Green Crassier and the supporting Fosse St Louis and Alpaca Trench positions between the railway station and Canal de Lens. If they were taken, Lens would be encircled on three sides and it might have precipitated a German withdrawal from the town, but it would also leave 44th Battalion dangerously exposed. The attack started well at 3 a.m. and the top of the Green Crassier was reached, but the troops attacking the Fosse were caught in heavy machine gun fire. Although they reached the objective, they were weak and were forced back again. The Fosse changed hands a number of times, but daylight on the 24th found the troops on the Green Crassier isolated. They were counterattacked repeatedly and by late afternoon the Germans had retaken it after a desperate defence by 44th Battalion, which suffered 257 casualties in this action.

During the 44th Battalion attack on Green Crassier on 23rd August, a party of 47th Battalion under Captain DB Weldon assisted by raiding a machine gun post in a tunnel in the vicinity of Puits 4. In the approach it is claimed that Konowal was surprised by an enemy reconnaissance patrol and was taken prisoner, but turned on his captors and killed them to make his escape. This is not mentioned in official histories or the VC citation. The party closed with the machine gun post and destroyed part of the tunnel by throwing in two ammonal charges. Konowal displayed bravery and leadership, mopping up cellars, craters and machine gun nests in his sector with his section. He made a snap decision to take on a nearby machine gun post on the right flank single-handedly: *I was so fed up standing in the trench with water to my waist that I said to hell with it and started after the German Army.* Armed only with a couple of grenades and a rifle, he leaped out of the flooded trench and moved towards the enemy position. Later he claimed that the wounded captain at first thought he was deserting and fired at him. Konowal entered a bombed out cottage and, finding no one within it, jumped down into the cellar, where he was fired at by three Germans. They missed him and he bayoneted all three to death in a confused struggle in the dark. Konowal then continued his stealthy advance on the machine gun post, which was located in a large crater just east of the Lens-Arras road. As he reached it, it was clear that the Germans were attempting to pull back. Without hesitating he threw in his hand grenades, then shot three Germans dead before charging in and bayoneting the remaining four members of the machine gun crew. He returned to the Canadian lines with the captured machine gun on his shoulders.

These gains had to be given up later in the face of heavy enemy counterattacks, of which six were held by the troops on the Lens–Arras road. Heavy losses were inflicted on the enemy. It is claimed that Konowal commanded his company until

The 47th Battalion attack came over the road on the left into Puits 4, which was to the right of the trees in the centre. The right turn leads to Parc de la Glissoire, the Green Crassier in 1917.

relieved by an officer later that day, but again this is not mentioned in official histories or the VC citation. Having escaped serious injury in the fighting, Konowal was standing in a trench being debriefed by a newly arrived officer when he was hit in the face and neck by a sniper and had to be evacuated.

On 25th August there was better news when 50th Battalion secured the northern half of Aloof Trench at a cost of only six men wounded. Patrols pushed eastwards almost to the objectives set for 21st August. This was just about the last action in this short campaign. When 10th Canadian Brigade came out of the line on 26th August it had suffered 1,115 casualties, including 157 killed and 147 missing. One hundred and thirty-eight prisoners were taken.

The seizure of Hill 70 was a major success and it remained in Allied hands until the end of the war. Five German divisions had been severely mauled and were unable to relieve battle-worn formations in Flanders. Total Canadian Corps losses in these operations from 15th to 25th August were 9,198. A plan was developed to complete the capture of Lens in mid October, but lack of troops meant it never took place.

20th/21st August 1917

250 2Lt Hardy Parsons, 14th Gloucestershire (105th Brigade, 35th Division), Near Épehy, France

While the main fighting during the late summer of 1917 was concentrated in Flanders, small actions were fought elsewhere. On 15th August the Canadian Corps (First Army) launched an attack at Lens, while on the Somme Third Army made

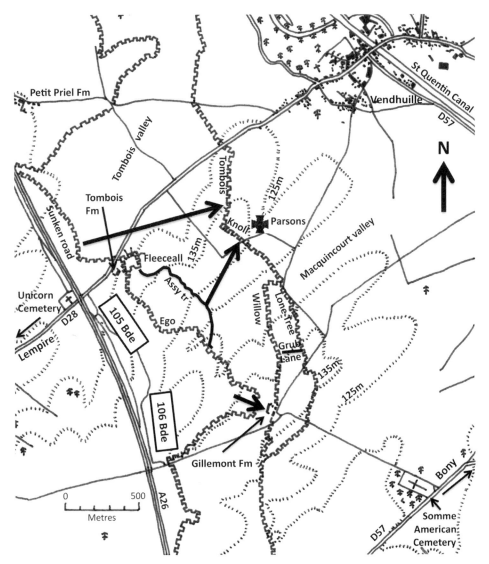

Leave Vendhuille on the D28 and drive southwest towards Lempire. Go over the brow of the hill and start to drop down towards the A26. After 600m turn left onto a gravel track. Follow it for 600m to the southeast. It swings left and after another 300m there is a distinct turn to the right. Stop on this corner. The bombing post held by Hardy Parsons was in the field on the left at the head of the re-entrant.

a series of small attacks near Épehy. During the latter operations 35th Division attacked near Lempire on 19th August.

105th Brigade was tasked to take the Knoll on the high ground northeast of Lempire, while 106th Brigade seized Gillemont Farm. Two battalions were detailed for the 105th Brigade attack; 15th Cheshire on the right and 15th Sherwood Foresters on the left. 16th Cheshire held the line and supplied two companies as carriers, while 14th Gloucestershire remained in reserve. The preparations were meticulous and rehearsals were held on replica positions constructed by the divisional pioneers.

Taken from the bombing post held by Hardy Parsons. The Knoll is far left. Vendhuille is at the bottom of the re-entrant right of centre and the Macquincourt Valley is far right.

The attack was well supported by artillery. The assault battalions moved into an assembly trench in front of Ego and Fleeceall posts on the right and in the sunken road on the left. Fifteen minutes before zero they crept out to lie on tapes in no man's land. At 4 a.m. they swept forward and within fifteen minutes the objective had been taken. Support waves began mopping up and by 5.40 a.m. the assault companies were back in their own lines. Enemy resistance had been weak, with the whole operation costing the Brigade 131 casualties.

Consolidation work began immediately on a new trench on the forward crest of the slope about 200m in advance of the old German line. The work was covered by a smoke screen until 7 a.m. The support companies brought up canvas crates that were stretched out on arrival at the new line and filled with earth dug out of the new trench, thus providing instant cover.

A small counterattack was driven off at 6 a.m., but at 9 a.m. the Knoll was shelled heavily. At 9.40 a.m. the enemy was seen massing in Macquincourt Valley and the SOS barrage was called for on and off until 11 a.m. From 7.37 p.m. until 9.30 p.m. heavy shelling fell on the Knoll and the SOS was put up on several occasions. Two enemy companies attacked from Macquincourt Valley, but were hit by heavy shellfire and machine guns, leaving many dead behind. Another counterattack later against both flanks was also driven back with heavy loss. Overnight a communication trench from the Knoll back to the sunken road in front of Fleeceall Post was dug by 19th Northumberland Fusiliers (Pioneers), while 14th Gloucestershire put out wire defences in front of the new line.

At 9 a.m. on 20th August the Knoll and Fleeceall positions were shelled heavily and Germans were seen assembling to attack in Willow Trench and Grub Lane. The fire increased at 9.45 a.m., but the attackers were dispersed by artillery and machine guns and it quietened down from 10 a.m. However, at 10.51 a.m. the SOS was put up from the Knoll, which was under heavy artillery fire. The enemy was again collecting in Macquincourt Valley, but the artillery was sufficient to prevent

an attack developing. More counterattacks were threatened during the day, but were not pressed home and, despite heavy enemy shelling, the position was fairly secure. Another bombardment from 7.45 p.m. until 8.10 p.m. was silenced by the British artillery and machine guns fired on likely enemy assembly areas.

At 1.30 a.m. on 21st August, 14th Gloucestershire took over the line and continued the work of consolidation. At 3.51 a.m. the Germans made a much more determined effort. Parties of about forty each attacked the left and right bombing posts and the left and right forward companies. The British artillery support was weak, as many of the guns massed for the original attack had already been thinned out to support further raids to the north.

Second Lieutenant Hardy Parsons was commanding the southern-most (right) bombing post forward of the trenches. The bombers were the first to encounter the flamethrowers and were forced back, except for Parsons, who refused to retreat. He remained in the post alone and, although badly scorched, held up the enemy with bombs until he was severely wounded. His gallant example of self-sacrifice delayed the enemy long enough for the bombers to reorganise. Lieutenant Baker led the counterattack, which killed four of the Germans and wounded many more. At the same time another party of the enemy in front of the right company was engaged with rapid small arms fire and forced back. Stokes trench mortars were directed against the enemy on both flanks and helped to disperse them. Meanwhile both attacks on the left were driven back by small arms fire and rifle grenades before reaching the British trenches. By 4.35 a.m. the enemy fire had quietened. The right bombing post was later named Dolan Bombing Post.

Parsons died soon afterwards, one of seven fatalities resulting from this action. Three are buried in Villers-Faucon Communal Cemetery with Parsons, three are commemorated on the Thiepval Memorial and the seventh is buried in Templeux-le-Guerard British Cemetery. On the night of 22nd/23rd August, 14th Gloucestershire was relieved on the Knoll by 15th Cheshire and fell back to the battle line. When 105th Brigade was relieved on 27th August it had suffered 393 casualties, including the 131 in the initial assault.

The Germans were not content to allow the British observation from the Knoll over the St Quentin Canal crossings at Vendhuille. On 30th August the position was shelled heavily and in the mist early next morning, covered by smoke and artillery and trench mortar fire, a strong attack ejected 17th West Yorkshire from the position. A counterattack got to within eighty metres of the top, but was forced back and the brief occupation of this position was over.

26th August 1917

253 Cpl Sidney Day, 11th Suffolk (101st Brigade, 34th Division), East of Hargicourt, France

During the offensive in Flanders, 34th Division was many miles to the south holding part of Third Army's front near Bellenglise. On 24th August, 101st Brigade took over from 102nd Brigade in preparation for a brigade attack on Malakoff Farm and the trench system in front of Hargicourt. 11th Suffolk took over the front northeast of Hargicourt, including Hussar and Valley Posts, Valley Trench and the Quarry.

At 5.20 a.m. on 25th August the artillery fired a barrage to entice the German guns to respond and reveal their positions. The rest of the day was spent in wire cutting, with a break from 2 p.m. to 2.30 p.m. to allow photographs to be taken of the German wire to identify where it had yet to be cut. By 4 a.m. on 26th August the assault troops were in their start positions.

The attack was on a four-battalion frontage, with 20th Northumberland Fusiliers in reserve and a party of 23rd Northumberland Fusiliers told off to occupy Rifle Pit Trench on the left flank (both 102nd Brigade). From left to right the assault battalions were: 11th Suffolk, 10th Lincoln, 16th Royal Scots and 15th Royal Scots. There were two objectives. The first, the Black Line, ran from the northern end of Malakoff Trench southwards along Sugar, New, Pond and Railway Trenches. The second objective, the Red Line, ran along Malakoff Support from its junction with Malakoff Trench, through the Sugar Factory, Bait Trench and then southwards to the Railway Triangle.

11th Suffolk was the left assault battalion and advanced with three companies (from the left, A, B and D) with C in support. Its objectives were Rifle Pit Trench, Malakoff Trench, Sugar Trench north of Enfilade Trench, Malakoff Farm and Malakoff Support Trench. The start line was the sunken road between Unnamed Farm and Hussar Post. A covering party deployed a little over one hundred metres in front and the Battalion was in position at 2.30 a.m.

The advance started at 4.30 a.m. behind a creeping barrage and a machine gun barrage. The attack was a complete success except on the right, where 15th Royal Scots was checked by machine guns at the junction of Railway and Junction Trenches. Counterattacks forced the Battalion back on the right. It remained under

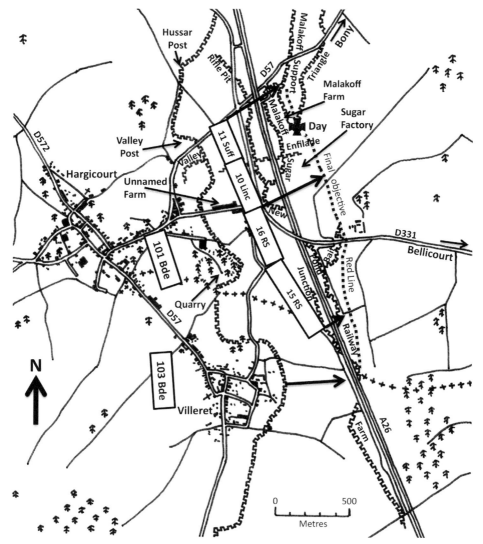

Leave Hargicourt on the D57 to the northeast towards Bony. Just after going under the A26 park on the left where there is a track running north parallel with the Autoroute. Follow it on foot for 350m then stop and turn back. Sidney Day's VC action was on the opposite hillside to the south of the D57. The depression of the road that once led to Malakoff Farm can be seen and Sidney Day's VC action was to the left of it as you look from this vantage point.

Alternatively, just before going under the Autoroute, turn left on the D58/332 towards Ronssoy. After 450m stop on the hard standing on the right just before the top of the hill. Look back to Malakoff Farm on the far side of the Autoroute. The road that marks 11th Suffolk's start line is to the right of the Autoroute.

pressure and found it difficult to bring up stores. A brigade reserve company was brought up in support.

On the left, 11th Suffolk had reached its objectives in contact with 10th Lincoln. Rifle Pit Trench was found to be empty and Malakoff and Sugar Trenches were seized quickly. There was hand to hand fighting at the junction of Sugar and

The site of Malakoff Farm east of the A26 Autoroute. The former road leading to the farm is shown as a dashed line.

Malakoff Trenches and a machine gun there caused a number of casualties before the crew was killed. The second wave passed through to its objective. In the centre, B Company fell behind while it fought through Malakoff Farm. However, this had been anticipated and the flanking companies turned inwards and bombed down Malakoff Support Trench so that the Red Line objective was taken on time. D Company greatly assisted in the consolidation of this part of the line by seizing

The most likely location for Sidney Day's VC action is around the junction of Triangle and Malakoff Support Trenches.

the adjacent portion of Triangle Trench, taking thirty prisoners in the process. A block was established thirty metres north of the junction of Malakoff and Malakoff Support Trenches. Vickers machine guns were set up in Sugar Trench and Stokes trench mortars kept down the enemy fire.

Corporal Sidney Day, commanding a bombing section in D Company, was detailed to clear a maze of trenches still held by the enemy. This he did, killing two machine gunners and capturing four others. Pressing on, he came to a portion of the trench that had been levelled. He proceeded alone from this point and bombed his way to the left to join up with the troops there. On returning to his section a stick grenade landed in the trench close to where two officers and three soldiers were located. Day acted instantly, seizing the grenade and flinging it over the parapet where it exploded immediately. His prompt action undoubtedly saved the lives of those in the trench, one of whom was severely wounded and unable to move. After this incident Day finished clearing the trench and established himself in an advanced position in which he remained for sixty-six hours. Throughout this time he was constantly subjected to shell, grenade and small arms fire. As the citation says, he was an inspiration to all.

The situation at noon found 11th Suffolk, 10th Lincoln and 16th Royal Scots on their objectives, as were the left and centre companies of 15th Royal Scots. However, the right had been fighting hard all morning against counterattacks and bombing parties coming from Farm Trench. It was difficult to bring up ammunition owing to snipers and machine guns.

Elsewhere the Germans were seen massing for counterattacks, but they were dispersed by artillery or small arms fire. At 1.25 p.m., HQ 34th Division ordered 103rd Brigade to attack Railway and Farm Trenches as soon as it was dark. 15th Royal Scots was to gain ground on its right and join up with 103rd Brigade. The attack was launched at 3 a.m. on 27th August and was not successful. 15th Royal Scots made another attempt to progress along Railway Trench to get into Farm Trench. There was some success, but the attack bogged down in rain and the

Germans counterattacked in force. Early on 28th August, 15th Royal Scots was relieved by 20th Northumberland Fusiliers.

101st Brigade's war diary mentions a sergeant and a sniper in 11th Suffolk attacking a machine gun in Triangle Trench that was causing problems for the troops in Malakoff Support. The sergeant killed four men and the sniper shot the machine gunner, putting it out of action. The identity of the sergeant is not known, but may have been Sidney Day. 101st Brigade was relieved by 5 a.m. on 29th August.

Chapter Three

Battle of Langemarck

11th August 1917

240 Pte Arnold Loosemore, 8th Duke of Wellington's (West Riding) (32nd Brigade, 11th Division), South of Langemarck, Belgium

The Third Battle of Ypres had opened on 31st July 1917, but that evening and for the next three days the rain continued without a break. Operations planned for 2nd August were cancelled as the swollen streams overflowed and turned the shelled area into a 3,500m wide marsh. To allow time for the ground to dry, operations were postponed until the 9th, but a violent storm on the 8th caused another day's delay.

Haig was determined to press on, not least to keep pressure off the French Army while it rebuilt its fragile morale following the spring mutinies. In addition to the rain, preparations were also severely hampered by the German artillery. As a consequence it took until 8th August just to move the guns forward into their new positions. Prior to reopening the general offensive, II Corps carried out a preliminary operation on 10th August to clear the crucial Gheluvelt plateau. The attack met with some success, gaining most of its objectives, including the village of Westhoek, but on the right the Germans held on to Glencorse Wood and Inverness Copse.

To the north, in XVIII Corps' area, 11th Division relieved 51st Division south of Langemarck on 8th August. As part of this relief, 8th West Riding took over a section of the front line the previous day from 4th Gordon Highlanders. While in the line 32nd Brigade's role was to reconnoitre the strength and dispositions of the Germans and to advance the line of posts beyond the Steenbeek, in order to establish a forming up position for the forthcoming renewal of the offensive. A third task was to prepare for the coming offensive by making roads and tracks to allow units to concentrate in the forward areas and set up dumps.

On the night of 9th/10th August, 9th West Yorkshire on the right of 32nd Brigade advanced its posts to Maison Bulgare and Maison du Rastu by 'peaceful penetration'. The Germans appeared to be forming for a counterattack at one time, but were dispersed with Lewis guns. The approaches to Maison Bulgare were periodically shelled with shrapnel to discourage a repeat.

To the north of 32nd Brigade, XIV Corps intended to establish a new line of posts 200m east of the Steenbeek on 11th August, with zero hour at 4.15 a.m. The

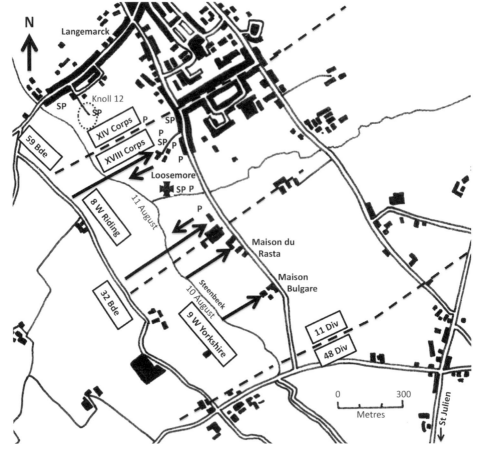

Drive towards Langemarck from Pilkem. Pass Cement House Cemetery on the right and 350m beyond turn right for Langemarck and then immediately sharp right. After 100m turn left and head southeast, parallel with the Steenbeek to your left. After 450m there is a farm on the right. Pull over somewhere safe and look across the Steenbeek towards Langemarck and the scene of Arnold Loosemore's VC action. SP = German strongpoints and P = a post to be established as a result of the attack.

Looking northeast across the Steenbeek, which runs across the middle of the picture and is marked by a line of bushes on the left. This is the area of 8th West Riding's attack. Knoll 12 is the slight rise in front of the houses to the left of Langemarck church.

attack was to be made by 20th Division on the right and 29th Division on the left. 32nd Brigade was to take advantage of this by attacking in conjunction with 59th Brigade (20th Division, XIV Corps) on the left to continue the line of advanced posts to the south. Prior to the attack commencing, existing posts were withdrawn 200m southwest of the Steenbeek to allow the artillery to commence the barrage from the line of the stream, moving forward twenty metres per minute. 8th West Riding, on the left of 32nd Brigade, made the main attack with Y and Z Companies.

8th West Riding encountered heavy resistance from strongpoints to its front and also from Knoll 12 on the left flank. During the attack, 12 Platoon was checked by heavy fire from a blockhouse and the enemy then counterattacked in strength. **Private Arnold Loosemore** crawled forward through uncut wire, dragging his Lewis gun with him. He reached a shell hole, where he dealt with a strong enemy party single-handedly killing about twenty of them. His Platoon was then able to capture the position, but they were ahead of the other attacking troops and had to fall back slightly, covered by Loosemore. The Lewis gun was blown up by a bomb and three of the enemy rushed Loosemore's position, but he shot them all with his revolver. While the position was being consolidated by his Company, Loosemore shot five snipers, exposing himself on each occasion to heavy fire. At another time he threw German grenades in defence of the gains.

The attackers held their positions until 4 p.m., when they were forced to withdraw to the northeast bank of the Steenbeek due to heavy machine gun fire and a superior enemy force. While returning to the original line, Loosemore brought back a wounded comrade under heavy fire and at great risk to his own life. The rest of the attacking force also fell back due to the strong enemy resistance. 8th West Riding was ordered to clear up the situation of its forward troops. This was carried out and the Battalion was relieved next day by 6th Yorkshire, having sustained 120 casualties since going into the line on 7th August.

16th August 1917

243 LCpl Frederick Room, 2nd Royal Irish Regiment (49th Brigade, 16th Division), Frezenberg, Belgium

244 Sgt Edward Cooper, 12th King's Royal Rifle Corps (60th Brigade, 20th Division), Langemarck, Belgium

245 Pte Wilfred Edwards, 7th King's Own Yorkshire Light Infantry (61st Brigade, 20th Division), Langemarck, Belgium

246 CQMS William Grimbaldeston, 1st King's Own Scottish Borderers (87th Brigade, 29th Division), Wijdendrift, Belgium

247 CSM John Skinner, 1st King's Own Scottish Borderers (87th Brigade, 29th Division), Wijdendrift, Belgium

Despite setbacks to his plans in Flanders, Haig's priority remained to relieve pressure on the French. Offensive operations resumed on 10th August, with II Corps launching an abortive attack on the Gheluvelt plateau. Meanwhile the German artillery did its utmost to disrupt British preparations for a resumption of the general offensive, particularly in the II and XIX Corps areas. Bad weather continued to hamper aerial reconnaissance and it proved impossible to keep track of the German batteries.

All the reserve divisions were, or had been, in the line and there was no opportunity for proper rest. The heavy rain caused a rapid deterioration in the condition of the troops and led to the next major attack being delayed until 16th August. The night before this attack was pitch black and ground conditions were appalling, but by 4.45 a.m., when the barrage opened, all assault brigades were on their start lines.

II Corps was to take the original German Third Line from Polygon Wood to the Ypres–Roulers railway. 56th Division's attempt to establish the southern defensive flank turned into a shambles when the leading battalions were hit by artillery and heavy machine gun fire from Inverness Copse. The centre and left gained the first objective in Glencorse Wood and along the edge of Nonne Boschen, but the support battalions ran into increasingly heavy fire and soft ground and lost the barrage. Only isolated parties reached the objective in Polygon Wood and along Anzac Farm Spur. On the left, 8th Division crossed the Hanebeek and swept on to the objective, with only the left being delayed. However, the barrage was weak and isolated groups on the objective were soon surrounded. By 7 a.m. most survivors were back in Glencorse Wood, where they halted a German counterattack. At 9.30 a.m. the Germans attacked again and forced the Division back to a line a few hundred metres west of the Hanebeek. At about 4 p.m. a counterattack forced 56th Division back to its start line and, to avoid casualties from enfilade fire, 8th Division also withdrew to its start line in the evening. At the end of the day, II Corps had gained a few yards of insignificant ground and was nowhere near its objectives.

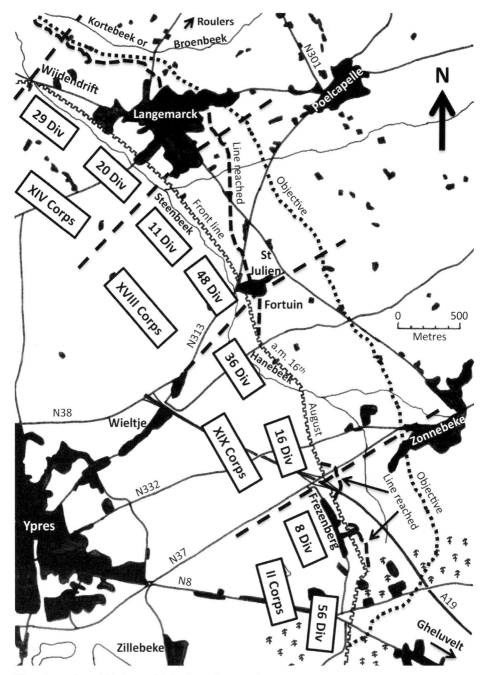

The gains made on 16th August fell far short of expectations.

XIX Corps' objective was the Third Line on Anzac and Zonnebeke Spurs, about 1,600m from the start line. This attack was an all Irish affair, with 16th Division on the right and 36th Division on the left. Both formations were exhausted and wet through, having been in the quagmire of the Hanebeek and Steenbeek valleys

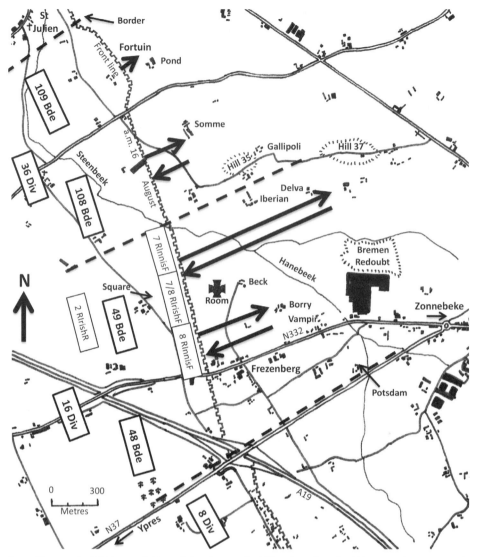

Leave Ypres on the N332 towards Zonnebeke. Go over the A19 and continue for 900m to a minor crossroads. Turn left into a dead end and follow the road for just over 500m to a dump on the right on the site of Beck Farm. Look left over the road to the site of Square Farm.

for a fortnight. Some units were down to half strength. In 36th Division, 108th Brigade on the right was halted by fire from Gallipoli and Somme Farms, while 109th Brigade lost the barrage advancing through the swamp of the Steenbeek. It came under heavy fire from Pond Farm and Border House, but the left managed to occupy Fortuin, a slight rise 350m from the start line.

16th Division's advance on the right was led by 48th and 49th Brigades. In 48th Brigade on the right, small parties got to within one hundred metres of the objective, but came under very heavy machine gun fire from Borry, Vampir and

Potsdam Farms. The artillery failed to neutralise many of the enemy shelters and the leading waves were also fired on from behind as they advanced.

On the left, 49th Brigade's experience was similar. It advanced on a frontage of 900m, led by 7th Royal Inniskilling Fusiliers on the left, two companies of 7/8th Royal Irish Fusiliers in the centre and 8th Royal Inniskilling Fusiliers on the right. In support, three companies of 2nd Royal Irish Regiment (from the right D, C and A) occupied the old British front line when the advance began, while B Company remained in reserve. In Brigade reserve at Vlamertinghe, west of Ypres, was 6th Connaught Rangers, attached from 47th Brigade.

The attack commenced at 4.45 a.m. The right was held up by the Borry Farm blockhouse, garrisoned by 300 men with three machine guns, against which many unsuccessful efforts were made. The left overran Iberian and Delva Farms, but was checked 350m from Hill 37. The 2nd Royal Irish Regiment CO established his HQ at Square Farm at about 7.30 a.m., and at 8.45 a.m. it was learned from 8th Royal Inniskilling Fusiliers that Borry Farm was still holding out. D Company was ordered to attack the Farm and B Company was to replace it in the front line, but when it was learned that 7th Royal Inniskilling Fusiliers already had a company at the Farm, the attack was cancelled.

At 9 a.m. a massive counterattack forced the right of 36th Division to retire and the left of 16th Division had to comply. The retirement spread to the whole of the XIX Corps front. All the gains made during the morning were lost and at 10.15 a.m. the Corps commander reluctantly ordered the barrage back to the start line, although it was known that parties of friendly troops were still fighting their way back.

In the original front line 2nd Royal Irish Regiment was joined by small parties of 7th Royal Inniskilling Fusiliers and 7/8th Royal Irish Fusiliers. This composite force held 49th Brigade's front for the rest of the day in the face of terrific shelling. At 5 p.m. two platoons of C Company, 2nd Royal Irish Regiment, were sent to form a post at Beck House, which had been captured by 7/8th Royal Irish Fusiliers. They suffered heavy casualties on the way and remained in the location until 10 p.m., when the survivors were ordered back to the old front line, where they were attached to B Company.

The Battalion suffered 116 casualties in this action, mainly in the C Company platoons sent to Beck House. **Lance Corporal Frederick Room**, in charge of his company's stretcher-bearers, worked his way along the line of shell holes and short sections of trench, tending the wounded unceasingly and helping to organise their evacuation. He totally disregarded the fire around him and due to his efforts many lives were saved.

At midnight the whole front of 49th Brigade was relieved by 6th Connaught Rangers with 6th Royal Irish Regiment in support (both 47th Brigade). The rest of the Brigade, including 2nd Royal Irish Regiment, withdrew into the old German and British front lines. Next day 49th Brigade was relieved by 45th Brigade and

The ground over which 49th Brigade attacked on 16th August.

moved back to No.3 Area at Vlamertinghe. Total casualties in the Brigade since 1st August had been 1,533, mostly in the period 15th-16th August. 2nd Royal Irish Regiment's share of the total was 228, including twenty-two killed and twenty-four missing, although CWGC records only show sixteen men died in this period.

XVIII and XIV Corps formed the northern defensive flank with the French. There were three objectives, the Blue, Green and Red Lines. Preparations were not as badly affected by the German artillery in this area and local actions on 11th-14th August established outposts on the far bank of the Steenbeek. The leading companies therefore had the advantage of forming up east of the stream. XVIII Corps attacked with two brigades; 145th Brigade of 48th Division on the right and 34th Brigade of 11th Division on the left. On the right the north of St Julien was cleared, but there was little further progress. The left enjoyed more success and the final objective was almost reached near the White House.

Reverse view of the previous picture from the dump on the site of Beck House. Frederick Room rescued numerous wounded from the exposed slope between here and Square Farm.

XIV Corps advanced with two brigades in each of the two forward divisions; 20th Division was on the right and 29th Division on the left. Arrangements had been made to pass forward clean rifles during the advance to replace those choked by mud. The barrage was very effective and in many instances was sufficient to put the enemy to flight. The objective was reached in many places and in others the troops were not far short.

20th Division advanced on a narrow frontage, led by 60th Brigade on the right and 61st Brigade on the left. 61st Brigade advanced on a two battalion frontage against Langemarck, but 60th Brigade's front was only wide enough for one battalion. If 61st Brigade ran into problems in Langemarck, 60th Brigade was to assist by advancing around the village from the south. The artillery plan included a smoke screen at each objective to allow the infantry time to reform before continuing.

Forming up for the attack on the east bank of the Steenbeek was an extremely delicate operation, with the enemy within 130m of the stream and only seventy metres at Au Bon Gite. The sappers laid sixteen canvas covered bridges over the stream and, despite heavy shellfire, the approach was made without alerting the Germans. By 3.30 a.m. the men were in position.

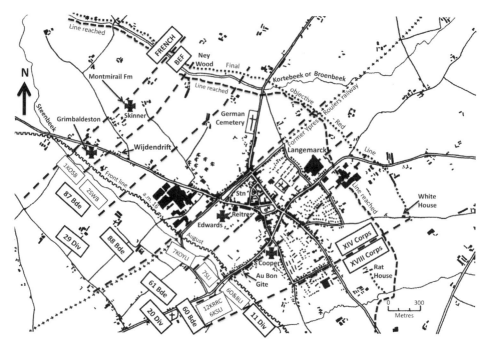

Access to anywhere with a view of the area in which Edward Cooper won his VC is difficult. Two options allow limited views. Drive towards Langemarck northeasterly from Pilkem. Pass Cement House Cemetery on the right and 350m after it turn right for Langemarck and then immediately sharp right. One hundred metres on turn left and head southeast, parallel with the Steenbeek to the left. After 350m, just before a farm on the right, pull over somewhere safe and look left across the Steenbeek towards Langemarck. There is a small knoll on the far side of the stream and the VC action was beyond it. Alternatively, continue into Langemarck and take the first right into Cayennestraat, with a café on the corner. After 250m pull over where there is a dead-end road on the right leading to Cayennestraat 20, 20A, 22, 30, 32. Walk along it to the end and look right towards Langemarck, if the crops allow, into the area where Edward Cooper captured the strongpoint.

From the church in the centre of Langemarck drive northwest towards Bikschote. After 500m, at the roundabout turn left onto the course of the old railway. Park immediately on the right on the cobbled area. A little further on is the fire station, which should not be impeded. Cross the road to the southeast side and look back towards Langemarck and the rebuilt farm on the site of Reitres, where Wilfrid Edwards earned his VC. The former farm pond is still there.

Return to the roundabout and turn left. After 1,200m, stop in front of a row of houses on the right. There is plenty of room to park here. On the left side of the road is the site of the pillbox captured by William Grimbaldeston.

Turn round and head back towards Langemarck. After 350m turn sharp left into Mangelaarstraat. Continue past a row of houses on the right for 450m and park on the roadside where safe. Look right to a row of low trees around the pond of Montmirail Farm. There are no other remains of the buildings attacked by John Skinner.

60th Brigade was led by 6th Oxfordshire and Buckinghamshire Light Infantry. Its first wave set off from east of the stream to take the first and second objectives. The support battalions, consisting of 6th King's Shropshire Light Infantry on the right and 12th King's Royal Rifle Corps on the left, were to cross the Steenbeek during the initial advance and go on to take the final objective. 12th Rifle Brigade was in reserve. In order to give 6th Oxfordshire and Buckinghamshire Light Infantry a clear run for the assault, B Company, 11th Rifle Brigade (59th Brigade), and some sappers were detailed to take Au Bon Gite.

At zero hour the barrage fell like a curtain in front of the advancing troops. 11th Rifle Brigade's bombers masked Au Bon Gite with smoke grenades while the rest of B Company rushed forward and took the position after a short fight. By 5.40 a.m., 6th Oxfordshire and Buckinghamshire Light Infantry was on the first objective (Blue Line), having overcome relatively light opposition, and five minutes later the second wave advanced to reach the second objective (Green Line) with little loss.

6th King's Shropshire Light Infantry and 12th King's Royal Rifle Corps followed over the Steenbeek. On the way to the first objective, which was 275–350m short of Langemarck, 12th King's Royal Rifle Corps was held up by heavy fire from a large pillbox in a ruined farmhouse about 225m away on the left flank. It caused heavy casualties and also held up the right battalion of 61st Brigade (12th King's). The CO was wounded and Captain Lycett, the Adjutant, assumed command. He ordered **Sergeant Edward Cooper**, who was commanding 1 Platoon in A Company after his officer had been killed, to deal with the pillbox.

Cooper rushed forward with twelve men, but when they were still one hundred metres from the pillbox only four of them had not been hit. Cooper ordered the survivors to take cover and to engage the pillbox slits with their rifles. This failed to subdue the enemy and three of his four remaining companions were killed. Cooper realised there was a point beyond which the enemy machine guns were unable to traverse. Armed with his officer's revolver, Cooper charged directly at the pillbox with a lance corporal, who was hit on the way. Cooper reached the pillbox unharmed and fired through one of the slits while shouting to the Germans to surrender. He fired through the other slits to give the impression that the pillbox was surrounded. The occupants began to come out, but Cooper had not seen a second entrance and

Looking across the Steenbeek towards Langemarck from the south. Edward Cooper's VC action was to the right of the church, beyond the white house.

he was surprised when other Germans emerged from it to surrender. The revolver went off accidentally and killed the leading German. Somewhat upset by this, the rest rushed back inside and Cooper had to repeat the process to persuade them to come out again. To avoid further accidents he thrust the revolver into his belt and used his rifle and bayonet instead. Eventually forty-five Germans surrendered and seven machine guns were taken. The first man out was an officer and Cooper boxed his ears and kicked him up the backside to encourage the others. It worked. The rest came quietly and he kept them together while he waved the Battalion forward. Cooper's action allowed the advance to continue and undoubtedly saved many lives. The German fire from further back did not decrease and some of those who surrendered were hit and killed.

At first the Adjutant gave Cooper a roasting for going in the wrong direction, but changed his mind when he realised what had been achieved. The advance to the second and third objectives was made more difficult by the ground conditions and fire from a number of pillboxes. Despite heavy opposition, in particular against the left company, the final objective was taken at 7.50 a.m. Cooper was almost killed by a grenade thrown by one of his own men and later a shell buried him. However, he managed to dig himself out and rescued another man, but a third man suffocated before he reached him.

The view from the end of Cayennestraat 20, 20A, 22, 30, 32 can be very restricted by maize, as illustrated here. Edward Cooper captured the pillbox beyond the clump of trees in the centre.

As early as 8.00 a.m. reports from spotter aircraft were being received of a German division concentrating 2,250m east of Langemarck. Orders were issued for the Green and Red Lines to be held at all costs. Behind 60th Brigade, 12th Rifle Brigade moved to dead ground east of the Steenbeek and a section of 60th Brigade Machine Gun Company moved up to the Red Line behind the right flank.

At 4.10 p.m. a counterattack forced 12th King's (61st Brigade) back, allowing the enemy to attack 12th King's Royal Rifle Corps in the left flank. The left company resisted almost to the end and only five men returned. A defensive flank was hurriedly thrown back and at one time about 200m of this critical flank was held by only sixteen men. A company of 6th Oxfordshire and Buckinghamshire Light Infantry was sent up to support 12th King's Royal Rifle Corps, while a company of 12th Rifle Brigade went forward into the Green Line and a platoon of the same battalion strengthened the Brigade's right flank, held by 6th King's Shropshire Light Infantry. The Germans were halted and the Green Line was consolidated overnight, which passed relatively quietly, apart from continuous sniping.

Orders were issued to retake the portions of the Red Line lost in the German counterattack. Zero hour was set for 6.30 p.m. on the 17th, with 60th Brigade's advance being led by two companies of 12th Rifle Brigade. As the barrage lifted at 7 p.m., the attacking troops were met by heavy enfilade machine gun fire from a pillbox on the right flank at Rat House. The advance was halted after one hundred metres and the line reached was held in conjunction with 61st Brigade on the left, which reached about the same approximate line. 60th Brigade was relieved by two battalions of 114th Brigade on the night of 18th/19th August. 12th King's Royal Rifle Corps had suffered 246 casualties.

At a parade soon after the battle, Cooper was very nervous while being questioned by the divisional commander about manhandling the German officer. He relaxed when it became clear that the GOC really did not mind about the breach of military etiquette in the circumstances.

61st Brigade was led by 7th Somerset Light Infantry on the right and 7th King's Own Yorkshire Light Infantry on the left. After the capture of the second objective (Green Line), the advance was to be taken up by 12th King's on the right and 7th Duke of Cornwall's Light Infantry on the left. During the forming up a screen was maintained by 59th Brigade. Moving forward was made more difficult by the Germans at Au Bon Gite continuously firing flares. 7th Somerset Light Infantry was spotted crossing the Steenbeek and a brief enemy barrage fell, but casualties were light due to the shells falling into the deep mud. 7th King's Own Yorkshire Light Infantry moved forward of the taped start line and risked the British barrage. By 3.30 a.m. all were in position and ready. The barrage when it opened was very accurate.

Opposition to the front was not serious, but fire from Au Bon Gite on the right flank caught the leading waves as they struggled over the boggy ground. 7th King's Own Yorkshire Light Infantry was held up by two pillboxes at Reitres Farm, west of

Reitres Farm from the former railway line. The pond of the old farm can just be made out in front of the buildings. 7th King's Own Yorkshire Light Infantry attacked from right to left.

Langemarck, and another at the Station, which was supported by crossfire from Au Bon Gite on the right. The leading companies (C and D) were held up one hundred metres from the first objective (Blue Line), by which time about half the Battalion had become casualties.

The fire from Reitres Farm threatened to stall the advance altogether. Except for one subaltern, all officers in D Company had been hit. Without hesitation and on his own initiative, **Private Wilfred Edwards** crawled forward. He reached a pillbox, where a German officer fired at him but missed. Edwards threw in three grenades and the German officer then asked him to climb in through the loophole. Edwards responded with more bombs. Soon afterwards thirty Germans surrendered to him, except for the machine gunner, who had to be brought out at bayonet point.

Nearby 14015 Lance Corporal A Powell (DCM for this action) got into a position from where he could fire his Lewis gun through the loophole of another pillbox. Once both pillboxes had been secured, Edwards climbed onto the roof of the one he had captured to wave his comrades on. The advance had been delayed by about fifteen minutes. They charged forward and reversed a very critical situation. Four machine guns and forty-two prisoners were taken here, including a battalion commander, and many more were killed. The German officer Edwards had sparred with said that he deserved the Iron Cross for his actions. Edwards acted as a runner for the rest of the day, giving invaluable service.

The Station pillbox fell soon afterwards with the capture of thirty-three more prisoners and this allowed the second wave to go forward, but the ground from here onwards was an almost impassable swamp. The men had to move around it in file on the right but, once the Station pillbox had fallen, a party of B Company managed

to advance along the railway to the left of the swamp. The mud and isolated pockets of resistance were eventually overcome with the assistance of 60th Brigade on the right, and 61st Brigade reached the far side of Langemarck. The second objective (Green Line) was taken, albeit almost an hour late, on the right in 7th Somerset Light Infantry's area.

12th King's on the right and 7th Duke of Cornwall's Light Infantry on the left passed through to take the third objective (Red Line). They suffered a number of casualties, mainly from flanking fire, and were at times forced to advance in file due to the nature of the ground. The Red Line was secured at about 9 a.m. and 12th King's and 7th Duke of Cornwall's Light Infantry consolidated along it. 7th Somerset Light Infantry and 7th King's Own Yorkshire Light Infantry dug in on the Green Line. C and D Companies, 7th King's Own Yorkshire Light Infantry also established strongpoints at Reitres Farm and near the Station on the only patch of hard ground in the area.

At 5 p.m., 12th King's on the right reported an enemy concentration and it was dispersed by an artillery barrage. However, about 6.30 p.m. the right company of 12th King's fell back about 175m to conform to the left of 60th Brigade. The refused flank was extended to the right until contact was regained with 60th Brigade. About the same time 15th Welsh, attached to the Brigade, arrived and was ordered to move forward to support 12th King's. By 11 p.m. a continuous line had been restored. At 7.30 p.m. an enemy concentration in front of 7th Duke of Cornwall's Light Infantry was engaged with artillery and small arms fire.

For an unexplained reason at 2 a.m. the following morning the centre company of 12th King's fell back from the Red Line. The company had no officers and was commanded by a sergeant, who was subsequently killed. A patrol went forward to investigate and found Germans in that portion of the Red Line. At 7 p.m. on 17th

Looking southwest over the Langemarck – Bikschote road. 1st King's Own Scottish Borderers attacked towards the camera position. The pillbox captured by William Grimbaldeston was in the field on the other side of the road.

August, 12th King's moved forward, supported by 7th Somerset Light Infantry and the right company of 7th Duke of Cornwall's Light Infantry. They reoccupied the Red Line with little opposition on the left, but the right suffered heavy casualties from Rat House on the right flank and was unable to hold on. It pulled back and dug in on the ground held.

61st Brigade was relieved by elements of 114th Brigade by 10 a.m. on the 18th. When 7th King's Own Yorkshire Light Infantry came out of the line, it had taken a total of seventy prisoners, twelve machine guns, including four from Reitres Farm, and three 4.2″ howitzers.

North of the railway, 29th Division was responsible for about one mile of XIV Corps' front, its objective being a block of land between the Steenbeek and the Kortebeek (Broenbeek on modern maps). 88th Brigade on the right took the strongpoints along the Langemarck–Wijdendrift road and assisted 61st Brigade with enfilade fire to the south before pressing on to just short of the final objective.

87th Brigade on the left was led by 2nd South Wales Borderers on the right and 1st King's Own Scottish Borderers on the left, next to the French. Each battalion had a frontage of 350m and was to take the first two objectives, each about 450m distant. 1st King's Own Scottish Borderers formed up on tapes at 2 a.m. with

The low line of bushes left of centre marks the pond that is all that remains of Montmirail Farm. The complex of blockhouses there in 1917 was captured by John Skinner, leading parties of men of A Company.

D Company on the left and B Company on the right leading. A and C Companies followed ten metres behind. When the advance commenced the Battalion was slowed by heavy resistance and the situation was not helped by the French failing to start on time. However, the French soon caught up, assisted by 1st King's Own Scottish Borderers' enfilade fire.

B Company was held up by a pillbox on its left and the way ahead seemed to be impassable. **Sergeant William Grimbaldeston** resolved to capture the pillbox. He arranged for covering fire by rifle grenadiers and a rifleman. Despite the heavy fire from the pillbox, he managed to make his way to the rear and threatened the garrison with a grenade held aloft. Thirty-six enemy surrendered to him, along with six machine guns and a trench mortar. The advance to the first objective was then completed.

While waiting for the advance to the second objective to begin, **CSM John Skinner** and his men in A Company took advantage of a twenty minutes halt in the creeping barrage for a rest. When the barrage lifted, A Company moved off, but quickly ran into heavy opposition, especially on the left flank from the three blockhouses near Montmirail Farm. The French had been delayed, so no help could be relied upon from that direction. The Company was pinned down, but continued to creep forward by short rushes.

Skinner was wounded in the head, but despite this he took six men and worked round the left of the three blockhouses. There is some evidence that the company commander, Captain Currie, was with them at this stage. About sixty metres away they took cover and fired their rifles through the weapon slits, knocking out two of the machine guns. Skinner went on alone and after ten minutes succeeded in reaching the rear of the pillbox on the extreme left. He bombed the garrison with grenades and forced them to surrender. His small team did their best to cover him as he went to the second pillbox. A few bombs through the weapon slits caused this pillbox to surrender as well. At this the company commander ordered the rest of the company forward and, after suffering heavy casualties, the third pillbox was also secured. In total, Skinner took sixty prisoners, six machine guns and a few trench mortars. This action allowed the second objective (Green Line) to be reached at 7.50 a.m. and consolidated.

The whole Division was on the final objective by 8.30 a.m. To the north the French also reached their objectives. In the evening a counterattack from the direction of Ney Wood was broken up by artillery. 87th Brigade was relieved by 86th Brigade, except for 1st Royal Inniskilling Fusiliers, which was left behind to hold the new line. The Brigade had suffered 613 casualties, including 197 in 1st King's Own Scottish Borderers.

Chapter Four

Local Operations September 1917

8th September 1917

254 Sgt John Carmichael, 9th North Staffordshire (Pioneers) (37th Division), Klein Zillebeke, Belgium

The incident for which **Sergeant John Carmichael** was awarded the VC did not occur during a major action. On 2nd September 1917, 37th Division extended its front north and as a result the Pioneer Battalion was allocated extra tasks. A Company was to construct a new communication trench, Imperial Avenue, through Battle and Fusilier Woods. It was a huge undertaking, involving digging and revetting 2,700m of trench. The other companies worked on other communication trenches and one was allocated the task of constructing a mule track. All this work was in preparation for the forthcoming resumption of the offensive in Flanders.

Drive through Zillebeke to the southeast, towards Zwarteleen and Zandvoorde. Pass the turning to Hill 60 on the right and continue 800m to Fusilier Wood on the right. There is a house on the roadside and room to park there. Walk past the house and turn immediately right along a grass path and follow it left and right around the outside of the Wood to the southwest. About thirty metres after entering the Wood there is a track on the left. This is about where Imperial Avenue crossed the main track and continued eastwards along the edge of the Wood. John Carmichael stood on the grenade somewhere about here.

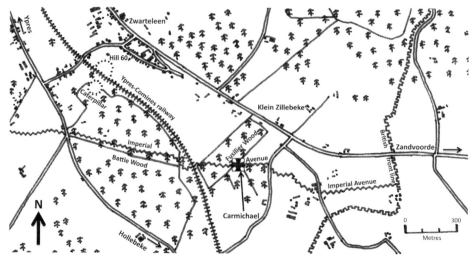

Imperial Avenue crossed the path in the foreground at this point. This is approximately where John Carmichael stood on the grenade and saved his comrades.

Work on Imperial Avenue commenced on the 2nd and it moved closer to the front each day. By 6th September, A Company was revetting the new trench east of the railway. On the 8th a man deepening the trench in preparation for it to be revetted dislodged a grenade from the trench wall and the fuse started to burn. Carmichael, a bombing instructor, rushed to the spot and shouted to his men to get clear, knowing they only had a few seconds in which to do so. There was time to throw the grenade out of the trench and this would have saved the lives of those around him. However, he realised he could not do this because of the men working outside the trench, so he took off his steel helmet, placed it over the grenade and stood on it.

The explosion blew him out of the trench shattering both legs and injuring his right arm, but his quick action saved many lives. Only one other man was injured. Carmichael was carried back to No.53 Casualty Clearing Station at Bailleul for treatment. Work continued on Imperial Avenue and on the 10th it reached the support line. Next day it progressed to the front line, but it was not until the 17th that the last work was carried out and this involved padding the last 200m with sandbags to deaden sound. This is but one example of the enormous efforts made routinely by the pioneer battalions in this war.

13th–16th September 1917

> 255 LSgt John Moyney, 2nd Irish Guards (2nd Guards Brigade, Guards Division), Northwest of Langemarck, Belgium
>
> 256 Pte Thomas Woodcock, 2nd Irish Guards (2nd Guards Brigade, Guards Division), Northwest of Langemarck, Belgium

On the afternoon and evening of 12th September, 2nd Irish Guards relieved 3rd Coldstream Guards in the front line along the Broenbeek at the junction with the French. It was part of the relief of 1st Guards Brigade by 2nd Guards Brigade. The stream was swollen, the banks were swampy and, although the water was only a metre at the deepest, below it was a layer of mud of varying depth. The bottom was also liberally strewn with barbed wire. On the far bank was a small exposed lodgement held by outposts within one hundred metres of the enemy lines. In the 450m stretch between Ney Copse and Ney Wood there were only two crossing points; a wooden bridge and a series of duckboards laid as stepping stones at the western corner of Ney Copse.

On the way to the front 2nd Irish Guards was attacked by a dozen low flying aircraft, which caused twenty casualties as well as cutting the Battalion transport to pieces. Fortunately there were no fatalities. To make matters worse, the guides lost their way and it was not until midnight that the weary troops reached their positions. Six platoons were sent over the Broenbeek to hold the lodgement; No.2 Company on the right held the eastern edge of Ney Copse as far as the southeast corner of Ney Wood and two platoons of No.3 Company held posts in Ney Copse. Two advanced posts in Ney Copse were held by **Sergeant John Moyney**'s platoon. The men settled into their new positions and for about three hours all was peaceful. Then at 2.40 a.m. the enemy opened a barrage on the forward posts. After twenty-five minutes it drifted back to the stream and then on to the British front line west of it.

As the barrage lifted two companies of Württembergers (about 200 strong in total) attacked. Some of them were wearing body armour. All the posts east of Ney Copse were bombed out and lost. The barrage hit the posts so suddenly that no SOS signals were sent up and it was some time before the support companies realised that an attack had been made.

A spirited defence of the south of Ney Copse by Captain William Redmond (son of the Irish MP) and No.2 Company prevented the whole lodgement being overturned. Redmond received the DSO for this action. Two hours after it started the barrage fell again to cover the withdrawal of the Württembergers. Redmond formed a post on the eastern edge of Ney Copse and prevented the enemy from rushing it during the night. This prevented the remaining posts in Ney Copse being surrounded from the south. 2nd Irish Guards suffered about eighty casualties in this attack and those surviving in Ney Copse were not contactable. It is not surprising

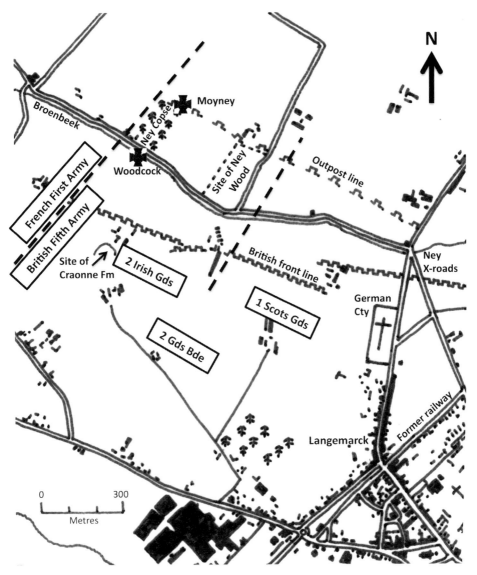

Leave Langemarck northwards on Klerkenstraat. Pass the German War Cemetery on the left and 300m beyond turn left into Hanebeekstraat, with the Broenbeek on the left of the road. Follow it for 650m, passing the 34th Division Artillery and Engineer memorial. At the junction with Kleine Merkemstraat there is space to park on the left side of the road, but do not go too far as the Broenbeek is only five metres away! This road junction is at the southeast corner of the former Ney Wood. Walk a little way up Kleine Merkemstraat and look northwest along the Broenbeek to the site of Ney Copse and the VC actions of John Moyney and Thomas Woodcock.

that the posts were lost, there being no wire to the front, whilst the Broenbeek behind prevented rapid support. During the day 1st Scots Guards took over the right sub-sector from 1st Irish Guards.

The CO of 2nd Irish Guards realised that the lodgement was untenable and asked to withdraw the survivors south of the Broenbeek, but Brigade HQ was not

From the southeast corner of the former Ney Wood looking northwest to Ney Copse, the trees right of centre. The Broenbeek follows the road running across the picture from bottom left. Moyney's party was trapped around the prominent tall trees on the far right. Craonne Farm is to the left of the poplars on the left beyond the road and Broenbeek.

convinced. He had to send his written appreciation of the situation before authority was given to proceed with the withdrawal. Two platoon-sized officers' patrols were sent out after dusk to locate the posts holding Ney Copse and clear up the situation. One patrol was tasked to work southeast from Ney Copse. It was to make good the ground between the original posts and the Broenbeek, proceeding as far as Ney Wood. If it was unable to clear up the situation as far as Ney Wood, a second patrol was to cross the Broenbeek and endeavour to make good the posts in Ney Wood and join up with the first patrol.

The first patrol was fired on from Ney Wood while crossing the Broenbeek and found the southern edge of the Wood was held strongly. The second patrol reached the northern edge of Ney Copse, where it was held up by a strongly held post. It turned east along the line of the original posts until reaching the eastern edge of Ney Copse, where it was fired on by a machine gun. It was then forced to withdraw, covering the retirement of the remaining posts in Ney Copse as it went. However, the Copse was not properly searched and Moyney's posts of two NCOs and fifteen men were overlooked and reported as missing.

The patrols returned as it was growing light. Throughout the early morning of the 13th the enemy shelled the Irishmen vigorously. Despite the heavy fire, some survivors of No.2 Company made their way in through the enemy posts. Another patrol went out that night and discovered that the enemy were holding the two crossing points over the Broenbeek in force. They were also holding Ney Wood and had posts between it and Ney Copse. They did not find Moyney's men, but other remaining posts in the area were withdrawn. On the morning of the 14th the Brigade commander visited the Battalion and left no one in any doubt as to what he

Ney Copse

thought of their patrolling skills. As the regimental history put it, …*with a missing patrol in front…and a displeased Brigadier in rear, life was not lovely…*

The heavy artillery fired a concentrated bombardment on Ney Copse and Wood during the morning and that night two creeping barrages were laid down by the 18 Pounders. A post north of the Broenbeek near Ney Crossroads was withdrawn successfully during the night.

15th September passed in comparative quiet, with two creeping barrages each of eight minutes being fired at 9.10 p.m. and 9.30 p.m. and again at 3 a.m. and 3.07 a.m. next morning. At 4.30 a.m. on the 16th a terrific barrage fell on the front line of 2nd Irish Guards in the Brigade's left sub-sector. This was followed by SOS rockets from the left and also from in front of 1st Scots Guards on the right. The British guns responded and very quickly the whole front was being plastered by both sides with every means available. Brigade HQ had information from a prisoner captured at St Julien that the enemy would attack at 6.00 a.m., although by 5 a.m. most of the front was quiet again. Firing continued on the right for some time longer and an attack was made against 61st Brigade. As the time of the expected attack arrived, Moyney and the missing platoon turned up at Battalion HQ to announce that they had just returned from Ney Copse. He was then able to fill in the missing details.

On the 12th Moyney had been put in command of two advanced shell-hole posts in Ney Copse; he commanded one and Corporal Fitzgerald the other. His orders were to hold and under no circumstances to break into the iron rations. The Württembergers' attack cut him off from the rest of the Battalion and, although he wanted to withdraw, he noticed a machine gun in a commanding position between his location and the Broenbeek duckboard crossing. Wisely, he decided not to attract attention and kept his men quiet while awaiting events to unfold.

They had iron rations for two days and a bottle of water each, but as instructed the iron rations were not touched. The Germans knew they were there, but not exactly

Reverse view of the previous picture. Craonne Farm is on the right on the other side of the Broenbeek. The bridge is approximately where Moyney's party escaped across the Broenbeek and where Thomas Woodcock rescued Patrick Hilley.

where and, since they had other problems, they largely left the Irishmen alone. As a result Moyney was shelled by both sides. At dawn on the 16th the situation changed dramatically when a company of about 250 men was sent to flush him out.

Moyney waited until the Germans were less than twenty-five metres away and then ordered his men to jump out and attack. This unexpected action caught the enemy unawares and within a few seconds three drums of Lewis gun ammunition and four boxes of grenades had been expended against the attacking Germans. They attacked again and received the same treatment, but the Lewis guns were knocked out by grenades. Moyney realised he was surrounded and ordered his men to turn about and charge straight through the advancing Germans and across the Broenbeek.

They plunged into the swampy waters and struggled through the barbed wire under constant machine gun fire and amid a shower of bombs. Moyney with his rifle and **Private Thomas Woodcock** with his Lewis gun covered the withdrawal. Woodcock continued to fire until the enemy were only a few metres from his position. He then jumped into the water and was almost across when he heard cries for help behind him. Returning through a shower of bombs he fished out 6015 Private Patrick Hilley, who had a broken thigh. Woodcock brought Hilley to the far bank and then carried him over open ground to safety close to Craonne Farm whilst under very heavy machine gun fire. Moyney was the last over, crossing under very intense bombing and machine gun fire. Corporal Fitzgerald's post was not heard of again. Patrick Hilley died on 7th November 1918 (Glasgow (St Kentigern's) Roman Catholic Cemetery, Lanarkshire – VII 289).

Seeing troops dashing towards them, the front line posts initially thought this was an enemy attack and sent up SOS rockets, which accounts for the rockets seen

on the left at 4.30 a.m. By good fortune this fire covered Moyney's withdrawal and also caught the enemy preparing for the 6.00 a.m. attack. Heavy casualties were inflicted as a result, but it could just as easily have ended in disaster.

A survivor of the platoon later explained why Moyney had taken such a draconian stance on opening the iron rations. *Twas a bad mix up first to last. We ought never to have been that side the dam' river at that time at all. Twas not fit for it yet.... And why did Moyney not let the men break into their ration? Because in a tight place if you do one thing against orders ye'll do anything. An' 'twas a dam' tight place that that Moyney man walked them out of.* Whatever his reasoning, it worked; for four days Moyney kept his head and by determination, endurance and skill brought his men back unscathed.

Later that day the Battalion was relieved. Having marched out of the line, Moyney's platoon celebrated their deliverance with a round of beer.

Chapter Five

Battle of the Menin Road

20th September 1917

257 2Lt Hugh Colvin, 9th Cheshire (58th Brigade, 19th Division), Northeast of Hollebeke, Belgium

258 Sgt William Burman, 16th Rifle Brigade (117th Brigade, 39th Division), East of Klein Zillebeke, Belgium

259 Cpl Ernest Egerton, 16th Nottinghamshire and Derbyshire (117th Brigade, 39th Division), East of Klein Zillebeke, Belgium

260 2Lt Montagu Moore, 15th Hampshire (122nd Brigade, 41st Division), West of Gheluvelt, Belgium

261 2Lt Frederick Birks, 6th Battalion AIF (2nd Australian Brigade, 1st Australian Division), Glencorse Wood, northwest of Westhoek, Belgium

262 Pte Reginald Inwood, 10th Battalion AIF (3rd Australian Brigade, 1st Australian Division), Polygon Wood, southwest of Zonnebeke, Belgium

263 Capt Henry Reynolds, 12th Royal Scots (27th Brigade, 9th Division), Frezenberg, Belgium

264 LCpl William Hewitt, 2nd South African Infantry (South African Brigade, 9th Division), Northwest of Zonnebeke, Belgium

265 Sgt Alfred Knight, 2/8th London (174th Brigade, 58th Division), Northeast of St Julien, Belgium

Following the Battle of Langemarck on 16th August, the next major British effort was the Battle of the Menin Road on 20th September. Although the French mutinies were dying out, Pétain was not optimistic about the offensive capabilities of his forces. In the east the Russians were collapsing and little could be expected from the Americans until well into 1918. The onus therefore remained on the British to maintain pressure on the enemy.

Haig reasoned that if the Germans were worn down in Flanders they would reduce support to their allies, who would collapse. Once the rot started Germany's own collapse would soon follow. Lloyd George held the opposite view; the Russians were almost finished and the French needed time to recover, so the remainder of 1917 should be a period of consolidation. He also wanted heavy artillery transferred to support the Italians. Haig maintained that withdrawing resources from Flanders would allow the Germans freedom of action. On 4th September the War Cabinet

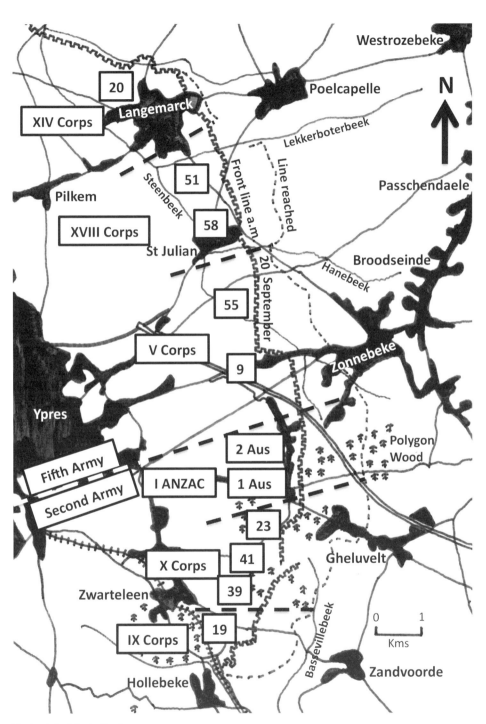

Battle of the Menin Road.

compromised by agreeing to Haig's approach, but also ordered some heavy artillery to Italy.

In the next attack Second Army was to throw its weight against the Gheluvelt plateau in a series of limited steps which, if successful, would assist Fifth Army as it struggled over the swampy land to the north. Second Army's attack was carried out by X and I ANZAC Corps, with II ANZAC Corps in reserve. IX Corps secured the southern flank, while further south VIII Corps remained on the defensive. The attack was to unfold in four steps, each separated by six days to allow the artillery to be brought forward and to absorb German counterattacks. Assault divisions had frontages of only 900m; a concentration four times that of 31st July. Reserves were kept close at hand for consolidation and to meet the inevitable counterattacks.

The number of guns was doubled and the concentration of shells quadrupled; for the first seven days alone there were 1,296 guns and 3,500,000 shells. The artillery plan concentrated upon systematic pinpointing and destruction of pillboxes. A screen of fire 900m deep, comprising five belts, was to precede the infantry; two each of heavy and field artillery and one of machine guns. Beyond this belt of fire 222 other guns were ready to neutralise enemy batteries as they opened fire. The infantry also adopted new tactics; the leading troops were to skirmish to identify centres of resistance, which were to be outflanked by follow–on troops.

The attack was to be a three–phase operation. The first objective (Green Line) was about 725m through the outpost zone. It was to be taken by one battalion per brigade, supported by a barrage lifting fifty metres every two minutes. After a halt of forty-five minutes for mopping up, a fresh battalion would continue to the second objective (Red Line), 450m beyond the first. Thereafter the barrage would slow to ninety metres every six minutes and the rate of fire halved. This was the area of the main pillbox belt. After a two hour pause for consolidation, the advance to the third objective (Blue Line), another 275m on, would be made by the remaining two battalions (in some cases only one was used). Throughout, one quarter of the troops was to be held as immediate reserves.

Artillery preparations began as early as 31st August, but the main bombardment did not commence until 13th September. Full rehearsals of the attack barrage were carried out from 15th September onwards up to three times per day to wear down the enemy, during which raids were launched. In the last few days the artillery concentrated on counter-battery work. Having lost observation over the battlefield during the August battles, the Germans made little impact on the preparations.

During September the ground dried out, although the deepest hollows and craters remained waterlogged. The move to the assault positions on 19th September commenced in sunshine. However, at midnight heavy rain fell until just before zero hour, drenching the troops as they struggled into position. The leading waves moved into no man's land and lay on white tapes within 140m of the barrage line. The troops for the second objective were to clear the front line within minutes of

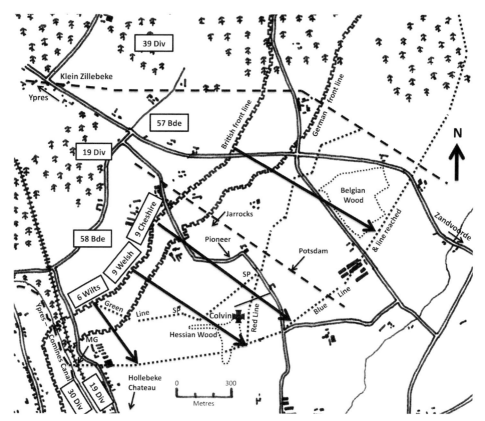

Drive through Zillebeke to the southeast towards Zwarteleen and Zandvoorde. Pass the turning to Hill 60 on the right and continue for just under a kilometre. Turn right and immediately left with a rather surprising vineyard on the right. The road swings round a number of corners. After just over a kilometre there is a sharp right bend and 250m after it a farm on the left. At the far end of the farm is a track on the right. You should be able to park here for a few minutes. Walk up the track for 225m. Hugh Colvin's VC action was to the left. The corner of the next field is where the northeast corner of Hessian Wood was in 1917.

the attack starting to avoid the counter-barrage. Those for the third objective were held back 900m to move forward two hours after zero.

The assembly was completed without incident, except in the ANZAC area, where two severe bombardments were received. The British barrage opened by hitting enemy batteries with gas shells. Zero hour at 5.40 a.m. coincided with the first traces of dawn. The fighting will be described from the southern defensive flank northwards.

In IX Corps, 19th Division advanced with two brigades (57th and 58th) on a frontage of 1,450m. On the right, 58th Brigade had three battalions in line – 6th Wiltshire on the right, 9th Welsh in the centre and 9th Cheshire on the left, with 9th Royal Welsh Fusiliers in reserve. Even though the route to the start line had been clearly marked with tape, it was extremely difficult in the near total darkness to find the way, but most of the troops reached their positions around 1.45 a.m. They then had four hours to wait, lying in the cold wet mud. In front were standing patrols to prevent

German patrols discovering the assembly. Those men detailed to go through to the final objective had yellow patches and each platoon was issued with two coloured flags. In 58th Brigade these were black and yellow diagonally. They were to be displayed from time to time in the advance to show their position to the artillery observers. 9th Welch and 9th Cheshire had engineers attached to them with charges to deal with stubborn dugouts. At the final objective 82nd Field Company RE was to construct two strongpoints in the areas held by 9th Welsh and 9th Cheshire, each reinforced by one or two Brigade machine guns. The Company was also to construct a post on the railway embankment for the machine guns attached to 6th Wiltshire.

The advance commenced as soon as the barrage fell to avoid the counter-barrage. A smoke barrage masked off Zandvoorde Ridge. 58th Brigade came under fire from the railway embankment and Hollebeke Chateau on the right and the centre was checked by frontal fire from Hessian Wood. 6th Wiltshire reached the Red Line on time, which coincided there with the final objective, but 9th Welsh and 9th Cheshire were held up with heavy casualties and lost touch with flanking units and the barrage.

9th Cheshire's advance was well covered initially by smoke and mist, which screened enemy fire from Zandvoorde Hill. The Battalion overcame strongpoints at Jarrocks Farm and Pioneer House and the intermediate position was carried relatively easily. Although casualties were light they included two company commanders and so **2nd Lieutenant Hugh Colvin** (D Company) found himself in command of D and C Companies. As they consolidated on the Red Line prior to the next move forward, enemy fire intensified; but despite this 9th Cheshire made up the lost ground and established contact on the flanks. However, in the centre 9th Welsh was held up by machine gun fire from the northern corner of Hessian Wood.

From the end of the track mentioned in the map caption. Hugh Colvin led the two D Company platoons from right to left across the picture into Hessian Wood, which stood in the field beyond the fence in the centre. The northern tip of Hessian Wood is marked by a few bushes on the left side of the field. On the right skyline is the church in Hollebeke.

The move forward to the final objective commenced at 6.44 a.m. Colvin led his companies forward with great dash. Potsdam Farm on the left fell after a furious struggle but on the right machine guns in Hessian Wood continued to hold up 9th Welsh and threatened the success of the whole operation. Colvin became aware of this predicament and detached two platoons to reinforce C Company, which was held up by snipers. He led the other two D Company platoons in a flanking attack through the northeast corner of Hessian Wood.

Colvin approached the nearest strongpoint with only two men, who covered him from the top as he went in. He came out with fourteen prisoners and then went to the next strongpoint, which was manned by machine gunners, riflemen and bombers. This position was the main cause of the delay in the centre. He gained the top of the post and it too surrendered after a few of the garrison had been killed. Colvin's tiny party was then set upon by about fifteen Germans emerging from a nearby dugout. One of his companions was killed and the other wounded, but he grabbed a German rifle, shot five of the enemy and took a sixth prisoner, using him as a human shield to force the rest to surrender. Colvin went on, assisted by only one man, to clear a number of other dugouts, taking fifty prisoners in all. The way was open for 9th Welsh to sweep on to its final objective, where it joined 9th Cheshire at the northern edge of Hessian Wood. Contact was also established with 6th Wiltshire at the southwest corner.

Colvin returned to D Company to consolidate the position, which he did with great skill. He personally wired his front after others had been killed in the attempt, all the time under close range sniper fire. He was completely buried by shellfire and his clothing and equipment were hit by bullets several times. The complete success of the attack in this area was entirely due to his efforts. On the left, 57th Brigade lost the barrage whilst struggling through deep mud in front of Belgian Wood, but by 8.10 a.m. its objectives had been taken, albeit with heavy losses.

The main Second Army attack was led by five divisions. From south to north these were 39th, 41st and 23rd Divisions in X Corps and 1st and 2nd Australian

Divisions in I ANZAC Corps. In effect these five divisions had the same frontage as three divisions on 31st July. The effect of the artillery in this area was devastating and although many pillboxes outwardly appeared intact their occupants were often too stupefied to offer resistance. The mist also greatly assisted the attackers in closing with them quickly.

39th Division, on the right of X Corps, continued the southern flank guard northwards. The attack was made by 117th Brigade, with the advance to the first objective (Red Line) being led by 16th Rifle Brigade on the left and 17th Sherwood Foresters on the right. Assembly was not completed until 5 a.m. due to the rain, darkness and some shelling of the duckboard approach tracks. One of the battalions was also delayed by using the wrong track.

At zero the assault battalions set off in perfect order into the fog on compass bearings. The initial German artillery response generally fell ineffectually behind

Drive south into Zillebeke from Ypres. At the t-junction in Zillebeke turn left and follow the priority road round to the right. After 100m turn left, signed for Maple Copse Cemetery. After 1,800m turn right at a farm on the corner. Go on another 800m through Lower Star Post (LSP) and enter the Cutting. As you emerge from the other end there is a small grassy area on the left suitable to stop for a few minutes. Opposite is the gate to a house (Kattebos). Look along Forest Road to the east. Just beyond the house gate the road is ditched, banked and hedged on the right. This is where William Burman, CSM Bean and the lance corporal cleared the forty Germans enfilading 16th Sherwood Foresters. Bulgar Wood can be seen beyond the road bank. Walk east along the road for seventy meters and turn right into a wide footpath heading south. Look along it to the tip of the wood. Just to the right is a slight rise in the ground, beyond which was the strongpoint at Welbeck Grange. Ernest Egerton attacked it from this side, i.e. the north. The Wood does not extend as far west as it did in 1917, when Welbeck Grange was on the edge of it rather than in the open today.

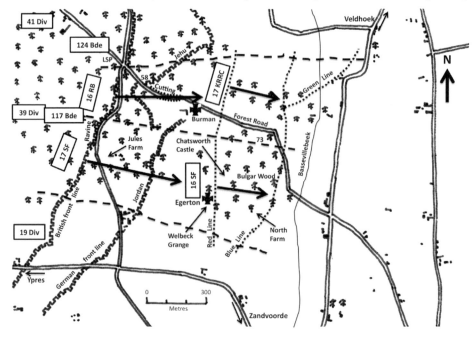

the attacking troops, except on the right where it came down just thirty seconds after zero. 16th and 17th Sherwood Foresters suffered casualties as a result. Enemy machine guns were active across the Brigade front from the outset.

16th Rifle Brigade attacked with D (right) and B (left) Companies leading, each with three of its four platoons in line. C and A Companies followed in support on the right and left respectively. At zero hour the troops set off into thick fog and the left became involved immediately in fighting for a strongpoint near Lower Star Post. The position was overcome after being bombarded with rifle and phosphorus grenades and trench mortars, but in doing so it had to be outflanked and many casualties were suffered from flanking machine gun fire. The Battalion then turned its attention to the strongpoint at Point 58 in the sunken road leading to the Cutting. This was taken and many casualties were inflicted on the Germans as they fell back towards the Red Line. A and C Companies, advancing behind the leading companies, came under heavy fire from the left flank and a party was sent across the divisional boundary to deal with it as 10th Queens (124th Brigade, 41st Division) was still some way behind.

By then B Company on the left had lost about seventy-five men and all its officers. It was under heavy fire from a strongpoint just over the divisional boundary in Jehu Trench and was unable to reach the Red Line. This was due to 124th Brigade (41st Division) on the left being well behind the barrage. B Company was forced to throw back its left to cover this open flank. In complete contrast, on the right, D Company took the Red Line eighteen minutes after zero. German snipers used incendiary bullets, which set the clothes of some men alight; the only solution was to roll them in mud to extinguish the flames before their wounds could be dealt with.

C Company, in support on the right, was held up by a machine gun firing at point blank range. **Sergeant William Burman** shouted to the men near him to wait and went on himself to what appeared to be certain death. He reached the post, killed the gunner and two others and carried the machine gun on to the Company's objective. There he put it into use against its previous owners. His action assured the success of that part of the attack.

About fifteen minutes later, OC C Company noticed that the left of 16th Sherwood Foresters was held up at Bulgar Wood by about forty Germans lying along Forest Road. He sent a party to clear them. Burman, 7001 CSM HW Bean and a lance corporal ran forward and got behind the enemy. They killed six, wounded two others and captured a further thirty-one. CSM Bean, a South African War veteran, was awarded the DCM for this action.

At 7.30 a.m., two battalions of enemy were seen massing for a counterattack and were broken up by the SOS barrage. The Battalion then settled down to consolidate its position on the Red Line. Fifty-eight prisoners, four machine guns and a trench mortar had been taken, but the attack cost 16th Rifle Brigade 208 casualties. During the night the Battalion was withdrawn into support in the Ravine and the Cutting while 1/6th Cheshire took over the left of the Brigade front.

This is the section of Forest Road cleared by William Burman, CSM Bean and the lance corporal. Bulgar Wood is in the background.

On the right of 117th Brigade, 17th Sherwood Foresters encountered enemy shell-hole posts between Jules Farm and Bulgar Wood as well as snipers in Jordan Trench. This opposition was overcome by the Lewis gunners. The next resistance came from the northwest of Bulgar Wood and Welbeck Grange. Despite this, the centre company advanced well and was able to support the flanking companies in reaching the Red Line.

At 7 a.m. the advance to the Blue Line was continued by the support battalions. 16th Sherwood Foresters was on the right, with 17th King's Royal Rifle Corps on the left. 16th Sherwood Foresters assembled in the Ravine behind 17th Sherwood Foresters. As soon as the leading battalions advanced, 16th Sherwood Foresters followed to avoid the enemy counter-bombardment. Although serious casualties were avoided, a Lewis gun team was lost in the centre. In the thick mist, A Company lost direction and drifted left. B Company conformed to the movement, but the error was discovered and corrected while 17th Sherwood Foresters was consolidating the Red Line.

16th Sherwood Foresters was raked by machine guns on the left from Point 73 and from dugouts to the south throughout its advance to the Red Line, but the fog reduced the effectiveness of this fire. Keeping close to the barrage, 16th Sherwood Foresters advanced from the Red Line. At first it surprised the enemy in their dugouts, but as the advance swept on through Bulgar Wood the fog began to clear. It was discovered that dugouts at Welbeck Grange had not been cleared and sniper and machine gun fire was received from the rear. C Company was detailed to sort out the mess. Covering fire was provided by a Vickers machine gun from 57th Brigade Machine Gun Company on the right and a party, led by **Corporal Ernest Egerton**, dashed forward to take the dugouts from the north. Egerton was spurred on by recent news of his brother's death in action. Despite the heavy

From Forest Road looking south, with Bulgar Wood on the left. Welbeck Grange was just beyond the slight rise to the right of the edge of the wood.

fire he was soon well ahead of his comrades. He shot a rifleman, a bomber and a gunner and single handedly took a machine gun post. C Company caught up and completed the capture of the position, taking twenty-nine prisoners and a machine gun. Egerton's action resolved a very difficult situation in a matter of seconds. The advance continued despite opposition from North Farm, which was overcome.

Two Lewis guns were set up on the left edge of the wood and enfiladed the enemy holding up 17th King's Royal Rifle Corps on the left flank. The Germans immediately went to ground and when two rifle grenades were fired into them they bolted. Many were cut down by the Lewis guns and thirty-three prisoners were taken. The advance then moved on quickly to the Blue Line, where several more prisoners were taken. The Battalion was well ahead of both flanking units.

A and B Companies came under heavy machine gun fire from a concrete strongpoint sixty-five metres in front of the Blue Line. The firefight was won by machine guns and rifle grenades and one German gun was put out of action. At this the Germans abandoned their other machine gun and got into the dugout; thirty prisoners, two machine guns and a trench mortar were taken. Lewis guns were established on the strongpoint to command the Bassevillebeek. Chatsworth Castle was taken around this time, along with thirty-four prisoners. During the consolidation phase severe casualties were inflicted on the enemy as they attempted to run away. In view of the heavy casualties sustained by the Battalion, two Lewis guns and a company of 17th Sherwood Foresters moved up into close support.

Reverse view of the previous picture, taken from the south on the Ypres – Zandvoorde road looking north. Bulgar Wood is on the right and Welbeck Grange was just to the left of the edge of the wood.

At 5.38 p.m. a strong counterattack was seen massing and was repulsed by murderous artillery and machine gun fire. At 6.55 p.m. the enemy massed again but were once more dispersed by the SOS barrage and machine guns. After that it was a quiet night, except for intermittent shelling and machine gun fire. The Battalion gained thirty-one other gallantry awards in addition to Egerton's VC.

While the right made steady progress, on the left 17th King's Royal Rifle Corps' left and centre were seriously delayed in reaching the Blue Line by the failure of 41st Division to keep up. A strongpoint was seized in Jehu Trench, but at heavy cost. The Battalion was forced to establish a defensive flank to await 41st Division. A company of 1/6th Cheshire was sent up to support this flank at 7.40 a.m. By the time 17th King's Royal Rifle Corps reached the Blue Line, casualties were so severe that two companies were commanded by corporals. The left flank continued to be held back to comply with 124th Brigade's (41st Division) failure to cross the Bassevillebeek to the north. Despite this, a strongpoint in the Green Line was taken. A second company of 1/6th Cheshire was sent up.

A renewed attack by 41st Division in the afternoon was to be supported by the two 1/6th Cheshire companies against the Green Line. At the same time 17th King's Royal Rifle Corps was to concentrate on clearing up the Blue Line and establishing contact with 41st Division along it. At 6.30 p.m. the attack appeared to have succeeded in taking the objective, but it soon became clear that 41st Division had failed to advance further than the Bassevillebeek. A 1/6th Cheshire company had seized the Green Line in its area, but was isolated and compelled to withdraw. 41st Division tried again at 9.30 a.m. next morning without success.

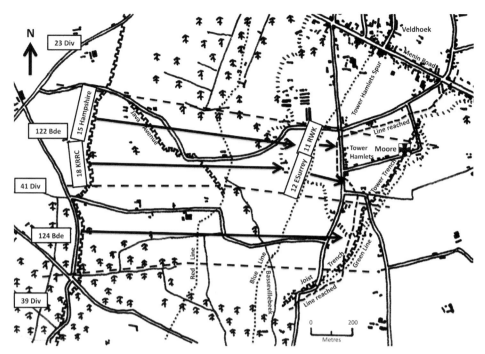

Drive east from Ypres along the Menin Road (N8). Pass the 18th Division memorial on the right and continue for 1,700m. Turn right into Waterstraat, opposite a shrine on the left. Continue south for 500m to a crossroads. Turn left and after 350m turn right. Continue 125m and stop. This is where Tower Trench crossed the road, running southwest to northeast. Montagu Moore held Tower Trench in the fields on the right of the road.

117th Brigade was relieved by 118th Brigade on 21st September. It had captured 376 prisoners, twenty-four machine guns and two trench mortars. However, its losses had been thirty-two officers and 770 other ranks, of whom about 120 were known to have been killed.

41st Division faced the difficult crossing of the Bassevillebeek valley and then the Tower Hamlets Spur, whereas the other assault divisions were already on high ground. The Red and Blue Lines, west and east of the Bassevillebeek respectively, were to be captured by the leading battalions in each of the two assault brigades. Then the reserve battalions were to continue the advance to the Green Line (Tower Trench on Tower Hamlets Spur). The attack was made by 124th Brigade on the right and 122nd Brigade on the left. In 122nd Brigade, 15th Hampshire (left) and 18th King's Royal Rifle Corps (right) were to lead to the Blue Line, where 11th Royal West Kent (left) and 12th East Surrey (right) were to pass through and continue the advance to the Green Line.

Despite the dreadful conditions caused by the rain, the assembly was carried out uneventfully, although the Brigade Major had to redirect 12th East Surrey after it deployed too far to the left. 124th Brigade's attack began promptly at zero, but stiff resistance was encountered from the outset from machine guns hidden in the Bassevillebeek valley. The barrage was lost in the confusion, but the stream

Looking across the Bassevillebeek valley along the axis of advance of 15th Hampshire towards Tower Hamlets, the high ground in the centre distance.

was crossed and the men advanced up the eastern slopes of the valley. Here the fire intensified and the advance was checked, the main opposition coming from a quadrilateral area of ninety metres by 365m at the southern tip of the spur.

In 122nd Brigade, 15th Hampshire was held up at Java Avenue by pillboxes missed by the barrage. All four of the company commanders were hit, as well as many of the men. The resistance was eventually overcome with the assistance of 11th Royal West Kent, following on behind for the advance to the Green Line. The Red Line was secured and the Blue Line was also reached after pushing on over the swampy depression of the Bassevillebeek. Consolidation commenced immediately and a counterattack threatening from northeast of the Menin Road was dispersed by small arms fire. The reserve battalions continued the advance up the Tower Hamlets Spur to the Green Line. Despite flanking fire from the right, where 124th Brigade's attack had failed, Tower Trench was reached. However, in the face of the curtain of fire from the flank it could not be held and the attackers fell back to the Blue Line.

Late in the afternoon, 15th Hampshire and 11th Royal West Kent were ordered to take the Green Line. 11th Royal West Kent was still disorganised from the attack in the morning and only 150 men from 15th Hampshire could be found for the attack. Amongst them was **2nd Lieutenant Montagu Moore**, leading a party of seventy men. Although met by heavy machine gun fire from a flank, Moore reached the objective with a sergeant and four others. Undaunted, he bombed a large dugout and took twenty-eight prisoners (only eight according to a letter he wrote later), a light field gun and two machine guns. Some of the defenders surrendered too late and were shot out of hand. Eventually about sixty men arrived and contact was made for a time with 23rd Division to the north, but they failed to locate the survivors of 11th Royal West Kent from the morning attack. 123rd Brigade in reserve attacked three times on the right, but could not come up on Moore's flank and he was totally isolated. However, he set about consolidating the position and several counterattacks were repulsed during the night. All this was achieved without artillery support, since it was not known where the surviving attackers were.

Looking northeast. Tower Trench ran from the camera position through the prominent tree in the centre foreground towards the bushy topped tree just to the right of it in the background. This is the section defended by Montagu Moore until he was forced to abandon it and pull back.

Next morning at about 10 a.m. the British artillery fell on the Green Line to support an attack by 123rd Brigade, which managed to cross the Bassevillebeek but failed to reach the objective. This was again due to fire from 124th Brigade's area to the south. Moore was now the senior officer in the Green Line. He demonstrated great resourcefulness by withdrawing his men a short distance during the bombardment and rushing back to the trench again when it ended. When the enemy attacked at 3.30 p.m. he put up an SOS flare and the British barrage fell on his position. This was extremely uncomfortable, but it succeeded in driving off the enemy, who then attacked the Blue Line from the southeast. This move was halted by small arms fire

Reverse of the previous view. Tower Trench ran from this position through the tree in the centre distance.

and a German carrying a flamethrower was seen to burst into flames. The artillery on both sides bombarded this position again at 6.30 p.m.

By the early morning of the 22nd Moore had only ten men left, all armed with German weapons. At 4 a.m. another British barrage fell on his position and he was forced to pull back at 7 a.m., having arranged for the wounded to be removed. Reluctantly abandoning the captured field gun and machine guns, he withdrew under cover of thick mist to the Blue Line. All the survivors with Moore were decorated; 6225 Sergeant Henry George Gannon received the DCM and the rest MMs. Another twenty-four decorations were awarded to the Battalion for this action. It was relieved at 11 a.m., having suffered 349 casualties since the attack commenced on the 20th.

Further north, 23rd Division encountered strong resistance all the way to the final objective, which was taken. Counterattacks in the evening were driven off mainly by the artillery.

Drive east along the Menin Road (N8) from Ypres. Pass Hooge Crater Cemetery on the right and Bellewaerde Park on the left. The road bends to the right and after 200m turn left into Oude Kortrijkstraat. Continue for just over 700m to a crossroads. The turning on the left is the sunken road. Look north from the crossroads. Frederick Birks' VC action was to the left of the sunken road, just behind the fence and about where the building now stands. There are a couple of café/restaurants along Oude Kortrijkstraat.

Continue along Oude Kortrijkstraat over the A19 to Black Watch Corner (BWC) and turn left, keeping Polygon Wood on the right. Continue to the next junction, with the restaurant on the corner, and turn right still keeping Polygon Wood on the right. After just over a kilometre is a car park on the left. Walk back from it and cross the road to gain the top of the Butte in Polygon Wood and the 5th Australian Division memorial. Look southwest over Buttes New British Cemetery and the New Zealand Memorial to the Missing to the site of Reginald Inwood's VC action beyond.

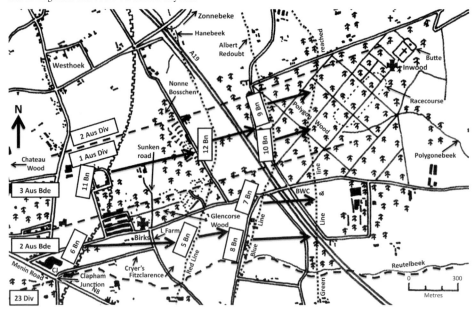

I ANZAC Corps attacked with 1st and 2nd Australian Divisions on a frontage of about 1,800m north of the Menin Road. This area had been occupied and lost twice in August. 1st Australian Division was to seize the main ridge and 2nd Australian Division the appropriately named Anzac Spur. The narrow frontage made assembly difficult and some roads in flanking corps' areas had to be used. Four tracks, one per assault brigade, were also constructed to facilitate the move forward to the start positions.

In 1st Australian Division, 2nd Australian Brigade was on the right and 3rd Australian Brigade was on the left. Each followed the pattern elsewhere of one battalion each for the first and second objectives and two battalions for the final objective. In 2nd Australian Brigade, 6th Battalion was assigned the Red Line, 5th Battalion the Blue Line and 7th (left) and 8th (right) Battalions the Green Line. Similarly, in 3rd Australian Brigade, 11th Battalion was assigned the Red Line, 12th Battalion the Blue Line and 9th (left) and 10th (right) Battalions the Green Line.

As the final stages of the assembly were being completed in 1st Australian Division, the German artillery opened fire. Elements of 2nd Australian Brigade were hit by an enemy barrage at 5.20 a.m. at Clapham Junction. Just twenty-five minutes before the attack started, the Germans attempted a flammenwerfer attack at Cryer's Farm. Sergeant HA Flatman, commanding a 1st Battalion covering post there, managed to hold off the attack and destroyed the flammenwerfer, but a machine gun was set up less than fifteen metres away. Flatman alerted Lieutenant RFH Green of 6th Battalion, who with Lance Corporal Knight bombed it into silence and returned to their unit to prepare for the attack. Had they not removed this post the machine gun would have been able to fire into the right flank of the advancing Australians.

In 3rd Australian Brigade, 11th Battalion formed up in no man's land in front of Glencorse Wood, seventy metres in advance of the front line. By so doing it escaped an enemy barrage on the front line at 4.30 a.m. with few casualties. In support, 12th Battalion moved forward and to the left to avoid this barrage. Coming up behind was 3rd Australian Machine Gun Company and 9th and 10th Battalions. As they arrived at Chateau Wood they were caught by the enemy barrage and suffered heavy losses. The two rear companies of 10th Battalion were thrown into confusion, but sorted themselves out and continued moving forward. Counter-battery fire eased the enemy fire by 5.15 a.m., but it started again at 5.20 a.m.

At 5.40 a.m., when the attack started, the troops were keen to get on through the enemy barrage quickly. The rear lines pressed forward and caught up with the leading lines, making a dense crowd. Fortunately the barrage had stupefied the German survivors and most pillboxes were captured quickly, often with little resistance. There were some stiff fights, but by and large the advance went according to the timetable. On reaching each objective every field gun involved in the creeping barrage fired one smoke shell as a signal to the infantry. Reports on the effectiveness of this measure vary. Some say it was effective, while others say the smoke needed to be more distinctive to differentiate it from the other smoke and dust created by the barrage.

The debris of Glencorse Wood was expected to cause delays to 2nd Australian Brigade, but when the assault commenced it proved little impediment. 6th Battalion advanced with A Company on the right and D Company on the left, supported by C and B Companies respectively. Two or three pillboxes on the southern edge of the Wood offered some resistance, but were quickly surrounded and surrendered. A machine gun in one checked 6th Battalion's advance. **Lieutenant Frederick Birks MM** and Corporal W Johnston (Lance Corporal King in the Battalion war diary, but Johnston in every other account) rushed the pillbox and were met with a shower of bombs. Johnston was badly wounded, but Birks continued and reached the rear of the pillbox. He killed the machine gun crew with a bomb and captured the gun.

Shortly afterwards there was some resistance from posts on the line of the sunken road running north from L Farm through Glencorse Wood. These were dealt with and a number of Germans were bayoneted in the skirmish. On the right, at Fitzclarence Farm, there was a short fight; but while some men fired on the pillbox loopholes, others worked round the rear and forty Germans surrendered. At about the same time Birks led a small party in attacking a series of dugouts held by about twenty-five Germans along the edge of Glencorse Wood. They killed ten and captured the other fifteen. On the left, Lance Corporal King and a small party bombed four or five dugouts, captured some prisoners and shot a number of those retreating. Lieutenant McLachlan's party secured two dugouts at the eastern end of the position, killing or capturing twelve Germans.

The Red Line was reached by 6th Battalion on time and mopping-up and consolidation proceeded immediately. It was noted that one 18 Pounder field gun was firing short in the advance to the Red Line. Despite reports being sent back, it continued to do so throughout the operation, resulting in some casualties.

In 3rd Australian Brigade, 11th Battalion had a fierce fight in the sunken road north of Glencorse Wood. A light machine gun on the roof of a pillbox swept

The crossroads on Oude Kortrijkstraat, with the sunken road leading into Glencorse Wood on the right. Frederick Birks' VC action was to the left of the sunken road, in the trees behind the road sign.

the advancing troops and held them up. As a result the supporting 10th Battalion closed up and became intermingled. It had been specially trained for this action and organised into two storm companies and two of carriers. The CO of the 10th, Lieutenant Colonel Wilder-Neligan, saw the hold up and sent Lieutenant GH Leaver with one of the storm platoons to get round the pillbox. Leaver was within a few metres of the machine gun when he was shot through the head. At this his men went mad. A combined party of 11th and 10th Battalion men swarmed into the road and set about the enemy. A frenzy of killing followed until only an officer and forty men remained to be taken prisoner.

The Red Line was reached between 5.57 a.m. and 6.09 a.m. along the entire ANZAC front. The troops were much intermingled and needed some time to sort themselves out. At 7.08 a.m. the advance continued to the Blue Line. It was a similar story to the first advance; the Germans were generally stupefied and surrendered. Some resistance from machine gun posts was overcome quickly. Between 7.30 a.m. and 7.45 a.m. the Blue Line was reached. The strongly defended neck of the plateau between the Bassevillebeek and the Hanebeek, that had defied the August attacks, had fallen. While consolidation progressed, pillboxes in front opened fire and were overcome by local initiatives, including one at Black Watch Corner in the Wilhelm Line and Garter Point to the north in 2nd Australian Division's area, which was almost on the final objective. Even after this there was still considerable sniping to contend with while digging-in. Some of the fire came from the Butte in Polygon Wood, which overlooked most of the ANZAC area.

A two-hour pause followed before the final advance. Some thought it too long but, despite a relatively easy advance, some units were glad of the break to reorganise. At the same time the heavy machine guns and trench mortars were brought forward and positioned to meet the expected German counterattacks. On arriving at the Blue Line 10th Battalion discovered that there was an unoccupied gap 175m long on the right and the support and mopping up companies were pushed forward to fill the void, assisted by two platoons of 7th Battalion on the flank.

In the advance to the Green Line in 3rd Australian Brigade, 10th Battalion was on the right with 9th Battalion on the left. At 9.53 a.m. the final short advance commenced. Some of the pillboxes ahead of the Blue Line had already been captured and were therefore in the line of the advancing barrage. The artillery in front of Polygon Wood was falling short and at Black Watch Corner the advanced troops had to dash back to avoid it. Despite a few challenges, in general the final advance took just a few minutes and at Garter Point it was a matter of simply handing over to the fresh troops as they arrived. By 10.14 a.m. the advance was completed except where the troops were held back by their own barrage. As soon as the artillery lifted the final advance was made without difficulty. In a few places pillboxes in advance of the final line had to be seized to avoid their fire during consolidation. The final objective was held by three lines of posts with strongpoints at specified locations

Looking southwest from the top of the Butte in Polygon Wood over Buttes New British Cemetery and the New Zealand Memorial into the wood where Reginald Inwood captured the strongpoint.

behind. By nightfall the Blue and Green Lines had been dug to 5′6″ deep and wire put out in front.

There were reports of enemy forces moving forward and movement was seen, but nothing happened and at 1.48 p.m. the barrage ended. From 2 p.m. onwards further movement was seen and the artillery was called for at intervals, but no coordinated counterattacks took place. German barrages were largely ineffective, as they seemed uncertain where the forward Australian troops were. It was intended to bring up the

Reverse of the previous view looking northeast out of Polygon Wood towards the Butte and the 5th Australian Division memorial. Reginald Inwood's VC action was in this area.

reserve brigades to take over the Red Line, but the forward area was already crowded and Lieutenant General Birdwood, commanding I ANZAC Corps, countermanded this. The forward troops were thinned out and the lines of posts were linked into continuous trenches. Further German activity developed soon after 7 p.m., but was stopped by the artillery before it could develop.

The night was quiet and strong patrols were pushed forward into Polygon Wood. In one patrol **Lance Corporal Reginald Inwood** in 10th Battalion went forward alone 550m through the barrage and found some Germans in shelters near the Butte. He captured the strongpoint, killing several Germans and taking nine prisoners. Early the next morning, with a soldier of 7th Battalion, he again went forward and bombed a machine gun crew, killing all but one, who he made bring back the gun.

At dawn on 21st September (4.30 a.m.) the barrage and machine gun fire came down as arranged until 5.39 a.m. and swept forward 1,800m to discourage any planned German counterattack. Before dawn RFC aircraft had flown low over the lines and machine gunned the German forward positions. New posts were pushed out ahead of the Green Line in Polygon Wood and the Reutelbeek valley. German aircraft tried to harass the forward troops with little effect, but German shelling was more accurate. One shell hit a post held by D Company, 6th Battalion in the Red Line, killing Lieutenant Birks and four other ranks and wounding two others. Birks was trying to dig out some soldiers who had been buried by a previous shell. There was heavy artillery action by both sides, but no counterattacks occurred and by 8.15 p.m. the shelling ceased. That night the assault troops were relieved by 1st and 6th Australian Brigades. Losses in 1st Australian Division amounted to 2,754, including 258 in 6th Battalion and 223 in 10th Battalion.

Next along to the north, 2nd Australian Division attacked with 5th and 7th Australian Brigades astride the Westhoek–Zonnebeke road. Opposition at the first objective was overcome quickly. Thereafter resistance stiffened; but the assault was determined and many Germans surrendered without firing a shot. On reaching the top of Anzac Spur the attackers came under heavy fire from Albert and Iron Cross Redoubts in the Wilhelm Line. They were smothered by smoke grenades and the garrisons fled under Lewis gun fire. The two-story Anzac House pillbox was overcome as two machine guns were being moved out into open positions.

Fifth Army's V and XVIII Corps each attacked with two divisions, while XIV Corps formed the northern defensive flank. V Corps had the hardest task. Its final objective, 1,100m away, had twice been attacked unsuccessfully in the August battles. Pillboxes and fortified farms were intact and special parties were organised to take and hold each one as the advance progressed. The assault divisions had frontages twice as long as in Second Army and the artillery support was spread more thinly; three belts of artillery fire instead of four elsewhere. In this area there were only two objectives. 27th Brigade refers to them as the Red Dotted and Green Lines. However, the South African Brigade appears to have inserted its own intermediate objective, the Yellow Line, between the Red Dotted and Green Lines.

On the right, 9th Division faced the crossing of the flooded Hanebeek valley. Two brigades, 27th on the right and the South African on the left, went into the attack, each with two battalions leading. Here the creeping barrage consisted of HE and smoke, rather than shrapnel. This allowed lanes to be left for company groups to infiltrate behind the enemy positions, so that when the barrage lifted they could

From Ypres travel northeast towards Zonnebeke on the N37, the former railway line. Go over the A19 and take the first left. After 100m there is a small lay-by on the right. Park there and look right towards Zonnebeke and the site of the Potsdam group of pillboxes (P P P). 12th Royal Scots advanced parallel with the N37 from 100m in front of this road.

There is no access to the area where Hewitt won his VC. The best view can be obtained from the north on Hill 37. Drive out of Zonnebeke to the northwest towards St Julien. Just before Dochy Farm Cemetery on the left, turn left and follow this road for 600m to the start of a gravel track leading to a farm on the left. Pull over here and look south towards the massive Steenbakkerij building on the other side of the Zonnebeek. Hewitt won his VC on the rough ground between the stream and the factory where Zevenkote used to stand.

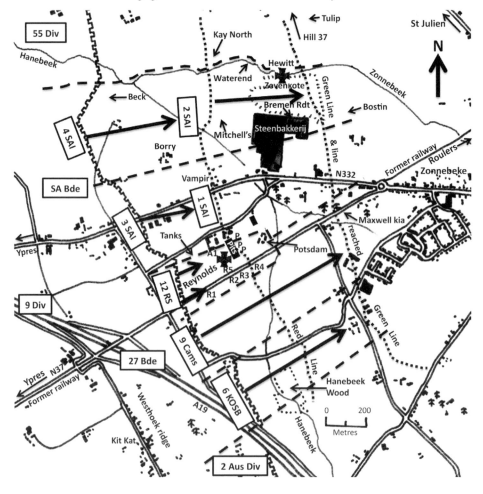

be attacked from front and rear simultaneously. Moppers-up were trained to deal with pillboxes in which the garrisons had locked themselves in and could not be dealt with immediately. They carried shovels with which to blind the defenders by throwing up earth banks in front of the loopholes.

27th Brigade was led by 6th King's Own Scottish Borderers on the right, 9th Cameronians in the centre and two companies of 12th Royal Scots on the left. The remainder of 12th Royal Scots was the Brigade reserve on the left. 11th Royal Scots was the Brigade reserve on the right. The forming up positions on the forward slope of Westhoek Ridge were laid out with string on the night of 18th/19th September and the following night the string was replaced with white tape. Two tracks were allocated for the four battalions to reach their forming up positions. Despite these being well marked with tape and lamps, it proved a difficult task to get into position on time, but it was achieved with only a few casualties from enemy artillery fire. Five minutes before zero the German artillery fired a barrage on Kit Kat ridge, but little damage was caused further forward.

6th King's Own Scottish Borderers successfully infiltrated Hanebeek Wood and captured the pillboxes, together with fifty prisoners and four machine guns. 9th Cameronians had mixed fortunes. The right swept forward almost without a check, but the left struggled against heavy machine gun fire from the R1 pillbox on the railway and other machine guns about 150m southeast of it. However, both battalions gained the final objective successfully. Consolidation consisted of establishing a line of shell hole posts and then connecting these into short lengths of trench, covered by advanced posts of Lewis gun teams.

12th Royal Scots' task was to take a series of pillboxes around the railway line, after which it would take no further part in the attack. The pillboxes were the R group (R1–R5), A1 and the Potsdam group. R1–R4 were grouped south of the railway, with R1, the closest, being 180m from the front line. R5 was on the north side, 275m beyond the front line, flanked by A1; and 230m beyond it was the fortified Potsdam Farm.

C Company on the right, detailed to take R1–R5, advanced with 9, 10 and 11 Platoons south of the railway and 12 Platoon to the north. 11 Platoon was checked by fire from R1 as it approached from the south. As the barrage lifted the Germans behind R1 threw grenades onto the railway, which stopped 9 Platoon from rushing straight along the line. 12 Platoon tried to rush the pillbox, but was stopped by a machine gun slightly behind the pillbox. While 10 Platoon went to reinforce 12 Platoon, the CO sent two platoons of D Company to attack from the south. This distracted the Germans sufficiently to allow 10 and 12 Platoons on the railway to rush in and overcome the garrison of about forty. Three machine guns were also taken. A machine gun on top of the railway was put out of action when the gunner was sniped. The remainder of the R group had either been destroyed by shellfire or they were flooded and there was little further resistance. C Company arrived soon after at the Red Line.

Looking along the axis of 12th Royal Scots' advance. The start line was about 100m into this field. Potsdam is behind the large glasshouse left of centre and Zonnebeke church is right of centre. The tree lined former railway line (N37) is on the right.

A Company on the left, commanded by **Captain Henry Reynolds**, was detailed to capture the Pits at A1 and the Potsdam group. The attack was made in two lines of section columns close behind the barrage. The defenders of A1 poured forth very heavy fire. It looked at one point as if the defenders had been subdued, but when the attackers approached the pillbox it burst into life again. They went to ground and only Reynolds' intervention averted a panic. Having settled the Company, he and six men dodged from shell-hole to shell-hole and reached the base of the pillbox where they were out of the line of fire. Reynolds attempted to throw a bomb through a weapon slit, but the Germans blocked the gap with a pack and carried on firing. Reynolds' own account says he threw five grenades. The enemy reacted violently and every weapon in the area was turned upon him. Taking cover he again wriggled forward and forced a rifle smoke grenade (No.27) past the pack, which set fire to the interior, killing three of the garrison and forcing the remaining seven to surrender

From the site of R1 on the former railway line looking north across the ground over which 12th Royal Scots advanced.

with two machine guns. Although he was not hit, Reynolds' tunic, belt and pack were shredded by near misses.

Reynolds hastily reformed his men and continued the attack towards the three pillboxes at Potsdam, where two machine guns were in action; one mounted just north of the pillboxes and the other between the two northern pillboxes. The creeping barrage here halted on the Pits for six minutes and then lifted 135m beyond onto the Potsdam position. This was to allow time for the frontal attack platoons to go in through a gap in the barrage between the railway and the Pits to attack from the rear. Beforehand the Pits were bombarded by 4.5″ Howitzers for twenty minutes, which then switched to Potsdam.

Reynolds led A Company in the attack. One platoon and half a South African platoon worked round the north while another platoon moved round from the south. The remaining two platoons attacked frontally. They got to within seventy-five metres when the barrage lifted, but just as they were about to mount the final rush, the barrage came down again and the defenders re-opened fire. As the barrage died away Reynolds and his men charged, shot the gunners and the other defenders could not resist the converging attack from three sides. Seventy Germans were accounted for, killed or taken prisoner, together with two machine guns.

By 9.40 a.m., 12th Royal Scots Battalion HQ was established in R1 with A Company at Potsdam, B Company at the Pits, C Company in railway dugouts and D Company on the line of the Hannebeek. It became the left support battalion in the new position and minor changes were made to the dispositions overnight. Early on 21st September the commander of 27th Brigade, Brigadier General Francis Maxwell VC CSI DSO, on a tour of his positions with his Brigade Major, was shot dead by a sniper (Ypres Reservoir Cemetery – I 37). The Brigade was relieved on the night of 22nd/23rd September by 9th Brigade, 3rd Division. Casualties for 19th–22nd September were 739, including one hundred known dead.

The South African Brigade was led by 3rd South African Infantry on the right and 4th South African Infantry on the left, supported by 1st and 2nd South African Infantry respectively. The support battalions were to seize the second and third objectives. In reserve was 5th Cameron Highlanders, attached from 26th Brigade. 7th Seaforth Highlanders, also 26th Brigade, was added during the operation. Moving into the forming up positions was particularly difficult in this marshy area and was restricted to duckboard tracks, but it was achieved on time, mainly due to thorough reconnaissance and clear signs and tapes.

4th South African Infantry took Beck House and Borry Farm and by 6.30 a.m. was on the first objective. A party continued beyond the objective through the barrage to seize Mitchell's Farm, killing most of the garrison. A machine gun across the stream at Kay North was causing trouble, so a platoon crossed and seized the position, together with twenty prisoners.

3rd South African Infantry's left took Vampir Farm and reached the objective, but the right was held up by delays in 27th Brigade. The ground was swept by machine gun fire from Potsdam and casualties were heavy. The CO of 1st South African Infantry, Lieutenant Colonel Heal, believed 27th Brigade had fallen back and ordered Captain Sprenger of 3rd South African Infantry to collect whatever men he could find of both battalions and capture Potsdam. Two Lewis guns and a Vickers machine gun provided covering fire and at 6.55 a.m. Sprenger's party advanced by rushes from shell-hole to shell-hole against Potsdam from the northwest and west. The Germans began to bolt towards the railway and after fifteen minutes the position was taken, with up to thirty prisoners and seven machine guns. After another fifteen minutes a subaltern leading a party of 12th Royal Scots arrived and took over the position. This version of the taking of Potsdam is somewhat at variance with that of 27th Brigade's.

The South African Brigade had previously arranged to send half a platoon along the north bank of the railway after Potsdam had been taken to maintain contact. This party moved forward at zero and close to Potsdam came under heavy machine gun fire. With no other troops nearby, they pulled back to some derelict tanks and then turned southeast and reached the railway. They found some men of 1st South African Infantry who had lost their way and a single Royal Scot clearing a small dugout on the south side. They killed four Germans there and continued along the railway to bomb a large dugout on the south side. Twenty Germans surrendered and others escaped along the railway.

Ten minutes before the advance resumed to the second objective, Sergeant Frohbus of 1st South African Infantry led a combined party of both battalions against a large concrete shelter. Up to forty medics surrendered, but others inside refused to come out. A grenade set the inside alight and thirty men tried to escape, but were all shot down.

At 7 a.m. the support battalions passed through and continued the advance to the second objective. 1st South African Infantry on the right was on the second objective quickly. 2nd South African Infantry on the left had a harder task. It attacked with three companies in line – D on the right, C in the centre and B on the left. A Company in support had a platoon behind each of D and B Companies and the other two behind C Company.

Mitchell's Farm had already been taken by 4th South African Infantry, but fire was being poured in from the left flank from Waterend Farm, Tulip Cottages and Hill 37 in 55th Division's area. The barrage at Mitchell's Farm lasted longer than anticipated and held up C Company in the centre but, despite this, the right and centre companies reached their objectives by 8.30 a.m. On the left, the left of B Company was halted, but the right moved ahead and then turned north. Bremen Redoubt, Zevenkote and Waterend Farm were captured, together with seventy prisoners and three machine guns. Even with the second objective secured, the situation on the left was still of concern. 55th Division was held up in front of Hill 37, leaving an exposed left flank for 2nd South African Infantry. In addition, B Company was not in contact with C Company in the centre. The CO, Major Cochran, sent up seventeen men to reinforce B Company while C Company extended to the left and turned its left flank back to connect with B Company. Cochran established contact

From Hill 37 looking south to the Steenbakkerij, the large building on the other side of the Zonnebeek, which runs across the middle of the picture in the low ground. William Hewitt's VC action was just beyond the stream in front of the building.

with 55th Division and set up a defensive flank from Kay North to a point 175m north of Bremen Redoubt. He was knocked down and was thought to be killed, but rose unhurt and continued. A platoon of 5th Cameron Highlanders was also sent up to reinforce the left flank. It was not until the late afternoon that 55th Division took Hill 37 and thus allowed B Company to advance to the final objective.

The night before the attack **Lance Corporal William Hewitt** was in the party laying out the start line tapes for 2nd South African Infantry. He then rushed back to guide his company into position. Soon after the attack started a small pillbox surrendered and the occupants made their way to the rear without escorts. However, a larger pillbox beyond was holding up the advance. The platoon commander, Lieutenant Walsh, sent his runner to fetch Hewitt. Walsh explained the situation to Hewitt and ordered him to take it. Returning to the large shell hole where his section was sheltering, he discovered it had been hit by a shell. Only Private Ziess was capable of carrying on. Undaunted, Hewitt made for the pillbox and discovered a low doorway on the right side. He threw in a grenade and shouted for the occupants to come out.

As they came out two Germans fired at him from point blank range, but missed. Another threw a stick grenade, which blew off his gasmask, tore much of his clothing, smashed four of his teeth, broke his nose and gave him two black eyes. The blast threw him back into a shell hole, but he was not seriously injured. Undeterred and understandably angered by the situation, he picked himself up and moved to where he could see a loophole. He threw a grenade at it, which missed and he narrowly escaped further serious injury when it exploded close by. He crawled forward and dropped his final grenade through the loophole, but was shot through the hand. He heard the grenade explode and moved back to the doorway. As he rushed down the steps, he was confronted by an escaping German with his hands up but, remembering his last encounter, he bayoneted the soldier. As he struggled to withdraw the bayonet he was grabbed from behind, but fought himself clear before losing consciousness. When he regained his senses he was leaning against a Cameron Highlander officer and saw three Germans with their hands up. A British sergeant coming out of the pillbox told him there were fifteen dead inside.

Hewitt retrieved his helmet and rejoined his company, but soon after was sent for medical assistance. On the way he relieved a private escorting forty-eight prisoners, but struggled to keep up with them as they were very keen to get away from the German barrage. Having handed over the prisoners, he realised that he was at his Battalion's old HQ where he had delivered some jars of rum a few days before. He explained this to a Cameron Highlander officer who told a corporal to get some rum for Hewitt. Having downed a full mug of rum and not having eaten since midday the previous day, he believed he was invincible and he had to be restrained before he continuing to the rear to an aid station. As he arrived the supply of soup and tea ran out, so he relieved a prisoner of his portion of soup before being loaded onto an ambulance. He fell asleep on the floor and awoke to hear an orderly asking another man to help him remove the 'stiff'.

An enemy concentration at 9.45 a.m. near Bostin Farm was dispersed by small arms fire and the artillery. Three times during the day parties of Germans were seen working forward to reach assembly points for a counterattack. On each occasion they were checked by rifle fire and then hit by the artillery. At about 6 p.m. a large enemy counterattack force was seen approaching, but the SOS barrage, which lasted for forty minutes, destroyed it completely. By nightfall all objectives had been taken and consolidated.

It was customary in the South African Brigade HQ for every man who arrived there during a battle to be given a cup of tea with a dash of rum. On the night of 21st September alone the cook and waiter served 690 cups of tea using a single teapot and eight cups. The South African Brigade was relieved early on 22nd September, having suffered 1,258 casualties, including sixty-one killed in 2nd South African Infantry, which also had 224 other casualties.

On the left of V Corps, 55th Division had a terrible ordeal. The troops were hit by the enemy before the attack began and then ran into heavy small arms fire as they picked their way forward. In the mist a number of strongpoints were missed and the supporting troops were checked. The barrage was lost and then the mist lifted to aid the defenders. While the rest of the Corps swept on to the final objective, 55th Division struggled towards its first with little artillery support. Not until the whole of the reserve was committed were Hills 35 and 37 taken and touch gained with the South Africans on the right at 5 p.m. However, the left and centre were 450m short of the objective.

XVIII Corps' assault divisions, 58th on the right and 51st on the left, had difficulty assembling east of the Steenbeek between Langemarck and St Julien due to the appalling ground conditions. 58th Division had an advance of 900m to the strongpoints on the western extremity of the Gravenstafel spur. On the right 173rd Brigade was to take the Winnipeg crossroads. Its attack was led by 2/4th London. With the experience of two previous unsuccessful frontal attacks, it was decided that the main attack by 174th Brigade on the left would be a left flanking movement. The objective was Langemarck ridge between Wurst and Quebec Farms. The attack was to be made by three battalions; 2/8th London was to make the initial assault to the first objective and then 2/5th London would pass through to the second. 2/6th London was to take the final objective. In this area the three objectives were named the Dotted Blue, Brown and Blue Lines. 2/7th London in reserve was to counter any enemy attempts to counterattack. 2/8th London was allocated a section of four tanks from 15 Company, E Battalion and 2/6th London a section of three tanks from 13 Company. Sixteen bridges were laid across the Steenbeek in the Brigade's area.

2/8th London had a frontage of 730m, but only seventeen officers and 433 men with which to make the attack on the Dotted Blue Line. The CO decided to concentrate on taking the strongpoints, reasoning that when these fell the ground between would also fall. All four companies attacked in line, each with two platoons

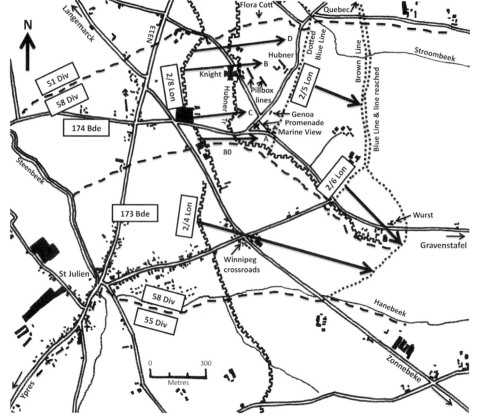

From Zonnebeke drive northwest towards St Julien, passing Dochy Farm Cemetery on the left. Keep going for 2,800m and turn right just before the large glasshouses. Drive east for 400m and turn left at the windmill (Promenade) and 100m beyond turn left into Keerzelaarstraat. You can usually pull over here for a few minutes. Look northwest along Keerzelaarstraat to the houses on the right. This is where B Company crossed the road from left to right and captured Hubner Trench just beyond it. Look right towards Hubner Farm. The lines of pillboxes were in the field between Hubner and the houses.

leading. Each company was preceded by two sections of skirmishers. D Company on the left was to advance to the north of Hubner Farm, while the strongpoints on the Wurst Farm Ridge were allocated to the other companies. B Company in the centre left was allocated Hubner Farm and a group of ten pillboxes in front of it. C Company in the centre right was to capture the Promenade (windmill) and Genoa Farm while A Company on the right tackled Marine View. The move forward to the start positions was difficult, with the single duckboard crossing over the Steenbeek under constant fire. However, although the Battalion was ninety minutes late reaching the start line, only one casualty was sustained en route.

When the attack commenced the state of the ground made for slow progress, but the leading troops kept within thirty metres of the creeping barrage and accepted a few inevitable casualties from it. The first opposition was encountered just under one hundred metres before Hubner Trench. Heavy small arms fire was received mainly from the left flank. The enemy posts were rushed with great determination

Looking northeast from Promenade over the ground crossed by B, C and A Companies, 2/8th London.

and many defenders were bayoneted. Some posts were engaged with rifle grenades and Lewis guns while other parties worked round and took them from the rear. Hubner Trench was hardly recognisable, but a few posts survived and caused problems, particularly the Promenade and Point 80. There was a check at the northern pillbox of the Promenade, but the garrison of about fifty surrendered as soon as they realised they had been outflanked. A chain of fortified shell-holes at Point 80 was rushed by an officer and three men. The advance continued and the pillboxes behind Hubner Trench were mopped up without great difficulty.

A Company on the right took its objectives within forty-five minutes, but with heavy casualties from flanking fire from Genoa Farm. One platoon was wiped out save for five men. C Company lost all its officers but slogged on. One hundred metres from the Promenade it was hit by all manner of fire, including liquid fire bombs, but the opposition was overcome and Genoa Farm was captured with the assistance of covering fire from A Company.

B Company took Hubner Trench with little difficulty, but thereafter the enemy in numerous shell-holes had to be dealt with individually. In places the troops got to within ten metres of the barrage to overcome the dogged resistance of these isolated posts. The advance continued and the Company detached a Lewis gun to provide covering fire for C Company's attack on Genoa Farm. Two groups of pillboxes were taken and by 6.10 a.m. B Company had secured all its objectives.

Sergeant Alfred Knight commanded 6 Platoon (B Company) and the remnants of others in the attack. Early on his platoon came under heavy machine gun fire while attacking a strongpoint. Knight rushed through the British barrage, bayoneted the gunner and captured the position single-handed. A little later twelve Germans were encountered in a shell-hole. He again rushed forward on his own, bayoneted two of them and shot a third, while the rest fled. Knight had to interrupt the advance at one point, due to members of 51st Division straying across the left boundary, causing him to pull one party back before pressing on. Reinforced by Company

HQ and the Battalion reserve he advanced on the pillboxes on the left and took them, adding more prisoners to the bag. Finally he assisted in the attack on Hubner Farm. Noticing that D Company was held up close to the Farm he collected some men and took up a position on the flank to bring down supporting fire. He became stuck in mud up to his waist at the same time as he saw a large number of Germans firing on his troops. He immediately opened fire, without trying to extricate himself first, and killed six of them. All platoon officers in B Company were casualties and Knight took command while tirelessly organising the consolidation. Throughout the fighting his single handed actions prevented numerous casualties and were instrumental in securing the objectives. Although not wounded, his kit was hit several times. He had a hole in his helmet, part of a book in his pack was shot away and his cigarette case deflected a bullet under his armpit.

D Company secured Hubner Trench and pushed on to Hubner Farm, but sustained heavy casualties from Flora Cott on the left. Resistance at Hubner Farm reduced the platoon allocated to take it to a corporal and four soldiers with a Lewis gun. They engaged the entrances to the farm while B Company on the right also opened Lewis gun fire. Under cover of this fire four soldiers of 9th Royal Scots who had strayed across the boundary and five men from 2/5th London worked around the rear from the left flank. As soon as they were surrounded the garrison of between seventy and one hundred surrendered. Inside were two MOs, eight stretcher-bearers and thirty wounded Germans. Around the Farm were many dead.

The Battalion swept on to its objective by 6.30 a.m. and a strong chain of posts was established on the line Marine View–Genoa–Hubner–Flora Cott. The tanks had been of little assistance due to the slippery ground. Four machine guns were brought forward to strengthen the new line, two each at Marine View and Hubner Farm. Although the attack was a resounding success, it was not achieved without heavy loss. 2/8th London suffered 247 casualties (57% of those taking part) by the time it was relieved early on 23rd September. It took at least 185 prisoners and fifteen machine guns and also killed a large number of the enemy. In addition to Knight's VC, the Battalion received another thirty-nine gallantry awards.

The two rear battalions passed through and swung half right up the rise of the spur. They were well supported by the barrage and smoke shells mixed with the mist to screen the enemy fire. Keeping to the high ground, they took several strongpoints on the spur in reverse. Once a pillbox was outflanked it was as good as captured. Each had a section or platoon allocated to it. 2/5th London suffered numerous casualties, particularly officers, before reaching the Dotted Blue Line and the rifle companies had only one officer left. In the advance the right met some opposition in Dimple Trench, but the centre and left met little opposition in reaching the Brown Line. 2/6th London took over and reached its objective on the Blue Line beyond Wurst Farm on time, having encountered little serious opposition. Outposts were pushed out to the left divisional boundary. 2/7th London deployed two companies at Hubner and Stroppe Farms in case of counterattack.

At 2.30 p.m. groups of enemy were seen advancing from the direction of Winchester and Albatross farms towards the Brigade's left front. They were broken up by small arms fire. About 5.30 p.m. an enemy force of about 2,000 was seen massing for an attack. About 6 p.m. the enemy force was engaged by the machine guns when 1,400m away. At 600m the riflemen joined in, but only when the enemy was 140m away did the artillery open fire. The effect was devastating. An observer commented, *The effect of this was beyond description; can make no estimates of enemy losses as dust precluded good observation, but he stampeded.* 174th Brigade was relieved by 3 a.m. on 23rd September, having suffered 798 casualties.

In 51st Division, 154th Brigade, which had swept on to the final objective by 8.25 a.m., became involved in the enemy counterattack at 5.30 p.m. On the left the defenders ran out of ammunition and fell back. They rallied at Pheasant Trench and went forward again, regaining as far as the first objective, but were 550m short of the original gain. This was the only successful enemy counterattack all day.

The northern defensive flank was to be secured by 20th Division of XIV Corps, but only the left battalion of the left brigade reached the final objective. The right flank of the right brigade made some progress but the inner battalions in both brigades failed to overrun Eagle Trench, which did not fall until early on 23rd September.

Although not realised immediately, particularly at home, the attack on 20th September 1917, with a few minor exceptions, had been a great success. The new tactics had proved a match for the German defence and the majority of the Gheluvelt plateau had fallen. Significantly, the troops were pleased with their performance.

25th/26th September 1917

266 LCpl John Hamilton, 1/9th Highland Light Infantry (100th Brigade, 33rd Division), Veldhoek, north of the Menin Road, Belgium

Following the success of the first step of the Menin Road operations on 20th September, Haig issued instructions for the second step to be made across the Gheluvelt plateau. The main part of this attack was to be carried out by I ANZAC Corps, while the right flank was secured by two divisions of X Corps (33rd and 39th) and the left flank by elements of Fifth Army. Zero was set for dawn on 26th September.

On the right of X Corps, 39th Division side slipped from the south to relieve 41st Division south of the Menin Road, while on the left 33rd Division came up from reserve to relieve 23rd Division north of the Road. During the night of 24th/25th September, while the assault brigades of 33rd Division concentrated for the attack between the southwest corner of Polygon Wood and the Menin Road, the rest of the Division completed taking over from 23rd Division. During the relief and move

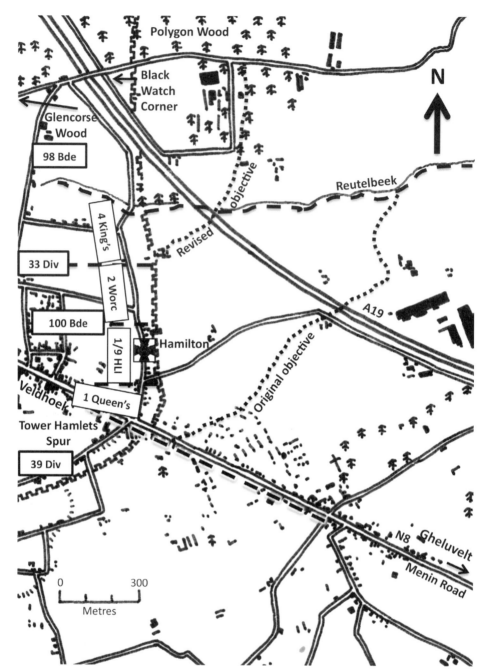

Drive east from Ypres on the Menin Road (N8) towards Gheluvelt. Pass the 18th Division memorial at Clapham Junction on the right and continue 2.2 kilometres, then turn left into Polygonestraat and pull over where it is safe to park. Walk north along this road to the junction with Poezelhoekstraat on the right. This was 1/9th Highland Light Infantry's right boundary. From here northwards the front line was to the right of Polygonestraat and the support line to the left. John Hamilton was active all over this area and crossed the road numerous times to keep the front line supplied with ammunition.

into battle positions there was a great deal of enemy artillery activity, resulting in many casualties.

33rd Division's attack was to be led by 98th Brigade (less one battalion) on the left and 100th Brigade (reinforced by a 98th Brigade battalion) on the right. 100th Brigade's front rested on the Menin Road on the right and the Reutelbeek on the left. Its front line battalions from right to left were 1st Queen's, 1/9th Highland Light Infantry, 2nd Worcestershire and 4th King's (98th Brigade). 16th King's Royal Rifle Corps was in reserve. The front consisted of hastily constructed trenches with no wire in front. The enemy still held Tower Hamlets ridge and the continuation of the Veldhoek spur south of the Menin Road.

At 5.15 a.m. on the 25th the Germans opened an intense HE, gas and shrapnel bombardment against the front of 33rd Division, which paralysed the British and made it impossible to move troops behind the lines. SOS signals sent up from the front line could not be seen by the British artillery through the thick mist and telephone cables to the rear were cut by the shellfire. The British artillery eventually replied with a tremendous counter-bombardment, but it did not deter the Germans from hurling a strong force (wildly overestimated at six divisions in some sources, in reality the majority of 50th Reserve Division) against 33rd Division's front at 5.30 a.m.

The German attack was arranged hurriedly and many shells fell amongst their own troops, but they rushed forward, supported by numerous flame-throwers and many aircraft. Desperate fighting ensued. On 100th Brigade's right, the posts held by 1st Queen's were overwhelmed and the Battalion was forced back 175m. 1/9th Highland Light Infantry's A and D Companies managed to hold the attackers at first and covered across to the right to assist 1st Queen's. At the same time the remnants of 2nd Worcestershire, badly battered by the bombardment, moved forward from Inverness Copse to fill the gap that had opened between the left of 1/9th Highland Light Infantry and 4th King's. As a result no ground was lost on the left of the Brigade front.

At 9 a.m. 1st Queen's launched a counterattack and regained its support line. About the same time 1/9th Highland Light Infantry counterattacked and recovered part of its lost ground. Rapid rifle and Lewis gun fire from the battalions on the right, together with the concentrated fire of the Brigade Machine Gun Company, caused horrific casualties to the Germans. 2nd Worcestershire sent one of its companies to form a flank on the right and this helped to relieve pressure on 1/9th Highland Light Infantry.

On the left, in 98th Brigade, 1st Middlesex fell back 550m, except for one company that held its position. This left 4th King's left flank in the air, but it was secure. The only serious casualties were suffered in the reserve company, which lost heavily in the shelling. 2nd Argyll & Sutherland Highlanders went up to reinforce the line and established a new front during the afternoon from Black Watch Corner southwards.

On 1/9th Highland Light Infantry's front the fighting swayed back and forth and in several places the enemy broke through the Battalion. Elements of B and C Companies in support were pushed forward to plug the gaps. From 12.30 p.m., when the German barrage resumed its former intensity, there was a major problem keeping the front line supplied with ammunition. The supply was only maintained by a few heroic individuals. At one time the Battalion HQ personnel had to secure rations and water from Jackdaw Dump. Communication by runner was the only viable means of passing messages and this was fraught with danger and delay.

On a number of occasions when ammunition supplies were dangerously low, **Lance Corporal John Hamilton** in B Company acted on his own initiative by carrying ammunition bandoliers from the support to the front line through the enemy barrage. He moved along the front line distributing ammunition in full view of enemy snipers and machine gunners firing at very close range. When supplies ran low again he scavenged from the dead and badly wounded to keep the defenders supplied.

By the end of the morning the line had been pushed back 360m. As a result, 33rd Division's part in the 26th September offensive had to be curtailed to allow for the losses. 98th Brigade was to cover I ANZAC Corps' right flank; while in 100th Brigade, 4th King's was to gain the Red Line, while the other battalions regained the ground lost on the 25th.

A company of 16th King's Royal Rifle Corps was sent forward to reinforce 2nd Worcestershire and later in the afternoon another reserve company was sent to 1st Queen's, which was preparing to counterattack to retake its former front line. During the night 98th Brigade made up some lost ground. 1st Cameronians

Looking north along Polygonestraat from 1/9th Highland Light Infantry's right boundary.

was made available to 100th Brigade and one company reinforced 4th King's for the attack on the 26th and another was sent to assist 1st Queen's. The other two companies formed a reserve for 100th Brigade. The last uncommitted company of 16th King's Royal Rifle Corps was sent to reinforce 1/9th Highland Light Infantry.

Zero hour on 26th September was at 5.50 a.m. 1st Queen's, with two companies of 16th King's Royal Rifle Corps, advanced to recover its original front line and got within fifty metres of it by 7 a.m. It was held there by a strongpoint holding out between the left flank and 1/9th Highland Light Infantry. Nevertheless, by 9.10 a.m., 1st Queen's reported success and contact was established with both flanking units. However, 1/9th Highland Light Infantry's right flank was still thrown back and portions of its original front line were still held by the Germans.

At 2.30 p.m. the Germans attempted to get around the left of 1st Queen's, between it and 1/9th Highland Light Infantry. However, this move was seen and coincided with 1/9th Highland Light Infantry completing arrangements for its own attack. About seventy Germans left their trench to attack 1st Queen's flank and were met by two platoons of 1/9th Highland Light Infantry. The Germans turned and fled, but passed the right flank of 2nd Worcestershire, where two Lewis guns had been positioned. Only four of the seventy are reported to have escaped. The 1/9th Highland Light Infantry platoons continued and recovered another portion of the lost front line. Then only one pillbox on the Menin Road remained in enemy hands. At 4 p.m. an attack was launched against the pillbox by a 1st Cameronians party reinforcing 1st Queen's. It was taken at bayonet point and twenty-nine prisoners were taken, as well as many Germans being killed in the assault. The Germans launched another major attack at 5 p.m. However, the SOS barrage came down almost as soon as the German artillery commenced and the infantry assault came to nothing.

On the left of 100th Brigade, 4th King's advance was delayed because it was pointless to extend forwards when there was no support on the left flank. 100th Brigade had been caught by a heavy German barrage around Glencorse Wood at 4.45 a.m. as it assembled and could not set off at zero hour as planned. At 2.20 p.m., 98th Brigade reported that 5th Cameronians had gone forward and was in contact with the Australians on the left. 4th King's was ordered to push forward one company to the northeast across the Reutelbeek to gain touch with 5th Cameronians. By nightfall contact had not been established. At 11 p.m. it was reported that 4th Suffolk and 2nd Royal Welsh Fusiliers were on the Red Line and 5th Cameronians was trying to gain touch with 4th King's. By 9.30 a.m. on 27th September contact had been made between 4th King's and 2nd Royal Welsh Fusiliers. Due to the state of the ground it was not possible to consolidate on the intended objective and the new line was a little short of it.

By the time 100th Brigade was relieved it had sustained 1,517 casualties, including those in attached units. Of these, 386 were suffered by 1/9th Highland Light Infantry.

Chapter Six

Battle of Polygon Wood

26th–28th September 1917

267 Pte Patrick Bugden, 31st Battalion AIF (8th Australian Brigade, 5th Australian Division), Polygon Wood, Zonnebeke, Belgium

268 Sgt John Dwyer, 4th Company, Machine Gun Corps AIF (4th Australian Brigade, 4th Australian Division), Zonnebeke, Belgium

269 Lt Col Philip Bent, 9th Leicestershire (110th Brigade, 21st Division), Near Reutel, east of Polygon Wood, Belgium

Following the success of the first step of the Menin Road operations on 20th September, Haig issued instructions for the second step to be made across the Gheluvelt plateau. The main part of this attack was to be carried out by I ANZAC Corps, which was to push the line forward another 1,100m, including the whole of Polygon Wood and the southern part of Zonnebeke. The right flank was to be secured by two divisions of X Corps (33rd and 39th) and the left flank by elements of Fifth Army. Zero was set for dawn (5.50 a.m.) on 26th September.

The prospects for success were good and plans were made for the rest of the campaign. Assuming the second step was a success, the third step would secure the Broodseinde sector and the fourth was aimed at the main ridge, including Passchendaele. With the right flank thus secured by Second Army, Fifth Army would be able to continue the advance north-eastwards. In case of a German collapse, all five cavalry divisions were assembled and Fourth Army on the coast was to be ready to attack across the Yser.

The artillery began moving forward on specially constructed roads as early as the afternoon of the 20th. The barrage programme and counter-battery fire followed the pattern of the first step, while the guns of VIII and IX Corps attempted to divert attention by simulating preparations for an attack against Zandvoorde to the south. During the artillery preparation, which included practice barrages at least once per day, the assault divisions moved up and took over their sectors.

South of the Menin Road, 39th Division failed to complete the capture of Tower Hamlets Spur, mainly because of fire from the Quadrilateral, which had thwarted 41st Division on 20th September. 116th Brigade on the left did capture Tower Hamlets by 6.30 a.m., but 118th Brigade on the right lost the barrage and was delayed while crossing the morass of the Bassevillebeek valley. The Quadrilateral

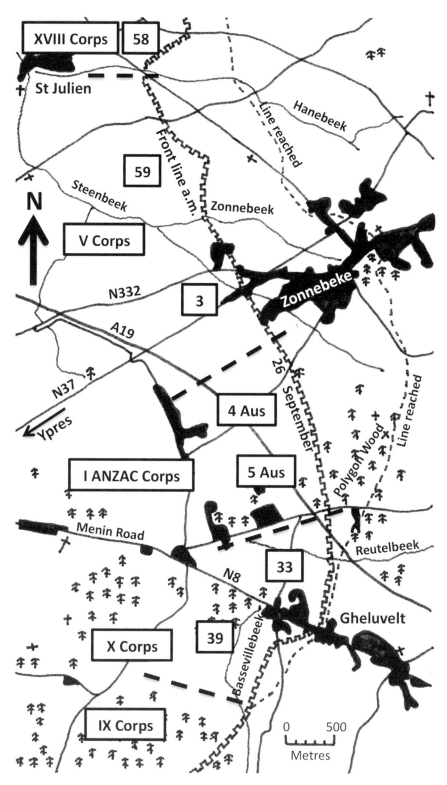

The Battle of Polygon Wood.

was entered, but before consolidation could commence the assault troops were swept by machine guns at close range from the south and southeast and were then counterattacked. They fell back into the ravine to the west and established a new line there.

In 33rd Division two battalions of 98th Brigade (1/4th Suffolk and 5/6th Cameronians attached from 19th Brigade) were detailed to attack to protect the right flank of 5th Australian Division. They had 450m to cover just to reach the start line by 5.50 a.m., where they were to pick up the remnants of the Brigade holding out at Black Watch Corner. Neither battalion had seen the ground previously, the moon had set and there was a mist. One battalion lost its way to the assembly position and the Germans shelled it at 5 a.m. The start was delayed from 5.15 a.m. to 5.30 a.m., but the German shelling strengthened into an intense barrage and the troops were forced into cover. When the British barrage opened at 5.30 a.m., it was lost and the battalions were unable to proceed beyond Black Watch Corner. They were 900m short of the objective.

On the night of 22nd/23rd September in I ANZAC Corps, 5th and 4th Australian Divisions took over from 1st and 2nd Australian Divisions. The former had been rested for four months, but the latter had been relieved at Messines three weeks before. Each Australian division had two brigades forward, each using one battalion for the first objective (Red Line) and two for the second (Blue Line).

5th Australian Division's plans had to be modified at the last minute to take account of the German attack to the south the previous day, during which 98th Brigade (33rd Division) had been pushed back. This resulted in 15th Australian Brigade on the right having to protect the long southern flank. The effect of the German attack on 33rd Division was not appreciated by the Australians at the time. In countering the German attack and maintaining the right flank, 15th Australian Brigade had used most of the troops assigned for the assault on the 26th. As a result, 29th and 31st Battalions of 8th Australian Brigade in reserve were allocated to 15th Australian Brigade for the second objective. 59th Battalion, one of the two 15th Australian Brigade battalions for the second objective, became the assault battalion for the first objective. 31st Battalion on the right was warned that the right flank where 33rd Division had been pushed back might be open. 14th Australian Brigade was on the left of the Division.

The barrage fell as planned at 5.50 a.m. on 26th September. The ground was very dry and a dense cloud of dust added to the smoke of the exploding shells. The Australians thought it resembled a bushfire and direction could only be maintained by compass. Early morning mist added to the obscuration.

15th Australian Brigade's 59th Battalion set off three minutes after the barrage commenced with a thin screen in front. 29th and 31st Battalions (A Company leading with B Company behind, followed by C Company and D Company in reserve) followed very close behind to avoid the enemy barrage. As a result units became mixed as they pressed on together in a thick line. Up to eighteen German

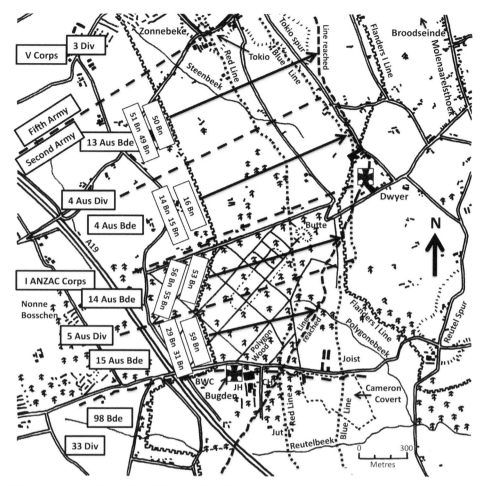

Drive east along the Menin Road (N8) from Ypres. Pass Hooge Crater Cemetery on the right and Bellewaerde Park on the left. The road bends to the right and after 200m turn left into Oude Kortrijkstraat. Continue over the A19 passing Black Watch Corner (BWC) and keeping Polygon Wood on the left. Five hundred metres after the Black Watch memorial turn right into Oude Kortrijkstraat 87-89-91-93 and after 150m pull over. Look back towards Polygon Wood. Cameron House (CH) was on the right of this track and Jerk House (JH) was on the other side of the farm buildings on the left. Bugden attacked from that direction.

Return to BWC and turn right, keeping Polygon Wood on your right. After 675m turn right at the restaurant, still with Polygon Wood on the right. Continue 1,200m to the car park at the northern end of the Wood. Dwyer's VC action was about 300m northeast of the easternmost point of the car park. It is difficult to get a closer view because buildings and trees obscure it from just about every other angle. Depending on the height of the crops it is possible to view the area from the road running northeast from this point (Spilstraat).

machine guns were firing through the barrage, but as each was identified the troops surged towards them. Notable resistance came from two pillboxes at the southwest corner of Polygon Wood and another on the 'racecourse', the driving track of the Belgian artillery school. Fire was also received from the Butte in 14th Australian Brigade's area. There was some confusion when most of 59th Battalion mistook the 'racecourse' for the final objective, but the left continued in conjunction with 14th Australian Brigade to the correct first objective some 135m further on.

Half an hour later Captain Neale noticed the mistake and he led the right of the Battalion forward at about the same time as the advance to the second objective commenced elsewhere. When the main body of 31st Battalion reached the first objective it was fired upon from Cameron House, close by on the right. Two Lewis guns were detailed to keep the strongpoint engaged. Posts were also established on the left, where contact had yet to be made with 29th Battalion.

The right company of 31st Battalion swung quarter right towards the fire coming from a group of pillboxes down the slope inside 33rd Division's area at Cameron House. The company commander was killed and Lieutenant R Thompson assumed command. A determined fight took place for each of them and **Private Patrick Budgen** led several of these attacks through heavy machine gun fire. He silenced the pillboxes with bombs and captured the garrisons at bayonet point. After gaining the objective a party on the right was ordered to retire due to 33rd Division being held up. Corporal Alf Thomson, sheltering in a shell hole, did not receive the order and continued firing on the Germans, killing two. Three Germans tumbled into his shell hole and disarmed him. A young German put his revolver to Thomson's head, but an order from an older soldier forced the young man to back off. The older German then jumped into an adjoining shell hole, where he was shot in the stomach by Bugden. Bugden charged the remaining two Germans, killing them with his bayonet. Thompson kept the identity disc of the older German who had saved his life.

A local counterattack from pillboxes beside the Polygonebeek was launched against posts of 59th and 31st Battalions on the first objective. They knocked out a Lewis gun post and captured two officers and about twenty men, fourteen of whom were wounded. The Germans were forced back to the pillboxes, from where they continued to fire. As Neale's advance reached the first objective, a party detached

Looking north along Oude Kortrijkstraat 87-89-91-93 towards Polygon Wood. The building to the right of the road is on the site of Cameron House. Jerk House was just behind the cluster of farm buildings on the left and that is the direction from which Patrick Bugden attacked.

itself and immediately rushed the German held pillboxes, working round from the south. About sixty Germans were taken prisoner. At about 9.45 a.m., 29th Battalion took over the captured post and was in contact with a portion of 31st Battalion on the right. A high priority was to ensure proper contact was made between 29th and 31st Battalions. Meanwhile the reserve company of 31st Battalion reported 33rd Division on the right appeared to be retiring. This flank was swung back and a line was organised facing south.

A company of 57th Battalion was to have safeguarded the right flank, but it was hit by the German barrage falling behind the leading troops a few minutes after zero and could not get through. 60th Battalion, holding the front line prior to the attack commencing, had to cover the flank instead. CO 31st Battalion decided not to advance from the first objective with the flank wide open. Less rationally, this decision was also taken for the 29th Battalion on the left, leaving 14th Australian Brigade's right flank open in turn. However, 29th Battalion's left company did go forward with 14th Australian Brigade. The decision to remain on the first objective did not reach the companies before the barrage moved forward and they set off towards the final objective as planned. When they had advanced about 135m the order not to attack arrived and they came back to the first objective. Part of 31st Battalion's rear company was sent back and with part of 60th Battalion formed several tiers of fire out towards Jerk House. However, the leading platoons of 31st Battalion had not received the order and went on following the barrage. The commander of 15th Australian Brigade reversed CO 31st Battalion's order and told him to get on.

The advance to the final objective coincided with a renewed attack by 98th Brigade on the right. 2nd Royal Welsh Fusiliers was sent through 15th Australian Brigade's area to attack towards Joint and Jut Farms, while a frontal assault was launched from Black Watch Corner. There was no artillery assistance because it was known that some men were holding out in the forward area. When 2nd Royal Welsh Fusiliers attacked 98th Brigade's first objective with two companies of 60th Battalion in support, 29th and 31st Battalions were ordered to attack the second objective. However, 29th Battalion was already on it.

The advance to the final objective by 31st Battalion came under fire from the right flank and rear. Ammunition was running short across the Australian front, due mainly to the destruction of a forward dump the day before. The men of the right company were eventually forced into the cover of shell-holes about one hundred metres from Jerk House. Most of the officers were casualties, including the company commander. While this company had extended almost 200m into 33rd Division's area, most of 31st Battalion continued on the correct course. By 9.45 a.m., 15th Australian Brigade had reached its intended positions in contact with 14th Australian Brigade on the left. When the barrage ended at 11.17 a.m. the position was consolidated.

Despite heavy machine gun fire, most of the ground lost by 98th Brigade the previous day was recovered but not before 2 p.m. Jerk House was abandoned by the Germans when they saw the attack forming up and it was occupied.

Over the next two days Budgen went out on five separate occasions under heavy fire to bring in wounded men. He was killed on 28th September while attempting to rescue another wounded man. The CO 31st Battalion also recommended 4000 Private WO Wilson for the VC, but the DCM was awarded instead.

14th Australian Brigade was led by 53rd Battalion to the first objective. It had caught the full weight of the German barrage on 25th September and lost 150 men in Nonne Bosschen. The ration party was gassed and many men had to break into their emergency rations and fill their water bottles from filthy shell-holes. Despite this, the Battalion was ready to move forward to the start line tapes at midnight. To ensure the attacking troops avoided the enemy barrage, all twelve waves were compressed into only 55m depth. As a result the German barrage fell harmlessly to the rear. 53rd Battalion followed the barrage closely, with 56th and 55th Battalions following for the attack on the second objective.

Pillboxes were quickly outflanked and the advance was almost unhindered in the 450m advance to the first objective. The important OP on the Butte in Polygon Wood was captured before 9 a.m. About sixty of the garrison, mainly medics, surrendered in the dugouts on the reverse side. The advance by 56th and 55th Battalions commenced at 7.30 a.m. and they hardly recognised the battered Flanders I Line as they passed over it to the second objective. Pillboxes fell easily, but there was considerable fire from the right flank until 29th Battalion in 15th Australian Brigade caught up. They were fired on from two pillboxes, but both fell, with about forty-five prisoners being taken. Both pillboxes were then abandoned as they were within the barrage line. Consolidation and preparations to meet counterattacks commenced. The Brigade had taken 200 prisoners and thirty-four machine guns. Casualties had been light.

From Spilstraat looking north. The northeastern tip of Polygon Wood is on the left, with the car park behind it and Zonnebeke church is just to the right in the background. John Dwyer's VC action was in the centre in front of the buildings. On the right Spilstraat leads to Molenaarelst on the N303 Beselare–Passchendaele road.

4th Australian Division advanced with 4th Australian Brigade on the right (16th Battalion to take the Red Line and 14th (left) and 15th (right) Battalions the Blue Line) and 13th Australian Brigade on the left. Although the Division was overlooked from the ridge at Broodseinde, it reached its objectives without any serious holdups. Crossing the source of the Steenbeek was achieved with few casualties and the new front was established along Tokio Spur. 4th Australian Brigade faced Molenaarelsthoek and 13th Australian Brigade's left was in the ruins of the southern outskirts of Zonnebeke. While the front was being consolidated harassing machine guns were fired on by 4th Australian Brigade's Stokes mortars.

4th Company Australian Machine Gun Corps established four guns in and around the Blue Line and two in the Red Line. As **Sergeant John Dwyer** reached the final objective, he rushed his gun forward to within thirty metres of a German machine gun that was enfilading troops on the right flank. He opened fire at point blank range, killed the detachment and brought back the German gun, which was put to use alongside his own. He also commanded his guns with great coolness and effect while repelling counterattacks that day and the next. Two machine guns in 4th Company were destroyed about 7.20 p.m. and requests were sent back to the Company HQ for replacements and extra men to man German machine guns, one each in the Red and Blue Lines. The Company suffered twenty-three casualties, including nine killed or died of wounds.

From noon onwards reports began to come in of German troops moving towards the attack front. The high ground of Tower Hamlets and Polygon Wood was vital to the Germans and they were prepared to take desperate measures to regain it. Artillery observers were well established on Tower Hamlets Spur and the Butte in Polygon Wood and from 1 p.m. onwards they could see the enemy columns approaching. The approaches and likely assembly areas for German counterattacks had been worked out ahead of the attack. They were bombarded heavily, resulting in severe disorganisation to the enemy formations before they deployed into battle formations. As a result the attacks that were launched were disjointed.

At 3.25 p.m. Captain Albert Jacka VC in 4th Australian Division put up the SOS signal north of Polygon Wood. The fire was so effective that the counterattack either side of the Molenaarelsthoek never materialised. At 4 p.m. waves of German infantry were seen coming over the Reutel Spur, about 900m from the fronts of 98th Brigade and 5th Australian Division. Protective artillery and machine gun barrages were put down, including gas shells. Some forward 2nd Royal Welsh Fusiliers and 31st Battalion companies were out of ammunition and fell back in good order to the Black Watch Corner support line around Jerk House and the first objective. For the most part the barrage was sufficient to break up the counterattack. Enemy aircraft flew low, firing their machine guns and were engaged. One was shot down beside the Australian trench.

Soon after 4 p.m. another force approaching 100th Brigade was so severely battered by the artillery that the few who reached the front line were dealt with by small arms fire and the bayonet. Further concentrations were reported opposite Tower Hamlets at 5 p.m., 6 p.m. and 6.40 p.m., but again the artillery and machine gun barrages prevented any counterattacks materialising. A final German effort at 6.50 p.m. across the whole front from Tower Hamlets to north of Polygon Wood was battered by the barrage and survivors were annihilated by small arms fire.

At dusk it became clear that 98th Brigade was only slightly ahead of the original line. It was arranged for patrols from 98th and 15th Australian Brigades to meet to reconnoitre 98th Brigade's first objective. They failed to make contact, but the Australian patrol from 57th Battalion found that 98th Brigade's line was at Jerk House and Cameron House on the first objective was held by Australian troops.

By 8 a.m. on 27th September, 60th Battalion had move forward against light opposition to the next spur at Cameron Covert, forward of the second objective. This was in 33rd Division's area and covered the Polygonebeek and Reutelbeek valleys. 31st Battalion moved up on the left under heavy machine gun fire. In the afternoon 2nd Royal Welsh Fusiliers came down the Reutelbeek valley in the face of heavy artillery and machine gun fire and seized the whole objective, thus finally securing this difficult and dangerous open flank. That night 30th and 32nd Battalions of 8th Australian Brigade relieved 15th Australian Brigade. Total losses in I ANZAC Corps were 5,785, including 1,729 in 4th Australian Division and 3,723 in 5th Australian Division. 31st Battalion had 430 casualties.

Brigadier General Harold 'Pompey' Elliott commanding 15th Australian Brigade was very critical of 33rd Division's performance. Although he believed many of his statements to be true, he was incorrect and at times unfair in his judgements. Lieutenant General William Birdwood, commanding I ANZAC Corps, refused to accept the report and did not include it in the official records.

The northern flank of the attack was secured by Fifth Army's V Corps and part of XVIII Corps. 3rd Division attacked with 76th Brigade on the right, in contact with 4th Australian Division. It established itself in the western outskirts of Zonnebeke. 8th Brigade on the left, north of the railway, faced the marshy Zonnebeek valley halfway to the objective. In places it was impassable and the mist caused some confusion. The barrage was lost and the Brigade was halted by machine guns near the foot of Hill 40, still 550m from its objective. At 6.30 p.m. another effort was made just as a German counterattack moved down the slope of the Broodseinde–Passchendaele Ridge. As a result of the clash no progress was made by either side. Hill 40 remained in German hands. 3rd Division suffered 3,532 casualties.

59th Division advanced steadily with 176th Brigade and 178th Brigade. The final objective was reached in contact with the barrage, having suffered few casualties. On the right of 58th Division, 175th Brigade advanced in cooperation with 59th Division. However, it lost direction in the mist and was 400m short of the objective.

From 8.30 p.m. the front was relatively quiet. The results of the second step battle were again very encouraging. Three or four German counterattack divisions had been committed to support three line holding divisions and had been very severely handled. Indeed they had been expended quicker than they could be replaced in the line. German counterattack tactics were working against them. As a result they changed tactics and decided not to commit counterattack (eingrief) divisions until the following day, when the situation in the forward area would be clearer. However, to achieve this the line holding divisions had to have sufficient strength to stop the initial surge of the assault. They were therefore reinforced with more machine guns. The line divisions were to make the initial counterattacks while the assault troops were still disorganised and had not been able to consolidate.

1st October 1917

While the British were preparing to make the third step of the operation to capture the Gheluvelt Plateau on 4th October, the Germans launched a series of spoiling attacks. Early on the morning of 30th September they attacked 70th Brigade in thick mist between the Reutelbeek and the Menin Road. The SOS signals were not seen and it was two hours before the artillery came down. In the meantime the enemy was driven back by the small arms fire of the two forward battalions. A second attack at 6 a.m. suffered the same fate.

Next morning at 5.25 a.m. a hurricane bombardment saturated the front from the Reutelbeek to Polygon Wood to a depth of 900m. It included a smoke screen on the front line. Three brigades were holding this sector; from south to north 69th (23rd Division), 110th (21st Division) and 22nd (7th Division). At 5.27 a.m. the first wave of German infantry appeared in strength, particularly in front of Polygon Wood, where 1st Royal Welsh Fusiliers, holding 22nd Brigade's front, held on stubbornly.

A 9th Leicestershire company (110th Brigade) observed German infantry advancing out of the smoke. The SOS signal was sent up and the first enemy wave was driven off. A few minutes later a second enemy wave was also driven off except on the right flank, which was forced to give ground near Joist Farm. This caused 9th Yorkshire (69th Brigade) to swing back its left flank in Cameron

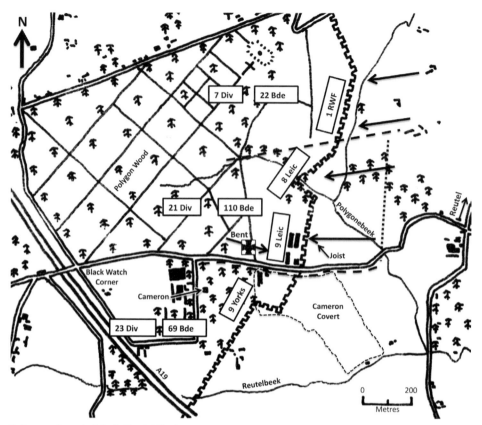

Drive east along the Menin Road (N8) from Ypres. Pass Hooge Crater Cemetery on the right and Bellewaerde Park on the left. The road bends to the right and after 200m turn left into Oude Kortrijkstraat. Continue over the A19, passing Black Watch Corner and keeping Polygon Wood on the left. Almost 800m after the Black Watch memorial pull over on the roadside at the Nicholas VC memorial. On the other side of the road is Polygone Vallei farm. Look north along the east side of the farm. This is where the British front line ran. Philip Bent led the counterattack from Polygon Wood through the farm to restore the front line in front of Joist Farm, which stood seventy-five metres east of the current buildings.

Covert. **Lieutenant Colonel Philip Bent**, CO 9th Leicestershire, realised that the situation was critical and immediate action was required to avoid a catastrophe in the confusion. He issued detailed instructions for the defence of the position. He then personally collected two platoons from D Company in reserve and with B Company in support launched a counterattack at 5.40 a.m. The original line was regained and the enemy driven out, but in the final charge Bent was killed as he reached the objective, calling out, *Come on, the Tigers*.

Although the immediate crisis had passed, the Germans continued to try to make progress on the right flank. The third wave was launched against the Battalion's front and two platoons of C Company counterattacked on the right flank. By 6.00 a.m. the enemy had been driven off, but losses meant that the line had to fall back about one hundred metres to the eastern edge of Polygon Wood. Casualties continued to mount from enemy shelling, which went on all day. C Company established a

The scene of the counterattack led by Philip Bent. He led his men out of Polygon Wood on the left, through the modern farm buildings in the centre and on to restore the front line on the right.

defensive flank in front of Cameron House, but the Germans attacked twice more in the next three hours. They were driven back to their original positions by Lewis gun and rifle fire and the new line held firm. All the ground lost in the morning was regained, except for a couple of pillboxes in Cameron Covert. Fresh enemy units assembling for further attacks were broken up by combined small arms and artillery fire.

At 9.30 a.m. reinforcements from 7th Leicestershire arrived on the right. A little later an enemy airplane was shot down over no man's land and then destroyed by the shelling. Although 7th Leicestershire took over the line, 9th Leicestershire remained until being relieved at 11.00 p.m. on 2nd October. The survivors were merged into two companies and amalgamated with 8th Leicestershire.

Chapter Seven

Battle of Broodseinde

4th October 1917

270 Pte Thomas Sage, 8th Somerset Light Infantry (63rd Brigade, 37th Division), Tower Hamlets, West of Gheluvelt, Belgium

271 Capt Clement Robertson, Royal West Surrey Regiment attached A (or 1st) Battalion Tank Corps, near Reutel, east of Polygon Wood, Belgium

272 Lt Col Lewis Evans, Black Watch attached 1st Lincolnshire (62nd Brigade, 21st Division), Near Reutel, east of Polygon Wood, Belgium

273 LCpl Walter Peeler, 3rd Pioneer Battalion AIF (3rd Australian Division), East of Ypres, Belgium

274 Sgt Lewis McGee, 40th Battalion AIF (10th Australian Brigade, 3rd Australian Division), East of Ypres, Belgium

275 Pte Arthur Hutt, 1/7th Royal Warwickshire (143rd Brigade, 48th Division), Southeast of Poelcapelle, Belgium

276 Sgt Charles Coverdale, 11th Manchester (34th Brigade, 11th Division), Poelcapelle, Belgium

277 Cpl Fred Greaves, 9th Nottinghamshire and Derbyshire (33rd Brigade, 11th Division), Poelcapelle, Belgium

278 Sgt James Ockendon, 1st Royal Dublin Fusiliers (86th Brigade, 29th Division), Northeast of Langemarck, Belgium

Taking stock after the successful attacks across the Gheluvelt Plateau on 20th and 26th September (first and second steps), Haig's HQ believed the Germans were close to breaking point. There was optimism that, if the fine weather held, the Passchendaele–Staden Ridge could be gained by the end of October. Haig believed the fourth step could lead to a breakthrough and reserve formations were moved to Flanders in readiness for rapid exploitation. However, the Army commanders believed this optimism was somewhat premature.

In the meantime preparations for the third step (Battle of Broodseinde) on 4th October continued. The main attack by Second Army involved twelve divisions in four Corps on a frontage of ten kilometres. Each assault division retained a lightly equipped brigade to follow up if the initial attack was particularly successful, and each Corps held a division in readiness to arrive within seven hours. Haig also wanted to secure the southeast of the Gheluvelt Plateau, which had held out during the second step, and 5th Division was added to X Corps for this operation. South of

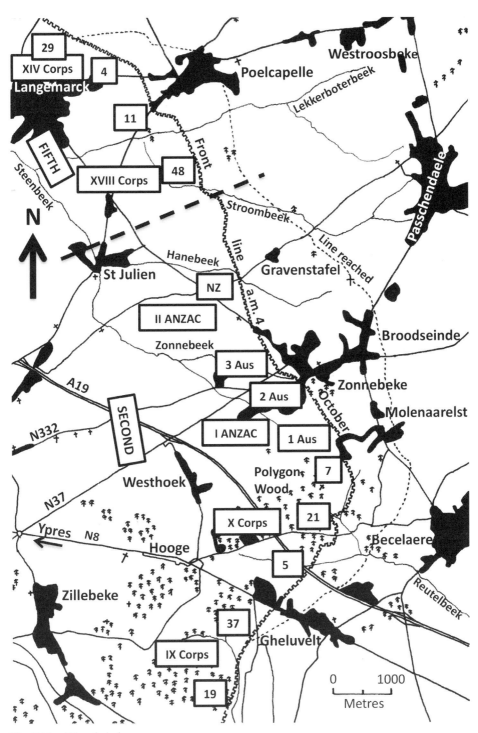

The Battle of Broodseinde.

the Menin Road, 37th Division (IX Corps) secured the southern flank. On the left, Fifth Army launched a supporting attack towards Poelcapelle with four divisions on a frontage of five kilometres.

The artillery had to move forward up to 1,400m, which entailed the construction of many new plank roads. There were no overt artillery preparations apart from normal counter-battery work, the deliberate destruction of strongpoints and a number of rehearsal bombardments. As the assault troops began moving up at dusk on 3rd October a violent storm blew up. The rain made the ground slippery, but it was not saturated at this stage and in places it was still so hard that shells skipped off it. However, the campaign had entered a new phase in which bad weather would become the norm again. By 4 a.m. on 4th October the troops were on their start line tapes.

At 5.20 a.m. the German artillery opened fire, the heaviest barrage causing many casualties in the two ANZAC Corps. At 6 a.m. the British artillery crashed down in a 900m deep belt. At the same time the infantry shook out into their attack formations and set off towards the enemy through the rain, poor visibility and strong southwesterly wind.

Second Army attacked with IX, X, I ANZAC and II ANZAC Corps. South of the Menin Road IX Corps' 37th Division faced the Tower Hamlets Spur with 63rd Brigade on the right and 111th Brigade on the left. 63rd Brigade was led by two companies of 8th Somerset Light Infantry on the right, with a company of 10th York and Lancaster in support. There were three companies of 8th Lincolnshire on the left, with two companies of 4th Middlesex in support. The remaining companies of the leading battalions were disposed in depth in the British lines.

In 8th Somerset Light Infantry's area the objective was east of the north–south road through Jute Cotts, which coincided with the German outpost line. There were no landmarks on which to fix a position and communication with the front line was only possible at night. It had been intended to have a single objective, but due to the difficulties of the ground and forward enemy positions, it was decided to have an initial objective on the high ground before continuing to the final objective. The Battalion reached the assembly positions by 5 a.m. without major incident but, as often happened, the enemy put down a heavy bombardment an hour before zero causing a number of casualties.

At 5.30 a.m. the forward posts were withdrawn and at 6 a.m. the British barrage came down. However, it was very thin and fell beyond the first objective, making it impossible for the assault troops to follow close behind. At first only the left and centre of 8th Somerset Light Infantry had to advance, since the right was already well forward. As the leading companies came over the crest they came under heavy small arms fire. The advance continued by section rushes and the Battalion reached its objective. It attempted to consolidate the position under intense machine gun fire from a strongpoint on the right front and from three machine guns in Jager Trench 400m away on the right flank. The Germans launched heavy bombing

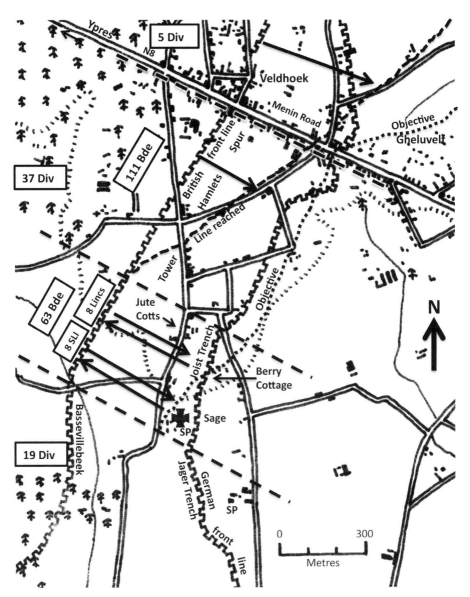

Drive east from Ypres along the Menin Road (N8). Pass the 18th Division memorial on the right and continue for 1,700m. Turn right into Waterstraat opposite a shrine on the left. Continue south for 800m and at the fork keep right on the main route. After another 250m turn right into Passendaleveldstraat and 300m later cross the Bassevillebeek. One hundred metres further on pull in at the track junction on the left and look back eastwards up the slope attacked by 8th Somerset Light Infantry. Return to the t–junction and turn right for 225m to a right bend. There is space to pull over on the left for a few minutes opposite a prominent knoll on the right. Look north along the road you have just driven along. Thomas Sage saved the lives of his comrades just beyond the first buildings on the right.

Early on a misty September morning looking southeast along the axis of advance of 8th Somerset Light Infantry. The Bassevillebeek runs across the picture in the low ground. Above it is Tower Hamlets Spur. Thomas Sage's VC action was in the area of the large clump of trees on the skyline left of centre.

counterattacks and the right company was pinned down by fire from the right and was unable to assist the other companies. Casualties mounted and a gap opened between the Battalion and 8th Lincolnshire, which Major JHM Hardyman MC filled with a Lewis gun team (Lieutenant Colonel John Hay Maitland Hardyman DSO MC was killed commanding 8th Somerset light Infantry on 24th August 1918– Bienvillers Military Cemetery – XIX F 11). Reinforcements were rushed forward, but enemy shelling and the appallingly muddy conditions in the Bassevillebeek valley prevented their arrival. Meanwhile two attempts were made to capture the strongpoint, one led by Second Lieutenant NH Crees and the second by Second Lieutenant Henry James Smith who was killed (Tyne Cot Memorial).

During one of these attacks **Private Thomas Sage** and eight others, including a captain and a sergeant, took shelter in a shell-hole. Sage was shot through the head near the right eye. Movement in any direction was almost impossible due to the close proximity of the strongpoint, but eventually they decided they had to do something. The sergeant rose to throw a bomb and was promptly shot. The grenade fell back into the shell-hole and Sage threw himself upon it to save the lives of his comrades. He was very seriously injured by at least seventeen pieces of shrapnel and his left thigh was torn to shreds, but the remaining six occupants of the shell-hole were uninjured.

Reverse of the previous view from Tower Hamlets Spur with the Bassevillebeek in the low ground on the far left. Thomas Sage's VC action was in the large clump of trees just right of centre.

Miraculously Sage was still conscious. The rest decided to make a run for it and the captain left Sage a water bottle and his revolver. From the war diary it is known that Second Lieutenant Crees brought back three survivors that night, having held out in shell-holes all day. Crees may be the 'captain' mentioned in other accounts. A little later Sage decided he must try to get away and, despite his horrific injuries, managed to drag himself back to an aid station before passing out. The Reverend Theodore Hardy (VC 1918) helped to care for him. He lost the sight of his right eye and pieces of shrapnel remained in him for the rest of his life, but in the circumstances it was a miracle that he survived at all.

8th Lincolnshire was forced back on the left around Joist Trench and Berry Cottage and 8th Somerset Light Infantry was ordered back. When the original front line was secured the CO sent in another attack against the strongpoint, but it also failed. Meanwhile the right was held against persistent bombing attacks, having been reinforced by the reserve company. By nightfall 8th Somerset Light Infantry was back on its original start line. The operation resulted in 63rd Brigade suffering 400 casualties (seventy two killed, 268 wounded and sixty missing).

On the left, 111th Brigade advanced south of the Menin Road. It suffered the same problems as 63rd Brigade, being swept by machine guns, but its left managed to keep up with 5th Division's advance north of the Menin Road.

The southern flank of X Corps was to be established between Polygon Wood and the Menin Road by 5th Division on the right and 21st Division in the centre. The attack area was crossed by the Polygonbeek and the Reutelbeek, both swollen by rain into belts of mud hundreds of metres wide. 5th Division occupied Cameron

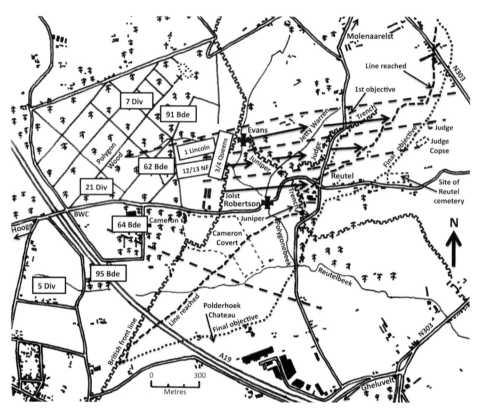

Drive east along the Menin Road (N8) from Ypres. Pass Hooge Crater Cemetery on the right and Bellewaerde Park on the left. The road bends to the right and after 200m turn left into Oude Kortrijkstraat. Continue over the A19 passing Black Watch Corner (BWC) on the right and keeping Polygon Wood on the left. When Polygon Wood runs out, continue past Polygone Vallei farm on the left and the Nicholas VC memorial on the right. Just under 200m beyond is a turning on the left into a footpath, part of a circuit around Polygon Wood. You can pull over here for a short time. Look along the Reutel road to the east to see the route taken by Clement Robertson in guiding his tanks over the Polygonbeek and up the far slope, where he was killed. Walk north along the footpath for 200m. Look north through gaps in the trees along the Polygonbeek to the slope in front of Juniper Trench where Evans cleared the pillbox. As an alternative you can walk north along the track on the eastern side of Polygon Wood. Cross the Polygonbeek and continue for 100m until clear of the trees on the right. Look right across the valley to where Juniper Trench ran into the wood on the far side. Evans' VC action was in the fields in front of the wood.

There is another more time consuming option to see the site of Lewis Evans VC action from the north. Return to your vehicle and continue east over the Polygonbeek, noting the pillbox in the field to the left on the line of Juniper Trench. On entering Reutel note the memorial to Clement Robertson and Cyril Allen on the wall of the Merlijn Restaurant. Continue to the crossroads in Reutel, turn left and continue for 600m, then turn left into Oude Wervikstraat 24–32 after a group of houses. Follow this lane for 400m to a t-junction. Parking is very restricted, but if the crops allow it is possible to park one car on the corner here. A permissive path, part of the Polygon Wood circuit, goes off to the right. Follow it past the house and round to the left. After 200m it emerges from the trees after crossing a small stream. Look left along the wood line. Lewis Evans' VC action was about 300m along a line from this point to Polygone Vallei farm in the distance. Without trespassing on private land it is not possible to get any closer from any direction.

Covert on its left, but the right had less success against Polderhoek, although some gains were made.

21st Division attacked with two brigades, each employing one battalion for the first objective and two for the follow through. On the right, prior to 64th Brigade's attack, **Captain Clement Robertson** and his batman, 200195 Private Cyril Sheldon Allen (DCM for this action), spent three days and nights under heavy shellfire reconnoitring the ground over which the four tanks (A56, A58, A59 and A60) of 12 Section, 3 Company, A Battalion were to advance against Reutel. The approach route from Observatory Ridge to Stirling Castle was completed first before Robertson personally guided the tank commanders over every inch of the route to their start point at Black Watch Corner. Taping the route from Stirling Castle to Black Watch Corner was only completed at 9.30 p.m. on 3rd October.

The tanks began moving forward at 3 a.m. when it was still very dark and misty. Robertson led them on foot under very heavy fire and brought them to the start line in time for zero hour. The attack began at 6 a.m., but the ground was very difficult and the road had been demolished for the first 450m. Knowing that the tanks would lose their way and become stuck in the bog between the Polygonbeek and the Reutelbeek, Robertson continued to lead them on foot despite the very heavy fire. He lost A60 (2nd Lieutenant FS Hunnikin) to shellfire within a few minutes. While A60's crew tried to fix the damage, Robertson pressed on, with A58 leading followed by A56 and A59. He took them along the remains of the Hooge–Reutel road between Cameron House and Joist Farm.

A58 engaged the enemy in front of the British start line on both sides of the road, inflicting heavy losses and helping the infantry to advance. After crossing the bridge over the Reutelbeek, the road had been blown away for a distance of 450m by the artillery, and on either side there was a morass of mud. Robertson was well

Clement Robertson directed his tanks on foot along this road to get them over the Polygonbeek, which runs across the middle of the picture in the low ground. Reutel is on the high ground on the right. On the far side of the Polygonbeek the course of the road is marked by a series of white posts. On the far left is the start of the footpath that leads to one of the viewing points for Lewis Evans' VC action. Above the path just in front of the tree line in the background a few horses can be seen around a surviving pillbox on the line of Juniper Trench.

aware of the importance of the tanks to the infantry and so, with total disregard for his own safety, he continued to guide them forward on foot. They attracted every form of fire imaginable. Just before the leading tank reached the firm road again he was shot in the head and killed. However, none had ditched and they were able to fight a most successful action.

Allan had been guiding the rearmost tanks and came forward to find Robertson on his hands and knees in a shell-hole. Allen recovered Robertson's

Private Cyril Sheldon Allen DCM.

papers and maps and then sought shelter in one of the tanks. Cyril Allen was killed at Cambrai on 20th November 1917 (Cambrai Louveral Memorial).

A58 stopped to cool its engine for twenty minutes just below the top of the ridge. When the infantry caught up Lieutenant VHG Foxwell proceeded over the ridge while A58's gunners shot up a number of strongpoints on both sides of the road. The tank was under heavy fire and armour piercing bullets caused splinters to fly around inside, injuring all the crew except for one man. There was no one in sight when they reached Reutel cemetery. After shooting up a number of machine gun posts, A58 returned to the Red Line, where four boxes of small arms ammunition were handed over to the infantry. Continuing back along the road, it was hit west of

Reverse of the previous view from the roadside just west of Reutel. Joist Farm stood just in front of the modern farm (Polygone Vallei) right of centre on the far side of the Polygonbeek. Polygon Wood is behind and right of Polygone Vallei.

the Reutelbeek on the right sponson. South of Glencorse Wood the secondary gears went wrong and the tank was left with one man as a guard while the rest of the crew carried back the three undamaged Lewis guns.

A59 assisted the infantry by silencing the machine guns at Juniper Cottages. It then attempted to head east to another post, but the ground was too bad and the tank ditched. The crew fitted the unditching gear under heavy fire, but it broke. A59 continued firing, but eventually it had to be abandoned. The Lewis guns were recovered and the crew joined the infantry for two hours. When the Lewis gun ammunition was expended the crew made its way back, having handed over the ammunition boxes it carried for the infantry. 77058 Private Thomas Bellamy carried one of the Lewis guns but went missing in the retirement (Tyne Cot Memorial).

A56 also engaged the enemy in front of the start line, but only on the left and directly ahead. The enemy fell back and some surrendered. Targets were also engaged on the right in the advance. The infantry caught up at the cutting just before the Reutelbeek bridge. Just below the ridge on the far side, the tank stopped to cool its engine for twenty minutes while the infantry moved on to consolidate the top of the ridge. When the advance resumed the tank was soon ahead of the infantry, picking up targets on both sides. About 230m from the cemetery it came under fire from it and engaged machine gun posts there. It continued to Judge Cott, where some Germans were silenced. After a while circling looking for targets, the tank returned to the infantry to hand over the ammunition boxes. It waited a while, but did not seem to be required and returned by the same route to the rally point at Gunners Lodge. Three Lewis guns were damaged and the unditching beam was lost.

A60 was restarted at 10.30 a.m. just as the other crews were returning from the action and it took no part in the battle. Lewis guns from A58 were put inside and they continued to Clapham Junction, where they reported to the company commander.

62nd Brigade on the left was led by 3/4th Queen's to the first objective, followed by 12/13th Northumberland Fusiliers on the right and 10th Yorkshire on the left to the second. 1st Lincolnshire, commanded by **Lieutenant Colonel Lewis Evans**, was in reserve. While moving into position enemy artillery shells exploded a number of ammunition dumps. The resultant fires silhouetted the men moving forward and probably alerted the Germans that an attack was coming.

Evans selected a position on the eastern edge of Polygon Wood for 1st Lincolnshire and the evening before the attack the Battalion moved forward from Scottish Wood. The men were in position by midnight and, while they dug in, Evans went forward to reconnoitre, returning one hour before zero. At that time it was not known what had become of 10th Yorkshire. Brigade HQ ordered 1st Lincolnshire to take up position on the left of 12/13th Northumberland Fusiliers as the left assault battalion for the second objective. 10th Yorkshire had been caught in two heavy barrages in Glencorse Wood and while passing Black Watch Corner. It suffered heavy casualties and was badly disorganised, not arriving at its intended starting position until fifteen minutes after zero.

By a masterpiece of organisation Evans had his men formed up and ready to move five minutes before zero. D Company was on the left and C Company on the right, supported by B and A Companies respectively. In the move forward some casualties were caused by machine guns and a few shorts from the British artillery. However, the battalions were so closed up that an enemy barrage at 5.30 a.m. landed behind them.

From the eastern edge of Polygon Wood north of the Polygonbeek, looking east to the site of Lewis Evans' VC action in front of the trees in the centre distance.

In the advance Evans noticed some gaps in the ranks of 3/4th Queen's and pressed his men forward to fill them and keep up with the barrage. CO 12th/13th Northumberland Fusiliers did the same on the right. The slough of the Polygonbeek slowed the advance and the barrage was lost even though the artillery was moving forward at only ninety metres every six minutes. The morass appeared impassable, but a few mud mats and some trench boards were brought up with great difficulty and some lightly equipped troops got over. They faced heavy fire from a number of unsuspected pillboxes on the east side of the Polygonebeek and in enfilade from the valley on the right. These pillboxes were manned by twenty to thirty men each and had three machine guns in separate compartments.

3/4th Queen's had trained hard in the techniques required to overcome pillboxes and this proved invaluable. Assisted by one of the tanks moving along the Hooge–Reutel road, the Battalion captured the strongpoints. At 6.40 a.m. the first objective was taken by 3/4th Queen's, assisted by both support battalions. 1st Lincolnshire took cover in Judge Trench, in touch with 12th/13th Northumberland Fusiliers on the right and 91st Brigade (7th Division) on the left.

When the leading waves had moved on, a machine gun opened fire from a pillbox just in front of Juniper Trench, northeast of Joist Farm. The pillbox was on fire, but one compartment on the north side was unaffected. Evans organised a two pronged attack, assisted by a Machine Gun Corps officer, and personally rushed the pillbox. He fired his revolver through the loophole and forced the garrison to come out. The Battalion war diary says that the garrison surrendered, but none was taken prisoner.

Evans passed his two leading companies (D on the left and C on the right) through the northern part of 3/4th Queen's. They struggled over the swamp of Jetty Warren to help rush the next objective, where large numbers of the enemy were killed. On the right, 12th/13th Northumberland Fusiliers reached Judge Trench at the same time. It was found that the enemy line was held by 19th Reserve Division

From the footpath running north from the Reutel road. On the far right in front of the tree line is the remaining pillbox on the line of Juniper Trench. Left of centre through the trees growing along the Polygonbeek is the hillside where Lewis Evans' VC action took place. The attack came from the left. In the distance on the left is the northeastern point of Polygon Wood.

Looking south from the northern viewing option. Juniper Trench ran along the tree line on the left. Lewis Evans silenced the pillbox just beyond the lone tree in the centre. To the right of the tree in the distance is Polygone Vallei farm on the Reutel road.

recently arrived from Riga on the Eastern Front. The bayonet was used freely and strongpoints were cleared by explosive and phosphorus grenades, while shell-hole posts were dealt with by rifle grenades and any escapers were shot down by the riflemen. About 500 prisoners were taken, in addition to numerous enemy dead.

Evans moved A Company forward between C and D Companies to form a frontage of three companies, with B Company remaining in reserve. The pause of 100 minutes on the first objective was covered by a standing barrage, which included some smoke shells. Although these obscured the view for enemy machine gunners, their fire from Cameron Covert and Polderhoek Chateau increased in volume and continued to cause casualties, including the CO of 3/4th Queen's and all four company commanders. All three leading battalions had lost about forty percent of their strength and none had more than six officers left. Although contact was made with both flanking formations, it was clear that 5th Division on the right had been held up at Polderhoek Chateau and this resulted in a great deal of enfilade fire from that flank.

The attack resumed at 8.10 a.m. in the face of heavy enemy shellfire. 12th/13th Northumberland Fusiliers had its right in the air and was raked by machine guns on that flank. After 135m the Battalion was halted and dug in.

1st Lincolnshire had some protection from the fire due to the curve of the spur. However, it still received indirect fire from the Chateau and direct fire from

Judge Copse, isolated pillboxes and numerous snipers in shell holes. The Battalion also continued to suffer from 'friendly' shells dropping short. However, the final objective was reached, although the line was not continuous and it had strayed into 7th Division's area. 3/4th Queen's threw back a defensive flank on the right in expectation of a counterattack, while the Germans shelled Polygon Wood and the rear areas heavily.

Although wounded in the shoulder early in the attack, Evans refused to be bandaged. Having reformed his men on the first objective, he waited for the next phase of the attack to begin. As they advanced from their positions near Judge Trench, they ran into heavy machine gun fire from Judge Copse. A reserve platoon from B Company was brought up to reinforce the right flank. Evans was again badly wounded, but refused treatment until the second objective was reached. While it was being consolidated he collapsed from loss of blood. When he came to he refused treatment until other casualties had been attended to. Evans then made his own way back to the dressing station. The Battalion, much weakened in the advance, established touch with its flanking units and consolidated the posts it held during the night.

At 3 p.m. the Germans were seen massing in Cameron Covert to counterattack. A pigeon message (the only viable means of communications) brought down heavy artillery fire, causing heavy casualties and breaking up the German attack before it could start. There was heavy shelling by both sides during the night; although enemy counterattacks appeared to threaten, none materialised.

Early on the morning of 5th October, 1st Lincolnshire and 12th/13th Northumberland Fusiliers were relieved by 6th Lincolnshire and moved back to Zillebeke Lake. 3/4th Queen's and 10th Yorkshire remained in the line until relieved the following night. That night 6th Leicestershire pushed forward the outpost line and reached the intended final objective for 4th October. 62nd Brigade suffered heavy losses – seventy-four of the eighty-six officers committed and 1,279 other ranks were casualties. At least thirty-seven machine guns and fifteen trench mortars were captured. In 1st Lincolnshire only 325 of the 570 who went into the line came out unscathed, but in view of the weight of enemy artillery fire the Battalion's war diary considered the casualties were comparatively light.

The success of 21st Division's attack gave observation over the Reutelbeek valley. Later in the day constant machine gun and artillery fire from Polderhoek spur against the right flank forced a slight withdrawal to more sheltered ground. The final objective was not taken, but the advance was sufficiently successful to secure the southern flank of the main Broodseinde battlefront. 7th Division on the left, attacking with two brigades, fell just short of the final objective, but still overlooked the German rear areas and was able to see preparations for a counterattack.

To the north of X Corps, both ANZAC Corps fought side by side. At 5.20 a.m. intense German artillery fire opened across the front of both Corps, but was particularly heavy on I ANZAC Corps. It was thought the assembled troops had been detected and they pressed even closer forward to the German outposts. Despite these precautions, there were heavy casualties along the whole line. I ANZAC Corps' losses amounted to one in every seven men. In reality the German barrage was preparation for an attack by three battalions of 212th Reserve Regiment to retake the observation areas lost on 26th September.

At zero, despite their losses, the infantry stood up, shook out into formation and set off into the drizzling rain. Visibility at twilight was only thirty metres. There were two objectives. The first was 90–175m short of the crest of the ridge and the second was 175–350m beyond it. Each division attacked with two brigades, with the by now usual method of one battalion for the first objective and two for the second.

In I ANZAC Corps, 1st and 2nd Australian Divisions started from Tokio Spur before crossing the upper Zonnebeek and then up Broodseinde Ridge. The barrage was noticeably weaker than in the attack on 26th September. As the assault troops advanced they had a most unusual experience when men rose in front of them with bayonets fixed. They were the German troops awaiting the start of their own attack. It was one of those rare occasions when both sides attacked simultaneously. The Australians drove off the enemy and swept all before them, with only a slight delay.

1st Australian Division ran into numerous strongpoints. Some surrendered easily, but others resisted strongly. On the right, 1st Australian Brigade lost heavily and slipped into 2nd Australian Brigade's area. Machine guns at Retaliation Farm caused losses to 2nd Australian Brigade before it was cleared. Both brigades arrived at the first objective at 7.15 a.m. Rather than halt as planned, some companies flushed with victory rushed on. The next phase was to advance over Broodseinde Ridge. Bombers cleared the pillboxes and the support battalions were soon on the final objective.

2nd Australian Division also encountered Germans preparing to attack and forced them back. 6th Australian Brigade on the right and 7th Australian Brigade on the left passed either side of Zonnebeke Lake. Many machine gun posts in the village were overcome; and some troops failed to stop on the first objective and were brought back. Broodseinde village was taken easily but, having cleared Zonnebeke, 7th Australian Brigade ran into withering machine gun fire as it topped the crest. It was halted just east of the highway and a British trench line from the winter of 1914–15 was consolidated 200m short of the objective.

II ANZAC Corps' task was to capture the Zonnebeke and Gravenstafel spurs. The first part of the advance was up open slopes against numerous strongpoints. The final objective was to be consolidated as the start line for the final advance on the Broodseinde–Passchendaele Ridge. As its front was 900m wider than I ANZAC Corps, it had additional artillery support; half as many heavies and double the number of field guns.

3rd Australian Division had the Flanders I Line lying diagonally across its front. The Germans had strongpoints in various places, including Windmill Cabaret,

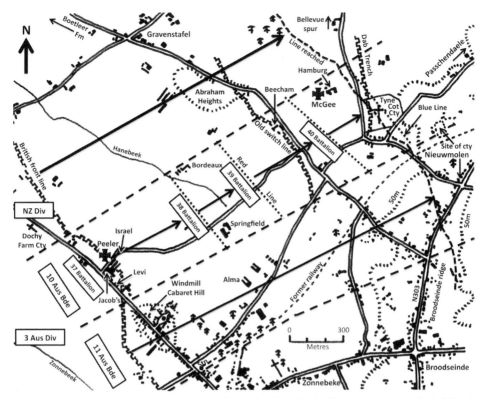

From Zonnebeke drive northwest towards St Julien and park at Dochy Farm Cemetery on the left. Look back towards Zonnebeke. The first buildings on the left are on 10th Australian Brigade's left boundary and the front line ran almost parallel with the road one hundred metres northeast of it. Walter Peeler's VC action was northeast of the road in this area.

Turn round and go back towards Zonnebeke for just over 400m and turn left into Maarlestraat. Follow this road for 1,350m and turn right then left after 275m. Continue northeasterly and follow signs to the car park behind Tyne Cot Cemetery. Follow the visitor's route to the Cemetery entrance along the outside of the northern wall. At the northwest corner of the Cemetery, where the wall meets the north-south road, look half right to the rebuilt Hamburg Farm in the trees, slightly southeast of the original. Lewis McGee captured the pillboxes on the far side. You can get closer by walking north along the road for sixty metres and turning left into the entrance track to the farm. Continue along the track past the farm to the end and look right into the fields where the pillboxes stood.

Jacob's Cottages, Alma, Springfield, Bordeaux Farm, Beecham, Hamburg and also in Dab Trench, in addition to numerous shell-hole positions between them. The difficulties of assembling in the marshy ground, particularly around the Zonnebeek, were eased by the engineers laying duckboard bridges and paths. As the men moved into position they had to halt frequently when flares were put up by the Germans on Windmill Cabaret Hill.

Each assault brigade was allocated eight Vickers machine guns; the remaining forty-eight guns in the Divisional Machine Gun Battalion were for barrage work. Engineers were to follow closely behind the assault battalions to construct strongpoints during consolidation, while a company of the Pioneer Battalion was to dig a new communications trench up to the Blue Line to enable movement to continue in daylight. Two pioneer companies were allocated to CRA for the construction and maintenance of artillery roads. The remainder of the Pioneer Battalion, with a few exceptions, worked under CRE.

On the right, the whole of 11th Australian Brigade was crowded into a belt only ninety metres deep. It moved off sharply at zero, with 43rd Battalion leading, and met stiff resistance from several pillboxes. When the advance was held up, parties outflanked them, covered by showers of rifle grenades. One pillbox near Zonnebeke station on the right opened up with a machine gun while another post on the left threw bombs from the top of Windmill Cabaret Hill. As the pillboxes were overcome, one was found to house a battalion HQ and fifty prisoners were taken. More prisoners were taken while mopping up the dugouts in the banks of the railway cutting. After a short halt, the Brigade pressed on with 42nd Battalion leading. Its right crossed the railway and reached the Red Line after some fighting to clear the numerous pillboxes and dugouts along it. The left was held up by fire from behind Alma and a gap appeared in the line. This was filled by the two platoons of the reserve company and three pillboxes were seized. At the Red Line there was a planned halt until 8.10 a.m., when the advance resumed towards the final objective. Crossing the swamp north of the railway, 44th and 41st Battalions lost the barrage and came under heavy machine gun fire and a number of pillboxes had to be overcome. 41st Battalion led to the final objective near Nieuwemolen crossroads soon after 9 a.m. and 11th Australian Machine Gun Company quickly set up two guns there.

On the left, 10th Australian Brigade had four objectives, each allocated to a single battalion. 37th Battalion was to take the first, 38th Battalion the second (Red Line), 39th Battalion the third and 40th the fourth and final objective (Blue Line). 37th, 38th and 40th Battalions were allocated two Stokes mortars each. Those with 37th and 38th Battalions were to join 40th Battalion as it passed through them. 38th, 39th and 40th Battalions wore coloured patches below the collar on the back of their

From Dochy Farm Cemetery looking southeast towards Langemarck. 37th Battalion attacked from the far side of the road into the low ground on the left. The four prominent poplars in the far left distance are at Tyne Cot Cemetery.

tunics to identify which objective they were responsible for – white, red and blue respectively.

37th Battalion crept forward to within thirty metres of the British barrage in front of the pillboxes at Levi Cottages in order to avoid enemy shelling. 40th Battalion had to assemble in the swamp east of the Zonnebeke due to the overcrowding and was not able to shake out into formation until the move forward commenced at zero. The Brigade was criticised for making too much noise in the early stages of the advance. It seems that a rabbit tried to escape through the waves of advancing troops as they set off and this was too much temptation for those with a sporting instinct. After eluding the three forward battalions, 40th Battalion captured it and this raised a cheer from the whole Brigade.

Machine guns opened fire from Levi Cottages against 37th Battalion when the advance commenced, but they were overcome quickly. Large numbers of enemy were bayoneted and at least 350 dead Germans were counted in the first 450m of the advance. Attached to 37th Battalion was **Lance Corporal Walter Peeler** from 3rd Australian Pioneer Battalion. He was one of twenty-four Lewis gunners from the Pioneer Battalion attached to 10th Australian Brigade for anti-aircraft protection. However, Peeler went ahead of the first wave and accounted for over thirty Germans in shell-hole positions, including a number of snipers and a machine gun that was firing at the advancing troops.

Further resistance was encountered from pillboxes at Israel House until they were outflanked and screened by a smoke grenade. The first objective fell at 6.17 a.m. At this intermediate objective the barrage halted for twelve minutes to allow extra time for the New Zealand Division to cross the marsh to the north. However, in front of 10th Australian Brigade the pause of twelve minutes was inexplicably extended by the artillery to twenty-six minutes and the assault troops were delayed.

As 38th Battalion advanced down the boggy rear of Windmill Hill and over the Hanebeek, the Germans were seen running back through the barrage, which was

Reverse of the previous view from Maarlestraat. The large tree behind the farm on the far right can also be seen right of centre on the far side of the road in the previous picture. The buildings running across the middle of this view are on the Langemarck – St Julien road. The site of Jacob's Cottages is in the centre and Levi Cottages is on the far left.

described by one observer as 'a wall of flame'. The Battalion reached the Red Line with only a few casualties at 7.15 a.m.

At the Red Line there was a planned halt until 8.10 a.m., during which the German artillery became more active and effective. 39th Battalion was too close to the standing protective barrage and had to fall back slightly, which caused it to collide with the rear battalions as they pressed forward and forcing them to fall back in turn. When the advance continued, 39th Battalion was checked by fire from an old switch line in front and also from machine guns on Abraham Heights in the New Zealand Division's area. Casualties were heavy. A platoon of D Company, 40th Battalion, following behind with a Stokes mortar, moved into the New Zealand sector and dealt with the machine guns in the old switch line. A company of 39th Battalion worked round some sheltered ground and outflanked the position in front. The third objective was taken at 8.40 a.m. after overcoming resistance at Beecham.

The barrage had moved on and 40th Battalion pressed ahead for the final bound, but could not catch it up. The ground was very boggy and the leading companies (B on the right and D on the left) moved over to the flanks to avoid the worst part in the centre, leaving a gap of about 275m, which was filled by a party of A Company following behind to mop up. The Battalion came under heavy fire from the Flanders I Line (Dab Trench) in front and also from Hamburg on the left and as far away as Bellevue Spur. Ten machine guns were identified and progress could only be made by short rushes. To add to the difficulties there was a thick belt of barbed wire in front of Dab Trench. Casualties were heavy as the men tried to dash through the few gaps that existed. Captain William Cyril Gentry Ruddock (first winner of the King's Medal shooting competition in Australia in 1924) worked D Company on the left around the German position through some half sheltered ground in the New Zealand Division's sector. Opening fire from there, Ruddock's men suppressed the

Hamburg Farm from the southwest. In the far right in the distance is Tyne Cot Cemetery. The attack came from the left and the pillboxes attacked by Lewis McGee were in the field to the left of the farm in the area of the wind generator.

Germans in Hamburg and Dab Trench and a series of gallant actions against the pillboxes commenced.

Sergeant Lewis McGee's platoon in B Company suffered heavy casualties from a machine gun on the roof of a pillbox immediately in front of Hamburg. The survivors were pinned down in shell holes. Armed with only a revolver, he rushed forward fifty metres, shot some of the detachment and captured the rest. In the subsequent advance he organised a bombing attack on another pillbox. The next blockhouse at Hamburg was charged by A Company in a flanking movement and the position was seized with twenty-five prisoners and four machine guns being taken. Meanwhile D Company on the left had worked forward onto the objective and in a final rush by D, A and B Companies there was a short but bloody fight to secure the Blue Line.

Because of heavy casualties, B Company on the right had to be strengthened by two platoons of C Company in reserve. In conjunction with 41st Battalion (11th Australian Brigade) on the right, pillbox after pillbox was taken until the objective was reached by 40th Battalion at 9.12 a.m. Mopping up parties operated forward of the Blue Line up to the standing barrage and overcame more opposition. CSM H Boden and two men captured a pillbox containing a German battalion HQ, along with seventy prisoners, without firing a shot. Lewis gun teams were positioned 175m in front of the Blue Line. At 8.50 a.m. two platoons of 39th Battalion were sent forward to reinforce 40th Battalion for the next two hours. Two more platoons were sent up at 6 p.m. and remained with 40th Battalion until it was relieved. Ammunition in the forward area was in short supply and parties of 37th Battalion were detailed to carry small arms ammunition to the Blue Line at 12.15 p.m. and 1.05 p.m. A captured machine gun kept three German field guns from firing freely into the new line. Eventually the British artillery silenced these guns. The captured pillboxes were found to contain all manner of 'souvenirs', and good use was made of abandoned German cigars and beer.

40th Battalion was relieved at 11 p.m. on 5th October by 2/7th Manchester. The rest of the Brigade was relieved by other units of 199th Brigade (66th Division).

Hamburg Farm

The Battalion suffered 253 casualties in this action, including fifty killed, but took 200–300 prisoners, fifteen machine guns and two trench mortars. The Battalion war diary entry for 6th October merely states, 'The Battalion slept'.

From 10.30 a.m. various German parties began advancing against the new line, but they were driven off. One force was dispersed from the cemetery near Tyne Cot, another was seen advancing from Passchendaele and settled in old trenches about 200m from 41st Battalion, which charged and the Germans bolted. Other counterattacks threatened throughout the day, but none was pressed home and they were dispersed by artillery or mortar fire. 3rd Australian Division suffered 1,810 casualties and recorded 1,038 prisoners passing through the cages.

The New Zealand Division on the left carried all before it. 4th New Zealand Brigade overran Abraham Heights and Gravenstafel was mopped up with many prisoners being taken. On the left, 1st New Zealand Brigade took Boetleer Farm on Hill 32. The advance continued over the spur into the upper Stroombeek valley and on to the final objective near the Ravebeek. Bellevue Spur, the objective for the next big attack, could be seen across the valley.

Fifth Army's XVIII Corps employed three brigades from two divisions (48th and 11th) in the attack. On the right, 143rd Brigade covered the whole of 48th Division's front. It led with three battalions – 1/5th Royal Warwickshire on the right, 1/6th Royal Warwickshire in the centre and 1/7th Royal Warwickshire on the left. 1/8th Royal Warwickshire was in reserve. Specially designated parties were to capture specific strongpoints at Burns House and Kronprinz and Stoke Farms. On the right, 1st New Zealand Brigade was prepared to assist in the capture of Vale House and Winzig and Albatross Farms.

There were two objectives – the Red Dotted Line and the Red Line. On reaching the Red Dotted Line, strongpoints were to be constructed at Albatross and Winchester Farms and at Tweed House. On the Red Line the strongpoints were to be at Wellington Farm, an unnamed house 450m southeast of it, Burns House, and Terrier Farm. Vickers machine guns were allocated to most of these strongpoints. Behind the left and right battalions was a Stokes mortar from 143rd Trench Mortar Battery, ready to deal with any stubborn strongpoints. Two more Stokes mortars were to set up at York Farm to assist the final advance onto Winchester Farm ridge; they would be supported by 145th Trench Mortar Battery.

Officers and NCOs from all battalions spent time in the forward trenches in the days before the attack to learn their objectives and take compass bearings. The start line was well marked and assembly went ahead with hardly a hitch and only a handful of casualties. All were in place by 1.30 a.m. The Brigade was hit by the German barrage at 5.00 a.m. and there were several casualties, mainly in 1/5th and 1/6th Royal Warwickshire. Some Lewis guns were lost.

On the right, 1/5th Royal Warwickshire took Vale House after encountering only slight resistance. However, taking Winzig involved a more severe fight in which twenty prisoners were taken. A machine gun post north of Vale House caused

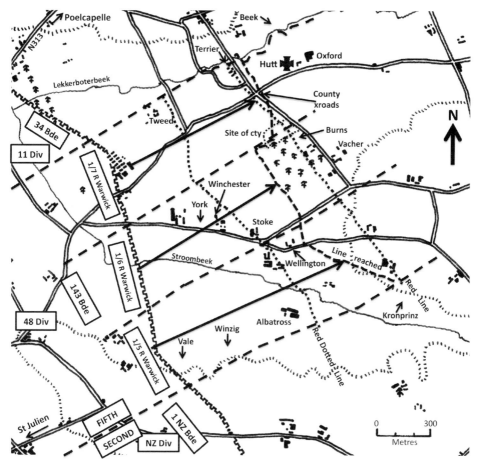

From the large roundabout in the centre of Langemarck drive southeast on Wallemolenstraat for just under 1,200m to a crossroads (County Crossroads). Two hundred metres before the crossroads you will cross the Lekkerboterbeek and pass Terrier Farm on the right. At the crossroads turn left into Steenstraat and continue for 200m. On the left, about fifty metres into the field in front of the house, is the site of the pillbox captured by Arthur Hutt.

considerable casualties to the left company and by the time it had been overcome the company was reduced to only thirty effectives. As the advance progressed direction was lost due to the New Zealanders edging down the slope from the right. Wellington was occupied, but the troops holding it were wiped out by shelling. The New Zealanders took up a line from Wellington south-eastwards for 500m towards Kronprinz and 1/5th Royal Warwickshire took it over at dusk and pushed on further on the right.

In the centre, 1/6th Royal Warwickshire overran the enemy posts along the west bank of the Stroombeek with few casualties. As the advance continued heavy small arms fire was received from the right and the high ground and road in front of York and Winchester Farms. There were many losses, particularly amongst the officers, and D Company on the left was drawn towards York, leaving a gap of 175m before

1/7th Royal Warwickshire on the left. All the officers in B Company were killed and the CSM took a platoon to fill the gap. The rest of B Company and D Company became mixed up on the right, but they pressed on and reached the positions in front of York Farm. On the far right, A Company seized the high ground west of Winchester and many prisoners were taken. It pressed on to Winchester, which was also attacked by D Company, but it was found to be empty. A party moved towards Wellington, but was stopped by the protective barrage. A party of 1/5th Royal Warwickshire came up and took over on the right. This allowed 1/6th Royal Warwickshire to move left and dig in east of Winchester.

The support companies became involved. C Company came up behind A Company, but lost direction crossing the Stroombeek and drifted to the right, where it became involved in the fight in front of Winchester. There was considerable confusion before it was taken. The barrage had moved on from the Red Dotted Line before it could be captured and it took a huge effort to reorganise sufficiently to continue the advance to the final objective. Eventually a line 275m west of the Vacher Farm road was reached, but the strength of the Battalion had been so reduced that it was unable to press on to Burns House and Vacher Farm. At 1.30 p.m. two companies of 1/8th Royal Warwickshire in reserve arrived to seize the final objective, but the fire against them was too heavy and they failed to pass the front line. After 5 p.m. a counterattack got to within 150m of the line held, where it was driven off by small arms fire.

On the left, 1/7th Royal Warwickshire was commanded by Lieutenant Colonel James Meldrum Knox DSO (died of wounds 23rd September 1918 – Granezza British Cemetery, Italy), brother of Second Lieutenant Cecil Leonard Knox, who was awarded the VC for his actions on 22nd March 1918. D Company was on the left and C Company on the right for the advance to the first objective. They were supported by A and B Companies respectively. Assembly was completed with only four casualties and on arrival at the start line the men rolled themselves in their

From Steenstraat looking north. The pillbox captured by Arthur Hutt was in the centre, about fifty metres from the camera position, with Poelcapelle in the distance beyond. County Crossroads is on the far left at the cottage.

County
Crossroads

oil sheets and tried to sleep. Rum was served at 5 a.m., about the same time as the German barrage fell.

On the right, C Company was hampered by the poor ground conditions but, although it suffered many casualties, after half an hour's fight it managed to overcome a machine gun post on the right boundary just short of the objective. The Company pressed on, overcame another strongpoint and reached the edge of the cemetery before realising where it was. It was within the barrage and had to fall back to dig in just in front of the barrage line. On the left, D Company overcame a machine gun post at Tweed House and consolidated a line after joining up with C Company on the right and 9th Lancashire Fusiliers (11th Division) on the left.

A and B Companies then took over the advance and initially made good progress behind the barrage. On the left, A Company captured Terrier Farm, but as it continued the platoon commander and all the NCOs in 2 Platoon were hit. **Private Arthur Hutt** took command. The platoon was held up by a strongpoint on the right. Hutt ran forward alone, shot an officer and three men in the pillbox and took the remaining forty to fifty occupants prisoner. A Company pressed on but ran into the protective barrage and was forced to withdraw. Hutt covered the withdrawal of his party by sniping at the enemy, killing a number of them. When it was his turn to fall back he carried a wounded comrade to shelter. Having consolidated the new position, Hutt learned there were still wounded lying out in front. He went out four times under heavy fire to bring in injured men, as there were no stretcher-bearers available at the time. Elements of A Company worked forward as far as Beek Houses and the rest of the Company pushed on to a line between Terrier and Oxford Houses.

B Company on the right pushed fifty metres east of the cemetery. However, with both flanks in the air and being in the middle of the barrage, both companies had to withdraw a little and a line was consolidated. B Company made contact with 1/6th Royal Warwickshire on the right and A Company linked up with 9th Lancashire Fusiliers (11th Division) on the left. A counterattack was spotted heading for 9th Lancashire Fusiliers and all the Lewis guns were turned to that flank and inflicted heavy losses on the enemy. Three small counterattacks from around Beek Houses

Poelcapelle

Pillbox

were also broken up by the Lewis gunners. Another two counterattacks from east of the cemetery were similarly dispersed and fifty prisoners were taken. Two Vickers machine guns were set up at Tweed House to cover the new front.

At 12.38 p.m. two battalions of 145th Brigade (5th Gloucestershire and 4th Oxfordshire & Buckinghamshire Light Infantry) were ordered forward to exploit the success of 143rd Brigade. The attack was timed for 5 p.m., but it proved impossible to move 4th Oxfordshire & Buckinghamshire Light Infantry forward in time. Instead 1/8th Royal Warwickshire was ordered to attack on the left to take Burns House and Vacher Farm, supported by all available troops of 1/6th and 1/8th Royal Warwickshire. 5th Gloucestershire was on the right. The barrage fell behind a considerable number of German defenders and little progress was made. As a result the centre and right of 143rd Brigade were 250m short of the final objective. In total 400 prisoners were taken, together with fifteen machine guns and two anti-tank guns.

11th Division faced an advance up the gradual slope of the Poelcapelle Spur. It was supported by ten tanks. 33rd Brigade was on the left. On the right, 34th Brigade led with 9th Lancashire Fusiliers on the right and 11th Manchester on the left. 5th Dorset was in reserve to deal with counterattacks if necessary. As with 48th Division, the objectives were the Red Dotted and Red Lines. Each forward battalion was allocated one Vickers machine gun, while the remaining guns in the Machine Gun Company were held in readiness to hold the ground gained. Six Stokes mortars of the Brigade Trench Mortar Battery were positioned to bombard the enemy positions at zero and the remaining two were ready to move forward to a position from where they could fire on Gloster Farm.

Parties were detailed to deal with specific strongpoints during the advance and on reaching the Red Line a patrol was to investigate if Meunier House was held. Each forward battalion was to construct a series of strongpoints during consolidation. There were to be three of them fifty to one hundred metres in front of the Red Line and another three the same distance behind. Another strongpoint was to be in the support position and two platoons of 8th Northumberland Fusiliers, in divisional reserve, were to work on them under the CRE, assisted by a platoon of 11th Manchester. There were to be two more strongpoints in the rear.

Assembly was completed by 4.45 a.m. without incident, but thick cloud and drizzle meant it was darker than expected at zero. The barrage was thickened for the first three minutes by Stokes mortars firing on strongpoints close to the start line, including Malta House. The Brigade operation order states that anyone using the word 'retire' was to be shot or bayoneted. The going was heavy, particularly near the Stroombeek, but there was only weak resistance and the Red Dotted Line was reached on time. The pause there allowed reorganisation to take place and 11th Manchester was able to correct a slight deviation to the right. A feeble counterattack against the Battalion was disposed of by small arms fire.

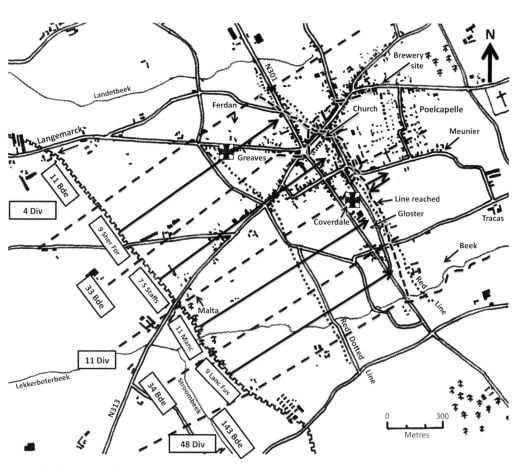

At the large roundabout in the centre of Poelcapelle take the Langemarck road to the west. After 350m, pull over on the right where there are spaces to park just before a bus shelter. The pillbox captured by Fred Greaves was just behind No.31 on the opposite (south) side of the road. Continue for 175m and turn left into Langemarktstraat 45–47. Continue for 275m to the left bend where there is a pull-in on the right. Look left to the rear of the houses on Langemarktstraat where the pillbox stood in 1917.

Continue to the t-junction and turn left onto the N313 towards Poelcapelle. After 175m turn right and follow this round to the left to a crossroads. Turn right and just over 300m later there is a raised section of road with a small area to pull-in on the right just beyond. Walk back a few metres and look through the gap in the buildings to the northeast. Charles Coverdale's VC action was in the foreground and 650m beyond in this direction is the site of Meunier House.

In the advance to the Red Line, 9th Lancashire Fusiliers met almost no opposition, but 11th Manchester faced resistance from a number of pillboxes sweeping the area with fire and causing casualties. The garrison of Gloster Farm put up a fight until a Stokes mortar was brought into action as two tanks approached and a party of 11th Manchester rushed the position, killing or capturing the whole garrison. The advance was hampered by machine gun fire from Poelcapelle church and the brewery and also by snipers. **Sergeant Charles Coverdale** dashed forward. He killed an officer and took two men prisoner who were sniping into the flank of his unit. He then rushed two machine gun posts, disposing of both teams.

Charles Coverdale's VC action was in the centre foreground. Beyond it, behind the long building is Meunier House. On the far left is Poelcapelle with the church tower above the houses on the right side of the road. On the far right is the raised section of road beyond which it is possible to park for a short period.

The Red Line was reached and consolidation began behind the protective barrage as patrols were pushed out as far as the barrage would allow. In front, Beek Houses and Meunier House appeared to have been abandoned. Coverdale's platoon had lost its formation in the final advance. Having reorganised it he attempted to capture Meunier House. However, after covering one hundred metres he ran into the barrage. After suffering nine casualties he had to give up. By the time the barrage ended the Germans had reoccupied both positions.

A post was pushed out to the northeast of Tracas Farm, but it was isolated and had to be withdrawn. Although overall casualties were comparatively light, losses in officers had been heavy, particularly in 11th Manchester, which had kept too close to the barrage. By the time the Red Line was secured, 9th Lancashire Fusiliers had lost its CO and all four company commanders and 11th Manchester had lost three company commanders and seven other officers. Major Meugens, commanding 11th Manchester, was hit in the arm by a sniper during the night and had to leave the Battalion next morning.

As consolidation proceeded, contact was maintained with flanking units, but the enemy interfered throughout. Plans to continue the advance were cancelled due to a German counterattack against 33rd Brigade on the left about 1 p.m. When the shelling died down at about 1.30 p.m., Coverdale led five men forward for another attempt on Meunier House, but after covering a short distance he noticed a German party preparing to advance. He sent his men back one by one, being the last to leave, and then reported the enemy build-up. Coverdale's inspiring and gallant leadership was a major contributory factor in the success of the day's operations.

The concentration of enemy troops became more apparent around 4 p.m. and fifty Germans behind Meunier House were dispersed by small arms fire. A

Meunier

verdale

counterattack by 300–400 enemy was launched at 6.30 p.m. from the ridge northeast of Beek Houses. The SOS signal brought down the artillery, which combined with rapid small arms fire to break up the attack.

During the night a pillbox captured by 11th Manchester just inside 33rd Brigade's area was handed over to 7th South Staffordshire. Next morning a portion of 11th Manchester's front was also handed over. On the night of 5th/6th October, 5th Dorset relieved 9th Lancashire Fusiliers and 11th Manchester in the front line. The latter fell back into the support position and the former went into reserve. The Brigade was relieved on 8th October having suffered 779 casualties. 11th Manchester had the lion's share, with 328 casualties, including thirty-nine killed and twenty-six missing.

On the left of 11th Division, 33rd Brigade attacked with 7th South Staffordshire on the right and 9th Sherwood Foresters on the left. 6th Border was in support and 6th Lincolnshire was in divisional reserve. A half section of sappers was attached to each forward battalion to construct key strongpoints in the support positions. Both battalions were in position by 5.10 a.m.

The Red Dotted Line was reached having encountered only a little resistance. B Company, 9th Sherwood Foresters reached it having cleared two machine gun posts, but A Company encountered more serious problems. The company commander, CSM and two platoon sergeants were hit and many others were casualties. Three machine gun posts were encountered and from two of these the enemy fell back, taking their guns with them. However, at the third they stood their ground. This was a large concrete emplacement, south of the Poelcapelle–Langemarck road, just over 350m west of the road junction in the centre of Poelcapelle. The pillbox had two machine guns in the upper part and two others on the flanks outside. **Corporal Fred Greaves'** platoon was checked by this strongpoint and the platoon commander and sergeant were both hit. Greaves knew that it was vital to keep up with the barrage so he rushed to the rear of the emplacement with Sergeant Terry and bombed it.

From the Poelcapelle–Langemarck road looking south, with Poelcapelle to the left. The single storey building in the centre is No.31 and the pillbox captured by Fred Greaves (removed post-war) was in the garden behind, which can be glimpsed through the gap in the fence.

The occupants were either killed or wounded. Five Germans surrendered and the four machine guns were captured, but in the confusion another twenty Germans managed to escape.

Due to Greaves' courage heavy losses were avoided and the attack swept on to Ferdan House and the final objective. At about 1.00 p.m. on the left flank, 1st Somerset Light Infantry (11th Brigade, 4th Division), gave way temporarily in the face of a heavy counterattack and fell back 350m. By then all the officers in A Company were casualties. Greaves grasped the situation, collected his men, threw out extra posts on the threatened flank and opened up rifle and machine gun fire into the flank of the enemy advance. Although the Germans attacked repeatedly

Reverse of the previous view from Langemarktstraat 45–47. No.31 is just left of centre with a chimney on the right and tall trees beyond it. Poelcapelle church is on the far right.

they were held on every occasion. The Battalion's war diary also mentions 13016 Sergeant Fred Carlisle (DCM for this action) of D Company led a party forward under heavy machine gun fire to clear some ruined houses. When the left flank came under attack Carlisle organised the defence and the objective was secure.

6th Border took over whole Brigade front on the night of 5th/6th October. 7th South Staffordshire went into the support line and 9th Sherwood Foresters into reserve. 33rd Brigade was relieved by 32nd Brigade on the night of 7th/8th October.

XIV Corps formed the northern flank. On the right, 4th Division was halted a few hundred metres short of its objective. The survivors were raked by machine gun fire and forced to withdraw slightly. On the left, 29th Division's task was to smooth off the northern flank. 1st Royal Dublin Fusiliers on the right and two platoons of 1st King's Own Scottish Borderers on the left were the only units involved. This operation was to be 1st Royal Dublin Fusiliers' swansong with the 29th Division, as it transferred to 16th (Irish) Division a few days later. The Battalion faced an advance of 900m with its frontage gradually narrowing to the right, where it was to

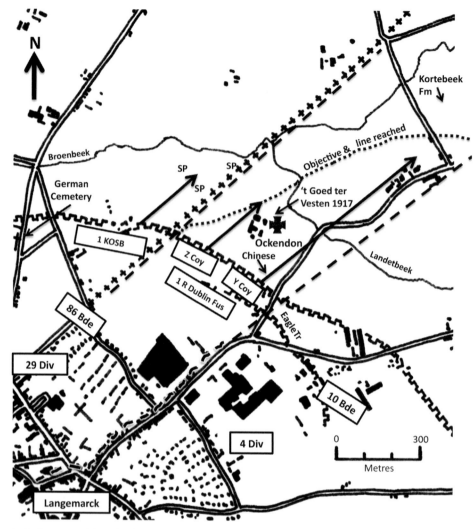

At the large roundabout in the centre of Poelcapelle take the Langemarck road to the west. After 1,900m, where the road bends left at a factory, turn right into Schreiboomstraat. Follow this road for almost 400m to the entry track to 't Goed ter Vesten on the left. There is space to park for a few minutes at this junction. There were two pillboxes in the 't Goed ter Vesten complex captured by James Ockendon, both to the right of the entrance track to the modern farm about 125m from the junction. The modern farm is about fifty metres southwest of where it was in 1917. Vestiges of the moat that almost surrounded the earlier farm remain as a pond nearby.

The farm at 't Goed ter Vesten from the entrance track on Schreiboomstraat looking northwest. 1st Royal Dublin Fusiliers attacked from left to right.

establish contact with 10th Brigade (4th Division). Two strongpoints had to be taken on the way, at Chinese House and 't Goed ter Vesten Farm on the final objective.

The Irishmen were in fine form, singing Republican songs on their way to the front. When the GOC visited, he asked who was to win a VC in the coming attack. A sergeant is reputed to have jumped up and said he would, *or leave his skin in dirty old Belgium*. The move forward was carried out with few casualties, while the artillery paid particular attention to the strongpoints. The Battalion took over from 16th Middlesex during the night, with the leading companies assembling in Eagle Trench. A welcomed mug of tea and rum was served just prior to zero.

The advance was led by Y Company on the right and Z Company on the left, with W Company in support and X Company in reserve. Following behind Y Company was a section of trench mortars and two platoons of 16th Middlesex with two machine guns to form the flank guard.

The 1st King's Own Scottish Borderers platoons reached their objective successfully and took three isolated strongpoints, one on the railway and two others northwest of it. 1st Royal Dublin Fusiliers' advance was steady, deliberate and unstoppable. The first objectives were gained and the Battalion pressed on towards the Broembeek valley. Y Company lost all its officers and the CSM, but gained its objective and maintained contact with 4th Division on the right. Z Company took Chinese House and swept on before coming under heavy fire from its final objective at 't Goed ter Vesten Farm.

Sergeant James Ockendon was acting as CSM of Z Company during the attack. In the initial advance he saw one of the platoon commanders shot down on the right of the company and the platoon was held up by machine gun fire. Having identified the gun position he rushed it, killed two of the crew and chased the third a long way forward of the Battalion's front, where he bayoneted him to death. The rest of the men rose up despite the heavy fire to give him a cheer. In his own account Ockendon mentions turning the captured machine gun on the enemy before he came under fire from another machine gun, which he rushed and killed the crew. Later while leading the Company forward they came under fire from the 't Goed ter Vesten Farm strongpoint. He rushed forward, again, calling to the garrison to surrender, but instead was fired upon. He returned the fire, killing four of the garrison before the remaining sixteen surrendered. Z Company was then able to reach its objective.

A counterattack at 1.30 p.m. from the direction of Kortebeek Farm forced Y Company and a flanking unit back, but the lost ground was recovered. Ockendon

't Goed ter Vesten 1917

Pond
Pillbox

Pillbox

conducted a number of dangerous patrols to bring back valuable information on the enemy's dispositions and intentions.

By noon it was clear that the main objectives had been taken by Second Army. A few counterattacks developed in the afternoon, but none came to much. The only exception was on the southern flank, where the enemy reoccupied Reutel and Cameron Covert and reinforced the garrison at Polderhoek Chateau. The main German reaction was to shell the captured ground, particularly on the Gheluvelt Plateau and Broodseinde Ridge. The indications were that the Germans had suffered a major and demoralising defeat and the possibility of decisive exploitation arose. Indeed the German official history describes it as 'the black day of October 4th'. Some felt that further rapid blows should be struck immediately provided the weather held. However, because the enemy still had reserve divisions in the area, it was decided that the original plan should be adhered to, at least until these formations had been engaged and worn down. Those in the front line, particularly around Broodseinde, saw that they could simply walk into Passchendaele, but the window of opportunity soon passed.

Chapter Eight

Battle of Poelcappelle

9th October 1917

279 Cpl William Clamp, 6th Yorkshire (32nd Brigade, 11th Division), Poelcapelle, Belgium

280 Sgt Joseph Lister, 1st Lancashire Fusiliers (86th Brigade, 29th Division), Northwest of Poelcapelle, Belgium

281 Sgt John Molyneux, 2nd Royal Fusiliers (86th Brigade, 29th Division), Northwest of Poelcapelle, Belgium

282 Pte Frederick Dancox, 4th Worcestershire (88th Brigade, 29th Division), Northwest of Poelcapelle, Belgium

283 LSgt John Rhodes, 3rd Grenadier Guards (2nd Guards Brigade, Guards Division), South of Houthulst Forest, Belgium

Following the success of the attack on 4th October, Haig was keen to launch the next step without delay. The plan was for Second Army to force the Germans off the main ridge beyond Passchendaele, while Fifth Army gained the Flanders I line about Spriet. Intelligence indicated that the only German reserves in the area were divisions that had been withdrawn for rest following 4th October. It was assessed that another two blows in quick succession would create a breakthrough. Accordingly Haig brought forward the next steps to 9th and 12th October.

Rain set in on the afternoon of 4th October and continued until the 7th. The Army Commanders were of the opinion that the campaign should be wound up, but Haig was not ready to close it down for three reasons. First, he wanted to clear the Passchendaele–Westroosbeke section of the main ridge before winter. Second, there was the tantalising prospect of what the next steps might achieve and third, the continuing requirement to divert attention from other theatres and fronts. However, the British were desperately tired and the pressure on them was increased by the need to take over six divisional frontages from the French in order to allow them to take leave.

The ground was so badly torn by three months of fighting that the construction of roads and gun positions became increasingly difficult. There was also no prospect of the weather improving in the short term. As a result the artillery would have to fire at extreme range as the assault troops approached the final objective around Passchendaele. The effort involved in preparing the guns defies imagination;

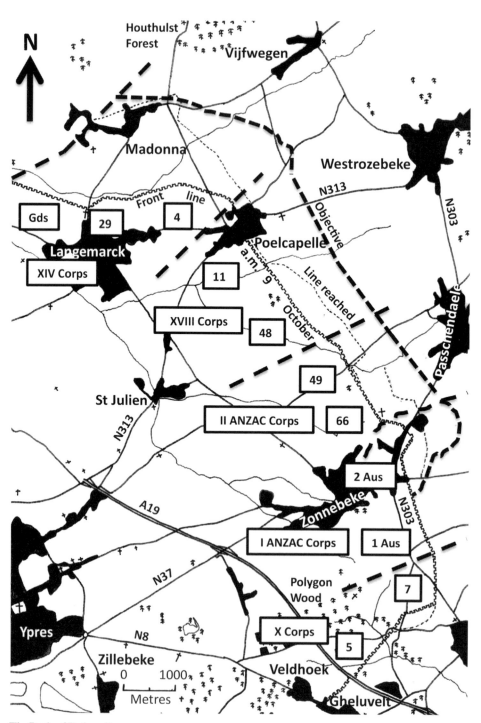

The Battle of Poelcapelle.

batteries took up to sixteen hours to resupply with ammunition although they were less than 150m from main roadways. When the barrage opened it was much reduced, due to the specially constructed gun platforms slipping in the mud and the exhaustion of the crews.

On the evening of 8th October the assault brigades began their approach marches, each relying on a single track to get within a mile of the start line. Thereafter they followed staked routes marked with lamps. The final move to the assault positions was made in pitch darkness and heavy rain. Many soldiers did not reach their positions before zero, which was at 5.20 a.m.

On the right of Second Army a barrage simulated a general offensive and X Corps attacked with two divisions to hold the enemy reserves about Becelaere and Polderhoek. Another attempt to take Polderhoek Chateau made little progress in the face of enfilade fire from Gheluvelt, but on the right the final objective of the 4th October attack, including Reutel village, was secured.

I ANZAC Corps' left brigade reached the final objective, but was forced back by the time II ANZAC Corps came up on its left. A line was established on the first objective and a counterattack was checked at 5.10 p.m. II ANZAC Corps' left managed to negotiate the swollen Ravebeek, but ran into heavy machine gun fire and thick belts of wire in front of the Flanders I Line. By the afternoon most assault brigades were not much further forward than their start lines, although some progress was made on the left. The right enjoyed more success since the Flanders I Line in this area had been captured on 4th October. The brigade on the extreme right was on higher and drier ground and, although it lost the barrage, it reached the final objective about 10 a.m. A patrol found Passchendaele deserted beyond the Flanders II Line, but when the rain stopped the improved visibility allowed the enemy machine gunners to sweep the leading units.

Fifth Army employed XVIII and XIV Corps in the attack, with a brigade of tanks in support. XVIII Corps faced an advance of 1,100m up the Poelcapelle Spur and the main ridge towards Westroosebeke. 48th and 11th Divisions each attacked with one brigade, 144th and 33rd respectively. The assault battalions took over fourteen hours to struggle through the mud and rain to reach their start positions and were consequently exhausted even before the attack. As soon as the advance commenced the leading units were raked by machine gun and sniper fire and were checked. The barrage was lost and it is not surprising that they made little progress.

33rd Brigade attacked with three battalions; 6th York & Lancaster on the right, 9th West Yorkshire in the centre and 6th Yorkshire, attached from 32nd Brigade, on the left. They went into the line on 7th October. Eight tanks were allocated to the Brigade.

A and B Companies, 6th Yorkshire were in the outpost line and C and D Companies were in support near Pheasant Farm Cemetery. The Battalion moved up to the start line early on the morning of 9th October and the companies were not briefed on the details of the attack until 1 a.m. Ground conditions were so atrocious that the

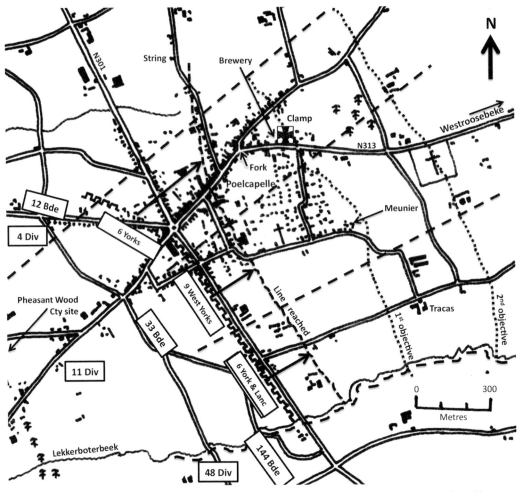

At the large roundabout in the centre of Poelcapelle take the N313 road towards Westroosebeke. After 400m the road bends right. Follow it round and park on the left where there are spaces. Walk on for another hundred metres, passing a shrine on the left. Just after it is where the Brewery pillboxes were in 1917.

Looking west along the Westroosebeke road into Poelcapelle. The brewery pillboxes were across the road and behind the fence.

start line tapes disappeared into the mud and had to be put out a second time. At 2 a.m. a heavy enemy barrage fell and the British response, which fell short, was ineffective. The British forward posts had been withdrawn to allow for the barrage and it seems that these were occupied by German troops, who thereby avoided the British barrage. The barrage was not very effective, falling short in places and inaccurate elsewhere. When the advance commenced at zero, the advancing troops were hit immediately by fire from their former posts and also from String Houses, Tracas Farm and Meunier House.

In the face of heavy fire, no tank support, appalling ground conditions and poor artillery support, the right and centre battalions only succeeded in reaching the line of abandoned posts. 9th West Yorkshire was reinforced by two companies of 8th Duke of Wellington's. Contact on the left with 6th Yorkshire was lost when the latter's right company inclined inwards towards Poelcapelle. The gap was not filled properly until that night.

On the right, 6th Yorkshire entered Poelcapelle with relative ease supported by a company of 8th Duke of Wellington's. The Battalion took over 150 prisoners and there was little opposition in the village until the fork in the road was reached near the brewery. Here the second line pressed forward, went through the first to reach the brewery and four concrete dugouts were taken. Tanks had been included in the plan to subdue this position, but did not make it due to the state of the ground.

Corporal William Clamp dashed forward with two other men and attempted to rush the largest pillbox. The two others became casualties and Clamp came back to collect some bombs. With two more men he rushed forward again, reached the pillbox first and hurled his bombs inside, killing many occupants. Entering the pillbox alone, he captured twenty prisoners and a machine gun and brought them back under heavy sniper fire. Several pillboxes northwest of the Brewery were taken in the face of terrific fire from strongpoints at Meunier House and String House, but further advance was halted by enfilade fire from the left. By 8 a.m. a rudimentary line had been established and at 11.05 a.m., W Company, 8th Duke of Wellington's came up in support on the left of the village.

As the troops dug in casualties continued to be caused by machine guns along the spur. Trench mortars attached to the Battalion were destroyed by shelling before they could come into action. Clamp went forward again, encouraging the men around him to subdue sniper posts in ruined buildings close to the Battalion's positions. He tackled a number of positions, but as he went to hunt out another machine gun he was killed by a sniper.

At 4 p.m. reports were received of a counterattack assembling at Meunier House and 6th Lincolnshire was brought up into support. Around 5 p.m. the enemy began to reoccupy their former positions near the Brewery. An advanced post of seven men was forced to withdraw and a partial withdrawal of the whole line was made a little later. 33rd Brigade suffered 751 casualties in this action, including 231 in 6th Yorkshire.

The northern flank of the whole operation was formed by XIV Corps advancing towards the southern edge of Houthulst Forest, with the French cooperating on the left. Although the ground was swampy it was not as badly damaged by shellfire as further south; and the Broenbeek, although an obstacle, was fordable. In consequence, most of the troops reached their start lines without difficulty. The final objective was well within artillery range and there were no problems with ammunition supplies. On the right, 4th Division was held back by the failure of XVIII Corps on its right flank, but a line was eventually established astride the Poelcapelle–Houthulst road.

In the centre, 29th Division employed 86th and 88th Brigades on the right and left respectively. Taping the start line was hazardous, but there was an amusing incident in 88th Brigade's area. The officer leading the taping party returned to the Brigade HQ dugout, where he mentioned to one of the COs that his men were in need of musketry practice. The indignant CO demanded to know why. It transpired that the taping party had been mistaken for a German patrol and was fired upon by three outposts of this battalion from less than fifty metres. Not one man had been hit. Needless to say the other battalion commanders enjoyed the jibe.

Due to the ground conditions it was decided to move forward the leading battalions on the night of 7th/8th October. Even so, one battalion took six hours to move four and a half miles and reached the start line just before zero at 5.20 a.m. Operations on 4th October had advanced the right of the Division much more than the left. As a result 88th Brigade faced an advance of 2,300m, while the 86th had only 1,500m to cover to its final objective. The attackers faced a number of problems. First, Bear Copse on the Division's northern boundary had been spared proper artillery attention in the earlier fighting due to mist. Second, the Broenbeek in this area, although not impassable, was still a major obstacle. Third, the left would be under enfilade fire from Koekuit; and finally, there were a number of very strongly defended locations to be overcome, mainly along the railway line.

The plan was for two companies of the leading battalions to take the first objective (Green Dotted Line) and after a pause of one hour the other two companies were to take the second objective (Blue Dotted Line). Another hour was allowed for

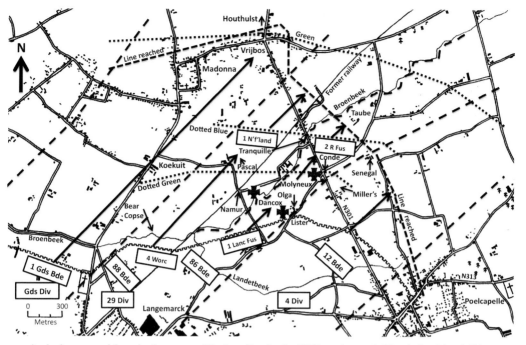

At the large roundabout in the centre of Poelcapelle take the N301 road towards Houthulst. After 1,400m turn left at Conde House crossroads into Schreiboomstraat and park where safe. Walk back to the crossroads to consider the action fought here by John Molyneux.

Continue southwest along Schreiboomstraat for 675m from Conde House crossroads. Pass Olga Farm on the right and at the next t-junction on the left there is usually space to halt for a few minutes. Walk back to Olga Farm, the site of Joseph Lister's VC action. In 1917 there were two pillboxes just to the southwest of the buildings and another a little further away to the northeast of the Farm.

Continue from the t-junction southwest of Olga Farm along Schreiboomstraat for another 200m and turn right into Koekuitstraat. Follow it northwest for 600m and cross the former railway (cycle track) to park on the far side. Walk back over the railway, passing the Frederick Dancox memorial, take the lane to the left and follow it for 135m. On the right of the lane at this point is the site of the pillbox attacked by Dancox.

consolidation under cover of a smoke screen, while the artillery bombarded the third and final objective about 650m beyond the second, which was to be taken by the support battalions. The barrage fell promptly at zero. At the same time Bear Copse was neutralised by Stokes mortars and the garrison surrendered.

86th Brigade on the right did not have to cross the Broenbeek. 1st Lancashire Fusiliers attacked with A and B Companies leading on the right and left respectively. They were to take the first objective. C and D Companies were then to take over the advance to the second objective on the line Senegal Farm to Tranquille House. By coincidence, 2nd Lancashire Fusiliers (12th Brigade, 4th Division) was on 1st Lancashire Fusiliers' right flank. 2nd Royal Fusiliers was in support to continue to the final objective. 1st Lancashire Fusiliers had a number of problems to overcome, including an awkward angle of attack, shortage of tape to mark the start line and confusion caused by the loss and later discovery of two of B Company's leading platoons. The Battalion met stubborn resistance from a series of pillboxes, south

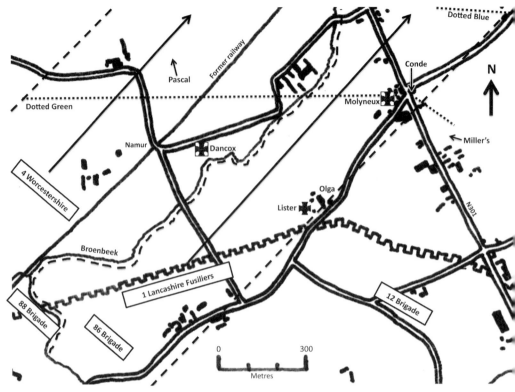

Larger scale map of the area around the three 29th Division VC actions on 9th October 1917.

and north of Olga House. After these had been cleared, A Company was confronted by Olga House itself, which stopped it dead.

While the company commander was deliberating on whether to risk a costly but rapid frontal assault or a potentially more costly delayed flanking attack, the decision was taken for him. **Sergeant Joseph Lister** realised that delay would lead to loss of contact with the barrage. He went ahead of his men to silence a machine gun post in a shell-hole in front of the pillbox. He shot the gunners and then shouted to the pillbox garrison at Olga House to give up. One hundred Germans appeared from it

Olga Farm from the southeast. 1st Lancashire Fusiliers attacked from the left, parallel with the road (Schreiboomstraat). Two pillboxes stood in the field just to the left of the farm buildings.

and nearby shell-holes. One man who refused to surrender was shot dead, but the rest came quietly. This action allowed the Battalion to continue its advance behind the barrage and the first objective was taken at about 5.58 a.m.

While A and B Companies were consolidating, C and D Companies went on. Because of the heavy casualties, 2nd Royal Fusiliers reinforced 1st Lancashire Fusiliers with two platoons from Y Company. Stragglers from a number of other units were also picked up on the way. The combined force advanced by short rushes towards Conde House. D Company reached Senegal Farm, although some shells falling short caused a number of casualties. Some troops also reached Tranquille House and dug-in with elements of 1st Newfoundland and 4th Worcestershire (both 88th Brigade).

The Germans counterattacked in eight lines and were met with small arms fire. At 8.55 a.m. the barrage fell for the attack on the third objective, hitting the counterattack force and driving it back. A combined force of 4th Worcestershire, 1st Newfoundland, 1st Lancashire Fusiliers and some Guardsmen set off for the final objective. Because 12th Brigade (4th Division) had been held up on the right, a flank party was organised by 1st Lancashire Fusiliers. At 10 a.m. the enemy resistance suddenly collapsed and the objective was taken.

2nd Royal Fusiliers had a difficult time following 1st Lancashire Fusiliers. Y Company led on the right and X Company on the left, with Z and W Companies in support respectively. The Battalion was held up for fifteen minutes near Olga House until 1st Lancashire Fusiliers advanced another 135m, but by then it had lost the barrage.

1st Lancashire Fusiliers in front of Y Company, 2nd Royal Fusiliers, veered to the left except for thirty men who continued in the correct direction. These men halted on the first objective between Olga and Conde Houses; but when the advance should have resumed to the second objective nothing happened. Two platoons of Y Company passed through and came under heavy fire from Senegal Farm. They advanced 175m, suffering twenty casualties on the way, and halted, with the right on Miller's Farm. Some Lancashire Fusiliers were seen in front firing to the left, but there was no one to the right. A patrol discovered a gap of 275m before the nearest troops of 4th Division were found on this flank. A line was established 225m in front of Conde House to ninety metres north of Miller's House. As the second objective had not been secured and there was no support, no attempt was made to reach the third objective.

On the left, X Company was in contact with 4th Worcestershire and the advance proceeded well until Olga House was reached. The Company was delayed there for fifteen minutes until 1st Lancashire Fusiliers in front advanced another ninety metres and reached the first objective. At the appointed time X Company passed through the survivors sheltering in shell holes. The barrage fell short at Conde House and when it lifted the troops were forced to advance without protection.

Looking northeast along Schreiboomstraat to Conde House crossroads, the same direction as the attack by John Molyneux.

Sergeant John Molyneux in W Company realised the attack was in danger of being checked by a machine gun in a trench in front of Conde House. He and Sergeant Day tried to work their way around the post, but Day was hit twice. This made Molyneux extremely angry. Making his way further around the flank, he came across a trench containing six or seven Germans and at once organised a bombing party to clear them. Many were killed and the machine gun was captured. He then jumped out of the trench and called on some men to follow him as he rushed Conde House. By the time his men arrived, Molyneux was in the thick of hand-to-hand fighting. The struggle was short lived due to the impetus of the assault. A number of enemy were killed and wounded and twenty to thirty prisoners were taken. Finally, Molyneux captured a pillbox at the rear of the House. The Battalion's left was then able to continue the advance towards the final objective, but it soon petered out and a line was established at Tranquille House. 86th Brigade was relieved by 51st Brigade (17th Division) on the night of 10th/11th October.

Conde House, in the centre on the far side of the N301 Poelcapelle – Houthulst road.

88th Brigade's attack on the left was led by 4th Worcestershire to the first two objectives (Dotted Green and Dotted Blue Lines), where 1st Newfoundland was to take over for the advance to the final objective (Green Line). A detachment of 1st Newfoundland, with a Lewis gun section and two guns of 88th Machine Gun Company, were to protect the left flank, moving 175m behind the leading troops. 2nd Hampshire was poised to deal with any German counterattacks and 16th Middlesex was in reserve, with 1st Essex back on the canal bank. The heavy rain the night before the attack helped to cover the move forward and the laying out of tapes on the start line. All were in position by 2.30 a.m. Due to a mix up, hand carried bridges to cross the Broenbeek were misdirected and only one arrived with 4th Worcestershire, but once the advance commenced two intact German bridges were discovered and, although swollen, the Broenbeek was fordable. Hot tea and rum was served, in one instance only five minutes before zero.

4th Worcestershire attacked astride the railway from old German trenches (Bear and Leopard). In crossing the Broenbeek elements of 1st Newfoundland in support became intermingled. The advance proceeded in spite of opposition from numerous pillboxes along the railway embankment and the first objective beyond Namur Crossing was reached at 5.50 a.m. The Battalion was in contact with 2nd Coldstream Guards (1st Guards Brigade) on the left and 2nd Royal Fusiliers (86th Brigade) on the right. Losses had been light and the troops began to dig in under cover of a smoke screen.

One pillbox continued to fire. Casualties were heavy and little could be done until trench mortars were brought up to silence the position. **Private Frederick Dancox** had other ideas. He was the sanitary orderly in Battalion headquarters and had overheard much talk about taking pillboxes by entering them through the back door. He asked to take part in the attack with his company and was allocated to one of the mopping-up parties. During the consolidation on the first objective his party was detailed to search the ground in front, but remain on the 'friendly' side of the protective barrage. However, the pillbox causing the problem was beyond the

The former railway line is in the foreground with Koekuitstraat running away to the southeast in the centre. Frederick Dancox's memorial is to the left of Koekuitstraat alongside the railway line. The pillbox he attacked was in the light coloured field slightly above and to the left of the memorial just beyond the fence posts.

barrage and lay at the midpoint between the railway and the Broenbeek. Risking his life, Dancox passed through the barrage and got behind the pillbox undetected. He entered the strongpoint, threatening the occupants with a Mills bomb, which he held up high and slowly backed out, beckoning the Germans to follow; forty surrendered. Once they were heading towards the British lines he went back inside and dismounted the machine gun. As the barrage lifted, he was seen returning with his prisoners and the machine gun tucked under his arm. The Brigade report on the operation states that a mortar did come into action just south of the Broenbeek and, at a range of 275m, landed four direct hits on the blockhouse following which the infantry attacked.

From the site of Frederick Dancox's pillbox, looking southwest, with Langemarck church on the far left and the former railway line on the right. Namur Crossing is right of the prominent tree in the centre.

4th Worcestershire's support companies took over the advance to the second objective, which was achieved by 8 a.m., with less opposition than the first objective. There was a hold up at Pascal Farm until mortars engaged it with twenty-five bombs. This, combined with the infantry's fire, resulted in about fifty Germans surrendering. Touch was gained with 1st Irish Guards on the left and 2nd Royal Fusiliers on the right. Dancox kept the captured machine gun in action all day.

88th Brigade's advance to the final objective was taken over by 1st Newfoundland, which was well supported by 1st Irish Guards on the left. However, the right flank was open as 86th Brigade was halted by marshy ground. German attempts to organise counterattacks from near Taube Farm were broken up by the artillery. About 5.30 p.m. enemy pressure on the left necessitated the line being pulled back a little. Around the same time a separate operation was launched to capture a farm in the angle formed by the railway and the Poelcapelle–Houthulst road. 2nd Hampshire took over the front line from 1st Newfoundland and the two forward companies of

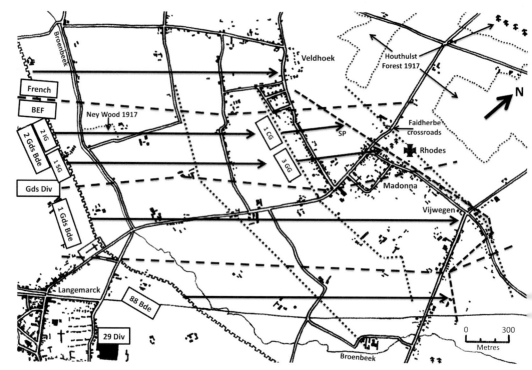

Drive northeast out of Langemarck, passing the German War Cemetery on the left and continue for 1,850m to the roundabout in Madonna. Turn right. There is a track on the left after 350m. Park on the side of the main road and walk north along the track for 125m and then turn left for another 100m. The pillbox captured by Rhodes was just to the right/north of the track at this point. If you hear the sound of exploding shells, don't be alarmed. The Belgian Army disposes of WW1 artillery ammunition found on the battlefields in Houthulst Forest to the northeast.

4th Worcestershire. The final line held was just east of the Poelcapelle–Houthulst road. 4th Worcestershire was relieved by 7th Lincolnshire and pulled back to Harrow Camp. It suffered 174 casualties, but took over 200 prisoners. In addition to Dancox's VC, another thirty-eight gallantry awards were received by the Battalion.

The view northwest from the track north of Madonna, with the site of the pillbox captured by John Rhodes right of centre.

On the left, the Guards Division was supported by an intense and accurate artillery barrage, which kept the defenders occupied until the attackers were upon them. 1st Guards Brigade was on the right and 2nd Guards Brigade was on the left. At the end of the day 1st Guards Brigade was on its objective or very close to it.

2nd Guards Brigade's attack was led by 1st Scots Guards on the right and 2nd Irish Guards on the left. These battalions were to take the first two objectives, while the third and final objective was allocated to 3rd Grenadier Guards on the right and 1st Coldstream Guards on the left. At the Broenbeek the 200 light bridges provided were found to be largely unnecessary. A machine gun in Ney Wood caused a slight delay, but the first objective was taken on time; and the French on the left reached the first objective at about the same time. The support companies passed through and took the second objective by 8.15 a.m. Meanwhile at 7.30 a.m. the support battalions had crossed the Broenbeek. As 3rd Grenadier Guards neared the second objective it shook out into attack formation, deploying No.3 Company on the right and No.4 Company on the left, with Nos.1 and 2 Companies in support. The support battalions passed through to the third objective on the heavily defended southern fringe of Houthulst Forest.

Lance Sergeant John Rhodes, 3rd Grenadier Guards, was in charge of a Lewis gun section covering the consolidation of the right forward company (No.3). He had already accounted for a number of the enemy when he saw some Germans leave a pillbox ninety metres ahead of the line being consolidated. He went out on his own through the British and hostile fire to enter the pillbox. He captured ten occupants, including a forward observation officer still connected by telephone with his battery, and brought them and much valuable information back.

On the left of the Brigade, 1st Coldstream Guards was held up by a strongpoint between Veldhoek and Madonna. It was not taken until the early afternoon. The final objective along the western extremity of the Veldhoek–Vijwegen spur was not reached, but 2nd Guards Brigade was close to it and consolidation commenced. A counterattack from the southwest corner of Houthulst Forest in the late afternoon was driven back by 1st Coldsteam Guards at Faidherbe crossroads and the French.

Reverse of the previous view, with the site of the pillbox in the foreground.

By the time 2nd Guards Brigade was relieved on 12th October it had suffered 544 casualties.

Overall the main gains of the day were confined to near Reutel, in front of Passchendaele and near Houthulst Forest. In general, final objectives had not been reached.

Chapter Nine

The Battles of Passchendaele

First Battle of Passchendaele

12th October 1917

284 Capt Clarence Jeffries, 34th Battalion AIF (9th Australian Brigade, 3rd Australian Division), Passchendaele, Belgium

285 Pte Albert Halton, 1st King's Own (Royal Lancaster) (12th Brigade, 4th Division), Poelcapelle, Belgium

The attack on 9th October had been far from successful. It was believed at the higher levels of command that this was due mainly to the mud. Despite the lack of progress, General Plumer, commanding Second Army, considered that a position had been reached by II ANZAC Corps (66th and 49th Divisions) from where a successful attack against Passchendaele could be launched. Having achieved that, the recently arrived Canadian Corps would take over the line on the Passchendaele–Westroosebeke Ridge with a view to continuing the advance towards Moorslede and Becelaere. Haig was anxious to take Passchendaele village before closing down the campaign for the winter.

Plumer's optimism was based on inaccurate information. The position was not as advantageous as believed and there were hundreds of wounded still lying out from the attack on 9th October. The survivors of that attack were utterly exhausted as they clung on to their meagre gains. In most cases it had not been possible to resupply them with food and ammunition.

Mud was a serious problem, but not the only one. There were only three days to prepare after the previous attack on 9th October. Patrols in front of II ANZAC Corps detected two belts of wire thirty metres wide protecting the Flanders I Line. The artillery found it almost impossible to cross the Steenbeek and the specially constructed gun platforms slipped when the guns fired. Rain fell throughout 10th and 11th October, holding up work on the plank roads and further delaying the move forward of the batteries. Resupply of ammunition was slow and shells arrived coated in mud. In consequence there was little counter-battery fire.

In I ANZAC Corps, 4th Australian Division was to protect the southern flank of the main attack. Two battalions of 12th Australian Brigade gained their objectives

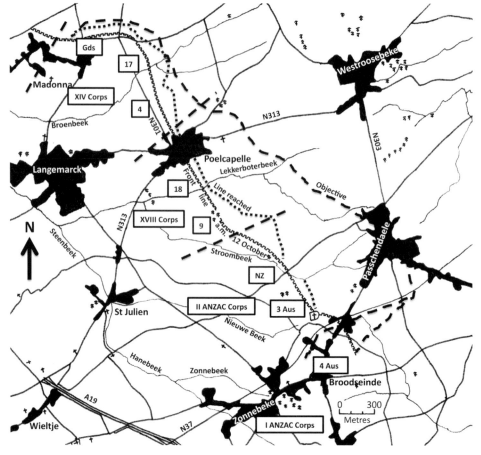

The First Battle of Passchendaele, 12th October 1917.

with some difficulty and loss, but later had to abandon them due to the withdrawal of 3rd Australian Division north of the railway.

The main attack on 12th October was made by 3rd Australian Division and the New Zealand Division in II ANZAC Corps, the former to capture Passchendaele village while the latter concentrated on Bellevue and Goudberg on the Wallemolen Spur. The objectives were similar to those on 9th October. As the assault troops made their way forward on the evening of 11th October, they found it difficult to keep direction due to the pitch darkness and rain. They had to hang on to the equipment of the man in front. The Ravebeek was crossed using five coconut-matting bridges and by 3 a.m. the lead battalions were on the start line.

On taking over the front, 3rd Australian Division discovered that the front line was well behind where it was reported to be. In the days prior to the attack 11th Australian Brigade had to establish a line amongst the chaotic and shattered remnants of 66th Division. It wasn't until 11th October that the reality was fully known. By then it was too late to alter the barrage orders for 12th October. All that could be done was to start the barrage 325m behind the planned line and advance

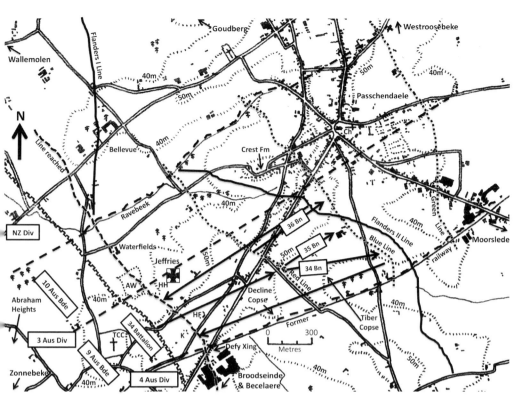

Follow signs for Tyne Cot Cemetery (TCC) and park in the car park at the rear. Go back onto the road and walk northeast for thirty metres northeast to the right bend. Stop here and look northeast towards Passchendaele church (Ch). Clarence Jeffries' VC action was about 400m away on the next spur to the one you are standing on, down the slope from the farm buildings. A few trees mark the site of Augustus Wood. There is no trace of Heine House (HH). A number of other abbreviations are used on the map – K = Keerselaanhoek, HF = Hillside Farm and AW = Augustus Wood.

it more quickly over the first 450m to catch up with the rest of Second Army. The attacking troops faced having to advance at twice the recognised practicable speed over very difficult ground, something that had not even been attempted in the dry conditions in September.

3rd Australian Division attacked with 9th Australian Brigade on the right against the main ridge and 10th Australian Brigade south of the Ravebeek. There were three objectives. The first, the Red Line, was about 1,100m from the start line and was almost the same as the second objective on 9th October. The second objective, the Blue Line, was 800m further on, whilst the final objective, the Green Line, about another 800m further on, was to be reached at 12.11 p.m. Each assault battalion had two Vickers machine guns and two Stokes mortars attached. Assault battalions were to attack with three companies forward and one in support.

In 9th Australian Brigade the Red, Blue and Green Lines were allocated respectively to 34th, 35th and 36th Battalions. 33rd Battalion was in reserve. The support company of 35th Battalion was to move behind the Battalion's left rear to assist 10th Australian Brigade in Passchendaele. 9th Australian Brigade was at Winnezeele until 10th October and had very limited time for preparations. There were no forward dumps of ammunition, food and water and there was no time to dig communication cables forward of Brigade HQ. No final written operation orders could be issued and instructions were dictated to battalion commanders and adjutants. Battalion strengths varied between 450 and 550.

In 10th Australian Brigade, 38th Battalion was allocated to seize Passchendaele. If the village was not taken, 33rd Battalion in 9th Australian Brigade was to enclose the village from the south, while the New Zealand Division had troops ready to enclose it from the north.

The approach march commenced at 6 p.m. on 11th October. All went well initially. The duckboard tracks had been extended from where they ended for 66th Division. However, from Zonnebeke station onwards they were shelled, including with gas. Fortunately the wind was strong enough to disperse the gas and there were few casualties in the leading battalion, but 36th Battalion suffered a hundred. The shelling also destroyed the track in places and the tape was lost. The rain started again at 1.30 a.m. and by 3.30 a.m. was falling heavily.

On reaching the Broodseinde railway cutting, the two leading company commanders in 9th Australian Brigade, Captains Jeffries and Gilder of 34th Battalion, went ahead to check where the line was so that their men did not walk into the Germans. However, all was well and they found the white tape at Keerselaarhoek. The speed of the approach march had averaged just 1,200m per hour. Whilst lying out waiting for zero there were numerous casualties from hostile shelling.

At 5.20 a.m. the Germans fired a barrage on the start line and there were about 150 casualties before it was cleared at zero five minutes later. As the troops advanced it was clear that the barrage was weak; even heavy shells did little more than splash the pillboxes with mud.

From the right bend in the road northeast of Tyne Cot Cemetery looking northeast. This is about the closest viewpoint available over the site of Clarence Jeffries' VC action without straying onto private, cultivated land.

9th Australian Brigade had no opportunity to shake out into proper formation before the undisturbed German machine guns were turned upon them. Men sank into the mud and had to be helped out, which delayed progress. The advance proceeded in some confusion. It was impossible to catch up with the rapidly advancing barrage, such as it was. Three positions with machine guns caused the main problems. They were in a ruined house at Defy Crossing, Hillside Farm and Augustus Wood/Heine House. The advance was delayed for an hour. More delay was imposed by another pillbox close to the Passchendaele road near the first objective, close to the highest point of the ridge.

There was no cover on the left, where the position east of Augustus Wood and northeast of Heine House was holding up the advance in the centre. **Captain Clarence Jeffries** organised a small party from his company, including Sergeant James Bruce (later Lieutenant J Bruce MC DCM, killed in action 17th July 1918 – Villers-Bretonneux Military Cemetery), another NCO and twelve men. They outflanked the post and rushed it, seizing four machine guns and thirty-five prisoners. He then led his company to seize fifty metres of trench held by twenty to thirty Germans about 150m behind the pillboxes. Jeffries' efforts ensured the centre of the advance could continue.

Two machine guns were mopped up at Decline Copse on the railway on the right. The advance was then able to resume and the first objective was taken. 34th Battalion began consolidation there. The Battalion had only three officers left and there were big gaps in the line. The right flank had swung away from the railway and 4th Australian Division, leaving a gap. The line on the left was in contact with 10th Australian Brigade, but heavy fire was being received from Bellevue Spur. In the advance the trench mortars and machine guns had either been destroyed, the ammunition carriers did not arrive, or the weapons could not be manhandled in the conditions. Many Lewis guns and rifles became so clogged with mud that they were unusable.

The advance to the second objective started almost immediately because of delays in reaching the first. About one hundred men of 35th Battalion passed

Tyne Cot Cemetery

through with most of 34th Battalion joining them. It was difficult to ascertain where the barrage was and the weather and visibility had improved considerably. Machine guns opened fire from the gap on the right, about 200m from the railway. Jeffries and Bruce led a small party from the first objective and made for this position. Moving between bursts of fire, they managed to close with it. As the gun swung to fire to the north, they dashed in from the west. However, the gun was swung back and Jeffries was killed. His men went to ground, but continued to work round the position. They rushed in and two machine guns and more than twenty-five prisoners were taken.

35th and 36th Battalions, augmented by 34th Battalion, overcame resistance in Tiber Copse. Once over the crest on the eastern side the men were exposed to artillery firing over open sights. 35th Battalion reached what it took to be the second objective. On the left the line was where 66th Division had reached on 9th October. Passchendaele church was ahead and there appeared to be no resistance. However, heavy fire from the left had all but wiped out the left company in the advance. By the time the Blue Line was reached all three assault battalions were involved. 36th Battalion was largely on the left, 35th Battalion was in the centre and 34th Battalion was largely on the right. However, 9th Australian Brigade was in a precarious position. It was clear that 4th Australian Division on the right was some way ahead, but, on the left, 10th Australian Brigade was some way behind.

10th Australian Brigade's leading battalion, 37th, met strong resistance from Augustus Wood and Waterfields. The advance was slowed to hopping from shell-hole to shell-hole. 40th and 38th Battalions following became hopelessly intermingled with 37th Battalion. However, Augustus Wood and Waterfields were eventually taken. Casualties had been heavy. One of those killed was Sergeant Lewis McGee, who had earned the VC on 4th October. Fire increased from Bellevue on the left flank, where the New Zealanders had been held up. A party sent to subdue it was not heard from again. Just short of the first objective the advance degenerated into a number of small individual parties and a slight fold in the ground was chosen to dig in. With only about 150 men reaching the first objective, Major Giblin decided not to advance until reinforcements arrived. However, a party of about twenty men, mainly 38th Battalion, had gone ahead through the Ravebeek valley. It met no resistance until it climbed onto a spur jutting into the end of the valley. At Crest Farm a large pillbox surrendered immediately. On the Bellevue Spur the Germans could be seen retreating. The party pressed on and reached Passchendaele church; the village was deserted. However, due to being unsupported on both flanks, the party turned back and withdrew to the left flank of 9th Australian Brigade. As they fell back it was noted that the Germans were going forward to reoccupy their former positions, including Crest Farm. Another small party on the left of 10th Australian Brigade made some progress, getting over the Ravebeek at a road crossing and overcoming some German positions. However, it was unable to suppress the fire from Bellevue Spur.

At 10.50 a.m. Major General Monash, at HQ 3rd Australian Division, ordered an enveloping attack with 33rd Battalion, the reserve battalion of 9th Australian Brigade, passing the west side of Passchendaele. The New Zealand Division was requested to bombard Bellevue with everything available. However, the latter had been ordered by Commander II ANZAC Corps to attack again at 3 p.m. 33rd Battalion was instead ordered to cooperate by pushing forward around Crest Farm. Well before 3 p.m. the situation had changed considerably. 10th Australian Brigade had been raked continuously by fire from Bellevue and had suffered heavy losses. The senior surviving officer realised that nothing could be gained and ordered a withdrawal back to the start line. This left 9th Australian Brigade isolated on the ridge. It too was lashed by heavy fire from guns over open sights, as well as machine guns and snipers. Faced with annihilation, its senior officer also ordered a withdrawal almost to the start line. The Corps Commander cancelled the renewed attack.

9th Australian Brigade suffered 964 casualties in this operation. 34th Battalion was not relieved until 5 p.m. on 14th October and moved into support on the reverse side of Abraham Heights.

The New Zealanders ran into uncut wire and the artillery support was weak. Despite valiant attempts, few gains were made except on the left. The Division suffered 2,735 casualties.

Fifth Army was to establish the northern flank. XVIII Corps (9th and 18th Divisions) attacked with the intention of advancing 1,800m onto the main ridge. The artillery and machine gun support was ineffective and the Germans opened heavy fire on the attackers as they struggled through the deep mud. The barrage was lost and even advancing by short rushes died out as losses mounted; but touch was maintained with the New Zealanders on the right. Although isolated parties neared the final objective, the majority advanced very little.

Further north, XIV Corps attacked in the Houthulst Forest area, where the artillery and machine guns had fewer problems. In the days before the attack, enemy aircraft, artillery and snipers were very active, but the night before was quiet. Zero in this area was at 5.30 a.m., with the assault troops setting off three minutes after the barrage fell. 12th Brigade, commanded by Brigadier General Adrian Carton de Wiart VC, carried out the attack on the front of 4th Division, starting from east of the Poelcapelle–Miller's House road. The Brigade was led by the Household Battalion on the right and 1st Royal Warwickshire on the left, both units attached from 10th Brigade. 1st King's Own was in support to oppose counterattacks, with 1st Rifle Brigade (11th Brigade) and 2nd Duke of Wellington's was in reserve. There were two objectives, the Green and Red Lines, the latter also described as the Purple Line. The leading battalions were to take both objectives and each was allocated two Vickers machine guns.

The final objective was to be consolidated with posts up to ninety metres in front. The support battalions were to establish a depth line from Requete Farm to Bower

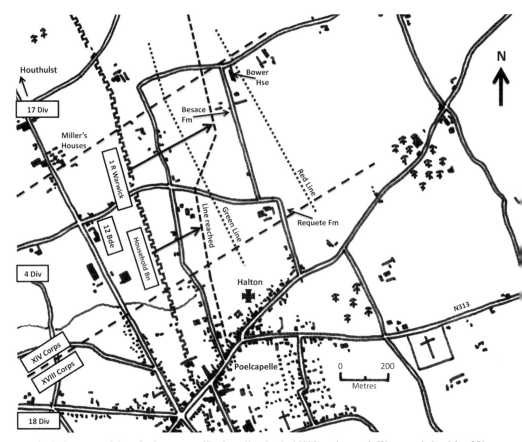

Houthulst

17 Div

Miller's Houses

Bower Hse

Besace Fm

Red Line

1 R Warwick

Line reached

Green Line

Requete Fm

12 Bde

Household Bn

Halton

4 Div

N313

XIV Corps

XVIII Corps

Poelcapelle

0   200
Metres

18 Div

N

At the large roundabout in the centre of Poelcapelle take the N313 road towards Westroosebeke. After 250m, turn left into Poorterstraat and drive along it for just over 400m, to where it bends slightly to the right. Park where safe to do so and look back along the road towards Poelcapelle. About 200m away half left is a football pitch, which is about where Halton captured the machine gun post.

House. Patrols were to probe forward to gain information about the enemy and special parties were detailed to maintain contact with flanking units.

1st Royal Warwickshire met little resistance and almost gained its objective at Besace Farm. A counterattack was driven off. However, a heavy enemy barrage on the front line and flanking machine gun fire from Poelcapelle on the right, which

The football pitch where Albert Halton captured the machine gun crew is on the left, beneath the crane. Poelcapelle church is on the right.

18th Division had thus far failed to capture, caused many casualties in the Household Battalion. Despite the resistance, its objective at Requete Farm was captured when 18th Division secured part of the village to the south. A protective right flank was formed on the outskirts of Poelcapelle by a company each from 1st King's Own and 1st Rifle Brigade. A counterattack later in the day made a withdrawal necessary at Requete Farm.

While the protective flank was being consolidated heavy fire was received from the right. **Private Albert Halton** went forward 275m on his own and captured the crew of a machine gun that had been causing heavy casualties. He went out again and returned with twelve prisoners.

12th Brigade was relieved by midnight on 13th October and on the 14th the Household Battalion and 1st Royal Warwickshire returned to 10th Brigade. Further north the 17th and Guards Divisions encountered less resistance and gained most of their objectives.

26th October 1917

286 Lt Robert Shankland, 43rd Battalion CEF (9th Canadian Brigade, 3rd Canadian Division), Passchendaele, Belgium

287 Capt Christopher O'Kelly, 52nd Battalion CEF (9th Canadian Brigade, 3rd Canadian Division), Passchendaele, Belgium

288 Pte Thomas Holmes, 4th Canadian Mounted Rifles (8th Canadian Brigade, 3rd Canadian Division), Passchendaele, Belgium

On 13th October further attacks were postponed until the weather improved and roads could be constructed to bring forward the artillery. However, the aim of securing the main Passchendaele Ridge as a winter position remained. There were two other imperatives that ensured the offensive in Flanders would continue. The BEF needed to divert German attention and tie down reserves prior to a French attack in Champagne on 23rd October. Preparations for a new offensive to be carried out before winter at Cambrai were well advanced and its chances of success would be improved the longer the Flanders offensive continued.

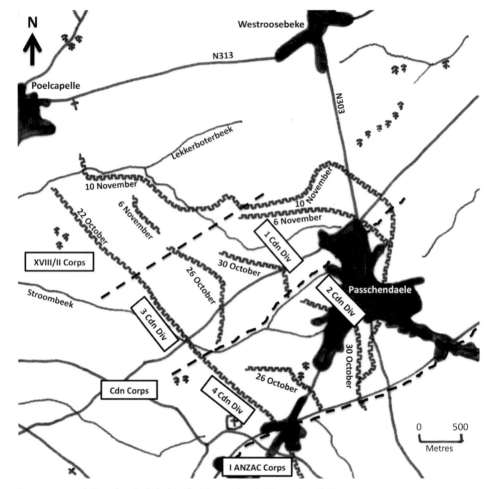

Progress towards Passchendaele in late October and early November 1917.

Ground conditions in front of Passchendaele were appalling. The Ravebeek valley was impassable and split the front of the Canadian Corps, which had been in the Lens–Vimy area until it replaced II ANZAC Corps on 18th October. It was to seize Passchendaele in three short advances, with three or more days between each to allow for reliefs. Fifth Army was then to take Westroosebeke to secure the position for the winter. While the Canadians made the main attacks the flanks would be protected by I ANZAC Corps on the right and Fifth Army on the left.

The immediate priority for the Canadians was to take over existing artillery pieces from the outgoing ANZACs in situ. Although the total number of guns in the area was impressive, the reality was somewhat different. Two hundred and fifty heavy guns were taken over, but only 227 could be found and of these only 138 were serviceable and in action. Field guns were in a similar situation. Of 306 18 Pounders, less than half were in action and many were where they had bogged in rather than in ideal positions to support the forthcoming resumption of the offensive. Many guns required workshop attention, but the Australians had been unable to move them back because of the risk of blocking the tracks, which were needed to bring forward reinforcements and materiel. Because of the ground conditions most of the guns were closely bunched into four clusters, two each of heavy and field guns. These made ideal targets for the German gunners. However, by the time the attack was launched on 26th October the situation had improved considerably and the Canadian Corps was supported by an increasing number of guns of all types, many provided by the Australians, British and New Zealanders. While tracks were pushed forward for the field artillery, the heavy guns commenced bombarding the enemy wire and pillbox positions.

German tactics had evolved again. To the end of September the Germans had tended to hold the forward areas lightly and rely on rapid and closely based counterattack forces to push back attacks. However, the British had limited their advances to short steps and used their artillery to devastating effect to destroy counterattack forces before they could be committed properly. As a result, in front of Passchendaele 11th Bavarian Division deployed its three regiments, each with a single battalion forward, another in support and a third in reserve. The concept was to commit separate counterattack forces the day after a British advance, or maybe even two days. The forward battalions had an outpost line in craters, short sections of trench and pillboxes with light machine guns. Five hundred to a 1,000 metres to the rear was the main line of resistance. Each front line division had a counterattack division behind it with which it rotated periodically. German artillery was ranged on the outpost line and could be moved back and forth depending upon the tactical situation. This change meant that the forward area was once again relatively strongly held in order to defeat the enemy advance early on.

The weather improved towards the middle of the month. The German artillery hindered progress on laying plank roads and other preparations, which were in view from Passchendaele Ridge. A combination of sneezing gas, which forced men to remove their respirators, followed by mustard gas in nightly bombardments caused numerous casualties and rendered some areas unusable for battery positions or bivouacs. Construction of the plank roads and battery positions involved the daily commitment of nine infantry and pioneer battalions and twenty-three engineer and labour companies.

Fifth Army cooperated with the French in an attack towards Houthulst on 22nd October. At 5.35 a.m. the artillery of Second and Fifth Armies opened fire along the whole front to simulate a large scale offensive. Only XVIII and XIV Corps in Fifth Army attacked and made some gains, although in places these were lost later in the day. Next day the Canadian 50th Battalion pushed posts forward 300–400m along the top of the ridge towards Passchendaele.

From 23rd October the bombardment of the enemy wire and strongpoints intensified. There was also a considerable amount of counter-battery work and preparatory barrages were fired morning and afternoon in the four days before the attack. Orders for the forthcoming attack emphasised the need to have muzzle

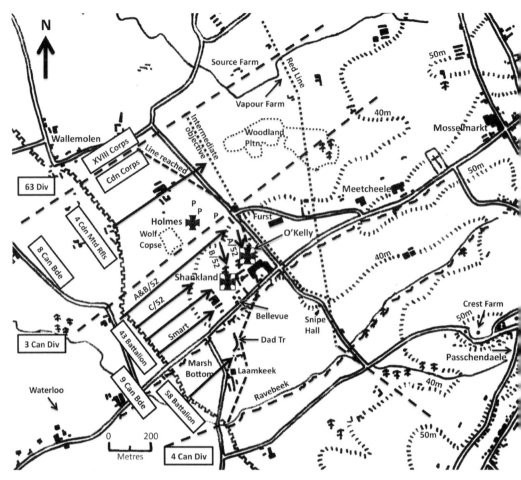

From the Canadian Memorial at Crest Farm, on the southwestern edge of Passchendaele, drive southwest off the ridge. After 475m turn right and cross over the easy to miss Ravebeek, but in 1917 it made this area an impenetrable swamp. After 600m, at the crossroads go straight over, pass a right turn after 300m and continue another 250m to a wide turning into a farm complex on the left. There is space to park here for a few minutes. Look back the way you came. The field in front is where Thomas Holmes captured the machine gun posts, attacking up the slope from the right. Further up the slope to the right of the road is where Christopher O'Kelly's attack took place towards the line of trees on the skyline. Robert Shankland's position was at the western (right) end of the same line of trees. Return to the crossroads, turn right and after the factory pull in where safe. Between gaps in the houses here you can see the end of the line of trees where Robert Shankland defended the line.

protectors and breech covers for infantry weapons. It was found that the rubber caps for 18 Pounder shells fitted neatly over the muzzle of the Lewis gun.

The first Canadian Corps attack was launched at 5.40 a.m. on 26th October. The day before (and the day after) had been clear, fine and warm, with a strong wind drying the ground between shell-holes. However, as the assault troops moved into position the rain returned. Just to reach the start positions for the attack was a major task. The swampy conditions did not allow communications trenches to be dug. Forward of the plank roads and light railways movement was confined to narrow duckboard paths winding between shell-holes. In places even the duckboards were knee deep in mud. The tracks were also under enemy observation, so movement was only possible at night. To ensure that the assault troops had some rest before the attack, they moved up to the support lines two to four days before zero. This also allowed time for officers and NCOs to acquaint themselves with the ground over which they would advance. While they waited the men huddled in shell-holes under their groundsheets. The night before the attack, forward companies pushed posts out into no man's land to ensure that the Germans could not move forward to get inside the barrage.

The 26th started misty, but this changed to rain for the rest of the day. Simultaneous attacks on the flanks gave the impression of a wider offensive and helped pin down enemy reserves. On the right flank, X Corps' 7th and 5th Divisions attacked to capture Gheluvelt and Polderhoek Spurs. Polderhoek Chateau was taken, but progress across the waterlogged plateau was extremely difficult and all gains had to be given up later in the day. X Corps suffered 3,321 casualties.

The Canadian Corps front was split by the Ravebeek swamp, necessitating a two-pronged attack either side of the impassable ground in the valley. The objective, the Red Line, was 1,100m away. The barrage moved forward at only forty-five metres every four minutes, allowing time for the struggling infantry to negotiate the difficult ground conditions.

On the right, 4th Canadian Division's attack was made by 46th Battalion (10th Canadian Brigade) from 350m south of the Ravebeek. The Battalion crept forward to assemble just behind the forward posts of 50th Battalion holding the line. 46th Battalion's main obstacle was Decline Copse, which was strongly defended by Bavarians. Despite the conditions, the Battalion reached its objective with a I ANZAC Corps battalion alongside. One company was 225m ahead of its objective. The line was consolidated under heavy German artillery fire and two counterattacks were driven off, but the forward posts had to be pulled back and a defensive left flank was established. However, in the afternoon enfilade fire from Laamkeek and a heavy barrage resulted in 70% casualties to the 420 men in the position. A third counterattack and a misunderstanding between the Canadians and Australians at Decline Copse resulted in the survivors pulling back to within one hundred metres of the start line. 44th and 47th Battalions came up later and on the night of 27th/28th October the gains made by 46th Battalion were retaken.

On the left, 3rd Canadian Division had 9th Canadian Brigade on the right and 8th Canadian Brigade on the left. 9th Canadian Brigade assembled north of the Ravebeek and all were in position an hour before zero. They advanced initially through broken wire, but 58th Battalion on the right was checked about 225m in front of Snipe Hall and by fire from Crest Farm. By 8 a.m. the German artillery and machine gun fire, combined with a counterattack, had stopped the advance 350m short of the objective and most of the Battalion was back on the start line. D Company, 52nd Battalion attached to 58th Battalion, was sent forward to support

Panorama of the area of the attacks made by 43rd Battalion, 52nd Battalion and 4th Canadian Mounted Rifles. The main pillboxes and multiples are indicated by white boxes with a 'P'.

the attack. At 10 a.m. it was holding the 58th Battalion start line in Marsh Bottom with some of 58th Battalion. It advanced through the remnants of 58th Battalion and took Dad Trench about midday after suffering heavy casualties.

On the left of the Brigade, 43rd Battalion was led by B Company on the right and C Company on the left to the first objective. D Company was to pass through to take the final objective, with A Company following to consolidate a support line.

From the roadside at Bellevue looking north to the western end of the strip wood where the three pillboxes stood in 1917. Robert Shankland established his small force on the crest just beyond the pillboxes.

D Company had four Vickers machine guns attached with which to hold the Red Line. C Company, 52nd Battalion was on call.

B Company, 43rd Battalion lost its company commander wounded while forming up. His replacement was hit early in the attack and soon after the Company was being commanded by Corporal Hainstock. Similarly C Company lost three officers early on, but continued up the slope as planned. By 6.30 a.m. elements of the Battalion had reached the crest north of Bellevue and started moving round the pillboxes there. In D Company, **Lieutenant Robert Shankland DCM** rallied his own platoon (he had arrived from the Transport Lines on the 24th to replace a casualty) and gathered elements of other companies, together with two Vickers detachments of 9th Machine Gun Company. His small force of about forty men held on to the positions gained on the crest to the left of the three pillboxes situated just north of the Mosselmarkt road for about four hours. Shankland held off some counterattacks and gained time for support troops to arrive. Meanwhile by 10 a.m., most of 58th and 43rd Battalions had pulled back in some confusion almost to the start positions.

Shankland left the wounded Lieutenant Ellis of 9th Machine Gun Company in command while he went back to Battalion HQ situated in a pillbox near Waterloo, to ensure that the CO was aware of the situation. As a result a party of 43rd Battalion under Lieutenant Smart was sent to the right of Shankland's party and C Company, 52nd Battalion to the left. Both parties were ordered to connect with Shankland in the centre and with flanking units.

Although wounded, Shankland rejoined his party. Two scouts with him returned with a German officer and two soldier prisoners. The officer spoke good English and reported that he had expected to find his company on the ridge after a counterattack. Shankland eventually handed over command to Captain Galt, who had tried to take the strongpoint on the crest and had worked round the left side of it, but could not penetrate to the right due to a tangle of wire and iron rods. The Germans were able to continue firing into 58th Battalion on the right. As he came away with his small party, Galt lost two men and their Lewis gun jammed. They took cover from machine gun fire until 52nd Battalion came forward across his front and relieved Shankland's post.

A Company, 52nd Battalion was sent to extend the line further left to link up with 8th Canadian Brigade. B Company, 52nd Battalion also passed through on the left and pushed across the front of the line established to take the enemy positions in flank on the left front, then Bellevue and on to some strongpoints on the right front. By then Smart's party had pushed forward on the right onto the ridge. These moves took a few hours to complete and there was hard fighting, but it ended with the pillboxes on the spur being overcome.

In this advance **Captain/Lieutenant Christopher O'Kelly** led A Company, 52nd Battalion across 900m of open ground without artillery support. The soil on the ridge was sandy and the going was found to be easier on top. O'Kelly's force fought southwards to outflank the remaining pillboxes near Bellevue and Laamkeek and he organised a series of attacks on the pillboxes. A Company had seized two when B Company came up on the right and the two companies continued the advance. They seized all the ground west of the road, including three more pillboxes and Bellevue Farm. Over 200 prisoners were taken with ten machine guns.

By 3.30 p.m. the German defences in the Flanders I Line north of the Ravebeek to Wolf Copse had been taken and contact established with 8th Canadian Brigade on the left. A, B and C Companies, 52nd Battalion established the new front line, including a strongpoint. A company of 116th Battalion in reserve was sent forward by Brigade HQ to support the left, the right being held by Galt's party. At 4.30 p.m. about 500 Germans were seen massing southwest of Meetcheele, but they were dispersed by machine gun fire. Another counterattack threatened from the same area in the evening and was similarly broken up. 43rd, 58th and 52nd Battalions were relieved in the forward area at 6 p.m. on 27th October by 116th Battalion. By then 43rd Battalion had suffered 351 casualties.

Christopher O'Kelly led A Company, 52nd Battalion up this slope from right to left.

Crossroads

8th Canadian Brigade attacked with 4th Canadian Mounted Rifles. The assembly of the Battalion, although exhausting, went ahead without interference and was completed within forty-five minutes at 5.15 a.m. The start line was seventy metres in advance of the front line. C Company was on the left and D Company on the right for the advance to the intermediate objective. B and A Companies followed to pass through and seize the final objective, the Red Line. Two Vickers machine guns were attached to D Company and four Stokes trench mortars were also attached to the Battalion. Another four Vickers followed behind the Battalion, with a roving commission to engage targets of opportunity. C Company, 1st Canadian Mounted Rifles followed behind.

The machine gun barrage opened at 5.38 a.m. and two minutes later the artillery crashed down. This included the Stokes mortars firing eighty rounds at pillboxes and wire on the intermediate objective. The German barrage in reply was light, but the British barrage was erratic in places, causing some casualties. At 5.48 a.m. the Battalion moved off against strong opposition. The first line of pillboxes was overcome and the advance moved on to tackle the Wallemolen-Bellevue line of pillboxes. There was hard fighting, but a line close to the intermediate objective was reached on time. When the barrage moved on at 7.38 a.m., the advance was stopped by fire from Furst Farm, north of Bellevue, on the right and Wallemolen and Source Trench on the left. Parts of two platoons of C Company on the left managed to get to the western edge of Woodland Plantation, but heavy resistance and mounting casualties forced them to return. Even if the attacking force had been strong enough to continue, the troops on both flanks were some way behind and holding any further gains would have been impossible.

In the advance **Private Thomas Holmes** ran forward on his own initiative and threw two bombs, killing the crews of two machine gun posts that were holding up the advance. Later he again went forward alone and threw a bomb into the entrance to a pillbox, resulting in nineteen defenders surrendering. As a result the Battalion

Shankland's position

The area through which 4th Canadian Mounted Rifles attacked looking northwest. Thomas Holmes' VC action was in this field near the solitary tree just left of centre.

reached its objective and waited for the troops on both flanks to catch up. Little else is known of these actions, which are not mentioned in the Brigade or Battalion war diaries. Given the available evidence, it seems likely that they took place on the right of the Battalion, near Wolf Copse, and in front of the intermediate objective. Trench maps show three pillboxes just short of the line reached.

C Company, 1st Canadian Mounted Rifles moved up to support 4th Canadian Mounted Rifles at 8.20 a.m. and, if possible, was to continue the advance. A and D Companies, 1st Canadian Mounted Rifles occupied the original front line at 9.10 a.m. On arrival in the forward area C Company, 1st Canadian Mounted Rifles found 4th Canadian Mounted Rifles in disarray, having suffered heavy casualties. It was clear that further advance was impossible and the company commander reorganised the line. Up to 11 a.m. the Germans tried to dislodge the line and prevent consolidation, but thereafter the artillery fire died down. A trench was dug and connected with the flanks.

At 2 p.m. 52nd Battalion (9th Canadian Brigade) came up on the right flank and contact was made. During the afternoon large numbers of Germans coming forward behind Woodland Plantation, Source Farm and Vapour Farm were dispersed by the artillery. During the day 175 unwounded and twenty-five wounded prisoners were brought in, 120 of them being used as stretcher-bearers to evacuate the wounded. At dusk forward posts were pushed out about fifty metres from the front line. A counterattack at 10 p.m. from the area of Source Trench was beaten back by small arms fire. By midnight the line was being held from left to right by C Company, 1st Canadian Mounted Rifles, then C, B, A and D Companies, 4th Canadian Mounted

Rifles. A Company, 1st Canadian Mounted Rifles was in immediate support. 4th Canadian Mounted Rifles was relieved by 2nd Canadian Mounted Rifles on the night of 27th/28th October. It had suffered 291 casualties and another twenty-nine men were evacuated with chills and trench feet.

Despite these successes, in which 3rd Canadian Division advanced on average 450m, it was still 450m short of its final objective. The Canadian Corps suffered 2,481 casualties up to 28th October, but it was established on the higher, drier ground southwest and west of Passchendaele, in a better situation to deliver the next attack.

Supporting attacks by Fifth Army on the left flank made no progress. In the Lekkerboterbeek valley, XVIII Corps' advance by 63rd and 58th Divisions slowed to a metre per minute as the men tried to move through knee-deep mud. The barrage was lost, weapons were clogged with mud and survivors made their way back to the start line. XIV Corps attacked with 57th and 50th Divisions and was also unable to progress. Fifth Army suffered 5,402 casualties for no gain. On the extreme left the French First Army made a little progress towards the southwestern corner of Houthulst Forest.

Late on 26th October Haig received instructions from Prime Minister Lloyd George to send two divisions to Italy immediately. The Italians had collapsed at Caporetto and needed support. At this crucial time in Flanders the BEF could ill afford to lose two divisions, but by the evening of the 28th the advance parties of 23rd and 41st Divisions (X Corps) were on their way. Before the end of November another three divisions had been sent to Italy (7th and 48th Divisions on 8th November and 5th Division on 14th November).

30th October 1917

289 Sgt George Mullin, Princess Patricia's Canadian Light Infantry CEF (7th Canadian Brigade, 3rd Canadian Division) Passchendaele, Belgium

290 Lt Hugh McKenzie, 7 Company, Canadian MGC (7th Canadian Brigade, 3rd Canadian Division) Meetscheele Spur, Belgium

291 Pte Cecil Kinross, 49 Battalion CEF (7th Canadian Brigade, 3rd Canadian Division) Passchendaele, Belgium

292 Maj George Pearkes, 5 Canadian Mounted Rifles CEF (8th Canadian Brigade, 3rd Canadian Division) Passchendaele, Belgium

No further progress could be contemplated after the partial success of the attack on 26th October until the forward troops had been resupplied with rations, ammunition and trench stores. The Canadian Corps organised a train of 250 pack animals per forward brigade and corduroy tracks were pushed forward again. These tracks could only be used at night and many animals lost their footing, slipped into the mud and drowned. Artillery ammunition also had to be brought up to the battery positions and dumps before another advance could commence. Many casualties were suffered in this work, but there was no lack of materiel when it was needed.

The weather improved and 10th Canadian Brigade managed to push forward posts on the night of 27th October. The RFC took advantage of the clear weather to carry out observed artillery shoots on 116 enemy batteries, photograph the forward areas and bomb various targets. Although the 28th was dry there was a lot of fog and the Germans shelled the battery positions with mustard gas at night. The 29th was quiet except for some aerial bombing by the Germans in the British rear areas.

The Canadian Corps attacked at 5.50 a.m. on 30th October to complete the objectives of 26th October and establish a position on the southern edge of Passchendaele for the final assault. On the right it was to link up with I ANZAC Corps on the railway south of Vienna Cottage and with XVIII Corps (Fifth Army) on the left flank at Vapour Farm. The night before was clear and cold, with bright moonlight and a strong drying westerly wind, but the assembly went ahead without interference. Advanced posts were withdrawn and the barrage fell on time. The day dawned cold and clear with a strong wind, but at 11 a.m. the rain returned once again. It took the Germans eight minutes to commence their barrage, which allowed the Canadians time to get clear before it fell.

4th Canadian Division on the right attacked with 12th Canadian Brigade to reach the outskirts of Passchendaele on both sides of the ridge highway (N303). The advance was carried out from right to left by 85th, 78th and 72nd Battalions. There was no intermediate objective in this area, but the final objective was reached on time, including seizing Crest Farm, which 9th Australian Brigade had been unable to hold on 12th October. In the attack 85th Battalion lost half its strength. 78th

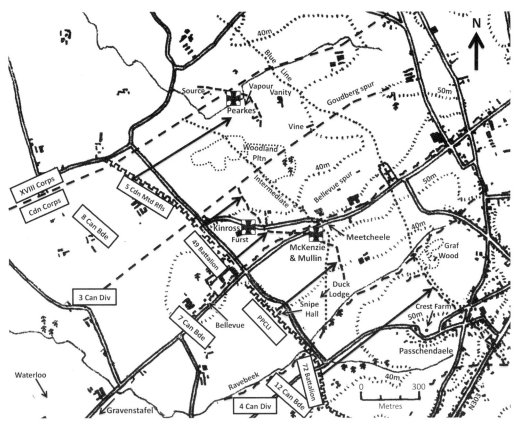

From the centre of Passchendaele drive northwest along 4e Regiment Karabiniersstraat. At the t-junction turn left, passing Passchendaele New British Cemetery on the right. Drive southwest for 500m to the right turn into Wieltjestraat. The pillbox attacked by Hugh McKenzie and George Mullin was on the left/south of the main road on the knoll opposite the turning. It is possible to park here for a short time, but beware traffic on the main road. Continue along Wieltjestraat for just over 400m to the farm on the left, where there is space to park. Look back the way you came. The farm on the left/north side of the road is on the site of Furst Farm. Cecil Kinross probably rushed the machine gun post at the western end of these farm buildings. Look north across the road. If the crops are not too high it is possible to see Source Farm and the site of Vapour Farm just over 600m away. Drive on for just over 200m to the t-junction and turn right for 550m, then turn right for another 350m to a clump of trees on the right. From here there is a good view to the east to Source Farm and the site of Vapour Farms, the line defended by George Pearkes and his small party.

Battalion encountered less opposition, crossed the road to the east of Passchendaele and sniped Germans trying to organise a new defensive line. On the left 72nd Battalion rushed Crest Farm before the defenders could man their guns and patrols went on into Passchendaele. The Brigade gained all its objectives except north of Crest Farm, where it was so badly flooded that consolidation had to take place just short of the Blue Line. Here the left flank had to be dropped back to allow for 3rd Canadian Division's right not being as advanced.

3rd Canadian Division on the left attacked with 7th Canadian Brigade on the right and 8th Canadian Brigade on the left. 7th Canadian Brigade took over the line from 9th Canadian Brigade on the night of 28th/29th October. Immediately the relief was completed, No.4 Company, Princess Patricia's Canadian Light Infantry pushed forward its line on the right to come up alongside 49th Battalion and seized the Snipe Hall pillbox that had held up 9th Canadian Brigade on 26th October. Eight Vickers machine guns of 7th and 8th Canadian Machine Gun Companies were to follow behind the attacking battalions for a short distance. They were then to set up in rear of them on high ground to bring direct fire to bear as they advanced.

Lieutenant Hugh McKenzie DCM commanded the 8th Canadian Machine Gun Company guns. He had two with him behind Princess Patricia's Canadian Light Infantry, the right assault battalion, and Sergeant Henry Howard MM the other two behind 49th Battalion, the left assault battalion.

The two assault battalions each had two platoons of the Royal Canadian Regiment in close support and a company as carriers. The last Royal Canadian Regiment company was in the Gravenstafel Ridge area on short notice to work for the engineers. 42nd Battalion was further back in reserve. All were in position by 5.30 a.m. despite the difficulties and enemy shelling.

At zero both battalions were subjected to heavy small arms fire and the enemy barrage fell at 5.52 a.m. From zero onwards communication forward of Waterloo Farm was by runner and Lucas Lamp only. Information was sketchy at first, but it was known that the capture of Crest Farm by 72nd Battalion had secured the right flank.

Princess Patricia's Canadian Light Infantry was led by No.2 Company on the right and No.3 Company on the left, with Nos 4 and 1 Companies in support respectively. Each leading company had a Vickers machine gun and Stokes mortar attached. Before the attack started one of the company commanders, Major Talbot Papineau, remarked that the task was suicidal. By the time his company reached the intermediate objective he was dead (Ypres (Menin Gate) Memorial) and the forty

The pillbox attacked by Hugh McKenzie and George Mullin up this slope stood on the highest point in the centre and to the right of the electricity distribution tower, which is on the far side of the Grafenstafel – Mosselmarkt road.

men remaining were commanded by the CSM and later by a corporal. A pillbox beside the main road running through Meetcheele was causing serious casualties and had to be taken before the intermediate objective on the left could be reached.

Three of the longest serving members of the Battalion intervened. Lieutenant JM Christie dashed to the left, from where he could bring fire to bear on the pillbox and snipers positioned around it. Lieutenant Hugh McKenzie of 7th Canadian Machine Gun Company (formerly PPCLI) left his guns in charge of Corporal Hampson while he went to rally and take command of No.2 Company, Princess Patricia's Canadian Light Infantry. He carried out a quick reconnaissance, dashing from shell-hole to shell-hole, and then led the Company in an attack. As they rushed up the slope McKenzie was with a small party twenty metres ahead of the rest and was killed while drawing enemy fire. **Sergeant George Mullin MM** went on and rushed a sniper's post in front of the pillbox, which he destroyed with bombs. He then gained the top of the pillbox, shot two machine gunners with a revolver and rushed to the entrance, where he forced the rest of the garrison of ten to surrender. His clothes were shredded by bullets, but he was unscathed.

The attack was slowed by the mire, but after the pillbox fell it was able to press on. Duck Lodge was taken on Princess Patricia's Canadian Light Infantry's intermediate objective, but after an hour of fighting the Battalion had lost almost all of its junior officers. The advance continued and at 11.15 a.m. a line was being consolidated on the crest in contact with 49th Battalion to the left rear, but not with 4th Canadian Division on the right due to the separation imposed by the marsh of the Ravebeek valley. Reinforcements were called for and the two Royal Canadian Regiment platoons moved up. Ammunition and stretcher-bearers were also summoned. Officer losses had been heavy, so three officers held back were called forward and arrived in the evening.

The machine gunners also suffered heavy losses. Sergeant Howard was killed (Ypres (Menin Gate) Memorial), as were a number of others; and reinforcements had to be sent forward to keep the machine guns in action. Of the twenty-eight members of the Company in the attack, seventeen were casualties, over half killed.

On the left, 49th Battalion suffered casualties moving into the line and the QM was killed bringing forward the rations. When the barrage map was issued on the afternoon of 29th October, it was clear that the positions held were too far forward and had to be withdrawn slightly after dark. The British barrage was light and some shells dropped short. On the right, B Company was all but wiped out before it reached the road running southeast to northwest east of Bellevue. This road was also bombarded by the Germans. C Company was on the left. It captured Furst Farm, 450m west of the Meetcheele crossroads. **Private Cecil Kinross** rushed a machine gun post alone, killed the six man crew and captured the gun.

The intermediate objective was not reached and there were heavy losses. Four officers left out of battle had to be called forward. A line was established astride the Meetcheele road in contact with Princess Patricia's Canadian Light Infantry on

Reverse of the previous view, giving an impression of the superb field of fire of the pillbox. The Ravebeek valley is to the left with two clumps of prominent poplars beyond at Tyne Cot Cemetery. The Grafenstafel – Mosselmarkt road is on the right with the right turn to Furst Farm just after the tower and house.

the right, but not with 5th Canadian Mounted Rifles on the left. Enemy shelling continued heavily.

Reinforcing companies of the Royal Canadian Regiment were sent forward with the intention of completing the advance, but orders to continue were cancelled later. After dusk shelling diminished and a company and a half of the Royal Canadian Regiment reinforced the line. By nightfall Princess Patricia's Canadian Light Infantry was down to about 180 men and had a company of the Royal Canadian Regiment in the front line and in close support. 49th Battalion was down to 130 all ranks and had two platoons of the Royal Canadian Regiment in support. The other two companies of the Royal Canadian Regiment were holding the start line. 42nd Battalion moved up to Gravenstafel ridge.

Looking east along Wieltjestraat, with Furst Farm on the left. The machine gun post captured by Cecil Kinross was somewhere in this area.

Counterattacks against 7th Canadian Brigade were driven off at 8 a.m., 10 a.m. and 11.15 a.m. For the rest of the day the Germans shelled the area heavily. The wounded were recovered and evacuated the next day and later both assault battalions were relieved. Princess Patricia's Canadian Light Infantry had suffered 355 casualties and 49th Battalion another 443, out of a Brigade total of 1,221.

8th Canadian Brigade's attack was led by 5th Canadian Mounted Rifles with a strength of 590 all ranks. It assembled successfully but the artillery on both sides was active and there were several casualties. A Company was on the right, with C Company on the left. In support were B and D Companies respectively and D Company, 2nd Canadian Mounted Rifles was behind to occupy the vacated front line. The forward companies were to go through to the final objective, while the support companies were to mop up and establish a support line on the intermediate objective. The impassable swamp at Woodland Plantation was to be bypassed by the companies to the north and south.

One minute after zero the enemy barrage fell on the front and support lines. There were difficulties negotiating the swampy areas around Woodland Plantation, but by 7 a.m. large numbers of the enemy were falling back in some disorder. Despite this, A Company failed to reach the objective and suffered severe casualties. It had no contact with 49th Battalion on the right. However, by 6.37 a.m. on the other flank, C Company had reached the intermediate objective, albeit with both flanks in the air. There were only fifty men of C and D Companies to hold the line gained. A footing was gained at Vapour, Source and Vanity (later lost) Farms on the western tip of the Goudberg Spur. **Major George Pearkes MC** was wounded in the thigh early in the day. He was deliberating whether or not to go for treatment when he noticed that his men were becoming restless and indecisive. He stood up and moved forward, calling on them to follow. Assisted by Sergeant Charles Smith Rutherford (MM for this action and VC on 26th August 1918), he led an attack on a strongpoint, which was captured. He held Vapour and Source Farms against repeated counterattacks with just a handful of men. To the north of him, XVIII Corps struggled to keep up in the swamp of the Lekkerboterbeek valley.

From Furst Farm, looking north towards the line of farms held by George Pearkes and his small party of men.

At 8.50 a.m. two companies of 2nd Canadian Mounted Rifles began moving forward to reinforce 5th Canadian Mounted Rifles. At 9.12 a.m. CO 5th Canadian Mounted Rifles directed one platoon of B Company, 2nd Canadian Mounted Rifles to Source Farm. The rest of the Company was sent to reinforce A and B Companies on the right where they were to clear up the situation and contact 49th Battalion. They advanced either side of Woodland Plantation and suffered heavy casualties. Despite this a platoon on the right reached the intermediate objective. On the left the survivors took cover in shell-holes when the officer and NCOs became casualties and returned the enemy fire. Meanwhile, at 9.15 a.m. HQ 8th Canadian Brigade had

Reverse of the previous view, looking south.

Site of Vapour Farm

Vanity Farm

ordered A Company, 2nd Canadian Mounted Rifles also to move forward in support of 5th Canadian Mounted Rifles.

By 10.15 a.m. C Company, 5th Canadian Mounted Rifles was holding a line of shell-holes in front of Vapour and Source Farms, partly inside 190th Brigade's area on the left. Both flanks were open and at that time there were only about twenty-five men left and with ammunition dwindling. However, the situation improved when sixty men of 2nd Canadian Mounted Rifles arrived.

At 11.30 a.m., A Company, 2nd Canadian Mounted Rifles was ordered to reinforce C and D Companies, 5th Canadian Mounted Rifles and establish a defensive flank facing north to include Source and Vapour Farms. By 1 p.m. there were up to one hundred men of C and D Companies, 5th Canadian Mounted Rifles and B Company, 2nd Canadian Mounted Rifles holding the line at Source and Vapour Farms, but they were under pressure and casualties continued to mount. There was

Bellevue
- behind trees

Source Farm

no news of A and B Companies, 5th Canadian Mounted Rifles on the right, but C and D Companies, 2nd Canadian Mounted Rifles were holding the old front and support lines.

A Company, 2nd Canadian Mounted Rifles did not leave the start line until 2.30 p.m. A platoon each headed for Vapour and Source Farms, with a third covering them. On arrival at Source Farm that platoon had its officer, a Lewis gun and a few riflemen to reinforce the four men of 5th Canadian Mounted Rifles with a Lewis gun that they found there. Despite the weakness of this party it pressed on seventy metres north of Source Farm to set up a shell-hole post. A wounded officer and three more men with a Lewis gun were found there. By 4.30 p.m. a strongpoint with three Lewis guns had been established. The other platoons reached Vapour Farm and reported to Major Pearkes, who put them into position on the right of the Farm.

At 1.45 p.m. Major Pearkes reported the Germans were digging-in about 200m away. By then his combined force amounted to twenty men with little ammunition. At 6.55 p.m. patrols from C and D Companies, 2nd Canadian Mounted Rifles still in the original front line were ordered to make contact with the flanks, ascertain where they were, gain touch with the force at Vapour and Source Farms, locate other parties holding ground and round up those who were lost. Around 7 p.m. contact was established with 49th Battalion on the right. During the night the line was connected with 190th Brigade on the left, which had only advanced about fifty metres on that flank.

That evening 2nd Canadian Mounted Rifles and a company of 1st Canadian Mounted Rifles took over 5th Canadian Mounted Rifles' gains. 5th Canadian Mounted Rifles moved back to the area of the intermediate objective only fifty strong and next day went back to the rest camp at Watou. It had suffered 416 casualties. During the night 4th King's Shropshire Light Infantry established a line of posts from Source Farm to link up with the right flank of 190th Brigade. Counterattacks continued against the Canadians until early on 31st October, but they were isolated and uncoordinated. Vanity House was captured early on 2nd November by 3rd Canadian Mounted Rifles, but an attempt to seize Vine Cottage at the same time failed. Before any further attacks could be made the two assault divisions had to be relieved.

6th November 1917

293 Pte James Robertson, 27 Battalion CEF (6th Canadian Brigade, 2nd Canadian Division)
     Passchendaele, Belgium
294 Cpl Colin Barron, 3 Battalion CEF (1st Canadian Brigade, 1st Canadian Division)
     Passchendaele, Belgium

On 31st October, General Plumer took XVIII Corps under command to ensure that future operations all came under HQ Second Army. On 2nd November, HQ XVIII Corps was replaced by HQ II Corps under Lieutenant General Claud Jacob.

Meanwhile preparations for the final attacks on Passchendaele progressed. From 31st October vigorous counter-battery work was carried out by the Canadian Corps and II Corps. Field guns were moved forward wherever possible. The next attacks were planned for 6th and 10th November to allow time for reliefs. On 3rd November, 2nd Canadian Division relieved 4th Canadian Division and the following day 1st Canadian Division relieved 3rd Canadian Division.

The next stage of the offensive was launched at 6 a.m. on 6th November to seize the Green Line. The objective of the Canadian Corps was an arc east and northeast of Passchendaele. The Canadians attacked with two divisions, while its flanks were protected by other corps. II Corps on the left was only to participate with artillery, while I ANZAC, IX and VIII Corps on the right simulated attacks as a diversion. On the evenings of 1st, 2nd and 3rd November artillery fire was more concentrated in depth. On the nights of 1st/2nd and 3rd/4th November small attacks were launched to improve the Canadian Corps' starting positions. A number of strongpoints were seized against strong opposition. On the night of 2nd/3rd November the Germans launched an attack around the junction of the Canadian and I ANZAC Corps, which succeeded in recapturing a small wood in the Ravebeek valley. At 5 a.m. on 3rd November, just after 2nd Canadian Division took over the line, a German attack on the ridge north of the Roulers railway pushed the Canadians back in a few places, but by 11 a.m. the line had been restored.

The weather started clear and fine on 6th November, but became overcast with showers later. The Canadians formed up in no man's land and avoided a German barrage at 4.30 a.m. The initial assault moved forward quickly, avoided the German retaliatory fire and kept well up with the barrage. The defenders in many instances had no time to man their machine guns before the Canadians were upon them.

On the right, 2nd Canadian Division advanced with 5th Canadian Brigade on the right and 6th Canadian Brigade on the left. 5th Canadian Brigade used only 26th Battalion to form a flank and its attack was entirely successful. 6th Canadian Brigade advanced with, from right to left, 27th, 31st and 28th Battalions, on a frontage of 700m, each with a Stokes mortar attached. 29th Battalion in reserve was to take over the front line on the night of 4th/5th November. Each attacking battalion averaged 800 strong and left three officers and sixty-three men out of battle at the transport

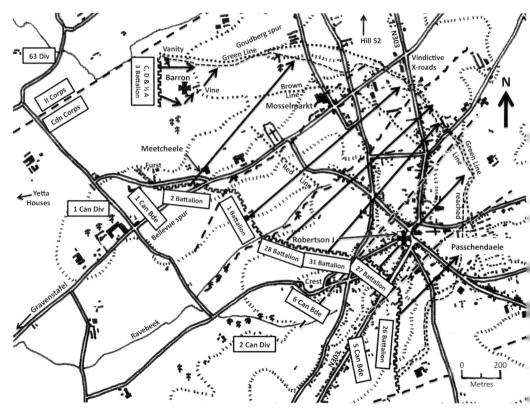

From the centre of Passchendaele drive northwest along 4e Regiment Karabiniersstraat. At the t-junction turn right and then after 300m turn left into Haringstraat. Follow it for 350m then turn left into Paardebosstraat. After 550m the road swings right and the house in front is Vine Cottage. Follow the road to the end where there is a house and turn back to look the way you came. The house on the left of the road is Vanity Farm, but the view across to Vine Cottage on the right is obscured by trees. An alternative viewpoint is from Furst Farm. Retrace your steps and pass Passchendaele New British Cemetery on the right. Continue 400m then turn right into Wieltjestraat and after another 400m there is a farm on the left with space to park. Look northeast across the road. If the crops are not too high it is possible to see Vanity Farm just over 600m away. The church at Westroosebeke is beyond it on the horizon. Unfortunately Vine Cottage is obscured by a copse of tall poplars. However, you do get a feel for the shape of the ground from here.

lines. It was decided to carry packs rather than haversacks in order to allow the men to take their greatcoats.

By 5 a.m. on 5th November 29th Battalion had pushed forward a line of posts to within forty metres of the enemy to protect the assembly area. This move was not detected. During the day on 5th November enemy aircraft swooped down periodically and one was shot down. That evening the assembly area was taped for the attacking battalions. Ten guides were provided to each incoming battalion by 29th Battalion to ensure that they found their correct positions. The 6th Canadian Brigade move forward commenced at 5.00 p.m. Moving over Hill 37, 27th Battalion suffered some casualties due to enemy shelling. It was the last battalion in position at 12.30 p.m.

The barrage fell on time and was intense. The attack started immediately and it was clear that the Germans were surprised. The German barrage fell three minutes later and although it was heavy it was also erratic, falling mainly behind the advancing troops. The first line of resistance was overwhelmed and the advance swept on. Thereafter resistance stiffened.

On the right, 27th Battalion advanced with D Company on the right, C Company in the centre and B Company on the left, with A Company in reserve. The forward companies advanced on a frontage of two platoons each. 27th Battalion was the first unit to enter Passchendaele. As it reached the main street a machine gun opened fire from the ruins of a building on their left. The position was surrounded by uncut barbed wire and resisted several attempts to outflank it with the support of other positions in the ruins of nearby houses.

Private James Robertson decided to tackle the machine gun post. While his comrades engaged the position he dashed across the open ground, outflanked the machine gun post and jumped over the wire. He bayoneted four of the crew singlehandedly, and the rest fled. He then turned the gun on the retreating enemy, inflicting many casualties amongst them. He carried the machine gun while his platoon progressed to the objective, overcoming other strongpoints on the way. The Germans were driven from the village and the final objective was captured. Robertson set up the German machine gun and covered the consolidation, suppressing troublesome German snipers. Later two Canadian snipers positioned forward of the line were wounded and Robertson went out alone under small arms and artillery fire to carry in the man furthest away. He went out again and picked up the second man. On the way back he was hit by rifle fire and fell, but got up and again lifted the injured sniper onto his shoulder. Robertson staggered back and had almost reached safety when a shell exploded nearby and he was killed, one of 261 casualties suffered by 27th Battalion.

31st Battalion was hit by heavy machine gun and rifle fire from pillboxes, which delayed but did not halt its progress. German aircraft swept low to engage the troops, but the mist limited their vision and on one occasion they strafed a line of abandoned greatcoats on 31st Battalion's start line. 28th Battalion on the left had the hardest time. It was under heavy machine gun fire as it struggled out of the Ravebeek valley, with the men often up to their knees in mud and sometimes up to their waists.

By 7.10 a.m. the Brigade was streaming through and around Passchendaele, with the defenders falling back in disarray. Resistance from pillboxes was overcome by teams employing rifle grenades and Lewis guns. By 7.40 a.m. 27th and 28th Battalions had reached the final objective, but 31st Battalion was delayed temporarily by pillboxes. By 8.45 a.m. the whole objective along the eastern crest had been captured and Passchendaele village, so long the objective of the BEF's efforts, had fallen.

6th Canadian Brigade had 949 casualties and took 245 prisoners, including two battalion commanders in a pillbox cleared at 3 p.m. They commanded the forward and reserve battalions in the area. The reserve battalion CO had gone forward to liaise with the forward battalion and could not get back. As a result the battalion did not counterattack as intended and this helped the Canadians in consolidating the gains. Evacuation of the wounded was not completed until 7th November, but many were killed or injured again as they were being carried back, as were many of the German prisoners.

On the left, 1st Canadian Division advanced north of the village. Large areas of ground were too badly flooded to negotiate and therefore the Division's front was reduced to the width of the Bellevue–Meetcheele Spur. The task was allocated to 1st Canadian Brigade's 1st and 2nd Battalions, astride the Meetcheele–Mosselmarkt road, while a flanking attack along Goudberg Spur was carried out by 3rd Battalion. 4th Battalion was in reserve around Gravenstafel. 1st and 2nd Battalions were in position by 4 a.m., each with two Stokes mortars attached.

1st Battalion attacked on a two-company frontage, each of two platoons. At the Red Line the two supporting companies were to pass through to the Brown Line and seize Mosselmarkt. Then one company from the Red Line was to pass through to the final objective, the Green Line. 2nd Battalion attacked with only one company to the Red Line, where two supporting companies were to pass through to the Brown Line. The fourth company was then to pass through to the Green Line.

Both battalions met opposition from machine gun posts immediately, but they were overrun. Mosselmarkt's garrison was surrounded and a shell-hole position behind it was outflanked and silenced by trench mortars. Two field guns, four machine guns and fifty-four prisoners were taken there alone. By 7.45 a.m. the objectives had been seized and the inner flanks of both Canadian divisions had met on the main highway along the ridge just north of Passchendaele. Enemy reinforcements were seen advancing at 9.30 a.m., but were dealt with by artillery fire. German artillery and machine gun fire made resupply of the forward positions and communications difficult, but every effort to regain the lost ground was pushed back. At 12.50 p.m. one Canadian flag per battalion was sent forward from Brigade HQ to be planted in the captured ground.

From the end of Paardebosstraat looking east. Vanity Farm is on the left and Vine Cottage can just be made out in a gap in the trees just to the right of the road.

3rd Battalion had two roles. The attack on the left was carried out by C Company (Captain JK Crawford) and half of A Company, supported by D Company (Captain KC Brooke) on call at Yetta Houses. This force was commanded by Major DHC Mason DSO from an advanced Battalion HQ. B Company and the other half of A Company were in support to 2nd Battalion, with two and a half companies of 4th Battalion attached to make 3rd Battalion up to full strength.

The part of 3rd Battalion commanded by Major Mason was isolated from the rest of the Brigade by the swamp at Furst on the right. A start line running north–south through Vanity House was organised with some difficulty. The plan was for three platoons to lead the assault from Vanity, where one platoon was to remain as the garrison. Two platoons on the left were to clear from the northern divisional boundary to Vine Cottage, while a third platoon attacked the pillboxes at Vine Cottage itself. At 1 a.m. a great deal of enemy movement was observed east of Vanity House and north of Vine Cottage. The CO gave Major Mason authority to use four platoons in the attack if he thought it necessary.

The two platoons on the left moved forward with the barrage, which was supplemented by two Stokes mortars. They were in contact with the Hood Battalion (63rd Division) on the left. The right platoon, under Lieutenant HT Lord (wounded), had to move southeast initially instead of east in order to avoid the very marshy ground. The advance was in two lines. The first line skirmished ahead to find the best route for the second, which consisted of the assault sections. The whole attack was a left wheeling movement, pivoting on Vanity House.

Lord's platoon appears to have approached Vine Cottage from an unexpected direction as the defenders were surprised. As the barrage lifted, the German sentries were disposed of swiftly and the attackers pressed on. There was no wire to slow them down. The garrison of one pillbox, an officer and forty men, surrendered. Two other posts seem to have been silenced by the barrage or the mortars, but another machine gun post in a pillbox caused serious problems. It inflicted many casualties and brought the advance to a halt. Riflemen engaged the post and caused some casualties amongst the defenders, but this on its own was not enough to shift the blockage.

Corporal Colin Barron used a Lewis gun to neutralise three machine guns. He then wriggled forwards almost a hundred metres to within throwing range and tossed in some bombs, which silenced the machine guns. He charged in, killed four crewmen and captured the remainder singlehandedly before turning one of the guns on the retreating enemy. His action enabled the advance to continue. Vine Cottage was taken and the objective facing north was reached, in contact with 2nd Battalion on the right. Forty prisoners were retained at Vine Cottage to carry back the wounded that night. Casualties had been heavy and two reinforcement platoons of D Company were sent up after dark.

At 5.30 p.m. German shelling intensified and at 6.45 p.m. the SOS signals went up along the whole Canadian Corps front. Although German patrols were seen, no attack developed and by 7.30 p.m. the front was quiet once again.

When 1st Canadian Brigade was relieved the boundary on the left was changed and part of the area to the north was taken over by B Company, 2nd Welsh (3rd Brigade), while the remainder was handed over to 3rd Canadian Brigade. By the time 3rd Battalion was relieved on the night of 7th/8th November it had suffered 263 casualties, including seventy-eight killed, died of wounds or missing.

The Canadian Corps suffered 2,238 casualties, but had gained a great victory. By the following day the captured positions had been consolidated into outpost, front, support and main lines, with reserve positions behind. While preparations went ahead for a further advance there was little activity along the Passchendaele front. On 8th November General Plumer handed over command of Second Army to General Sir Henry Rawlinson (Fourth Army) and departed Flanders to take command of British forces in Italy.

From 250m north of Furst Farm. This is private land, so it is not recommended to try reaching this point without permission. Vine Cottage can be seen right of centre amongst the trees. Vanity Farm is the next set of buildings to the left of it.

On 10th November the final attack was carried out by 1st Canadian Division in heavy rain. It was to extend the hold on the ridge for another 450m northwards to Vindictive Crossroads and Hill 52, the highest point on the northern end of the ridge. 2nd Canadian Division and 1st Division (II Corps) protected the flanks. The objective was gained by 7.45 a.m. and counterattacks were held. 1st Division managed to gain the main ridge north of Goudberg, but the right battalion veered right, leaving a large gap between the two leading battalions. The Germans counterattacked into the gap, cutting off most of the left battalion and the gains were lost. The main objective on the ridge was retained by the Canadians despite being exposed to extremely heavy artillery fire. Forward posts were pushed out and counterattacks were broken up by small arms and artillery fire. The day's fighting resulted in another 1,094 casualties for the Canadians; by the time the Canadian Corps was relieved on 11th November it had suffered 12,924 casualties.

The loss of five divisions to Italy and the threat of another three being required reduced the BEF's available reserves considerably. The Cambrai offensive was looming and the four divisions of Fourth Army were diverted from the coastal area to take over another forty miles of the French front south of the Somme. It was clear that the intention to continue the capture of the whole ridge northwards to Westroosebeke could not be achieved. On 20th November, Haig closed down the offensive and switched attention to Cambrai, where operations had already started.

The 1917 Flanders campaign cost the British 244,897 casualties over 105 days, an average of 2,332 per day. By comparison, the 141 days of the 1916 Somme offensive resulted in 419,654 casualties, an average of 2,976 per day. Of the Flanders casualties, 64% eventually returned to front line duty and another 18% to lines of communication and other less strenuous duty. German losses are more difficult to calculate, but the Official History concluded they were around 400,000. Despite the apparent disparity in casualties, it was still not enough for the British to produce a breakthrough.

Vine

The Belgian coast was not cleared, but the aim of relieving pressure on the French had been achieved and the British had seized possession of the ridge from Messines in the south to north of Passchendaele. If Haig had been able to launch the Flanders offensive earlier in the year the results might have been considerably different. Although not known at the time, the exhaustion of many German divisions in Flanders was one of the reasons for the failure of the German offensives in the spring of 1918.

Much criticism has been levelled at Haig for continuing the campaign in the mud. In places and at times the mud was terrible, but it has to be seen in perspective. Worse conditions were encountered during the war around the Lys, north of the La Bassée Canal and indeed, on the Somme. Similar conditions were encountered in the Netherlands in 1944 and in Italy in the winters of 1943/44 and 1944/45. Fourteenth Army endured mud for years in Burma, but no one criticised General Bill Slim for continuing that campaign in atrocious weather conditions. Although the mud around Ypres caused a few delays, it was not until 5th October that it had a significant effect on operations. By then there was no option other than to continue the offensive for reasons that have already been explained.

Biographies

CAPTAIN HAROLD ACKROYD
Royal Army Medical Corps attached 6th Battalion, Princess Charlotte of Wales's (Royal Berkshire Regiment)

Harold Ackroyd was born at 26 Roe Lane, Southport, Lancashire on 18th July 1877. His father, Edward Ackroyd (1833–91), was a tailor and outfitter, living at 25/27 Gutta Percha Depot, Market Square, Bolton in 1861, with his sister Anne acting as his housekeeper. He married Ellen née Holden (1842–1908), a bleacher, at Birkdale, Lancashire in June 1866. Edward became Chairman of Southport and Cheshire Lines Extension Railway Company. The family was living at Bank House, Halliwell, Lancashire in 1868, at 9 Back o' the Bank, Bolton in 1871 and at 26 Roe Lane, North Meols, Southport in 1881. Harold had five siblings:

- Annie Holden Ackroyd (1868–1949) married Gerrard Septimus Peck (1868–1945) in 1898 and they emigrated to Calgary, Alberta, Canada in 1919. They had four children – Hubert Gerard Peck 1900, Edward Finch Peck 1901, Oswald Ackroyd Peck 1903 and David Ackroyd Peck 1904. Stillborn triplets were born and died in 1915.

Edward Ackroyd was Chairman of the Southport and Cheshire Lines Extension Railway Company. Its Southport Lord Street station, which opened in 1884 and closed in 1952, was the northern terminus of the line.

- Elizabeth Ackroyd (1869–1914) married Francis Edward Fish (1876–1915) in 1912 at St Luke's, Southport and they lived at New Manor Farm, Winterslow, Wiltshire. Francis was commissioned in 2nd Volunteer Battalion, Alexandra, Princess of Wales's Own (Yorkshire Regiment) in 1901 and was a lieutenant on transfer to the 3rd Battalion on 7th May 1904. He last appears in the Army List in July 1909. He was recalled to 3rd Battalion as a captain on 30th September 1914 and employed initially on coastal defence. He was blown off his feet when a shell exploded close to him during the bombardment of Hartlepool on 16th December 1914. On 19th March 1915 he embarked for France and was attached to the 2nd Battalion. He was killed in action on 17th May 1915 at Festubert and is buried in Guards Cemetery, Windy Corner, Cuinchy, France (V K 4). There were no children.

Harold's brother-in-law, Captain Francis Edward Fish, was killed on 17th May 1915 at Festubert and is buried in Guards Cemetery, Windy Corner, Cuinchy.

- Samuel Percival Ackroyd (1870–73).
- Robert Holden Ackroyd (1873–81).
- Edward Ackroyd (1875–1956), a barrister, married Ellen Johanna Stewart (1881–1942) in 1904 and they had three children – Edward Stewart Ackroyd 1905, Margaret Ellen Ackroyd 1908 and Guy Stewart Ackroyd 1916. They were living at 8 Mosley Road, Southport in 1911.

Harold's paternal grandfather, Samuel Ackroyd (c.1803–84) was a tailor and draper born at Sileby, Leicestershire. He married Ann (c.1802–68) and they were living at 69 Deansgate, Bolton, Lancashire in 1851, at Fleetwood Street, North Meols, Lancashire by 1861 and at 2 Hesketh Street, North Meols by 1871. In addition to Edward they had two other children – Anne Ackroyd c.1837 and Elizabeth Ackroyd 1838.

His maternal grandfather, Robert Holden (c.1801–65), was a rag and waste dealer born at Bolton, Lancashire. He married Ann née Pilkington (born c.1805) in 1840 at Bolton Le Moors, Lancashire. They were living at 8 Knowsley Street, Bolton in 1851, when Ann was listed as Mary in the census return. They had moved to 5 Lark Street, Bolton by 1861. In addition to Ellen they had a son, Edward Pilkington Holden (1838–67),

Deansgate in Bolton, where Harold's paternal grandparents were living in 1851.

Knowsley Street in Bolton where Harold's maternal grandparents were living in 1851.

a waste manufacturer who, in 1859, patented an invention, 'improvements in machinery for opening, carding, and cleaning cotton and other fibrous materials, when in a manufactured or partially manufactured state'. He was a partner in Richard Pollit & Co, Boiler Makers at Rose Mill Boiler Works, Bolton and was also a partner in Jonathon Dearden & Co, Cotton Spinners, Little Bridge Mill, Bolton. In 1866 he and Jonathon Dearden patented an invention of, 'certain improvements in carding engines'. Both patents became void within a few years due to non-payment of additional Stamp Duty. Edward married Agnes Longworth (born c.1838) in 1858. They were living at 77 Florence Street, Bolton in 1861 and they had five children – Robert Percy Pilkington Holden 1859, Mary Ellen Pilkington Holden 1860, Harold Pilkington Holden 1862, Annie Pilkington Holden 1863 and Edward Pilkington Holden 1868.

Harold was educated at:

- Shrewsbury School in Chance's House and was a member of the OTC.
- Mr Clough's School (Mintholme College) Southport.
- Gonville and Caius College, Cambridge from October 1896 (BA Natural Sciences 1899 & MA 1904).
- Guy's Hospital October 1900–April 1903 (MB BCh 1904 & MD 1910).

Harold Ackroyd married Mabel Robina née Smythe (12th November 1877–17th April 1947), born at Newport, Shropshire, on 1st August 1908 at St Luke's Church, Southport. In 1901 she was a governess in the home of Clarence Wilson at 10 Grosvenor Square, Westminster, London and at the time of her marriage was the matron of Strangeways Hospital, Cambridge. They lived at Brooklands, 46 Kneesworth Road, Royston, Hertfordshire and had three children:

Shrewsbury School was founded in 1552 and moved to its present site, a former workhouse, in 1882. Old Salopians include naturalist Charles Darwin, the novelist Nevil Shute, the actor and TV presenter Michael Palin and the politician Lord Heseltine. In addition to Harold Ackroyd, the school had another First World War VC, Thomas Tannatt Pryce.

Gonville and Caius College was founded as Gonville Hall by Edmund Gonville in 1348. In 1557 it was refounded as Gonville and Caius College by John Caius who extended the buildings. Caius did not accept payment, but imposed unusual rules of entry, insisting that the College admit no scholar who is *deformed, dumb, blind, lame, maimed, mutilated, a Welshman, or suffering from any grave or contagious illness, or an invalid, that is sick in a serious measure.* Caius founded the College as a centre for the study of medicine, which continues to this day. The College has thirteen Nobel Prize laureates, including in 1962 Francis Crick, co-discoverer of the structure of DNA. Other noted alumni include Harold Abrahams, the Olympic athlete portrayed in the film *Chariots of Fire*, the comedian Jimmy Carr, Kenneth Clarke, Chancellor of the Exchequer in John Major's government in the 1990s, David Frost the broadcaster and Titus Oates of the Popish Plot. Professor Stephen Hawking, the theoretical physicist, is a fellow.

- Ursula Ackroyd (1909–93), born at Great Shelford, Cambridgeshire, married Captain Guy Malet de Carteret (1901–72) at Malvern, Worcestershire in 1930. He was born at St Leonards, New South Wales, Australia, the son of Captain Reginald Malet de Carteret, Seigneur of St Ouen, Jersey, and Anne Frances, daughter of Commander Richard Ramsay Armstrong RN. Guy was educated at Victoria College in Jersey and Exeter College, Oxford, where he was in the Oxford University Contingent (Senior Division) OTC. He was commissioned in 4th Lincolnshire on 25th June 1926 and transferred to Malvern College Contingent (Junior Division) OTC on 9th October 1926 (35316). Promoted lieutenant 25th June 1929 and captain 23rd February 1936. He ceased serving in the OTC on 31st July 1945 and resigned his commission on 20th October 1946. Appointed to the Order of St John as Serving Brother (LG 2nd January 1953), Officer (LG 8th January 1957) and Commander (LG 14th July 1959). Awarded the Efficiency Decoration with Territorial brooch, LG 14th July 1961. He succeeded his father as Seigneur of St Ouen in January 1935.

Guy's Hospital was founded in 1721 by Thomas Guy to treat incurables discharged from St Thomas' Hospital. Sir Alexander Fleming (1881–1955), discoverer of penicillin, worked there.

St Luke's Church, Southport, founded in 1879, where Harold Ackroyd married Mabel Smythe in August 1908.

Ursula was appointed to the Order of St John as Officer (LG 14th July 1959) and Commander (LG 12th January 1965). They had three children:

St Ouen is one of the twelve parishes of Jersey. St Ouen's Manor has been the home of the de Carteret family for over eight centuries.

- Philip Malet de Carteret (1932–2013) lost the sight in his right eye after a tennis accident while a student at Gonville & Caius College, Cambridge. He became a stockbroker and married Patricia May Burke (1928–98) in 1957 at Westminster Cathedral, London. She was born at Glencar, Co Sligo and was a ward sister at Moorfields Eye Hospital, London where they met. They had five children including – Charles Guy Malet de Carteret 1960, Edward Francis Malet de Carteret 1961, Elizabeth Malet de Carteret 1965 and Robert Helier Malet de Carteret 1967. Philip later married Adele. He was Seigneur of St Ouen, Jersey and President of Le Cercle De Carteret.

- Reginald Malet de Carteret (born 1935) married Carole Chiswell (born 1937) at Banff, Canada in 1956. They had three children – Nicola Malet de Carteret 1959, Guy Malet de Carteret 1961 and John R Malet de Carteret 1968. They divorced and he married Shirley.

- Genette Malet de Carteret (born 1938) returned to Jersey in November 1945 and was educated at Jersey College for Girls 1946–51 and Prior's Field School, Godalming, Surrey 1951–55. She read law at Lady Margaret Hall, Oxford (MA 1959). She married Podromos Dagtoglou (born 1929) in 1963 at St Ouen, Jersey. He was born in Athens, Greece. They had three children – Miranda Dagtoglou 1966, Ion Demetrios Dagtoglou 1968 and Olive Dagtoglou 1969. Genette was called to the Bar in 1973. She held a number of appointments – Treasury Solicitor's Department in Jersey 1974, ten years in European Law Litigation Department, two years as EEC Cabinet Office Legal Adviser, one year in Company Law Department and one year in Planning Department conducting litigation on behalf of the Department of the Environment.

• Stephen Ackroyd (1912–64) was educated at Middlesex Teaching Hospital, London (MRCS (Eng) & LRCP 1939). He married Jacqueline Drummond (died 1975) and they were living at Blue Cottage, Sumner Place Mews, London in 1956.

• Anthony Ackroyd (1914–88) was educated at Gonville & Caius College, Cambridge (BA 1936, MA 1946, MB & BChir 1947) and Middlesex Teaching Hospital (MRCS (Eng) & LRCP (London) 1940). He held various appointments – Junior Assistant Pathologist, London County Council; House Surgeon, Middlesex Hospital Sector (Emergency Medical Service); and Obstetrics and Gynaecology House Surgeon, Lewisham London County Council Hospital.

Tony was commissioned in the RNVR as a temporary surgeon lieutenant on 18th December 1940 and served until May 1945. He married Mary Patricia Jean Dixon (1914–2004) in 1940 and they had two children – Christopher Edward Ackroyd 1942 and Robert Barry Ackroyd 1946. They lived at St Christopher's, Harsfold Road, Rustington, West Sussex.

Mabel's father, John Fennel Smythe (1849–1920), born at Carlow, Ireland, was an Inland Revenue officer with the Excise Branch. He married Louisa née Howle (1852–1935), born at Newport, Shropshire in 1877. They were living at Park Lane, Newmarket All Saints, Cambridge in 1881 and at Repps Road, Martham, Norfolk in 1901. In addition to Mabel they had three other children – Bertha Lillian Smythe 1880, Cyril Montague Smythe 1888 and Dorothy Mildred Smythe 1891.

Queen's Hospital, Birmingham dates to 1840 and was extended in 1845 and 1871. It was a military hospital during the First World War and closed in 1938. It reopened in 1941 as Birmingham Accident Hospital and Rehabilitation Centre and in 1974 became the Birmingham Accident Hospital. It closed in 1993 and is now student accommodation.

Harold was appointed House Surgeon at Queen's Hospital, Birmingham, Warwickshire, and then at David Lewis Northern Hospital, Liverpool, Lancashire. He received a BMA research scholarship for Downing College Laboratory, Cambridge in 1909, pioneering research into vitamins and human metabolism. Initially he was attached to the Department of Pharmacology and later transferred to the School of Agriculture, where he accepted a post in the newly formed Institute for the Study of Animal Nutrition. He was engaged mainly in research into purine metabolism and later in the study of nitrogenous constituents of root crops. He wrote a paper on this subject, but it was not published until December 1916. Harold received the Thurston Medal and Medical Scholarship (Caius & Gonville College) in 1911 for his scientific research work.

He was commissioned in the RAMC as a lieutenant on 15th February 1915

The twenty-bed Northern Hospital opened at Leeds Street, Liverpool in 1834. By 1838 it had expanded to 106 beds, but more accommodation was required. In 1845 a purpose-built hospital opened in Great Howard Street. With the financial support of the David Lewis Trust a new hospital was built, opening in 1902 as the David Lewis Northern Hospital. It was evacuated to St. Katherine's College, Childwall 1939–47 and closed in 1978 with the opening of the new Royal Liverpool Hospital.

and attached to 6th Royal Berkshire as the RMO. The Battalion trained at Colchester, Essex and Codford St Mary in Wiltshire. Harold was not popular with the troops during training due to his intolerance of malingerers, who he could spot by instinct. The Battalion went to France on 25th July 1915 and Harold was promoted captain on 15th February 1916.

Awarded the MC for his actions during intense fighting in Delville Wood on the Somme 19th–21st July; he tended the wounded, working with coolness, purpose and method in clearing the entire Wood of more than 700 British and German wounded, which was fraught with difficulty due to the conditions and the confused nature of the fighting. Often under sniper and heavy shellfire, he was once blown up and eleven officers in other units submitted recommendations for the VC, LG 20th October 1916.

His tireless devotion to easing the suffering of the wounded caused him to spend hours in no man's land at night. The mental strain took its toll and he suffered a nervous breakdown and nervous exhaustion, compounded by blindness brought on by shell shock. He was invalided home for six weeks leave on 11th August. A

Codford St Mary in Wiltshire was the site of fifteen military training camps during the First World War and from 1916 became a major ANZAC depot.

The shattered remains of Delville Wood. In July 1916 Harold Ackroyd cleared it of more than 700 wounded under very difficult and dangerous conditions.

Harold Ackroyd seated on the right with the other officers of 6th Royal Berkshire prior to the opening of the Ypres offensive (Ned Malet de Cartaret).

medical board on 3rd October passed him fit and he returned to France to rejoin the Battalion.

Awarded the VC for his actions at Ypres, Belgium on 31st July/1st August 1917, LG 6th September 1917. On 11th August, following the repulse of an enemy attack at Jargon Trench, Glencorse Wood, he set about locating casualties behind the firing line, moving from shell hole to shell hole alone. Having dressed the wounds of one man he had found in a forward crater, he got up to fetch the stretcher-bearers and was shot through the head and killed. His body was discovered in the shell hole with six others by his batman, Private A Scriven, and was brought back for burial behind the lines. Alfred Clark, an officer in HQ 18th Division, wrote to Mabel, *All of our medical officers are wonderfully brave, but your husband was quite in a class by himself.* Harold Ackroyd is believed to be buried in Birr Cross Roads Cemetery (Special Memorial No. 7). The VC and MC were presented to his wife and son, Stephen, by the King outside Buckingham Palace on 26th September 1917. Harold left £39,748/4/5 in his will. He is commemorated in a number of places:

* Ackroyd Road, Royston, Hertfordshire.
* Royston War Memorial, Trinity and Priory Church, Melbourn Street, Royston, Hertfordshire, unveiled on 26th March 1922 by Lieutenant Colonel ECM Phillips.
* Southport War Memorial, Lord Street, Southport, Lancashire unveiled on 18th November 1923 by the Earl of Derby.
* Memorial stone tablet to the five Southport VCs in Southport Garden of Remembrance, Lord Street. Nearby in Christ Church, Lord Street is a cabinet displaying a replica VC with photographs and citations of the five VCs.

Royston War Memorial.

Harold Ackroyd's Special Memorial headstone in Birr Cross Roads Cemetery.

Guy's Hospital Memorial Arch at St Thomas Street, Southwark, London was dedicated in 1921. It has since been moved to the Memorial Gardens.

Southport War Memorial.

- Wooden memorial panel in the antechapel of Gonville & Caius College, Trinity Street, Cambridge dedicated to the members, fellows and staff who fell in the Great War.
- Memorial plaque in Room C9, Tree Court, Gonville & Caius College, Cambridge.
- Named on the Memorial Arch, Guy's Hospital, St Thomas Street, Southwark, London unveiled by The Duke of York on 16th July 1921, dedicated to the medical students and staff who fell in the Great War. It stood at the entrance to the hospital grounds until moved to the Memorial Gardens. It was rededicated on 11th November 1994.
- Blue plaque on his home at Brooklands, 46 Kneesworth Road, Royston.
- Memorial in Shrewsbury School Chapel, Shropshire.

King George V and Queen Mary arriving for the dedication ceremony for the British Medical Association House Memorial on 1st July 1925.

- A VC plaque marks an Acer 'Crimson King' tree dedicated to him in the RAMC Memorial Grove at the National Memorial Arboretum, Alrewas, Staffordshire.
- Memorial plaque in St George's Church, Ypres, Belgium.
- Named on the British Medical Association House Memorial, Tavistock Square, Bloomsbury, London unveiled by King George V on 1st July 1925 and dedicated to the 574 BMA members who fell in the Great War.
- Named on the Malet de Cartaret family grave, St Ouens Churchyard, Jersey.
- The Department for Communities and Local Government decided to provide a commemorative paving stone at the birthplace of every Great War Victoria Cross recipient in the United Kingdom. A commemorative stone for Harold was dedicated at Lord Street, Southport on 8th September 2017 to mark the centenary of his award.

Mabel moved to Link Lodge, Malvern, Worcestershire in the 1930s and subsequently lived at 'Les Landes', Christchurch Road, Malvern. She died at St Ouen, Jersey.

In addition to the VC and MC he was awarded the 1914–15 Star, British War Medal 1914–20 and Victory Medal 1914–19. Mabel bequeathed the VC and 1914–15 Star to her son Stephen and the MC, British War Medal, Victory Medal and Thurston Medal to her son Anthony in her will dated 16th December 1940. After Stephen died the medals were owned by Anthony and passed to his son, Dr Christopher Ackroyd, orthopaedic surgeon of Bristol, in 1988. All the medals were loaned to the Army Medical Services Museum, Keogh Barracks, Ash Vale, Aldershot, Hampshire until being returned to the family on 12th April 1994. They were sold for £110,000 in October 2003 to Lord Michael Ashcroft. The proceeds from the sale were donated to Gonville and Caius College, Cambridge to fund four annual medical scholarships for undergraduates and an annual lecture by a medical professor. The medals are held by the Michael Ashcroft Trust, the holding institution for the Lord Ashcroft Victoria Cross Collection and are displayed in the Imperial War Museum's Lord Ashcroft Gallery.

11795 CORPORAL LESLIE WILTON ANDREW
2nd Battalion, Wellington Regiment NZEF

Leslie Andrew was born on 23rd March 1897 at Ashhurst, Manawatu-Wanganui, near Palmerston North, New Zealand. His father, William Jeffrey Andrew MA (1865–1949), born at Ballarat, Victoria, Australia, emigrated to New Zealand and settled at Wanganui. He was a teacher in Westland at Ross School 1880–84, Gillespie Beach School 1884–85 and Blue Spur School 1885–87, then at Masterton 1887–88 and Avenue School, Wanganui 1888–92. He was headmaster at Longburn School in Palmerston North

(FA Swaine)

1892–95, Ashhurst School 1895–1909 and Wanganui East School 1909 until his retirement in July 1924. William married Frances Hannah Neil (1869–1941) at the Wesleyan Church, Pitt Street, Auckland in 1891. Leslie had six siblings:

Manawatu River at Ashhurst.

- Hazel Jane Andrew (1893–1940) married James Douglas Campbell (1894–1946) in 1924.
- Elsie Frances Andrew (1894–1917) was a teacher.
- Edith Tangye Andrew (born 1899).
- James Rogers Neil Andrew (born 1902) married Alice Whitford in 1930.
- Clarice Edna Andrew (born 1905) married Harry Skelton in 1928.
- Jeffery Mervyn Andrew (1908–80).

His paternal grandparents, James Andrew and Jane née Jeffrey, lived at Ballarat, Victoria, Australia. In addition to William they had six other children – James Andrew 1867, Hannah Andrew 1869, Edward James Andrew 1870, Ellen Andrew 1870, Mary Ann Andrew 1871 and Henry Andrew 1871.

His maternal grandfather, Hugh Neil (c.1830–1901), born in Glasgow, was a baker. He married Jane Alexander (died 1867) in 1851 and they had three children – Elizabeth Jane Neil 1852, John Rodger Neil 1855 and Mary Jane Neil 1857. He later married Hannah Dixon née Rogers. He emigrated to New Zealand and was living with his family at Halswell Street, Manawatu-Wanganui in 1900.

Leslie was educated at:

- Ashhurst Primary School, near Palmerston North.
- Sedgebrook School, (later Wanganui East School), Wanganui from February 1909.
- Wanganui District High School.
- Wanganui Collegiate School until 1913.

After school he worked in a solicitor's office until joining the Railway Department in Wellington as a clerk. He served in the Avenue School Cadets, in which his father was a company commander, and also in a Territorial unit, No.7 Company, Railway Engineers. Leslie enlisted in the New Zealand Expeditionary Force on 26th October 1915 (11795 later 30250).

The opening of the new Wanganui Collegiate School buildings in 1912.

On 1st May 1916 he left New Zealand with the 12th Reinforcements aboard HMNZT 51 *Ulimaroa*, landing at Suez, Egypt on 9th June 1916 as a sergeant. He reverted to private to join 2nd Wellington and sailed for England in July before proceeding to France in August. He was wounded for the first time on the Somme in September. Promoted corporal on 12th January 1917.

The Railway Department headquarters building in Wellington.

Awarded the VC for his actions at La Basse Ville, Belgium on 31st July 1917, LG 6th September 1917. He was the youngest New Zealander to win the VC. Leslie was promoted sergeant on 1st August and was wounded again and buried three times by high explosive shells before attended officer training in England. He received the VC from the King at Buckingham Palace on 31st October 1917. Leslie was commissioned on 1st March 1918, but remained in England and led a Victory Day parade contingent through London. He departed Britain for New Zealand in August 1919 and was demobilised on 21st October.

SS *Ulimaroa* (5,777 tons) was a passenger vessel built by Gourlay Bros & Co of Dundee for Huddart Parker & Co of Melbourne. Her first voyage as HMNZT 42 commenced on 5th February 1916. Six more voyages followed as HMNZT 51, 60, 74, 90, 100 and 108. The last voyage arrived in London on 4th October 1918. She was scrapped at Kobe, Japan in July 1934.

Leslie Andrew married Bessie Mead Ball (1894–1986), a VAD nurse, on 12th November 1918 at Basford, Nottinghamshire. She was a milliner improver in 1911. They returned to New Zealand and lived at 28 King's Drive, Levin before moving to 47 King's Drive. Leslie and Bessie had five children:

• Leslie Wilton Andrew (born and died 1920).
• Elsie Andrew (born 1921) married AD Arcus of Levin.
• Joan Andrew married EP Bielski of Apiti.
• Bruce Andrew (born 1928 at Basford, Nottinghamshire).
• Donald Andrew.

Bessie's father, Thomas Ball (born 1863 at Greasley, Nottingham), was a coal miner contractor. He married Mabel née Lewis (born c.1866) in 1888 at Northleach, Gloucestershire. In addition to Bessie they had five other children – Frank Joseph

Three of the key New Zealand commanders during the Battle for Crete at Helwan, Egypt on 21st July 1941. On the left is Lieutenant Colonel Andrew VC, CO 22nd Battalion, in the centre Brigadier Hargest CBE DSO** MC, Commander 5th New Zealand Brigade, and on the right Major General Bernard Freyberg VC CMG DSO**, GOC 2nd New Zealand Division.

Two doomed ships. RMS *Empress of Britain* passes HMS *Hood* in the Clyde. RMS *Empress of Britain* was lost in October 1940 and HMS *Hood* was sunk by the *Bismarck* on 24th May 1941.

Sergeant Keith Elliott VC.

Ball 1888, Jack Ball 1890, Amelia Ball 1892, Owen Ball 1898 and Colin Ball 1908. They were living at Broad Lane, Brinsley, Nottinghamshire in 1911.

Leslie served in the Permanent Army. He was lieutenant and Adjutant of the Taranaki Rifles 1920–23 and was promoted captain the following year. In 1927–29 he was attached to 2nd Highland Light Infantry in India. On returning to New Zealand he served as Adjutant of 1st Wellington. On 11th May 1937 Leslie commanded a New Zealand party mounting guard on Buckingham Palace and the following day he attended the coronation of George VI with fellow New Zealand VCs Captain Samuel Frickleton and Staff Sergeant James Crichton.

Promoted major in 1939 and lieutenant colonel and CO 22nd Battalion, 2nd New Zealand Expeditionary Force on 29th January 1940. He became known as 'Old February' due to twenty-eight days detention being his standard punishment. Sergeant Keith Elliott, who was awarded the VC for his actions in the Western Desert in 1942, served in 22nd Battalion throughout Leslie Andrew's tenure as CO. The Battalion departed New Zealand on RMS *Empress of Britain* in May 1940 and disembarked at Gourock, Scotland the following month. It served in Kent as part

RMS *Empress of Britain* (42,348 tons) was launched in 1931 in Scotland for the Canadian Pacific Steamship Company. At the time she was the largest, fastest and most luxurious ship on the Britain to Canada route. She is seen here entering the King George V dry dock at Southampton with RMS *Olympic* in the background. Her captain 1934–37 was Ronald Niel Stuart VC. In June 1939, she sailed from Halifax to Southampton with her smallest ever passenger list of only forty people – King George VI, Queen Elizabeth, thirty-five staff, a photographer and two reporters. She was requisitioned as a troopship on outbreak of war, initially bringing Canadian troops to England. Then she went to Wellington, New Zealand returning to Scotland in June 1940 as part of the 'million dollar convoy' of seven luxury liners. The others were

Empress of Canada, *Empress of Japan*, *Queen Mary*, *Aquitania*, *Mauretania* and *Andes*. On 26th October 1940, about seventy miles off the Irish coast she was strafed and bombed by a long-range German Condor. There were few casualties, but fires broke out and most of the 623 crew and passengers were picked up by other ships, leaving a skeleton crew. Next day tows were attached, but she moved very slowly and was intercepted by U-32 and torpedoed. There was a massive explosion and she sank on 28th October, the largest liner lost in WW2 and the largest ship sunk by a U-boat.

of the anti-invasion defences for the rest of that year. While Leslie was away, Bessie was living at 1 Ranui Crescent, Khandallah, Wellington.

In March 1941, 22nd Battalion moved to Egypt and three weeks later to Greece. It was evacuated to Crete where it deployed around Maleme airfield, particularly on Hill 107. On 20th May Leslie lost touch with his widely dispersed companies as lines were cut and runners failed to get through. Radio communications with HQ 5th New Zealand Brigade were maintained, but when Leslie appealed for help it was refused, because the other battalions were also heavily engaged. In the middle of the afternoon Leslie counterattacked with a reserve platoon and two tanks, which broke down, forcing the survivors to fall back. By nightfall Leslie believed that three of his companies had been destroyed. A company from 23rd Battalion arrived, but was insufficient to restore the balance and he decided to withdraw during the night to the area held by 21st and 23rd Battalions. At daylight the 'missing' companies realised that the rest of the Battalion had withdrawn and followed. Leslie realised too late that the position was stronger than envisaged and the Germans occupied the airfield, a significant factor in their eventual victory.

Leslie served in North Africa during Operation Crusader (8th November–30th December 1941)

Maleme airfield on Crete from Hill 107.

in the Libyan Desert. HQ 5th New Zealand Brigade was overrun and captured on 25th November, but this was not known for certain for thirty-six hours. Leslie Andrew tried all means possible to contact the HQ and other units. On 1st December with food, water and ammunition running low he decided to move the Battalion and join the Indian Division, which was achieved by 4 a.m. the following morning. The Battalion was ordered to Musaid to strengthen the Sollum-Capuzzo Line, while he was to form a new Brigade HQ with himself in command. On 3rd December the Brigade was ordered to Menastir to occupy the line previously held by 22nd Battalion. There it defeated several attacks, inflicting heavy losses on the enemy. After three days it was ordered back to the Sollum-Capuzzo Line. This was a difficult move on a single track below an escarpment, requiring engineers to blast a way through to make it passable for vehicles. However, this was achieved successfully and the Sollum-Capuzzo Line was taken over again. He handed over command of the Brigade on 9th December. **Mentioned in War Office Despatches, LG 30th December 1941. Awarded the DSO for his outstanding courage, skill and leadership in bringing the Brigade through a very difficult fourteen days, LG 19th March 1942.**

Leslie was replaced as CO 22nd Battalion in February 1942 and returned to New Zealand in April. He ceased expeditionary service in October 1943 and in November was promoted colonel and appointed Officer Commanding Wellington Fortress Garrison. He returned to Britain and commanded the New Zealand Contingent during the Victory Parade in 1946 and in 1946–47 attended the Imperial Defence College in London. Appointed ADC to the Governor General of New Zealand, Sir Cyril Newell. Promoted brigadier in 1948 and appointed Commandant of the Central Military District, New Zealand.

Leslie retired in 1952 and was asked on several occasions to stand for Parliament, but he refused. He was a member of the Legion of Frontiersmen and attended the VC Centenary Celebrations at Hyde Park, London on 26th June 1956. Leslie Andrew died after a short illness at Palmerston North Hospital on 8th January

A post-WW2 group of eleven New Zealand VCs. From left to right; back row – Leslie Andrew, Reginald Judson, James Crichton, Henry Laurent and Cyril Bassett; front row – John Hinton, Keith Elliott, Charles Upham, Clive Hulme, Samuel Frickleton and John Grant.

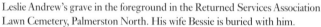

Leslie Andrew's grave in the foreground in the Returned Services Association Lawn Cemetery, Palmerston North. His wife Bessie is buried with him.

1969. He is buried in the Returned Services Association Lawn Cemetery, Tiro Tiro Road, Palmerston North (Row 13 Plot 158). He is commemorated in a number of other places:

- 22nd New Zealand Battalion L.W. Andrew VC Bursary was established by former members of the Battalion. It is awarded annually for one year's tertiary study to a student from Horowhenua College, Levin for service and academic excellence.
- Andrew Barracks, 60 Field Engineers, Linton Military Camp, near Palmerston North, Manawatu-Wanganui.
- Andrew Avenue, Roslyn, Palmerston North.
- Andrew Street, Waiouru Military Camp, Manawatu-Wanganui.
- Named on Victoria Cross Memorial, Queens Gardens, Dunedin.
- Plaque at Victoria Cross Corner outside the Dunedin Branch of the Returned Services Association of New Zealand.
- An obelisk sundial in the centre of the War Memorial Wall, Caroline Bay, Timaru bears the names of eleven New Zealand VCs, including Leslie Andrew.
- Plaque at Rue Faubourg de Lille, La Basse Ville, Comines-Warneton, Belgium, unveiled by the New Zealand Ambassador to Belgium, Peter Kennedy, on 26th October 2008.
- An issue of twenty-two 60c stamps by New Zealand Post entitled 'Victoria Cross – the New Zealand Story' honouring

The Victoria Cross Memorial, Queens Gardens, Dunedin.

Victoria Cross Corner, Dunedin Returned
Services Association Memorial Hall.

Memorial plaque at La Basse Ville, Comines-Warneton,
Belgium, unveiled in October 2008. It is only a few
metres from the former In den Rooster Caberet inn.

New Zealand's twenty-two Victoria Cross holders was issued on 14th April 2011.

- Named on one of eleven plaques honouring 175 men from overseas awarded the VC for the Great War. The plaques were unveiled by the Senior Minister of State at the Foreign & Commonwealth Office and Minister for Faith and Communities, Baroness Warsi, at a reception at Lancaster House, London on 26th June 2014 attended by The Duke of Kent and relatives of the VC recipients. The New Zealand plaque was unveiled on 7th May 2015 to be mounted on a wall between Parliament and the Cenotaph. The ceremony was attended by Defence Minister Gerry Brownlee, Defence Force Chief Lieutenant General Tim Keating and Corporal Willie Apiata, New Zealand's only living VC.

The plaque presented to New Zealand by the people of the United Kingdom on 7th May 2015, honouring the sixteen New Zealanders awarded the VC for the First World War.

- The Secretary of State for Communities and Local Government, Eric Pickles MP announced that Victoria Cross recipients from the Great War would have commemorative paving stones laid in their birthplace as a lasting legacy of local heroes within communities. The stones would be laid on or close to the 100th anniversary of their VC actions. For the 145 VCs born in Australia, Belgium,

Canada, China, Denmark, Egypt, France, Germany, India, Iraq, Japan, Nepal, Netherlands, New Zealand, Pakistan, South Africa, Sri Lanka, Ukraine and United States of America, individual commemorative stones were unveiled at the National Memorial Arboretum, Alrewas, Staffordshire by Prime Minister David Cameron MP and Sergeant Johnson Beharry VC on 5th March 2015.

In addition to the VC and DSO he was awarded the British War Medal 1914–20, Victory Medal 1914–19, 1939–45 Star, Africa Star, Defence Medal, War Medal 1939–45 with Mentioned in Despatches Oakleaf, New Zealand War Service Medal 1939–45, George VI Coronation Medal 1937, Elizabeth II Coronation Medal 1953 and New Zealand Long & Efficient Service Medal. The VC is held by the Queen Elizabeth II Army Memorial Museum, Waiouru, New Zealand. On 2nd December 2007, ninety-six medals were stolen from the Museum by James Joseph Kapa and Ronald van Wakeren, including nine VCs (Andrew, Elliott, Frickleton, Grant, Hinton, Hulme, Judson, Laurent and Upham) and two GCs. A $300,000 reward was offered by medal collector Lord Michael Ashcroft and Nelson businessman Tom Sturgess and the collection was recovered on 16th February 2008. The medals returned to the Museum in October 2008. Kapa was jailed for six years and van Wakeren for eleven years for this and other crimes. Upgrades to security at the Museum cost NZ$1.4 million.

Leslie Andrew's commemorative paving stone at the National Memorial Arboretum, Alrewas, Staffordshire. It is one of 145 stones unveiled by Prime Minister David Cameron MP and Sergeant Johnson Beharry VC on 5th March 2015 to commemorate the First World War VCs born outside the United Kingdom.

404017 CORPORAL COLIN FRASER BARRON
3rd Battalion (Toronto Regiment), Canadian Expeditionary Force

Colin Barron was born on 20th September 1893 at Baldavie, Boyndie, Banff, Banffshire, Scotland. His father was identified following an action by Barron's mother on 31st January 1894, the findings of which were recorded by the Sheriff at Banff on 1st February 1894. He was William Cowie, a soldier, of Seafield Farm, Cullen, Banffshire. When Colin attested in the Canadian Army he recorded his father as Joseph Barron and when he married, his parents were recorded as Joseph Barron and Mary Reid, but they were actually his maternal grandparents. His mother, Margaret Walker Barron (1870–1958), a domestic servant, was born at Church Lane, MacDuff, Gamrie, Banffshire. Colin had three half siblings:

Seafield Farm, Cullen, Banffshire, one time home of Colin Barron's father, William Cowie.

- Isabella Raffan Barron (born 1889) was the illegitimate daughter of Margaret Barron and George Raffan Riddle.
- Alexander Barron (1891–1916), whose father may also have been William Cowie. He emigrated to Canada and enlisted in 28th Battalion (North West), Canadian Expeditionary Force (424552) on 3rd July 1915. He was

Alexander Barron's name on the Ypres (Menin Gate) Memorial.

described as 5′ 6″ tall, with medium complexion, brown eyes, black hair and his religious denomination was Presbyterian. He was killed in action on 6th June 1916 during the Battle of Mount Sorrel in Belgium and is commemorated on the Ypres (Menin Gate) Memorial, Belgium.
- Margaret Stevenson Barron (born 1898) was the illegitimate daughter of Margaret Barron and John Stevenson, a mason, of 17 Constitution Street, Inverurie.

Colin's paternal grandparents are not known. His maternal grandfather, Joseph Barron (1836–1925), was living with his parents at Duff Street, Gamrie in 1841. By 1851 he was a farm servant at the farm of Robert and Isabel Bruce at Glenhouses, Aberdour, Aberdeenshire. He was living at Montbletton, Gamrie in 1860 when he married Mary née Reid (1841–1907), also a farm servant, at Church of Boyndie, Banffshire. They were living at Blairmaud Cottage, Mill of Boyndie, Banffshire in 1881. At various times Joseph was employed as a wood labourer, agricultural labourer and a mason's labourer. In addition to Margaret they had nine other children:

- Mary Ann Barron (1861–1916) had a daughter, Maria Lawrence Barron, in 1884.
- John Barron (1862–63).
- Margaret Barron (1863–64).
- Helen Barron (born 1865) married James Innes and had two children, James and Rebecca Innes.
- Joseph Barron (born 1868).

- Alexander Walker Barron (1873–1949) served in the Royal Field Artillery (543 later 636389) and was discharged time expired. He married Christina R Seivwright (1882–1979) in 1905 at Rathven, Banffshire. He re-enlisted in the RFA on 28th August 1914 at Aberdeen (3750). Christina was living at 21 Bristo Street, Edinburgh, Midlothian in 1917. They had eight children – John Barron 1905, Mary Barron 1907, Alice Barron 1909, George Brian Tore Barron 1914, Joseph Barron 1917 and Anne Barron. They emigrated to Canada. He died on 19th February 1949 at Toronto, Ontario and she died on 7th February 1979 at Owen Sound, Simcoe, Ontario.
- James Barron (born 1875).
- John Reid Barron (1878–1949) was a farm servant working as a blacksmith's labourer for John and Ann Hay at Dubiton, Marnoch, Banffshire in 1891. He enlisted in the Gordon Highlanders at Aberdeen (5995) on 23rd December 1896 and joined 2nd Battalion on 8th April 1897. He was described as 5′ 5¾″ tall, weighing 127 lbs, with fresh complexion, grey eyes, fair hair and his religious denomination was Presbyterian. He achieved 3rd Class Education on 3rd May 1898 and was granted Good Conduct Pay of 1d per day on 23rd December. On 30th April 1899 he transferred to 53rd Battery, Royal Field Artillery (9029) and served throughout the South Africa War 1899–1902. He was awarded the Queen's South Africa Medal with four clasps (Defence of Ladysmith; Orange Free State, Belmont and Laing's Nek) and the King's South Africa Medal with two clasps (South Africa 1902 and 1902). He was appointed acting bombardier on 19th December 1900 and was granted Good Conduct Pay of 2d per day on 23rd December 1902. He was promoted bombardier on 5th February 1903, passed the corporal's examination on 8th April, was posted to No.1 Depot on 16th October, achieved 2nd Class Education on 24th October and re-engaged to complete twelve years on 28th October. From 1st April 1904 he received Class 1 Service Pay and was promoted corporal on 18th November 1905. He was posted to 42nd Battery on 10th March 1906 and attended the Short Course of Gunnery on 6th December. On 31st October 1907 he re-engaged to complete twenty-one years. He was promoted sergeant on 23rd May 1908 and was posted to 53rd Battery on 10th June. Postings followed to 95th Battery on 29th November 1909 and C Battery, 15th Brigade at Kilkenny, Ireland on 1st December 1914. On 15th March 1915 he was promoted warrant officer class 2 and appointed battery sergeant major and was posted to B Battery, 75th Brigade on 8th May and went to France on 2nd September. He was awarded the Long Service and Good Conduct Medal in 1915 with gratuity. He was posted to 5C Reserve Brigade at Charlton Park on 13th March 1916 and to 1A Reserve Brigade at Newcastle upon Tyne on 13th July. He went to France on 25th July 1917 and joined 6th Divisional Ammunition Column on 16th August. He volunteered for an extra year's service on 12th April 1919 and returned to Britain on 8th September, where he was posted to 68th Battery, 14th Brigade on 25th September and to 61st Battery, 14th Brigade on 10th November.

He was demobilised on 22nd January 1920 and was discharged on completion of his engagement on 19th February 1920. John married Florence Maud Watchman (1897–1975) at 35 (possibly 85) Hutcheson Street, Glasgow in May 1916 by declaration. She was born at Houghton, Co Durham and was living at Struan Cottage, Old Meldrum, Aberdeenshire at the time of her marriage. They were living in Northumberland in 1917 before moving to Buchan, Aberdeenshire in the early 1920s, but their last child was born in Northumberland in 1927. They had seven children including – John Joseph Reid Barron 1917, Joseph Reid Barron 1920, Alexander Mathers Barron 1921, Florence Margaret Reid Barron 1922, Agnes Mary Barron 1925 and Heather Barron 1927. They emigrated to Canada, arriving at Quebec on 6th May 1927. Florence married Alexander Ogilvie (1891–c.1960) c.1939 at Gravenhurst, Muskoka, Ontario.

• Elizabeth MacKay Barron (1880–1949) had two children – Mary Ann Mitchell Barron 1896 and Gertrude Maria Chalmers Barron 1900. The children were living with their grandparents, Joseph and Mary Barron, in 1901.

Colin was educated at Blairmaud, Boyndie, Banff. He emigrated to Canada in March 1910 and settled in Toronto, where he worked on the railways as a teamster. He enlisted in 48th Highlanders (Militia) on 16th May 1913 and served in H Company. He enlisted in D Company, 35th Battalion on 25th January 1915 (A/4017 also seen as 9/4017 and corrected later to 404017). The unit became 35th Reserve Battalion on 9th February. On 5th April he attested for the Canadian Overseas Expeditionary Force at Toronto. He was described as 5′ 7½″ tall, weighing 170 lbs, with dark complexion, dark brown eyes, black hair and his religious denomination was Presbyterian. He sailed for Britain aboard SS *Metagama* from Montreal on 4th June and was taken on strength of 23rd Battalion on 20th June at Dibgate Plain, near Shorncliffe, Kent. On 12th July he forfeited one days' pay for absence and on 17th July proceeded to Boulogne, France to join 3rd Battalion.

He was in hospital with bronchitis 20th-23rd August and was attached to 1st Canadian Brigade Machine Gun School 9th-23rd November. He was admitted to 2nd Canadian Field Ambulance with an infected left foot 29th December 1915–2nd January 1916. On 1st May he was granted nine days leave and was attached to 1st Canadian Machine Gun Company 2nd-4th June. He was admitted to 4th Canadian Field Ambulance with gastro enteritis 8th-13th September. He was admitted to 39th General Hospital, Le Havre with gonorrhoea 28th January–18th February 1917 and 22nd February–20th April 1917. Colin was promoted lance corporal on 9th April and corporal on 1st July. He was granted ten days leave to England from 7th September.

Awarded the VC for his actions at Vine Cottage on Goudberg Spur, Passchendaele Ridge, Belgium on 6th November 1917, LG 11th January 1918. He was attached to the Canadian Corps School on 7th February 1918 and was appointed acting sergeant with pay on 12th February while employed as an instructor. On 13th March he went on leave to England for fourteen days, extended to 8th April for private family affairs. He received a gold watch and a wallet of Treasury notes from the Duke of Richmond and Gordon at Whitehills, Banff, Scotland in March 1918. While in Scotland he became a Freemason, being Initiated into Saint Andrew Lodge No.52, Banff on 21st March. The VC was presented by the King at Buckingham Palace on 6th April 1918.

Colin was Initiated into Saint Andrew Lodge No.52 at Banff on 21st March 1918.

Colin attended Lewis gun instruction on 2 May to become an instructor at the Canadian Corps School. On 30th December he was taken on strength of the Canadian Army Base Depot and rejoined 3rd Battalion on 22nd February 1919. He returned to England on 23rd March and was posted to 1st Central Ontario Regimental Depot. On 12th April he was struck off the strength of 3rd Battalion and embarked at Southampton for Canada on RMS *Olympic* on 15th April. On 23rd

April he was demobilised at No.2 District Depot, Toronto giving his intended place of residence as 56 Robina Avenue, Toronto. His occupation was recorded as a blacksmith. Colin rejoined 48th Highlanders of Canada on 4th November 1921. He was discharged on 22nd May 1931, having been promoted to company sergeant major.

Colin and Helen lived at 396 Rhodes Avenue, Toronto. (*Ferris Virani*)

71 Hamilton Street, Toronto was where Helen lived prior to her marriage to Colin in 1921. (*Ferris Virani*)

Sumach Street, Toronto where Colin was living when he married in 1921.

Colin Barron married Helen Milne (born 1892 in Aberdeen, Scotland) on 23rd September 1921 at York, Toronto, Ontario. She was described as an operator. Colin was living at 9 Sumach Street, Toronto and Helen was living at 71 Hamilton Street, Toronto at the time. They lived at 396 Rhodes Avenue, Toronto and had two children:

• Helen Barron married DC Kerr.
• Marjory Barron married as Thompson.

Helen's parents were William Milne of Aberdeen and Margaret née Brown.

Colin joined the Provincial Police and served at Kitchener, Orangeville and Niagara Falls. He attempted to join the National Force but was rejected for being too short. He worshipped at Davenport Presbyterian Church and was an honorary member of many Toronto military clubs. He ran his own transport business while also employed with the Ontario Department of Highways, but during the Depression he was out of work for two years. He eventually found employment as a guide at the Provincial Government building and was then on the staff of Don Jail. On 9th November 1929 he attended the VC Dinner at the Royal Gallery of the House of Lords, London. He was one of seven VCs presented to King George VI and Queen Elizabeth during their tour of Canada at Queen's Park, Toronto on 22nd May 1939. The other VCs presented were Benjamin Geary, Walter Rayfield, Henry Robson, Thomas Holmes, William Merrifield, and Charles Rutherford.

Wychwood-Davenport Presbyterian Church, Toronto.

At the outbreak of the Second World War he enlisted in the Royal Regiment of Canada and took part in the occupation of Iceland. He was later appointed Provost Sergeant Major of HQ 1st Canadian Division in England. After the war he returned to his job as a security guard at Don Jail. He joined the Toronto Corps of Commissionaires, serving at the Canadian Broadcasting Commission television studios, Hester How School and Sunnybrook Hospital.   He was present at the Coronation of Queen Elizabeth II in 1953 and attended the VC Centenary Celebrations

Don Jail in 1949. It was built to the east of the Don River in Toronto in 1864 and was reputed to be the largest jail in North America at the time.

Hester How School in 1952.

Colin Barron's gravestone in Prospect Cemetery, Toronto.

at Hyde Park, London on 26th June 1956. Colin Barron died at Sunnybrook Hospital, Toronto on 15th August 1958 and is buried in Prospect Cemetery, Toronto (Veteran's Section 7 Grave 3562). He is commemorated in a number of other places:

- Named on a Victoria Cross obelisk to all Canadian VCs at Military Heritage Park, Barrie, Ontario dedicated by The Princess Royal on 22nd October 2013.
- Named on one of eleven plaques honouring 175 men from overseas awarded the VC for the Great War. The plaques were unveiled by the Senior Minister of State at the Foreign & Commonwealth Office and Minister for Faith and Communities, Baroness Warsi, at a reception at Lancaster House, London on 26th June 2014 attended by The Duke of Kent and relatives of the VC recipients. The Canadian plaque

The Colonial Auxiliary Forces Long Service Medal was instituted in 1899 for part-time members of all ranks of military forces throughout the Empire. It gradually superseded the Volunteer Long Service Medal for India and the Colonies. In 1930 it was superceded by the Efficiency Medal, along with the Volunteer Long Service Medal, Volunteer Long Service Medal for India and the Colonies, Militia Long Service Medal, Special Reserve Long Service and Good Conduct Medal and the Territorial Efficiency Medal.

was unveiled outside the British High Commission in Elgin Street, Ottawa on 10th November 2014 by The Princess Royal in the presence of British High Commissioner Howard Drake, Canadian Minister of Veterans Affairs Julian Fantino and Canadian Chief of the Defence Staff General Thomas J Lawson.
- Two 49 cents postage stamps in honour of the 94 Canadian VC winners were issued by Canada Post on 21st October 2004 on the 150th Anniversary of the first Canadian VC's action, Alexander Roberts Dunn VC.
- Plaque on a memorial to the ninety-nine Canadian VCs in York Cemetery, Toronto.

In addition to the VC he was awarded the 1914–15 Star, British War Medal 1914–20, Victory Medal 1914–19, Defence Medal, Canadian Volunteer Service Medal 1939–45 with Maple Leaf clasp, War Medal 1939–45, George VI Coronation Medal 1937 and Elizabeth II Coronation Medal 1953. Some sources include the 1939–45 Star and Colonial Auxiliary Forces Long Service Medal in the group. The medals are held privately.

LIEUTENANT COLONEL PHILIP ERIC BENT
9th Battalion, The Leicestershire Regiment

Philip Bent was born at Halifax, Nova Scotia, Canada on 3rd January 1891. His father, Franklin Pierce Bent (1856–1941), was a 1st class clerk in 1872 and was working for the railway department in the 1881 Census of Canada. By 1888 he was working for the Halifax Post Office, living at Pugwash, Cumberland, Nova Scotia. By 1891 he was a money order clerk at the Post Office Department and was later a superintendent of railway mail services. He married Sophia 'Sophy' née Harvey (1856–1930), on 15th December 1885 at Edinburgh, Midlothian, Scotland and they sailed for Canada. She was born at Childe Okeford, Dorset. Sophia returned to England without her

Halifax was founded in 1749. During the War of 1812, in a naval engagement off the Halifax station, HMS *Shannon* captured the frigate USS *Chesapeake*. The invasion force that landed at Washington in 1813 and burned the Capitol and White House set out from Halifax. Although Nova Scotia joined the Canadian confederation, Halifax retained a British garrison until 1906 and the Royal Navy remained until 1910, when the newly created Royal Canadian Navy took over the dockyard. In 1912 Halifax was the hub for recovery operations following the sinking of *RMS Titanic*. One hundred and fifty victims of the disaster are buried there. During the First World War the port became a major departure point for Canadian forces going to Europe. In both world wars it was a key assembly point for trans-Atlantic convoys. On 6th December 1917 the town suffered a devastating explosion when the French SS *Mont-Blanc*, carrying high explosives, collided with the Norwegian SS *Imo* in the Narrows. About 2,000 people were killed and 9,000 were injured.

Pugwash is small village on the Nova Scotian coast, known for fishing, salt mining and small-scale manufacturing. Many of its early settlers were Highland Scots and the village still celebrates its Scottish heritage every July. In 1957 it hosted an international conference of scientists from both sides in the Cold War organized by Bertrand Russell. In 1995 the Nobel Prize was awarded to the International Pugwash conferences, *for their efforts to diminish the part played by nuclear arms in international politics and in the longer run to eliminate such arms.*

husband after 1901 and settled in Leicestershire. By 1911 she was living at Flat 6, Clyde House, Surbiton Road, Kingston upon Thames. During the war she lived at 218 Woodstock Road in Oxford, 7 Bouverie Avenue in Salisbury and moved to 26B South Terrace, Littlehampton, Sussex before October 1917. By 1923 she had moved to Hindhead, Surrey. She travelled to Australia aboard the P&O liner *Mooltan*, leaving London on 15th November 1929 bound for Sydney. She died on 6th March 1930 at King Street Hospital, Rotorua, New Zealand leaving effects valued at £2,093/2/8d to her children, Muriel and Lionel. On 12th April 1929 Frank departed Sydney, Australia on SS *Canadian Highlander* bound for the USA. He died on 2nd December 1941 at Halifax, Nova Scotia. Philip had two siblings:

• Lionel Lorraine Bent (1889–1961) was born in Nova Scotia. He was a surveyor and travelled to the United Kingdom with his mother or followed her there. He returned to Canada and enlisted in 11th Battalion CEF on 23rd September 1914 at Valcartier. He was described as 6′ 1″ tall, with fair complexion, blue eyes, light brown hair and his religious denomination was Church of England. Lionel

Clyde House, Surbiton Road, Kingston upon Thames, where Philip's mother was living in 1911.

Woodstock Road, Oxford where Philip's mother lived during the First World War.

was appointed temporary honorary lieutenant on 3rd August 1915 and was later promoted captain. His name was brought to the notice of the Secretary of State for War for valuable service on 26th October 1916. He married Jessie Bell Cardiff (c.1879–1960) in November 1915 at the Parish Church, Bloomsbury, London. She was born in Ontario, Canada. They were living at Bedford Gardens House, Kensington, London in 1930 with Gladys Ethel Cardiff (born 1883), probably Jessie's sister. By 1939 he was a secretary to a public company living with his wife at Gloucester Terrace, Paddington, London. Lionel was living at Elmcroft, 33 The Green, West Drayton, Middlesex at the time of his death on 31st July 1961 at Thorney Weir Mill, West Drayton. He left effects valued at £717/8/1 to Gladys Cardiff.

- Muriel Bent (born 1888 in Nova Scotia).

Philip's paternal grandfather, James Bent, was born c.1809 in Nova Scotia. He married Ellen possibly née Jones (born 1828). James was a farmer living with his family at Pugwash, Nova Scotia in 1871. Ellen was living with her son-in-law, William, and his family in 1891. In addition to Frank they had two other children:

- Maggie L Bent (born c.1859) married William McNutt (born c.1835) and they had a daughter, Madeline, c.1890.
- Evelyn Bent (born c.1862).

His maternal grandfather, Edwin Harvey (1816–91), was born at Childe Okeford, Dorset. He married Ann née Hatcher (born c.1815 at Marnhull, Dorset) on 28th January 1839 at Childe Okeford. Edwin was a farmer in Childe Okeford in 1851, innkeeper at Worthy's Royal Hotel, Templecombe, Somerset by 1861 and the Warwick Arms at Clutton, Somerset by 1871, with his children Edward, Matilda and Fanny. By then Ann was a room keeper at Abbas and Templecombe, Somerset with her children David, Thurza and Sophia. By 1881 Edwin was running the Railway Hotel, Shillingstone Street, Shillingstone, Dorset with his second wife, Elizabeth (born c.1841), and was also farming four acres. In addition to Sophia they had nine other children:

- Louise Hatcher Harvey (born and died 1839).
- Anne Amelia Harvey (1840–92) married Thomas Dennington in 1864. He was a bank clerk (1840–94) born at Ashton, Lancashire. She was living at Ash Villa, Vicarage Road, King's Heath, King's Norton, Warwickshire at the time of her death on 13th May 1892. They had four children – Hugh Dennington 1865, Jessie Augusta Dennington 1868 and twins Bertha and Lilian Dennington 1871.
- Juliana Harvey (1842–99) married Charles Green (1843–1907), a screen finisher, in 1862. They had emigrated to Hamilton City, Ontario, Canada by 1877. They had ten children – Margaret Jane Harvey Green 1863, Sidney Charles Green

1864, Ernest Edward Green 1865, Bertie Frederick Green 1867, Hedley Reginald Green 1868, Agnes Ida J Green 1870, Victor Maurice Green 1872, Ivor Horace Green 1873, Gertrude Ethel Harvey Green 1877 and Earl Trevor Green 1881.

- David John Harvey (1843–82) died at The Woodbine Inn, Gough Street, Birmingham, Warwickshire.
- Henry 'Harry' James Harvey (1845–1919), a domestic gardener and servant, married Sarah Jane Thompson (1845–1907) in 1868. In 1871 they were living at Childe Okeford. By 1901 he was the caretaker at a high school and they were living at 13 Avenue Road, Trowbridge, Wiltshire. Henry married Fanny Young (1856–1924) in 1908. Fanny had two children prior to her marriage – Alan Young c.1890 and Hazael [sic] Alexander Young 1897.
- Edward Harvey (born 1847).
- Matilda Harvey (1849–1922) married George Edwin Chappell (born 1848) in 1871 at Clutton. They had five children – Florence Chappell 1874, Minnie Chappell 1875, Ethel May Chappell 1877, Arthur Chappell 1881 and Emily Chappell 1886. Matilda was a widowed dairywoman by 1901, living with her children Florence, Arthur and Emily at 21 Prince of Wales Avenue, Reading, Berkshire.
- Frances 'Fanny' Harvey (1851–1939) was a needlewoman in 1911, living with her niece, Emily Chappell, at 25 Holdsworth Road, Halifax, Yorkshire.
- Thurza Louisa Harvey (c.1855–1931) never married.

Philip was educated at:

- Ashby de la Zouch Boys Grammar School 1904–07, where he was head boy. His mother donated his boxing gloves to the school in 1918.
- Royal High School Edinburgh, Midlothian. Also attended by Harcus Strachan VC.

Ashby de la Zouch Boys Grammar School was founded in 1567 by Henry Hastings, 3rd Earl of Huntingdon. A girls' grammar school opened in 1901 and they merged in 1972 to become a comprehensive, Ashby School. On 1st October 2012 it became an Academy.

One of the teachers at Ashby de la Zouch Boys Grammar School after Philip Bent left was Bernard William Vann, who was also awarded the VC during the Great War.

The Royal High School is one of the oldest schools in the world, dating back to at least 1128. By 1378 it was the Grammar School of the Church of Edinburgh. In 1566 Mary Queen of Scots transferred control from Holyrood Abbey to the Town Council of Edinburgh and James VI granted it royal patronage about 1590. By the early 19th century the School had gained an international reputation and attracted foreign students. It was the model for the English High School of Boston, the first public high school in the USA in 1821. The school had many locations in Edinburgh, the most famous on Regent Road was in use from 1829 until 1968, when it moved to its current site at Barnton. During the First World War 1,024 former members served in the armed forces of whom 180 died. The school gained over 100 gallantry awards, including two VCs, the other being awarded to Harcus Strachan. Another VC was awarded to John Cruikshank in the Second World War. The school has numerous famous alumni, including architect Robert Adam, inventor Alexander Graham Bell, Labour politician and Foreign Secretary Robin Cook, comedian Ronnie Corbett and author Walter Scott. The building on Regent Street was to be the site of a devolved legislature for Scotland, but it failed to gain sufficient support in 1979. The building was subsequently used for various political committees and as offices for Edinburgh City Council. Following the introduction of Scottish devolution in 1999, the former school was considered for the Scottish Parliament, but it was established on a new site at Holyrood. Since then a number of proposals have been made for its use, including home for a Scottish National Photography Centre and a luxury hotel.

Philip joined HMS *Conway*, the Merchant Navy training ship in the Mersey, in 1909 to gain sea-going experience and education. He was a senior cadet captain and a boxing champion in his final year. In December 1910 he left to become an apprentice on the steel four-masted barque *Vimeria* (2,233 tons), owned by John Hardie & Co of Glasgow. He qualified as 2nd mate in early 1914.

Philip was ashore when war broke out and enlisted as a private in A Company, 15th Battalion (1st Edinburgh), Royal Scots on 2nd October 1914 (17209). He was described as 5′ 8″ tall, weighing 144 lbs with fresh complexion, blue eyes, brown hair and his religious denomination was an unspecified form of Protestantism. There was a tattooed frog on his left forearm. Philip was commissioned on 30th November in the Leicestershire Regiment and joined A Company, 7th Battalion at Aldershot in April 1915. He also trained at Perham Down on Salisbury Plain. He was promoted lieutenant on 1st June and transferred to 9th Battalion in July. Philip went to France on 31st August 1915. He was the Battalion Grenade Officer when he applied for a regular commission in March 1916. He was appointed temporary captain on 21st April 1916 and was granted a permanent regular commission in the Bedfordshire Regiment on 3rd May 1916 with seniority from 4th April 1916. **He was mentioned in General Sir Douglas Haig's Despatch dated 30th April 1916, LG 15th June 1916.** Philip transferred to the Leicestershire Regiment

HMS *Conway*, a naval training school was founded in 1859 and for most of its life was housed aboard 19th century wooden ships of the line. It was created to satisfy a growing demand for merchant navy officers and operated under the Mercantile Marine Service Association. There would be three Conways over the years and they were moored in the Sloyne off Rock Ferry on the Mersey. By the time Philip Bent joined her in 1909, HMS *Conway* was the former HMS *Nile*, a ninety-two gun second-rate line-of-battle ship, launched in 1839 and served in the Royal Navy until 1875. In 1941 she was moved out of the Mersey to Anglesey to avoid the bombing raids on Liverpool. In 1953 she was being towed to Birkenhead for a refit when an eddy drove her ashore. As the tide fell she sagged and her seams opened letting in huge amounts of water. On the next high tide she failed to refloat and was judged to be a total constructive loss. The school was rehoused in tents in the grounds of Plas Newydd, the seat of the Marquess of Anglesey, then in a temporary hutted camp until permanent premises were built in the grounds in the 1960s. The school closed in 1974 and the buildings are now used by the Conway Centre for arts and outdoor education. Three other trainees were awarded the VC – Lieutenant Charles George Bonner, Lieutenant Ian Fraser and Captain Edward Unwin. Other famous alumni include: Captain Matthew Webb, the first man to swim the English Channel; John Masefield, Poet Laureate 1930–67; Buster Crabb, the Royal Navy frogman who disappeared while diving near a Soviet warship in 1956; Iain Duncan Smith MP, leader of the Conservative Party 2001–03; and Sir Clive Woodward, the 2003 World Cup winning England rugby union coach.

on 5th July 1916 and his regular commission was backdated to 30th August 1915. He joined 9th Battalion as temporary major and second in command on 13th July. He was wounded on 29th September, but remained at duty. On 17th October he suffered a gunshot to the neck and was treated at 7th Stationary Hospital, Boulogne, returning to duty on 25th October. Appointed acting lieutenant colonel on 26th October to

The barque *Vimeira*.

command 9th Battalion and temporary lieutenant colonel on 1st February 1917 with seniority from 26th October 1916. His permanent regular commission was transferred to the Leicestershire Regiment on 24th February 1917 with seniority

Philip Bent's name on the Tyne Cot Memorial.

from 30th August 1915. **Awarded the DSO in the Birthday Honours, LG 4th June 1917.** Promoted lieutenant 1st July 1917 while retaining the rank of temporary lieutenant colonel. **Awarded the VC for his actions east of Polygon Wood, Zonnebeke, Belgium on 1st October 1917, LG 11th January 1918. Mentioned in Field Marshal Sir Douglas Haig's Despatch dated 9th April 1917, LG 22nd May 1917.**

Philip was killed during his VC action at Polygon Wood on 1st October 1917. He has no known grave and is commemorated on the Tyne Cot Memorial, Belgium. As he never married, the VC and DSO were presented to his mother by the King at Buckingham Palace on 2nd March 1918. He is commemorated in a number of other places:

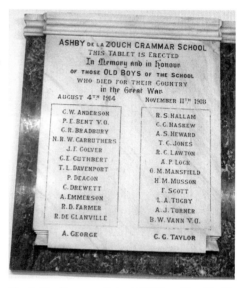

The Ashby Grammar School Old Boys First World War memorial including the names of Philip Bent VC and Bernard Vann VC.

- Canadian Book of Remembrance.
- Two memorials at Ashby School (formerly Ashby Boy's Grammar School), Ashby-de-la-Zouch, Leicestershire:
  - Named on a marble tablet in memory of the Old Boys who lost their life in the Great War.
  - A framed replica VC with his VC citation in School House unveiled on 19th November 2009.
- Named on the War Memorial, Royal High School, Edinburgh, Scotland.
- Named on the Honours Board of HMS *Conway* in the Memorial Chapel, Birkenhead Priory, The Wirral.
- Portrait and mementoes of his days on HMS *Conway* in the Army Museum in Halifax, Nova Scotia, Canada.
- His sword hangs in the Cathedral Church of All Saints in Halifax, Nova Scotia.
- Named on the War Memorial outside St Alban's Church, Hindhead, Surrey.

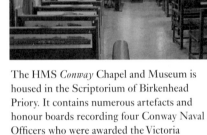

The two 49 Cent postage stamps commemorating ninety-four Canadian VCs issued by Canada Post on 21st October 2004.

The HMS *Conway* Chapel and Museum is housed in the Scriptorium of Birkenhead Priory. It contains numerous artefacts and honour boards recording four Conway Naval Officers who were awarded the Victoria Cross – Philip Bent, Charles Bonner, Ian Fraser and Edward Unwin.

- Named on a Victoria Cross obelisk to all Canadian VCs at Military Heritage Park, Barrie, Ontario dedicated by HRH The Princess Royal, Princess Anne on 22 October 2013.
- Two 49 Cent postage stamps in honour of the ninety-four Canadian VCs were issued by Canada Post on 21st October 2004 on the 150th Anniversary of the first Canadian VC's action, Alexander Roberts Dunn.
- A wooden plaque bearing fifty-six maple leaves each inscribed with the name of a Canadian-born VC holder was dedicated at the Canadian Forces College, Toronto on Remembrance Day 1999.
- Named on one of eleven plaques honouring 175 men from overseas awarded the VC for the Great War. The plaques were unveiled by the Senior Minister of State at the Foreign & Commonwealth Office and Minister for Faith and Communities, Baroness Warsi, at a reception at Lancaster House, London on 26th June 2014 attended by The Duke of Kent and relatives of the VC recipients. The Canadian plaque was unveiled outside the British High Commission in Elgin Street, Ottawa on 10th November 2014 by The Princess Royal in the presence of British High Commissioner Howard Drake,

Philip Bent's sword in the Cathedral Church of All Saints in Halifax, Nova Scotia. (*Memorials to Valour*)

Canadian Minister of Veterans Affairs Julian Fantino and Canadian Chief of the Defence Staff General Thomas J Lawson.

- The Secretary of State for Communities and Local Government, Eric Pickles MP announced that Victoria Cross recipients from the Great War would have commemorative paving stones laid in their birthplace as a lasting legacy of local heroes within communities. The stones would be laid on or close to the 100th anniversary of their VC actions. For the 145 VCs born in Australia, Belgium, Canada, China, Denmark, Egypt, France, Germany, India, Iraq, Japan, Nepal, Netherlands, New Zealand, Pakistan, South Africa, Sri Lanka, Ukraine and United States of America, individual commemorative stones were unveiled at the National Memorial Arboretum, Alrewas, Staffordshire by Prime Minister David Cameron MP and Sergeant Johnson Beharry VC on 5th March 2015.
- Named on a plaque at Ashworth Barracks Museum, Doncaster, South Yorkshire unveiled by Lord Lieutenant Andrew Coombe on 22nd June 2015.

In addition to the VC he was awarded the DSO, 1914–15 Star, British War Medal 1914–20 and Victory Medal 1914–19 with Mentioned-in-Despatches Oakleaf. His mother presented his medals to Ashby Boys' Grammar School in 1923 with a covering letter stating, *I'm hoping that they will serve as a lasting stimulant to high ideals to following generations.* In 1972 the medals passed on permanent loan to the Royal Leicestershire Regiment Museum Collection. They are held by the Royal Leicestershire Regiment Museum, New Walk Museum & Art Gallery, Leicester.

LIEUTENANT COLONEL BERTRAM BEST-DUNKLEY
2/5th Battalion, The Lancashire Fusiliers

Bertram Best-Dunkley (Best Dunkley at birth) was born at York on 3rd August 1890. His father, Alfred Corah Dunkley (c.1837–1900), was a baker in 1851, later a commercial traveller and by 1891 was an agent in the hop trade. He married Eliza Jane Drury (c.1830–87) in 1862 at Worcester and they were living at Severus Place, Holgate, York in 1881. Eliza died in February 1887 and Alfred married Bertram's mother, Augusta Martha 'Edith' née Draper (1854–1907) that November at St Paul's, York. Her name was recorded as Augusta Mary in the 1891 Census and when her second marriage and death were registered. In 1891 they were living at Mount Vale, York. Alfred suffered epilepsy and sunstroke and became wild and violent towards Augusta, even threatening to shoot her. They had separated in July 1899, but Alfred persuaded her to take him back. She did not want to put him in an asylum and hired two male attendants to protect her, one by day and the other by night. On 17th August 1900, Commissionaire George Harris went to their home at 82 Kensington Garden Square, London to serve Alfred with a notice for a judicial separation instituted in the Divorce Court by Augusta. Harris had to protect her from Alfred, who then went into the lavatory and shot himself a number of times with a revolver. Alfred died at St Mary's Hospital, Paddington the following day. At the inquest it was revealed that he was ruined financially. The jury returned a verdict of 'suicide while of unsound mind', and expressed regret that steps had not been taken to restrain the deceased in an asylum.

Bertram had four brothers from his father's two marriages:

- Thomas Henry Dunkley (1862–63).
- Alfred 'Fred' Edmund Dunkley (1864–1944), born at King's Norton, Worcestershire, married Ada Harriet Fletcher (1865–1954) in 1889 at Cardiff, Glamorgan. He was a brewer, living at 16 St Andrews Street, Cardiff in 1901 and at 103 Henley Road, Reading, Berkshire in 1939. They had three children:
  - Charles Stewart Dunkley (born 1891) was commissioned in the Welsh Regiment, serving from 1908 until 1912 and 1914 to 1923. When his CO was killed, he took command of a battalion on the Somme. He was seriously wounded in the head and body and was evacuated home (MC and Bar, LG 1st January 1917 and 16th November 1917). He also served as a staff captain and brigade major and at the end of the war was posted to India. On 23rd June 1923 he retired on account of ill health caused by war wounds and went into partnership in a motor business at Eastbourne until August 1930 when it was annulled due to a dispute. In May 1931 he was sentence to eighteen months' hard labour at the Old Bailey having pleaded guilty to two charges of demanding money with menaces from a man and woman at Eastbourne. He was living in a hotel in the Strand, London at the time and arranged for the money to be handed over at two other hotels, the Strand Palace and the Regent Palace. The police became involved and he was arrested on the Strand with Eva Smith, who was not prosecuted. Dunkley claimed he needed the money to go abroad because 'I just hate the country and the idiots who govern it'. He was married with a child at the time. His family believed the head wound during the war had affected his mind. As a result of the conviction he was removed from the Army on 12th May 1931.
  - John Douglas Dunkley (born 1898) enlisted in 7th (Cyclist) Battalion, Welsh Regiment (1088) at Bridgend, Glamorgan on 5th September 1914 and served at the Depot until joining the Battalion on 26th September. He was described as 5′7″ tall and variously as a student, farmer and clerk. He applied for a commission on 1st May 1915 giving his address as 'Hurstleigh', 29 Ninian Road, Cardiff, South Wales. He gave his date of birth as 19th November 1896 and claimed four years and three months service in the ranks of 7th Welsh (Cyclists), including three and a half years as a bugler. He was commissioned

with seniority backdated to 2nd May 1915 in 13th Welsh, but was cashiered from 21st Welsh on 25th October 1916 following trial by a general court martial at Reading on 4th October. He had claimed that two cheques had been stolen from his cheque book, but he had used them himself. He enlisted again on 27th December 1916 in the Gordon Highlanders (S/15989), described as 5' 10" tall and weighing 133 lbs. He was hospitalised with measles in Edinburgh, Midlothian 3rd-12th March 1917 and joined A Company, 8/10th Gordon Highlanders in France on 2nd May. Promoted corporal on 14th May and was gassed on 15th July. He was admitted to 46th Field Ambulance before being transferred to No.12 Casualty Clearing Station and then by 21 Ambulance Train on 21st July to 1st Australian General Hospital, Rouen. He was evacuated to Britain on 27th July and admitted to No.5 Auxiliary Hospital, Exeter before being transferred to Barnstaple VAD Hospital until 10th October and then back to Exeter until 19th October. Following convalescence he was sent on sick leave. Promoted lance sergeant 2nd February 1918 and returned to France from Folkestone to Boulogne on 9th May, but reverted to corporal at the Infantry Base Depot. He joined 1st Battalion on 4th June and was promoted sergeant on 8th June, but his stay was short as he received a gunshot wound to the right forearm causing a compound fracture to the ulna on 15th June at La Bassée. He was admitted to 7th Field Ambulance, No.4 Casualty Clearing Station and Base Hospital No.5 (also known as No.5 American Hospital) at Boulogne. On 29th June he was evacuated to Britain on HS *Jan Breydel* and treated at Keighley Auxiliary Hospital, Yorkshire until 12th August and Reading War Hospital, Berkshire until 12th May 1919. He was discharged on 19th May 1919 with 60% disability. In March 1922 the Colonial Office sought a character reference from the War Office and was informed of his dismissal in 1916. John applied to be enrolled in the Officers' Emergency Reserve on 10th May 1937 but was not accepted. He was fined 15/- at Bow Street Court on 21st May 1939 for failing to conform to an automatic traffic signal on Regent Street, London on 10th May. His address was Garden Flat, 6 Lancaster Drive, Hampstead, London.

○ Violet Nellie Dunkley (born 1908) was a mannequin in 1939. She married George William Edwin Airey (born 1910) in 1941. He was an officer cadet in the Cambridge University OTC and was commissioned in 69th (West Riding) Field Brigade RA on 18th July 1931. By 1955 he was a company director.

• William Draper Dunkley (born 1888 at York) was boarding at 13 Upper Bedford Place, Bloomsbury, London in 1911.

• Eric Julian Dunkley (1898–1958) was born at Kensington, London. He served as a temporary midshipman in the Royal Naval Reserve on the armoured cruiser HMS *Donegal* with seniority from 13th February 1916. He was cautioned for twice exceeding the limit of his monthly wine bill. He was appointed lieutenant commander in the Burma Royal Naval Volunteer Reserve on 1st December 1941. He married Ellen Mayflower Crisp (1893–1966) in November 1918 at Rangoon

Cathedral. She was born at Monkey Point, Rangoon, Burma. They had three children including, James Desmond Dunkley. Eric and Ellen were living at Flat 4, 3 Carlton Drive, Putney Hill, Putney, London prior to his death.

By 1901 Augusta was running a boarding house at 82 Doreck College, Paddington, London. She married Baron Hans Bjorn-Graesse (born c.1863), Vice-Consul for Uruguay, in September 1906 at Dover, Kent. Bjorn-Graesse had been a privy councillor to the Kings of Saxony and had also served the Greek government. He had been married previously to Helena Manuela Verrier in 1888 at Philadelphia, USA. Her father was Cuban and her mother was a wealthy woman from Philadelphia. Following the wedding, the couple left for Washington DC by train and stopped off at Wilmington, Delaware, where it was discovered that their luggage had been misplaced. Helena went to see her sister and Bjorn-Graesse left the country, possibly for the West Indies. The wedding expenses had not been paid and Helena was left to clean up the mess. Augusta died in 1907, but Hans appears to have remained in Britain. He was convicted at Hastings on 22nd December 1914 for failing to register as an enemy alien under the Aliens Restriction Order and was sentenced to six months imprisonment. He claimed to be the Uruguayan Vice Consul in Folkestone, but had never resided there and was not known in the town. In any case his appointment as a foreign representative was invalidated when Britain declared in August 1914 that enemy nationals could not be recognised, even if acting for a third power.

Bertram's paternal grandfather, Edmund Dunkley (c.1800–66), was an agricultural labourer born at Harborough, Leicestershire. He married Sarah née Corah (c.1807–76), born at Bagworth, Leicestershire. They were living at Leicester Road, Loughborough, Leicestershire in 1841. She was a shirt maker in 1871, living with her daughter Elizabeth at 42 Regent Street, Loughborough. In addition to Alfred they had six other children:

• Eliza Dunkley (born 1831).
• Emma Dunkley (c.1833–1911) was a dressmaker. She married Joseph Chapman (c.1824–89), a grocer, in 1852 at Loughborough. They were living at Albert Street, Loughborough in 1861, at Station Street, Whitwick, Leicestershire in 1871 and at Abbott's Lane, Glen Parva, Leicestershire in 1881. She was living at 115 Park Road, Loughborough at the time of her death in June 1911 at Loughborough, leaving effects valued at £157/14/- to Ernest Chapman, a commercial traveller. Emma and Joseph had ten children including – John Ernest Theophilus Chapman 1854, Edmund W Chapman 1858, Lucy Chapman 1859, Joseph W Chapman 1861, Albert Chapman 1862, Charles Henry Chapman 1864, Samuel Chapman 1867, Clarence Chapman 1868 and Annie Marianne Chapman 1875.
• Thomas Dunkley (born c.1837) was living with his sister, Emma, in 1911.
• Ann Dunkley (born 1842).

- Elizabeth Dunkley (born 1849).
- Mary Ann Dunkley (born 1851).

His maternal grandfather, William Best Draper (c.1824–1902) was born at Langport, Somerset. He was descended from Lieutenant General Sir William Draper (1721–87), who was involved in setting the first rules of cricket, and William Draper Best, 1st Baron Wynford (1767–1845), who was Lord Chief Justice 1824–29. He married Augusta Martha née Jackson (c.1821–98) in 1850 at Nottingham. She was born in Marylebone, London. William was a stationer in 1851, a master printer by 1861 and an engineer by 1871. They were living at Parliament Street, Nottingham in 1851, at 32 Cromwell Street, Nottingham by 1871 and at Walnut Grove, Radcliffe-on-Trent, Nottinghamshire in 1902. In addition to Augusta they had two other children:

- William Henry Best Draper (1852–84) was a printer. He was unemployed at the time of the 1881 Census, lodging with John and Ann Smith at Thyme Bank Cottage, Epperstone, Nottingham.
- Alice Martha Draper (1858–1931) married Julius Kaufmann (born c.1852) in 1877 at Nottingham. He was born in Prussia and in 1881 was a foreign correspondent in lace manufacturing. They were living at 21 Regent Street, Nottingham in 1881 and Alice's mother, Augusta, was visiting at the time.

Bertram's maternal grandparents were living on Parliament Street, Nottingham in 1851.

Bertram was educated in Switzerland or possibly Germany. He worked as an assistant teacher in Ireland and by 1911 was a tutor at Gore Court Preparatory School, Tunstall, Sittingbourne, Kent. Later he was a teacher at Tientsin Grammar School in China. He took leave from his teaching job in Tientsin when war broke out and had an eventful journey home through Siberia to St Petersberg, then on to Stockholm, Christiania and Bergen to Newcastle upon Tyne. Bertram later received a letter of grave displeasure from the Army Council as a result of a letter intercepted by the censors. He wrote it on 15th September 1914 and inadvertently revealed minor military facts to one of his fellow travellers, Mr WJ Gunn, an American staying in Christiania, in contravention of the Defence of the Realm Act 1914. However, it was accepted that he acted out of ignorance of the Act rather than a genuine attempt to assist the enemy.

Bertram was commissioned in 6th (4th (Extra Reserve) from 1908 when he became a Special Reservist) Lancashire Fusiliers on 1st November 1907. He was promoted lieutenant on 14th June 1909 and was the Machine-Gun Officer at one time. He rejoined 4th Battalion at Barrow-in-Furness on 13th September 1914 and at the end of the month was admitted to hospital for an appendectomy. He transferred to 2nd Battalion in May 1915 and was later seconded to the King's Own (Royal Lancaster Regiment). He went to France in July 1915 and was appointed acting captain on 6th July 1916.

Bertram Best-Dunkley married Marjorie Kate née Pettigrew (1890–1980) at Barrow-in-Furness, Lancashire in October 1916 and they had a son, Bertram Eric Lorimer Best-Dunkley (19th July 1917–15th November 2004). Marjorie lived at Risedale, Abbey Road, Barrow-in-Furness and by early 1922 was living at The Manor House, Oldmixon, Uphill, near Weston-super-Mare, Somerset. She died

Tientsin School was founded in 1905 to educate English-speaking children of Tientsin and the country dependent on Tientsin, in preparation for attending public schools in England and for business careers in the Far East.

on 26th January 1980 at Walhatch Country Hotel, Forest Row, Sussex. Bertram junior married Katherine Middleton née Muncaster (1921–2003) in 1940 at Richmond, Yorkshire and they had three children – Gaye V Best-Dunkley 1942, Alexandra K Best-Dunkley 1948 and Andrew L Best-Dunkley 1963. He was granted an Emergency Commission in Royal Signals on 1st March 1941 and was promoted war substantive lieutenant on 1st September 1942. He last appears in the Army List in October 1946.

Marjorie's father, William Frank Pettigrew M.Inst.CE (c.1858–1942), born at Glasgow, Lanarkshire, was a civil engineer boarding with his mother, brother and sister at 9 Deanery Terrace, Deanery Road, West Ham, London in 1881. He married Alice Maud née Tuckett (1861–1938) in 1888 at St Mary's, Bathwick, Bath. She was born at Llanelly, Breconshire and was living with her parents at 18 Daniel Street, Bathwick, Somerset in 1881. By 1891 William was the manager of a railway works in London and in 1916 he was chief locomotive engineer with the Furness Railway Company. They were living at 42 Guildford Road, Lambeth, London in 1891 and by 1901 had moved to Friar's Dene, Abbey Road, Barrow-in-Furness, Lancashire. In 1899, William published *A Manual of Locomotive Engineering*. In addition to Marjorie they had two other daughters:

• Nellie Maud Mary Pettigrew (1888–1969) married George Westlake Vickers (born 1884) in 1909. George was an engineering draughtsman for an electrical engineering firm, born at Waverley, New South Wales, Australia. In 1911 they were living at Totley Brook Road, Sheffield, Yorkshire and at 23 Broomgrove Road, Rotherham, Yorkshire by 1939. Nellie and George had six children – Valerie C Vickers 1911, Nigel W Vickers 1913, Yvonne Vickers 1916, Sonia Vickers 1917, Fernandé A Vickers 1920 and Ann V Vickers 1924.
• Flora Edith Mary Pettigrew (1891–1974) died unmarried.

Bertram Best-Dunkley's grave at Proven before his remains were moved to Mendinghem Military Cemetery (Australian War Memorial).

Bertram's grave in Mendinghem Military Cemetery.

The damaged memorial to Bertram Best-Dunkley in No. 20 Tianjin High School, Tianjin, formerly Tientsin Grammar School.

Bertram acted as adjutant for a few months and transferred to 2/5th Battalion in October 1916. Appointed acting major on 10th October and temporary lieutenant colonel and CO 2/5th Battalion on 20th October. Promoted captain 1st November. **Bertram was mentioned in Sir Douglas Haig's Despatch of 9th April 1917, LG 22nd May 1917.**

Awarded the VC for his actions at Wieltje, Belgium on 31st July 1917, LG 6th September 1917. Marjorie was unable to travel to London to receive the VC from the King. Colonel Pedley CB, Commander Barrow Garrison, pinned it on the shawl of the infant Bertram at Risedale House, Barrow-in-Furness on 27th October 1917. Bertram was not well liked by his fellow officers and was described as, *a brilliant young man endowed with a remarkable personality, an imperfect hero, a petty tyrant.* A senior officer reported that Best-Dunkley was determined to gain the premier gallantry award. However, despite imperfections in his character, nobody could doubt his fearless leadership.

Bertram died of wounds at a casualty clearing station (probably No.46) at Proven, near Ypres, Belgium on 5th August 1917 and was originally buried there. His remains were later moved to Mendinghem Military Cemetery, Belgium (III D 1). There is a memorial in Tientsin Grammar School, now No. 20 Tianjin High School, Tianjin.

In addition to the VC he was awarded the 1914–15 Star, British War Medal 1914–20 and Victory Medal 1914–19 with Mentioned-in-Despatches Oakleaf. His medals have been sold at auction on three occasions – for R27,000 by Alex Kaplan on 1st November 1982, for R22,500 at Chimperie Agencies on 1st August 1984 and for an estimated £12,500 at Spink's in June 1986. They were owned by a Canadian collector, Jack Stenabaugh, at one time and are now held by the Fusilier Museum, Bury, Lancashire.

SECOND LIEUTENANT FREDERICK BIRKS
10th Australian Infantry Battalion AIF

Frederick 'Fred' Birks was born on 31st August 1894 at Garden Cottage, Lane End, Buckley, Flintshire, Wales. His father, Samuel Birks (1852–99), a groom/coachman, was born at Great Boughton, Cheshire. He married Ann Dodd in Manchester, Lancashire in 1871, but she died on 29th November 1872 in Chester. Samuel married Mary née Williams (c.1859–1917) in 1877 at Chester. He was a collier at Messrs George Watkinson and Sons' Mountain Colliery when a rock fall seriously injured his neck and back on 7th November 1899. He died at Mold Cottage Hospital on 17th November. Mary was a shopkeeper after her husband's

death and was living at Lane End, Buckley with her sons Samuel, John and Fred in 1911. Fred had seven siblings:

- George Henry Birks (1872–1956), a coal miner hewer, married Ellen Holland (1872–1954) in 1892 and they had ten children – Samuel Birks 1892, Annie Birks 1893, Mary Agnes Birks 1896, Samuel Birks 1898, Charles Birks 1900, Sarah Birks 1902, James Birks 1904, Elizabeth Alice Birks 1908, George Birks 1911 and Ellen Birks 1913. The family was living at 7 Bank Street, Wigan, Lancashire in 1911. James Birks (1904–88) emigrated to Australia where he married Jane Gavaghan (1905–95) in 1935 and they had three children.

Lane End Road, Buckley.

- Mary Ann 'Polly' Birks (born 1879) married William Jones (c.1875–1937) in 1900.
- Emily Birks (1881–1960), a midwife, married Richard Isaac Springall (1881–1940), a ship's painter, in 1907. They were living at 32 South Hill Road, Liverpool in 1911.

Mountain Colliery where a rock fall on 7th November 1899 resulted in the death of Fred's father ten days later.

- Beatrice Birks (born 1882), a domestic servant in 1901, married Ernest Henry Jones, a goods porter, in 1903. They were living at 2 Central Mission Yard, Market Place, Chesterfield, Derbyshire in 1911. They had four children – John Ernest Jones 1904, Dorothy Beatrice Jones 1905, Annie Elizabeth Jones 1907 and Irene Mary Jones 1910.
- Martha Jane Birks (1883–1954) was a domestic cook in 1911 at Highland Tower Road, South Heswall, Cheshire. She married Samuel Beavan (1886–1967), a pottery labourer, in 1920. They had two children – Mary Beavan 1921 and Frederick S Beavan 1924.
- Samuel Birks (1888–1960), was a coal miner hewer in 1911 and was working at Bullcroft Main Colliery, Carcroft, Doncaster in 1914. He served in the Royal Engineers Volunteers and 3rd Welsh Brigade RFA from April 1908 (462 later 840310). He was embodied at Coventry on 1st September 1914 in the Ammunition Column of 4th South Midland (Howitzer) Brigade RFA. He was described as 5′ 7″ tall with dark complexion, brown eyes and black hair. Samuel was appointed

temporary acting bombardier on 22nd March 1915, acting bombardier on 1st April and corporal on 25th September. He embarked at Southampton on 30th March 1915 and landed at Le Havre the following day. He was granted leave 19th–28th November 1915 and was posted to 48th Divisional Ammunition Column on 16th May 1916. Promoted acting sergeant on 30th December 1916 and sergeant on 1st May 1917. His leave from 12th to 22nd September 1917 was later extended. He joined the Base at Le Havre on 10th January 1918 and rejoined his unit in Italy on 28th January, where he was admitted to a field ambulance 6th–7th March 1918 with a cut hand. He was admitted to hospital on 16th October, a convalescent depot on 1st November and rejoined his unit from the Base Depot, Arquata on 15th November to join No.2 Section. Samuel was posted to the Base in Italy on 1st November 1918 and was disembodied on demobilisation on 11th January 1919. He was awarded the Meritorious Service Medal, LG 31st May 1918. Fred's medals passed to Samuel and he displayed them to the pupils and staff of St Matthew's Church School, Buckley every year on the anniversary of his brother's death. Samuel married Sarah Ellen 'Sally' Jones (c.1884–1962) in 1919 and they had four children – Helen 'Nellie' Mary Birks 1920, Frederick Hayes Birks 1922, Elizabeth 'Bessie' Hayes Birks 1924 and Nancy P Birks 1926. Bessie emigrated to New Zealand, where she married Valentine Brinsley Brown.

• John Birks (1890–1959) was a labourer in a clay hole in 1911.

Fred's paternal grandfather, Samuel Birks (1803–80), was a firebrick labourer. He married Catherine Ellis (c.1803–47) in 1829 and they had six children – Ann Birks c.1830, Elizabeth Birks c.1832, George Birks c.1834, Ellis Birks c.1837, Jane Birks 1839 and John Birks c.1843. Samuel married Mary née Jones (c.1811–85) in 1851 at Great Boughton, Cheshire. In 1861 they were living at Lane End, Buckley.

Fred's maternal grandfather, William Williams (1807–59), was a cotton spinner when he enlisted in the 7th Regiment of Foot (Royal Fusiliers) at Salford, Lancashire on 8th January 1825 (306). He was described as 5′7″ tall with fair complexion, hazel eyes and sandy coloured hair. He was promoted corporal on 21st March 1833 and sergeant on 1st September 1835. During his service he was eleven years in the Mediterranean and eighteen months in Gibraltar. Having been discharged at his own request at Naas, Ireland on 6th May 1846 he became a police constable. William married Anne, who was born c.1820 in Ireland, and they had nine children – Emma Williams c.1839, James Williams c.1841, John Williams c.1845, William Williams c.1848, Thomas Williams c.1850, Henry Williams c.1852, Charles Williams c.1855, Anne Williams c.1857 and Mary Williams c.1859. The family was living at the police office, Hawarden, Flintshire in 1851. William also served in the Flintshire Militia and was a sergeant by 1857. In 1861 Anne was a mangle woman, living with her family in New Street, Mold, Flintshire.

Fred was educated at St Matthew's Anglican Parish School, Buckley, Flintshire until 1908. He was a member of St Matthew's Church Lads' Brigade and for a

SS *Otway* (12,077 tons), one of six ships built for the Orient Steam Navigation Co around 1909 for the fortnightly service to Australia and New Zealand. She was requisitioned by the Royal Navy as an armed merchant cruiser and on 23rd July 1917 she was torpedoed and sunk by UC-49 off the Hebrides, with the loss of ten lives.

period was the drummer. He was a mischievous teenager. During a play in Buckley's Central Hall, *Face at the Window* (released as a film in 1939), an actor's face appeared at regular intervals at the scenery window causing some mirth amongst the audience. Fred told his chums, *If he comes again, he'll cop it*. When the face next appeared he threw an orange hitting the actor full in the face. Amid the resulting uproar he fled the theatre. Despite his misbehaviour Fred was a devout Christian.

Fred was employed as a labourer and steel-roller man at John Summers Steelworks annealing plant at Shotton, Flintshire. By 1911 he was a brick setter's labourer. On 29th August 1913 he emigrated alone to Australia, sailing on the Orient Line's SS *Otway*, arriving in Melbourne, Victoria. He was employed as a waiter in Tasmania and Melbourne, where he stayed with relatives of his mother's.

He enlisted in Melbourne in 2nd Australian Field Ambulance, Australian Army Medical Corps on 18th August 1914 (47). He was described as 5′ 9½″ tall, weighing 168 lbs, with dark complexion, hair and eyes. His address at the time was with Mrs E Cornelius, 18 King Street, Norwood, South Australia, possibly a relative. Fred claimed two years service in the Welsh Royal Artillery TA before emigrating to Australia. It is known that he falsified his age and may have made up some previous service to give himself an advantage when so many others were also attempting to join.

He trained at Broadmeadows Camp, Melbourne, Victoria and embarked with the unit from Melbourne aboard HMAT A18 *Wiltshire* on 18th October. He disembarked at Alexandria, Egypt and proceeded to camp at Mena. He embarked at Alexandria for Lemnos on 5th April 1915 and landed at Gallipoli on 25th April 1915. On 8th May at Krithia he brought in some wounded under fire. In June 1916 he was recommended for the MM for this action, but it never materialised. He was wounded by shrapnel at Anzac Cove on 26th June, but it was minor and he was back at duty next day. He was evacuated on 9th December aboard HMS *Clacton*, in the preliminary stage of the evacuation of Anzac. He arrived at Lemnos next day and embarked for Alexandria aboard the troopship SS *Tunisian* on 30th December, arriving on 2nd January 1916. He was at Tel-el-Kebir and Serapeum until embarking at Alexandria on HMT *Briton* on 23rd March 1916, disembarking at Marseille, France on 30th March.

Fred was promoted lance corporal on 21st April 1916. **Awarded the MM for leadership and service with a team of stretcher-bearers while under heavy**

shellfire at Pozières on 26th July 1916, LG
16th November 1916. The immediate award
was promulgated in I ANZAC Routine Orders
on 4th October 1916, the ribbon having been
presented by Lieutenant General Sir William
Birdwood at Reninghelst, Belgium on 27th
September 1916.

Fred was appointed temporary wagon
orderly corporal on 5th August and was
promoted corporal on 10th August. In
December he was granted leave and went
back to Buckley, Flintshire. On 9th February
1917 he reported sick with pyrexia and was
admitted to hospital until 14th February.
On 28th February he was detached to 1st
Australian Division School in France and

Broadmeadows Camp, Melbourne.

on 26th April he was commissioned. Fred was posted to 6th (Victoria) Australian
Infantry Battalion on 10th May and was taken on strength on 12th May.

Awarded the VC for his actions at Glencorse Wood, Belgium on 20th
September 1917, LG 8th November 1917. Fred Birks was killed by a German
shell exploding in a D Company post in Glencorse Wood on 21st September 1917.
He had been working to rescue a number of soldiers who had been buried by a
previous shell. He was buried where he fell, but his body was later moved to Perth
(China Wall) Cemetery, Zillebeke, Belgium (I G 45). His mother received a parcel
of Fred's personal effects including a notecase, photograph, visiting card, MM
medal ribbon, a button, five coins, two studs, a metal watch and a handkerchief. She
also received an illuminated address on 17th October from 2nd Field Ambulance
signed by over a hundred of his former colleagues. The Rector of Flint, Canon

Lemnos in 1915.

HMS *Clacton* (820 tons), a steam passenger ship built in 1905 at Hull for the Great Eastern Railway Co, was requisitioned by the Royal Navy as an auxillary minesweeper. On 3rd August 1916 she was sunk by U-73 in Kavalla Bay in the Aegean Sea.

Fred Birks' grave in Perth (China Wall) Cemetery, Zillebeke.

SS *Tunisian* (10,576 tons) was built for the Allan Line in 1900. In 1914 she was used as a troopship transporting the Canadian Expeditionary Force to Europe. In 1915 she was an accommodation ship for prisoners of war off Ryde, Isle of Wight and later that year returned to trooping to India and Gallipoli. In 1917 the Allan Line was taken over by the Canadian Pacific Line. *Tunisian* was renamed *Marburn* in 1922 and was scrapped in 1928.

Nicholas, offered £10 to the first Flintshire elementary schoolboy to win the VC and handed the money to Fred's mother on 12th November 1917. As Fred never married, the VC was presented to his brother, Sergeant Samuel Birks RFA, by the King at Buckingham Palace on 19th December 1917. Fred is commemorated in a number of other places:

- Panel 46, Roll of Honour, Australian War Memorial, Canberra.
- Named on one of eleven plaques honouring 175 men from overseas awarded the VC for the Great War. The plaques were unveiled by the Senior Minister of State at the Foreign

Australian War Memorial, Canberra.

& Commonwealth Office and Minister for Faith and Communities, Baroness Warsi, at a reception at Lancaster House, London on 26th June 2014 attended by The Duke of Kent and relatives of the VC recipients. The Australian plaque is at the Australian War Memorial.

Victoria Cross Memorial, Queen Victoria Building, George Street, Sydney. (*MaritimeQuest.com*)

- Victoria Cross Memorial, Campbell, Canberra dedicated on 24th July 2000.
- Victoria Cross Memorial, Queen Victoria Building, George Street, Sydney, New South Wales dedicated on 23rd February 1992 to commemorate the visit of Queen Elizabeth II and Prince Philip on the occasion of the Sesquicentenary of the City of Sydney. Sir Roden Cutler VC, Edward Kenna VC and Keith Payne VC were in attendance.
- VC memorial at Springvale Botanical Cemetery, 600 Princes Highway, Springvale, Victoria commemorates the thirty-three Australian and six British VCs associated with Victoria.
- Birks Drive, Wodonga, Victoria on White Box Rise estate built on land formerly part of Bandiana Army Camp.
- 'Local Heroes 2015', a series of concerts at the Melbourne Recital Centre, honoured individual Victoria men and women in the Great War, including sixteen VCs. Fred Birks' concert, 'Powerhouse', was performed by 'Benaud Trio Ten Not Out' on 7th March 2015.
- In Buckley, Flintshire:
  - Named on his parents' grave in St Matthew's Churchyard.
  - Roll of Honour and War Memorial inside St Matthew's Church.
  - Memorial initially in St Matthew's schoolyard, later moved to St Matthew's Churchyard.
  - Memorial at the Royal British Legion Club.
  - Blue Plaque on the house where he was born at Lane End.
  - Buckley War Memorial, Mill Lane, Hawkesbury.
- Twenty two Berberis shrubs represent the 22 members of the Church Lads' Brigade who were awarded the VC at the Church Lads

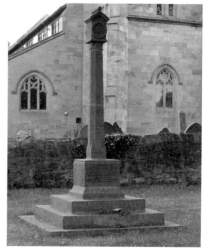

Memorial initially in St Matthew's schoolyard, later moved to St Matthew's Churchyard. (*Memorials to Valour*)

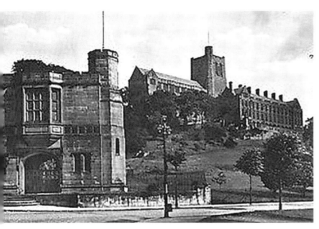

North Wales Heroes Memorial at Bangor, Gwynedd, on the left, was completed in 1923. Above the archway the room is lined with wooden panels listing 8,500 people from the region who died on active service during the First World War. Prime Minister David Lloyd George was a patron and students at Bangor University helped with fund-raising. The Memorial was opened by the Prince of Wales (later Edward VIII) on 1st November 1923.

& Church Girls Brigade Memorial Plot at the National Memorial Arboretum, Alrewas, Staffordshire.

• North Wales Heroes Memorial, Bangor, Gwynedd.

In addition to the VC and MM he was awarded the 1914–15 Star, British War Medal 1914–20 and Victory Medal 1914–19. The medals are held on loan and are displayed in the Hall of Valour, Australian War Memorial, Treloar Crescent, Campbell, Australian Capital Territory.

226353 PRIVATE HARRY BROWN
10th Battalion (Canadians), Canadian Expeditionary Force

Harry Brown was born on 11th May 1898 at Gananoque, Frontenac County, Ontario, Canada. It is understood he was originally John Henry Brown, but this was shortened to just Harry. His father, Henry Brown (born 1869) of Irish extraction, was a brass-moulder. He married Adelaide 'Addie' Helen née Ledger (1872–1919), a cook. They were living at Gananoque, Ontario in 1901. Henry died before 1911 as Adelaide married Patrick McAuliffe, a widowed  farmer, that November at St Peter's Cathedral, Peterborough, Ontario. They lived at Lot 17, Concession 7, East Emily Township, Omemee, Victoria County, Ontario. Harry had three siblings:

• Irene M Brown (born 1892) was a bookbinder in 1911. She married Charles Luther Egelton (1894–1976) in 1914. They were living at 283 Hyman Street, London, Ontario in 1917 and had a son, Albert Maxwell Egelton that year.

- Marie Loretta Brown (1899–1934) was raised by her grandmother, Elizabeth Ledger, after the death of her father. She married Edward John Henry (1902–63) in 1928 at St Peter's Cathedral, London, Ontario and they had a child.
- Lawrence Patrick McAuliffe (1912–62) was a Catholic priest in St Martin's Parish, Ennismore, Ontario. Later he worked in China, Bombay in India and Santo Domingo in the Dominican Republic. He died in Haiti.

London, Ontario.

Harry's paternal grandfather, John Brown, a cabinetmaker, married Mary Ann (possibly née Ainsley). His maternal grandfather, Osimus James Ledger (c.1842–1911), was a factory hand in 1891. He married Elizabeth Louise Leveque née Bishop (c.1846). In addition to Adelaide they had ten other children:

- Mary 'Minnie' Ledger (c.1867–96).
- Elizabeth Ledger (born 1868) married Thomas J Bedard in 1886.
- Osimus 'Osie' Ledger (born 1873) married Charlotte L Sullivan in 1899 and they had a daughter, Genevieve Elizabeth Ledger in 1909.
- Emma Ledger (born c.1873) married Philip Heffernan in 1898.
- Alexander Ledger (born 1877) married Ida Villeneuve (born c.1884) in 1907 and they had at least three children – Doris Beatrice Ledger 1907, Earl Ledger 1908 and Samuel Ledger 1909.
- Monica Cecelia Ledger (born 1879).
- John Baptiste Ledger (c.1883–1909) married Clara Graham (1888–c.1977) in 1908.
- Nettie Ledger (born c.1885).
- George Samuel Ledger (1890–1949) married Capitolia Dingman (1891–1981) c.1910 and they had a son, Riley Ledger, in 1911.
- John Thomas Ledger (born 1892).

Harry was educated at Peterborough, Ontario and began working on his mother's farm at East Emily Township, Omemee c.1910. He moved to London, Ontario where he worked in a munitions factory in 1916 and lived with his married sister, Irene. Harry enlisted in the Depot Regiment, Canadian Mounted Rifles CEF at London on 18th August 1916. He was described as 5′ 6½″ tall with dark complexion, dark hazel eyes, dark brown hair and his religious denomination was Roman Catholic. He gave his address as 164 Bruce Street, London. Harry sailed for Britain on RMS *Mauretania* on 25th October as part of the 6th Overseas Draft, Canadian Mounted

Moore Barracks, Shorncliffe.

Omemee, Ontario.

Rifles, arriving on 31st October. He was taken on strength of Lord Strathcona's Horse Reserve Regiment at Shorncliffe, Kent on 1st November and transferred to 11th Reserve Battalion, 4th Canadian Training Brigade on 3rd November. He was admitted to Moore Barracks Canadian Hospital with tonsillitis 23rd November– 10th December. He transferred to 202nd Battalion at Witley on 5th February 1917 and sailed for France on 17th May, joining the Canadian Base Depot the same day until 13th June. Harry joined 10th Battalion in the field on 27th June.

Shorncliffe Military Hospital.

Awarded the VC for his actions on Hill 70, Lens, France on 16th August 1917, LG 17th October 1917. Harry was very seriously wounded during his VC action and died at No.7 Casualty Clearing Station the following day. He is buried in Noeux-les-Mines Communal Cemetery, France (II J 29) and is commemorated in a number of other places:

Harry Brown's grave front row extreme right in Noeux-les-Mines Communal Cemetery. The leftmost grave in the row behind is that of Major Okill Learmonth VC.

- Harry Brown VC Royal Canadian Legion Branch No.497, 46 King Street, Omemee, Ontario.
- Memorial outside Coronation Hall on the corner of King Street and Sturgeon Road, Omemee, Ontario.
- Omemee District War Memorial outside Coronation Hall.

- Plaque in front of Colonel Russel Britton Legion Branch 92, Gananoque, Ontario.
- Gananoque War Memorial.
- Memorial cairn unveiled in front of the Town Hall in Gananoque Town Park on King Street on 16th August 2007 to mark the 90th anniversary of his VC action.
- Peterborough War Memorial, Confederation Square, Ontario, Canada.
- Two 49 Cent postage stamps in honour of the ninety-four Canadian VCs were issued by Canada Post on 21st October 2004 on the 150th Anniversary of the first Canadian VC's action, Alexander Roberts Dunn.

Gananoque War Memorial outside the town hall, with Harry Brown's memorial in the foreground.

- Victoria Cross obelisk to all Canadian VCs at Military Heritage Park, Barrie, Ontario dedicated by The Princess Royal on 22nd October 2013.
- Named on one of eleven plaques honouring 175 men from overseas awarded the VC for the Great War. The plaques were unveiled by the Senior Minister of State at the Foreign & Commonwealth Office and Minister for Faith and Communities, Baroness Warsi, at a reception at Lancaster House, London on 26th June 2014 attended by The Duke of Kent and relatives of the VC recipients. The Canadian plaque was unveiled outside the British High Commission in Elgin Street, Ottawa on 10th November 2014 by The Princess Royal in the presence of British High Commissioner Howard Drake, Canadian Minister of Veterans Affairs Julian Fantino and Canadian Chief of the Defence Staff General Thomas J Lawson.
- The Secretary of State for Communities and Local Government, Eric Pickles MP announced that Victoria Cross recipients from the Great War would have commemorative paving stones laid in their birthplace as a lasting legacy of local heroes within communities. The stones would be laid on or close to the 100th anniversary of their VC actions. For the 145 VCs born in Australia, Belgium, Canada, China, Denmark, Egypt, France, Germany, India, Iraq, Japan, Nepal, Netherlands, New Zealand, Pakistan, South Africa, Sri Lanka, Ukraine and United States of America, individual commemorative stones were unveiled at the National Memorial Arboretum, Alrewas, Staffordshire by Prime Minister David Cameron MP and Sergeant Johnson Beharry VC on 5th March 2015.
- A wooden plaque bearing fifty-six maple leaves each inscribed with the name of a Canadian-born VC holder was dedicated at the Canadian Forces College, Toronto on Remembrance Day 1999.
- Plaque on a memorial to the ninety-nine Canadian VCs in York Cemetery, Toronto.

As he died on operational duty, his next-of-kin is eligible to receive the Canadian Memorial Cross. As he never married, the VC was sent to his mother but was recorded as undeliverable and was re-addressed to his sister, Mrs Charles Egelton, 283 Hyman Street, London, Ontario. In addition to the VC he was awarded the British War Medal 1914–20 and Victory Medal 1914–19. The VC passed to his half-brother, Father Lawrence McAuliffe, on the death of their mother. When he went to the Dominican Republic, he left the VC in the care of a fellow priest at Omemee, Ontario. It was retained in a vault until after the death of Lawrence McAuliffe and his fellow priest, when it passed to the Scarboro Foreign Mission Society near Toronto, Ontario. In 1970 the Society donated the VC to the Canadian War Museum, General Motors Court, 330 Sussex Drive, Ottawa, Ontario, Canada where it is still held.

3774 PRIVATE PATRICK JOSEPH BUGDEN
31st Australian Infantry Battalion, AIF

Patrick Bugden was born on 17th March 1897 at Gundurimba, near Lismore, New South Wales, Australia. His father, Thomas Joseph Bugden (1869–1903), born at Coraki NSW, was a dairy farmer at Tatham NSW. He was also one time licensee of the Farmer's Home Hotel, Gundurimba and then leased a hotel at Bangalow. He married Annie May Teresa née Connolly (1874–1949), born at Grafton NSW, in 1896 at Casino NSW. Patrick had seven siblings:

(*Australian War Memorial*)

• Rose Cecilia Bugden (born 1899) married Albert Clarence Elliott (1896–1949) in 1926. He was a junior clerk in the public service when he enlisted in 9th Battalion AIF (650) on 27th August 1914 at Casino, NSW. He was described as 5′ 9″ tall, weighing 140 lbs, with dark complexion, brown eyes, brown hair and his religious denomination was Church of England. Promoted lance corporal on 31st August 1914 and sergeant on 10th September 1914. He deployed to Gallipoli and reverted to corporal on 3rd July 1915. He was evacuated to Cairo and admitted to 1st Australian Hospital with influenza on 1st September and evacuated to Australia aboard HMAT A60 *Aeneas* on 31st October. On 11th February 1916 he was discharged as medically unfit due to dysentery and neurasthenia and awarded a disability pension. He worked as an articled clerk with Hynes & Elliott, solicitors, Murwillumbah and later as a partner in Smith & Son, estate agents at Tweed Heads. Rose and Albert had a son, William G Elliott, in 1928, who was killed in a car accident with his grandparents in 1949. Rose was living at Tweed Street, Coolangatta, NSW in April 1952.

- Monica Mary Bugden (1900–75) married Joseph John Knapp (1892–1987). He was a motor engineer when he enlisted in the Australian Flying Corps (1470) on 15th October 1916 at Roma, Queensland. He was described as 5′ 7½″ tall, weighing 153 lbs, with dark complexion, grey eyes, auburn hair and his religious denomination was Roman Catholic. He sailed for Britain from Melbourne, Victoria aboard HMAT A9 *Shropshire* and was appointed voyage only corporal on 11th May 1917. On arrival at the AFC Training Depot, Halton Park, Wendover, Buckinghamshire he reverted to 2nd aircraft mechanic on 19th July. Promoted extra duty pay sergeant on 20th July, but reverted to private on posting to 69 Squadron AFC on 13th August. Promoted flight sergeant on 14th August and deployed to France on 21st August. Appointed chief master mechanic on 17th May 1918. He was admitted to 1st Australian Auxiliary Hospital, Harefield, London with acute appendicitis on 9th November and was discharged on 11th December. He returned to Australia aboard SS *Kaiser-i-Hind* and was discharged to 1st Military District, Queensland on 20th July 1919. Monica and Joseph were living at Wondai, Wide Bay, Queensland in 1936.
- Bernard 'Barney' John Bugden (1902–48) enlisted in 2/15th Battalion (QX667) on 3rd November 1939 at Annerley, Queensland and served in Papua New Guinea, where he was seriously wounded. He was discharged on 12th September 1945, but never recovered from his wounds and died on 26th September 1948 at Tweed Heads NSW.
- Ellen M Kelly (born 1908).
- Bridget V Kelly (born 1910).
- William Lennard Kelly (born 1912) enlisted in the 2nd Australian Imperial Force on 2nd September 1941 at Brisbane, Queensland (QX23563). He married Jean Armour Milne in 1942 at West Maitland, NSW and they were living at Park Avenue, Wynnum, Brisbane in September 1951.
- Nancy Kelly (born c.1914) married as Nunan and lived in Toowoomba, Queensland.

After Thomas died, Annie moved her family to the Farmer's Home Hotel, Gundurimba and later to the Billinudgel Hotel. Annie married James Joseph Kelly, a hotelier in the Brunswick District, in 1906. They were living at Hotel Wells, Tweed Heads NSW when Patrick's medals were issued on 30th May 1921. On 21st January 1949, they were travelling with Annie's eldest grandson, William G Elliott, when the car was forced to swerve by a bolting horse near the Mount Gravatt Showground, Queensland. The car overturned in a ditch, killing all three passengers.

The Wells Hotel at Tweed Heads NSW.

Patrick's paternal grandfather, John Bugden (1839–1911), married Margaret Jane née Smith (1837–1909), born at Knockbride, Co Cavan, Ireland, in 1837 at Brookfield, Maitland, NSW. She was an assisted immigrant, departing Liverpool on the barque *China* on 28th May 1854 and arriving at Sydney on 24th August. In 1867 a reward of £20 was offered for information leading to the conviction of whoever shot two of John's working bullocks. The following year he settled on the Richmond River at Gundurimba, where he remained for the rest of this life. In 1871 he was farming forty acres and by 1875 was a timber cutter. In 1877 he was granted a slaughtering licence and by 1885 he was farming 297 acres and had ten horses and sixty cattle. He grew sugar cane until the sugar industry declined and retired around 1901. Margaret was thrown from a sulky on 13th October 1909 and, despite appearing to suffer no serious consequences, died on 16th October at Gundurimba. In addition to Thomas they had six other children:

- Mary Bugden (1859–1941). She married Edward Flaherty in 1883 and they had nine children – Margaret G Flaherty 1884, John Flaherty 1886, Mary C de L Flaherty 1888, Edward B Flaherty 1890, Robert J Flaherty 1892, Martin Flaherty 1894, Agnes D Flaherty 1894, Annie E Flaherty 1899 and Bridget E Flaherty 1902.
- Alice Bugden (1861–1932) married Thomas Francis Flaherty (1856–1934) in 1881. He was born at Shannonbridge, Co Offaly, Ireland. He arrived in Australia with his widowed father and siblings, Patrick, Edward and Mary, on 13th December 1866 aboard the *Sir Robert Sale* from Plymouth, Devon. They had eleven children – John Flaherty 1882, Patrick James Flaherty 1884, Mary Cecelia Flaherty 1886, Thomas E Flaherty 1887, Bridget Alice Flaherty 1889, Bernard M Flaherty 1891, Margaret Jane Flaherty 1892, Annie Theresa Flaherty 1895, Robert Bernard Flaherty 1898, Elaine Julie Flaherty 1903 and Hugh Kevin Flaherty 1909.
- Margaret Jane Budgen (1863–1943) married William T Byrne in 1912.
- Anne A Bugden (1865–1938) married John Gooley (1861–1926) in 1889 and they had eight children – Margaret Gooley 1890, Mary Gooley 1892, John Gooley 1894, William Gooley 1897, Rose A Gooley 1900, Bridget A Gooley 1903, Agnes J Gooley 1906, Edward B Gooley 1909.
- John Budgen (1867–68).
- Julia Elizabeth Bugden (1872–1953) married Joseph Timothy George Cooper (1864–1944) in 1896. They had seven children – Margaret Sarah Cooper 1897, James Clive Cooper 1899, John Joseph Jack Cooper 1901, Monica Julia Cooper 1903, Mary Dorothy Cooper 1906, Thomas G Cooper 1908 and Ellen Therese Cooper 1910.
- Robert James Bugden (1874–1935) married Margaret Ellen Nilon (1876–1929) in 1904. They had five children – Margaret Mary Mollie Bugden 1905, John T Bugden 1908, Winifred Agnes Bugden 1910, Ellen Bugden 1912 and Roberta P Bugden 1914.

- John Bernard Bugden (1876–1943) married Maude MP Fryer in 1900 and they had eight children – Stephen Bugden 1901, Vera M Bugden 1903, Eileen P Bugden 1905, Doris B Bugden 1909, Margaret P Bugden 1911, Maud M Bugden 1913, Bernard J Bugden 1914 and Dardanella Bugden 1916.

His maternal grandfather, James Lawrence Connolly (1837–1915), born at Tullamore, Laois, Ireland, married Bridget Doherty née O'Doherty (1845–1913). In addition to Annie they had twelve other children:

- James Patrick Connolly (1867–1943) joined the police and eventually became a sergeant in the Mounted Police at West Wyalong NSW. He married Mabel Caroline Mary Greenham (1876–1954) in 1896. They had seven children – Clarence James Connolly 1895, Patrick R Connolly 1899, Adrian George Connolly 1900, Leslie Tennyson Connolly 1902, Vincent Connolly 1917, Alvia Mervyn Connolly 1918 and Ronald Patrick Connolly 1925.

Tullamore, Laois, Ireland where Patrick's maternal grandfather was born in 1837.

- Patrick Joseph (1868–1940) married Maud Monica Edwards in 1908. They had eight children – Gertrude Connolly, Maisie Connolly, Mary Connolly, Philip Connolly, Walter Connolly, Monica Maud Connolly 1909, James Lawrence Connolly 1910 and Daniel Francis Connolly 1917.
- Mary Ann Connolly (1870–1946) married James Allen McDonald (1862–1946) in 1893. They had six children – Mary Justina McDonald 1898, Felix J McDonald 1900, Patrick Aloysius McDonald 1903, Laurence Angus McDonald 1905, Hilary Matthew McDonald 1907 and Ann Therese McDonald 1909.
- Thomas Augustine Connolly (1872–1948) married Mary Magdalen Hughes (1878–1967) in 1908.
- Elizabeth Mary Agnes Connolly (1875–1958) married John Frederick Boyle (1884–1955) in 1907. They had three children – John F Boyle 1908, Edward Boyle 1911 and Bridget Boyle 1914.
- William Stanislaus Connolly (1877–1949) married Catherine Mary McDonald (died 1964) in 1908. She was the sister of James Allen McDonald who married William's sister Mary above. They had at least two children – Mary P Connolly 1912 and Joseph W Connolly 1914.
- Martin Connolly (1879–1952) married Florence Ethel Sweeney (1898–1977) in 1918.

- Philip Urban Connolly (1881–1960) married Elizabeth Rose Reynolds (1889–1929) in 1909. They had two children – Margaret Bridget Connolly 1909 and Thomas Vincent Connolly 1918.
- Matthew Connolly (1883–1949).
- John Francis Connolly (1885–1949), a twin with Michael, married Louisa Elizabeth Lenholm (1893–1974) in 1915 at Newcastle, NSW. Her father was Swedish.
- Michael Benedict Connolly (1885–1957), a twin with John, married Mary Jane Reynolds (1884–1949) in 1910. They had a son, James Reynolds Richmond Connolly, in 1911.
- Daniel Vincent Connolly (born 1889).

Patrick was educated at:

- Convent School, Tatham NSW.
- Gundurimba Public School NSW.
- A local public school at Billinudgel NSW, where he excelled at shot-putt, rugby league and cricket.

Patrick worked at the Post Office at Mullumbimby, which appears at the far end of the street on the left side with the light coloured roof.

The Federal Hotel, Alstonville was purchased by the Kellys in 1914 and Patrick worked there for a short time.

He worked in the Post Office at Mullumbimby, on the New South Wales coast, before the family business at the New Brunswick Hotel, Billinudgel NSW. He later worked at the Federal Hotel, Alstonville NSW, which the family purchased in 1914. Patrick played cricket and rugby league for Billinudgel 1911–14.

Patrick served for twelve months under the Compulsory Service Obligation scheme. He enlisted in the Australian Imperial Force at Adelaide Street, Brisbane, Queensland on 25th May 1916, giving his age as twenty-one years and one month. He was described as 5′ 10½″ tall, weighing 180 lbs, with fair complexion, brown eyes, light brown hair and his religious denomination was Roman Catholic. He was posted to 11th Depot Battalion at Thompson's Paddock, Enoggera, Queensland and

HMAT A49 *Seang Choon* (5,807 tons) was built in 1891 by Harland & Wolff, Belfast as SS *Cheshire* for the Bibby Line, Liverpool. In 1900 she was used as a Boer War troopship and in 1910 was sold to Lim Chin Tsong, Rangoon and renamed *Seang Choon*. She was taken over as a troopship in 1915 and took part in the Dardanelles campaign and also sailed the India – Britain route. In March 1917 she was taken over under the Liner Requisition Scheme, but on 10th July she was torpedoed and sunk by *U-87* off the Fastnet Rock south of Ireland en route from Sydney to London. Nineteen lives were lost.

Thompson's Paddock Camp, Enoggera, Queensland in 1915.

embarked at Brisbane for England with 9th Reinforcement Group for 31st Battalion aboard HMAT A49 *Seang Choon* on 19 September. He arrived at Plymouth, Devon on 9th December and joined 8th Training Battalion at Codford on Salisbury Plain, Wiltshire on 11th December. He reported sick at Hurdcott, Wiltshire and was admitted to the isolation hospital from 17th to 31st December.

On 16th January 1917 he embarked at Folkestone, Kent aboard *Princess Victoria*, arriving next day at 5th Australian Divisional Base Depot, Étaples. He was taken on strength of 31st Battalion on 19th March. His size and physique earned him the nickname 'The Tank' by his colleagues. He was a keen sportsman, winning most of the awards for

Looking along the Salisbury road through Codford Camp, where 8th Training Battalion was based in December 1916.

gymnastics in his unit and also boxed regularly. He took part in an obstacle race during a visit by the King. The race was filmed and a copy is held by the Imperial War Museum, London. He also took part in a drill competition, ceremonial escort duty and the Battalion football and tug of war teams on the same day. Before going into the line for the first time he wrote to his mother, … *we are going into the firing line tomorrow, if by chance anything happens I feel that I shall gain a place of happiness for I have never done a deed in my life that I am ashamed of. So I fear nothing.*

Patrick reported sick with influenza on 3rd May and was admitted to 15th Australian Field Ambulance before being transferred to the Divisional Rest Station.

Ronald Craufurd Munro Ferguson, 1st Viscount Novar KT GCMG (1860–1934), a Scottish politician, was the sixth Governor General of Australia from 1914 until 1920. On 4th April 1918 he presented Patrick's VC to his mother. Back in Britain he became Secretary for Scotland 1922–24.

Folkestone harbour was the embarkation point for most cross-Channel troop movements. Millions of troops passed through it.

He rejoined his unit on 15th May. **Awarded the VC for his actions at Polygon Wood, Belgium on 26th-28th September 1917, LG 26th November 1917.** He was killed during the VC action on 28th September 1917 and was buried just south of the southeastern corner of Glencorse Wood. The grave was fenced off and a wooden Celtic cross was placed over it. His body was exhumed after the war and re-interred at Hooge Crater Cemetery near Ypres (VIII C 5). His military will, dated 9th June 1917, left everything to his mother. The VC was sent to Australia from Downing Street, London on 12th December 1917. As Patrick never married, the VC was presented to his mother by the Governor General of Australia, Sir Ronald Craufurd Munro-Ferguson GCMG, at Admiralty House, Sydney, New South Wales on 4th April 1918. Patrick is commemorated in a number of other places:

- Named on the Roll of Honour, Panel 118, Australian War Memorial, Canberra, ACT.
- Display in the Hall of Valour, Australian War Memorial, Canberra, ACT.
- Bugden Avenue, Canberra, ACT.
- Bugden Bridge, South Gundurimba, NSW.
- Patrick Bugden VC Gardens, Retirement Home, Suffolk Park, NSW.

Patrick Bugden's grave in Hooge Crater Cemetery near Ypres. In the background is the chapel housing the Hooge Crater Museum. There is a café attached to it.

- Bugden Avenue and Bugden Lane, Alstonville, NSW.
- A sandstone cross memorial on a concrete base was raised by the Returned and Services League on Bugden Avenue, Alstonville in 1948 and became a focus for Anzac Day observances. It was replaced by the Paddy Bugden Memorial on Bugden Avenue, unveiled by the Governor of Queensland, Major General Peter M Arnison AO (who was born and raised in Alstonville) on 28th September 1997 on the 80th anniversary of Bugden's death and in the 100th year of his birth.

Admiralty House is the official Sydney residence of the Governor General of Australia on the northern foreshore of Sydney Harbour. It was the residence of the Commander-in-Chief of the Royal Navy's Australia Squadron 1885–1913.

- Budgen Street in Enoggera Barracks, Brisbane, Queensland.
- Bugden VC Club has a Paddy Bugden Bar in Lavarack Barracks, Townsville, Queensland.
- Bugden Street, Wodonga, Victoria on White Box Rise estate built on land formerly part of Bandiana Army Camp.
- Named on the Victoria Cross Memorial, Campbell, Canberra dedicated on 24th July 2000.

The memorial wall at Alstonville, unveiled on 28th September 1997.

- Named on the Victoria Cross Recipients Wall at the North Bondi War Memorial, NSW dedicated on 27th November 2011.
- Victoria Cross Memorial, Queen Victoria Building, George Street, Sydney, NSW dedicated on 23rd February 1992 to commemorate the visit of Queen Elizabeth II and Prince Philip on the occasion of the Sesquicentenary of the City of Sydney. Sir Roden Cutler VC, Edward Kenna VC and Keith Payne VC were in attendance.
- Named on one of eleven plaques honouring 175 men from overseas awarded the VC for the Great War. The plaques were unveiled by the Senior Minister of State at the Foreign & Commonwealth Office and Minister for Faith and Communities, Baroness Warsi, at a reception at Lancaster House, London on 26th June 2014 attended by The Duke of Kent and relatives of the VC recipients. The Australian plaque is at the Australian War Memorial.
- The Secretary of State for Communities and Local Government, Eric Pickles MP announced that Victoria Cross recipients from the Great War would have commemorative paving stones laid in their birthplace as a lasting legacy of local

The overseas VC commemorative stones at the National Memorial Arboretum, Alrewas, Staffordshire unveiled by Prime Minister David Cameron MP and Sergeant Johnson Beharry VC on 5th March 2015.

Queensland Museum, Brisbane where Patrick's VC is displayed.

heroes within communities. The stones would be laid on or close to the 100th anniversary of their VC actions. For the 145 VCs born in Australia, Belgium, Canada, China, Denmark, Egypt, France, Germany, India, Iraq, Japan, Nepal, Netherlands, New Zealand, Pakistan, South Africa, Sri Lanka, Ukraine and United States of America, individual commemorative stones were unveiled at the National Memorial Arboretum, Alrewas, Staffordshire by Prime Minister David Cameron MP and Sergeant Johnson Beharry VC on 5th March 2015.

In addition to the VC he was awarded the British War Medal 1914–20 and Victory Medal 1914–19. His mother kept the VC in her handbag. After her funeral the family searched everywhere for it, but it could not be found. Finally they returned to the crash site where she was killed and found the VC lying in grass by the side of the road. The VC was presented to the Board of Trustees of the Queensland Museum, Brisbane on 14th June 1980 by his eldest surviving sister, Mrs Rose Elliott, and it remains there.

P/649 SERGEANT WILLIAM FRANCIS BURMAN
16th Battalion, The Rifle Brigade (The Prince Consort's Own)

William Burman was born at 5 Baker Street, Stepney, London on 30th August 1897. His father, George Burman (1865–1940), was a vanguard – carman. He married Agnes Elizabeth née McGuire (1862–1926), a cork fitter, on 25th December 1889 at St Philip's, Stepney, East London. They were living at 5 Baker Street, Mile End Old Town, London in 1891 and she was living as a widow at 3 Walter Street, Ratcliff, London in 1911. William had four siblings:

- Agnes Burman (born c.1888).
- George Robert Burman (1890–1919), a general printer, married Sarah AG Cotter in 1914. They had a son, William L Burman, in 1916. He married Phyllis M Wren in 1945 and they had two children – Jane E Burman 1948 and Andrew J Burman 1955. Sarah is understood to have married John Fairbairn in 1945.
- James William Burman (1892–1971) was a horse driver carman in 1911. He lived a very varied life, becoming a merchant seaman in 1912 and settling temporarily in Australia, where he ventured deep into the outback and also working on coastal vessels. He spent fifteen years in New Zealand as a shepherd, but by 1939 he was working at the Royal Mint. James went back to sea, serving on SS *San Farey*, a British run American ship handed back to the Americans after the Japanese surrender in 1945. He suffered from alcoholism later in life and was assisted by the Reverend James Martin MBE of the Bow Mission, London. James made significant progress and Martin recommended him for the award of Maundy Money, which he received from Queen Elizabeth II in 1968.
- Jane Elizabeth Burman (1894–1976) was a bookbinder in 1911. She married Frederick Self in 1926.

William's paternal grandfather, George Burman (1835–89), a weaver, married Ann née Dowles (c.1837–65), a trimming maker, on 13th April 1857 at St Jude, Bethnal Green, London. In 1871 they were living at 22 Thomas Street, Bethnal Green. In addition to George they had four other children:

- Ann Elizabeth Burman (1857–1928) married James Ellensworth (1850–1915), a labourer, in 1875.
- Ellen Burman (1859–1901) married Edward Andrew Hudson (born 1857), a groom and later a carman, in 1880. They were living at 5 Brunswick Place, Hoxton New Town, London in 1881, at 6 Church Row, St Luke, London in 1891 and at 97 Old Church Road, Mile End Old Town, London in 1901. They had five children – Ellen Hudson 1882, Florrie Hudson 1884, Edward Andrew Hudson 1887, Edith Annie Hudson 1893 and Maude Louisa Hudson 1895.

Saint Jude's Church was constructed 1842–46 and quickly developed a full range of church functions and groups, including a young men's association, provident society, library, soup kitchen, mission services, brigades, temperance classes, clubs, penny bank and holidays for mothers and children. It was damaged in the Blitz in 1940 and had to be demolished.

- Mary Ann Burman (born 1861) was a confectioner's assistant in 1881 living with her sister Ellen.
- Elizabeth Burman (1863–79).

George Burman married Maria née Smith (1841–89), a weaver and his sister-in-law, on 21st December 1872 at St James, Shoreditch. Maria was married previously to George's brother, John Burman (1839–71), a weaver, in 1864 at St James, Shoreditch. John and Maria had three children – Elizabeth Burman 1865, Maria Mary Ann Burman 1867 and John Burman 1869. By 1881 George was a dock porter, living with his family at 22 Baker Street, Mile End Old Town. George and Maria had five children:

- William Joseph Burman (1873–74).
- William Thomas Burman (1875–94).
- Joseph Burman (1877–1939), a carman, was boarding with M Seeney at 55 Lucas Street, St George in the East in 1901. John Seeney married Joseph's sister Harriett. Joseph married Elizabeth Condell (1876–1958) in 1901. By 1911 they were living at 35 Lucas Street, East London. They had at least four children – Charlotte Elizabeth Burman 1901, Maria Mary Burman 1903, George Thomas Burman 1909, William R Burman 1914.
- David James Burman (1879–1958), a twin with Harriet, was a printer, living with his brother-in-law, Robert Samuel McGuire in 1901 and his sister Harriet in 1911. He married Annie Maria Lorman (1879–1938) in 1913.
- Harriet Burman (1879–1959) was a jelly maker in 1901, living with her brother-in-law, Robert Samuel McGuire. She married John Seeney (1873–1931), a stevedore and later a farrier's assistant, in 1901. They were living at 55 Lucas Street, East London in 1911. John enlisted in the Army Service Corps on 14th August 1894 (11898) in the rank of driver. He was serving in 4th East Surrey (Militia) at the time. He was described as 5′ 3¼″ tall, weighing 120 lbs with fair complexion, grey eyes, fair hair and his religious denomination was Church of England. He had a number of tattoos. John deserted on 19th January 1895 and rejoined on 19th February. As a result he was imprisoned for twenty-eight days from 1st March and his previous service was forfeited. He was discharged on 10th August 1896 for misconduct and all service towards pension was forfeited. Harriet and John had seven children – Polley Seeney c.1902, Margaret Maria Seeney 1903, John Frederick Seeney 1906, Fred Seeney c.1909, Robert Seeney 1912, Joseph Seeney 1915 and George Seeney 1919. Harriet was living at 11 Barnardo Street, Stepney in 1939.

William's maternal grandfather, Robert William McGuire (1840–1915), a carman, married Elizabeth née Harris (1844–1900) in 1862 at St James, Westminster. In 1871 they were living at 2 Baker Street, Mile End Old Town, London. In 1891 he was a patient in the London District Hospital, Whitechapel and by 1911 he was lodging at 38 Baker Street, Leighton Buzzard, Leicestershire. In addition to Agnes they had eight other children:

- Robert Samuel McGuire (1865–1934) was a printer's lad in 1881. He married Maria Mary Ann Burman (1867–1921) in 1887. They were living at 126 Lucas Street, St George in the East, London in 1901 and at 16 Taylors Place, Limehouse, London in 1911. They had nine children including – Robert John McGuire 1888, possibly Alice McGuire (born and died 1890), Maria Elizabeth McGuire 1894, Joseph McGuire 1896, George Robert McGuire 1899, William John McGuire 1901 and Richard Charles McGuire 1903. It is understood that Robert married Ellen D Albone in 1923.
- James Thomas McGuire (1869–1927), a printing machine minder, married Elizabeth Alice Darnell (1868–1942) in 1890. In 1901 they were living at 5 Ramsey Street, Bethnal Green and by 1911 they had moved to 16 Atlas Road, Plaistow, Essex. They had ten children by 1911 including – Beatrice Elizabeth McGuire 1891, Maud Matilda McGuire 1893, Sydney James McGuire 1895, Frederick Albert McGuire 1897, Violet Gladys McGuire 1901, Alice Elizabeth McGuire 1904, William Thomas H McGuire 1906, Victor Albert C McGuire 1909 and Lilian V McGuire 1911.
- Louisa Jane McGuire (1871–1941) married Samuel Francis Fox (1872–1945), a porter, in 1892 and they lived at 2 Baker Street, Mile End Old Town, London. They had eleven children by 1911 including – Robert James Fox 1893, Alfred William Fox 1895, Charles Frederick Fox 1898, Francis Henry Fox 1899, Cecilia Louise Fox 1901, Elizabeth Agnes Fox 1903, George Fox c.1907, Ellen Margaret Fox 1909 and Lily L Fox 1910. In 1939 they were living at 48 Florence Road, Deptford, London. Samuel was a street trader in grocery.
- William Henry McGuire (1875–1904).
- Frederick Arthur McGuire (1877–1947) was a carman in 1901, living with his sister Louisa.
- Alfred Albert McGuire (1879–1965).
- Charles Sidney McGuire (1881–1971) was a carman in 1901, living with his sister Louisa Samuel. By 1911 he was living with his sister Agnes and her family at 3 Walter Street, London. It is understood that he married Elizabeth J Penning (1885–1956) in 1918. By 1939 they were living at 8 Normandy Road, Lambeth, London and he was a bus driver.
- Emily Louisa McGuire (1885–1925) married Henry Frederick Smail (1885–1927) in 1905. They had two children and both were living with their maternal aunt Agnes at 3 Walter Street, Ratcliff, London in 1911 – Henry Frederick Smail 1905 and William Adam Smail 1906.

William was educated at Stepney Red Coat School until 1911. It is not clear what he did next, but he may have assisted his father as a carman. He was a member of

D Company, 1st Cadet Battalion The Queens (later North East London), affiliated to the Rifle Brigade. He enlisted on 23rd March 1915 and went to France about 8th March 1916. He was promoted sergeant on 20th April 1916. **Awarded the VC for his actions southeast of Ypres, Belgium on 20th September 1917, LG 26th November 1917.** The VC was presented by the King at Buckingham Palace on 19th December 1917. He was presented with an illuminated testimonial by the Mayor of Stepney on 2nd August 1918 and £220 from public subscriptions. He also received a presentation bayonet and scabbard and a gold watch from the London Borough of St Pancras. William was demobilised on 7th March 1919.

He was a candidate for the Mile End Ward in the November 1919 Stepney Borough Council elections and was a member of the VC Guard at the Interment of the Unknown Warrior on 11th November 1920. William Burman married May Violet née Watts (10th March 1899–12th July 1961) at St Mary Magdalene, Peckham on 4th March 1922. At the time he was living at 2 Devonshire Place, Childs Hill and May was at 156 Hollydale Road, Peckham. They lived at 1 Temple Grove, Temple Fortune, London and had two sons:

William Burman married May Watts at St Mary Magdalene, Peckham on 4th March 1922. It was one of a number of new parishes created in Peckham to serve the growing population. The first church was consecrated in May 1841. A Church Day School, now St Mary Magdalene Church of England Primary School, was built in 1856. On 21st September 1940 the church was destroyed by a bomb with the loss of five lives. A new church was consecrated on 3rd November 1962 in the presence of HM Queen Elizabeth, the Queen Mother. Unfortunately the building had many design defects and it was demolished in 2010. A new church and community centre was consecrated in May 2011, 170 years after the consecration of the first church.

• Donald Francis Burman (28th February 1928–February 2004) married Vera M Sands in 1953.
• David W Burman (born 1934) married Hilary J Beckett in 1953.

William attended the VC Dinner at the Royal Gallery of the House of Lords, London on 9th November 1929. As a result of the draw for positions, he sat to the right of The Prince of Wales, who had Viscount Gort VC to his left. In 1939, William was a chauffeur living at the Garage, Bracknell Way, Frognal Gardens, Hampstead, London.

May's father, Edward Edgar Watts (1868–1929) was a furniture remover. He married Elizabeth Mary A née Smith (1870–1932) in 1889. In 1901 they were living at 57 Bournemouth Road, Camberwell, London. In addition to May they had twelve other children:

- Edith Elizabeth Watts (born 1890).
- Edward Albert Watts (born 1892).
- Ethel Maud Watts (born 1893) was a domestic servant in 1911.
- Rose Emily Watts (born 1895) was a domestic servant in 1911.
- Elizabeth May Watts (born 1896) was a domestic servant in 1911.
- Florence Beatrice Watts (born 1897) is understood to have married Henry Charles Ambrose in 1918 and they had three children – Ronald H Ambrose 1920, Joyce C Ambrose 1924 and Peter J Ambrose 1933.

May Watt's family lived on Bournemouth Road, Camberwell.

- Elsie Pretorius Watts (born 1900) married John Thompson in 1921.
- Lilian May Watts (born 1902).
- Agnes Dora Watts (born 1903).
- Beatrice Mabel L Watts (born 1905).
- Walter William Watts (born 1906).
- Edwin Charles J Watts (born 1909) married Daisy V Smith in 1928.

After the war William was employed as a chauffeur to the Managing Director of the Daily Mirror for thirty years. He then ran his own car hire business in Temple Grove, Golders Green until retiring in 1964. The effects of Phosgene gas prevented him from serving during the Second World War.

William Burman died at the Royal British Legion Home, Halsey House, Cromer, Norfolk on 23rd October 1974. He was cremated at St Faith's Crematorium, Horsham St Faith, Norfolk and his ashes were scattered in Section 2–5 at Golders Green Crematorium, London. He is commemorated on the Rifle Brigade Memorial in Winchester Cathedral, Hampshire and on a bench at the Royal British Legion Home, Cromer, Norfolk.

In addition to the VC he was awarded the 1914–15 Star, British War Medal 1914–20, Victory Medal 1914–19, George VI Coronation Medal 1937 and Elizabeth II Coronation Medal 1953. His VC is held in the Lord Ashcroft Gallery, Imperial War Museum, Lambeth Road, Kennington, London.

Halsey House was built in 1901 as a private home and was bought by the British Legion in 1947. It opened the following year and now cares for more than eighty reside (Northmetpit).

17/1280 PRIVATE WILLIAM BOYNTON BUTLER
17th Battalion, The Prince of Wales's Own (West Yorkshire Regiment)
attached 106th Trench Mortar Battery

William Butler was born at 29 Back Stanley View, Armley, Leeds, Yorkshire on 20th November 1894. His birth was registered as William Boynton Butler, but the name of his father was not recorded. His father, William Ellis Boynton (1874–1923), was a coal miner in 1891, a colliery banksman in 1894 and a bricklayer's labourer in 1901. He married Caroline née Butler (1873–1953), a woollen weaver, at Leeds in the 4th quarter of 1894. They were living at 2 Goodwin Street, Wortley, near Leeds in 1901 and at 5 Royal Terrace, Royal Road, Hunslet Carr, Leeds in 1911. William had five siblings:

- Nellie Boynton (born 1900) married James 'Jack' H Abbott in 1922 and they had two daughters – Kathleen Abbott 1924 and Margaret Abbott 1926.
- Gwendoline May Boynton (1903–70) married Samuel Jowitt (1905–74) in 1927 and they had a son, Brian Jowitt, in 1933.
- Mary Alice Boynton (1908–95).
- Edith Annie Boynton (born and died 1911).
- Mark Boynton (1916–2001) married Doris Smith (1919–94) in 1946. They had a daughter, Sheila Boynton (1949–2004), who married William J Harper in 1970 and had a daughter, Caroline, in 1972.

William's paternal grandfather, William Ellis Boynton (1839–1909), was a wool carder and by 1891 was a machine fitter. He married Martha née Hargraves (1845–82) in 1862. They were living at 8 Far Fold, Armley in 1881 and by 1891 were at 5 Akeroyd Yard, Armley. In addition to William they had eight other children:

- Samuel Boynton (1864–1930) was a boot maker. He married Annie Shaw (1867–1932) in 1886. They were living at 17 Hill End, Armley in 1891 and by 1901 had moved to 25 Eastern Street, Armley. They had six children – Martha Elizabeth Boynton 1887, Louis Boynton 1889, Florence Constantine Boynton 1892, Annie Boynton 1899, George Arthur Boynton 1901 and Harry Boynton 1904.
- Mary Ann Boynton (born 1866) was a wool filler in 1881.
- William Ellis Boynton (1867–68).
- Walter Boynton (1870–1944) was a coal miner in 1891.

- Arthur Boynton (1872–1952) was a coal miner in 1891. He married Julia Holmes (1881–1974) in 1899. They were living at Gomersal in 1911. They had two children, including Nellie Boynton 1910, one of whom did not survive infancy.
- Sarah Emma Boynton (1876–1925) married John William Swift (1876–1941), a coal miner, in 1898. They were living at 8 Cabul Row, Armley in 1911. They had six children including – George Ellis Swift 1899, John William Swift 1899, Frederick Swift 1902, Florence Hannah Swift 1902 and Edward Swift 1905.
- Ada Alice Boynton (1878–96).
- Jesse Boynton (1881–1934) married Eliza Dyson (1879–1946) in 1905 and they were living at 5 Ely Street, Armley, Leeds in 1911. He was a bricklayer's labourer and she was a tailoress machinist.

His maternal grandfather, James Butler (born 1847), was a scrapler in a stone quarry. He married Harriet née Brooksbank (born 1854) in 1871. They were living at 10 Hayfield Street, Wortley in Bramley in 1881, at 1 Goodwin Place, Wortley in 1891 and by 1901 had moved to 18 Hayfield Street, Wortley. In addition to Caroline they had eight other children:

- Mary Elizabeth Butler (born 1871) was a filler in a cloth mill in 1891.
- Rose Alice Butler (1875–1925) was a tailoress in 1891. She married George Medley (born 1873), a miller in a woollen mill, in 1895. They were living at 4 Grace Terrace, Armley in 1901.
- Florence Norah Butler (born 1877) was a piecer in a mill in 1891. She married Harry Smith Mortimer (born c.1871), a coal miner hewer, in 1894. They were living at 1 Hayfield Street, Wortley in 1901 and at 7 Firth Mount, Beeston, Leeds in 1911 and had eight children – Ivy Mortimer 1899, Lily Mortimer 1902, Rose Hannah Mortimer 1906, Nellie Mortimer 1909, Harry Smith Mortimer 1912, James TS Mortimer 1914, Charles Mortimer 1915 and Robert Mortimer 1918.
- Mark Butler (born 1879) was a miner in a clay pit in 1901.
- Matilda Butler (1882–92).
- James Butler (born 1884) was a miner in a clay pit in 1901.
- Nellie Butler (1887–1971) married John Kenyon (1887–1971) in 1912 and they had three children – John Butler 1914, Ivy Butler 1915 and Alfred Butler 1917.
- Louie Butler (born 1896).

William was educated at St Oswald's School, Hunslet Carr, near Leeds, leaving in about 1907. He was employed as a coal miner (pony driver below ground) at No.2 Middleton Pit, near Leeds. William enlisted on 14th January 1915 as a bantam in 17th West Yorkshire, having previously been rejected due to his height. He was described as 5′ 2½″ tall and weighed just 110 lbs. He went to France on 1st February 1916 and was admitted to 133rd Field Ambulance on 17th June (cause not known). He transferred to 106th Trench Mortar Battery on or shortly after its formation in April 1916. Promoted lance corporal 4th September and reverted to private on 29th September. He returned to England on leave on 23rd November. On 22nd January 1917 he attended the School of Mortars, returning to his unit on 29th January. William was admitted to 106th Field Ambulance with dental caries on 25th June, to 107th Field Ambulance with conjunctivitis on 28th June and 103rd Field Ambulance, also with conjunctivitis, on 3rd July.

Awarded the VC for his actions east of Lempire, France on 6th August 1917, LG 17th October 1917. He was on leave in England 2nd-16th December 1917. He arrived home on 4th December to find that his parents had already left for the investiture. The VC was presented by the King at Buckingham Palace on 5th December 1917. On returning to Leeds he was given a civic reception in the Town Hall on 6th December. Wilfrid Edwards VC was also a guest. William then went to his old school at St Oswald's, where he received a china clock from the citizens of Leeds and a gold medal from Mr W Owen. In addition £300 had been subscribed and was invested on his behalf.

William returned to France on 17th December and transferred to 15/17th West Yorkshire on 19th December. On 11th December 1918 he transferred to the Corps Demobilisation Camp and returned to Britain on 15th December on MT *Lydia*. **Awarded the French Croix de Guerre for coolness and gallantry in the execution of exacting and perilous duties as a despatch rider, LG 19th June 1919.** He was demobilised to the Class Z Reserve on 13th January 1919 and discharged on 31st March 1920.

Leeds Town Hall, where William Butler was received on 6th December 1917 after the VC investiture.

William Butler married Clara Johnson (1895–1964), a winder in a mat works, in the 1st quarter of 1920 at Hunslet. A daughter, Nellie Boynton Butler (born

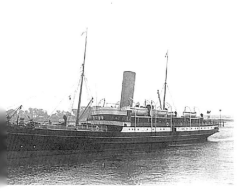

SS *Lydia* was built for the London & South Western Railway's fast service between Southampton and the Channel Islands. Her maiden voyage to the Channel Islands was on 7th October 1890. On 6th May 1891 she hit La Rond Rock off Guernsey and limped into St Peter Port before running aground. In 1901 she had a furnace blowback at St Helier and the fire took an hour to extinguish. She was requisitioned by the Admiralty in 1915 and survived a submarine attack in 1915 with the torpedo missing by fifty metres. In 1915 she moved German prisoners to Jersey for the camp at Blanches Banques and in 1919 returned Guernsey troops home. She returned to civilian service in 1919 and was sold a number of times before being scrapped in 1933.

1921), married Joseph H Howe in 1939 and they had a daughter, Moya J Howe in 1941. William and Clara were living at 324 Belle Isle Road, Leeds at the time of his death in 1972.

William was a member of the VC Guard at the Interment of the Unknown Warrior on 11th November 1920. He was employed as a spray painter by Leeds Corporation/North Eastern Gas Board, as was George Sanders VC and Wilfrid Edwards VC. William and George Sanders both served in the Gas Board Home Guard in Leeds during the Second World War. William attended a number of significant occasions:

Belle Isle Road, Leeds in the 1950s, where the Butlers lived. (*Leeds Library & Information Servic*

- Opening of the Regimental Headquarters at York by The Princess Royal.
- VC Garden Party at Buckingham Palace on 26th June 1920.
- Dedication of the West Yorkshire Regiment Chapel at York Minster in March 1926 with three other West Yorkshire Regiment VCs (Mansel-Jones, Traynor and Sanders).
- VC Dinner at the Royal Gallery of the House of Lords, London on 9th November 1929.
- He was introduced to the future King George VI when he visited Leeds on 27th September 1932. Wilfrid Edwards VC and George Sanders VC were also there.
- Victory Day Celebration Dinner and Reception at the Dorchester Hotel, London on 8th June 1946.
- VC Centenary Celebrations in Hyde Park, London on 26th June 1956.
- Naming of the Prince of Wales's Own Regiment of Yorkshire D55 Deltic Class engine at York Station on 8th October 1963.
- The funerals of John Raynes VC on 16th November 1929, George Sanders VC on 6th April 1950 and Albert Mountain on 12th January 1967.

William Butler was one of 319 VCs to attend the V Dinner at the Royal Gallery of the House of Lord London hosted by Edward, Prince of Wales, the future King Edward VIII, on 9th November 1929.

William Butler died at Leeds General Hospital in March 1972. It was opened on 19th May 1869 by the Prince of Wales, later King Edward VII, and h been extended several times since. The hospital is leading centre for neurosurgery.

The French Croix de Guerre was first awarded in 1915 to individuals or units distinguishing themselves by acts of heroism. Some notable recipients include:

Josephine Baker – American born French dancer, singer and actress for her work in the Resistance.

Jacques Cousteau – pioneer diver and underwater filmmaker.

General Dwight D Eisenhower – Supreme Allied Commander during Operation OVERLORD.

Noor Inayat Khan and Violette Szabo – British SOE agents awarded the George Cross and executed by the Nazis.

Audie Murphy – American actor and the most decorated US soldier of WW2, including the Medal of Honor.

General George S Patton – commander of US Third Army in the Second World War.

Theodore Roosevelt – son of President Theodore Roosevelt, awarded the Medal of Honor for his actions on 6th June 1944 on Utah Beach.

James Stewart – American actor for his role in the liberation of France as a USAAF Colonel.

Major Richard D Winters – Easy Company, 506th Parachute Infantry Regiment, made famous by the TV series and book *Band of Brothers*.

Sergeant Alvin C York – American First World War Medal of Honor winner and subject of a film in 1941 starring Gary Cooper.

William Butler's grave in Hunslet Cemetery. (*Dave Blyth*)

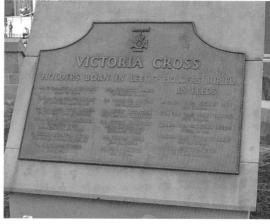

This memorial outside Leeds City Art Gallery commemorates the seventeen VCs born and buried in the city.

William Butler died at Leeds General Infirmary on 25th March 1972 and is buried in Hunslet Cemetery (Section 3 Grave 48). On his death certificate he is described as a retired spray painter. He is commemorated in a number of other places:

- Plaque outside the City Art Gallery, Leeds to VCs born and buried in Leeds.
- The Department for Communities and Local Government decided to provide a commemorative paving stone at the birthplace of every Great War Victoria Cross recipient in the United Kingdom. A commemorative stone for William was dedicated at Hunslet War Memorial, Hunslet Cemetery, Middleton Road, Leeds on 7th August 2017 to mark the centenary of his award.

In addition to the VC he was awarded the British War Medal 1914–20, Victory Medal 1914–19, George VI Coronation Medal 1937, Elizabeth II Coronation Medal 1953 and the French Croix de Guerre. The VC is held in the Lord Ashcroft Gallery, Imperial War Museum, London.

939 SERGEANT ROBERT JAMES BYE
1st Battalion, Welsh Guards

Robert Bye was born at 13 Maritime Street, Graig, Pontypridd, Glamorgan, Wales on 12th December 1889. Both parents were married previously:

- Father – Martinore (also seen as Mortimer) Bye (1848–1902), was a collier. As Martin Bye he married Hester Hicks (1849–79) in 1868 at Bristol and they were living at Jefferies Hill, Bitton in 1871. They had two children:
  ○ Martin Bye (born 1869).
  ○ Elizabeth 'Eliza' Bye (born 1870).
- Mother – Sarah Ann née Edwards (1858–1927) married James Dungey (1842–82), a coal miner, born at St Austell, Cornwall, in 1875 at Merthyr Tydfil, Glamorgan. Her middle name has also been seen as Jane. They were living at 9 Rheola Street, Llanwonno, Glamorgan in 1881. Sarah and James had three children:
  ○ Annie Elizabeth Dungey (c.1876–1973) married Charles Wilde (1871–1904), a platelayer, in 1899 and they had three children – Reginald Charles Wilde 1899, William John Wilde 1901 and Ethel Elizabeth Wilde 1903. At the time of their marriage she was living at 7 Vaughan Terrace, Penrhiwceiber and he was at 13 Springfield Terrace. Reginald Charles Wilde enlisted in 2nd County of London Regiment (2692) and later transferred to the Labour Corps (362011). Annie married John Oakley (born 1874), a coal miner haulier, in 1907. They were living at 35 Caemain Street, Ynysboeth Llanwonno, Mountain Ash in 1911 and at 195 Abercynon Road, Mountain Ash in 1939. They had a son, Harry George, in 1907.

- ○ William John Dungey 1877.
- ○ Sarah Jane Dungey (born and died 1880).

On 4th January 1881 Martin Bye appeared before a magistrate at the Shire Hall, Taunton, Somerset for stealing a sheep from Farnham Rich at Brislington, Somerset between the evening of 27th and the morning of 29th November 1880. He pleaded guilty to killing a sheep and stealing part of the carcass. He was sentenced to three months imprisonment at Corn Hill Gaol, Shepton Mallet, Somerset.

Looking over the railway station into Penrhiwceiber. Woodfield Terrace, Glanlay Street and Church Street, all associated with Robert Bye's early life are in this photograph.

Martin and Sarah married in 1883 at Pontypridd and were living at 21 Woodfield Terrace, Penrhiwceiber in 1893. The majority of the family appears in the 1901 Census with the surname Smith, although William J Dungey retained his original name. The reason for the name change is not known. In 1911 Sarah was living at 64 Glanlay Street, Penrhiwceiber. By 1916 she was blind and was again living at 21 Woodfield Terrace. Martin and Sarah had five children:

- David Gordon Bye (1892–1945) enlisted in the Welsh Regiment Special Reserve (95) for six years at Mountain Ash on 6th May 1908. He was a collier at the time described as 5′ 2¼″ tall, weighing 108 lbs, with brown eyes, dark brown hair and his religious denomination was Church of England. He was confined to barracks for five days for improper conduct on sentry duty on 28th June and was discharged on 2nd July 1908 having made a misstatement as to age on enlistment. He enlisted in 18th Hussars (7107) on 6th March 1911 and served during the Great War in France from 15th August 1914. He served with the Mediterranean Expeditionary Force 7th November 1915–12th November 1917, then returned to the BEF until 9th January 1919. David married Georgina Wheeler (1892–1972) in October 1915 at Pontypridd. She was born at Andover, Hampshire. David transferred to the Labour Corps on 7th April 1918 (519485) and to the Section B Army Reserve on 7th February 1919. He transferred to 18th Hussars Section B Army Reserve on 2nd April 1920. His address was 169 New Street, Andover. He rejoined 10th Hussars on 23rd July 1920 and was discharged from Canterbury on 18th February 1924 as a lance corporal with Exemplary character. He re-enlisted in Section D Army Reserve, Cavalry Pool at Winchester on 2nd April 1925 (537809) and was discharged on 1st April 1927. He enlisted in the Royal Engineers TA on 5th May 1938. David served as a bombardier in 231st Searchlight Regiment RA (537809) during the Second World War and died on 20th May 1945 at Abercynon, Wales. He is buried in Llanfabon Cemetery, Glamorgan (Row 37 Grave 22). David and Georgina had six children:

- Marion Georgina Bye (born 1918) married Watkin Bevan (born 1912) in 1938 and they had four children – Marlean Bevan 1939, Marion M Bevan 1941, June Bevan 1945 and Curigwyn Bevan 1949.
- David Gordon Bye (1919–86) married Mabel HP Stearn (born 1919) in 1942 and they had a daughter, Patricia A Bye in 1944.
- Philip Raymond Bye (born 1922) married Marjorie L Calkin in 1953 and they had three children – Philip D W Bye 1953, Robert Bye 1956 and Kevin Raymond Bye 1969.
- Oswald Llewellyn Bye (1925–94) married Dorothy M Crocker (born 1927) in 1951 and they had two sons – Gordon F Bye 1954 and Douglas G Bye 1958.
- Marjorie P Bye (born 1928) married John Youngs in 1948 and they had two sons – David J Youngs 1948 and Peter J Youngs 1950.
- Eric E Bye (born 1931) married Joan Moore in 1952 and had a daughter, Christine S Bye, in 1954.

- Margaret May (born 1893) married Herbert F Bath (1893–1945) in 1910 and they had two children – Herbert C Bath 1913 and Zena M Bath 1915.
- Vivian George Bye (1896–1947) enlisted in the Royal Welch Fusiliers and served in the Dardanelles. He married Margaret Jane Nicholas (1896–1926) in 1919 and they had two children – Vivian G Bye 1920 and Bronwen Bye 1922. Vivian senior married Sarah E Jones in 1928 at Pontypridd and they had a daughter, Margaret Ellen Bye, in 1929.
- Macdonald 'Donald' Claremont Bye (1900–66) enlisted in the Welsh Regiment aged fourteen and went to France, but his true age was discovered and he was sent home. He enlisted in an Irish regiment three years later. He married Margaret Mary Connelly (1899–1983) in 1920 and they had five children – Lilian May Bye 1922, Donald Bye 1924, Gordon Bye 1927, Olga Bye 1929 and Patricia Philomena M Bye 1938. They were living at 94 Woodfield Terrace, Mountain Ash, Glamorgan in 1939, when he was a colliery surface platelayer. Donald suffered a heart attack during his brother Robert's funeral on 28th August 1962.
- Martin Henry Bye (1902–62) married Clara Muxworthy (1903–75) in 1921 and they had three children – Ruby M Bye 1922, Thomas H Bye 1924 and Ann S Bye 1938. In 1939 they were living at 159 East Barnet Road, East Barnet, Hertfordshire. Martin was a fitter's labourer (central heating).

Sarah married David Coates in 1916 and continued to live at 21 Woodfield Terrace, Penrhiwceiber. She died at Mountain Ash, Glamorgan in 1927.

Robert's paternal grandfather, James Bye (1800–73), was born at Preston Candover, Hampshire and was baptised on 1st December 1805 at Heckfield, Hampshire. He attested on 30th May 1815 and enlisted in 5th Regiment of Fusiliers at Windsor, Berkshire on 1st June (96). He came of age on 30th May 1818 and was promoted corporal on 4th September 1822 and sergeant on 25th December

1824. However, he was permitted to resign his rank without trial by court martial and reverted to private on 26th April 1827. The alleged offence was not recorded. Promoted corporal on 1st April 1836. He was awarded the Good Conduct Badge with pay on 1st September 1836, but was deprived on 21st September 1836. It was restored on 22nd September 1837. Robert served in France for two and a half years and the West Indies from 3rd April 1819 to 14th April 1826. He was assessed by a medical board at Dublin, Ireland and declared unfit for service due to chronic rheumatism and general debility. He was discharged on 24th June 1839, described as 5′ 8″ tall with brown hair, grey eyes and fresh complexion. His employment was labourer. His conduct was Very Good. Robert married Bridget née Connor (c.1810–75) in 1824. She was born at Roscommon, Ireland. They were living at 27 Lewins Mead, St James, Bristol, Gloucestershire in 1851. In addition to Martinore they had four other children:

- James Bye (1831–73) was born at Banagher, Co Leitrim, Ireland. He married Elizabeth 'Betsy' Bryant (c.1833–91) in 1852 at Bedminster, Somerset and they had three children – James Bye 1853, Sarah Bye 1856 and Matilda Bye 1856.
- Mary Bye (1836–59).
- Stephen Bye (1846–1927) was born at Devizes, Wiltshire. He was a labourer in a distillery and married Sarah Ann Atkins (1846–1934) in 1866 at Bristol. They were living at Elm Tree Cottage, Bristol in 1911. They had nine children – Mary A Bye 1867, Betsy Bye 1869, Ann Bridget Louisa Bye 1871, Albert Cornelius Bye 1874, Stephen Bye 1876, Kate Bye 1878, Sarah Ann Bye 1880, James Bye 1883 and Robert Gilbert Bye 1885.
- Robert Bye (1851–63).

His maternal grandparents are believed to be Henry Edwards (c.1832–78), born in Somerset, and Margaret, born c.1832 in Swansea, Glamorgan.

Robert Bye was educated at Penrhiwceiber School and was employed as a miner at Deep Dyffryn Colliery, Mountain Ash and at other pits. He married Mabel Annie née Lloyd (28th March 1891–17th December 1974), a waitress, at Pontypridd on 14th October 1912 and they lived in Church Street, Penrhiwceiber. By 1939 they were living at 120A Sherwood Street, Warsop, Nottinghamshire. Robert and Mabel had five children:

- Robert Edward Bye (1st November 1912–1973), a colliery hewer, married Clara Holmes in 1940 at Mansfield, Nottinghamshire. They had six children – David H Bye 1940, John E Bye 1941, Vivien Bye 1943, Anne Bye 1947, Robert Bye 1951 and Trefor M Bye 1959. They were living at 1 Elkesley Road, Welbeck Colliery Village, Warsop, Nottinghamshire in 1962.
- Jenny Bye (21st July 1915–1985), married John G Ridley (born 1914), a gas and electrical welder, in 1937 and they had three children – June Ridley 1937, Hazel

M Ridley 1938 and John G Ridley 1949. They were living at 2 Emmerson Square, Derby in 1939 and at 51 Vickers Street, Warsop in 1945.

- Mabel Bye, born and died 1919.
- Desmond James Bye (5th February 1922–2000) enlisted in the Royal Artillery (14374936) and served in North West Europe, where he was wounded in 1944. He was found guilty of larceny by a court martial and sentenced to eighteen months imprisonment. He was a colliery surface worker in 1946. Desmond married Irene M Drzewiecka (née Abbott) (1925–79) in 1952. Irene was previously married to Jan Drzewiecka (registered as Drzwiecki) (c.1922–52) in 1946. They divorced and Jan married Edna Needham 1949.
- Mary Bye (born 1928) married George E Moody (born 1920) in 1948 and they had a son, Robert C Moody in 1949. They were living at 49 Hammerwater Drive, Warsop, Nottinghamshire in 1962.

Penrhiwceiber Primary School opened in 1881 and still serves the village. A mosaic memorial to Robert Bye was dedicated on 13th March 2015 (Jaggery).

Deep Dyffryn Colliery, Mountain Ash commenced sinking in 1850. On 27th April 1861, 400 tons of its coal was loaded onto the Royal Yacht *Victoria & Albert* at Portsmouth to conduct comparison trials with northern coal; the Welsh coal proved better quality. By 1918, Deep Dyffryn was employing 2,684 men. It closed in 1979 and the site is now Parc Dyffryn Pennar, home of Mountain Ash Rugby Football Club, which opened in 1994.

Mabel's father, Edward Lloyd (born c.1859), a coal hewer, married Jane née Evans (born c.1856), a general servant, in 1886. Jane had three children prior to her marriage – George Maldwyn Evans 1879, David Parry Evans 1880 and Thomas Watkin Evans 1883. Edward and Jane were living at 14 Perthygleison Crescent, Merthyr Vale, Merthyr Tydfil, Glamorganshire in 1901 and at 51 Church Street, Penrhiwceiber, Llanwonno, Glamorganshire by 1911. It is understood that they had fourteen children, but this may include Jane's three prior to their marriage. Six did not survive infancy, but by 1911 they had also adopted Harold James Whitford born in 1908. Their known children are:

- Edward Lloyd (born 1887) was an army blacksmith in 1911 stationed at Dublin, Ireland.
- William John Lloyd (born 1889) was a coal miner in 1911.

- Louisa Jane Lloyd (born 1893) was a domestic servant in 1911.
- Edith Blodwen Lloyd (born 1895) was a domestic servant in 1911.
- Idris Lloyd (born 1898).
- Beatrice Alice Lloyd (born 1900) married George Whitcombe in 1913 and they had a daughter, Enid Whitcombe, in 1914.
- Ivor Lloyd (born 1901).

3rd Grenadier Guards about to depart for the front from Wellington Barracks. 1st Welsh Guards moved into the barracks in June 1915, which have been in use since 1833. The façade remains very much as it was in 1915, but the rest of the site was redeveloped in the 1960s. Wellington Barracks also houses the Guards Chapel and Museum.

Robert Bye receives his VC from the King in the Buckingham Palace forecourt on 26th September 1917. (*Gillian James*)

Robert Bye enlisted in the Welsh Guards on 3rd April 1915 and was stationed initially at White City, London before moving to Esher, Surrey, where the Battalion was quartered in the grandstands at Sandown Park racecourse. In June 1915 it moved to Wellington Barracks in London and paraded at Buckingham Palace on 3rd August to receive its Colours from the King. Robert went to France with the Battalion, departing Waterloo Station on 17th August and landing at Le Havre next day via Southampton. Promoted lance corporal 13th March 1916, corporal 21st September 1916 and sergeant 4th April 1917.

Awarded the VC for his actions east of the Yser Canal, Belgium on 31st July 1917, LG 6th September 1917. He was the first Welsh Guards VC, the Regiment only forming on 26th February 1915. The VC was presented by the King outside Buckingham Palace on 26th September 1917. He was discharged on 1st February 1919, but re-enlisted in the Sherwood Foresters (127176) on 21st August, joining 1st Battalion on 5th November 1919. He served with the Battalion at the Naval Academy, Flensburg-Mürwik, Germany during the Schleswig Plebiscites of 1920. Robert was a member of the VC Guard at the Interment of the Unknown Warrior on 11th November 1920. He was discharged on 2nd July 1921 for medical reasons.

The family moved to the Warsop area of Nottinghamshire, where Robert returned to mining at Warsop Main, Firbeck and Welbeck Collieries. He was a member of the Warsop

The German Naval Academy was established at Flensburg-Mürwik by Kaiser Wilhelm II in 1910. In 1920, 1st Sherwood Foresters was based there while supervising the Schleswig Plebiscites mandated by the Treaty of Versailles. They were held on 10th February and 14th March and resulted in the northern portion voting to join Denmark, while the smaller southern portion voted to remain in Germany. In the dying days of the Second World War, Grand Admiral Karl Dönitz succeeded Adolf Hitler as Reichspräsident and established his government in the sport school at the Naval Academy.

The VC recipients at the investiture on 26th September 1917. From left to right – Lieutenant Gilbert Insall RFC, Sergeant Robert Bye WG, Sergeant Edward Cooper KRRC, Sergeant Alexander Edwards Seaforth Highlanders, Sergeant Ivor Rees South Wales Borderers, Lance Corporal Wilfred Edwards KOYLI and Private William Ratcliffe South Lancashire.

British Legion and a founder member of the Warsop Vale Branch, often acting as parade marshal on Remembrance Day parades. During the Second World War he was a sergeant major in the Sherwood Foresters guarding a prisoner of war camp in Derbyshire until medically discharged in 1941. He then served in the Home Guard and was a temporary police constable in Mansfield at some time.

Just before Christmas 1945, Robert turned the family out of the overcrowded home at 120a Sherwood Street, Warsop. It transpired that married life had not been happy since 1917, owing to allegations (unknown) made by Robert about Mabel. When Mabel, Desmond and Mary asked Robert if they could return, the old quarrel was revived. Desmond claimed his father had always treated his mother poorly. While Robert quarrelled with Mabel he was stabbed in the back by Desmond, who was committed for trial, but released on bail.

Robert retired from the mines in 1955, already showing signs of pneumoconiosis. Prolonged exposure to coal dust had a serious effect on his health and he moved to his daughter Mary's house at 49 Hammerwater Drive, Warsop, near Mansfield, which was on a hill and considered to be more airy. He lived there for only a few days before he suffered a heart attack and died on 23rd August 1962. The cause of death was recurrent coronary thrombosis and atheroma. He is buried in Warsop Cemetery (Grave 2129) and is commemorated in a number of other places:

• Roll of Honour in the Guards Chapel, Wellington Barracks, London.
• A painting by David Rowlands, commissioned by the Warrant Officers and Sergeants Mess, 1st Welsh Guards, was unveiled by his great-granddaughter, Claire Armstrong, and his great-grandson, Guardsman Paul Bye WG, in 1988.

The Victoria Cross Memorial in the grounds of Nottingham Castle commemorates the recipients born or buried in Nottinghamshire.

- Plaque at Mansfield Civic Centre, Nottinghamshire.
- Plaque at his birthplace at 13 Maritime Street, Graig, Pontypridd, Wales, unveiled on 26th September 1999 by his niece, Gillian James.
- Mosaic memorial at Penrhiwceibr Primary School dedicated on 13th March 2015. The ceremony was attended by his niece, Gillian James.
- Victoria Cross Memorial, Nottingham Castle Grounds, Nottinghamshire.
- The Secretary of State for Communities and Local Government, Eric Pickles MP, announced a campaign to honour Victoria Cross recipients from the Great War by laying commemorative paving stones in their birth place as a lasting legacy of local heroes. Robert Bye's commemorative stone was dedicated at Ynysangharad War Memorial Park, Rhondda Cynon Taff, Pontypridd, Wales on 10th July 2015.

In addition to the VC he was awarded the 1914–15 Star, British War Medal 1914–20, Victory Medal 1914–19, Defence Medal, George VI Coronation Medal 1937 and Elizabeth II Coronation Medal 1953. The VC is held by RHQ Welsh Guards, Wellington Barracks, Birdcage Walk, London.

34795 SERGEANT JOHN CARMICHAEL
9th Battalion, The North Staffordshire Regiment (Pioneers)

John Carmichael was born at Stoneybrae Cottages, Glenmavis, New Monkland, near Airdrie, Lanarkshire, Scotland on 1st April 1893. His father, Alexander Carmichael (c.1847–1916), was a mason in 1871, living with his mother at Mulindry, Kilarrow, Argyll. He married Janet née Harrison (born 1856) in 1877, by when he was a stonedresser. By 1881 he was a whinstone quarryman. They lived at Upper Houses, Bonawe Quarries, Ardchattan & Muckairn, Argyll and moved to Stoneybrae Cottages, Glenmavis before 1891. John had nine siblings:

- Mary Carmichael (1878–1900) was a domestic servant and died unmarried.
- William Carmichael (1879–1957) was a sett maker in 1901 and later a farm labourer. He married Mary Pitman (c.1879–1935), a weaver in a cotton mill, in 1906. They had three children – Helena Carmichael 1907, Janet Harrison Carmichael 1909 and Alexander Carmichael 1913.
- James Carmichael (born 1881) was a sett maker in 1901. He married Jessie Young (1887–1972) in 1909. They had five

Glenmavis and New Monkland church.

children – Alexander Carmichael 1910, Alison Douglas Carmichael 1913, Janet Carmichael 1915, John Young Carmichael 1920 and James Carmichael 1923.
- Donald Carmichael (1884–1906) was a stonebreaker in 1901 and a sett maker at the time of his death.
- Alexander McPherson Carmichael (1886–1954) was a stonebreaker in 1901, a steel dresser in 1916 and later a whinstone sett maker. He married Margaret Gilmour Milligan (born c.1889), a domestic servant, in 1916. They had at least two children – Alexander Carmichael 1923 and Alistair McPherson Carmichael 1925.
- Sarah Ann Carmichael (1888–1973) married John Kellock (c.1892–1954), a machine man in a boiler works and later a motor driver, in 1920. They had a daughter, Janet Carmichael Kellock, in 1922.
- Anne Haston Carmichael (born 1890).
- Thomas Carmichael (born 1897) was a whinstone quarryman living at Greenwood Terrace, Glenmavis when he married Christina Middleton Brown (born c.1893),

a cotton mill worker, in 1921. They had five children – Helen Brown Carmichael 1922, Alistair McPherson Carmichael 1925, Janet Harrison Carmichael 1928, David Brown Carmichael 1929 and Morag Carmichael 1934.

• Janet Harrison Carmichael (1898–1996), a grocer's assistant, married Thomas Alexander Cross Stirrat (1895–1980), a motorbus driver, in 1924. Thomas was later a caretaker. They lived at 15 Blairhill Street and 6 Tossisdale Street both in Coatbridge. They had a daughter, Janet Harrison Stirrat, in 1926.

John's paternal grandfather, Donald Carmichael (c.1810–65), was a private watchman in 1861 and later a slate quarryman. He married Mary née McPherson (1816–91) and they lived at 3 Little Hamilton Street, Glasgow, Lanarkshire. In addition to Alexander they had eight other children – Alexander Carmichael 1838, John Carmichael 1840, Donald Robertson Carmichael 1843, James Carmichael 1847, Sally Carmichael 1849, Donald Carmichael 1852, James Robertson Carmichael 1854 and Archibald Carmichael 1860. Mary was living with her sons Donald and James at Brackenbrae Cottage, Glassary, Argyll in 1881. By 1891 she was living at Clachan Point, Parish of Kilninver, Argyll at the home of her son James and his family.

His maternal grandfather, William Harrison (born c.1828), was a stone dresser. He married Ann née Haston (born 1830) in 1854. They were living at Goatfield, Cumlodden, Kirkliston, Linlithgowshire and by 1881 had moved to Lower Houses, Bonawe Quarries, Ardchattan and Muckairn, Argyll, by when he was a causeway dresser. In addition to Janet they had eight other children – Henry Harrison c.1854, Ann Harrison 1860, William Harrison 1862, Isabella Harrison 1864, James Harrison 1867, Thomas Brash Harrison 1870, William Aitkenhead Harrison 1873 and Alexander Harrison 1877.

John was educated at New Monkland Parish School, Glenmavis and was then employed by Messrs More & Co Quarrymasters alongside his father. He enlisted in 415th (Lowland) Field Company, Royal Engineers (62nd Division) at Coatdyke, near Airdrie on 8th June 1915. With little prospect of early action he transferred to 8th Sherwood Foresters in 46th Division and went to France in 1916. He transferred to 9th North Staffordshire in early 1917.

Awarded the VC for his actions in Imperial Avenue, near Hill 60, Zwarteleen, Belgium on 8th September 1917, LG 17th October 1917. He was seriously wounded in his VC action and was evacuated to No.53 Casualty Clearing Station at Bailleul. He wrote of the incident:

'We were on Hill 60, digging a communication trench, and I was detailed off with a party of men to get it done quick… One of the chaps was deepening the trench when his spade struck an unexploded grenade, just lodged there in the side of the trench, and it started to fizz… I knew that there would be seven seconds before it went off unless I did something. I couldn't throw it out, because there were men working

outside the trench as well as the blokes in it. So I shouted at them to get clear and I had some idea of smothering it, to get the thing covered, keep it down until they were out of range. All I had was my steel helmet. So I took it off my head, put it over the grenade as it was fizzing away, and I stood on it. It was the only way to do it. There was no thought of bravery or anything like that... Well, it did go off. They tell me it blew me right out of the trench, but I don't remember that. The next thing I remember is being carried away. That's how I got this thing....'

He was visited by the Divisional Commander, Major General Hugh Bruce Williams:

'... he was very nice to me. They'd put me in clean pyjamas, and he patted me on the shoulder and called me 'my boy' and then he told me about the medal. I suppose I was pleased, but I've never been more surprised. And I was more pleased yet when my platoon came – the whole lot of them. I don't know how they did it... but they came into the ward and they lined up at the foot of the bed and every one of them saluted me. Oh, I was embarrassed, but it was a great feeling. It was very good of them. They said I'd saved their lives, but I was there and I was in charge of them. I didn't think I was doing anything extraordinary.'

In St James's Park with his mother and sister, Annie, following his investiture on 22nd June 1918. (*Mrs E Dunlop & Mr J Carmichael*)

When he wrote to his mother, who had heard of his wounds, he told her that he was recovering well, but mentioned nothing of his award. The VC was presented by the King in the Quadrangle of Buckingham Palace on 22nd June 1918. His injuries were so severe that he never returned to the front and spent most of the next two years in a Liverpool hospital. He was discharged on 13th September 1918 and was awarded the Silver War Badge (B12565) on 2nd October.

John invested £1,000 presented to him by the citizens of Airdrie in a small chicken farm at New Monkland. He branched out into public transport, starting with one vehicle, and his fleet grew to forty buses operating between Airdrie, Helensburgh-on-the-Clyde, Kilsyth and Stirlingshire. He also expanded his agricultural interests by taking on two other farms.

Outside his home in Carluke with his mother and sister, Annie, while convalescing. (*Mrs E Dunlop & Mr J Carmichael*)

John Carmichael married Margaret née Aitken (c.1901–10th February 1978) on 22nd April 1931. There were no children. He served in 2nd Lanarkshire Battalion Home Guard and was promoted lieutenant on 1st August 1942. John also served as President of the Coatbridge branch of the Royal British Legion. He sold his bus company in 1967 and retired. He and his wife, accompanied by Lieutenant Commander Horace Taylor GC MBE, as representatives of the VC and GC Association, attended the requiem mass for Thomas McAvoy GC at the Church of the Immaculate Heart of Mary, Glasgow on 24th May 1977.

John in later life. (*Mrs E Dunlop & Mr J Carmichael*)

John died at his home Hurstmain, Glenmavis, Lanarkshire on 26th December 1977, the last surviving North Staffordshire VC. He is buried in Landward Cemetery, New Monkland, Airdrie (Section K, Grave 21–22). His wife died six weeks later and is buried with him. John is commemorated in a number of other places:

- Carmichael Close, one of five streets in Boley Park, Lichfield, Staffordshire, named after Staffordshire Regiment VCs.
- Memorial plaque in the Garrison Church, Whittington Barracks, Lichfield, Staffordshire.

John Carmichael's headstone in Landward Cemetery, New Monkland.

The North Staffordshire Regiment's VC memorial in the Garrison Church, Whittington Barracks, Lichfield, Staffordshire. John Carmichael's name is at the bottom (Memorials to Valour).

- Memorial arch in Hamilton, Lanarkshire to the fifteen Lanarkshire VCs. The other VCs commemorated are – Frederick Aikman, William Angus, Thomas Caldwell, Donald Cameron, William Clamp, William Gardner, John Hamilton, David Lauder, Graham Lyall, David MacKay, William Milne, John O'Neill, William Reid and James Richardson.

In addition to the VC he was awarded the British War Medal 1914–20, Victory Medal 1914–19, Defence Medal, George VI Coronation Medal 1937, Elizabeth II Coronation Medal 1953 and Elizabeth II Silver Jubilee Medal 1977. His

The memorial arch in Hamilton, Lanarkshire to the fifteen Lanarkshire VCs. John Carmichael's name is on the top stone of the right column. (*Memorials to Valour*)

medals were presented to the Staffordshire Regiment by his sister in May 1978 at the Drill Hall, Airdrie. The VC is held by the Staffordshire Regiment Museum, Whittington Barracks, Lichfield, Staffordshire.

CAPTAIN NOEL GODFREY CHAVASSE
Royal Army Medical Corps att'd 1/10th (Scottish) Battalion, The King's (Liverpool Regiment)

Noel Chavasse was born at 36 New Inn Hall Street, St Peter-le-Bailey Rectory, Oxford on 9th November 1884. He was the younger twin with Christopher. The twins were very frail at birth and contracted a form of typhoid fever as infants. However, during their long recovery they spent much time outdoors and this helped them develop considerable athletic ability.

His father was Francis James Chavasse (1846–1928), a rather diminutive man, who graduated from Corpus Christi College, Oxford with a First in Law and Modern History in 1869. He was ordained in the Church of England at Manchester in 1870 and was a curate at St Paul's, Preston until 1873. He was then Vicar of St Paul's, Upper Holloway until 1877 and Rector of St Peter-le-Bailey, Oxford until 1889, when he became Principal of Wycliffe Hall, living with his family at Wycliffe Lodge, 52 Banbury Road, Oxford. Francis was consecrated 2nd Bishop of Liverpool, succeeding Bishop John Charles Ryle on 25th April 1900. The family lived at 19 Abercromby Square, Liverpool, just a few doors away from

Robert Alexander and family, father of Ernest Wright Alexander VC. Francis was effectively the founder of Liverpool Cathedral, although the project started under his predecessor. On 19th July 1904, King Edward VII and Queen Alexandra laid the foundation stone. The Lady Chapel was opened in 1910, but the Cathedral was not completed until 1978. Francis retired in 1913 and moved to St Peter's House, Oxford, where he was elected an honorary fellow of Corpus Christi College. He was

New Inn Hall Street, Oxford.

a major influence in the creation of St Peter's Hall (later St Peter's College). He died on 11th March 1928 and is buried in Founder's Plot at Liverpool Cathedral. Christ Church at Norris Green was dedicated to him.

Noel's mother was Edith Jane née Maude (1851–1927). She and Francis were married at Overton-on-Dee near Wrexham on 27th September 1881. The service was conducted by the Reverends LT Chavasse and S Maude (her brother). She was a devout and compassionate woman who took a great interest in missionary work. Noel had six siblings:

Noel's father, Francis James Chavasse 1846–1928.

- Dorothea Chavasse (1883–1935) married the Reverend George Foster-Carter (1876–1966), Rector of St Aldate's, Oxford in 1908. They had four children:

Abercromby Square, Liverpool, home to the Chavasse family while Noel's father was Bishop there.

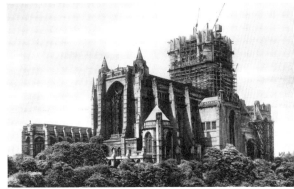

Liverpool Cathedral under construction.

The seven Chavasse children.

St Peter's Hall later St Peter's College, Oxford.

- ○ Aylmer Francis Foster-Carter (1911–79) was a chest physician and expert on tuberculosis. He married Ethna Josephine McDermott (1914–2005) in 1947 and they had two children – Aidan G Foster-Carter 1947 and Clare F Foster-Carter 1950.
- ○ Lois Marguerite Foster-Carter, born 1916. She was commissioned as 2nd Subaltern in the ATS (W/242314–350580) on 29th June 1945.
- ○ Pamela Mary Foster-Carter (1918–67).
- ○ Felicity J Foster-Carter, born 1923. She was a Franciscan Tertiary who moved to Singapore in 1955, teaching scripture and carrying out pastoral work at St Margaret's Primary School. She moved to mission schools in Singapore and Malaysia and was appointed Assistant Boarding Mistress before retiring to Oxford in 2000, where she lived with her sister Lois. She wrote, *All Things to All People – An Exciting Life in Singapore and Malaysia* in 2011.
- • Christopher Maude Chavasse (1884–1962) was Noel's elder twin by twenty-eight minutes. He was educated as the same schools as Noel. While at Trinity College, Oxford he gained blues for lacrosse and athletics. Christopher became a curate at St Helens, Lancashire. He was commissioned as chaplain to the forces 4th class on 20th August 1914 and was chaplain to 10th General Hospital at St Nazaire. He was at the bedside of William Rhodes–Moorhouse VC when he died at No.6 or No.7 Casualty Clearing Station at Merville on 27th April 1915 and about the same time he was at the execution of a soldier, which affected him deeply. Christopher became Senior Chaplain of 62nd Division in 1916. For attending to the wounded under fire at Bullecourt in April or May 1917, he was recommended for the DSO, but received the MC, LG 25th August 1917. In 1918, he became Deputy Assistant Chaplain General of IX Corps as temporary chaplain 2nd class, 30th September 1918. He was also awarded the French Croix de Guerre, LG 7th October 1919.

Christopher was wounded sometime during the war and last appears in the Army List in June 1920. After the war he was Vicar of St George's, Barrow-in-Furness until 1922, when he returned to Oxford as Rector of St Aldates and later St Peter-le-Bailey. He helped found St Peter's Hall at Oxford with his father and was appointed its first master in 1929. He was a tenacious opponent of proposals to revise the Book of Common Prayer and risked his advancement in the Church. Christopher was Proctor in Convocation for Oxford University 1936–39. He was appointed a chaplain in the Territorial Army Reserve from 2nd May 1930. Appointed chaplain to the forces 3rd Class (major) on 29th November 1931 and attached to Oxford UOTC until 9th November 1944 (OBE, LG 23rd June 1936 and TD 1940). On 18th August 1939, he and his wife were sailing aboard a whaler near the Giant's Causeway, Northern Ireland when it was capsized by a huge wave. Christopher's leg was crushed against a rock and he was rushed to Portrush Cottage Hospital in a baker's van. The leg was saved, but continued to trouble him and in February 1942 it was amputated at St Nicholas Hospital, Pyrford, Surrey. He said, *The boys were becoming too good for me at tennis. Now I can always claim: 'If only I had my other leg, I'd show you!'* Christopher was consecrated Bishop of Rochester on 25th April 1940 and chaired the commission, that produced the report *Towards the Conversion of England* in 1945. He wrote a number of publications including *The Meaning of the Lessons and of the Psalms*, *A Letter from the Catacombs*, *Christ and Fairies*, *Five Questions before the Church* and *This is Our Faith*. He was appointed Deputy Lieutenant of Kent in 1959 and retired the following year to 14 Staverton Road, Oxford. He became an honorary fellow of St Peter's College in 1949 and Trinity College in 1955. St Peter's was fully incorporated into the University in 1961. Frost Crescent, Wayfield Road, Wayfield, Chatham, Kent was named Chavasse Terrace in his honour. Christopher married Beatrice Cropper née Willink (1896–1977) in 1919 at Toxteth Park, Liverpool and they had five children:

- Noel Willink Chavasse, born 1920, was awarded the MC during the Second World War. He married Janet Eleanor Davidson in 1951.
- Michael Louis Maude Chavasse (1923–83) graduated from Trinity College, Oxford. He enlisted in the Royal Armoured Corps in October 1941 and was commissioned in the Buffs (Royal East Kent Regiment) in 1942, seeing service in Italy with the Royal Norfolk Regiment 1943–45. He was called to the Bar, Inner Temple, in 1949 and was Recorder of the Crown Court 1972–77, a QC and a circuit judge. He married Rose Ethel Read (born 1925) in 1951, daughter of

Christopher Maude Chavasse (1884–1962) when Bishop of Rochester.

Vice Admiral Arthur Duncan Read CB and the Honorable Rosamond Vere née Monckton. They had three daughters. His publications include *A Critical*

Annotation of the RIBA Standard Forms of Building Contract 1964 and *Rights of Light* with Bryan Anstey 1959.

○ John Chavasse, born 1925, married Mary EA née Vaughan in 1965 and they had three children.

○ Anna Chavasse, born 1927, married Richard Charles Chalinor Watson (born 1923) in 1955. He was the son of Colonel Francis William Watson and Alice Madeline née Collings-Wells, the sister of John Stanhope Collings-Wells VC DSO. They had two children. Richard was commissioned in the Indian Army Artillery and served as a captain in South East Asia 1942–45. He became a curate in Stratford, East London 1952–53 and was Tutor and Chaplain at Wycliffe Hall, Oxford 1954–57. In 1957 he became Chaplain of Wadham College and Oxford Pastorate and was Vicar of Hornchurch, Essex 1962–70. He was also Examining Chaplain to the Bishop of Rochester 1956–61, Examining Chaplain to the Bishop of Chelmsford 1962–70, Assistant Rural Dean to Havering 1967–70, Rector of Burnley, Lancashire 1970–77 and Bishop Suffragan of Burnley 1970–87.

Rochester Cathedral where Christopher was Bishop 1940–60.

Christopher Chavasse with members of St Peter's Hall in 1929–30.

○ Susan M Chavasse, born 1931.

• Edith Marjorie Chavasse (1886–1987) was a twin with Mary. She worked for Dr Barnardo's and represented England at hockey.

• Mary 'May' Laeta Chavasse (1886–1989) was a twin with Edith. She was a nurse at Liverpool Merchant's Mobile Hospital, Étaples (6th British Red Cross Society Hospital) and was Mentioned in Sir Douglas Haig's Despatches in May 1917. She joined the Queen Alexandra's Imperial Military Nursing Corps in the Second World War and served aboard the Elder Dempster Company Hospital Ship *Aba*. She was later a nurse in Oxford.

• Francis Bernard Chavasse (1889–1941), known as Bernard, graduated from Balliol College, Oxford and

Mary 'May' Laeta Chavasse.

became a doctor (MRCS (Eng) 1915, LRCP (London) 1915). Commissioned in the RAMC on 1st May 1915, he was appointed MO of 17th King's. Promoted captain on 1st May 1916 and was awarded the MC for tending the wounded at great personal risk for four days while wounded himself at Hooge, Belgium during the Third Battle of Ypres, LG 9th January 1918. Later served with No.11 Casualty Clearing Station. Appointed acting major on 6th November 1918. After the war, he was Honorary Ophthalmic Surgeon at the Liverpool Eye and Ear Infirmary and lecturer in Ophthalmology at Liverpool University living with his family at 39 Rodney Street, Liverpool. He edited a new edition of Claud Worth's *Worth's Squint* regarding binocular reflexes and the treatment of strabismus. Bernard challenged Worth's theory, applied his own ideas to new developments in physiology and pathology and almost rewrote the book. The seventh edition, published in 1939, became *Worth and Chavasse's Squint*. Bernard went on to invent several surgical instruments, but his best-known device was the eponymous lens. He died in a car accident in 1941. Francis married Anita née Reeves-Thomas in 1923 and they had three children:

○ Edgar FJ Chavasse (born 1924).
○ Evadne Chavasse (1928–97) married Donald Louis Nicholas (1909–73) in 1950 and they had three children.
○ Thomas A Chavasse (born 1932) married Barbara AJ Beyer (born 1938) in 1960 and they had two children.

• Aidan Chavasse (1891–1917) was commissioned on 22nd August 1914 and promoted lieutenant on 1st January 1915. He served in 17th King's. On the night of 3rd/4th July 1917, he was with a patrol of eight men on Observatory Ridge, near Hooge, Belgium when they met a German patrol. In the ensuing encounter, Aidan was wounded by a bullet in the right thigh. Lance Corporal W Dixon MM was with him, but was unable to move Aidan alone. As it was getting light and they were only ten metres from a German sap, Aidan sent Dixon back. Next night he and Aidan's brother Francis went out, but found no trace of Aidan, or on the next night. He was listed as missing until early 1918, by when there had been no notification through the Red Cross and he was presumed dead officially. He is commemorated on the Ypres (Menin Gate) Memorial, Belgium.

Francis Bernard Chavasse.

Noel's paternal grandfather was Thomas Howard Chavasse FRCS (1800–84). He married Catherine Margaret Grant (1807–42) in 1827 and they had eight children – Ludovick Thomas Chavasse 1829–92, Nicholas Horace Chavasse

Aidan Chavasse.

1830–1918, Jane Ann Chavasse 1832–63, Catherine Henrietta Chavasse c.1834–1915, Howard Sidney Chavasse 1835–63, Margaret Elizabeth Chavasse 1838–1927, Charles Edward Chavasse c.1841–93 and Emily 1842. In 1844, he married Miriam Sarah née Wyld (1817–84). The family was living at Wylde Green House, Sutton Coldfield, Warwickshire in 1851 and 1861. Thomas and Miriam had four more children in addition to Francis:

- Miriam Sarah Chavasse (1848–1935) married (as Miriam Theresa Chavasse) the Reverend Percival Ewen Wilson (1853–1948) in 1879 at Aston, Warwickshire.
- Ada Martha Chavasse (1850–1922) married the Reverend Henry Charles Squires (c.1847–1910) in 1878. They had five children – Herbert C Squires 1880–1964, Elsie C Squires 1883–1946, Francis 'Frank' Chavasse Squires 1885–1915, Winfred C Squires 1888–1962 and Mildred Christian Squires 1892–1963. Captain Francis Chavasse Squires was Adjutant of 1/23rd Sikh Pioneers when he died on 7th July 1915 (Maala Cemetery, Aden – C 137).
- Thomas (later Sir Thomas) Frederick Chavasse FRCS LRCP (1854–1913) was a Doctor of Medicine, Master of Surgery and Consulting Surgeon to the General Hospital, Birmingham. Thomas published various papers on surgical subjects in the *Transactions of the Royal Medical Chirurgical Society*, *Transactions of the Pathological Society* and the *Lancet*. He married Frances Hannah Ryland (1848–1928) in 1885 and they had six children – Gwendoline L Ryland Chavasse 1885, Arthur Ryland Chavasse 1887–1916, Frederick Ryland Chavasse 1889, Francis Ryland Chavasse 1890, Frances Gladys Ryland 'Gaggie' Chavasse 1893 and Esmé Margaret Ryland Chavasse 1895. Frances Gladys Ryland Chavasse was engaged to Noel in April 1916. Captain Arthur Ryland Chavasse RAMC BA MA MB MRCS LRCP was serving at 2nd General Hospital when he died of pneumonia on 12th March 1916 (Ste Marie Cemetery, Le Havre – 19 T 3).
- Joseph Hodgson Chavasse (1856–1906) married Mary Elizabeth Gilman (1859–92) in 1880 and they had a son, Thomas John Chavasse, in 1881. Joseph married Alice Maria Nation (1867–1962) in 1895.

Noel's maternal grandfather was Canon Joseph Maude (1805–74), Curate of Newport, Isle of Wight in 1851 and later Vicar of Chirk, Denbighshire. He married Mary Fawler/Fowler née Hooper (1820–1913) in 1841 and they had six more children in addition to Edith:

- Samuel Maude (1845–1912) was Curate of Holy Trinity, St Pancras in 1881, Vicar of Needham Market in Suffolk in 1891 and had moved to Lyncombe, Guildford Road, Woking, Surrey by 1911.
- Mary Julia Maude (1847–1934).
- Margaret Esther Maude (1848–49).

- Joseph Hooper Maude (1852–1927) was a clerk in holy orders. He married Louisa Frederica Grey Fuller (1864–1938) in 1884 and had two children – Cecily Margaret Evadne Maude 1887–1958 and Louis Edward Joseph Maude 1891–1916, who served as a lieutenant in 11th King's Own Yorkshire Light Infantry and was killed in action on 1st July 1916 (Gordon Dump Cemetery, Ovillers-la-Boisselle, France – Special Memorial B 7).
- Daniel Edward Maude (1855–56).
- Grace Fawler Maude (born and died 1858).

Noel and Christopher were identical in looks and manner, so were often made to wear a different item of clothing or a coloured ribbon to identify them in class and on the sports field. They took great amusement swapping these items to cause confusion. They were very close to each other and also with their twin sisters.

Christopher (left) with Noel at an athletics event.

Until they were twelve, Noel and Christopher were educated by their governess and a tutor. They then went to Magdalen College School in Oxford 1896–1900, where they won numerous athletics trophies and produced a number of small publications for their classmates. In 1900 they moved to Liverpool College, where Noel won the Earl of Derby's History Prize in 1901 and the Routhwaite Prize for Reading and Recitation in 1902. The twins were very active in debating, often taking opposing sides. They continued to excel at sports, with Noel taking first place in Neat Diving for Beginners in 1900. Both played for the Cricket 2nd XI in 1902 and the Rugby 1st XV in 1904. Noel broke the school records for the 100 yards, quarter mile and mile races in 1903. The

Magdalen College School in Oxford on the right, where Noel and Christopher were educated 1896–1900.

same year, a knee injury prevented him playing rugby. Instead, during his games afternoons and summer vacations, he helped to organise sports and annual camps for Holy Trinity Certified Industrial School for Boys, Grafton Street, Liverpool. He also led Bible reading and singsongs. Also attending Liverpool College was future VC Ronald Niel Stuart.

At Trinity College, Oxford 1904–09 (BA 1st Class Physiology 1907, MA 1909) the twins shared rooms in Kettle Hall. Noel was a member of the medical section of Oxford

Royal Southern Hospital, Liverpool.

Trinity College, Oxford.

UOTC January–May 1909 as a lance sergeant, but gave it up due to his studies. Noel and Christopher gained blues in 1907 for running against Cambridge. Noel gained a first in Physiology in 1909, but Christopher failed his exams. Noel was awarded a post-graduate exhibition in medicine at Oxford, but deferred it until his brother passed his examinations. Instead he decided on a course at Liverpool University (Royal Southern Hospital) to be at home and able to help his brother prior to the examinations.

At Liverpool University 1910–12, he qualified as MBChB MRCS LRCP. The placement part of the course was at the Rotunda Hospital, Dublin in the summer of 1911. On 15th March 1912, the committee of the University's Medical Faculty awarded him their premier prize, the Derby Exhibition. During his time at Oxford Noel spent his weekends learning the skills of orthopaedic surgery at the surgeries of his friend and mentor, Dr Robert Jones. He was registered as a doctor with the General Medical Council on 22nd July 1912.

As talented athletes, Noel and Christopher were both invited to trials for the British team for the Fourth Olympic Games in London, 13th–25th July 1908. Noel pulled a muscle and could not take part and Christopher also pulled out. They wrote to the authorities explaining that they could not run due to injuries, but would be fit for the Games. Their times for the quarter mile and 100 yards were included, some of which were the best in England since 1906. They were invited to run in front of King Edward VII and the French President, but had to decline. However, their times were good enough and on 2nd June, PL Fisher, Secretary of the Amateur Athletic Association invited them to take part in the Games. They were both entered in the 400 metres. Noel came third in Heat VII and Christopher was second in Heat VIII, but

Rotunda Hospital, Dublin.

The Great Britain team at the opening ceremony of the Olympics in 1908.

Poster advertisement for the London Olympics of 1908. The athletics events were at the White City in July as shown, but the Games lasted for a record 187 days. Great Britain emerged with the largest number of medals – 146, including 56 Gold, with the USA closest with 47 medals including 23 Gold.

neither time was good enough to go through to the next round. Strangely the press made no mention of twin brothers running in the same event.

After university, Noel researched blood plasma at the Radcliffe Infirmary, Oxford. He became a house physician and resident house surgeon to Mr Douglas Crawford at the Royal Southern Hospital in Liverpool 4th October 1912–31st March 1913, which was extended for a further six months. He specialised in orthopaedics under Sir Robert Jones, the leading orthopaedic surgeon of the day.

On 2nd June 1913, Noel was commissioned in the RAMC (TF) and was attached to 10th King's as its MO. On 2nd August 1914, the Battalion went to Hornby Camp, Lancashire for annual training, but was ordered to return to Liverpool next day. Noel and his brothers did not want to wait to get to the front, so on 5th August they travelled to the War Office in London to volunteer for immediate service overseas. The Battalion was recalled on 7th August and Noel was ordered to Chester Castle next day to perform medical examinations on recruits. He rejoined the Battalion in early September at King's Park, Edinburgh, where the unit formed part of the Forth Defences. The Battalion moved to Tunbridge Wells, Kent on 10th October, where in kitted out and undertook exercises prior to going overseas.

The Liverpool Scottish Battalion Headquarters in Liverpool.

Noel embarked with the Battalion at Southampton on SS *Maidan* on 1st November. The ship missed the tide and did not put in to Le Havre until the following night. The Battalion disembarked on the morning of 3rd November. It arrived at St Omer on 5th November and then spent two very cold weeks training at Blendecques. On 20th November it reached Bailleul and on the 22nd crossed the border into Belgium.

Noel quickly developed strong concern for the health and condition of the men and obtained whatever he could for them. He earned a reputation for being able to get hold of the impossible. He was one of the first doctors to use anti-tetanus serum on wounded men. This was a great success and very few developed tetanus as a result. The Battalion moved into the front line for the first time on 27th November near Kemmel. Noel's first patient was Captain Arthur Twentyman, who was hit in the chest by a bullet next day and died of his wound on 29th November (Rue-Petillon Military Cemetery, Fleurbaix – II A 63).

Noel returned to Britain for a few days leave in early February 1915. Over the next few months the Battalion was in the Ypres Salient and at St Eloi. Noel's dressing station was in the infantry barracks in Ypres, 10th March–2nd April. On 16th June, the Battalion took part in Second Army's attack on Bellewaarde as part of 9th Brigade, 3rd Division. Of the twenty-three officers and 519 other ranks who went into action, twenty-one officers and 379 other ranks became casualties. Noel scoured the ground between the opposing lines to provide aid to the wounded. In his search for one officer he visited all hospitals in the area by bicycle in the hope of finding him, but to no avail. **Awarded the MC for clearing no man's land of the wounded around Hooge during this attack, LG 14th January 1916.**

The CO, Major GA Blair, had submitted a list of recommendations for awards, but it never reached Division Headquarters and was probably destroyed in a fire at Brigade Headquarters. However, believing that the recommendations had been approved, he announced them at a church parade in a barn near Ouderdoum. None of those who subsequently received awards for 16th June resulted from recommendations made by the Battalion. Noel had been told earlier of his award and was absent from the parade. He was found later weeping in a wood. **Mentioned in Sir John French's Despatch of 30th November 1915 for his part in an attack on Sanctuary Wood on 30th September, LG 1st January 1916.**

The Battalion transferred to 166th Brigade, 55th (West Lancashire) Division under Major General Sir H

A remarkable picture taken under fire by a wounded soldier of the Liverpool Scottish, Private FA Fyfe, a pre-war newspaper photographer, during the attack at Bellewaarde and Hooge on 16th June 1915. A number of wounded and dead can be seen. It was in this area that Noel earned his MC (FA Fyfe).

Jeudwine on 1st January 1916. Noel was arrested as a spy by a vigilant military policeman because his uniform was unusual; he was wearing a RAMC uniform with Corps insignia and a Glengarry cap with the Liverpool Scottish badge, but the Battalion wore the khaki Balmoral. Early in April 1916 he was chosen from hundreds of other officers to receive his MC from the King, but his leave was postponed. As a result he was not decorated with the MC until 7th June, almost a year after the action at Bellewaarde.

Noel had a few days' leave in Britain and returned to the Battalion at Busselboom, Belgium on 9th July. **Awarded the VC for his actions at Guillemont, France on 9th August 1916, LG 26th October 1916.** He was promoted captain in August, backdated to 1st April, and in November was transferred temporarily to a field hospital. He attended the start of a six-day course on hygiene and sanitation in December, but he and the Battalion were sent for rest at C Camp, Brandhoek for Christmas, following which he completed the course.

Noel was granted fourteen days leave to attend his VC investiture at Buckingham Palace on 5th February 1917. The medal was taken back to Liverpool for safekeeping by his sister Marjorie. A miniature version was carried by Noel. On 20th July, the Battalion left St Omer and moved by train to Poperinghe for a short rest, before marching up to the lines in front of Wieltje. Up to 24th July, the Battalion suffered 145 casualties from a mustard gas attack combined with heavy shelling. It was relieved that day and rested at Derby Camp, between Poperinghe and Ypres, where it re-equipped and prepared for the forthcoming offensive.

Awarded a Bar to the VC for his actions at Wieltje, Belgium 31st July–2nd August 1917, LG 14th September 1917. His was the only Great War double VC. He was very seriously wounded by a shell exploding in his dugout at 3 a.m. on 2nd August and was eventually taken to No.32 Casualty Clearing Station at Brandhoek. On the way the ambulance stopped briefly at 46th Field Ambulance, commanded by Lieutenant Colonel Arthur Martin-Leake VC and Bar. He was seen by Dr Colston who wrote, *An ambulance came up late tonight and in it was Captain Chavasse VC RAMC of the King's Liverpool Battalions* [sic] *of the 55th Division. His face was unrecognizable, all blackened from a shell burst very near and he seemed to be unconscious.*

As he had an abdominal wound besides I did not take him out of the Ambulance, which was sent on direct to 32 CCS where he will probably die. Despite a successful operation to

Noel Chavasse with the stretcher-bearers of the Liverpool Scottish in Flanders shortly before the opening of the Third Battle of Ypres in July 1917.

remove shell fragments, his condition worsened on 4th August and he died of wounds at 1 p.m. He was nursed in his final hours by Sister Ida Leedam, who had worked with Noel at the Royal Southern Hospital in Liverpool. Noel was buried next day (his brother Bernard did not manage to get there until 6th August) in Brandhoek New Military Cemetery – III B 15. His CWGC gravestone is unique as it carries two Victoria Crosses. His will was administered by his father; he left £603/8/4.

The Bar to the VC was presented privately to his father by Lieutenant General Sir William Pitcairn Campbell KCB, GOC Western District in late 1917. Noel became engaged to his cousin, Frances Gladys Ryland Chavasse in April 1916. She was a volunteer worker with the Church Army at Euskirchen, Germany, where she met the Reverend James 'Pud' Ferguson Colquhoun (c.1881–1937). Their marriage was registered in the 4th quarter of 1919 at Bromsgrove, Worcestershire. Christopher Chavasse was one of the officiating clergy. James has been Chaplain to 12th York & Lancaster and later was Senior Chaplain of 31st Division. Gladys ran a canteen for troops and was evacuated from Dunkirk in 1940. She was Mentioned in Despatches for gallant and distinguished services at Monte Cassino, Italy. She visited Noel's grave every year until she was knocked over in France in September 1962 and killed; she was very deaf and probably never heard the car.

Noel Chavasse's unique headstone in Brandhoek New Military Cemetery south of the busy N38 Ypres–Poperinghe road.

Noel is related distantly to three other VCs:

- Captain Charles Hazlitt Upham VC and Bar – his aunt-by-marriage was the wife of Noel's second cousin.
- Lieutenant Neville Josiah Coghill VC – his paternal aunt, Anne Georgina Coghill, was married to Pye Henry Chavasse, Noel's great uncle.
- John Stanhope Collings-Wells VC DSO – Noel's niece, Anna Chavasse, married Collings-Wells' nephew, Richard Charles Chalinor Watson.

Private Rudd's grave in Brandhoek New Military Cemetery.

In addition to the VC & Bar and MC he was awarded the 1914 Star with 'Mons' clasp, British War Medal 1914–20 and Victory Medal 1914–19 with Mentioned-in-Despatches Oakleaf. The VC passed to his brother, Christopher, who left it to the trustees of St Peter's College, Oxford in the 1930s. It was displayed on the main staircase, but the insurers became concerned about the location and a replica set replaced the originals, which were locked in a bank vault for about fifteen years. They were presented on permanent loan to the Imperial War Museum on 22nd February 1990 in the presence of Queen Elizabeth The Queen Mother, Colonel-in-Chief RAMC. In November 2009 the medals were purchased by Lord Ashcroft, reputedly for £1.5M. They are now held by The Michael Ashcroft Trust in the Lord Ashcroft Victoria Cross Collection and are displayed in the Ashcroft Gallery of the Imperial War Museum. Christopher's medals are displayed alongside Noel's.

Gladys in later life.

Noel is commemorated in a considerable number of places, including:

- Chavasse House, 208 (Liverpool) Field Hospital, Territorial Army Centre, Sarum Road, Liverpool. The unit also holds a competitive twenty-one kilometres march annually, with the winner receiving a medal inscribed, "Chavasse March" "208 R.A.M.C.".
- 207 (Manchester) Field Hospital (Volunteers) Officers' Mess, The Castle Armoury, Castle Street, Bury, Lancashire was dedicated to him in February 2009.
- A memorial plaque at Forbes House, Liverpool, dedicated in 1979, was the idea of Great War Liverpool Scottish veteran, Brigadier Tom Robbins.
- A bronze bust of Noel is next to the Liverpool Book of Remembrance in Liverpool Cathedral.
- He was one of six VCs commemorated on a set of stamps published by the Royal Mail to commemorate the 150th Anniversary of the Victoria Cross on 21st September 2006. The other VCs were Jack Cornwell, Agansingh Rai, Charles Lucas, Albert Ball and Charles Upham.
- A tree and plaque in the RAMC Memorial Grove at the National Memorial Arboretum, Alrewas, Staffordshire, as part of a tribute to every VC & GC recipient within the Corps. The Grove was dedicated on 18th October 2000.
- RAMC Great War Book of Remembrance in Westminster Abbey. His entry wrongly records that he was awarded the DSO.
- Blue plaque unveiled on 30th September 2005 at Magdalen College School, Oxford by the Oxfordshire Blue Plaques Board.
- Blue plaque on the wall of the former Bishop's Palace, 19 Abercromby Square, Liverpool.
- A memorial unveiled opposite 19 Abercromby Square, Liverpool in July 2008, depicts Noel helping a wounded soldier accompanied by a stretcher-bearer. Fifteen other VCs associated with Liverpool are included on the memorial.

The commemorative Chavasse VC stamp issued by Royal Mail in September 2006.

- Portrait painting in the dining room and portrait photograph in the snooker room of the Officers' Mess, Defence Medical Services Training Centre, Keogh Barracks, Aldershot, Hampshire.
- Named on the Army Medical Services VC & GC Roll of Honour in the Army Medical Services Regimental Headquarters at the former Army Staff College, Camberley, Surrey.
- As the son of a Bishop, his name is on the House of Lords memorial.
- Chavasse Trophy – awarded annually by Oxford University Athletic Club to the winning college in the inter-college athletics competition based on aggregated points from the two 'cuppers' competitions. 'Cuppers' in Hilary Term is dedicated to Noel Chavasse and in Michaelmas Term to his brother, Christopher. They both competed for Oxford in the 1906 and 1907 Varsity matches.

The Chavasse memorial in the grounds of Brandhoek Church on the northern side of the N38 Ypres–Poperinghe road. Inset on the left is an enlargement of the memorial.

- Chavasse VC House, Colchester, Essex, a Personnel Recovery Centre funded by Help for Heroes and The Royal British Legion for wounded, injured and sick service personnel, was opened on 8th May 2012.
- Chavasse Ward, MOD Hospital Unit Frimley Park, Surrey established in February 1996. The other military ward is named after Martin-Leake VC and Bar.
- Liverpool College has memorials to Noel and Aidan.
- Noel is named in the rolls at Liverpool Town Hall's Hall of Remembrance. For an unknown reason his brother Aidan is missing.
- The Merseyside Branch of the Western Front Association and the King's (Liverpool) Regiment published a limited edition first day cover on the 80th Anniversary of his first VC.
- The Department for Communities and Local Government decided to provide a commemorative paving stone at the birthplace of every Great War Victoria Cross recipient in the United Kingdom. Noel has three stones. One was dedicated at St Peter's College, New

Basil Rathbone (1892–1967) served as a private with the London Scottish until commissioned in 2/10th King's early in 1916. He was the intelligence officer. 2/10th King's amalgamated with 1/10th King's early in 1918. Basil became adept at daylight reconnaissance, using camouflaged suits, fresh foliage and hands and face blackened with burnt cork. After the war he had a full career on stage and in films. His most famous role was Sherlock Holmes in fourteen films between 1939 and 1946.

Inn Hall Street, Oxford on 9th August 2016 and another at Magdalen College School, Oxford on 5th September 2016 to mark the centenary of his first award. A third stone was dedicated in Abercromby Square, Liverpool on 29th August 2017 to mark the centenary of his second award.
• Memorial at Brandhoek Church, Belgium.

Members of the British Olympic Association, including the Chairman, Lord Colin Moynihan, conducted a memorial service at Noel's grave at Brandhoek on 11th November 2011. Dr Jacques Rogge, President of the International Olympic Committee, also attended, as did representatives of the Belgian, French and German National Olympic Committees and several Olympic medalists.

42537 CORPORAL WILLIAM CHARLES CLAMP
6th Battalion, Alexandra, Princess of Wales's Own (Yorkshire Regiment)

William Clamp was born at 2 Bridge Street, Motherwell, Lanarkshire, Scotland on 28th October 1892. His father, Charles Henry Clamp (1868–1947), born at Daisy Bank, Staffordshire, was an iron bundler. He was working at Craigneuk Borland's Ltd in 1871. He married Christina née Dundas (1874–1934), born at Square of Woodhall, Old Monkland, Lanarkshire, on 27th May 1892 at Motherwell, Lanarkshire. She was living with the family of her sister-in-law, Isabella Fisher, at 149 George Street, Back Land, Paisley, Renfrewshire in 1891 and was working as a bleachfield worker at the Bowfield Women Houses, Lochwinnoch, Renfrew. Later Charles worked at the Etna Iron & Steel Co and the family lived at 13a Reid Terrace, Shields Road, Flemington, Motherwell. They returned briefly to Worcestershire c.1897 before again settling in Lanarkshire, but by 1901 they were living at 13 Palmerston Street, Thornaby, Yorkshire. William had fifteen siblings:

Advertisement for the Etna Iron & Steel Company in Motherwell.

• Hannah Tunnicliff Clamp (1894–1933), at Holytown, Motherwell, married James Henderson (born c.1888), a colliery wagon shunter, in 1912. They lived at 23 Flemington Street, Motherwell.

- Jessie Clamp (1895–1971) at Holytown, Motherwell), married James Kelly (born c.1887), a crane trigger, in 1919. They later lived at 15 Cowley Road, Wyken, Coventry, Warwickshire.
- Grace Clamp (born and died 1896).
- James Clamp (born 1898 at Wolverhampton, Staffordshire), a hammer man, was living at 13 Reid Terrace, Motherwell in 1921. He married Agnes Campbell (born c.1901) in 1921 at 7 Netherton Terrace, Netherton, Cambusnethan, Lanarkshire. They moved to England after 1925 and lived at 35 Henrietta Street, Coventry, Warwickshire. They had six children – Helen Campbell Clamp 1921, Charles Henry Clamp 1922, Robert Campbell Clamp 1925, William C Clamp 1929, James A Clamp 1931 and Albert Clamp 1937.
- John Clamp (1899–1963), born at Gas Works Row, Motherwell, married Elizabeth Ferguson, a tweed mill worker, in 1928 at Gretna Green, Dumfries (no marriage record found). They had two children – Charles Henry Clamp 1925 and Christina Dundas Clamp 1930.
- Annie Clamp (1902–84), born at 31 Overjohnstone Place, Craigneuk, Lanarkshire, married Robert Hendrie, a steelworks labourer, in 1925. Robert became an engineer's fitter and predeceased his wife. They had at least three children – Robert Barclay Hendrie 1926, William Hendrie 1927 and Doreen J Hendrie 1934. Her sister Grace also married a Hendrie in 1936. Thereafter there were six Hendrie/Clamp births that could be to either marriage. When she died at Carluke, Annie's permanent address was 31 Cowley Road, Wyken, Coventry, Warwickshire.
- Elizabeth Clamp (1903–06).
- Albert Clamp (born and died 1904 at Craigneuk, Lanarkshire).
- Albert Clamp (1905–1974), born at Craigneuk, was a hammer driver, living at 13 Shields Road, Motherwell in 1924. He married Margaret Craig (c.1905) in 1924 at 4 Leslie Street, Motherwell. They had six children – Charles Henry Clamp 1924, William Craig Clamp 1926, Albert Clamp 1928, James Clamp 1931, John Clamp 1937 and Valerie C Clamp 1945.
- Charles Henry Clamp (1910–11) born at Ravenscraig, Dalziel.
- Emily Clamp (born and died 1907).
- Christina Clamp (1911–20).
- Clara Clamp (1914–2001), born at 13c Reid Street, Motherwell, was a domestic servant living at 8 Jack Street, Motherwell in 1932. She married John McAllister (born c.1913), a steel worker, in 1932 at 67 Cadzow Street, Hamilton, Lanarkshire and they had two children in Coventry – Christina DC McAllister 1936 and John McAllister 1939. Clara married secondly Ronald Frankland in Cleveland in 1959. She married thirdly Ian George McDonald Reid (1911–82) in 1968 in Glasgow. She married fourthly, Robert Gow (1919–2009), a steel worker, in 1982 in Glasgow and they lived at 500 Old Shettleston Road, Glasgow.
- Grace Clamp (born 1915) married William Hendrie in 1936 and they lived at 31 Cowley Road, Coventry, Warwickshire. Her sister Annie also married a Hendrie in Coventry. The following children belong to the two marriages – Jean C Hendrie

1937, Gordon A Hendrie 1937, Ann CCK Hendrie 1939, John W Hendrie 1944, Raymond Hendrie 1951 and Brenden Hendrie 1952.
- Alfred Jacob Clamp (born 1917) was born at 13c Reid Street, Motherwell. He lived at 15 The Boxhill, Stoke Aldermoor, Coventry and is understood to have married Matilda Bamford in 1937. They had eight children – Ronald H Clamp 1938, Sylvia Clamp 1939, Alfred Clamp 1941, Robert Clamp 1942, June Clamp 1944, Patricia A Clamp 1946, Raymond Clamp 1951 and William J Clamp 1955.

William's paternal grandfather, William Clamp (1848–1927), was born at Sedgley, Staffordshire. He married Hannah née Tunnicliff (1852–1930) in 1867. She was born at Hill Top, near Leek, Staffordshire. William was a labourer in an ironworks and the family was living at 2 Chapel Street, Wolverhampton, Staffordshire in 1881. They moved to Lanarkshire, Scotland between 1871 and 1875, but returned to Wolverhampton c.1880. They moved back to Lanarkshire c.1888 and he was working as an ironworker at Craigneuk Borland's Ltd. They again returned to England and he was working as a bundler at an iron works alongside his son Charles in 1901 and the family was living at 10 Skinner Street, Thornaby, Yorkshire. By 1911 they were living at Stockton-on-Tees. In addition to Charles they had eleven other children:

- Hannah Clamp (1871–1956) is understood to have had a son, William, in 1886. She married William Thomas Allford (1869–1952), an iron puddler, born in Shropshire, England, in 1894 at Motherwell. They lived at 4 Carmichael Street, Law, Lanarkshire and 65 Young Street, Wishaw, Lanarkshire. They had two children – Hannah Tunnicliffe Allford 1897 and Mary Wynn Allford 1898.
- William Thomson Clamp (1873–74).
- Emily Clamp (c.1875–1963) married William Gebbie (1871–1931) in 1892 at Craigneuk, Lanarkshire. They were living at 8A Hornsea Place, Craigneuk in March 1918. They had ten children – James Gebbie 1892, Elizabeth Gebbie 1893, Janet Gebbie 1894, William Gebbie 1896, John Gebbie 1900, Claire Gebbie 1901, Margaret McKinlay Gebbie 1904, Robert Gebbie 1906, Mary Gebbie 1908 and Agnes Gebbie 1910. James served as a private in 4th Gordon Highlanders (S/19698) and was killed in action on 25th March 1918 (Arras Memorial, France).
- William Thomson/Thomas Clamp (1876–1942).
- Mary Clamp (1878–1951) married Joseph Murphy (born 1871 at Coalisland, Co Tyrone, Ireland), a coal miner, in 1900. They were living at 178 Wellington Street, Motherwell in 1901 and later at 128 Watson Street, Motherwell. They had at least a daughter, Hannah Murphy, in 1900.
- John Clamp (1880–1962).
- Clara Clamp (1883–1963) married Philip Hutchinson (1884–1939) in 1911 at Stockton-on-Tees. He was a driller in a shipyard in 1911, living with his brother-in-law, William Thomas Elkins, at 42 Hume Street, Stockton-on-Tees.
- Samuel Clamp (1885–88).
- Sarah Clamp (1887–88).

- Albert Clamp (1889–1966) married Ethel Selby (1886–1966) in 1910 at Stockton-on-Tees. He was an ironworker in a pig iron factory in 1911 and they were living at Pearson Street, Stockton-on-Tees. They had eight children – Alfred Clamp 1910, Albert Clamp 1913, Clara Clamp 1915, John T Clamp 1917, Wilfred Clamp 1920, Ethel M Clamp 1922, Hannah Clamp 1925 and Edna Clamp 1927.
- Alfred Clamp (1891–1961) was an ironworker in 1911 living with his parents. He married Caroline Southall (born 1893) in 1912 at Stockton-on-Tees. They had twelve children – Caroline Clamp 1912, Violetta Clamp 1914, Alfred Clamp 1916, Albert Clamp 1919, William Clamp 1920, Charles H Clamp 1923, Hannah Clamp 1924, Clara Clamp 1927, John Clamp 1929, Mavis Clamp 1932, Jean Clamp 1934 and Derek Clamp 1936.

His maternal grandfather, James Dundas (c.1838–98), was born in Ireland. He married Janet 'Jessie' née Waldie (c.1844–88), born at Old Monkland, Lanarkshire, in 1864. James was a coal miner and they were living at 22 Hillhead Row, Old Monkland in 1871. They were living at 74 Scott Row, Dalziel, Lanarkshire in 1881, at 8 Russell's Row, Craigneuk in 1888, at 15 Cowie's Square, Craigneuk in 1891 and later at 22 McAndrews Row, Craigneuk. In addition to Christina they had fifteen other children:

- James Dundas (born 1865) died in infancy.
- Isabella Dundas (born 1865) married William Fisher (born 1863), a bricklayer's labourer. They were living at 149 George Street, Back Land, Old Monkland in 1891. She died on 3rd April 1934 at Vancouver, Canada. They had two children – James Fisher 1887 and William Fisher 1890.
- Annie Dundas (1867–1951) married John McIntyre, a coal miner, and they lived at 118 Meadowfield Road, Craigneuk.
- Jessie Dundas (born 1869).
- James Dundas (1870–1942), a coal miner, enlisted in 2nd Argyll & Sutherland Highlanders on 9th April 1890 at Stirling (3502). He was described as 5′ 4¼″ tall, weighing 122 lbs, with fresh complexion, grey eyes, fair hair and his religious denomination was Presbyterian. He went to India on 25th November 1891 and was granted Good Conduct Pay at 1d per day from 8th April 1892. This was forfeited on 3rd June 1892, restored on 3rd June 1893, forfeited on 26th September 1893, restored on 1st July 1894, forfeited on 19th October 1895 and restored on 19th April 1896. He was in action on the Punjab Frontier in June 1897 and returned to Britain on 29th March 1898. He took part in the Second Boer War in South Africa from 27th October 1899. He returned to Britain on 10th August 1902 and was discharged the following day. James married Annie Hunt (born c.1880) in 1904. They lived at 108 Waverley Drive, Wishaw.
- Elizabeth Nisbet Waldie Dundas (twin with Malcolm) (1871–73).
- Malcolm Waldie Dundas (twin with Elizabeth) (1871–72).
- Martha Dundas (born and died 1873).
- Grace Dundas (twin with Christina) (1874–1949) was born deaf and dumb. She was a housekeeper in her father's house in 1891 and 1901. She married Archibald

McMahon (c.1859–99), an ironworker, in 1892 and John Syme (c.1876–1924), a crane driver, in 1903.

- William Dundas (1876–1943) married Susan/nah Graham (1881–1916) in 1900 and they were living at 7 Old Ravenscraig, Dalziel in 1901. They had a son, William Dundas, the same year.
- Malcolm Waldie Dundas (1878–88).
- David Dundas (1881–1937), a coal miner stripper, was boarding at 30 Cowie's Square, Wishaw Road, Craigneuk in 1901. He married Jeanie Young Scott (1889–1970) in 1908 and they lived at 102 Laurel Drive, Wishaw.
- Janet Dundas (1883–1943) married Walter Menzies (1882–1948) in 1900.
- Margaret Stewart Dundas (born 1884) married Francis McMahon (1879–1956) in 1901. He was a steelworker when he enlisted in 8th Cameron Highlanders on 19th May 1915 at Inverness (18198). He was described as 5′5″ tall and weighed 112 lbs. He had a moderate spinal curvature and suffered from chronic rheumatism, resulting in him being discharged on 1st June 1915 on medical grounds. They were living at 67 Scotts Row, Craigneuk in 1915. They had eight children – Francis McMahon 1901, Annie Dundas McMahon 1904, Margaret Cameron McMahon 1907, Grace Dundas McMahon 1910, Alexander McLellan McMahon 1913, James Dundas McMahon 1915, Margaret Dundas McMahon 1917 and Isabella Dundas McMahon 1920.
- Elizabeth Dundas (1886–96).

William was educated at Craigneuk Primary School, Wishaw and also attended the Motherwell Salvation Army Sabbath School and played cornet in the Motherwell Corps Band. He was a member of the Good Templar Lodge. William was employed by Messrs Hurst, Nelson and Co at their wagon works in Flemington. He enlisted in 6th Cameronians (Scottish Rifles) TF (1889) on 2nd January 1914. He was mobilised when war broke out and went to France on 20th March 1915 with 1/6th Cameronians. William was wounded twice and after the second time he transferred to 6th Yorkshire on 10th January 1917. He returned to duty just before his last action. In his last letter to his mother he wrote, *Don't worry about me, Mother, for, whatever happens, my soul is right with God.*

  Awarded the VC for his actions at Poelcapelle, Belgium on 9th October 1917, LG 18th December 1917. He was killed during his VC action and is commemorated on the Tyne Cot Memorial, Belgium. As he never married, the VC was presented to his parents by the King at Buckingham Palace on 2nd March 1918. William is commemorated in a number of other places:

- Named on the war memorial in Duchess of Hamilton Park, Motherwell, Lanarkshire.
- Clamp Road, Motherwell, Lanark.
- Clamp Memorial Prize – Gold medal awarded annually by Craigneuk Public School, to the 'Dux of the School'. The medal is in the shape of the VC.

- Memorial arch in Hamilton, Lanarkshire to the fifteen Lanarkshire VCs. The other VCs commemorated are – Frederick Aikman, William Angus, Thomas Caldwell, Donald Cameron, John Carmichael, William Gardner, John Hamilton, David Lauder, Graham Lyall, David MacKay, William Milne, John O'Neill, William Reid and James Richardson.

William Clamp's name on the Tyne Cot Memorial.

- His name was added to a new plaque when the Craigneuk War Memorial was restored and dedicated on 27th August 2011.
- Named on a plaque at Ashworth Barracks Museum, Doncaster, South Yorkshire unveiled by Lord Lieutenant Andrew Coombe on 22nd June 2015.
- The Department for Communities and Local Government decided to provide a commemorative paving stone at the birthplace of every Great War Victoria Cross recipient in the United Kingdom. A commemorative stone for William was dedicated at Motherwell War Memorial, Duchess of Hamilton Park on 9th October 2017 to mark the centenary of his award.

Motherwell War Memorial in Duchess of Hamilton Park. William's name appears incorrectly under the Cameronians (Scotland's War).

In addition to the VC he was awarded the 1914–15 Star, British War Medal 1914–20 and Victory Medal 1914–19. When his parents died the VC passed to his brother, James. When he died it passed to his sister, Jessie Kelly, who sold it to the Regiment in 1967. The VC is held by the Green Howards Museum, Richmond, Yorkshire.

In September 2005, William Clamp's great-great-nephew, Junior Bombardier Carl Clamp, graduated from the Army Foundation College, Harrogate. The Green Howards Museum allowed him to carry the VC on parade in his pocket. His father, Billy, a Territorial Army sergeant with D (KOSB) Company, 52nd Lowland Regiment (Volunteers), completed a tour in Iraq alongside his cousin, Corporal John Clamp, a regular soldier serving in 1st King's Own Scottish Borderers. Carl's two cousins were also serving – Kevin in the Royal Engineers and Charles in the Royal Artillery.

The restored Craigneuk War Memorial with the plaque to William Clamp in the foreground (Scottish Military Research Group).

BRIGADIER GENERAL CLIFFORD COFFIN
Corps of Royal Engineers, Commanding 25th Brigade

Clifford Coffin was born at 9 St John's Park South, Blackheath, London on 10th February 1870. His father, Isaac Campbell Coffin (1801–72), was born on Nantucket off the coast of Massachusetts. He entered military service with the East India Company on 3rd June 1818 and arrived in India on 12th January 1819, where he was posted as a lieutenant to 21st Madras Pioneers in 1821. He was appointed Adjutant of 12th Madras Native Infantry from 4th June 1824 and served in Burmah, including the attack on Rangoon on 9th and 15th December. His next appointment was Quartermaster, Interpreter and Paymaster to 12th Madras Native Infantry on 27th October 1826. Promoted captain on 26th July 1828 and appointed Paymaster to the Nagpore Subsidiary Force on 30th June 1829. Appointed Paymaster in Mysore 7th January 1834. Promoted major 24th July 1840 and lieutenant colonel 15th September 1845. Isaac assumed command of 3rd Palamcottah Light Infantry, Madras Native Infantry on 7th October 1845. Promoted colonel 20th June 1854 and, with the rank of 1st class brigadier, he commanded the Hyderabad Subsidiary Force from 6th November 1855 throughout the Indian Mutiny. Promoted major general 29th May 1857 and commanded a division of the Madras Army from 28th March 1859 until 28th March 1864. Promoted lieutenant general 18th July 1869 and retired soon afterwards to 9 St John's Park South, Blackheath. He was created Knight Commander of the Order of the Star of India, LG 25th May 1866. Isaac married Marion St Helena Elizabeth Harrington (1800–64) on 12th February 1824 at Prince of Wales Island, Bengal. She died at Nellore, Madras in February 1864. Isaac married the VC's mother, Catherine 'Kate' Eliza née Shepherd (1834–1903), on 23rd October 1866 at the British Embassy in Berlin. She was living at Frimley, Surrey on her own means in 1901 and at 8 St Stephen's Crescent, Westbourne Park, Paddington, London in 1903. Clifford had eleven siblings from his father's two marriages:

Clifford Coffin's father, Lieutenant General Sir Isaac Campbell Coffin (1801–72).

- Francis Somerset Sinclair Coffin (born 1828).
- George Henry Somerset Coffin (1830–33).
- Frederick Malcolm Coffin (1832–33).
- George Lennox Coffin (born and died 1833).
- Marian Isabella Coffin (1835–1906) was born in Bangalore, India. She married William McAdam Steuart (1824–84) of Glenormiston, Peeblesshire in February

1853 at Ootacamund, India. William was an East India silk manufacturer. They were living at 31 Seagrove Road, Fulham, London in 1881. William died on 21st May 1884 at 91 Princes Street, Edinburgh, Midlothian. Marian was living at 128 Queen's Gate, Kensington, London as a manageress in 1901 and died there in 1906. Marian and William had three children all born in Calcutta, India:

- ○ Isabella Grace Steuart (c.1854–1927) was with her grandparents and her sister Marian at West Wickham, Kent in 1861. She died unmarried at Brighton, Sussex.
- ○ Marian Emily Steuart (1855–1905) was at boarding school with her sister Mary at 233 Belmont Belvedere, Hove, Sussex in 1871. She died unmarried at Poona, India.
- ○ Mary Helena Steuart (1856–95) was boarding at 13 New Bridge Street, Chelmsford, Essex in 1881. She died unmarried at Maidstone, Kent.
- Cecilia Rebecca Coffin (born and died 1836).
- Isaac Campbell Coffin (c.1837–38).
- Louisa Coffin (born c.1838) married Edward Holwell Short (1807–83) in October 1854 in Madras. Edward was a captain in 29th Madras Native Infantry and was later a coffee planter. They had twelve children – Thurston Holwell Short 1852, Edward Woodville Bernard Short 1853, Laurence Beresford Sebright Short 1856, Frederick D'Arcy Harcourt Short 1859, Charles Kirkby Short 1862, Octavius Holwell Hunter Short 1863, Louisa Eleanora Jane Short 1866, Bruce Norton Short 1867, Amy Holwell Short 1869, Isabella Martin Short 1870, Herbert Holwell Short 1872 and Charlotte Danby Short 1875.
- Kenneth Douglas Coffin (1839–73) was commissioned in 105th Regiment of Foot (Madras Light Infantry) on 20th September 1856. Promoted lieutenant and appointed adjutant on 28th May 1858. He was in action with 3rd Madras (European) Regiment (108th Regiment of Foot (Madras Infantry) from 1862 at Bundhelkand, Kabri, Banda and the surrender of Kirsole. Promoted captain 27th March 1868 and sold his commission in 1870. Kenneth married Eliza Seely Kenworthy (1842–1917) in 1860 at Trinchinopoly (now Tiruchirappalli), Madras. The marriage ended in divorce after a petition lodged by Eliza due to her husband's adultery and cruelty on 10th June 1869; decree nisi 17th January 1871. Eliza reverted to her maiden name and was living at 74 Coburg Road, Upper Teddington, Middlesex at the time of her death. Kenneth married Jessie Margaret Groves (c.1835–1914) at All Saints, Coonoor, Tamil Nadu, India in 1871. Kenneth was superintendent of a coffee plantation at Washermanpettah, Madras when he died of a lung disorder on 12th January 1873. Jessie moved to England. Kenneth and Eliza had five children:
  - ○ Eliza Marian Coffin (born 1861) married Thomas John Duncan (born c.1859) of Dublin, Ireland. He was secretary of the Stephen's Green Club in Dublin, a gentlemen's club founded by, among others, Daniel O'Connell, an early campaigner for Catholic emancipation in Ireland. By the time of the 1911

Census, the family was living at 29 Northumberland Avenue, Kingstown, near the port of Dun Laoghaire. Thomas was a widower and lived into his nineties. They had two daughters – Marion Isabelle Lottie Duncan 1888 and Ida May Coffin Duncan (1892–1975). Marian developed a passion for motorcycle scrambling in Ireland, taking part in events in the 1920s with the Ramblers Motorcycle and Light Car Club, riding an Enfield. She was in business in Ulster as a poultry breeder with a partner, Violet Charlotte Wood Fishbourne, living at Portledge Cottages, Hillsborough, Co Down. It is understood she never married. Ida graduated from Trinity College, Dublin (BA Hons Law 1915) and Middle Temple, London, becoming one of the first female barristers in England in January 1923. She was the first woman to argue a case in the Court of Criminal Appeal and won. In 1931 she became a commissioner on the Board of Control (previously the Lunacy Commission); OBE 1959. She never married.

○ Kenneth Douglas Coffin (c.1862–1907) moved to Mackay, Queensland, Australia where he was a bank clerk. He married Ida Harden (born 1866) in 1890. She was born in Queensland. They lived at 106 Archer Street, Rockhampton, Queensland and had at least one son, Carl Douglas Coffin (1894–1915). Carl enlisted in the Australian Imperial Force on 22nd September 1914 at Brisbane, Queensland (583) and was allocated to D Company, 15th Battalion. He sailed from Melbourne, Victoria aboard HMAT A40 *Ceramic* and was killed in action on 26th April 1915 at Gallipoli (Lone Pine Memorial, Turkey).

○ Edward Harington Coffin (born 1863).

○ Minnie Coffin (born 1864).

○ Eva Coffin (born 1865).

• Helena Beatrice Coffin (1841–78) married Brevet Major Edward Long Grant (1822–1907), Madras Fusiliers in 1859 at St Mark's Church, Bangalore, India. He was commissioned in the Madras Infantry 11th June 1841, arrived in Madras on 20th September and joined 1st Madras (European) Fusiliers on 1st November. Promoted lieutenant 1845, captain 22nd August 1854, major in the army 24th March 1858, major in the regiment 16th July 1864 and lieutenant colonel 22nd February 1866. He saw action in Burmah 1851–56, where he was severely wounded. He was also wounded twice during the Indian Mutiny and was eventually invalided out on 1st October 1867. CB, LG 5th January 1888. Helena and Edward had two daughters:

The Lone Pine Memorial, Turkey where Clifford's great-nephew, Carl Douglas Coffin, is commemorated.

○ Helena Marian Grant (1860–91) married Julian D'Arcy Evezard (1862–1943) in 1885 at Wellington, Madras. Julian was the son of Edwin D'Arcy Evezard, Surgeon Major Indian Army, and Mary Juliana Haviland Burke, great niece of Edmund Burke, the politician and author. They had two children – Edith Helena Evezard 1887 and Edward Grant Evezard 1888. Julian married Alice Martha Martin (1862–1945) in 1892. They had a son, George Evezard (c.1894–1916), born at Darjeeling, India. He was commissioned in the Royal Warwickshire Regiment on 19th May 1915 and died of wounds serving with 1st Battalion on 9th May 1917 (Aubigny Communal Cemetery Extension, France – VI G 7).

○ Mary Edith Grant (1862–1934) died unmarried.

• Campbell Coffin (1867–1952) was born at 51 Oxford Terrace, Hyde Park, London. He was educated at Haileybury College and the Royal Military Academy, Woolwich. He was commissioned in the Royal Engineers on 17th February 1886. Promoted captain 1896, major 1904, lieutenant colonel 1912 and colonel 1916. He arrived in France on 26th August 1914 (CMG, LG 23rd June 1915) and went to Mesopotamia in 1916 (MID, LG 22nd June 1915 and 19th October 1916) with 3rd (Lahore) Division. He served in India 1917–22, where he retired from the post of Deputy Director of Military Works at Army Headquarters. Appointed Companion of the Order of the Indian Empire in connection with operations against Afghanistan, LG 3rd August 1920. Campbell married Ethel Lilian Ffinch (1875–1966) in 1895 at Brentford, Middlesex. They were living at 19 Hartington Mansions, Eastbourne, Sussex in 1939. It is understood they did not have children.

Clifford's paternal grandfather, Rear Admiral Francis Holmes Coffin RN (1768–1842), was born at Boston, Suffolk, Massachusetts. He served in the Royal Navy and was a lieutenant on HMS *Rattler* on 13th July 1791. He also served on HMS *Bulldog* June 1792–January 1794, HMS *Medusa* July–September 1794, HMS *Rattlesnake* September 1794–October 1795, HMS *Monarch* October 1795–August 1796 and HMS *Hope* before commanding HMS *Sphinx* 22nd August 1796–6th May 1797. Promoted commander 23rd August 1797 and captain 29th April 1802. He commanded HMS *Arethusa* 23rd January 1811–26th June 1813 and HMS *Gloucester* 6th August 1829–31st March 1831. Promoted rear admiral of the white on 17th August 1840. Francis married Rebecca Huddlestone née Mawby (c.1781–1842) on 25th June 1798 at Chatham, Kent. In addition to Isaac they had nine other children:

• Isabella Anne Coffin (c.1799–1882) married Thomas Leech Lennox Galloway (1794–1842), 10th Foot, and they had eleven children – Isabella Mary Ann Galloway 1824, Stewart Campbell Coffin Galloway 1825, Isabella Mary Anne Bertie Galloway 1826, Mary Ann Bertie Galloway 1829, William Francis Galloway 1830, Frederick Adam Galloway 1831, Sebright Freer Galloway 1833, Thomas Edward Galloway 1835, Jane Anna Galloway 1838, John Mawby Clossy Galloway (1840–1916) and Frank Lennox Galloway 1842. John was commissioned as a cornet on 1st September 1857 and served with 4th Madras Cavalry from 15th December. He served in the Indian Mutiny and Burmese Expedition 1886 and rose to major general on 25th May 1894.

- Maria Sarah Coffin (c.1806–78) died unmarried.
- Emily Coffin (born c.1810) married, as his second wife, Captain Carteret George Scott (born 1803),1st Regiment Madras Native Infantry, of Malleny, Midlothian on 21st August 1833 at St Mary's Church, Madras. Carteret had married Charlotte McDougall in 1830 at Edinburgh. Emily and Carteret had at least three children – Francis Cunningham Scott c.1835, Emily Scott c.1838 and George Scott c.1840.
- Frances Wilmot Coffin (c.1812–83) married John Murray and they had a daughter, Augusta. Frances died at Christchurch, New Zealand.
- Sebright Sheaffe Coffin (1814–93) married Charlotte Isabella Grant Martin (1820–1904) on 16th July 1840 at Boulogne-sur-Mer, France. Sebright retired as a lieutenant colonel Madras Light Infantry. They had eight children – Frances Jane Coffin 1841, Sophia Grant Coffin 1842, Mary Coffin 1844, Roger Pine Coffin 1847, Eleanor Coffin 1850, Sebright Edward Coffin 1852, Annie Grant Coffin 1853 and Isabella Susan Coffin 1860. Roger served in the Royal Marine Light Infantry 1864–1912, rising to general. Sebright Edward Coffin had a son of the same name (1886–1915), who was a planter in India and served in the Calcutta Light Horse and Bihar Light Horse as a trooper. He applied for a commission on 22nd May 1915 and was described as 5′ 4″ tall, weighing 184 lbs. He was commissioned in 3rd attached 2nd Royal Scots and served in France, where he received a gunshot wound to the abdomen on 18th December 1915. He was treated at No.10 Casualty Clearing Station, but died two days later (Lijssenthoek Military Cemetery, Belgium – II A 17). His mother was living at Prince of Wales Hotel, De Vere Gardens, Kensington, London and his father was in India at the time.
- Francis Holmes Coffin (1815–16).
- Rebecca Coffin (c.1816–94) died unmarried.
- Caroline Coffin (born c.1818) married James Thompson Macky (born 1800) on 4th July 1843 at Carrigans, Co Donegal. He was JP and DL, Co Londonderry, High Sheriff 1860 and JP Co Donegal. They had three children – William Macky 1844, Francis Coffin Mackey 1847 and Caroline Macky.
- Henry Townsend Coffin (born and died 1819).

His maternal grandfather, Major John Shepherd CB (1804–53), born at Westminster, London served in the Honourable East India Company Service and the Madras Army. He married Catherine Elizabeth Shepherd née Colley (1814–93) in 1831 at Gopalpur, Madras, India. He died in September 1853 at Cawnpore, India. She was living at 4 Sion Place, Bathwick Hill, Bath in 1858 and at 8 St Stephen's Crescent, Westbourne Park, Paddington, London in 1891. She died there on 31st January 1893, leaving £9,382/3/3 to her sons William and George. In addition to Catherine they had eleven other children:

- John Shepherd (born and died 1832).
- Louisa Mary Shepherd (1836–95), born at Secunderabad, India, married Henry Philip Hawkes (1834–1900) in 1855 at Bangalore. He was commissioned on 3rd March 1850, rising to lieutenant general on 9th January 1894 (CB, LG 25th November 1887). They had four children – Henry Phillip Hawkes 1856, Edith Louisa Hawkes 1857, Phillip Hawkes 1866 and Lilian Hawkes 1872. She died in February 1895 at The Old Rectory, Goring-on-Thames, Oxfordshire. Henry married Sarah Anne Dewrance (1856–1932) in 1897 at Farnham, Surrey. He died at the Porthminster Hotel, St Ives, Cornwall.
- Jane Shepherd (born and died 1837).
- William John Shepherd (1838–40).
- Harriet Jane Shepherd (1839–81) was born at Madras, India. She died unmarried in April 1881 at 92 Gloucester Crescent, London.
- William Shepherd (1842–1919) was born at Bangalore, India. He was commissioned as a lieutenant in the Bengal Engineers on 9th December 1859. He rose to lieutenant colonel on 10th January 1889 and retired on 12th February 1892. One of his appointments was Consulting Engineer for Railways Central Provinces. He was living at Thames Chambers, 12 York Buildings, Adelphi, London at the time of his death in August 1919, leaving £22,570/16/8 to his brothers Charles and George.
- Charles Edward Shepherd (1843–1923) was born at Chepanth, Madras, India. He was commissioned in the Indian Army on 19th December 1860. Promoted lieutenant 1st January 1862, captain 19th December 1872, major 19th December 1880, lieutenant colonel Bengal Staff Corps 19th December 1886 and colonel 19th December 1890. In 1895 he was Deputy Consulting Engineer for Railways Lucknow. He retired on the Unemployed Supernumerary List on 22nd March 1900. Charles married Eliza Kendall McDougall (1843–1925) in October 1874 at St John the Evangelist, Blackheath, London. He was badly mauled by a tiger in India, contracted malaria and suffered from lumbago. He suffered severe bouts of depression and committed suicide by cutting his throat on 19th March 1923 at his home at Stanhope Gardens, Kensington. The inquest verdict was, 'Suicide whilst of unsound mind'. Eliza was living at Iddesleigh, Granville Road, Sevenoaks, Kent at the time of her death in December 1925, leaving £3,773/14/4. Charles and Eliza had four children – Catherine Shepherd 1875, Charles Edward Shepherd 1878, Amy Dare Shepherd 1880 and Irene Martin Shepherd 1880.
- George Hutchinson Shepherd (1845–1928) was born in Singapore. He married Camilla Leonie Dolores formerly Drake née Metherall (1856–1941) in September 1910 at St Saviour, Paddington, London. Camilla was married previously to Reginald Drake (c.1844–1904) of the Indian Civil Service in 1875 at Mozufferpore, India. Reginald and Camilla were living at 3 Manor Park Crescent, Ealing, London in 1901. By 1911 George was a banker, living with his wife at Stansgate, Steeple, Essex. They were living at Becton Gouse, Barton-on-Sea, New Milton,

Hampshire at the time of George's death in April 1928. He left £77,389/15/11. Camilla was living at 33 West Cliff Road, Bournemouth, Hampshire at the time of her death in April 1941, leaving £17,170/13/- to her son, Lieutenant Colonel (Ret'd) Reginald John Drake (1876–1948). Reginald was commissioned in the North Staffordshire Regiment on 29th February 1896 and served in the Second Boer War 1900–02 and during the Great War. He was employed under the Military Governor Johannesburg June 1900–January 1901 and was Assistant Provost Marshal and Intelligence Officer Wakkerstroom November 1901–May 1902. He retired in April 1921, having been Mentioned in Despatches twice (LG 11th December 1917 and 5th July 1919). He was awarded the DSO, American Distinguished Service Cross, Belgian Order of the Crown 4th Class, Belgian Croix de Guerre and French Legion d'Honneur 4th Class.

- Mary Grace Shepherd (1847–1921) was born in Singapore. She lived at 18 Newton Road, Bayswater, London and died unmarried at a nursing home at 16 Grange Road, Ealing, Middlesex in July 1921, leaving £6,236/12/1 to her brother George.
- Helen Augusta Shepherd (1849–51) was born at Gopalpor, Tamil Nadu, India.
- Herbert Henry Shepherd (born and died 1852).

Clifford was educated at Haileybury College 1884–86 and the Royal Military Academy, Woolwich. He was commissioned on 17th February 1888 and promoted lieutenant 17th February 1891, serving with the Submarine Miners in Jamaica December 1891–March 1894. Submarine Miners oversaw observation and electro-mechanical defensive minefields in harbours.

Clifford Coffin married Helen Douglas née Jackson (4th March 1869–30th November 1949) on 22nd August 1894 at St Bartholomew's, Grays Inn Road, London. Helen was born at

Haileybury began in 1806 as the East India College, training administrators for the Honourable East India Company. It closed in 1858 and in 1862 a public school opened on the site, but close links remained with the East India Company. In 1942 Haileybury merged with the Imperial Service College, which had already merged with the United Services College, to become Haileybury and Imperial Service College, but was known simply as Haileybury. Among the school's many notable alumni are the dramatist Alan Ayckbourn, Bruce Bairnsfather the creator of 'Old Bill', Erskine Childers, author of 'The Riddle of the Sands', Field Marshal Lord Edmund Allenby, Air Chief Marshal Sir Trafford Leigh-Mallory, Prime Minister Clement Attlee and Sir Stirling Moss, the Formula 1 driver. The school has eighteen VCs and three GCs, including another brigadier general from the First World War, George William St George Grogan VC CB CMG DSO & Bar.

Kensington, London. They were living at The Terrace, Royal Dockyard, Devonport, Devon in 1901, at 17 Carmalt Gardens, Putney, London in 1911 and at Rystcot, Forest Row, near East Grinstead, Surrey in 1937. Clifford and Helen had four children:

17 Carmalt Gardens, Putney, London, where Clifford and his family were living in 1911.

- Geoffrey Coffin (born 1898) was educated at Stubbington House Preparatory School, Stubbington, near Fareham, Hampshire and emigrated to Canada in March 1924.
- Kathleen Coffin (25th December 1904–February 1998) was born at Standerton, Transvaal, South Africa. She was a governess c.1929 and died unmarried at Eastbourne, Sussex.
- Damaris Coffin (16th February 1906–8th May 1975) was born at Ealing, Middlesex and died unmarried at Heathfield, Sussex.
- Humphrey Coffin (30th December 1907–5th March 1973) was born at East End Manor Farm, Durrington, near Amesbury, Wiltshire. He was commissioned in the Worcestershire Regiment on 1st September 1927, rose to temporary major on 8th March 1942 and last appears in the Army List in June 1943.

Helen's father, Thomas Sturges Jackson (1842–1934), was the son of Reverend Thomas Jackson, Prebendary of St Paul's Cathedral (1812–86) and Elizabeth Prudence Fiske (1814–1907). He entered the Royal Navy in April 1856 and was appointed to HMS *Calcutta* as a midshipman. He was at the capture of the Peiho Forts in 1858 and was ADC to Captain WK Hall during the Second China War. Promoted sub-lieutenant July 1862 and lieutenant March 1864. He served on HMS *Marlborough* March–April 1864, HMS *Gibraltar* April–June 1864 and HMS *Orlando* June 1864–January 1866. He was appointed to the gunnery training ship HMS *Cambridge* at Devonport January 1866–June 1868. Having served on HMS *Lord Warden* June 1868–November 1870, he was appointed First Lieutenant of HMS *Excellent'* until November 1873. Promoted commander 1st November 1873 and attended the Naval College in July 1874, where he was awarded a £50 prize. He was appointed commander of the frigate HMS *Topaze* on detached service July 1874–May 1877 and HMS *Agincourt* July 1877–November 1879. He then commanded the training ship HMS *Implacable* at Devonport November 1879–June 1881. Promoted captain 14th October 1881 and was appointed to the Admiralty in June 1884 for special service as Naval Adviser at the War Office. Appointed captain of the corvette HMS *Comus* on the North America Station in 1886. He commanded the battleship HMS *Colossus* in the Mediterranean May 1890–September 1892 and was then appointed Commodore and Naval Officer in Charge Jamaica. He returned to Britain in October 1896. Promoted rear admiral and appointed Admiral-Superintendent of Devonport Dockyard July 1899–July 1902. In that appointment he was President of the Devonport Rifle Club. Promoted vice admiral 24th January 1902. Thomas was created KCVO during the Royal Visit to Devonport on 8th March 1902 for the launch of the battleship HMS *Queen*, the laying down of HMS *King Edward VII* and the laying of the foundation stone of Britannia Royal Naval College, Dartmouth. Promoted admiral 5th July 1905 and retired the same month. Thomas was a prominent member of the Navy Records Society and in 1889–1900

Clifford's father-in-law, Admiral Thomas Sturges Jackson (1842–1934).

edited the two-volumes *Great Sea Fights*, dealing with the logs of vessels involved in Nelson's and other operations 1794–1805. He was also a regular contributor to the Times. In April 1867, he married Helen Louisa née Gordon (1845–84) at St Barnabas, Kensington. Thomas was living at Cherries, Colchester, Essex when he died in September 1934. In addition to Helen they had seven other children:

• Thomas Jackson (1868–1945) entered the Royal Navy and attended Britannia Naval College July 1881–July 1883. Appointed midshipman 15th July 1883 and served on HMS *Achilles* in the Channel Squadron until April 1885. He then served on HMS *Bacchante*, flagship of Admiral Sir Frederick Richards, in the East Indies April 1885–November 1887 and saw action with the Naval Brigade during the Burmah War 1885–87. Promoted sub lieutenant 14th January 1887 and lieutenant 14th January 1889. He served on HMS *Monarch* May 1889–January 1890 and HMS *Rodney* January–September 1890 before HMS *Excellent* to qualify for Gunnery September 1890–July 1893, including an attachment to HMS *Barracouta* June–August 1891. In April 1893 he took unnecessary risks resulting in a collision between HMS *Excellent* and HMS *Enchantress*. He was appointed Gunnery Lieutenant on the cruiser HMS *Magicienne* in the West Indies August 1893–August 1895, followed by HMS *Excellent* January–March 1897 to requalify in Gunnery. His next appointments were the battleship

HMS *Colossus* (9,520 tons), launched in 1882 was the first modern battleship. Her armament consisted of four 12″ breechloaders and five 6″ guns. Several features in her design became standard thereafter for warships, including all steel construction, main armament mounted in turrets and propelled only by steam engines. She served with the Mediterranean Fleet 1886–93 and was broken up in 1908.

HMS *Victorious* in China June 1897–March 1900, during which he was promoted commander on 31st December 1899, HMS *Revenge* March 1903 and HMS *Rosario* March 1903–December 1904, during which he was lent to the legation in Tokyo for special service from 15th April 1904. He was selected for special service during the Russo-Japanese War in November 1904 and his cool gallantry was noted by Admiral Togo during the naval battle between the Russian and Japanese fleets in the Tsushima Straits. He was promoted captain on 1st January 1905 and appointed Naval Attaché in Tokyo January 1906. For his good work in Japan he was awarded the MVO 4th Class (LG 15th May 1906), CB (LG 9th November 1906) and the Japanese Order of the Sacred Treasure 2nd Class (LG 12th October 1906). The MVO was for his work during the special mission of Prince Arthur of Connaught to invest the Emperor of Japan with the Order of the Garter. Thomas returned to Britain to command the cruiser HMS *Cressy* in May 1907 and attended the Signal and War Course in September 1909.

In January 1912 he became Director of the Intelligence Division, Naval War Staff. He commanded the battleship HMS *Thunderer* November 1913–December 1914 in the Grand Fleet, then succeeded Rear Admiral AC Leveson as Director of the Operations Division at the Admiralty in January 1915. Promoted rear admiral 9th June 1916 and was appointed Senior Naval Officer Egypt and Red Sea 5th July 1917–31st December 1918. For his services during the Great War he was Mentioned in Despatches six times (LG 16th January 1918, 7th October 1918, 16th November 1918, 29th March 1919, 11th August 1919

Clifford's brother-in-law, Vice Admiral Sir Thomas Jackson (1868–1945).

and 15th December 1919). He was also awarded the Japanese Order of the Rising Sun 2nd Class (LG 2nd November 1917), Russian Order of St Stanislaus 1st Class, Egyptian Order of the Nile 2nd Class, French Legion d'Honneur (LG 27th May 1919) and the American Distinguished Service Medal (LG 12th December 1919). Promoted vice admiral 26th March 1920 and was created KBE (LG 23rd June 1923). He retired at his own request on 7th October 1923 and was promoted admiral on the Retired List on 8th May 1925. Thomas married Mona Anna

HMS *Cressy* was an armoured cruiser built around 1900. She served on the China Station until 1907 when she transferred to the North American and West Indies Station. Placed in reserve in 1909, she was recommissioned at the outbreak of the First World War and was involved in the Battle of Heligoland Bight. On 22nd September 1914 she and HMS *Aboukir* and *Hogue* were torpedoed and sunk by U-9. Cressy lost 560 of her crew.

Murray (1884–1945) in 1907 at Kensington, London. She was born at St Peter Port, Guernsey daughter of Colonel Henry Murray, Royal Munster Fusiliers. They lived at Waterside, Uplyme, Devon and had four children – Nancy Caroline Jackson 1909, Thomas Jackson 1911, Henry Murray Jackson 1913 and Prudence Barbara Jackson 1916.

- Charles Sturges Jackson (born 1871) was commissioned in the Royal Naval Reserve and was confirmed as sub-lieutenant on 24th December 1895. Appointed temporary lieutenant 16th November 1916 and served as Transport Officer Grade 1 at HMS *President VI*, the London accounting base for Coastguard ships and the Reserves 1918–26. He was living at 15 Disraeli Road, Putney, London in 1891. Charles was awarded his 2nd Mate Certificate 30th March 1894, 1st Mate 20th September 1895 and Master's 29th May 1897. He married Annie Mary Clara Brooks in 1900 at Cardiff, Glamorgan and they had two children – Evelyn Maud Jackson 1901 and Thomas Sturges Jackson 1903.
- Esther Louisa Jackson (1873–1949) married Commander Hugh Robert Evans RN (1852–1941) on 31st March 1894 in Jamaica. Hugh entered Britannia Naval College on 2nd May 1866 and served on HMS *Warrior* July 1867–July 1870. Appointed midshipman 30th January 1868 and served on the following ships/ establishments thereafter – HMS *Narcissus* July 1870, HMS *Excellent* October 1872 including Haslar Hospital 21st December 1872–30th January 1873, HMS *Amethyst* March 1873 including landing with the Naval Brigade 27th December 1873–27th January 1874, HMS *Cambridge* February–May 1875, HMS *Excellent* for Torpedo Course 2nd-11th May 1875, HMS *Duncan* October 1875, HMS *Terror* April 1877, HMS *Bullfinch* August 1877, HMS *Duncan* September–October 1878, HMS *Cambridge* February 1879–April 1879, HMS *Vestal* July 1879, HMS *Vernon* May–July 1880, HMS *Magpie* December 1880, HMS *Adelaide* July–August 1884, HMS *Vernon* April 1885, HMS *Cambridge* June 1885, HMS *Shannon* October 1885, Half Pay 22nd October 1887–23rd April 1888, HMS *Swiftsure* April 1888 including command of the ship as acting commander 20th May–2nd August 1889, HMS *Vivid* for HMS *Black Prince* as 1st Lieutenant 4th October–3rd November 1890, Half Pay 4th-20th November 1890, HMS *Vivid* for HMS *Black Prince* 21st November 1890; HMS Swiftsure as 1st Lieutenant May 1891, Half Pay 1st September–23rd October 1892, HMS *Urgent* in Jamaica October 1892, HMS *Pembroke* at Chatham January 1896–December 1897 and HMS *Alexandra* on coastguard duties. He was promoted sub lieutenant 29th July 1872, lieutenant 31st March 1874 and commander 30th June 1892, having been recommended by the Duke of Edinburgh. He transferred to the Retired List as a captain on 24th July 1902 and was granted a pension of £65 per annum from 8th May 1913. He applied for active service at the outbreak of the Great War but was considered too old. They were living at 6 Penare Road, Penzance, Cornwall in 1901 and at Belvoir House, Alphington, Devon in 1911. She was living at Crosslands, Alphington, Devon when she died. They had nine children –

Thomas Hugh Evans 1895, Robert Henry Evans 1897, Bertha Helen Evans 1898, Margaret Esther Evans 1900, Clara Joan Evans 1901, Douglas Frederick Evans 1904, Ursula Marian Esme Evans 1905, Leslie Ernest Olding Evans 1909 and George B Evans 1911.

- Harold Gordon Jackson (1875–1950) was a Naval Cadet at Britannia Naval College 15th January 1890–14th January 1892. He served on the following ships/establishments thereafter – HMS *Victory* January 1892, HMS *Blake* February 1892 including attachment to HMS *Cleopatra* December 1892, HMS *Tourmaline* August 1894, HMS *College*, *Vernon*, *Excellent* and *Victory* until December 1896, HMS *Duke of Wellington* January 1897, HMS *Wanderer* March 1897, HMS *Revenge* October, HMS *Excellent* to qualify for Gunnery September 1898 including attachment to HMS *Vindictive* for manoeuvres, HMS *Cambridge* July 1900, HMS *Sans Pareil* January 1901 during which he was relieved of duties as Gunnery Officer on 25th November 1901, HMS *Jupiter* March 1902 during which he was allowed to resume Gunnery duties, HMS *Revenge* December 1902, HMS *Prince of Wales* April 1904, Portland Hospital 7th July–5th October 1906 and HMS *Excellent* 16th April–2nd September 1907 to requalify in Gunnery. He was appointed to the Superintendent Staff, Woolwich 13th September 1907 and was an inspector at Sheffield in January 1911. He was promoted midshipman 15th January 1892, sub lieutenant 14th July 1895. lieutenant 14th January 1896 and lieutenant commander in January 1904. He retired at his own request on 1st January 1912 and was raised to captain. On 5th December 1914 he was appointed acting commander (retired) as Naval Ordnance Inspector. Promoted commander (retired) in July 1915 and awarded the OBE, LG 1st January 1919. On 5th March 1919 he was appointed Superintendent of Design, Design Section No.2. He was treated at Osborne Convalescent Home 4th-20th February 1924 and 27th-30th January 1926. From September 1925 he was Superintendent of Design, Design Department, Woolwich and was awarded the CBE, LG 3rd June 1929. He was appointed Naval Member Ordnance Committee as captain 15th August 1929–1st January 1932. Harold married Louisa Browne in August 1901 at Holywood, Co Down, Ireland and they had three children – Elizabeth M Jackson 1904, Robert Gordon Jackson 1908 and Gwendoline OL Jackson 1913. They were living at 31 Thornsett Road, Sheffield in 1911, at 5 Cambalt Road, Putney, London in 1920 and later at 1 Greenhill, Weymouth, Dorset.

- Esme Margaret Jackson (1878–1944) married Arthur Reuben Stannard (c.1890–1980) in July 1910 at St Paul's Church, Elk Lake, Nipissing, Ontario, Canada. She died at Victoria and he at Campbell River, both in British Columbia. They had four children – Esther Esme Juanita Stannard 1911, Aileen Violet Stannard 1916, Stella Stannard 1919 and Philip Stannard 1922.

- Maud Edith Jackson (1880–1972) married Major Norton Francis (1871–1939) in 1907. He had previously married the youngest daughter of Michael Studholme of Te Waimate in 1896, and she died in September 1902. Norton worked for two years in London at Lloyd's before moving to New Zealand in 1893 for health reasons and was a cadet on the Waimate Estate for two years. He purchased Point Bush block from the Waimate Estate and later increased his holding to 2,300 acres. A number of appointments followed – partner in Guinness and Le Cren in August 1901, Mayor of Waimate, chairman of Waimate Saleyards Co and President of A&P Association. During the Great War he served in Samoa and later took charge of the Base Records Office at Wellington (CMG, LG 1st January 1918). He was appointed a director of the Central Bank, Christchurch. They were living at 71 Rossall Street, Christchurch, New Zealand in 1935 and had four children including – George Norton Francis 1908, Phyllis Maud Francis 1909 and Marjorie Helen Francis 1912.

- Kate Duguay-Trouin Jackson (c.1882–c.1913). She was born aboard the boy's training ship, HMS *Implacable*, formerly the French ship *Duguay-Trouin*, in Devonport. She died in Cairo, Egypt.

Thomas Sturges Jackson married, secondly Marian Crane (c.1852–1920), in November 1892 at St Stephen, Kensington. She was born in New Brunswick, Canada. They had a daughter, Rose Marian Jackson, c.1895 in Jamaica. They were living at 7 The Terrace, HM Dockyards, Devonport, Devon in 1901 and at Ablington, Lansdown Road, Cheltenham, Gloucestershire in 1911. After the death of Admiral Claude E Buckle in 1930 Thomas was the senior officer of his rank on the Retired List and was regarded as the 'Father' of the Navy. Thomas died on 9th September 1934 at his home in Colchester, Essex.

Clifford Coffin served with 1st Fortress Company at Cork Harbour, Ireland. Promoted captain 17th February 1899. He was a French interpreter and attended the Staff College in 1899, graduating early due to the South African War 1900–02. He was Assistant to the Commander Royal Engineers (CRE) of 6th and 10th Divisions and was involved in actions during the relief of Kimberley, Paardeberg, Poplar Grove, Dreifontein and Zillikat's Creek. Clifford commanded a composite field company in Lord Roberts' final operations after the fall of Pretoria. **Mentioned in Lord Robert's Despatch of 4th September 1901 for leading a composite force of 9th and 7th Field Companies in Sir Ian Hamilton's column pursuing De Wet, LG 10th September 1901.** Appointed CRE Standerton until returning to Britain in September 1904. Appointed GSO3

The Staff College Camberley grew out of the Senior Department of the Royal Military College formed in 1802. In 1858 the Senior Department became the Staff College and in 1870 it separated from the Royal Military College. Except for during the two world wars, it operated until 1997, when it merged with its Royal Navy and Royal Air Force equivalent colleges to form the Joint Services Command and Staff College.

in the Intelligence Section, Army HQ 6th September 1904–31st March 1907. Promoted major 18th January 1907. He commanded 56th Field Company at Bulford and was GSO2 Sierra Leone 7th June 1911–6th June 1914.

Clifford was appointed CRE 21st Division August 1914–10th January 1917, including at Loos and on the Somme. Appointed temporary lieutenant colonel 9th June 1915 and promoted lieutenant colonel 22nd June. He went to France on 10th September 1915. He was temporary commander of 64th Brigade 18th–31st March 1916 and was appointed Chief Engineer XV Corps 22nd April–8th May 1916. **Awarded the DSO for distinguished services in the field while CRE 21st Division, LG 1st January 1917. Awarded the Russian Order of St Stanislaus 3rd Class with Swords while serving with the Canadian Engineers, LG 15th February 1917.** Appointed temporary brigadier general on 11th January 1917 to command 25th Brigade, which he did until 4th May 1918. In that time he was also temporary commander 50th Division 23rd February–17th March 1918.

Awarded the VC for his actions at Westhoek, Belgium on 31st July 1917, LG 14th September 1917. He was the first general officer to be awarded the VC. Appointed brevet colonel 1st January 1918. The VC was presented by the King at Buckingham Palace on 2nd January 1918. **Awarded a Bar to the DSO in March 1918 during the German spring offensive on the Somme; displaying personal courage and example during a long period of active operations. He handled his Brigade with great skill especially while covering the withdrawal of the remainder of his Division. On one occasion he also commanded the infantry of the Division with marked success, LG 26th July 1918.** Appointed temporary major general to command 36th Division, 6th May 1918–23rd March 1919.

The Russian Order of St Stanislaus 3rd Class with Swords, presented to Clifford Coffin in 1917.

Awarded the CB, LG 1st January 1919. Clifford was also awarded the Belgian Commandeur de l'Ordre de la Couronne LG 24th October 1919, Belgian Croix de Guerre LG 24th October 1919 and the French Officier de la Legion d'Honneur LG 15th December 1919. He was MID five times in Sir Douglas Haig's Despatches (LG 15th June 1916, 4th January 1917, 11th December 1917, 20th December 1918 and 5th July 1919).

Clifford was appointed temporary brigadier to command 1st Brigade, Western Division, British Army of the Rhine 24th March–15th September 1919. Promoted colonel 2nd

Clifford Coffin with his family after the VC investiture on 2nd January 1918.

June 1919. He remained a temporary brigadier while commanding 16th Brigade in Ireland 16th September 1919–17th April 1920. Appointed Commander Troops Ceylon 8th June 1920–1924 and ADC to the King 27th July 1920–1924. He went on Half Pay on 10th July 1924 and retired as honorary major general on 29th November 1924.

Clifford worked for the British Empire (Commonwealth) Ex-Service League and was Chairman of the Executive Council during the Second World War. He was Colonel Commandant Corps of Royal Engineers 1936–10th February 1940. In 1936 he managed to return a Dutch Bible he had brought back from South Africa to its previous owner, having traced the name written within it.

Clifford Coffin towards the end of his life.

Clifford Coffin died on holiday at Whitbourne, Museum Road, Torquay, Devon on 4th February 1959 and is buried in Holy Trinity Churchyard, Coleman's Hatch, East Sussex. He left £34,620 gross. His grave fell into complete disrepair and was renovated by members of the Victoria Cross Trust in 2013. He is also commemorated on:

- Royal Military Academy, Woolwich VC Memorial Board in the Royal Military Academy, Sandhurst library.
- For Valour board at the Royal Engineers Museum.
- Memorial plaque at Lewisham Shopping Centre, London unveiled by Philip Gardner VC in May 1995, commemorating fourteen VCs with local connections.
- The Department for Communities and Local Government decided to provide a commemorative paving stone at the birthplace of every Great War Victoria Cross recipient in the United Kingdom. A commemorative stone for Clifford was dedicated at Lewisham War Memorial, High Street on 31st July 2017 to mark the centenary of his award.

In addition to the VC he was awarded the Companion of the Order of the Bath, Distinguished Service Order and Bar, Queen's South Africa Medal 1899–1902 with four clasps (Relief of Kimberley, Paardeberg, Driefontein & Transvaal), King's South Africa Medal 1901–02 with two clasps (South Africa 1901 & South Africa 1902), 1914–15 Star, British War Medal 1914–20, Victory Medal 1914–19 with Mentioned-in-Despatches Oakleaf, George VI Coronation Medal 1937, Elizabeth II Coronation Medal 1953, Russian Order of St Stanislaus 3rd Class with Swords, French Officer of the Legion of Honour, Belgian Commander of the Order of the Crown and Belgian Croix de Guerre. Clifford stipulated in his will, *My full-sized orders, decorations and medals to be placed for the use of my brother officers of the Corps of Royal Engineers in any place the Chief Royal Engineer may from time to time consider suitable.* A memorial service was held in the Garrison Church, Chatham, Kent on 9th April 1959, following which his medals were presented to the Royal Engineers Museum, Brompton Barracks, Chatham, Kent, where they are held.

SECOND LIEUTENANT HUGH COLVIN
9th Battalion, The Cheshire Regiment

Hugh Colvin was born at Rose Grove, Burnley, Lancashire on 1st February 1887. His father, also Hugh Colvin (1856–1941), was born in Aberdeen, Scotland. He was a master gardener and was lodging with Mary Sexton at Ankerwyke Lodge, Wraysbury, Buckinghamshire in 1881. He married Jane née Stables (1856–1936), a domestic servant, on 12th June 1884 at Crofts of Clova, Kildrummy, Aberdeenshire. She was employed in the home of William and Rachel Cameron at Auchindoir and Kearn in 1881. They lived at various addresses:

- 1885 – Logie Buchan, Aberdeenshire.
- 1889 – Kildrummy, Aberdeenshire and then 3 Greenhill Yard, Gannow Lane, Burnley.
- 1893 – 33 Larkhill Road, Cheadle, Cheshire.
- c.1896 – Romiley, Cheshire.
- 1901 – 4 High Hatherton, Bredbury, Manchester, Lancashire.
- 1911 – 56 Lower Bents Lane, Bredbury.
- 1917 – 11 Moor Street, West Didsbury, Manchester.
- Before 1936 – Co Antrim, Northern Ireland.

Hugh had three siblings:

- Thomas Colvin (born 1893) was an assistant greengrocer in 1911. He married Annie McAuley (possibly born 1901) in 1919 and they had two children – Hugh Colvin 1920 and Gordon Colvin 1922.

Lower Bents Lane, Bredbury where the Colvin family was living in 1911.

The Gannow Lane area of Burnley.

- Margaret Colvin (1885–1951) was a felt hat trimmer. She married William Swindells (1880–1934) in 1908. They were living at 11 Tates Avenue, Lisburn Road, Belfast, Northern Ireland at the time of his death in January 1934. They had seven children – Kathleen Swindells 1909, David Swindells 1911, Ruth Swindells 1913, Jean Swindells 1915, Seth Swindells 1920, Victor Swindells 1922 and William Swindells 1925.
- Mary Helen Colvin (1889–1971) was a seasoner, incandescent mantles in 1911 and later qualified as a State Registered Nurse.

West Didsbury, Manchester.

Hugh's paternal grandfather is not known for certain, but when his father married in 1884 he recorded his father as Hugh Colvin, a deceased boilermaker. His paternal grandmother was Margaret Colvin (born c.1833), daughter of Hugh Colvin and Barbara Ogston (1792–1865). Margaret was a mill spinner.

Kennethmont, Aberdeenshire, where Hugh's maternal grandfather, John Stables, was born.

His maternal grandfather, John Stables (1824–1902), a farm servant and general labourer, was born at Kennethmont, Aberdeenshire. He married Jane née Thain (1823–78) in 1849 and they lived at Crofts of Clova, Kildrummy, Aberdeenshire. Jane had a son, John Stewart, born c.1847. John Stables committed suicide by drowning on 3rd November 1902 at Clova. In addition to Jane they had seven other children:

- Margaret Stables (born 1849) had a son, William Robertson, in 1867 with William Robertson (born c.1844), a police constable. Margaret married William Robertson in 1869. He was a shore porter by 1881. They were living at 10 Hanover Street, Aberdeen in 1881, 19 Hanover Street in 1891 and by 1901 were at 60 Rosemount Viaduct, Aberdeen by when William was a stevedore. They had nine children – Jane Robertson c.1870, John Robertson c.1872, Andrew Robertson 1873, Margarct Robertson c.1876, George Robertson c.1878, Christina Robertson 1880, Mary A Robertson c.1882, Alexander Robertson c.1884 and Williamina Robertson 1887. After Margaret died William married Margaret Dyker in 1888 and they had two children – Margaret Smith Robertson 1888 and Helen Yeats Robertson 1890.
- George Stables (1852–1939), a farm overseer, married Jessie Miller (1862–1939) in 1893. They had five children – John Alexander Stables 1894, Mary Ann Stables 1897, Donald George Stables 1898, William Stables 1900 and George Stables 1904.

- Ann Forbes Stables (1854–1928), a domestic servant, married John Sutherland (born c.1846), a farm servant, in 1875. They had nine children – Margaret Sutherland 1877, Mary Jane Sutherland 1879, Elizabeth Sutherland 1882, Helen Sutherland 1883, John Sutherland 1885, Jessie Ann Sutherland 1888, Annabella Sutherland 1890, Adam Sutherland 1892 and Dorothy Dickie Sutherland 1895.
- Mary Stables (born 1858) was living with her sister Helen in 1891. She was a housekeeper caring for her father at Crofts of Clova, Kildrummy in 1901.
- James Thain Stables (1860–1928) died at Vancouver, British Columbia, Canada.
- William Stables, a twin with Helen (1864–1912), was a draper's assistant, living with his father and sister Mary in 1901. He became a commercial traveller and never married.
- Helen Stables (1864–99) was living with her aunt, Margaret Thain, at Croft of Clova in 1881. She had an illegitimate daughter, Alice Mary Stables, in March 1889. Helen was a domestic servant when she married John Henderson (born c.1866), a butler, in August 1889. They were living at 24 Hanover Street, Aberdeen in 1891. He became a tobacconist and they moved to 9 Gilbert Crescent, Bucksburn, Aberdeenshire. They had five children – Helen 'Nellie' Henderson c.1890, Ion Francis Henderson 1894, Dorothy C Henderson c.1896, Annabella Henderson 1896 and Patricia Henderson c.1899. John Henderson married Susan Watt in May 1900 and they had twins – Katherine Elizabeth Henderson and James Burr Henderson in June 1900.

Hugh was educated at Hatherlow Day School, Romiley, Cheshire. He was keen on athletics, distance running and gymnastics. He was employed as a gardener in Lancaster and later moved to Belfast to live with his sister.

Hugh enlisted on 21st May 1908 in 8th (King's Royal Irish) Hussars (2919). He served in England for a year and then went to India with the Regiment in 1909. He was at Campbell Barracks, Dilkusha, Lucknow in 1911 and then at Ambala until 16th October 1914. He went to France with the Regiment as a lance corporal, landing at Marseille on 11th November 1914. He was promoted to lance sergeant and was commissioned in the Cheshire Regiment on 13th April 1917 and attached to 9th Battalion. **He received a GOC's commendation for patrol work near Messines on 15th-16th June 1917 – having searched the enemy positions his party mopped up a series of concrete dugouts hidden in a hedge and returned with valuable information about the location of enemy posts.**

Awarded the VC for his actions near Klein Zillebeke, east of Ypres, Belgium on 20th September 1917, LG 8th November 1917. The VC was presented by the King at Buckingham Palace on 28th November. Hugh received a civic reception at Chester on 3rd December and returned to France on the 7th. He became a company commander in March 1918 and was promoted lieutenant on 13th October. On 5th February 1919 he was appointed Supervisor of Physical and Bayonet Training, Army Gymnastic Staff and on 12th April was appointed

The promenade near Sandhurst Avenue, Blackpool.

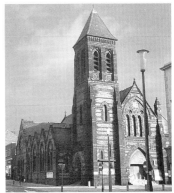

Hugh Colvin married Lilian Elsie Croudson at Christ Church, Blackpool in December 1920.

Assistant Superintendent and Chief Instructor, School of Physical Training, Army of the Rhine. He held the latter appointment until 24th October 1919 as a temporary major. Hugh served with 2nd Cheshire from November.

While gardening after the war he almost cut off his nose with a scythe. He pushed it back into place before going for medical assistance. It healed, leaving only a slight ridge at the tip. Hugh Colvin married Lilian Elsie née Croudson (9th August 1887–1960) at Christ Church, Blackpool, Lancashire on 29th December 1920. At the time he was living at 11 Moor Street, West Didsbury and she was living at 96 Cocker Street, Blackpool. They moved to 1 Sandhurst Avenue, Bispham, Blackpool and had a daughter, Marjorie Jean Marcie Colvin (5th October 1923–1951), known as Jean.

Lilian's father, William Henry Croudson (1859–1929) was a clerk in a gas office in 1891 and a rate collector in 1920. He married Mary Jane née Ash (1859–1927) in 1885. They were living at Cooper Street, Hook, Yorkshire in 1891 and at 12 Mount Pleasant, Atwick Road, Hornsea, Yorkshire in 1929. In addition to Lilian they had a son, William Henry Croudson (1891–1960), who was a shipbroker's clerk in 1929. He lived at 43 Marlborough Avenue, Kingston upon Hull, Yorkshire.

Hugh transferred to the 1st Battalion in India, where he escaped serious injury when a lorry overturned and fell twenty-five metres down a hillside. Promoted captain 17th October 1927 and retired on Half Pay on 1st February 1935. However, he was not out of uniform for long. He became a recruiting officer for North-Western Division in Chester and Preston as a local major with effect from 1st June 1938, working under Lieutenant Colonel Harry Daniels VC, Chief Recruiting Officer North-Western Division. Hugh retired again in 1947 and returned to Northern Ireland. In 1939 Lilian was living with her daughter at Edgewater, Pool Brow, Fylde, Lancashire. Hugh was boarding at 55 Upper Parliament Street, Liverpool due to his duties as a recruiting officer.

Hugh Colvin's grave in Carnmoney Cemetery.

The memorial to Hugh Colvin in Chester Cathedral. Note the incorrect spelling of Klein.

Hugh worked under Harry Daniels VC MC (1884–1953), Chief Recruiting Officer North-Western Division. Harry was awarded the VC for his actions at Neuve Chapelle France on 12th March 1915.

Hugh Colvin died at Bangor Hospital, Co Down, Northern Ireland on 16th September 1962 and is buried in Carnmoney Cemetery, Newtonabbey, Bangor, Northern Ireland. He is commemorated in a number of other places:

- Memorial chair and a memorial tablet set into the floor of the Regimental Chapel in Chester Cathedral.
- Blue Plaque at St Johns Court, Wordsworth Street, Burnley, Lancashire.

In addition to the VC he was awarded the 1914 Star with 'Mons' clasp, British War Medal 1914–20, Victory Medal 1914–19, Defence Medal, George VI Coronation Medal 1937 and Elizabeth II Coronation Medal 1953. The VC is held by The Soldiers of Cheshire, Cheshire Military Museum, The Castle, Chester, Cheshire.

CAPTAIN THOMAS RIVERSDALE COLYER-FERGUSSON
2nd Battalion, The Northamptonshire Regiment

Thomas Colyer-Fergusson was born at 13 Lower Berkeley Street, London on 18th February 1896. He was known as Riv. His father, Sir Thomas Colyer Colyer-Fergusson (1865–1951), assumed the additional surname of Colyer on marriage to Beatrice Stanley née Müller (c.1864–1902) on 30th January 1890. Sir Thomas held a number of appointments – Warden of Rochester Bridge, JP 1896 and High Sheriff of Kent 1906. He was elected life member of Kent Archaeological Society 1889 and served as Honorary

Treasurer 1903–04, Council Member and Vice-President 1946 until his death. He was also a Fellow of the Society of Antiquaries. The family lived at Ightham Mote, a moated medieval manor house, near Sevenoaks, Kent, which he purchased in 1889 (acquired by the National Trust in 1985). He also inherited Wombwell Hall, Northfleet, Gravesend, Kent from his mother. Sir Thomas married Mary Freda Cohen (1872–1964) on 28th July 1914 at Bramshott, Hampshire. Her father, Arthur Cohen PC KC, was Counsel to the Secretary of State for India 1893–1914. Sir Thomas succeeded as 3rd Baronet on the death of his father on 28th October 1924. Riv had five siblings:

Ightham Mote dates back to 1320. The house was in the Selby family from 1591 until sold to Thomas Colyer-Fergusson in 1889. He carried out extensive repairs and restoration. On Sir Thomas's death, the property passed to his grandson James, but the cost of upkeep and repair forced him to sell in October 1951. Three local men purchased the freehold to ensure it was not demolished or converted into flats. In 1953 the house was purchased by Charles Henry Robinson, an American, who made many repairs and partly refurnished it. When he died in 1985, Ightham Mote and its contents were bequeathed to the National Trust.

• Max Christian Hamilton Colyer-Fergusson (1890–1940) married Edith Jane White Miller (c.1881–1936), a singer, in 1913. She was born in Manitoba, Canada. They lived at Jacob's Knoll, Brimscombe, near Stroud, Gloucestershire. Max was commissioned in the Army Service Corps on 1st December 1914 and was promoted captain on 25th April 1916. He relinquished his commission, retaining the rank of captain, on 13th June 1919. Max was recalled to serve in the Royal Army Service Corps as a lieutenant (108042) on 2nd December 1939. He was killed during an air raid near Ludgershall, Wiltshire on 13th August 1940 and is buried in the churchyard of St Margaret's Church, Ifield, Kent. Max and Edith had a son, James Herbert Hamilton Colyer-Fergusson (1917–2004), who became the 4th Baronet on the death of his grandfather on 7th April 1951. He was an officer cadet in 163rd Officer Cadet Training Unit and was commissioned in The Buffs (Royal East Kent Regiment) on 25th February 1940 (121552). Promoted war substantive lieutenant 25th August 1941. He was a prisoner-of-war 1940–45 and last appears in the Army List in October 1946. James joined the Great Western Railway Traffic Department in 1947, later the Operating Department of Western Region, British Railways. Other appointments followed – Operating Superintendent's Office, Paddington Station (Western Region); Personal Assistant to Chairman of British

Riv's mother, Mary.

Transport Commission 1958–62; Passenger Officer, South-East Division of Southern Region, British Railways 1962; Parliamentary and Public Correspondent, British Railways Board 1967 and Deputy to Curator of Historical Relics, British Railways Board 1968. He created 'The Colyer-Fergusson Charitable Trust' in 1969.

The churchyard of St Margaret's Church, Ifield, Kent where Riv's brother, Max Christian Hamilton Colyer-Fergusson, is buried. He was killed during an air raid on 13th August 1940, 'Eagle Day' during the Battle of Britain.

- Mary Adelaide Somes Colyer-Fergusson (1892–1964) married Walter Turner Monckton (1891–1965) in 1914 and they had two children (see below). He was educated at Harrow and was the wicketkeeper in the famous Fowler's cricket match against Eton at Lord's in July 1910. One of the other team members was Harold Alexander, later Field Marshal Earl Alexander of Tunis. Of the twenty-two players, at least nine died in the two world wars. Walter went up to Oxford (BA & MA 1918), where he was President of the Oxford Union in 1913 and wicketkeeper for the Combined Oxford and Cambridge Universities team. He applied for a commission on 25th May 1915 and was described as 6' 1½" tall and weighed 160 lbs. He was commissioned in 4th Queen's Own (Royal West Kent Regiment) on 7th June. Appointed temporary lieutenant 24th December 1915, adjutant 1st June 1916–14th November 1917 and acting captain 10th November 1916. Promoted lieutenant 1st February 1917. Appointed acting major while second-in-command of 9th West Yorkshire 28th November 1917–12th June 1918. MID, LG 21st December 1917. Appointed temporary captain while employed as Education Officer, HQ 17th Division 14th December 1918–7th February 1919, when he was released. Awarded the MC, LG 3rd June 1919. He transferred to the TF Reserve on 7th September 1920 as a lieutenant. Promoted major in 4th Royal West Kent on 20th October 1920. His address on demobilisation was 20 Cliveden Place, Eaton Square, London. Walter qualified as a barrister (Inner Temple) 1919 and was appointed KC on 18th February 1930. He held a number of senior appointments – Recorder of the Borough of Hythe 1930–37; Commissioner of Assize on Midland Circuit 1943; Attorney-General to the Prince of Wales 1932–36, including during the abdication crisis; Attorney-General to the Duchy of Cornwall 1936–47 and 1948–51; Director-General, Ministry of Information & Deputy Under-Secretary of State for Foreign Affairs 1940; Head of Propaganda & Information Services, Cairo 1941; Solicitor-General May–July 1945. He was MP for Bristol West 1951–57, Minister of Labour and National Service 1951–55, Privy Counsellor 1951, Minister of Defence December 1955–October 1956 and Paymaster-General October 1956–January 1957. He was also President of

Surrey County Cricket Club 1950–52 and 1959–65, Chairman of Midland Bank 1957–64, Chairman of Iraq Petroleum Co 1958–65 and Chairman of the Advisory Commission on Central Africa 1960. Honorary DCL Oxford 1951 and LLD Bristol 1954 and Sussex 1963. Chancellor of the University of Sussex 1961–65. KCVO (LG 1st February 1937), KCMG (LG 1st January 1945) and GCVO (LG 1st January 1964). He was created Viscount Monckton of Brenchley on 11th February 1957 (LG 12th February 1967). Mary's marriage to Walter ended in divorce on 23rd June 1947 on the grounds of his adultery with the Countess of Carlisle. Walter married Bridget Helen Hore-Ruthven CBE (1896–1982), Baroness Ruthven of Freeland, Co Perth (formerly Countess of Carlisle) on 13th August 1947. She was the daughter of Major General Walter Patrick Hore-Ruthven CB CMG DSO JP DL, 9th Baron Ruthven of Freeland, and niece of the Earl of Gowrie VC PC GCMG CB DSO. Bridget joined the Auxiliary Territorial Service in 1938 and was commissioned as second subaltern (192026) on 30th September 1941. She was appointed controller in 1941 and senior controller as Director of Women's Auxiliary Corps, India 1944–46 (CBE, LG 1st January 1947). She succeeded as 10th Baroness in her own right on the death of her father in 1956. Her previous marriage to George Josslyn L'Estrange Howard, 11th Earl of Carlisle, in 1918 ended in divorced on the grounds of her adultery with Sir Walter Monckton. Walter's and Mary's two children were:

○ Gilbert Walter Riversdale Monckton (1915–2006) was commissioned in 5th Royal Inniskilling Dragoon Guards on 27th January 1938 and was awarded the MC for his actions in Belgium on 18th May 1940, LG 20th December 1940). Appointed GSO3 at the HQ of an armoured division 24th August 1940–20th October 1941. Acting captain 25th August–24th November 1940, war substantive lieutenant 25th November 1940, temporary captain 25th November 1940–20th October 1941 and lieutenant 1st January 1941. He attended Staff College at Camberley in 1941. Temporary captain 12th March–2nd September 1942. Appointed GSO3 at the HQ of an armoured division 12th March–20th May 1942. Appointed brigade major of an armoured brigade 21st May 1942–21st January 1943 and 26th February–22nd July 1943. Acting major 3rd June–2nd September 1942, war substantive captain 3rd September 1942 and temporary major 3rd September 1942–9th December 1943. He attended the Command and General Staff School in the USA, then transferred to 3rd (King's Own) Hussars and served in Palestine and Italy in 1944

Riv's sister, Mary Adelaide Somes Colyer-Fergusson, married Walter Turner Monckton, who held a number of senior government positions in the 1940s and 1950s. As a result of his opposition to Anthony Eden's policy over Suez in 1956, he was moved from the Ministry of Defence to be Paymaster-General.

and later in Germany. Temporary major 14th January 1944–26th January 1951, local lieutenant colonel 7th February–28th October 1944 and captain 27th January 1946. He attended the Royal Air Force Staff College in 1949 and was then GSO2 HQ 7th Armoured Division 3rd January 1950–15th July 1951. Major 27th January 1951. During the Korean War 1951–52 he rejoined 3rd (King's Own) Hussars and was appointed second-in-command. Temporary lieutenant colonel and GSO1 War Office 26th November 1953–8th January 1956. Lieutenant colonel 9th January 1956. Commanded 12th Royal Lancers in Germany. Temporary brigadier 7th July 1958–20th February 1963. Appointed Commander RAC with an infantry division 7th July 1958–3rd November 1960. Promoted colonel 21st February 1959 and brigadier 21st February 1963. Appointed Deputy Director of Personnel Administration, War Office 10th January 1962–31st January 1963. Promoted major general 10th April 1963 and appointed Army Director of Public Relations the same day until 7th February 1965, including during the Profumo Affair. His last appointment was Chief of Staff, HQ British Army of the Rhine in 1965 and he retired in 1967. He was appointed Colonel 9th/12th Royal Lancers 1967–73. He received numerous British and foreign awards – BStJ 1948, OBE 1956, OStJ 1964, Belgian Order of the Crown 1965, CB 1966, Grand Officer of the Belgian Order of Leopold II 1978, Bailiff Knights Grand Cross in Obedience of the Sovereign Military Order of Malta, Member of the Sacred Military Constantinian Order of Saint George, Knight Grand Cross of Justice and Knight Grand Cross of the Royal Order of Francis I. Gilbert married Marianna Laetitia Bower (born 1929) in 1950 and they had five children – Christopher W Monckton 1952, Rosamond Mary Monckton 1953, twins Jonathan St Quintin Riversdale and Timothy David Rober Monckton 1955 and Anthony Leopold Colyer Monckton 1960. He became the 2nd Viscount on the death of his father in 1965. In addition to running a 350–acre farm near Maidstone, Kent, he was on the board of Anglo-Portuguese Bank, Burberrys and Ransomes and attended the House of Lords regularly as a Conservative and later as a crossbencher. He was appointed DL Kent 1970 and was President of the Institute of Heraldic and Genealogical Studies 1965–2000. Marianna was appointed High Sheriff of Kent 1981–82 and Dame of Malta.

- Valerie Hamilton Monckton (1918–2003) joined the First Aid Nursing Yeomanry and the Auxiliary Territorial Service during the Second World War. She married Irish fertiliser manufacturer and art collector Sir 'William' Basil Goulding, 3rd Baronet, in 1939. He moved to England at the outbreak of the Second World War, was commissioned as a pilot officer in the RAF on 16th August 1940 (84407) and rose to wing commander. They returned to Ireland after the war. Valerie was an ardent campaigner for disabled people and co-founded the Central Remedial Clinic with Kathleen O'Rourke in 1951 to provide non–residential care for the disabled. She remained its chairman and managing director until 1984. She was nominated by the Taoiseach, Jack Lynch, to Seanad Éireann in 1977 and sought election to the Dáil twice as Fianna Fáil candidate, both times unsuccessfully. She was a possible candidate for the Irish Presidency in 1983, but Patrick Hillery was re-elected.

- William Porteous Colyer-Fergusson (1893–1974) enlisted in 16th Battalion, Middlesex Regiment (Public Schools) (901) at 24 St James' Street, London on 23rd September 1914. He was described as 5′ 6″ tall, weighing 140 lbs, with medium complexion, hazel eyes, light brown hair and his religious denomination was Church of England. Posted to 24th Battalion on 7th July 1915 and was awarded twenty-eight days detention and forfeited twenty-one days pay on 27th October. William was posted to 17th Middlesex in France on 21st April 1916 and arrived at 33 Infantry Base Depot, Étaples on 22nd April. He joined the Battalion on 4th May and was appointed unpaid lance corporal on 1st August. He received a gunshot wound to the back on 8th August and was treated at XIII Corps MDS and No.21 Casualty Clearing Station before being evacuated to England on 12th August. He was at the Convalescent Hospital, Woodcote Park, Epsom 6th–23rd September and was posted to B Company, 6th Battalion at Chatham on 2nd October. He applied for a commission on 20th October, by when he had grown to 5′ 7½″ and 150 lbs, and was posted to 16th Officer Cadet Battalion, Kinmel Park on 1st December. He was commissioned in 3rd Northamptonshire (Special Reserve) on 26th April 1917 and was attached to 2nd Battalion in France. On 26th July he was severely wounded when a dugout was blown up and he was crushed. He was evacuated via a casualty clearing station to hospital in Boulogne and embarked on HMHS *St Denis* at Boulogne on 1st August for Dover. He was treated at Prince of Wales' Hospital, Marylebone, London. From 23rd August he attended a number of medical boards and on each occasion was unfit for General Service for periods of two to six months. He was treated in an officers' convalescent hospital and on 3rd July 1918 was again found unfit for General Service, but fit enough for Home Service with 52nd (Graduated) Battalion, Northumberland Fusiliers. Promoted lieutenant on 26th October 1918. He was released on 12th February 1919 and was living at 25 Ball Road, Hillsborough, Sheffield at the time. He relinquished his commission on 1st April 1920 and was discharged from the Special Reserve on 9th November 1920, while living at 20 Oxford Street, London. William married Doris Dunstan Ford-Smith (1899–1986) in 1919. The marriage ended in divorce in 1938. Doris married Alfred Gustav von Kampf (1893–1986) in 1946 and they were living in Saxony, Germany 1947–48. William married Isobel Mary Fairbairn in 1964 and they lived at Barrhill House, Gourock, Renfrewshire and also on the Isle of Coll, Argyll and Bute. At one time he was Honorary Japanese Consul at Manchester, Lancashire.
- Phillis Katherine St Ledger Colyer-Fergusson (born 1900) married Captain John Naylor Hodgson-Wilson in 1922. They had two daughters – Rosemary Janet St Leger Hodgson-Wilson 1923 and Marjorie Cecile Mary Hodgson-Wilson 1925.

The marriage ended in divorce in 1934. Phillis married Theobald Henry Hinkson in 1938, but that marriage also ended in divorce in 1947.

- Beatrice Helen Valentine Colyer-Fergusson (1902–63) married Leonard Riddle (1887–1963) in 1930 and they had two children – Jane A Riddle 1932 and Ann B Riddle 1939.

Riv's paternal grandfather, Sir James Ranken Fergusson (1835–1924), 2nd Baronet, was the son of Sir William Fergusson, 1st Baronet, Surgeon to Queen Victoria. James married Mary Ann Somes née Colyer (1844–68) in 1862. In addition to Thomas they also had William Hamilton Colyer Fergusson (1864–73). They lived at Spitalhaugh, West Linton, Peeblesshire and Bordlands, Dolphinton, Lanarkshire. Sir James married Louise Forbes (born c.1845) in 1877 and they had a son, Louis Forbes Fergusson (1878– 1962), who was Clerk of the Council and Keeper of the Records of the Duchy of Lancaster 1927–45 (KCVO 1945). He wrote *Old Time Music Hall Comedians* in 1949. Louis married Elizabeth Frances Ethel Lewis (1898–1986) in 1922 and they had a daughter, Christine Forbes Fergusson, in 1934. They lived at 44 Combe Lea, Grand Avenue, Hove, Sussex. Sir James married for the third time, Alice Fanny Simpson (1857–1926), in 1886 and they had four children:

Riv's paternal great-grandfather, Sir William Fergusson, was a Scottish surgeon who accepted the professorship of surgery at King's College London in 1840. In 1849 he was appointed surgeon in ordinary to Albert, Prince Consort, and in 1867 sergeant-surgeon to Queen Victoria. In 1866 he was created a baronet and was President of the British Medical Association in 1873.

- Margaret Alice Hamilton Fergusson (1889–1969) married Cuthbert Archibald Lambton (c.1871–1946) in 1913. Cuthbert was the son of Lieutenant Colonel Francis William Lambton of Brownslade, Pembroke and Lady Victoria, daughter of 2nd Earl of Cawdor and the aunt of John Vaughan Campbell VC. They lived at Five Trees, Oatlands Chase, Weybridge, Surrey and had a son, John Ronald Lambton (1915–98).
- Helen Hamilton Fergusson (1890–1970) married Arthur Julian de Spiganovicz MD (1876–1925) in 1919. He was commissioned as surgeon lieutenant in 6th Volunteer Battalion, Royal Scots on 1st March 1907. Helen married Allan Rigden Finn MD (1879–1971) in 1933 and they had a daughter, Patricia A Finn, in 1934. Allan trained at St Mary's Hospital Medical School (MRCS LRCP 1904, MB BS London 1905, MD London 1907, FRCS England 1912) and became a ship's medical officer on a P&O liner. He was commissioned as a temporary lieutenant RAMC on 29th March 1915 and served with a field ambulance at Ypres and on the Somme. After the war he ran a medical practice in southwest London before joining Dr Simmons' practice near Newbury in 1923. He carried out general surgery at Newbury District Hospital and Sandleford Hospital, Newbury until

The La Ferté-sous-Jouarre Memorial commemorates 3,740 members of the BEF who fell at the Battles of Mons, Le Cateau, the Marne and the Aisne from August to October 1914, who have no known grave. It stands on the banks of the River Marne. It was unveiled by Sir William Pulteney, Commander of III Corps in 1914, on 4th November 1928.

joining the National Health Service in 1948. He was also doctor to Newbury race course for thirty years. He had been married to Jeanie V Bates (c.1883–1927) in 1913 and they had four children – Allan R Finn 1914, Jeanie V Finn 1916, Anthony J Finn 1918 and Audrey V Finn 1920.

- James Adam Hamilton Fergusson (1892–1914) was commissioned in the Highland Light Infantry on 14th February 1912 and was killed in action during the Battle of the Aisne on 20th September 1914 whilst serving with 2nd Battalion. He is commemorated on the La Ferte-sous-Jouarre Memorial, France. His lost grave was described as being *right of road leading to fallen caves on Verneuil Ridge*.
- Charles Hamilton Fergusson (1894–1953) served in 3rd (Reserve) attached to 6th Northamptonshire during the Great War. Promoted lieutenant 1st July 1917 and last appears in the Army List in July 1920. He emigrated to Kenya, where he and Richard Bingley were murdered by a gang of Mau Mau insurgents on his farm near Thomson's Falls on 1st January 1953.

Riv's maternal grandfather, Professor Friedrich Maximilian Müller (1823–1900), was born at Dessau, Leipzig, Germany, the son of the poet Wilhelm Müller (1794–1827) and Adelheid von Basedow, daughter of Präsident von Basedow, Prime Minister of the duchy of Anhalt-Dessau. He studied at the Universities of Leipzig and Berlin before emigrating to Paris and in May 1848 came to England and settled at Oxford. He was appointed Deputy Taylorian Professor of Modern European Languages at Oxford 1850, Professor 1854 and Curator of the Bodleian Library 1856–63 and 1881–94. He published *History of Ancient Sanskrit Literature* in 1859 and other works, which were known to Queen Victoria and the Royal Family. He was acquainted with Emperor Frederick of Germany, King of Sweden, King of Roumania and the Sultan of Turkey. He received numerous foreign awards – Prussian Pour le Mérite, Knight of the Corona d'Italia, Swedish Northern Star 1st Class and Grand Cordon, French Legion of Honour, Bavarian Maximilian, German Albert the Bear and the Turkish Medjidieh. He was an honorary doctor of Berlin, Bologna, Buda-Pesth, Cambridge, Dublin, Edinburgh, and Princeton Universities.

He was a foreign associate of the Institute of France, the Reale Accademia dei Lincei of Rome, the Royal Berlin, Sardinian, Bavarian, Hungarian, and Irish academies, member of the Imperial Academy of Vienna, the Royal Society of Upsala and the American Philosophical Society. Honorary member of the Royal Asiatic Society of Great Britain and Ireland, the German Oriental Society and more than twenty other societies. In Britain he became a Privy Counsellor in 1896. Frederick married Georgina Adelaide née Grenfell (c.1835–1916), great-aunt of Francis Octavus Grenfell VC, in 1859. They were living at 7 Norham Gardens, Oxford in 1881. In addition to Beatrice they had three other children:

- Adelaide Ashley Müller (1861–76).
- Mary Emily Müller (1862–86) was a translator of Wilhelm Scherer (1841–86), the philologist and historian of literature. She married Frederick Cornwallis Conybeare (1856–1924) in 1883. He was a British Orientalist, Professor of Theology at Oxford and Fellow of University College, Oxford. Frederick became a bishop in the Catholic Order of Corporate Reunion in 1894. He wrote a book on the Dreyfus case in the 1890s and translated the Testament of Solomon and other early Christian texts. He carried out influential work on Barlaam and Josaphat, was an authority on the Armenian Church and a member of the Rationalist Press Association 1904–15. One of his best-known works, *Myth, Magic, and Morals* 1909 was reissued as *The Origins of Christianity*. Frederick married Jane MacDowell (born c.1860 at Belfast) in 1888 and they were living at 13 Norham Gardens, St Giles, Oxford in 1891. Jane and Frederick had three children – John Josias Conybeare 1888, Irene Helena Conybeare 1890 and Edith Conybeare 1895.
- William Grenfell Max-Müller (1867–1945) was educated at Eton, where he won the Prince Consort's 1st German Prize, and at University College, Oxford (Hons in Jurisprudence 1889). He entered the Diplomatic Service and was assigned to Constantinople 1892–98, then The Hague, Washington and Madrid. After a spell in the Foreign Office 1902–05, he served in Mexico, was appointed Head of Chancery at Christiania in Denmark 1907, then to Peking, China as Counsellor and was often Head of Legation. In 1913 he was appointed Consul-General to Budapest, Hungary and was at the Foreign Office in London throughout the Great War. In 1920 he was appointed British Minister to the Polish Republic in Warsaw. He received a number of honours and awards – MVO 1908, CB 1911, KCMG 1922 and GBE 1928. William married Wanda Maria Heiberg (1883–1970) in Denmark in 1908 and they had two sons.

Riv was educated at Summerfields School, Oxford and Harrow 1909–14, where he was a sergeant in the Rifle Corps. He developed a passion for following the hounds and was an accomplished shot. He was due to go up to Oriel College, Oxford when war broke out. Instead Riv enlisted in 16th Middlesex (Public Schools) (1021) on 25th September 1914 at 24 St James Street, London. He was described as 5′ 4″

tall, weighing 139 lbs, with medium complexion, light hazel eyes, brown hair and his religious denomination was Church of England. He joined at Kempton Park on 27th September and was serving in I Company at Woldingham on 5th February 1915 when he applied for a temporary commission. He was posted to 3rd (Reserve) Northamptonshire at Weymouth on 19th February and received a temporary commission in the Special Reserve on 21st February.

Riv's maternal grandfather, Professor Frederick Maximilian Müller.

Francis Octavus Grenfell VC was Riv's maternal grandmother's great nephew.

Riv went to France to join 2nd Battalion on 5th December. He applied for a permanent commission on 25th February 1916, which was granted on 29th July with seniority from 4th July. Meanwhile he had received a gunshot wound to the right arm at Contalmaison on 7th July and was evacuated to England, embarking on SS *Maheno* at Boulogne on 9th July and arriving at Southampton on 10th July. A medical board at Tidworth on 2nd August found him unfit for service for three weeks and he was sent on leave until 23rd August. A medical board at the Military Hospital, Edinburgh on 1st September found he was unfit for

General Service for a month, but was fit for Home Service and he was attached to 3rd (Reserve) Northamptonshire at Gillingham, Kent. A medical board at the Military Hospital, Fort Pitt, Chatham on 6th October passed him fit for General Service and he returned to the front in November. Appointed acting captain on 8th December to command B Company. In February 1917 he led an attack on the ridge overlooking Bouchavesnes as the Germans pulled back to the Hindenburg Line. The attack swept across two lines of enemy trenches and into a third before it was realised the advance was beyond the objective. The line was pulled back and consolidated in the newly won position, where it was held against five counterattacks.

Awarded the VC for his actions at Bellewaarde, Belgium on 31st

Harrow School, founded in 1572, is one of the original ten public schools regulated by the 1868 Public Schools Act. Amongst its alumni are seven British Prime Ministers, including Robert Peel, Henry Palmerston, Stanley Baldwin and Winston Churchill, members of various royal families, Jawaharlal Nehru first Prime Minister of India and twenty VC and one GC winners. Other notables include Lord Byron, Wimbledon champions Spencer Gore and Frank Hadow, FA Cup founder Charles W Alcock, actor Benedict Cumberbatch, singer/songwriter James Blunt, rugby international Billy Vunipola and racing pundit John McCirick.

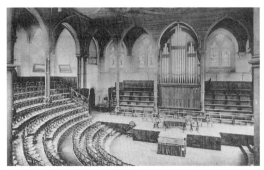

Harrow School's Old Speech Room is also a gallery and museum. It was completed in 1821 to encourage public speaking. The school's twenty VCs are commemorated there.

Bangour Hospital accepted its first mental patients from the Royal Edinburgh Asylum in 1904, although it did not open officially until October 1906. In 1915 Bangour Village Hospital was taken over by the War Office as the Edinburgh War Hospital and the staff and number of beds were increased to cater for the influx of wounded. By 1918 it had a capacity of 3,000 patients in wards, huts and marquees. Bangour reopened as a psychiatric hospital in 1922, but in 1939 again became the Edinburgh War Hospital. In 1989, St John's Hospital opened nearby in Livingston and services were transferred from Bangour General Hospital until it closed in the early 1990s. The Village Hospital closed in 2004.

July 1917, LG 6th September 1917. He was wounded during his VC action and died at 24th Field Ambulance later the same day. He is buried in Menin Road South Military Cemetery, Belgium (II E 1). On 21st August his prismatic binoculars in a case with sling and gold wristwatch and strap were sent to his father. Riv left £3,001/9/5 in his will. As he never married, the VC was presented to his father at Buckingham Palace on 20th October 1917. A war gratuity of £63 and £5 for his commissioned and non-commissioned service respectively was paid to his father on 14th November 1919 in accordance with the Royal Warrant of 10th February 1919. Riv is commemorated in a number of other places:

Riv's grave in Menin Road South Military Cemetery, Belgium.

Ightham War Memorial. (*Marathon*)

- Harrow School Speech Room with the other School VCs.
- War memorials at:
  - Ightham, Kent.
  - St Peters Church, Ightham, Kent and a plaque in St Catherine's Chapel.
  - Ivy Hatch Mission Church, now at Kent Life Museum, Sandling, Kent. The Ivy Hatch Roll of Honour is at Igtham Mote.
  - St Margaret's Church, Ifield, Kent.
  - Northfleet, Kent.
  - All Saints Church, Perry Street, Northfleet, Kent and memorial plaque inside.
  - Perry Street, Northfleet, Kent.
  - Old Town Hall, High Street, Gravesend, Kent.
  - Clarence Place, Gravesend, Kent.
  - West Linton Section, Peebles, Borders, Scotland.
- His original wooden grave marker is in Ightham Mote new chapel.
- Colyer Road, Northfleet, Kent.
- The Department for Communities and Local Government decided to provide a commemorative paving stone at the birthplace of every Great War Victoria Cross recipient in the United Kingdom. A commemorative stone for Riv was dedicated at Embankment Gardens, Whitehall, London on 26th June 2017 to mark the centenary of his award.

Memorial plaque in St Peters Church, Ightham, Kent. (*Michael Garlick*)

Riv's wooden grave marker in the chapel at Ightham Mote.

In addition to the VC he was awarded the 1914–15 Star, British War Medal 1914–20 and Victory Medal 1914–19. The VC passed to Sir James Herbert Hamilton Colyer-Fergusson, 4th Baronet, following the death of Sir Thomas Colyer Fergusson, before being presented to the Regiment. It is held by the Northamptonshire Regiment Museum, Abington Park, Northampton.

R/2794 SERGEANT EDWARD COOPER
12th Battalion, The King's Royal Rifle Corps

Edward Cooper was born at 38 Saint Ann's Terrace, Portrack, Stockton-on-Tees, Co Durham on 4th May 1896. He was known as Ned. His father, William Edward Cooper (1859–1925), was a labourer and a steelworker, born at Dudley, Staffordshire. He married Anne née Mackie (born 1864), a stocking knitter, born at Nether Sunnyside, Drumoak, Aberdeenshire, in 1882. They lived at 38 St Anne's Terrace, Portrack, Stockton-on-Tees and by 1901 had moved to 15 Barrett Street and to 12 Barrett Street by 1911. Ned had eight siblings:

(*Gazette Live*)

- Alexander John Cooper (1884–1968) was a shipyard labourer in 1901 and a steelworks labourer in 1911. He married Rose Hannah Crawford (1891–1966) in 1913. She was born at Sacristan, Co Durham as Rose Anna Crawford and was a general servant in 1911, working at Lydford House, Crossgate Peth, Durham. They had three children – an unnamed male (born and died 1914), Irene Cooper 1915 and Alexander Cooper 1917.
- Jane Cooper (born 1886) was living with her aunt, Esther Muter, at 26 Gallant Terrace, Howdon in 1911.
- Annie Cooper (born 1888) was a dressmaker in 1911.
- Jessie Cooper (born 1890).
- Emma Cooper (born 1893).
- Arthur Cooper (born 1899).
- Edith Cooper (born 1902).
- Martha Cooper (born 1909).

Ned's paternal grandfather, John Cooper (c.1832–1908), an oil merchant, was born at Much Wenlock, Shropshire. He married Jane née Brandon (c.1834–97) in 1857 at Stourbridge, Staffordshire. She was born at Sutton Coldfield, Warwickshire. They moved to 2 Cardigan Street, Stockton-on-Tees. John was living with his son William in 1901. In addition to William, John and Jane had five other children:

- John H Cooper (born c.1861) was a labourer in 1881.
- Emma Jane Cooper (1866–71).
- Sarah Louisa Cooper (1868–1950) married Robert Hird (1868–1958) in 1890. He was a rolleyman with the North Eastern Railway Company in 1911. They lived at 36 Hartington Road, Middlesbrough and had five children including – Albert Hird 1891, Edith Jane Hird 1892, Evelyn Blanche Hird 1897 and Robert Hird 1906.
- Mary Elizabeth Cooper (1870–1956) married Henry Matthew Oxborough (c.1869–1929) in 1888. He was born at Deeson, India and was a manager in a pawnbroker's shop in 1911. They lived at 3 Melville Street, Darlington and had ten children – John Henry Oxborough 1889, Annie Oxborough 1891, William Matthew Oxborough 1891, Margaret Jane Oxborough 1893, Louisa Oxborough 1895, Frederick Oxborough 1899, Florence Elizabeth Oxborough 1902, Ethel Blanche Oxborough 1904, Thomas Arthur Oxborough 1907 and Albert H Oxborough 1911.

- Thomas Arthur Cooper (c.1873–1937) was a butcher. He married Helen Elizabeth Forsyth (1879–1938) in 1898. They were living with her mother at 5 Station Street, Stockton-on-Tees in 1911. Thomas and Helen had five children – Alice Elizabeth Cooper 1899, Mabel Cooper 1902, George William Cooper 1904, Catherine Cooper 1910 and Thomas A Cooper 1912.

Ned's maternal grandfather, Alexander Mackie, was born at Fochabers, Moray, Scotland.

His maternal grandfather, Alexander Mackie (c.1831–98), a shoemaker, was born at Fochabers, Moray, Scotland. He married Jane L née Souter (c.1830–89), born at Kincardine, in 1857 at Banchory Ternan, Kincardineshire. They were living at 23 Florence Street, Stockton-on-Tees in 1871 and at 22 Mitre Street in 1881. He was living at 41 Cecil Street, Stockton-on-Tees in 1891. In addition to Anne they had six other children:

- Alexander Gordon Mackie (1858–1915) was a clerk in a fruit shop in 1871, an accountant's clerk in 1881, a clerk in an iron works by 1901 and a traffic manager in a blast furnace in 1911. He married Lina Edith Croft (1868–1918) in 1895. She was an assistant schoolmistress by 1911. They had three children – May Mackie 1895, Madge Mary Mackie 1898 and Alexander Croft G Mackie 1900.
- Mary Jane Mackie (1860–1947) married Featherstone Tutty (1851–1922), a miller grinder, in 1884. They were living at 3 Providence Place, Thornes Lane, Wakefield, Yorkshire in 1911 and had three children – Robert Henry Tutty 1885, Margaret Gertrude Tutty 1889 and Harry Tutty 1896.
- Jane 'Jinnie' Elizabeth Mackie (1862–1940) married William Bland (1869–1947), a general labourer in a marine engineering works, in 1895. They were living at 11 Millbank Street, Stockton-on-Tees and by 1911 had moved to 12 Albert Road. They had at least three children – Florence Leah Bland 1896, Edith Mary Bland 1898 and Margaret Esther M Bland 1901.
- John James Mackie (1866–1937) was a telegraph messenger in 1881. He married Elizabeth Jane Watson (1868–99) in 1894 and they had three children – Elspeth Mackie 1895, John James Mackie 1897 and Florence Mackie 1899. Elizabeth died in November 1899, almost certainly linked to the birth of her daughter, Florence, who also did not survive. John married Emily Jane Boot (1873–1927) in 1902. By 1911 he was a postman with the General Post Office, living with his family at 7 Buckingham Street, Stockton-on-Tees. John and Emily had five children – Donald Mackie 1904, twins James and John Mackie 1906, Ronald Mackie 1911 and Jean Mackie 1914.
- Esther Beattie Mackie (1867–1911) married Isaac Muter (c.1855–1930), a ship's plater, in 1893. They lived at 26 Gallant Terrace, Howdon and had three children

including – Alexander Spence Muter 1895 and Isaac Muter 1903.
- Margaret Ogg Mackie (born 1869) married John George Sparke in 1899. They lived at 41 Cecil Street, Stockton-on-Tees and had two children – John Mackie Sparke 1901 and Elsie Mackie Sparke 1903.

Ned was educated at Bailey Street Council Schools until aged thirteen. He played football for the school team for two years and for local clubs on leaving school. He was employed as an errand boy in his uncle's, Thomas Cooper, butcher's shop. After about a year he became assistant fruit carter with the local Cooperative Society and in 1911 got his own cart. When war broke out the Army commandeered most of the horses and he found himself without a job. He enlisted on 7th September 1914 and spent six months in a camp at Bisley, Surrey. Ned went to France on 23rd July 1915 and was promoted sergeant on 13th March 1917.

Edward Cooper receives his VC from the King on 26th September 1917.

Awarded the VC for his actions at Langemarck, Belgium on 16th August 1917, LG 14th September 1917. The VC was presented by the King outside Buckingham Palace on 26th September 1917. He returned to the Battalion in time for the Battle of Cambrai in November 1917. **Awarded the French Médaille Militaire for rescuing wounded men under fire on the Menin Road, LG 10th October 1918.** Ned claimed he had no idea what the award was for. Having returned to England for officer training, he was commissioned on 26th June 1918 into the same Battalion and returned to France on 4th September. Ned was demobilised on 27th January 1919 and returned to work for the Cooperative Society.

Ned Cooper married Iris Kate née Morris (born 1897) on 6th November 1919 and they eventually lived at 113 Whitton Road, Stockton-on-Tees. They had three sons:

- Maurice born 4th June 1920.
- Keith born 18th March 1922.
- Harry born 20th September 1926.

Iris' father, David Edward Morris (c.1875–1946), was living with his parents at 44 Thornaby Road, Thornaby in 1881. He married Margaret Elizabeth A née Picken (c.1876–1958) in 1895. She was living with her parents at 50 & 52

The French Médaille Militaire, awarded for meritorious service or bravery in action, is the third highest award of the French Republic. During the First World War 230,000 were awarded. Foreign recipients include the black American fighter pilot Eugene Jacques Bullard, Winston Churchill, Dwight D Eisenhower, and Field Marshal Bernard Montgomery (Fdutil).

Hymer Street, Ormesby, Yorkshire in 1881. By 1901 David was a ship's boilermaker and they were living at 23 St Martins Avenue, East Ham, Essex.

Ned became the Cooperative warehouse manager in Sunderland in 1926 and returned to Stockton as the fruit department manager in 1938, a post he retained until he retired in 1961. He was very active in the community, being a JP for over twenty years and helped with various church, youth and ex-service organizations, including President of the Thornaby Royal British Legion, President of the Thornaby Citizens Advice Bureau and Secretary of the local Soldiers', Sailors' and Airmen's Families Association. He was also a Sunday school teacher, superintendent, deacon and elder of the United Reformed Church for forty-five years.

Edward Cooper towards the end of his life. (*Gazette Live*)

Ned was a Freemason, being Initiated into Saint John's Lodge No.80 on 14th May 1929 while working in Sunderland. On returning to Stockton-on-Tees, he joined the Lodge of Unity No.6003 on 22nd October 1945. In 1957 he was presented with a silver salver by the Stockton Freemasonry Lodges to mark the centenary of the inauguration of the VC. His son Harry was initiated into the Lodge of Unity in May 1958, as was Keith in February 1965. Ned, Harry and Keith were founder members of the Lodge of Justice No.8361 on 20th March 1971. Ned also proposed his grandson Graham for Initiation to the Lodge of Unity in April 1974. In May 1979 about 200 Brethren assembled in Saint John's Lodge No.80 in Sunderland to celebrate the fiftieth anniversary of Ned's Initiation. In 1983 he was appointed Past Assistant Provincial Grand Pursuivant for Durham.

Ned attended every VC reunion until his death, including the Garden Party at Buckingham Palace in June 1920, the House of Lords dinner in November 1929, the Victory Day Celebrations Dinner in June 1946, the VC Centenary Celebrations in June 1956 and every VC & GC Association Reunion from the first, on 24th July 1958, until the thirteenth, on 6th October 1983.

During the Second World War he helped to set up the Thornaby Home Guard and was appointed captain in 3rd North Riding (Thornaby) Battalion on 1st February 1941. He was promoted major to command G Company, 9th North Riding (Middlesborough) Battalion at Thornaby on 8th December 1943. On 13th May 1944, Ned Cooper VC and Tom Dresser VC were granted the Freedom of Middlesbrough. Ned was granted the Freedom of Stockton-on-Tees on 24th July 1985.

Edward Cooper taking the salute at a passing out parade at Winchester in the 1970s. (*Ted Cooper*)

Ned Cooper was admitted to North Tees Hospital, Stockton-on-Tees and watched a documentary on his life on television, but five hours later he suffered a heart attack and died on 19th August 1985. The place of death was recorded as the General Hospital. He was cremated at Teesside Crematorium and his ashes were scattered there in the August plot of the Garden of Remembrance. His name is recorded in the Book of Remembrance. He is also commemorated in a number of other places:

- Bronze commemorative plaque in Stockton Library dedicated on 16th August 1977.
- King's Royal Rifle Corps Regimental Memorial in Winchester Cathedral, Hampshire.
- Cooper Room, Masonic Hall, Stockton-on-Tees opened on 19th May 1997.
- Cooper Square, Durham.

In addition to the VC he was awarded the 1914–15 Star, British War Medal 1914–20, Victory Medal 1914–19, Defence Medal, George VI Coronation Medal 1937, Elizabeth II Coronation Medal 1953, Elizabeth II Silver Jubilee Medal 1977 and French Médaille Militaire. The VC is owned privately and is loaned to Preston Hall Museum, Stockton-on-Tees, having previously been displayed at the Green Dragon Museum, Stockton-on-Tees until 2009.

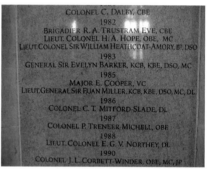

The King's Royal Rifle Corps Memorial in Winchester Cathedral records distinguished members of the Regiment by the year of their death. (*Memorials to Valour*)

4926 SERGEANT CHARLES HARRY COVERDALE
11th Battalion, The Manchester Regiment

Charles Coverdale was born at 53 Clifford Street, Brooks' Bar, Old Trafford, Manchester, Lancashire on 21st April 1888. He was known as Harry. His father, John Yates Coverdale (1851–1915), an upholsterer, was born at Kirkleavington, Yorkshire. He was lodging at 69 Warwick Street, Hulme, Lancashire prior to his marriage to Emily née Goddard (1853–1923) in 1881. In 1871 she was a nurse working with her sister Martha, a housemaid, for James Fort at Beaumont Manor, Cheshunt, Hertfordshire. By 1881 she was a cook working for Charles Hilditch Richards at 2 The Beeches, Seymour

Grove, Stretford, Manchester. She was working for Mary J Chesworth at 581 Stretford Road, Stretford, Manchester in 1901 and she was still there in 1911 as a housekeeper. They also lived at 7 Skirton Road, Old Trafford, Manchester. Harry had six siblings:

Oxford Street, Old Trafford, where it intersected Clifford Street.

- Emily Ann Coverdale (1882–1929) was a clerk in 1901 and 1911. She married Thomas G Whittle in 1926 at Leeds, Yorkshire (1895–1967). He married Miriam Collinge (1904–43) in 1931 and they had two daughters – Adrienne Whittle 1932 and Joan Whittle 1939.
- Mabel Mary Coverdale (1884–1944) was a dressmaker in 1901. She married Harry Denton Davies (1874–1936) in 1906. He was a commercial traveller working for warming and ventilating engineers in 1911, when they were living at 58 Cromwell Avenue, Didsbury, Chorlton, Lancashire. They had three children – John Denton Davies 1907, Harry Coverdale Davies 1909 and Stanley E Davies 1915.
- John William Goddard Coverdale (1887–1929) was a clerk in 1911. He married Ada England in 1916 and they had two children – John Goddard Coverdale 1917 and George Coverdale 1918.

Warwick Street, Hulme, where Harry's father, John Coverdale, lodged prior to his marriage.

- Edward Percy Coverdale (1890–1949) was a compositor in 1911. He married Laura Jones in 1924.
- Florence Sunniva Coverdale (1892–1969) was an upholstress in 1911. She was the beneficiary of her brother Harry's home and contents at 37 Ingfield Avenue, Dalton, Huddersfield following his death in 1955 and she subsequently lived there. She died unmarried.
- Frances Ella Coverdale (1893–1946) was a clerk in 1911. She married George Stevens in 1924.

Harry's paternal grandfather, John Coverdale (c.1822–1904), born at Crathorne, Yorkshire, was a master carpenter. He married Ann née Lamb (c.1821–95), born at Kirkleavington, Yorkshire,

Beaumont Manor, Cheshunt, Hertfordshire, where Harry's mother, Emily Goddard, was a nurse working for James Fort in 1871 (Christine Matthews).

in 1846 at Stockton, Co Durham. She was a general servant in 1841 working at the home of Robert Bell at Kirkleavington. In 1861 they were living at Kirkleavington. By 1871 they had moved to 15 Southampton Street, Darlington, Co Durham. In 1881 they were at 8 Southampton Street, by 1891 at 6 Fern Street and by 1901 at 5 Peel Street. In addition to John they had five other children:

- Elizabeth Coverdale, born in 1847 and believed to have died in 1864.
- James Coverdale (1854–1919) was a bolt maker in 1871. He married Elizabeth Ellen Sowerby (1860–1934) in 1881. By 1911 he was a blacksmith on the railway and they were living at 38 Osborne Road, West Hartlepool, Co Durham. They had three children – Ethel Lamb Coverdale 1883, John Edwin Coverdale 1886 and Charles Coverdale 1888.
- Robert Thomas Coverdale (1858–1930), a carpenter and joiner, married Mary Ellen Rudge (1862–1939) in 1889. She was born at Tipton, Staffordshire and was a dressmaker in 1881. Mary's sister, Alice Florence Rudge, was living with them at Stephenson Street, Tynemouth in 1891 and at 76 Norfolk Street, Tynemouth, Northumberland in 1901. Robert and Mary (recorded as Thomas and Ellen) were still living there in 1911, by when he was a wagon wright for a railway company. They had two children, including Maud Coverdale, in 1892.
- William Coverdale (1861–1931), a painter in 1881, married Hannah Arrowsmith (1867–1945) in 1890. They were living at 46 Dickinson Street, Darlington in 1891 and at 46 Harrison Street, Darlington in 1911. They had two children – John W Coverdale 1892 and Hilda Coverdale 1895.
- Jane Ann Coverdale (1865–1926) looked after her parents until at least 1901. She married John Wetherell (born 1858), a joiner with the North Eastern Railway Company, in 1905. They were living at 23 Stanley Terrace, Darlington in 1911.

His maternal grandfather, William Goddard (1821–87), born at Harborough Magna, Warwickshire, was a bricklayer. He married Mary née Collier (c.1818–95), a dressmaker, in 1842 at Rugby, Warwickshire. They were living at Pennington Street, Rugby in 1861. She was living alone at Badby, Northamptonshire in 1891. In addition to Emily they had six other children:

- Elizabeth Frances Goddard (1843–1922) was a dressmaker in 1861. She married Thomas Walton (born 1839) in 1867. She was living with her unmarried daughter Florence at New Villa, Badby, Northamptonshire in 1911. She was recorded as married, but her husband was not with her and his whereabouts are unknown.

Harry's maternal grandparents, William and Mary Goddard, were living at Pennington Street, Rugby in 1861.

They had seven children – Thomas W Walton 1868, Charlotte Elizabeth H Walton 1869, Florence Emily Walton 1871, John G Walton 1873, Edward Harry Walton 1875, Mary Ann Walton 1878 and Ellen Frances Walton 1883.

- Edward Goddard (1845–1918) was a bricklayer in 1861. He married Sarah A Moss (1840–1914) in 1866. They often lived apart due to his work commitments. She was living with her daughter, Sarah, at 62 James Street, Rugby in 1871. By 1881 he was a builder's foreman, boarding at Melton Mowbray, Leicestershire. They were living at 7 Spencer Terrace, Fulham, London in 1891. Edward was living at 89 Elsham Road, Kensington, London in 1901 with Euphemia (c.1849–1907) who was recorded as his wife, but no marriage record has been found. Sarah was living at 32 Lowestoft Road, Watford, Hertfordshire with her daughter, Sarah, in 1911. Her husband was not present, but she was recorded as married. They had three children – Sarah Elizabeth Goddard 1867, John Edward Goddard 1875 and Katie Goddard 1883.
- Martha Goddard (1848–1928) was a housemaid in 1871 working for James Ford and his family at Beaumont Manor, Cheshunt, Hertfordshire. She married William Saville (born 1848), a labourer, in 1872. They were living at Heronfield, Hertfordshire in 1881 and at Church Green, Badby, Northamptonshire in 1911. They had five children, including Ernest William Saville 1874, John A Saville 1876 and Sydney Harry Saville 1880.
- Mary Ann Goddard (1851–1933) was a servant in 1871, working with her sister Emily. She married George Beeston (1852–1915) in 1879. They had four children – Mary Ann Beeston 1880, Emily Beeston 1882, Martha Hall Beeston 1885 and William George Beeston 1889.
- John Goddard (born 1856).
- William Goddard (1858–1932) married Mary Elkington (1858–1915) in 1885. He was a builder's foreman in 1891 and they were living at London Road, Weedon Beck, Northamptonshire. By 1911 he was a clerk of works (building) and they were living at Heath Villa, Virginia Waters, Berkshire. They had a daughter, Emily F Goddard, in 1888.

Harry was educated at a local church school in Manchester and at Bangor Street Board School, Hulme, Manchester. He was employed as an engineering fitter at Galloway's Boiler Works, Knott Mill, Manchester. Harry wanted to join the Royal Engineers, but had to wait, so on 7th September 1914 he enlisted in 4th (Extra Reserve) Manchester and was engaged on coastal defence duties at Riby, near Grimsby, Lincolnshire. He was promoted lance corporal on 3rd April 1915 and was charged with neglect of duty on 10th August while in charge of No.4 Blockhouse at Killingholme, for which he received a severe reprimand. He transferred to 11th Battalion and served with it at Gallipoli from 20th September. The Battalion was evacuated on 15th December on the *Carron* and ferried to Mudros. He went to Egypt on 30th January 1916 and embarked at Alexandria on the *Transylvania* or *Toronto* on

3rd July, disembarking at Marseilles, France on 8th July. He was appointed acting corporal on 27th October and acting sergeant on 16th December (later confirmed in the rank with the same seniority date). **Awarded the MM for holding an objective 200m north of the cemetery on the Langemarck–Zonnebeke road after all the officers and senior NCOs had been killed on 16th August 1917, LG 2nd November 1917.** The award appeared in XVIII Corps Routine Orders on 12th September. He was presented with the DCM ribbon in the field in error and this was replaced by the MM a fortnight later.

Harry was educated at Bangor Street Board School, Hulme, Manchester. It has since been demolished.

Awarded the VC for his actions southwest of Poelcapelle, Belgium on 4th October 1917, LG 18th December 1917. He was posted to the Depot on 14th January 1918 and to Depot West Lancashire Reserve Brigade, Oswestry as a candidate for a commission on 29th January. He trained at No.16 Officer Cadet Battalion, Kinmel Park, Rhyl from 22nd March, but severely sprained his left knee in a football match on 10th April and was in hospital 12th April–5th June. He was commissioned in the Manchester Regiment on 9th October 1918 and attached to 11th Battalion, but was posted to 3rd (Reserve) Battalion at Cleethorpes. The VC was presented by the King at Buckingham Palace on 31st October 1918. Harry was demobilised on 5th February 1919 from 4th Manchester and relinquished his commission, retaining the rank of second lieutenant, on 1st September 1921. He was presented with a silver rose bowl by Stretford Council in 1919. On 7th July 1921 he was presented to the Prince of Wales outside Manchester Town Hall in

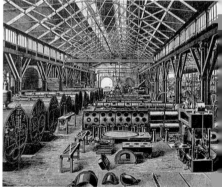

W & J Galloway and Sons was a major manufacturer of steam engines and boilers, established in 1835 by William and John Galloway. The company went into receivership in 1932. The sketch shows the inside of the workshops in 1894.

Albert Square together with fellow VCs George Evans, John Readitt, and George Stringer.

Harry returned to engineering work and on 29th October 1919 he married Clara Florence Travis née Riley (1889–1940) at Barton upon Irwell, Lancashire. Clara's surname changed from Riley to Baron when her mother married in 1895. She was a mantle presser in 1911 and married Frederick Robert Travis, a packer, on 28th September 1912. They had a son, George Travis, in 1913 and were living at 17 Rudyard Street, Queens Park, Harpurhey, Manchester in October 1915. Frederick enlisted in the Royal Garrison Artillery on 26th October 1915 (60232), described as 5′ 10″ tall and weighing 119 lbs. He joined at Brockhurst, Gosport on 28th October. He was posted from the Heavy Artillery Depot to 3rd Reserve Battery on 24th February 1917, to the Siege Artillery School, Deepcut on 3rd October and then to 452nd Siege Battery RGA. He served in Britain with X Bty, 2nd Reserve Brigade RGA in Manchester until going to France on 5th February 1918 to the RGA Base Depot. He was appointed acting lance bombardier next day and was posted to 22 Observation Group, 4th Field Survey Company on 24th February. He was attached to 1st Field Survey Company on 10th May and was admitted to No.11 Casualty Clearing Station with a cyst on his neck 9th July–1st August. He died of pneumonia at the New Zealand Stationary Hospital, St Omer, France on 3rd November 1918 and is buried at Longuenesse (St Omer) Souvenir Cemetery, France (V E 20).

SS *Carron* (1017 tons) was launched in 1894. She was sunk as a blockship in Holm Sound, Scapa Flow in 1940.

Harry was one of the VC Honour Guard at the burial of the Unknown Warrior at Westminster Abbey on 11th November 1920. Harry and Clara were living at 7 Skirton Road, Old Trafford, Manchester in March 1920 and had moved to 17 Spring Lane, Radcliffe, near Manchester by January 1930. In 1955 they were living at 37 Ingfield Avenue, Dalton, Huddersfield. They had two sons:

- Charles Harry Coverdale (born 1922) married Freda M Marsden (1923–77) in 1946. They had two children – Stephen R Coverdale 1947 and Judith S Coverdale 1951.
- David Coverdale (born 1927).

Marseilles was the arrival port in France for most of the troopships arriving from Egypt after the end of the Gallipoli campaign.

Clara's father, Joseph Baron (1866–1911), a locksmith, was living with Mary Ellen née Riley (c.1872–1963) in 1891 at 10 Ely Terrace, Mile End Old Town, London. She was born at Burton-on-Trent, Staffordshire. They had moved to Manchester by 1893 and married there in 1895 having had two children already. In 1901 they were living at 26 Law Street, Manchester. In 1911 he was a bookmaker's clerk and they were living at 29 Turkey Lane, Queen's Park, Manchester. Mary was living at 3 Romily Street, Queens Park, Manchester in 1914. She married Arthur Isherwood in 1921. In addition to Clara, Joseph and Mary had three other children:

- William Riley (born 1894). His surname had changed to Baron by 1901. He was a porter in 1911 and a labourer when he enlisted in 21st Manchester on 11th December 1914 (19568), described as 5' 6" tall and weighing 141 lbs. On 16th July 1915 he was confined to barracks for four days for causing a disturbance in the lines and using obscene language to an NCO. He served in France from 10th November and was employed as a batman from 23rd January 1916 with 21st Field Ambulance and HQ 91st Brigade. He was wounded in October 1917 and evacuated to England. More disciplinary problems followed, including being absent on 18th January 1918. On 6th May he was sentenced to twenty-eight days detention to be served at Mold for being absent at Knowsley Park. He received four days remission and rejoined 4th Manchester on 30th May, but went absent again from Tetley Lock on 13th June and was declared a deserter next day.
- Mark Baron (born 1896) was a grocer's assistant in 1911. He was killed in action serving with 21st Manchester (19885) on 29th August 1916 and is commemorated on the Thiepval Memorial, France (Pier and Face 13 A & 14 C).
- Mary Ellen Baron (1901–47) had a son, William Baron, in 1921. She married Nathan Webster (1902–55) in 1924 and they had two children – Thomas Webster 1924 and Brian Webster 1937.

Harry attended the VC Garden Party at Buckingham Palace on 26th June 1920, the VC Dinner at the Royal Gallery of the House of Lords, London on 9th November 1929 and the Victory Day Celebration Dinner and Reception at The Dorchester, London on 8th June 1946. He moved his family to Yorkshire in 1930, where he became chief engineer of four mills owned by Joseph Lumb's & Sons in Huddersfield. They lived at 37 Ingfield Avenue, Dalton, Huddersfield.

During the Second World War Charles joined the Home Guard and was commissioned in 26th West Riding (Huddersfield) Battalion on 1st February 1941. He was promoted lieutenant on 1st August 1942 and served until the Home Guard stood down on 3rd December 1944. When the Home Guard was resurrected against the growing Soviet threat, he was appointed lieutenant on 8th May 1952 in 25th West Riding Battalion, Huddersfield Sector, East and West Riding District Home Guard. He was promoted captain on 13th May 1955.

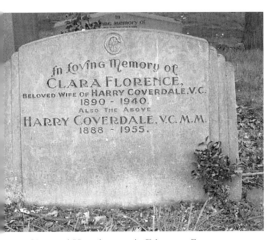

Clara and Harry's grave in Edgerton Cemetery, Huddersfield. (*Memorials to Valour*)

The memorial to Harry Coverdale and Ernest Sykes in Huddersfield Town Hall. (*Memorials to Valour*)

Harry Coverdale died at Huddersfield Royal Infirmary on 20th November 1955 and is buried in Edgerton Cemetery, Huddersfield (5G 105). He is also commemorated on a plaque dedicated to him and Ernest Sykes VC at Huddersfield Town Hall.

In addition to the VC and MM he was awarded the 1914–15 Star, British War Medal 1914–20, Victory Medal 1914–19, Defence Medal, George VI Coronation Medal 1937 and Elizabeth II Coronation Medal 1953. The VC is held privately.

21654 PRIVATE FREDERICK GEORGE DANCOX
4th Battalion, The Worcestershire Regiment

Frederick Dancox was born at Crown Lane, Claines, Worcester on 19th March 1878 as Frederick John Dancocks. The family name, Dancocks, was corrupted to Dancox when he enlisted. His father, William Dancocks (1840–80), a general labourer, married Louisa née Chance (1853–1929), a glove maker, on 12th July 1875 at St Martin, Worcester. They lived at St Stephen's Terrace, Claines and by 1880 were at Perdiswell Terrace, Droitwich Road, Claines. In 1881 she was living with her father and three sons at 24 Droitwich Road, Claines. Louisa married William Whittle (1851–1937), a labourer and widower, on 19th August 1883 at Holy Trinity Church, Worcester. He lived at Tolladine Road, Worcester and in 1881 was living with his widowed mother, Eliza, at Rose Cottages, Claines. William Whittle's age varies widely between census returns and his surname is also seen as Whittall and Whittal. William and Louisa were living at 35 St George's Lane, Claines in 1891 and at 59 Hylton Road, Worcester in 1901, by when he was a domestic groom. By 1911 he was a carter and they were living at 1 Hood Street, Worcester. They were living at 6 Court, Carden Street, Worcester in the early 1920s. William had three sons from his previwous marriage:

The Thiepval Memorial built between 1928 and 1932, originally commemorated 73,077 men from the United Kingdom and South Africa who died on the Somme before 20th March 1918 and have no known grave. It also serves as an Anglo-French memorial to the joint 1916 Somme offensive. Over the years names have been added and remains have been identified, resulting in a net reduction of the total commemorated to 72,245. It was designed by Sir Edwin Lutyens to straddle the main Albert – Bapaume road at Pozieres, but it was decided to move it to Thiepval. The memorial was unveiled by the Prince of Wales on 1st August 1932, in the presence of the French President. The missing of other Commonwealth countries who have no known grave are commemorated on national memorials elsewhere.

- William John Whittle (1874–1918) served as a private in 2/8th Worcestershire (240625) and was killed in action on 31st March 1918 (Pozières Memorial, France).
- Herbert Whittle (1875–1927) was a labourer in 1891.
- Thomas Whittle (born 1877) may have served in 1/7th Worcestershire (20723) and was killed on 21st August 1916 (Thiepval Memorial, France).

Frederick had eight siblings:

- William Thomas Dancocks (1875–1914) served in South Africa during the Boer War and was a hay trusser in 1911. He was a private in 3rd Worcestershire (4304) when he was killed in action on 23rd October 1914 (Le Touret Memorial, France).
- Henry 'Harry' George Dancocks (1880–1907) was a hay trusser in 1901. When he married Rosina 'Rose' Fletcher (1878–1960), a glove maker, in 1900, he was registered as George Henry Dancox. They had a son, William Henry Dancocks, in 1900. Rosina married Ernest C Ledbury (1876–1937) in 1919 and they had two children – Eva MD Ledbury 1919 and Ernest HC Ledbury 1921.

- Elizabeth Annie Whittle (born 1883) was a general domestic servant in 1901 and 1911. She married Walter Purnell Rodway (born 1888) in 1913 at Worcester. He was a farmer

The Le Touret Memorial with inset William Dancocks' name.

who emigrated to Canada and applied for a homestead at Calgary, Alberta on 23rd August 1909. He returned to Britain, married Elizabeth and they both emigrated to Canada. They had a daughter, Nina Rodway, in 1915 in Canada and were living at Bow River, Alberta in 1916.

- John Arthur Whittle (born 1886), registered as John Arthur Whittell, was a hay trusser in 1901.
- Alice Jane Whittle (1888–1950), registered as Whittell, was a domestic servant in 1911. She married Disney Randolph Reynolds (1883–1963) in 1912 at Worcester. He was an apprentice baker in 1901 living with his parents at Holly Cottage, Malvern, Worcestershire. He was assisting his sister Ermina Amanda Marshall and her husband William Edwin Marshall with their dairy and greengrocer's business at St John's, Worcester in 1911. They had two daughters – Gladys E Reynolds 1913 and Norah E Reynolds 1920.
- Agnes Whittle (born 1891), registered as Sarah Agnes Whitall, was a bristle brush maker in 1911.
- Dorothy Whittle (born c.1893).
- Lucy Mabel Whittle (born 1895), registered as Whittall, married Arthur F Attwood (1896–1962) in 1937.

Frederick's paternal grandfather, Thomas Dancocks (1815–1905), an agricultural labourer, married Mary 'Maria' née Glover (c.1811–66) in 1838. In 1841 and 1851 they were living at White Ladies Aston, Worcestershire. In 1861 they were at Low Hill, Stoulton. In 1901 he was in Pershore Workhouse. In addition to William they had George Dancocks (born c.1839).

His maternal grandfather, William Chance (c.1808–87), an agricultural labourer, married Elizabeth née Footman (c.1815–63) in 1845. She was a dressmaker in 1851 and a glove maker in 1861. They were living at Fordraft Lane, Tibberton, Worcestershire in 1851 and 1861. By 1871 he was living with his daughter, Louisa, at Old Barn Lane Cottages, Hindlip and was still there in 1881. In addition to Louisa they had two other children:

- Rose Ellen Chance (1845–1909) was recorded as Rosaline in the 1851 Census. She was a glove maker in 1861 and married John Rutter (1844–76) in 1866. They had four children – Elizabeth Ellen Rutter 1867, Julia Rose E Rutter 1868, Caroline Fanny Rutter 1872 and Henry George Rutter 1874. Rose was living with her children at 14 Spa Row, Worcester in 1881 and James Robinson (born c.1856), a general labourer, was boarding with the family. Rose married James in 1888 and they had moved to 6 Askew Square, Little Charles Street, Worcester by 1901, by when James was a bricklayer's labourer. James and Rose had three children – Beatrice Robinson 1889, Ethel Robinson 1893 and Albert Robinson 1896.
- John Chance (born 1849).

Frederick was educated at St Stephen's School, Worcester and was then employed as a hay trusser. Frederick married Ellen née Pritchard (1884–1967), registered at Pershore, Worcestershire in the first quarter of 1915. Ellen was a shop assistant living with her parents in 1901. They lived as husband and wife long before they married. In the 1911 Census they were boarding with James and Charlotte

Pershore Poor Law Union formed in September 1835 and the workhouse was built the following year. In the 1930s it became a Public Assistance Institution and later an old people's home.

Harris at 1 Church Square, Merrivale, Worcester and declared that they had been married for twenty years, which was not possible given their ages. It appears that they legalised their union about the time of his enlistment in order that she would be eligible for allowances and a widow's pension in the event of his death. Initially they lived at 12 Court, Dolday, Worcester. They had five children:

- Frederick George Dancocks was born c.1899 at Worcester according to the 1911 Census, but does not appear in the 1901 Census. The birth of a Frederick Herbert Dancox was registered in Worcester in the first quarter of 1902. This birth matches the death of a Frederick G Dancox in the first quarter of 1962. Frederick married Phoebe Bills (1900–72) in 1922. She was living with her parents at 5 Willow Place, Dent Street, Worcester in 1911. They had five children – Vera C Dancox 1922, Irene R Dancox 1925, Eleanor Dancox 1928, Frederick T Dancox 1932 and William R Dancox 1935.
- Florence May Dancocks (born 1906) married William A Cox in 1929. They had three daughters – Eileen S Cox 1929, Jessica H Cox 1932 and Patricia L Cox 1936.
- Harry Dancocks (born 1909) was living with his paternal grandparents in 1911. He is understood to have married Carrie Webb (born 1914) in 1934 at Worcester. They had a daughter, Marian F Dancocks, in 1939.
- Ellen 'Nell' Dancocks (born 1913) married John Henry Brookes (1918–74) in 1947 and they had a daughter, Vivienne C Brookes, in 1950.
- George Dancocks (1915–16).

Ellen's father, William Pritchard (born 1862), was born at Cleobury Mortimer, Shropshire. He was a tailor living with his mother and stepfather, Frederick and Hannah Norton, at 67 Mill Street, Kidderminster in 1881. He married Sarah Jane née Flavell (1862–1923) in 1881. She was a redoubler in spinning mills, boarding with William S Barnett and his family at 125 Wood Street, Kidderminster, Worcestershire. By 1891 they were living at 25 Chapel Street, Kidderminster and at 57 Oxford Street, Kidderminster in 1901 and 1911, by when he was a master tailor. In addition to Ellen they had seven other children, but four died prior to 1911. Those known are:

- William Pritchard (born 1885) was a tailor.
- Albert Henry Pritchard (born 1888) was a tailor living with his parents in 1911.
- Arthur Pritchard (1890–1908).
- Edmund/Edward Pritchard (born 1894) was a tailor living with his parents in 1911.

Frederick enlisted in March 1915 and served at Gallipoli from 19th September. He was evacuated to Egypt on 14th January 1916 and disembarked in France on 20th March. **Awarded the VC for his actions at Namur Crossing, near Poelcapelle, Belgium on 9th October 1917, LG 26th November 1917.** He was granted fourteen days leave to return to England for the investiture, but was delayed by a German counterattack during the Battle of Cambrai. He was killed instantly by a piece of shrapnel in the head near Masnières, France on 30th November 1917 and is commemorated on the Cambrai Memorial. Preparations were well advanced for a civic reception and welcoming party at home when the news of his death arrived. The VC was presented to his widow by the King outside Buckingham Palace on 31st July 1918. Frederick is commemorated in a number of other places:

- Dancox Sheltered Housing, St Clements Gardens, Worcester.
- Memorial information board unveiled at Namur Crossing on 9th September 2006. The ceremony was attended by Frederick's great grandson, John Jones-Newton, together with Fred, Bill and Stuart Dancox and Lance Corporal Jones-Newton.
- Memorial at the Deansway entrance to CrownGate [sic] Shopping Centre, Worcester dedicated on 13th May 2010 with his grandson, Fred Dancox, in attendance.
- Named on the war memorial at All Saints Church, Deansway, Worcester.
- A painting of the VC action by Captain Gilbert Halliday is held by the Museum of the Worcestershire Soldier.

Ellen moved to a small house in Bull Entry, Worcester and struggled financially. The house was demolished during slum clearance in the 1930s. The City of

The Cambrai Memorial to the Missing with Frederick Dancox's name inset.

Dancox Sheltered Housing in Worcester.

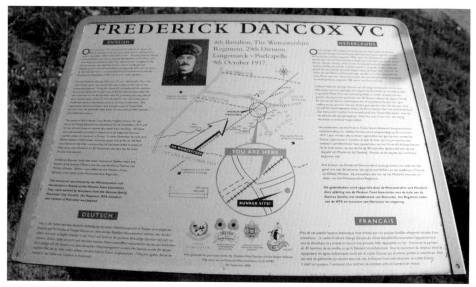

The Dancox memorial at Namur Crossing.

Worcester established a public fund for her and made an initial donation of £50. In February 1918 the Council was concerned that, *subscriptions were not coming in very satisfactorily*, but eventually £451 was raised. Ellen laid a wreath of poppies at the City's war memorial in 1932 in the presence of the Prince of Wales (later King Edward VIII).

In addition to the VC he was awarded the 1914–15 Star, British War Medal 1914–20 and Victory Medal 1914–19. Ellen was forced to sell the VC in the early 1920s due to financial difficulties. It was originally displayed with the King's letter to her in the foyer of Worcester Guildhall. It is now held by the Museum of the Worcestershire Soldier, City Museum & Art Gallery, Foregate Street, Worcester Worcestershire.

All Saints Church, Worcester where Frederick is commemorated on the war memorial as Frank Dancox.

31161 CORPORAL JAMES LLEWELLYN DAVIES
13th Battalion, The Royal Welsh Fusiliers

James Davies was born at 14 Lethbridge Terrace, Victoria, Ebbw Vale, Glamorganshire, Wales on 16th March 1886. His father, John Davies (1856–1942), spoke Welsh fluently and worked in a steelworks and later in a coalmine. He married Martha née Llewellyn (1861–1937) at the English Wesleyan Chapel, Tredegar, Monmouthshire on 26th December 1880. She was born as Martha Wellings (also seen as Welings/Welling), but the reason for the change of her surname is not known. They were living at 14 Lethbridge Terrace, Victoria, Ebbw Vale in 1881, at 18 Fronwen Terrace, Llangeinor, Glamorgan by 1891, at 16 Fronwen Terrace by 1901, at 46 North Vale, Nant-y-Moel by 1911 and at 42 Vale View, Nant-y-Moel in 1919. They also lived at Wyndham, Ogmore Vale and at 8 Nant-y-Moel Row, Nant-y-Moel. James had nine siblings:

- Thomas Henry Davies (born 1880) was a coal miner hitcher in 1911.
- Mary Alice Davies (born 1884) married Benjamin James in 1902 and they were living at 28 Nant-y-Moel Row, Nant-y-Moel in 1911. They had five children – Mary Ethel James 1902, Reginald John James 1904, Edwin Clifford James 1906, Annie Maud James 1908 and Bertie James 1910.
- George Edward Davies (1890–1960), was a coal hewer. He married Alice Maud Saunders (1890–1955) in 1910. They had two daughters – Cecilia G Davies 1912 and Iris G Davies 1914.

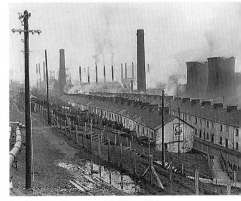

Lethbridge Terrace with Ebbw Vale steelworks in the background.

- Susan Davies (1892–1936) married Charles Harry Saunders (1892–1970) in 1913.
- Richard Edwin Davies (1893–1980) was a coal miner hewer in 1911. He married Hannah Mary Hughes (1898–1971) in 1921.
- William John Davies (born c.1896) was a coal miner hewer in 1911.
- Alfred Davies (born 1898).
- Stanley Davies (1901–1972) was a labourer in a colliery. He married Elizabeth Jane Edwards (1906–92) in 1923. They had two sons – Granville Royston Davies 1924 and John David Davies 1931.
- Silwyn Davies (born 1910).

James' paternal grandfather, Henry Davies (c.1819–93), was a railman and later a locomotive lamp cleaner. He married Margaret née Owens (c.1817–85) in 1841. In 1861 they were living at 131 Briery Hill, Bedwelty, Monmouthshire and by 1881 were at 34 Library Row, Bedwelty. In addition to John they had five other children:

• David Davies (born c.1842) was a puddler in 1861.
• Thomas Davies (born c.1844) had a son, Johnny Gwynne Davies (1888–1957), whose mother is not known.
• Anne Davies (born c.1846).
• Joshua Davies (born 1849).
• Sara Davies (born c.1851).

His maternal grandfather, Thomas (Llywellyn) Wellings (c.1832–1911) was a labourer in a limeworks in 1861 and later an ostler. He married Susan née Breeze (c.1836–1901) in 1859 and they lived at Gwestydd, Montgomeryshire. In addition to Martha they had three other children:

• Mary Wellings (c.1864–1919) married William Scandrett (1859–1944), a colliery timberman, in 1884. They were living at 47 Meadow Street, Llanhilleth, near Newport, Monmouthshire in 1911. Mary's sister-in-law Martha and her husband John Davies (VC's parents) were visiting at the time of the 1911 Census.
• Thomas Wellings, born 1867.
• George Edward Wellings (1870–1900).

James was educated at Wyndham School of the Ogmore Vale and Nant-y-moel Formal Education Council School. He was employed as a miner at Wyndham Colliery, Ogmore Vale. On 24th March 1906 he married Elizabeth Ann née Richards (born 1887) at Bridgend Registry Office and they were living at 8 Nant-y-Moel Row, Nant-y-Moel in 1911. They had four children:

• William John Davies born on 2nd April 1907.
• Morgan James Davies (27th February 1909–1976).
• Alcwyn George Davies, born on 9th June 1911, married Edna M Edwards in 1938.
• Priscilla Maud Davies, born on 11th November 1913, married Ronald G John in 1937.

Wyndham Colliery, Ogmore Vale where James Davies was employed.

Elizabeth's father, William Richards (born c.1849), was a colliery timberman. He married

Elizabeth (born c.1853). They were living at 8 Nant-y-Moel Row, Nant-y-Moel, Glamorgan in 1871 and at 9 Nant-y-Moel Row in 1891. In addition to Elizabeth they had seven other children – Gwenllian Richards 1870, William Richards c.1873, Charlotte Richards 1878, Margaret Richards 1881, Joanna Richards 1885, Sarah Richards 1889 and Jane Richards 1892.

James enlisted in the Royal Garrison Artillery on 12th October 1914 (44304). He was described as 5′ 6¼″ tall, weighing 139 lbs, with fair complexion, blue eyes, brown hair and his religious denomination was Baptist. He served at the Royal Citadel, Plymouth and transferred to 3rd (Reserve) Battalion, Royal Welsh Fusiliers (31161) at Litherland, Liverpool on 5th June 1915. James joined the Mediterranean Expeditionary Force on 28th August 1915 and joined 8th Battalion at Gallipoli on 9th September. He was evacuated to Alexandria, Egypt with enteric fever in December and returned to Britain on 23rd February 1916 on the strength of the Depot. Having recovered at Stobhill Hospital, Scotland he joined 3rd (Reserve) Battalion on 7th June and transferred to 5th (Home Service) Garrison Battalion at Wrexham on 21st August. James went to France on 16th December to 5th Infantry Base Depot and joined 13th Battalion on 1st January 1917. He was treated at 129th Field Ambulance for a foot injury 27th May–5th June and was promoted corporal on 10th July.

Before leaving for the assembly trenches ahead of the opening of the Third Battle of Ypres, he wrote home:

Dear Wife,
You will see by the address that I have been made a corporal – two stripes instead of one. If I am spared I hope to be made serjeant soon. I am glad to hear that Priscilla Maud is a good girl and going to school. Tell her that daddy thinks of her

James Davies on the right after transferring to the Royal Welsh Fusiliers. (*Mark Davies*)

The Royal Citadel, Plymouth in the 1890s. It was built over the earlier Drake's Fort of the late 1660s. The Citadel is still occupied by the military, being the base of 29 Commando Regiment RA, part of 3 Commando Brigade.

James Davies, seated front row left, while recovering in hospital. (*Mark Davies*)

Stobhill Hospital, Glasgow opened in 1904. In September 1914 it was taken over by the War Office and redesignated 3rd and 4th Scottish General Hospitals. The wounded arrived by hospital trains at a temporary platform within the hospital grounds. The hospital returned to civilian use in the spring of 1920.

often. We are about going over. Don't vex, as I hope to go through it all right, and if I do not you will know that I died for my wife and children and for my King and country.

Awarded the VC for his actions at Pilkem, Belgium on 31st July 1917, LG 6th September 1917. He died of wounds at a 131st Field Ambulance dressing station (believed to be at Canada Farm) on 31st July 1917 officially, but his platoon commander stated that he died on the evening of 1st August. He is buried in Canada Farm Cemetery, Elverdinghe, Belgium (II B 18). He is also commemorated at:

The original wooden cross over James Davies' grave in Canada Farm Cemetery. (*Mark Davies*)

Alcwyn visits his father's grave in the 1920s. (*Mark Davies*)

James Davies' headstone as it appears today.

- Davies Road, Barracksfield Estate, Wrexham.
- Nant-y-Moel War Memorial, Glamorgan.
- Portrait in Nant-y-Moel Memorial Shelter.
- The Department for Communities and Local Government decided to provide a commemorative paving stone at the birthplace of every Great War Victoria Cross recipient in the United Kingdom. A commemorative stone for James was dedicated at Nant-y-Moel Memorial Shelter, Ogwr, Mid Glamorgan, South Wales on 30th July 2017 to mark the centenary of his award.

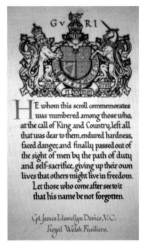

The VC was presented to his wife and eldest son by the King at Buckingham Palace on 20th October 1917. In addition to the VC he was awarded the 1914–15 Star, British War Medal 1914–20 and Victory Medal 1914–19 with MID Oakleaf. The VC is held by the Royal Welch Fusiliers Museum, Queen's Tower & Chamberlain Tower, Caernarfon Castle, Gwynedd, Wales.

The scroll that accompanied James Davies' memorial plaque. (*Mark Davies*)

Elizabeth was awarded a pension of £1/10/- per week from 11th February 1918. In the 4th quarter of 1918 she married Eli Darby (1878–1963) and had another five children – Lilian Darby 1920, Peter G Darby 1922, Ronald Darby 1925, Grenville Darby 1927 and Iris Darby 1930.

15092 CORPORAL SIDNEY JAMES DAY
11th Battalion, The Suffolk Regiment

Sidney Day was born at 4 St Anne's Lane, off King Street, Conisford, Norwich, Norfolk on 3rd July 1891. His father, William Day (1856–1924), was a labourer in 1881 and later was head cellarman of Morgan's Brewery, King Street, Norwich. He married Elizabeth née Plowman (1849–1931) in 1877 and they lived at various places in Norwich:

- 1881 – Jays Square, Mountergate.
- 1901 – 64 Hall Road.
- 1911 – 119 Ber Street.
- Later he was the landlord of the Jolly Butchers public house and lodging house at 125 Ber Street.
- 1924 – 5 Carshalton Road.

Morgan's Brewery dates back to 1563. By 1904 the Morgan family had expanded the business to include about 600 public houses. In June 1942 the brewery suffered bomb damage and operations shifted to the Lady Bridge Brewery in King's Lynn, also owned by the Morgans. Brewing in King Street recommenced in 1950, but in 1961 the company went into voluntary liquidation. It was taken over by Bullards and Steward & Patteson who shared the tied estate between them and sold the brewery to Watney Mann. The brewery was demolished in the winter of 1989/90.

Sidney had seven older siblings:

- William John Day (born 1878) married Susannah Hardisty (1878–1965) in 1911. She was living at 109 Cecil Road, Norwich in 1939. Also present was Ronald J Goodwin (born 1915), a married civil engineer. William and Susannah had two children:
  - Marjorie SH Day (born 1912) married Leslie A Bayfield (born 1913), a ledger keeper with Barclay's Bank, in 1938. They were living at 3 Kingston Park Lane, Wymondham, Norfolk in 1939 and had two children – Ann Bayfield 1941 and John L Bayfield 1947.
  - Dorothy S Day (1915–42) was a shorthand typist in 1939, living with her mother. She died unmarried.
- Harry Day (1879–1974) was a printer in 1901. He married Mary Cox (born 1878) in 1907 at Halifax, Yorkshire. By 1911 he was a compositor, living with his family at 96 Ber Street, Norwich. He served in the Norfolk Regiment during the Great War. They had a daughter, Rose Mary Day

The Jolly Butchers included Day's Lodging House in the rear. The pub was later known as 'Black Anna's' after the landlady from 1935 to 1976, Antoinette Hannent, who sang and held jazz sessions there, starting in the Second World War with American servicemen. The pub was sometimes so crowded that Anna lifted doors off their hinges to make more space. The Jolly Butchers closed in 1989 and the building was converted into offices. (George Plunkett).

(1909–43), who married Reginald M Weight (1901–67), a commercial traveller in wholesale groceries, in 1934 and they had a son, John R Weight, in 1935. They were living at 8 Belvoir Street, Norwich in 1939.

- Edith Sarah Day (1881–1969) married John E Harrison in 1911.
- Lilian 'Lilley' Elizabeth Day (1883–1959) married George Beales in 1915 and they had two children – Doris E Beales 1918 and Dennis E Beales 1921.
- Ethel Day (born 1885) was an elementary school teacher in 1911. She married Charles Fryer in 1919 and they had a daughter, Betty J Fryer, in 1927.
- Alice Jane Day (born 1887) married Samuel James Bowler or Richard Grimmer in 1909.
- Agatha Day (1889–1932).

Sidney's paternal grandfather, James Day (c.1835–96), was a blacksmith in 1861 and a smith in a railway works in 1871. He married Charlotte née Thorpe (c.1830–92) in 1854 and they lived at Turner's Square, Conisford, Norwich. In addition to William they had three other sons:

- James Day (1854–1904) was a labourer in 1871. He married Alice Butler in 1885 and they were living at 17 Turner's Square, Conisford, Norwich in 1891. By 1901 he was a railway fitter living at Station Cottages, Mundford Road, Weeting, Norfolk.
- Henry Day (1859–93) married Lucy Bland (1866–1928) in 1884 and they had four children – Lucy Ada Day 1885, Henry Day 1889, Alfred Ernest Day 1892 and James Day 1894. They were living at William Street, Norwich in 1891. Lucy moved in with James O'Connor Graver (1876–1934), a fish hawker, at 44 Mariner's Lane, Norwich, and in 1901 was recorded as his wife. They had seven children – Wilfred O'Conner Graver 1896, Arthur George Graver 1898, Elsie Graver 1899, Alice Graver 1901, George Graver 1903, Charles William Graver 1905 and Sidney Graver 1907. By 1911 Lucy was recorded as Lucy Day, a widow, still living with James Graver at 4 Lower Square, Shorne Lane, Norwich.
- Alfred George Day (1862–1926) married Eliza Temperance Claxton (1861–1922) in 1890. He was a brewery labourer in 1901 when they were living at East Wymer, Norwich and at 5 Abbey Lane, King Street, Norwich in 1911.

Fairland Street, Wymondham where Sidney's maternal grandparents were living in 1851.

His maternal grandfather, John Spanson Plowman (c.1821–1902) was a master butcher. He married Rebecca née Mann (c.1829–1907), a dressmaker, in 1847. They were living at Fairland Street, Wymondham, Norfolk in 1851 and at Vicar Street, Wymondham in 1891. In addition to Elizabeth they also had Rebecca Plowman (1850–1930) who was unmarried and living with her sister Elizabeth and family in 1911.

Sidney was educated at St Mark's School, Lakenham, Norwich and was also a member

St Mark's church was built in the 1840s and the south chapel is the local war memorial. (*George Plunkett*)

St Mark's School, Lakenham, Norwich has been converted into flats. (*Eastern Daily Press*)

St Catherine's Plain, Norwich. (*George Plunkett*)

of St Mark's Company, Church Lads' Brigade. He was employed as an apprentice butcher with Mr Miller of St Catherine's Plain and later at Saxmundham, Suffolk. He enlisted on 14th September 1914 and was allocated to 9th Suffolk at Shoreham on 21st September. He was described as 5′ 7¼″ tall, weighing 131 lbs, with sallow complexion, brown hair, blue eyes and his religious denomination was Church of England. Appointed unpaid lance corporal 14th August 1915 and went to France with the Battalion on 31st August.

At Loos on 26th September he rescued Lieutenant Thomas Tearle Stevens, but the officer was shot dead in his arms as he was being carried to safety (Loos Memorial). Promoted lance corporal 1st December. He received four gunshot wounds to the

Norfolk War Hospital, Yarmouth Road, Thorpe St Andrew, near Norwich 1915–19. It was the Norfolk County Asylum from 1814 and was expanded to eventually take more than 1,000 patients. In 1919 it became the Norfolk Mental Hospital and in 1923 was re-named St Andrew's Hospital. It closed in 1998 and most of the buildings were demolished, but the main building was converted into housing.

left chest, side, thigh and buttock on the Somme on 18th September 1916. He was evacuated to Britain next day on the strength of the Depot and was treated at Norfolk War Hospital, Thorpe Road, Norwich. Transferred to 3rd Battalion on 19th March 1917 and returned to France (15th Base Depot and 9th Battalion) on 9th June. He transferred to 11th Battalion on 2nd July and was promoted corporal on 17th August.

Awarded the VC for his actions east of Hargicourt, France on 26th August 1917, LG 17th October 1917. He wrote to his parents on 4th September:

> *… In about six weeks' time you will, I hope, be informed of great news, which will make you the proudest parents in Norwich. I am recommended for the coveted honour, the V.C., the first one in the battalion up to the present. Now I know you want to hear all about it, and what I did to get it. Shall be able to tell you more about it when I come home. Am sure it cannot be a greater surprise to you than it has been to me. You cannot imagine how honoured I feel to break the news to you all. Last Sunday week, August 26th, we went over to the attack. Everything went off successful, and, thanks to God's mercy and care, I came through untouched. When we got back to our billets my platoon officer, who is a perfect gentleman, broke the news to me.*
>
> *He called me aside, and told me that he was very pleased with what I had done in the attack, and was recommending me for a reward. At first, he said I was in for a M.M., but the captain and himself decided on a D.C.M., but initially the colonel and captain thought me worthy of the Victoria Cross, as he told me personally I thoroughly deserved it, and he hoped I would get it. Well, when my officer told me that, you might have knocked me down with a feather, for little did I dream that I should ever be the one to gain that much coveted honour … The colonel congratulated me personally. He came to my billet, and said, 'Corporal, I have come to congratulate you on the splendid work you did last Sunday. I am very pleased with and proud of you…'….*

Sidney was granted leave in England 14–28th December 1917, which was extended by the War Office to 11th January 1918 due to his wounds and also to attend the investiture. He was given a hero's welcome in Norwich and a civic reception at the Guildhall, where he was presented with an illuminated address. He was the guest of St Mark's School on 19th December, accompanied by his sister, and was presented with a clock. He also attended a Church Lads' Brigade social at St Mark's Mission Hall in Trafalgar Street. On 23rd December he attended a service at St

Sidney Day had a civic reception at Norwich Guildhall in January 1918. It was constructed 1407–13 and was the seat of local government until 1938. Magistrates Courts continued to use the Guildhall until 1977. It is now the office of Norwich Heritage Economic and Regeneration Trust.

Helen's before marching with the Church Lads' Brigade to the Market Place.

The VC was presented by the King at Buckingham Palace on 9th January 1918. The following day Sidney was admitted to Lakenham Military Hospital, Norwich and moved via the Eastern Command Depot, Shoreham to the Regimental Depot, Bury St Edmunds on 12th January. He was admitted to Bury St Edmunds Military Hospital on 26th January. Sidney returned to 11th Battalion on 7th April and was posted missing on 10th April, having been wounded by a bullet through the right thumb at Erquinghem, France. His next of kin was notified officially that he was missing on 15th May and that he was a prisoner of war on 7th June. He was held at a camp at Langensalza (now Bad Langensalza), having initially been in hospital after capture. He was repatriated through Hull on 23rd December and held on the strength of the Depot.

Sidney outside Buckingham Palace with his parents and wife following his investiture. The picture has a German stamp on the back and was probably sent to him after he was taken prisoner (Michael Day).

The prisoner of war camp at Langensalza opened in 1914 and held 10,000 men.

Having transferred to 3rd Battalion on 26th February 1919, he was demobilised to the Class Z Reserve on 19th April. He was assessed as 30% disabled and was awarded a pension, but the precise details are indistinct in his service record. He was given a warm welcome in May 1919 by the Loyal Amicable Lodge of Oddfellows at a meeting held at the Cricketer's Arms in Red Lion Street, Norwich. Sidney was a member of the VC Guard at the Interment of the Unknown Warrior on 11th November 1920. He returned to butchery and was later employed by Norwich Electricity Department. In the early 1930s he moved to Portsmouth, Hampshire and took out a lease on the Arcade Restaurant at 12 The Arcade, Edinburgh Road, Portsea, Portsmouth, which he renamed the Sidney Day VC Tearoom.

On 21st June 1939 Sidney Day married Doris Ena Gray (née Ellis) (13th July 1906–18th June 1982) at Portsmouth. Doris had been married previously to Arthur E Gray in 1929. Sidney and Doris had a son, Michael David Day, born on 24th February 1943. He served in the RAF from September 1959 until February 1998, including in Borneo, Malta and Cyprus as a warrant officer in Supply Branch and later in Movements.

Doris' father, John Ellis (1874–1938), born at Tiverton, Devon, was a bricklayer's labourer. He married Lucy Alice née Eames (born 1874 at Beacon Hill, Hampshire) in 1894 at Havant, Hampshire. In 1911 they were living at 43 Fratton Grove, Portsmouth, Hampshire. In 1939 Lucy was living with her daughter Victoria and family. In addition to Doris they had five other children:

Sidney outside the Arcade Restaurant.

• Victoria Maud Ellis (born 1903) married George Henshaw (born 1898 at Salford, Lancashire) in 1926 and they had three children – Kenneth G Henshaw 1928, Avis J Henshaw 1934 and Jean P Henshaw 1937. George was a miller in an iron works when he joined the Royal Navy as a boy and was assigned to HMS *Impregnable* on 18th January 1915. He was promoted to boy 1st class on 13th March. George was assigned to various ships and shore establishments – HMS *Digby* 7th September 1915, HMS *Pembroke I* 21st November 1915 & 19th December 1918, HMS *Amaryllis* 22nd January 1916, HMS *Hannibal* (*Amaryllis*) 16th July 1917, HMS *Commonwealth* 25th March 1919, HMS *Victory I* 28th August 1920 & 6th June 1924, HMS *Champion* 14th October 1920, HMS *Columbine* (*Vivacious*) 2nd January 1922, HMS *Vernon* 27th June 1925 & 31st October 1925, HMS *Dido* (*Seymour, Tilbury, Stronghold*) 14th October 1925 and HMS *Tiger* 3rd June 1926. He signed on for twelve years as an ordinary seaman on 12th November 1916 (J33741), described as 5′ 3¾″ tall, with brown hair, grey eyes and fresh complexion. He spent seven days in the cells from 25th March 1917 and on 2nd April 1917 was sentenced to twenty-eight days detention for sleeping on duty. Despite these misdemeanours he was promoted to able seaman on 1st September 1917 and qualified for Good Conduct Badges on 7th December 1919 and 13th December 1924. He completed a mining course on 10th May 1926. Victoria and George were living at 42 Fritton Grove, Portsmouth in 1939. Living with them was Arthur Ellis (born 1920), a brewery worker.
• Hilda Louise Ellis (born 1905) married Augustus Farminer (1903–66), a plumber, in 1932 and they had a son, Ronald G Farminer in 1933. They were living at 205 Chatsworth Avenue, Portsmouth in 1939.
• Flora Ellis (born 1908) married Charles Mawer in 1927.
• Lucy Alice Ellis (born 1910) married Charles F Palmer (born 1905), a brewer's fitter maker, in 1929 and they had five children – Doreen E Palmer 1929, Raymond C Palmer 1930, Betty Palmer 1935, Julia Palmer 1938 and Brian D Palmer 1940. They were living at 1 Hythe Road, Portsmouth in 1939.
• Elsie Ellis (1913–46) married William J Bowles (born 1904), a general labourer excavator, in 1935 and they had three children – Edward J Bowles 1938, Margaret R Bowles 1941 and Sandra C Bowles 1946. They were living at 19 Park Mansions,

Portsmouth in 1939. William married Mabel V Fraser née Small (born 1923) in 1951. She had married John Fraser in 1941 and it is assumed that they divorced, having had a son, Peter A Fraser, in 1946. William and Mabel had six children – Thomas W Fraser/Bowles 1948, William N Bowles 1950, Angela M Bowles 1952, Susan A Bowles 1953, Julie E Bowles 1956 and Stephen J Bowles 1957.

Sidney and Doris lived above the Tearoom until 10th January 1941, when it was destroyed in the Blitz. They moved to rented accommodation at 182 Kirby Road, North End, Portsmouth before moving to a prefabricated house at 37 Penhale Road, Fratton. Their final move was to 18 Fraser Road, Bedhampton, Havant, Hampshire in 1956. Following the loss of the Tearoom, Sidney worked as a dockyard messenger until suffering from tuberculosis and retired on 9th March 1956. He died at Queen Alexandra's Hospital, Cosham, Hampshire on 17th July 1959 and is buried in Milton Cemetery, Portsmouth (R 11 6). He is commemorated in two other places:

- A memorial was erected in St Mark's School, Hall Road, Lakenham by former pupils. When it disappeared a replacement was placed in the memorial chapel at St Mark's Church in October 1971 together with Sidney's portrait and a copy of his citation.
- Twenty-two Berberis shrubs, one for each members of the Church Lads' Brigade who has been awarded the VC, were planted in the Church Lads & Church Girls Brigade Memorial Plot at the National Memorial Arboretum, Alrewas, Staffordshire. None of the shrubs are dedicated to individual VCs.
- The Department for Communities and Local Government decided to provide a commemorative paving stone at the birthplace of every Great War Victoria Cross recipient in the United Kingdom. Sidney's stone is to be dedicated at Norwich War Memorial, City Hall, Norwich on 26th August 2017 to mark the centenary of his award.

Queen Alexandra's Hospital, Cosham, Hampshire was originally a military hospital, named after Edward VII's consort, Alexandra of Denmark. It was built in 1904–08 and replaced an earlier hospital in Portsea, Portsmouth. In 1926 it passed to the Ministry of Pensions to care for disabled former servicemen. Capacity was increased during the Second World War and the first civilian patients were admitted. In 1951 all but one hundred of the 640 beds were transferred to the National Health Service. In the 1960s it became a district general hospital and several new buildings were constructed. A major redevelopment took place in the 1980s and a major rebuilding project was completed in 2009.

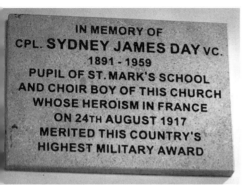

The memorial in St Mark's Church, Norwich
(Eastern Daily Press).

Sidney Day's gravestone in Milton Cemetery,
Portsmouth.

Doris moved to 43 Thrush Walk, Wecock Farm, Havant and died at Queen
Alexandra's Hospital, Cosham on 18th June 1982. She is buried beside her husband.

In addition to the VC he was awarded the 1914–15 Star, British War Medal 1914–
20, Victory Medal 1914–19, George VI Coronation Medal 1937 and Elizabeth II
Coronation Medal 1953. It is understood that the VC passed to Norman 'Norrie' S
Day (born 1930 in Norwich, son of Sidney Frank and Mabel L Day), who emigrated
to New Zealand in the 1950s. Norrie's relationship to Sidney Day VC is not known.
The current whereabouts of the medals are unknown.

2060 SERGEANT JOHN JAMES DWYER
4th Australian Machine Gun Company, AIF

John Dwyer was born on 9th March 1890 at Lovett, Port
Cygnet, Tasmania. He was known as Jack. His father,
Charles Aaron Dwyer (1860–1946), known as Red Charlie,
was a farmer of Alonnah, Bruny Island, Tasmania. He
married Mary Anna née Scanlon (1860–1935) in 1884.
John had ten siblings:

- Jeremiah Patrick Dwyer (1885–1904).
- Alice Genevieve Dwyer (1886–1945) married Frederick
  William Beltz (1882–1965) in 1910. His father, Louis
  Beltz (1841–1912), was German born. Frederick was a
  waterside worker at the outbreak of the Great War and his

(*Australian War Memorial*)

employment was terminated when he registered as an alien with the Intelligence
Section, General Staff, 6th Military District. He was living at 32 Patrick Street,

Alonnah (formerly Mills Reef) from the air (Australia for Everyone).

The first European settler in the Cygnet area was William Nichols in 1834. His grandson, John Wilson, established a shipbuilding business and the town was known as Port Cygnet until 1895, Lovett until 1915 and then Cygnet.

Hobart at the time and requested permission to travel to Melbourne, Victoria on 29th October 1917. He was regarded as being of excellent character and was granted permission. He returned to Tasmania on 9th November and was living with his family at Mount Stuart Road, North Hobart. He also owned a house and seven acres at Alonnah and fifty acres selected from the Crown at Adventure Bay, Tasmania. They had a daughter, Margaret Beltz (c.1912–75).

- Eileen Kathleen 'Kate' Dwyer (1887–1973) married Ernest Charles Whitehouse (1882–1973), possibly in 1914 at Sydney, New South Wales. They had three children – Bernard Charles Whitehouse 1915, Thomas Desmond Whitehouse 1923 and Dorothy Mary Whitehouse c.1926. Thomas enlisted on 3rd August 1944 at Enoggera, Queensland (NX193600) and served with No.32 Company, Australian Army Service Corps. He was discharged as a private on 7th June 1946.
- Adeline Margaret 'Maggie' Dwyer (1889–1911).
- Charles Aaron Dwyer (1891–1904).
- Clara May Dwyer (1894–1964) married Henry Edmund Dillon (1893–1935) in 1919. They had four children – Edmund Charles Dillon 1920, Gerald Joseph Dillon 1921, Denis Henry Dillon 1923 and Kevin 'Sandy' James Dillon 1925. Kevin enlisted as a stoker in the Royal Australian Navy on 11th October 1943 at Moonah (H2665) and was discharged from HMAS *Australia* on 3rd October 1946.
- Thomas Vincent Dwyer (1896–1960) enlisted in C Company, 26th Battalion (863) at Claremont on 27th February 1915. He was described as a labourer, 5′ 10½″ tall, weighing 162 lbs, with fresh complexion, grey eyes, brown hair and his religious denomination was Roman Catholic. He embarked at Brisbane on 29th June on HMAT A60 *Aeneas*. On 6th September he was admitted to 19th General Hospital, Alexandria with influenza and again on 25th September with measles. He embarked at Alexandria on HMAT A30 *Borda* on 18th October and disembarked on Gallipoli on 25th October. On 24th December he transferred to 15th Battalion at Mudros and disembarked at Alexandria on 9th January 1916. He was admitted to No.1 Australian General Hospital and later No.4 Auxiliary Hospital at Abbassia

from 12th February until 22nd March with scarlatina. Having rejoined his unit at Serapeum on 2nd April, he embarked at Alexandria on 1st June and disembarked at Marseille on 8th June. He transferred to 4th Machine Gun Company on 27th June and was appointed driver next day, but reverted to private at his own request on 29th April 1917. Promoted lance corporal 28th September 1917 and corporal 1st April 1918. Thomas was awarded the MM on 4th July 1918 for engaging the enemy with his machine gun from an exposed position while under heavy enemy machine gun fire and continued to give covering fire while his men dug in (LG 21st October 1918). He was granted leave in Britain 18th August–9th September and was appointed temporary sergeant 3rd December 1918–9th January 1919. He transferred to No.1 Command Depot, Sutton Veny, Wiltshire on 16th January and joined 2nd Training Brigade at Codford on 7th February 1919. On 5th April he embarked on SS *Warwickshire* at Liverpool and returned to Australia, where he was discharged on 14th August 1919. In July 1949 he applied for assistance under the War Service Homes Act. The same year he married Phyllis Dympner Pegler (died 1968) and they are understood to have had four children – Janice Dwyer, Aileen Dwyer, Charles Dwyer and Rosalie Dwyer.

- Denis Paul Dwyer (1898–1975), a farmer, enlisted at Claremont on 23rd February 1916 and was assigned to A Company, 40th Battalion (179). He was described as 5′ 11″ tall, weighing 147 lbs, with medium complexion, grey eyes, dark hair and his religious denomination was Roman Catholic. On 7th May he was absent without leave at Claremont and confined to camp for three days. He sailed for England aboard HMAT A35 *Berrima* from Hobart, Tasmania on 1st July 1916, disembarking at Devonport on 22nd August.

He went to France on 23rd November and was in hospital 16th–21st March 1917. On 22nd May he was promoted lance corporal and on 7th June he was wounded by a gunshot to the face, which fractured his jaw. He was admitted to No.2 Australian Casualty Clearing Station the same day, transferred to Boulogne on 11th June, then to England on HMHS *St Andrew* on 12th June. He was admitted to 1st London General Hospital later that day and transferred to 1st Auxiliary Hospital, Harefield on 20th October. Denis was granted leave 27th October–10th November, then moved to No.1 Command Depot, Sutton Veny on 11th November. He transferred to the Overseas Training Brigade, Sandhill Camp, Longbridge Deverill on 2nd February 1918. He returned to France via Southampton on 13th March and rejoined his

Thomas Dwyer, standing extreme right, with other members of 4th Machine Gun Company in France, including his brother, John Dwyer, seated on the right (juliebird).

unit on 19th March, but his stay was short. On 28th March he received a gunshot wound to the left arm. He embarked for Britain on HMHS *Antrim* on 1st April and was admitted to 3rd Southern General Hospital, Oxford later that day. On 9th April he transferred to 3rd Auxiliary Hospital and to No.3 Command Depot on 12th April. He moved to 1st Australian Dermatological Hospital, Bulford on 9th May and to Parkhouse Camp nearby on 10th July. He was severely reprimanded for being in Bulford village on 18th July without a pass and transferred to No.1 Command Depot, Sutton Veny on 23rd July. While there he was admitted to the Military Hospital with an abscess on the right hand, 25th August–7th September. Denis transferred to the Army Provost Corps and reverted to private at his own request at Bhurtpore Barracks, Tidworth on 28th November. He was promoted 2nd corporal on 10th February 1919. On 2nd December he embarked on HMAT A9 *Shropshire* and returned to Australia, disembarking on 22nd January 1920. He was discharged from 6th Military District on 24th March 1920. Denis married Ardis Cowan (1895–1975) in 1925 in Queensland. In 1927 he lost all his personal belongings in floods at Bemerside and applied for a new certificate of discharge in 1944. His address at the time was 113 Taylor Street, Lakemba, Sydney. In 1930 he applied for assistance under the War Service Homes Act. They had two children – Kevin V Dwyer 1929 and Lawrence Dwyer 1936, both of whom died soon after birth.

• Maud Joanna (or Hanorah Johanna 'Nora' or Honora) Dwyer (1900–92) married Walter Francis Dillon (1894–1951) in 1925. They had eight children – Veronica Dillon 1926, Nora Dillon 1927, Michael Francis Dillon 1930, Pauline Clare Dillon 1932, twins Mary Bernadette Dillon and Gregory Thomas Dillon 1934 (Gregory died the day he was born), Daniel Ignatius Dillon 1938 and Brendon Charles Dillon 1940. Walter was an engine driver when he enlisted in 14th Battalion, 24th Reinforcements AIF on 31st July 1916 at Melbourne, Victoria (7230). He was described as 6′ tall, weighing 151 lbs, with fair complexion, blue eyes, fair hair and his religious denomination was Roman Catholic. He embarked at Melbourne aboard HMAT A70 *Ballarat* on 29th February 1917, arriving at Devonport, Devon on 25th April. He was immediately admitted to Devonport Military Hospital and was posted to 4th Training Battalion, Codford, Wiltshire thereafter. He went to France on 23rd July, but was evacuated to Norfolk War Hospital, Thorpe, Norfolk with trench feet on 20th October. He transferred to the Overseas Training Brigade, Sandhill Camp, Longbridge Deverill, Wiltshire on 7th March 1918, to 4th Division Signal School from 13th Training Battalion on 22nd March and to 16th Battalion on 13th September. On 16th September he returned to France. He was back in England on 13th May 1919 and returned to Australia aboard HMT *Main* on 23rd July, disembarking at 3rd Military District on 11th October. He was discharged there on 24th January 1920.

• Timothy Martin Dwyer (1902–14) died in an accident on a dray in Bruny Island.

John's paternal grandfather, Jeremiah Dwyer (1819–64), married Ellen née Brereton (1830–1905) in Ireland. Both were born in Tipperary, Ireland and they emigrated to Australia aboard the *Blanche Moore*, arriving at Sydney before moving on to Hobart, Tasmania aboard the *City of Hobart*, arriving on 15th June 1855. They settled in Cygnet, Tasmania. In addition to Charles they had five other children:

- Catherine Agatha Dwyer (c.1853–1929) married James Patrick Sullivan (c.1834–93), born in Ireland, in 1867. They had twelve children – Margaret Sullivan 1868, Ellen Sullivan 1870, Mary Kate Sullivan 1872, Hanora [sic] Sullivan 1873, John Sullivan 1875, Catherine Sullivan 1877, John Bernard Sullivan 1880, Angela Sullivan 1883, Alice Bridget Sullivan 1885, James Sullivan 1887, Christina Sullivan 1889 and James Patrick Sullivan 1891. Catherine married James Cleary in 1895.
- Patrick Dwyer (c.1855–86).
- Honora or Hanorah Dwyer (1856–1900) married Phillip O'Rourke (1852–1938) in 1874. They had fourteen children – Catherine O'Rourke 1875, Phillip John O'Rourke 1877, Jeremiah O'Rourke 1879, Daniel Francis O'Rourke 1880, William Charles O'Rourke 1882, Frederick James O'Rourke 1883, Alexander James O'Rourke 1884, Mary Ellen O'Rourke 1885, Herbert Patrick O'Rourke 1887, John Douglas O'Rourke 1889, Christina May O'Rourke 1891, Albert Raymond O'Rourke 1893, Martin O'Rourke 1894 and Joseph Henry O'Rourke 1897. John Douglas O'Rourke served as a corporal in 49th Battalion AIF (1663) and died on 5th April 1917 (Villers-Bretonneux Memorial, France).
- John Jeremiah Dwyer (1858–1934) married Julia Cleary (1865–1904) in 1884. They had eight children – May Dwyer 1886, Ellen Dwyer 1888, Lillian Winifred Dwyer 1889, Olive May Dwyer 1893, Jeremiah Dwyer 1895, John Thomas Dwyer 1896, Thomas Dwyer 1898 and James Rowland Dwyer 1902. Thomas Dwyer served as a private in 19th Battalion AIF (5566) and died on 23rd May 1918 (Beacon Cemetery, Sailly-Laurette, France – I F 8).
- Ellen Dwyer (born 1862) married Timothy William Mackey (1862–1919) in 1882 and they had three children – William Mackey 1885, Michael Mackey 1886 and Jeremiah Mackey 1887.

Ellen senior married Martin Coy (c.1822–84) in 1870. He was born in Co Clare, Ireland. They had two children:

- Mary Coy (1868–1946) married John Hanrahan in 1892 and they had nine children – William Hanrahan 1892, Isabel Hanrahan 1893, Ellen Doris Hanrahan 1894, John Hanrahan 1896, Ethel May Hanrahan 1898, Oscar Bernard Hanrahan 1899, Martin Eric Hanrahan 1901, Stella Hanrahan 1902 and Mary Margaret Hanrahan 1904.

- Martin Joseph Coy (1871–1940) married Annie May Markey (died 1944) in 1906. They had ten children – Keith Joseph Coy 1907, Martin Claver Coy 1908, Ellen Mary Coy 1909, Norah Mary/May Coy 1911, Patrick John Coy 1912, John Joseph Coy 1914, Dennis Douglas Coy 1915, Bernard Charles Coy 1917, Alan William Coy 1922 and Hazel May Coy 1925.

His maternal grandfather, Thomas Scanlon (c.1833–76), married Alice née Hanlon (c.1833–1903) in 1856. In addition to Mary they had six other children:

- Michael John Scanlon (1856–1935) married Ellen Brereton (c.1857–97) in 1881 and they had ten children – Thomas John Scanlon 1882, Jane Theresa Scanlon 1883, Dennis Scanlon 1885, Alice Scanlon 1886, Mary Ellen Scanlon 1887, James Scanlon 1889, Martin Scanlon 1890, Margaret Frances Scanlon 1892, Johanna Kathleen Scanlon 1894 and Patrick Michael Scanlon 1896. Patrick was serving as a private in 12th Battalion AIF (772) when he was killed in action on 23rd August 1918 (Heath Cemetery, Harbonnières, France – VII E 1).
- James William Scanlon (c.1861–88).
- Margaret Scanlon (1863–1935) married Michael Boyle (born 1872) in 1906 and they had a son, Percy Andrew Boyle, in 1907.
- Thomas Scanlon (1865).
- Alice Scanlon (1868–76).
- Denis Cornelius Scanlon (born c.1869) married Mary Sylvia Jones and they had seven children – Thomas Jerasisus Scanlon 1883, Denis Boniface Berna Scanlon 1887, Alice Maude Scanlon 1891, Ida Anna Scanlon 1893, James Michael Scanlon 1896, Basil Scanlon 1897 and Roy Joseph Scanlon 1898.

John was educated at Mills Reef State School, Alonnah, Bruny Island, Tasmania until 1910. He worked as a cane cutter in Queensland until 1913, then worked on the Mount Lyell Company's Lake Margaret Hydro–Electric Scheme. He returned to Tasmania where he worked as a labourer and axeman at Queenstown. On 4th February 1915 he enlisted in the Australian Imperial Force at Queenstown, Tasmania. He was described as 5′ 11″ tall, weighing 170 lbs, with fair complexion, brown eyes, brown curly hair and his religious denomination was Roman Catholic. He trained at Claremont, Tasmania and embarked at Melbourne on HMAT A20 *Hororata* with 5th Reinforcement Group for 15th Battalion on 15th April. He disembarked at Alexandria, Egypt and moved to Camp Heliopolis. From

Mills Reef School became Alonnah State School in 1900 when the community adopted this name. In this grainy picture Jack Dwyer is in the front row second from the left, with his brother Charlie to the right.

The Upper Lake Margaret Power Station was constructed by the Mount Lyell Mining & Railway Co 1911–14 for its smelting operations in Queenstown. The power station uses water from Lake Margaret, which was dammed in 1914 to raise the level by six metres. The water is transported to the power station by a 2,200m woodstave pipeline constructed by the Australian Woodpipe Co using Oregon Pine imported from Canada. This pipeline deteriorated and in 1938 was replaced by local King Billy Pine wood, which was still in service when the power station was decommissioned in 2006. Following a major refit it was recommissioned in 2009 by Hydro Tasmania with a new pipeline of Alaskan Yellow Cedar.

The area around Queenstown has been known for mining since the 1860s. The discovery of alluvial gold led to the formation of the Mount Lyell Gold Mining Company in 1881, which became the Mount Lyell Mining & Railway Co.

Troops training at Claremont Camp.

HMAT A20 *Hororata* (9,400 tons) departing Melbourne in 1916. She was a passenger/cargo steamship built by W Denny & Sons in Glasgow and completed on 23rd May 1914 for the New Zealand Shipping Co of London. She was leased by Australia until 11th September 1917 and, having completed six trooping voyages, was taken up next day under the Liner Requisition Scheme until 12th April 1919. She was laid up in London and then Falmouth from August 1930 and was used as a cadet training ship. On 6th June 1939 she was sold to the British India Steam Navigation Co, London and renamed *Waroonga*. She was requisitioned on 7th March 1940. On 5th April 1943 she was bound for London from Sydney and New York in Convoy HX231 when she was torpedoed in mid-Atlantic and sank next day. Nineteen members of the crew and passengers were lost out of 132 aboard (Australian War Memorial).

2nd August he was on operations with 15th Battalion on Gallipoli.

On 13th September he was admitted to No.13 Casualty Clearing Station at Anzac with influenza and was transferred to No.25 Casualty Clearing Station on Imbros. He transferred to the Base on 16th September and was attached to the police at Anzac on 18th September. Next day he was admitted to 4th Australian Field Ambulance and evacuated to Mudros on Lemnos. He transferred to No.24 Casualty Clearing Station on 24th September and to the Convalescent Depot next day until 31st October. He returned to Heliopolis on 29th December aboard HMAT A11 *Ascanius*. On 1st January 1916 he was appointed driver and posted to 4th Machine Gun Company on 9th March at Serapeum, Egypt. On 1st June he embarked on HMT *Haverford* at Alexandria and disembarked at Marseille on 10th June. Operations at Pozières and Guedecourt on the Somme followed.

The camp at Heliopolis.

John reverted to private at his own request on 16th September and was promoted lance corporal on 31st December. On 28th March 1917 he reported sick to 5th Australian Field Ambulance with mumps and was treated until 14th April at the Corps Mumps Stationary Hospital. Rejoined his unit and was appointed temporary corporal on 16th April, promoted corporal on 22nd April and appointed temporary sergeant the same day. On 9th June he received a gunshot wound to the left shoulder near Messines and was evacuated through 3/2nd West Lancashire Field Ambulance and No.53 Casualty Clearing Station to 26th General Hospital, Étaples and reverted to corporal. He transferred to 39th General Hospital, Le Havre on 11th June and to 4th Convalescent Depot, Le Havre on 18th July. He rejoined his unit on 22nd August, having passed through the Australian Corps Base Details on 10th August, the Machine Gun Corps Depot at Rouelles on 12th August and the Machine Gun Corps Base Depot at Camiers on 13th August. On 29th August he was promoted sergeant.

Awarded the VC for his actions near Zonnebeke, Belgium on 26th September 1917, LG 26th November 1917. He was granted leave to England 18th January–3rd February 1918. The VC was presented by the King at Buckingham Palace on 23rd January 1918. John was appointed temporary RSM on 9th April and on 20th May he was commissioned. He attended the Corps Gas School 22nd–29th June and returned to England on

HMT *Haverford* was built for the American Line for transatlantic service by John Brown & Co on Clydebank in 1901. She operated on the Southampton – New York and Liverpool – Philadelphia routes. She was used as a troopship from 1915 and in 1917 was damaged in a torpedo attack by U-94 off Ireland. She was attacked and damaged again in 1918. In 1921 she was bought by the White Star Line, but was decommissioned in 1924 and scrapped the following year.

Mudros in 1915.

31st July. Having been promoted lieutenant on 20th August, he embarked on HMAT D21 *Medic* on 24th August to return to Australia to support recruiting, arriving on 11th October. On board were fellow VCs John Carroll, Reginald Inwood, Joergen Jensen, Thomas Kenny, Leonard Keysor, Stanley McDougall, Walter Peeler, William Ruthven and John Whittle. John's appointment was terminated on 15th December 1918 and he transferred to the Reserve of Officers in 6th Military District.

John Dwyer married Myrtle Mary Ivy née Dillon (20th October 1898–5th October 1981) on 24th September 1919 at St Brendan's Catholic Church, Alonnah, Tasmania. They were living at 88 Coleman Street, Glenorchy, Tasmania in 1962. They had six children:

- Iris Patricia Dwyer (30th October 1920–3rd December 2006) married Charles Leonard Burnett (1910–76) in November 1951. They had three children – Cecily Mary Burnett 1953, Kathryn Anne Burnett 1955 and Michael Joseph Burnett 1961.
- Molly Lois Dwyer (18th September 1922–22nd August 2010) married John 'Jack' Edward Goggins (1912–88) in September 1945. They had four children – Pauline Mary Goggins 1946, Margaret Goggins 1948, John Goggins 1952 and Peter Goggins 1954.
- Noreen Mary Dwyer (14th September 1924–11th March 2010) married Sidney Arthur Riley (born 1914) in July 1948. They had three children including, Patricia Mary Riley in 1951.
- John James Dwyer (1st January 1926–10th December 2008) married Molly Grace Triffitt (born 1928) in December 1949. They had a son, David John Dwyer, in 1950.

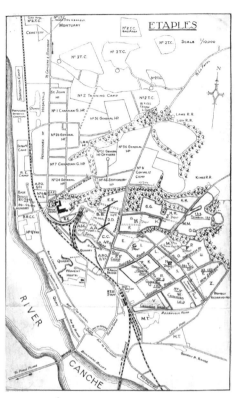

Map of the Étaples area showing the various medical facilities, including 26th General Hospital where John Dwyer was treated in June 1917 (University of Oxford).

St Brendan's Catholic Church, Alonnah where John Dwyer married Myrtle Dillon on 24th September 1919. The church was built in 1906 of weatherboard construction. There are seven arched windows, two of them of stained glass installed in 1997. The interior is of tongue and groove pine (Linc Tasmania).

- Kathleen Mary Dwyer (born 3rd September 1928) married Leslie John Brooks (1927–96) in January 1956. They had a daughter, Bernadette Anne Brooks, in 1965.
- Margaret Dwyer (born 9th May 1930) married Trevor Lloyd Williams (born 1928) in April 1955. They had twins, Maree and Therese Williams, in March 1956.

Myrtle's father, John Joseph Dillon (1862–1931), a farmer, married Mary née Burns (c.1873–c.1968) in 1893. They were living at Franklin, Tasmania in 1926. In addition to Myrtle they had eight other children:

- Elizabeth Magdeline Dillon (1893–1976) married Arthur John 'Bunny' Reynard (1897–1972) in 1921. They had five children – Phyllis Reynard 1922, Hilary Reynard 1923, Kathleen Reynard 1925, Josephine Alice Reynard 1930 and Arthur Reynard 1933.
- Timothy Sylvester Dillon (1895–1946) married Edith Talbot Robinson in 1921.
- William Dillon (1896–99).
- Annie A Dillon (1900–84) married Augustus Andrew Hansson (1893–1952) in 1918. They had eight children – Raymond John Hansson 1920, Elsie Myrtle Hansson 1922, twins Victor Andrew Hansson and Annie 'Joan' Hansson 1928, Mary Hansson 1929, Sheila Hansson 1934, Robert Hansson 1936 and Beryl Hansson 1938.
- Catherine 'Kit' Mary Dillon (1903–76) married Clarence Edward 'Tal' Hawkins (1901–71) in 1925. They had four children – Maureen Hawkins 1926, Maxwell Hawkins, Leo Hawkins and Peter Hawkins.
- Edward Joseph 'Ned' Dillon (1905–83).
- Mary Agnes Dillon (1907–89) married Kenneth Hume 'Toge' Hawkins (1904–89) in 1925. They had five children – Patricia Hawkins, Kenneth Rupert Hawkins, Elizabeth Hawkins, Janice Hawkins and John Hawkins.
- John Maurice Dillon (1910–80) married Alice Beatrice 'Beat' Beltz (1915–82) in 1933. They had four children – Lesley Alice Dillon 1934, John Desmond Dillon 1936, Joanne Delores Dillon 1949 and Dion Joseph Dillon 1956.

On leaving the Army John established an orchard on Bruny Island, Tasmania under the Soldier Settlement Scheme. He then worked for his father-in-law at his sawmill near Alonnah. From 1924 John was on the Council of the Bruny Municipality for three and a half years and was appointed JP at the same time. He then moved to New Norfolk and established his own saw mill at Moogara. Encouraged by his father-in-law he stood for the Tasmanian Legislative Assembly as a Labor Member and was elected to the seat of Franklin on 9th May 1931. He remained in the State Parliament for thirty years, being Speaker 1941–48, Minister for Agriculture and Fisheries 1948–61 and Deputy Premier August 1958–May 1959. He was also a member of the New Norfolk licensing court and an official visitor to Lachlan Park

Bruny Island is in reality two islands joined by a narrow isthmus. It is named after the French explorer, Bruni d'Entrecasteaux, who discovered it was an island in 1792. However, the first European to land there was Tobias Furneaux in 1773. Captain James Cook visited in January 1777 and William Bligh of HMS *Bounty* fame stayed in the Adventure Bay area in 1788 and 1792. Settlers came mainly for the timber industry and since the 1920s it has been a holiday destination noted for its surfing beaches and national parks.

The Tasmanian Legislative Assembly in Hobart consists of the House of Assembly or Lower House and the Legislative Council or Upper House. The Assembly, founded in 1856, currently has twenty-five members, but had thirty in 1931 when John Dwyer was elected (Linc Tasmania).

Mental Hospital. John sold his sawmill in 1949 and moved to Glenorchy. He was forced to retire through ill health on 19th September 1961.

John was a member of the New Norfolk Golf Club and the Buckingham and Claremont bowling clubs. He took part in the Anzac Commemoration Service on 25th April 1927 at the Exhibition Building, Melbourne, Victoria in the presence of the

John Dwyer while serving as a Member of the House of Assembly. (*Parliament of Tasmania*)

The Tasmanian Parliament building in 1869. (*S Clifford*)

Duke of York. In the march past the twenty-three VCs present conceded pride of place to blinded soldiers who insisted on marching. An Anzac Dinner was held two nights before, hosted by Lieutenant General Sir John Monash GCMG KCB VD, and attended by the same twenty-three VCs, but for an unknown reason the Duke of York was not invited. John attended the VC Centenary Celebrations at Hyde Park, London on 26th June 1956, travelling on SS *Orcades* with other Australian VCs who were amongst of the 301 recipients from across the Commonwealth to attend.

In later years John was known as 'Old Silver' and he retained his interest in the land. He was always committed to helping others and served on the Boards of the Fire Brigade and hospitals. He was hospitalised in 1961 with dermatitis, probably a legacy of exposure to mustard gas during the Great War. John Dwyer died at Bruny Island on 17th January 1962. He was given a State Funeral with 2,000 mourners attending, including three VC recipients. He is buried in Alonnah Cemetery, Cornelian Bay, Hobart, Tasmania in the Catholic section (ND Grave 220). He is commemorated in a number of other places:

The grave of John and Myrtle Dwyer in Alonnah Cemetery, Cornelian Bay, Hobart, Tasmania.

- Display in the Hall of Valour, Australian War Memorial, Canberra, ACT.
- Victoria Cross Memorial, Campbell, Canberra dedicated on 24th July 2000.
- Victoria Cross Memorial, Hobart Cenotaph, Tasmania, dedicated on 11th May 2003.
- Dwyer Club, Tasmania Command Ordnance Depot, Tasmania.
- John James Dwyer VC Maiden/Class 1 Plate, a Tasmanian Turf Club horse race over 1,600m held annually on Anzac Day at Launceston Racecourse, Mowbray, Tasmania. It is one of four Anzac Day races at Launceston named after Tasmanian-born VCs (the others are named after McDougall, Murray and Statton).
- J. J. Dwyer VC Memorial Green, Glenorchy Returned & Services League Bowls Club, 320 Main Road, Glenorchy, Tasmania.
- Dwyer Lane, Wodonga, Victoria on White Box Rise estate built on land formerly part of Bandiana Army Camp.
- Dwyer Street, Macleod, Victoria, Australia.
- Victoria Cross Memorial, Queen Victoria Building, George Street, Sydney, New South Wales dedicated on 23rd February 1992 to commemorate the visit of Queen Elizabeth II and Prince Philip on the occasion of the Sesquicentenary of the City of Sydney. Sir Roden Cutler VC, Edward Kenna VC and Keith Payne VC were in attendance.

- Named on one of eleven plaques honouring 175 men from overseas awarded the VC for the Great War. The plaques were unveiled by the Senior Minister of State at the Foreign & Commonwealth Office and Minister for Faith and Communities, Baroness Warsi, at a reception at Lancaster House, London on 26th June 2014 attended by The Duke of Kent and relatives of the VC recipients. The Australian plaque is at the Australian War Memorial.
- The Secretary of State for Communities and Local Government, Eric Pickles MP announced that Victoria Cross recipients from the Great War would have commemorative paving stones laid in their birthplace as a lasting legacy of local heroes within communities. The stones would be laid on or close to the 100th anniversary of their VC actions. For the 145 VCs born in Australia, Belgium, Canada, China, Denmark, Egypt, France, Germany, India, Iraq, Japan, Nepal, Netherlands, New Zealand, Pakistan, South Africa, Sri Lanka, Ukraine and United States of America, individual commemorative stones were unveiled at the National Memorial Arboretum, Alrewas, Staffordshire by Prime Minister David Cameron MP and Sergeant Johnson Beharry VC on 5th March 2015.
- Memorial Plaque, Alonnah District School, Bruny Island, Tasmania dedicated on 2nd November 2014.

In addition to the VC he was awarded the 1914–15 Star, British War Medal 1914–20, Victory Medal 1914–19, George VI Coronation Medal 1937 and Elizabeth II Coronation Medal 1953. His son presented the medals to the Australian War Memorial on 27th September 1982. They are displayed in the Hall of Valour, Australian War Memorial, Treloar Crescent, Campbell ACT.

265473 SERGEANT ALEXANDER EDWARDS
1/6th Battalion, Seaforth Highlanders (Ross-shire Buffs, The Duke of Albany's)

Alexander Edwards was born at High Street, Branderburgh, Lossiemouth, Morayshire, Scotland on 4th November 1885. His father, Alexander Edwards (c.1851–1933), was a fisherman. He married Jessie née Smith (c.1851–1912), a fisherman's servant, on 3rd October 1873 at the United Presbyterian Church, Lossiemouth. They were living at 7 Shore Street, Lossiemouth in 1881, at Briar Cottage, Drainie in 1891, at Stotfield, Lossiemouth by 1901 and in 1912 at Honeysuckle Cottage, Stotfield, Lossiemouth. When he died on 26th January 1933, Alexander senior was living at 1 Union Street, Lossiemouth. Alexander junior had seven siblings:

- Ann Souter Edwards (born 1874).
- William Edwards (born 1876) was living at Ivy Cottage, Stotfield, Lossiemouth, Moray in 1912 and at Seaview, Commerce Street, Lossiemouth in 1933.
- Margaret Jane Edwards (born 1879).
- Jemima Edwards (1881–1968) was living at Lilac Cottage, Stotfield, Lossiemouth in 1911. She married John George King (born c.1882), a fisherman, in 1911.
- James Edwards (born 1883) was lost at sea.
- John Edwards born 1891, served as a company sergeant major with 1/6th Seaforth Highlanders (1853). He was awarded the MM as a sergeant, LG 3rd June 1916.
- Jessie Edwards born 1888.

Originally built in 1841 as a United Secession Church, in 1847 it united with the Relief Church to form the United Presbyterian Church. In 1881 the congregation moved to James Square, then Prospect Terrace. The building became a drill hall and is still in use by the Highland Reserve Forces. (*Anne Burgess*)

Alexander's paternal grandfather, James Edwards (1829–87), was living at Stotfield, Lossiemouth in 1841. He married Ann Souter (c.1829–67) and they had a daughter, Jane Edwards, c.1866. After Ann died, he married Annie Buchan (born c.1844). James died of apoplexy on 5th June 1887 at the Lunatic Asylum, Elgin. His maternal grandfather was William Smith, a fisherman who died before 1881. He married Margaret née Farquhar (born c.1826).

Lossiemouth.

Moray Golf Club opened in March 1889. The old course was designed by Old Tom Morris, the St Andrews professional. A new course, designed by Sir Henry Cotton, opened in 1979. Ramsay MacDonald, the Labour politician from Lossiemouth, played there, but in 1915 his anti-war stance caused a group of members to move for his expulsion from the club. The club council took no action, but in 1916 a new motion was carried by seventy-three votes to twenty-four. Attempts to reverse the decision in 1924, by when MacDonald was Prime Minister, and in 1929 failed to gain the necessary two-thirds majority.

Alexander was educated at Lossiemouth School. He was employed as a cooper, being apprenticed to Thomas Jenkins, a fish curer of Burghead. He later worked for James Gerry of Buckie and just before the war for Thomas Davidson of Aberdeen. He also caddied at Moray Golf Club.

He enlisted on 1st September 1914 (1828) and was promoted lance corporal prior to disembarking in France on 1st May 1915. He was later promoted sergeant. In October 1916 he was hospitalised with a throat infection and after six weeks was evacuated to Britain. He spent two weeks in Lossiemouth, following which he was posted to a reserve battalion. On 1st March 1917 his number became 265473 and in June he volunteered to return to France.

Awarded the VC for his actions near Langemarck, Belgium on 31st July/1st August 1917, LG 14th September 1917. He was wounded during his VC action and evacuated to a base hospital. The VC was presented by the King outside Buckingham Palace on 26th September 1917. On 4th October at Lossiemouth Town Hall he was presented with a wallet containing National War Loan Bonds for £100, War Saving Certificates for £27/13/-, £4/10/- in bank notes and a gold watch and chain. He later received an Address of Appreciation from the Seaforth Highlanders Association.

Alexander became a freemason on 3rd January 1918 when he was Initiated into Pitgaveny Lodge No.681, meeting at Lossiemouth, Moray. On 24th-27th March 1918 he was in action near Loupart Wood, Bapaume when he was reported wounded and missing. His body was never recovered and his death was presumed to have occurred on or since 24th March 1918. He is commemorated on the Arras Memorial. Alexander never married, but was at one time engaged to Bella Christie of Aberdeen. He is also commemorated:

Alexander Edwards receives his VC from the King outside Buckingham Palace on 26th September 1917.

- On the Lossiemouth War Memorial on Clifton Road.
- With his cousin George on a sundial alongside the last green at Moray Golf Club, where both were caddies.
- His VC action featured in Issue 358 of the Victor Comic on 30th December 1967.
- The Department for Communities and Local Government decided to provide a commemorative paving stone at the birth place of every Great War Victoria Cross recipient in the United Kingdom. Alexander's stone was dedicated at Lossiemouth War Memorial, Pitgaveny Street on 30th July 2017 to mark the century of his award.

In addition to the VC he was awarded the 1914–15 Star, British War Medal 1914–20 and Victory Medal 1914–19. The VC is held by the Highlanders Museum, Fort George, Ardersier, Inverness-shire.

Alexander's cousin, Captain George Eric Edwards DSO, is buried in Orival Wood Cemetery, Flesquières, France.

Alexander Edwards' name on the Arras Memorial.

His cousin, Second Lieutenant (Acting Captain) George Eric Edwards, A Company, 1/6th Seaforth Highlanders, was awarded the DSO for the attack on Beaumont Hamel on 13th November 1916. He seized the south cave entrance by rushing through a barrage to reach the objective. He captured a complete enemy staff and kept 400 others in the cave with only six men, four of whom were wounded, LG 13th February 1917. He was killed on 20th November 1917 and is buried in Orival Wood Cemetery, Flesquières, Nord, France (I B 8).

13303 PRIVATE WILFRID CLAUDE EDWARDS
7th Battalion, The King's Own (Yorkshire Light Infantry)

Wilfrid Edwards was born at 76 Vauxhall Street, Heigham, near Norwich, Norfolk on 16th February 1893 as Wilfrid Claude Fox. His father, Charles Edward Fox (1873–1957) was a tailor's improver, boarding with Arthur Tayler at Arborfield Street, Newland, Wokingham, Berkshire in 1891. By 1893 he was a master tailor. Charles married Kate Mary née Kelter (born 1874), a tailoress, in January 1892 at St Clement's Chapel, Colegate Street, Norwich. They were living at 15 Theatre Street, St Peter Mancroft, Norwich. Charles and Kate had five children, but two did not survive infancy and as a result Wilfrid had only two sisters:

- Kate Louisa Fox (born 1892) was a tailoress in 1911. She changed her surname to Edwards after 1911 and married Herbert Collinson in 1918.
- Amy Lilian Fox (born 1895) was working in the boot trade in 1911. She changed her surname to Edwards after 1911 and married James Marshall (born 1895) in 1915. They had three children – George Marshall 1915, Wilfred J Marshall 1919 and Kathleen Marshall 1921. They were living at 17 Potternewton Mount, Leeds, in 1939. James was a labourer at a cabinet works and Amy was a vest machinist.

Kate was living with her family, but not her husband, at 73 Rosebank Grove, Leeds, Yorkshire in 1901, by when her surname was Edwards. In 1911 she was a housekeeper living at 32 Corporation Street, Leeds with her children, by when their surname had reverted to Fox. It is understood that Charles ran into financial difficulties, changed his surname to Edwards and left his family before moving to Tunbridge Wells, Kent to start a new business. By the time of the 1911 Census he was known as Clare Charles Edwards and was living with his 'wife' Clarice and two sons at 35 Cliffe Street, Keighley, Yorkshire. He gave his birthplace as Reading, Berkshire. Charles married Clara 'Clarice' Smithson (born 1872), a seamstress/milliner, as Charles Edward Fox-Edwards, a widower, at Gillingham Parish Church, Kent in January 1917. They were both living at 16 Linden Road, Gillingham at the time. By 1939 Charles was living alone at 77 St John's Road, Tunbridge Wells, Kent, as Charles E Edwards. He was recorded as a master tailor and married. Charles and Clara had four children:

- Frank Douglas Edwards (1906–93) married Vera Marguerita Jinks (1908–96) in 1929 at Tonbridge, Kent. They were living at 37 Dynevor Road, Tunbridge Wells in 1939. Frank was an oil company clerk and served in the RAF during the Second World War. They had three children – John Douglas Edwards 1929, Bryan F Edwards 1932 and Carole E Edwards 1943.

Rosebank Grove, Leeds where Kate Fox/Edwards was living with her family, but not her husband, in 1901. (*Eric Jaquier*)

Gillingham Parish Church, Kent where Wilfrid's father, Charles Fox, married Clara Smithson in January 1917. He was recorded as a widower, although his first wife, Kate, was still alive. (*D Price*)

- Geoffrey Edwards (1908–87) had a tailor's shop which he lived above at 17a Vale Road, Tonbridge. He married Marjorie Irene Nash (1913–96), a sewing machinist, in 1934. By 1939 he was a master tailor. He also served in the RAF during the Second World War. They had a son, Geoffrey M Edwards in 1947.

- Primrose Marjorie Edwards (1911–2006) married the Reverend Charles Eric Waters (1914–2003) in 1940 and they had a son, Robert HE Waters, in 1942. Charles was Vicar of St Hilda at South Shields, Rural Dean of Jarrow and Honorary Canon of Durham until July 1957, when he moved to the living of Witton-le-Wear, Co Durham.

Wilfrid's paternal grandfather, John William Fox, was from Coltishall, Norfolk. It was the site of RAF Coltishall, which was built as a bomber base in 1939–40, but operated fighters during the Second World War. It closed in 2006 and is now a prison, HMP Bure.

- Henry 'Harry' Ernest Edwards (born 1916) served as a lance bombardier in the Royal Artillery during the Second World War (1552055P). He was captured by the Japanese and interned at one of the numerous PoW camps at Fukuoka.

Wilfrid's paternal grandfather, John William Fox (1847–1925) was born at Coltishall, Norfolk. He married Sarah Anne née Stearman (1850–1930) in 1871, by when he was an

Wilfrid's paternal grandparents were living on Prince of Wales Road, Norwich in 1901.

organist. By 1881 he had become a tailor, living with his family at Flowers Court, Norwich. They were living at St Peter Mancroft, Norfolk by 1891 and by 1893 he was a woollen draper. They were living at 69 Prince of Wales Road, East Wymer, Norwich by 1901. In addition to Charles, they had eight other children:

- Georgiana Blanche Fox (born 1872) was a tailoress in 1891.
- George Fox (born 1875) was an apprentice tailor in 1891 and a tailor in 1901.
- Edward Stearman Fox (1877–1956), a tailor, married Elizabeth Mary Ann Bridges (1882–1968) in 1899. They had two children – Gladys Blanche E Fox 1902 and Doris Rosanna H Fox 1907.
- Susannah Louisa Fox (1880–1976) was a tailoress in 1901. She married Horace Alfred Carr (1877–1951) in 1945. Horace had previously married Florence Alice Munday (1874–1930) in 1902 and had a daughter, Flora Amanda Carr, in 1904. He was a salesman and wholesale grocer in 1911 and they were living at 6 Saxon Road, Great Yarmouth.

- Ernest William Fox (1882–1904) was a grocer's assistant in 1901.
- Fred Fox (born 1885) was a tailor's apprentice in 1901 and a tailor in 1911.
- John William Fox (born 1887) was a printer in 1911.
- Sidney Herbert Fox (born 1890) was a clerk in 1911.

His maternal grandfather, James William Kelter (c.1838–1918), born at Wood Dalling, Norfolk, married Mary Ann née Steward (c.1835–1914), born at Trunch, Norfolk, in 1863. He was a coachman for the family of John Barwell, a wine merchant, living at The Lodge, Hoveton Hall, Smallburgh, Norfolk in 1881. In 1891 he was still working for the Barwells, but had moved to the Coachman's House, St Catherine's Close, Norwich. He was the innkeeper of the King's Arms, Foulsham, Norfolk from October 1899 until May 1913. In addition to Kate they had five other children:

- Blanche Emma Kelter (1864–1945) married William Hannant (1864–1940), a servant, in 1889. They had eleven children – Louisa Christine Hannant 1890, Kate Elizabeth Hannant 1891, William Kelter Hannant 1892, Alice Mary Hannant 1894, Ethel Nora Hannant 1896, Blanche Helen Hannant 1898, Jack Hannant 1900, Miriam Hannant 1901, Margaret Annie Hannant 1903, Winifred E Hannant 1905 and Wilfred Robert Hannant 1906.
- Frederick James Kelter (1866–1939) married Elizabeth March (1855–1937) in 1888.
- Florence Fanny Kelter (born 1867) married Charles Vanderstein (born 1864) in 1888. They had five children – Violet Florence Vanderstein 1889, Arthur Charles Vanderstein 1891, Walter James Vanderstein 1892, Francis George Vanderstein 1893 and Gertrude E Vanderstein 1902.
- Arthur George Kelter (1869–1937) married Sally Elizabeth Shingles (1866–1947) in 1891 and they had four children – Kate Frances Kelter 1891, Arthur James Kelter 1893, Albert George Kelter 1897 and Arthur James Kelter 1900.
- William Kelter (1871–1936) married Edith Emma Pease (1869–1903) in 1894. He was a butcher in 1901. They had two children – James William Kelter 1895 and Hilda Florence Kelter 1898. William married Rosanna Seppings (1871–1956) in 1904 and they were living at 136 Magdalen Street, Norwich in 1911.

Wilfrid was educated at Park Lane Council School, Leeds. He was employed as a tailor and from the summer of 1914 as a miner at Waterloo Main Colliery, Leeds. He enlisted on 4th September 1914 (13303) and carried out basic training at Albuhera Barracks, Aldershot, Hampshire. He went to France on 26th August 1915, was wounded in October and was evacuated to Hoddesdon Military Hospital, Rose Hill, Hertfordshire. Having returned to the front in February 1916, he was wounded again in July and sent to hospital in Colchester, Essex. Wilfrid rejoined his unit in January 1917.

Awarded the VC for his actions at Langemarck, Belgium on 16th August 1917, LG 14th September 1917. He received a card from his CO congratulating him on his 'fine behaviour', but wrote to his wife in frustration:

Park Lane Council School, Leeds on the right in the 1940s. It was used by Leeds College of Technology before it moved to Cookridge Street in 1956 (Leodis).

Men in my battalion keep getting honours, but I have not heard a word about mine. The officer tells me that I shall have to wait for my honour, as it will have to pass through a lot of hands before it is settled. The officers have congratulated me upon my work, and one has presented me with a watch. Other officers have promised me something, so I look like being well off when I come home.

Waterloo Main Colliery, where Wilfrid worked for a short time in the summer of 1914 before enlisting.

His wife was besieged by reporters following the announcement of his VC, but insisted that she knew no details of the action, *You see my husband is a quiet, homely fellow, and in his letters to me he has had very little to say about his deed.* The VC was presented by the King in the forecourt at Buckingham Palace on 26th September 1917. He was nervous about meeting the sovereign and forgot to salute, which caused the King some amusement. On 10th October 1917 he received a hero's welcome in Victoria Square, Leeds and was handed a cheque for £200 raised by public subscription, together with a framed photograph. Next day he was presented with an inscribed silver watch at his old school.

The staff of Hoddesdon Military Hospital, Hertfordshire.

Victoria Square, Leeds with the Town Hall in the background, scene of a hero's welcome for Wilfrid on 10th October 1917 (Leodis).

Wilfrid returned to Britain in December 1917 for officer training and was entertained at the Town Hall, Leeds together with Private W Boynton Butler VC. He was commissioned in 4th King's Own Yorkshire Light Infantry on 31st July 1918, but relinquished his commission on 17th June 1919 due to ill health caused by his war wounds. He was awarded the Silver War Badge on 16th June 1919.

Wilfrid Edwards married Belinda née Timlin (1891–1976) at Mount St Mary's Church, Richmond Hill, Leeds, Yorkshire on 20th February 1915. She was a press feeder in the printing trade in 1911 and a munitions worker during the war. They lived at 27 Harry Crescent, South Accommodation Road, Leeds and by 1939 were at 33 Greenhill Crescent, Leeds. Due to his war wounds, Wilfrid was unable to have children and they adopted two daughters:

Mount St Mary's Church, Richmond Hill, Leeds where Wilfrid Edwards married Belinda Timlin on 20th February 1915. The church was dedicated in 1857 to serve Irish migrants living in the east of Leeds. It became known as the Famine Church because it was built during the recovery of the Irish population from the Great Famine. From the 1930s onwards the local population moved away to new houses and by 1979 the population it served had reduced from 6,000 to under 800. The cost of maintaining the church became increasingly prohibitive and in 1996 it was sold, since when it has been unused and has gradually deteriorated.

- Winifred Joan born on 17th May 1922 and adopted on 21st April 1927. She married Jack Craven in 1948 and they had a son, David Craven, in 1954.
- Valerie Blodwen Edwards born on 13th October 1926 and adopted on 18th May 1936. She married Alan Scriven in 1950 and was living at 1 Whinmoor Way, Leeds at the time of her father's death in January 1972.

Belinda's father, Stephen Timlin (c.1867–1910), a labourer and plasterer, was born in Co Mayo, Ireland. He married Bridget née Brislane (c.1865–1913), also born in Co Mayo, in c.1887. They were living at 429 Warrington Road, Ince in Makerfield, Lancashire in 1891 and 33 Devon Street, Leeds in 1901. By 1911 she was living with her children at 26 Devon Terrace, Pontefract Lane, Leeds. In addition to Belinda they had six other children:

- Patrick Timlin (1888–1947) was born in Ireland and was a painter in 1901 and a plasterer in 1911. He married Blanche Maud Warne (1888–1953) in 1911 and they had four children – John Timlin 1912, James Timlin 1913, George Timlin 1915 and Margaret Timlin 1921. By 1939 Blanche was living with her children John, George and Margaret at 6 Harry View, Leeds, while Patrick was living at 19 Cross Monkston Street, Leeds.

- Mary Kate Timlin, born 1889 at Wigan, Lancashire, was a sewing machinist in 1911.
- William Timlin, born c.1894 in Co Mayo, was a brass finisher in 1911.
- Annie Timlin, born 1897 at Normanton, Yorkshire.
- John Timlin, born 1898 at Leeds.
- Sarah Ellen Timlin, born 1900 at Leeds, married Alfred Harding in 1930. They were living at 9 Northrops Field, Pudsey, Yorkshire in 1939.

After the war Wilfrid returned to mining, although he was assessed as 60% disabled. He then worked for Leeds Gas Department showrooms in Vicar Lane, as did William Butler VC. On 16th November 1929 he attended the funeral of John Crawshaw Raynes VC with fellow VCs George Sanders, Fred McNess, Charles Hull, Albert Mountain, Frederick Dobson, Arthur Poulter, William Butler, Sam Meekosha, Albert Shepherd and John Ormsby.

Wilfrid during the Second World War. (*David Craven*)

Wilfrid was granted a Regular Army Emergency Commission in the Royal Army Ordnance Corps as a lieutenant (163562) on 2nd January 1941. He was promoted war substantive lieutenant on 11th March 1941 and temporary captain on 29th February 1944. Immediately after the war he ran a Ford factory in Germany and after demobilisation he worked for a firm of accountants and later at David Brown's factory at Farsley, near Pudsey, Yorkshire. He was granted the Freedom of Leeds in 1950. On 12th January 1967 he attended the funeral of Albert Mountain VC at Garforth Parish Church, Leeds.

Wilfrid Edwards died at St James's Hospital, Leeds, Yorkshire on 2nd January 1972, the last surviving KOYLI VC. His employment on his death certificate was retired switchboard operator. He is buried in Upper and Lower Wortley Cemetery, Oldfield Lane, Wortley, Leeds (M 42). He is also commemorated on a plaque to all Leeds VCs at the Garden of Rest, Victoria Gardens, The Headrow, Leeds.

In addition to the VC he was awarded the 1914–15 Star, British War Medal 1914–20, Victory Medal 1914–19, Defence Medal, War Medal 1939–45, George VI Coronation Medal 1937 and Elizabeth II Coronation Medal 1953. In his will he left the VC to York Castle Museum, but the other medals are on loan to the King's Own Yorkshire Light Infantry Museum, Doncaster, Yorkshire.

Wilfrid Edward's grave in Upper and Lower Wortley Cemetery.

71130 CORPORAL ERNEST ALBERT EGERTON
16th Battalion (Chatsworth Rifles), The Sherwood Foresters
(Nottinghamshire and Derbyshire Regiment)

Ernest Egerton was born at Meir Lane, Caverswall, Longton, near Stoke-on-Trent, Staffordshire on 10th November 1897. The surname also appears as Edgerton in some records. His father, Thomas Henry Egerton (1864–1933), was a potter's engine fitter in 1881. He married Sarah Ann née Keay (1867–1900) on 25th December 1886 at St Michael's, Stone, Staffordshire. By 1891 they were living at Meir Lane, Caverswall. In 1897 he was a die fitter and a potter's engine fitter in 1901, by when the family was living
at 7 May Place, Fenton, Staffordshire. Thomas married Annie Baxter (c.1861–1920) in 1902 at Stone, Staffordshire. They were living at 24 Kildare Street, Longton, Stoke-on-Trent in 1911. Ernest had six siblings:

Caverswall, where Ernest Egerton was born in 1897.

- Thomas Edwin Egerton (1887–1929) was a potter's attendant in 1901 and later a miner. He married Florence Beard (1889–1952), a potter's thimble maker, in 1911 and they boarded at 8 Meir View, Meir, Stoke-on-Trent. He enlisted in the North Staffordshire Regiment on 2nd September 1914 (12575), but was discharged on medical grounds on 21st October. They had two sons – Norman Egerton 1916 and Ernest Egerton 1923. In 1939 Florence was living at 107 Heathcote Road, Stoke-on-Trent with her son Ernest.
- William Charles Egerton (1888–1917) was a labourer in 1911 boarding at Tiley Cottages, Blurton, near Longton, Staffordshire when he married Hannah Seabridge (1891–1943), a stilt maker in a pottery. They lived at 12 Cross Goodfellow Street, Tunstall, Staffordshire and later at 30 Foley Street, Fenton, Staffordshire. They had a daughter, Ivy A Egerton, in 1914, who married Arthur Goodwin in 1940. William enlisted in 12th Rifle Brigade (S/6419) and was promoted acting corporal before he was killed in action on 17th August

Ernest's parents were married on Christmas Day at St Michael the Archangel, Stone, Staffordshire built between 1753 and 1758. It stands on the site of Stone Priory.

1917 (Panel 145–147 Tyne Cot Memorial, Belgium). Hannah married Elijah Henry Hodgkinson (1889–1937) in 1920 and they had three sons – Reginald Hodgkinson 1920, Harry Hodgkinson 1922 and George Hodgkinson 1923. In 1939 Hannah was the licensee of the Farmer's Arms, 117 High Street, Tunstall, Stoke-on-Trent.

Ernest's brother, William Charles Egerton is commemorated on the Tyne Cot Memorial.

* Percy Egerton (1890–97).
* Agnes Ann Egerton (1892–1963) married John William Birks (1883–1945) in 1921. They were living at 67 Westminster Road, Leek, Staffordshire in 1939, when he was a labourer with Leek Urban District Council.
* Lizzie Egerton (1893–1966) married William Henry F Steele (1893–1956) in 1924 and they had a daughter, Elaine Steele in 1937. They were living at 42 Drubbery Lane, Stoke-on-Trent in 1939.
* Harold Egerton (1900–74) married Eliza Jane Brain (born 1902) in 1923. They had two children – Betty Egerton 1929 and Harold W Egerton 1933. They were living at 31 Kildare Street, Stoke-on-Trent in 1939, when he was an omnibus conductor.

Ernest's paternal grandfather, William Egerton (c.1824–76) married Sarah Anne née Barnes (c.1823–90) on 18th March 1846 at Cheadle Parish Church. William was an engineer in 1851 when the family was living at Old Wall Street, Stoke-on-Trent. By 1871 he was a writing clerk and they had moved to 28 Wise Street, Blurton and Trentham, Staffordshire. In addition to Thomas they had eight other children:

* William Barnes Egerton (1847–95) was a die cutter at a kiln works. He married Harriett Ann Moore Eastwood (1849–92) in 1867 and they were living at 60 Edensor Road, Stoke-on-Trent in 1871. By 1881 he was a fitter and turner and they were living at 44 Grove Road, Stoke-on-Trent. They had two children – Florence Egerton 1868 and Ernest Albert Egerton 1870.
* Sarah Elizabeth Egerton (1849–1920) married Sampson Bridgwood Boden (born 1848), a potter turner, in 1873. They emigrated to Canada and had a daughter, Caroline Gertrude Boden (1877–1951), born at Trenton, Canada. Sarah returned to Britain with her daughter before 1881, by when she was a potter's

Ernest's paternal grandparents married at Cheadle Parish Church of St Giles the Abbot in 1846. It was built 1837–39 on the site of an older parish church. Nearby is the more famous Roman Catholic Church of St Giles designed by AW Pugin.

burnisher and was living with her mother. It is not known what happened to Sampson Boden. Sarah married John Keay (1842–1913), a builder's labourer, in 1898 at Stoke-on-Trent. They were living at 28 Kildare Street, Longton in 1901. By 1911 Sarah was living with her daughter at 46 Peel Street, Dresden, Stoke-on-Trent.

- Martha Egerton (1851–1923) was a china burnisher in 1871 and a potter at the time of her marriage to Vernon Phillips Cash (1850–90), a shoemaker, in 1875. He was a cordwainer in 1881 by when they were living at 6 Ricardo Street, Trentham, Staffordshire. She was living at 36 Ronald Street, Longton in 1901. They had six children – Catherine Cash 1877, John Cash 1879, Maud Cash 1881, Ernest Cash 1883, Martha Cash 1886 and Amelia Cash 1889.
- Charles Arthur Egerton (1854–88) was a china warehouseman in 1871.
- Louise Caroline Egerton (1856–1927) was a potter's burnisher in 1891. She married Richard Millward, (c.1830–1906) a warehouseman, in 1892. By 1901 he was living on his own means with his wife at 29 Belgrave Road, Longton.
- Susan Ann Egerton (1859–1941) was a potter's burnisher in 1881. She died unmarried.
- Amelia Gertrude Egerton (1862–1910) was a potter's burnisher in 1881 and was living with her sister Louise in 1901. She died unmarried.
- James Oswald Egerton (1867–1928) was an errand boy in 1881 and a house painter in 1891. He married Sarah Ann Brown (1868–98) in 1889 and they lived at 51 Kildare Street, Trentham. By 1901 they had moved to 22 Dundee Street, Longton. They had four children – Albert Edwin Egerton 1891, Elsie May Egerton 1892, Hilda Egerton 1893 and Charles Egerton 1898. James married Sarah Alice Elizabeth Loffill (1859–1941), a potter's gilder, in 1900. They were living at 1 Kildare Street, Longton in 1911.

Sarah was living with her children at 31 Wise Street, Trentham in 1881. She married William Turner in 1883.

Ernest's maternal grandfather, Thomas Keay (born c.1841) was a drayman and later a farmer. The surname has also been seen as Key. He married Elizabeth née Thorley (1841–1931) in 1862. In 1871 they were living at 6 Marsh Street, Stoke-on-Trent and by 1881 they had moved to Belgrave Road, Trentham, Staffordshire. In 1911 they were living at Draycott Lane, Forsbrook, Staffordshire. In addition to Sarah they had seven other children including:

- Edwin Keay (1863–1946) was a printer in 1881.
- Thomas Keay (1866–1950) was an errand boy on 1881.
- Mary Elizabeth Keay (1871–1941) married Charles Leonard Gimbert (1872–1931), a railway porter, in 1893. Charles was also Ernest Egerton's father-in-law. He was a drayman in 1911, living with his family at the home of his parents-in-law at Draycott Lane, Forsbrook. They had five children – Frances Lilian

Gimbert 1896, Elsie May Gimbert 1899, Wilfred Leonard Gimbert 1901, Gertrude Elizabeth Gimbert 1906 and William Thomas Gimbert 1909. Mary was living at 105 Uttoxeter Road, Cheadle, Staffordshire in 1939 with her incapacitated son Wilfred and two evacuees – Annie I McCarthy (born 1914) and her son Wilfred N McCarthy (born 1938).

Ernest's maternal grandparents were living in Belgrave Road, Trentham, Staffordshire in 1881.

Ernest was educated at Queen Street School, Cooke Street School and Blurton Church School near Longton. He was employed by Florence Coal and Iron Company, Longton as a haulage hand, but he declared that he was a miner when he enlisted in 3rd North Staffordshire at Shelton on 27th November 1915 (19399). He was described as 5′ 2½″ tall and weighed just 112 lbs. He joined at Lichfield on 28th November and underwent basic training at Wallsend-on-Tyne from 1st December. He was promoted lance corporal, but was reduced to private on 29th May 1916 for being drunk and creating a disturbance at 9.30 p.m. roll call at Forest Hall. On 21st October he was allocated to 1st North Staffordshire and arrived at 12th Infantry Base Depot, Boulogne, France on 23rd October. He transferred to 16th Sherwood Foresters on 8th November and joined the Battalion on the 11th.

Ernest was admitted to 131st and 129th Field Ambulances with diarrhoea on 14th January 1917 and return to the Battalion next day. He was promoted lance corporal on 21st February and admitted to hospital with pain next day. He was admitted to 132nd Field Ambulance 8th-20th March with influenza and with anaemia 27th April–17th May. Promoted corporal 23rd August.

Awarded the VC for his actions southeast of Ypres, Belgium on 20th September 1917, LG 26th November 1917. Among many congratulatory letters was one from the Duke of Devonshire, who took a special interest in the Battalion, which was named after his family's seat at Chatsworth. Ernest was granted leave in England 1st-15th December, extended to the 19th by the War Office. The VC was presented by the King at Buckingham Palace on 5th December 1917. He arrived at Stoke station on 8th December and was met by the Mayor, Alderman WE Robinson, and taken for lunch at the North Stafford Hotel. He was then escorted by the Mayor and Deputy by train to Longton. On arrival he was greeted by the bells of St John's church and was carried shoulder high through a cheering crowd to an open carriage for a triumphal tour of the town with a mounted escort. They arrived at the Town Hall for tea and he was later taken to his grandparents home in Blythe Bridge. Next morning he attended Edensor Church, where a few weeks earlier there had been a memorial service for his brother. He left for Manchester on 11th December and on to London on 14th December to go back to the front. However,

Chatsworth House, seat of the Dukes of Devonshire, after which 16th Battalion (Chatsworth Rifles), The Sherwood Foresters was named. The estate pre-dates the Norman conquest. In 1549 it was purchased by Sir William Cavendish, husband of Bess of Hardwick. Mary, Queen of Scots was held there several times from 1570. The 4th Earl, later the 1st Duke, helped put William of Orange on the throne and began the rebuilding of Chatsworth in 1687. The 4th Duke made great changes to the house and gardens, which were designed by Capability Brown. In the 19th Century guests at the numerous house parties included Queen Victoria and Charles Dickens. The 6th Duke also made extensive changes to the house and gardens. The death of the 10th Duke resulted in a charge of £7,000,000 in death duties and it seemed inevitable that the estate would be transferred to the nation. However, the 11th Duke was determined to retain the family home and sold some major works of art, thousands of acres of land and transferred Hardwick Hall to the National Trust in lieu of tax. In the 1950s the house was comprehensively restored and brought up to modern standards. In 1981 it came under The Chatsworth House Trust.

The North Stafford Hotel was built for the North Staffordshire Railway opposite Stoke-on-Trent station in 1849 and extended in 1878. It was designed to resemble an Elizabethan manor. In 1923 it was taken over by the London Midland and Scottish Railway and was sold by British Rail in 1953. It is now owned by Britannia Hotels and is Grade II* listed.

in the meantime Mr S Barber, manager of Florence Colliery, had arranged for his leave to be extended so that he could attend another presentation at Longton Town Hall on 17th December. The directors, managers and workers at Florence Colliery presented him with an inscribed silver cigarette case and £85/10/- mainly in War Bonds.

Ernest returned to France and was granted Class 1 Proficiency Pay on 4th December. He was gassed at Heudicourt, France on 21st March 1918. He was admitted to 132nd Field Ambulance with anaemia and inflamed connecting tissue on the arm 25th April–6th May. Promoted sergeant 11th May 1918. He left France on 20th August for officer training and that evening was presented with an illuminated testimonial at Longton Town Hall by the Mayor, Alderman WE Robinson. A total of £262/9/3 had been raised by the townsfolk, of which £24 had already been handed to Ernest. The Mayor presented him with a further £39 that evening and the balance of £200 was retained for his future use. He decided against taking a commission and was held by No.1 Reception Battalion at Ripon until joining 3rd Battalion at Sunderland as an instructor on 15th October.

Ernest Egerton married Elsie May née Gimbert (14th August 1899–5th July 1988) on 1st September 1918 at Forsbrook Parish Church and they lived at 105 Chapel View, Blythe Bridge, Staffordshire. They had three daughters:

A memorial service for Ernest's brother was held at St Peter's Church, Edensor in 1917 and the Colours of 16th Sherwood Foresters were laid up there in 1922. St Peter's is the parish church for Chatsworth House, home of the Devonshires, many of whom are buried and commemorated there. The original village was next to Chatsworth House, but the 6th Duke had it moved out of sight between 1838 and 1842. Sir Joseph Paxton planned the new village and church, which was rebuilt between 1867 and 1870. Paxton was the architect of the Crystal Palace designed for the Great Exhibition of 1851. Amongst those buried in the churchyard is Kathleen Cavendish, Marchioness of Hartington (1920–48) who was killed in a plane crash. She was the sister of US President John F Kennedy, who visited the grave. Kathleen's husband was destined to be the 11th Duke, but was killed in action in Belgium in 1944. A window in the eastern chapel is dedicated to Lord Frederick Cavendish, murdered in Phoenix Park, Dublin in 1882.

Longton Town Hall was the centre for local administration from 1865 to 1910, when it came under Stoke-on-Trent. The building was due for demolition in 1986, but an injunction saved it (The Potteries).

Forsbrook Church where Ernest Egerton married Elsie Gimbert in 1918.

- Dorothy M Egerton (17th September 1919–1975) died unmarried. She was registered as incapacitated and living with her parents in 1939.
- Sylvia VJ Egerton (born 20th July 1925) was a cotton machinist living with her parents in 1939. She married Harry Funge (born 1922) in 1949. They had two children – Susan Funge 1952 and Peter E Funge 1954.
- Margaret R Egerton, birth registered during the 4th quarter of 1930, married Frederick Porter in 1953 and they had two sons – Gary M Porter 1956 and Stephen J Porter 1964. They were living at 291 Oxford Gardens, Stafford in 1966.

Elsie's father, Charles Leonard Gimbert (1872–1931), a railway porter, married Mary Elizabeth née Keay (1871–1841), Ernest Egerton's maternal aunt, in 1893.

Charles was a drayman in 1911 and the family was living at the home of his parents-in-law at Draycott Lane, Forsbrook. In 1939 Mary was living at 105 Uttoxeter Road, Cheadle, Staffordshire. In addition to Elsie they had four other children:

- Frances Lilian Gimbert (born 1896), registered as Frances Lydia Gimbert, was an apprentice gilder in 1911. She married Joseph Davies (born 1882) a motor mechanic and driver, in 1915 and they had four children – Albert J Davies 1921, Irene D Davies 1923, Rose L Davies 1925 and John D Davies 1928. They were living at 45 Vaudrey Crescent, Congleton, Cheshire in 1939.
- Wilfred Leonard Gimbert (born 1901) was incapacitated and living with his mother in 1939.
- Gertrude Elizabeth Gimbert (born 1905) married George Webb (1901–60) a potter's biscuit presser, in 1922 and they had six children – Michael GA Webb 1933, Cynthia D Webb 1936, Roy Webb 1938, George Webb 1941, Howard Webb 1943 and Sylvia Webb 1944. They were living at 17 Regent Street, Stoke-on-Trent in 1939. Gertrude married Robert Wright in 1961.
- William Thomas Gimbert (born 1909), an omnibus driver, married Fanny James (1909–99) in 1930 and they had two children – Beryl F Gimbert 1933 and Keith T Gimbert 1944. They were living at 24 Guildford Street, Stoke-on-Trent in 1939.

Ernest contracted tuberculosis as a result of being gassed in March 1918 and reported sick on 16th February 1919. He was admitted to Sunderland War Hospital on 19th February and later spent time in a sanatorium in Staffordshire. As a result he was discharged on 25th April 1919, unfit for further military service and was assessed as 100% disabled. He was awarded the Silver War Badge (B 185577) on

Preston Hall dates back to the 12th Century and was owned by the Culpepper family for over 400 years. In 1848 it was bought by Edward Betts, a railway contractor, who had the old house demolished and rebuilt in the current Jacobean style. The Brassey family bought it in 1867. Henry Brassey was MP for Sandwich 1868–85 and was later Deputy Lieutenant and High Sheriff of Kent. By the outbreak of war in 1914, the house was owned by the Saubers, who let the Hall and estate to the Red Cross for use as a hospital and convalescent home for wounded servicemen. It specialised in treating gas victims and tuberculosis sufferers. It was recognised that tuberculosis would continue to be a major problem after the war and Preston Hall remained a treatment centre. Industrial Settlements Incorporated acquired the estate as a sanatorium and village settlement known as the Preston Hall Colony. The British Legion took over the running in 1925. The Hall was headquarters of Maidstone Health Authority 1983–2012 and in 2014 was sold to Weston Homes for conversion into residential apartments.

The Simplex Electric Company Creda Works at Blythe Bridge in 1947. It was originally a Rootes factory and is now Meir Park housing estate. Early in the Second World War Rootes, like most other car manufacturers, became involved with the Government's shadow factory scheme. The Blythe Bridge site constructed 1,202 Blenheim and Beaufighter aircraft. During the war Rootes built one in every seven British bombers. (*Britain from above*)

The Potteries Electric Traction Company was incorporated in 189 to extend the existing tramway through the Potteries. A coal-fired power station was constructed at the depot at Woodhouse Street, Stoke-on-Trent and the first electric trams ran from Stoke to Longton on 16th May 1899. By 1902 the Company had 105 trams carrying over fourteen million passengers per year. Ernes became a conductor in 1924 and an inspector in 1928, the same year that the system closed (The Potteries).

16th May. He escorted the Battalion Colour when it was laid up in Edensor Church, Chatsworth Park, Derbyshire in January 1922.

Ernest retrained under the Ministry of Pensions (later British Legion) at Preston Hall, Aylesford, Kent as a gamekeeper and the outdoor life aided his recovery. He settled at Leigh near Uttoxeter, Staffordshire and became an agent for a firm marketing ex-servicemen's handicrafts. This did not go well and in 1924 his old headmaster got him a job as a bus conductor with the Potteries Electric Traction Company. He became an inspector in 1928. They were living at 186 Uttoxeter Road, Cheadle, Staffordshire in 1939. During the Second World War Ernest served in the Local Defence Volunteers and later the Home Guard.

Ernest worked as a security officer for Rootes Aircraft Works at Blythe Bridge and was later a lodge man for The Staffordshire Potteries, Meir Heath for fourteen years. Ernest died at his home at 350 Uttoxeter Road, Blythe Bridge, Staffordshire on 14th February 1966 and he is buried in St Peter's Churchyard, Forsbrook, Cheadle Road, Blythe Bridge. He is also commemorated at:

Ernest Egerton's grave in St Peter's Churchyard, Forsbrook. (*Military Images*)

- Ernest Edgerton [sic] Close, Tunstall, Stoke-on-Trent built in 2003, one of four roads named after VCs on Swallows Rise estate in Bankeyfields. The road names were dedicated on 27th January 2004.
- Egerton Close, Uttoxeter Road, Blythe Bridge, dedicated in 2009, part of a housing development built opposite the family home in Uttoxeter Road.
- Egerton Wing (East), Victoria Block, Army Training Centre, Alexander Barracks, Pirbright, Woking, Surrey. Victoria Block, completed in April 2007, accommodates instructor course students and comprises four VC named wings. The others are Nelson Wing (North) after David Nelson, Speakman Wing (South) after William Speakman and White Wing (West) after Archie White.
- A plaque unveiled by his daughter, Margaret Porter, at 350 Uttoxeter Road, Blythe Bridge on 20th September 1997.
- A tablet on the Lodge at Staffordshire Tableware in Meir Park, Staffordshire.
- A portrait of him in St Bartholomew's Church, Burton, Staffordshire.

Ernest's former home at 350 Uttoxeter Road, Blythe Bridge with the plaque unveiled by his daughter in September 1997 to the left of the front door. (*Open Plaques*)

In addition to the VC he was awarded the British War Medal 1914–20, Victory Medal 1914–19 with Mentioned-in-Despatches Oakleaf, George VI Coronation Medal 1937 and Elizabeth II Coronation Medal 1953. After he died the family presented the VC to the Regiment and it is held by the Sherwood Foresters Museum, Nottingham Castle.

LIEUTENANT COLONEL LEWIS PUGH EVANS
The Black Watch (Royal Highlanders) attached 1st Battalion, The Lincolnshire Regiment

Lewis Evans was born at Hen-Blâs, Abermâd, Llanilar, Ceredigion, near Aberystwyth, Cardiganshire, Wales on 3rd January 1881. His father, Griffith Humphrey Pugh Evans (1840–1902), studied medicine but changed careers and became a barrister-at-law in 1867 (Lincoln's Inn). He practised at the Indian Bar and was a member of the Viceroy of India's Legislative Council for twenty years, for which he was knighted (KCIE 24th May 1892). He inherited Lovesgrove, Llanbadarn Fawr, Cardiganshire and built a mansion there in

The family home, Lovesgrove, at Llanbadarn Fawr, Cardiganshire.

1883. He was a JP and DL Cardiganshire. Griffith married Emilia Savi née Hills (1848–1938), born at Neechindipore, India, on 4th September 1873. Emilia was living with her brother, James Hills-Johnes (VC in the Indian Mutiny on 9th July 1857), at Dolancothy, Pumpsaint, Llanwrda, Llandovery, Carmarthenshire in 1911. Her brother-in-law was William George Cubitt (VC in the Indian Mutiny on 30th June 1857). Lewis had six siblings:

• Alice Mary Pugh Evans (1874–1955) was born at sea. She married Richard Townsend Greer (1854–1942) of Dolau, Aberystwyth in 1901. He was the son of the Reverend George Greer, Rector of Ballyhulbert, County Down and was educated at Trinity College, Dublin. He played rugby for the College, Wanderers, North of Ireland and for Ireland.

In 1877 he entered the Indian Civil Service and his appointments included Chairman of the Calcutta Corporation, Commissioner of Behar and Orissa, Inspector General of the Police of Bengal and member of the Council of the Lieutenant-Governor of Bengal for making Laws and Regulations (CSI, LG 1st January 1904). He became a Freemason and was Deputy Grand Master of Bengal. A prominent figure in Calcutta he set up the Indian Youth Athletic Club. In 1912 the couple returned to Llanbadarn Fawr to live at Dolau and he became a JP in 1917. They had four children, including Gladys Gwendolyn Alice Greer 1902 and George Griffith John Greer 1905.

Lewis' uncle, Lieutenant General Sir James Hills-Johnes VC GCB (1833–1919), served during the Indian Mutiny and was awarded the VC for his part in the Siege of Delhli on 9th July 1857. He also took part in the Second Afghan War 1878–80 and was military governor of Kabul.

• Gladys Pugh Evans (1876–1955), born at Calcutta, India, married Harry Arthur Clifton (1874–1947) in 1903. He was commissioned in

7th Dragoons on 19th May 1900 and during the South African War 1899–1902 he served with Béthune's Horse. He was recalled from the Reserve of Officers as a captain on 2nd September 1914 and served in 1/1st Scottish Horse. Promoted major backdated to 23rd August 1914. He served at Gallipoli and in Egypt (MID). Appointed a Deputy Assistant Adjutant General in the Department of the Adjutant General to the Forces on 5th June 1917. Appointed brevet lieutenant colonel 3rd June 1918 and last appears in the Army List in January 1921. They had two children – Cuthbert Clifton 1906 and Gladys Elizabeth Clifton 1911.

- Griffith/Gruffydd Pugh Evans (1879–1946), born at Calcutta, India, was educated at Magdalen College, Oxford (BA History). He was struck by paralysis in 1892, but overcame it to lead an active life as a keen huntsman with the Gogerddan Hounds. He became a barrister-at-law in 1909 (Lincoln's Inn). During the Great War he served as a temporary lieutenant in the Royal Naval Volunteer Reserve from 25th August 1915. He was with Commander Oliver Locker-Lampson's RNAS armoured cars, but by late 1915 there was little use for them in Belgium. Three squadrons were sent to Murmansk as the Armoured Car Expeditionary Force (Russian Armoured Car Division) under Locker-Lampson. They operated with the Russian Army in Galicia, Romania and the Caucasus. Griffith worked under the Military Attaché to Romania from 18th June 1917 and was recommended for good services by Locker-Lampson for his work in France, Russia and Romania and also by General Henri Berthelot, Chief of the French Mission in Romania and Russia, on 23rd January 1919. Griffith was demobilised on 22nd March 1919. He was awarded the Russian Order of St Stanislaus, Belgian Officer of the Crown, Chevalier of the Star of Roumania and the French Croix de Guerre with Palm. He became a farmer at Home Farm, Lovesgrove, and supported local agricultural shows. Griffith was active in local life with the church, in politics, as a JP from 1904, President of the Trefeurig Branch of the British Legion, member of the Council of the Church in Wales, the Territorial Army Association, the Parish Council and DL from 1931. He was living at 36 Buckingham Gate, London in 1911 and died unmarried on 26th July 1946 at Lovesgrove.

- Betha 'Betty' Millicent Pugh Evans (1882–1954) never married. She took a keen interest in the Red Cross Hospital in Aberystwyth during the Great War and helped to run the Woman's Voluntary Service for the Aberystwyth area with her sister Gwyneth. Betha also supported the Girl's Friendly Society and for over fifty years worked on behalf of the Soldiers and Sailors Family Association (Soldiers, Sailors, Airmen and Families Association from 1919).

- James John 'Jim Jack' Pugh Evans (1885–1974) was educated at Eton College and the Royal Military College, Sandhurst. He was commissioned in the Royal Welch Fusiliers on 16th September 1905 and served in India from 9th November. He transferred to the Reserve on 2nd March 1910 and was mobilised with the Territorial Force for 215 days before being appointed lieutenant Welsh Guards on 2nd April 1915. Appointed temporary captain 1st January 1916–5th January 1917 and was promoted captain on 5th March 1917. He was appointed Staff Captain, 1st Guards Brigade 30th April–26th August 1917 and then Brigade Major, 1st Guards Brigade until 3rd February 1919. On 4th February 1919 he was appointed temporary major while Deputy Assistant Adjutant General, Guards Division until 9th May and next day was appointed Regimental Adjutant Welsh Guards until 31st October 1920. He was awarded the MC (LG 3rd June 1916) and Bar (LG 3rd Jun 1918). He was once again Brigade Major, 1st Guards Brigade at Aldershot, Hampshire 30th October 1920–21st January 22. Promoted major on 14th December 1920 and last appears in the Army List in July 1922. He was active locally as a JP 1926–65, High Sheriff of Cardiganshire 1927, DL Carmarthenshire 1943–65, member of the County Agricultural Executive Committee 1948 and Secretary of the Cardigan and Carmarthen Territorial Army Associations. He was awarded the MBE for services in the Carmarthen Sector Home Guard (LG 15th December 1944). James married Viola Murielle Robinson (born 1891) in 1916 and they had two children:

○ Ieuan Lionel Threipland Pugh (1919–36) was educated at Eton College.

○ Humphrey Ap Evans (later Drummond of Megginch (born 1922) was educated at Eton College and Trinity College, Cambridge. He was commissioned on 22nd April 1942 and served in 1st Mountain Regiment, Royal Artillery. He was promoted war substantive lieutenant on 25th October 1942 and temporary captain on 25th November 1943. He was awarded the MC, LG 10th July 1945 and last appears in the Army List in December 1946. In 1952 he married Hon Jean Cherry (1928–2005), later Baroness Strange, eldest daughter of 15th Baron John (Drummond) Strange of Tholt-Y-Will, Sulby Glen, Isle of Man. They had six children – Adam Humphrey Drummond Evans 1953, Charlotte Cherry Evans 1955, Humphrey John Jardine Evans 1961, Amélie Margaret Mary Evans 1963, John Humphrey Hugo Evans 1966 and Catherine Star Violetta Evans 1967. Humphrey was Lord of the Hundred of Shropham and Manors of Banham and Wilby in Norfolk, General Secretary of the Council for the Preservation of Rural Wales 1947–52 and a representative on the National Trust for Wales 1949–54.

• Gwyneth Veronica Pugh Evans (1888–1951) never married. She assisted her sister Betha in the Red Cross Hospital and also worked on behalf of the Girl Guides.

Lewis' paternal grandfather, John Evans JP (c.1804–74) was a lime merchant with a shop in Commerce House, Bridge Street, Aberystwyth. He married Elizabeth née Pugh (c.1808–1902) in 1830 and adopted the middle name of Pugh. He purchased 'Lovesgrove', Llanbadarn Fawr, Cardiganshire for £7,500 in 1843 and was Mayor of Aberystwyth in 1842 and 1844. In addition to Griffith they had five other children:

• Elizabeth Pugh Evans (c.1831–73) married the Reverend Howell Powell Edwards (c.1827–97), Vicar of Caerleon, Monmouthshire in 1852. They had thirteen children – Mary Elizabeth Edwards 1853, Howell Powell Edwards 1855, Sarah Powell Edwards 1856, Margaret Sophia Edwards 1857, Edith Julia Edwards 1858, Elizabeth Clara Edwards 1860, William Rice Edwards 1862, Lewis Pugh Edwards 1864, John Herbert Vaughan Edwards 1866, Elizabeth Agnes Edwards 1867, Ethel Constance Edwards 1869, Arthur Llewelyn Edwards 1870 and Alice Mabel Edwards 1872.

- Lewis Pugh Evans (born and died 1833).
- John Pugh Evans (c.1834–1908) became a clergyman and was Rector of Efenechtyd. He married Ellen Fairclough (born c.1830) in 1864. They had at least three children – Anne Beever Pugh Evans 1870, Sarah Alice Pugh Evans 1872 and John Owen Griffith Pugh Evans 1875.
- Lewis Pugh Evans (1837–1908) was educated at Winchester and Corpus Christi College, Oxford (BA 1859, MA 1868). He married Veronica Harriet née Hills (1844–1931) in 1864 at St Paul's Cathedral, Calcutta, India. She was born at Neechindipore, India, daughter of James Hills and Charlotte Mary Savi, the VC's maternal grandparents. Lewis was a barrister from 1862 (Lincoln's Inn), an additional Member of Council of the Government of India, a member of the Council of the Lieutenant Governor of Bengal, officiated as Standing Counsel to the Government of India and was Attorney General of Bengal. He inherited Abermâd following the death of his bachelor uncle and assumed the surname of Pugh by Royal Licence in accordance with his late uncle's will. He was elected Liberal MP for Cardigan 1880–85 and also served as a JP, High Sheriff and DL Cardiganshire. Lewis died on 6th January 1908 at 2 Theatre Road, Calcutta, India leaving £14,246/6/11 to his widow. He is buried at Llanbadarn Fawr, Cardiganshire. They had ten children:
  ○ Lewis Pugh Evans (later Lewis Pugh Evans Pugh) KC (1865–1940) married Adah Emily Sophia née Chaplin (1867–1953) in 1896, eldest daughter of Thomas Chaplin MD of the English Mission Hospital, Jerusalem. He was a barrister-at-law in the High Court, Calcutta and was appointed Puisne Judge 1910–14. They had six children – Veronica Alice Pugh 1897, Gwladys Mary Pugh 1898, Phyllys Betha Pugh Evans Pugh 1901, Georgina Gwyneth Rosamunde Pugh 1907, Lewis Griffith Cresswell Evans Pugh 1909 and Ruth Myfanwy Pugh 1910. Gwladys Mary Pugh married Ion Percy Fitzgerald Campbell and had a son, Ion Lewis FitzGerald Campbell (1925–50), who served in the Black Watch and with the Malayan Police 1948–50. He died on 17th February 1950 in Malaysia leading a jungle patrol. Lewis Griffith Cresswell Evans Pugh (1909–94) became a doctor. He skied in the World Championships in the downhill and was selected for the cross-country in the 1936 Winter Olympics but could not compete because of injury. He served in the RAMC in the Second World War in Britain, Greece, Crete, Egypt, Ceylon, Iraq, Jerusalem and the School of Mountain Warfare in the Lebanon. In 1953 he was part of the British Everest expedition led by John Hunt during which Edmund Hillary and

Tensing Norgay made the first ascent. Pugh insisted on the provision of adequate oxygen and fluid for the climbers. In 1956–57 he was with the New Zealand team crossing Antarctica. In 1960–61 he spent nine months at 5,800m in the Himalayas on an expedition led by Hillary, studying the physiological effects on the heart and lung in prolonged periods of low oxygen. Later in the 1960s he investigated deaths in young people from hypothermia in the British Isles.

Lewis Griffith Cresswell Evans Pugh.

o Veronica Charlotte Evans Pugh (1867–1969) married John Frederick Macnair (1846–1908) in 1891. They had three children – James Lewis Pugh MacNair 1893, John Hamilton MacNair 1895 and Veronica Janet Macnair 1902.

o Alice Evans Pugh (1868–69).

o James Griffiths Evans Pugh (born 1869).

o Archibald John Pugh CDE VD ADC MLC (1872–1923) married Marian 'Nina' Fraser Arundel (1881–c.1967) in 1894 at Calcutta and they had six children, including Archibald John Pugh, in 1908. He was appointed Adjutant of the Calcutta Light Horse on 22nd March 1901. Promoted captain 26th May 1903, major 22nd February 1908 and was appointed Commandant on 1st October 1920 as a lieutenant colonel. He was Honorary ADC to the Viceroy and Governor-General of India 3rd April 1921–2nd April 1926. He founded Pugh & Son, Solicitors of Calcutta.

o Elinor Pugh (1873–1949) married Ernest William Ormond (c.1863–1930), a judge, in 1896. They had three children – Ernest Charles Ormond 1896, Herbert Edward Ormond 1900 and John Evelyn Ormond 1902. Ernest junior married Nancy Edith Magor in 1930 and had three children – Martin Ormond 1930, Roessa Ormond 1932 and Charmian Ormond 1942. Ernest was commissioned in the Royal Artillery and while serving in France was severely wounded. In 1925 he was called to the Bar (Gray's Inn) and practiced in the High Court, Calcutta. He served again in the Second World War until 1944 and became a Judge of the Calcutta High Court. Ernest was author of *The Law of Patents in India* 1936 and *The Rules of the Calcutta High Court*. He was Judge of the High Court, Dakka, Pakistan 1947–50.

o Herbert Owain Pugh DL (1874–1954) became a merchant in India in 1891–1900. He was commissioned in the Indian Mounted Infantry Corps (Lumsden's Horse), Volunteer Corps (Bengal) on 1st February 1900 and was promoted lieutenant on 16th February. He served in South Africa with Lumsden's Horse and was appointed Assistant District Commissioner, Heilbron. He joined the South African Constabulary in 1901 (DSO, LG 19th April 1901). He was commissioned in 72nd Punjabis on 3rd April 1907 with seniority from 24th January 1906. The date he relinquished this commission is not traceable, but he was appointed honorary lieutenant in the Army with seniority from 12th January 1901. In 1908 he was appointed Secretary to the Territorial Force Associations of the Counties of Carmarthen, Cardigan and Pembroke. Appointed major in the Welsh Horse 30th August 1914. He embarked at Liverpool on 23rd September 1915, disembarked at Mudros on 1st October and landed at Gallipoli on 10th October. He disembarked at Alexandria, Egypt on 25th December. On 25th August 1916 he was granted five weeks home leave, rejoining his unit on 27th October. He was admitted to hospital with lumbago 8th-15th February 1917. On 23rd February he transferred to 1/1st Berkshire Yeomanry from 25th Royal Welsh Fusiliers (formed from 1/1st Welsh Horse and 1/1st Montgomeryshire Yeomanry) to be second-in-command. On 19th April 1917 in the Second Battle of Gaza he received multiple wounds. A bullet fractured the seventh cervical vertebra and there were numerous shrapnel wounds to the back, loins, thigh and both knees. He was admitted to the Anglo-American Hospital, Cairo on 22nd April, listed as dangerously ill with paraplegia of the lower limbs. He was removed from the list on 24th June and transferred to the British Red Cross Hospital, Giza, Cairo. A medical board at Nasrieh Schools Military Hospital on 13th June recommended he be moved to Britain and he was evacuated on HMHS *Kaylan,* arriving on 24th October. He was treated at Lady Carnarvon's Hospital, Bryanston Square, London and a medical board at Caxton Hall on 10th December recommended he be transferred to a south coast convalescent hospital. As a result he was at the Central Military Hospital for Officers, Brighton from January to April 1918 and at Mrs Frank Porter's Convalescent Home for Officers, Woodlyn, Branksome Park, Bournemouth from May to November. On 25th August 1918 he applied to the War Office for his pension to be reconsidered. He had been awarded a £300 wound gratuity and a temporary wound pension of £100 p.a. on the basis that his condition would improve. At the time of writing he still had a bullet lodged in the left knee joint, was able to move short distances only with a walking machine and there was very little movement in the right leg and the foot dropped. He had practically no sense of temperature below the middle, two fingers on the right hand were useless and he had severe pain in the forearm. His eyes were weak, and his bowels alternated between constipation and diarrhoea. He was invalided out of the Army on 7th May 1918, but continued to receive treatment. A medical board at Carmarthen on 26th March 1920 found he still had difficulty using his legs and had limited control of his bladder and bowels. On 4th December 1921 he was awarded constant attendance allowance of £200 p.a. and comforts allowance of £26 p.a. On 5th April 1923 he received retired pay of £-/10/- per day and a wound pension of £400 p.a. His legs never recovered, but he gradually gained control of his arms and his eyes improved, allowing him to continue as Secretary to the Territorial Force Associations of Carmarthen, Cardigan and Pembroke until 1932. Herbert married Edith Mary née Smith (1879–1943) and had two children, including Lewis Henry Owain Pugh (1907–81). Lewis was commissioned in the Royal Artillery on 29th January 1927 and served in Germany between the wars and on the North West Frontier of India. Promoted lieutenant 29th January 1930 and captain 30th January 1938. Later he joined the Special Branch Intelligence Department of the Bengal Police. In the Second World War he returned to the Army and by 1943 was Director of Country Sections with SOE's Force 136 in Calcutta, placing agents and trained saboteurs behind enemy lines in Burma and Malaya. He was appointed temporary lieutenant colonel on 8th January 1943 and on 9th March he led the 'Last Action of the Calcutta Light Horse'. The target was a German merchant ship, *Ehrenfels*, transmitting Allied shipping positions to U-boats from Mormugao harbour in Portugal's neutral territory of Goa. The incident was revealed in the 1978 book *Boarding Party – The Last Action of the Calcutta Light Horse*, and in the 1980 film, *Sea Wolves*, starring Gregory Peck as Pugh. Promoted major 29th January 1944, acting colonel 18th June 1945, temporary brigadier 20th November 1949, colonel 29th January 1951 and major general 1st March 1957. He was appointed Brigadier General Staff, Department of the Chief of the Imperial General Staff on 25th September 1952 and Chief of Staff HQ Far East Land Forces on 14th January 1956. He was Colonel of 2nd King Edward VII's Own Gurkha Rifles from 20th March 1956. Lewis retired to the family estate in 1961 as a major general CB CBE and DSO with three Bars.

o Evelyn A Pugh (1875–1952) married Captain Thomas James Sellar (c.1878–1924) in 1902 at St Paul's Cathedral, Calcutta.

o Roland Anthony Evans Pugh (born c.1879–1946) married Nina Easter Lilian Bowen (1895–1974) in 1923. They had four children – Elizabeth EJ Pugh 1929, Anthony CR Pugh 1932, Marjorie FF Pugh 1936 and another daughter.

o Marjorie Pugh (1880–1936) married Alexander Cox Patterson (1872–1948) in 1905 and they had three children – Lewis David Malcolm Patterson 1906, John Alec C Patterson 1908 and Veronica Helen Emileen Patterson 1910. Alexander played cricket for Crystal Palace 1892, Old Cliftonians 1894 and Calcutta Cricket Club 1897–1903. He was an East India merchant when he attested in the RAF on 16th August 1918 (285282). He was appointed Sheriff of Merionethshire.

Lewis Henry Owain Pugh during a publicity event for the 1980 film, *Sea Wolves*, in which he was played by Gregory Peck (Rob Bogaerts).

- David Pugh Jones Evans (c.1840–97) married Martha Jane Owen (1846–1929) in 1887. He was Rector of Trefonen, Salop 1874–78, Vicar of Carmarthen 1878–85 and Vicar of Lampeter Velfrey from April 1885.
- Mary Margaret Evans (1845–1929) married Charles Gunning (c.1812–87), a surgeon, in 1885. He had been married previously to Ann Fisher in 1850 and Eliza Coakley in 1876.

His maternal grandfather, James (later Sir) Hills (1801–72), was one of the largest landowners and indigo planters in Bengal, India. He was living at Dean Bank House, Edinburgh 1851–53. James married Charlotte Mary (or Marie) née Savi (1813–50), born at Chandernagore, India, in 1831 at St Andrew's Church, Calcutta, India. In addition to Emilia they had nine other children:

- Archibald Hills (1832–96) was born at Chandernagore, West Bengal, India. He was educated at Edinburgh Academy 1843–47 and the Scottish Naval and Military Academy 1848–49, intending to serve in the Indian Army, but changed his mind in order to inherit his father's businesses in Bengal in 1851. He married Emma Louisa Erle White (1839–93) in 1860 at Rampore, Bengal. She was the daughter of Dr William White, Indian Medical Department. Archibald was passionate about hunting wild boar and was described by Lord William Beresford VC as the *Prince of Pig-stickers in Bengal.* They had several children including – James William Gordon Hills 1862, Archibald Hills 1863, Elliot Brownlois Hills 1864, Charlotte Mabel Hills 1867, Archibald Chalmers Hills 1868, Sybil May Hills 1870 and Lilian Julia Alice Hills 1875. Emma was living with her daughter Lilian at Grosvenor, Esplanade, Isle of Wight, Hampshire in 1891. Archibald was living at Patkabari, Moorshedabad, Bengal when he died.
- John Hills (1834–1902) was born at Bombay, Maharashtra, India. He was educated at Edinburgh Academy 1844–47 and Edinburgh University, where he was awarded the Straton Gold Medal. He entered the East India Company Military Seminary (Addiscombe College) in August 1852 and was commissioned in the Bombay Engineers on 8th June 1854. After some basic instruction at Brompton Barracks, Chatham, Kent, he arrived at Bombay in August 1856. He passed a course in Hindustani and was appointed Assistant Field Engineer with 2nd Division of the Persian Expeditionary Force under Major General Sir James Outram on 14th January 1857 and was present at the capture of Mohamrah. Promoted lieutenant 5th November 1857, captain 1st September 1863, major 5th July 1872, lieutenant colonel 1st October 1877 and brevet colonel 1st October 1881. He was elected a Fellow of the Royal Society of Edinburgh on 21st March 1859. John held a number of appointments – Garrison Engineer at Fort William Calcutta, Assistant to the Chief Engineer of the Public Works Department in Lucknow in January 1862 and Executive Engineer in Rajputana 1865. He joined the Abyssinian Expedition under Major General Sir Robert Napier in 1867, where he was Field

Engineer at Kumeyli camp and assisted in sinking wells for water supply and the construction of roads from the railhead at Kumeyli to Senafeh (MID). He returned to Lucknow and commanded the Bombay Sappers and Miners at Kirkee 1871–83. During the Second Anglo-Afghan War 1879–80, he commanded a division in the Kandahar Field Force and the South Afghanistan Field Force and took part in the defence of Kandahar (MID and CB, LG 22nd February 1881). John commanded the expeditionary force to Burmah in 1886–87 and retired on 31st December 1887 as honorary major general (KCB May 1900). He was an all-round sportsman, excelling at cricket, swimming, swordsmanship and shooting. He published *The Bombay Field Force, 1880* and *Points of a Racehorse* in 1903. He died unmarried at 50 Weymouth Street, London on 18th June 1902 and is buried in the family vault at Kensal Green. Effects valued at £585/8/6 were left to Sir James Hills-Johnes VC.

• George Scott Hills (1835–92) was born at Neechindipore, Bengal. He was educated at Edinburgh Academy 1844–47 and the East India Company Military Seminary (Addiscombe College) 1853–55. He was living with his uncle Robert and aunt Jackina Barton at Dean Bank Lodge, Edinburgh in 1851. He was commissioned in the Bengal Engineers in 1855 and served during the Indian Mutiny 1857–58. He was in action during the capture of Forts Dehgar and Tirhoul and with the Sobraon Field Force. Promoted lieutenant 1858, captain 1867, major 1873, lieutenant colonel 2nd March 1881 and colonel 2nd March 1885. He transferred to the Royal Engineers in 1861 and took part in the Bhootan Expedition 1864–65 and the Second Anglo-Afghan War 1879–80. He died at 33 Regent's Park Road, London on 11th May 1892.

• Robert Savi Hills (1837–1909) was born at Neechindipore, Bengal. He was educated at Edinburgh Academy 1850–53 and Winchester College, where he played rugby in the first match against Marlborough in 1855. He played professional cricket for Marylebone Cricket Club 1867–76. Robert married Agnes Leonore Hay (c.1860–1940) in 1896. She was born at Bothwell, Lanarkshire, daughter of William Hay, distiller and Susanna Glennie Doulton. At the time of his marriage Robert was living at Rattray House, Crimond, Aberdeenshire. They lived at Keith Hall, Inverurie, Aberdeenshire. She was living with her children at Frimley, Surrey in 1911. They had eight children – Nora Agnes Hills 1896, Charlotte Alice Hills 1898, Eileen Constance Hills 1899, Lucy Hills 1901, Robert Savi Hills 1902, James Hills 1903, John Hills 1905 and George Ker Hills 1906. John Hills served as a squadron leader in the RAFVR on the Allied Control Mission in Italy. He died of blood poisoning in Rome on 5th July 1945 (Rome Cemetery – I C 30).

• Elizabeth Scott Hills (1838–97) was born at Kishnagur, Bengal. She married Captain Jenkin Jones, Bombay Engineers, in July 1857 at All Saint's Church, St John's Wood, London. He was commissioned in the Royal Bengal Engineers on 9th December 1844 and was promoted lieutenant 9th October 1848, captain 24th May 1856, lieutenant colonel 1st September 1863, colonel 1st September

1868, major general 24th August 1878 and lieutenant general 31st December 1878. He retired by 1881. They had eleven children – Charlotte Mary Jones 1860, Jenkin Jones 1861, Florence Henrietta Jones 1863, Harry Jones 1864, Lizzie Emilia Augusta Jones 1864, William Ellanan Jones 1867, James Hills Jones 1869, Veronica Christine Jones 1872, Violet Frances Jones 1876, a stillborn son 1877 and Charles Angelo Jones 1879.

- Charlotte Isabella Hills (1840–1916) married William George Cubitt VC (1835–1903) on 19th May 1863 at Fort William Church, Calcutta, West Bengal. They were living at Greenhill, Harrow-on-the-Hill, Middlesex in 1881 before moving to Collingwood House, Eastfield, Camberley, Surrey. They had five children – William Martin Cubitt 1864, James Edward Cubitt 1865, Ethel Mary Cubitt 1868, Lewis Hills Court Cubitt 1872 and Helen A Cubitt 1874.
- Elliot Macnaghten Hills (1842–43) was born at Neechindipore.
- Veronica Harriet Hills (1844–1931) was also born at Neechindipore. She married Lewis Pugh Evans, paternal uncle of Lewis Pugh Evans VC, in 1864 – see above.
- Charles Richard Hills (1847–1935) was born at Kishenagur.

Lewis was educated at Eton College January 1895–December 1898 and the Royal Military College, Sandhurst from January 1899. He had hoped to join the Royal Welsh Fusiliers but was instead commissioned in the Black Watch on 23rd December 1899. He served in the South African War with 2nd Battalion February 1900–January 1902. He was involved in operations in:

St Andrew's Church, Calcutta, India, where Lewis Evans' maternal grandparents married in 1831.

Eton College in Berkshire was founded by King Henry VI in 1440. It has produced nineteen British Prime Ministers, the latest being David Cameron. Numerous members of the Royal Family have been educated there, including Princes William and Harry. Other notable Old Etonians include Aldous Huxley, George Orwell, Ian Fleming, Beau Brummell, John Maynard Keynes, Ranulph Fiennes, Bear Grylls and Hubert Parry. The College has produced numerous TV presenters and actors including Ludovic Kennedy, Eddie Redmayne, Damian Lewis, Hugh Lawrie, and Michael Bentine. Thirty-seven Old Etonians have been awarded the VC, the largest number for any school.

Orange Free State February–May 1900, including at Poplar Grove, Driefontein (10th March 1900) and Vet River.

Transvaal May–June 1900, including actions at Johannesburg (31st May 1900), Pretoria and Diamond Hill (11th-12th June 1900).

Transvaal (east of Pretoria) July–29 November 1900, including action at Belfast (26th-27th August 1900).

Orange River Colony November 1900–January 1902.

He was promoted lieutenant on 1st May 1901. During operations around Ladybrand he was captured and held prisoner for a short period. He suffered from diptheria and rheumatism and was in hospital for two months. After South Africa he served in India, where in 1905 he was taken dangerously ill with enteric fever. Promoted captain 27th October 1906 and returned to Britain in 1913. He enrolled at the Bristol Flying School, Brooklands, near London and learned to fly under Mr Merriman. He went solo on 7th August 1913 and gained Royal Aero Club certificate No. 595 on 20th August flying a Bristol Biplane. Lewis passed out of the Staff College, Camberley in the summer of 1914 and was appointed GSO3 at the War Office, London on 20th August. His Medal Index Card records him proceeding to France with 1st Black Watch on 14th August 1914, but he was employed in the War Office from 20th August 1914 to 15th September 1914 in the Army List, which shows he went to France on 16th September. He was posted to the RFC at Netheravon, Wiltshire and went to France on 16th September 1914, arriving at Fère-en-Tardenois, France as an observer in No.3 Squadron RFC on 22nd September. James B McCudden, later VC DSO & Bar and MC & Bar, was also in the Squadron. Lewis was engaged on reconnaissance work. At that time mechanical defects were more of a threat than the Germans. Flying with his pilot, Sergeant Reggie Carr, they suffered engine failure over the German lines but managed to make the French lines before landing. Carr repaired the fault and they flew back to their base.

Lewis applied to return to his Regiment and was posted as a company commander to 1st Black Watch on 13th December. He was appointed Brigade Major of 7th Brigade 3rd May 1915–29th February 1916. **Awarded the DSO for his actions at Hooge, Belgium on 16th June 1915, when the troops became mixed up he moved up and down the line under continuous heavy fire from 10 a.m.**

A 1913 advertisement for the Bristol flying schools. Lewis Evans trained at Brooklands. The airfield on Salisbury Plain was at Larkhill, close to Netheravon, where Lewis joined the RFC in September 1914.

until midnight reorganising units and bringing back their reports, LG 24th July 1915. Promoted major 1st September 1915 and was appointed GSO2 HQ 6th Division 1st March 1916–5th March 1917. On 23rd March 1917 he was appointed temporary lieutenant colonel and CO 1st Lincolnshire.

Awarded the VC for his actions near Reutel, Belgium on 4th October 1917, LG 26th November 1917. He relinquished his acting rank on 5th October and was evacuated to England on 16th October. The VC was presented by the King at Buckingham Palace on 2nd January 1918. Lewis returned to resume command of 1st Lincolnshire on 4th January 1918, but took command of 1st Black Watch on 23rd January as acting lieutenant colonel, which he held until 9th June. **Awarded a Bar to the DSO for his actions at Givenchy 18th-20th April 1918; on the first day he moved about all over the forward areas, the next day he personally conducted a reconnaissance for a counterattack, which he led on the third day, driving the enemy out of the forward system, LG 16th September 1918.** He was appointed temporary brigadier general to command 14th Brigade 10th June 1918–17th February 1919, succeeding VC winner Frederick Lumsden. **Lewis was Mentioned in Field Marshal Sir John French's Despatch dated 30th November 1915 (LG 1st January 1916) and in Field Marshal Sir Douglas Haig's Despatches dated 9 April 1917 (LG 15th May 1917), 8th November 1918 (LG 20th December 1918) and 16th March 1919 (LG 5th July 1919). He was awarded the CMG for services in command of 14th Brigade, LG 3rd June 1919.** He was also awarded the Belgian Officier de l'Ordre de Leopold (LG 24th September 1917) and the Belgian Croix de Guerre (LG 11th March 1918).

Netheravon airfield just before the First World War.

Holy Trinity Church, Sloane Square, London, where Lewis Pugh Evans married Dorothea Margaret Segrave Vaughan-Pryse-Rice on 10th October 1918. It was built in 1888–90 in arts and crafts style by 5th Earl Cadogan, replacing an earlier Gothic style church. The new church was attended by Liberal politician and four times Prime Minister, William Ewart Gladstone (1809–98). During the Blitz it was badly damaged by incendiary bombs, but had been restored by the early 1960s. The church authorities wanted to demolish the building, but a successful campaign to retain it was led by John Betjeman and the Victorian Society.

On 10th October 1918 Lewis married Dorothea Margaret Segrave née Pryse-Rice (1894–1921) at Holy Trinity Church, Sloane Square, London. Colonel the Hon Maurice Drummond DSO Black Watch was best man. Dorothy, as she was known, and her sisters Nest and Faith were living with their great aunt, Louisa Stewart, at Machonochie House, Gloucester Road, Bognor, Sussex in 1901. She served as a nurse in the Red Cross from 1914–19 and she and her sister, Nest, are commemorated on the Llandovery (Carmarthenshire Red Cross) Memorial. Dorothy died of influenza at St Thomas, Devon on 5th December 1921 and she is buried at Llandingat Church, Llanymddyfri, Carmarthenshire.

Dorothea is buried at Llandingat Church, Llanymddyfri.

They had a son, Griffith Eric Carberry Vaughan-Pryse-Rice Evans (19th February 1920–3rd July 1950), known as Eric, was born at Chelsea, London. He was educated at Eton College and Trinity College, Cambridge. He received a Regular Army Emergency Commission in the Black Watch on 1st October 1939 and was promoted war substantive lieutenant on 1st April 1941. He was appointed staff captain and acting captain on 1st May 1942 and last appears in the Army List in early 1945. He succeeded to the estate of Aberglasney on the death of his great aunt, Mary Ann Emily Jane Mayhew, in 1939. Griffith married Barbara Noel née Rogers (born 1924) on 26th July 1943 and they had two sons:

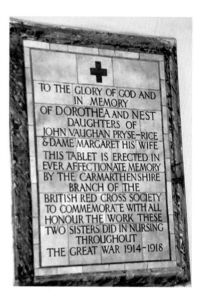

The Llandovery (Carmarthenshire Red Cross) Memorial to Dorothea and Nest (teaserbox).

- Christopher Lewis Vaughan Pryse Evans (born 5th December 1945), educated at Stowe and the Royal Agricultural College Cirencester, inherited the Lovesgrove Estate on the death of his grandfather. He married Prudence CM Winter-Blyth (born in Bombay, India 1947) in 1971.
- Roger David Loveden Evans (born 23rd June 1947) was educated at Eton College, Berkshire. He married Karen J Sinclair in 1973 and they had two daughters – Polly Beatrice Evans 1973 and Charlotte Imogen Evans 1975. Roger and Karen were directors of ACE Debt Recovery Ltd, Ruffe House, Fountains, Ripon, North Yorkshire.

Barbara married Michael Andrew Lyndon Skeggs (born 1926) on 8th April 1953 and they had two daughters – Victoria IL Skeggs 1954 and Marianne EL Skeggs 1955.

Dorothy's father, John Carbery Pugh Vaughan-Pryse-Rice (1859–1937) was born as Vaughan-Pryse. He assumed the additional name of Rice by Royal Licence on 26th July 1887 in compliance with the last will and testament of his maternal uncle, George Watkin Rice-Watkins. John was a keen hunter with hounds. He was appointed DL Cardiganshire, Mayor of Llandovery 1905–12 and re-elected 1913, High Sheriff Carmarthenshire 1891 and JP. He married Margaret Ker née Stewart (1869–1948) in 1887 at St George Hanover Square, London. She hunted the counties of Carmarthenshire and Brecknockshire with the Hare Hunting Harriers and was a member of the Hunter Improvement Society. She was created DBE for services during the war as President of the Carmarthenshire Branch of the British Red Cross Society, LG 7th January 1918. In addition to Dorothea they had three other children:

- Carine Evelyn Nest Pryse-Rice (1896–1921) served as a nurse in the Red Cross as a staff nurse at Llandovery Auxiliary Hospital 1914–19. She was killed in a railway accident at Abermule, Montgomeryshire on 26th January 1921.
- Faith Viola Alison Pryse-Rice (1899–1913) died on 11th August 1913 following an operation for appendicitis.
- George Carbery Pryse-Rice (1904–71) married Celia Blanche Steward (1912–2002), daughter of Captain Rupert Donald Stewart, 7th Dragoons, in 1933 and they had a daughter, Rosemary A Pryse-Rice, in 1934.

Lewis' sister-in-law, Carine Evelyn Nest Pryse-Rice, was one of seventeen people killed in a railway accident at Abermule, Montgomeryshire on 26th January 1921. Another thirty-six were injured. One of the others who died was Lord Herbert Lionel Vane-Tempest, a Director of Cambrian Railways, whose estate was inherited by Winston Churchill.

After the war Lewis was appointed temporary brigadier general and Base Commandant Rotterdam 18th February–6th November 1919. He reverted to temporary lieutenant colonel and was appointed an instructor at the Senior Officers School 18th January 1920–23rd May 1921. On 7th June 1921 he was appointed brigade major and on 16th February 1923 GSO2 Scottish Command until 15th April 1925. Promoted lieutenant colonel and CO 2nd Black Watch 15th September 1926–15th September 1930. Appointed brevet colonel 1st January 1928 and promoted colonel 5th September 1930. Appointed Assistant Adjutant General, Eastern Command on 15th May 1931 and commanded 159th (Welsh Border) Infantry

Brigade TA on promotion to brigadier 18th May 1933–18th May 1937. On 28th January 1936 he was a pall-bearer at King George V's funeral. He went onto Half Pay on 19th May 1937 until retiring on 3rd January 1938 as honorary brigadier. **Awarded the CB on retirement, LG 9th June 1938.**

Lewis had inherited the Lovesgrove Estate on the death of his father in 1902 and took an active part in the life of the community. He was made a Freeman of the Borough of Aberystwyth. His appointments included:

Chairman of the Royal British Legion at Llanbadarn Fawr.

President and later patron of Aberystwyth Royal British Legion Branch for twenty-five years.

President of the Royal British Legion for Cardiganshire.

County Commissioner of St John's Ambulance Brigade (**OStJ, 27th June 1941 and CStJ, LG 8th July 1947**).

President of the Jersey Cattle Society (Wales).

JP Cardiganshire 1943 and Chairman of the Llanbadarn Fawr Bench.

Churchwarden at Llanbadarn.

Member of the Governing Body of the Church in Wales. DL Cardiganshire from 1st November 1937 – he declined the Lord Lieutenancy of Cardiganshire in 1952 on the grounds of age.

He served as Military Liaison Officer Western Command with Regional Commissioner Wales 1939–6th December 1941 and was chairman of a selection board for granting Home Guard commissions in December 1940. He was appointed Honorary Colonel 16th (Welsh) Parachute Battalion from 1947 and Honorary Colonel Cardiganshire Cadet Force. He attended a number of VC reunions:

VC Garden Party at Buckingham Palace on 26th June 1920.

VC Dinner at the Royal Gallery of the House of Lords, London on 9th November 1929.

VC Centenary Celebrations at Hyde Park, London on 26th June 1956.

The 3rd VC & GC Association Reunion at the Café Royal, London on 18th July 1962.

On 30th November 1962 Lewis left Aberystwyth to attend his grandson's confirmation and died of a heart attack after stepping off the train at Paddington Station, London. He is buried in St Padarn's Churchyard, Llanbadarn Fawr, Cardiganshire (Section E1–E13). He is commemorated in a number of other places:

Lewis Pugh Evans is buried in the churchyard of St Padarn's, Llanbadarn Fawr, Cardiganshire. (*Ian Capper*)

Lewis Pugh Evans' gravestone.

- Plaque at Llanbadarn Fawr war memorial, Cardiganshire unveiled in October 1991 by Major General Dick Gerard-Wright CB CBE.
- Named on the Eton College Cloisters For Valour Memorial, unveiled by the Queen on 27th May 2010.
- His VC action featured in Issue 485 of the Victor Comic, entitled 'Man of Steel', dated 6th June 1970.
- A portrait of him by S Morse Brown held by the National Museum of Wales.
- The scroll and sword presented to him by the civic leaders at the end of the war are displayed in Aberystwyth town museum.

In addition to the VC he was awarded the CB, CMG, DSO & Bar, Commander of the Order of the Hospital of St John of Jerusalem, Queen's South Africa Medal 1899–

Llanbadarn Fawr war memorial with inset the Lewis Pugh Evans VC memorial, mounted on the wall behind (Memorials to Valour).

The Eton College Cloisters For Valour Memorial commemorating the thirty-seven VC winners from the school.

1902 with five clasps (Cape Colony, Laing's Nek, Johannesburg, Diamond Hill & Belfast), King's South Africa Medal 1901–02 with two clasps (South Africa 1901 & South Africa 1902), 1914 Star with 'Mons' clasp, British War Medal 1914–20, Victory Medal 1914–19 with Mentioned-in-Despatches Oakleaf, Defence Medal, George V Delhi Durbar Medal 1911, George V Silver Jubilee Medal 1935, George VI Coronation Medal 1937, Elizabeth II Coronation Medal 1953, Belgian Order of Leopold and Belgian Croix de Guerre 1914–18. The VC was acquired by Lord Ashcroft's VC collection in 2009 and is displayed in the Imperial War Museum's Lord Ashcroft Gallery.

The George V Delhi Durbar Medal 1911 was awarded mainly to the officers and men of British regiments who took part in the Durbar. About 26,800 medals were issued.

23715 CORPORAL FRED GREAVES
9th Battalion, The Sherwood Foresters (Nottinghamshire and Derbyshire Regiment)

Fred Greaves was born at Killamarsh, Derbyshire on 16th May 1890. His father, Jude Greaves (1867–1937), a coal miner hewer, married Edith Louisa née Rodgers (1868–1944) at St John's Church, Ridgeway on 25th December 1889. They were living at Netherhope, Killamarsh in 1891, at 44 Arkwright Town, Sutton-cum-Duckmanton by 1901 and at High Common, Barlborough, near Chesterfield in 1911. Fred had eleven siblings:

- Edith Greaves (1892–1970) married James William Hutchings (1881–1943) in 1914. He was a colliery hewer in 1939 and the family was living at 3 Bell House Lane, Staveley, Derbyshire. They had two daughters – Joyce Hutchings 1915 and Barbara Hutchings 1921.
- Harry Greaves (1894–1945) was a coal miner pony driver below ground in 1911. He enlisted in the Sherwood Foresters (15523) on 9th September 1914 and joined the Depot at Derby next day. He was described as 5' 6" tall, weighing 146 lbs, with fair complexion,

Barlborough High Street.

blue eyes, light brown hair and his religious denomination was Primitive Methodist. Posted to 11th Battalion on 19th September and appointed drummer 1st November. He embarked at Folkestone for France on 27th August 1915. Awarded seven days Field Punishment No.1 for disregarding Battalion orders on 23rd November. He was admitted to 25th Field Ambulance with impetigo 2nd-5th February 1916. Promoted lance corporal 5th July, corporal 17th September 1916 and lance sergeant 1st March 1917. He applied for a commission on 7th April, returned to Britain on 17th April and joined No.9 Officer Cadet Battalion at Gailes on 6th July. Harry was commissioned in the Sherwood Foresters Special Reserve on 31st October 1917, reported to the 3rd Battalion on 3rd November and was attached to 1st Battalion in France. He was awarded the DSO for his actions near Oppy, France on 6th-7th October 1918, when he led his platoon to their objective on two occasions in the face of heavy fire and stubborn resistance, capturing twenty-three prisoners and two machine guns (LG 8th March and 4th October 1919). He was also awarded the MC and two Bars (LG 16th September 1918, 2nd December 1918 and 11th January 1919). He was demobilised on 23rd February 1919 and relinquished his commission with effect from 1st April 1920 on 10th November 1920, retaining the rank of lieutenant. He is understood to have married Mary Ellen Atkin (1893–1972) in 1918 at Worksop, Nottinghamshire. They had two children – Dorothy M Greaves 1921 and Margaret Wendy Greaves 1926. Dorothy served in the WAAF as a corporal in the Second World War.

- Jude Greaves (born and died 1897).
- Frank Greaves (1897–1968) was a coal miner pony driver below ground in 1911. He married Stella Howells (born 1898) in 1924. They had six children – Nellie Greaves 1925, Doreen Greaves 1929, Audrey Greaves 1933, twins Derek and Peter Greaves 1934 and Margaret Gillian Greaves 1936. They were living at Co-op House, Clowne, Derbyshire in 1939.
- Jude Greaves (1899–1967) married Kate Gee-Pemberton (born 1906) in 1931. They had a son, Michael Greaves, in 1937. He was a colliery deputy in 1939 and the family was living at Poplars, High Common, Clowne, Derbyshire.
- Olive Greaves (1901–85) married Lawrence William Howells (1897–1980) in 1925. They had a son, Ian Howells, in 1939 and had moved to Blackpool, Lancashire by 1967.
- Louie Greaves (1902–68) died unmarried.
- John Greaves (1905–79) married Annie Brown (born 1900) in 1932. He was a colliery hewer below ground in 1939 and the family was living at High Common, Clowne in 1939. They had two children – John P Greaves 1934 and Pamela Greaves 1943.

Fred and Harry Greaves – a VC, DSO and three MCs between them. (*Hazel Greaves*)

- Ellen Greaves (born 1907).
- Jessie Greaves (born 1908).
- Harvey Greaves (born 1910) was a grocery provisions and cattle feed dealer in 1939 living with his sisters Edith, Louie and Jessie at 4 Barlborough Road, Clowne. He married Ivy C Turner (born 1916), a ladies hairdresser, in 1942. They had four children – Jennifer Greaves 1946, Sharon Greaves 1956, Ian Greaves 1960 and Paul William Greaves 1966.

Fred's paternal grandfather, John Greaves (c1825–89), a coal miner, was lodging at Cresswell at Elmton, Derbyshire in 1851. He married Sarah née Mallender/Mallinder (c.1833–1902) on 17th October 1852 at the Church of St Peter & St Paul, Sheffield, Yorkshire. In 1851 Sarah Mallinder was a servant at Killamarsh, boarding with her brother James, a coal miner. By 1861 John and Sarah were living at Netherthorpe Lane, Killamarsh with his widowed father. In 1871 and 1881 John was a farmer of thirty-four acres and they were living at Forge Lane, Killamarsh. He was living at Nether Moor, Killamarsh at the time of his death. In 1891 Sarah was living at Netherthorpe Lane, Killamarsh with four of her children and two grandchildren. She was still there in 1901 with her grandson Samuel. In addition to Jude they had eleven other children:

- John Greaves (1852–1915) was boarding with his brother Samuel in 1901.
- George Greaves (1854–1919), a colliery labourer, married Harriet French (1854–1911) in 1873. He was living with his children at 57 Bonds Main, Temple Normanton, Derbyshire at the time of the 1911 Census. They had eleven children – John Greaves 1874, Harvey Greaves 1876, Edward Greaves 1878, Luke Greaves 1880, Wilfred Greaves 1882, Walter Greaves 1884, Annie Greaves c.1888, Charles Greaves 1889, Nellie Greaves 1891, Ernest Greaves 1893 and Rhoda Greaves 1894.
- Hannah Greaves (1857–59).
- Daniel Greaves (1860–1939), a coal miner, had a relationship with Jane Plant (1863–1956), a dressmaker, and they had two children – Samuel Greaves 1882 and Lucy Greaves c.1884. Jane Plant married James William Simpson Gray (1876–1959), in 1901. By 1911 he was a police constable and they were living at Myrtle Cottages, Flaxpiece Road, Clay Cross, Derbyshire. Daniel married Mary Ann Bartlett (1872–1930), a vocalist, in 1914 at Dover, Kent giving their address as 19 Chapel Place there. Mary had a daughter, Lily Holmes Bartlett, born in 1899. In 1901 Daniel and Mary were living with his sister, Eliza, at Rotherham, Yorkshire, giving his age as twenty-nine and married. In 1911 they were living as husband and wife at 39 Bolton Street, Denaby Main, Yorkshire, giving his age as forty-six and declaring they had been married for eleven years. They had nine children – William Greaves 1901, Horace Greaves 1903, Joseph Greaves 1904, Harold Greaves 1906, Paul Greaves 1908, Jeanie Greaves 1910, Rose Greaves 1912, James Greaves 1914 and another child who did not survive infancy.

- Rachel Greaves (1861–1942) married Frederick Wilkins (c.1861–1934) in 1882. They had six children – Louisa Wilkins 1888, Nellie Wilkins 1892, Jude Wilkins 1897, Albert Wilkins 1902, Thomas Wilkins 1905 and William Wilkins 1907. She was living at 15 Lansbury Road, Chesterfield in 1939.
- Harvey Greaves (born and died 1864).
- Samuel Greaves (born 1865), a coal miner stone man, married Betsy Kirkland (1868–1930) in 1887. They were living at 101 Ark Town, Chesterfield in 1901 and at 57 The Park, Brodsworth, Doncaster by 1911. They had nine children – Alice Greaves 1892, Sarah Greaves 1894, Wilfred Greaves 1895, Jude Greaves 1897, Betsy Greaves 1899, Samuel Greaves 1900, Isaac Greaves 1902, Kathleen Greaves 1907 and Elizabeth Greaves 1909.
- Charles Greaves (born 1870), a coal miner hewer, married Elizabeth Turner (born 1871) in 1892. She had a daughter, Rose Turner, in 1889. They were living at Thornleigh Cottages, Barlborough Common, Derbyshire in 1911. They had five children – Joseph Greaves 1893, Nellie Greaves 1893, James Greaves 1895, Frank Greaves 1897 and Herbert Greaves 1901.
- Eliza Greaves (born 1873) married Matthew James (born 1869 at Newport, Monmouthshire), a coal miner stone cutter, in 1893. They were living at 27 Sherwood Crescent, Rotherham, Yorkshire in 1901 and at 76 Station Road, Halfway, Eckington, Derbyshire in 1911. They had six children including – Ellen James 1895, Doris James 1898, Maggie James 1899, Edith Annie James 1901 and Matthew James 1904.
- Alice Greaves (born 1874) was a domestic servant in 1891, working for George Leah, a farmer, and his family. She married James William Bennett (born 1870) in 1892 at Leicester. They had four children, but only two survived by the time of the 1911 Census – Gordon Masters Bennett 1895 and Marjorie Alice Bennett 1899.
- Rhoda Greaves (1877–1967) married Herbert Wesson (1871–1961), a shopkeeper, in 1901 at Leicester. They were living at 28 Checketts Road, Leicester in 1911 and at 110 Willow Street, Leicester in 1939. They had three children – Florence Gertrude Wesson 1901, Rhoda Wesson 1904 and Robert Wesson 1906.

His maternal grandfather, George Rodgers (1840–1900), a coal miner, was living at 125 Lightwood Lane, Eckington, Derbyshire in 1871. He married Sarah née Bunting (1842–1918) in 1875 and they were still at 125 Lightwood Lane in 1891. She was living at Eckington, Derbyshire in 1901. In addition to Edith had five other children:

- Albert Thomas Rodgers (1864–1949), a coal miner, married Louisa Frost (1863–1930) in 1887. They were living next door to his parents at Lightwood Lane, Eckington in 1891. By 1901 he was a deputy in a coal mine, living with his family at Bole Hill, Marsh Lane and at 83 Bonds Main, Chesterfield by 1911. They

had five children including – Florence Rodgers 1892, Lily Rodgers 1895, Maggie Rodgers 1897 and Arthur Rodgers 1899. He was living at 83 Sycamore Street, Chesterfield in 1939.
- Frederick Rodgers (born 1870) was a coal miner in 1891.
- Ellen Rodgers (born 1874).
- Mary Emma Rodgers (born 1876) was an assistant at home in 1891. She married Joseph Shaw (born 1880), a coal miner, in 1907. They were living at 68 South Street, Ardwick-le-Street, Yorkshire in 1911 and at 9 Doncaster Road, Ardwick-le-Street in 1939. They had four children – Joseph Arthur Shaw 1909, Charles Bernard Shaw 1910, Mavis M Shaw 1913 and Grace Shaw 1921.
- George Rodgers (born c.1878) was a coal miner, living with his mother in 1901.

Fred was educated at Bonds Main Council School. He was employed as a miner at Bonds Main and later at Barlborough No.2 Pit and Markham Colliery. He survived a number of accidents and suffered a broken jaw and ribs. At Barlborough No.2 Pit he was run over by a coal truck, which broke both his legs and crushed his pelvis. He spent two years in Chesterfield Hospital recovering and when he was discharged had to walk nine miles to get home because his parents could not afford the bus fare. For the rest of his life part of a bone protruded under his skin, causing him some discomfort, which he relieved by tightly binding his leg. Doctors suggested that he take up cycling to rebuild his wasted muscles. Fred joined the Sheffield Cycling Club and excelled in the saddle despite his injuries. He thought nothing of cycling to Skegness and back in a day, a round trip of over 140 miles. In August 1913 the Club presented him with a medallion for covering 190 miles in twelve hours. He was the Club's twenty-five miles championship in May 1914 in a time of one hour fifteen minutes and forty-nine seconds, and that year he became the Derbyshire fifty and one hundred miles champion.

In 1896 the Staveley Coal & Iron Co sank a new pit northeast of Barlborough. Officially it was named Barlboro No.2, but was known as Peggers Pit, Pebley Pit or Oxcroft No.4. The last seam worked was abandoned in September 1928, but the pit was used as an upcast shaft for Bariboro No.1 Pit until April 1949.

Bond's Main operated at Temple Normanton, near Chesterfield from 1895 until 1949. It was sunk initially by Staveley Coal & Iron Co, but closed after the 1921 strike and was re-opened by the Clay Cross Co in 1923.

Fred was turned down for service in September 1914 due to the severity of the injuries he received in the pit, but was accepted on 26th February 1915. He served at Gallipoli from 20th July 1915, in Egypt from 1st February 1916 and France from 6th July. He was wounded at the end of 1916 and on his return to the unit was put in a Lewis gun section. A bullet remained embedded in his back until 29th January 1952, when he winced as he climbed into a coal wagon and exclaimed, *"Ouch, that'll be my bullet"*. His colleagues assumed that he was joking until he had it removed at Chesterfield Royal Hospital later in the day.

Fred was recommended for the MM for rescuing wounded men under heavy shellfire, but it was not granted. It was not an isolated incident as a fellow NCO recorded, *Before the acts that won him the Cross, he had already come under the notice of his superiors for his coolness and dash. On one occasion … he rushed a machine-gun post single-handed, and on another occasion he risked his life to bring a comrade out of action.* At some time he was captured by the Germans whilst on a patrol and they jabbed him so often with their bayonets that his uniform ended up in tatters. He thought the end was near until he heard the voice of the officer in charge of the patrol behind him, *Keep still Greaves*, and he then shot the two captors.

Awarded the VC for his actions at Poelcapelle, Belgium on 4th October 1917, LG 26th November 1917. On his way to London by train to attend the VC investiture, he was in civilian clothes to protect his worn uniform. He was presented with a white feather by a lady and simply smiled at her. His uniform was in such a state of disrepair that the RSM at Wellington Barracks ordered him to get a new one. The VC was presented by the King at Buckingham Palace on 2nd January 1918. At a Sheffield garden party in June 1918 he was presented with £100 by General Jackson on behalf of friends and admirers for the conspicuous bravery he had displayed on the battlefield. Fred was later promoted sergeant and was demobilised to the Class Z Reserve on 28th January 1919.

Fred returned to the mines and became a pit deputy and later a safety officer at Markham Colliery, where he was also a member of the colliery's St John's Ambulance Division. The Duke of Devonshire granted him free fishing rights in Chatsworth Park. On 10th May 1938 at Markham Colliery some tubs ran out of control down an incline and were derailed, cutting an electrical cable, which caused a spark and ignited the coal dust. Seventy-nine miners were killed and Fred spent a week working tirelessly to dig men out and help the injured. He retired in 1955.

Markham Colliery has been the scene of two major mining disasters. At about 5.30 a.m. on 10th May 1938, just before the end of the night shift, an explosion killed seventy-nine miners and seriously injured forty more, out of the 171 men below ground. On 30th July 1973 a cage crashed to the bottom of the shaft, killing eighteen men and seriously injured eleven more. The mine closed in 1994.

Fred Greaves married Harriett Hallam née Broughton (1890–1927) on 2nd April 1923 at Barlborough Church. Harriett had married Charles Hallam (1884–1917), in 1913 at Worksop, Nottinghamshire. Harriett was born at Stanground, Huntingdonshire. They had a daughter, Beatrice Phoebe Hallam (1913–14). Charles served as an acting bombardier in A Battery, 175th Brigade RFA (90548) and died on 29th March 1917 (Barlborough (St James) Churchyard NE 15 1). Fred and Harriett lived at Woodland Villas, Barlborough and had two children:

The grave of Charles Hallam and his daughter Beatrice in Barlborough churchyard. Fred Greaves married Harriett Hallam in St James' church in the background in 1923.

• Cyril Greaves (23rd May 1924–14th November 1982) served in the Royal Navy during the Second World War. He married Kathleen Margaret Davis (1930–2001) in 1958 and they had two children – Julie Greaves 1963 and Stephen Peter Greaves 1966.
• Hazel Greaves (born 6th September 1925) lived at 11 Renishaw Road, Mastin Moor, near Chesterfield. She never married.

Harriett's father, Charles Daniel Broughton (1869–1937), a brickyard labourer, married Harriett née Lee (1872–1934) in 1889 at Peterborough, Northamptonshire. In 1901 they were living at 34 St Margaret Road, Fletton, Huntingdonshire. By 1911 he was a brick burner and they were living at Westfields, Barlborough, near Chesterfield. At the time of his death at 87 North Street, Stanground, Huntingdonshire he was living at Marsh Leys Cottage, Kempston, Bedfordshire. In addition to Harriett they had three other children:

• John William Broughton (born 1892) was a colliery loader below ground in 1911.
• Beatrice Ellen Broughton (1894–1974) was a domestic servant in 1911. She married Arthur E Bullock (c.1894–1950) in 1918 and they had a daughter, Joyce H Bullock in 1920.
• Albert Reginald Broughton (born 1901).

Harriet died on 28th April 1927 and Fred married Gladys Maria Jepson née Bilham (1886–1970) on 20th October 1930 at Harthill Church, Chesterfield. Gladys had married Charles Jepson (1885–1924) in 1909. Fred and Gladys lived at Whitelands, 48 Ringwood Road, Brimington, Chesterfield. There were no children to this marriage. Gladys' father, William Bilham (c.1849–1930), a coal miner, married Mary née Presswood (1848–1925) in 1873. In 1891 they were living at Main Street, Harthill. By 1901 he was a labourer on the highways and they were living at Fir Vale Street, Harthill. In addition to Gladys they had nine other children:

- John Henry Bilham (1874–1922), a coal miner hewer, married Eliza Stirland (1880–1942) in 1900 at Basford, Nottinghamshire. They were living at 122 Midland Road, Royston in 1911.
- George Edward Bilham (1876–1958), a mason's labourer, married Sarah Elizabeth Caswell (1878–1942) in 1900. By 1911 he was a greengrocer living with his wife at Midland Road, Royston. They had a son, George William Bilham, who was born and died in 1902. By 1939 he was a bus proprietor and driver, living at 110 High Street, Royston and Sarah was a patient at Beckett Hospital, Barnsley.
- Lavinia Ann Bilham (1877–1965) married John French (born 1872), a gardener, in 1912 at Newton Abbot, Devon. They had two children – Catherine French 1913 and Gladys Mary French 1915.
- Frederick Bilham (1879–1956), a coal miner, married Emma Jones (1884–1965) in 1906 at Barnsley, Yorkshire. They were living at Army Row, Royston in 1911 and at 18 Calder Avenue, Royston in 1939. They had a child who did not survive infancy.
- Horace Bilham (1880–1964), a coal hewer, married Florence Stubbings (born 1887) in 1919. By 1939 he was a railway ganger living with his wife at 151 Firvale, Harthill, Kiveton Park, Yorkshire.
- Sarah Elizabeth Bilham (1882–1958) married Frank Newton (1881–1958), a colliery weighman, in 1906. They lived at 44 Ringer Lane, Clowne, near Chesterfield and had moved to 32 The Haven, Church Street, Clowne by 1939. They had two children – Richard Newton 1907 and Jessie Newton 1911.
- Frances Mary Bilham (1888–1963) married Francis William Bingham (1888–1958) in 1912. They had a son, Sydney Gordon Bingham, in 1916. He worked at a stone works and they were living at 178 Fourth Avenue, Southwell, Nottinghamshire in 1939, by when he was a colliery engine fitter.
- Alec Presswood Bilham (1891–1977), a coal miner pony driver underground, married Charlotte Bagshawe Jones (born 1893) in 1914. By 1939 he was a milk and poultry farmer living at 2 Winny Land, Harthill, Kiveton Park.
- Sydney Presswood Bilham (1893–1979) married Kathleen Meek (1910–1973) in 1930. They had three children – Norman Bilham 1931, Patricia M Bilham 1934 and Edith Bilham 1937. He was a bookmaker, living with his family at 19 Thorpe Road, Kiveton Park in 1939.

Fred was a quiet and reserved man, a teetotaller and a prominent member of Barlborough Primitive Methodist Church. He served in the Markham Colliery St John's Ambulance. **Appointed Serving Brother of the Most Venerable Order of St John of Jerusalem on 22nd December 1948 for services to Markham Colliery St John's**

Barlborough Primitive Methodist Church was built in 1913, although there was a preacher and a congregation there by 1820.

Ambulance Division, LG 4th January 1949. The Order was presented by Lord Wakehurst on behalf of the Duke of Gloucester at Preston, Lancashire on 15th May 1949. He was also awarded the St John's Ambulance Brigade Long Service and Good Conduct Medal with two bars for twenty-five years service. During the Second World War he served in Civil Defence.

Fred attended the VC Garden Party at Buckingham Palace on 26th June 1920, the VC Dinner at the Royal Gallery of the House of Lords on 9th November 1929, the Victory Day Celebration Dinner and Reception at The Dorchester, London on 8th June 1946 and the VC Centenary Celebrations at Hyde Park, London on 26th June 1956. He also attended six of the first eight biennial VC & GC Association reunions at the Café Royal, London between 1958 and 1972. Approaching Buckingham Palace in a taxi prior to one of these events, the cab driver asked Fred which entrance he would like to be dropped at. Fred replied that any would suffice, but the driver glanced back to see Fred putting on his medals. As soon as he saw the VC, the driver said, *You're definitely going in the main entrance, mate!* Fred attended the presentation of new colours to the Sherwood Foresters by the Duke of Devonshire at Hyderabad Barracks, Colchester on the 20th Anniversary of VE Day in July 1965.

Fred Greaves died at his home, Whitelands, 48 Ringwood Road, Brimington, Chesterfield on 8th June 1973. He was cremated at Chesterfield and District Crematorium, Chesterfield Road, Brimington, where his name appears in the Book of Remembrance. His ashes were buried in Brimington Cemetery. Fred is commemorated in a number of other places:

Barlborough war memorial.

- Fred Greaves VC memorial park bench was dedicated next to the war memorial in Chesterfield on 30th October 2010 with his daughter, Hazel, in attendance.
- Plaque in Chesterfield FC Memorial Garden at the Proact Stadium dedicated on 2nd August 2014.
- Inscription on the war memorial at Barlborough, Derbyshire.

In addition to the VC and the Order of St John of Jerusalem he was awarded the 1914–15 Star, British War Medal 1914–20, Victory Medal 1914–19, Defence Medal, George VI Coronation Medal 1937, Elizabeth II Coronation Medal 1953 and St John of Jerusalem Service Medal (with two bars). In accordance with Fred's wishes, his son presented the medals to the Trustees of the Sherwood Foresters Collection on 8th December 1973. They are held by the Sherwood Foresters Museum, Nottingham Castle. For an inexplicable reason the group includes the 1914 Star with 'Mons clasp' instead of the 1914–15 Star.

The Order of St John of Jerusalem.

13531 COMPANY QUARTERMASTER SERGEANT WILLIAM HENRY GRIMBALDESTON
1st Battalion, The King's Own Scottish Borderers

William Grimbaldeston was born at 58 Hickory Street, Blackburn, Lancashire on 19th September 1889. His father, Thomas Grimbaldeston (1860–1929), was a carder in a cotton mill in 1881, a labourer at an iron foundry in 1889 and a cotton doubler in 1911. He married Isabella née Davis (1863–1934) in 1884. They were living at 20 Daisy Street in 1891, 58 Hickory Street by 1889, 68 Hickory Street by 1911 and 193 Beaumont Terrace by 1914. William had nine siblings:

(*Mrs Mary Grimbaldeston*)

- Grace Grimbaldeston (1891–1964), a cotton weaver in 1911, married Walter Haworth in 1919. She was living at 6 Cromwell Terrace, Barrowford, Lancashire, in 1939.
- Ellen Grimbaldeston (1895–1940) was a cotton weaver in 1911. She married William Parker in 1919 and they had a son, William Parker, in 1920. She was living with her son William, a motor driver, at 28 Whalley Old Road, Blackburn in 1939.
- Rose A Grimbaldeston (born 1896) married George Rostron (1883–1914), a blacksmith's striker, in 1910. They were living at 84 Harwood Street, Blackburn in 1911. She married William Eccles in 1917. By 1939 she was recorded as a single cotton weaver under her maiden name and was living with her sister Theresa.
- Joseph Grimbaldeston (born 1899) was a part-time cotton weaver in 1911.
- Winifred Grimbaldeston (born 1901), a cotton weaver, married Arthur Evans (born 1901), a hydraulic packer, in 1925. By 1939 they were living at 7 Boland Street, Blackburn.
- Theresa Grimbaldeston (1903–91) was a cotton weaver in 1939 living at 193 Whilley Lane, Blackburn. She died unmarried.
- Edward Grimbaldeston (born 1905) was a twin with Annie. He was recorded as Edmund in the 1939 Census, living with his sister Theresa and working as a cotton weaver.
- Annie Grimbaldeston (born 1905). She was incapacitated in 1939, living with her sister Theresa.
- George Grimbaldeston (1910–61).

William's paternal grandfather, Henry Grimbaldeston (c.1835–1900), was a labourer in 1871 a farm worker by 1881. He married Mary née Davis (1841–1911) in 1862. They were living at 48 Cavendish Street, Dalton, Lancashire in 1871 and at 13 Long Row, Catterall, Lancashire in 1881. In addition to Thomas they had six other children:

- Ann Grimbaldeston (born 1862).
- Richard Grimbaldeston (1866–1932) married Mary Ann Wooler (c.1857–1913) in 1896 and they had a daughter, Janey Wooler Grimbaldeston, the same year. Richard married Ellen Ashton (1882–1955) in 1916 and they had six children – John H Grimbaldeston 1916, Francis Grimbaldeston 1917, Richard V Grimbaldeston 1918, Mary E Grimbaldeston 1919. Joseph Grimbaldeston 1921 and Robert Grimbaldeston 1923. Ellen was living with her sons Richard and Robert at 3 Aintree Cottage, Blackburn in 1939.
- Robert Grimbaldeston (1868–1940).
- Ralph Grimbaldeston (1871–1962) married Agnes Farrant (1874–1942) in 1915.
- William Grimbaldeston (1877–1959) married Mary Elizabeth Merrick (1878–1942) in 1911. He was a cotton weaver living with his wife at Delemere, Lytham Road, Fylde, Lancashire in 1939.
- Edward Grimbaldeston (1879–1954) married Grace Bell (1876–1942) in 1903 and they had a son, Henry Grimbaldeston, in 1904. They lived at 185 Walter Street, Blackburn before moving to 28 June Street, Blackburn by 1939. He attested on 10th December 1915 and transferred to the Class B Reserve the same day. His occupation was given as size mixer and he was described as 5′ 8½″ tall and weighed 152 lbs. He was called up on 23rd March 1917 (38092) and joined 3rd East Lancashire on 25th March. At Saltburn he overstayed his leave from tattoo on 9th June until 6 p.m. on 11th June, for which he forfeited three days pay. He went to France on 12th June, joining 30 Infantry Base Depot and then 2nd East Lancashire. He transferred to 9th Lancashire Fusiliers (40141) on 29th June from 22 Infantry Base Depot and received a mild gunshot wound to the right leg on 17th August. He was admitted successively to 35th Field Ambulance, No.64 Casualty Clearing Station and a general hospital at Wimereux. He transferred to 23 Infantry Base Depot at Étaples on 2nd September from Base Depot Boulogne and to the 1st Battalion on 11th September, joining the following day. He transferred to the Royal Engineers (360209) on 16th April 1918 and joined 254th Tunnelling Company next day (Sapper William Hackett was awarded the VC serving with this unit in June 1916). He was demobilised to the Class Z Reserve on 17th March 1919.

His maternal grandfather, William Davis (1842–1915), was a coachman. He married Ann née Nixon (c.1841–1909) in 1861. In 1871 they were living at 3 Dalton Clough Cottages, Bleasdale, Lancashire. By 1891 they were at 56 Hickory Street, Blackburn and by 1901 at 59 St James Road, Blackburn. William was living at 11 Boxwood Street, Blackburn with his unmarried sons, Henry and Edward, in 1911. In addition to Isabella they had eleven other children:

- Joseph Davis (born 1861).
- Rosanna Davis (1866–74).
- Elizabeth Ann Davis (1869).
- Grace Davis (1871–1949), a weaver, married John Walmsley (born c.1868), also a weaver, in 1893. They were living at 29 Boxwood Street, Blackburn in 1911. They had three children – Ethel Walmsley 1896, Ada Walmsley 1900 and another who died in infancy.
- Dorothy Davis (born 1873–1957) married Alexander Ormerod (born 1875), a dental mechanic, in 1899. They had a son, Alexander Ormerod in 1906 and were living at 29 Boxwood Street, Blackburn in 1911.
- Theresa Davis (born 1875), a cotton weaver, married Thomas Miller (born c.1876) in 1897. They had five children – Richard Miller 1904, William Miller 1905, Jane Miller 1909, Henry Miller 1910 and Edward Miller 1913. They were living at 10 Daisy Street, Blackburn in 1911.
- William James Davis (1877–1958) was a cotton weaver.
- Henry Davis (born 1879) was a corporation labourer in 1911.
- Edward Davis (1882–1952) was a corporation labourer in 1911.
- Alice Davis (born 1884), a cotton weaver, married John Hoyles (born 1877), a rural district council road labourer, in 1902. They were living at High Road, Garstang in 1911 and had seven children – Robert Hoyles 1904, Thomas Edward Hoyles 1906, John Hoyles 1909, Sarah Hoyles 1910, Dora Hoyles 1912, Margaret Hoyles 1915 and Rose Hoyles 1918.
- Norah Davis (1886–1955) married Thomas Charles Watkinson (1874–1945) in 1918.

William was educated at St Alban's School, Blackburn until the age of thirteen. The school was also attended by James Pitts, who was awarded the VC for his actions in South Africa in 1900. William worked as a cotton weaver at Cicely Street Mill, Cherry Tree Mill and for Messrs Greenwood Bros Ltd of Rockford Mill. He was a noted amateur boxer and appeared at the Palace Theatre. He also won several trophies as a weightlifter and athlete, regularly attending the YMCA gymnasium in Blackburn.

Before the war he served in 4th East Lancashire Brigade RFA (TF) and became an orderly to his CO, Lieutenant Colonel TP Ritzema. He enlisted in the King's Own Scottish Borderers on 3rd September 1914 and was described as 5′ 10″ tall, weighing 140 lbs, with fresh complexion, hazel eyes, dark hair and his religious denomination was Roman Catholic. He joined B Company, 7th Battalion next day. Appointed acting lance corporal on

Private James Pitts, 1st Battalion, The Manchester Regiment was awarded the VC along with Private Robert Scott during the Second Boer War. At Caesar's Camp, Natal on 6th January 1900 they held a sangar for fifteen hours without food or water, under heavy fire throughout. Pitts also served in the First World War and was awarded the MSM in 1918.

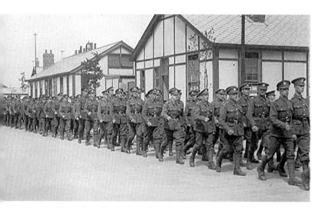

Chiselden Camp in Wiltshire.

The Palace Theatre, Blackburn opened in 1899 and saw performances by Gracie Fields and Harry Houdini. It was a cinema 1936–57 and in the 1960s became a bingo hall. By 1975 it was in dual use as a cinema and bingo hall until it closed in 1984. It was demolished in 1989.

22nd September, corporal on 8th December and acting sergeant on 30th December. He was reprimanded at Chiselden, Wiltshire on 21st May 1915 for being absent from tattoo roll call until 9.50 p.m. William went to France with the Battalion on 9th July and was promoted sergeant on 17th September. He was wounded by a gunshot at Loos on 25th September, resulting in a finger being amputated on his left hand. Piper Daniel Laidlaw was awarded the VC for the same action. Having been evacuated to England on 26th September, William was taken on the strength of the Depot next day and was granted leave 12th–21st February 1916.

William married Sarah Ellen née Woodcock (born 1896) at the Chapel Street Congregational Church, Blackburn on 17th February 1916. They were living at 17 Woodbury Street, Blackburn in 1919, at 6 Holland Street in 1935 and at 49 Bold Street in 1959. They had a son, also William (born 18th October 1918), who married Mary L Clarke in 1949 at Aldershot, Hampshire. They were living at 11 Northumberland Road, Leamington Spa, Warwickshire in 1959 and at 48 Palmerston Way, Alverstoke, Gosport, Hampshire by 1966.

Sarah's father, Thomas Woodcock (1853–1921), was in the Fulwood Workhouse, near Preston, Lancashire in 1881. By 1891 he was a carter. He married Elizabeth Jane née Holliday

Piper Daniel Laidlaw was awarded the VC serving with 7th King's Own Scottish Borderers at Loos on 25th September 1915. William Grimbaldeston was with the Battalion that day and was wounded in the left hand.

(1867–1919) in 1885. They were living at 11 Brunswick Place, Preston in 1891, at 119 Kent Street in 1901 and at 21 Miles Street by 1911. In addition to Sarah they had three other children:

- Thomas Woodcock (1888–91).
- Mary Jane Woodcock (1902–75) married Ralph Dimascio (1894–1948), a terrazo polisher, in 1928 and they had a daughter, Violet F Dimascio, the following year who died aged one. They were living at 16 Ellerton Road, Kingstanding, Birmingham, Warwickshire in 1939.
- Henry Woodcock (born 1905).

William was posted to 9th Battalion on 25th February 1916 and was admitted to Kinghorn Auxiliary Hospital 5th–8th June with a mild case of herpes gastes. Having been posted to 3rd Battalion on 1st September, he returned to France to join 1st Battalion on 5th October. Appointed acting CQMS 16th April–16th August 1917. **Awarded the VC for his actions at Wijdendrift, Belgium on 16th August 1917, LG 14th September 1917.** William was gassed on 17th August and was evacuated to Warrington Whitecross Hospital, England on 26th August. As a result he was taken on the strength of the Depot and reverted to sergeant next day. He and his wife were caught in a Zeppelin raid on London the night before his investiture, but they were not injured. The raid, which was the last Zeppelin attack on London, left thirty-three people dead and many more injured. The VC was presented by the King at Buckingham Palace on 20th October 1917. **William was also awarded the French Croix de Guerre in September 1917, LG 17th December 1917.**

He returned home on 11th January 1918 and was given a civic reception twelve days later, receiving a cheque for £200 raised by public subscription and an illuminated address decorated with the town's coat of arms and his regimental crest. He was posted to 3rd Battalion on 6th April and appointed acting CQMS on 31st May. William was demobilised to the Class Z Reserve on 21st February 1919 and was awarded a weekly pension of 10/6d plus an allowance of 2/- for his child. His pension was temporarily increased by 20% to be reviewed after thirty-nine weeks. He was discharged from the Reserve on 31st March 1920.

William worked as a clerk at Blackburn Employment Exchange and later in 1919 became steward of New Public Halls (King George's Hall) in Northgate. This included being the mace-bearer for the town. In 1937 he was a porter of the Trustees Savings Bank on Lord Street West and retired in 1949, having suffered poor health attributed to gas poisoning. He was Provincial Grand Sword Bearer in Freemason Lodge De Lacy (No.4591) at Clayton-le-Moors, Lancashire and was Chairman of the 15th (Scottish) Division Old Comrades Association (South of the Border Branch).

William collapsed and died at his home at 49 Bold Street, Blackburn on 13th August 1959, having just taken a glass of water to his semi-invalid wife. He was cremated at Pleasington Crematorium, Blackburn and his ashes were scattered in

The New Public Halls, better known as King George's Hall, in Northgate, Blackburn, where William Grimbaldeston was steward from 1919. (*Wikipedia*)

The Trustees Savings Bank on Lord Street West, Blackburn, where William was a porter from 1937 until retiring in 1949.

Plot G. A piper played *Flowers of the Forest*. Donald Ross of Edinburgh, who was with William when he won the VC, attended. He is also commemorated on a plaque in the Old Town Hall, Blackburn dedicated on Armistice Day 1956 to commemorate the town's four VCs – Percy Dean, William Grimbaldeston, James Pitts and John Schofield.

Plaques inside the Old Town Hall, Blackburn commemorate the town's four VCs – Percy Dean, William Grimbaldeston, James Pitts and John Schofield.

In addition to the VC he was awarded the 1914–15 Star, British War Medal 1914–20, Victory Medal 1914–19, George VI Coronation Medal 1937, Elizabeth II Coronation Medal 1953 and the French Croix de Guerre with Bronze Star. His medals were presented to the Kings Own Scottish Borderers Regimental Museum at a ceremony in Berwick-on-Tweed on 17th August 1960, the forty-third anniversary of the action at Wijdendrift.

241475 PRIVATE ALBERT HALTON
1st Battalion, The King's Own (Royal Lancaster Regiment)

Albert Halton was born at 22 Albert Street, Millhead, Warton, Carnforth, Lancashire on 1st May 1893. His father, Jonathan Halton (1849–1921), was born at Lower Kellet, Bolton le Sands, Lancashire. He was a labourer living with his parents in 1871 and was a farm servant at Thomas and Ellen Hilton's farm at Timrigg, Over

Kellet, in 1881. His future wife, Sarah Farrer (c.1857–1945), was also working there as a farm servant. They married in May 1882 at the Church of St Cuthbert, Over Kellet. Sarah may have been the illegitimate daughter of Agnes Farrow (born 1839). In 1861 Sarah was living at Lindale Village, Lancashire with her great grandfather James Keith (born c.1789). Also in the household were his son James Keith (c.1808–97), daughter Margaret (born c.1812), son-in-law Henry Woodburn (born 1838) and his wife Mary née Keith (born c.1840), granddaughter Agnes Keith (born c.1844) and grandson James Farrow (born 1848). By 1871 Sarah was living with James Keith (c.1808–97) and his sister Margaret (born c.1812) as their niece. Also in the household were James Farrow (born 1848) and James Keith (born c.1865), recorded as a grandson, but neither James nor Margaret was married. Jonathan was a furnace charger in 1891 and they were living at Nether Kellet, Lancashire. By 1901 he was a blast furnace man at Carnforth Ironworks and the family was living at 19 Highfield Terrace, Carnforth. Albert had five siblings:

- Maggie Halton (1883–1965) was a domestic servant at the home of John Swindells, manager of a cotton mill, at 1 Laurel Bank, Lancaster in 1911. She married Richard Wilding (1879–1951) in 1912 and they had a son, Harry Wilding, in 1916.
- George Halton (1884–1928) was an ironworks labourer in 1901 and a blast furnace man in 1911.
- Herbert Halton (1887–1852) was a paper shop errand boy in 1901. He was a farm labourer at the time of his enlistment in the Westmorland and Cumberland Yeomanry (2973) at Penrith on 29th May 1915. He was described as 5′ 4⅛″ tall, weighing 136 lbs, with fresh complexion,

Albert's parents married at St Cuthbert's, Over Kellett, in 1882. The church dates back to 1215.

grey eyes, black hair and his religious denomination was Church of England. He went to France via Southampton on 4th December where the unit served as XI Corps Cavalry Regiment. He attended 39th Division Bombing School 16th-23rd July 1916 and was admitted to 93rd Field Ambulance for an unknown reason on 30th September. He was granted leave in Britain in March 1917. On 30th July he was admitted to 2/2nd West Riding Field Ambulance and transferred to 6th British Red Cross Hospital at Étaples on 7th August. On 21st September 1917 he transferred to 7th Border (260433) when it absorbed 260 men officers and men of the Westmorland and Cumberland Yeomanry and was renamed 7th (Westmorland

and Cumberland Yeomanry) Battalion. Herbert was granted leave in Britain 10th–24th January 1918 and was appointed unpaid lance corporal on 30th April. He was awarded the DCM (LG 2nd December 1919) for his actions in the attack on the Fôret de Mormal on 4th November 1918 – he was a scout moving ahead of his platoon when the enemy opened fire as he neared the objective, but worked his way forward under heavy fire and rushed the enemy post single-handed, capturing the gun and twelve prisoners. Appointed acting corporal 11th November 1918 and was granted leave to Britain 10th–24th January 1919, coincidentally exactly the same dates as in 1918. He transferred back to the Westmorland and Cumberland Yeomanry on demobilisation on 4th March 1919. Herbert married Jane Barr (1899–1975) in 1926 and they had a son, John C Halton, the same year.

- Walter Halton (1896–1953).
- Ethel Halton (1889–1957) was a domestic housemaid in the home of Edward Cardwell and his family at 3 Laurel Bank, Lancaster in 1911. She married John Hird (1886–1919) in 1912 and they had a daughter, Doris Hird, in 1918.

Albert's paternal grandfather, Thomas Halton (c.1813–90), married Elizabeth 'Betty' née Wilson (c.1816–94) in 1839. He was an agricultural labourer in 1851 living with his family at Nether Kellet. By 1861 he was a farmer of sixty-one acres at Nether Kellet and in 1871 he was a carter. In addition to Jonathan they had eleven other children:

- John Halton (1840–1935) was a farmer in 1861 living with his parents.
- Thomas Halton (1841–1908) was a farmer in 1861 living with his parents. He married Sarah Jane Carr (1851–83) in 1870 at Kendal, Westmorland. In 1881 he was a railway engine driver and the family was living at 1 Jackson Terrace, Warton with Lindeth, Lancashire. They had four children – Agnes Halton 1873, John Thomas Halton 1875, Elizabeth Halton 1877 and Joseph Halton 1880.
- Joseph Halton (1842–1921) married Mary Ann Wilson in 1874. In 1881 he was an iron miner and the family was living at 4 Castle Street, Lower Kellet. They had a son, Thomas Halton, in 1880.
- Lawrence Halton (1844–54).
- Elizabeth Halton (1846–1908) married Robert Towers (c.1851–89) in 1874. She was a confectioner in 1891, living with her son, John Towers (born 1876), at 20 New Street, Carnforth, Lancashire.

Albert's paternal grandparents lived at Nether Kellet. It is one of fifty-three villages in England and Wales from which all members of the armed forces returned. Nether Kellet is one of the fourteen 'doubly thankful' villages, as it also lost no service personnel during the Second World War.

- Robert Halton (born 1848).
- Charles Halton (1851–1923) was a labourer living with his parents in 1871. He married Sarah Jane Cowperthwaite (1856–1910) in 1876. They had two children – Bell Halton 1882 and Harriet Halton 1890. In 1901 he was a steamroller driver and the family was living at Stone Terrace, Grange, Lancashire. By then Sarah was an invalid. Charles was still living at Stone Terrace, Grange in 1911 with his daughter Harriet.
- Margaret Halton (born 1854).
- Isabella Halton (1855–1941) married Fidelio Tyldesley (c.1854–1942) in 1880. He was an asylum attendant and they were living at 24 Adelphi Street, Lancaster in 1891. They had moved to 54 Gregson Road, Lancaster by 1911. They had seven children – Ruth Halton Tyldesley 1880, Robert Fidelio Tyldesley 1882, Thomas Edgar Tyldesley 1884, Ben Allic Tyldesley 1885, Florence Tyldesley 1887, Alfred James Tyldesley 1892 and Hebe Tyldesley 1894.

Carnforth National School attended by Albert Halton.

- Lawrence Halton (1856–1939) married Elizabeth Relph (1850–1913) in 1879. They had three children – Lawrence Halton 1884, Elizabeth Halton 1887 and Ernest Halton 1890. He was a farmer and innkeeper in 1901, running the Red Well Hotel, Over Kellet. Ernest was serving as a private (1416) in 1/5th King's Own when he was killed on 30th September 1914 and is buried in Calder Vale (St John) Churchyard, near Garstang, Lancashire. He was patrolling the railway line between Steventon Station and Causeway Crossing near Didcot, Berkshire with 1091 Private James Walton when both men were struck by a train at about 10 p.m. and died at the scene. The coroner's inquest concluded that they stepped from the up line to avoid a milk train and were hit by a down line express. Both men were sober and the coroner's jury returned a verdict of 'accidentally killed'.
- George Halton (1858–62).

Albert worked for the London and North Western Railway and one of its stations was at Carnforth. It opened in 1846 with a single platform and was enlarged several times over the years. In 1945 it became famous when David Lean's *Brief Encounter*, starring Celia Johnson and Trevor Howard, was filmed there. Part of the station is a Heritage Centre and includes the Brief Encounter Refreshment Room. This view shows the famous clock above the subway.

Storey Avenue in Westfield War Memorial Village. It was built for war veterans on land donated by the industrialist Herbert Storey in 1919–24. (*Humphrey Bolton*)

A wartime photograph of Albert seated left.

His maternal grandparents are not known. Albert was educated at Carnforth National School until 1906 after which he was employed as a farm labourer at the farm of Thomas Hilton at Over Kellet. By 1911 he was employed by George Phizacklea at Plumpton Cottage, near Ulverston, Lancashire. Later he worked for the London and North Western Railway and finally joined John Rigg & Sons, building contractors, as a labourer.

Albert enlisted in 5th King's Own on 15th August 1915. He was wounded on the Somme on 22nd October 1916 and was evacuated to hospital in Aberdeen. He returned to France on 1st March 1917 and joined the 1st Battalion. **Awarded the VC for his actions near Poelcapelle, Belgium on 12th October 1917, LG 26th November 1917.** The VC was presented by the King at Buckingham Palace on 2nd January 1918. Albert was discharged in May 1919.

Albert Halton married Emily née Tatman (1893–1969) in November 1918 at Lancaster. She was born at Farnhill, near Skipton, Yorkshire and was a general servant living in the home of Annie Davis, a widow, at Westfield, Gargrave, near Skipton, Yorkshire in 1911. They were living at 19 Highfield Terrace, Carnforth, near Lancaster in 1921 and had moved to 20 Storey Avenue, Westfield War Memorial Village, Lancaster by 1939. They had four children:

• Victor Halton (born and died 1920).
• Elsie Halton (1921–22).
• Joan Halton (born 1923) is understood to have married Frederick Swift at Lancaster in 1946.
• Dorothy Halton (born 1924) married Frank Bromley in 1952. They lived at 13 Brantwood Drive, Scotforth, Lancaster and had a son, Granham H Bromley, in 1959.

Emily's father, Jonathan Lightfoot Tatman (1873–1946) was born at Great Barford, Bedfordshire. He married Ellen née Smith (1872–1955), born at Cross Hills,

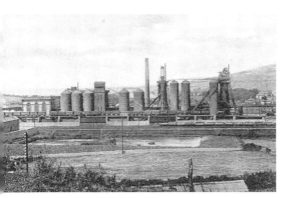

Cranforth Ironworks was established in 1846. In 1864 the Carnforth Haematite Co took it over and vastly increased production. The works closed in 1929. The site was then used by the War Department as an ordnance depot until the 1960s. It is now an industrial estate.

The gateway into Lansil Works during a visit by the King and Queen in 1917.

Yorkshire, at Keighley, Yorkshire in 1893. He was a railway signalman in 1901. That year they were living at Water Street, Gargrave, Yorkshire and at High Street, Gargrave in 1911. In addition to Emily they had two other children:

- Eleanor Tatman (1895–1928), born at Hornby, Lancashire, married Tom Bradley Hirst (1887–1957) in 1917. They had four children – Elizabeth E Hirst 1920, Florence M Hirst 1922, Richard Hirst 1924 and William Hirst 1927. Tom married Mary J Leatherbarrow (1881–1949) in 1930.
- John Tatman (1905–70) was born at Gargrave, Yorkshire. He was a farm labourer in 1946 and a council employee in 1955.

After the war Albert was employed by Carnforth Ironworks until it closed in 1929 and was then a gateman at Lansil Works, Lancaster until retirement in 1961. He served in the Lancaster Home Guard in the Second World War.

Albert Halton died at Lancaster Moor Hospital on 24th July 1971. He was cremated at Lancaster and Morecombe Crematorium and his ashes were scattered in Plot 38/6. He is commemorated in a number of other places:

Albert died at Lancaster Moor Hospital in 1971. It opened in 1816 as the Lancaster County Lunatic Asylum, later renamed the Lancaster County Mental Hospital. It closed in 2000 and some of the buildings have been converted into apartments. (*Daily Mail*)

- Memorial plaque on his former home at 20 Storey Avenue, Westfield War Memorial Village.
- Plaque on a park bench at Lancaster and Morecambe Crematorium.

In addition to the VC he was awarded the British War Medal 1914–20, Victory Medal 1914–19, George VI Coronation Medal 1937 and Elizabeth II Coronation Medal 1953. The VC is held by the King's Own (Royal Lancaster) Regiment Museum, City Museum, Market Square, Lancaster.

331958 LANCE CORPORAL JOHN BROWN HAMILTON
1/9th Battalion, The Highland Light Infantry

John Hamilton was born at 190 High Street, Dumbarton, Scotland on 26th August 1896. He was known as Jack or Hammy. His father, Thomas Hamilton (1854–1936), a journeyman steel moulder, was living at Glassford, Lanarkshire in 1861 and at Lower Bushyhill, Cambuslang, Lanarkshire by 1871. He was living at The Square, Cambuslang when he married Agnes née Brown (1855–1935), on 1st January 1878. She was a handloom weaver in 1871 and a power loom weaver at the time of her marriage. Thomas was later a foreman steel moulder with Messrs Hardie & Gordon's Levenbank steel foundry. The family was living at 7 Gladden Place, Colebrook Street, Cambuslang in 1881 and at 190 High Street, Dumbarton by 1896. Thomas was living at 13 Howieshill Avenue, Cambuslang when he died in 1936. John had five siblings:

- Agnes Orr Hamilton (1880–1908), a dressmaker in 1901, married Gabriel Wingate (1876–1936), a journeyman iron ship plater, in 1904. Gabriel was boarding at 3 McKenzie Street, Greenock when he married Jessie Neil Ness (1878–1959), a knitter, in 1911. He was living at 29 Bannerman Street, Clydebank, Dunbartonshire when he died in 1936.
- Alexander Hamilton (born 1882) was an apprentice engineer in 1901.
- James Hamilton (born c.1886 in England).
- William Brown Hamilton (born 1891), a steel moulder, married Elizabeth Marshall Black Purnell (born 1892), a sewing machinist, in 1913.
- Thomas Hamilton (born 1894).

John's paternal grandfather, Alexander Hamilton (1830–1912), married Agnes née Orr (c.1831–1906) in 1853. He was a dairyman in 1861, a carrier by

John Hamilton was born at 190 High Street, Dumbarton.

1871, a master carter by 1881 and a road surface man in 1891. The family was living at Howhole, Glassford, Lanarkshire in 1861, at Lower Bushyhill, Cambuslang, Lanarkshire by 1871 and at Chapel Park, Cambuslang in 1881. In addition to Thomas they had six other children:

Main Street, Cambuslang.

- Sarah Hamilton (born c.1854) died before the 1861 Census.
- Ann Hamilton (1855–1920), a domestic servant, married James Thomson (born c.1852), a coal miner, in 1877. James was recorded as a flesher in 1878 and a butcher by 1891, when they were living at 3 Coalgate, Alloa, Clackmannanshire. They were living at 5 Commercial Street, Methil, Fife when she died in 1920. Ann and James had seven children – John Thomson 1878, Agnes Orr Thomson 1881, Robert Thomson c.1883, Marion Thomson c.1885, James Thomson c.1886, Daniel Thomson c.1887 and David Thomson c.1889.
- Marion Hamilton (1856–1925) married Robert McLintock (1846–1909) in 1881. They had four children – Elizabeth McLintock 1881, William McLintock 1886, Marion Stewart McLintock 1891 and Robert McLintock 1896.
- James Hamilton (born 1858) married Mary Wilson (1845–1925) in 1880. He was a carter in 1881, a roadman in 1891 and a general labourer in 1901. They were living at Peasweep Row, Blantyre, Lanarkshire in 1891 and at 8 Dogwell Wynd, Linlithgow, West Lothian in 1901. They had two children – Alexander Hamilton 1882 and Agnes Orr Hamilton c.1887.
- Mary Hamilton (born 1864).
- Janet Hamilton (born 1869).

Alexander married Margaret Mitchell or McRorie (c.1843–1922), a widow, in 1908. They were living at 5 Tabernacle Street, Cambuslang when he died in 1912.

John's maternal grandfather, James Brown (1826–1901) was a cotton handloom weaver and a road surface man. He married Mary née Jenkins (c.1827–79) in 1849. They were living at Chapel Park, Cambuslang in 1871 and at 2 Oakfield Place, Cambuslang when he died in 1901. In addition to Agnes they had eight other children:

- Christina Brown (c.1849–98), a handloom weaver in 1871, married John Smith (born c.1849), a coal miner, in 1872. They lived at 18 Lilybank Buildings, Cambuslang and had a son, Robert Smith, in 1889.
- Isabella Brown (born c.1850) was a handloom weaver in 1871.
- Unnamed son born before 1854 who died in infancy.

- Mary Brown (born 1859).
- Janet Brown (born 1861).
- John Brown (born 1863).
- Elizabeth Brown (born 1867).
- James Brown (born 1869).

John was educated at a Dumbarton Burgh school, probably West Bridgend School, and later at Dumbarton Academy, although there are no surviving records of him having attended the latter. He was a sergeant in 2nd Dumbarton Company Boys' Brigade. Having left school in 1912, John was an apprentice electrical fitter at Leven Shipyard in Dumbarton. Later he was employed at the Steel Company of Scotland's Works, Hallside, Newton, Cambuslang and in 1914 he joined the Electrical Company in Pitt Street, Glasgow for six months. He played for Cambuslang Rangers Football Club and was an energetic lifetime supporter of the Club.

Dumbarton Academy is one of the oldest educational establishments in Scotland, dating back to the 1600s. Another former pupil was Sir Jackie Stewart OBE, who won three Formula One championships between 1965 and 1973.

John Hamilton married Mary Love Weir née Maxwell (28th December 1895–July 1963) on 15th November 1915 at the United Free Church Manse, Hallside, Cambuslang, where they were both choristers. The marriage was in defiance of their parents, who thought them too young. He was living at Burnbank, Croft Road, Cambuslang and she was living at 10 Overtown Terrace, Hallside, Cambuslang, where they settled and had four children:

There has been shipbuilding along the River Leven at Dumbarton since the 15th century. Denny's Yard constructed over 1,500 ships between 1844 and 1963. *Cutty Sark* was completed by Denny's in 1870 after the liquidation of her contracted builders. The company was renowned for innovation. In 1878 *Rotomahana* was the first all steel merchant ship and in 1901 *King Edward* was the first commercial turbine steamer. In 1934 *Robert the Bruce* was the first all welded vessel as well as the first diesel-electric paddle. It also pioneered stabilisers in conjunction with Brown Brothers and experimented in hovercraft and helicopter-type aircraft. Much of the success was due to the Ship

Model Experiment Tank constructed in 1883, which can still be seen as part of the Scottish Maritime Museum. The company was well known for producing top quality ferries and in 1905 began working on Admiralty projects building torpedo boats, destroyers, sloops, minesweepers, gunboats, submarines, a tank transporter and river hospital ships plus 150 fighter aircraft. The Company went into liquidation in 1963.

- John Brown Hamilton (born 16th August 1915) died during the flu epidemic after the Great War in 1919.
- Jessie Horn Hamilton (born 6th October 1918), a bookkeeper, married John Crerar Rogers (1916–2003), an insurance collector, in 1940. John Rogers was born at Ripon, Yorkshire and was serving as a lance corporal in the Gordon Highlanders at the time of their marriage. He was granted an Emergency Commission in the Pioneer Corps on 1st January 1943 (256707), was promoted war substantive lieutenant on 1st July and transferred to the Indian Army. He was a staff captain in the Adjutant-General's Branch of the Headquarters Staff of the Army in India as a temporary captain 1st Pioneer Corps on 1st July 1946. He transferred to the Reserve as honorary captain on 1st January 1949 and ceased to belong to the Reserve of Officers Royal Pioneer Corps on 21st June 1967, having reached the age limit. They had two children – Meryle Maxwell Rogers 1944 and Gordon Hamilton Crerar Rogers 1948.
- A son who died during the flu epidemic after the Great War.
- Ian Hamilton (21st April 1926–24th October 1983).

Mary's father, Andrew Maxwell (1869–1951) married Jessie née Horn (1870–1915) in 1891. He was a steel moulder in 1901 and later became an engineer turner. When Mary married, he was described as an electrical engineer. The family lived at 20 Burnside, Cambuslang then at 30 Clyde Street. In 1901 they were at 75 Hallside, Cambuslang, at 65 Hallside in 1907 and at 67 Hallside in 1911. In addition to Mary they had six other children:

- Andrew Fyfe Maxwell (1895–1900).
- William Maxwell (born and died 1897).
- Janet Hill Maxwell (1898–1900).
- James Horn Maxwell (1901–02).
- John Maxwell (born 1907).
- Elizabeth Horn Maxwell (1911–59) married William Sandilands in 1939.

After Jessie died, Andrew married Jeanie Anderson née Waugh (1874–1955) in 1920. She had married Peter Anderson (c.1871–1914) in 1899 and they had three children – Peter Anderson 1900, David Anderson 1901 and Jeanie Anderson 1905.

John enlisted in 3/9th Highland Light Infantry at the Drill Hall, Greendyke Street, Glasgow on 21st October 1915 (4876) and was promoted lance corporal in February 1916. He went to France in April. Having been wounded near High Wood on the Somme in July 1916, he did not return to his unit until September 1917. **Awarded the VC for his actions north of the Ypres–Menin Road at Veldhoek, Belgium on 25th/26th September 1917, LG 26th November 1917.** He was posted to 5th Reserve Battalion and became a sergeant instructor. The

VC was presented by the King at Buckingham Palace on 23rd January 1918. John was granted the Freedom of the Borough of Dumbarton and Cambuslang.

John returned to his job with the Electrical Company, Pitt Street, Glasgow work. He and William Connor were seriously burned when a blowlamp burst at Newton Steel Works, Cambuslang on 28th April 1923. In 1934 John appeared in the documentary film *Forgotten Men – The War as It Was*.

He remained in the TF/TA, but became seriously ill with influenza in 1939 and was declared unfit for overseas service. As a result he was discharged. However, the outbreak of the Second World War changed the situation and on 18th December 1940 he was granted a Regular Army Emergency Commission in the Pioneer Corps (154598). He served in 260th Company 6th February–18th December 1941, then transferred to No.12 Centre at Prestatyn, Wales commanded by Lieutenant Colonel Harry Greenwood VC

John Hamilton pictured at the time of the filming of *Forgotten Men – The War as It Was* in 1934.

DSO OBE MC. Promoted war substantive lieutenant on 11th April 1942, acting captain on 26th August 1942 and war substantive captain on 1st October 1944. He later commanded a prison camp of Italians in the Middle East. Arriving at the camp, he was angered by the prisoners wandering about with their hands in their pockets, so he ordered all trouser pockets to be sewn up. He believed that *idle hands lead to trouble* and set them to work. One young soldier was trying to paint or draw, but without proper materials, so Hamilton bought paints for him out of his own money. At the end of the war, when the prisoners were going home, he was presented with a painting at a farewell concert. It now hangs in his daughter's home. John retired as honorary major about September 1945.

After the war he became the first probation officer in Lanarkshire and when he retired in 1962 he was Principal to Lanark Joint Probation Committee with a staff of twenty. He gained tremendous satisfaction from seeing young offenders make good. He also fought for pensioner's rights and even when dying of cancer continued to petition political and union leaders for bigger pensions. In July 1971 *The Sunday Post* arranged a reunion between John and his old platoon sergeant, Jimmy Dickson, at the latter's home at 22 Albury Road, Aberdeen. It was the first time they had met since the VC action, fifty-four years previously.

John Hamilton died at Hairmyres Hospital, East Kilbride, Strathclyde on 18th July 1973. He was cremated at Daldowie Crematorium, Broomhouse, Glasgow and his ashes were scattered there. John is commemorated in a number of other places:

John Hamilton during the Second World War.

- A memorial to the fourteen Lanarkshire VCs dedicated on 19th April 2002 in Hamilton, Lanarkshire following a public appeal by the Hamilton Advertiser and South Lanarkshire Council. The VCs commemorated are – Frederick R Aikman, William Angus, Thomas Caldwell, Donald Cameron, John Carmichael, William C Clamp, William Gardner, John B Hamilton, David R Lauder, David MacKay, William J Milne, John O'Neill, William Reid and James C Richardson.

The National War Museum of Scotland in Edinburgh Castle.

- The Department for Communities and Local Government decided to provide a commemorative paving stone at the birthplace of every Great War Victoria Cross recipient in the United Kingdom. John's stone is to be dedicated at Cambuslang Remembrance Garden, Glasgow in September 2017 to mark the centenary of his award.

In addition to the VC he was awarded the British War Medal 1914–20, Victory Medal 1914–19, War Medal 1939–45, Defence Medal, George VI Coronation Medal 1937 and Elizabeth II Coronation Medal 1953. His Victory Medal ribbon bears the Mentioned-in-Despatches Oakleaf, but no trace could be found in the London Gazette. The medals were held by the Glasgow Highlanders Regimental Club until his daughter presented them to the Scottish United Services Museum (later renamed the National War Museum of Scotland), where they remain.

75361 COMPANY SERGEANT MAJOR ROBERT HILL HANNA
29th Battalion (Vancouver), Canadian Expeditionary Force

Robert Hanna was born on 6th August 1886 (1887 on gravestone and death certificate) near Hanna's Close, Aughnahoory, Kilkeel, Co Down, Ireland. His father, also Robert Hill Hanna (born c.1864), was a farmer. He married Sarah (born c.1865) in c.1885. In 1901 they were living at 7 Aughnahoory, Kilkeel and by 1911 had moved to 18 Aughnahoory. Robert had ten siblings:

- William Hanna (born c.1886) was a farmer in 1911.
- Sarah Hanna (1889–1969) emigrated to Canada c.1907 and married Adam Stevenson (born c.1885 in Ireland), a logger, at Vancouver in 1908. They divorced and she married Henry Duncan Mann (born c.1882 at Prince Edward Island), a lumberman, in 1912 at First Presbyterian Church, Vancouver. They lived at 3793 West 23rd Avenue, Vancouver.

- Margaret Jane Hanna (1891–1969) emigrated to Canada c.1919 and married Montague Elsworth Munn (1886–1945), born at Prince Edward Island, brother of Henry, who married Margaret's sister Sarah. They had a son, Robert Elsworth Duncan Munn (1931–87). Margaret was living at 2239 West First Avenue, Vancouver when she died.

Kilkeel, a small fishing port in the shadow of the Mourne Mountains in Co Down. On 30th May 1918 a fishing fleet from the town was sunk by U-*64* twelve miles offshore. Two boats were not sunk and the crews of the other eight returned to port on them.

- Samuel John Hanna (born c.1893) was a farmer in 1911.
- Elizabeth Hanna (c.1894–1977).
- Annie Hanna (born c.1898).
- Catherine Amelia Hanna (1900–35) married as Vaughn and was a logging camp cook when she drowned on 18th May 1935.
- Susan Florence Hanna (1901–2001) married William Henry Curtis (1900–88), who was born at Alresford, Hampshire. They had three children, all registered at Portsmouth – Patricia OF Curtis 1927, Maureen Curtis 1932 and James R Curtis 1935. Susan and William both died at Winchester, Hampshire.
- Minnie Irvine Hanna (born 1903).
- Essie Hanna (born c.1910).

Robert was educated at Ballinran School, near Kilkeel. He emigrated to Canada in 1905 and took up farming initially before working as a logger in British Columbia. He enlisted at Vancouver, British Columbia on 1st November 1914. He was described as 5′ 5¾″ or 5′ 7½″ tall with fair complexion, blue eyes, light brown hair and his religious denomination was Presbyterian. He was posted to 29th Battalion and sailed with it for Britain on 20th May 1915 on RMS *Missanabie*. He was fined one day's pay for being absent 22nd–23rd August. Robert sailed with the Battalion to France on 17th September, arriving in Boulogne the following day. He was a member of a wood cutting party, returning to the Battalion on 6th January 1916. Having contracted German measles, he was admitted to 6th Canadian Field Ambulance on 31st March and No.7 General Hospital, St Omer on 1st April until being discharged on 13th April. On 24th June he was slightly wounded on the cheek by shrapnel, but returned to the Battalion the same day. He attended a bombing course 24th–30th July and was promoted lance corporal on 20th August. Having been promoted sergeant on 9th October, he was granted leave from 25th October until 3rd November. Robert attended the Canadian Corps Training School from 29th January to 24th February 1917. He was appointed acting company sergeant major of B Company on 21st August.

Awarded the VC for his actions at Hill 70, Lens, France on 21st August 1917, LG 8th November 1917. He was promoted company sergeant major on 27th August. The VC was presented by the King at Buckingham Palace on 5th December.

Robert returned to England via the Base Depot in France, arriving on 23rd September. He attended officer training and was also granted leave in Ireland to visit his family home at Kilkeel. He received a hero's welcome in the square from over 3,000 people, who marked the occasion with a presentation of gifts. A presentation was also made to him by Crimean veteran Sergeant Thomas Hanna of the 14th Regiment of Foot. On 10th November 1917 he was posted to the Canadian Training School Bexhill pending commissioning, which

RMS *Missanabie* (12,469 tons) was launched by Barclay Curle & Co, Glasgow for the Canadian Pacific Railway Company on the Liverpool – Canada route. Her maiden voyage commenced on 7th October 1914. During the First World War she was a defensively-armed passenger liner. On 9th September 1918 she was torpedoed by UB-*87*, fifty-two miles off Daunts Rock, Ireland. Forty-five lives were lost.

occurred on 26th January 1918. The following day he joined 1st Canadian Reserve Battalion and was appointed temporary lieutenant on 12th February. On 24th August he joined the Canadian Forestry Corps at Sunningdale and on 16th October joined 51st District CFC, 107th Company at Inverness. He served with 138th Company at Inverness from 4th January until 29th April 1919, then rejoined the CFC Base Depot Sunningdale, reverting to 29th Battalion next day. Robert sailed for Canada on 10th May and was on the strength of District Depot XI, Hastings Park, Vancouver until being demobilised in Ottawa, Ontario on 24th May 1919.

He returned to the lumber industry and managed a logging camp at Aldergrove, British Columbia. In 1930 he married Hannah May Gillis, of Scottish origin, and went back to farming, settling at Bradner Road, Mount Lehman, British Columbia. Robert and Hannah had two sons:

• John Hanna (born and died 1st June 1941).
• Robert HA Hanna. He was living at 311 Dixon Road, Weston, Ontario in 1967. Robert was a member of the Aughnahoory Loyal Orange Lodge No.343B and the Ontario LOL No.2226 Vancouver, British Columbia. Along with fellow Canadian

Canadian soldiers training near Bexhill. The Canadian Training School moved there from Crowborough in March 1917 and was joined by the Canadian Trench Warfare School in May. In January 1918, Cooden Camp was converted into Princess Patricia's Canadian Red Cross Hospital and many other buildings in and around the town were taken over by the Canadians.

member of LOL 2226, Lieutenant Harold Rose, he joined Royal Black Preceptory 208. Due to it being wartime they had special permission to receive all their Black degrees in a single night from the Grand Master of Co Down, Sir William Annett, a process that in peacetime usually took eleven months. Robert was a Freemason, initiated into Canada Lodge No.3527, London, England. He was affiliated with Lions Gate Lodge No.115, Vancouver on 6th October 1938 and that Lodge consolidated with Keystone Lodge No.121 in 1996.

Huge quantities of wood were required to support the war on the Western Front. The Canadian Forestry Corps was formed at first to fell trees in Canada, but the lumber required too much space aboard the hard pressed merchant fleet. It was then decided to use the Canadians in Europe to cut lumber in Britain and France. A number of infantry battalions were converted into lumberjack units instead. Eventually 35,000 Canadians served in the Forestry Corps. Its companies were occasionally used as labour units.

Robert attended the VC Centenary Celebrations at Hyde Park, London on 26th June 1956. He died at Mount Lehman, British Columbia on 15th June 1967 and is buried in the Masonic Cemetery, Burnaby, British Columbia (Plot 49, Section C, Grave 2). He is commemorated in a number of other places:

- WOII Robert H Hanna VC Memorial Bursary awarded annually by the British Columbia Regiment (Duke of Connaught's Own) Association to a serving member of the Regiment for academic achievement and loyalty to the Regiment. It is one of five bursaries ($500 in 2007) honouring the VCs of units perpetuated by the Regiment.

Robert Hanna's grave in the Masonic Cemetery, Burnaby, British Columbia.

- Display in Beattie Street Armouries, Vancouver, British Columbia.
- Memorial bench outside the Regimental Museum, Beatty Street, Vancouver, British Columbia.
- Named on the memorial bench to the VCs of the Orange Order at Ulster Tower, Thiepval, France.
- Plaque on the war memorial, Kilkeel, Co Down, Northern Ireland.
- Plaque on Chemin Des Croisettes, Loos-En-Gohelle, France.
- Two 49 Cent postage stamps in honour of the ninety-four Canadian VCs were issued by Canada Post on 21st October 2004 on the 150th Anniversary of the first Canadian VC's action, Alexander Roberts Dunn.
- Victoria Cross obelisk to all Canadian VCs at Military Heritage Park, Barrie, Ontario dedicated by The Princess Royal on 22nd October 2013.
- Named on one of eleven plaques honouring 175 men from overseas awarded the VC for the Great War. The plaques were unveiled by the Senior Minister of State

Robert Hanna's memorial plaque on Chemin Des Croisettes, Loos-en-Gohelle, France on the lower slopes of Hill 70. Also commemorated there is Private Michael James O'Rourke VC. The view is looking towards Loos, with the top of Hill 70 behind the camera.

Kilkeel war memorial, Co Down. (*Irish War Memorials*)

at the Foreign & Commonwealth Office and Minister for Faith and Communities, Baroness Warsi, at a reception at Lancaster House, London on 26th June 2014 attended by The Duke of Kent and relatives of the VC recipients. The Canadian plaque was unveiled outside the British High Commission in Elgin Street, Ottawa on 10th November 2014 by The Princess Royal in the presence of British High Commissioner Howard Drake, Canadian Minister of Veterans Affairs Julian Fantino and Canadian Chief of the Defence Staff General Thomas J Lawson.

- The Department for Communities and Local Government decided to provide a commemorative paving stone at the birthplace of every Great War Victoria Cross recipient in the United Kingdom. Robert's stone was dedicated at Cross of Sacrifice, Glasnevin Cemetery, Dublin, Ireland on 12th May 2017 to mark the centenary of his award.
- Plaque on a memorial to the ninety-nine Canadian VCs in York Cemetery, Toronto.

In addition to the VC he was awarded the 1914–15 Star, British War Medal 1914–20, Victory Medal 1914–19, George VI Coronation Medal 1937 and Queen Elizabeth II Coronation Medal 1953. His medals are understood to be held by the family.

SECOND LIEUTENANT DENIS GEORGE WYLDBORE HEWITT
2nd attached 14th Battalion, The Hampshire Regiment

Denis Hewitt was born at 103 Park Street, Mayfair, London on 18th December 1897. His father, Hon George Wyldbore Hewitt JP (1858–1924), was born in Ireland and was a tea planter. He married Elizabeth Mary Rampini (c.1871–1959) in Calcutta, Bengal in January 1891. The family was living at 12 College Street,

Winchester, Hampshire in 1901 and later at Field House, Hursley, near Winchester.

Denis had a brother, Alan William Wingfield Hewitt (1900–87). When he applied for a commission on 25th October 1918, he was 5′ 10″ tall and weighed 132 lbs, but his chest was ½″ under the required girth and he was accepted subject to growing during training. Alan joined the Royal Military College, Sandhurst on 17th January 1919 and was commissioned into The Hampshire Regiment on 24th December 1920. He was injured by the accidental discharge of a pistol late on 10th September 1921 at Cork, Ireland and was in hospital for three weeks. A Court of Enquiry, convened at Victoria Barracks, Cork on 20th September, learned that Alan and some other officers were walking over St Patrick's Bridge. Lieutenant JL Leith MC was armed with a .32 Colt Automatic in his right overcoat pocket in accordance with orders. The pistol slipped in the pocket and turned over with the muzzle pointing upwards. As Leith turned it back, he accidentally pressed the trigger and the round hit Alan in the left foot. The others took him to the Central Military Hospital for treatment and remarkably no bones were broken. No blame was attached to Leith. Hewitt resigned his commission on 29th November 1921 and resigned from the Regular Army Reserve of Officers on 17th December 1930. He became a farmer and succeeded his cousin in 1954 as 8th Viscount Lifford. He married Alison Mary Patricia Ashton (1910–2010) in 1935 and they had four children:

• Lydia M Hewitt (born 1938) married Sir Michael Christopher Swann (born 1941) in 1965. He was commissioned in 3rd Green Jackets (468651), promoted lieutenant 3rd February 1963, transferred to 4th Battalion, captain 1st April 1967, major 1st March 1970, awarded ED (LG 12th July 1977) and brevet lieutenant colonel 1st April 1979. He last appears in the Army List in 1979. They had three children – Jonathan Christopher Swann 1966, Tessa Margaret Swann 1968 and Toby Charles Swann 1971. The marriage ended in divorce in 1983. Sir Michael married Marilyn Ann Morse in 1988. He was Chairman of Gabbitas Truman and Thring 1987, General Commissioner of Income Tax 1988, Director GVG Financial Services 1988–92 and a partner in Smith Swann & Company 1992–97.

College Street, Winchester. The Hewitt family was living at No.12 in 1901. The house on the right is No.8, where Jane Austen died on 18th July 1817.

• Belinda Anne Hewitt (born 1939) married Reverend Piers Eliot de Dutton Warburton (1930–2015) in 1963 and they had two children – Piers Richard Grove Warburton 1964 and Elizabeth Jane Warburton 1967.

- Flora E Hewitt (born 1947) married Edward Bell Henderson in 1965 and they had two children – Samantha Elizabeth Henderson 1967 and Victoria Amanda Henderson 1971. The marriage ended in divorce in 1975.
- Edward James Wingfield Hewitt (born 1949), 9th Viscount Lifford, inherited the family home at Field House, Hursley, Hampshire. He married Alison Mary Law in 1976 and they had three children – Annabel Louise Hewitt 1978, James Thomas Wingfield Hewitt 1979 and Alice Mary Hewitt 1990.

Denis's paternal grandfather was James Hewitt (1811–87), 4th Viscount Lifford, born in Merrion Square, Dublin, Ireland. One of his mother's nephews was Lieutenant General Sir Frederick Stanley Maude KCB CMG DSO (1864–1917), who was responsible for capturing Baghdad in Mesopotamia in March 1917. The lineage began with James Hewitt, 1st Viscount Lifford, former Lord Chancellor of Ireland during the 18th Century, who was elevated to the peerage of Ireland in 1768 as Baron Lifford and was created a viscount thirteen years later. He owned over 11,000 acres of prime land at Meenglas, Ballybofey, Co Donegal. With Sir Samuel Hayes, of Drumboe Estate, Stranorlar, James helped to expand Ireland's railways. Their representations to Parliament helped to secure funding for what became the Finn Valley Railway Company in May 1860. James married Mary Acheson (1809–50), daughter of Archibald Acheson (1776–1849), 2nd Earl of Gosford, and Mary Sparrow (1777–1841), in 1835. They had seven children:

- James Wilfrid Hewitt (1837–1913) was commissioned in 4th Regiment of Foot 1856, transferred to 3rd Regiment of Foot on 16th January 1857 and was promoted lieutenant the same year. Honorary Colonel, Donegal Royal Field Reserve Artillery. He married Annie Frances Hodgson in 1867 and succeeded as 5th Viscount Lifford on the death of his father. JP Co. Donegal.
- Mary Anne Hewitt (1840–1913) married John Gathorne Wood (c.1839–1929) in 1866.
- Evelyn John Hewitt (1842–67) served as a lieutenant in the Royal Artillery.
- Archibald Robert Hewitt (1844–1925) married Helen Blanche Geach (1859–1942) in 1878. He succeeded as 6th Viscount Lifford and they lived at Hill House, Lyndhurst, Hampshire. They had four children:

James Hewitt, 1st Viscount Lifford (1712–89), the son of a Coventry draper, began as an attorney's clerk and by 1742 was a barrister. He was MP for Coventry 1761–66, but the culmination of his career was being appointed Lord Chancellor of Ireland 1767–89. He married Mary Rhys Williams (died 1765) c.1749 and they had four sons. He married his second wife, Ambrosia Bayley, in 1766 and they a son and two daughters.

○ Norah Hewitt 1879.
○ Evelyn James Hewitt (7th Viscount) (1880–1954), served in the South African War on operations in Cape Colony January to 31st May 1902. He was commissioned in the Dorsetshire Regiment from the Militia on 26th August 1903. Promoted lieutenant 9th April 1905 and captain 26th May 1910. During the Great War he was appointed Staff Captain 34th Brigade 2nd April 1915–15th August 1916. Appointed acting major 16th-21st August 1916, acting lieutenant colonel 22nd August–22nd October 1916, acting major 22nd December 1916–8th April 1917 and temporary lieutenant colonel to command 6th Duke of Cornwall's Light Infantry 9th April 1917–2nd June 1918. Promoted major 22nd October 1917 and appointed temporary lieutenant colonel to command 4th East Lancashire 3rd June 1918–5th January 1920. He was awarded the DSO (LG 3rd June 1916) and Bar (LG 3rd June 1918) and was MID three times (LG 13th July 1916, 18th December 1917 and 24th May 1918.
○ Archibald Rodney Hewitt (1883–1915) was commissioned in the East Surrey Regiment on 22nd October 1902. Promoted lieutenant 18th June 1904 and captain 18th May 1910. Appointed adjutant 1st June 1911–31st May 1914. During the Great War he serving with 2nd East Surrey and was awarded the DSO (LG 9th November 1914). He was killed in action on 25th April 1915 (Ypres (Menin Gate) Memorial, Belgium).
○ Anne Rachel Millicent Hewitt 1885.
• Cornwallis Charles Hewitt (1847–89), Prebendary of Tuam in Co Galway, Ireland, married Maria Hayes (c.1848–82) in 1881 at Calcutta, India. She died the following year at Darjeeling, India.
• Edward Hewitt (1848–1931) married Evelyn Frances Charlotte Stronge (c.1866–1956) in 1890. He was appointed JP Wiltshire and Denbighshire.
• Isabella Hewitt (1850–1924) married Richard Southby (1838–1921) in 1879. They had four children – Richard Southby 1879, Olivia Mary Ann Southby 1881, Evelyn John James Southby 1882 and Archibald Richard James Southby 1886.

James married Lydia Lucy, late Purdon-Coote, née Wingfield-Digby (1828–1919) in 1851. She was the daughter of Reverend John Digby Wingfield-Digby and Ann Eliza Wyldbore-Smith and was the widow of Charles Purdon-Coote of Ballyclough Castle, Co Cork (died 1848). In addition to George they had five other children:

• Lettice Lucy Hewitt (c.1853–1939) married Captain Alexander William Maxwell Clark-Kennedy, Coldstream Guards (1851–94) in 1875. His grandfather, General Sir A Clark Kennedy KCB KH, fought at Waterloo and captured the eagle of the 105th Regiment. They lived at Knockgray, Carsphairn, Galloway, Scotland. By 1881 they were living at Henbury House, Sturminster Marshall, Dorset and by 1891 had moved to 72 Eaton Place, St George, Hanover Square, London. He was DL Kircudbrightshire and JP for Dumfries and Dorsetshire. He was a

Fellow of the Linnaean Society, Royal Geographic Society, Zoological Society, Society of Actuaries and Society of Actuaries (Scotland). The author of several works on science, travel and poems, he was also Secretary of the Colonial Mutual Life Assurance Society, West End Branch, 29 Cockspur Street, London. Lettice was living at 41 Albany Street, Edinburgh during the Great War. They had eight children:

- John William James Clark-Kennedy (1876–1939) emigrated to South Africa, where he married Phyllis Elizabeth Ashburnham (born 1895) in 1918. John served as a lieutenant colonel in the South African Police Force.
- Alexander Clark-Kennedy (born and died 1876).
- Lettice Eleanor Clarke-Kennedy (c.1878–1926).
- William Hew Clark-Kennedy (1879–1961) worked for Standard Life Assurance Company from 1896. He served as a trooper in the Imperial Yeomanry, Rhodesian Horse and Paget's Horse in the South African War 1899–1902 and was Mention in Despatches. He emigrated to Canada in 1902 and continued working for Standard Life, later becoming Assistant Manager, Canada. He joined the Canadian Militia. In 1910 he transferred to Standard Life in Johannesburg, South Africa but later returned to Canada. He married Katherine Florence Reford (1877–1966) in Canada in 1914. On the outbreak of war, he joined 13th Battalion CEF as a captain and sailed to England with the 1st Canadian Contingent, arriving in October 1914. He went to France and was in action during the German gas attacks at Ypres in April 1915 during which he was buried and knocked unconscious (French Croix de Guerre). At Festubert in May 1915 he was awarded the DSO. MID, LG 1st January 1916. He was appointed brigade major in October 1916 and was involved in the capture of Vimy Ridge in April 1917. Promoted lieutenant colonel and assumed command of 24th Battalion CEF in February 1918. For his actions at Wancourt on 27th-28th August 1918 leading his Battalion, he was awarded the VC, LG 14th December 1918. After the war he became manager of Standard Life Canada until retiring in November 1945. He was also a director of Guardian Insurance of Canada from 1927, chairman in 1943 and was also chairman of the Advisory Board of the Guardian-Caledonian group of insurance companies.

William Hew Clark-Kennedy VC CMG DSO was Denis Hewitt's cousin.

- Leopold James Clark-Kennedy (1881–1932).
- Alice Arthur Clark-Kennedy (1882–1961).
- Alexander Kenelm Clark-Kennedy (1883–1917) was a civil servant in the Factory Department of the Home Office. He served in 1/5th King's Own Scottish Borderers and

was appointed temporary captain on 11th May 1915. He landed at Gallipoli on 6th June and suffered from diarrhea, but continued at duty until 15th September when he was hospitalised. On 30th September he was evacuated from Lancashire Landing with rheumatism and enteritis to Mudros, then to Malta on HMHS *Grantully Castle* on 6th October. A medical board there next day sent him home on HMHS *Panama*, arriving at Southampton on 16th October. A medical board at Caxton Hall, London on 22nd October noted he had lost lots of weight and was weak. As a result he was not fit for General Service for three months and was sent on leave until 22nd December. A medical board at Caxton Hall on 3rd January 1916 found him fit for light duties at Home and a medical board at Ripon Military Hospital on 9th February found him fit for General Service. He embarked on HMS *Aragon* at Devonport on 4th April and disembarked at Alexandria, Egypt on 15th April for the Base Depot, Mustapha. He was admitted to 19th General Hospital, Alexandria with pyrexia 19th–29th April and rejoined the Battalion at Kantara on 4th May. Alexander was killed in action

Denis' cousin, Archibald Douglas Hewitt Clark-Kennedy, is buried in Quéant Road Cemetery, Buissy, France.

during the Second Battle of Gaza on 19th April 1917 and is buried in Gaza War Cemetery (XVIII A 3). He left £1,243/18/2 to his mother.

- ○ Archibald Douglas Hewitt Clark-Kennedy (1888–1918) served in 4th Royal Scots (Queen's Edinburgh Rifles) from 1910 and the Bombay Light Horse in 1912. He was commissioned in 1/5th Royal Scots Fusiliers on 12th July 1915. A medical board at 3rd Scottish General Hospital, Glasgow found him fit for duty following an operation to rectify an internal derangement of the right knee. He went to France on 6th June and was MID, LG 16th January 1918. He died of wounds near Moeuvres on 18th September 1918 and is buried in Quéant Road Cemetery, Buissy, France (VII D 20). He left £890/9/11 to his mother.
- Alice Anne Hewitt (1854–1943) married Sir Samuel Hercules Hayes (1840–1901), 4th Baronet, of Drumhoe Castle, Co Donegal, Ireland in 1878. He died on 6th November 1901 at Funchal, Madeira.
- William James Hewitt (1856–1948) married Evelyn Frances Carey (1862–1946), daughter of Lieutenant General Francis Carey, in 1887. They had two sons:
  - ○ James Francis Hewitt (1888–1914) served as a lieutenant in 1st Cameronians. He embarked at Southampton and joined the

Another cousin, Lieutenant James Francis Hewitt, was killed in action at La Boutillerie on 26th October 1914 and is commemorated on the Ploegsteert Memorial, Belgium.

Battalion in the field on 22nd September 1914 and was killed in action at La Boutillerie on 26th October 1914 (Ploegsteert Memorial, Belgium). He left £1,927/14/5 to his father.

○ William George Hewitt (1892–1914) served as a Second lieutenant in 3rd attached 2nd Royal Scots and was killed in action on 14th October 1914 (Vieille-Chapelle New Military Cemetery, La Couture, France – V C 10). He left £1,269/5/4 to his father.

• Georgina Rosamund Hewitt (1857–87) married John Kenelm Digby Wingfield-Digby (1859–1904) in 1883. John married Charlotte Kathleen Digby (1863–1935) in 1890 and they had a son, Frederick James Bosworth Digby Wingfield-Digby (1885–1952).

• Anne Elizabeth Hewitt (1860–1957) never married.

His maternal grandfather, Charles Joseph Galliari Rampini (1840–1907), was born at Edinburgh, Midlothian, son of Joseph Charles Rampini (1805–63) and Eliza Fulton (1811–85). Charles was a banker's clerk in 1861, living with his parents at 10 Gloucester Place, Edinburgh and was later a barrister. He married Anne née Burness (1846–1929), born at Montrose, Angus, in 1867 at Kingston, Jamaica, West Indies. The family was living at Independent Manse, High Street, Lerwick and Gulberwick, Shetland in 1881, where he was Sheriff Substitute for Zetland. By 1891 they were living at Springfield House, Elgin where he was Sheriff Substitute for Inverness, Moray and Nairn. By 1901 they were living at 'Vancouver', Paignton, Devon. He was DL Hampshire and Sheriff of Dumfries and Galloway. In addition to Elizabeth they had five other children:

• Frederick Charles Rampini (1868–1941) was born in Jamaica. He served in the Army, attending the Royal Military College, Sandhurst and was commissioned in The South Staffordshire Regiment on 22nd August 1888. He served at Gibraltar from 2nd November 1888 and was promoted lieutenant on 27th October 1889. On 13th March 1891 he transferred to the Indian Staff Corps and was appointed Supply and Transport Officer 4th Class on 12th May 1893. He was promoted captain on 22nd August 1899 and was posted to Port Blair on 12th May 1901. On 12th May 1905 he was appointed Supply and Transport Officer 3rd Class and promoted major on 22nd August 1906. He was granted leave outside India for eight months from 27th February 1910. He later changed his name to Rampini Fulton.

• Isabella Burnet Rampini (born 1873) married John Manson in 1894 at St James's, Piccadilly, London. They had five children – Charles Claude Edmonstone Manson 1895, Gerald P Manson 1897, John A Manson 1898 and twins George Wilfred Manson and Nanette Manson 1899. She was living with her children at 2 Burgess Terrace, Edinburgh in 1901.

• Maud Florence Rampini (c.1878–1953), born in Jamaica, was living with her uncle and aunt Arthur and Mary Dickson and her sister Clara Rampini at 103 High Street, Montrose in 1891.

- Clare Rampini (1880–1967) was born at Hillhead, Lerwick, Shetland. She married Harold Cotterell Adams (1874–1964), a medical practitioner, in 1904 at Totnes, Devon. In 1911 they were living at Palmeira, Paignton, Devon. They had two children – Louise Maud Adams 1907 and Phyllis Clare Adams 1910.
- Edward Arthur Craig Rampini (1888–1968) was born at Elgin, Morayshire and changed his name to Fulton. He married Maud Georgina May Forsdyke (1890–1969) in 1940 at Totnes. Her father, Frederick Walewski Forsdyke (1857–1941) graduated as a veterinary surgeon in 1879 and served in the Army – captain 25th May 1889, major 24th May 1899, lieutenant colonel 22nd August 1902 and colonel 22nd August 1907. He served with the Kyber Line Field Force in the Afghan War 1880, Bozdar Expedition 1881 and Chitral Relief Force 1895. He was with the Tirah Expeditionary Force on the North West Frontier 12th October 1897–28th April 1898 (MID) as Inspecting Veterinary Officer on the Lines of Communication. He also served throughout the South African War, 1899–1903. Other appointments included Principal Veterinary Officer II Corps 12th January 1903–19th June 1906, Principal Veterinary Officer Southern Command 20th December 1906–4th February 1908, Inspecting Veterinary Officer HQ India 1st October 1911–4th February 1913 and Assistant Director of Veterinary Services, Northern Scotland & Western Commands 10th March 1913 until his retirement in April 1914.

Denis was educated at The Old Malthouse School, Langton Matravers, near Swanage, Dorset and Winchester College September 1911–1915. When he applied for a commission on 5th May 1915, he was 6′ 1″ tall and weighed 161 lbs. He trained at the Royal Military College, Sandhurst and was commissioned in 2nd Hampshire on 7th April 1916. Attached to 14th Battalion, he went to France in September 1916. He suffered debility after tonsillitis and a medical board at Boulogne on 8th June 1917 found him unfit for any service for two weeks and recommended home leave. **Awarded the VC for his actions at St Julien, Belgium on 31st July 1917, LG 14th September 1917.** He was killed during the VC action and is commemorated on the Ypres (Menin Gate) Memorial. The location of his grave was recorded as, *150 yards west of the St Julien–Poelcapelle road*. As he never married, the VC was presented to his parents by the King at Buckingham Palace on 19th December 1917. Most of his personal effects were recovered by Sergeant Skinner, Lance Corporal Harding and Private Sparks, but

The Old Malthouse, a preparatory school, was founded by Rex Corbett, a former England footballer, in Langton Matravers in 1906. It closed in 2007, but was reopened the following year by the Cothill Educational Trust to run week-long practical science courses for children aged ten to thirteen.

The Royal Military College was established in 1802 in Great Marlow to train gentleman cadets for the infantry and cavalry of the British Army and the Presidency armies in India. In 1812 the College moved to purpose-built buildings at Sandhurst, Berkshire. In 1947 it became The Royal Military Academy, having merged with the Royal Military Academy, Woolwich when the latter closed. It continues to train officers for all arms and services of the British Army to this day.

Winchester College was founded in 1382 by William of Wykeham, Bishop of Winchester, hence members of the college are known as Wykehamists. It was to act as a feeder for New College, Oxford and the buildings of both colleges were designed by William Wynford. It has been expanded over the centuries and now has about 700 pupils. Its long list of famous and diverse alumni include author Anthony Trollope, Edward Grey, the Foreign Secretary 1905–16, senior Second World War commanders Hugh Dowding, Charles Portal and Archibald Wavell, George Mallory, who was lost on Everest in 1924, politicians Stafford Cripps, Hugh Gaitskill and Geoffrey Howe, British fascist leader Oswald Mosley, comedian Tim Brooke-Taylor and the extraordinarily diverse sportsman Maxwell Woosnam, who won Olympic gold and silver in tennis at the 1920 Games, the 1921 Wimbledon doubles title, captained the British Davis Cup team, had a maximum break of 147 in snooker, made a century at Lords and captained Manchester City FC and the England football team.

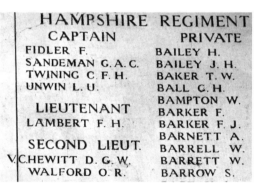

HAMPSHIRE REGIMENT	
CAPTAIN	**PRIVATE**
FIDLER F.	BAILEY H.
SANDEMAN G. A. C.	BAILEY J. H.
TWINING C. F. H.	BAKER T. W.
UNWIN L. U.	BALL G. H.
	BAMPTON W.
LIEUTENANT	BARKER F.
LAMBERT F. H.	BARKER F. J.
	BARNETT A.
SECOND LIEUT.	BARRELL W.
V.C.HEWITT D. G. W.	BARRETT W.
WALFORD O. R.	BARROW S.

Denis Hewitt's name on the Menin Gate Memorial to the Missing.

The War Memorial Cloister at Winchester College commemorates the Wykehamists lost in the two World Wars. Designed by Sir Herbert Baker, it was dedicated in 1924 and 1948.

some items were lost. Sergeant Skinner returned a ring and watch personally to his father, who tried to recover a missing cigarette case and some papers, mainly photographs, through the Depot, but without success. As he was legally a minor, Denis left no will and died intestate. Denis is also commemorated at:

The memorial to Denis Hewitt in All Saints' Church, Hursley, Hampshire.

The Old Malthouse School war memorial in St George's Church, Langton Matravers, Dorset.

- War Memorial Cloister, Winchester College, Hampshire.
- Memorial at All Saints' Church, Hursley, Hampshire.
- Old Malthouse School War Memorial in St George's Church, Langton Matravers, Dorset.
- Regimental Memorial and VC Memorial, Memorial Chapel, Sandhurst, Camberley, Surrey.
- Victoria Cross Memorial, Hampshire Regiment Museum, Winchester, Hampshire.
- The Department for Communities and Local Government decided to provide a commemorative paving stone at the birthplace of every Great War Victoria Cross recipient in the United Kingdom. Commemorative stones for Denis were dedicated at Embankment Gardens, Whitehall, London on 26th June 2017 and at Hursley War Memorial, Winchester on 2nd August 2017 to mark the centenary of his award.

In addition to the VC he was awarded the British War Medal 1914–20 and Victory Medal 1914–19. The VC is held privately.

8162 LANCE CORPORAL WILLIAM HENRY HEWITT
2nd South African Infantry Regiment (Natal & Orange Free State Regiment)

William Hewitt was born on 19th June 1884 at Copdock, near Ipswich, Suffolk. His father, also William Henry Hewitt (1830–1915), was born at Paddington, London. In 1851 he was a farmer of eighty acres at Preston Farm, Harrow-on-the-Hill, Middlesex. He is believed to have married Mary Shipman (1845–76), born at Chorlton, Lancashire, at Northampton in 1868. By 1871 William was a butcher and the family was living at 61 Bishops Road, Paddington. William married Mary Elizabeth née Marsh (1856–1929),

born at Holcot, Northamptonshire, in 1881 at Kensington, London. By 1891 William was living with his family at New Hall, Copdock, Suffolk. They had moved to West Hill House, Copdock, Suffolk by 1901. William senior left £17,663/17/6 when he died on 15th April 1915. Mary was living at 15 Portland Road, Hove, Sussex at the time of her son's enlistment in 1915. William junior had six siblings:

St Peter's Church, Copdock where George Hewitt is commemorated. (*Richie Wisbey*)

- George Robarts Hewitt (1872–1900) served as a private in the Cape Mounted Rifles (3249) and was killed in action at Labusch Nek, South Africa on 4th March 1900. There is a brass memorial plaque to him in Copdock Church.
- Maud Mary Hewitt (1870–1957) was a sculptor in 1901, living with her widowed aunt, Hannah Robarts (née Hewitt), at 29 Cromwell Road, Hove, Sussex. She married Quintin Waddington (1867–1945), an archaeologist, in 1902 and they lived at Little Ash, Ditchling, Sussex. They had a son, James Hilary Sheffield Waddington (1903–89), who became an Architect Inspector of Antiquities. He married Ruth Elizabeth Florence Pollard (1905–78) in 1932 in Jerusalem, Palestine and they had three children.
- Helen Annie Hewitt (1874–1958) was an artist in 1901.
- Evelyn Hewitt (1881–1958).
- Marian Hewitt (born 1882).
- Mabel Mary Hewitt (1887–1971) married Edwin Gordon in 1935.

William's paternal grandfather, Henry Hewitt, was a butcher living with his family at John Street West, Marylebone, London in 1830. He married Phoebe née Couzens on 16th February 1829 at St George, Bloomsbury, London. Phoebe had a daughter, also Phoebe Couzens, born on 28th February 1822. Phoebe junior married Henry Elmore (c.1820–53) in 1845 and they had three children – Lydia Elmore 1846, Charlotte Elmore 1848 and Anne Elmore 1850. Phoebe senior was a widow in 1861 living with her brother, William, as his housekeeper, together with her daughter Annie. A relative of Henry's, John Elmore, possibly his father, was the winning owner of the Grand National in 1839 with Lottery and in 1842 with Gaylad.

William's maternal grandfather, the Reverend Samuel Laundon Marsh (c.1820–81), was an independent minister. He married Mary née Cockerill (born 1829) in 1854 and in 1871 they were living at Old, Northamptonshire. In addition to Mary they had four other children:

- Annie Devrieux Marsh (1857–1943).
- Samuel Laundon Marsh (1861–99).
- Louisa Sarah Marsh (born 1862).
- Emily A Marsh (born c.1867).

In 1897 St Joseph's Roman Catholic College, Church Lane, Tooting Graveney was taken over by the Wandsworth Board of Guardians to provide extra workhouse accommodation. It was renamed the Tooting Home for the Aged and Infirm. Hill House, the original manor house on the site, became the nurses' home and was once the home of the author Daniel Defoe. By 1901 the Home housed 605 inmates and in 1903 it was expanded to accommodate 204 more. During the Great War the establishment was taken over by the War Office as the Church Lane Military Hospital and was also known as the Tooting Military Hospital. It had 712 beds. After the war the Ministry of Pensions used it as a neurological hospital until 1923. After a period of dereliction the site was purchased by London County Council and it opened in 1931 as St Benedict's Hospital for long-stay patients. It closed in 1981 and the site was turned over to housing.

Framlingham College, founded in 1864 by public subscription, was originally named the Albert Memorial College. A former pupil was Percy Charles Pickard DSO and two Bars DFC, whose squadron dropped the paratroopers on the Bruneval Raid in 1942. He went on to fly numerous covert missions over Europe and was killed leading the Amiens prison raid in 1944. In addition to William Hewitt, two other VCs attended the College – Lieutenant Gordon Flowerdew (1885–1918) and Captain Augustus Agar RN (1890–1968). Another old boy, Commander Henry Tupper, was awarded the Albert Medal, later replaced by the George Cross.

William was educated at Framlingham College, Woodbridge, Suffolk 1894–1900. Two other pupils were also awarded the VC – Gordon Flowerdew and Augustus Agar. He emigrated to South Africa in 1905 and served in the South African Constabulary and later the Natal Police, including during the Zulu Rebellion in 1906. He later became a farmer in Natal. William enlisted on 24th November 1915 and was posted to the Depot. He went to

Gordon Muriel Flowerdew emigrated to British Columbia and became a rancher. He enlisted as a private in Lord Strathcona's Horse and was commissioned in 1916. At the end of March 1918 he led a desperate cavalry charge to capture Moreuil Wood and stem the German advance. The action resulted in him being awarded the VC posthumously.

France on 12th July 1916 and was taken on strength of 2nd South African Infantry on 15th July. He fought at Delville Wood and later at the Butte de Warlencourt as a Lewis gunner in 2 Platoon, B Company. Having been wounded in the leg on 12th October, he was evacuated to England on 24th October, where he was treated at Tooting Military Hospital, London. William returned to France in April 1917 and was promoted lance corporal on 17th May.

Awarded the VC for his actions at Zevencote, near Zonnebeke, Belgium on 20th September 1917, LG 26th November 1917. William was evacuated to Richmond, Surrey on 1st October. He was presented with the VC by the King at Buckingham Palace on 16th January 1918 and was appointed acting sergeant on 1st April.

William Hewitt married Lily Ollett (born 1894 at Hackney, London) in October 1918. She was a shorthand typist in 1911. They met while he was a patient at Tooting Military Hospital in October 1916. William returned to South Africa on RMS *Durham Castle* on 22nd April 1919 and was discharged the next day. He continued farming in Natal until 1925, when they moved to East Africa. He ran a coffee farm there until he sold it in 1939. William and Lily had four daughters, including Diana Kathleen Violet Hewitt (1921–22). Another daughter emigrated to Australia in 1968 with her husband and daughters.

Lily's father, Arthur Frederick Ollett (1861–1926), was a printer/compositor. He married Sarah Ann née Waller (1862–1937) in 1882 and in 1901 they were living at 10 The Grove, Hackney, London. They later moved to 48 Ainslie Wood Road, South Chingford, London. In addition to Lily they had three other children:

- Arthur Joseph Ollett (1887–1915) served as 17352 Lance Corporal Arthur Joseph Ollett, 7th Field Company RE and died on 12th November 1915. He is buried in Cité Bonjean Military Cemetery, Armentières (IX D 39).
- Sarah Ann Ollett (1892–94).
- Violet Ollett (1900–52).

RMS *Durham Castle* was built for the Union-Castle Mail Steamship Co in 1904 for the Cape of Good Hope – Mombasa service. During the war she was occasionally used as a troopship. She returned to the East African route until being replaced by RMS *Pretoria Castle* in 1939. During the Second World War she was requisitioned by the Admiralty. On 26th January 1940, while being towed to Scapa Flow to be used as a base accommodation ship, she struck a mine off Cromarty, probably laid by U-57, and sank.

During the Second World War William served as a major in Mombasa, East Africa as a liaison officer and later as assistant provost marshal. William and Lily were living in Nairobi, Kenya in 1952.

When his health began to fail in 1950, he retired to Hermanus on the Cape Coast and became a South African citizen in 1955. He returned to Britain to attend the VC Centenary celebrations in Hyde Park, London on 26th June 1956. By the late 1950s he could hardly speak due to cancer of the larynx. When surgeons removed his larynx at Groote Schuur Hospital in Cape Town, they found pieces of shrapnel embedded there and shortly afterwards he developed Parkinson's disease. Lily took him to Britain in 1961 in an attempt to find a cure through a Parkinson's specialist in Edinburgh. He fell badly during his final years and twice suffered pneumonia. Although crippled, unable to speak and latterly completely helpless, William continued as best he could without complaint.

William died at Delancey Hospital, Cheltenham, Gloucestershire on 7th December 1966. The causes of death were recorded as uraemia, malnutrition, an old laryngectomy and carcinoma of the larynx. He was cremated at Cheltenham Crematorium, Gloucestershire on 10th December and his ashes were scattered at sea off Hermanus Cliffs, South Africa on 2nd January 1974. William is commemorated in number of other places:

- A bench dedicated to his memory near his former seaside cottage at Hermanus.
- Memorial plaque in Framlingham College Chapel.
- Named on the South African Memorial, Delville Wood, France.
- The Commonwealth Memorial Gates on Constitution Hill, London, commemorate the armed forces of the British Empire that served Britain in the World Wars from the Indian subcontinent, Africa and the Caribbean. The memorial was inaugurated on 6th November 2002 by the Queen in her Golden Jubilee year. The ceiling of a memorial pavilion on the Green Park side of the Gates lists the names of seventy-four VC and GC recipients – twenty-three First World War VCs and twelve GC and thirty-nine VC recipients from the Second World War.
- The Department for Communities and Local Government decided to provide a commemorative paving stone at the birthplace of every Great War Victoria Cross recipient in the United Kingdom. William's stone is to be dedicated at Copdock, near Ipswich, Suffolk on 17th September 2017 to mark the centenary of his award.

Delancey Hospital was established in 1874 for fever and other infectious disease cases. In 1950 its use changed to the care of the elderly. It closed in 2011.

The Castle of Good Hope, Cape Town where the South African VC memorial plaque is located.

The Natal Rebellion Medal 1906 was awarded to 9,622 soldiers and policemen who served for at least twenty days between 11th February and 3rd August 1906. Most recipients were members of the Natal colonial military and police forces. The rebellion was over taxation and was sparked in February 1906 when two British tax collectors were killed, resulting in martial law being declared. The revolt was led by Chief Bambatha kaMancinza, who launched guerrilla attacks from the Nkandia Forest area. By the time the rebellion had been put down up to 4,000 Zulus had been killed. Another 7,000 were imprisoned and 4,000 were flogged.

• Named on one of eleven plaques honouring 175 men from overseas awarded the VC for the Great War. The plaques were unveiled by the Senior Minister of State at the Foreign & Commonwealth Office and Minister for Faith and Communities, Baroness Warsi, at a reception at Lancaster House, London on 26th June 2014 attended by The Duke of Kent and relatives of the VC recipients. The South African plaque is at the Castle of Good Hope, Cape Town.

Lily ended up living at The Hut, Greenway Cottage, Greenway Lane, Charlton Kings, near Cheltenham, Gloucestershire. In addition to the VC, William was awarded the Natal Rebellion Medal 1906, British War Medal 1914–20, Victory Medal 1914–19, 1939–45 Star, Africa Star, War Medal 1939–45, George VI Coronation Medal 1937 and Elizabeth II Coronation Medal 1953. The VC was presented to Framlingham College by his widow in May 1967. It was held in the Chapel until the College loaned it indefinitely (and the VC of Gordon Flowerdew) to the Imperial War Museum on 23rd April 2004. It is displayed in the Lord Ashcroft VC Gallery. The Castle Military Museum, Cape Town holds four of Hewitt's campaign medals – Natal Rebellion Medal 1906, British War Medal 1914–20, Victory Medal 1914–19 and King George VI Coronation Medal 1937. The location of his other medals is not known.

57113 SERGEANT FREDERICK JOHN HOBSON
20th Battalion (Central Ontario), Canadian Expeditionary Force

Frederick Hobson was born on 23rd September 1873 at Norwood, South London, England. His father, John Hobson, married Sarah née Wallace (born c.1851 in Dublin, Ireland). She was living at 27 Henley Street, Hardingstone, Northamptonshire in 1881. Frederick had two siblings:

• Florence Louisa Hobson (1877–1975) emigrated to Canada with Frederick and married as Brown. She lived at 1381 Lansdowne Avenue, Toronto, Ontario. She became Frederick's next of kin after his wife remarried.

- George Henry Hobson (born 1879).

Frederick was educated at Norwood School, Elder Road, South London, while under the care of the Lambeth Board of Guardians. What he did after school is not known until he enlisted and served with 2nd Wiltshire from 1897. He went to South Africa in 1899 and saw action in Cape Colony, the Transvaal and Wittebergen during the Second Boer War. He was promoted to corporal before being discharged in 1903.

Lansdowne Avenue, Toronto, where Frederick's sister Florence lived (City of Toronto Archives).

Frederick is reputed to have married Louise Alice Esther née Moses (29th September 1884–July 1965) on 12th June or 1st September 1904, but there is no trace of such a union. She was born in Kensington and they met in 1903. They emigrated to Canada in 1904 and lived at 69 South Street, Galt (now Cambridge), Ontario. Frederick and Louise had five children, all born in Ontario:

- George Henry Hobson (1905–76) was a cabinetmaker. He married Winifred Irene Veale (1911–90) in 1928 at Stratford, Ontario. Frederick was a witness. Winifred was born at Braunton, Devon.
- Frederick John Hobson (1909–92) married Thelma Evangeline Lynch (1912–91) in 1930 at Stratford and they had four children. She was born Thelma Evangeline Lester at Middlesex, Ontario and was later adopted by Duncan Elder Lynch and his wife Jane Ann in 1923 at London, Ontario.
- Albert Edward Hobson (1911–86) married Margaret Druce in 1931 and served as a corporal in The Perth Regiment, Canadian Army during the Second World War.
- Florence Louisa Hobson (1913–73).
- John 'Jack' French Hobson (1915–91) worked in the furniture trade at Stratford, Ontario, firstly with Globe-Wernicke (became Preston-Noelting in 1926) and

2nd Wiltshire travelling by train during the South Africa War (Underwood & Underwood).

Galt in 1894.

later with Adams Furniture. He married Rita Deakin (1921–2003) and they had five children.

Louise's father, Frederick Thomas Moses (1847–1927), was a coach painter in 1891. He married Elizabeth née Taylor (1851–98) in 1874 and they lived at 36 Hewer Street, Kensington, London. In addition to Louise, they also had Florence Ellen Moses (1883–1958), who married George Porter in 1910 and they had at least four children – Nellie F Porter 1911, George J Porter 1912, Frederick Porter 1914 and Hilda E Porter 1922. Frederick senior married Martha A Shaw in 1916.

Frederick was employed as a labourer by Dominion Canners and later became a storekeeper employed by the Galt City authorities. Early in the war he enlisted in 39th Regiment Norfolk Rifles in Ontario (his number was probably 557). He attempted to enlist in the CEF at Galt, but was rejected and travelled to Toronto and enlisted in 20th Battalion on 10th November 1914. He was described as 5′ 11″ tall with fair complexion, blue eyes, light brown hair and a scar on the back of his head. He gave no religious denomination. Frederick sailed with 20th Battalion on RMS *Megantic* on 15th May 1915, arriving in England on 24th May.

Frederick sailed with 20th Battalion from Folkestone, arriving at Boulogne, France on 14th September. He was granted seven days leave in England between 31st January and 10th February 1916. On 30th June he was promoted sergeant, backdated to 1st January 1915. He completed a will on 23rd July 1916 leaving all his property and effects to his sister Florence. In September 1916 he received a gunshot wound to his right hip and he was admitted to No.4 Canadian Field Ambulance on 16th September. However, it must have been fairly minor as he was back with the Battalion on 19th September. From 16th October until 4th December he was attached to 255th Tunnelling Company and then to Res Company until 9th February 1917. Res may stand for Reserve, but no such organisation could be found within 2nd Canadian Division's order of battle. From 1st April until 2nd June he was attached

RMS *Megantic* (14,878 tons), built by Harland & Wolff in Belfast, was launched on 10th December 1908. She was operated by the White Star Line, but was originally ordered by the Dominion Line as the *Albany*. Her maiden voyage from Liverpool to Montreal commenced on 17th June 1909 and she remained on that route, and briefly the Liverpool – New York service, until taken over as a troopship in 1915. In 1910, after being arrested in Canada, Dr Crippen was returned on the *Megantic* to England for trial and subsequent hanging for murder. She was attacked by U-43 in 1917, but escaped unharmed. She underwent refits in 1919 and 1924 and continued in service from Liverpool to Canada until 1928 and then also operated out of London and Southampton. In the 1930s she was used for Caribbean cruises from New York. *Megantic*'s last Atlantic crossing was in May 1931, then she was laid up until 1933 and sold for scrap in Osaka, Japan.

The front of the Ontario Legislative Building in Toronto where Frederick's VC was presented to his sister, Florence Brown, by the Governor General of Canada on 8th May 1918. Construction of the building commenced in 1886 and it was opened in 1893. A fire broke out in 1909 while an extension wing was being added, resulting in the destruction of much of the interior. Repairs and reconstruction took until 1912.

The Canadian National Vimy Memorial. Frederick Hobson is one of 11,162 Canadians commemorated on the Memorial who were killed in France and have no known grave.

to 2nd Division Training Company. From 12th until 24th July he was granted ten days leave in England.

Awarded the VC for his actions near Hill 70, Lens, France on 15th-18th August 1917, LG 17th October 1917. He was killed during his VC action and is commemorated on the Canadian National Vimy Memorial, France. The VC was presented to his sister Florence by Victor Cavendish, 9th Duke of Devonshire (1868–1938), Governor General of Canada 1916–21, in front of the Ontario Legislative Building, Toronto on 8th May 1918. Frederick is commemorated in a number of other places:

• Royal Canadian Legion, Frederick Hobson VC Branch 79, West Street, Simcoe, Ontario.
• Heritage Foundation plaque unveiled by his grandson, Albert Hobson Thorn, in 1995 in Valour Square, beside the Armoury in Cambridge, Ontario.
• Named on the war memorial, Queen's Square, Cambridge, Ontario.
• Frederick Hobson VC Drive, Simcoe, Ontario.

Cambridge War Memorial, Ontario, where Fred Hobson is commemorated. (*Memorials to Valour*

Victor Christian William Cavendish, 9th Duke of Devonshire KG GCMG GCVO TD KStJ PC JP FRS (1868–1938), while Governor General of Canada. He served in the Derbyshire Yeomanry 1890–1911 and in 1891 became the youngest MP in Parliament at the time, winning his father's former seat of West Derbyshire. Numerous parliamentary positions followed, including appointment to the Privy Council in 1905. In 1892 he married Lady Evelyn MitzMaurice, daughter of the Viceroy of India. In 1907 he became a deputy lieutenant of Derbyshire and the following year Lord Lieutenant and also Honorary Colonel of 5th Sherwood Foresters (TF). Cavendish inherited his uncle's dukedom in 1908 and took his place in the House of Lords. In 1916 he was appointed Governor General of Canada to replace Prince Arthur and was succeeded by Lord Byng in 1921. Devonshire was Secretary of State for the Colonies 1922–24. He is buried in St Peter's Churchyard, Edensor. In the church are the colours of 16th (Chatsworth Rifles) Battalion, The Sherwood Foresters, in which served Corporal Ernest Albert Egerton VC, who features elsewhere in this book. (Dupras & Colas)

- Hobson Street, Cambridge, Ontario.
- Two 49 Cent postage stamps in honour of the ninety-four Canadian VCs were issued by Canada Post on 21st October 2004 on the 150th Anniversary of the first Canadian VC's action, Alexander Roberts Dunn.
- Victoria Cross obelisk to all Canadian VCs at Military Heritage Park, Barrie, Ontario dedicated by The Princess Royal on 22nd October 2013.
- Named on one of eleven plaques honouring 175 men from overseas awarded the VC for the Great War. The plaques were unveiled by the Senior Minister of State at the Foreign & Commonwealth Office and Minister for Faith and Communities, Baroness Warsi, at a reception at Lancaster House, London on 26th June 2014 attended by The Duke of Kent and relatives of the VC recipients. The Canadian plaque was unveiled outside the British High Commission in Elgin Street, Ottawa on 10th November 2014 by The Princess Royal in the presence of British High Commissioner Howard Drake, Canadian Minister of Veterans Affairs Julian Fantino and Canadian Chief of the Defence Staff General Thomas J Lawson.
- Plaque on a memorial to the ninety-nine Canadian VCs in York Cemetery, Toronto.

The Queen's and King's South Africa Medals as issued to Fredrick Hobson for his service with 2nd Wiltshire in the South Africa War 1899–1902.

While Frederick was away, Louise became involved with a widowed neighbour, Thomas

George Thorn (1866–1949), of Stratford, Perth, Ontario. He was born at Staines, Middlesex, England. When they married on 15th April 1916, she was declared to be a spinster. Frederick's army Separation Allowance account was closed on 26th May, indicating that he knew she had left him and remarried. All five of Frederick's children were later adopted by Thomas Thorn and assumed his surname. In Frederick's service record is a War Service Gratuity form, which describes his wife as *Mrs Louisa AE Thorn née Hobson, unmarried wife and guardian of five children.* It also states that his wife was not eligible for a pension. Louise and Thomas had four children, including, Donald Thorn (1928–93), who married Constance Brousseau (1928–93) and they had three children. Donald and Constance lived in California, USA.

In addition to the VC he was awarded the Queen's South Africa Medal 1899–1902 with three clasps (Cape Colony, Transvaal, Wittebergen), King's South Africa Medal 1901–02 with two clasps (South Africa 1901, South Africa 1902), 1914–15 Star, British War Medal 1914–20 and Victory Medal 1914–19. As he died on operational duty, his next-of-kin is eligible to receive the Canadian Memorial Cross. Florence Brown presented her brother's VC to Fort Malden National Historic Park, Amhertsburg, Ontario in 1959. The Queen's and King's South Africa Medals were donated by Florence to a charity auction held by Eaton's of Toronto. Several appeals in the national press for their recovery went unanswered. In June 1974 the other medals were acquired by the Canadian War Museum, Vimy Place, Ottawa, Ontario where they are held. The British Ministry of Defence presented the Canadian War Museum with duplicate Queen's and King's South Africa Medals.

The Canadian Memorial Cross was instituted on 1st December 1919 and was awarded to mothers and widows of Canadian service personnel who died on active duty or whose death was consequently attributed to such duty.

838301 PRIVATE THOMAS WILLIAM HOLMES
4th Battalion, Canadian Mounted Rifles CEF

Thomas Holmes was born on 14th October 1898 at Montreal, Quebec, Canada. He was known as Tommy. His father, John Robert Holmes (born 1865), was a labourer. He married Edith Mary née Scarff (1871–1937) in 1891. They were living in Montreal in 1901 and by 1903 had moved to Owen Sound, Ontario. Edith was living at 380, 9th Street East, Owen Sound, Grey, Ontario in 1915 when she was nominated as Tommy's next of kin. She was living at 643 (also seen as 634), 7th Street East, Owen Sound when she died. Thomas had three siblings:

- Charles John Holmes (1892–1953) married Anne Maude Augusta Thompson (1889–1974) in 1911. They had nine children – Mary Eileen Holmes 1912, Marguerite Sarah Bernice Holmes 1914, Frederick Charles Holmes 1917, Thomas Elmer Holmes 1919, Allister Cullen Holmes 1920, James Robert Holmes 1922, Betty Ruth Holmes 1924, Shirley Ann Holmes 1928 and Harold Marshall Holmes 1931.
- Anna Elizabeth Holmes (born 1894) married as King and was living at 765, 3rd Avenue East, Owen Sound in 1937.
- Almer Roy Holmes (born 1896) attested in the Canadian Army on 25th June 1915 at Niagara Camp. He was described as a labourer, 5′ 4″ tall, with fair complexion, blue eyes, dark hair and his religious denomination was Church of England. He joined 58th Battalion (451236) on 30th June and was wounded at Sanctuary Wood, Belgium in June 1916, losing an eye. He was evacuated to a hospital at Hastings, Sussex.

Tommy's paternal grandparents are not known. His maternal grandfather, John Scarff (1843–1918), was born at Hartismere, Suffolk, England. He emigrated to Canada with his parents and they settled at Owen Sound, Ontario. He married Anne née Taylor (born 1835) in October 1868 at Derby, Grey County, Ontario. She may have been born in Scotland. John was a labourer in 1871. He was a fish trader by 1901 and they were living

A settlement named Sydenham was established in 1841 and was renamed Owen Sound in 1851. Its seaport made for a busy and somewhat rowdy town and it became known as *Corkscrew City, Chicago of the North* and *Little Liverpool*. One intersection of streets was known as 'Damnation Corner' as it had taverns on all four corners and a block away was 'Salvation Corner' as it had four churches. A reputation for vice led to the city authorities banning drinking establishments for several decades; it was 'dry' until 1972.

Looking east along 9th Street East in Owen Sound where Tommy's mother was living in 1915.

at North Grey. Anne predeceased her husband. In addition to Edith they had three other children:

* Thomas F Scarff (born 1873).
* William John Scarff (born c.1875) married Alice Ann Applegarth (born 1874) in October 1899 at Grey. She was born at Houghton le Spring, Co Durham, England. They had three children including William John Scarff 1901 and Elizabeth Ester Scarff 1902.
* Sarah Ann Scarf (1877–1957) married Thomas Ross Shaw (1877–1946) in September 1897 at Owen Sound. They had three children – John Lloyd Shaw 1898, Annie Evelyn Shaw 1906 and Ross Shaw 1910.

Tommy was educated at Ryerson School, Owen Sound. He worked for JR Boyd, a butcher, then as a poulterer at Templeton Farm, Annan, Ontario. When he enlisted he gave his employment as chicken picker and also as labourer. Thomas enlisted on 12th December 1915 and his date of birth is variously recorded as 17th and 27th August 1897 and 27th October 1898. He was described as 5′ 5½″ tall,

weighing 130 lbs, with fair complexion, blue eyes, fair hair and his religious denomination was Salvation Army. He attested in 147th (1st Grey) Battalion on 20th December at Niagara Camp, where he carried out basic training and also at Camp Borden, near Barrie, Ontario. A diphtheria outbreak delayed the Battalion's departure and it eventually sailed from Halifax, Nova Scotia on RMS *Olympic* on 14th November 1916. It arrived in Britain on 20th November.

Recruits on kit inspection at Niagara Camp in 1915. The Commons was used for military training from the 1870s and many attempts were made to close it and move it to the larger facilities at Petawawa. In 1908 the government purchased more land and moved the rifle range outside town. Sir Sam Hughes described the training at the Camp in 1914 as, ... *first-class for little picnic affairs, but the troops get no real training whatever at Niagara*. Despite this, 14,000 troops were trained there in the First World War. It was also the winter training camp for Canadian and American Poles who were attached to the French Army and helped to re-establish an independent Poland after the war. Niagara Camp remained open until the Korean War.

   Tommy transferred to 8th Reserve Battalion at Shorncliffe, Kent on 1st January 1917 and to 4th Canadian Mounted Rifles on 7th February. He went to France on 9th February and was attached to 3rd Entrenching Battalion 9th March–1st April. He was in action with his machine-gun section at Vimy Ridge on 9th April. On 11th April he was wounded by a gunshot to the left arm, which fractured the ulna. He was admitted to No.2 Australian General Hospital, Wimereux and was then evacuated to England to 2nd Southern General Hospital, Bristol on 15th April. On 30th April he transferred to the Canadian Convalescent Hospital, Hillingdon

Aerial panoramic view of No.2 Australian General Hospital at Wimereux.

A military camp was first established at Shorncliffe in 1794. In 1803 Sir John Moore trained the Light Division there to fight in the Peninsula under Wellington. In the First World War it was a staging post for troops going to the Western Front and in 1915 the Canadians established a training camp there as well as some general hospitals in 1917–18. This picture shows the area known as 'Tin Town'. The camp later became Sir John Moore Barracks and is currently the home of the Royal Gurkha Rifles. Shorncliffe Military Cemetery has three VCs of the Victorian era, 471 First World War burials, including over 300 Canadians and eighty-one burials from the Second World War.

2nd Southern General Hospital was based on Bristol Royal Infirmary and eventually had 200 beds for officers and 1,350 for other ranks.

Hillingdon House was originally built in 1717 and the current building dates to 1844. The government purchased it in 1915, intending it for use as a prisoner of war camp, but local objections prevailed and it became a Canadian Convalescent Hospital instead. It opened on 20th September 1915 and closed on 12th December 1917, when the remaining patients and staff transferred to other Canadian hospitals in England. In 1917 the RFC Armaments School moved in and the estate later became RAF Uxbridge. TE Lawrence trained there in 1922. Most famously it was the HQ of No.11 Group RAF during the Battle of Britain and the Grade 1 listed operations bunker is in the grounds. RAF Uxbridge closed on 31st March 2010 and the site is under development for housing and commercial use.

House, Uxbridge, Middlesex and on 1st May to Woodcote Park Military Convalescent Hospital, Epsom, Surrey.

Tommy returned to 8th Canadian Reserve Battalion at Shorncliffe on 28th May and while there travelled to Hastings to meet his brother Roy. Tommy transferred to 4th Canadian Mounted Rifles on 23rd September and returned to France on 30th

William Avery 'Billy' Bishop VC CD DSO & Bar MC DFC ED (1894–1956) was also born in Owen Sound. He was the top Canadian ace of the First World War, credited with seventy-two victories, although some historians believe the true total may be as low as twenty-seven. He was one of the few aviators to survive an encounter with the Red Baron. The award of the VC was somewhat controversial as it was based on his own testimony in violation of the VC Warrant. In the Second World War he played a major role in setting up the British Commonwealth Air Training Plan.

Tommy with two comrades. The VC ribbon shows up clearly on his left breast. The vertical stripe on his left forearm denotes he has been wounded.

The Royal Automobile Club purchased the Woodcote Park estate in 1913. The War Office requisitioned it and requested the Chairman of the RAC, Arthur Stanley, to form a brigade of infantry. A camp was built in the grounds but in 1915 it was decided that the camp would be better utilised as a convalescent hospital. The Canadian Convalescent Hospital opened on 5th September 1915, initially with 500 beds but later increased to 1,000. The first patients to arrive were ANZAC troops from Gallipoli, later joined by British troops. Pictured here is the visit of King George V and Queen Mary in July 1916, by when there were over 3,000 patients, 2,500 of them in the Canadian section. In August 1916 the entire Hospital was handed over to the Canadian Army and became its main convalescent hospital, with a total of 3,800 beds, the largest convalescent hospital in the country. On 10th November 1918 there were 4,142 patients. In June 1919 a riot took place in Epsom following the arrest of a Canadian soldier after a fight in a pub. A mob of Canadians stormed the police station, freed their comrades, destroyed part of the police station and the station sergeant died from a blow to the head. Five men were sentenced to five months in prison but no one was ever charged with the murder. On 30th June 1919 the Canadian hospital closed and it became Queen Mary's Convalescent Centre for the treatment and training of ex-servicemen. In 1923 the estate returned to the RAC. In the Second World War it was used as a training centre and today is a RAC country club and golf course.

Tommy Holmes was sent to the Canadian Concentration Camp at Kinmel Park in North Wales prior to being repatriated to Canada. Two weeks before he arrived the troops in the camp rioted for two days in protest over delays in being sent home. Five men were killed. Seventy-eight men were arrested and of these twenty-five were convicted of mutiny, receiving sentences from ninety days to ten years.

SS *Saturnia* (8,611 tons) was built in Glasgow for the Donaldson Line. Her maiden voyage on 11th June 1910 was from Glasgow to Quebec and Montreal. In August 1911 she collided with an iceberg near Belle Isle, but completed her voyage. In 1921 she was chartered by the Anchor Line. Her last voyage was in March 1925 from Glasgow to Portland and she was scrapped in 1929.

September to the Canadian Corps Reinforcement Camp. He rejoined his unit on 9th October.

Awarded the VC for his actions at Wolf Copse, near Passchendaele, Belgium, on 26th October 1917, LG 11 January 1918. At the time Thomas was the youngest VC in the Canadian forces and the second from Owen Sound, the first being air ace Billy Bishop. Thomas was granted fourteen days' leave in the UK from 25th November 1918, which was extended by fourteen days on 16th December to cover the investiture. The VC was presented by the King at York Cottage, Sandringham, Norfolk on 31st December 1918.

Tommy was appointed acting sergeant on 24th January 1919. He was attached to the Canadian Concentration Camp, Kinmel Park, Rhyl, North Wales on 20th March and sailed from Glasgow aboard SS *Saturnia* on 30th March. He was taken on strength No.2 District Depot, Toronto on arrival in Canada on 10th April and was discharged on 14th April 1919. As a result of his time in the trenches he developed tuberculosis and had to fight several federal government departments before he was granted a pension.

Thomas Holmes married Annie Middaugh and they had two children:

• Roy Holmes served in the Royal Canadian Naval Volunteer Reserve during the Second World War.
• June Holmes.

Tommy worked as a secretary for the Northern Business College Veteran's Club in Toronto, Ontario. He then worked as a pilot for the Toronto Harbour Commission.

In 1936 he and another officer rescued three persons whose auxiliary cabin boat had capsized in the harbour. In 1942 he narrowly escaped death when his launch exploded and he was hospitalised with burns. Tommy became a chauffeur for the Toronto Harbour Commission for fourteen years until ill health forced him to retire. He attended the VC Dinner at the Royal Gallery of the House of Lords, London on 9th November 1929. On 22nd May 1939 he was presented to King George VI and Queen Elizabeth at Queen's Park, Toronto, along with fellow VCs Colin Barron, Benjamin Geary, Walter Rayfield, Henry Robson, William Merrifield and Charles Rutherford. Tommy was a long-term sufferer with tuberculosis and was in Queen Alexandra Hospital, Toronto for many years. He contracted cancer and spent the last three months of his life at Sunnybrook Hospital, Toronto, where he died on 4th January 1950. He was buried with full military honours in Greenwood Cemetery, Owen Sound, Grey County, Ontario. Every Remembrance Day a firing party from the Grey & Simcoe Foresters, Canadian Forces pay their respects and place a wreath on his grave. He is commemorated in a number of other places:

The Toronto waterfront, with the six-storey Toronto Harbour Commission building at the end of the jetty. It is now several hundred metres inland.

Sunnybrook Hospital, Toronto.

Tommy Holmes' grave in Greenwood Cemetery, Owen Sound. Also buried there are Billy Bishop VC and David Currie, a Second World War VC, whose wife was from Owen Sound.

• Thomas Holmes VC Memorial Armouries, Owen Sound, Ontario.

The Thomas Holmes VC Memorial Armouries, Owen Sound, Ontario.

Plaques to the three Owen Sound VCs in Queen's Park, with Tommy Holmes' plaque inset bottom right.

- Plaque in Queen's Park, 1st Avenue, West and 8th Street West, Owen Sound, Toronto, Ontario erected by the Ontario Archaeological and Historic Sites Board and unveiled by his sister Annie in 1959.
- Named on a Victoria Cross obelisk to all Canadian VCs at Military Heritage Park, Barrie, Ontario dedicated by The Princess Royal on 22nd October 2013.
- Named on one of eleven plaques honouring 175 men from overseas awarded the VC for the Great War. The plaques were unveiled by the Senior Minister of State at the Foreign & Commonwealth Office and Minister for Faith and Communities, Baroness Warsi, at a reception at Lancaster House, London on 26th June 2014 attended by The Duke of Kent and relatives of the VC recipients. The Canadian plaque was unveiled outside the British High Commission in Elgin Street, Ottawa on 10th November 2014 by The Princess Royal in the presence of British High Commissioner Howard Drake, Canadian Minister of Veterans Affairs Julian Fantino and Canadian Chief of the Defence Staff General Thomas J Lawson.
- Two 49 cents postage stamps in honour of the 94 Canadian VC winners were issued by Canada Post on 21st October 2004 on the 150th Anniversary of the first Canadian VC's action, Alexander Roberts Dunn VC.
- A wooden plaque bearing fifty-six maple leaves each inscribed with the name of a Canadian-born VC holder was dedicated at the Canadian Forces College, Toronto on Remembrance Day 1999.
- The Secretary of State for Communities and Local Government, Eric Pickles MP announced that Victoria Cross recipients from the Great War would have commemorative paving stones laid in their birthplace as a lasting legacy of local heroes within communities. The stones would be laid on or close to the 100th anniversary of their VC actions. For the 145 VCs born in Australia, Belgium,

Canada, China, Denmark, Egypt, France, Germany, India, Iraq, Japan, Nepal, Netherlands, New Zealand, Pakistan, South Africa, Sri Lanka, Ukraine and United States of America, individual commemorative stones were unveiled at the National Memorial Arboretum, Alrewas, Staffordshire by Prime Minister David Cameron MP and Sergeant Johnson Beharry VC on 5th March 2015.
- Plaque on a memorial to the ninety-nine Canadian VCs in York Cemetery, Toronto.

In addition to the VC he was awarded the British War Medal 1914–20, Victory Medal 1914–19 and George VI Coronation Medal 1937. The medals were stolen from his home in 1935 and were never recovered. A replacement VC was issued on 6th August 1935. His daughter donated it and his other medals to the Royal Canadian Legion Branch in Owen Sound. In August 1978 the replacement VC was also stolen, but was eventually recovered. The replacement VC is held by Royal Canadian Legion Branch 6, 1450, 2nd Avenue West, Owen Sound, Ontario, Canada.

267110 PRIVATE ARTHUR HUTT
1/7th Battalion, The Royal Warwickshire Regiment

Arthur Hutt was born at 1 Court, 4 New Buildings, Earlsdon, Coventry, Warwickshire on 12th February 1889. His father, Samuel Hutt (born 1854), a timber labourer, married Jane née Knibb (1854–1914), a silk winder, on 8th July 1876 at St Michael's, the Old Cathedral, Coventry. They were living at 55 New Buildings, Holy Trinity, Coventry in 1881, at 10 Court, 4 House, Jordan Well, Coventry in 1901 and at 7 Gulson Road, Coventry in 1911. Arthur had nine siblings:

- Mary Ann Hutt (1872–1943) married George Warner (c.1876–1935), a cycle machinist, in 1897. He was born c.1876 at Coventry. They were living at 1 House, Court 1, Palmer Lane, Coventry in 1901 and at House 33, The Jetty, Broad Street, Coventry in 1911 by when George was a labourer at Courtaulds Silk Works. They had nine children – Winifred Warner 1897, Bertie Warner 1899, Harriet Warner 1901, Lily Warner 1906, Alice Warner 1908, Florence E Warner 1911, Ellen Warner 1913, Beatrice V Warner 1918 and Lilian M Warner 1919. It is understood that another three children may have died in infancy.
- William Hutt (1876–1954) married Martha McDonagh (1879–1944), in 1897. In 1911 he was a grocer's porter in 1911 and the family was living at 3 Court, 13 House, Gulson Road, Coventry. William served during the Great War. They were living at 34 Gulson Road, Coventry in 1939 and at the time of his death. They had

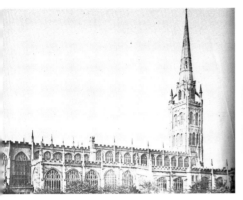

Arthur's parents, Samuel Hutt and Jane Knibb, were married at St Michael's Church, Coventry on 8th July 1876. It dates back to the late 14th Century and was one of the largest parish churches in England when it was elevated to cathedral status in 1918. On 14th November 1940 it was razed to the ground in the Coventry Blitz, but the spire and outer walls survived. A new cathedral was consecrated alongside the ruins on 25th May 1962. Benjamin Britten composed *War Requiem* for the occasion.

six children – Horace Hutt 1897, William Samuel Hutt 1900, Harold Ernest Hutt 1901, Edward Hutt 1904, Doris 'Dolly' Hutt 1906 and Arthur Hutt 1910. Horace was employed by Triumph Cycle Co, Coventry as a motorcycle repairer when he enlisted in 7th Royal Warwickshire (3480 later 266146) on 24th July 1914. He was 5' 7" tall and weighed just 98 lbs. He served in 2/7th Royal Warwickshire from 24th November and went to France on 22nd May 1916. He received a gunshot wound to the left leg and was evacuated to Britain on 22nd July, where he was treated at Reading War Hospital until 22nd September. He also suffered deafness as a result of being wounded but recovered. During his service he also had a fractured right thumb and a hernia operation. He embarked at Southampton on 15th April 1917 and arrived at Rouen on 18th April. He was allocated to 1/5th Royal Warwickshire that day and transferred to 1/8th Royal Warwickshire on 4th May. Appointed unpaid lance corporal 27th September and paid on 7th

Jordan Well, Coventry, where the Hut family was living in 1901.

By 1911 the family had moved to Gulson Road.

November. He was reduced to private for a breach of discipline on 5th December. Admitted to 1/1st South Midland Field Ambulance with tonsillitis on 14th April 1918, No.24 Casualty Clearing Station on 25th April and 62nd General Hospital with diphtheria on 27th April. He was admitted to 62nd General Hospital again in June and 38th Stationary Hospital, Genoa. Italy on 21st September with influenza and 51st Stationary Hospital, Genoa on 4th November. His disciplinary record was very poor, with offences spanning from 18th February 1915 until 5th December 1917 committed at Epping, Northampton, Chelmsford, Catterick, Danbury, Perham Down and in the field. They included overstaying his pass, having a dirty cot, insolence and using obscene language to an NCO, absence from parades, not complying with orders, filling a water bottle while on the line of march, smoking on the march and refusing to put it out, neglect of duty while a sentry and absence. He returned to a dispersal centre in Britain on 22nd January 1919 and was disembodied on 19th February, assessed as 35% disabled. His address was 3 Court, 13 House, Back of Gulson Street, Coventry. Horace married Hilda Alice Poulter (1899–1979) in 1921 and they had four children.

• Elizabeth Hutt (born 1881) married Joseph Lenton in 1915. They had two children – Winifred M Lenton 1921 and Joyce M Lenton 1926.

• Henry Hutt (1884–1946) was a labourer in a cycle factory in 1901. He married Mary Ellen Marston (1886–1918) in 1906. In 1911 they were living at 3 Court, 21 House, Gulson Road, Coventry and he was a silk spinner. He was a millwright in 1939 at the same address. They had two children – Gladys Elizabeth Hutt 1908 and Thomas H Hutt 1913. Henry married Violet Sayers (born 1896) in 1920 and they had three children – Violet E Hutt 1920, Edward Hutt 1922 and Harold Hutt 1925.

• Thomas Hutt (1886–1946) was a labourer in a cycle factory in 1901 and an artificial silk spinner in 1939, living at 5 Weston Road, Coventry.

• Alfred Hutt (1891–1918), an engine fitter, married Priscilla Peabody (1891–1930) in 1910. They had three children – Albert George Hutt 1911, Elsie M Hutt 1914 and Priscilla Hutt 1915. Alfred enlisted in 2nd Dorsetshire (25029) and later transferred to the Labour Corps (436795). He died in service after being kicked in the head by a horse on 27th November 1918 (Coventry (London Road) Cemetery – Grave 199 152). Priscilla married Henry Preston Reynolds Elkington (born Henry Preston Reynolds) (1893–1945), a general labourer, in 1919. They lived at 20 Howard Street, Coventry.

• Bertie Hutt (1892–1917) was a polisher in 1911. He married Lucy Oldham (1891–1955) in 1912. She was a cycle spoke nippler in 1911, living with her parents at 7 Vauxhall Terrace, East Street, Coventry. They had three children – Alice E Hutt 1912, Lucy Jane Oldham 1913 and Helen M Hutt 1916. He was rejected by the Royal Navy in 1910 for not being tall enough and was only 5′ 3″ tall when he enlisted in 7th Royal Warwickshire (TF) on 16th October 1911 (1437 later 330755). He was embodied on 5th August 1914 and served in 81st Provisional

Battalion. He re-engaged on 23rd June 1916 and was appointed acting unpaid lance corporal on 26th September. He had a consultation at Bath War Hospital on 15th December due to chronic diarrhoea. It was also discovered that his tympanic membrane had disappeared resulting in chronic deafness. Appointed paid lance corporal 23rd December. He was graded B1 by No.5 Travelling Medical Board in February 1917 and went to France on 16th June, reverting to private. He was posted to 2/8th Battalion on 20th June and joined 2/7th Battalion on 10th July. He was admitted to 2/2nd South Midlands Field Ambulance on 28th July, 10th Stationary Hospital at St Omer on 1st August and 1st Stationary Hospital at Rouen on 2nd August with venereal disease. He was released to the Depot on 23rd September and forfeited fifty-eight days pay. Bertie was wounded on 13th December, died of wounds at 12th General Hospital on 25th December 1917 and is buried in St Sever Cemetery Extension, Rouen (P V H6A). His wife received pension of £1/5/5 per week from 1st July 1918 for herself and her two surviving children. She was living at 2 Court, 5 House, Gulson Road, Coventry. Lucy married Frederick C Rowley (born 1895 as Hine) in 1919 and they had a son, Percy W Hutt, the same year.

- Walter Hutt (born 1895), a polisher in 1911, served in the Royal Warwickshire Regiment from 20th May 1914 (265410) and was seriously wounded. He was discharged on 11th May 1918 and was awarded the Silver War Badge (No.347175) on 16th April 1918. He lived at 220 Stoney Stanton Road, Coventry. He married Julia Rogers (1897–1969) in 1918 and they had seven children – Evelyn M Hutt 1920, Florence J Hutt 1924, Alfred H Hutt 1928, Reginald W Hutt 1930, Julia M Hutt 1934, Ernest J Hutt 1938 and Dennis E Hutt 1941. In 1939 they were living at 61 The Moorfields, Coventry, by when he was a stores labourer at an airfield.
- Joseph William Hutt (1896–1954), a labourer in 1911, married Violet Beatrice Garratt (1900–84) in 1920. He died within twenty-four hours of his brother Arthur. They had nine children – Walter T Hutt 1921, George Hutt 1922, Joseph W Hutt 1924, Elizabeth D Hutt 1927, Arthur Hutt 1929, Stanley Hutt 1931, Henry Hutt 1934, Violet Hutt 1937 and Ida Hutt 1940.

Arthur's paternal grandfather, Jesse Hutt (1815–83), was a coal dealer at Foleshill. He married Mary née Woodman (1818–98), a servant, at Holy Trinity Church, Coventry on 29th May 1849. They were living at Court 2, House 4, Sherbourne Street, Coventry in 1861. By 1881 he was a labourer in a gas works and they were living at 11 Park Street, Coventry. In addition to Samuel they had a daughter, Selina Hutt (1850–98), a domestic servant in 1881. She married Thomas Charles Cox (1846–1930), a watch finisher, in 1883 and they had two children – John Cox 1883 and James Cox 1888. Thomas married Annie Gutteridge (born 1883), a servant, in 1899. He was a green grocer at the time, living at 90 Much Park Street and Annie was living at 98 Much Park Street. Thomas was a watch finisher in 1911 and they were living at 8 Court, 11 House, Garden Well, Coventry. They had four children

Arthur's grandparents, Jesse Hutt and Mary Woodman, were married at Holy Trinity Church, Coventry on 29th May 1849. It is now the only medieval church in Coventry and dates back to 1113. It is thought to have originated next to St Mary's Priory as a side chapel. The original Norman church was destroyed in a fire in 1257 and only the North Porch survives today. The rest was rebuilt in the 13th Century and the walls were painted with biblical scenes. One example of this artwork from the 1430s has suvived above the tower arch. Mary Ann Evans, the 19th Century novelist better known as George Eliot, attended Holy Trinity for many years. During the Coventry Blitz, Holy Trinity survived due to the efforts of Rev Graham Clitheroe, vicar of Holy Trinity, and a few others. They used hydrants and ladders to stop fires taking hold and on the night of 14th November 1940 they extinguished fires around the building and pushed bombs off the church roof to stop further damage. The church was not unscathed but it did survive largely intact as a result of their efforts.

including – Charles Cox 1903, Walter Cox 1906 and Rosa Cox 1909.

His maternal grandfather, Joseph Knibb (c.1824–97), an agricultural labourer, married Martha née Twaites (c.1828–86), a silk winder, in July 1850 at Coventry St Michael. They lived initially with his widowed mother, Ann (born c.1787) at Hertford Street, Coventry. He was recorded as Josiah in 1861, living with his family at 11 Brick Kiln Lane, Coventry. By 1871 he was a gardener and they had moved to 1 Court, House 3, Hertford Street, Coventry. In 1881 they were living at 3 Court, 7 House, Little Park Street, Coventry. In 1891 he was still living there as a general labourer and a widower with sons John and Henry. In addition to Jane they had nine other children:

- William Knibb (born 1851) was a plumber and glazier in 1871.
- Charles Knibb (1852–54).
- Fanny Knibb (1857–1935), a silk winder, married William Henry Foster (c.1857–1900), a watchmaker, in 1876. They were living at 7 Court, 9 Much Park Street, Coventry in 1881 and at 7 Court, 3 House, Coventry St Michael in 1891. They had five children – Amy Foster 1879, John Foster 1880, Frances Fanny Foster 1885, Alfred Foster 1886 and Sidney Foster 1893. Fanny was a greengrocer in 1901 living with her children at 38 Much Park Street, Coventry. She married James Thomas Lowe (1858–1935) in 1907 at Coventry. He was a machinist with a cycle manufacturer in 1911. James had married Julia Palmer (1865–1905) in 1884 and they had four children – Emily Lowe 1886, Flora Lowe 1887, James J Lowe 1890 and Charles Frederick Lowe 1892.
- Alfred Knibb (1859–1941), an assistant in a bicycle works in 1881, married Mary Bale (1854–1903) in 1883. She was born at St John's, Newfoundland. They had four children – Amy Jane Knibbs 1884, Annie Elizabeth Knibbs 1885, Alfred Knibbs 1888 and Alice Knibbs 1891.

- Josiah 'Joseph' Knibb (1861–1934), a bicycle fitter, married Alice Reaves (1865–1950) in 1884. They were living at 38 Russell Street, Coventry in 1901. By 1911 he was a motor fitter. They had six children – Florence Alice Knibbs 1889, Ethel Maud Knibbs 1896 and Edith May Knibbs 1897, plus three others who died in infancy.
- Mary Ann Knibb (1864–66).
- John Knibb (1866–67).
- John Knibb (1868–1935) an errand boy in 1881 and a bicycle machinist fitter in 1891.
- Henry Knibb (1870–1943), a bicycle machinist fitter in 1891, married Susannah Charlotte Burr (1872–1952) in 1892. Henry was an iron turner in the motor trade by 1911 and they were living at 14 Spring Street, Coventry. They had three children – Walter Francis Knibbs 1893, Gladys Lottie Knibbs 1897 and Lilian May Knibbs 1900.

Arthur was educated at Holy Trinity School, Coventry. He was employed by Courtaulds artificial silk works, Foleshill, Coventry 1910–15. He enlisted in 7th Royal Warwickshire (TF) when Courtaulds raised B Company (1006). Arthur married Alice M née Lenton (30th January 1890–1977) in the 1st quarter of 1913 in Coventry. They lived at 8 Caludon Road, Earsldon, Coventry, Warwickshire and had a daughter, Victoria Constance Hutt, in 1920. She married Sydney FG Taylor in 1947 and they were living at 70 Sussex Road, Coventry in 1954. They had two children – Stephen F Taylor 1951 and David P Taylor 1953.

Alice's father, Henry Lenton (1845–1902), a bricklayer, married Hannah née Hirons (1847–1911), in 1866. Her birth was registered as Hiorns. In 1871 they were living at 3 House, 1 Court, Cook Street College, Coventry. By 1891 they were at 55 Cox Street, Coventry and at 49–51 Cox Street by 1901. In addition to Alice they had eight other children:

- Henry Lenton (1870–1925) married Gertrude Bonham (1871–1953) in 1892. He was the publican of the Hare and Hounds Inn, Keresley, Coventry in 1911.

Arthur's maternal grandparents were living on Little Park Street, Coventry in 1881. Much of it was destroyed in the 1940 Blitz.

Courtaulds opened an artificial silk works in Foleshill in 1904. In 1941 it became the first British firm to produce nylon yarn. At its peak in the 1950s and 1960s the Little Heath Works employed 5,000 people, but its fortunes waned and by 1992 the workforce was down to 450. Production ceased in 2007 and the factory was later demolished to make way for housing.

- Emma Lenton (born 1871).
- John Lenton (born 1874) was a shoeing smith in 1911, living as head of household with his siblings Ada, William, Annie and Alice at 49 & 51 Cox Street, Coventry. He married Ellen Beesley (1878–1952) in 1912. She was a booking clerk at the Empire Theatre, Coventry in 1911, living with her widowed mother, a provision dealer, at 9 Matlock Road, Coventry. Ellen had a son, Frank Guppy Beesley, born in 1906. By 1939 John Lenton was a turner (incapacitated), living alone at 16 Upper Well Street, Coventry.
- Ada Lenton (1876–1962) was a silk weaver in 1901 and a shop assistant in 1911. She was living at 14 Old Road, Coventry in 1939. She died unmarried.
- Thomas Arthur Lenton (1878–99).
- Ellen Lenton (born 1880) was a silk weaver in 1901.
- William Lenton (1883–1951) was a bricklayer in 1901 and a builder in 1911. He married Mary Ann Barnes (born 1886) in 1914. By 1939 he was a licensed victualler, living with his wife at 57 Gosford Street, Coventry.
- Annie Victoria Lenton (1887–1979), a shop assistant in 1911, married Alec Kelham (1889–1928) in 1911. They had two children – Marjorie B Kelham 1921 and Winifred M Kelham 1926. She was a general shopkeeper in 1939 living at 12 Mowbray Street, Coventry.

Arthur was at annual camp at Rhyl, North Wales when war broke out and the Battalion was embodied on 4th August 1914. He sailed from Southampton, Hampshire to Le Havre, France on 22nd March 1915. In the spring of 1916 he returned to Britain to his old job. His service record no longer exists, making it difficult to ascertain the reason for his discharge. He may have been recalled due to the shortage of skilled labour in Britain or he may have reached the end of his term of service in the Territorial Force.

Arthur was recalled in September 1916. **Awarded the VC for his actions at Terrier Farm, southeast of Poelcapelle, Belgium on 4th October 1917, LG 26th November 1917.** His Division served in Italy from November 1917. He had been promoted corporal by 12th January 1918 when he returned to Coventry. He was met at the station by the Mayor and driven through the streets to the Council House for a civic reception, during which he received an illuminated address and learned that a mayoral fund opened on his behalf had already raised nearly £500. Neighbours and friends presented him with a silver cigarette case. That evening there was a reception at the Drill Hall, Queen Victoria Road, during which he was presented with £250 of War Bonds by his employers. The following Saturday, at Courtaulds, he and his wife were both presented with gold watches. The VC was presented by the King at Buckingham Palace on 16th January 1918. In February he was involved in starting off Coventry Tank Week during the visit of Tank 119 'Old Bill'. Arthur was discharged in early 1919. He received the Freedom of Coventry.

Arthur returned to work at Courtaulds. Between the wars he had a number of jobs and suffered unemployment just before the Second World War. He attended the

Arthur being escorted by Mayor Alick Sargeant Hill to the civic reception on 12th January 1918.

Arthur standing next to the Mayor alongside Tank 119 *Old Bill* during Coventry Tank Week 11th-16th February 1918. The appeal raised over £1,370,000 (£107M today). *Old Bill* was one of six tanks touring the country to raise funds for the war effort.

VC Garden Party at Buckingham Palace on 26th June 1920 and the VC Dinner at the Royal Gallery of the House of Lords, London on 9th November 1929. At the opening ceremony for Coventry's War Memorial Park on 8th October 1927 he was seated next to Eliza Bench, who lost five of her six sons in the war. In November 1938 he volunteered for the Auxiliary Fire Service and was serving with it when war broke out, but later joined the Home Guard. He was working for an engineering firm in Coventry in 1939–40. His last job before retirement was in the packing department of the Standard Motor Company. On 1st February 1941 he was a lieutenant in 13th Warwickshire (Coventry) Battalion Home Guard.

After the Second World War Arthur drifted away from his immediate family, but did not divorce Alice. He lived at 35 Weston Street, Coventry. Arthur may have had more children; a daughter, Jeannie, attended his funeral and mention has been made of a son named Joseph. However, the latter has almost certainly been mixed up with his nephew Joseph Hutt. He attended the Victory Day Celebration Dinner

The Standard Motor Co was founded in Coventry in 1903. During the First World War it produced over 1,000 aircraft. A new works opened at Canley in 1916, which became the main centre of manufacturing. In 1919 civilian car production restarted and by 1924 Standard's market share was about the same as Austin. The late 1920s saw a slump, but in the 1930s new models were introduced and by 1939 Canley was producing 50,000 cars a year. In the Second World War some production was switched to aircraft, including 1,100 Mosquitos, 750 Oxfords, 20,000 Bristol Mercury VIII engines and 3,000 Beaufighter fuselages. In 1945 Standard bought Triumph Motor Co and production of the small Ferguson tractor helped fill some of the large wartime factory space. The famous Vanguard car was introduced in 1948 and overseas assembly plants were opened in Australia, Canada, India and South Africa. By 1950, 97,000 vehicles were being produced. Standard-Triumph International was bought by Leyland Motors in the 1960s and further mergers resulted in the formation of British Leyland Motor Corporation in 1968.

The Cornish–granite memorial dedicated to Arthur Hutt on 17th April 1955 in Coventry's War Memorial Park

Coventry's War Memorial in War Memorial Park, where Arthur Hutt's ashes were scattered.

and Reception at The Dorchester, London on 8th June 1946. Arthur was a keen supporter of ex-service organizations and was a member of the 7th Royal Warwickshire Old Comrades' Association and the Royal Warwickshire Regimental Association. He was one of ten Vice Presidents of the Royal Warwickshire Association appointed in 1935. Arthur Hutt died at his nephew's home at 277 Sewall Highway, Coventry on 14th April 1954. More than 350 people attended his funeral service on 20th April 1954, including William Beesley VC, Arthur Procter VC and Henry Tandey VC. Arthur was cremated at Canley Crematorium and his ashes were scattered in War Memorial Park, Stivichall, Coventry. Arthur is commemorated in a number of other places:

- A plaque on a Cornish–granite memorial dedicated in Coventry's War Memorial Park on 17th April 1955.
- Named on a plaque on a tree at Canley Crematorium.
- Named on a plaque on Coventry War Memorial.

In addition to the VC he was awarded the 1914–15 Star, British War Medal 1914–20, Victory Medal 1914–19, Defence Medal, George VI Coronation Medal 1937, Elizabeth II Coronation Medal 1953 and Territorial Efficiency Medal. The VC is held privately.

The Territorial Efficiency Medal, awarded for a minimum of twelve years service in the Territorial Army (war service counted double), replaced the Territorial Force Efficiency Medal when the Territorial Force became the Territorial Army in 1921. It was superseded by the Efficiency Medal in 1930.

506 PRIVATE REGINALD ROY INWOOD
10th Australian Infantry Battalion, AIF

Reginald Inwood, known as Roy, was born on 14th July 1890 at North Adelaide, South Australia. His father, Edward Inwood (1866–1922), a labourer, married Mary Ann née Minney (1868–1952) in 1887. They were living at 233 Cornish Street, Broken Hill in 1916 and at Beryl Street in March 1918. Roy had six siblings:

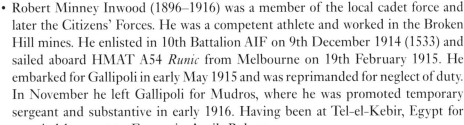

- Lilly Gertrude Inwood (1888–89).
- Albert Edward Inwood (1893–1970) married Rachel M Ward (born 1898) in 1916 and they had a child. Albert married Eustella Myrtle Francis née Winkler (1890–1963) in 1947. She had previously been married to Harkless Albert Walton Francis (1901–39).
- Robert Minney Inwood (1896–1916) was a member of the local cadet force and later the Citizens' Forces. He was a competent athlete and worked in the Broken Hill mines. He enlisted in 10th Battalion AIF on 9th December 1914 (1533) and sailed aboard HMAT A54 *Runic* from Melbourne on 19th February 1915. He embarked for Gallipoli in early May 1915 and was reprimanded for neglect of duty. In November he left Gallipoli for Mudros, where he was promoted temporary sergeant and substantive in early 1916. Having been at Tel-el-Kebir, Egypt for a period he went to France in April. Robert was with Lieutenant Arthur Blackburn during the latter's VC action at Pozières on 24th July 1916. It was reported that a German threw a grenade into Robert's trench. He immediately threw it back only to have it returned by the enemy. The grenade exploded in Robert's hand as he tried to throw it a second time and he was killed. His body was not recovered until 1929 and was reinterred in Serre Road Cemetery No.2, France (XXIV M 6).

Robert Inwood's grave in Serre Road Cemetery No.2, France.

- Harold Ray Inwood (1898–1974) was a mill hand and served for four years in the Senior Cadets. He enlisted at Adelaide on 14th January 1916 (320) giving his address as Wolfram Street, Broken Hill. He was assigned to E Company, 2nd Depot Battalion and to B Company, 1st Depot Battalion on 4th February. He was described as 5′ 8¼″ tall, weighing 124 lbs, with medium complexion, brown eyes, brown hair and his religious denomination was Church of England. On 7th March he transferred to B Company, 43rd Battalion at Morphettville Camp and embarked at Adelaide on HMAT A19 *Afric* on 9th June for Britain. At Larkhill, Salisbury Plain on 30th October he was absent without leave from midnight until 1 p.m. the following day. As a result he was confined to barracks for four days and forfeited a day's pay. Harold went to France via Southampton on 25th November. He received a gunshot wound to the left shoulder on 6th July 1917 and was treated at 9th Australian Field Ambulance, No.11 Casualty Clearing Station and 22 Ambulance Train. On 16th July he was evacuated to Britain on HMHS *St Denis* from 2nd Australian General Hospital at Wimereux and was admitted to Lakenham Military Hospital, Warwick the same day. He transferred to 1st Auxiliary Hospital on 25th July and to the Depot at Weymouth on 8th August. Harold embarked on HMAT A38 *Ulysses* on 10th September and returned to Australia, where he was discharged on 23rd November 1917. He subsequently joined the Royal Australian Navy on 27th April 1921 and married in 1922. In 1957 he was living at 8 Broadway Street, Port Lincoln, South Australia. Harold had at least one son, Murray Charles Inwood (born 1931), who served in the Australian Army (4/751) from 27th July 1950 until 26th July 1956. He was in Japan with the British Commonwealth Occupation Force from 19th July 1951 and transferred to the British Commonwealth Base Signals Regiment on 10th December 1951 as a dispatch rider. Murray was later Secretary of the Korean Veterans Association of Australia.

• Myrtle Edith Inwood (1902–41) married Cyril Walter Hurtle Ocean Steele (1894–1962) in 1924 and they had four children – Robert Cyril Steele 1925, Roy Steele, Margaret Steele and Dulcy Steele. Robert enlisted in the Australian Military Forces at Adelaide on 29th September 1939 (S212222) and was discharged from 4th Garrison Battalion on 3rd November 1941. He enlisted in the Royal Australian Air Force on 5th July 1943 at Adelaide (442399) and served as a wireless air gunner, flying several sorties in Beaufort bombers. He was posted to the Air and Ground Radio School, Ballarat, Victoria before being discharged on 4th March 1946 as a warrant officer.

• Clarence Leslie Inwood (1905–1990) married Irene Muriel Watkinson

Harold Inwood was based at Larkhill on Salisbury Plain before going to France in November 1916. Tented camps for units training on the Plain were set up there from 1899. In 1910 the first army airfield was established, but it closed in 1914. In its short life it saw the formation of No.3 Squadron RFC, the first RFC unit to be equipped with airplanes. In August 1912 the first Military Aeroplane Trials were held on the airfield, the competition being won by Samuel Cody. The original hangars still exist and are Grade II listed. During the First World War thirty-four battalion sized hutted camps were constructed, served by a light military railway from Amesbury. Most new divisions finalised their training in this area before departing for the front. Post-war a permanent camp was established at Larkhill for the Royal Artillery (TL Fuller).

(born 1908) in 1934. He enlisted in the Australian Army on 13th November 1941 at Keswick, South Australia (S39435) and was promoted to lance corporal before being discharged on 24th February 1943.

Roy's paternal grandfather, Edward Inwood (c.1834–79) married Ann née Jenkins (born c.1838) in 1861. His maternal grandfather, Isaac Sutton Minney (1828–99), a shoemaker, was born at Yardley Hastings, Northamptonshire. He married Eliza née Ashley (1828–77), a lace maker, born at Eaton Socon, Bedfordshire, in 1850 at Hardingstone, Northamptonshire. They were living at Grendon, Northamptonshire in 1851 and subsequently emigrated to South Australia.

Roy was educated at North Adelaide Public School in South Australia and Broken Hill Model School in New South Wales. He worked as a miner and labourer at the British and North Mines, Broken Hill. On 24th August 1914 he enlisted in the Australian Imperial Force at Morphettville, South Australia. He was described as 5′ 8½″ tall, weighing 142 lbs, with fair complexion, brown eyes, light brown hair and his religious denomination was Church of England.

North Adelaide Public School, now North Adelaide Primary School was attended by Roy Inwood.

Australia, in common with the other dominions, had little military infrastructure when war broke out. Some temporary training camps were established on racecourses and Morphettville Camp was one (Australian War Memorial).

On 20th October 1914 Roy embarked on HMAT A11 *Ascanius* at Adelaide with H Company, 10th Battalion bound for the Middle East. He embarked at Alexandria for Lemnos on HMT *Ionian* on 2nd March 1915, but was evacuated sick to 1st Australian General Hospital, Heliopolis, Egypt on 17th April. He joined 10th Battalion on Gallipoli on 9th May and was promoted lance corporal on 25th August. Roy reported sick with gastritis and debility to 3rd Field Ambulance and later No.1 Australian Casualty Clearing Station on 14th September. He was evacuated to No.25 Casualty Clearing Station at Mudros and transferred to Alexandria, Egypt aboard HMHS *Formosa* on 16th September with rheumatism. He moved to 1st Auxiliary Hospital, Cairo on 21st September, to Helouan Convalescent Depot on 2nd October and the Base Garrison Section at Zeitoun, Egypt on 10th October.

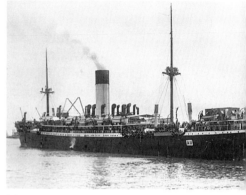

SS *Ionian* was built in Belfast in 1901 for the Allan Line. She was sunk by a mine laid by UC-*51* off Milford Haven on 21st October 1917. This view was taken on 1st March 1915 alongside at Alexandria whilst awaiting to embark 10th Battalion (Australian War Memorial).

SS *Ascanius* (10,048 tons), completed in December 1910 as a steam passenger ship for the Ocean Steam Ship Co, had an eventful career. As HMAT A11 *Ascanius* she was the first troop carrying ship to leave Fremantle and joined the first ANZAC convoy on 3rd November 1914. After leaving Colombo she rammed HMAT A9 *Shropshire*, but both ships were able to continue to Aden. She returned to her owners in 1920, but in 1940 was again requisitioned for war service. On 30th July 1944 she was torpedoed and damaged by U-*621* in the English Channel, but was repaired. She had been bound for Normandy to be used as a depot ship. Later she carried Jewish emigrants from Marseille to Haifa and in 1949 was sold to an Italian company and renamed *San Giovannino*. She was broken up at La Spezia in 1952.

Having recovered Roy joined 3rd Training Battalion, Tel el Kebir on 13th May 1916 and moved to France, where he reported to 1st Divisional Base Depot on 20th June. He was appointed temporary corporal on 16th August, but was absent from parade on 19th October and was reduced to private again. He reported sick again on 10th December and was transferred to 141st Field Ambulance on 13th December, returning to his unit on 26th December.

Awarded the VC for his actions at Polygon Wood, east of Ypres, Belgium 19th-22nd September 1917, LG 26th November 1917. Roy was promoted lance corporal on 28th September and was granted leave to England the same day until 16th October. He was promoted corporal the following day and was

1st Australian General Hospital in the Heliopolis Palace Hotel.

detached to the Brigade School until 11th November. He was again granted leave to England 9th-22nd December. The VC was presented by the King at Buckingham Palace on 19th December 1917.

HMAT D21 *Medic* (11,985 tons) was built in 1899 by Harland & Wolff in Belfast for the Oceanic Steam Navigation Co. In 1928 she was renamed *Hektoria* by her new owners of the same name and was converted to a whale factory. She was sunk by U-*211* and U-*608* on 11th September 1942 en route from Liverpool to New York.

Australian soldiers being instructed in grenade throwing at Rollestone Camp on Salisbury Plain. Similar throwing bays would have been used at the Southern Command Bombing School at Lyndhurst, which began in 1915 and eventually covered 190 acres. A Trench Mortar School was established in 1917 (Australian War Memorial).

The YMCA at Greenhill House used by Australian troops while training at Sutton Veny.

Roy was posted to 1st Training Battalion, Sutton Veny, Wiltshire on 29th April 1918 and was taken on strength on 2nd May. He attended a course at the Southern Command Bombing School at Lyndhurst 5th-22nd June. On 24th August he boarded HMAT D21 *Medic* for Australia to support recruiting with fellow VCs John Carroll, John James Dwyer, Joergen Jensen, Thomas Kenny, Leonard Keysor, Stanley McDougall, Walter Peeler, William Ruthven and John Whittle. Roy was discharged on 12th December 1918 at Keswick Barracks, Adelaide. His intended place of residence was 65 Third Avenue, Forestville, South Australia.

When Roy left Broken Hill in 1914 the contingent was hooted, *by socialists and red-raggers*, and he claimed he was ... *stoned by mongrels at the train*. Although he returned to a hero's welcome the memory of his departure was evident as he spoke to the waiting crowd, ... *those mongrels were the first to shake me by the hand. If the boys stick together like they did in France there will be no Bolshevikism in this town.... I would like to be at one end of the street with a machine-gun and have them at the other end.* He was subsequently accused by local Member of the House of Representatives, Michael P Considine, of inciting trouble between returned soldiers and the working class. Roy found the atmosphere uncomfortable and moved to Adelaide.

Roy was one of several Australian VCs to be presented with a fifteen carat gold life pass to Tivoli Theatres by the Hon Hugh Donald McIntosh MLC. Roy Inwood married three times, but had no children:

Flinders Street, Adelaide, where Roy Inwood lived at a number of addresses.

- Mabel Alice Collins, née Weber, a widow. They married on 31st December 1918 and divorced in 1921. In 1924 Roy was living at 233 Cornish Street, Railway Town, Broken Hill and later at 234 Main North Road, Prospect.
- Evelyn Owens in 1927. They were living at 6 Argyll Street, Prospect when he enlisted in 1939, but he changed his address to 310 Flinders Street, Adelaide later. Evelyn died before 1942.
- Louise Elizabeth Gates on 28th March 1942. They lived at various addresses:
  43 Grove Street, Unley Park.
  35 Robert Street, North Unley.
  12 Barkley Street, Wayville.
  319 Flinders Street, Adelaide.
  48 Sheldon Street, Norwood.

43 Grove Street, Unley Park, where Roy lived with his third wife, Louise Elizabeth Gates.

In 1919 Roy was charged with assault, resulting in a fine. Following his divorce in 1921 he spent a short time mining at Queenstown, Tasmania and then worked at a eucalyptus distillery on Kangaroo Island. He returned to Adelaide and secured employment as an attendant and painter with Adelaide City Council in 1928, retiring in 1955.

Roy re-enlisted in the Australian Military Forces in Adelaide on 29th September 1939 and was posted to B Company, the Garrison Battalion (S212249). He was described as 5' 9" tall, weighing 161 lbs, with brown hair and eyes. He was promoted sergeant on 4th October and transferred to HQ Company on 23rd October. He transferred to the Australian Provost Corps, was posted to the Provost Section (Military Police) Adelaide on 29th March 1940 and was promoted staff sergeant on 5th April. He was posted to 4th Military District Barrack Detention Staff on 19th November 1941, was promoted temporary warrant officer class two on 25th November and appointed temporary warrant officer class one on 2nd April 1942. On 11th August he transferred to the South Australian Lines of Communication Area Detention Barracks and was attached to 2nd Australian Detention Barracks 10th–17th October. He transferred to the Military Prison and Detention Barrack Service on 4th June 1943 and was attached to 2/2nd Australian Detention Barracks from 9th Australian Detention Barracks 5th-27th August 1943. A medical board on 10th September classified him as Class B (Constitutional). He was promoted warrant officer class one on 9th November. Roy was reprimanded and forfeited one days' pay for being absent without leave 5th-9th July 1944. He was discharged on 30th November 1944 as unsuitable for further military service. His intended place of residence was 319 Flinders Street, Adelaide. Roy was one of 25,000 Diggers inspected by Queen Elizabeth II at a rally on Adelaide University Oval in March 1954. He was in an official party of VC and GC holders introduced to Her Majesty. He attended the VC Centenary Celebrations at Hyde Park, London on 26th June 1956, travelling on SS *Orcades* with other Australian VCs who were part of the 301 VC recipients from across the Commonwealth. Roy attended the funeral of Arthur Blackburn VC in November 1960. In 1964, with seventeen other VCs, he attended the opening of the VC Corner at the Australian War Memorial by the Governor General, Lord De L'Isle VC. Roy was described as a rugged, independent, well-built man, *with the rough corners still on him*. He often gave the impression that *his VC had not done him much good*.

SS *Orcades* was the Orient Line's third ship of that name. Her maiden voyage from Tilbury to Australia commenced on 14th December 1948. In 1955 she began a world service westwards, departing London to New Zealand and Australia via the Panama Canal and returning to Britain via the Suez Canal. During the November 1956 Olympic Games in Melbourne she was used as an accommodation ship. She sailed her last cruises in 1972 and was broken up in 1973.

Roy Inwood in 1965.

Roy Inwood died at Tara Private Hospital, St Peters, Adelaide on 23rd October 1971 and is buried in the Australian Imperial Forces Cemetery, West Terrace, Adelaide, South Australia (5–N 1E), one of four First World War VCs buried there. He is commemorated in a number of other places:

• Inwood Place, Canberra, Australian Capital Territory.
• Inwood Crescent, Wodonga, Victoria on White Box Rise estate built on land formerly part of Bandiana Army Camp.

- Inwood Road, Elizabeth East, South Australia.
- Roy Inwood Club, 10th Battalion, Torrens Parade Ground, Adelaide.
- Roy Inwood VC House (Returned and Services League), Argent Street, Broken Hill, New South Wales opened on 4th February 1996.
- Victoria Cross Memorial, Campbell, Canberra dedicated on 24th July 2000.
- Hall of Valour, Australian War Memorial, Canberra.
- Victoria Cross Memorial, Queen Victoria Building, George Street, Sydney, New South Wales dedicated on 23rd February 1992 to commemorate the visit of Queen Elizabeth II and Prince Philip on the occasion of the Sesquicentenary of the City of Sydney. Sir Roden Cutler VC, Edward Kenna VC and Keith Payne VC were in attendance.

Roy Inwood's grave in the Australian Imperial Forces Cemetery, West Terrace, Adelaide (Memorials to Valour).

- Named on one of eleven plaques honouring 175 men from overseas awarded the VC for the Great War. The plaques were unveiled by the Senior Minister of State at the Foreign & Commonwealth Office and Minister for Faith and Communities, Baroness Warsi, at a reception at Lancaster House, London on 26th June 2014 attended by The Duke of Kent and relatives of the VC recipients. The Australian plaque is at the Australian War Memorial.
- The Secretary of State for Communities and Local Government, Eric Pickles MP, announced that Victoria Cross recipients from the Great War would have

The Australian VC plaque at the Australian War Memorial unveiled at Lancaster House, London on 26th June 2014.

Information board about the four VCs buried in the Australian Imperial Forces Cemetery, West Terrace, Adelaide (Anthony Staunton).

commemorative paving stones laid in their birthplace as a lasting legacy of local heroes within communities. The stones would be laid on or close to the 100th anniversary of their VC actions. For the 145 VCs born in Australia, Belgium, Canada, China, Denmark, Egypt, France, Germany, India, Iraq, Japan, Nepal, Netherlands, New Zealand, Pakistan, South Africa, Sri Lanka, Ukraine and United States of America, individual commemorative stones were unveiled at the National Memorial Arboretum, Alrewas, Staffordshire by Prime Minister David Cameron MP and Sergeant Johnson Beharry VC on 5th March 2015.

In addition to the VC he was awarded the 1914–15 Star, British War Medal 1914–20, Victory Medal 1914–19, War Medal 1939–45, Australia Service Medal 1939–45, George VI Coronation Medal 1937 and Elizabeth II Coronation Medal 1953. He left his VC to the 10th Battalion Ex-Servicemen's Association, which in turn donated it to Adelaide Town Hall at 128 King William Street on 19th September 1972, where it was displayed in the Council Chambers. The VC group was loaned to the Australian War Memorial on 10th March 2016.

CAPTAIN CLARENCE SMITH JEFFRIES
34th Australian Infantry Battalion AIF

Clarence Jeffries was born on 26th October 1894 at Wallsend, New South Wales, Australia. He was known as Jeff. His father, Joshua Jeffries (1872–1943), was the manager of Abermain Collieries. He married Barbara née Steele (1873–1954) in 1894. Joshua retired in January 1924 and later he and his wife visited most of the leading coal mining countries in Europe. They were living at Main Road, Charlestown, NSW around 1937. Clarence was an only child.

Clarence's paternal grandfather, Joshua Jeffries (c.1832–1901) married Susan Laura née Brown (c.1835–1922) in 1864 in Sydney, New South Wales. In addition to Joshua they had seven other children:

• John Jeffries (1867–1950) married Hannah Euphemia Brooks (1874–1953) in 1896. John was a mine manager at Abermain, Weston, Hunter, NSW in 1930. They were living at 4 Fitzsimmons Street, Port Kembla, Werriwa, NSW in 1936 and at Kings Road, Moss Vale, Eden Monaro, NSW in 1943. They had a daughter, Millicent Elizabeth Brooks Jeffries in 1897.
• Francis H Jeffries (1871–1928) married Emily Dalhousie Hunter (1876–1952) in 1892. They had two children – Jane M Jeffries 1893 and Charles R Jeffries 1900.

- James Thomas Jeffries (born and died 1874).
- James Jeffries (1878–1940).
- Alfred Isaac Jeffries (c.1880–1932), a school-teacher, married Catherine 'Kate' Edith Morgan (1882–1959) in 1905 and they lived at 6 Norfolk Street, Paddington, Sydney. They had two children – Eileen E Jeffries 1905 and Winnie Z Jeffries 1907. He enlisted on 1st March 1916 (816) and was described as 5′ 3″ tall, weighing 129 lbs, with dark complexion, brown eyes and light balding hair. He was in E and C Companies, 1st Battalion, but was discharged on 24th June as medically unfit for service with neurasthenia. He had been involved in a dynamite accident four years before. He enlisted again at Moore Park on 2nd March 1917 as a driver in the Engineer Reinforcements in 2nd Military District (75503). His wife was living at Queen's Road, New Lambton and his weight had increased to 140 lbs. He was admitted to the garrison hospital on 18th March and was discharged from the Army on 20th March.
- Gertrude S Jeffries (born and died 1882).
- Clara M Jeffries (1884–1942) married George Williams in 1911. They had at least one child, Alexander J Williams, in 1914.

His maternal grandfather, Thomas Gleghorn Steel (1841–1908), was born in Northumberland, England. He emigrated to Australia and settled at Pitt Town, Wallsend, New South Wales. He married Hannah née Dronsfield (1850–1931) in 1868. She was born at Chadderton, Lancashire, England. In addition to Barbara they had eleven other children:

- Andrew Steel (1869–70).
- Mary Jane Steel (1871–1947) married Joseph James Trotter (1866–1952) in 1893. They had four children – Albert Joseph Trotter 1894, Horace Albert Trotter 1894, Elsie E Trotter 1901 and Carl Raymond Trotter 1910.

Wallsend was named after Wallsend on Tyneside in England by Alexander Brown in the 1850s when he purchased land in the area. He formed the Newcastle-Wallsend Coal Company to operate the colliery that opened in January 1861.

Abermain No.1 Colliery began production in November 1903 and was followed by Abermain No.2 in November 1910 and Abermain No.3 in December 1917. In October 1922 Abermain Collieries Ltd merged with Seaham Collieries to become Abermain Seaham Collieries Ltd. A further merger in 1931 resulted in the formation of J & A Brown Abermain Seaham Collieries Ltd. The Abermain Colliery Railway was constructed to carry coal from the three mines. Abermain No.2 was the last to cease production in April 1964. The picture shows Abermain No.3.

- Roger Gleghorn Steel (1875–1953) married Margaret A O'Hare (died 1929) in 1904. They had four children – Thomas Steel 1907, Owen Steel 1908, Margaret Steel 1912 and Roger Steel 1913. He married Elizabeth Hirst in 1933 and in 1935 they were living at Robert Street, Belmont, by when he was a weighman. By 1942 they had moved to George Street, Belmont.
- Margaret Ellen Steel (1878–c.1950) married James Leitch in 1900. They had three children – Hannah D Leitch 1900, George Leitch 1903 and Alexander Leitch 1905.
- Joseph Dronsfield Steel (1880–1956) married Elizabeth Hodge (1880–1961) in 1907. They had three children – Thomas Gleghorn Steel 1908, Christina Ross Steel 1909 and Archibald H Steel 1914.
- Andrew Steel (1882–1957) married Jane Whitelaw West (died 1959) in 1906. He was a shot-firer in 1935 and they were living at George Street, Belmont. They had two children – Bertha M Steel 1906 and Roy Steel 1910.
- Thomas Gleghorn Steel (1884–1963) married Isabella Florence Conn (1893–1981) in 1913. He was a shot-firer in 1935 and they were living at Blacksmith's, Swansea, NSW.
- James Coubourne/Colbourne Steel (1886–1956), a carpenter, married Violet Wilson Weston (1890–1979) in 1915. They had five children – Gertie Evelyn Steel 1916, Olive Clarice Steel 1918, James Coubourne Steel 1920, Marjory Steel 1923 and Leslie Allen Steel 1927. They were living at Haig Street, Belmont by 1935.
- Sarah Anne Steel (1888–1971) married Percy Alexander Abell (1887–1953), a clerk, in 1911. They were living at Stockton Street, Newcastle in 1913. Percy was a member of the Loyal Orange Lodge 137, Maryborough, Queensland and Royal Black Perceptory 480, Gympie, Queensland. They had two children – Thomas Abell 1913 and Eric Abell 1915.
- Oswald Oliver Steel (1890–1917) married Irene Hamilton Johnston (1894–1959) in 1915. He enlisted at Newcastle on 27th November 1915 (903) in C Company, 35th Battalion. He was a labourer and had been an apprentice carpenter for four years with Seaham Company, West Wallsend. He was described as 5′ 5″ tall, weighing 129 lbs, with fair complexion, brown eyes, brown hair and his religious denomination was Church of England. He was promoted sergeant on 1st May 1916, embarked on HMAT A24 *Benalla* at Sydney on 12th May and disembarked at Plymouth on 9th July. He went to France via Southampton on 21st November and reported sick with influenza on 20th February 1917. He was admitted to 10th Australian Field Ambulance on 22nd February and returned to the Battalion on 7th March. Oswald received shrapnel wounds to the shoulders, knee and buttock on 7th June and was evacuated through 9th Australian Field Ambulance and a casualty clearing station to 14th General Hospital, Wimereux on 8th June. His family was informed that he was dangerously ill on 18th June and progressing favourably on 22nd June. He was evacuated on HS *David* on 14th July to 1st London General Hospital, Camberwell. His family was informed that he had

been removed from the seriously ill list on 24th July, but he died of wounds on 10th August. He is buried in the Australian Military Burial Ground, Brookwood Cemetery, Surrey (XI D 13). Irene was living at Clearly Street, Hamilton and later at Wyee, Carrington Street, Mayfield, Newcastle. She married Thomas Featherston in 1920 and lived at Manning Street, Taree, NSW. They had moved to 58 The Avenue, Strathfield, Sydney by 1922. She gave up her rights to Oswald's medals and plaque in favour of his mother. Irene died in June 1959 and is buried at Middle Village Cemetery, Queen's County, New York, USA.

• George Clyde Steel (1895–1966) enlisted at Show Ground Camp Sydney on 4th November 1916 (838 later 56078), having been medically examined on 24th September. He was described as a railway employee, 5′ 8″ tall, weighing 120 lbs, with medium complexion, hazel eyes, brown hair and his religious denomination was Church of England. He attested at Addison Road Camp on 9th November in 9th Reinforcements, 1st Anzac Cyclist Battalion. He had served three years in the Militia (15th Infantry). He embarked at Sydney on 24th January 1917 on HMAT A33 *Ayrshire*, disembarked at Devonport on 12th April and was based at No.3 Camp, Parkhouse on Salisbury Plain. On 21st April he joined the Cyclist Battalion at Chiselden. On 28th June he transferred to Engineer Details at Brightlingsea and was absent for nine hours on 21st-22nd July, for which he was awarded four days Field Punishment No.2 and forfeited five days pay. He was at Colchester Hospital on 5th August. On 21st October he proceeded to France via Southampton and reported to the Base Depot, Rouelles on 23rd October. He departed France from Le Havre on 12th November and reported to No.3 AIF Command Depot, Weymouth next day. He embarked on HMAT A54 *Runic* on 20th December and disembarked in Australia on 14th February 1918. He was discharged from 2nd Military District on 15th March as unfit for service. George married Rebecca Laverick (1897–1973) in 1919. They had three children – Raymond Steel 1919, Oliver Clarence Steel 1921 and Joan Ferry Steel 1926.

Clarence was educated at:

• Dudley Public School, Boundary Street, Dudley, New South Wales, where he excelled at cricket. William Currey VC was also a pupil there.
• Newcastle Collegiate School, Newcastle, New South Wales.
• Newcastle High School, Newcastle, New South Wales.

Clarence was employed as a mining surveyor at Abermain Collieries, where his father was

Clarence Jeffries VC and William Currey VC both attended Dudley Public School.

the manager, and also undertook an apprenticeship as a mining engineer. He was interested in breeding thoroughbred horses, although not in racing, and had a fine collection of breeding stock. He served in 14th Infantry, Citizen's Military Forces (later 14th (Hunter River) Infantry) from 1st July 1912 under the compulsory training scheme. He was promoted corporal in January 1913 and sergeant on 1st July 1913. He was mobilised and commissioned on 22nd August 1914 for home defence duties, described as 5′ 10½″ tall and weighing 136 lbs. Having attended the School of Instruction, Duntroon 9th-20th November, he was appointed to instruct volunteers for the Australian Imperial Force at Newcastle and Liverpool Camps, New South Wales.

He passed No.17 School and was appointed provisional lieutenant on 1st July 1915. On 1st February 1916 he transferred as a second lieutenant to the AIF and embarked for Britain with C Company, 34th Battalion on 2nd May aboard HMAT A20 *Hororata* from Sydney. He disembarked from HMT *Aragon* at Plymouth, Devon on 23rd June 1916 and was based initially at Larkhill on Salisbury Plain, Wiltshire. Promoted lieutenant on 1st August and attended the Officer's School at Chelsea, London 1st-21st October. Clarence embarked at Southampton for Le Havre, France on 21st November. He attended the Gas School 27th-30th December and the Snipers' School 12th January–22nd April 1917.

Having been attached to the School of Instruction 2nd-13th May he rejoined the Battalion and received a gunshot to the left thigh on 9th June at Messines. He was treated at 9th Australian Field Ambulance before being transferred to No.2 Australian Casualty Clearing Station and 2nd Red Cross Hospital at Rouen on 11th June. On 15th June he was evacuated to England on HMHS *Pieter de Coninck* from Rouen and admitted to 3rd London General Hospital next day. Promoted captain on 26th June and transferred to Cobham Hall on 12th July. He was declared fit for General Service on 2nd August, discharged to Perham Down Depot, Wiltshire on 16th August and then to Tidworth, Wiltshire. He embarked for France

RMS *Aragon* (9,588 tons) was the first of the Royal Mail Steam Packet Company's transatlantic mail ships. She was built in Ireland in 1905 and in 1913 became the first defensively equipped merchant ship, know as DEMS. When war broke out she became a troopship and took part in the Gallipoli campaign in 1915. She entered Alexandria harbour on 30th December 1917, but there were no berths and she was ordered out into the Roads. While awaiting permission to re-enter harbour she was torpedoed by UC-*34* ten miles off Alexandria. The destroyer HMS *Attack* pulled alongside to take people off, but *Aragon* went down before everyone got away. Many went into the water, including Battery Sergeant Major Ernest Horlock VC, who helped rescue others until picked up by *Attack*. However, *Attack* was also torpedoed and he was killed instantly. Of the 2,500 men and women (160 VAD nurses) aboard *Aragon*, 610 were lost, including the Captain and six VADs. Ernest Horlock is buried in Alexandria (Hadra) War Memorial Cemetery, Egypt.

Le Havre was a vital port for the BEF in the First World War, with almost two million troops passing through it. Five infantry base depots formed there and there were six hospitals at various times, as well as a number of supply depots.

The 3rd London General Hospital started life in in 1859 as the Victoria Patriotic Asylum for orphan daughters of soldiers, sailors and marines. It was renamed the Royal Patriotic School and in 1914 became a Territorial Force hospital, with the staff being provided by the Middlesex, St Mary's and University College Hospitals. It originally only had 200 beds, but was eventually expanded to almost 2,000. A temporary railway enabled wounded to be brought from the south coast ports. The Hospital had its own newspaper, *The Gazette*, run by RAMC orderlies drawn from the Chelsea Arts Club. It closed in August 1920 having treated almost 63,000 patients. In recent times the Royal Victoria Patriotic Building was converted into apartments, studios, workshops, a drama school and a restaurant.

Pieter de Coninck (1,767 tons) was built in 1910 and was one of four Belgian mail steamers used as ambulance transports. Each could accommodate 377 casualties and they were in war service from March 1917 to March 1919.

on 27th August and rejoined his unit on 2nd September from 3rd Division Base Depot.

Awarded the VC for his actions southwest of Passchendaele, Belgium, on 12th October 1917, LG 18th December 1917. Clarence was killed during his VC action on 12th October and was buried on the battlefield about 135m northwest of Heine House. The VC was presented to his mother by the Governor General of Australia, Rt Hon Sir Ronald Craufurd Munro Ferguson GCMG, at Admiralty House, Sydney, New South Wales on 4th April 1918. His father confirmed in a letter his desire that his wife should receive the decoration. Joshua Jeffries assisted the family of James Bruce, who was with Clarence during his

Clarence Jeffries' grave in Tyne Cot Cemetery, Passchendaele. Behind is a preserved German pillbox, one of the few that remain in the area from the fighting in 1917.

Officers playing croquet while recovering at Cobham Hall. The first house on the site of the current Cobham Hall dates back to 1208. Elizabeth I visited in 1559, by then home of Sir William Brooke, 10th Lord Cobham. In 1613 James I granted the estate to his cousin Ludovick Stuart, 2nd Duke of Lenox, having confiscated it from the Brookes following their involvement in the plot to put Arabella Stuart on the throne. Charles I and Henrietta Maria spent their honeymoon night at Cobham Hall in 1625. In 1725 the then owner, John Bligh, was created first Earl of Darnley. The 1882 English cricket team travelling to Australia to regain the Ashes was captained by Ivo Bligh, later 8th Earl of Darnley. During the First World War Cobham Hall was a military hospital, initially for British and later Australian officers. Ivo Bligh's Australian wife, Florence, was the Commandant and was later created DBE. The Prime Minister of Australia and Mrs Hughes spent Christmas 1918 with Lord and Lady Darnley at Cobham Hall and it ceased to be a hospital at the end of the year. When Ivo Bligh died, Lady Darnley presented the Ashes urn to the MCC for safekeeping and it is now in the MCC Museum. During the Second World War the Hall housed evacuees, then RAF officers based at nearby Gravesend. In 1962 a school for girls opened at the Hall.

VC action, by appointing his two eldest sons as trainee mining surveyors at his mine.

Joshua travelled to Belgium in July 1920 to try to find his son's grave, but was unsuccessful and returned to Australia. However, in January 1921 he was informed that his son's remains had been exhumed on 14th September 1920 and interred in Tyne Cot Cemetery, Passchendaele, Belgium (40 E 1A). The body was identified by the captain's stars and the initials 'C.S.J.' on the ground sheet in which it was wrapped. The Australian Graves Service confirmed that no other Australian captain with those initials had been killed near Passchendaele. Joshua and Barbara visited the grave in Tyne Cot Cemetery in 1924. Clarence is commemorated in a number of other places:

- Roll of Honour, Panel 124, Australian War Memorial, Canberra, Australian Capital Territory, Australia.
- Display in the Hall of Valour, Australian War Memorial, Canberra.
- Named on the Victoria Cross Memorial, Campbell, Canberra dedicated on 24th July 2000.

- Jefferis (sic) Street, Canberra, dedicated on 8th February 1978.
- Named on one of eleven plaques honouring 175 men from overseas awarded the VC for the Great War. The plaques were unveiled by the Senior Minister of State at the Foreign & Commonwealth Office and Minister for Faith and Communities, Baroness Warsi, at a reception at Lancaster House, London on 26th June 2014 attended by The Duke of Kent and relatives of the VC recipients. The Australian plaque is at the Australian War Memorial.
- Jeffries Currey Memorial Library, Dudley Public School, corner of Boundary Street and Ocean Street, Dudley, New South Wales, was dedicated on 1st May 1976 by Sir Roden Cutler VC, Governor of New South Wales. The Currey-Jeffries Mural in the quadrangle was completed in 1986.
- Memorial Plaque, Newcastle Primary School Library, Newcastle, NSW, Australia.
- Captain Clarence Smith Jeffries VC and Private William Matthew Currey VC Memorial Wall erected by Sandgate Cemetery Trust at Newcastle, NSW. It was dedicated by Keith Payne VC and Edward Kenna VC on 16th April 2000.
- A Defence Housing Association development named after him at Adamstown, near Newcastle by the Parliamentary Secretary to the Minister of Defence, Teresa Gambaro, on 26th April 2005.
- A carved memorial chair presented to Holy Trinity Anglican Church, Abermain, Newcastle, NSW by his uncle and aunt.
- Captain Clarence Smith Jeffries Memorial Park, Abermain, together with a bronze plaque commemorating Jeffries and a transcription of the Victoria Cross citation.
- Plaque in Federal Park, Wallsend incorrectly spells his name as 'Jeffreys'.
- Memorial dedicated on 24th June 1919 in the survey room of the superintendent's offices at Abermain Collieries. Lieutenant Colonel Edward Nash unveiled a full size portrait of Jeffries, who had been in charge of the survey department. When the colliery closed the portrait was transferred to Abermain Bowling Club.
- St Luke's Church of England Church, Wallsend installed a lead glass window dedicated to the deceased servicemen of the District at the eastern end of the church with £200 bequeathed by his mother.
- Jeffries VC Club, Singleton Camp, NSW.
- Victoria Cross Memorial, Queen Victoria Building, George Street, Sydney, New South Wales dedicated on 23rd February 1992 to commemorate the visit of Queen Elizabeth II and Prince Philip on the occasion of the Sesquicentenary of the City of Sydney. Sir Roden Cutler VC, Edward Kenna VC and Keith Payne VC were in attendance.
- Named on the Victoria Cross Recipients Wall at North Bondi War Memorial, NSW

Holy Trinity Anglican Church, Abermain, Newcastle, New South Wales.

erected by the Returned & Services League of Australia and dedicated on 27th November 2011.

• Jeffries Crescent, Wodonga, Victoria on White Box Rise estate built on land formerly part of Bandiana Army Camp.

• Clarence Smith Jeffries Award established in 2006 by the Australian Institute of Mine Surveyors and awarded annually to the best mining surveying candidate performance in the Institute's examinations.

• The Secretary of State for Communities and Local Government, Eric Pickles MP announced that Victoria Cross recipients from the Great War would have commemorative paving stones laid in their birthplace as a lasting legacy of local heroes within communities. The stones would be laid on or close to the 100th anniversary of their VC actions. For the 145 VCs born in Australia, Belgium, Canada, China, Denmark, Egypt, France, Germany, India, Iraq, Japan, Nepal, Netherlands, New Zealand, Pakistan, South Africa, Sri Lanka, Ukraine and United States of America, individual commemorative stones were unveiled at the National Memorial Arboretum, Alrewas, Staffordshire by Prime Minister David Cameron MP and Sergeant Johnson Beharry VC on 5th March 2015.

In addition to the VC he was awarded the British War Medal 1914–20 and Victory Medal 1914–19. The VC was bequeathed by his mother in her will dated 3rd October 1950 to the Dean and Chapter of Christ Church Cathedral, Newcastle to be kept in the Warrior's Chapel. The VC was handed over following her death in January 1954 and remains in the Warrior's Chapel. The whereabouts of his other two medals are unknown.

Clarence Jeffries' commemorative paving stone at the National Memorial Arboretum, Alrewas, Staffordshire (Memorials to Valour).

437793 PRIVATE CECIL JOHN KINROSS
49th Battalion (Edmonton Regiment), Canadian Expeditionary Force

Cecil Kinross was born on 17th February 1896 at Dews Farm, Harefield, near Uxbridge, London, England. His father, James Stirling Kinross (1864–1954), was born at Gannochan Farm, Ardoch, Perth, Scotland. He went to Texas in the USA and became a cowboy for a period before returning to Britain. He took over Flanders Farm, Hurley, Warwickshire in 1888 when his brother moved to Mount Farm. James lived at 32 Flanders Hall, Tamworth, Staffordshire with his sister Isabella before moving to Harefield, Middlesex in 1891, where he was in partnership with his brother John until 1894. He married Emily/Emilie Alice née Hull (1871–1921), who was born at Hurley, Kingsbury, Warwickshire, in 1891. They were living at Dews Farm, Harefield by 1894 and at Hollies Farm, Lea Marston 1904–11. He became a parish councillor in Lea Marston. They emigrated to Canada aboard RMS *Empress of Ireland* from Liverpool, Lancashire, arriving at St John, New Brunswick on 12th March 1911. They settled on a farm near Lougheed, Alberta and he became a JP. James retired in 1937 and spent the last five years of his life living with his daughter, Nancy Kennedy, at 622 Third Avenue West, Prince Rupert, British Columbia. Cecil had four siblings:

- James Hector Kinross (1900–10) was a diabetic and died at Hollies Farm on 10th March 1910.
- Mary Kinross (1892–96) died from food poisoning on 26th August 1896.
- Elizabeth 'Ellie' Stirling Kinross (1894–1986) was educated at Hurley Girls' School, Kingsbury and Coleshill Grammar School, near Birmingham. She married George Arthur Edward Keward (1886–1937) in 1919, in Lougheed, Alberta, Canada. He was born at 15 Bolsover Street, Marylebone, London.
- Isabella 'Nancy' Annie Kinross (1903–c.1984) married as Kennedy and they had at least a son, John Kinross-Kennedy, who eventually inherited his uncle's VC. Nancy was living at 622 Third Avenue West, Prince Rupert, British Columbia when she died.

RMS *Empress of Ireland* (14,191 tons) was built on the Clyde in 1906 for the Canadian Pacific Steamships' service from Quebec to Liverpool. She collided with the Norwegian collier SS *Storstad* in the Saint Lawrence River early on 29th May 1914 and sank in fifteen minutes. The loss of 1,012 lives was the worst maritime disaster in Canadian history.

Cecil's paternal grandfather, John Kinross (1822–1916), was born at Ardoch, Perthshire. He was a farmer of 235 acres at Gannochan Farm, Ardoch, Perthshire employing four labourers, a boy and a girl. He married Elizabeth Graham Stiraham née Stirling (1830–1922) in 1852 at Craighead, Dunblane, Perthshire. They lived at Sauseway Head, Stirling. In addition to James they had six other children:

- Mary Kinross (born 1854) married Thomas Miller (born 1858), a farmer, in 1883 at Hillend House, Clackmannan and they had three children – John Miller 1887, James Stirling Kinross Miller 1890 and Elsie Miller 1893. They were living at Craigluscar, Fife in 1891, at Stanhope Park Farm, Stanwell, Middlesex in 1901 and at Bodymoor Heath, Kingsbury, Staffordshire in 1911. They sailed from Liverpool, Lancashire aboard RMS *Empress of Ireland*, arriving at Quebec, Canada on 24th April 1914, just a month before the liner sank in the St Lawrence River with the loss of 1,012 lives. They settled at Qu'Appelle, Saskatchewan.

- Isabella Eadie Kinross (born 1857) married Thomas Kyle (c.1846–1920), a civil engineer, in 1893 at Hillend House, Clackmannan. Thomas had been married twice before. He married Maria Morris and had two children. He then married Margaret Reid Stewart (1851–91) in 1873 at Edinburgh, Midlothian and had ten children. Thomas and Isabella had three children – Donald Alexander Kyle 1894, Mary Helen Kyle 1895 and Andrew Wingate Kyle 1897. In 1901 they were living at Ferry Port on Craig, Fife with their children and the following from his previous marriages – Elizabeth Kyle c.1880, Margaret Jane Kyle c.1884, James B Kyle c.1886 and John B Kyle c.1890. They were still living there in 1911.
- An unnamed child born on 8th June 1859, who died the next day.
- John Kinross (1861–1936), a farmer, married Isabella Miller (1865–1913), sister of Thomas Miller above, in 1884 at Beannie, Ardoch, Perthshire. They were living at Mount Farm, Grendon, Warwickshire in 1888 before moving to Flanders Hall and Rushy Flanders, near Tamworth, Staffordshire. They were back at Mount Farm, Grendon by 1891. In 1892 he took over four farms at Harefield, Middlesex with his brother James, but the partnership was dissolved two years later. They then lived at Riding Court Farm and Ditton Park, near Windsor, Berkshire in 1894, leased from the Duchess of Buccleuch and later purchased from her grandson, Lord Montagu of Beaulieu. He also ran several other farms in the area, including Yeoveney Manor, totalling 1,500 acres. John was a Buckinghamshire County Councillor for thirty years and a JP from 1907. He ran a herd of Shorthorn cattle and joined the Royal South Bucks Agricultural Association, winning nine cups over twenty-seven years presented by Queen Victoria, King Edward VII and King George V for best all-round root crops. He eventually became chairman. He also co-founded the South Buckinghamshire branch of the National Farmers' Union and was chairman for seven years. John and Isabella had six children – Janet Kinross 1886, Elizabeth Kinross 1887, John Kinross 1890, Isabella Frances Kinross 1891, Margaret May Kinross 1896 and Dorothy Kinross 1899. John had a relationship with Lilian Winifred Sinnock (1890–1938) and they had two children – Lillian Graham Stirling Sinnock Miller 1912 and Winifred Cordelia Miller 1914. Lilian married Aaron Ford in 1923. John Kinross married May Violet Henriette Purser (1892–1959) in 1914 at Paddington, London. During the Great War John was an agricultural representative on the Appeal Tribunal and was Chairman of the Slough branch of the County War Committee. John and May lived at Grove Ley, Feltham Hill, Middlesex from 1930. May married Frank Oscar Pidduck (1882–1964) in 1947 at Staines, Middlesex.

- Donald Alexander 'Sandy' Kinross (1867–1942), also seen as Alexander Donald Kinross, was a farmer at Hillend House, Clackmannan. He married Margaret Alexander (1874–1911) in 1895 at Loanside, Clackmannan. They had eight children – Catherine Emily Kinross 1898, William Christie Kinross 1899, Elizabeth Kinross 1901, Donald Alexander Kinross 1903, James Kinross 1904, Austen Coubrough Kinross 1905, Margaret Kinross 1907 and Thomas Kinross 1911. Donald married Margaret McEwen Weir Allan in 1913 at Clackmannan. William Christie Kinross was called up 10th October 1917 and served in 53rd (Young Soldier) Battalion, Gordon Highlanders (TR/1/19453) at Tillycoultry, Clackmannanshire. He was a cash clerk, described as 5′ 2″ tall, weighing 96 lbs and his religious denomination was Presbyterian. He was attached to No.1 Officer Technical Training Wing RFC, St Leonards until 5th January 1918. He was found to be medically unfit for service as a flying officer, but was recommended for a commission elsewhere. Posted to 52nd (Graduated) Battalion, Gordon Highlanders at Colchester 6th April. Applied for a commission on 7th May in the Tank Corps, Royal Artillery, Argyll & Sutherland Highlanders or Gordon Highlanders. Appointed unpaid lance corporal 19th May. He commenced training at No.7 Officer Cadet Battalion, Fermoy on 5th July, was commissioned in the Gordon Highlanders on 3rd March 1919 and transferred to the Class Z Reserve the same day. He relinquished his commission on 1st September 1921, retaining the rank of second lieutenant.
- Elizabeth Jane Kinross (1872–1966) married Francis Maxwell Thomson (1871–1946), a farmer, in 1900 at the Royal Hotel, Friars Street, Stirling. They lived at Canon Court Farm, Fetcham and Lynton, Banstead Road, Banstead, Surrey. Elizabeth was living at 79 Hillside Avenue, Worthing, Sussex at the time of her death. They had two daughters – Elizabeth Frances Thomson 1901 and Mary Corrie Thomson 1902.

His maternal grandfather, John Hull (1839–1927) was born at Rugeley, Staffordshire. He married Mary née Stafford (1843–1910) in 1866 at Atherstone, Warwickshire. He was a butcher and farmer of seventy acres in 1871 and they were living at Kingsbury, Hurley, Staffordshire. By 1881 his farm had reduced to thirty acres. In addition to Emily they had five other children:

Cecil's maternal grandparents were living at Kingsbury, Hurley, Staffordshire in 1871.

- Harry Stafford Hull (1867–1942) was a butcher. He married Eleanor Gertrude Rudge (1874–1918) in 1897 at Solihull, Warwickshire and they were living at Hurley, Warwickshire in 1911. One of Harry's employees, Sydney Allton (1893–1974), stole a diamond ring belonging to Eleanor some time before March 1912 and gave it to his girlfriend, Annie Elizabeth Deeming, a domestic servant. Allton had been living with the Hull family as assistant butcher for nine years. Eleanor reported the loss to the police and the ring was discovered by PC Marston on 15th July and returned. Allton was found guilty of theft and placed on probation for two years, ordered to pay £1 costs and was dismissed from Hull's staff. Harry and Eleanor had a son, John Henry Hull, in 1900. Harry married Olive Ethel Marriott (1908–91) in 1932 at Nuneaton, Warwickshire. Harry owned several properties, including six houses at Knowle Hill, and nearly four acres of pasture. Harry and Olive had a daughter, Beryl K Hull, in 1933.

- Annie Hull (1868–1941) married William Breeden (1860–1922), a farmer, in 1891 at Kingsbury, Warwickshire. They were living at Hurley Village, Kingsbury in 1891, at Grass Yard Farm, Kingsbury in 1901, at Hurley, Atherstone in 1911 and later at Dunton Hall, Curdworth, Warwickshire. William had married Emma Slater (1857–90) in 1884 at Cannock, Staffordshire. She died following complications with the birth of their son, Eric Slater Breeden (1890–1971). Three previous children had died at birth – Annie Maria Breeden 1884, William Henry Breeden 1886 and Samuel Percy Breeden 1888. William was living at Hurley Village with his mother-in-law, Annie Slater, at the time of the 1891 Census and his son Eric was being cared for by John and Hannah Lawrence at Hurley Cottage. William and Annie had seven children – John Samuel Breeden 1892, Nellie Breeden 1894, twins Gladys and Mary Breeden 1897, Harry Stafford Breeden 1899, William Breeden 1902 and Annie Breeden 1907.

- George (1874–1959) was a farmer and milk seller. He married Amelia Mary Hollick (1880–1962) in 1902 at Kingsbury, Warwickshire. She was living at The Hills, Hurley, Atherstone. They had six children – Dorothy Mary Hull 1905, Annie Elizabeth Hull 1907, John William Hull 1910, George Hull 1916, Cecil James Hull 1918 and Beatrice S Hull 1921.

- Jessie Willetts Hull (1877–1955) married John Averill (1874–1955), a farmer, in 1900 at Tamworth. They had five children – John Averill 1901, Marjorie Averill 1903, Dorothy Averill 1905, Mary Averill 1906 and Frederick George Averill 1909.

- Mary Hull (born 1882) married Adam Dale (born 1874), a farmer, in 1910 at Tamworth. He was born at Cardross, Dumbarton, Scotland. They were living at Blackgreaves, Lea Marston, Warwickshire in 1911. They had three children – Adam D Dale 1913, John S Dale 1915 and Cecil Dale 1918.

Cecil was educated at:

- Hurley School, Kingsbury, Warwickshire.
- Lea Marston Boys School, Warwickshire from 8th May 1905.
- Coleshill Grammar School, near Birmingham, Warwickshire.

As a young man Cecil was injured by a plough, which scarred both shins for life. He was working as a farmer when war broke out and he enlisted in 51st Battalion in Calgary, Alberta on 21st October 1915. He was described as 5′ 11½″ tall, weighing 150 lbs and his religious denomination was Church of England. He embarked for England aboard RMS *Missanabie* on 18th December as part of the third reinforcing draft and was posted to 9th Reserve Battalion at Shorncliffe, Kent on 28th December. On 13th February 1916 he was hospitalised with German measles until 3rd March.

Coleshill Grammar School, now The Coleshill School, was also attended by Charles George Bonner VC DSC (1884–1951).

On 15th March Cecil went to France to the Canadian Base Depot and joined 49th Battalion in divisional reserve near Kemmel on 19th March. His platoon sergeant regarded him as a disgrace to the platoon, which brought a wry smile to Cecil's face. He became a runner in D Company and gained a reputation for dodging bullets. As a result he was nicknamed Hoodoo. When newcomers were assigned to him, bets were taken on how long they would last. He was attached to 7th Canadian Trench Mortar Battery from 23rd May until 25th August. His luck ran out in an attack on Regina Trench on the Somme on 8th October, when he was hit by shrapnel in the right arm and side. Cecil was admitted to 3rd Canadian General Hospital, Boulogne on 10th October and transferred to No.7 Convalescent Depot on 13th October. He rejoined his unit on 6th November. He took part in the capture of Vimy Ridge in April 1917 and was attached to 7th Field Company, Canadian Engineers from 18th May until 24th July. Having returned to his unit in August, he took part in the fighting around Lens and was granted leave 28th August–15th September.

Awarded the VC for his actions at Furst Farm, Passchendaele on 28/29th October and 31st October/1st November 1917, LG 11th January 1918. Cecil was admitted to 149th Field Ambulance and No.12 Casualty Clearing Station on 30th October with gunshot wounds to the right arm and left temporal region. He was transferred to 8th Stationary Hospital, Wimereux the following day. Having been evacuated to Britain on HMHS *Jan Breydel* he was admitted to No.2 Military Hospital, Old Park, Canterbury, Kent on 3rd November on the strength of the Alberta

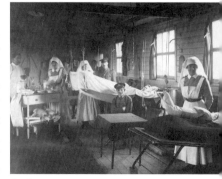

Cecil was treated at 3rd Canadian General Hospital, Boulogne in October 1916. The Hospital was commanded by Lieutenant Colonel John McRae, author of *In Flanders Fields*.

8th Stationary Hospital, Wimereux.

Pantages Theatre in Edmonton hosted a civic
reception for Cecil shortly after he was discharged
from the army.

Regimental Depot, Bramshott. He transferred to No.16 Canadian General Hospital (Ontario Military Hospital), Orpington, Kent on 16th November. On 15th February 1918 he transferred to 21st Reserve Battalion. The VC was presented by the King at Buckingham Palace on 6th April. He was arrested shortly afterwards by military policemen who assumed he was impersonating a VC winner, but was released when he produced the VC with his name on it.

On 7th December he transferred to the Canadian Concentration Camp at Kinmel Park in North Wales and on 20th January 1919 sailed for Canada. He was declared medically unfit and was discharged on 17th February. He had partial ulnar paralysis and suffered recurring headaches from the gunshot wounds received at Passchendaele. A few days after his discharge many Edmontonians packed into Pantages Theatre for a civic reception during which Cecil was presented with a purse of gold.

Despite the effects of his injuries, Cecil resumed farming at Lougheed, Alberta, having been given 160 acres of land there by the Canadian Government. He attended the VC Dinner at the Royal Gallery of the House of Lords, London on 9th November 1929 and the VC Centenary celebrations at Hyde Park, London on 26 June 1956. He was presented to King George VI and Queen Elizabeth at Edmonton during the Royal Tour of Canada in 1939. Cecil was a confirmed bachelor and was well known for his eccentric behaviour. When he was admitted to hospital to have his tonsils removed he insisted on going through the operation without any anaesthetic. On another occasion he was teased about the amount of courage it took to win a VC compared to jumping into a frozen lake. Cecil immediately removed his coat and plunged through a hole in the ice.

Cecil died alone in his hotel room in Lougheed, Alberta on 21st June 1957. He is buried in the Soldiers' Plot of Lougheed Cemetery. Among the pallbearers was Alex Brereton VC. Cecil is commemorated in a number of other places:

• Kinross Road, Griesbach, Edmonton, Alberta was named in 2005.
• C.J. Kinross V.C. Branch No.180, Royal Canadian Legion (Alberta/Northwest Territories Command), Lougheed, Alberta. Cecil was Honorary President.

C.J. Kinross V.C. Branch No.180, Royal Canadian Legion at Lougheed, Alberta.

Cecil Kinross' gravestone in Lougheed Cemetery.

- C.J. Kinross V.C. Memorial Playground, Lougheed, Alberta.
- Mount Kinross (2640m) in Jasper National Park was named after him in 1951.
- Named on a Victoria Cross obelisk to all Canadian VCs at Military Heritage Park, Barrie, Ontario dedicated by The Princess Royal on 22nd October 2013.
- Named on one of eleven plaques honouring 175 men from overseas awarded the VC for the Great War. The plaques were unveiled by the Senior

The plaque on Cecil's birthplace at Dews Farm, Harefield, Middlesex.

Minister of State at the Foreign & Commonwealth Office and Minister for Faith and Communities, Baroness Warsi, at a reception at Lancaster House, London on 26th June 2014 attended by The Duke of Kent and relatives of the VC recipients. The Canadian plaque was unveiled outside the British High Commission in Elgin Street, Ottawa on 10th November 2014 by The Princess Royal in the presence of British High Commissioner Howard Drake, Canadian Minister of Veterans Affairs Julian Fantino and Canadian Chief of the Defence Staff General Thomas J Lawson.
- Two 49 cents postage stamps in honour of the 94 Canadian VC winners were issued by Canada Post on 21st October 2004 on the 150th Anniversary of the first Canadian VC's action, Alexander Roberts Dunn VC.
- A Heritage Blue Plaque was placed on his birthplace at Dews Farm, Harefield, Middlesex on 17th February 2011. The ceremony was attended by the Deputy

City Hall, Edmonton, Alberta, where Cecil's medals are displayed at the entrance to the Mayor's office.

Cecil's commemorative paving stone at Harefield War Memorial, Middlesex (Memorials to Valour).

High Commissioner for Canada, Claude Boucher, along with members of the Loyal Edmonton Regiment.

• The Department for Communities and Local Government decided to provide a commemorative paving stone at the birthplace of every Great War Victoria Cross recipient in the United Kingdom. Cecil's stone was dedicated at Harefield War Memorial, Middlesex on 4th November 2014 to mark the centenary of his award.

• Plaque on a memorial to the ninety-nine Canadian VCs in York Cemetery, Toronto.

In addition to the VC he was awarded the British War Medal 1914–20, Victory Medal 1914–19, George VI Coronation Medal 1937 and Elizabeth II Coronation Medal 1953. The medals were handed over on permanent loan to the City Hall in Sir Winston Churchill Square, Edmonton, Alberta on 9th November 2015 by John Kinross Kennedy, Cecil's nephew. The group is displayed at the entrance to the Mayor's office.

370995 SERGEANT ALFRED JOSEPH KNIGHT
2/8th (City of London) Battalion The London Regiment (Post Office Rifles)

Alfred Knight was born at 12 Clifton Terrace, Friston Street, Ladywood, Birmingham on 24th August 1888. His father, Joseph Knight (1866–1931), was an apprentice in a lamp factory in 1881, a glasscutter in 1887, a glass fitter in 1901 and a confectioner by 1911. He married Annie Maria née Rowbottom (1867–1949) on 30th October 1887 at St John's, Ladywood, Birmingham. They lived at various addresses:

Friston Street, Ladywood. Clifton Terrace, where Alfred was born, is the third gap on the left (Irene Smith).

St John's Church, Ladywood, where Alfred's parents were married in 1887.

299 St Vincent Street, Ladywood.
12 Clifton Terrace, Friston Street, Birmingham 1888–91.
3 Claines Place, St Vincent Street, Ladywood.
41 Islington Row, Edgbaston by 1911.

Alfred had two siblings:

• Doris 'Dolly' Mary Knight (1898–1979) married John Charles Newey (1889–1962) in 1925.
• Philip Anthony Knight (1903–83) married Frances Hilda Downey (1909–2000) in 1929. They had a son, Anthony G Knight, in 1936.

Alfred's paternal grandfather, Joseph Knight (1827–76), was born at Stretton on Dunsmore, Warwickshire. He was a servant in 1847 and a box maker in 1851. He married Anne née Scales (c.1822–96), born at Barton Seagrave, Northamptonshire, in 1847 at Leek Wootton, Warwickshire. In 1851 they were living at 56 Wharf Lane, Birmingham. By 1861 they had moved to 5 Back of 15 Granville Street, Ladywood and to 5 Bakers Buildings, Granville Street by 1871. Anne was a charwoman in 1881, living with her daughter, Harriet, at the home of John Baker Lythall at 347 Bristol Road,

St Vincent Street, Ladywood (Irene Higgins).

Edgbaston, Warwickshire. By 1891 she was an office minder, living with her daughter, Ellen Griffiths, at 1 Back of 15 Granville Street, Ladywood. In addition to Joseph they had six other children:

Bristol Road, Edgbaston.

- Sarah Ann Knight (born 1848).
- James Henry Knight (born and died 1850).
- Harriet Elizabeth Knight (born 1855) was a nurse in 1871.
- Alice Ellen Knight (born 1857) married David Griffiths (born 1856) in 1881 and they had a son, William John Griffiths, the same year. Alice was a laundress in 1891.
- John Knight (1860–98), a house painter, married Emily Milbrough (or Milbrew) Jones (1860–1955) in 1885. They had four children – John Henry Knight 1887, Bertha Christina Knight 1888, William Harold Knight 1890 and Emily Milbrough Knight 1892.
- Mary Maud Knight (born 1863) was a cleaner in a lamp factory in 1881.

His maternal grandfather, Robert Rowbottom (1843–1922), a gun maker, reportedly married Septima née Ball (1845–1905) in 1861. She was born at Chew Magna, Somerset. In addition to Annie they had four other children:

- William Rowbottom (born c.1861).
- Laura Rowbottom (1864–1932) married John MacQueen (1851–1933), a tailor and draper, in 1884. They lived at 32 Summer Hill Terrace, Ladywood and had ten children – John James MacQueen 1887, Mary Hamilton MacQueen 1889, William Stewart MacQueen 1890, Gordon MacQueen 1892, Norman MacQueen 1893, Doris Elizabeth MacQueen 1894, Annie Laura MacQueen 1898, Ian Hamilton MacQueen 1900, Andrew Stewart MacQueen 1903 and Roy Stewart MacQueen 1907.
- Thomas R Rowbottom (1866–1935), registered as Roubottom.
- Alfred Rowbottom (born 1868 as Roubottom).

Septima died in July 1905 at 41 Islington Row, Edgbaston, Warwickshire. Robert married Amy Miles née Cheslin (1861–1949), in September 1913. Amy had married Adrian George Miles (born 1858) in 1882.

Alfred was educated at St Philip's Grammar School, Edgbaston 1900–03. He was employed as a clerical assistant and then clerk in the engineering department of the General Post Office in Birmingham from 1909 and at Carrington Street Post Office in Nottingham after it moved in 1912. He enlisted on 26th October 1914 (original number 3000).

Birmingham's General Post Office.

St Philip's was founded in 1887 when two Birmingham Oratory priests took over an existing Catholic Grammar School. It became St Philip's Roman Catholic Sixth Form College in 1976 and closed in 1995. St Philip's had a number of famous alumni, including Julian Fellowes the actor, novelist, director and screenwriter, best known for the TV series *Downton Abbey*. The future Field Marshal William Slim attended the School 1903–10. He commanded Fourteenth Army in Burma during the Second World War. JRR Tolkien, author of *The Hobbit* and *Lord of the Rings*, and his brother Hilary were also educated there.

Recruiting poster for the Post Office Rifles.

Boroughbridge Road, York, where Alfred and Mabel lived in the late 1930s and early 1940s.

Alfred Knight married Mabel née Saunderson (14th February 1890–25th December 1988) on 8th May 1915 at The Oratory, Hagley Road, Edgbaston, Warwickshire. Mabel was born at 8 Goldsmith Square, Goldsmith Street, Nottingham and worked for Jesse Boot, founder of Boots the Chemist, at Boots Pure Drug Co Ltd in Nottingham. They lived at various addresses:

The Birmingham Oratory was founded in 1849 by John Henry Newman with the authority of Pope Pius IX. Newman also founded the Oratory School, which moved to near Reading in 1922. The current Oratory Church was completed in 1910. JRR Tolkien was a parishioner for nine years as a child. On 19th September 2010 Pope Benedict XVI visited the Oratory, having conducted the first ever beatification ceremony in England for Newman at Cofton Park, Birmingham.

Balfour Street, Birmingham.
204 Monument Road, Edgbaston 1925–31.
63 Severus Avenue, York.
244 Boroughbridge Road, York 1937–41.
45 Elvetham Road, Edgbaston from 1941.

Mabel and Alfred had three children:

- Marjorie Mary Knight (28th October 1916–17th May 2000) married Horace F Carey (1913–97) in 1946. They had a son, Michael J Carey, in 1946.
- Geoffrey Joseph Knight (born 21st April 1924) married Georgina C Hearn (born 1923) in 1951. They had three children – Christopher J Knight 1952, Rosemary AB Knight 1956 and Fiona S Knight 1965.
- Valerie Mary Knight (1st April 1927–8th December 1993) married Brendan Francis Walsh (1920–2008) in 1950. He was born at Caragh Lake, Kerry, Ireland. They lived at 16 Wheeleys Road, Edgbaston before moving to 6 Norfolk Road, Edgbaston by 1960 and Harborne, Birmingham by 1965. They had three children – Anne CM Walsh 1955, Bernadette Mary Walsh 1958 and Paul F Walsh 1961.

Mabel's father, William Robert Saunderson (1848–1925), born at Lord Mills Street, Chesterfield, Derbyshire, was an insurance agent and later a fruit merchant. He married Eliza Ann née Walker (1850–1908), a lace warehouse overlooker, in 1872. She was a lace finisher by 1905. They were living in Nottingham at 11 Allan Terrace, Sherwood Street in 1882, at 8 Goldsmith Square, Goldsmith Street in 1891 and at 41 Albert Grove in 1908. In addition to Mabel they had seven other children:

- Herbert William Saunderson (1873–1964), a lace designer, married Kate Oscroft (1874–1952) in 1899. By 1901 he was an insurance inspector and they were living at 14 Derby Grove, Nottingham. By 1911 they had moved to Everslea, 8 Esher Grove, Mapperley Park, Nottingham, by when Kate was a secretary in an insurance company. They had two children – Herbert Cecil Saunderson 1901 and Kathleen Mary Saunderson 1907.
- Ellen Saunderson (1875–1963) married Joseph Charles Dickinson (1884–1936) in 1908. They were living at 100 Barcombe Avenue, Streatham, London at the time of his death. They had two children – Charles Reginald Dickson 1909 and Dorothy Dickinson 1911.
- Florence Saunderson (1876–1955) was a lace clipper in 1891 and a clerk in a furniture shop in 1901. She married Henry James Potterton (1878–1965) in 1902 at Balham St Mary, London. They were living at 93 Upper Grosvenor Road, Tunbridge Wells, Kent in 1911 and later moved to 9 North Side, Streatham Common, London. They had two children – Nellie Dorothy Smithers Potterton 1903 and May Potterton 1905.

- Arthur Saunderson (1878–1936) was a fruit salesman and by 1911 was a potato merchant. He married, probably, Gertrude Barker (1879–1944), in 1903. In the 1911 Census he was living alone at 48a Silverdale Road, Tunbridge Wells, Kent.
- Henry Saunderson (1882–1963) was a clerk in a drapery house in 1901. By 1911 he was a lay reader, boarding at 79 Green Lane, Small Heath, Aston. He graduated (LTh) from the University of Durham in 1916 and was appointed Curate of St Andrews, Bordesley 1916–19 and Curate of St Asaph, Birmingham 1921–24. Henry was Organising Secretary of the Church of England Temperance Society for Birmingham and Coventry 1924–37 and was appointed Curate, The Quinton 1927–32 and Vicar of St Matthias, Handsworth. He served at Douglas, Isle of Man 1936–63.
- Thomas Saunderson (1883–1959) was a fitter when he enlisted in the Army Service Corps on 28th May 1915 at Aldershot (M2/113342). He was described as 5′ 7″ tall, living at 38 Balfour Road, Nottingham. He volunteered for Home Service only and served in 52nd Company (MT Depot) in the workshops at Aldershot until 5th April 1917. Admitted to Cambridge Military Hospital, Aldershot 28th February–11th March 1916 with impetigo and again 28th March–9th May with a hernia. He embarked at Folkestone and disembarked at Boulogne on 5th May 1917 and embarked at Marseille on 21st May on HMT *Menominee* and disembarked in Salonica on 30th May. He joined 910th Company. He was admitted to 21st Stationary Hospital 3rd–5th June with scabies and to 43rd General Hospital 20th June–18th July with dysentery, recovering at No.1 Convalescent Depot until rejoining his unit on 2nd August. He was admitted to 43rd General Hospital 13th–19th June 1918 and recovered at No.2 Convalescent Depot until rejoining his unit on 10th July. From 29th August until 5th October he was attached to HQ MT Units. He was admitted to 33rd Stationary Hospital 14th 27th October and again in November and December. He was moved to 63rd General Hospital until embarking on 25th January 1919 for return to Britain via Taranto, arriving on 25th February. Discharged to the Class Z Reserve on 25th March 1919. Thomas married Florence Elizabeth Turton (1887–1962) in 1916 and they lived at 55 Broad Oak Street, Nottingham, later moving to 82 Chandos Street. They had a daughter, Florence Beryl Saunderson in 1920.
- Hilda 'Lilla' Saunderson (1892–1970) married Arthur Southern (1884–1946) in 1918. Arthur was a pawnbroker and inherited the family business after his mother died.

Alfred moved with the Battalion to Sutton Veny, Wiltshire in July 1916 and served in France from 4th February 1917 until 27th February 1918. He rescued a wounded man under heavy fire at Bullecourt on 14th May 1917 for which he received the Divisional Commander's certificate for gallant conduct and was promoted sergeant soon afterwards.

Awarded the VC for his actions at Hubner Farm, Ypres, Belgium on 20th September 1917, LG 8th November 1917. He was employed as a training instructor in France after the VC action. The VC was presented by the King at Buckingham Palace on 2nd January 1918. Alfred was commissioned in the Sherwood Foresters on 17th March 1919 and relinquished it on 1st September 1921, although he does not appear in the Army List after May 1920. He was the only member of the Post Office Rifles to be awarded the VC, but another Birmingham Post Office employee, Albert Gill, was awarded the VC during the Great War. Nottingham presented Alfred with an ornate silver tea service and a £100 War Bond, while postal workers bought him an inscribed marble clock. Birmingham presented him with an illuminated address and another clock.

Sergeant Albert Gill (1879–1916) was serving with 1st King's Royal Rifle Corps when he was awarded the VC posthumously for his actions at Delville Wood, France on 27th July 1916. Albert worked for the Post Office for seventeen years, initially as a town sorter at Birmingham Head Post Office in Pinfield Street and later as a delivery postman in Hockley. He left a widow, Rosetta, and two sons, Albert and Henry.

Alfred returned to the Post Office and in 1920 he moved to the Ministry of Labour and National Service. He was manager of the York Employment Exchange 1931–37 and then Manager of the Trade Board Section in Leeds. He returned to Birmingham in 1941 as the Senior Wages Inspector in the Ministry of Labour. In 1945 he travelled to India to talk to servicemen about resettlement arrangements. **Awarded the MBE while Senior Wages Inspector, Minister of Labour and National Service in recognition of his service to the Ministry of Labour 1920–51, LG 7th June 1951.** Alfred retired in November 1951 from his post as Deputy Regional Director of the Ministry of Labour in the Midlands. He returned to work briefly as a clerical officer at Handsworth Labour Exchange until suffering a stroke, which forced him into permanent retirement. He was also one time President of the City of Birmingham and York Circles of the Catenian Society, a Roman Catholic professional and businessmen's organisation.

Alfred Knight at a ceremony outside Birmingham Town Hall. The official party appear to be standing on top of a Mark IV Tank.

Alfred Knight died at his home at Elvetham Road, Edgbaston, Birmingham on 4th December 1960 and is buried in Oscott College Road Roman Catholic

Cemetery, Sutton Coldfield, West Midlands. He is commemorated in a number of other places:

Handsworth Labour Exchange (Birmingham Post & Mail).

- Alfred Knight Way on the Park Central residential development in Birmingham opened on 9th November 2006. Four of his grandchildren attended the naming ceremony.
- A painting of his VC exploit by Terence Cuneo was unveiled at the Royal Engineers Postal Depot, Inglis Barracks, Mill Hill on 17th March 1979. Mabel was in attendance.
- Named on a plaque commemorating 'The Post Office At War' in the General Post Office Memorial Garden at the National Memorial Arboretum, Alrewas, Staffordshire.
- The Department for Communities and Local Government decided to provide a commemorative paving stone at the birthplace of every Great War Victoria Cross recipient in the United Kingdom. Alfred's stone was unveiled at the Walk of Heroes, Hall of Memory, Centenary Square, Birmingham on 7th December 2015 by The Duke of Cambridge.
- Named on the Rifle Brigade Roll of Fame, Winchester Cathedral, Hampshire.

Alfred and Mabel's grave in Oscott College Road Roman Catholic Cemetery, Sutton Coldfield (Findagrave).

Mabel was living at 16 Wheeley's Road, Edgbaston in 1961, at 39 Bryanston Road, Solihull, Warwickshire in 1969, at Woodleigh Avenue, Birmingham in 1984 and 34 Redfern Avenue, Hounslow, Middlesex in 1984.

In addition to the VC he was awarded the MBE, British War Medal 1914–20, Victory Medal 1914–19, George VI Coronation Medal 1937 and Elizabeth II Coronation Medal 1953. His medals were purchased by the Post Office Museum for £13,600 at a Spink auction on 9th June 1992. The VC is held by The Postal Museum, Freeling House, Phoenix Place, London.

144039 CORPORAL FILIP KONOWAL
47th Battalion (British Columbia), Canadian Expeditionary Force

Filip Konowal was born on 15th September 1886 (25th March 1887 in his service record) at Kutkivtsi, (also seen as Kedeski or Kutcowce), Province of Podolia (also seen as Podeske, Podolskoy or Podolski), Guberny, Ukraine, which was then part of Russia. Kutkivtsi in now described as being in the Chemerivtsi Raion (district) of Khmelnytskyi Oblast in western Ukraine. His father, Miron/Myron/Meron Konowal, was a stonecutter. He married Eudkice, who had died by July 1915. Filip was educated at Kutkivtsi and worked on the family farm and in his father's stone quarry.

Filip married Anna Stanka on 25th July 1909 and they had a daughter, Maria/Marichka (1909–86). He was conscripted into the Imperial Russian Army in 1909 and became a bayonet instructor in the Russian Imperial Guards. After four years he finished his service in eastern Siberia and was selected as a lumberjack by a Canadian lumber company. He emigrated to Canada via Vladivostok, arriving at Vancouver, British Columbia in April 1913. Filip had to leave Anna and Maria behind when he went in search of work. Anna was his next of kin in his service records and payments were assigned to her from his military pay. He was unable to make contact with Anna after the war and in the Soviet era it was impossible to gain any information about his family. He was informed that they had died, possibly during the Great Famine of 1932–33, but it is now understood that Anna lived well into the 1940s. Maria married and she had a daughter, Hanna Vasylyivna Motsna, c.1936, who was living in Kutkivtsi in 2007, by when she was a grandmother.

Filip became a stonecutter and then a lumberjack in Western Canada for four months before moving to Eastern Ontario to work in the Ottawa Valley and l'Outaouis Regions, where there was a shortage of manpower for lumbering. However, the good times did not last long and he was soon working part time. On 12th July 1915 Filip enlisted in the Canadian Army. As he was born east of the Zbruch river, he had been a Russian citizen and was regarded as an ally in the war against the Central Powers. Thousands of other Ukrainians were interned because they had been born in Austro-Hungarian territory and were therefore regarded as enemy aliens. He was assigned to 77th Battalion, serving under Lieutenant Colonel DR Church. He was described as 5' 6½" tall with medium complexion, brown eyes, brown hair and his religious denomination was Ukrainian Greek Catholic. He gave his wife's address as P/O Husiatin, Podolsky, Gubernia, Selo, Kulkovtse/Kutcowce, Russia; there were a number of variations of spelling in his service record. He was admitted to hospital in Ottawa with an injured eye 15th–22nd February 1916.

After ten months training at Ottawa and Valcartier, Quebec he embarked on RMS *Missanabie* at Halifax, Nova Scotia on 19th June 1916, arriving at Liverpool, Lancashire on the night of 28th/29th June. He moved to Bramshott Camp, Hampshire, where he transferred to 47th Battalion on 6th July. On 22nd July he was promoted lance corporal and the same day he filled out a Military Will leaving everything to his wife (mother crossed out).

Until 1918 the Zbruch River, a 247 kms long tributary of the Dniester, was the border between Austria-Hungarian Galicia to the west and Imperial Russia to the east. The Treaty of Riga, which ended the Polish–Soviet War in March 1921, established the river as part of the Polish – Soviet border until 1939. Today it is the boundary between the Ternopil and Khmelnytskyi regions of Ukraine.

Filip sailed for France with the Battalion on 10th August, arriving the following day. He was wounded on the Somme on 16th September when a tendon in his right hand was severed. However, it cannot have been very serious as he was back on the Battalion's strength on 23rd September, although he was attached to No.4 Canadian Sanitary Section from 18th September until 23rd October. He was attached to 10th Canadian Field Company from 26th January 1917, but was admitted to 10th Canadian Field Ambulance with complicated diarrhoea on 13th February. He was transferred to 13th Canadian Field Ambulance with suspected dysentery on 14th February and later that day to No.1 Canadian Casualty Clearing Station. On 20th February he was admitted to 4th Stationary Hospital at St Omer and rejoined the Battalion on 1st March.

Bramshott Camp on Bramshott Common in Hampshire was used by the Canadian Army in both world wars.

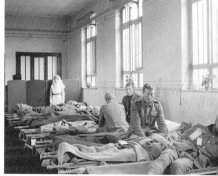

No.1 Canadian Casualty Clearing Station was at Bailleul from January 1916 until March 1917. This photograph was taken there in July 1916 and would have looked much the same when Filip Konowal passed through it in February 1917.

Filip was appointed acting corporal on 6th April and took part in the attack on Vimy Ridge on 9th April, during which he led a group of Canadian Japanese soldiers. **Awarded the VC for his actions at Lens, France on 22nd/23rd August 1917, LG 26th November 1917.** Having been seriously wounded during the VC action, Filip was admitted to No.6 Casualty Clearing Station on 23rd August and transferred to the St John's Ambulance Brigade Hospital, Étaples on 25th August. He was evacuated to Britain on 27th August on the strength of the British Columbia Regiment Depot, Seaford and was admitted to Beaufort War Hospital, Bristol on 30th August. On 12th September he was transferred to the Canadian Convalescent Hospital at Bearwood, Wokingham, Surrey, where his head wound was examined by Dr CK Wallace, a neuro-specialist. The wound had left a large jagged scar from just below his right eye down the cheekbone to his upper jaw, but at that time no lasting mental damage was suspected. He was discharged to 3rd Canadian Command Depot, Seaford on 22nd September and was sent on sick leave until 2nd October.

Queen Mary visiting the St John's Ambulance Brigade Hospital at Étaples in July 1917, a month before Filip was treated there for serious gunshot wounds to the head and neck.

Filip was taken on the strength of 16th Reserve Battalion on 1st November. The VC was presented by the King at Buckingham Palace on 5th December. The following day he was appointed to the Military Attaché at the Russian Embassy, London and on 30th December was appointed acting sergeant without pay and allowances. From 15th February 1918 he was on the strength of 1st Reserve Battalion and completed his tour of duty at the Russian Embassy on 8th July, when he reverted to acting corporal. On 1st August he was transferred to the Base Depot, Canadian Forestry Corps at Sunningdale, but on 10th September he returned to Canada and was taken on the strength of the Base Headquarters Unit of the Canadian Siberian Expeditionary Force

The camp at Seaford where the British Columbia Regiment Depot and 3rd Canadian Command Depot were based.

The Canadian Convalescent Hospital at Bearwood, Wokingham opened on 26th October 1915 and closed on 15th March 1919. The estate was purchased about 1830 by John Walter (1776–1847), owner of *The Times*, and his son John had the mansion built between 1865 and 1874. In March 1921 it was taken over by the Royal Merchant Seaman's Orphanage (Royal Merchant Navy School from 1935) when it moved from Snaresbrook. In 1961 it became the fee-paying Bearwood College (Reddam House).

on 18th September. The main function of the CSEF was to help guard the Trans-Siberian Railway from Vladivostok to Omsk in Western Siberia. Interpreters and translators were essential and Filip was one of more than one hundred serving Ukrainian-Canadians who volunteered for duty in Siberia.

On 1st October he was appointed acting sergeant and sailed from Vancouver, British Columbia on 11th October on RMS *Empress of Japan*, arriving at Vladivostok on 26th October. He was found guilty of being absent without leave from 11.00 p.m. on 14th December until 10.30 a.m. on 15th December, resulting in him reverting to acting corporal and forfeiting of one day's pay. He served with a small liaison group at Omsk, the main Allied base about 2,700 miles west of Vladivostok, from 28th March until 1st June 1919. Filip rejoined the main body of the CSEF and departed Vladivostok for Vancouver on SS *Monteagle* on 5th June, arriving on 20th June. He was discharged on 4th July 1919. His final medical inspection noted a number of mental and physical

Filip Konowal outside Buckingham Palace.

RMS *Empress of Japan* (5,905 tons) approaching Vancouver in 1893. She was built in 1890–91 at Barrow, England for the Canadian Pacific Railway and was known as the 'Queen of the Pacific'. She had made 315 trans-Pacific crossings by 1922 and held the record for crossing the Pacific for over two decades. Her sister ships were RMS *Empress of China* and RMS *Empress of India*. During the First World War she was refitted as an armed merchantman and later as an armed auxiliary cruiser. After the war she was the only one of the three *Empress* ships to return to the trans-Pacific route. She ceased service in 1922 and was scrapped in 1926. A second RMS *Empress of Japan* was built in 1929.

In Imperial days, Omsk was the seat of the Governor General of Western Siberia and later of the Governor General of the Steppes. It grew significantly as a result of the construction of the Trans-Siberian Railway in the 1890s and became a major logistics centre. Soon after the 1917 October Revolution, anti-Bolshevik White Russians took control of Omsk and the Provisional All-Russian Government was established there in 1918. Omsk became a major objective for the Red Army and the White Russians were eventually forced to abandon the city and retreat eastwards along the Trans-Siberian Railway.

Omsk railway station during the First World War.

SS *Monteagle* (5,498 tons) was built for the Canadian Pacific Line in 1898 at Jarrow-on-Tyne. She was scrapped in 1926.

problems. He suffered partial paralysis of a facial muscle on the left side as a result of bullet wounds received at Lens and his left hand was partly crippled as a result of wounds received at Ypres. He also suffered from fluttering of the heart and periodic pains on exertion.

On 19th July 1919 Filip led the Peace Parade of Veterans through Ottawa to the Parliament Buildings. The following evening, Filip and Leonti Diedek, a fellow veteran from France and Siberia, went to an area of downtown Hull known as 'Little Chicago' that was notorious for bootleggers, brothels and gambling dens. They were to inspect some bicycles at the house of William (Vasyl) Artich, a bicycle salesman and small-time bootlegger. They stopped at a restaurant/store operated by Mike Romaniuk. Filip ordered supper while Diedek went to Artich's. A fight broke out. Artich punched and kicked Diedek, who tried to flee, but Artich stunned him with a large stone. Filip heard the struggle and left the restaurant to find that Artich had dragged the stunned Diedek into the house. Filip forced the front door and Artich released Diedek. According to Henri Simard, a neighbour, Artich struck Filip on the head and then slashed his hand and wrist with a butcher's knife. In the ensuing struggle, Filip gained control of the knife and killed Artich with a thrust to the heart. Constables Coté and Meranger arrived and Filip admitted he had killed Artich in self-defence and commented, *I've killed fifty-two of them, that makes it the fifty-third*. Filip and Diedek were arrested on suspicion of murder. A coroner's jury convened on 22nd July. The constables gave their testimony then the wife of the deceased, Sophie, and members of his gang were questioned. Sophie had not seen Filip kill her husband. John Pavliuk saw Artich stagger into the house and collapse dead on the living room floor, but did not see the stabbing. Jacques Ouellette supported Diedek's claim that Artich had struck him with a large stone. The most damaging testimony came from Romaniuk who alleged that Filip had taken a large knife from his restaurant. Filip was formally charged with murder the following day while Diedek was released with a suspended sentence for disturbing the peace.

At the preliminary hearing, Sophie Artich and members of the Artich gang changed their testimony. She stated she had seen Konowal kill her husband in cold blood and had obtained the weapon at Romaniuk's restaurant. George Wright discredited her story and destroyed the credibility of the other gang members. Romaniuk admitted that he ran the restaurant/store as a front for Artich's bootlegging and could not identify the weapon as one of his knives. Between July 1919 and April 1921, Filip's trial was postponed three times. Veterans and others raised $8,000 to have him released on bail on 18th October. He was suffering recurring problems from the gunshot wound to his head and underwent a series of X-rays and other tests at Saint Luke's Hospital, Ottawa. He was examined by Dr CK Wallace, who had last seen him in England in 1917. A fracture of the skull had not properly

Hull is the oldest part of Gatineau, on the opposite bank of the Ottawa River from Ottawa city. It was famous for its nightlife from 1917 to 2000. Prohibition on alcohol began in 1916 in Ontario and continued until 1927. Hull enacted local prohibition laws in 1918, which led to an enormous increase in bootlegging and the town becoming known as 'Little Chicago'. Crime rates soared and in 1919 Hull's prohibition laws were repealed, making the town attractive again for people in neighbouring Ontario, but the area's notorious reputation continued.

healed and was putting increasing pressure on his brain. By early 1920 he was experiencing long periods of acute pain followed by memory loss for hours or even days. During these periods he had flashbacks to the war, believing he had to defend his men and assumed individuals around him were the enemy. Colonel Church and the veterans retained the services of George C Wright KC as defence counsel and added Alban Germain KC, a noted Montreal defence lawyer, and R MacDonald, a leading Hull lawyer, to the defence team.

The trial commenced on 15th April and the defence did not contest that Filip had killed Artich. Diedek and Simard confirmed that Artich had struck Filip on the head and then stabbed him in the arm. Specialist witnesses, including Dr Wallace, were unanimous that the skull fracture had rendered Filip mentally unstable and not responsible for his actions. Artich's blow to Filip's head had triggered the mental episode that resulted in the victim's death. Summing up, Judge Cousineau instructed the jury that justice would be served if Filip were found not guilty by reason of insanity. The jury complied. However, medical experts advised that Filip posed a potential danger to himself and others. As a result Judge Cousineau ordered him to

Saint Luke's Hospital, Ottawa where Dr CK Wallace discovered Filip's fractured skull had not healed properly.

be detained until he could be placed in an asylum. Although found not guilty, he was confined for the next seven years, firstly in Hull Jail until 27th April 1921 and then at Saint Jean de Dieu Hospital (now Louis Hippolyte Lafontaine Hospital) in Montréal. From about 1927 he was in the Hospital for the Criminally Insane in Bordeaux, Quebec.

St Jean de Dieu Hospital, where Filip was an inmate for six years, opened in 1873. It was affiliated with the Faculty of Medicine at Montréal University to look after people with severe mental health problems. On 16th May 1890 about one hundred people were killed in a fire that almost completely destroyed the building. In 1976 it became the Louis Hippolyte Lafontaine Hospital.

Filip was released in 1928 and found it difficult to find work, but secured employment on the maintenance staff of the Ottawa Electrical Company building. The Depression of the mid-1930s led to staff reductions and Filip was unemployed until he was offered a job as a junior caretaker in the Canadian House of Commons in 1936 by Milton Gregg VC MC, the Sergeant-at-Arms. One of Filip's duties was to clean the Hall of Fame. When asked about his employment, he commented, *I mopped up overseas with a rifle, and here I must mop up with a mop.* The Prime Minister, William Lyon Mackenzie King, spotted the crimson ribbon of the VC on Filip's uniform and had him assigned as a special custodian in the Prime Minister's Office. The position was a combination of caretaker, messenger and commissionaire. He continued working there until his death.

In 1928, Filip enlisted in No.4 Company, Governor General's Foot Guards in Ottawa, under the command of Major Milton Fowler Gregg VC MC. In 1934 he married a French-Canadian widow, Juliette Leduc–Auger (1900–87). She had two children from her first marriage – Roland Auger, who married and had at least two children, and Albert Auger. Juliette was also caring for an invalid brother. They lived at 75 Rue Demontigny, Hull, Ontario during the 1930s and 1940s and moved to 24 Spadina Avenue, Ottawa on 3rd July 1956. There were no children.

When the Vimy Memorial was due to be dedicated in 1936, Thomas Wayling, President of the Parliamentary Press Gallery and one of the reporters covering Filip's trial in 1921, wrote to Prime Minister Mackenzie King requesting that the government assist in sending Filip to the dedication ceremony. The request, forwarded to the Minister

The Canadian Parliament building in 1927.

of National Defence, was rejected and he was left behind. He was presented to King George VI and Queen Elizabeth at Rideau Hall in Ottawa during the Royal Visit to Canada in 1939. The King shook hands with Filip during the dedication of the National War Memorial. Filip enlisted briefly in Le Regiment de Hull at the outbreak of the Second World War, but was considered too old for active service. He joined the Legion de Hull, Branch No.30, Royal Canadian Legion on 20th December 1945 and the Montgomery Branch No.351 of the Royal Canadian Legion and the Army, Navy and Air Force Association in 1956 after moving to Ottawa.

William Lyon Mackenzie King OM CMG PC (1874–1950) was Prime Minister of Canada 1921–30 and 1935–48.

Milton Fowler Gregg VC PC OC CBE MC ED CD (1892–1978) was awarded the VC for his actions during the Battle of the Canal du Nord on 28th September 1918. He was Sergeant at Arms of the House of Commons 1934–39. In the Second World War he served in the West Nova Scotia Regiment before commanding training centres in Canada as a brigadier. He was a MP 1947–57, then became UN representative in Iraq, UNICEF administrator in Indonesia and Canadian High Commissioner in British Guiana. His medals were stolen from the Royal Canadian Regiment Museum in London, Ontario in 1978 and have never been recovered.

Filip was guest of honour of the Ukrainian Canadian Veterans Association at their convention at the Chateau Laurier Hotel in Ottawa on 4th/5th December 1954. During the banquet he was appointed Honorary President of the Association and was presented with a gold watch engraved with the VC and 'For Valour'. When he was invited to attend the VC Centenary celebrations in London in 1956, the cost of travel was paid by the Canadian Federal Government, but he was unable to raise sufficient finances for clothing and living expenses. He requested assistance and the President of Royal Canadian Legion Branch 360, Stephen Pawluk, appealed for help and over $400 was raised. Juliette ensured that he had a new suit, coat and hat for the trip. Filip was one of nine VC winners to fly to England on 23rd June 1956, while the remainder travelled by sea. In a letter to Pawluk, Filip expressed his thanks in his usual humble manner:

Please be kind enough to extend my thanks to every Ukrainian Canadian Legion Branch who have contributed to the large sum of money sent to me lately. I was very surprised and I was not expecting that much. I knew I had friends amongst the Ukrainian people but I never thought they could do so much for a poor fellow like me. This will certainly help me to enjoy my trip in England and will be glad to tell you about it when I return. Thanks again to all of them and specially you Mr Pawluk as I am sure it is through you I received so much.

Filip's health deteriorated, but he continued working until 21st April 1959, when he became seriously ill. He was admitted to the Veterans Pavilion, Ottawa Civic Hospital, where he died on 3rd June 1959. His funeral, with full military honours, was held at St John the Baptist Ukrainian Catholic Church, Ottawa and he is buried in Notre Dame de Lourdes Cemetery, Montreal Road, Ottawa (Section A, Lot 502). His original headstone was replaced with a granite CWGC style headstone in 1996, which was consecrated in a Ukrainian religious ceremony. There was an honour guard and a bugler and piper from the Foot Guards. Filip is commemorated in a number of other places:

Filip Konowal meeting King George VI in 1939 during the dedication of the Canadian National War Memorial.

- Konowal VC Branch No.360, Royal Canadian Legion (Ontario Command), 326 Queen Street West, Toronto, Ontario. Filip became its Patron on 7th November 1953. It was also known as the Ukrainian Canadian Veterans Branch, unofficially CLUB 360 (Canadian Legion Ukrainian Branch 360). On 15th September 1996, the Branch established the Konowal Prize, an annual scholarship to support Ukrainian officer cadets at the Royal Military College, Kingston or to finance research at a Canadian university in Ukrainian and Ukrainian-Canadian military history. The Minister of National Defence announced the establishment of the Prize on 21st August 1996, the 69th anniversary of Filip's VC action. He also unveiled a trilingual plaque in the presence of Claudette Wright, Filip's step-granddaughter, her daughter Lynne and Claudette's brother Brian. The Branch closed when the Ontario Command suspending its Charter on 7th June 2005.

- His VC action was featured in Issues 786 and 1313 of the Victor Comic entitled *A True Story of Men at War* dated 13th March 1976 and 19th April 1986.
- Filip Konowal VC Memorial Award for Lifetime Achievement established in 1995 by the Ukrainian-Canadian Professional and Business Association of Ottawa. It is awarded annually to those who have made

Filip's grave in Notre Dame de Lourdes Cemetery, Montreal Road, Ottawa, with his second wife's grave on the left.

substantial contributions over their lifetime to the development of the Ukrainian-Canadian community.

* Plaque unveiled in Cartier Square Drill Hall of the Governor General's Foot Guards, Ottawa on 15th July 1996.
* Plaque unveiled on 23rd November 1996 at New Westminster, British Columbia, home of the Royal Westminster Regiment.
* Cairn unveiled at Selo Ukraina in the Ukrainian Centennial Memorial Park, Dauphin, Manitoba in 1997.
* Commemorative bust by Petro Kulyk, unveiled in Kutkivtsi, Ukraine in 2000.
* A 46 Cent postage stamp featuring Filip's portrait was authorised in limited quantities in July 2000, but it was not a regular Canada Post stamp.

The memorial plaque to Filip Konowal at Cartier Square Drill Hall of the Governor General's Foot Guards, Ottawa. The Foot Guards perpetuate 2nd Canadian Battalion (Eastern Ontario Regiment) and Filip's original unit, 77th (Ottawa) Battalion CEF.

* The Order of Merit of the National Council of Veteran Associations in Canada was presented by Cliff Chadderton, chief of the War Amputees Association, to Filip's step-granddaughter, Claudette Wright, in Ottawa in August 2000.
* Two 49 Cent postage stamps in honour of the ninety-four Canadian VCs were issued by Canada Post on 21st October 2004 on the 150th Anniversary of the first Canadian VC's action, Alexander Roberts Dunn.
* Plaque at 242 Route de Béthune, Lens, France, unveiled on 22nd August 2005.
* Victoria Cross obelisk to all Canadian VCs at Military Heritage Park, Barrie, Ontario dedicated by The Princess Royal on 22nd October 2013.
* Named on one of eleven plaques honouring 175 men from overseas awarded the VC for the Great War. The plaques were unveiled by the Senior Minister of State at the Foreign & Commonwealth

Filip's memorial plaque on Route de Béthune (N43), Lens set into the front wall of No.242 behind a demarcation stone, which marks the limit of the German advance during the 1918 offensives. The plaque is northwest of the memorial to 906 employees of Lens Mining Company who died during the war. Rather unusually the plaque is 1,700m as the bullet flies from where the VC action took place.

Office and Minister for Faith and Communities, Baroness Warsi, at a reception at Lancaster House, London on 26th June 2014 attended by The Duke of Kent and relatives of the VC recipients. Filip is named on two plaques. The Canadian plaque was unveiled outside the British High Commission in Elgin Street, Ottawa on 10th November 2014 by The Princess Royal in the presence of British High Commissioner Howard Drake, Canadian Minister of Veterans Affairs Julian Fantino and Canadian Chief of the Defence Staff General Thomas J Lawson. The Ukrainian plaque is at the British Embassy, Kiev and his great granddaughter, Valentyna Bortniak, was present at the unveiling in November 2014.

- The Secretary of State for Communities and Local Government, Eric Pickles MP, announced that Victoria Cross recipients from the Great War would have commemorative paving stones laid in their birthplace as a lasting legacy of local heroes within communities. The stones would be laid on or close to the 100th anniversary of their VC actions. For the 145 VCs born in Australia, Belgium, Canada, China, Denmark, Egypt, France, Germany, India, Iraq, Japan, Nepal, Netherlands, New Zealand, Pakistan, South Africa, Sri Lanka, Ukraine and United States of America, individual commemorative stones were unveiled at the National Memorial Arboretum, Alrewas, Staffordshire by Prime Minister David Cameron MP and Sergeant Johnson Beharry VC on 5th March 2015.
- Plaque at St John the Baptist Ukrainian Catholic Church, 952 Green Valley Crescent, Ottawa.
- Plaque at the Armoury of The Royal Westminster Regiment, Richmond, British Columbia.
- Bronze plaque at the Royal Canadian Legion Building, Ottawa, Ontario.
- An oil painting of him by Major Ambrose McEvoy hangs in the Canadian War Museum, Ottawa, Ontario.
- Plaque on a memorial to the ninety-nine Canadian VCs in York Cemetery, Toronto.

In addition to the VC he was awarded the British War Medal 1914–20, Victory Medal 1914–19, George VI Coronation Medal 1937, Elizabeth II Coronation Medal 1953 and the Russian Cross of St George 4th Class. He was granted permission to wear the Russian award on 19th January 1918. When he died his medals passed to his widow and it is possible that she sold them to a medal collector/dealer in the Ottawa-Hull area before or in 1969. Former Flight Lieutenant GR Bohdan Panchuk, a RCAF Second World War veteran and prominent member of the Ukrainian Canadian Veterans' Association, looked after them for a brief period until the medals were acquired by the Canadian War Museum in 1969 for $3,750. The VC went missing about four years later. In the 1990s a woman took a Hawaiian silver dollar and a VC to a coin/medal dealer who compared the VC with a picture of a Canadian Victoria Cross (instituted in 1993), which bears the words 'Pro Valore' instead of 'For Valour'. He declared the medal and the coin were both fakes and paid her just $20 for the pair. The Cross was placed in a drawer and forgotten until a representative of the Jeffrey Hoare Auction House in London, Ontario asked if he had anything interesting for the next auction. The VC was remembered and authentication was carried out, resulting in the Cross being listed in the April 2004 catalogue with an estimated value of $120,000. Joe Geurts, senior vice-president of the Canadian War Museum, was alerted, together with the Ukrainian Canadian Civil Liberties Association, Branch 360 of The Royal Canadian Legion (Konowal Branch), Ron Sorobey co-author of *Konowal*, Inky Mark MP for Dauphin-Swan River, the Metropolitan Ottawa Police, the news media of Canada and the Royal Canadian Mounted Police. They combined efforts to remove the Konowal VC from the sale and have it returned to the Canadian War Museum, 1 Vimy Place, Ottawa, Ontario on 28th June 2004, where it is still held.

ACTING MAJOR OKILL MASSEY LEARMONTH
2nd Battalion (Eastern Ontario Regiment), Canadian Expeditionary Force

Okill Learmonth was born on 20th February 1894 at St Louis Road, Quebec, Montreal, Canada. He was an only child. His father, William Learmonth, a stenographer, married Martha Jane née Richardson. She was living at 43 Murray Avenue, Quebec in 1916 and was Okill's next of kin in August 1917. By 1918 William was Deputy Lieutenant Governor of the Province of Quebec.

Okill was educated at St George's School, Quebec and Quebec High School. He worked for the Union Bank of Canada in Quebec and then on a private estate on Anticosti Island, Quebec, before being appointed to the Provincial Treasury Department at Quebec. He was elected a member of the Literary and Historical Society of Quebec on 11th March 1914.

Okill enlisted in 8th Regiment Royal Rifles on 1st October 1912. He enlisted in the Canadian Expeditionary Force at Valcartier, Quebec on 29th August 1914 (22893), described as 5′ 8″ tall, with fair complexion, blue eyes, fair hair and his religious denomination was Presbyterian. He had a birthmark on his left leg and a scar on his nose. He also bore the scar of a recent varicocele operation. He was attested on 22nd September and sailed for Britain on SS *Scotian* with 12th Battalion on 3rd October, arriving on 15th October.

He transferred to 2nd Battalion and sailed for France on 8th February. In his will, dated 20th February 1915, he left everything to his mother. He was promoted lance corporal on 4th June. On 2nd November he reported sick and was transferred to 2nd Canadian Field Ambulance and No.3 Canadian Casualty Clearing Station where he was found to be suffering from acute gonorrhoea. He was moved by 5

SS *Scotian* (10,322 tons) was built by Harland and Wolff as SS *Statendam* for the Holland America Line. She was launched in 1898 and was sold to the Allan Line in 1911 and renamed *Scotian*. In 1917 the Allan Line was taken over by Canadian Pacific Line. In 1922 she was renamed SS *Marglen* and was scrapped in 1927.

The Royal Free Hospital was founded in 1828 to provide free care to those of little means and it moved to Gray's Inn Road in the 1840s. In 1974 the Royal Free moved to its current location on the site of the former Hampstead General Hospital and the North Western Fever Hospital.

Ambulance Train on 6th November and was admitted to 24th General Hospital, Étaples on 7th November. He was transferred to 9th Stationary Hospital, Le Havre on 9th November. He transferred to No.1 Camp Details on 2nd December and to No.19 Camp Hospital, Rouelles near Le Havre on 16th December, before returning to the Battalion on 26th December.

Okill was granted leave 10th–18th April 1916 and was promoted corporal on 6th May. He was in action in the Observatory Ridge sector near Ypres and received gunshot wounds to his right index finger and leg on 13th June. He was admitted to 7th Stationary Hospital, Boulogne next day and was evacuated to Britain on HMHS *Jan Croydel*, where he was admitted to the Royal Free Hospital, Gray's Inn Road, London on 15th June.

Okill Learmonth (right) in France in 1915 (Library & Archives Canada).

A ward at 7th Stationary Hospital, Boulogne.

In the meantime Okill was commissioned as a temporary lieutenant on 12th June. On 30th June a Medical Board at the Department of Medical Services, Canadians at 86 Strand, London found him unfit for service due to his injuries and the strain of constant duty. He was granted leave in Canada from 30th June to 28th September. Okill travelled home to Canada on RMS *Empress of Britain* 5th-14th July. On his return he was attached to 12th Reserve Battalion at Shorncliffe, Kent on 29th September and transferred to 2nd Battalion on 16th October. He attended a Lewis gun course 10th-17th December.

RMS *Empress of Britain* (14,189 tons) was built by Fairfield Shipbuilding at Govan, Glasgow and was launched on 11th November 1905. Her maiden voyage to Quebec left Liverpool on 5th May 1906. At the time she and her sister ship, RMS *Empress of Ireland*, were the fastest ships on the Canadian run. A few weeks after RMS *Titanic* sank, *Empress of Britain* also struck an iceberg, but the damage was minor. In July 1912, she rammed and sank the collier SS *Helvetia* in fog off Cape Magdelene in the St Lawrence River estuary. In 1914 she became an armed merchantman in the South Atlantic. In 1915 she changed role to troop transport and that December collided with and sank a Greek steamer in the Straits of Gibraltar and next night she collided with an empty French troopship, the *Djuradjura*, cutting it in half. She returned to trans-Atlantic traffic after the war and was used to return CEF troops from England to Canada. In 1924, she was renamed SS *Montroyal* and underwent a major refit and again in 1926. Her final voyage of 190 return trips across the Atlantic commenced from Antwerp on 7th September 1929. In 1930 she was sold for scrap.

Okill was involved in the storming of Vimy Ridge on 9th April 1917 and was appointed temporary captain the following day. On 15th April he was appointed acting major and assumed command of No.3 Company. **Awarded the MC for his actions during a frontal assault on 3rd May at Fresnoy-en-Gohelle – he found himself the senior officer of his Battalion after reaching the objective where he directed the consolidation and made personal reconnaissances under heavy fire. In addition to taking a number of prisoners he was involved in silencing many pockets of resistance, passed through the village and reached the final objective to the east of it, LG 16th August 1917.** He was granted ten day's leave in Paris from 25th May.

He is believed to have been engaged to Nursing Sister Irene Winifred Lamarche (born 1881 at Mattawa, Ontario). He changed his will on 21st March 1917 to make her the beneficiary, except for £10 to his batman, 412123 Private Ernest Alfred Insley (killed on 9th April 1917 and buried in Écoivres Military Cemetery, Mont St Eloi, France – V D 8). Irene was attached to HQ Canadian Army Nursing Service, 133 Oxford Street, London and also served at 8th Canadian General Hospital at St Cloud, Paris. It is possible they planned to marry in Paris and from 1st July 1917 he assigned $50 per month to Mrs OM Learmonth (wife) at 25 Midland Road, Gloucester. However, Okill visited the Consulate-General in Paris and postponed the ceremony. Irene was released

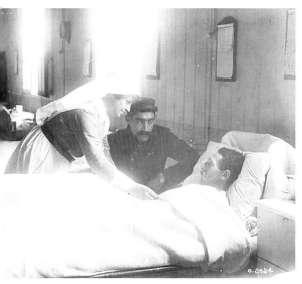

8th Canadian General Hospital began treating French wounded in November 1915 at St Cloud, Paris and continued until January 1919.

133 Oxford Street, London was CAMC Headquarters during the First World War (Jerry Latter).

on medical grounds and returned to North Bay, Ontario sometime in 1917. It is possible that the wedding was cancelled due to Irene being repatriated.

Awarded the VC for his actions at Hill 70, east of Loos, France, on 18th August 1917, LG 8th November 1917. He died of wounds sustained in the VC action on 19th August at No.7 Casualty Clearing Station and is buried in Noeux-les-Mines Communal Cemetery, near Lens, France (II K 9). His medals, plaque and scroll were sent by post to his mother at 65 Murray Avenue, Quebec in 1921 and 1922. He is commemorated in a number of other places:

25 Midland Road in Gloucester had a sinister later history when Fred and Rose West lived there. Rose West murdered Fred's eight-year-old stepdaughter Charmaine there in 1971, but her remains were not discovered until 1994. In the meantime the Wests moved to 25 Cromwell Street, where they killed another ten women.

• Learmonth Avenue, Quebec.
• A wooden plaque bearing fifty-six maple leaves each inscribed with the name of a Canadian-born VC holder was dedicated at the Canadian Forces College, Toronto on Remembrance Day 1999.
• Memorial and painting by James Quinn at the Canadian War Museum, Ottawa, Ontario.

- Two 49 Cent postage stamps in honour of the ninety-four Canadian VCs were issued by Canada Post on 21st October 2004 on the 150th Anniversary of the first Canadian VC's action, Alexander Roberts Dunn.
- Victoria Cross obelisk to all Canadian VCs at Military Heritage Park, Barrie, Ontario dedicated by The Princess Royal on 22nd October 2013.
- The Secretary of State for Communities and Local Government, Eric Pickles MP, announced that Victoria Cross recipients from the Great War would have commemorative paving stones laid in their birthplace as a lasting legacy of local heroes within communities. The stones would be laid on or close to the 100th anniversary of their VC actions. For the 145 VCs born in Australia, Belgium, Canada, China, Denmark, Egypt, France, Germany, India, Iraq, Japan, Nepal, Netherlands, New Zealand, Pakistan, South Africa, Sri Lanka, Ukraine and United States

Okill Learmonth's grave in Noeux-les-Mines Communal Cemetery, near Lens.

of America, individual commemorative stones were unveiled at the National Memorial Arboretum, Alrewas, Staffordshire by Prime Minister David Cameron MP and Sergeant Johnson Beharry VC on 5th March 2015.
- Named on one of eleven plaques honouring 175 men from overseas awarded the VC for the Great War. The plaques were unveiled by the Senior Minister of State at the Foreign & Commonwealth Office and Minister for Faith and Communities, Baroness Warsi, at a reception at Lancaster House, London on 26th June 2014 attended by The Duke of Kent and relatives of the VC recipients. The Canadian plaque was unveiled outside the British High Commission in Elgin Street, Ottawa on 10th November 2014 by The Princess Royal in the presence of British High Commissioner Howard Drake, Canadian Minister of Veterans Affairs Julian Fantino and Canadian Chief of the Defence Staff General Thomas J Lawson.
- Plaque on a memorial to the ninety-nine Canadian VCs in York Cemetery, Toronto.

In addition to the VC and MC he was awarded the 1914–15 Star, British War Medal 1914–20 and Victory Medal 1914–19. The VC is held by the Governor General's Foot Guards Museum, 2 Queen Elizabeth Drive, Ottawa, Ontario.

8133 SERGEANT JOSEPH LISTER
1st Battalion, The Lancashire Fusiliers

Joseph Lister was born at 65 Fenney Street, Higher Broughton, Salford, Manchester, Lancashire on 19th October 1886. His father, also Joseph Lister (1854–1907), was born at Tibbermore, Perthshire. Joseph senior set up a bookkeeping business at Burnage, Manchester, before moving to Hayfield, Derbyshire. He married Nancy née Gee (1856–1909) at Hayfield in 1877 and they were living at Market Street in 1881. By 1891 they had moved to 1 Conway Street, Broughton, Lancashire and by 1896 they were at 17 Ash Street, Harpurhey, Manchester. By 1901 they were living at 20 Prenton View, Reddish, Cheshire. Joseph junior had three sisters:

- Esther Eva Lister (1882–1858) was a jam potter in 1901. She married Herbert Hodson (1881–1959), a warehouseman in a jam factory, in 1901 and they were running a fish and chip shop in 1911, living at 83 Broadstone Road, Reddish. Living with them were Esther's three siblings.
- Nancy Lister (1890–1955) was a maker up in a jam works in 1911. She married Peter Dootson Dean (1888–1946), a piecer in a cotton mill, in 1911. He was living with his parents at 43 Davies Street, Ancoats, Manchester. He was a mule minder in a cotton mill in 1939 and they were living at 13 Prenton View, Reddish. They had two children – Noah Dean 1913 and Harold Dean 1914.
- Florence Maud Lister (1896–1989) married Alfred Smith (1898–1949), a cotton spinner, in 1918. They were living at 10 Bedford Street, Stockport in 1939. They had two children – John Smith 1921 and Clarence Smith 1925. Florence married Samuel Walker in 1956.

Joseph's paternal grandfather, John Lister (1819–90), married Nancy née Savage (c.1819–72) in 1840 at Blackburn, Lancashire. They were both born at Oswaldtwistle, Lancashire. In 1861 he was a madder dyer at a print works and they were living at Lucas Terrace, Scotch Row, Hayfield, Derbyshire. By 1871 they had moved to South View, Hayfield and their grandson, Walter (born 1868), was living with them. In addition to Joseph they had five other children:

- William Lister (born 1842) was a labourer at a print works in 1861.
- Elizabeth Lister (born 1845) was a sewing machinist at a print works in 1861.
- John Ramsden Lister (1847–1917) was a labourer at a print works in 1871. He married Amelia Ashdown (c.1855–1903) in 1878. By 1881 he was a calico dyer and

they were living at Church Street, Bollington, Cheshire and had moved to 2 Platt Street, Newton, Cheshire by 1901. They had two children – Gordon Lister 1885 and Doris Lister 1895.

- Nancy Lister (1850–51).
- Thomas Lister (born 1851) was a labourer in 1871.
- Richard Lister (born 1858).

Joseph's grandparents, John and Nancy Lister, were both from Oswaldtwistle, Lancashire.

His maternal grandfather, John Gee (c.1818–90), married Esther née Mason (c.1814–79) in 1840. They were both born at Hayfield, Derbyshire. He was a machine printer calico and they were living at Top of Mill, Hayfield in 1841. By 1851 they were at 23 Back Grosvenor Street, Hayfield and at Bridge End, Hayfield in 1861. In 1871 they were at Church Street, Hayfield and in 1881 he was living with his son William and his family. In addition to Nancy they had six other children:

- John Gee (born c.1841).
- Joseph Gee (born 1843) was a joiner in 1861. He married Mary Storer (born c.1844) in 1866 at Chapel en le Frith, Derbyshire. They were living at Fishers Lane, Hayfield in 1881. He was a carpenter and joiner in 1911 and they were living at Hazel Villas, Hayfield. They had seven

Joseph's maternal grandparents, John and Esther Gee, lived on Church Street, Hayfield in 1871.

children including – Martha Gee 1869, Annie Gee 1874, Esther Gee 1870, Mary Gee 1876, Joe Gee 1878, Edith Gee 1879.
- George Gee (1845–71) was a labourer in a print works in 1861.
- Mary Ann Gee (1847–68) was working in a cotton band mill in 1861. She probably had a son, Walter Gee, born in 1868, who was living with his grandparents in 1871.
- William Gee (1850–83) was a butcher in 1871. He married Nancy Pollard (born 1852) in 1877. They were living at Market Street, Hayfield, Manchester in 1881 with their nephew, Walter, probably the son of William's sister Mary Ann.
- Esther Gee (born 1852).

Joseph was educated until 1899 probably at Broughton and Harpurhey. He was a member of St Elizabeth's Boys' Brigade in Reddish, near Stockport and was employed as a labourer at Lowe's Chemical Works in Reddish.

Joseph Lister married Harriet née McAulay (7th January 1888–17th December 1962), registered in the second quarter of 1911 at Stockport. They lived at Prenton View, Reddish, Stockport before moving to 25 David Street. She was a daily cleaner in 1939. They had seven children:

- Eva Lister (born 9th November 1911) married John Ellis (born 1908), a general labourer at a brickworks, in 1934. They were living at 3 Prenton View, Reddish in 1939. They had three children – Joseph Ellis 1935, Jean Ellis 1936 and Neil Ellis 1939.
- Neil Lister (born 25th October 1913) lived at 11 Victoria Avenue, Manchester, Lancashire. He was a grinder in an engineering works in 1939. He married Muriel Wheatley (born 1917) in 1942 and they had a son, Neil Lister, the same year.
- Victor Lister (1919–30).
- Mary Lister (born 26th June 1920) was a doubler in a cotton mill in 1939. She married John Wright in 1946 and they had two children – Eric Wright 1946 and Joan Wright 1949.
- Esther Lister (14th December 1922–18th May 2003) was a doffer in a cotton mill in 1939. She married Henry Timperley in 1949. They had two daughters – Elaine Timperley 1953 and Susan Timperley 1955.
- Joan Lister (19th April 1925–1980) married George Bernard Harrison (1925–2005) in 1948 and they had a son, Christopher Harrison, in 1950.
- Jack Lister (born 22nd March 1931) married Mavis A Gibson in 1954. They had three children – Janet Lister 1955, Keith Lister 1959 and David Lister 1960. It is understood that the marriage ended in divorce. Jack married Nora Cherry in 1965 and Mavis married Herbert Duffin 1963.

Harriet's father, Neil Macaulay/ McAulay (c.1845–92) was born in Dunbartonshire, Scotland. He married Emily née Twenlow (1861–1943) in 1879 at Chorlton, Lancashire. In 1891 he was a machine calico printer and they were living at 1 Florence Grove, Levenshulme, Lancashire. She

St Elisabeth's Church in Reddish was built by William Henry Houldsworth, a mill owner in Reddish, and was named after his wife. It was consecrated in 1883.

was living at 2 Seddon Street, Reddish by 1917 and was still there in 1939. In addition to Harriet they had six other children:

- Mary Elizabeth McAulay (1880–1933) is believed to have married Joseph Heywood in 1913.
- John McAulay (c.1882–1917) served as 25594 Private J Macaulay, 11th Lancashire Fusiliers and died on 4th August 1917 (Lijssenthoek Military Cemetery – XVII G 10A).
- Agnes McAulay (born 1884).
- Annie McAulay (1885–1940) married Robert Adshead (1887–1961), a general labourer in an iron foundry, in 1909 and they had two children – Arnold Adshead 1909 and Agnes Adshead 1913. They were living at 6 Sneddon Street, Reddish in 1911.
- Florence McAulay (born 1890).
- Neil McAulay (1891–1923) served in the First World War.

Joseph enlisted on 7th September 1914 and trained with 11th Battalion at Codford on Salisbury Plain, at Boscombe, Dorset and Malplaquet Barracks, Aldershot, Hampshire. He went to France on 25th September 1915. He was evacuated with trench fever in early 1917, returned to France ten weeks later and may have transferred to 1st Battalion at that time. Joseph was recommended for the DCM before the VC action. **Awarded the VC for his actions near Poelcapelle, Belgium on 9th October 1917, LG 26th November 1917.**

Joseph returned to England in December 1917. The VC was presented by the King at Buckingham Palace on 19th December. He was given a civic reception in Reddish, including a torchlight procession to the Town Hall, and was presented with gifts of money from his former workmates. **Also awarded the Belgian Médaille Militaire, LG 15th April 1918.** He was wounded four times in the mouth, shoulder and leg, although none was serious enough to warrant evacuation. Later he recovered from gassing at Temple Road Military Hospital, Birkenhead, an external ward of 1st Western General Hospital. He returned home in May 1918 to further receptions, during which he was presented with £150 in War Bonds from public subscription. He also received a gold medal from St Elizabeth's Church Lads' Brigade. He was discharged in 1919.

Post-war Joseph became a postman in Reddish and later was a watchman at Craven's works. By 1939 he was

The Belgian Médaille Militaire was established in December 1873 for non-commissioned officers and other ranks for gallantry or long service. Gallantry awards have the ribbon shown here, but long service awards have a different pattern.

Stockport Infirmary was founded as a dispensary in 1792 and the Infirmary opening in 1833. It closed in 1996 and is now Millennium House, home of the government's Pension Service.

Houldsworth Working Men's Club (Reddish Houldsworth School Archives).

a chief watchman there. He was a life member of Houldsworth Working Men's Club. He attended the VC Garden Party at Buckingham Palace on 26 June 1920 and the VC Dinner at the Royal Gallery of the House of Lords, London on 9th November 1929.

Joseph became a school-crossing attendant after retiring from full-time work.

He served in the Lancashire Fusiliers in the Second World War and afterwards worked as a school-crossing attendant until forced to retire due to his wife's ill health. He attended the Victory Day Celebration Dinner and Reception at The Dorchester, London on 8th June 1946 and the VC Centenary Celebrations at Hyde Park, London on 26th June 1956.

Joseph Lister died at Stockport Infirmary on 19th January 1963. He is buried in Willow Grove Cemetery, Reddish, Stockport (Section P, Grave 9931) and is named on the Roll of Honour in St Elisabeth's Church, Reddish.

In addition to the VC he was awarded the 1914–15 Star, British War Medal 1914–20, Victory Medal 1914–19 with MID Oakleaf, Defence Medal, War Medal

Joseph Lister's grave in Willow Grove Cemetery, Reddish.

1939–45, George VI Coronation Medal 1937, Elizabeth II Coronation Medal 1953 and Belgian Médaille Militaire. The VC was listed for sale by Eugene G Ursal of Ottowa, Canada for $C26,500 on 1st April 1986. It was purchased privately by Michael Ashcroft in 1991 and is displayed in the Imperial War Museum's Lord Ashcroft Gallery.

The Imperial War Museum in Lambeth, London, home of Lord Ashcroft's VC Gallery.

15805 PRIVATE ARNOLD LOOSEMORE
8th Battalion, The Duke of Wellington's (West Riding Regiment)

Arnold Loosemore was born at 3 Dyson Lane (now Dyson Place), Sharrow, Sheffield on 7th June 1896. The surname has also been seen as Loosmoore, Lucemoore and Loosemoor. His father, George Henry 'Harry' Loosemore (1860–1933), was a farm servant in 1871 and was later head gardener at the General Cemetery, Sheffield. He married Selina née Hoyland (1859–1925) in 1882. They were living at 3 Dyson Lane, Ecclesall, Sheffield in 1901, before moving to 1 Lescar Lane, Sharrow Vale Road, Sheffield. Arnold had seven siblings:

• Joseph Joshua Loosemore (1883–1934) was a shoeing-smith. He married Jane Elizabeth Turner (1888–1956) in 1906 and they were living at 7 Stone Terrace, Stewart Road, Sheffield in 1911 and at 35 Eastwood Road in 1914. He served for a period in the West Yorkshire Militia and enlisted in the Army Service Corps on 10th August 1914 (MS/2657), joined at Avonmouth with medical category B1 and was employed as a blacksmith. He was described as 5′ 4″ tall, weighing 154 lbs, with fresh complexion, brown eyes, brown hair and his religious denomination was Church of England. He served in France from 15th August with 4th Ammunition Park. Joseph's disciplinary record was poor. He was confined to camp for fourteen days for being in a café/public house in prohibited hours and absent from billets whilst being a prisoner at large on 5th December at St Omer. He was awarded three extra guards for not complying with an order on 15th December at Wardecques and was again confined to camp for six days for being absent from roll call on 26th December. On 10th March 1915 he was confined to camp for seven days for being absent from roll call at

Flêtre and on 21st March was confined to camp for seven days for breaking out of camp and being absent for over twelve hours. He was confined to camp for six days for being absent from roll call on 16th June. Joseph was on leave 4th-9th August and returned to 4th GHQ Ammunition Park on 10th August. He was awarded twenty-eight days Field Punishment No.1 for breaking out of camp, being absent and found in a private house and giving a false name and number to the Mounted Military Police on 10th September. On 27th October he was again awarded twenty-eight days Field Punishment No.1 and forfeited a day's pay for breaking out of camp while undergoing medical treatment and being absent from billets. He was absent from roll call on 15th January 1916 (punishment unclear) and was confined to camp for five days for being absent from roll call on 23rd April. On 29th June he was absent and drunk, for which he forfeited fourteen days pay. Having been sent on leave 10th-21st December and being treated in hospital for an eye complaint 22nd-23rd December, he was posted to 50th Auxiliary (Motor Transport) Bus Company on 28th January 1917. His next leave was 1st-15th January 1918, but he was awarded twenty-eight days Field Punishment No.1 for overstaying his leave, failing to entrain at Victoria Station on 16th January and remaining absent until 24th January. He was awarded four days Field Punishment No.2 and had to pay for a new cap and ASC badge for being absent without leave for ten hours on 19th-20th May. He forfeited fourteen days pay for being absent from roll call for fifteen minutes on 2nd August, but despite repeated instances of absence, he was appointed acting corporal on 30th September and paid from 2nd October. He was on leave 20th December 1918–3rd January 1919 and returned to Britain permanently on 30th April until transferred to the Class Z Reserve on 29th May 1919. Joseph became a senior mechanic with the Commonwealth War Graves Commission at St Omer, France and died there on 12th February 1934 (Longuenesse (St Omer) Souvenir Cemetery – CWGC Grave 5). Joseph and Jane had seven children:

- Leonard Loosemore (1907–08).
- Nita/Neta Loosemore (1908–81) married Louis Rhodes (1906–75) in 1928 and they had four children – Betty Rhodes 1929, Louis Rhodes 1930, Dennis Rhodes 1931 and Patricia A Rhodes 1942. He was a general labourer in an armament works and they were living at 94 Halliwell Close, Sheffield in 1939.
- Annie Loosemore (1911–63) married Cyril Shaw (1906–68) in 1930. He was a conductor with Sheffield Corporation Transport and by 1939 was a master plasterer, when they were living at 27 Eastwood Road, Rotherham. They had two children – Jean Shaw 1930

Joseph's grave in the Commonwealth War Graves Commission plot of Longuenesse (St. Omer) Souvenir Cemetery.

and David Shaw 1940. David married Norma Hayley (born 1954) in 1985. Norma is third cousin once removed of Francis Arthur Jefferson VC.

○ Lily Loosemore (1912–78) married Cyril Baxter (1912–90) in 1937 and they were living at 35 Eastwood Road, Rotherham in 1939, close to her sister Annie at No.27. Cyril was a strop steel furnace man. They had two children – Dawn Baxter 1939 and Anthony J Baxter 1945.

○ Joseph Loosemore (1915–86) married Emily Bolan (born 1914) in 1940. Emily was living at 84 Halliwell Close in 1939 and was a spoon and fork buffer. Joseph was living as a single man at 94 Halliwell Close and was a roadworks labourer. At the same address was his sister Nita and her husband, Louis Rhodes. Emily married John C Wood in 1950 and Joseph reportedly married Ruby Jane Wilson (born 1918) in 1966.

○ Selina Loosemore (born 1917) married William F Sykes (born 1913) in 1938 and they had two children – Beryl Sykes 1940 and Howard W Sykes 1942.

○ Eva M Loosemore (born 1921).

After Joseph died, Jane married Septimus Inman Sellers (1872–1935) in 1935. Septimus had married Florence Edith Graves (born 1860) in 1896 at Salford, Lancashire. He enlisted in 6th York and Lancaster at Pontefract, Yorkshire on 23rd January 1915 (6/18578) giving his age as thirty-seven years and nine months and his employment as painter. His wife was recorded as Edith Greaves (sic) crossed out and replaced with Ada Elizabeth Baker. Septimus had a poor disciplinary record, including absence, overstaying his pass and drunkeness. He was posted to Malta on 2nd July, where he was hospitalised with diarrhoea and evacuated to England, arriving on 30th October. He was absent from the Depot on 17th January 1916 (forfeited eight days' pay) and was declared a deserter on 11th February 1916. It is not clear what became of Florence, although she may have married James Laming in 1912, as a Florence E Laming of about the right age died in Sheffield in 1929. Septimus married Ada Elizabeth Baker (1880–1928) on 3rd April 1915 at Leeds Register Office and they were living as husband and wife at 22 Chad Street, Newtown, Leeds in 1911, declaring they had been married for eight years. He was recorded as James Sellars. Septimus and Ada had six children, four of them before they married – Ada Sellers 1904, Sydney Sellers 1905, Lena Sellers 1907, Thomas Nicholson Sellers 1912, Agnes Sellers 1917 and Ernest Sellers 1918. Ada, Sydney, Lena and Thomas are confirmed by Septimus' service papers in 1915. Sydney and Lena are recorded with their parents in the 1911 Census and Ada was with her maternal grandparents, Albert and Mary Baker. Jane was living at 139 Neill Road, Sheffield in 1939.

• George Arthur Hoyland Loosemore (1885–1951) worked in a brickyard and married Ethel Linacre (1889–1940) in 1913. He served in the King's Own Scottish Borderers for eight years before the war and re-enlisted in the Royal

Engineers in September 1914. They were living at 12 Court, 3 House, Portland Street, Sheffield in 1939, by when George was a plasterer's labourer. They had nine children:

- George Loosemore (born 1914) married Alice Johnson in 1941 and they had six children – June Johnson 1949, Carole A Johnson 1951, Malcolm G Johnson 1953, Diane Johnson 1954, Anthony C Johnson 1956 and Glenn Johnson 1957.
- Ethel Loosemore (1915–17).
- Cyril Loosemore (born 1916) married Mary E Lishman (born 1928) in 1947 and they had four children – Keith J Loosemore 1948, Lorraine Loosemore 1950, Ian Loosemore 1952 and Michelle Bernadette Loosemore 1967.
- Edna Loosemore (born 1918) married Albert H Gray (born 1915) in 1937 and they had two children – Patricia Gray 1939 and Janet R Gray 1942.
- Fanny Loosemore (born 1920) married Edward Yeardley (born 1912) in 1942 and they had two children – Margaret Yeardley 1947 and Graham Yeardley 1948.
- Herbert Loosemore (1924–44) served as a private (4698891) in 16th Durham Light Infantry and died on 7th March 1944 (Cassino Memorial, Italy).
- Edith Loosemore (born 1926) married Bernard Holland (born 1924) in 1948 and they had two children – Judith Holland 1952 and David Holland 1955.
- Arthur Loosemore (born 1928) married Norma Groom (born 1935) in 1955 and they had a son, Martin W Loosemore in 1961.
- Wilfred Loosemore (1930–94) married Mavis Lee (1936–95) in 1953 and they had six children – Brian Loosemore 1954, Michael Loosemore 1956, Angela Loosemore 1960, Andrew Loosemore 1962, Lynne Loosemore 1965 and Dawn Loosemore 1969.

- John William Loosemore (1887–1964) was a dray boy and served in the Royal Engineers during the war. He married Emma Walker (1893–1978) in 1919 and they had two children – William Loosemore 1920 and Dinah Mary Loosemore 1921, who married Denys Weare in 1944 and they had twins, Denys M Weare and Robin D Weare in 1947.
- Harry Loosemore (born 1890) enlisted in the King's Own Scottish Borderers in 1906 but his discharge was delayed by the war, during which he was slightly wounded.
- Mary Loosemore (1892–93).
- Frank Loosemore (1894–1956) enlisted in the Royal Engineers in September 1914.
- Ernest Loosemore (1898–1955) joined the York and Lancaster Regiment in October 1914, lying about his age. He was slightly wounded and later became a prisoner of war. He married Elsie Caswell (1899–1971) in 1919 and they had seven children:
  - Kenneth Ernest Loosemore (1923–88) married Irene Alice Gregory (1925–97) in 1946 at Southwark, London and they had two children – Robert P Loosemore 1947 and Pauline SJ Loosemore 1950.

- Donald Edward Loosemore (1925–76) married Elizabeth Boyle Wright (born 1927) in 1948 at Saltcoats, Ayrshire and they had two children – Joyce Mary Loosemore 1951 and Donald James Loosemore 1955.
- Audrey J Loosemore (1926–30).
- William A Loosemore (born 1928) married Teresa C Arundell (born 1938) in 1968 at Maidstone, Kent and they had three children – Stephen William Loosemore 1968, Mark Sidney Loosemore 1969 and Kerry Jane Loosemore 1972.
- Dorothy Ivy Loosemore (born 1931) married Stanley W Loosemore (born 1921) in 1959.
- Ronald Loosemore (born 1934) married Rita A Wilson in 1960 and they had two children – Stephen John Loosemore 1966 and Jacqueline Anne Loosemore 1968.
- John Loosemore (1935–79) married Jean Helen Reader (born 1934) in 1953 at Tonbridge, Kent and they had three children – Kenneth J Loosemore 1953, Graham N Loosemore 1954 and Alan B Loosemore 1956.

Ernest was a motor driver in 1939, living at 3 Deacon Street, Southwark with Florence M Loosemore (1907–87), an unpaid domestic. She was showed as being married, but crossed out and replaced with single. Ernest and Florence married in 1951 at Southwark. She was born as Florence Maud Nash and married Edward Barlow in 1928 at Stepney, London. It is assumed that the marriage failed, as Edward married Rosetta Stow in 1946.

Arnold's paternal grandfather is not known. His grandmother, Hannah Charlotte Loosemore, was born at Whitestaunton, Devon in 1841. She was a charwoman, living with her father at Brinsworth, Sheffield in 1861 and 1871. In addition to George she had two other children:

- James Frederick Loosemore (born and died 1863).
- Clara Loosemore (1867–85) was a servant at the home of William Graves and his family at Angel Inn, Brinsworth in 1881.

Charlotte married James Lever (c.1839) in 1875. He had married Sarah Westnidge (c.1837–73) in 1863. Charlotte was working as a servant/manager of a lodging house at 33 & 35 Westgate, Rotherham in 1881. Charlotte and James had a son, William Lever (1876–1947), a painter and paperhanger, who married Lucilla Gertrude Woollen (1866–1936) in 1897. They may also have had Rose Lever (1878–79).

Rotherham's Westgate in the early 1900s.

His maternal grandfather, Joshua Hoyland (c.1827–84), was an agricultural labourer and by 1881 was a stone quarryman. He married Mary née Hinchliffe (c.1830–1909), a charwoman, in 1855. They were living at 3 Mill House, Rails Road, Bradfield, near Sheffield in 1861, at 124 Lansdowne Road, Ecclesall Bierlow, Sheffield in 1871 and at Greystones Road, Ecclesall Bierlow in 1881. In addition to Selina they had six other children:

- John Arthur Hoyland (1856–80).
- Clara Hoyland (born c.1862).
- William Henry Hoyland (1861–1905) was a brickyard labourer in 1881.
- Alice Hoyland (1867–80).
- George Hoyland (born 1868).
- Sarah Hannah 'Annie' Hoyland (1871–1924) married John Johnson (c.1868–1931), an engineer, in 1895. John was a stationary engine driver by 1901 and a cutlery factory engineer in 1911. They were living at Crosspool in 1891, at 165 Rockingham Street, Sheffield in 1901 and 1911 and at 118 Gell Street, Sheffield in 1924. They had a daughter, Evelyn Johnson, in 1896, who died nine weeks later. John Johnson was living at 44 Selbourne Road, Sheffield when he died in September 1931.

Arnold was educated at Clifford Church of England School, Psalter Lane, Sheffield. By 1911 he was living and working as a cowboy on Samuel Clarke's Lowfields Farm, Fulwood, near Sheffield. When war broke out he tried to enlist, but was rejected for being in poor physical shape and took a job as a carter with a coal merchant to build himself up. Arnold enlisted in the York and Lancaster Regiment (18746) on 2nd January 1915, adding a year to his age. He joined the 3rd Battalion on 9th January and was awarded five days' duties for being absent from parade on 17th March. He transferred to the West Riding Regiment Depot on 19th March and departed England on 1st September, arriving in the Mediterranean theatre on 9th September. He served at Gallipoli with 8th Battalion from 11th September. The Battalion moved to Mudros in December, to Egypt on 7th February 1916 and to France on 7th July. He was confined to barracks for seven days for being absent from billets on 7th July 1917. After training as a Lewis gunner he is reputed to have shot down a German aircraft.

Clifford Church of England School, Psalter Lane, Sheffield has been there since 1832, but the majority of the buildings date from 1896 (Ray Howard).

Awarded the VC for his actions south of Langemarck, Belgium on 11th

August 1917, LG 14th September 1917. He wrote home, *You will be having a great surprise one of these days.* Promoted corporal soon after the VC action. The VC was presented by the King at Buckingham Palace on 2nd January 1918. On his return to Sheffield on 3rd January he was greeted by a crowd of 2,000, but war weariness had set in and there was a lack of bands and the normal pomp and ceremony of such occasions. He was accompanied by his father and two of his brothers as the other four brothers were serving in France and Italy. The Lord Mayor, Alderman A Cattell, used the occasion to shame those who chose to work in munitions factories rather than fight for their country.

Arnold returned to France on 12th January. 8th West Riding disbanded on 13th February and he transferred to 1/4th West Riding on 1st May. Promoted sergeant 6th May. **Awarded the DCM for his actions at Langemarck on 19th/20th June 1918; on a fighting patrol his officer was wounded and the platoon was scattered by enemy bombs, he rallied the men and brought them back in good order with all the wounded. On a subsequent occasion he handled his platoon with great skill and complete disregard for his own safety under heavy machine-gun fire. Owing to his determination and powers of leadership the platoon captured the enemy post they were attacking, LG 3rd October 1918.** He was reprimanded for being absent from tattoo roll call on 3rd October until reveille on the 4th. Arnold received a gunshot wound to the left leg on 13th October 1918 near Villers-en-Cauchies, France. The leg was amputated and he was evacuated to England on 27th October and held on the Depot strength from the 28th. The DCM was presented by the King at Victoria Hall, Sheffield on 20th May 1919. Arnold was discharged unfit for war service on 13th May 1920. He was assessed as 60%

Victoria Hall is the main Methodist building in Sheffield, standing on the site of the original Wesleyan Chapel consecrated in 1780 by John Wesley. It was demolished in 1906 and the current building opened in September 1908. In September 1909 the Trades Union Congress held its annual conference there and it was the main concert venue in Sheffield until the City Hall opened in 1932. During both World Wars it was used to care for members of the armed forces.

Arnold Loosemore with CSM John Williams, 10th South Wales Borderers, who was awarded the VC for his actions at Villers Outreaux, France on 7th-8th October 1918.

Redmires, near Sheffield, at almost 1,000′ above sea level can be a bleak and inhospitable place in winter. The camp seen in this view was the first base of the famous Sheffield City Battalion (12th Battalion, The York & Lancaster Regiment).

The Lescar Hotel on Sharrow Vale Road, Sheffield, where Amy Morton lived before she married Arnold Loosemore in 1920.

disabled and was awarded a pension payable until 16th August 1921. Sheffield raised £1,000 to be invested on his behalf.

He tried running a poultry farm at Redmires near Sheffield, but it proved to be too physically demanding. He took up photography and got about in a pony and trap purchased for him with a helper-driver to assist his mobility, but he lived in a three-storey court house and could not cope with the stairs. The Rotary Club added a large hut at the rear for him to work and sleep in.

Arnold Loosemore married Amy née Morton (1st August 1897–10th February 1956) on 24th August 1920 at St Andrew's Church, Sharrow. She was living at the Lescar Hotel, Sharrow Vale Road, Sheffield. They had a son, Arnold Loosemore, born on 28th April 1921, who served in the Royal Engineers in North Africa in the Second World War. He married Audrey Sellers in 1947 and they had three children – Andrew D Loosemore 1947, Andrea V Loosemore 1950 and Kevin V Loosemore 1954.

Amy's father, Joseph Morton (1849–1922), was a knife cutter. He married Emma née Linnaker (1856–1910) in 1883. They were living at 8 Court, 1 House, Hoyle Street, Sheffield in 1901 and by 1911 Joseph had moved to 1 & 3 Fornham Street, Sheffield. In addition to Amy they had five other children:

St Andrew's was the Anglican parish church in Sharrow from 1869. Despite its fine appearance, the foundations were inadequate and by 1996 it was unsafe. The congregation moved into the Church Centre next door (St Andrew's Hall) and in 1998 joined with Psalter Lane Methodist Church to form a local ecumenical partnership. The old parish church was demolished in 2000.

- Joseph Morton (1883–1937) was a warehouse assistant in 1901.
- Sarah Ann Morton (born 1885) was a spoon and fork polisher in 1901.
- Mary Anise Morton (born 1890).
- Edith Annie Morton (1892–1938) married George Brooham (1888–1944) in 1911. He was a messenger on the Midland Railway in 1901 living with his father at 6 Cuthbert Road, Nether Hallam, Yorkshire. They had a son, Frank Brooham, in 1914, who became a schoolteacher. George married Ethel Thompson (1889–1951) in 1941. She was living at 61 Morgan Avenue, Sheffield in 1939 as Ethel Brooham, but George was living at 554 Bellhouse Road, Sheffield with his son Frank. At the time George was a widower, employed as a vertical press assistant.
- Ellen Morton (born 1895).

Hoyle Street, Sheffield, where the Mortons were living in 1901. The whole area has been redeveloped and Hoyle Street's cobbles and three storey court houses have given way to a dual carriageway.

Arnold was confined to bed for the last year of his life, during which his health continued to deteriorate as a result of the war and he contracted miliary tuberculosis. He battled the disease for a few weeks, but died at his home at 11 Court, 3 Stannington Road, Stannington, Sheffield on 10th April 1924. His death came only four days after his maternal aunt, Sarah Hannah Johnson. They were both buried in the Johnson family plot at Ecclesall New Churchyard, Sheffield, Yorkshire with full military honours on 15th April 1924. The funeral cortege started at Stannington and concluded at Ecclesall. The gun carriage was drawn by six horses ridden by war veterans. The guard at the gate of Hillsborough Barracks presented arms as the cortege passed. The firing party was provided by 30th Battery RFA. The Lord Bishop of Sheffield, Canon Houghton, and the Reverend W Seldon Morgan officiated. Because the grave is in the old part of the churchyard and difficult to find, Brass Founders (Sheffield) donated three cast bronze signage plaques to direct visitors from the church door. Arnold is commemorated in a number of other places:

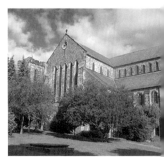

All Saints Church, Ecclesall, Sheffield. Arnold Loosemore is buried in the churchyard.

The guard at the gate of Hillsborough Barracks presented arms as Arnold's funeral cortege passed by.

- Memorial tablet unveiled at St Andrew's Church, Sharrow by his former CO, Lieutenant Colonel

The Rotary Club hut (on the right) built for Arnold is still in use at the Rotary Centre in Castleton, Derbyshire.

Arnold Loosemore was buried with his maternal aunt, Sarah Hannah 'Annie' Johnson, who died four days previously. The grave is signed from the church door.

AL Mowat DSO MC. It is now at Clifford Church of England School, Psalter Lane, Sheffield.

- Loosemore Drive, Sheffield was named in 1983 following a lengthy campaign by his son Arnold. In December 2014 the Lord Lieutenant of South Yorkshire and the Lord Mayor of Sheffield unveiled a bronze plaque to replace the original stolen in 1986.
- The hut erected for Arnold by the Rotary Club was moved to Shatton, Derbyshire and later to the Rotary Centre in Castleton, Derbyshire, where it still provides holiday accommodation for disadvantaged children.
- An English oak donated by Norman Armstrong-Kersh MBE, director of 'Life for a Life', was dedicated to Arnold Loosemore and fourteen other First World War servicemen in Ecclesall Churchyard on Remembrance Sunday 2014.
- The Department for Communities and Local Government decided to provide a commemorative paving stone at the birthplace of every Great War Victoria Cross recipient in the United Kingdom. A commemorative stone for Arnold was dedicated at Sheffield War Memorial, Barker's Pool on 11th August 2017 to mark the centenary of his award.

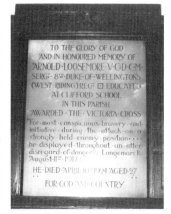

The memorial to Arnold formerly in St Andrew's Church, Sharrow is now at Clifford Church of England School, Psalter Lane, Sheffield (Ray Howard).

Amy struggled financially following her husband's premature death and was presented with many of the costs of his funeral. The government refused to pay her a war widow's pension because Arnold was not serving at the time of their marriage and she was fully aware of his injuries when she married him. She was restricted to drawing interest from the civic trust fund, about £25 per year, and was forced to take another job. In 1942 Amy met Sergeant J Hannah VC on

The Forum Cinema on Herries Road, Sheffield opened in September 1938. In 1942 Amy Loosemore appeared on stage there with Sergeant John Hannah VC. It closed in 1969 and was briefly a bingo hall before being demolished and replaced with a supermarket, where the author had a holiday job stacking shelves in the early 1970s.

the stage of the Forum Cinema, Sheffield and talked about her husband and son then serving in North Africa.

In addition to the VC and DCM he was awarded the 1914–15 Star, British War Medal 1914–20 and Victory Medal 1914–19. The VC and DCM were sold at Sotheby's for £1,080 on 1st May 1969 to Kenneth R Thomson (later 2nd Lord Thomson of Fleet), Chairman of Times Newspapers. In 1986 the VC was sold to John Marskell of Toronto, who is understood to have sold it to fine arts and antiques valuer Wayne Gardiner of Perth, Western Australia. The medals were displayed at the Army Museum of Western Australia 28th–29th October 2006 with two other loaned VC groups – Frederick William Bell VC (Western Australian Museum, Perth) and Cliff Sadlier VC (St George's Cathedral, Perth). The current location of the VC is not known.

200717 LANCE SERGEANT TOM FLETCHER MAYSON
1/4th Battalion, The King's Own (Royal Lancaster Regiment)

Tom Mayson was born at Silecroft, Cumberland on 3rd November 1893. His father, William Mayson (1853–1915), was a farm servant at Town Ends, Whitbeck, Cumberland in 1871. Tom's mother, Annie late Raw née Kneebone (1851–1896), married John Raw (c.1852–77) in 1873. Annie married William Mayson in 1879. By 1881 he was a pit worker at the Hodbarrow iron ore mine. The family was living at 3 Commerce Terrace, Whicham, Cumberland in 1881 and at 3 Kiln End, Whicham in 1891. William married Elizabeth Mason (1870–1956) in 1900. She was the licensee of the John Bull Inn at Silecroft and by 1918 was the publican of the Prince of Wales Hotel, Foxfield near Ulverston, Lancashire. Tom had ten siblings from his parents' three marriages:

• Eleanor Ann Raw (born 1874) married Abraham Hartley (born 1875) in 1902. He was a farm servant in 1881, a ploughman in 1901 and later a domestic gardener. They were living at Ramsden Cottage, Little Mill, Dalton-in-Furness, Lancashire in 1911. They had two children – Arthur Harry Hartley 1904 and Abraham Francis Hartley 1910.

- Daniel Raw (1876–1962), a general farm labourer, married Margaret Crosthwaite Maxwell (1888–1973) in 1908. They were living at Holmrook, Cumberland in 1911. They had five children – Isabella Raw (born and died 1908), Eleanor 'Nellie' Ann Raw 1910, Isabella Raw 1912, Daniel Raw 1913 and John C Raw 1916.

Tom's father worked at Hodbarrow, one of the largest West Cumbrian iron mines, in production 1848–1968. It produced 25M tons of ore and at its peak about 1902 was producing almost 1.9 M tons annually.

- John Mayson (1880–81).
- Charles Mayson (1884–1968), registered as Mason at birth, was a farm worker. He married Ruth Singleton (1891–1972) in 1913. They had six children – Charles Mayson 1913, Dorothy Mayson 1915, Mary H Mayson 1918, Tom F Mayson 1920, Daniel Mayson 1925 and Frank Mayson 1929.
- Martha Mayson (1887–96).
- Frank Burney Mayson (born 1891) was a horseman on a farm at Holm Gate, Whitbeck, Cumberland in 1911. He emigrated to Poplar Point, Manitoba, Canada and enlisted in 1st Depot Battalion, Manitoba Regiment on 16th

Tom's stepmother, Elizabeth Mason, was the publican of the Prince of Wales Hotel, Foxfield in 1918 (Robert Gale).

July 1918 at Winnipeg (D3348243). He was described as 5′ 4¾″ tall with ruddy complexion, blue eyes and light coloured hair.

- John Mayson (born c.1893). His relationship is confirmed only by his presence in the family in the 1901 Census. No birth record has been found.
- Percy Harold Mayson (1901–70) enlisted in the Border Regiment (30129). He married Elizabeth A Towers in 1925 and they had a son, William A Mayson in 1930.
- Doris Mayson (1903–89) married John N Harrison in 1921. They had five children – Marjorie Harrison 1923, William B Harrison 1924, Joan Harrison 1927, John Harrison 1928 and Doris Harrison 1935.
- Stanley Dodgson Mayson (1908–64) married Nora Murray in 1931. They had four children – Eileen Mayson 1932, Sheila A Mayson 1934, Stanley IG Mayson 1939 and Kathleen E Mayson 1942.

Tom's paternal grandfather's name is not known, but he is understood to have been born c.1830 and died before 1861. Tom's paternal grandmother, Hannah née Barton (born c.1832), was a widow living with her brother John Barton and his family at Waterloo Street, Cockermouth in 1861.

Tom's maternal grandfather, Daniel Kneebone (c.1826–92), was born at Redruth, Cornwall. He was a labourer in an iron mine and by 1871 was a mine captain. He married Ann née Charnley (c.1831–73) in May 1849 at Ulverston and the family was living at Oubas Hill, Ulverston, Lancashire in 1851. In addition to Annie they had five other children:

- Harriet Kneebone (1850–91) married Richard Henry Bennetts (1852–94) in 1874. He was born at Pinks Moor, Cornwall. They had seven children – Richard Henry Bennetts 1876, Elizabeth Ann Bennetts 1878, Alice Grace Bennetts 1879, William Bennetts 1881, Daniel Bennetts 1882, Francis Kneebone Bennetts 1887 and Edith Bennetts 1889.
- Francis Kneebone (1854–58).
- Margaret Kneebone (born 1857) married Henry Parker in 1880.
- Daniel Kneebone (born 1862) was an iron miner in 1881.
- Ellen Kneebone (born 1864).

Daniel senior married Susannah Walker (born 1845) in 1875 and they were living at Lindal Moor, near Dalton-in-Furness, Lancashire in 1881. Susannah married John Langford in 1895 at Ulverston.

Tom was educated at Whicham School and was then employed as a labourer on Mr Dawson's Gutterby Farm at Whitbeck. He enlisted on 16th November 1914 (2950) and went to France on 3rd May 1915. Having been admitted to 1/3rd Highland Field Ambulance at Hillencourt on 16th November, he passed through No.51 (Highland) Casualty Clearing Station at Villers Bocage north of Amiens next day, 6 Ambulance Train on the 19th and arrived at St John's Ambulance Brigade Hospital, Étaples later that day. Tom was evacuated to England on SS *Stad Antwerpen* on 10th December. Having recovered, he embarked at Southampton on 18th April 1916 and joined 55th Division Base Depot at Rouen next day. He rejoined the Battalion on 4th May and was attached to Brigade on 20th May until returning to the Battalion again on 1st June. He was sentenced to ten days' Field Punishment No.1 on 2nd June for making a false statement to the CO and having a dirty rifle in the trenches. However, this indiscretion does not appear to have held him back as he was promoted to lance corporal on 11th July and corporal on 8th August.

Tom received a gunshot wound to the hand on 25th September and was admitted to No.15 Casualty Clearing Station at Hazebrouck before transferring to 6th General Hospital at Rouen next day. He moved to 23rd Infantry Base Depot, Étaples on 30th September and rejoined the Battalion on 18th October. He was admitted to 2/1st Wessex Field Ambulance on 9th December, moved to No.2

2nd Australian General Hospital at Wimereux near Boulogne (Australian War Memorial).

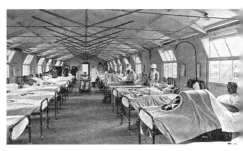

A surgical ward at St John's Ambulance Brigade Hospital, Étaples.

Canadian Casualty Clearing Station at Remy Siding on the 13th and 2nd Australian General Hospital at Wimereux near Boulogne on 15th December, before being evacuated to England on 27th December. He returned to France on 20th March 1917, joined 23rd Infantry Base Depot next day and rejoined the Battalion on 21st April. Appointed unpaid lance sergeant on 15th July.

Awarded the VC for his actions at Wieltje, Belgium on 31st July 1917, LG 14th September 1917. When he heard that he had been recommended for the VC, he wrote to his mother, enclosing a card from Major General Hugh Jeudwine, GOC 55th Division:

I have been recommended for a great honour, as you will see by the card, but I have not got it yet. It will be a surprise to a good few if I get it, which I think I will, but I will not tell you what it is because I have not got it yet, but you might be able to guess what it is. I expect to be home in a few weeks if this decoration comes through.

Major General (later Lieutenant General KCB KBE) Hugh Jeudwine was commissioned in the Royal Artillery in 1882. During the First World War he commanded 41st Brigade and 55th Division from 1916. After the war he became Chief of General Staff, HQ British Army of the Rhine and then commanded 5th Division in Ireland. His last appointment before retiring was Director General of the Territorial Army 1923–27.

SS *Stad Antwerpen* was sister ship to *Ville de Leige*. Tom Mayson was evacuated to Britain on both ships during the course of the war. *Stad Antwerpen* was built in 1913 at Hoboken, Belgium and her maiden voyage was Antwerp to Plymouth, but her normal route was Ostend to Dover/Folkestone. She was used as a troop and hospital ship 2nd October 1915 – 12th December 1919 and was scrapped in 1935.

Tom was promoted sergeant on 20th August and returned to England on leave 18th November–3rd December. Millom and Silecroft gave him a great welcome before his investiture, raising £200 in cash and £169 in war savings certificates. The VC was presented by the King at Buckingham Palace on 28th November 1917.

Back in France, Tom was admitted to 33rd Field Ambulance with myalgia on 28th December. He was moved to No.1 Casualty Clearing Station at Chocques on 2nd January 1918, to 22nd General Hospital at Camiers on the 4th and was evacuated to England on 11th January on the *Ville de Liège*. Held on the strength of the Depot from 12th January, he joined 3rd (Reserve) Battalion at Harwich on 31st January. Having recovered, he embarked at Folkestone and disembarked at Boulogne on 6th April. He reported to the Base Depot at Étaples the same day and rejoined the Battalion on 14th April. The onset of winter seems to have caused a recurrence of myalgia and he was admitted to 1/3rd West Lancashire Field Ambulance on 2nd October, moved to 12th Stationary Hospital at St Pol on the 5th and to 83rd General Hospital at Boulogne on the 12th. Tom moved to 3rd Infantry Base Depot at Rouen on 4th November and 3rd Employment Base Depot on 25th November. He transferred to the Labour Corps (471805) on 4th December and was posted to the Chinese Labour Corps Base Depot. He served in 186th Company, Chinese Labour Corps until returning to England via Dieppe on 29th January 1919. Tom was disembodied from Heaton Park

SS *Ville de Liège* entered service in January 1914 for the Ostend – Folkestone service. During the war she was a troop and hospital ship and was involved in the evacuation of Ostend 10th-14th October 1914. In January 1919 she and *Stad Antwerpen* brought Belgian refugees back from Britain. On 11th February 1929 *Ville de Liège* sank on rocks inside Dover harbour, but was refloated, repaired and the opportunity was taken to refit her to take cars as well as foot passengers. In June 1940 she carried refugees to Britain. In February 1941 she was taken up by the Royal Navy as HMS *Ambitious*, a minesweeper depot ship. In June 1944 she was involved in the Normandy landings and from 19th June was inside the Mulberry harbour at Arromanches directing minelaying and minesweeping operations. After renovation she reopened the Ostend service on 22nd October 1945 and was scrapped in 1950.

The Chinese Labour Corps was recruited to free troops for front line duty by performing support work and manual labour. About 100,000 worked for the British and another 40,000 for the French. About 2,000 died in service, mainly from influenza, but some by enemy action. Over 5,000 remained in France after the war and started the Chinese community in Paris.

Dispersal Centre on 5th March 1919 with 20% disability due to myalgia. His address was given as Prince of Wales Hotel, Foxfield, Lancashire.

Tom returned to farm labouring and was later a greenkeeper on a local golf course. He married Sarah Eleanor Sharp (1886–1946) at St Mary's Church, Whicham registered in the 4th quarter of 1935. Sarah had a daughter, Dorothy Sharp (1910–66), whose father is understood to be William Leavens Hodgkin (born 1890), who emigrated to Victoria, British Columbia, where he married Maggie Williamson in 1915. Dorothy was living with her grandparents, Harry and Ruth Sharp, at the time of the 1911 Census. Dorothy married Edward Postlethwaite Barker (1911–79) in 1936 and they had a daughter, Elizabeth Barker, in 1944.

St Mary's Church, Whicham, where Tom Mayson married Sarah Sharp in 1935 (Andrew Hill).

Sarah's father, Harry Sharp (1865–1914), was an agricultural labourer. He married Ruth née Satterthwaite (1864–1934) in 1886. The family was living at Stubble, Drigg, Cumberland in 1891 and was still there in 1901. In addition to Sarah they had eleven other children:

- William Henry Sharp (1888–1959).
- John Sharp (born 1889).
- Jane Sharp (1890–1969) married John B Mawson in 1917 and they had three children – Elsie Mawson 1918, Harry S Mawson 1920 and Ruth Mawson 1923.
- Ruth Sharp (1892–1967) married Gilbert Towers Hartley (1895–1977) in 1920 and they had three children – Nancy Hartley 1920, Tyson Hartley 1924 and Ruth M Hartley 1926.

Four King's Own Royal Regiment VCs at a reunion at Bowerham Barracks in 1932. From left to right – Albert Halton, James Hewitson, Tom Mayson and seated Harry Christian VC.

- Isaac Sharp (1894–1968).
- Jonathan Sharp (1895–1961).
- Anthony Sharp (twin with Isabel) (1899–1986).
- Isabel Sharp (1899–1921) married Harry Bertram Hunter (1889–1956) in 1920 and they had a son, William Hunter, also in 1920. Harry married Annie Williamson in 1925 and they had two children – Ivor HB Hunter 1926 and Ian H Hunter 1928.
- Joseph Sharp (1905–53).

Tom lived at the Miner's Arms at Silecroft while employed by the Atomic Energy Authority at Sellafield in the 1950s.

The Sellafield nuclear power station and reprocessing plant, also known as Windscale.

North Lonsdale Hospital was constructed in 1885–87 and another wing was added in 1899. It was Barrow's main hospital for almost a century, closing in 1989 after services transferred to Furness General Hospital. Despite being listed, it was demolished to make way for a retirement home.

The memorial to Tom Mayson VC and Jack White VC at The Priory, Lancaster.

- Annis Sharp (born 1906) married Isaac Satterthwaite (1901–73) in 1928 and they had a son, Norman Satterthwaite in 1935.
- Elizabeth Sharp (born 1910) married Arthur Rowland Moore (1904–58) in 1932 and they had a son, Brian Moore in 1938.

Tom served in HM Coastguard during the Second World War and was also a special constable. He was also a Freemason (Whitwell Lodge No. 1307). By the 1950s he was living at the Miner's Arms at Silecroft while employed by the Atomic Energy Authority at Sellafield. He retired early in late 1957 due to ill health. Tom Mayson died at North Lonsdale Hospital, Barrow-in-Furness on 21st February 1958. He is buried in St Mary's Churchyard, Whicham, near Silecroft. The funeral was attended

Tom Mayson's medals are held by the King's Own Royal Lancaster Regiment Museum, Lancaster.

Tom Mayson's grave in St Mary's Churchyard, Whicham, in the shadow of Black Combe (Memorials to Valour).

by Harry Christian VC, during which three rifle volleys were fired over the grave while a snowstorm swirled around nearby Black Combe. Tom is commemorated in a number of other places:

- Memorial at Millom Museum, Cumbria.
- Memorial at The Priory, Lancaster, Lancashire.
- The Department for Communities and Local Government decided to provide a commemorative paving stone at the birthplace of every Great War Victoria Cross recipient in the United Kingdom. Tom's stone was dedicated at Whicham and Silecroft War Memorial, Hodgson Green, Silecroft, Cumbria on 30th July 2017 to mark the centenary of his award.

In addition to the VC he was awarded the 1914–15 Star, British War Medal 1914–20, Victory Medal 1914–19, George VI Coronation Medal 1937, Elizabeth II Coronation Medal 1953 and Special Constabulary Long Service Medal. The VC was held by St Mary's Church, Whicham but, because of its value, it passed on long-term loan to the King's Own Royal Lancaster Regiment for security. A replica VC displayed at St Mary's Church, and labelled as such, was stolen, as was a replacement. The VC is held on loan by the King's Own Royal Lancaster Regiment Museum, Lancaster City Museum, Market Square, Lancaster. His other medals are owned by the Museum.

Harry Christian VC attended Tom Mayson's funeral.

The Special Constabulary Long Service Medal was established in 1919 to recognise the service of members of the Special Constabulary for three years unpaid service during the First World War. Thereafter it was awarded after nine years of service in the Special Constabulary, with service in both world wars counting as triple.

456 SERGEANT LEWIS McGEE
40th Australian Infantry Battalion, AIF

Lewis McGee was born on 13th May 1888 at Verwood, Campbell Town, Tasmania, Australia. His father, John Dedman McGee (1842–1929), was a labourer and later a farmer. He married Mary née Green (1848–95) on 12th December 1867 at Ross, Tasmania. Mary died on 30th May 1895 during an operation to remove a tumour on her lung, which was complicated by pleurisy. John later moved his family to Snow Hill, near Avoca, Tasmania. Lewis had ten siblings:

- Mary Ellen McGee (1868–71).
- Harriet McGee (1870–75).
- John James McGee (1872–1947) married Clara Jane Todd (c.1875–1937) in 1895. They had at least eight children – Clifford James McGee 1897, William McGee 1899, Ernie Albert McGee 1901, Elsie Isabel McGee 1904, Leslie Arthur McGee 1905, Sidney John McGee 1908, Daisy McGee and Eric McGee. At least three of the sons had military service:

Campbell Town, Tasmania.

  - Clifford James McGee (1905–78), a miner, enlisted on 5th September 1915 (10970) and served in 6th Field Artillery Brigade, departing Melbourne aboard HMAT A19 *Afric* on 5th January 1916. He was described as 5′ 8″ tall, weighing 154 lbs, with fair complexion, grey eyes, fair hair and his religious denomination was Church of England.
  He returned to Australia from France aboard SS *Ypiringa* on 15th May 1919 and was discharged at Anglesea Barracks, Hobart on 21st September 1919. Clifford married Gladys Doreen Hollingsworth (c.1908–77) and they had four children. He applied for a ground position in the Royal Australian Air Force on 10th August 1942.

  - Leslie Arthur McGee (1905–73) enlisted at Campbell Town on 14th May 1942 (T34383) and served as a corporal in 2nd

Lewis' father, John Dedman McGee, with his grand-daughter.

Lewis' mother, Ma McGee.

Battalion, Volunteer Defence Corps until 7th December 1945. He married Doris Eileen.

○ Sidney John McGee enlisted on 7th November 1939 at Brighton, Tasmania (TX469) and was discharged on 3rd May 1944 from Camp Staff Goondwindi.

• Albert William McGee (1874–1954) married Julia Gertrude Rigby Parker (1881–1931) in 1900. They had seven children – Ruby Emily Parker McGee c.1900, Mary Ellen McGee 1901, Albert Roy McGee 1904, Amy Gertrude McGee 1907, Ernest John McGee 1908, Edward Charles McGee 1910 and Raymond Henry McGee 1913. Raymond married Alice Lillias Lewis (1935–2006 in 1935. He enlisted on 29th January 1942 at Evandale, Tasmania (T21614) and was discharged from 10th Australian Auxiliary Horse Transport Company, Australian Army Service Corps on 30th July 1943.

• Percival Charles McGee (1876–1952).

• Frances Amy McGee (1878–83/84).

• Ada May McGee (1880–1961) married John Rubenbach (1871–1944) in 1911. They had five children – John Wilfred Herman Rubenach 1912, Phillip Clement Rubenach 1914, Barbara Rubenach, Bernard Frederick Rubenach 1916 and Everline Rubenach. John Wilfred Herman Rubenach enlisted in the Royal Australian Air Force at Alphington, Melbourne, Victoria (119989) on 22nd October 1942 and was discharged from 6th Recruit Depot on 26th September 1944 as a corporal. Bernard enlisted on 24th September 1942 at Lewis Hill, Tasmania (TX11176) and was discharged as a driver from 12th Australian Field Ambulance Transport Detail on 9th April 1944.

• Frederick Arthur McGee (1882–1961) married Florence Clarke (born c.1884) in 1908. They had seven children – Constance McGee, Elvie McGee, Arthur Percival McGee 1911, Roy Vernon McGee 1913, Maisie McGee, John Frederick

SS *Ypiranga* (8,142 tons) was operated by the Hamburg-America Line from 1908. She was notoriously unsteady and this was resolved by adding two water tanks near the fore and after masts. The flow between them helped to stabilise the ship in rough weather. *Ypiranga* had an eventful career. In September 1910 she brought the crews of the battleships SMS *Kurfürst Friedrich Wilhelm* and *Weissenburg* back to Germany after the ships had been delivered to the Ottoman Navy. On 31st May 1911 she embarked the ousted Mexican dictator Porfirio Diaz at Veracruz and took him to exile in France. On 15th April 1912 she was one of the ships in contact with RMS *Titanic* as she sank. She was fined by the USA for delivering arms to the government of Victoriano Huerta in Mexico in April 1914. On the outbreak of war in Europe she was laid up in Hamburg and fitted out to carry cavalry in the event of an invasion of Britain. In 1919 she was ceded to the United Kingdom as a war reparation and was managed by the White Star Line, initially to repatriate troops and then operated on the Australia route. In 1921 she transferred to the Anchor Line as the *Assyria*, initially on Atlantic routes and later on the Bombay run. In 1923 during Prohibition in the USA $1,000,000 worth of alcohol was confiscated from her, but was later returned. The Portuguese company, Companhia Colonial de Navegação, bought her in 1929 and she was renamed *Colonial*. She was to be scrapped in 1950, but on the way she broke her tow and was wrecked near Campbeltown in Scotland.

McGee and Robert McGee 1915. Frederick senior enlisted on 15th May 1942 at Avoca (T34337) and was discharged from 3rd Battalion as a lieutenant on 1st January 1944. John Frederick enlisted on 15th May 1942 at Launceston (TX6631) and was discharged from 281st Light Aid Detachment as a corporal on 19th March 1946. Arthur enlisted on 4th July 1936 at Fingal, Tasmania (T42719) and was discharged as a sergeant from 22nd Light Horse Regiment on 27th October 1941. Roy enlisted on 16th October 1942 at Mona Vale (TX11956 & T42718) and was discharged from 1st Australian Division as a sergeant on 20th March 1944.

- Leslie Rochester McGee (1884–1970), a labourer, married Beatrice Vera May Smith (c.1893–1967) in 1913. They had five children – Rupert Arthur Rochester McGee 1914, Cyril Donald Norman McGee 1916, Ivy May McGee 1918, Iris Joan McGee 1920 and Keith Gordon McGee 1922. Leslie enlisted on 15th May 1943 at Campbell Town, Tasmania (T155146). Rupert enlisted on 7th November 1939 at Brighton, Tasmania (TX470) and was discharged from 2/12th Battalion as a sergeant on 13th November 1944. Keith enlisted on 13th August 1942 at Mona Vale, Tasmania (TX12257 (T20583)) and was discharged as a lance corporal from 1st Australian Parachute Battalion on 19th February 1946.
- Everline Emma McGee (1885–1970) married Allan Tasman Rubenach (c.1885–1958) in 1919.

Lewis' paternal grandfather, James Dedman McGee (c.1816–99), was born at Liverpool, Lancashire and his surname has also been seen as Magee and Mac Gee. He was apprehended for stealing two gowns and a shawl and appeared before the General Quarter Session of Peace at Lancaster on 12th January 1829. He had two prior convictions and was sentenced to be transported for fourteen years. James embarked on the *David Lyon*, departing London on 2nd May 1830 and arrived at Van Dieman's Land (now Tasmania) on 19th August. In 1837 permission was granted for him to marry Eleanor Elizabeth née Presnell (1819–91), which they did on 24th September 1838 at Oatlands, Tasmania. Eleanor was born at St Luke's Old Street, London and was the daughter of free settlers. James received a conditional pardon on 30th July 1840 and a Free Certificate (No.771) in 1845. In addition to John they had eight other children:

- James Dedman McGee (1838–39).
- Eleanor Elizabeth McGee (born 1840) married William Smith (born c.1832) in 1873. They had four children – unnamed female 1874, unnamed female 1876, William Arthur Smith 1879 and Peter Smith 1882.
- Caroline Dedman McGee (1844–1908) had a daughter, Rose Ellen McGee (1863–86), and the father is understood to have been Richard William Ingle Fryer. Caroline married John Presnell (born 1843) in 1870. They had eight children – Elizabeth Emma Presnell 1871, Harriett Amelia Presnell 1873, Caroline Mary

Presnell 1875, John William Presnell 1877, Fanny Louisa Presnell 1879, Ann Presnell 1881, George Presnell 1883 and Grace Presnell 1886.
- Henry Dedman McGee (1846–85) married Annie Appleyard (born 1851) in 1869 and they had eight children – William Henry McGee 1870, James Edward McGee 1871, Charles McGee 1874, Eleanor Ann McGee 1876, Albert John McGee 1878, Rose McGee 1879, Mary McGee 1881 and Robert McGee 1883.
- William Dedman McGee (born 1848).
- Jane Dedman McGee (1851–54).
- James Dedman McGee (1853–1924).
- Mary Isabella McGee (born 1860) married John Kerr (c.1859) in 1892 and they had two children – Isabella Rose Kerr 1892 and Ruby Kerr 1898.

His maternal grandfather, John Cutler Green (born c.1815), married Harriet née Presnell (1827–57). In addition to Mary they had three other children:

- Christiana Green (1846–70).
- John Cutler Green (1851–1914) married Annie Elizabeth Standaloft née Found (1853–1935), born in Yorkshire, England, in 1877. They had eight children – Thomas John Green 1878, Hadley Laurence Green 1882, Clement Cutler Green 1884, Blanche Edith Green 1887, Grace Evelyn Green 1890, Alfred Allen Green 1892, Albert Cyril Green 1895 and Jane Emma Green 1897.
- Harriet Cutler Green (1855–1934).

Lewis was employed by the Tasmanian Department of Railways as an engine driver. He was an accomplished cyclist, winning numerous events as a member of the Avoca Cycling Club. On 15th November 1914 he married Eileen Rose Bailey (2nd September 1897–21st June 1985) at St Thomas' Church, Avoca, Tasmania. They had a daughter, Nada Mary McGee (2nd November 1915–19th April 1993) at Snow Hill, Avoca, Tasmania. Nada lived at Cosgrove Park Nursing Home, South Launceston, Tasmania for some years until her mother's death, then lived with her half-sister, Dawn Saunders, until she was admitted to Nazareth House, Station Road, St Leonard's, Tasmania in January 1987, where she later died.

   Eileen's father, Thomas Henry Bailey, married Mary Ellen née Hill (born c.1876) in 1894. In addition to Eileen they had ten other children – Beryl Lucy Bailey 1895, Corrie Patricia Bailey c.1901, Thomas Elliott Bailey c.1903, Jessie Agnes Bailey c.1906, Frederick William Bailey c.1908, Roy Robert Bailey c.1910, Robert George Bailey c.1913, George Francis Bailey c.1916, Georgina Lewis Bailey c.1918 and Bernard Bailey c.1920.

   Lewis enlisted in the Australian Imperial Force at Avoca, Tasmania on 1st March 1916. He was described as 5′ 8¾″ tall, weighing 187 lbs, with dark complexion, grey eyes, dark hair and his religious denomination was Methodist. He was posted to Claremont, Hobart, Tasmania and allocated to 40th Battalion on 1st May. He

Lewis with Eileen and Nada.

Avoca with St Thomas' Church on top of the hill.

was promoted lance corporal on 22nd May and embarked with B Company, 1st Reinforcements, 40th Battalion at Hobart, Tasmania aboard HMAT A35 *Berrima* on 1st July. He disembarked at Devonport, Devon on 22nd August and was based at Larkhill on Salisbury Plain until embarking at Southampton, Hampshire for France on 23rd November 1916. Lewis was promoted corporal on 4th December 1916 and sergeant in 6 Platoon, B Company on 12th January 1917. He was attached to the 3rd Australian Division School of Instruction 25th February–4th March and took part in the Battle of Messines in June 1917.

Awarded the VC for his actions on Broodseinde Ridge, east of Ypres, Belgium, on 4th October 1917, LG 26th November 1917. On 12th October, in the advance on Augustus Wood, his platoon came under heavy machine gun fire and Lewis was shot in the head and killed instantly. He is buried in Tyne Cot

SS *Berrima* (11,137 tons) was launched in 1913 for P&O for the carriage of immigrants to Australia via Cape Town. She was requisitioned by the RAN in 1914 as HMAS *Berrima*, initially as an auxiliary cruiser. She transported two battalions of the Australian Naval and Military Expeditionary Force to the German New Guinea colonies in September. In October she was in the second ANZAC convoy to the Middle East and towed the submarine *AE2*. On 18th February 1917 she was torpedoed off Portland, Dorset, but was towed ashore and repaired, following which she was used to carry stores and munitions. *Berrima* returned to P&O service in 1920 until 1929 and she was broken up in 1930.

Cemetery, Belgium (XX D I). Lewis is commemorated in a number of other places:

- Display at the Hall of Valour, Australian War Memorial, Canberra, ACT, Australia.
- Named on Roll of Honour, Australian War Memorial, Canberra.
- McGee Place, Canberra, Australian Capital Territory.

- Named on the Victoria Cross Memorial, Campbell, Canberra, dedicated on 24th July 2000.
- McGee Street, Wodonga, Victoria on White Box Rise estate, built on land formerly part of Bandiana Army Camp.
- Named on the Honours Board, St Thomas Church of England, Avoca, Tasmania, Australia.
- McGee Soldier's Club, Anglesea Barracks, Hobart, Tasmania.
- Named on the War Cenotaph at Ross, Tasmania.
- Named on a plaque on the Returned Services League Cenotaph in Boucher Park, Avoca, Tasmania, unveiled by the Governor of Tasmania, Sir James Plimsoll, on 19th March 1984. His widow, Eileen, and daughter, Nada, attended the ceremony.

Lewis McGee's grave in Tyne Cot Cemetery. Hamburg Farm is in the trees in the distance.

- Named on the Victoria Cross Memorial, Hobart Cenotaph, Tasmania, dedicated on 11th May 2003.
- Victoria Cross Memorial, Queen Victoria Building, George Street, Sydney, New South Wales, dedicated on 23rd February 1992 to commemorate the visit of Queen Elizabeth II and Prince Philip on the occasion of the Sesquicentenary of the City of Sydney. Sir Roden Cutler VC, Edward Kenna VC and Keith Payne VC were in attendance.
- Named on one of eleven plaques honouring 175 men from overseas awarded the VC for the Great War. The plaques were unveiled by the Senior Minister of State at the Foreign & Commonwealth Office and Minister for Faith and Communities, Baroness Warsi, at a reception at Lancaster House, London on 26th June 2014

Ross War Memorial, with Lewis McGee's plaque at the top.

St Thomas' Anglican Church, Avoca, Tasmania, where Lewis married Eileen and where he is commemorated.

attended by The Duke of Kent and relatives of the VC recipients. The Australian plaque is at the Australian War Memorial.

- The Secretary of State for Communities and Local Government, Eric Pickles, MP announced that Victoria Cross recipients from the Great War would have commemorative paving stones laid in their birthplace as a lasting legacy of local heroes within communities. The stones would be laid on or close to the 100th anniversary of their VC actions. For the 145 VCs born in Australia, Belgium, Canada, China, Denmark, Egypt, France, Germany, India, Iraq, Japan, Nepal, Netherlands, New Zealand, Pakistan, South Africa, Sri Lanka, Ukraine and United States of America, individual commemorative stones were unveiled at the National Memorial Arboretum, Alrewas, Staffordshire by Prime Minister David Cameron MP and Sergeant Johnson Beharry VC on 5th March 2015.

McGee had an Iron Cross, presumably removed from a dead German. It was enclosed in a letter of condolence to his wife written by a 40th Battalion officer. The posthumous VC was presented to his wife by The Governor General of Australia, Sir Ronald Craufurd Munro-Ferguson GCMG, at York Park, Launceston, Tasmania on 2nd March 1918. Eileen remarried as Heyward in 1929 but remained in Avoca and had two more children – Dawn Heyward and a son, who died as a teenager.

In addition to the VC he was awarded the British War Medal 1914–20 and Victory Medal 1914–19. His VC was purchased by the Tasmanian Government at Spinks Australia on 1st May 1984 for $A36,000. It is displayed in Queen Victoria Museum & Art Gallery, Royal Park, 2 Wellington Street, Launceston, Tasmania.

265579 PRIVATE GEORGE IMLACH MCINTOSH
1/6th (Banff and Donside) Battalion, The Gordon Highlanders

George McIntosh was born at 80 Portessie, near Buckie, Banffshire, Scotland on 22nd April 1897. His father, Alexander McIntosh (1864–1951), was a fisherman and ship's carpenter. He married Mary Jane née Reid (1871–1932), a domestic servant living at Seaview Road, Buckie, on 14th September 1894. They were living at 107 Shore Street, Portessie in 1901. The family moved to Buckie in 1910 and was living at 79 Seatown in 1911 and at 10 Cathedral Street in 1932. Alexander was employed on Admiralty service (DA 5962) from 12th April 1915. He was described as 5' 6½" tall, with a 39" chest, fresh complexion and grey eyes. He gave his date of birth as 20th October 1870 and his address as 24 Seaview Road, Buckie. Alexander served on a number of boats, including *Liberty*, a transport formerly in

P&O service, *Osiris II* a depot ship for trawlers and drifters at Mudros, *Deal Castle*, *Fisher Boy* (*White Oak* – depot ship for net drifters at Poole) and *Thalia*, an Auxiliary Patrol parent ship at Cromarty. He was discharged on 7th March 1918 to return to his civilian employment as a carpenter with Messrs Jones of Buckie. A war gratuity of £16/10/- was paid on 30th April 1919. He was also awarded prize money of £12/10/- on 20th July 1920 and a final award of £18/15/- on 24th October 1922.

Portessie.

George had a brother, Alexander Reid (later McIntosh), born to Mary Jane Reid on 6th September 1894, whose natural father is not known, but may have been Alexander McIntosh. He was a wood sawyer in 1911. He served in 2nd Gordon Highlanders during the war and was badly wounded at Neuve Chapelle. It is understood that a second sibling did not survive infancy.

George's paternal grandfather, Alexander McIntosh (c.1835–1920), was a boat carpenter. He married Elizabeth Brodie née Coull (1832–1910) in 1854. In addition to the VC's father, they had nine other children:

Buckie, from Seatown.

George McIntosh's cousin, James, is commemorated on the Ploegsteert Memorial.

- Ann McIntosh (1854–1905) married George Imlach (1856–1931) in 1878 at St Nicholas, Aberdeen. They had four children including William John Imlach 1883. Ann died at Fraserburgh, Aberdeenshire and George in Toronto, Canada.
- Elizabeth McIntosh c.1855.
- Peter McIntosh 1856.
- William McIntosh 1858.
- John McIntosh 1860.
- Elizabeth Brodie McIntosh 1869.
- Jane M McIntosh 1874.
- Margaret McIntosh 1876.
- James McIntosh c.1877.

Alexander and Elizabeth McIntosh had at least four other grandsons who served during the war, but their parents are unknown:

- George McIntosh, a cycle repair mechanic, was a seaman.
- Alexander McIntosh, an insurance agent, was a gunner.
- John McIntosh, a farm servant, was a private.
- James McIntosh, a farm servant at Smerack in the Enzie, was a private in 6th Gordon Highlanders (1204) and was killed in action on 24th December 1914 (Ploegsteert Memorial). He was the first Buckie Territorial to be killed. He was the son of Mr McIntosh and his wife Maggie.

His maternal grandfather, William 'Rosie' Reid (c.1840–97) was master and owner of the *Bethany* (BF 1443), a thirty-ton fishing vessel. He married Margaret née Cowie (1835–77), a domestic servant, in 1864. In addition to Mary Jane they had five other children:

- Alexander Reid (1865–89), a fisherman, was sailing with his father aboard the *Bethany* when he was thrown overboard by a mizzen sheet five miles off Copinshay, Orkney on 31st January 1889. His body was never recovered.
- Mary Jane Reid (1867–69).
- Margaret Reid (1869–74).
- James Reid (1873–97), a fisherman, was aboard the *Bethany* with his father on 9th June 1897 when she was lost on the Pentland Skerries, Orkney.
- Margaret Ann Reid born 1875.

Rosie married Ann Farquhar, a thirty-two year old spinster of Port Gordon, and they had five children – Jessie Reid 1880, Nelly Reid c.1881, Rebecca Reid 1884, Rachel Reid 1885 and Alexander Reid c.1889. *Bethany* was carrying a cargo of wood from Stornoway to Shetland on 9th June 1897 when she was lost on the Pentland Skerries, Orkney, with the loss of six lives, including Rosie and his son James. Ann died in 1917.

George was educated at Fraserburgh Academy before being employed as an apprentice nipper with wood merchant Tom Jones & Son in 1910. He also worked with John Barclay, a slater, and on the Cluny dock extension to Buckie Harbour. He enlisted in D Company, 6th Gordon Highlanders (TF) in 1913 (10789 and 265579 from 1917) and was mobilised on 4th August 1914. George went to France with the Battalion on 10th November 1914 and was evacuated with trench foot early in the war.

Awarded the VC for his actions north of St Julien, Belgium on 31st July 1917, LG 6th September 1917. He had no idea he had been recommended until he received a

Fraserburgh Academy old building.

congratulatory message from GOC 51st (Highland) Division, Major General GM Harper CB DSO. He returned to Britain on leave on 12th September and arrived unannounced at his parent's home. His pre-war employers presented him with a purse of fifty gold sovereigns. The VC was presented to him by the King at Ibrox Park, Glasgow on 18th September. For a while George was appointed batman to a senior officer, but it did not suit him and he returned to the Battalion for the rest of the war.

Ibrox Park, home of Glasgow Rangers FC, as it looked when it was the venue for the investiture on 18th September 1917.

George returned to Buckie in July 1919 and worked as a herring runner for Thomson & Brown, a fish sales company. His work took him back to Fraserburgh. On 27th April 1923, George McIntosh married Alexanderina née Sutherland (25th June 1897–23rd May 1981), a dressmaker, at the Station Hotel, Elgin, Moray. He was living at 24 Seaview Road, Buckie and she was living at 26 Main Street, Buckie at the time. They were living at School Cottage, South Pringle Street, Buckie in 1951 and she was living at Grant Eden, Wilson's Land, Buckie at the time of her death at Seafield Hospital, Buckie in 1981. They had two children:

George McIntosh receives his VC from the King.

Fraserburgh Harbour packed with fishing boats.

- George Imlach McIntosh born on 4th June 1924. He died unmarried on 23rd March 1992 at the Royal Infirmary, Aberdeen, usual residence Grant Eden, Wilson's Land, Buckie.
- Grace Grant McIntosh, was born mute on 2nd February 1929. She appeared on BBC TV programme *See Hear* on 9th November 1997.

Alexanderina's father, Alexander Sutherland (1862–1933), was a cooper. He married Grace née Grant (1862–1933), in 1883. In addition to Alexandrina they had six other children – Grace Sutherland 1884, Mary Ann Sutherland 1887, Isabella Sutherland 1889, Georgina Sutherland 1891, Robert Grant Sutherland 1893 and Margaret Jane Sutherland 1895.

George enlisted in the Royal Air Force (370531) on 21st August 1925 as an Aircraftman/Armourer. He was based at RAF Leuchars, Fife and at No.3 Flying Training School, RAF Spitalgate near Grantham. He transferred to the Reserve on 21st August 1932. Thereafter he was employed as a green-keeper at Buckie bowls club until July 1939, when he became the janitor and groundsman at Buckie High School. On 26th August 1939, he was recalled to the RAF and served at RAF Sullom Voe on Shetland, RAF Mount Batten, Plymouth and RAF St Eval in Cornwall as a temporary corporal. He was appointed temporary sergeant in July 1940 and was **Mentioned in Despatches, LG 1st January 1941**. In May 1941 George was promoted flight sergeant and served with the Anti-Aircraft Flight at RAF St Eval until 1st October. On one occasion a 100 lbs bomb just missed him and failed to explode. He then spent until 5 a.m. the following day putting out fires. Air Commodore AP Revington CB CBE wrote, *We were subject to a very heavy air attack ... and 'Mac' was in his element – an inspiration and an example to everybody. He matched up to every situation, however hazardous, and seemed to welcome danger, and was indeed a very brave man of great resource.*

George was posted to Reykjavik, Iceland as a ground gunner and was appointed acting warrant officer in November 1941. He joined No.2848 Squadron RAF Regiment at RAF Angle, South Wales on 2nd July 1942 and served with No.4054 Anti-Aircraft Flight from November. In March 1943 he remustered as an Aircraftman/General Duties and moved to RAF Biggin Hill, Kent. In September 1943 he joined No.3017 Servicing Echelon at RAF Lympne. He reverted to flight sergeant in the latter part of 1943. George joined No.6001 Servicing Echelon at RAF North Weald in April 1944 and remained there until the end of the war. He was discharged at Ludham, Norfolk on 17th September 1945.

RAF Leuchars around the time George McIntosh served there.

George returned to his janitor job, eventually becoming head janitor, and was granted the Freedom of Buckie on 21st December 1955. On 4th February 1960 he became the only Gordon Highlanders NCO to take the salute at a passing-out parade at Bridge of Don

Buckie High School, where George McIntosh was the janitor and groundsman from July 1939.

Woodend Hospital, Aberdeen, where George McIntosh died in 1960. The picture shows the hospital when it was a military hospital during the First World War.

George McIntosh while serving in the RAF in the Second World War.

Buckie High Street.

Barracks, Aberdeen. In his earlier years he played for Buckie Thistle Football Club. Later he became the first Honorary President of the town's British Legion branch and was also President of Buckie Bowls Club and a kirk elder for Buckie North Church.

George McIntosh died following a series of heart attacks and two operations at Woodend Hospital, Aberdeen, Scotland on 20th June 1960. He is buried in the family plot at New Cemetery, Buckie, Banff and

George McIntosh's memorial and headstone in Buckie New Cemetery (Alan Beedham).

there is a memorial plaque on the wall behind his grave dedicated in September 2004. He is commemorated in a number of other places:

- McIntosh Avenue, Craigbo, Portessie, Buckie.
- Off High Street, Buckie is Steinbeck Road, a corruption of Steinbeck, which George crossed to win the VC.

- The Department for Communities and Local Government decided to provide a commemorative paving stone at the birthplace of every Great War Victoria Cross recipe in the United Kingdom. George's stone was dedicated at Buckie War Memorial, Cluny Square, on 29th July 2017 to mark the centenary of his award.

In addition to the VC he was awarded the 1914 Star with 'Mons' clasp, British War Medal 1914–20, Victory Medal 1914–19 with Mentioned-in-Despatches Oakleaf, Defence Medal, War Medal 1939–45 with Mentioned-in-Despatches Oakleaf, George VI Coronation Medal 1937 and Elizabeth II Coronation Medal 1953. The medals were purchased for £32,000 by Lord Michael Ashcroft's VC Trust through dealer Michael Naxton at Spink's on 6th November 1996. They are held by the Michael Ashcroft Trust and displayed in the Imperial War Museum's Lord Ashcroft Gallery.

LIEUTENANT HUGH McDONALD McKENZIE
7th Canadian Machine Gun Company, Canadian Expeditionary Force

Hugh McKenzie was born on 5th December 1885 at Liverpool, Lancashire, England. His birth was registered there as Hugh Mac Donald Mackenzie and that form of the surname has been seen in other documents. When he enlisted in the Canadian Army he gave his birthplace as Inverness, Scotland. His father, James McDonald McKenzie (c.1850–85), was born at Cargill, Perthshire and was a confection packer in 1877, living at 6 St Peter Street, Dundee. He married Jane née McDonald (born c.1853 at

Inverness), a domestic servant, on 13th June 1877 at 24 Rose Street, Dundee. Jane became a midwife at 23 James Street, Dundee. They were living at 28 Crescent Street, East Greenock, Renfrewshire in 1881, by when he was a sugarhouse engineman in a confectionery factory. James joined the Merchant Marine as a fireman and was serving aboard SS *Arabic* when he died at sea, presumed drowned in Trieste harbour, on 1st October 1885. His body was never found. Jane returned to Inverness with her family and was living with her aunt Jane MacDonald at Blackpark of Muirtown, Inverness in 1891. Hugh had five siblings:

- Robert Gillies McKenzie (1877–1965) was born at 54 Drumfochar Road, Greenock, Renfrewshire. He served in the Army Service Corps during the Great War (S/25549) and was in Montreal and Halifax, Canada June 1921–February 1934. He died at Calderhead, Lanarkshire.
- James McKenzie (1879–99), born at 116 Drumfochar Road, Greenock, was a carter. He died at Blackpark of Muirtown, Inverness.

Hugh's father was living on St Peter Street, Dundee (on the left) in 1877.

His mother was living on Rose Street, Dundee in 1877.

Hugh attended Rosebank Primary School in Dundee (Alexander Wilson).

SS *Arabic* was the first steel-hulled ship built for the White Star Line in 1881 as a cargo/passenger freighter. Her maiden voyage was from Liverpool to New York on 10th September 1881. In 1882 she was chartered to the Occidental & Oriental Steamship Co for the San Francisco – Hong Kong route. She returned to Britain in 1886 and made one London – Melbourne – Sydney via Cape Town voyage for Occidental & Oriental. She ran White Star's London – Queenstown – New York route in March 1887 and resumed the Liverpool – New York route in May. In May 1888 she resumed charter service with Occidental & Oriental and in February 1890 was sold to Holland America Line and renamed SS *Spaarndam* for the Rotterdam – New York service. Her final voyage was in February 1901 and she was then broken up at Preston.

- Alexander McKenzie (born c.1888) was born at Inverness. He served in the Cameron Highlanders during the Great War and was captured by the Germans.
- Isabella Ferguson McKenzie (born 1881) was born at 26 Crescent Street, Greenock, Renfrewshire.
- Jeannie McDonald McKenzie (born 1884) was born at 15 Main Street, Greenock. She married Robert Colville in 1906 at St Andrew, Dundee.

Hugh's paternal grandfather, John McKenzie, a farm servant, married Marjory née Small. His maternal grandfather, Hugh McDonald (c.1811–84), a shipwright, married Agnes née Collins (c.1812–95) on 20th October 1827 at Inverness. She was admitted to the Poor House, Inverness after her husband's death and died there on 20th January 1895.

Hugh was educated at Leachkin Public School, Assynt Road, Inverness and at Rosebank Primary School, Rosebank Road, Dundee, Angus. He worked for the Highland Railway Company as a cleaner before returning to Dundee around 1905. He then worked for Messrs Watson & Sons of Seagate, Dundee and later for the Caledonian Railway Company as a carter. Hugh was a noted sportsman and a founder member and instructor of the Dundee Amateur Boxing and Wrestling Club at Dudhope Castle. He won the North Scotland Wrestling Championships and a number of other wrestling trophies.

Hugh McKenzie is understood to have married Marjory née McGuigan (23rd October 1884–24th May 1959) c.1911, but no record of

The Caledonian Railway Company's station at Dundee. The Railway formed in the early 19th Century to link the English railways with Glasgow and the network was extended to Edinburgh and Aberdeen. The Dundee and Perth Railway opened in 1847 and was taken over by Scottish Central Railway. Its network was taken over by Caledonian Railway in 1865. It was absorbed into the London, Midland & Scottish Railway in 1923.

it can be found in either the Scottish or England and Wales records. Marjory was a jute spinner in 1901, living with her parents. They had two children:

* Elizabeth McKenzie, born prior to 1912, is understood to have remained in Dundee when her parents emigrated to Canada. She joined them once they were settled and later married as McAndrew.
* Alexander McKenzie.

Dudhope Castle, where Hugh was an instructor in the Dundee Amateur Boxing and Wrestling Club. The castle dates back to the 13th Century and was in the Scrymageour family until 1668, when Charles II granted the castle and office of Constable to Charles Maitland. It passed through the Graham and Douglas families until 1795, when it was leased to the Board of Ordnance as accommodation for 400 soldiers until 1881. The castle was used as a barracks during both world wars. It is now used as offices, a conference centre, and by Dundee Business School. In 1998 a dinner was held there by the Scrimgeour

Clan Association to commemorate the 700th anniversary of a charter to the Scrimgeours signed by William Wallace and reaffirmed by Robert Bruce. Captain Francis Alexander Carron Scrimger VC, Canadian Army Medical Corps (see the second book in this series), had a distant ancestor, Alexander Carron, who fought for King Alexander I of Scotland in the Battle at the Spey in 1106. During the battle he caught the falling royal standard, rallied the troops and saved the day. He was knighted on the spot and became the standard-bearer of Scotland until 1124, when the appointment became hereditary. The title later included the post of Constable of the Castle and town of Dundee. Alexander was also granted the right to add 'Skirmisheour' to his name. Over the years this became Scrymgeour and when Francis' family emigrated to Canada it was simplified to Scrimger.

Marjory's father, Charles McGuigan (c.1849–1919), was born at Dundee, Angus. He married Elizabeth née Colgan (c.1849–1921), also born at Dundee, on 26th November 1877 at St Mary's Roman Catholic Chapel, Dundee. Charles was a general labourer in 1891 and they were living at 25 James Street, Dundee and were still there in 1901, by when he was a mason's labourer. In addition to Marjory they had five other children:

- James McGuigan (1878–1905) was a mill worker in 1891 and later a journeyman mason of 25 James Street, Dundee. He married Margaret née Mellen (1878–1910), a jute winder, on 1st January 1900. She previously lived with her parents at 19 Powrie Place, Dundee. They had twin daughters, Margaret and Elizabeth McGuigan, in 1901.

- Mary Ann McGuigan (1880–1941) was a mill worker in 1891. She married William Walls (c.1880–1950), a calendar worker, living at 229 Hilltown, Dundee, in June 1900. He was later an electric crane man. They had five children – Margaret Walls 1900, James Walls 1902, Elizabeth Walls 1905, Charles Walls 1906 and Mary Walls 1910. He married Ann McQuillan (c.1887–1975) in 1942 and they were living at 81 Sandeman Street, Dundee in 1950.

Joseph McGuigan's grave in New Munich Trench British Cemetery, Beaumont-Hamel, France

- John McGuigan (1886–90).
- Charles Edward McGuigan (1889–1910) was a journeyman brush maker. He died at 26 James Street, Dundee, usual residence 25 James Street.
- Joseph McGuigan (1891–1916) served in 17th Highland Light Infantry (43330) and was killed in action on 18th November 1916 (New Munich Trench British Cemetery, Beaumont-Hamel, France – C 8).

Hugh and Marjory emigrated to Canada and settled in Montreal, where he worked as a teamster on the railways. She was living at 297 Gertrude Avenue, Verdun, Quebec in 1914 when Hugh enlisted. When he attested for service in the CEF, Hugh declared four years previous service in the Garrison Artillery and two years in the Special Reserve Field Artillery. It is understood that both periods of service were in the Militia/Territorial Force in Britain. He enlisted in Princess Patricia's Canadian Light Infantry on 21st August 1914 (1158). He was described as 5′ 7″ tall, with fresh complexion, grey eyes, brown hair and his religious denomination was Presbyterian. He joined No.3 Company and sailed for England as part of the First Canadian Contingent on 3rd October, arriving on 18th October. The Battalion trained at Bustard Camp on Salisbury Plain and at Morn Camp, Winchester prior to joining the British 80th Brigade in 27th Division at Winchester on 20th November.

During November he forfeited two days' pay, but the reason in unclear. The Battalion sailed for France from Southampton on 20th December and became the first Canadian unit to serve on the Western Front.

On 21st January 1915 Hugh contracted dysentery and was admitted to a hospital at St Omer until returning to his unit on 2nd February. **Awarded the DCM for his actions on Bellewaarde Ridge 3rd-8th May during which Hugh was a member of a machine gun section. His gun team was killed or wounded on 4th May by enemy shellfire and he calmly stripped the wrecked gun of all undamaged parts and brought the survivors to safety. He then volunteered to carry messages to and from brigade headquarters under heavy fire, remaining in action until 8th May when he guided fresh troops to the relief of the Battalion, LG 14th January 1916 and details 11th March 1916. Awarded the French Croix de Guerre 1914–18, probably for the same action, LG 24th February 1916.** The Battalion's costly defensive action has gone down in regimental history. The Divisional Commander, Major General T D'O Snow, said, *No regiment could have fought with greater determination or endurance, many would have failed where they succeeded.*

Bustard Camp, near Larkhill on Salisbury Plain, was particularly cold, windswept and very wet in the winter of 1914–15.

The Princess Patricia's Canadian Light Infantry Memorial, with Bellewaarde Ridge beyond. The Battalion fought a costly action here in early May 1915, during which Hugh earned the DCM.

Hugh was promoted corporal on 22nd May and sergeant on 11th September 1915. On 22nd December Princess Patricia's Canadian Light Infantry joined 7th Canadian Brigade, 3rd Canadian Division. Hugh was granted ten days' leave in France from 27th March 1916. He transferred to 7th Canadian Machine Gun Company on 3rd September 1916 and was appointed acting company sergeant major the next day. He was struck off strength 7th Canadian Machine Gun Company on 22nd January 1917 and rejoined Princess Patricia's Canadian Light Infantry. He was commissioned temporary lieutenant on 28th January and was immediately seconded for duty with 7th Canadian Machine Gun Company.

His service record shows that he stopped his assigned pay to his wife with effect from 1st February 1917, due to her infidelity, and transferred payments to the Canadian Patriotic Fund, Drummond Building, Montreal. Hugh was granted leave 1st-11th April and 4th-14th October. **Awarded the VC for his actions on**

Meetscheele Spur, Passchendaele, Belgium on 30th October 1917, LG 13th February 1918. He was killed during his VC action and is commemorated on the Ypres (Menin Gate) Memorial (Panel 56). The VC was sent to his wife.

Marjory had moved to 1021 Clarke Street, Montreal by the time her husband was killed. She remarried as Smith on 6th January 1920 and lived at North Bay, Ontario. In his will dated 14th March 1915, Hugh left any outstanding pay and his watch to his mother and everything else to his wife. Despite her alleged infidelity, there does not appear to have been a legal separation. His scroll and plaque were sent to his widow in July 1921 and June 1922 respectively, but the plaque was returned on 3rd July 1922. Hugh is commemorated in a number of other places:

Poster for the Canadian Patriotic Fund, set up by Montreal manufacturer Sir Herbert Ames in August 1914. Although a private organization, the Governor General was patron and the Federal Minister of Finance was treasurer. It raised almost $50M for soldiers' families during the war (Library & Archives Canada).

- Plaque unveiled at Rosebank Primary School, Dundee in 1922. A new school was built in the 1970s, but the plaque was preserved and erected on the new building.
- A memorial unveiled opposite 19 Abercromby Square, Liverpool in July 2008, depicts Captain Noel Chavasse VC & Bar MC RAMC helping a wounded soldier accompanied by a stretcher-bearer. Fifteen other VCs associated with Liverpool are included on the memorial, including Hugh McKenzie.
- Named on a Victoria Cross obelisk to all Canadian VCs at Military Heritage Park, Barrie, Ontario dedicated by The Princess Royal on 22nd October 2013.
- Named on one of eleven plaques honouring 175 men from overseas awarded the VC for the Great War. The plaques were unveiled by the Senior Minister of

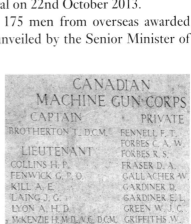

Hugh McKenzie has no known grave and is commemorated on the Ypres (Menin Gate) Memorial.

The Canadian War Museum holds Hugh McKenzie's medals.

The memorial in Abercromby Square, Liverpool to Captain Noel Chavasse VC & Bar MC RAMC and fifteen other VCs associated with Liverpool, including Hugh McKenzie.

State at the Foreign & Commonwealth Office and Minister for Faith and Communities, Baroness Warsi, at a reception at Lancaster House, London on 26th June 2014 attended by The Duke of Kent and relatives of the VC recipients. The Canadian plaque was unveiled outside the British High Commission in Elgin Street, Ottawa on 10th November 2014 by The Princess Royal in the presence of British High Commissioner Howard Drake, Canadian Minister of Veterans Affairs Julian Fantino and Canadian Chief of the Defence Staff General Thomas J Lawson.

* Two 49 cents postage stamps in honour of the 94 Canadian VC winners were issued by Canada Post on 21st October 2004 on the 150th Anniversary of the first Canadian VC's action, Alexander Roberts Dunn VC.
* Plaque on a memorial to the ninety-nine Canadian VCs in York Cemetery, Toronto.

In addition to the VC and DCM he was awarded the 1914–15 Star, British War Medal 1914–20, Victory Medal 1914–19 and French Croix de Guerre 1914–18 with Bronze Palm. As he died on operational duty, his next-of-kin is eligible to receive the Canadian Memorial Cross. His medals were in the possession of his widow when they were destroyed in a house fire at Amhertsburg, Lake Erie, Ontario, Canada on 24th May 1959, in which she died. Unaware of this, the Princess Patricia's Canadian Light Infantry Museum in Calgary appealed throughout Canada for the location of the VC. As a result contact was made with Hugh's daughter, Mrs Elizabeth McAndrew of Windsor, Ontario, in 1970 and who had her father's DCM and Croix de Guerre. The Museum arranged for official replacements of the missing medals and Hugh's daughter presented the complete group to the Canadian War Museum in Ottawa on 17th March 1979, where they are still held.

L/1817 SERGEANT JOHN MOLYNEUX
2nd Battalion, The Royal Fusiliers (City of London Regiment)

John Molyneux was born at 3 Marshall's Cross Road, Peasley Cross, St Helens, Lancashire on 22nd November 1890. His father, Joseph Molyneux (c.1864–1933), was a player and bandleader of Peasley Cross Concertina Club. He married Minnie Jane née Luckett (1863–1930) at Holy Trinity Church, Parr Mount, St Helens, Lancashire in 1886. She was born at Sheerness, Kent and in 1881 was a housemaid in the home of William R Stephens and his family at 3 Lee Road, Lee, Kent. They were living at 8 Manor Street, Sutton in 1891 and at 67 Ell Bess Lane, St Helens in 1901. In 1902 Ell Bess Lane was renamed Sherdley Road and Joseph and Minnie were living at No.81 in 1911. John had seven siblings:

- Lily Molyneux (born 1887) was a housemaid waitress domestic in 1911 at Hillside, St Helens, Lancashire, the home of Watkin Oppenheim, a solicitor, and his family.
- Grace Molyeux (1893–1952) was a kitchen maid in 1911 at 32 Westcliffe Road, Birkdale, Lancashire. She married John Richard Kerfoot (1899–1955) in 1922. He was born in Sheffield, Yorkshire. They had two sons – Peter J Kerfoot 1924 and Anthony Kerfoot 1926.

John's parents were married at Holy Trinity Church, Parr Mount, St Helens in 1886. The church is unique as it is built entirely of copper slag blocks and cement with walls being infilled with industrial rubble.

- Clara Luckett Molyneux (born 1895) married Thomas Chesworth in 1920. They had three children – Alice Chesworth 1920, Peter J Chesworth 1931 and Joan Chesworth 1937.
- Minnie Jane Molyneux (born 1898).
- Ada Frances Molyneux (born 1900, a twin with Henry).
- Henry Molyneux (1900–01), a twin with Ada.
- Fanny Molyneux (born 1909) married John Brown in 1933.

Marshall's Cross Road, Peasley Cross, St Helens where John Molyneux was born.

John's paternal grandfather, Joseph Molyneux (born c.1821, died 1891 or 1899) married Esther née Gleave (c.1827–95) in 1844. He was a collier in 1861 and they were living at Sutton, Lancashire. In addition to Joseph they had ten other children:

- Thomas Molyneux (born c.1845) was a collier in 1861.
- John Molyneux (born 1846) was a collier in 1861.
- Peter Molyneux (1848–49).
- Alice Molyneux (born 1853).
- Ann Jane Molyneux (1857–1920) married Robert Thomas Shaw (1856–1937) in 1878. He was a coal miner and she was a glass smoother in 1881 when they were living with her parents at 12 Manor Street, Sutton. They were living at 77 Derbyshire Hill Road, St Helens in 1911. They had two children – Albert Shaw 1885 and Kate Corbould 1895.
- William Molyneux (born c.1860).
- Esther Molyneux (born 1861).
- Ann Molyneux (born 1864).
- Hannah Molyneux (born 1866).
- Elizabeth Molyneux (born 1871).

His maternal grandfather, John Newnham Luckett (1829–93), served in the Royal Marine Light Infantry enlisting on 6th September 1842 aged thirteen. He was promoted corporal on 3rd November 1858 and sergeant on 18th September 1861, but was reduced to private on 10th September 1863. He was promoted corporal on 2nd January 1865 and sergeant on 12th September 1865. He served over sixteen years abroad or aboard HM Ships and was discharged from 69th Company on 3rd December 1868 with four Good Conduct Badges and conduct assessed as Very Good. He married Fanny Jane née Worger (c.1836–1908) in 1857 at Medway, Kent. She was born at Ordnance Place, Chatham, Kent. In 1881 they were living at 1 Greenhough Street, Sutton, Lancashire. By 1891 they were living at 10 Manor Street, Sutton, Lancashire, next door to their daughter Minnie and husband Joseph Molyneux. In addition to Minnie they had seven other children:

- John Samuel Luckett (1859–1936), a general labourer, married Cicely Potter (1872–1950) in 1895. They were living at 16 Manor Street, St Helens in 1901. John was a general labourer at Cannington Shaw Bottle Works in 1911, living with his family at 8 Mount Street, St Helens. They had at least eight children – Joseph Luckett 1896, John Newnham Luckett 1897, Philadelphia Luckett 1899, Harold Luckett 1901, Cicely Luckett 1906, William George Luckett 1910, Arthur Luckett 1912 and John S Luckett 1914. Cicely senior married David Bate in 1944.
- Thomas William Luckett (1861–1946) was a general labourer in 1881 and was working at Cannington Shaw Bottle Works by 1891. He married Laura Eliza Cantrill in 1892 (1866–1941). They were living at 4 Abbotsfield Road, St Helens

in 1901 and at 95 Edgeworth Street, St Helens in 1911. They had seven children – Mabel Luckett 1895, Edith Luckett 1896, Annie Luckett 1898, Grace Luckett 1900, Wilfred Luckett 1903. Minnie Luckett 1905 and Dorothy Luckett 1905.

- Ada Mary Luckett (1865–1953) was a domestic servant in 1901 living with her parents. She was a cook in 1911, living with her employer at Sherborne, Dorset. She never married.
- Grace Hannah Luckett (1869–1943) never married.
- Philadelphia Rebecca Luckett (1871–94), a dressmaker in 1891, never married.
- Clara Luckett (1873–94), a tailoress in 1891, never married.
- William George Luckett (1875–1943) was a glass bottle drawer in 1891. He married Fanny Louisa Smith (1877–1925) in 1899. He was a bricklayer in 1901 and they were living with her brother, Alexander Smith, at 39 Wilson Street, St Helens. By 1911 they were at 1 Cleveland Street, Peasley Cross, St Helens. They had seven children – David Luckett 1902, William Luckett 1904, John Luckett 1905, Fanny Luckett c.1909, William George Luckett 1909, Ellen Luckett 1911 and Thomas Luckett 1915.

John was educated at Holy Trinity Church of England School, St Helens until 1902. He was a nature lover and often skipped classes to go bird watching. He was also a fine athlete and enjoyed boxing. He was employed as a miner by the Sutton Heath and Lea Green Colliery Co at Sherdley Colliery. He was a member of Peasley Cross Concertina Club and performed on the radio.

John enlisted as a regular in the Royal Fusiliers on 7th September 1914. He trained at Dover, Kent and served with the 2nd Battalion at Gallipoli from 9th November 1915. He was slightly wounded and frostbitten about 26th November during the winter storms and was evacuated to Malta. He rejoined the unit in Egypt and moved with it to France, arriving on 22nd March 1916. Having been wounded in the left forearm on the Somme in November he was evacuated to England for treatment until after Christmas.

Sherdley Colliery was sunk by Bourne & Robinson c.1873. It closed around 1902, but had been reopened by Sutton Heath & Lea Green Collieries Co Ltd by 1905. It was worked until 1943, but was retained for some years for pumping water. The site is now a housing estate and part of Sherdley Business Park.

Awarded the VC for his actions north of Poelcapelle, Belgium on 9th October 1917, LG 26th November 1917. The VC was presented by the King at Buckingham Palace on 12th December 1917. After receiving the VC he received lots of mail, but he treasured one letter from a nurse who had cared for him the previous December:

I am glad to know that you have won such a coveted honour as the VC. Well done, 'Bed 34'. I feel quite a little reflected glory to think we had you here, and in our small way helped you back to health and strength, to go out and win your spurs. It is a grand thing you have done, sergeant. Deeds live on after we are gone, and inspire those who come after.

Returning home he was picked up by the Mayor and Mayoress of St Helens in an open carriage and kept his head bowed in embarrassment until a neighbour shouted out, *Lift thee 'ead up, Johnny!* He was presented with War Bonds and an illuminated address and addressed the crowd:

The Victoria Cross has not made me a proud man; not at all. I have seen thousands of men earn it, but they have not got it. I got mine because it was rather a high position, and I was seen by four or five others and I got four recommendations. I know the boys who were with me were all worthy of the VC. I am sorry to say most of them got wounded … The position we rushed was where the bullets were coming from that wounded our men. I set my teeth, and you know what it is when a British bulldog sets its teeth; it goes red-hot into it.

He concluded the reception by giving the crowd a rendition of *The Blue Bells of Scotland* on his concertina. He also received a gold watch and £50 in War Bonds from his workmates at Sherdley Colliery, a silver cigarette case from the management of a local theatre and a new concertina from the Peasley Cross Concertina Club.

Awarded the Belgian Croix de Guerre in February 1918, LG 15th April 1918. He was demobilized on 5th January 1919 and returned to work in the colliery. John Molyneux married Mary Agnes née Lyne (1896–1963) in the third quarter of 1919 at Stratford, Warwickshire. They had two children:

• Joyce Molyneux (born 1920).
• Joseph Molyneux (born 1921).

King George V and Queen Mary visited Liverpool on 19th July 1924 for the consecration of the new Cathedral. During the afternoon the King reviewed 55th West Lancashire Territorial Division at Wavertree Playground and John was one of nine VCs presented to the King and Queen. The others included Cyril Gourley, William Heaton, Arthur Procter, Ronald Stuart, Arthur Richardson and John Davies, a close friend of John Molyneux's. John Molyneux and John Davies also met the Prince of Wales (future King Edward VIII) at Victoria Park, St Helens in 1929.

From 1925 John worked for Pilkington Bros, the glassmakers, as a teazer and later as a gas producer in the sheet works. He remained with the company for thirty years until he retired. During the Second World War he served as a warrant officer in the West Lancashire Home Guard – probably in 75th or 93rd County of Lancaster (St Helens) Battalions.

John attended many VC reunions, including the VC Garden Party at Buckingham Palace on 26th June 1920, the VC Dinner at the Royal Gallery of the House of Lords, London on 9th November 1929, the Victory Day Celebration Dinner and Reception at The Dorchester, London on 8th June 1946 and the VC Centenary Celebrations at Hyde Park, London on 26th June 1956. He also attended the first four VC & GC Association Reunions at the Café Royal, London in July 1958, 1960, 1962 and 1964.

John Molyneux died at Ashton Green Hostel, Parr, St Helens, Lancashire after collapsing in the street on an errand for a neighbour on 25th March 1972. He was cremated at St Helens Crematorium, where his ashes were scattered. He is named on a plaque in the Royal Fusiliers Chapel in the Church of St Sepulchre, Holborn Viaduct, London.

John Molyneux meeting the Prince of Wales (future King Edward VIII) at Victoria Park, St Helens in 1929. His close friend, John Davies VC, is next in line to meet the Prince.

The Royal Fusiliers Museum within the Tower of London.

There has been a church on the site of St Sepulchre since Saxon times. The current building is the largest parish church in the City. During Mary 1's reign in 1555, the vicar, John Rogers, was burned as a heretic. In the 1666 Great Fire of London only the outer walls, tower and porch remained standing, but the church escaped with only minor damage during the Blitz. The church contains the Musicians' Chapel with windows commemorating, amongst others, the singer Dame Nellie Melba and the conductor Sir Henry Wood, who learned to play the organ in the church and went on to found the Promenade Concerts, which he conducted for fifty years and continue to this day. John Smith, governor of Virginia, famous for his association with Pocahontas, is buried there. The church bells are the *Bells of Old Bailey* in the nursery rhyme *Oranges and Lemons*. It also houses the Execution Bell, which was rung outside the condemned cell in nearby Newgate prison the night before an execution. The south aisle of the church is the Royal Fusiliers Chapel.

In addition to the VC he was awarded the 1914–15 Star, British War Medal 1914–20, Victory Medal 1914–19, George VI Coronation Medal 1937, Elizabeth II Coronation Medal 1953 and the Belgian Croix de Guerre. His service in the Home Guard may have qualified for the award of the Defence Medal, but it does not form part of the group held by the Royal Fusiliers Museum. The medals were purchased by the Royal Fusiliers at Sotheby's for £2,100 on 31st January 1973. They are held by the Royal Fusiliers Museum at the Tower of London.

2ND LIEUTENANT MONTAGU SHADWORTH SEYMOUR MOORE
15th Battalion, The Hampshire Regiment

Montagu Moore was born at 13 Montague Place, Worthing, Sussex on 9th October 1896. He was known as Monty. His father, Frederick William Moore (1862–1954), was a Queen's (India) Cadet at the Royal Military College, Sandhurst. He was commissioned in The King's (Shropshire Light Infantry) on 25th August 1883 and later became a barrister at law. Frederick married Gertrude Anne Seymour née Guscotte (1870–1952) on 27th February 1889. They were living at 13 Upton Farm, Sompting, West Sussex in 1901 and at 10 The Avenue, Bedford in 1911. They also lived at Goathland, Tower Road, Branksome Park, Bournemouth.

Monty had a sister, Evelyn Seymour Moore (1903–38). She married Charles Geoffrey Brook (1903–96), a shopkeeper, in 1925. They had a daughter, Caroline Jane Mabel Brook (1931–65), who died unmarried. Charles married Maria Eileen K De Sacadura in 1940 at Wandsworth, London. She was born in America c.1915. Charles and Maria had two sons – Peter Geoffrey Brook 1943 and James (or John) CW Brook 1945.

Monty's paternal grandfather, Charles Wilson Moore (1824–82), was commissioned in 6th Madras Native Infantry on 27th February 1841 and served in the China War 1842, being present at the storming of Chin Kiang Foo and operations before Nankin. He was promoted lieutenant 9th April 1844, captain 23rd November 1856, major 30th July 1862, lieutenant colonel 2nd November 1863, colonel 2nd November 1868 and major general 15th August 1869. Charles married Isabella née Atkinson (c.1835–79) in 1857 at

Montague Place in Worthing where Montagu was born. Worthing Pier in the background.

St George Hanover Square, London. They were living at 8 Landsdowne Crescent, Cheltenham, Gloucestershire in 1871. He and his daughter, Rose, were living at the home of his widowed sister-in-law, Eliza Robertson, at 4 Chester Street, St George Hanover Square, London in 1881. In addition to Frederick they had six other children:

- Charles Henry Hodgson Moore (1858–1920) was born at Ootacamund, Madras, India. He joined the Royal Navy on 15th July 1871. In 1881 he was serving aboard HMS *Bacchante* as a sub-lieutenant at the same time as Prince George and Prince Albert Victor, sons of the Prince of Wales, were serving on her as midshipmen. He was promoted lieutenant 30th June 1882, commander 1st January 1895, captain 31st December 1900 and rear admiral 27th April 1910. He commanded nine ships – HMS *Scylla* 18th July–24th August 1901, HMS *Sirius* 17th March 1903–20th October 1905, HMS *Argyll* 27th December 1905–29th January 1906, HMS *Monmouth* 30th January 1906–9th April 1906, HMS *Donegal* 10th April 1906–2nd May 1906, HMS *Hogue* 3rd–14th May 1906, HMS *St George* 15th May–8th August 1906, HMS *Trafalgar* 9th August 1906–14th April 1907 and HMS *Hood* 15th April–31st May 1907. Appointed Rear Admiral-in-Charge, North of Ireland Coast Guard District on 1st June 1907 while on the strength of HMS *President*. He was placed on the Retired List at his own request on 10th May 1913. Promoted to vice admiral on the Retired List on 24th October 1915 and admiral on 1st January 1919. Charles married Fanny Ponsonby (c.1863–1953), who was born at St Vincent, West Indies. They were living at 13 Ashburton Road, Portsmouth, Hampshire in 1891, at 151 Shooters Hill Road, Greenwich, London in 1901 and at 10 Western Parade, Southsea, Hampshire in 1911. Charles and Fanny had two children – Doris Isabel P Moore 1888 and Charles Dalrymple Moore 1890.
- Constance Isabel Moore (1860–1935). In 1881 she was head of household at 26 Royal Parade, Cheltenham with her siblings Herbert, William, Rose and Ethel. She married Francis Fitzgerald Haworth-Booth (1864–1935) in 1893. Francis, later Sir Francis (KCMG 1900), served in the Royal Navy from 15th July 1877. Promoted lieutenant 21st June 1887, commander 31st December 1899 and captain 30th June 1905. He served aboard HMS *Liberty, Active, Edinburgh, Alexandra, Warspite, Howe, Trafalgar, Redpole, Camperdown, Arrogant* and *President*. JP East Riding of Yorkshire 1900. Assistant Director of Naval Intelligence 1905–08. Commanded

HMS *Bacchante* (4,070 tons), second ship of the three-ship *Bacchante* class ironclad screw-propelled corvettes. She was launched in October 1876 and was armed with 14 x 7″ muzzle-loading rifle guns and two 64 Pounder torpedo carriages. During the Third Burmese War in 1885 most of her crew served on gunboats on the Irrawaddy River. In 1888 she went into reserve and was broken up in 1897.

HMS *Brilliant* 20th March 1908–1910. Chief of Staff Naval Mission to Australia 1911. He was placed on the Retired List at his own request on 1st July 1913 and was advanced to rear admiral on the Retired List on 3rd April 1917. Naval Advisor to the High Commissioner of Australia in London 1911–20. Constance and Francis had three children – Francis Adrian Blaydes Booth 1894, Osbert Moore Haworth-Booth 1895 and Constance Cordelia Haworth-Booth 1901. In 1901 Constance was living with her children at 1 Park Place, Devonport, Devon.

Prince Albert Victor on the left was the eldest son of the future King Edward VII and would have succeeded him, but he died of pneumonia in 1892. His brother, Prince George, on the right, became King George V in 1910. Both princes entered the Royal Navy in 1877 and on 17th September 1879 they were assigned to HMS *Bacchante*, part of a squadron to tour the Empire. They visited the Mediterranean, West Indies, South America, South Africa, Australia, China and Japan before *Bacchante* returned to Britain in August 1882. The Princes' diaries were published in 1886 as *The Cruise of Her Majesty's Ship Bacchante*.

- Herbert Moore (born c.1861) was a merchant seaman in 1881.
- Gerald Percy Moore (c.1864–1944), born at Secunderabad, India, was a clerk in a shipping office in 1901. He married Emily Hannah Guy (1864–1940) in 1890. They lived at Marston Villa, Oldfield Park, Bath, Somerset and had six children – Reginald Percy Moore 1892, Augustus Weston Moore 1893, John Atkinson Moore 1893, Gerald Wilson Moore 1895, Evelyn May Moore 1896 and Madeline Alice Moore 1899.
- John Ponsonby Moore (1865–90) was born at Ootacamund, India.
- Rose Gertrude Moore (1866–81) was born at Trimulgherry, India.

His maternal grandfather, John Guscotte (1838–1902), a solicitor, married Fanny née Reeve (c.1830–93) in 1862. They were living at 1 Pelham Crescent, Brompton, London in 1865 and at 47 Onslow Square, St Mary Abbotts, London in 1871. In addition to Gertrude they had six other children:

- Fanny Abigail Reeve Guscotte (1863–1937) married Evelyn Rothe Sandwith (1868–1942) in 1897. He was born at Ahmadabad, India. Evelyn was educated at Cambridge and played cricket for Norfolk. He was a stockbroker in partnership with his brother-in-law, Geoffrey Reeve Guscotte, at 7 Draper Gardens, Throgmorton Street, London. The partnership was dissolved by mutual consent on 15th August 1898. He was a Freemason and Brother of the United Grand Lodge of England. Evelyn was a member of the Dorking and Leatherhead Rural Council in 1909. They were living at The Studio, Holmwood, Dorking, Surrey in 1937.

- Leonard John Guscotte (1865–94) died at Magersfontein, Cape Colony, South Africa.
- Gerald Reeve Guscotte (born and died 1866).
- Geoffrey Reeve Guscotte (1867–1921) was a stockbroker in partnership with his brother-in-law, Evelyn Rothe Sandwith. He married Sybil Jeffery (1872–1941) in 1889 and they had two children – Gladys Reeve Guscotte 1890 and Geoffrey Claud Vivian John Guscotte 1894. Sybil was living at Thurston Lodge, Thurston Park, Whitstable, Kent at the time of her death.
- Lilias Louise Fisher Guscotte (1871–1937) married Charles Edward Bradbury (1866–1909), a solicitor, in 1899. They were living at 7 South Terrace, Surbiton, Surrey in 1901. They had three children – Frederick D Bradbury 1899, Phyllis Mary Bradbury 1904 and Ruth Louise Bradbury 1909. Lilias lived at Maltmans, South Cuckfield, Sussex before moving to Bankside Nursing Home, Wivelsfield, near Haywards Heath, Sussex, where she died.
- Ferrand Thomas Guscotte (1875–1918) married Eliza Chandler (1865–1933) in 1900. They were living at 3 Bedford Road, Hastings in 1901 and The Beacon, Lenham Heath, Hollingbourne, Kent in 1911.

HMS *Sirius* (3,600 tons), an Apollo-class cruiser of the Royal Navy in service from 1891 to 1918, was commanded by Montagu's uncle, Charles Henry Hodgson Moore, 1903–05. She was armed with two QF 6″ guns, six 4.7″ guns, eight 6 Pounder guns and a 3 Pounder. *Sirius* served off America 1892–95 and on the China Station 1903–05. She went into reserve in February 1912 in the training squadron. In October 1914 she was one of a number of obsolete warships supporting the Belgians with shore bombardments. *Sirius* was part of Nore Command until March 1915, and was then a guardship on the east coast until sent to West Africa.

In April 1918 HMS *Bacchante* (top) and HMS *Brilliant* were scuttled in the mouth of Ostend harbour during the failed raid to prevent U-boats transiting from their base at Bruges to the North Sea.

Monty was educated at Wykeham House School in Worthing, Bedford School 1906–13 and privately for a year at the Army coaching establishment, Stirling House, in Bournemouth, also attended by the future Lieutenant WL Robinson VC RFC. Monty was trained at the Royal Military College, Sandhurst from March 1915 and was commissioned in 3rd (Reserve) Battalion on 16th August 1916. He went to France on 20th September 1916 and was briefly attached to a brigade HQ before joining 15th Battalion. He was posted to 1st Battalion in January 1917, but returned to 15th Battalion in time for the attack on Messines in June 1917. He was wounded in the leg by shrapnel, evacuated to England and returned to the front in September 1917.

Wykeham House School on Wykeham Road, Worthing closed in 1934.

Stirling House on Manor Road, Bournemouth was a coaching establishment for those intending to go to Sandhurst.

Awarded the VC for his actions near Tower Hamlets, east of Ypres, Belgium on 20th September 1917, LG 8th November 1917. The VC was presented by the King at Buckingham Palace on 21st November 1917. He returned to the Battalion to train drafts from a Yeomanry unit and was later employed as a bombing instructor at the Divisional Reinforcement Camp. Awarded the French Croix de Guerre on 16th November 1917, for most brilliant military qualities and for rendering exceptionally good services during the battles in Flanders in September and October 1917, LG 16th January 1920. He was appointed acting captain on 3rd February 1918 while an assistant instructor at a school of instruction and later served as ADC to Lieutenant General Sir John Du Cane, commanding XV Corps. Promoted lieutenant 16th February 1918 and was posted to Fifth Army Infantry School. He took his trainees into action during the German March 1918 Spring Offensive.

Montagu attended Bedford School 1906–13. It was founded in 1552 and is one of four independent schools in Bedford run by the Harpur Trust. A member of staff in the early 1950s was John Durnford-Slater, who raised the first commando unit in the Second World War. The school has produced many famous alumni including; Dr Archer John Porter Martin (1910–2002), the 1952 Nobel Prize for Chemistry; five VC/GC recipients; twenty-four rugby internationals; seven Olympic gold medal winners, including Harold Abrahams, the winner of the 100m in 1924, whose story was told in the film *Chariots of Fire*; Alastair Cook the England cricket captain 2012–17; and Baron Paddy Ashdown, leader of the Liberal Democratic Party 1988–99. Most of the main school building was destroyed in a fire in March 1979, but the shell was restored and it reopened in September 1981.

Brigadier-General George Grogan VC CB CMG DSO. His story appears in the seventh book in this series, *The Lys to Amiens.*

Lieutenant Colonel John Sherwood-Kelly VC CMG DSO. His story appears in the sixth book in this series, *Cambrai to the German Spring Offensive.*

Montagu was ADC to Lieutenant General (later General) Sir John Du Cane (1865–1947), commander of XV Corps. He was commissioned in the Royal Artillery in 1884, served in the South African War and became CRA 3rd Division in 1911. As MGRA at GHQ BEF he laid the organisational groundwork for the expansion of BEF artillery. After a spell at the Ministry of Munitions in 1916 he took command of XV Corps. On 12th April 1918, during the crisis of the German spring offensives, he was appointed liaison officer between Haig and Foch. He was Master General of the Ordnance 1920, GOC-in-C Western Command 1923 and GOC-in-C British Army of the Rhine 1924–27. In 1927 he became Governor and C-in-C Malta on the death of General Sir Walter Norris Congreve VC KCB MVO DL.

After the war Monty served in 2nd Hampshire, commanded by Lieutenant Colonel John Sherwood-Kelly VC, in 238th Special Brigade, commanded by Brigadier-General George Grogan VC, in North Russia. The Battalion also served in Ireland. Monty transferred to the 1st Battalion, which served at Constantinople in the Army of the Black Sea 1920–21. He was attached to 2nd Nyasaland Battalion, King's African Rifles at Tabora, Tanganyika Territory, from 4th August 1921 and was promoted temporary captain in the King's African Rifles on 12th June 1924. Monty was restored to the establishment of the Hampshire Regiment as a lieutenant on 4th August 1926 and transferred to the Regular Army Reserve of Officers on 1st September with the rank of captain with seniority from 4th January 1925. His address given on his Medal Index Card in the National Archives was Horsa Lodge, Hengistbury Road, Southbourne, Hampshire.

Monty joined the Tanganyika Game Department and accompanied the Prince of Wales on a shooting trip in 1928. He returned to Britain to marry Audrey Yolande Penn née Milton (11th December 1903–1982), registered at Newton Abbot, Devon in the 3rd quarter of 1933. They had a son, Montague Charles P Moore, whose birth was registered in the 2nd quarter of 1936 at Newton Abbot. Montague junior was appointed Temporary District Officer (Kikuyu Guard), Meru District, Central Province, Kenya on 23rd June 1955. He married Jane M Acworth (born 1941) in

1967 and they had five children – Helen Rosamond Moore 1967, Sarah Veryan Moore 1969, Andrew James A Moore 1971, John Charles M Moore 1972 and Adam William P Moore 1973.

Audrey's father, John Penn Milton (1873–1923), married Alice Ellen née de la Condamine (1867–1935) from Edinburgh, Midlothian, in 1899 at Kingston, Surrey. They lived at Clifford

The Tanganyika Game Department staff in 1938. Monty Moore is centre right in the bush hat (rayhewlett.org).

Lodge, St George's Road, Babbacombe, Torquay and he worked at Devon County Council Sanatorium, Bovey Tracey. John served as a private in the Volunteer Medical Staff Corps c.1894–95 and on the outbreak of war volunteered to serve in the Sportsman's Battalions, Royal Fusiliers, but withdrew when he was offered a place in the RAMC. Appointed lieutenant in 2nd Wessex Field Ambulance RAMC on 11th October 1914 and joined the unit at Torquay. He was promoted captain on 11th April and served in France February–July 1917 with 2/2nd Wessex Field Ambulance. While in England on leave he was treated at Durnford Hospital, Plymouth for debility and anaemia. He was posted to 255th Infantry Battalion (later 52nd (Graduated) Battalion, Royal Sussex Regiment), 214th Brigade in the short-lived home based 71st Division in Colchester. He applied for a posting closer to his wife in Torquay, following the death of their only son. He was relieved in 71st Division on 19th September and posted to Southern Command on 28th September. A medical board on 23rd November found him unfit for General Service for three months but fit for Home Service. A medical board on 22nd February 1918 found him unfit for two months, but fit for duty at a base hospital. Posted to Egypt and Palestine in April 1918 and served with 137th Indian Stationary Hospital and 27th General Hospital, Cairo. He contracted paratyphoid in Cairo on 4th October 1919 and was treated at Nasrieh Officers' Hospital, Cairo before being evacuated to Britain on 8th December. He was admitted to Addington Park Military Hospital on 20th December. A medical board on 7th January 1920 sent him on three months' sick leave. Further medical boards at Devonport on 13th April and 6th May each sent him on leave for a month. A medical board at Tidworth on 6th May recommended discharge and he was demobilised on 10th May 1920. John retired on 29th September 1922, having reached the age limit. In addition to Audrey they had a son, also John Penn Milton (1900–17). He was a midshipman serving aboard HMS *Vanguard* when an accidental explosion occurred just before midnight on 9th July 1917 at Scapa Flow; 826 lives were lost according to CWGC records including John. There were only two survivors of this, the most catastrophic accidental explosion ever in the

UK. One of the casualties was Captain Kyosuke Eto, an observer from the Imperial Japanese Navy. John Milton is commemorated on the Chatham Naval Memorial, Kent.

Monty and Audrey settled in the Serengeti Game Reserve at Banagi Camp, a remote ranger station. She wrote *Serengeti*, published by Country Life in 1938, which did much to influence the preservation of wild life in East Africa. Monty became Tanganyika's Chief Game Warden in 1944, a post he held until 1951 when he retired to Kenya.

Monty Moore died at Kiganjo, Kenya on 12th September 1966 of renal failure. He was cremated at Langata Crematorium, Nairobi and his ashes were scattered by his son in Serengeti National Park, Tanzania and at Hyena Dam, Nairobi National Park. He is commemorated in a number of other places:

HMS *Vanguard* (20,000 tons), a St Vincent-class Dreadnought battleship in the Home and Grand Fleets launched in April 1909. She was armed with ten Mk XI 12″ guns, twenty Mk VII 4″ guns and three 18″ torpedo tubes. She underwent major alterations before the war. During the Battle of Jutland on 31st May 1916, she was in the 4th Division of the 4th Battle Squadron and engaged SMS *Wiesbaden*. On 9th July 1917 she exercised the routine for abandoning ship and anchored in the northern part of Scapa Flow. At 11.20 p.m. she was destroyed in a cataclysmic explosion. A court of inquiry learned that there was a small explosion between the foremast and 'A' turret followed, after a brief interval, by two much larger explosions. Although the main explosion resulted from the detonation of cordite charges in a main magazine, the cause is less clear.

- Memorial plaque at Bedford School.
- Victoria Cross Memorial, Hampshire Regiment Museum, Winchester.
- Stained glass window on Worthing Pier, Sussex dedicated in 2016, close to Montague Place, where he was born.

In addition to the VC he was awarded the British War Medal 1914–20, Victory Medal 1914–19 with Mentioned-in-Despatches Oakleaf, George VI Coronation Medal 1937, Elizabeth II Coronation Medal 1953 and French Croix de Guerre 1914–18 with Bronze Palm. The VC was on loan to the Royal Hampshire Regiment Museum, Serle's House, Southgate Street, Winchester, Hampshire until withdrawn by the family in 2011. It is held by The Michael Ashcroft Trust and displayed in the Lord Ashcroft Victoria Cross Collection in the Imperial War Museum.

Audrey Moore's book *Serengeti* was also published in French.

7708 LANCE SERGEANT JOHN MOYNEY
2nd Battalion, Irish Guards

John Moyney, known as Jack, was born at Rathdowney, Queen's County (now Co Laois), Ireland on 9th January 1895. His parents were James Moyney and Bridget née Butler. John had a brother. He was educated at Rathdowney School and worked on a local farm as a labourer. He applied to join the Royal Irish Constabulary, but an officer stated, *I do not consider the above-named a suitable candidate ... He joined the Irish Guards because he had seduced a young girl named Bowe of Moore Street, Rathdowney. Apart from this his people are of such a low class that the prestige of the Constabulary would be very much lowered in the eyes of the public...*

John enlisted in the Leinster Regiment on 6th April 1915 at Maryborough, Co Cork, but his attestation papers were amended to Irish Guards. He reported to the Depot (5th Company, 2nd Irish Guards) on 8th April and went to France on 5th October. He was promoted a number of times – unpaid lance corporal 17th February 1916, lance corporal 10th July, corporal and unpaid lance sergeant 18th September and lance sergeant 8th October.

The Square, Rathdowney.

Awarded the VC for his actions at Ney Copse, Broembeek, Belgium on 12th/13th September 1917, LG 17th October 1917. Promoted sergeant 27th September. The VC was presented to him and Thomas Woodcock by the King at Buckingham Palace on 9th March 1918. John Moyney married Bridget née Carroll (c.1892–26th June 1969) at Kilmartin, Roscrea, Queen's County on 17th March 1918. She was living at Nore View Cottage, Borris-in-Ossory at the time. John and Bridget had six children:

More than 200,000 prisoners of war passed through Stalag III-A. The population peaked in May 1944 at 48,600.

* Mary born on 2nd January 1919.
* James Moyney (c.1924–2008) enlisted in the Irish Guards and served during the Second World War in North Africa (2723468). He was taken prisoner in Italy and

held in Luckenwalde Prisoner of War Camp (Stalag III-A). He married Mary Kennedy (c.1925–2010) and they had a child.
• Four other daughters.

John and Thomas Woodcock were due to return to the Battalion on 20th March, but John did not arrive. His absence was almost certainly connected to his marriage three days before his leave ended. He returned on 2nd May after being absent for six weeks and was charged with breaking out of camp and being absent without leave while on active service. He was found guilty by a general court martial on 13th June 1918 and reduced to the ranks.

Awarded the French Medaille Militaire, LG 10th October 1918. John served in France and Germany until 1st March 1919. He was demobilised and transferred to the Class Z Reserve on 4th June 1919. Returning to Ireland, he felt disillusioned about the future, but refused to fight in the civil war with the Irish Republican Army, although many of comrades did. *Sure it was they who trained the IRA and why wouldn't you feel bitter: after fighting for the British, they send over the Black and Tans and start killing your people.*

John struggled financially and sought assistance on numerous occasions from a number of charitable organisations. He first appealed to the Irish Guards in October 1921 when a severe bout of trench fever prevented him from working consistently. This resulted in him being awarded a 20% Disability Pension of £-/8/- paid from 20th November 1921 until 30th January 1923. Financial problems continued and he made more appeals. The Irish Guards Charitable Fund responded, but it was barely sufficient. Captain Alfred Pollard VC MC DCM sought help for him from the VC Remembrance Fund, but the Irish Guards were reluctant to offer further assistance, *Moyney has already had more than his share from my funds. I can provide nothing, as my funds are so low, but if you will put up a concrete suggestion as regards the payment of Moyney's debts I will endeavour to help to a small extent, provided Moyney is made to understand clearly that it must be an absolutely final award as far as my funds are concerned.* Pollard suggest a better-paid job be secured for Moyney, but this brought an exasperated response, *I am very much afraid that Moyney is a hopeless case. He has had every chance. I have already assisted him to the extent of £20 and cannot make any further grant. Moyney, or rather his wife, does not want to come to this country. Knowing, as I do, what an improvident person Moyney is, I should be very sorry to recommend him for a job.* Despite all this John remained loyal and bequeathed his medals to the Irish Guards.

Alfred Pollard VC MC DCM (1893–1960) was one of two Honourable Artillery Company VCs at Gavrelle in April 1917. He served in the RAF in the 1920s and went on to become a prolific author of factual and fictional books. His autobiography, *Fire Eater*, was published in 1932.

John was employed as a porter by the Great Southern Railway in Ireland. He attended Dublin's Festival of Remembrance in November 1956 with fellow VCs Sir Adrian Carton de Wiart, James Duffy and Joseph Woodall, accompanied by Sir A Clutterbuck, the British Ambassador. John retired in 1960 as head porter at Roscrea Station. He watched Queen Elizabeth II present new Colours to the Irish Guards on 10th June 1966. He and Bridget were living at 9 Legion Villas, Ashbury, Roscrea at the time of her death in 1969. John was a devout Catholic and, despite his own financial problems, he raised thousands of pounds for St Joseph's Young Priests Society, a lay organisation that assisted students for the priesthood.

Roscrea Station, where John worked until 1960. The Great Southern Railways Company was formed by the amalgamation of the Great Southern and Western Railway Company, Midland Great Western Railway Company and the Cork, Bandon and South Coast Railway Company on 12th November 1924 and the Dublin and South Eastern Railway on 1st January 1925. Twenty-two smaller companies were absorbed and the new company operated all railways wholly within the Irish Free State. Cross-border railways remained separate (Turf Burner).

John Moyney died at Roscrea, Co Tipperary, Ireland on 10th November 1980 and is buried in Roscrea Roman Catholic Cemetery. He was the last surviving Irish VC. He is also commemorated on a plaque on his former home at 9 Legion Villas, dedicated on 27th June 2016. His VC action featured in Issues 682 and 1229 of the Victor Comic on 16th March 1974 and 8th September 1984, entitled *Open Fire!* and *A True Story of Men at War* respectively.

In addition to the VC he was awarded the 1914–15 Star, British War Medal 1914–20, Victory Medal 1914–19, George VI Coronation Medal 1937, Elizabeth II Coronation Medal 1953, Elizabeth II Silver Jubilee Medal 1977 and the French Médaille Militaire. The VC is held by the Irish Guards and is in the Guards Museum, Wellington Barracks, Birdcage Walk, London. A set of wire-cutters used by John during his VC action was mounted on a 4,800 year-old piece of Irish yew and presented to the Guards Museum in March 1999.

51339 SERGEANT GEORGE HARRY MULLIN
Princess Patricia's Canadian Light Infantry, Canadian Expeditionary Force

George Mullin was born on 15th August 1892 at Portland, Oregon, United States of America. His date of birth was recorded as 20th August 1891 in the 1901 Census of Canada and as 15th August 1891 on his attestation papers.

His father, Henry 'Harry' Mullin, was born c.1858 at St George, Brant County, Ontario, Canada. He was a blacksmith when he enlisted in 10th Infantry Regiment, US Army on 20th May 1878 at Buffalo, New Jersey, USA. He was described as 5′ 6¼″ tall, with grey eyes, dark brown hair and fair complexion. He was serving at Fort Holmes, Mackinac, Michigan in 1880 and later in Oregon, where he was discharged on 19th May 1883 at the end of a five-year engagement. Harry married Effie May née Kenedy/Kennedy (c.1870–1940), a dressmaker born at Benton, Oregon, USA, in 1888. They moved to Moosomin, Saskatchewan, Canada c.1893, where Harry took up farming. They had returned to Oregon by 1910 and were living at West Coquille Precinct, Coos County, where Harry was a shopkeeper. She was living at Kamloops, British Columbia by December 1914 and at 710 Kings Road, Victoria, British Columbia in 1916. Effie died on 5th February 1940 at New Westminster, British Columbia. Effie and Harry had had eight children by 1910, of whom five were still living, but only three of George's siblings are known:

George Mullin was born at Portland, Oregon in 1892.

- Gladys Mullin (born c.1893) was born in Canada. She was an actress with a travelling troupe in 1910.
- Roy Turner Mullin (1897–1916) was born at Flemming, Saskatchewan, Canada. He was a gas engineer when he enlisted in 10th Canadian Mounted Rifles on 23rd February 1915 (10382) at Moosomin, Saskatchewan. He was described as 5′ 8″ tall, weighing 145 lbs, with dark complexion, blue/grey eyes, dark brown hair and his religious denomination was Church of England. He gave his year of birth as 1896, probably to ensure he was accepted. He went to England and was taken on the strength of the Canadian Cavalry Depot, Shorncliffe. Kent on 10th September 1915. He transferred to 11th Reserve Battalion on 8th December 1915 and to the Princess

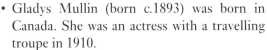

Moosomin was founded when the Canadian Pacific Railway arrived in 1882. It was named after Chief Moosomin, who led his band into treaty status. Several military units were based there, including 16th Light Horse, in which George served, and 10th Canadian Mounted Rifles, in which his brother Roy enlisted in 1915. The town's most famous son was General Andrew McNaughton, who commanded Canada's overseas army in the Second World War and then became Minister of Defence.

Patricia's Canadian Light Infantry (115079) on 15th March 1916. He landed at Le Havre the following day to join the Canadian Base Depot. He left it on 18th March and joined the Battalion on 19th March. Roy was reported missing in action 2nd–4th June, but rejoined his unit on 7th June. He was attached to 3rd Canadian Division Wiring Party 19th July–22nd August. He was killed in action near Courcelette, France on 15th September 1916 (Canadian National Vimy Memorial, France).

Main Street, Kamloops, British Columbia.

* William Valentine Mullin (born 1899) was born at Moosomin, Saskatchewan. He was a blacksmith's helper when he enlisted in 88th Battalion (Victoria Fusiliers) on 27th March 1916 (181156). He was described as 5′ 7″ tall, with fresh complexion, brown eyes, brown hair and his religious denomination

Roy Mullin's name on the Canadian National Vimy Memorial.

was Church of England. He emigrated to Washington, USA on 8th April 1941 and lived at Route 2, Kirkland, King County. He enlisted in the US Army on 4th December 1942 and was honourably discharged on 21st September 1943.

George's paternal grandfather, William A Mullin (1830–1910), was born in Ireland or at Long Island, New York, USA. He married Olivia née Johnson (c.1811–63), who was born in Ireland. She died following the birth of her fourth child at St George, South Dumfries Township, Brant County, Ontario. In addition to Harry they had four other children:

* John Mullin (born 1854) married in 1900 at Brant. He was a farmer in 1901 living with his younger brother, Turner, and nephew, Harry, at Assinobia, New Hastings.
* Hannah 'Isabella' Mullin (born c.1856) married in 1880 and died after 1930 at Beloit, Rock County, Wisconsin, USA.
* Robert Mullin (born c.1860).
* Turner Mullin (born 1863).

His maternal grandfather, George Washington Kenedy (1844–1922), was born at Liberty, Adams, Illinois, USA. He married Malinda née Johnson (1852–1922), born in Oregon, USA, in 1869 at Amity, Yamhill, Oregon. He was a blacksmith in 1880 and they were living at Corvallis, Benton, Oregon. In addition to Effie they had two other daughters:

- Grace Kenedy (born c.1873).
- Bertha Kenedy (born 1875) married Harland Robert Callison (born c.1866) in 1892 at Palouse, Whitman, Washington, USA. They had three children – George R Callison 1893, Lloyd Stanley Callison 1895 and Sarah Zada Callison 1897. Bertha married James Williamson McKee in 1901 and they also had three children – Clifford Harry McKee 1902, Lester McKee 1907 and Merle James McKee 1915.

William married Margaret Wallace (1834–1906) later in 1863 at Toronto, Ontario and they had a daughter, Jane Mullin c.1869, at St George, South Dumfries Township. William was an agent in 1871.

George was educated at Moosomin Public School and Moosomin Collegiate Institute, Saskatchewan. He became a farmer at Kamloops, British Columbia and also served with 16th Light Horse for five months. He enlisted in 32nd Battalion CEF at Winnipeg, Alberta on 14th December 1914. He was described as 5′ 7″ tall, weighing 155 lbs, with dark complexion, greyish brown eyes, dark brown hair and his religious denomination was Church of England. George was included in a draft transferred to Princess Patricia's Canadian Light Infantry in February 1915 and sailed for England on the 23rd. He went to France on 31st July and was selected as a sniper in October.

He was in action at Sanctuary Wood, near Ypres on 2nd-3rd June 1916 and received superficial shrapnel wounds to his right forehead, ear and penis (femur in some reports), which resulted in no lasting disability. He was treated at 3rd British Red Cross and 14th General Hospitals before being evacuated on HMHS *Jan Breydel* to Dartford War Hospital, Kent on 5th June. He was transferred to the VAD Hospital, Sidcup, Kent on 17th June and to the Canadian Division Convalescent Hospital, Woodcote Park, Epsom, Surrey on 8th July. He was discharged on 19th July and reported to the Canadian Casualty Assembly Centre, Folkestone, Kent on 22nd July and transferred to 1st Canadian Convalescent Depot on 26th July. Having been declared fit for duty on 30th August, he transferred

Moosomin Collegiate Institute, Saskatchewan.

HMHS *Jan Breydel* (1,767 tons) was a Belgian Goverment mail steamer built in 1909. She was in military service as a hospital ship from August 1915 until August 1919. She was broken up in 1933.

to the Royal Canadian Regiment & Princess Patricia's Canadian Light Infantry Depot at Caesar's Camp South, Cheriton, near Folkestone on 1st September. He was transferred to the strength of Princess Patricia's Canadian Light Infantry Overseas on 27th September, returned to France on the 29th and rejoined his unit on 4th October.

Awarded the MM for his actions on 16th December 1916 in the La Folie Sector on Vimy Ridge; he assisted Sergeant ND Dow (MM for this action) in a reconnaissance of an enemy post. George later accompanied Lieutenant AA McDougall's (MC for this action) party to the same spot at 3.20 a.m., killed the sentry, threw bombs down the communication trench to block the enemy supports and assisted in carrying his officer out of the crater. He also examined the enemy wire on numerous occasions after an artillery bombardment under very dangerous circumstances and his reports were always accurate, LG 19th February 1917.

George was promoted corporal on 16th March 1917 and acting sergeant on 9th April. He was granted ten days leave to Paris from 22nd May and was promoted sergeant on 15th July. **Awarded the VC for his actions on Meetscheele Spur, Passchendaele, Belgium on 30th October 1917, LG 11th January 1918.** George was granted fourteen days leave in Britain from 27th December 1917 and rejoined his unit on 12th January 1918. He assumed command of the snipers and scouts briefly and returned to England on 25th February. He was posted to the Eastern Ontario Regimental Depot, Seaford, East Sussex on 7th March prior to attending officer training and was attached to 6th (Reserve) Battalion the same day. The VC was presented by the King at Buckingham Palace on 16th March. On 3rd April George was granted authority to marry. He attended 9th Officers' Training Course at the Canadian Officers' Training School, Bexhill, Sussex from 11th May. George was commissioned as a temporary lieutenant on 6th August and was taken on strength of 6th (Reserve) Battalion. He was appointed Battalion Bombing Instructor on 1st September. He also coached and played baseball for the Battalion and maintained this interest throughout his life.

George was posted to No.3 Regimental Depot Group on 14th June 1919 and sailed for Canada on SS *Grampian* on 23rd June, arriving on 2nd July. He was struck off the strength of the CEF on general demobilisation on 6th July 1919.

George Mullin married Elizabeth 'Bessie' Dorothy née Gardner (1st February 1890–29th August 1983) on 13th April 1918 at St Thomas' Church, Heaton Chapel, Stockport, Cheshire. She was born at

Officer Cadet George Mullin on the right with Captain Thain MacDowell VC DSO on the left.

Brockville, Leeds, Ontario, Canada but moved to England and was living at Norville, Holly Road, Heaton Norris and later at Denmark House, Steyne Road, Seaford while George was based there. They returned to Canada and settled at Moosomin, Saskatchewan before moving to Regina in 1934. George returned to farming and was appointed Sergeant-at-Arms of the Saskatchewan Legislature in 1934. In that capacity he was a member of the Canadian Contingent at Queen Elizabeth II's Coronation in June 1953.

St Thomas Church was built in 1765 and gave Heaton Chapel its name. George Mullin married Elizabeth Gardner there in April 1918. There have been several extensions added to the building since.

Bessie's father, John Gardner (1865–1940), an engineer, was born at Levenshulme, Lancashire, England. He married Hannah Cooke née Walker (1866–1931) in 1889 at Stockport, Cheshire. Hannah was born at West Coast, New Zealand. He was an engineer, reportedly living at Waterstown, New York in 1900. She was living at 5 Coleman Grove, Heaton Norris, Stockport in 1901. By 1911 John was a traveller in the corn trade and they were living at 7 Hawthorne Grove, Stockport. In addition to Bessie they had three other children:

The Saskatchewan Legislature building in Regina, where George was Sergeant-at-Arms from 1934 (Global News).

- John Lawrence Gardner (1892–1950) was born at Waterstown, New York, USA. He was working with shorthand typewriters in 1911. He married Dorothy May Page (1899–1961) in 1918 at West Ashford, Kent, where she was born. He died on 15 September 1950 at Ashford, Kent. They had a daughter, Maisie D Gardner, in 1918. Dorothy is understood to have married Thomas Kennedy in 1960 at Folkestone, Kent.
- James Reginald Gardner (born 1895).
- Nellie Grace Gardner (1905–97) was born at 7 Hawthorn Grove, Heaton Norris, Stockport. She married Stanley Hodgson (1903–71) in 1931 at Heaton Norris and they had two children – Anne Hodgson 1933 and David G Hodgson 1937. In 1939 Stanley was a chief clerk in an assurance office and they were living at 6 Weston Avenue, Stockport.

George as Sergeant-at-Arms.

George was promoted major in 4th Battalion, South Saskatchewan Regiment on 1st October 1920. He transferred to 1st Assiniboia Militia on 31st May 1926 and to 110th Field Battery (Howitzers) on 15th December 1936. He volunteered for service at the outbreak of the Second World War and was appointed to the Veterans Guard of Canada as a lieutenant. He served until 1946 in command of an internment camp. George attended three VC reunions – the VC Dinner at the Royal Gallery of the House of Lords, London on 9th November 1929, the VC Centenary Celebrations at Hyde Park, London on 26th June 1956 and the 3rd VC & GC Association Reunion at the Café Royal, London on 18th July 1962. He joined the Canadian Division of the Legion of Frontiersmen about 1957.

George Mullin died at his home at Garnet Street, Regina, Saskatchewan on 5th April 1963. He is buried in a Canadian Legion plot of South Side Cemetery, Moosomin, Saskatchewan. He is commemorated in a number of other places:

At the outbreak of the Second World War many veterans of the previous conflict volunteered to serve again. Many of them formed the Veterans Home Guard, later renamed the Veterans Guard of Canada. They were organised into companies of both active and reserve companies. At its peak in June 1943 the Guard numbered 451 officers and 9,806 other ranks on active service. It served as a defence force, guarded military installations and also guarded internment camps. Thirty-seven active companies and seventeen internment camp staffs were raised for these duties. Most of the Veterans Guard remained in Canada, but a small number deployed overseas, most notably the General Duty Company attached to the Canadian Military Headquarters in London, England. The Guard was gradually reduced in size as its responsibilities ended and it was finally disbanded in 1947.

- Mullin Lake, North Saskatchewan, Canada.
- Two 49 cents postage stamps in honour of the 94 Canadian VC winners were issued by Canada Post on 21st October 2004 on the 150th Anniversary of the first Canadian VC's action, Alexander Roberts Dunn VC.
- Named on a Victoria Cross obelisk to all Canadian VCs at Military Heritage Park, Barrie, Ontario dedicated by The Princess Royal on 22nd October 2013.
- Named on one of eleven plaques honouring 175 men from overseas awarded the VC for the Great War. The plaques were unveiled by the Senior Minister of State at the Foreign & Commonwealth Office and Minister for Faith and Communities, Baroness Warsi, at a reception at Lancaster House, London on 26th June 2014 attended by The Duke of Kent and relatives of the VC recipients. The Canadian plaque was unveiled outside the British High Commission in Elgin Street, Ottawa on 10th November 2014 by The Princess Royal in the presence of British High Commissioner Howard Drake, Canadian Minister of Veterans Affairs Julian Fantino and Canadian Chief of the Defence Staff General Thomas J Lawson.

George Mullin's medal group.

George Mullin's grave
in South Side Cemetery,
Moosomin, Saskatchewan.

- The Secretary of State for Communities and Local Government, Eric Pickles MP, announced that Victoria Cross recipients from the Great War would have commemorative paving stones laid in their birthplace as a lasting legacy of local heroes within communities. The stones would be laid on or close to the 100th anniversary of their VC actions. For the 145 VCs born in Australia, Belgium, Canada, China, Denmark, Egypt, France, Germany, India, Iraq, Japan, Nepal, Netherlands, New Zealand, Pakistan, South Africa, Sri Lanka, Ukraine and United States of America, individual commemorative stones were unveiled at the National Memorial Arboretum, Alrewas, Staffordshire by Prime Minister David Cameron MP and Sergeant Johnson Beharry VC on 5th March 2015.
- Plaque on a memorial to the ninety-nine Canadian VCs in York Cemetery, Toronto.

Elizabeth may have died on 29th August 1983, but could have been as early as 1975. She is understood to have been buried at Wabash, Wabash County, Indiana, USA.

  In addition to the VC and MM he was awarded the 1914–15 Star, British War Medal 1914–20, Victory Medal 1914–19 with MID Oakleaf, Canadian Volunteer Service Medal 1939–45, War Medal 1939–45, George VI Coronation Medal 1937 and Elizabeth II Coronation Medal 1953. His medals were held in trust by the Princess Patricia's Canadian Light Infantry Museum, but were recalled by family members in 1975 and sold to the Canadian War Museum in Ottawa, Ontario for an undisclosed sum and are held there.

LIEUTENANT CHRISTOPHER PATRICK JOHN O'KELLY
52nd Battalion (New Ontario), Canadian Expeditionary Force

Christopher O'Kelly was born on 18th November 1895 at Winnipeg, Manitoba, Canada. His father, Christopher O'Kelly (1864–1936) was born at Pembroke, Ontario. He married Cecilia Mary née Morrison (1869–1928) at Pembroke, also of Irish extraction. In 1891 he was a furrier and they were living with his sister, Matilda, at Pembroke. He was working in real estate in Manitoba by 1911. They lived at Yale Avenue, Winnipeg and had moved to 2 Chelsea Court by 1916. In census returns her name appears as Mary Cecilia, Marion or Mary. She appeared as Mary O'Kelly in the 1911 Census of Canada. In 1920 she was living with her daughters in Hennepin, Minnesota, USA having emigrated there the previous year. It is understood that Cecilia and Christopher divorced in August 1925. Christopher junior had two sisters:

* Monica Marion O'Kelly (born 1894) was a commercial artist in 1920 at Hennepin, Minnesota. She married as Kiely and moved to Clearwater, Florida.

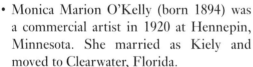
Patrick O'Kelly was born in Winnipeg, Manitoba in November 1895.

* Margaret Mary O'Kelly (born 1897) was a stenographer with a life insurance company in 1920, living with her mother and sister at Hennepin, Minnesota. She moved to Clearwater, Florida and married as Wall.

Christopher's paternal grandfather, Christopher O'Kelly, was born c.1816 in Ireland and emigrated to Canada. He married Elizabeth née Worrell, also born in Ireland. In addition to Christopher they had at least a daughter, Matilda O'Kelly, born c.1861 in Ontario. She was living with her brother Christopher and his wife in 1891 at Renfrew North, Ontario. She married as Roney and had at least two children – Percy Roney c.1886 and John Roney c.1888.

Christopher was educated in public schools and at St John's College in Winnipeg before becoming a gold prospector. He served in 90th Royal Winnipeg Rifles (Militia) and enlisted as a lieutenant in 144th Battalion (Winnipeg Rifles) CEF, the 'Little Black Devils', on 7th February 1916. He was described as 5' 11" tall, weighed 145 lbs and his religious denomination was Roman Catholic. He gave his address as Suite 1, 47 Kennedy Street, Winnipeg. Having trained at Camp Hughes,

St John's College in Winnipeg.

90th Royal Winnipeg Rifles (Militia) formed in November 1883 and served in the 1885 North-West Rebellion, during which it gained its nickname, Little Black Devils, due to wearing rifle green rather than traditional red coats. The Regiment raised several battalions during the First World War. In 1920 it became The Winnipeg Rifles and in 1935 The Royal Winnipeg Rifles. The Regiment landed in England in September 1940 and took part in the Normandy invasion in June 1944, serving in northwest Europe until the war's end. In 1955 the Winnipeg Light Infantry amalgamated with The Royal Winnipeg Rifles. In 2009 The Royal Winnipeg Rifles and the Queen's Own Cameron Highlanders amalgamated to form the Winnipeg Infantry Tactical Group.

Camp Hughes in August 1916. Camp Sewell was established west of Carberry and south of the Canadian Pacific Railway. The name changed in 1915 to Camp Hughes after Major General Sir Sam Hughes, Minister of Militia and Defence. Trench systems, grenade and rifle ranges and other military structures were constructed in 1915–16. More than 38,000 troops were trained there during the First World War and continued until 1934 when facilities moved to nearby Camp Shilo. Camp Hughes was used in a more limited way in the Second World War and as a communications station during the Cold War until 1991. Camp Hughes was designated a National Historic Site in 2011 and includes the only First World War trench system remaining in North America.

Manitoba he proceeded overseas with his unit, embarking on RMS *Olympic* at Halifax on 18th September, arriving in Liverpool, England on 25th September. He was promoted lieutenant the same day and was based initially at Whirley, near Macclesfield, Cheshire.

On 12th January 1917 he transferred to 18th Canadian Reserve Battalion at Seaford and was drafted to 52nd Battalion on 19th February. He sailed for France on 23rd February, joined the Canadian Base Depot next day and joined 52nd Battalion on 27th February to command 9 Platoon in C Company. Christopher attended the Canadian Corps School 2nd–22nd June.

Awarded the MC for his part in a minor action in the Avion-Méricourt sector on 28th June 1917, LG 26th September 1917 and details 8th January

1918. An attack on Avion Trench under Captain ERC Wilcox encountered uncut wire and a machine gun post. The attackers took cover in a nearby trench while O'Kelly led a bombing section against the gun. He threw a bomb just as one of the enemy threw a stick grenade. O'Kelly's bomb killed the machine gun crew and he turned it on the enemy. The enemy grenade wounded fatally one of his men. Christopher was granted leave 15th-28th August.

Awarded the VC for his actions at **Wolf Copse and Bellevue Spur near Passchendaele, Belgium on 26th October 1917, LG 11th January 1918.** Captain Theodore Roberts, who later edited a volume on Canadian VCs, met Patrick shortly after the Battalion came out of the line and noted, *He was very young. His manner was quiet and somewhat grim, as if he had looked too closely into a hundred faces of death.* Patrick was appointed temporary captain on 25th November and assumed command of A Company on 2nd December. Appointed acting captain on 4th December backdated to 25th August. He was granted leave to Britain 12th-29th December. On 22nd February 1918 he attended the GHQ Lewis Gun School at Le Touquet.

When his mother was seriously ill in the spring of 1918, he requested leave and returned to Britain on 15th March. The VC was presented by the King at Buckingham Palace on 23rd March and Christopher embarked for Canada on 26th March, arriving in Winnipeg on 9th April. A reception was organised by the local Catholic Club in his honour at Columbus Hall, Winnipeg, Manitoba on 14th April. He then visited his mother at Battle Creek, Michigan, where she was recovering in a sanatorium. His leave, originally granted until 26th May, was extended to 18th June. He

RMS *Olympic* (45,324 tons) arriving at New Yor on her maiden voyage on 21st June 1911. She wa the lead transatlantic liner of the White Star line Her sister ships, *Titanic* and *Britannic*, had shor and tragic careers. *Titanic* sank after striking an iceberg in April 1912 with the loss of 1,514 lives. *Britannic* struck a mine and sank in the Mediterranean in November 1916 with the loss of thirty lives. *Olympic*'s first voyage from Belfas to Liverpool coincided with the launch of *Titan* on 31st May 1911. On her maiden voyage on 14th June 1911 from Southampton to New York *Britannic* was captained by Edward Smith, mast of the *Titanic* on her maiden voyage the followin year. On 27th October 1914, off the north coast of Ireland *Olympic* went to assist the battleship HMS *Audacious*, which had struck a mine. *Olympic* took off 250 of *Audacious*' crew, but on the way to Lough Swilly the towing cable parted and *Audacious* sank later. In May 1915, *Olympic* was requisitioned as a troop transport. On 12th May 1918, en route to France with US troops, she sighted U-*103* surfaced 500m ahead and opened fire. U-*103* crash-dived, but *Olympic*'s port propeller sliced through the pressure hull. U-*103* surfaced and was scuttled and abandone by her crew. *Olympic* reached Southampton via Cherbourg with some damage, but her hull was not breached. USS *Davis* picked up thirty-one survivors from U-*103*. *Olympic*'s master, Captai Hayes, was awarded the DSO. During the war, *Olympic* carried 200,000 troops and travelled 184,000 miles. In 1920 she returned to passenge service, carrying many celebrities such as Charli Chaplin, Mary Pickford and the Prince of Wale The Depression and competition from new larger and faster liners had their effect and she left New York for the last time on 5th April 193! She was broken up in 1936–37, having complete 257 Atlantic crossings, transporting 430,000 commercial passengers and travelling 1,800,000 miles.

20th General Hospital at Camiers.

The Prince of Wales Hospital at 222 Marylebone Road, London opened in 1916 in the 700–bed Great Central Hotel and closed in July 1919. During its time as an officers' hospital it had a bad reputation. The food was poor and patients were not allowed to leave the hospital before 1 p.m. nor attend theatre matinees without permission. The Commandant required those fit enough to attend military lectures for two hours on alternate mornings or afternoons. The hotel was a convalescent hospital during the Second World War and later became headquarters of the British Railways Board; the staff knew it as the Kremlin. In the 1980s the building became a hotel again.

Christopher O'Kelly in a posed picture in the trenches (Library and Archives Canada).

was taken on strength of 18th Canadian Reserve Battalion, Seaford on 24th June. He returned to France on 26th August to the Canadian Corps Base Depot and rejoined the Battalion on 8th September. On 28th September he received a gunshot wound to the left groin and while lying out awaiting evacuation was hit by shrapnel in the left leg. He was treated at No.30 Casualty Clearing Station until 2nd October, then at 20th General Hospital at Camiers and on 5th October was transferred to the Prince of Wales Hospital, Marylebone Road, London. On 9th November he transferred to the Canadian Convalescent Officers' Hospital at Matlock Bath and was discharged the same day back to Seaford.

Christopher was granted leave 21st November–12th December and 30th December–7th January 1919. On 26th December 1918 he was admitted to 13th Canadian General Hospital, Hastings with a fractured fifth metatarsal on the right foot, having had a horse fall on him. On 28th February 1919 he transferred to the Canadian Convalescent Officers' Hospital, Matlock Bath and was discharged on

A ward in 12th Canadian General Hospital at Bramshott, Hampshire.

The Canadian Convalescent Officers' Hospital at Matlock Bath was based on the Royal Hotel. It suffered a disastrous fire in 1929 and had to be demolished.

5th March, but was then admitted to 12th Canadian General Hospital, Bramshott 8th-12th March with tonsillitis.

On 17th March 1919 Christopher embarked on RMS *Olympic* and returned to Canada on 25th March. He was struck off strength of the CEF at Port Arthur on 1st April 1919, giving his address as 601 McArthur Building, Winnipeg. Initially he returned to Winnipeg and sold real estate with his father before returning to prospecting. He rejoined 90th Royal Winnipeg Rifles (Militia) in 1921 as a major.

Christopher and a colleague, EL 'Bill' Murray, were prospecting in the region of Lac Seul, near Kenora, Ontario on 15th November 1922. Other prospectors on the shore saw them in a canoe on the lake as a storm broke. Their boat capsized and they were lost. Soon after the lake froze over and it was not until the spring that Murray's body was found. Christopher's body was never recovered and a hardwood cross was erected on nearby Goose Island in 1924, close to where the two men were lost. A silver plaque was attached to the

The McArthur Building in Winnipeg was constructed between 1909 and 1910. In 1974 it suffered extensive fire damage and in 1988 the remaining structure was demolished.

cross inscribed, *Erected to the memory of Major Christopher Patrick John O'Kelly, V.C., M.C., by his brother officers of the 90th Winnipeg Rifles. Ye who pass this way are asked to care for this monument.* A hydroelectric dam was built at Lower Ear Falls in 1929, causing Lac Seul to rise by sixteen feet and submerging the cross. The upright was found floating c.1969 and was donated to the Ear Falls Branch No.238 of the Canadian Legion. In 1992 Royal Canadian Legion Members from Ear Falls,

Sioux Lookout, Hudson and Dryden dedicated a new cross on Goose Island. Christopher is commemorated in a number of other places:

Lac Seul, Ontario, near Lower Ear Falls.

- O'Kelly School at the Canadian Force Base Shilo, Brandon, Manitoba opened in November 1957.
- Memorial plaque dedicated on 14th November 1965 at the Royal Canadian Legion Hall, Red Lake, Ontario. It is a replica of the one on Goose Island in 1924.
- Named on a Victoria Cross obelisk to all Canadian VCs at Military Heritage Park, Barrie, Ontario dedicated by The Princess Royal on 22nd October 2013.

O'Kelly School on Canadian Force Base Shilo at Brandon, Manitoba.

- Named on one of eleven plaques honouring 175 men from overseas awarded the VC for the Great War. The plaques were unveiled by the Senior Minister of State at the Foreign & Commonwealth Office and Minister for Faith and Communities, Baroness Warsi, at a reception at Lancaster House, London on 26th June 2014 attended by The Duke of Kent and relatives of the VC recipients. The Canadian plaque was unveiled outside the British High Commission in Elgin Street, Ottawa on 10th November 2014 by The Princess Royal in the presence of British High Commissioner Howard Drake, Canadian Minister of Veterans Affairs Julian Fantino and Canadian Chief of the Defence Staff General Thomas J Lawson.
- Two 49 cents postage stamps in honour of the 94 Canadian VC winners were issued by Canada Post on 21st October 2004 on the 150th Anniversary of the first Canadian VC's action, Alexander Roberts Dunn VC.
- A wooden plaque bearing fifty-six maple leaves each inscribed with the name of a Canadian-born VC holder was dedicated at the Canadian Forces College, Toronto on Remembrance Day 1999.
- The Secretary of State for Communities and Local Government, Eric Pickles MP, announced that Victoria Cross recipients from the Great War would have commemorative paving stones laid in their birthplace as a lasting legacy of local heroes within communities. The stones would be laid on or close to the 100th anniversary of their VC actions. For the 145 VCs born in Australia, Belgium, Canada, China, Denmark, Egypt, France, Germany, India, Iraq, Japan, Nepal, Netherlands, New Zealand, Pakistan, South Africa, Sri Lanka, Ukraine and United States of America, individual commemorative stones were unveiled at the

National Memorial Arboretum, Alrewas, Staffordshire by Prime Minister David Cameron MP and Sergeant Johnson Beharry VC on 5th March 2015.
- Stone cairn at Camp Morton on Lake Winnipeg erected by the St John's College Association in 1927.
- On 14 May 1990 the Thunder Bay Militia District Headquarters Armoury was designated 'The Major Christopher Patrick John O'Kelly, VC, MC Armoury'.
- On 4 July 2014 the Government of Manitoba named lakes after the fourteen Manitoban VC recipients. O'Kelly Lake is located at 51° 59′ 00″ N, 95° 50′ 11″ W.
- A painting by FH Varley is held by the Canadian War Museum.
- Plaque on a memorial to the ninety-nine Canadian VCs in York Cemetery, Toronto.

In addition to the VC and MC he was awarded the British War Medal 1914–20 and Victory Medal 1914–19. The VC and MC were donated to the Canadian War Museum in Ottawa, Ontario by his sister, Margaret, in May 1970. The campaign medals were missing but were replaced.

428545 PRIVATE MICHAEL JAMES O'ROURKE
7th Battalion (1st British Columbia), Canadian Expeditionary Force

Michael O'Rourke was born on 19th March 1878 in Limerick, Ireland. However, military records give his year of birth as 1879 and his death certificate records 3rd March 1874. His father was James O'Rourke and his mother was Catherine née Baker. Michael was an orphan by the age of eleven. He had two sisters:

- Sadie O'Rourke emigrated to Canada and married as King. She was looking after Michael at the time of his death, he having moved in with her during or after 1956.
- Name not known, but married as Mrs H Mack of 2564 Broadway Street, Montreal, Canada. She was listed as his next-of-kin in 1915. However, on one document in his service record his next-of-kin was recorded as Mrs Mary Ryan, Magee Avenue, Blackpool, presumably in Lancashire.

Michael served for four years in the Royal Munster Fusiliers before emigrating to Canada before 1914. He settled in Vancouver, British Columbia and became a lumberjack and later a tunneller working on the Connaught Tunnel in Rogers Pass for the Canadian Pacific Railway and the British Columbia Electric tunnel in Coquitlam. He also worked in mines at Fernie, British Columbia.

He enlisted in 104th Regiment Westminster Fusiliers of Canada at Revelstoke, British Columbia on 1st February 1915. On 26th February he enlisted in the CEF

The five miles long Connaught Tunnel carries the Canadian Pacific Railway under Mount Macdonald, replacing the previous route over Rogers Pass, which was susceptible to avalanches. Work commenced on 2nd April 1914 and the tunnel was in operation in December 1916. At the time it was the longest in North America and was perfectly straight, light being visible from one end to the other. It was named after the Governor General of Canada, Prince Arthur, Duke of Connaught.

Prospector William Fernie established the coal industry that continues to this day in the city named after him. He founded the Crows Nest Pass Coal Company in 1897.

The camp at Shorncliffe was first established in 1794 and in 1803 Sir John Moore trained the Light Division there. It became a staging post for the Western Front during the First World War and in April 1915 a Canadian Training Division formed there and Canadian hospitals from September 1917 onwards. The camp remains in use.

at Vancouver and joined 47th Battalion on 8th March. He was attested on 23rd March. Michael was described as 5′ 9¼″ tall with medium complexion, grey eyes, dark hair and his religious denomination was Roman Catholic. His address was 117 Oxford Street, Vancouver. He sailed for Britain with 7th Battalion on 22nd April, arriving on 6th May, and was posted to Shorncliffe, Kent. He transferred to 30th Reserve Battalion on 4th June and was fined seven days pay for drunkenness and abusive language on 28th June. He transferred to 7th Battalion on 28th August and sailed for France on 22nd August, joining the Battalion in the field on 29th August.

Michael was granted nine days leave on 30th May 1916 and saw action at Mount Sorrel in June. He was charged with drunkenness again on 29th June and sentenced to fourteen days Field Punishment No.1. **He was awarded the MM for his actions on 8th September at Mouquet Farm during the Battle of the Somme. He led the men in his sector over the parapet and maintained his position well in advance. He bombed the Germans for three hours from several points of vantage until he ran out of bombs and sent a Lewis gunner for more, but he was killed. A gunner from the 4th Battalion volunteered to go, but**

Michael O'Rourke sailed home on SS *Metagama*, leaving from Liverpool on 23rd December 1917. She was launched in Glasgow in 1914 and commenced service on the Canadian Pacific's North Atlantic service on 26th March 1915 from Liverpool to St John, New Brunswick. She carried Canadian troops throughout the war and afterwards ran the Glasgow – Canada service. From 1927 she also ran the Antwerp – Montréal route. *Metagama* collided with SS *Baron Vernon* in the Clyde in May 1923 and in June 1924 off Cape Race she collided with SS *Clara Camus*. In 1930, due to the Depression, she was laid up after 151 Atlantic roundtrips and was broken up in 1934.

Mouquet Farm, where Michael O'Rourke bombed the Germans for three hours on 8th September 1916, for which he was awarded the Military Medal.

he too was killed. O'Rourke spotted a German in a sap and killed him with a bomb found nearby. Taking his rifle and several bombs, he threw them into the enemy trenches, LG 9th December 1916.

The Canadian Discharge Depot was established in the Empire Hotel at Buxton in late 1916, having previously been at Shoreham and Bath. It arranged the return of discharged, disabled and injured Canadians back to Canada. The Depot dealt with up to 1,000 men at any time.

Following leave in England from 1st to 13th October, he was attached to 1st Canadian Division Train from 20th November to 2nd February 1917. He returned to the Battalion and took part in the Battle of Vimy Ridge 9th–12th April. **He was awarded the VC for his actions at Hill 70, near Lens, France 15th-17th August 1917, LG 8th November 1917.** Michael was admitted to hospital in September, probably suffering with the severe sciatica that was eventually to render him medically unfit to serve overseas. He was gassed during the Third Battle of Ypres in October and was granted fourteen days leave to Britain from 26th November. He was posted to the Canadian Discharge Hospital/Depot Buxton on 1st December and the British Columbia Regiment Depot at Seaford on 9th December. He received the VC from the King at Buckingham Palace on 5th December.

Michael sailed for Canada on SS *Metagama* from Liverpool on 23rd December 1917, arriving at St John on 6th January 1918 for ten weeks' furlough. He reported for duty on 14th March and was posted to the Special Service Company at

Vancouver on 2nd April and to 11th Battalion, Canadian Garrison Regiment CEF in Vancouver on 1st May. He took part in Liberty Bond drives across the western United States of America.

A medical board at Vancouver on 5th April found him fit for Home Service in Canada only (Class C3), having just been discharged from Royal Columbian Hospital after a nasal operation. He was granted a medical discharge on 16th July 1918 due to severe sciatica and a marked degree of disability, receiving a final payment of $416.80. By then he had grown to 5′ 10½″ and his dark hair was fair. His conduct and character was assessed as Very Good and his forwarding address was Georgian Hotel, 4th Avenue, Seattle, USA. Another document in his service record gives a c/o address as Mrs RJ McKenna, 1376 McAlister Street, San Francisco, California, USA.

Michael had a number of jobs in California and was hospitalised for bronchial pneumonia in San Francisco. He then worked in the fisheries in northern British Columbia. He became a longshoreman at Vancouver Docks, working the grain elevators and was known locally as the 'King of the Waterfront', but continued to suffer bouts of bronchitis from the grain dust. He was recommended for a ten percent disability pension in 1920, but a doctor stated the problem was exacerbated by his drinking habits and the review board rejected the proposal. He appealed and was awarded a pension of $10 per month for neurasthenia after the personal intervention of the Governor General of Canada, Field Marshal Lord Julian Byng. The Board of Pension Commissioners awarded him an additional five percent disability pension for chronic bronchitis in 1926. He also worked for the Coast Stevedoring Company of Vancouver as a swamper, responsible for loading and unloading trucks, and later as a watchman, before keeping a fruit stall by Vancouver Docks. Michael was a member of the Vancouver and District Waterfront Workers' Association. It seems likely he was suffering from what today is recognised as post-traumatic stress disorder and he became an alcoholic. It is said that he pinned his VC to the bar on occasion as surety for his drinks tab. He never married.

He refused to attend the 1929 VC Dinner in London hosted by the Prince of Wales because he didn't have a suit. His friends bought him a new one, but the day before the train was due to leave he disappeared for two weeks. His seat (No.260) on Table 9 was held open for him. He was admitted to the Shaughnessy Veterans Hospital for a month with severe stomach pains in 1930. On 18th June 1935, during the Depression, he led a parade of 1,000 striking dockworkers wearing his medals. The Battle of Ballantyne Pier with mounted police ensued, during which Michael, with a Union Flag in one hand and a brick in the other, ran into William

Vancouver Docks.

Michael O'Rourke (bottom left, carrying the Union flag) leading striking dock workers on 18th June 1935 in what became known as the Battle of Ballantyne Pier.

Field Marshal Lord Julian Byng (1862–1935) commanded the Canadian Corps during the Battle of Vimy Ridge in April 1917. He was elevated to the peerage in 1919 and in August 1921 was appointed Governor General of Canada, an appointment he held until August 1926.

Foster DSO, the Chief of Police (also the CO of the British Columbia Regiment (Duke of Connaught's Own Rifles) at the time). At least half of the special constables involved in the riot were also members of the Regiment, putting them in an awkward situation. Michael directed some foul language towards Foster, who ordered a Royal Canadian Mounted Police sergeant to charge the crowd and physically pick up and carry Michael away, in order to ensure that he was not seriously injured. The sergeant achieved his mission, despite Michael using the brick quite freely. Despite what transpired during the riot, Foster and Michael apparently got along quite well afterwards.

Michael was invited to meet Princess Elizabeth, the future Queen, and Prince Philip during the Royal Visit to Vancouver in 1951, but refused. From his Main Street hotel he said, *They wouldn't want to meet an old blatherskite like me. The seabag with all my clothes is being held at my last boarding house and I can't get it. Besides, my legs aren't so good, and I wouldn't be able to stand up for the whole ceremony.* In 1953 he was admitted to Shaughnessey Veterans Hospital again after becoming intoxicated. He had been badly beaten up and robbed and his optic nerves were damaged. He spent a month in the Hospital before being transferred under the Mental Health Act to the George Derby Facility in Burnaby, British Columbia, where he was diagnosed with senility and arteriosclerosis. As neither friends nor family was prepared to care for him, he signed over his power of attorney, pensions and VC gratuity to the hospital in exchange for his care.

By 1956 he was living with his sister, Sadie, and had been battling illness for some time. When he

Main Street, Vancouver.

was invited to attend the VC Centenary Celebrations in London he refused. In his confused mind he believed it was a ploy to have him committed to the Essondale Mental Hospital. He claimed that he was too tired to make the journey and by the time that his friends had convinced him that the offer was genuine, all available spaces had been booked. However, a Vancouver doctor, who had lost a leg during the 1942 Dieppe Raid, paid the airfare and Michael arrived just in time for the ceremonies in Hyde Park, London on 26th June 1956.

Michael O'Rourke died at his sister Sadie's home in Vancouver, British Columbia on 6th December 1957 following a long illness. His funeral was attended by a large number of dignitaries representing all levels of Government and the Army, as well as friends, dockworkers and 7th Battalion veterans. He is buried in Forest Lawn Memorial Park, Gilpin Street, North Burnaby, near Vancouver, British Columbia, Canada (Grave 6–13–3). He is also commemorated in a number of other places:

- Private Michael J O'Rourke VC MM Memorial Bursary awarded annually by the British Columbia Regiment (Duke of Connaught's Own) Association to a serving member of the Regiment for academic achievement and loyalty to the Regiment. It is one of five bursaries, worth $1,095 in 2010, honouring the VCs of units perpetuated by the Regiment.

Michael O'Rourke's turf-stone in Forest Lawn Memorial Park.

- A painting of him by Canadian war artist Ernst Fosberry is held at the Canadian War Museum, Ottawa, Canada.
- Two 49 Cent postage stamps in honour of the ninety-four Canadian VCs were issued by Canada Post on 21st October 2004 on the 150th Anniversary of the first Canadian VC's action, Alexander Roberts Dunn.
- Victoria Cross obelisk to all Canadian VCs at Military Heritage Park, Barrie, Ontario dedicated by The Princess Royal on 22nd October 2013.
- Named on one of eleven plaques honouring 175 men from overseas awarded the VC for the Great War. The plaques were unveiled by the Senior Minister of State at the Foreign & Commonwealth Office and Minister for

The Canadian VC memorial plaque (back right) outside the British High Commission in Ottawa (Memorials to Valour).

Faith and Communities, Baroness Warsi, at a reception at Lancaster House, London on 26th June 2014 attended by The Duke of Kent and relatives of the VC recipients. The Canadian plaque was unveiled outside the British High Commission in Elgin Street, Ottawa on 10th November 2014 by The Princess Royal in the presence of British High Commissioner Howard Drake, Canadian Minister of Veterans Affairs Julian Fantino and Canadian Chief of the Defence Staff General Thomas J Lawson.

- Memorial Plaque on Chemin Des Croisettes, Loos-en-Gohelle, France.
- Memorial Bench outside the Regimental Museum, Beatty Street, Vancouver, British Columbia.
- The Department for Communities and Local Government decided to provide a commemorative paving stone at the birthplace of every Great War Victoria Cross recipient in the United Kingdom. Michael's stone was dedicated at Cross of Sacrifice, Glasnevin Cemetery, Dublin, Ireland on 12th May 2017 to mark the centenary of his award.
- Plaque on a memorial to the ninety-nine Canadian VCs in York Cemetery, Toronto.

Memorial plaques to Michael O'Rourke VC and Robert Hanna VC on Chemin Des Croisettes, Loos-En-Gohelle. It is on the right side of the road leading towards Loos, just after the Hill 70 roundabout.

In addition to the VC and MM he was awarded the 1914–15 Star, British War Medal 1914–20, Victory Medal 1914–19, George VI Coronation Medal 1937 and Elizabeth II Coronation Medal 1953. His VC was reported stolen from his room at the Haden Hotel, Vancouver, British Columbia in May 1926. However, it seems more likely that he lost it or pawned it at a store on Main Street, Vancouver. The Regiment, part of the reserve, had many police officers in its ranks and an extensive search was made for the VC, without success. It is possible that the story of the VC being redeemed by the Regiment from a pawnshop was made up to spare embarrassment all round. The officers purchased a high quality unnamed replica, but it was not an official replacement. During the 1950s and 1960s the medals were displayed in a glass case in the Officers' Mess and were worn by Michael O'Rourke when he attended the 1956 VC Centenary celebrations in London. The replica VC was placed in a safety deposit box in a bank when the value of VCs started to rise, possibly because it was believed to be an original. It was later reunited with the rest of the medal group and is held by the British Columbia Regiment Museum (Duke of Connaught's Own), 620 Beatty Street, Vancouver, British Columbia, Canada. The location of the original is not known. Since 1926 it has never been sold openly and is possibly in a private collection, but more likely it was lost.

10605 SERGEANT JAMES OCKENDON
1st Battalion, The Royal Dublin Fusiliers

James Ockendon was born at 56 Alfred Street, Landport, Portsmouth, Hampshire on 10th December 1889. His surname is often seen incorrectly as Ockenden. His father, Alfred Robert Ockendon (1859–97), a general labourer, married Mary Anne Elizabeth née Verrall (1862–1907), in 1881. They were living at 58 Alfred Street, Portsea in 1891. James had four siblings:

- Alfred Ockendon (1881–1941) was living with his paternal grandparents in 1891 at 16 St Thomas Street, Portsea. He was a pawnbroker's assistant in 1901, living with his employer, Alfred R Jones, at 44–46 Greyhound Road, Fulham, London. Alfred married Eliza Bramble (1883–1976) in 1904 at Portsmouth. She had a daughter, Rose Emily (born c.1903), but no birth record has been found. Rose appeared with Alfred and Eliza as Rose Emily Ockendon in the 1911 Census. They were living at 62 Derby Road, Portsmouth in 1909 when his brother James enlisted and was declared as his next of kin. Alfred was a gas stoker in 1911 and they were living at 49 Knox Road, Portsmouth. They had two children – Violet May Ockendon 1904 and Alfred John Ockendon 1906.

- Alice Elizabeth Ockendon (1883–1942) was boarding at 40 River Street, Portsmouth in 1901 while working at a ginger beer factory. She married Harry James Pinhorne (1877–1960), a carman, in 1902 at Portsmouth, Hampshire. They were living at 17 Brighton Street, Portsmouth in 1911. There were no children.
- William Richard Ockendon (1886–1962) was serving on the Nautical Training Ship HMS *Formidable*, anchored off Portishead, Bristol, Gloucestershire in 1901.
- Elizabeth Ethel Ockendon (born 1888).

HMS *Formidable* was an eighty-four gun second-rate ship of the Royal Navy, launched in 1825 at Chatham. In 1869 she was leased from the Admiralty to become an Industrial School Ship anchored off Portishead. It could accommodate up to 350 boys aged 11 to 14, some committed by the courts. The opening ceremony was performed by the Reverend Charles Kingsley, author of *Westward Ho!* and *The Water Babies*. In 1906 she was damaged in storms and was replaced by the shore-based Incorporated National Nautical School at Portishead.

James' paternal grandfather, Richard Ockendon (c.1819–95), a dealer, married Sarah née Thompson (c.1824–99) in 1843. In 1881 they were living at 16 St Thomas Street, Portsea, Hampshire and were still there in 1891. In addition to Alfred they had five other children:

* George Henry Ockendon (1849–1915) was a tramcar driver in 1881 and a furniture remover in 1891. He was living with his sister Rosina and her family in 1901 and 1911. In 1911 he was helping his brother-in-law as an assistant dairyman.
* Sarah Ann Ockendon (1861–1934), an assistant in a dealer's shop in 1881, married Thomas Peter William Hatchard (1854–1923) in 1885. He was a coal hawker and they were living at 13 Clifton Street, Portsmouth in 1901 and 1911. They had three children – Florence M Hatchard 1890, Alice Amelia Hatchard 1897 and Thomas Peter Hatchard 1900, plus another child who did not survive infancy.
* Charles Ockendon (1863–1931) was a tramcar driver in 1881, a furniture dealer in 1891 and a furniture remover in 1901. He lived with Mary A (born c.1864 and died before 1901) as husband and wife, but no marriage record can be found. They were living at 24 George Street, Portsea in 1891 and at Vicar's Row, Portsmouth in 1901. He was living with his son, Charles, at 4 Blenheim Street, Southsea in 1911. They had four children – Mary A Ockendon 1885, Rosina Ockendon 1886, Charles Ockendon 1888 and George E Ockendon 1890.
* Clarissa 'Clara' Ockendon (1860–1955) married George Revans (1867–1940) in 1888. She was a mantle maker in 1891 living with her parents.
* Rosina Ockendon (1868–1939) married Walter Scott (1867–1915) in 1892. He was a dairyman in 1901 and they were living at 3 North Cross Place, Portsea. They had five children – Rosina Scott 1894, Olive Scott 1896, Hilda Scott 1899, Leonard Scott c.1900 and Doris Scott 1908.

His maternal grandfather, Charles Verrall (c.1831–1913) married Elizabeth née Towell (c.1830–78) in 1857. The surname is also seen as Verrell. He was a beerhouse keeper and bricklayer and they were living at 41 Hyde Park Road, Portsea in 1871. In addition to Mary they had three other children:

* William Verrall (1866–1939) married Emily Osmond (1862–1920) in 1888. He was a bricklayer living with his family at 12 Hyde Street, Hyde, Hampshire in 1891, at 33 Egbert Road, Winchester in 1901 and at 27 Egbert Road, Winchester in 1911. They had six children – twins Hetty Elizabeth and Nellie Verrall 1889, Frederick Harold Verrall 1892, William George Verrall 1893, Florence Emily Verrall 1895 and Egbert Verrall 1897.
* Elizabeth Charlotte Verrall (1870–1960) married Charles Abraham Wake (1871–1952) in 1893. He was a rabbit salesman in 1901 and they were living at 1 Montague Court, Portsea. By 1911 he was a green grocer hawker and they were living at 49 Jacob Street, Landport, Portsmouth. They had nine children – Lizzie Wake 1894, Martha Wake 1896, Charles Wake 1898, Harriett Wake 1900, Susan Wake

1906, Florence Wake 1908, Violet Wake 1911, George J Wake 1912 and Gladys EM Wake 1915.
• Frederick Charles Verrall (1874–1953), a bricklayer, married Hetty Ford née Osmond (1866–1929) in 1898. She was born at Lytchett Matravers, Dorset. Hetty had married George Woodnutt Ford (1865–95) in 1891. Frederick and Hetty were living at 29 Egbert Road, St Bartholomew Hyde, Winchester, Hampshire in 1901 and 1911. They had a son, Harold Frederick Verrall, in 1903.

Charles Verrall married Jane Mitchell (c.1835–94) in 1890 and they were living with her grandson, George Mitchell (born c.1888), at Eden Terrace, Market Street, South Stoneham, Hampshire in 1891. Charles was a resident at South Stoneham Union Workhouse, West End, Southampton, Hampshire in 1911.

James was educated at St Agatha's School, Portsmouth and was employed by Messrs GS Chalcroft & Son (Men's Outfitters) of Portsmouth as a shop porter. He enlisted in the Royal Dublin Fusiliers at Portsmouth on 22nd May 1909 and trained in Ireland. He was described as 5′ 6″ tall, weighing 115 lbs, with fresh complexion, grey eyes, light brown hair and his religious denomination was Church of England. He was posted to the 2nd Battalion at Naas, Co Kildare, Ireland on 3rd September 1909 and transferred to the 1st Battalion at Aldershot on 5th March 1910. He served in India and was at Ahmednuggur, Deccan in 1911. He landed at Gallipoli on 25th April 1915 and was appointed unpaid lance corporal on 21st June. James received a relatively minor gunshot wound to the forehead on 5th July and was treated at 3rd Light Horse Field ambulance, returning to the unit on 12th July. He picked splinters out for years after. Promotions followed rapidly – acting corporal on 29th August, corporal on 1st November and acting sergeant on 9th December.

He was evacuated to Egypt on 8th January 1916 and moved to France on 16th March. Promoted sergeant on 3rd May 1916. **Awarded the MM on 6th/7th August 1917 for his actions southwest of Wijdendrift, Belgium – the Battalion was relieving another when the enemy fired a heavy barrage causing many casualties and much confusion with many men becoming separated. He rallied the survivors and led them forward again, LG 28th September 1917.**

James married Caroline Ann née Green (1st November 1892–22nd June 1973) at St Luke's Church, Southsea on 20th August 1917. She was working in a stay factory in 1911. They lived at various addresses in Portsmouth and Southsea – 4 Bridport Street, 11 & 14 Nelson Square, 8 Sophia Place, 4 Durham Street, 15 Warwick Street and 5 Yorke Street. They had four children:

• Eileen V Ockendon (26th April 1919–21st April 2004) married Norman Harvey in 1939 and they had two children – Norman M Harvey 1943 and Carole D Harvey 1949.

- Irene Ruby May Ockendon (born 10th October 1920) married John AH Smith in 1942.
- James Richard Alfred Ockendon (born 29th April 1922) served in the Royal Navy on Atlantic convoys between August 1942 and November 1946 and at HM Dockyard Portsmouth. He married Joyce Parsonage (born 1934), a dressmaker, in 1953. He was Secretary of the Portsmouth Branch of the Royal British Legion in 1988. They had two children – Malcolm J Ockendon 1958 and Elaine A Ockendon 1962.
- Betty Doreen Ockendon (6th November 1924– 16th December 2007) married Edward Charles O'Donnell (1924–2000) in 1947. They had four children – Janice I O'Donnell 1948, Michael J O'Donnell 1953, Colin E O'Donnell 1958 and David P O'Donnell 1961.

James Ockendon and Caroline Ann Green married at St Luke's Church, Southsea on 20th August 1917.

Caroline's father, Richard Harris Green (1864–1942), a plasterer, married Caroline Ann née Faithful (1868–1956) in 1887. They were living at 15 Warwick Street, Southsea in 1911 and were still there in 1939. In addition to Caroline they had six other children:

- Alice Ellen Green (1888–1934) married William Charlie Pitman (born c.1885) in 1908. She was working in a stay factory in 1911 while living with her parents.
- Richard John Green (1890–1939), a general labourer, married Nellie Ayling (1895–1971) in 1921 and they had a son, Richard J Green, in 1921. Nellie married Henry J Kemp in 1942.
- Mary Jane Green (born 1896) was working in a stay factory in 1911. She married William John Beames (1894–1971) in 1918. They had three children – Joan D Beames 1919, Olive M Beames 1921 and Roy W Beames 1927.
- John William Green (1900–73) married Annie Charlotte Pitt (1901–76) in 1930. They had seven children – Raymond J Green 1932, David E Green 1934, Shirley I Green 1936, Rosemary Ann Green 1937, Richard J Green 1940, Jean CE Green 1946 and Diana J Green 1947.
- Lilian May Green (1905–49). In 1939 she was a kitchen maid living with her parents at 15 Warwick Street, Portsmouth. She married John Raby (1897–1952) in 1940.
- Ruby Florence Green (1907–40) married Frederick C Roberts in 1932 and they had two children – Daphne I Roberts 1933 and Frederick J Roberts 1936.

Awarded the VC for his actions east of Langemarck, Belgium on 4th October 1917, LG 8th November 1917. The VC was presented by the King at Buckingham

Palace on 5th December 1917. He received an illuminated address from Portsmouth Corporation and a silver casket from the Hampshire Telegraph & Post newspaper on 18th December. **Awarded the Belgian Croix de Guerre in January 1918, LG 12th July 1918.** He returned to Britain via Rouen and reported to the Royal Victoria Hospital, Netley on 7th February. He was discharged on 30th April 1918, no longer fit for war service as a result of being badly gassed. His character was Exemplary and he was awarded a pension of £1/12/6 per week, to be reviewed after a year.

Four VCs, from left to right, Private Michael O'Rourke 7th Battalion CEF, Sergeant James Ockendon 1st Royal Dublin Fusiliers, Private William Butler 17th West Yorkshire and Corporal Ernest Egerton 16th Sherwood Foresters. All four received their VCs from the King at Buckingham Palace on 5th December 1917 and the picture was probably taken that day. In the background is Tank 113 *Julian*, one of the six Tank Banks that toured the country from November 1917 to raise money for the war effort.

Post war James worked as a crane driver in HM Dockyard Portsmouth until aged sixty when he became a cleaner at No.3 Training Battalion RAOC at Hilsea. Despite being employed, in 1928 he was assessed as 100% disabled by the Ministry of Pensions and was granted a life pension. He attended the VC Garden Party at Buckingham Palace on 26th June 1920, the VC Dinner at the Royal Gallery of the House of Lords on 9th November 1929, the Victory Day Celebration Dinner and Reception at The Dorchester, London on 8th June 1946, the VC Centenary Celebrations at Hyde Park, London on 26th June 1956 and VC & GC Association Reunions at the Café Royal, London

HM Naval Base Portsmouth dates back to Tudor times. Nelson left Portsmouth for the last time on HMS *Victory* prior to the Battle of Trafalgar. In the 19th Century it expanded into the largest industrial site in the world. In the Second World War it was a major mounting base for the invasion of Normandy and in 1982 the Falklands Task Force assembled there. Today it is one of three remaining Royal Navy bases in Britain and the home of Portsmouth Historic Dockyard.

in 1960, 1962 and 1964. He was a Life Member of the Portsmouth British Legion Club and also belonged to the 29th Division Association. James served in the Home Guard in the Second World War.

James Ockendon died at his home at 5 Yorke Street, Southsea on 29th August 1966 and was cremated at Portchester Crematorium. His ashes were interred there at the North Border Post, Plot 20 and his name is in the Book of Remembrance. He is commemorated in a number of other places:

The Belgian Croix de Guerre was established in October 1915 for bravery or other military virtue on the battlefield, such as three years service on the front line and escaped prisoners of war. Noteable foreign recipients include Canadian General Harry Crerar, British Field Marshal Bernard Montgomery and Americans General George Patton, General Carl Spaatz, Major Dick Winters (Band of Brothers) and Lieutenant Audie Murphy (Medal of Honor and Holywood actor).

- Ockendon Close, Southsea, Hampshire.
- Plaque and portrait at Royal British Legion Club, Lucknow Street, Fratton, Portsmouth.
- Photograph in St Agatha's Church, Landport, Portsmouth.
- Commemorative bench in Burgoyne Gardens, Southsea restored by craftsmen from Portsmouth Craft and Manufacturing Industries in May 2011.
- The Department for Communities and Local Government decided to provide a commemorative paving stone at the birth place of every Great War Victoria Cross recipient in the United Kingdon. James' stone was dedicated at Portsmouth South Royal British Legion, 1–3 Lucknow Street, Fratton on 26th March 2017 to mark the centenery of his award.

In addition to the VC and MM he was awarded the 1914–15 Star, British War Medal 1914–20, Victory Medal 1914–19, Defence Medal, George VI Coronation Medal 1937, Elizabeth II Coronation Medal 1953 and Belgian Croix de Guerre. The VC is held privately.

SECOND LIEUTENANT HARDY FALCONER PARSONS
14th Battalion, The Gloucestershire Regiment

Hardy Parsons was born at Rishton, Great Harwood, Lancashire on 13th (also seen as 30th) June 1897. His father, the Reverend James Ash Parsons (1867–1963), married Henrietta 'Rita' Sophia née Falconer (1867–1949) in 1896. The family moved regularly and are known to have lived in the following places:

- Arnside, Westmoreland.
- London, when James worked at the Leysian Mission in City Road.
- 54 Salisbury Road, Redland, Bristol while James was minister of the Old King Street Wesleyan Chapel.
- 43 Drayton Park, Islington, London in 1901.

- 203 St George's Road, St Annes-on-Sea, Lancashire in 1911.
- Eversley, Stow Park Avenue, Newport, Monmouthshire in the early 1920s.

Hardy had two brothers:
- Ewart Moulton Parsons (1898–1918) became a member of Bristol University Officer Training Corps on 5th October 1916. Having served an engineer apprenticeship with Messrs Brecknell, Munro & Rogers of Bristol, he enlisted on 18th April 1917 and was commissioned in the Royal Flying Corps on 12th August. He was promoted lieutenant on 3rd November and served at Market Drayton from December. Ewart was serving with the RAF when he was killed in a flying accident near Eastbourne, Sussex on 17th July 1918. He is buried in Bristol (Canford) Cemetery (Plot 1194, Grave 5).
- Lyall Ash Parsons (1902–76) married Constance Mary Fortescue Hubbard (1909–99) in 1930. He was a Methodist minister. They were living at 86 Fairholme Avenue, Romford, Essex in 1939.

Hardy's paternal grandfather, Isaac Parsons (c.1821–1904), was a bookseller. He married three times, firstly to Mary Ann Vincett (1821–49) in 1843 and they had two sons:

- Frederick James Parsons (1844–1900) was the proprietor and publisher of the Hastings and St Leonards Observer. He married Sarah Crew in 1873 at Marylebone Church, London. They had ten children, including Frances Mary Parsons. When Frederick died he left effects valued at £38,648/7/2.
- William Parsons (1846–1911).

Isaac married his second wife, Hannah Vincett (c.1829–65) in 1850 and they had two daughters:

- Maria Parsons (born 1851) did not survive infancy.
- Fanny Parsons, who married Richard Bullymore in 1873 at St Peter's Church, Wisbech, Cambridgeshire.

Isaac married his third wife, Mary Anna Blackmore née Ash (1830–1902) in 1866 at the Wesleyan Chapel, Loudoun Square, Cardiff, Glamorgan. In 1873 Isaac was keeper of the Temperance Hotel, Wisbech. They later lived at 7 High Street, Rye, Sussex and by 1881 he was a hotelkeeper and Methodist local preacher at the Temperance Hotel, 63 Granby Street, Leicester. They were still there in 1891. In 1901 he was lodging at 19 Decimus Burton Road, Croydon, Surrey (possibly a nursing home) and she was living with her son James in Islington in 1901. In addition to James they had two other sons:

- Isaac Hardy Parsons (1868–1940) was an electrical engineer and inventor. He married Jane Birch Higson (1869–1937) in 1900. Her sister, Mary H Higson, married William Morgan Lewis (born c1856), a colliery and ship owner and coal merchant. They had three children, including Dorothy Perch Lewis (1888–1918), a war poet whose works were printed privately in Cardiff in 1919 under the simple title *Poems*. Isaac and Jane were living at The Croft, Kibworth, Leicestershire in 1911. They had two children – Hardy Kelvin Parsons 1902 and Christien Mary Swain Parsons 1905.

Hardy's paternal grandparents lived on High Street, Rye, Sussex.

- Christopher Hartley Parsons (1874–1914), a superintendent civil engineer (mechanical), married Marion 'Madge' Jane Ogle (1883–1959) in 1905. They were living at 92 Claude Road, Cardiff in 1911 before moving to Stockport, Cheshire. He was a delicate, highly-strung man who suffered from insomnia. He left home on business on 24th February 1914, but his wife became concerned when she had not heard from him by 6th March. He had booked into a temperance hotel in Tithebarn Street, Liverpool on 28th February. On the morning of 7th March a chambermaid knocked

The Temperance Hotel on Granby Street, Leicester, next door to the Old Wagon and Horses!

on his door, but received no response and returned about 1 p.m. and knocked again. Christopher called out, *I can't get up. I have shot myself.* A police constable found him sitting on the floor with a wound in the right temple and a revolver by his side with five spent cartridges. He was barely conscious, but managed to say, *This is a terrible business, isn't it?* He was rushed to David Lewis Hospital, but died later that day. A verdict of 'suicide whilst temporarily insane' was returned. Marion was living at 33 Belmont Road, Wallington, Surrey at the time of her death.

His maternal grandfather, Peter Falconer (c.1825–1900), a railway guard, married Mary née Milne (c.1825–99) in 1854 at Duns, Berwickshire, Scotland. In 1861 they were living at 20 Spencer Street, St Mary, Bishophill Senior, York. By 1881 he was a railway inspector and they had moved to The Poplars, 57 Holgate Terrace, York. He was a house furnisher at the time of his death. In addition to Henrietta they had five other children:

- Mary Ann Brown Falconer (1856–74).
- Janet Milne Falconer (1858–1940) married Charles Hale Hocken (1873–1933) in 1882 and they had a son, Donald Falconer Hocken in 1893. She was living at 27 Elgin Park, Bristol, Gloucestershire at the time of her death.

- Alexandrina Watson Falconer (1860–1918) married Henry Sidney Salter (1859–1938) in 1887. He was an Army agent's clerk in 1891 and a bank manager and secretary of a banking company by 1911. In 1901 they were living at 159 Fordwych Road, Hampstead, London and at 181 Willesden Lane, London by 1911. In 1915 they were at 68 Crediton Hill, Hampstead. They had three children – Reginald Charles Falconer Salter 1888, Ethel Maud Mary Salter 1889 and Ina Muriel Salter 1891. Reginald was educated at Merchant Taylors School, where he was in the school cadet corps, and was a trooper in 3rd County of London Yeomanry when he was commissioned in 7th County of London Battery, 3rd London Brigade RFA on 20th January 1909. He was 6′ 1″ tall and was employed as a bank clerk. He served as a captain in 2nd South Lancashire and on 12th January 1915 was admitted to 1st Field Ambulance with inflamed connecting tissue. He was killed in action on 8th June 1915 (Sanctuary Wood Cemetery, Belgium – II G 20).
- James William Falconer (1863–1936), a house furnisher, married Marianne Jones (1861–1912) in 1896 and they had a son, Peter Lyall K Falconer, in 1900.
- Elizabeth 'Lily' Eleanor Falconer (1865–1947) married William Stanley Ennals (1871–1961) in 1900. He was a flour traveller and they were living at The Avenue, Wolstanton, Staffordshire in 1901. They had a daughter, Dorothea Mary Ennals, in 1901.

Hardy was educated at:

- King Edward VII School, Lytham-St-Annes, Lancashire.
- Kingswood School, Bath September 1912–April 1915, he left a term early due to pneumonia.
- Bristol University from October 1915 – his intention was to train as a medical missionary.

Hardy was attested in the Gloucestershire Regiment (31273) on 30th November 1915 and transferred to the Army Reserve on 1st December under the Derby Scheme. He was 6′ ¾″ tall and weighed 149 lbs. He was a member of the Bristol University OTC from April 1916 and applied for a commission on 12th May 1916, declining a safe post in a government laboratory. Although rather

King Edward VII School, Lytham-St-Annes.

frail, he managed to persuade the doctors to pass him fit for service, despite two previous instances of pneumonia and spinal curvature. He was mobilised on 5th October 1916 and joined 6th Officer Cadet Battalion at Balliol College, Oxford next day. He was commissioned on 25th January 1917 and went to France in March.

Awarded the VC for his actions near Épehy, France on 20th/21st August 1917, LG 17th October 1917. He died of wounds sustained in his VC action on

Balliol College, Oxford.

The Orderly Room of 6th Officer Cadet Battalion at Balliol College, Oxford (Qualis Photo Co).

The family grave in Canford Lane Cemetery, Bristol where Hardy is commemorated and his brother Ewart is buried.

Hardy Parsons' grave in Villers-Faucon Communal Cemetery.

21st August 1917 and is buried in Villers-Faucon Communal Cemetery (A 16). He is also commemorated in a number of other places:

- Plaque in Hawkins Library, King Edward VII School, Lytham-St-Anne's, Lancashire.
- Brass memorial plaque at Kingswood School, Bath, Somerset and also on the school war memorial.
- The family grave in Canford Lane Cemetery, Bristol.
- War memorial, Wills Building, Bristol University.
- War memorial at the Methodist Church, Clifton Drive South, St Annes-on-Sea, Lancashire.
- Plaque at Wesley Memorial Church, New Inn Hall Street, Oxford.
- The Department for Communities and Local Government decided to provide a commemorative paving stone at the birthplace of every Great War Victoria Cross recipient in the United Kingdom. Hardy's stone was dedicated at Rishton War Memorial, Blackburn on 21st August 2017 to mark the centenary of his award.

As he never married, the VC was presented to his father by the King at Durdham Down, Bristol on 8th November 1917. In addition to the VC he was awarded the British War Medal 1914–20 and Victory Medal 1914–19. The VC is held by the Soldiers of Gloucestershire Museum, Custom House, Gloucester Docks, Gloucester.

CAPTAIN (ACTING MAJOR) GEORGE RANDOLPH PEARKES
5th Battalion, Canadian Mounted Rifles, Canadian Expeditionary Force

George Pearkes was born on 26th February 1888 at Watford, Hertfordshire, England. His father, also George Pearkes (1856–1929), a linen draper, was the junior partner in the family department store in Watford, WE Pearkes & Sons, a mixed clothing, drapers and furniture store. George ran the furniture side of the business. He married Helen Alexander Thompson (c.1859–83) in 1882 and Louise née Blair (born 1866) at Ashford, Kent in 1887. She was a milliner's apprentice in 1881. She separated from her husband, probably before 1906, and emigrated to Canada with her daughter, Hilda, to join sons George and Ted in Alberta in 1910. During the Great War, George senior was living at 14 Woburn Square, London and Helen was living at 1312 Stanley Avenue, Victoria, British Columbia. By 1924 she was living with her daughter, Hilda, on Mills Road, Sidney, Vancouver Island, British Columbia, where she managed a dairy farm. George junior had two siblings:

- William Edward 'Ted' Pearkes (1889–1967) emigrated to Canada with his brother George and attended Berkhamsted School Farm in Alberta. He then farmed 160 acres adjoining his brother. He died at Sacramento, California.
- Hilda Winifred Pearkes (1891–1963) was educated at Cheltenham Ladies' College. As a contribution to the war effort she purchased a cow, learned to milk and gradually built up a small herd of dairy cattle. After moving to North Saanich, British Columbia the herd grew to 200 Jerseys and she employed eight families.

Advertisement for Pearkes store in Watford.

George on the right with his mother, brother and sister.

George's mother, Helen, was living at 1312 Stanley Avenue, Victoria, British Columbia during the First World War (Newport Realty).

George's paternal grandfather, William Edward Pearkes (c.1818–85), was a linen draper. He married Mary Ann 'Marianne' née Bartholomew (c.1823–97) in 1849. They were living at 127 High Street, Watford, Hertfordshire in 1881. In addition to George they had seven other children:

• Edward Pearkes (1850–54).
• Arthur Pearkes (1851–54).
• Fanny Pearkes (1853–1931) married Walter Webb (1850–1927), a bank manager, in 1875. They had six children – Edith Fanny Webb 1879, George Reginald Webb 1880, Arthur Edward Webb 1882, Katherine Mary Webb 1883, Bernard Webb 1885 and Harold Webb 1890. They were living at 52 Market Street, Ashby-de-la-Zouch, Leicestershire in 1891, at Hinckley, Leicestershire in 1901 and at Elmfield, Loughborough, Leicestershire in 1911.
• Walter A Pearkes (1854–1925), a draper, married Catherine 'Kate' Mary Culshaw (1865–1926) in 1886. They were living at Lulworth, Upton Road, Watford in 1901. They had three children – Ethel Margaret Pearkes 1887, André Mellard Pearkes 1888 and Harry Cecil Pearkes 1890. Andre served in 9th West Yorkshire and was killed in action on 7th August 1915 at Helles Memorial, Gallipoli.
• Frederick Pearkes (1861–1939).
• Charles Herbert Pearkes (1862–63).
• William Andre Pearkes (1864–1927).

George's paternal grandparents lived on High Street, Watford.

His maternal grandfather, John Blair (c.1844–1917), was an engine fitter in the engineering department of the London, Brighton and South Coast Railway. He married Hannah Jane née Attrill (1843–1915) in 1865 at East Ashford. They were living at 93 Newtown, Willesborough, Kent in 1881. In addition to Louisa they had three other children:

- Charles Attrill Blair (1867–1932) was an engine fitter at the Royal Dockyard Sheerness, Sheppey, Kent. He married Rose Emma Dryland (1868–1943) in 1891 at West Ashford and they had two children – Nellie Blair 1892 and Donald Attrill Blair 1894.
- Alice Blair (1868–1954) married William Todd Holland (1869–1944), a carpenter, in 1899. They were living at 71 High Street, Gillingham, Kent in 1901 and had a son, Frank Edward Holland, in 1902. They emigrated to New Zealand and were living at 12 Church Street, Otahuhu, Auckland in 1938. Unusually, Alice was recorded as a widow in the 1935 and 1938 New Zealand Electoral Rolls.
- Ellen Blair (1873–1927) was a draper's assistant, boarding at 30 Sandgate Road, Folkestone, Kent in 1891 and at 65 High West Street, Dorchester, Dorset in 1901. She married Ernest Taylor Annett (1876–1958) in 1911 at Whitstable, Kent. He was born at Agra, India and was an assistant surveyor with Gillingham Borough Council at the time of the 1911 Census living with his mother, Bessie, at 167 Nelson Road, Gillingham. Ellen Blair was a visitor. Ernest was appointed temporary quartermaster as honorary lieutenant in the Kent RAMC (V) on 9th May 1918. He resigned his commission on 30th July 1919 and retained the rank of lieutenant. They moved to Bombay, India where he was a roads engineer with the Bombay Municipality and they lived at Ashmore House, Pedder Road. Ellen died of peritonitis on 22nd November 1927 at Jasmine Lodge Nursing Home, Outram Road, Bombay, leaving £2,151/5/1 to her husband. Ernest married Matilda Ellen Cullen née Russell (1886–1979) in 1928 in Bombay. They returned to England and were living at 21 Pashley Road, Eastbourne, Sussex in 1939.

George was taught initially by governesses before attending a local Dame School. He attended Berkhamsted School, Hertfordshire 1896–06 and joined the school cadet corps. He wanted to become a cavalry officer or a clergyman, but his father could not afford to put him through Sandhurst or university. He suggested that George emigrate to gain sufficient funds and return to England a few years later. George's old headmaster at Berkhamsted, Dr Thomas C Fry, moved to Canada and established Berkhamsted School Farm at Red Deer, Alberta. George left Berkhamsted during the Easter holidays in 1906, sailed from Liverpool aboard RMS *Virginian* and arrived in Quebec in June. He joined the Farm, where pupils were paid a small wage for tending the animals, ploughing, planting, harvesting, making hay, gathering wood and fencing the farm boundaries. He graduated in 1908.

George worked for George Root on his farm at Red Deer, Alberta. He bred Percheron horses and had a large herd of Shorthorn cattle. By 1909 George owned his own farm block of 160 acres near Dovercourt, Alberta. His brother Ted owned an adjoining block and they built a log cabin between them. When their mother and sister joined them in 1910, they built a better home to accommodate the family. To bolster their meagre finances, George earned money on other farms or in gangs working the forests. In 1911 he was a member of a land survey expedition to the Yukon and in 1913 he joined the Royal North-West Mounted Police as a constable (5529).

George was educated at Berkhamsted School, Hertfordshire 1896–1906. It originated as Berkhamsted Grammar School in 1541. In 1997 it amalgamated with Berkhamsted School for Girls and Berkhamsted Preparatory School to become Berkhamsted Collegiate School, but in 2008 was renamed Berkhamsted School. Amongst its numerous famous alumni are: Sir Algernon Methuen (1856–1924), founder and owner of Methuen publishers; Clementine Churchill (1885–1977), wife of Sir Winston Churchill; author Graham Greene (1904–91); Sir Hugh Greene (1910–87), Director-General of the BBC 1960–69; Sir Robin Knox-Johnston (born 1939), yachtsman; and Michael Meacher (1939–2015), politician. In addition to George the School has two other VCs – Arthur Mayo and Brett Cloutman (Daily Mail).

RMS *Virginian* (10,750 tons) was launched in 1904 for the Allan Line. In April 1912 she was one of several ships in wireless contact with RMS *Titanic*, passing on iceberg warnings. An erroneous message claimed that *Virginian* was towing *Titanic* to Halifax, Nova Scotia. During the First World War she was used as a troop transport and armed merchant cruiser. On 21st August 1917 she was damaged by U-*102*. In 1920 she was sold to the Swedish American Line and renamed SS *Drottningholm*. From March 1942 she was chartered by the US State Department. She carried Red Cross supplies for distribution to other nationals in Japanese controlled territory and travelled fully lighted at night. In March 1944 she docked in New York after an exchange voyage that took 750 Germans to Europe in exchange for 600 internees. In September 1944 she was used by the Red Cross to repatriate POWs and civilians from Germany to the UK via Sweden. Another voyage in April 1945 docked in Liverpool, including 212 interned Channel Islanders. From 1948 she sailed for the Home Lines of Italy as SS *Brasil* and from 1951 as SS *Homeland*.

The staff and students of Berkhamsted Farm School, Red Deer. George is the tall figure in the centre of the back row. Third from right in that row with the beard is Dr Fry. In the front row second from right is George Root for whom George worked for after leaving the School.

He was stationed at Whitehorse, Yukon. His brother looked after the joint farms during his absence. When war broke out in August 1914 George requested discharge by purchase, but the Police refused to release him until February 1915, when he informed his superiors that he was needed to tend his farm.

The house built on the Pearkes homestead in 1912 to replace the cabin George and Ted had previously lived in.

Instead he enlisted in 2nd Canadian Mounted Rifles at Victoria, Vancouver Island, British Columbia on 2nd March 1915 (107473). He was described as 5′ 11½″ tall, weighing 161 lbs with dark brown hair, brown eyes, fresh complexion and his religious denomination was Roman Catholic. He was promoted lance corporal on 16th April and became a rough rider, breaking in new mounts. He sailed for England on 12th June 1915 and continued training at Shorncliffe, Kent. He was appointed acting corporal on 13th September and qualified as a bomb thrower on the same day. He went to France on 22nd September and the unit was reorganised as infantry in November.

George attended a course at the Army Bombing School near Cassel 6th December 1915–30th January 1916. He was promoted sergeant on 4th March 1916 and was appointed Bombing Sergeant. On 26th March on the Menin Road near Hooge he was wounded slightly in the left arm and head by a German grenade. He was evacuated through 1st Canadian Field Ambulance, No.10 Casualty Clearing Station and 25 Ambulance Train to 1st Canadian General Hospital, Étaples for medical attention. He moved to No.6 Convalescent Depot on 28th March. On 3rd April he returned to his unit via the Canadian Base Depot, Le Havre and on 30th April he was commissioned as a lieutenant in the field to replace the deceased Bombing Officer. On 19th

George Pearkes while serving in the Royal North-West Mounted Police.

May he was wounded in the head and arm by the handle of an exploding German stick grenade, causing temporary blindness. He was evacuated through 10th Canadian Field Ambulance and No.10 Casualty Clearing Station to 14th General Hospital, Wimereux on 20th May. He was scheduled for return to England, but persuaded the medical staff to keep him in Boulogne and he returned to his unit on 8th June. In his absence there had been heavy losses in the fighting around Mount Sorrel and he instigated rigorous training for the reinforcements, interspersed with sports to bring them to the level of physical fitness required.

George was granted leave 21st–28th June and attended a bombing course 29th June–16th July. He was appointed Bombing Officer of 8th Canadian Infantry Brigade on 15th August and was responsible for the destruction of an enemy listening post. On 15th–16th September he was in the line at Courcelette on the Somme during an attack in the area of Mouquet Farm. He transferred to 5th Canadian Mounted Rifles and assumed command of C Company on 27th September. **Awarded the MC for his actions during the Battle of the Ancre Heights on 1st October – he led a bombing party in attacking the German trenches over a period of thirty-four hours, clearing 550m of Regina Trench and taking eighteen prisoners. It was only after his unit had been relieved that he admitted he had been wounded and was taken to a casualty clearing station, LG 21st December 1916.**

Tents of No.10 Casualty Clearing Station at Remy Siding near Poperinghe, Belgium.

14th General Hospital, Wimereux.

On 16th October George was appointed acting captain and acting major while commanding a company on 18th October. Promoted temporary captain on 15th January 1917. He took part in the attack on Vimy Ridge in April 1917 and remained in the region until the latter stages of the Third Battle of Ypres. He was admitted to 8th and 1st Canadian Field Ambulances 7th–9th July 1917 with pyrexia of unknown origin and was granted leave to Britain 16th–26th July. **Awarded the VC for his actions at Vapour Farm, Vanity House and Source Farm near Passchendaele on 30th/31st October 1917, LG 11th January 1918.**

He was treated for his wounded thigh at 11th Canadian Field Ambulance and No.17 Casualty Clearing Station and returned to duty on 4th November. He was readmitted for treatment to 10th Canadian Field Ambulance and No.2 Canadian Casualty Clearing Station 10th–17th November. Promoted temporary major on 30th November and transferred to 116th (Ontario County) Battalion CEF as the senior major. Appointed acting lieutenant colonel and commanding officer on 7th January 1918. Promoted temporary lieutenant colonel on 27th March 1918. He was granted fourteen days leave to Britain from 16th June, but returned on 25th June, having been presented with the VC and MC by the King in the Quadrangle at Buckingham Palace on 22nd June. **Awarded the DSO for his actions during the Battle of Amiens on 8th August – he led his Battalion in an enveloping movement** to overcome the enemy, then captured a wood on the final objective about 4,500m from the start. With his men on the point of exhaustion he went into the attack on his own, inspiring them to follow and resulting in the capture of about forty machine guns, breaking through the artillery lines and securing sixteen guns up to 8″ calibre and 450 prisoners, LG 11th January 1919. Mentioned in a War Office Despatch dated 31st December 1918, a continuation of Sir Douglas Haig's Despatch of 8th November 1918, submitting names deserving of special mention, LG 31st December 1918.

On 17th September at Guémappe his billets were shelled and he was severely wounded in the arm and side. He was treated at 9th Canadian Field Ambulance, No.1 Canadian Casualty Clearing Station and 10th British Red Cross Hospital, Le Tréport from 14th October. On 26th October he was evacuated to England for treatment at 2nd London General Hospital, King's Road, Chelsea and from 2nd November at the Imperial Order of the Daughters of the Empire Hospital for Officers, 1 Hyde Park Place, London. He was on the strength of 2nd Central Ontario Regimental Depot, Witley, Surrey. He was convalescing in London when the war ended and was

2nd London General Hospital in Chelsea was located at St Mark's College on King's Road and in the adjoining secondary school. It opened in September 1914 and provided sixty-six beds for officers and 995 for other ranks. A section of wall was demolished to make an entrance onto the platform at Chelsea station to allow casualties to be brought in more easily. There were 200 additional beds at St Thomas' Hospital and forty at the Great Northern Hospital, Holloway. Royal visits took place in October and November 1914 and February 1915. In 1915 it specialised in eye injuries and staff from St Dunstan's Hostel for Blinded Soldiers and Sailors visited daily to assist. 2nd London General Hospital closed in 1919. In 2000 much of the site was redeveloped for housing. The school is Grade II listed as London County Council's first purpose-built girls' school. It became Sloane Secondary School for Boys in 1919.

Many auxiliary military hospitals were established early in the war, but by 1915 there was a need for more hospital accommodation for officers. A 19th Century townhouse overlooking Hyde Park on Bayswater Road was obtained and Colonel and Mrs AE Gooderham of Toronto paid for its conversion into a hospital for Canadian officers; but other nationalities were also treated. There were twenty-five beds. It was run by the Daughters of the Empire (Mrs Gooderham was President), while the Canadian Red Cross was responsible for maintenance. The Hospital was opened by Princess Louise on 11th May 1916, although it had been receiving patients since February. It closed on 20th September 1919.

SS *Royal George* (11,146 tons) was built as SS *Heliopolis* for the Egyptian Mail Company on the Clyde in 1907. *Heliopolis* operated between Marseille and Alexandria until 1909 when she was dry-docked in Marseille. In 1910 the Canadian Northern Steamship Company bought the ship and renamed her *Royal George*, for the North Atlantic route. She served as a troopship during the First World War and became part of the Cunard Line afterwards. She resumed the North Atlantic passenger service in February 1919 but was retired in 1920 and used as a depot ship at Cherbourg, France to process emigrants before being scrapped in 1922.

The Staff College, Camberley was established for the British Army and what later became the Indian Army. It originated in the Royal Military College, High Wycombe, founded in 1799. In 1802 it became the Senior Department of the Royal Military College and in 1858 the name changed to Staff College, which in 1870 separated from the Royal Military College. The purpose-built premises at Camberley shown here were built in 1859–63 adjacent to the Royal Military College, Sandhurst. The number of students increased steadily and in 1903 colonial officers first joined the College and in 1905 the first naval officers. Apart from during the world wars, the Staff College operated until 1997, when it merged with the other two services' staff colleges into the new Joint Services Command and Staff College at Shrivenham.

granted leave 16th November–7th December, but returned to France on 23rd November to resume command.

George returned to Britain on 12th February 1919 and was admitted to 12th Canadian General Hospital, Bramshott 17th-19th February to have his appendix removed. He sailed for Canada on 17th March from Southampton on RMS *Olympic*. However, his stay in Canada was short. He transferred to Princess Patricia's Canadian Light Infantry and on 1st April began the return journey to England to attend the Staff College, Camberley (also attended by fellow VCs Foss, Gort, Freyberg and Hansen). He was struck off the strength of the CEF on 30th September on general demobilisation. He graduated from the Staff College on 16th January 1920 and returned to Canada on SS *Royal George*. In 1923 he was appointed to replace Colonel AH Borden as GSO1 at Winnipeg.

George was committed to the Boy Scout movement. He formed No.14 Troop in Calgary in 1921 and was appointed Assistant District Commissioner. Former officers of 8th Field Ambulance taught first aid and the Troop won the provincial and dominion titles in first aid and mine rescue work. The Troop's drum and bugle band was taught by an army bandmaster sergeant and an engineer officer taught the construction of simple bridges. George organised the Calgary Jamboree in 1923, which was attended by Chief Scout, Lord Baden Powell. George arranged for members of Lord Strathcona's Horse and veteran cowboys to teach the Troop

George with No.14 Troop. He is standing behind the back row to the left of the tree trunk in the centre.

to ride and Baden Powell was so impressed that he spoke of the display for months afterwards. He invited the Troop to put on the same display at the Imperial Scout Jamboree at Wembley, London the following year.

George Pearkes married Constance Blytha née Copeman (18th May 1902–25th August 1996) on 26th August 1925 at St Paul's Garrison Church, Esquimalt, British Columbia. She was born at her father's cattle ranch in the Bow River Valley, near Cochrane, Alberta. She was known as Blytha and they met during the summer of 1924 at a church service at the Anglican Chapel at Patricia Bay. They had two children:

St Paul's Garrison Church, Esquimalt, British Columbia, where George and Blytha married in August 1925. The church was originally built on the shores of Esquimalt harbour in 1866 as St Paul's Naval Church and was moved to its current location in 1899. The church has had many names – Admiralty Church, Esquimalt Church, Esquimalt Episcopal Church and the Naval and Garrison Church. It is now the parish church of St Peter & St Paul.

- Priscilla Edith 'Pep' Pearkes (1928–35) suffered an infection that resulted in large boils while still in hospital following her birth. She recovered but was weakened and she died in 1935 at Ottawa, Ontario.
- John Andre Pearkes (born 1931) became a lawyer in Vancouver, British Columbia and married Joyce Marilyn Pope in April 1958. They lived at No.4 – 5885 Yew Street, Vancouver. They had two sons – Anthony Pearkes and Timothy Pearkes. Timothy married Eileen Delehanty, an American who moved to Canada in 1985.

She became a writer focussing on the history of the Upper Columbia River and its tributaries. In 2014 she curated an exhibit on the history of the Upper Columbia River for the Touchstones Nelson Museum and the Columbia Basin Trust, resulting in an award of excellence from the Canadian Museum Association.

Blytha's father, William Frederick Utting Copeman (1872–1958), was born at Aslacton, Norfolk, England. He married Edith Harriette née Emerson (1873–1949) in 1898. She was born at Norwich, Norfolk. They emigrated to Canada in 1900 and took up cattle ranching in the Bow River Valley, near Cochrane, Alberta. They moved to Sidney, on the northern tip of the Saanich Peninsula, where he engaged in a profitable real estate business. They moved back to England in 1914, where he worked with the Royal Flying Corps as a materials workman constructing aeroplanes. They returned to Canada in the spring of 1918, settling initially at Vancouver, and resumed his real estate business in northern Saanich. He was also an accomplished artist. Two of his works included Burgess Mountain, Emerald Lake, British Columbia and a portrait of the British Conservative politician Richard Austen 'RAB' Butler. In addition to Constance they had two other children:

- John 'Jack' Utting Copeman (1900–62) married Alice Goff and they had a daughter, Edith Ann Montgomery Copeman, in 1935.
- Humphrey Copeman (born and died 1904).

In 1929 George was appointed Deputy Commandant, Royal Military College, Kingston, Ontario. While there he developed the Staff College Preparatory Course to prepare potential Canadian candidates for the entrance examination to the Staff College, Camberley, Surrey. To assist, a British staff officer was attached to RMC Kingston on an exchange basis. For the first year this was Major George Roupell VC and they worked closely together. Roupell later remarked, *He never courted publicity nor popularity, but his friendly, unassuming and cheerful character made him popular throughout the whole College and it was a great pleasure to work with him.* George attended the VC Dinner at the Royal Gallery of the House of Lords, London on 9th November 1929. The Prince of Wales made a speech after dinner and four VCs were invited to respond, two of them from Canada. Billy Bishop spoke for the Air Force and George was asked to respond for all overseas VCs. During his speech he said, *Holders of the Cross realised the Cross was never gained without the sacrifice of gallant lives. No matter whether it was won during some desperate assault or during some grim defence, the loss of gallant and faithful comrades went with the deed. It was natural, therefore, that they should think of those less fortunate than themselves, and it was with humble thankfulness for the miracle of their existence today that they joined in commending to the nation the cause of ex-Servicemen. We are simply the lucky ones…. There aren't enough VCs to go round, and the man who gets one is lucky, for there are tens of thousands as gallant as he.*

George attended the Senior Officers School in England in July 1933 and returned to Canada early in 1934. He was appointed Director of Military Training and Staff Duties at Ottawa in March 1934. At the beginning of 1937 he attended the Imperial Defence College in London. Blytha was in England during the Coronation of King George VI and was presented at Court shortly afterwards.

The Royal Military College of Canada was established in 1876 following the withdrawal of British forces from Canada to prepare cadets for both military and civil careers. In 1948 it became a tri-service institution.

At the end of the course George returned to Canada arriving at Halifax on 1st January 1938. On 1st February he was promoted colonel and brigadier and appointed Commander of 13th Military District at Calgary. In 1939 he accompanied King George VI in Edmonton during the Royal Visit to Canada. Shortly after the outbreak of the Second World War he assumed command of 2nd Canadian Infantry Brigade in 1st Canadian Division. He took it to England in December 1939 and was stationed at Aldershot, Hampshire. While visiting the BEF in France in February 1940 he contracted spinal meningitis and it was feared that he might not survive. His wife and son were sent for from Canada but by the time that they arrived he was well enough to meet them at the station.

George Roupell was awarded the VC whilst serving with 1st East Surrey on Hill 60, near Ypres on 20th April 1915. He retired from the army in 1946.

On 11th July he was promoted major general and assumed command of 1st Canadian Division. George was highly respected, but was critical of the planning and preparations for the Dieppe Raid on 19th August 1942: *I was anxious enough to get into battle – nothing would have given me greater pleasure at that time to have led the 1st Division into battle – but I was thankful my division wasn't asked to go....* His views caused friction with other commanders, including Lieutenant General HDG Crerar, who committed 2nd Canadian Division to the Raid. Just over a week after it Pearkes had an audience with General Andrew McNaughton, Commander Canadian First Army. Pearkes had hoped to command II Canadian Corps, but its formation was delayed. McNaughton informed Pearkes of the Japanese threat to the west coast of Canada and Pearkes was the preferred choice to command the defences of

George, on the right, in England during the Second World War.

British Columbia, Alberta and the Yukon. Pearkes would have preferred to remain with his Division, but McNaughton's appeal to his sense of duty was the deciding factor. On 1st September he flew back to Canada. There was no time to say farewell to his men and there was no space for his wife and son on the aircraft. They followed ten days later on RMS *Queen Elizabeth*.

George arrived at Esquimalt, Vancouver Island on 6th September and was appointed General Officer Commanding-in-Chief, Pacific Command, Canada with responsibility for protecting the western provinces. **Appointed Companion of the Order of the Bath (Military Division), LG 2nd June 1943. Appointed Commander Legion of Merit (USA), LG 25th April 1944.** In late 1944 the Canadian Government, under PM MacKenzie King, announced the intention to conscript men for overseas service. This reversal of policy caused a mutiny in British Columbia. George played a major role in quelling the mutiny in November; and under his direction the troops finally agreed to do their duty and were transferred eastwards in preparation for overseas duty. George resented the intolerable position he had been placed in of enforcing a policy that his experience warned him would have a deleterious effect on morale and discipline. He became further disillusioned when it became clear that the Canadian Government would not consider employing any force against the Japanese until the war in Europe ended. He began to see himself more as a senior recruiting officer than a commander-in-chief. He requested to be relieved in January 1945 and indicated his willingness to retire if another, more suitable, appointment could not be found. The Cabinet War Committee decided that there was no other employment for him in his present rank and he was retired with full pension on 7th April 1945.

George entered politics and in June 1945 was elected Progressive Conservative MP for Nanaimo, British Columbia and later for Esquimalt, Saanich. He attended the VC Centenary Celebrations at Hyde Park, London on 26th June 1956. He was appointed Minister of Defence when his party was returned to office on 21st June 1957 and he became a Canadian Privy Counsellor. He accompanied PM John Diefenbaker to London in 1957 for the meeting of Commonwealth leaders. At the State Dinner at Windsor Castle the Queen remarked that he was the only Commonwealth Cabinet Minister with the VC. As Defence Minister one of the crises he faced was the cancellation of the Avro Arrow interceptor aircraft. He helped approve the proposed agreement for the North Atlantic Air Defence Command (NORAD), which he considered one of the highlights of his political career. In 1959/60 he devised a policy for Canada to acquire nuclear warheads, but clashed with Howard Green, Secretary of State for External Affairs, who did not want Canada to become an atomic power. Green exerted pressure on PM Diefenbaker, who became reluctant to commit to the atomic policy. George stepped down in 1960 and was appointed Lieutenant Governor of British Columbia on 13th October. **Appointed Knight of Justice, Order of St John of Jerusalem, LG 11th July 1961.**

During his eight years as Lieutenant Governor he also served as Grand President of the Royal Canadian Legion, retiring from that post in 1976. One day while tending the rhododendrons in the grounds of Government House some American tourists passed by and one commented, *Isn't it dreadful that the government would employ a man of that age to work in the gardens.* George was highly amused. **Appointed Companion of the Order of Canada on 6th July 1967 for his services in the Armed Forces, as a Minister of the Crown and as Lieutenant Governor of British Columbia.**

The Avro Canada CF-105 Arrow was an advanced technical and aerodynamic delta-winged interceptor. It was capable of almost Mach 2 at 50,000′ and was intended for the Royal Canadian Air Force. Flight-testing began in March 1958, but on 20th February 1959 development was halted abruptly. The cancellation caused considerable political controversy and effectively put Avro out of business.

George retired as Lieutenant Governor on 2nd July 1968 and received The Order of the Dogwood from the Province of British Columbia, at that time its highest civilian honour for public service. Only thirteen individuals have ever been granted it. He was granted the Freedom of the City of Vancouver on 27th August. He either received the Keys or was granted the Freedom of eight other cities in British Columbia – Nelson 1961, North

Government House at Victoria, residence of the Lieutenant Governor of British Columbia.

Vancouver 1966, Kelowna 1967, Port Alberni 1967, Burnaby 1968, Central Saanich 1970, Vernon 1970 and Penticton 1973. George and Blytha lived for many years at 1268 Tattersall Drive, Saanich, British Columbia.

George suffered a bout of pneumonia during the autumn of 1982 and his health began to fail. He died following a stroke in a rest home at Victoria, British Columbia on 30th May 1984, having had an extraordinary life in which he went from trooper to major general and from homesteader to lieutenant governor. He was given a state and military funeral, the first such combined funeral in Canada's history. The funeral parade included thirty-two Mounties, 3rd Princess Patricia's Canadian Light Infantry, Canadian Scottish Regiment, British Columbia Dragoons and 50th British Columbia Field Regiment. The coffin was followed by a black, riderless horse named 'Major', with saddle draped in black and riding boots reversed in the stirrups, led by Constable Jack Emdall of the Vancouver Police Department. Two Canadian VCs attended – Charles Merritt and Smokey Smith. George is buried in

Section 4 – West of Holy Trinity Cemetery, West Saanich, Sidney, Victoria, British Columbia. He is also commemorated in a number of other places:

George Pearkes' grave in Holy Trinity Cemetery, West Saanich, Sidney, Victoria.

- General George R Pearkes Elementary School, Hudson's Hope, British Columbia 1968–86. It reopened in 1991 as Maranatha Christian Academy.
- George Pearkes Junior High School, Port Coquitlam, British Columbia opened in 1970 and was renamed Minnekhada Middle School in 1996.
- General George Pearkes Trophy awarded at the Cobble Hill Fair, British Columbia for the exhibitor attaining the highest aggregate score in the 'Vegetables Junior Division (13–16 years)'.
- George Pearkes Challenge Cup established in 1983 by the Vancouver Island Soccer League for the winning team in the League's Challenge Cup competition. The Gen. Pearkes Challenge Cup MVP Trophy was established in 1988 for the 'most valuable player' in the George Pearkes Challenge Cup competition.
- Major General GR Pearkes VC Scholarship awarded annually by the University of Victoria, British Columbia, to the student in the Department of History with the highest standing in three units of third or fourth year courses dealing with military history or defence studies.
- Major General George Randolph Pearkes Memorial President's Entrance Scholarship awarded to new students entering the University of Victoria directly from secondary school.
- Mount Pearkes, near Sechelt, British Columbia.
- George R Pearkes Arena, Saanich, British Columbia.
- George R Pearkes Centre for Children and the George R Pearkes Foundation for Children were set up to treat cerebral palsy. In 1986 they amalgamated with Queen Alexandra Hospital and the Queen Alexandra Solarium for Crippled Children Foundation to form the Queen Alexandra Centre for Children's Health, Victoria, British Columbia and the Queen Alexandra Foundation for Children. In 2012 it became the Children's Health Foundation of Vancouver Island.
- Pearkes Recreation Centre, Victoria, British Columbia.
- George Pearkes Royal Canadian Legion Branch No.56, Princeton, British Columbia, Canada.
- Royal Canadian Legion George R Pearkes VC Branch No.5, Summerside, Prince Edward Island. It awards an annual bursary to worthy students who are children or grandchildren of ex-military personnel.
- Pearkes Trophy established in 1957 for the winning team in the Canadian Forces tri-service soccer competition. George presented the trophy when he was Minister of National Defence.

- Patrol Vessel 'Pearkes' (30 tons) built in 1972 as a Class II Patrol Vessel for the Royal Canadian Mounted Police, West Coast Marine Service (Pennant MP90). She served in 'E' Division at Port McNeill until 1996 and was used as a Canadian Coast Guard Auxiliary 2001–04. In 2008 she was sold to Silver Prince Charters, Monterey, California, USA for use as a research vessel, dive boat and for film and TV charter work.

The icebreaker CCGS George R Pearkes.

- Light icebreaker CCGS George R Pearkes (3,809 tons), built in 1986 for the Canadian Coast Guard Service, has operated in the Pacific, Quebec and Newfoundland and Labrador Regions.
- Plaque at the former Royal Canadian Mounted Police Museum, Regina, Saskatchewan, Canada.
- Named on a Victoria Cross obelisk to all Canadian VCs at Military Heritage Park, Barrie, Ontario dedicated by The Princess Royal on 22nd October 2013.

The George R Pearkes Building in Ottawa.

- George R Pearkes Building, HQ Canadian Department of National Defence, Ottawa, Ontario.
- Named on one of eleven plaques honouring 175 men from overseas awarded the VC for the Great War. The plaques were unveiled by the Senior Minister of State at the Foreign & Commonwealth Office and Minister for Faith and Communities, Baroness Warsi, at a reception at Lancaster House, London on 26th June 2014

Plaques commemorating the three Mountie VCs on the wall of the combined mess and auditorium, formerly the RCMP Museum, in Regina, Saskatchewan.

The Order of Canada is the second highest honour for merit in Canada. It was established in 1967 to coincide with the centenary of the Canadian Confederation. Its award recognises outstanding merit or distinguished service through lifelong contributions in every field of endeavour.

The Most Venerable Order of the Hospital of Saint John of Jerusalem is a royal order of chivalry constituted in 1888. It evolved from a faction of the Order of Malta that moved to Britain in the 1830s and became associated with the founding of the St John Ophthalmic Hospital near Jerusalem in 1882 and the St John Ambulance Brigade in 1887.

The Canadian Forces Decoration is awarded to members of the Canadian Forces who have completed twelve years service and have a good record of conduct during the final eight years of claimed service. A bar denotes subsequent service for ten years. The decoration was initiated on 15th December 1949 and was first awarded on 1st September 1951.

attended by The Duke of Kent and relatives of the VC recipients. The Canadian plaque was unveiled outside the British High Commission in Elgin Street, Ottawa on 10th November 2014 by The Princess Royal in the presence of British High Commissioner Howard Drake, Canadian Minister of Veterans Affairs Julian Fantino and Canadian Chief of the Defence Staff General Thomas J Lawson.

- Two 49 cents postage stamps in honour of the 94 Canadian VC winners were issued by Canada Post on 21st October 2004 on the 150th Anniversary of the first Canadian VC's action, Alexander Roberts Dunn VC.
- Pearkes Sword donated to Berkhamsted School (formerly Berkhamsted Collegiate School), Hertfordshire, England by George and presented annually to the most outstanding male cadet in the CCF.
- Plaque on a memorial to the ninety–nine Canadian VCs in York Cemetery, Toronto.

In addition to the VC, DSO and MC he was awarded the Companion of the Order of Canada, Companion of the Order of the Bath, Knight of Grace of the Order of

St John of Jerusalem, 1914–15 Star, British War Medal 1914–20, Victory Medal 1914–19 with MID Oakleaf, Defence Medal, Canadian Volunteer Service Medal 1939–45 with Maple Leaf clasp, War Medal 1939–45, George V Silver Jubilee Medal 1935, George VI Coronation Medal 1937, Elizabeth II Coronation Medal 1953, Elizabeth II Silver Jubilee Medal 1977, Canadian Forces Decoration with three Bars, Canadian Centennial Medal 1967, French Croix de Guerre 1914–18 with Bronze Star and US Legion of Merit. His medals are held by the Canadian War Museum, Ottawa, Ontario, Canada.

The American Legion of Merit is a military award for exceptionally meritorious conduct in the performance of outstanding services and achievements. It was established by Congress on 20th July 1942.

The Canadian Centennial Medal commemorates the 100th anniversary of the Canadian Confederation. It was inaugurated on 1st July 1967 and 29,500 medals were issued, including 8,500 to Canadian Forces personnel.

114 LANCE CORPORAL WALTER PEELER
3rd Australian Pioneer Battalion AIF

Walter Peeler, known as Wally in the Army, was born on 9th August 1887 at Barker's Creek, near Castlemaine, Victoria, Australia. His father, William Peeler (1843–1926), a farmer/miner, married Mary Ellen née Scott (c.1851–1921) at Birkenhead, Victoria in 1870. They lived at 159 Cubitt Street, Richmond, Victoria. Walter had ten siblings:

- Elizabeth Annie Peeler (1871–1944) married Charles Berndt Schade (1912–1948) in 1894 and they had three children – Roy Wilhelm Schade 1895, Alfred Berndt Schade 1896 and Albert Edward Schade 1897. They were divorced in New Zealand in 1931.
- Charles Hubert Peeler (1873–1944) married Emma Eleanor Davies (c.1873–1956) in 1896. They had seven children – Lillian Rosalin Peeler 1896, Horace Peeler 1898, Arthur Walter Peeler 1902, Clifford Charles Peeler 1906, Mervyn Charles Peeler 1909, Ivan David Peeler 1913 and Esther Emma Peeler 1915.

159 Cubitt Street, Richmond, Victoria, where
the Peelers lived.

Castlemaine, Victoria.

- William John Peeler (1875–1947) married Ellen Sarah Murray (1876–1964) in 1898. They had eight children – Ellen Emma Peeler 1898, William John Peeler 1900, Ethel Florence Peeler 1902, Ernest Murray Peeler 1904, Esther Gertrude Peeler 1906, Alfred James Peeler 1907, Ivy May Peeler 1909 and Alan Leslie Peeler 1913.
- Edward Peeler (born and died 1878).
- Alfred Peeler (1879–1957) married Emma Matilda Elizabeth Schreck (1883–1959) in 1906.
- Harold John Peeler (1881–1968) married Elsie Pritchard (1888–1963) in 1907. They had two children – Rebecca Mary Peeler 1908 and Harold Pritchard Peeler 1913.
- Esther Amy Alice Peeler (1884–1961) married George Arthur Lupton (born c.1882) in 1905. They had three children – Alice Mary Lupton 1907, Eva Anne Lupton 1908 and Nellie Ethel Lupton 1909.
- Gertrude Jane Peeler (1885–1958) married William Charles McKindley (born 1878) in 1906. They had four children – Thomas McKindley 1906, Robert Archibald McKindley 1907, William Charles McKindley 1910 and Walter David McKindley 1914.
- Florence Mary Ellen Peeler (born 1889) married Albert Frederick Steiner (1884–1940) in 1911. They had two children – Florence May Steiner 1912 and Frederick James Steiner 1914.
- Edward Thomas Peeler (1891–1971) married Florence Mary Hewitt (1889–1976) in 1911. They had four children including – Gladys Peeler 1912, Mabel Peeler 1914 and Roy Peeler 1916.

Walter's paternal grandfather, William Peeler (1810–88) was born in Manchester, Lancashire. He was convicted of larceny in the Lancaster Quarter Sessions on 21st January 1828, sentenced to fourteen years and was deported to Van Dieman's Land from Portsmouth, Hampshire aboard Convict Ship *Woodford* on 29th April, arriving on 25th August 1828. He settled in Tasmania and married Mary née Bentley (1814–96), born at Linlithgow, Scotland, on 14th May 1839 at St David's Cathedral, Hobart. She was convicted of larceny and was deported to Van Dieman's Land from London aboard Convict Ship *Atwick* on 30th September 1837, arriving on 23rd January 1838. They later moved to Barkers Creek, near Castlemaine, Victoria. In addition to William they had seven other children:

St David's Church became a Cathedral when Hobart became a city in 1836. It was demolished after the current Cathedral was consecrated in 1874.

- Charles Peeler (1839–40).
- Ellen Peeler (1840–1925) married Edward Kimberley (1824–78) in 1862. His grandfather, also Edward Kimberley (c.1765–1829), was transported on the Convict Ship *Scarborough* arriving at Botany Bay with the First Fleet in January 1788. He was convicted of grand larceny at Coventry, Warwickshire on 20th March 1783 and sentenced to seven years. By 1805 he was a night watch member and was described by convicts in his charge as sadistic. He considered the convicts of Norfolk Island no better than heathens and women were born for the convenience of men. Edward junior and Ellen had eleven children – John Kimberley 1858, William Kimberley 1859, Robert Carl Kimberley 1862, Alfred Edward Kimberley 1864, Frederick Kimberley 1865, Amelia Mary Kimberley 1866, Hannah Jane Kimberley 1868, Alice Maude Kimberley 1871, Thomas Henry Kimberley 1872, Charles Edward Kimberley 1874 and Edward Kimberley 1876. Ellen married Charles McGennisken (born c.1852 in Co Leitrim, Ireland) in 1881 and they had four more children – Alfred Charles McGennisken 1880, Catherine Mabel McGennisken 1882, Thomas Erin McGennisken 1884 and Arthur James McGenniskin 1887.
- A male Peeler (born 1843).
- Thomas Peeler (1845–83) married Hannah McKindley (1839–1920) in 1868. She was born at Rathglass, Tullow, Co Carlow, Ireland. They had five children – Mary Ellen Jane Peeler 1869, Charlotte Anne Peeler 1871, Emily Maud Peeler 1872, Thomas Charles Peeler 1876 and William Archibald Peeler 1878.
- Jane Peeler (1847–1928) married Alfred Hampson (died 1934) in 1870. They had six children – Alfred Edward Hampson 1870, William Bentley Hampson 1872, John Harry Hampson 1874, Gilbert Hampson 1877, Minnie Maud Hampson 1882 and Gertrude Jane Hampson 1887.
- John Peeler (born 1851).
- Esther Peeler (1855–56).

His maternal grandfather, Allan Scott (1810–70) married Elizabeth née Rowland. In is not known where Walter was educated, but afterwards he worked in his parents' orchard at Barker's Creek, Castlemaine. In 1908 he was a wood carter there, then he worked at Thompson's Foundry, Castlemaine before working in the Leongatha district.

Walter Peeler married Emma Hewitt (2nd July 1887–2nd August 1964) on 10th July 1907 at the Congregational Parsonage, Castlemaine, Victoria. She was born at Chesterton, Cambridgeshire. They lived at 159 Cubitt Street, Castlemaine and had moved to Doveton Street by 1914. By 1917 they had moved to 45 Swan Street, Richmond and to 13 Chestnut Street by 1919, but appear to have retained their property at Doveton Street, Castlemaine. Walter and Emma had five children:

Thompson's Foundry in Castlemaine.

The complex of buildings forming the Congregational Church in Castlemaine were constructed between 1855 and 1862. It was purchased by the Presbyterian Church of Victoria in 1984 (Don Stephens).

- Walter Peeler (born and died 1908).
- Alice Peeler (1909–96) married Albert James 'Dick' Beck (1911–88) in 1930 and they lived at 48 Browning Street, South Yarra, Victoria. By 1943 they were living at 48 Wattletree Road, Armadale, Victoria, at 50 Wattletree Road, Armadale by 1949 and at 25 Cambridge Street, Armadale by 1972. They had at least three daughters – Shirley Alice Beck, Elaine Beck and Valerie Beck.
- Winifred Peeler (1912–51) married Keith Ernest Conquest (1911–49), a butcher, in 1933. They were living at 3 Burrindi Road, Caulfield East, Victoria in 1936. Keith was a storeman when he enlisted in 1st Corps Petrol Park, Westgarth, Victoria on 25th May 1940 (VX23617). He was described as 5' 8½" tall, with medium complexion, auburn

The railway crossing on Swan Street, Richmond. Walter Peeler's family was living there in 1917.

hair and blue eyes. He was classified a Group III Driver on 14th September, but reverted to General Duties on 24th November. Keith embarked at Melbourne on 29th December and arrived at Alexandria, Egypt on 30th January 1941. He was evacuated to 7th Australian General Hospital with a fractured radius on 6th January 1942. Having transferred to 109th General Transport Company, Australian Army Service Corps, he sailed for Java, arriving at Batavia on 18th February. He was reported missing on 7th March having been captured by the Japanese in Thailand. He returned to Australia from Singapore on 6th October 1945, arriving at Melbourne on 21st October and was discharged from 1st Australian Corps Petrol Park, Watsonia, Victoria on 21st January 1946, suffering from retrobulbar neuritis and a mal-united fracture of the left radius. Winifred served in the Australian Army Medical Women's Service during the Second World War, working in the office at Heidelberg Military Hospital, Victoria. She was living at 4 Redmond Street, Kew, Victoria in 1940, at 10 Venus Street, South Caulfield in 1945 and at 14 Laura Street, South Caulfield in 1946.

- Jean Peeler (1915–21).
- Kenneth Walter Peeler (1919–99), a labourer, enlisted in 37/39th Battalion (Militia) at Caulfield, Victoria on 24th September 1937 (324165). He had previously been a cadet in the same unit for eleven months. He was described as 5′ 7″ tall, weighing 140 lbs, with brown hair, blue eyes, fresh complexion and his religious denomination was Presbyterian. He was allocated to 14 Platoon, D Company and promoted lance corporal on 1st December, but was discharged on 13th April 1938. He enlisted in the Royal Australian Navy on 3rd August 1938 (22399) on a twelve-year engagement and was posted to HMAS *Cerberus* as an ordinary seaman. Appointed ordinary telegraphist on 24th November and posted to HMAS *Hobart* on 8th December. Promoted telegraphist on 22nd February 1940 and returned to HMAS *Cerberus* on 19th January 1941. Appointed acting leading telegraphist on 11th November. Posted to HMAS *Penguin* on 24th February 1942 and was promoted leading telegraphist on 1st November. He completed his service on 2nd May 1949 as a petty officer (telegraphist). Kenneth married Joan Mary Lewis (born 1921) in New South Wales in 1942. They lived at 28 Young Street, Armadale, Victoria, at 50 Wattletree Road, Armadale and 318 Parramatta Road, Stanmore, NSW. They had three children – Sharyn Kathleen Peeler 1945, Wayne Kenneth Peeler 1948 and Kerry Joan Peeler 1953.

Emma's father, John 'Jack' Hewitt (1852–1919), born at Smithy Fen, Cottenham, Cambridgeshire, married Sarah Ann née Peacock (1853–1933), also born at Cottenham, Cambridgeshire, on 19th October 1874. They ran a market garden and sold their produce at the Cambridge markets. They emigrated to Australia, leaving Gravesend on 13th January 1888 aboard SS *Waroonga* and arrived at Thursday Island on 28th February, but smallpox was declared on board and the passengers were in quarantine for three weeks. The Hewitts and other passengers for north Queensland disembarked at Magnetic Island for quarantine while *Waroonga* continued to Brisbane. When the quarantine ended SS *Bulimba* took the passengers to Townsville, arriving on 13th March. They had moved to Lyonville, near

Daylesford, Victoria by 1917, where they grew produce to sell at the Melbourne markets. In addition to Emma they had seven other children:

The station at Lyonville.

- John Hewitt (c.1875–1972) spent most of his life wandering around Australia and New Zealand.
- Esther Hewitt (1877–1947) moved to Western Australia with her sister Elizabeth in 1898 and she married Richard Yardley (1871–1940) in 1899 at Helena Valley WA. They had nine children – Esther Winifred Yardley 1899, Myrtle Elizabeth Yardley 1901, Edwin George Yardley 1903, Richard Yardley 1905, Alice May Yardley 1907, Doris Ethel Yardley 1909, Ruth Yardley 1911, Walter John Yardley 1913 and Gordon Leonard Yardley 1918.
- Elizabeth Mary Hewitt (1882–1957), born at Glossop, Derbyshire, moved to Western Australia, where she married Michael John King (died 1940), a horse driver, in 1911. In 1936 they were living at 92 Forrest Street, East Fremantle, WA. They had five children – Richard John King 1907, Ella May King 1912, Sheelah Mary King 1914, Michael George Henry King 1917 and Eva Elizabeth 1926.
- Charles Hewitt (1885–1961) married Lydia Atkinson (1888–1965) in 1908 in Tasmania and they had three children, including Margery Hewitt 1904 and Marjorie Hewitt 1915. They were living at West Mooreville Road, Burnil when he enlisted on 13th May 1915 at Claremont, Tasmania (4919), destined for 1st Australian General Hospital Convalescent Depot, Egypt. He was described as a farmer, 5′ 10½″ tall, weighing 154 lbs, with fair complexion, blue eyes, brown hair and his religious denomination was Church of England. He had previously served for two years in the Tasmanian Rangers as a corporal. He departed Melbourne on HMAT A62 *Wandilla* on 17th June and disembarked at Suez on 18th July. He was admitted to No.4 Auxiliary Hospital at Abbassia on 19th November with mumps and was discharged to his unit on 23rd December. On 9th February 1916 he embarked for Australia on HT *Nestor* at Suez with defective vision and was discharged from 6th Military District on 15th June 1916.
- Florence 'Flora' Mary Hewitt (1889–1976) married Walter's brother, Edward Thomas Peeler (1891–1971), in 1911. They had four children, including Gladys Peeler 1912, Mabel Peeler 1914 and Roy Peeler 1916.
- George Hewitt (1892–1915) served as a private in 5th Battalion AIF (1235 & 1361), joining at Broadmeadows, Victoria on 16th November 1914. He was described as a labourer, 5′ 11½″ tall, weighing 160 lbs, with dark complexion, dark grey eyes, black hair and his religious denomination was Church of England. He joined 5th Battalion, 2nd Reinforcements on 5th January 1915 and embarked on the *Novlan* at Alexandria, Egypt for Gallipoli on 4th April. He served in D Company and was

severely wounded in the back and abdomen in late April 1915. He was evacuated to HMHS *Derfflinger*, where he died on 29th April and was buried at sea (Lone Pine Memorial).

- Edwin Hewitt (1895–1929) enlisted on 26th May 1915 and joined at Claremont, Tasmania on 28th May. He was described as a labourer, 5′ 11″ tall, weighing 141 lbs, with fair complexion, hazel eyes, brown hair and his religious denomination was Church of England. He embarked on HMAT A30 *Borda* on 23rd June and disembarked at Suez on 18th July. Having been taken on strength of 12th Battalion (6th Reinforcements) at Gallipoli on 6th August, he was taken sick with diarrhoea on 24th August and was admitted to 1st Australian Field Ambulance. He was transferred to No.1 Casualty Clearing Station at Mudros next day. He disembarked at Alexandria from HMT *Nile* on 27th August and was admitted to 1st Auxiliary Hospital, Luna Park, Heliopolis and No.3 Auxiliary Convalescent Depot, Heliopolis next day with lung trouble. On 21st September he transferred to Ras El Tin Convalescent Home, Alexandria and was discharged to the Australian Base Details on 20th November. Edwin was admitted to 1st Australian General Hospital with bronchitis on 3rd March 1916 and was discharged from No.4 Auxiliary Hospital, Abbassia on 10th March. He was admitted and discharged from No.4 Auxiliary Hospital, Abbassia with diptheria on 5th April and was attached for duty in the men's mess as an orderly from 17th April. He embarked at Alexandria on 31st May, disembarked at Plymouth on 12th June and was assigned to 3rd Training Battalion at Perham Down until 25th July. Edwin rejoined 12th Battalion in France on 9th August. He received gunshot wounds to the hand and face in the period 19th-22nd August and was admitted to No.3 Casualty Clearing Station and 26th General Hospital, Étaples on 24th August. He embarked on HMHS *Brighton* at Calais on 14th September and was admitted to 1st Eastern General Hospital. He transferred to 1st Auxiliary Hospital on 29th December and was sent on leave on 12th January 1917. He reported to No.2 Convalescent Depot, Weymouth on 29th January and embarked on HMHS *Benalla* at Plymouth on 12th February. He returned to Melbourne on 10th April and was discharged from 6th Military District in Hobart as medically unfit on 10th May 1917. He had lost vision in his left eye and suffered from vertigo. Edwin married Rhoda Dora Maida Walters (1902–50) in Tasmania in 1919. They had three children – Lucy Verden Hewitt 1919, Jessie Merle Hewitt 1922 and Florence Victoria Hewitt 1926. He died at Kyneton, Victoria on 7th May 1929 of septic meningitis and cerebral compression, possibly caused by his head wound.

It is understood that Walter and Emma separated between 1919 and 1924, but no divorce has been traced. Emma was working as a shop assistant, living at 1 Primrose Street, Prahran, Victoria in 1931. When she died at Prahran in 1964, she was living at 135 Williams Road. Walter's second wife was Kathleen Emma McLeod (née Hewitt) (c.1886–1969), born at Bray, Co Wicklow, Ireland. Their relationship may have started before 1914, but no marriage certificate has been found. Her parents were William McLeod, a gardener, and Janet née Hay. Walter and Kathleen were living at Nicholson Street, Bairnsdale, Victoria by 1924 and in 1930 were at Oxford Road, Kilsyth, Victoria. By 1931 they were at 93 Devonshire Road, Sunshine, Victoria and at 10 Moore Street, Caulfield, Victoria by April 1938.

Kathleen had a son from a previous relationship, Alfred Harvey McLeod (1914–47), born at 43 Alfred Crescent, Fitzroy North, Victoria, who changed his name to Peeler later. He was a truck driver, living at 353 King Street, Melbourne at the time of his enlistment in Australian Military Forces on 7th May 1940 at Fitzroy, Victoria (VX14979). He was posted as a gunner to 2/4th Field Regiment on 14th May and sailed for the Middle East from Port Melbourne on 20th October via Bombay, arriving at Alexandria, Egypt on 26th November. He was graded a Group III Driver Mechanic on 7th March 1941. Alfred had a number of disciplinary problems. He was AWOL for ten hours on 12th–13th July for which he was fined 10/–. On 20th July he was AWOL for six hours and was confined to barracks for seven days and forfeited one day's pay. He returned to Australia aboard SS *Madras City*, arriving at 4th Military District on 23rd March 1942. On 9th August he was charged with an act to the prejudice of good order and military discipline in 1st Military District and confined to barracks for seven days. He sailed for Papua New Guinea aboard the *Tarooma* from Cairns, Queensland, arriving on 22nd July 1943. Alfred relinquished Group III Driver Mechanic and was graded Group II Signaller on 26th August. He was hospitalised with tonsillitis 20th–29th November and with malaria 6th–29th January 1944. He sailed from Port Moresby aboard USS *Orizaba* for Brisbane, Queensland, arriving on 16th February. On 17th October 1944 he changed his next of kin to his mother as his father was reported missing in action. Alfred was admitted to 2/2nd Australian General Hospital, Brisbane with a urinary infection 27th February–16th March 1945. He was discharged on 20th June 1945 suffering from bilateral osteosclerosis. He died in an accident on 28th October 1947 at Alexandra, Victoria.

Walter and Kathleen had four children:

• Jeanette Peeler (c.1922–2013) married W Baker and they lived at Lot 56, Acacia Road, Fern Tree Gully, Victoria.
• Margot Marie Peeler (born c.1924) married as Dunne and they had a son, Donald Dunne.
• Donald Peeler (1925–44) was a packing assistant when he enlisted at the Drill Hall, McWhae Avenue, Ripponlea, Victoria on 6th December 1943 (VX93902). He was described as having fair hair and brown eyes. He was allotted to 14th Australian Infantry Training Battalion on 12th February 1944 and transferred to 15th Battalion AIF on 30th October 1944 at Canungra, Queensland. He sailed from Brisbane for the Solomon Islands aboard SS *Cape Victory* arriving at Torokina, Bougainville on 27th November. Donald was killed in action on 31st December

1944 and was buried at Motupena Point. On 3rd March 1945 he was reinterred in Torokina Australian War Cemetery (B C 7) and later in Port Moresby (Bomana) War Cemetery, Papua New Guinea (A4 C 22).
- Elspeth Kathleen Peeler (born c.1927) married as Jude.

Walter enlisted in the AIF at Leongatha, Victoria on 17th February 1916 (114). He was described as 5′ 9″ tall, weighing 158 lbs, with dark complexion, brown eyes, brown hair and his religious denomination was Methodist. He embarked on HMAT A62 *Wandilla* at Melbourne with A Company, 3rd Pioneer Battalion on 6th June. He was charged with being AWOL at Cape Town, South Africa on 3rd July, but was admonished and forfeited one day's pay. He disembarked at Plymouth, Devon and was posted to Larkhill on Salisbury Plain on 26th July. Promoted lance corporal on 6th November. He embarked at Southampton, Hampshire on SS *Caesarea* for Le Havre, France on 25th November and attended a course at the Lewis Gun School, Le Touquet from 11th December. Walter was tried by field general court martial on

20th January 1917 for writing a letter contrary to censor regulations and forfeited one month's pay. He was severely reprimanded for having a loaded revolver in his billet on 30th March. On 8th May he was instructing a squad in the use of the Lewis gun. The butt, pistol grip, pinion group and gas regulator were stripped and the magazine was to one side when he was asked to demonstrate a stoppage. He loaded what he thought was a dummy cartridge in the magazine and pushed the cocking handle forward causing the cartridge to fire. The

SS *Wandilla* was operated by the Adelaide Steamship Co on the Fremantle to Sydney route from 1912. In 1915 she became a military transport and in 1916 a hospital ship. She was attacked by a U-boat in February 1918, but the torpedo failed to explode. In 1921 she was sold to the Bermuda & West Indies Steam Ship Company and renamed *Fort St George* in 1921. In 1924 she collided with RMS *Olympic* at New York. In 1935 she was sold to Lloyd Triestino and renamed *Cesarea* and *Arno* in 1938. In the Second World War she was used by the Regia Marina as a hospital ship, but was sunk by British aircraft on 10th September 1942. The British claimed a decoded German radio message indicated that the ship was carrying supplies to Benghazi and this justified the attack. Allegations that the attack was a war crime were not investigated after the war.

Larkhill was used as a tented camp from 1899 and in 1912 the first military aircraft trials were held there. On the outbreak of the First World War it expanded rapidly into a huge hutted town able to accommodate thirty-four battalions. It was served by a light railway system. Post-war it became the School of Artillery.

bullet seriously wounded 192 Private John Martin Fife (a forty-three year old plumber from Inverkeithing, Scotland) in the right buttock, resulting in him being discharged on 26th December 1917. As a result Walter was tried by field general court martial at HQ 36th Battalion and was severely reprimanded and reduced to the ranks. He was promoted lance corporal again on 30th May 1917.

Walter was wounded in the cheek near Messines on 7th June and rejoined his unit on 10th June. **Awarded the VC for his actions at Broodseinde, Belgium on 4th October 1917, LG 26th November 1917.** He received a gunshot to the right arm on 12th October near Zonnebeke, Belgium and was evacuated to hospital at Rouen. He was evacuated to England on HMHS *St Denis* on 15th October and admitted to Northampton War Hospital. He transferred to 1st Australian Auxiliary Hospital, Harefield, Middlesex on 30th October and was discharged to No.3 Convalescent Depot (Group Clearing Hospital), Hurdcott, Wiltshire on 12th November before moving to Longbridge Deverill, Wiltshire. On 9th January 1918 he was presented with the VC by the King at Buckingham Palace. He returned to France on 17th May and was appointed temporary corporal on 31st May. He attended the Corps Gas School 22nd–30th June. He was promoted sergeant on 30th July and returned to England next day. On 24th August he and nine other VCs embarked

SS *Caesarea* (1,504 tons) was built for the London and Southwestern Railway Co in 1910 for the Southampton – Channel Islands service. She saw service in both world wars. On 7th July 1923 she struck a rock off Jersey and sank just outside St Helier harbour, but was refloated and repaired. Later that year she was bought by the Isle of Man Steam Packet Co and renamed TSS *Manx Maid*. In August 1939 she was requisitioned as an armoured boarding vessel and in 1940 brought back 3,000 troops from Brest. In October 1941 she became a special duties vessel and was renamed HMS *Bruce*. From March 1942 until March 1945 she was used as a Fleet Air Arm target vessel, then returned to the Isle of Man Steam Packet Co. She was broken up in 1951.

The Lewis gun, designed by American Colonel Isaac N Lewis based on an earlier machine gun by Dr Samuel McLean, was developed by the British as a light infantry automatic weapon and for use in aircraft. It. It was gas operated, air cooled and fully automatic. The pan magazine held forty-seven or ninety-seven rounds and the gun could fire 500–600 rounds per minute. It weighed 28 lbs.

on HMAT D21 *Medic* to return to Australia to support recruiting. Walter was discharged on 10th December 1918.

After the war Walter worked as a labourer before securing employment with the Victorian Department of Lands for six years as a member of its Soldier Settlement

Branch. He resigned to run an orchard in Castlemaine, but later abandoned this venture and returned to Melbourne.

Walter attended an Anzac Dinner in Melbourne with twenty-two other VCs on 23rd April 1927 hosted by Lieutenant General Sir John Monash GCMG KCB VD. For an unknown reason The Duke of York (future King George VI) was not invited. Two days later Walter and the other VCs were at the Anzac Commemoration Service at the Exhibition Building, Melbourne, Victoria in the presence of The Duke of York.

He was a machinery assembler in 1931 and then joined HV McKay Harvester Works at Sunshine, Victoria, where Lawrence McCarthy VC was a commercial traveller. In 1934 Walter was appointed Custodian of Victoria's Shrine of Remembrance, Melbourne and remained in post for thirty years. In 1947 he became a member of the Victorian Corps of Commissionaires.

On 27th May 1940 Walter re-enlisted at Caulfield, Victoria, understating his age by fourteen years. He joined 2/2nd Pioneer Battalion (VX8345) and was posted to Puckapunyal, Victoria. He was appointed acting sergeant on 29th May and acting staff sergeant and CQMS on 1st August. He was promoted staff sergeant on 7th April 1941 and embarked at Sydney, New South Wales on RMS *Queen Mary* on 9th April for the Middle East, arriving at Suez on 3rd May. He took part in operations in Syria against Vichy

SS *St Denis* (2,570 tons) was constructed for the Great Eastern Railway as SS *Munich* in 1908 for the Harwich-Hook service. In the First World War she was used as a hospital ship and renamed *St Denis*, which was retained afterwards. In 1923 she was acquired by the London and North Eastern Railway. In 1940 she was scuttled at Amsterdam, but was raised by the Germans, renamed *Barbara* and was used for accommodation for Kiel university. She was scrapped in 1950.

The Northampton County Lunatic Asylum, later named St Crispin Hospital, opened in 1876 near Northampton. In October 1915 it became a war hospital until March 1919. It closed in 1995.

1st Australian Auxiliary Hospital at Harefield, Middlesex, England accepted its first patients in June 1915. It was accommodated in the home of Charles Billyard-Leake, an Australian resident in the United Kingdom. Capacity of the existing buildings was increased to 1,000 beds by the construction of numerous huts. It closed on 31st December 1918. Most patients were surgical cases and amputees were given special attention before returning to Australia.

The Shrine of Remembrance was built between 1928 and 1934 in remembrance of the 114,000 men and women of Victoria who served and the 19,000 who died in the Great War. Despite the financial difficulties of the late 1920s and 1930s, the money to build the Shrine was raised within six months of the opening of the appeal. The Duke of Gloucester opened the Shrine before a crowd of 300,000 in November 1934.

Lawrence Dominic McCarthy (1892–1975) was awarded the VC for his actions on 23rd August 1918 near Madam Wood, east of Vermandovillers, France. He killed twenty-two enemy, took fifty prisoners and captured three machine-guns and 450m of the German trench. He was employed by the Sunshine Harvester Works as a commercial traveler until 1934, when he was laid off due to the Depression.

French forces June-July 1941 with D Company. During the fighting at Merdjayoun in late June he led a party in front of the line at night looking for wounded and his missing company commander. The party recovered four wounded, but was unable to find their officer.

Walter embarked at Suez on SS *Orcades* on 31st January 1942 and disembarked at Batavia, Java on 18th February. He took part in operations with Blackforce, commanded by Brigadier AS Blackburn VC. On 7th March he was reported missing in action and was later confirmed to be a prisoner of war. He spent much of the rest of the war on the Burma Railway and was liberated in Siam on 18th August 1945. On 6th October he embarked at Singapore on SS *Highland Brigade* and disembarked at Melbourne on 21st October. He was treated at Heidelberg Military Hospital, Melbourne and was discharged from the Army on 11th December 1945.

Walter attended the VC Centenary Celebrations at Hyde Park, London on 26th June 1956, travelling on SS *Orcades* with other Australian VCs, part of the 301 VC recipients from across the Commonwealth. Walter maintained his interest in sport throughout his life, being a member of Castlemaine Cricket Club, secretary of Wesley Hill Football Club and captain of East Sunshine Cricket team, winning premierships in 1931 and 1932. He was also a member of the Richmond Returned and Services League, Victoria. In 1947 he became a member of the Victorian Corps of Commissionaires. **Awarded the BEM for his service as Custodian of the Shrine of Remembrance, Melbourne, LG 10th June 1961.** Walter Peeler died at his home at 10 Moore Street, South Caulfield, Victoria on 23rd May 1968 and is buried in Brighton

RMS *Queen Mary* entering the King George V drydock at Southampton. The installations were used to train the commandos who attacked the similar Normandie Dock at St Nazaire in 1942. *Queen Mary* entered service with Cunard-White Star Line (later Cunard) in 1936. She gained the Blue Riband in August 1936, lost it to SS *Normandie* the following year, but regained it in 1938 until 1952. During the Second World War she was converted into a troopship and was painted navy grey, resulting in her being known as the 'Grey Ghost'. Her interior fittings were stripped out to enable 16,000 troops to be

carried in a single journey (the record was 16,683). Her speed made her very difficult for U-boats to target. On 2nd October 1942 she accidentally sank one of her escorts, HMS *Curacoa*, off Ireland with the loss of 239 lives. She was carrying part of the US 29th Infantry Division at the time, destined to land on Omaha Beach on 6th June 1944. In December 1942, she was hit broadside on by a huge wave and rolled over fifty-two degrees, almost causing her to capsize. The incident inspired the novel, *The Poseidon Adventure*, which was adapted into a film of the same name in 1972. On 27th September 1967 she completed her 1,000th and final crossing of the North Atlantic, having carried 2,112,000 passengers over 3,792,227 miles. Her final voyage, starting from Southampton on 31st October 1967, took her around Cape Horn to Long Beach, California, where she is permanently moored as a hotel, museum and restaurant venue.

Cemetery, Melbourne, Victoria (Lawn Section, Grave 36, Compartment H). He is also commemorated in a number of other places:

- Display at the Hall of Valour, Australian War Memorial, Canberra, ACT, Australia.
- The Peeler VC Club at Casula, Moorebank, New South Wales, named in September 1959 with him as guest of honour.
- Peelers Road, Barkers Creek, Victoria.
- Peeler Place, Canberra, Australian Capital Territory.
- Peeler Close, Crib Point, Melbourne, Victoria.
- Peeler Street, Wodonga, Victoria on White Box Rise estate built on land formerly part of Bandiana Army Camp.
- Named on the Victoria Cross Memorial, Campbell, Canberra dedicated on 24th July 2000.

A post-Second World War photograph of Walter Peeler.

Walter Peeler's turfstone in Brighton Cemetery, Melbourne, Victoria.

- Named on a memorial in the Victoria Garden of Remembrance, Springvale, Victoria.
- Victoria Cross Memorial, Queen Victoria Building, George Street, Sydney, New South Wales dedicated on 23rd February 1992 to commemorate the visit of Queen Elizabeth II and Prince Philip on the occasion of the Sesquicentenary of the City of Sydney. Sir Roden Cutler VC, Edward Kenna VC and Keith Payne VC were in attendance.
- Named on one of eleven plaques honouring 175 men from overseas awarded the VC for the Great War. The plaques were unveiled by the Senior Minister of State at the Foreign & Commonwealth Office and Minister for Faith and Communities, Baroness Warsi, at a reception at Lancaster House, London on 26th June 2014 attended by The Duke of Kent and relatives of the VC recipients. The Australian plaque is at the Australian War Memorial.
- The Secretary of State for Communities and Local Government, Eric Pickles MP, announced that Victoria Cross recipients from the Great War would have commemorative paving stones laid in their birthplace as a lasting legacy of local heroes within communities. The stones would be laid on or close to the 100th anniversary of their VC actions. For the 145 VCs born in Australia, Belgium, Canada, China, Denmark, Egypt, France, Germany, India, Iraq, Japan, Nepal, Netherlands, New Zealand, Pakistan, Sri Lanka, South Africa, Ukraine and United States of America, individual commemorative stones were unveiled at the National Memorial Arboretum, Alrewas, Staffordshire by Prime Minister David Cameron MP and Sergeant Johnson Beharry VC on 5th March 2015.

The Australia Service Medal 1939–1945 was awarded to members of Australia's armed forces, mercantile marine and Volunteer Defence Corps. The qualifying period for those serving overseas was eighteen months full-time service or three years part-time service, but in 1996, the qualifying period was reduced to thirty days and ninety days respectively.

In addition to the VC and BEM he was awarded the British War Medal 1914–20, Victory Medal 1914–19, 1939–45 Star, Africa Star, Pacific Star, Defence Medal, War Medal 1939–45, Australia Service Medal 1939–45, George VI Coronation Medal 1937 and Elizabeth II Coronation Medal 1953. The Africa Star was awarded posthumously when service in Syria was recognised for this award. His medals are held in the Hall of Valour, Australian War Memorial, Treloar Crescent, Campbell, Australian Capital Territory, Australia.

20002 SERGEANT IVOR REES
11th Battalion, The South Wales Borderers

Ivor Rees was born at Union Street, Felinfoel, near Llanelly (Llanelli from 1966), Carmarthenshire, Wales on 18th October 1893. His father, David Edward Rees (1865–1937), was a tin plate worker and later an electrical engine driver (colliery engine worker) at Llanelly Steelworks. He married Ann née Bowen (1868–94) in 1888. They lived at 80 Tumble Row, Llannon, Llanelly before moving to Union Street, then 18 Long Row, Felinfoel before again moving to Pwll, Llanelly. David married Margaret Jane née Harry (1859–1941), a general servant, in 1899. They were living at Sailor's Row, Pwll in 1901 and at 38 Union Buildings, Llanelly in 1911. Ivor had six sisters:

- Mary Ann Rees, born 1884.
- Hannah Rees, born c.1889.
- Margaretta Rees, born 1890.
- Jane Rees, born 1893.
- Harriet Ann Harry, born 1896 between David's marriages.
- Helen 'Nellie' Rees, born 1901.

Ivor's paternal grandfather, Benjamin Rees (1840–1913), was a stonemason. He married Hannah née Owen (c.1830–71) in 1859 and Margaret Owens (1842–1908) in 1871. He was living with his family at Pentrepoeth in 1881 and at Union Buildings, Llanelly in 1891. By 1911 Benjamin was living with his daughter Annie and her husband. Benjamin had seven children from his two marriages:

Salamanca (later Station) Road in Llanelli. Llanelli was spelled in its anglicised form of Llanelly until the 1960s and should not be confused with the much smaller Llanelly in Monmouthshire. It expanded significantly in the 18th and 19th centuries as a coal mining town and was later a centre for the tinplate and steelmaking industries. Mine closures and reductions in steel production caused a significant economic decline from the 1970s onwards. The town's famous rugby union team has produced many Lions and Welsh international players.

- William Rees (born c.1860).
- Benjamin Rees (born 1869).
- Owen Rees (born c.1871) was a railway packer in 1891.
- Hannah 'Annie' Maria Rees, born 1872, was a tin plate opener in 1891. She married Thomas John (born c.1869), a steelworks labourer, in 1898. They were living at 17 Mount Pleasant, Llanelly in 1911.

- Edward Rees, born 1874, was a coal miner in 1891.
- Elizabeth Rees, born c.1877.
- Richard Rees, born c.1880.

His maternal grandfather, David Bowen (c.1831–94), a coalminer, married Harriet née Marks (c.1835–1905) in 1858. They lived at Bryncochfach Cottages, Llannon. In addition to Ann they had eight other children:

Felinfoel, a village of about 2,000 people to the north of Llanelli, is home to Felinfoel Brewery, the oldest in Wales.

- William Bowen (c.1859–1918) was living at Forest Fach, Swansea in 1894.
- Hannah Bowen (1861–1900) may have married Samuel Rees in 1886.
- Margaret Bowen (c.1862–80).
- Daniel Bowen (c.1864–1942).
- Elizabeth Bowen (born 1866).
- Sarah Bowen (born c.1871).
- Mary Bowen (born c.1874).
- Jane Bowen (1877–1957) was living at 28 Afon Road, Llangennech, Carmarthenshire when she died.

Ivor was educated at Pwll Council and Old Road Schools, Llanelly. He was originally employed as a steelworker in the South Wales Steelworks at Llanelly and was later a crane driver there. He enlisted

Ivor Rees receives a hero's welcome on returning home.

Ivor Rees receives his VC from the King.

on 9th November 1914. Promoted lance corporal 5th August and corporal 1st December 1915. He went to France on 4th December 1915. Promoted sergeant 19th September 1916. He was invalided home with trench fever in February 1917 and spent seven weeks at Cardiff Red Cross Hospital.

Awarded the VC for his actions at Pilkem, Belgium on 31st July 1917, LG 14th September 1917. The VC was presented by the King outside Buckingham Palace on 26th September. Ivor was later promoted to CSM and

One of the camps at Kinmel Park during the First World War, which were served by a railway from Rhyll. Practice trenches can still be seen there. In March 1919 there was a riot by Canadian troops angry at delays in being repatriated, during which five men were killed.

returned to Britain on 11th February 1918 to become an instructor in 53rd (Young Soldier) Battalion at Kinmel Park. He was fined £-/12/- for being drunk and disorderly at Llanelly on 11th March 1918. On 21st March 1919 he was discharged, but joined 4th Welch (TF) until being discharged on 30th December 1921.

Ivor was always humble about his exploits, but during one leave described to his father a narrow escape when he was with a party surprised by a group of Germans. In the close-quarter fight his bayonet broke off and he had to club his way out using his rifle butt. He received a gold watch and illuminated address from the villagers of Pwll, Llanelly. About 20,000 people lined the streets cheering the VC, including Sir James Hills-Johnes, who was awarded the VC during the Indian Mutiny. Ivor received a cheque for £156 raised by public subscription, £100 having been pledged by the late chairman of the South Wales Works to the first company employee to win a VC.

On 30th September 1917 Ivor Rees married Martha 'Mattie' Jenkins (born 1895) at Trinity Chapel, New Dock, Llanelly. Ivor was living at 5 Stradley Hill, Pwll and Martha was living at 12 St David's Street, Seaside, Llanelly at the time. They lived at 5 Craddock Street, St Paul's, Tyisha, Llanelly. Ivor and Martha had five children:

Lieutenant General Sir James Hills-Johnes VC GCB (1833–1919) joined the Bengal Artillery in 1853 and was awarded the VC for his gallantry in the Siege of Dehli during the Indian

- Lewis Jenkins Rees, born on 29th May 1915 at 12 Park View Terrace, Llanelly and registered as Lewis J Jenkins. The birth was registered again on 10th October 1917 as Rees. Lewis married Maggie M Harvey (born 1915) in 1940. He was living at 9 Waterloo Street, Llanelly in 1967.

Mutiny. He also fought in the Second Afghan War 1878–80 and became military governor of Kabul. In 1886 he became High Sheriff of Carmarthenshire.

- Meiriona Jenkins Rees, born on 11th December 1921.
- Aranwen Jenkins Rees, born on 25th December 1926, married James Grover in 1954.
- Annie Jenkins Rees, born on 3rd February 1929, is understood to have married John G Griffiths in 1955.
- Ifan Jenkins Rees, born on 27th September 1931, married Enid Thomas in 1959.

Trinity Chapel, Llanelli where Ivor Rees married Martha Jenkins in September 1917, a few days after the VC investiture. It was founded in 1858 (Jaggery).

Martha's father, Evan Jenkins (1863–1930), a carter for a coal merchant, married Sarah née Pughe (1868–1938) in 1887. They were living at 10 Maingwyn Street, Towyn, Merionethshire in 1891, at 13 Athelstan Road, Towyn in 1901 and at 11 Athelstan Road, Towyn in 1911, before moving to 12 St David Street, Llanelly in 1912. By 1917 Evan was a tin plate worker. In addition to Martha they had five other children:

- Sarah Mary Jenkins 1888.
- Isaac Lewis Jenkins (1890–1916) was a labourer in a tinplate works in 1911 boarding at Brynhenllan, Brgyn Road, Llanelly. He married Catherine 'Kate' Ellen Griffiths (born 1890), a domestic servant, later in 1911 and they lived at 6 Union Square, Dolgelly, Merionethshire. They had three children – Madeline R Jenkins 1912 and twins Evan H and Isaac L Jenkins 1916. Isaac served as a drummer in 10th Welsh (16425) and was killed in action at Mametz Wood on 12th July 1916 (Thiepval Memorial, France).
- Catherine Jenkins 1892.
- John David Jenkins (1898–1964).
- Evan Llewelyn Jenkins (1905–67).

Ivor returned to his job as a crane driver, then trained as a barber, but was unemployed for two years until being employed by Llanelli Borough Council as a water inspector and cleansing superintendent until retiring in 1959. He was charged at Carmarthenshire Assizes on 1st June 1921 with an attempted roadside sexual assault on fourteen-year-old Elsie Green. An all male jury reduced the charge to common assault and he was sentenced to four months' imprisonment with hard labour. During the Second World War he was a CSM in 2nd Carmarthenshire Battalion Home Guard. On 9th July 1953 Ivor was introduced to the Queen and Prince Philip at Swansea during their Royal Tour of the nation shortly after her Coronation.

Ivor Rees died at his home at 5 Craddock Street, Llanelli on 11th March 1967 and was cremated at Swansea Crematorium within Morriston Cemetery. His ashes were scattered in Section 5 of the Garden of Remembrance. He is also commemorated in a number of other places:

- Brass plaque on the wall of the entrance to Llanelli Town Hall.
- Blue plaque dedicated in People's Park, Llanelli on 31st July 2007 on the nineteenth anniversary of his VC action. The ceremony was attended by fifty-nine members of his family.
- Panel in Harvard Chapel, Brecon Cathedral, Powys dedicated to five South Wales Borderers VCs, including Ivor Rees.
- Victoria Cross Honours Board, Regimental Museum of The Royal Welsh (Brecon), The Barracks, Brecon, Powys.

The blue plaque dedicated to Ivor Rees in 2007 in People's Park, Llanelli, near the town hall and war memorial (Jaggery).

- The Department for Communities and Local Government decided to provide a commemorative paving stone at the birthplace of every Great War Victoria Cross recipient in the United Kingdom. A commemorative stone for Ivor was dedicated at Llanelli Town Hall, Town Square, Carmarthenshire on 31st July 2017 to mark the centenary of his award.

In addition to the VC he was awarded the 1914–15 Star, British War Medal 1914–20, Victory Medal 1914–19, Defence Medal, George VI Coronation Medal 1937 and Elizabeth II Coronation Medal 1953. The medals and illuminated address presented to him in October 1917 were loaned to the South Wales Borderers Museum in 1969 and the Regiment purchased them from his widow a few years later. They are held by the Regimental Museum of The Royal Welsh (Brecon), The Barracks, Brecon, Powys, Wales. The group includes the Victory Medal USA with three clasps (Meuse-Argonne, Aisne/Marne and Defensive Sector), but it is not known why he had it. Indeed the clasps Meuse-Argonne and Aisne/Marne were for battles fought months after he returned to Britain.

CAPTAIN HENRY REYNOLDS
12th Battalion, The Royal Scots (Lothian Regiment)

Henry Reynolds was born at Whilton Wharf, near Daventry, Northamptonshire on 16th August 1879. His gravestone shows his date of birth as 16th August 1883, but he appears in the 1881 Census aged one and the Army List agrees with 1879. Henry's father, Thomas Henry Reynolds (1838–1903), was born at Foleshill, Warwickshire. He married Tryphena née Gadsden (1840–1901), born at Nettleden, near Hemel Hempstead, Hertfordshire, in 1866 at Berkhampstead,

Hertfordshire. Thomas had a business based at Whilton Wharf and Daventry railway station retailing coal, lime, manure, seed and cattle cake. He was also a corn factor, a farmer of 350 acres employing two men and three boys and farm steward for John Craven at the Lodge, Daventry. Thomas was Mayor of Daventry four times. He was also a parish councillor, rural district councillor, guardian of the Daventry Poor Law Union, manager of Whilton School, a churchwarden and a colour sergeant in the Althorp Company of Volunteers. In the latter capacity he fired the first shots on the range at Brington when it was constructed in 1897. The family lived at Whilton Locks, but the house was later demolished and the Bannaventa public house was built in its place. Thomas left effects valued at £9,618/9/8. Henry had nine siblings:

Henry's nephew, Donald Richard Carey Smith, is buried in Calais Canadian War Cemetery.

- Tryphena Reynolds (1867–1922) married Alpheus Smith (1871–1959) in 1900. Alpheus was a Surveyor of Taxes for the Inland Revenue Department in 1911 and the family was living at 52 Tierney Road, Streatham Hill, London. They had three children – Tryphena Lucy Hope Smith 1903, Roy Norman Compton Smith 1907 and Donald Richard Carey Smith 1909. Alpheus was awarded the CBE (LG 29th December 1931). Donald served as a private in the Calgary Highlanders, Royal Canadian Infantry Corps (B/76152) and was killed in action on 8th September 1944 (Calais Canadian War Cemetery, Leubringhen, France – 7 C 9). Roy became a physician and surgeon.
- Thomas Reynolds (1868–1907) married Mary Elizabeth Montgomery (born 1872) in 1894 and they had a son, Thomas Henry Montgomery Reynolds, in 1901. Thomas senior's father's business passed to him in 1903 and from January 1904 he operated his own barge, *Harry*. There appears to have been a family dispute in 1905 and thereafter the business traded as 'Thomas and Henry Reynolds'. *Harry* was sold to Philip Mellor later that year and the coal business was purchased by Samuel Barlow of Glascote. Mary was proprietor of a café in 1911, living with her mother and son at Flore Hill, Northamptonshire.
- Mary Edith Reynolds (1869–1951) married John Henry Richard Collis (1867–1945) in 1905 and they had a son, John Patrick Douglas Collis, the same year. John senior was a clerk to the Surveyor of Taxes at the Inland Revenue Department in 1911 and the family was living at 75 Radbourne Road, Balham, London.
- Sarah Caroline (appears as Catherine in the birth registration but in all other documents as Caroline) Alice Reynolds (1870–1939) married John Henry Ivens (1876–1941), a wine merchant, in 1903. They had a son, John Henry Masters Ivens, in 1905. Sarah was living at Flat 31, Ideal Building, Mill Street, Kidderminster,

Worcestershire at the time of her death on 8th July 1939, leaving effects valued at £617/10/- to her son John.

- Ethel Reynolds (1872–1926) was living at 93 Palace Road, Tulse Hill at the time of her death.
- Clara Jane Reynolds (born 1874) married George Warren (born 1868), a leather merchant, in 1898. They were living at 14 St Michael's Avenue, Northampton in 1901. In 1911 he was a traveller in boots, boarding at 14 Finborough Road, Tooting, London.
- Martha Douglas Reynolds (1875–1963) married Richard Leigh (c.1842–1916) in 1905. She married Reginald Richard Frederick Cavendish (1857–1941) in 1922. Reginald was married previously to Mary Constance Dupuis (died 1914) in 1880.
- Florence Mabel Reynolds (1877–1959) married William Montague Marriott (1878–1943), an auctioneer, in 1905. They had two children – Miriam Mary Marriott 1906 and Delia Millicent Marriott 1908. In 1911 they were living at 109 Clarence Avenue, Northampton. The marriage ended in divorce and William married Alice Annie Bramsdon née Jones in 1921 (see mother-in-law below).
- Alfred Edward (1881–1920) married Maud Ophelia Marion Eliza Harper Boswell (1882–1972) in 1905. Maud was born in Sydney, Australia. After his brother, Thomas, died Alfred took over the family business, living at Braunston and trading as a corn, cake, coal, coke, lime, granite, gravel and sand merchant. Maud took over running the business, but it was declared bankrupt in the spring of 1914. When Alfred died Maud was living at Venture Lodge, Little Braunston. They had four children – Philip Edward Bowden Reynolds 1907, Alfred Donovan Douglas Reynolds 1908, Thomas Thorne Reynolds 1911 and Maud Joyce Primrose Gadsden Reynolds 1912. Maud senior married Albert E Hall in 1924.

Henry's paternal grandfather, Jeremiah Reynolds (c.1799–1863) was a farmer of fifty-six acres and a victualler. He married Mary née Pickard (c.1798–1887) in 1823 at Bedworth, Warwickshire. The family was living at the Elephant and Castle Inn, Foleshill, Warwickshire in 1861. In 1871 Mary was living with her daughter Jane at Bulkington Fields, Bulkington, Warwickshire. In addition to Thomas they had five other children:

- Mary Reynolds c.1824.
- Sarah Reynolds c.1828.
- Jeremiah Reynolds (c.1831–1913), a carpenter, married Elizabeth Spencer (c.1837–1916) in 1859. By 1881 Jeremiah was a farmer living with his family at the Elephant and Castle Inn, Foleshill. By 1901 he was Master of the Foleshill Workhouse, with his wife as Matron. They had three children – Mary Elizabeth Reynolds 1861, Sarah Jane Reynolds 1863 and Anne Alice Reynolds 1867.
- Jane Reynolds c.1834.

- Martha Reynolds (c.1836–1914) married Joseph Hood Clay (c.1825–84) in 1857. He was a farmer and they were living at Leicester Road, Nuneaton in 1881. They had nine children – Martha Reynolds Clay 1860, Richard Clay 1864, Alice Lucy Clay 1868, Joseph Henry Clay 1869, Mary Ethel Clay 1872, Jessie Reynolds Clay 1874, Frederick Septimus Clay 1876, Arthur Seymour Clay 1878 and George Reginald Clay 1880.

His maternal grandfather, Thomas Gadsden (1807–65) married Tryphena née Douglas (c.1809–77) in 1839. He was a farmer of 420 acres employing fifteen labourers in 1851 and the family was living at Nettleden Farm, Great Gaddesden, Hertfordshire. By 1861 the farm was 412 acres and employed twelve men and nine boys. In addition to Tryphena they had four other children:

- William Gadsden (1841–98) inherited his father's farm in 1865. He married Mary Lavinia Mead (1852–1907) in 1869. They had four children – Charles Thomas Gadsden 1873, Gertrude Mary Gadsden 1875, William Douglas Gadsden 1879 and Gladys Margaret Gadsden 1880. Mary was living at 'Beaufort', Paynesfield Road, Tatsfield, Surrey at the time of her death on 1st July 1907, leaving effects valued at £131/5/- to her unmarried daughter Gertrude.
- Thomas Gadsden (1843–85) married Mary Ann Caroline Anderson (1851–85) in 1870. He was a farmer of 252 acres at Woodlays Farm, Wavendon, Buckinghamshire in 1871, but by 1881 the farm had reduced to 170 acres. They had eight children – Douglas Anderson Gadsden 1871, James Herbert Gadsden 1873, Douglas Gadsden 1875, George Gadsden 1877, Tryphena Gadsden 1879, Arthur Harry Gadsden 1881 and twins Mary Evelyn Gadsden and May Coralie Gadsden 1883.
- George Gadsden (1845–84).
- Douglas Gadsden (1846–85) married Adelaide Sarah Ann Seymour (1848–1931) in 1876 and they had two children – Henry Seymour Gadsden 1879 and Percy George Gadsden 1881. They were living at 19 Newport Road, Bradwell, Buckinghamshire in 1881.

Henry was educated at Daventry Grammar School and was then employed in the family corn and coal merchant business, which included a coal wharf at Long Buckby. He served as a trooper in the Northamptonshire Yeomanry 1902–07. On 3rd October 1905 he married Gwendolen née Jones (1886–) at Brixworth, Northamptonshire and they had three children:

- Thomas Henry William Reynolds (1906–31) was commissioned in 2nd Royal Scots on 30th August 1926 and was promoted lieutenant on 30th August 1929. He was killed in a road accident at Quetta, India (now Pakistan) on 31st August 1931.
- Gwendoline Tryphena Alice Reynolds (1907–35) married John Cecil Melville Close (1908–83) in 1931. John was educated at Eton, where he was a cadet lance

A barge at Long Buckby Wharf. It was also known as Whilton Wharf.

Long Buckby.

corporal in the Junior Division Officer Training Corps. He was commissioned in the Royal Tank Corps on 31st January 1930 and was placed on the Supplementary Reserve of Officers. Gwendoline died on 24th May 1935 at Ranikhet, India. John subsequently rose to lieutenant colonel. He married Mary Eileen Ludgate Martin (died 2004) in 1939.

- Velia Rosemary Reynolds (1916–93) married Cyril Robert De Silva in 1941 (died 1995).

Gwendolen's father, William Jones (c.1846–1926), was born in Glamorgan. He married Alice Amelia née Incley (1858–1929) in 1880. He was a farmer and cattle dealer in 1891 and the family was living at Water's Lodge, East Haddon, Northamptonshire. By 1901 they had moved to The Grange Farm, East Haddon. Alice was living at The Grange, East Haddon with her grandson, Thomas Henry William Reynolds, in 1911. In addition to Gwendolen they had three other children:

- William Elias Jones (1882–1919), a twin with Alice.
- Alice Annie Jones (1882–1972), a twin with William, married Edgar Nevins Bramsdon (1882–1917) in 1905. They had three children – William John N Bramsdon 1907, Robert Edgar N Bramsdon 1908 and Alice MJ Bramsdon 1910. Edgar served as 47616 Lance Corporal EN Bramsdon, 9th Suffolk, and died on 16th March 1917 (Vermelles British Cemetery, France – V A 29). Robert was serving as a Trooper in 1st Royal Tank Regiment (7902491) when he died on 11th November 1942 (Halfaya Sollum War Cemetery, Egypt – 20 G 5). Alice senior married William Montague Marriot (1878–1943) in 1921 (see VC's sister, Florence Mabel Reynolds, above). They were living at 60 Deansgate, Northampton at the time of his death on 22nd January 1943. He left effects valued at £14,551/3/3.
- Ethel May Jones (born 1884) married Marshall Kerby Howe (born 1882), a farmer, in 1908. They had a daughter, Mary Beatrice Alice Howe, in 1910, and were living at Long Buckby, Northamptonshire in 1911. They emigrated to Kenya and he was elected to the South-East Ward of the Trans Nzoia District Council

on 17th April 1935. Ethel is understood to have married secondly as Ottaway and died in 1971 at Durban, South Africa.

Henry enlisted in the Northamptonshire Yeomanry on 5th October 1914 and was commissioned in 14th Reserve Battalion, Royal Scots on 8th July 1915. He went to France on 22nd August 1916 and joined A Company, 12th Royal Scots on 25th August. **Awarded the MC on 12th April 1917 for his actions in the attack on Greenland Hill near the chemical works at Roeux – he reorganised his company when all officers were casualties and led it into the attack with great courage and coolness; his fine example had a steadying effect on the men who had been badly shaken, LG 18th July 1917.** Henry was promoted lieutenant on 4th May and temporary captain on 2nd July.

Awarded the VC for his actions near Frezenberg, Belgium on 20th September 1917, LG 8th November 1917. He was wounded and hospitalised on 14th November and was evacuated to Britain on 22nd November. While recovering from his wounds he was employed by the Ministry of Labour 21st May 1918–20th March 1919. The VC was presented by the King at Buckingham Palace on 1st June 1918. Henry was demobilised on 3rd November 1919 and last appears in the Army List under the Royal Scots in May 1920. However, he rejoined as a captain in 2nd Loyal North Lancashire on 11th June 1921, with seniority from 1st January 1921. Having reached the age fixed for compulsory retirement, he transferred to the Regular Army Reserve of Officer on 16th August 1927 with a gratuity and the rank of captain with seniority from 8th February 1919.

Sir Frederick Milner MP PC (1849–1931) retired in 1906 due to deafness, but fought tirelessly to improve the treatment of injured troops. One result of this pressure was the formation of the Ministry of Pensions. Milner set up a hostel at Eden Lodge, Beckenham, created a number of village settlements and founded the Ex-Services Welfare Society. Henry Reynolds was the Superintendent and Steward 1930–33. After the Second World War it was taken over by Beckenham Council and was used by Scouts and Guides and as an experimental centre for Civil Defence. However, the property deteriorated and in 1960 it was demolished.

In 1926 the Ex-Services Welfare Society bought Long House at Leatherhead as its second rest and treatment centre. It was renamed The Sir Frederick Milner Home. Henry Reynolds was the Superintendent and Steward 1933–42. Milner House is now a private nursing home.

Henry was the Superintendent and Steward of Sir Frederick Milner Homes, Beckenham, Kent 1930–33 and at Leatherhead, Surrey 1933–42. He was granted the Freedom of Edinburgh and Northampton. He was keen on shooting, fishing,

Henry Reynolds' grave in St Giles' Churchyard, Ashtead, Surrey.

The King George VI Coronation Medal; 90,279 were awarded.

football, cricket and riding. General Lord Henry Horne, former command of First Army in the BEF, presented him with a gold watch on behalf of the people of East Haddon, Northamptonshire.

Henry Reynolds died at Carshalton, Surrey on 26th March 1948 and is buried in St Giles' Churchyard, Ashtead, Surrey. In addition to the VC and MC he was awarded the British War Medal 1914–20, Victory Medal 1914–19 and George VI Coronation Medal 1937. The VC is held by the Royal Scots Museum, Edinburgh Castle.

15122 LANCE SERGEANT JOHN HAROLD RHODES
3rd Battalion, Grenadier Guards

John Rhodes was born at Mellor Street, Packmoor, near Stoke-on-Trent, Staffordshire on 17th May 1891. His father, Ernest Rhodes (1862–1928), enlisted in the 38th Regiment (South Staffordshire Regiment from July 1881) (1252) on 18th January 1878 and joined at Dublin on 25th January. He was described as a labourer, 5′ 6¾″ tall, with fresh complexion, hazel eyes, brown hair and his religious denomination was Church of England. He transferred to 2/21st Regiment (Royal Scots Fusiliers from 1st July 1881) on 17th February 1879 (2356). He went to South Africa on 22nd February 1879 and served there during the Zulu War and First Boer War. Awarded Good Conduct Pay on 19th January 1880. He was in confinement 1st–3rd November 1880 awaiting trial for disobeying an order. He was imprisoned 4th November–15th December and forfeited his Good Conduct Pay. He served in the East Indies from 5th January 1882 and was awarded a certificate of education on 10th

March 1882. Good Conduct Pay was restored on 20th December 1883. He served in Britain from 26th February 1884 and was discharged on 18th January 1890. He became a coal miner hewer and married Sarah née Hanford (1866–1926) on 13th May 1886. She came from a family of Wesleyan Methodists and was a servant at Scholar Green, Odd Rode, Cheshire in 1881. He was an ironstone miner in 1891 and they were living at Packmoor. They were living at 21 Mellor Street, Packmoor in 1901 and were still there in 1911. Ernest enlisted in 14th West Yorkshire on 23rd November 1915 (23679) and joined at Brocton, Staffordshire next day. By then he was 5' 10¼" tall, living at 34 Thomas Street, Packmoor. He was discharged on 4th March 1916, having been in hospital throughout his service, no longer fit for war service. John was one of thirteen children, of whom ten survived infancy. Those known are:

* Florence Jane Rhodes (born 1887) was a domestic servant in 1901 living with her maternal grandfather. By 1911 she was a probationary nurse at Wolstanton and Burslem Union Workhouse, Turnhurst Road, Tunstall, Stoke-on-Trent.
* William Samuel Rhodes (1889–1959) was a coal miner hewer in 1911.
* Annie Dorothea Rhodes (1892–1919) was a dressmaker in 1911. She married Richard C Kemp (1890–1935) in 1914 and they had three children – John HR Kemp 1914, Charles F Kemp 1916 and Ernest Kemp 1919. Richard married Ellen 'Nellie' Barnett (1895–1957) in 1923 and they had three children – James W Kemp 1923, Gordon Kemp 1926 and Jean Kemp 1929. In 1939 Nellie was living with her children at 3 Mellor Street, Stoke-on-Trent.
* Jabez Rhodes (1898–1960) enlisted in the Army Service Corps on 19th November 1915 (263123) and transferred to the Reserve next day. He was mobilised on 6th October 1916, joined at Bradford on 9th October and embarked on SS *Viper* at Southampton on 18th November, disembarking next day at Le Havre. He was compulsorily transferred to 17th King's Royal Rifle Corps on 10th October 1917 (A203586), but retained ASC rates of pay. Jabez had a number of disciplinary and medical problems and was granted leave to Britain 18th–31st December. He received a gunshot wound to the right forearm and returned to Britain on 27th April 1918. He did not return to France and on 21st November moved to the Command Depot at Sutton Coldfield and was transferred to the Class Z Reserve on 5th February 1919. He was discharged on 31st March 1920. Jabez was assessed as 30% disabled and granted a pension of 8/3 for six months, then 20% disabled with a pension of 5/6 to be reviewed after a further six months. Jabez married Maria Hulme (born 1903) in 1926. They had a daughter, Florence Jane Rhodes, in 1927. In 1939 he was a dairy motor van driver and she was a fish and chip fryer, living at 14 May Avenue, Stoke-on-Trent. Florence married Jan T Wrobel (c. 1920–1961) in 1949 and they had four children – Aleksand M Wrobel 1950, Julian A Wrobel 1958, Jan M Wrobel 1959 and Joanna B Wrobel 1961.
* Alice Gertrude Rhodes (1899–1976) married George Arthur Biddulph (1898–1981), in 1930. They had two sons – Charles W Biddulph 1930 and Arthur

D Biddulph 1931. In 1939 he was a pottery caster and they were living at 13 Tennant Place, Newcastle-under-Lyme.
- Doris May Rhodes (1902–64) never married.
- Joseph Hanford Rhodes (born 1904).
- Beniah Rhodes (1906–57) served in the Grenadier Guards (26160) and was a reservist by 1939. He married Elsie Annie Phyllis May Drinkhill (née Watson) (born 1905) in 1938 at Willesden. Elsie had previously married William J Drinkhill (1902–64) in 1925 and they had a daughter, Barbara D Drinkhill, in 1925. They divorced in 1940 and William married Alice M Cook later that year. Beniah was a Metropolitan Police constable in 1939 and they were living at 94 Furness Road, Willesden, London. His brother, Cecil, was living with them. They were living at 11 Coverdale Crescent, Flixton, Lancashire in 1957.
- Cecil Stanley Rhodes (born 1911) was a night watchman at a police station in 1939, living with his brother, Beniah. He married Florence E Fisher (born 1903) in 1939 and they had a daughter, Margaret A Rhodes, in 1940.

John's paternal grandfather, Samuel Rhodes (1811–90), a hatter, married Charlotte Harrison (c.1816–56) c.1836. They had six children:

- James Rhodes (c.1831–74).
- Ann Rhodes (c.1836–1907) married Charles Wade (c.1836–83), a miner, in 1856. They had four children – George Wade 1859, Eliza Wade 1860, Charles Wade 1872 and Albert Wade 1874.
- Samuel Rhodes (born c.1837).
- Daniel Rhodes (born 1840).
- Mary Rhodes (born 1842) was a cotton doubler living with her father and stepmother, Sarah, in 1861.
- Eliza Rhodes (born 1847) was a cotton doubler living with her father and stepmother, Sarah, in 1861.

Samuel senior married Sarah née Gelshon (c.1827–72) in 1858. She was born at Manchester, Lancashire and was a cotton doubler in 1861. They were living at Foden Street, Newcastle-under-Lyme in 1861. By 1871 he was a gardener and they were living at 23 Deansgate, Newcastle-under-Lyme. In addition to Ernest they had Beniah Rhodes (1867–1908), who married Martha Fox (1866–1932) in 1888. Beniah was a potter's placer and Martha was an earthenware painter in 1891, lodging at New Street, Wolstanton. She was living with her sister, Amy Fox (born 1868), at 43 New Street, Wolstanton in 1911. Samuel senior married Eliza Betteley late Tunstall née Bennett (c.1819–85) in 1874. She was born at Rugby, Warwickshire and had previously married Ralph Tunstall in 1857 and George Betteley in 1868. She had several children, including William Bennett c.1858 and Samuel Tunstall c.1859. They were living with some of their children at May Bank, Wolstanton in 1881.

John's maternal grandfather, William Hanford (c.1837–1911), an iron stone miner, married Jane née Potts (1839–92) in 1864. They were living at Newchapel, Staffordshire in 1871 and at Packmoor, Staffordshire in 1881 and 1891. By 1901 he was living with his sons Joseph and Jabez and granddaughter Florence Rhodes at 11 Mellor Street, Newchapel. He was living with his daughter, Hannah, and her family in 1911. In addition to Sarah they had six other children:

- John Hanford (1867–1951), an ironstone miner, was living with his sister, Sarah and family, at 21 Mellor Street, Packmoor in 1901 and 1911.
- Joseph Hanford (1870–1945), an ironstone miner, married Hannah Shufflebottom (born 1872) in 1901.
- Mary Hanford (1872–1950) married Enoch Hood (1870–1950) in 1894. He was a boiler/fireman in 1901, boarding with his family at 24 Black Horse Lane, Hanley, Staffordshire. They had two children – Enoch Hood 1897 and Mary Ann Hood 1900.
- Annie Hanford (1874–98) never married.
- Jabez Hanford (1877–1950), an ironstone miner, married Zilpah Hancock (1883–1959 in 1905. They were living at Bull Lane, near Brindley Ford, Staffordshire in 1911. They had four children, three of whom survived infancy – Frank Hanford 1910, Annie Hanford 1912 and Joseph Hanford 1919.
- Hannah Hanford (1879–1959) married Thomas Henry Buckley (1873–1942), a joiner, in 1900. They were living at 26 Taylor Street, Goldenhill, Stoke-on-Trent in 1911. They had ten children, but only three were born alive – William Hanford Buckley 1900, Ethel Buckley 1902 and Annie Hanford Buckley 1905.

John Rhodes was educated at Church Schools, Newchapel near Packmoor. He was a bit of a daredevil and one night he and his brothers, Bill and Jabez, climbed through the back bedroom window, slid down the tiles and went across the street to a farmyard. They took two horses and rode them through the streets of Packmoor, two on one horse and one on the other, before returning them to the stable. They then re-entered the house and climbed into their beds without being missed. The following morning several neighbours spoke of the sound of galloping horses, but no one could explain it.

John was employed as a miner until he enlisted in the Grenadier Guards on 17th February 1911. He trained at the Guards Depot, Caterham, Surrey and served with the 3rd Battalion until transferring to the Reserve in February 1914. He returned to mining at Chatterley-Whitfield Colliery, Tunstall, near Stoke-on-Trent.

John was recalled on the outbreak of war to 5th (Reserve) Battalion at Windsor and was assigned to the 2nd Battalion. He went to France on 13th August 1914 and took part in the Retreat from Mons, including the actions at Landrecies and Villers Cotterêts. During the Battle of the Aisne in September he narrowly escaped death when a comrade stepped in front of him and was shot in the heart. At Ypres a shell fragment cut a tree he was chopping down to construct a dugout just above his head.

Entrance to the Guards Depot at Caterham built in 1877. It closed in 1995 and the site was redeveloped for housing.

Chatterley Whitfield Colliery was one of twenty-two in the Staffordshire coalfield. The area was known for its coal from the 14th Century. Mining started at Chatterley Whitfield in 1838 and in 1867 two collieries were bought by the Whitfield Colliery Co. In 1873 the company was bought by the Chatterley Iron Co. A serious fire and explosion at the colliery in 1881 killed twenty-four men. It closed in 1976 and operated as a mining museum for the National Coalmining Collection. The museum ran out of funds and closed in 1991, but the site was declared a Scheduled Ancient Monument by English Heritage. The Friends of Chatterley Whitfield open it once a year to the public, but there is no access to the underground workings.

On 24th December he was caught in a barrage in a water-logged trench and was partially buried, but his comrades dug him out. He was promoted lance corporal in January 1915. **Awarded the DCM for his actions at Rue du Bois, France on 18th May 1915 – he successfully conducted a patrol for a considerable distance to the front bringing back valuable information and subsequently twice volunteered to bring in wounded under heavy fire, which on each occasion wounded one of the men accompanying him, LG 5th August 1915.**

John Rhodes married Elizabeth née Meir (1892–1st March 1988) on 11th December 1915 and they lived at 27 New Street, Pitts Hill, Tunstall, near Stoke-on-Trent, Staffordshire, her parents' former home. She was a warehousewoman living with her widowed mother at 1 New Street, Tunstall in 1911. They had a son, John Rhodes, born on 13th May 1917.

Elizabeth's father, Aaron Meir (1863–1907), married Elizabeth née Callear (1867–1947) in 1886. Her birth was registered at Gallear. They were living at 7 Union Street, Chell in 1901 and later at 27 New Street, Pitts Hill. Elizabeth was a laundry maid at Wolstanton Union Workhouse in 1911, living with her daughters at 1 New Street, Pittshill,. In addition to Elizabeth they had three other daughters:

- Emma Meir (1887–1977), a warehousewoman in 1911, died unmarried.
- Alice Meir (1893–1941) was a patient in Staffordshire Mental Hospital, Cheadle in 1939.
- Mary A Meir (1900–04).

John was promoted corporal. **Awarded a Bar to the DCM for his actions at Givenchy, France on 6th August 1915 – when the sap heads and front line trench in the orchard near the shrine were blown in by a mine, he and 15529 Private T Barton (also awarded DCM) displayed great coolness and bravery in running forward and continuing to dig out the wounded until both were wounded, LG 11th March 1916.** John was evacuated to England with a wound in the right shoulder and was hospitalised for four months. He was presented with a purse of gold and a marble timepiece following the award of the DCM. On recovering he served as a lance sergeant instructor with 5th Reserve Battalion for a year.

John Rhodes' grave in Rocquigny-Equancourt Road British Cemetery, Manancourt and the original grave marker.

He returned to France on 19th January 1917. **Awarded the VC for his actions near Houthulst Forest, Belgium on 9th October 1917, LG 26th November 1917.** He was mortally wounded on 27th November and died of wounds at No.48 Casualty Clearing Station, Ytres, France. He is buried in Rocquigny-Equancourt Road British Cemetery, Manancourt (III E 1). His CO, Lieutenant Colonel Andrew Thorne DSO, made an attempt to notify him that he had been awarded the VC, but he arrived too late. The Battalion Chaplain wrote to John's widow:

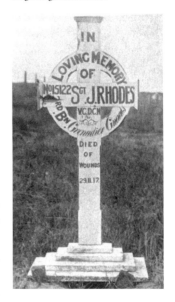

The other day I passed by the grave of your husband on the side of a hill facing the sun. And as we passed by we thought of you, of the tremendous loss we have suffered. It is one of the cruelest things of this war that just at the moment of great things the best are taken away. Your husband had won the greatest honour any soldier could have and had won it over and over again; yet he was always the same, quiet in his manner, never boastful, always doing his duty, a pattern to soldiers and a pattern to us all.

The VC was presented to his wife at her home on 15th July 1918. She never remarried. John is commemorated in a number of other places:

• John Rhodes Way, Tunstall, Stoke-on-Trent, Staffordshire is one of four VC named roads on

Newchapel Methodist Church, Packmoor

Swallows Rise Estate dedicated on 27th January 2004.
- Plaque on Millennium Green, Carr Street, Packmoor, Stoke-on-Trent, Staffordshire, unveiled in 2000.
- Named on a memorial at Newchapel Methodist Church, Packmoor.
- Named on a memorial plaque at Chatterley Whitfield Mining Museum, unveiled on 20th April 1984. It was moved to Packmoor School, Staffordshire when the Museum closed on 9th August 1993.
- Named on the war memorial, dedicated on 14th March 1928, and the memorial wall, dedicated on 12th September 2009, in Tunstall War Memorial Garden, The Boulevard, Tunstall, Stoke-on-Trent. Lance Sergeant John Daniel Baskeyfield VC is also commemorated there.
- Memorial Cross, Whitley Road, Ball Green, Staffordshire.
- Named on the war memorial, Congleton Road, Biddulph, Staffordshire.
- Named on the war memorial at Tunstall Methodist Church, Queens Avenue, Stoke on Trent, previously in the Primitive Methodist Church, St Michael's Road, Pitts Hill.
- A painting of the VC action was unveiled in the Sergeants' Mess, 1st Grenadier Guards, Queen Elizabeth Barracks, Pirbright on 5th March 1999.

Memorial on Millennium Green, Carr Street, Packmoor.

One half of the memorial wall in Tunstall War Memorial Garden.

In addition to the VC and DCM and Bar he was awarded the 1914 Star with Mons clasp, British War Medal 1914–20 and Victory Medal 1914–19. John Rhodes is the most highly decorated non-commissioned officer in the history of the Grenadier Guards. His VC is held by the Grenadier Guards.

CAPTAIN CLEMENT ROBERTSON
The Queen's (Royal West Surrey Regiment) attached A Battalion Tank Corps

Clement Robertson was born at Pietermaritzburg, South Africa on 15th November 1889 (also seen as 15th December 1890). His father, John Albert Robertson (1851–1928), trained at the Royal Military Academy, Woolwich and was commissioned as a lieutenant in the Royal Artillery on 6th January 1872. He was promoted captain 30th July 1881 and major 26th September 1888. In 1889 he was serving in Natal in the Mountain Artillery and retired on 6th May 1893. He was employed at Preston Barracks, Preston, Sussex in 1901 and during the First World War was living at Struan Hill, Delgany, Co Wicklow, Ireland. John married Frances Octavia Caroline née Wynne (1859–1949), born at Collon, Co Louth, Ireland, at St Matthias's Church, Dublin on 29th June 1881. Clement had four brothers:

• William Cairnes Robertson (1882–1950) attended the Royal Military Academy, Woolwich and was commissioned in the Royal Artillery on 15th May 1901. Promoted lieutenant 22nd February 1904, captain 15th May 1914, temporary major 26th March 1916 and major 27th April 1916 with seniority from 29th October 1915. He served in France from 28th June 1916 with the RGA and was awarded the DSO (LG 1st January 1918), French Croix de Guerre and was Mentioned in Despatches twice (LG 18th May and 14th December 1917). Appointed Assistant Superintendent of Experiments at Woolwich 2nd February 1920–26th December 1921, First Assistant Superintendent of Experiments Shoeburyness 27th December 1921–19th March 1923 and Deputy Superintendent (Class Z) Experimental Establishment Shoeburyness 20th March 1923–1st February 1924 and 24th May 1926–23rd May 1929. Promoted lieutenant colonel 24th May 1929. He also served during the Second World War. William married Norah Constance née Archer (1889–1972), daughter of Arthur Montford Archer MD JP, of Bellvue, Delgany, Co Wicklow, in 1912. They had five children:
  ◦ Constance Sheila Florence Robertson (born 1912) married Eric Arthur Levett

Pietermaritzburg around the time that Clement was born there.

The Royal Military Academy Woolwich was founded in 1741 to train artillery and engineer officers. New buildings came into use in 1806. From 1920 the Academy also trained Royal Signals officers. It closed in 1939 and its last Commandant was Major General Philip Neame VC. Thereafter all regular officers training was conducted at the Royal Military Academy, Sandhurst, which had previously only trained infantry and cavalry officers. The Woolwich site was sold in 2006 and was converted and extended into 334 houses and apartments.

(born 1907), of Tulagi, Kelly's Esplanade, Northwood, Sydney, New South Wales, Australia, in 1941 at Maidenhead, Berkshire. They had two daughters – Phoebe N Levett 1943 and Wendy N Levett 1945.

○ Arthur Albert Robertson (born 1914) of Sherwell, Wycliffe College, Stonehouse, Gloucestershire was educated at Clifton, and Balliol College, Oxford (BA).

○ Alice Joy Robertson (born 1919) married Thomas Albert Wels, of Seal House, Cansiron Lane, Ashurstwood, near Grinstead, Sussex, in 1941 and had at least two children – Ivan D Wels 1944 and Tania M Wels 1952.

○ Geraldine Patience Robertson (born 1923) married William BC Oswell, of 32 Beechwood Road, Sanderstead, Surrey, at Stroud in 1944 and they had a son and a daughter. Geraldine married Richard Lovell in 1970. She was appointed a company director in November 2001 and a company secretary in December 2003.

○ William Archer Robertson (born 1926), of 35 Gilbey Drive, Ottawa, Ontario, Canada, was educated at Clifton, Queen's University, Belfast (BSc 1952) and the Australian National University (PhD 1963). He served in the Royal Air Force 1945–48 (pilot officer 24th December 1944 and flying officer 24th June 1945) and was a research scientist with Dominion Observatory, Ottawa in 1964. He married Margaret Sheila Harris in 1953 and they had two sons and a daughter.

• Albert John Robertson (1884–1954) joined the Royal Navy as a naval cadet on 15th January 1899 and trained on HMS *Britannia* and *Duke of Wellington*. Appointed midshipman 15th June 1900, sub lieutenant 15th August 1903, lieutenant 15th February 1905, commander 30th June 1917, captain 31st December 1924 and rear admiral 3rd January 1936. He served on numerous ships and shore establishments including HMS *Mars, Illustrious, Hood, Venerable, Mercury, King Edward VII, Circe, Harrier, Dryad, Skirmisher, Highflyer, St George, Achilles, Minotaur, Victory* and

Clement's brother, Albert, trained on HMS *Britannia* (right) moored off Dartmouth before becoming a midshipman in 1900. She was the former HMS *Prince of Wales* and replaced an earlier HMS *Britannia* in 1869. HMS *Hindostan* (left) was connected by a gangway to provide extra accommodation and classrooms.

After war service with 2nd Cruiser Squadron, Albert became Navigating Officer on HM Yacht *Victoria and Albert* 1922–25. She entered service in 1901, the third yacht of her name. She served four sovereigns until being decommissioned as a royal yacht in 1939, but was used throughout the Second World War as a depot and accommodation ship and was broken up in 1954, when she was replaced by HMY *Britannia*.

HMY *Victoria and Albert*. During the Great War he served in 2nd Cruiser Squadron of the Grand Fleet aboard HMS *Achilles* and HMS *Minotaur*. He was Mentioned in Despatches for the engagement between HMS *Achilles* and the German auxiliary cruiser *Leopard* on 16th March 1917 in which the latter was sunk, LG 22nd June 1917. *Achilles* was commanded by Commander Francis Martin-Leake (DSO for this action), brother of the double VC, Arthur Martin-Leake. Albert was Navigating Officer on HM Yacht *Victoria and Albert* 1922–25 (MVO 1925). Appointed Captain of Dockyard and King's Harbour Master, Portsmouth 1931–33 and Aide de Camp to King George V 1935. He retired on 4th January 1936, but served again from 7th September 1939 to 31st March 1941 as Commodore of Convoys. Albert married Mary Alice Lorna Cardew (1883–1956), daughter of Colonel GM Cardew, Hampshire Regiment, in 1909 and they had six children:

- John Douglas Robertson (1910–85), a mechanical engineer, married Kathleen Pratt at Westminster in 1945 and they had three children – Caroline E Robertson 1948, Helen GF Robertson 1950 and John N Robertson 1952.
- Elizabeth Rosemary Robertson (born 1913), of Hill House, Scilly, Kinsdale, Co Cork, Ireland, married John G Conklin at Chelsea in 1944. She married John Kenneth Holcroft Lloyd–Blood (1910–59), of Wenonah, Winton Road, Dublin, at Chelsea in 1948. He was the son of Admiral Lloyd Lloyd-Blood.
- Clement Ronald Robertson (born 1915), of Killeen, Glencormac, Bray, Co Wicklow, Ireland, married Jill Keeble in 1950 and they had three children. He joined an officer cadet training unit at the outbreak of the Second World War and was granted an Emergency Commission in the Irish Guards on 4th July 1940 (138634). Promoted captain on 1st January 1949 and was granted the honorary rank of major on relinquishing his commission and transferring to the Reserve of Officers on 28th August 1965.
- Lorna Maureen Robertson (born 1918 at Exeter, a twin with Frances) married David Russell in 1951 and they had two daughters. The marriage ended in divorce. She married Peter Merricks at Chatham in 1962.
- Frances L Robertson (1918–97), a twin with Lorna, married Norman G Tee (1914–57) at Winchester in 1942 and they had two sons – Roger Tee 1945 and Philip Tee 1949.
- George Cardew Robertson (born 1920 at Portsmouth), of Killeen, Glencormac, Bray, Co Wicklow, Ireland. He was appointed probationary midshipman in the Royal Naval Reserve on 31st December 1937 and served aboard HMS *Loch Gorm* as a lieutenant (MID, LG 1st January 1946).

- Frederick Wynne Robertson (1885–1964) was educated at Charterhouse and Trinity College, Dublin (BA 1908). He served in the Indian Civil Service 1909–47 and his appointments included Settlement Officer at Bankura 1917, Secretary of the Board of Revenue in Bengal 1923, Commissioner of the Presidency Division in 1930, Commissioner of the Rajshahi Division 1933 (CIE 1935 and CBE, LG 3rd June 1935), Chairman of the Bengal Public Service Commission 1937 (CSI

1941) and Chairman of the Federal Public Service Commission 1942–47 (Knight Bachelor, LG 14th June 1945). He was commissioned in the Infantry Branch of the Indian Army Reserve of Officers on 5th August 1918. He married Gladys Veitch née Jerome (1886–1978) at Lanteglos-by-Camelford parish church, Cornwall in 1924. Gladys had married Harold Massyn Veitch (1883–1923) of the Indian Civil Service (District and Sessions Judge, Burdwan) in 1909 at the Cathedral, Calcutta, India and they had two sons – Douglas Harold Massyn Veitch 1911 and Kenneth Jerome Veitch 1912. Douglas held a Governor's Commission in the Sudan Defence Force and was granted an Emergency Commission on 12th June 1940 (254425).

- Charles Wyndham Robertson (born 1892) was educated at Haileybury and Trinity College, Dublin (BA and BAI 1919). He was commissioned in the Royal Monmouthshire Royal Engineers on 15th August 1914 and was described as 5′ 7½″ tall, weighing 145 lbs. He served at Gallipoli from 9th June 1915 and later in Palestine. Promoted lieutenant 19th September 1915, temporary captain 24th May 1917 and captain 3rd November 1917. He arrived in France on 7th May 1918 and served with 5th Field Company RE. He was granted leave 23rd June–7th July and embarked at Boulogne for Folkestone on the *Stranraer*, but was unable to rejoin his unit due to bleeding haemorrhoids. His leave was extended to 21st July and eventually to 2nd September on the recommendation of a medical board. He was admitted to King George V Hospital, Dublin on 2nd August and was operated on. Medical boards at Dublin on 1st August and 2nd September found him unfit for General Service, but the latter found him fit for Home Service. A medical board at Newport on 4th December found him fit for General Service. His last unit was 5th Provisional Company at Chatham and he was demobilised on 19th February 1920 (MID). He worked for the Sudan Irrigation Service 1920–27 and was later appointed a director of John Jameson & Son, Distillers of Dublin. Charles married Alice Mary Juliana née Bell (born 1904), daughter of Colonel Edward Bell CMG, of Lodge Park, Northleach, Gloucester, and granddaughter of Edward William Derrington Bell VC CB, in 1926. They had two daughters:
  - Barbara Robertson (born 1931) married William David Elliot Cairnes, son of Lieutenant Colonel Tom Algar Elliot Cairnes DSO, of Stameen, Drogheda, in 1953.
  - Elizabeth C Robertson (born 1935) married Hugh Crisp Fuller in 1961 and they had a son and a daughter.

Clement's paternal grandfather, John Jameson Robertson (1804–82), of Gledswood, Co Dublin, Ireland and Alloa, Clackmannanshire, Scotland, married Mary Anne née Cairnes (1815–99), daughter of William Cairnes, of Stameen, Drogheda, Co Louth, Ireland, in 1837. His father, William Robertson, married Margaret Jameson in 1801, daughter of John Jameson, founder of the Jameson's whiskey distillery, and Margaret Haig, sister of the Haig brothers who owned the Haig whisky distilleries. In addition to John they had six other children:

- William Robertson (1838–1929) was educated at Rugby and Trinity College Dublin. He married Margaret née Jameson (1851–1922), daughter of Henry Jameson, of Hermitage, Co Dublin, in 1872. They lived at 30 Fitzwilliam Square, South Dublin.
- James Jameson Robertson (1839–67), a twin with Robert, trained at the Royal Military Academy, Woolwich and drowned in the Medway in 1867.
- Robert Jameson Robertson QC (1839–94), a twin with James, was educated at Trinity College, Dublin and became a barrister. He married Minna Adeline Belcher (1850–1934) in 1873. They lived at 9 Fitzwilliam Place, Dublin and had eight children:
  - John Harold Robertson (born and died 1874).
  - Helen Mary Robertson (1875–1937).
  - Blanche Adeline Robertson (1877–1962) married Colonel Philip Cahill Sheridan CMG RE (1871–1949), son of Philip Sheridan, Postmaster General of Punjab, in 1906 and they had a daughter. He was appointed temporary captain on 13th April 1917 and as a temporary lieutenant colonel was awarded the CMG, LG 1st January 1919. Later he was a member of the Railway Board of India and officiating General Manager for East India Railway and was knighted for his services to the Railway Board, LG 3rd June 1929.
  - John Robertson (1878–1951) was educated at Clifton College (Cadet Corps corporal), and Trinity College, Dublin. He worked as a civil engineer on the railways in India and was commissioned in the East Indian Railway Volunteer Rifles on 10th March 1903. He passed Volunteer Proficiency in 1907 and was promoted lieutenant on 24th January 1908 and captain on 9th October 14 at Umbala. He passed the machine gun examination in June 1915 and was granted leave from the Volunteers to return to Britain. On 1st April 1916 he applied for direct entry as a captain in 12th Labour Battalion RE, which was forming in Ireland. He was

The John Jameson & Son Irish Whiskey Co was established in 1810 when John Jameson, a Scottish lawyer from Alloa, took over the Bow Street Distillery in Dublin. It had been built by his wife's cousins, the Steins, in 1780. John Jameson married Margaret Haig, a sister of the Haig brothers who owned Haig distilleries, in 1786. They moved to Dublin to manage the Stein's Distillery, which had been established in 1780. Production increased from 30,000 gallons annually to 1,000,000 by the turn of the 19th century. By 1805 Jameson's was the world's largest whiskey producer and today still ranks third. John Jameson is also known for being the great grandfather of Guglielmo Marconi, the Italian inventor and electrical engineer who pioneered long-distance radio transmissions and shared the 1909 Nobel Prize for Physics. In 1966 Jameson's merged with Cork Distillers and John Powers to form the Irish Distillers Group. In 1976 the Dublin distilleries in Bow Street and John's Lane closed and were replaced by the New Midleton Distillery in Cork. The Jameson brand was bought by the French company Pernod Ricard in 1988. The old Bow Street Distillery, seen here, in Dublin is now a museum.

5′ 8½″ tall and weighed 140 lbs. He served in France from 24th July. He was sick and left the unit on 6th January 1917 to be treated at Le Touquet until 21st January, when he embarked at Le Havre on HMT *Dunluce Castle* and arrived at Southampton on 22nd January. A medical board at Caxton Hall on 26th January found him unfit for General Service for two months. His address was Ashurst, Blackrock, Co Dublin. A medical board at Dublin on 21st February found him fit for General Service. Promoted major in the East Indian Railway Regiment 1st October 1918. Appointed temporary colonel on 1st July 1918 while Deputy Director Engineering Stores. He was released from service on 2nd August 1919 and granted the rank of colonel (MID, CBE 1919). John continued serving with the East Indian Railway Regiment and was promoted lieutenant colonel and appointed Commandant on 25th April 1925 (VD). Appointed Honorary ADC to the Governor of the United Provinces of Afra and Oudh on 14th May 1928 and last appears in the Indian Army List in 1929. John married Florence Emily née Hill (died 1982) in 1907 and they had two children – Joan Alice Robertson 1908 and Robert John Robertson 1909. Robert served as a lieutenant commander in the Royal Navy and was awarded the DSC. He was killed in action when HMS *Gloucester* was sunk by German dive-bombers during the Battle of Crete on 22nd May 1941 (Plymouth Naval Memorial).

○ Alice Maude Robertson (1879–80).
○ James Robert Robertson (1880–1963) was educated at Trinity College, Dublin. He was commissioned in the Royal Berkshire Regiment on 20th May 1905 and was promoted lieutenant on 9th March 1909. He transferred to the Bedfordshire Regiment on 7th July and served in the West African Rifles 20th March 1913–6th December 1915, including in Cameroon and Nigeria from September to December 1914. Promoted captain in the Bedfordshire Regiment on 7th May 1913. Appointed adjutant in the Machine Gun Corps 22nd April– 4th October 1916 and acting major in 8th Bedfordshire 5th October 1916–19th July 1917. He served in France from 10th September 1916. Appointed acting lieutenant colonel while commanded 8th Bedfordshire 20th July–5th August 1917 and 4th Leicestershire 6th August–14th November 1917. He returned to Britain on 10th October 1917 and commanded 2nd Training Battalion 15th November 1917–16th January 1918. He returned to France on 10th April and commanded 2nd York and Lancaster 22nd April–17th October, when he was wounded (DSO, LG 1st January 1919 and MID, LG 27th December 1918). He commanded a company at the Royal Military College, Sandhurst 13th January–8th May 1919 and was then appointed Brigade Major, School for Training Instructors, Berkhamsted 9th May 1919–26th April 1920. His next appointment was adjutant with a Territorial Army unit 27th April 1920–26th April 1923 and he was then employed under the Colonial Office as a staff officer with the Ceylon Defence Force from 3rd November 1923. Promoted major 3rd June 1925 and last appears in the Army List in July 1929. He married Winifred

Bryan in 1900 and they lived at Fairkytes, Hornchurch, Essex. He became a JP. They had at least a son, James Bryan Robertson, in 1906 who later served in the RAF as a flight lieutenant.

o Michael William Robertson (1885–1961) was educated at Malvern College and Trinity College, Dublin (BA 1907, MA 1911), where he was awarded the Silver Medal in History and Political Science. He was ordained in 1911 and was Chaplain of Elstree School, Hertfordshire 1911–13 and The Grange, Folkestone 1913–15. He served as a chaplain to the forces 4th class with 1/1st South Eastern Mounted Brigade from 15th September 1915. He was at Gallipoli October–December 1915, in Egypt until 21st December 1916, aboard HMHS *Essequibo* until 27th April 1917, with 5th Rifle Brigade at Minster-on-Sea, Sheppey 9th May–7th June 1917 and aboard HMHS *Araguaya* 7th June–5th September 1917. Home service followed until 17th December 1917. He was with 11th Division until 14th July 1918 and then No.6 Casualty Clearing Station until 15th July 1918. Michael was demobilised on 27th November 1919 as honorary chaplain to the forces 4th class. He was an assistant master at Epsom College 1921–45 and Curate of Fleet, Hampshire 1945–50.

o George Strafford Robertson (1886–1938) was educated at Malvern and Trinity College, Dublin (BA). He married Emmie Rainey (died 1933) in 1923.

• Mary Ann Robertson (1842–1901).

• Helen Robertson (1843–1926) married Canon Neligan in 1899.

• Susan Alice Robertson (1854–1943).

His maternal grandfather, John Wynne (1799–1884) of Wynnstay Roebuck, near Dublin, Ireland, was commissioned as a cornet in the Royal Horse Artillery on 16th December 1820. He was promoted lieutenant 1st August 1827, captain 13th August 1839 and placed on half pay on 28th September 1839. He married Anne née Warren (died 1874), daughter of Admiral Sir Samuel Warren KCB KCH, in 1838. Between February 1791 and February 1837 Samuel Warren served on HMS *Argo, Ramilles, Royal George, Alcmene, Vesuvius, Glory, Diadem, Bellerophon, President, Blenheim, Bulwark, Seringapatam and William & Mary*. He was promoted lieutenant 12th February 1791, commander 3rd March 1797 and captain 29th May 1805. In addition to Frances, John and Anne had eight other children:

• Robert Maxwell Wynne (1839–56).

• Katherine Frances Wynne (1840–57).

• Warren Richard Colvin Wynne (1843–79) served in the Royal Engineers and was promoted lieutenant 25th June 1862 and captain 3rd February 1875. He commanded 16th Company RE, Ordnance Survey, Reading. He married Eleanor née Turbett (1847–73), daughter of James Turbett of Owenstown, Co Dublin, and they had a son, Arthur Algernon Warren Wynne (1873–1961). Warren married

Lucy Parish (c.1852–1946), daughter of Captain Alfred Parish FRGS, in 1876. They had two children:

- ○ Henry Ernest Singleton Wynne (1877–1962) was commissioned in the Royal Artillery on 21st September 1896 and rose to lieutenant colonel on 11th June 1917. He served in the South African War and First World War and was put on Half Pay on 11th June 1921 and retired on 24th June 1922. He was awarded the DSO in 1916 and CMG (LG, 1st January 1919). He was later Secretary of the City of Edinburgh TF Association. Henry married Katherine Kennedy in 1911 and they had three children – Richard Warren Wynne, Audrey Christina Wynne 1914 and Beryl Kathleen Wynne 1919.
- ○ Charles Meredith Wynne (1878–1970) was educated at Uppingham and King's College, Cambridge from October 1897 (BA 1900, MA 1914). On 21st October 1901 he was appointed Clerk of the Higher Division at the War Office. On 10th January 1910 he was appointed Assistant Secretary at the Ministry of Pensions. Member of the National Health Insurance Commission 1912. Returned to the Ministry of Pensions in 1917. He lived at 31 Fitzjames Avenue, West Kensington, London and Blyton House, Weybridge.

- • Arthur Singleton Wynne (1846–1936) was commissioned as an ensign on 4th August 1865 with purchase. Promoted lieutenant 21st August 1867 with purchase, captain 22nd April 1871 with purchase, brevet major 22nd November 1879, major 1881, brevet lieutenant colonel 15th June 1885, colonel 15th June 1889, major general 25th January 1900 and lieutenant general 8th December 1905. He served in the East Indies 21st October 1863–13th April 1867 and was appointed adjutant 3rd June 1868–30th June 1871 at Aldershot, Portland, Waterford and the Curragh. He returned to the East Indies 15th October 1872 and was appointed Station Staff Officer Fyzabad 1st February–11th June 1874, Assistant Instructor in Musketry 20th October 1874–9th February 1875 and Station Staff Officer Naini Tal 14th May 1875–14th June 1877. He took part in the Jowaki Expedition 1877 (MID), the Afghan War 1878–79 (MID) and embarked for South Africa on 13th January 1881 to be Deputy Assistant Adjutant General of the Natal Field Force under Generals Sir George Colley and Evelyn Wood VC until December 1881. He took part in the Sudan Expedition 1884–85 and the South African War 1899–1901. Arthur was Keeper of the Jewel House, Tower of London 1911–17 (GCB 1914). He lived at Haybergill, Warcop, Westmorland and was appointed DL in 1921. He was Colonel of the King's Own Yorkshire Light Infantry. Arthur married Emily Mary Colville née Turner (1862–1959) (DStJ 1886). They had three children:
  - ○ Owen Evelyn Wynne (1887–1974) FRGS was commissioned in the Royal Engineers on 20th December 1905 and promoted lieutenant on 10th April 1908. He served on the Anglo-Belgian Boundary Commission in Northern Rhodesia 29th July 1911–15th March 1914. Appointed GSO3 at the War Office 16th March–4th August 1914 and then had a special appointment (GSO3 War Office) until 4th November 1914. He went to France on 5th August 1914.

Promoted captain 30th October 1914 and appointed GSO3 in France 30th July 1915–11th June 1916. Appointed brevet major 3rd June 1916 and brigade major 12th June 1916–31st January 1917. He returned to Britain on 9th February 1917 and was appointed GSO2 War Office as a temporary major next day. He returned to France as GSO2 1st February 1918–31st March 1919 (OBE LG 1st January 1919, MID LG 1st January 1916, 15th June 1916 and 20th December 1918 and Order of the Crown 5th Class). He was appointed GSO2 Peace Conference Paris as a temporary major 1st April–17th December 1919, Deputy Assistant Adjutant General Rhine Army 7th January 1922–21st January 1923 and GSO2 War Office 5th May 1927–20th January 1930. Promoted major 13th December 1922 and lieutenant colonel 1st June 1930. Appointed Staff Officer RE 1st Grade India 16th December 1931–24th September 1932 and Commander Royal Engineers India 25th September 1932–31st May 1934. He served in Baluchistan 1932–34 and went on Half Pay on 1st June 1934 as a colonel backdated to 1st June 1933. He was restored to full pay on 18th May 1936 as Deputy Chief Engineer Southern Command. During the Second World War he was Chief Engineer, Salisbury Plain District from 1942 and last appears in the Army List in April 1943. In 1926 he married Evelyn Jean Gordon Vernon Pirie (1895–1981), daughter of Lieutenant Colonel Duncan Vernon Pirie OBE, and they had two children – Evelyn Valerie Wynne 1928 and Robert Owen Wynne 1930. Owen was a Member of the British Ornithologists' Union and the author of a number of ornithological books.

○ Graeme Chamley Wynne (1889–1964) was commissioned in the King's Own Yorkshire Light Infantry on 9th October 1907 and was promoted lieutenant on 10th April 1912. He served in France 16th–26th August 1914 and was promoted captain on 6th February 1915. He was employed under the Assistant Secretary to the Committee of Imperial Defence from 1st April 1922 and last appears in the Army List in January 1927. He was awarded the OBE in 1956.

○ Arthur Meredyth/Meredith Wynne (1893–1967) gained the Royal Aero Club Aviator's Certificate on 15th October 1912 at the Graham White School, Hendon, Middlesex. He was commissioned in the Royal Flying Corps on 12th August 1914 and appointed acting captain while a flight commander 2nd April 1916. He transferred to the RAF on 1st April 1918 as an Aeroplane & Seaplane Officer and was promoted captain on 23rd January 1919 (AFC, LG 2nd November 1918). He last appears in the Air Force List in March 1920. He married Dorothy Leese (1899–1978) in 1926.

• Skeffington John Wynne (1849–1913) was commissioned in 103rd Regiment (Royal Dublin Fusiliers from 1881) on 4th February 1869 and was promoted lieutenant on 28th October 1871. Appointed instructor of musketry 11th October 1878 and paymaster 20th December 1881. Appointed honorary major 20th December 1891, staff paymaster 8th April 1897 and chief paymaster 8th April 1902. He married Emily Janet née Lloyd (c.1864–1931) in 1875 and they had a son, Warren Skeffington Wynne (1875–1956). Warren was a professional singer, living at Highbridge, Frimley Green, Surrey, when he applied for a commission on 16th August 1914. He served in 4th (Reserve) Battalion, attached 2nd Battalion, Highland Light Infantry. He was very seriously wounded on 13th November 1916 at Beaumont-Hamel. Bullets passed through his left cheek and left forearm. He was evacuated from Calais to Dover on 17th November on SS *Newhaven* for treatment at a hospital in London. Medical boards on 6th December 1916 and 6th March 1917 found him unfit for General Service. He was well enough to join 4th (Reserve) Battalion at Hawick on 19th March for light duties. Further medical boards on 19th April and 21st May found him unfit for General Service, but on 22nd June he was fit. Demobilised 7th October 1919 and relinquished his commission on 10th September 1920, retaining the rank of captain. Warren married Elizabeth Patterson (died 1973) in 1904 and they had two children.

- Sydenham Henry Wynne (1851–1942) served in the Indian Civil Service. He married Mary Kate née Lee (died 1957) in 1899 and they had a son, Robert Henry Skeffington Wynne (1899–1966), who was commissioned in 9th Lancers on 16th July 1919. Promoted lieutenant 16th July 1921 and resigned his commission on 1st August 1926. He was a member of the London Stock Exchange 1928–39. He was mobilised in 1939 from the Regular Army Reserve of Officers RAC 9th Lancers Class II. Promoted war substantive captain

Land for the East India Company College was purchased near Hertford Heath in October 1805, the foundation stone was laid in May 1806 and the buildings were occupied in 1809. The East India Company had existed since 1600, but by 1800 it was a de facto government. The College was set up to train administrators for the Indian subcontinent and became known as Haileybury. In January 1858 the college closed, but reopened as Haileybury public school in 1862. Although independent, it retained close links with colonial administration. In 1942 it merged with Imperial Service College.

Trinity College Dublin dates back to 1592. In the 18th Century it was regarded as a Protestant establishment. Catholics were allowed to apply for admission from 1793, but it was not until 1873 that religious tests were abolished. In the meantime the Irish Catholic bishops imposed a general ban on Catholics entering Trinity College, which was not rescinded until 1970. Women were admitted as full members in 1904. Following independence Trinity College had a cool relationship with the new Irish state, but thrives today, with student numbers doubling by the 1990s. In 1991 Thomas Noel Mitchell became the first Roman Catholic elected Provost of Trinity College.

on 26th June 1942 and temporary major on 30th October 1946. He served in France, Middle East, Western Europe and retired on 18th January 1949 (last in Army List in August 1948).

• Florence Anne Wynne (born 1853).
• Charles Wynne (1856–89).

Clement was educated at Hill House School, Filsham Road, Hastings, at the East India Company College (Haileybury College) 1904–06 and Trinity College Dublin (BA BAI Engineering 1909). He and his four brothers were keen golfers and were founder members of the Delgany Golf Club. Clement won the President's Cup in the first year it was played for in 1908. In 1911 he was a boarder at Croft House, part of Cotherston, Darlington while an articled pupil to a civil engineer

Clement Robertson's grave in Oxford Road Cemetery, Ypres.

engaged on waterworks. He was employed as a civil engineer with the Egyptian Irrigation Service for three years and returned to England on the outbreak of war.

Clement enlisted in 19th Royal Fusiliers (2nd Public Schools) on 8th October 1914 (826) and joined at Epsom. He was described as 5′ 9½″ tall, weighing 140 lbs, with ruddy complexion, grey eyes, dark brown hair and his religious denomination was Church of England. He applied for a commission on 30th December 1914 and was commissioned on 16th January 1915 in 3rd (Reserve) Battalion, The Queen's (Royal West Surrey Regiment). He appears to have served in France because he was admitted to 9th Stationary Hospital, Le Havre 12th–18th June 1915. According to the Army List he was employed with the Royal Engineers June 1916–February 1917, the Heavy Branch, Machine Gun Corps from March 1917 and was attached to the Tank Corps from September 1917. It is known that he was attached to A Battalion, Heavy Branch, Machine Gun Corps on 1st January 1917 and probably went to France on or about that date, although his Medal Index Card states 1st July 1917. He was not on A Battalion's nominal roll in December 1916, but was when the next roll was produced in May 1917. At Messines, Belgium on 7th June 1917 his tank A56 supported 140th Brigade (41st Division) and was hit by a 5.9″ shell, which killed 206121 Sergeant William Clegg (Dickebusch New Military Cemetery – III B 18) and wounded two other crewmen. Although A56 was heavily damaged, he brought it back to base and was

The South African Great War VC plaque at the Castle of Good Hope, Cape Town (defenceweb).

later appointed to command 12 Section in 3 Company.

Awarded the VC (the first by the Tank Corps) for his actions near Reutel, east of Polygon Wood, Belgium 30th September– 4th October 1917, LG 18th December 1917. He was killed during his VC action and is buried in Oxford Road Cemetery, Ypres (II F 7). He is commemorated in a number of other places:

- Named on one of eleven plaques honouring 175 men from overseas awarded the VC for the Great War. The plaques were unveiled by the Senior Minister of State at the Foreign & Commonwealth Office and Minister for Faith and Communities, Baroness Warsi, at a reception at Lancaster House, London on 26th June 2014 attended by The Duke of Kent and relatives of the VC recipients. The South African plaque is at the Castle of Good Hope, Cape Town.

Christ Church, Delgany, Co Wicklow (archiseek) and the memorial to Clement Robertson (Memorials to Valour).

- The Secretary of State for Communities and Local Government, Eric Pickles MP, announced that Victoria Cross recipients from the Great War would have commemorative paving stones laid in their birthplace as a lasting legacy of local heroes within communities. The stones would be laid on or close to the 100th anniversary of their VC actions. For the 145 VCs born in Australia, Belgium, Canada, China, Denmark, Egypt, France, Germany, India, Iraq, Japan, Nepal, Netherlands, New Zealand, Pakistan, South Africa, Sri Lanka, Ukraine and United States of America, individual commemorative stones

The Hall of Honour at Trinity College was opened in 1928 to commemorate 471 Trinity College staff, students and alumni who died in the First World out of 3,529 who served. The Hall was designed as the portico of the new reading room that opened in 1937. The Hall of Honour memorial stone was unveiled on the empty plinth seen at the front of the building on 26th September 2015.

were unveiled at the National Memorial Arboretum, Alrewas, Staffordshire by Prime Minister David Cameron MP and Sergeant Johnson Beharry VC on 5th March 2015.

- Memorial in Christchurch, Delgany, Co Wicklow, Ireland and named on the Roll of Honour.
- Robertson Road, Bovington Camp, Dorset.
- Named on the War Memorial, Trinity College, Dublin, Ireland.

Royal Barracks in Dublin (Collins Barracks following Partition in 1922), where Clement's mother received his VC from Brigadier General C Williams in March 1918.

The name panels in the Hall of Honour.

• Memorial plaque on the wall of the Merlijn restaurant at Reutel designed and installed by relatives of Clement Robertson VC and Cyril Allen DCM and the Tank Memorial Ypres Salient. It was dedicated on 29th April 2015. Ian Robertson, formerly Irish Guards, great nephew of Clement Robertson, is currently Vice President of TMYS.

As Clement never married, the VC was presented to his mother by Brigadier General C Williams CB, Commanding Dublin District, at the Royal Barracks Dublin on 27th March 1918. In addition to the VC he was awarded the British War Medal 1914–20 and Victory Medal 1914–19. The VC is held privately.

552665 PRIVATE JAMES PETER ROBERTSON
27th Battalion (City of Winnipeg), Canadian Expeditionary Force

James Robertson was born on 26th October 1883 (also seen as 25th or 26th December 1882) at Albion Mines, Stellarton, Pictou, Nova Scotia. He was known as Peter, Pete or Singing Pete. His father, Alexander Robertson (born 1852), was born in Nova Scotia of Scottish parents. He married Janet/ Janette (born 1856), also born in Nova Scotia of Scottish parents. They moved to Springhill, Nova Scotia c.1887 and to 656, 5th Street South East, Medicine Hat, Alberta in 1899. Alexander died before his son enlisted in 1916. Peter had eleven siblings:

- John D Robertson (born 1876) was a coal miner in 1891. He was rejected as unfit for service in the Canadian Army.
- Daniel Robertson (born 1877) was a miner at the Cumberland Railway and Coal Company's colliery at Springhill, Nova Scotia. On 21st February 1891 he was hauling empty coal boxes with his horse, Jenny, when an explosion occurred. The blast killed the horse and knocked him off his seat into the coal box. He ripped off his burning clothes, badly burning his hands and arms. As he moved towards the mine entrance he heard faint cries and discovered twelve-year old Judson Farris huddled in a corner, too afraid to move. Danny's hands were too painful to use so he told Farris to climb onto his back before making his way to safety. He was going to re-enter the mine to rescue his younger brother, Peter, but was placed in a container with other injured miners and taken to the pithead, where he found Peter waiting for him. One hundred and twenty five men and boys were killed in the disaster. Danny was awarded a gold cross by Sir Charles Tupper in recognition of his bravery. Danny married Lorna B before 1916.

Springhill, Nova Scotia.

Springhill was the scene of three disasters within the coalfield in 1891, 1956 and 1958, resulting in one hundred and twenty-five, thirty-nine and seventy-five deaths respectively.

She was born c.1882 in England and emigrated to Canada in 1905. Danny was a conductor with the Canadian Pacific Railway in 1916 and they were living at 547A, Sixth Avenue, Medicine Hat, Alberta. They had at least two children – Juanita Robertson c.1908 and Georgina R Robertson c.1914.
- Johanna 'Anna' Robertson (born c.1879).
- Margaret Robertson (born c.1880).
- Agatha 'Aggie' Robertson (born 26th June 1883). Her date of birth conflicts with the birth of her brother Peter on 26th October 1883. She was not with the family in the 1891 Census of Canada, when she would have been only eight years old. It is possible that she was adopted.
- Bessie Robertson (born 1885).
- Mary Robertson (born 1888).
- Alexander Murray Robertson (born 1889) was a clerk. He attested for the Canadian Expeditionary Force on 19th February 1916 at Medicine Hat and served in 175th Battalion (696236). He was described as 5′ 9½″ tall, with fair complexion, blue

eyes, brown hair and his religious denomination was Presbyterian. He transferred to 31st Battalion and was wounded in France and hospitalised for ten months.
- David R Robertson (born 1891) served in 175th Battalion and was assigned to the transport service.
- Janet 'Jennie' Robertson (born 1894).
- Christina 'Christie' F Robertson (born 1898).

Peter was educated at Springhill, Nova Scotia. He was employed as a fireman with the Canadian Pacific Railway at Medicine Hat, Alberta and later transferred to Lethbridge as a locomotive engineer. He enlisted in 13th Canadian Mounted Rifles at Fort Macleod, Alberta on 14th June 1915 (13665 later 552665). He was described as 6′ 1″ tall, weighing 180 lbs, with medium complexion, blue eyes, dark brown hair and his religious denomination was Presbyterian. Shortly after enlisting he was in uniform with several comrades near the military depot at Medicine Hat, Alberta, when a sneering pro-German bystander asked if they were wearing their uniforms for a meal ticket. Robertson stepped over to the man and knocked him down with his fist. He was treated for gonorrhoea on 9th June 1916. On 29th June he embarked on RMS *Olympic* and disembarked in England on 6th July. On 19th July he was taken on strength of Lord Strathcona's Horse Reserve Regiment, Canadian Corps Depot, Shorncliffe. He transferred to 11th Reserve Infantry Battalion, Shorncliffe on 17th September and arrived at the Canadian Base Depot, Le Havre, France on 28th September. On 10th October he transferred to 27th Battalion. He was treated for influenza and an ulcerated tongue at 1st and 6th Canadian Field Ambulances 23rd–26th November and at No.22 Casualty Clearing Station 26th November–7th December, when he was moved to 22nd General Hospital, Camiers. He was treated for syphilis at 39th General Hospital, Le Havre 10th December 1916–6th February 1917 and forfeited all field allowances in this period. On 7th February he transferred to the Base Depot, Le Havre and rejoined his unit on 24th February.

Lethbridge, Nova Scotia.

The Canadian Pacific Railway station at Medicine Hat.

He was stopped three days' pay for drunkenness and being in an estaminet during prohibited hours on 2nd July.

When not in hospital, Peter was in the thick of the action. On one occasion the dugout in which he was sheltering was collapsed by enemy artillery fire, burying him and his comrades alive. They remained trapped until their comrades arrived and dug them out. On another occasion there had been heavy losses and some men were sheltering in a

Fort Macleod was founded as a North-West Mounted Police barracks in 1874, named in honour of Colonel James Macleod. The town grew around it.

shell hole. When they began to give up hope, Peter jumped in amongst them and lifted their morale with jokes and lively banter.

Awarded the VC for his actions at Passchendaele, Belgium on 6th November 1917, LG 11th January 1918. He was killed by a shell during his VC action on 6th November 1917 and is buried in Tyne Cot Cemetery, Passchendaele (LVIII D 26). Tributes poured in after his death. In Cleveland, Ohio, 77,000 delegates at an international railway convention saluted his courage. The Canadian Pacific Railway displayed his photograph in Montreal Railway Station (believed to be the only person so honoured) and he has been included in the Canadian Railway Hall of Fame. The story of his sacrifice was published in *The Locomotive Engineer Journal*.

Peter Robertson's grave in Tyne Cot Cemetery.

As he never married the posthumous VC was presented to his mother by Robert George Brett, Lieutenant Governor of Alberta, at Medicine Hat, Calgary, Alberta on 25th April 1918. In his address Brett said, *This*

Robert George Brett (1851–1929) gained a medical degree at the University of Toronto. In the early 1880s he helped found the Manitoba Medical College and was also a physician at Banff Sanitarium, which he founded. In 1888 he was elected to the Legislative Assembly of the North-West Territories and chaired the Lieutenant Governor's Advisory Council. In 1898 he became the first leader of the official opposition. He was also a senior surgeon at Brett Hospital in Banff and in 1909 became President of the Alberta Conservative Party. He was appointed the second Lieutenant Governor of Alberta in 1915.

cross is only a small thing, its cost is very little, but it has engraved on it the words 'For Valour', which mean a great deal. Money can do much – with money titles can be bought, but money cannot buy the Victoria Cross. It must be won by valour and service. He is also commemorated in a number of other places:

The Royal Canadian Legion, Robertson Memorial Branch in Medicine Hat.

- Named on a family grave marker at Hillside Cemetery, Medicine Hat, Alberta.
- Robertson Way, Robertson Swimming Pool and Robertson Memorial Park in Medicine Hat, Alberta.
- Robertson Memorial Branch No.17, Royal Canadian Legion (Alberta/Northwest Territories Command), 702, 2nd Street SE, Medicine Hat, Alberta named on 13th December 1969.
- CCGS Private Robertson VC – one of nine Hero Class mid-shore patrol vessels (253 tons) ordered for the Canadian Coast Guard Service. She was built in 2011 by Halifax Shipyards Ltd (Irving Shipbuilding Inc) at Halifax, Nova Scotia and launched on 12th May 2012. She entered service on 30th April 2013 and is deployed on maritime security throughout the Great Lakes and St Lawrence Seaway.
- Private James P Robertson Memorial Park, Stellarton, Nova Scotia named in 2009.
- Named on the War Memorial, Stellarton, near Pictou, Nova Scotia, dedicated on 17th June 1967.
- Named on a Victoria Cross obelisk to all Canadian VCs at Military Heritage Park, Barrie, Ontario dedicated by The Princess Royal on 22nd October 2013.
- Named on one of eleven plaques honouring 175 men from overseas awarded the VC for

CCGS Private Robertson VC.

The War Memorial at Stellarton. The First World War names are on the panel on the left, including Pete Robertson.

the Great War. The plaques were unveiled by the Senior Minister of State at the Foreign & Commonwealth Office and Minister for Faith and Communities, Baroness Warsi, at a reception at Lancaster House, London on 26th June 2014 attended by The Duke of Kent and relatives of the VC recipients. The Canadian plaque was unveiled outside the British High Commission in Elgin Street, Ottawa on 10th November 2014 by The Princess Royal in the presence of British High Commissioner Howard Drake, Canadian Minister of Veterans Affairs Julian Fantino and Canadian Chief of the Defence Staff General Thomas J Lawson.

- Two 49 cents postage stamps in honour of the 94 Canadian VC winners were issued by Canada Post on 21st October 2004 on the 150th Anniversary of the first Canadian VC's action, Alexander Roberts Dunn VC.
- A wooden plaque bearing fifty-six maple leaves each inscribed with the name of a Canadian-born VC holder was dedicated at the Canadian Forces College, Toronto on Remembrance Day 1999.
- The Secretary of State for Communities and Local Government, Eric Pickles MP, announced that Victoria Cross recipients from the Great War would have commemorative paving stones laid in their birthplace as a lasting legacy of local heroes within communities. The stones would be laid on or close to the 100th anniversary of their VC actions. For the 145 VCs born in Australia, Belgium, Canada, China, Denmark, Egypt, France, Germany, India, Iraq, Japan, Nepal, Netherlands, New Zealand, Pakistan, South Africa, Sri Lanka, Ukraine and United States of America, individual commemorative stones were unveiled at the National Memorial Arboretum, Alrewas, Staffordshire by Prime Minister David Cameron MP and Sergeant Johnson Beharry VC on 5th March 2015.
- Plaque on a memorial to the ninety-nine Canadian VCs in York Cemetery, Toronto.

In addition to the VC he was awarded the British War Medal 1914–20 and Victory Medal 1914–19. As he died on operational duty his next-of-kin is eligible to receive the Canadian Memorial Cross. His Memorial Cross was sent to his mother on 17th December 1921. The VC is owned privately.

3/8614 LANCE CORPORAL FREDERICK GEORGE ROOM
2nd Battalion, The Royal Irish Regiment

Frederick Room was born at 42 Oak Road, Horfield, Bristol, Gloucestershire on 31st May 1895. His father, William James Room (1865–1920), born at Beaufort, Breconshire, was a railway labourer in 1881 living with his parents. He married Bertha Eaton née Rees (1865–1927) in 1889 at Bedminster, Somerset. In 1881 she was lodging as a scholar with Thomas and Mary Summerfield and their two daughters at 12 Spring Street Place, Bedminster, Somerset. William had a number of

different employments – in 1891 he was a warehouseman in a galvanised iron works, a master greengrocer in 1895 and a stay presser by 1901. The family was living at 12 Spring Street Place, Bedminster in 1891, at 7 Albert Road, Bristol by 1901 and at 24 Congleton Road, St George, Bristol by 1911. Frederick had four siblings:

- Edward James Room (1891–1948) was a corset presser in 1911 and served during the Great War. He married Winifred Matilda Sealley (1890–1958) in 1929.
- William Henry Victor Room (1898–1964) served during the Great War. He married Doris Cissie Boundy (1901–97) in 1925 and they had a daughter, Beryl D Room, in 1929.
- Winifred Irene Bertha Grace Room (born 1902) married Frederick Miles H Burnell (1904–72) in 1938. They had a daughter, Mollie G Burnell, in 1939. Mollie married David BK Kingscott (born 1940) in 1960 and they had at least two children – Andrew D Kingscott 1964 and Martyn James Kingscott 1967.
- Una Grace Theodora Room (1904–20).

Frederick's paternal grandfather, George Room (1841–1924), was born at Norton Malreward, Somerset. He married Elizabeth née Powell (1841–1914) in 1864. She was born at Wickwar, Gloucestershire. George was a porter in 1871 and a labourer in a flourmill in 1881. The family was living at 9 Nicholas Street, Bedminster, Somerset in 1871, at 1 Camden Terrace, Bristol St Mary, Redcliff, Gloucestershire by 1881 and at 11 Spring Street Place, Bedminster by 1891. In 1911 George and Elizabeth were living with their son Arthur. In addition to William they had seven other children:

- Ada Mary Room (1869–1930), birth registered as Rooms, was a stay machinist in 1891. She married Thomas Hodgson Bell (1870–1945) in 1892 and they had four children – Thomas George Bell 1893, Bertram Harold Bell 1895, Daisy Bell 1899 and William Bell 1900.
- George Henry Room (1871–1953), birth registered as Rooms, known as Henry, was a chocolate moulder. He married Rosa Maine (c.1874–1938) in 1894 at Bedminster. She was born in Chicago, Illinois, USA. They were living at Whitfield House, Bedminster in 1901 and at 89 Chessel Street, Bedminster in 1911. Henry and Rosa had five children – George William Room 1895, Albert Henry Room 1897, Victor Walter Room 1898, Percy James Room 1903 and Irene Grace Room 1905.
- Alice Elizabeth Room (1874–1935) was a stay machinist in 1891. She married Fred Musty (1873–1931), an elastic weaver, in 1897. They had six children – Alice Olive Musty 1900, Norman George Musty 1901, Edgar Raymond Musty 1903, Grace Mary E Musty 1908, Megan E Musty 1913 and Ivy O Musty 1919.
- Rosa Room (born 1876) married Walter Albert James (born 1875), a cocoa tin maker, and they had at least four children – Leonard Bramwell James 1901,

Douglas James 1906, Maurice James 1911 and Edith James 1916. They were living at 8 Newport Street, Bristol in 1901 and moved to Canada c.1903. He was a caretaker by 1916 at Winnipeg, Manitoba.
- Albert John Room (1878–1965), a machinist, married Florence Amy Foster (1882–1965) in 1911.
- Arthur Room (1880–1968), a tobacco blender, married Rose Florence Daniel (1883–1966) in 1907 and they had three children – Ivy May Room 1910, Kathleen M Room 1914 and Joyce M Room 1922. They were living at 89 York Road, Bristol in 1911.
- Walter Harold Room (1883–1955) married Ada Scobell (1883–1973) in 1908 at Bristol and they had at least two children – Harold L Room 1912 and Betty E Room 1921.

His maternal grandfather is not known, but his maternal grandmother is believed to be Anne Rees (c.1813–69). She was born at Haverfordwest, Pembrokeshire and was a housekeeper in 1861, living with her children at Castle Back, Haverfordwest. In addition to Bertha she had four other children:

- Thomas Rees (born c.1837) was a mariner in 1861.
- Mary Ann Rees (born c.1848) was a machinist in 1871 lodging with her siblings as head of the family at 3 Spring Street Place, Bedminster, Somerset. In 1881 she was lodging with her sisters Amelia and Bertha in the home of Thomas and Mary Summerfield and their two daughters at 12 Spring Street Place, Bedminster. In 1911 a married Annie Martin of the correct age was living with the Rooms in Bristol as a sister-in-law.
- Ellen Rees (born c.1853) was a dressmaker in 1871.
- Amelia Rees (1859–1916) was a dressmaker in 1871. In 1881 she was lodging with her sisters Mary Ann and Bertha in the home of Thomas and Mary Summerfield and their two daughters at 12 Spring Street Place, Bedminster. She married Joseph Phillips (born 1860) in 1882 and they had seven children – Phillip George Phillips 1886, Harold Charles Phillips 1887, Joseph S Phillips 1889, Edith P Phillips 1892, Mabel M Phillips 1894, Thomas A Phillips 1894 and Ivor Lewis Phillips 1899.

Frederick was educated at Whitehall Council School, Bristol and was a member of St Ambrose Company, 1st Bristol Cadet Battalion, Church Lads' Brigade, affiliated to the King's Royal Rifle Corps. He was employed by Mardon, Son & Hall's wagon works and later by the Western Engineering Co, Orchard Street, Bristol as a metal turner.

Frederick tried to join the Royal Engineers at Colston Hall, Bristol at the outbreak of the Great War, but was not accepted. He enlisted on 29th August 1914, joining Southern Command Cavalry Depot at Bristol on 1st September and 10th Reserve Cavalry Regiment (4th Hussars) on 3rd September (16158). He transferred to 3rd

Whitehall Primary School, Bristol.

Mardon's started out in 1823 as a small printing and engraving business in Bristol. James Mardon joined it in 1846. In 1849 the company began mass-producing labels. In 1888, Mardon's started printing packets for Will's, the tobacco producers, and rapid expansion followed. In 1902 it became part of Imperial Tobacco and by 1922 the company had eleven factories in Bristol. Despite many of its premises being lost to bombing in the Second World War, by 1979 it had nineteen factories in Bristol. A decade later, Mardon's was taken over by the Canadian group Lawson and the Bristol operation was run down. A much smaller business, Lawson Mardon Packaging continued.

Royal Irish Regiment on 2nd June 1915 and was posted to the Curragh and then to the 2nd Battalion in France on 26th July, joining it on 30th July as a stretcher-bearer. He received a gunshot wound to the right hand at Mametz on the Somme on 1st July 1916 and was treated at 23rd Field Ambulance, 11th Stationary Hospital at Rouen from 3rd July and 2nd Convalescent Depot at Étaples from 5th July. He was transferred to 16th Infantry Base Depot at Étaples on 8th July and returned to the Battalion on 20th July. Appointed unpaid lance corporal 11th September. Frederick suffered from boils and was treated at 113th Field Ambulance on 17th November and No.2 Casualty Clearing Station at Bailleul on 23rd November before rejoining the Battalion on 6th December. He was recommended for the MM for his actions during the Battle of Messines Ridge on 7th June 1917. Promoted lance corporal on 11th August 1917.

Awarded the VC for his actions at Frezenberg, Belgium on 16th August 1917, LG 17th October 1917. He was granted ten days' leave on 11th October and appointed unpaid acting corporal on 30th October. On 4th November he was granted one month's special leave, during which he was presented with the VC by the King at Durdham Down, Bristol on 8th November. Following the investiture he was given a civic reception even though he was determined to avoid any fuss. He repeatedly refused to be interviewed.

Frederick suffered from heart palpitations in January 1918. Appointed paid acting corporal on 30th August and paid lance sergeant on 20th September. In October he suffered shock from an aeroplane bomb that caused a reoccurrence of his heart palpitations and he also contracted influenza on 24th October. He was treated at 148th

A hut at 2nd Convalescent Depot celebrating Christmas 1917.

Field Ambulance before being admitted to 12th Stationary Hospital at St Pol, France on 28th October and later 22nd General Hospital at Camiers. Having been evacuated to Britain aboard HMHS *Princess Elizabeth* on 12th November, suffering from breathlessness and pain below the left nipple, he was admitted to Hulme Hall, Port Sunlight, Lancashire, a section hospital operating under 1st Western General Hospital, suffering from tachycardia.

The Curragh's history as a military assembly area goes back to before Elizabethan times. Training camps were set up there during the 19th Century and the first permanent wooden camp was built in 1855 during the Crimean War. Brick built structures started in 1879 with Beresford Barracks and six more barracks followed. The Home Rule Act of 1914 led to a number of officers threatening to resign in the Curragh Incident rather than enforcing Home Rule against the will of the Unionists. On 16th May 1922 the camp was handed over to the Irish Free State Army on the formation of the Irish Republic. Since then it has continued as a military camp, but has also been used as a detention centre on a number of occasions, including during the civil war, the Emergency 1939–46 and the 1950s. During the Second World War seperate sections of the camp were occupied by Allied, Axis and IRA personnel. The Curragh is now the Defence Forces Training Centre.

Hulme Hall was built in 1901 as a women's dining hall for Lever Brothers and became an art gallery in 1911 for some of the collection of William Lever. During the First World War the building housed Belgian refugees and was later a section hospital under 1st Western General Hospital at Fazakerley. The Beatles played at Hulme Hall on four occasions and it was where Ringo Starr made his first official appearance with the band on 18th August 1962. It is now a conference, banqueting and wedding centre.

The King during the Durdham Down investiture on 8th November 1917.

He relinquished the pay of lance sergeant and was posted to the strength of the Depot the same day. He was transferred to Netherfield Road Auxiliary Hospital, Liverpool (a seven bed specialist cardiac section of 1st Western General Hospital, Fazakerley) and later to the Military Hospital at Whittingham near Preston before being granted home leave 20th -31st December 1918.

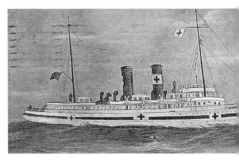

The *Princesse Elisabeth*, owned by the Belgian government, was built in 1905. During the war she became a 300-berth hospital ship on the cross-Channel service.

On 14th January 1919, Frederick was assessed as twenty percent disabled, which was likely to persist for twelve months, and was transferred to a military hospital at Bath, Somerset for dispersal on 24th January. He was one of five Bristol VCs to be presented with inscribed gold watches and illuminated addresses at a ceremony at Colston Hall on 15th February. Frederick was discharged to the Class Z Reserve on 5th March 1919 from Cork, Ireland.

Work began on Whittingham Asylum (from 1923 Whittingham Mental Hospital) in 1869 and it grew into the largest lunatic asylum in the country and the second largest in Europe. It opened in 1873 with 1,000 beds. During the First World War, St Margaret's Division was used as a military hospital and again during the Second World War. Four men are buried in CWGC graves in the hospital's cemetery. The hospital closed in 1995 except for a small secure psychiatric unit.

Frederick was employed by Thrissell Engineering Co, Easton Road, Bristol. He married Ellen Elizabeth Sargent (1895–1966) on 2nd August 1919 at St Michael's Church, Twerton, Bath. There were no children. They were both enthusiastic gardeners and had met before the war at the Twerton Flower Show. They lived at Gorse Hill, Fishponds, Bristol.

Ellen's father, Edwin George Sargent (1869–1926), born at Box, Wiltshire, was a carpenter in 1891, living with his parents at 9 Bridge Place, Lyncombe and Widcombe, Somerset. He married Ellen Elizabeth née Williams (1870–1940) later in 1891. By 1901 they were living at 59 Street, Lukes Crescent, Bristol, by 1911 at 20 Sladebrook Avenue, Bath, Somerset and had moved to Englishcombe Lane, Bath by 1919. Edwin was a house builder in 1911. In addition to Ellen they had

Thrissell Engineering Company's premises on Easton Road, Bristol.

The Church Lads' & Church Girls' Brigade Memorial Plot at the National Memorial Arboretum. The twenty-two Berberis shrubs are either side of the central walkway (Memorials to Valour).

Ham Green Hospital was based upon Ham Green House, which dates back to Queen Anne's reign. It was home to the Bright family for seventy years, including Dr Richard Bright (1789–1858), whose research led to the discovery of the kidney condition, Bright's disease. In 1899 the House became an isolation hospital for the treatment of infectious diseases and it was later enlarged into a Sanatorium. By 1927 the facility had grown to 235 beds, treating over 1,400 patients. The hospital closed in 1992.

two other children, including Gertrude Lilian Sargent (1892–1973) who married Alfred Harry Tavener (1895–1971) in 1925 and they had two children – Frederick E Tavener 1925 and Iris L Tavener 1929.

Frederick had to give up work in the early 1930s due to failing health. His lungs were severely affected by the war and he was hospitalised with pneumonia. Ellen

Bristol Fishponds District War Memorial.

Frederick Room's grave in Greenbank Cemetery, Bristol. His wife, Ellen, is buried with him (Memorials to Valour).

refused all offers of help and took a job while also nursing him at their home. He continued to deteriorate and was admitted to Ham Green Sanatorium/Hospital, Bristol towards the end of 1931, suffering from pneumonia and died there on 19th January 1932. The cause of death was recorded as pulmonary tuberculosis. He is buried in Greenbank Cemetery, Bristol. A marble headstone, provided by ex-service organizations, was unveiled on his grave in May 1933. Frederick's name was added to Bristol Fishponds District War Memorial on 18th March 2005. Twenty-two Berberis shrubs represent the twenty-two members of the Church Lads' Brigade who were awarded the VC at the Church Lads & Church Girls Brigade Memorial Plot at the National Memorial Arboretum, Alrewas, Staffordshire.

An appeal was launched by the Archdeacon of Bristol after Frederick's death to assist Ellen following rumours that she might be forced to sell her husband's medals. The appeal failed, so she secured a job making ladies' corsets.

In addition to the VC he was also awarded the 1914–15 Star, British War Medal 1914–20 and Victory Medal 1914–19. His medals were presented to the National Army Museum in 1966, where they are held.

33316 PRIVATE THOMAS HENRY SAGE
8th Battalion, Prince Albert's (Somerset Light Infantry)

Thomas Sage was born at Ham Lane, Tiverton, Devon on 8th December 1882. His father, Thomas William Sage (c.1856–59–1932), a stonemason, was born in New York, USA. He was working for Tiverton Town Council and living at Barrington Street, Tiverton in 1881. He married Jessie Laura née Osmond (1862–1907), a silk winder, in 1882. In 1881 she was living with her mother and stepfather at Saint Andrew Street, Tiverton. Thomas and Jessie were living at Ham Lane, Tiverton in 1891. Thomas was living with his daughter, Mabel, at 2 Ham Place, St Andrew Street, Tiverton in 1911. Thomas junior had two sisters:

• Jessie Laura Sage (1884–85).
• Mabel Sage (1886–1964) was working in a lace factory in 1911 and was also looking after her father. She married William H Aldridge (1872–1949), a lead worker, in 1933. William had been married previously to Eva Wreford (1875–1931) in 1897 at Tiverton. William and Eva had a daughter, Ivy Eva D Aldridge (1898–1970), who married George Vincent Laker (1894–1978) in 1925.

Thomas's paternal grandfather, John Sage (c.1822–95), a mason, married Elizabeth née Elliott (c.1820 – before 1861) in 1844 at South Molton, Devon. In addition to Thomas they had four other children:

Thomas's father lived on Barrington Street in Tiverton in 1881.

South Molton, Devon, where Thomas's paternal grandparents married in 1844.

- Kezia Ann Sage (born and died 1847).
- John Sage (1848–1911), a mason, married Amelia Melhuish (1857–1937) in 1883. They were living at 18 Topaz Street, Roath, Cardiff, Glamorgan in 1901. They had a daughter, Lily Sage, in 1884.
- George Sage (1850–95), a joiner, married Agnes McBride (1854–92) in 1874 at Newport, Monmouthshire. They were living at Devon Place, Aberystwyth, Monmouthshire in 1881 and emigrated to New Zealand soon afterwards. They had eight children – John Murdock Sage 1875, Mary Emily Georgia Sage 1876, Agnes Jemima Victoria Adelaide Sage 1879, George Albert Sage 1881, Arthur McBride Sage 1885, Alice Mabel Sage 1886, Ernest William Sage 1889 and Daisy Sage 1891.
- Emily Sage (born 1853) was living at home in 1871.

They moved to Canada and the USA after 1853 and Elizabeth died there before Thomas returned with the children by 1861, when he was living with his parents at Charity Lands, Chawleigh. Thomas married Mary Ann Govier (c.1823–84) in 1861. They had three children:

- William Sage (1861–1918), a mason, married Elizabeth Ann Norton (1866–1942) in 1897. They were living at 66 Cooks Cross, South Molton in 1911.
- Mary Jane 'Pollie' Sage (1864–1939) was a dressmaker in 1881 and was living with her brother Henry at Chawleigh in 1911. She married Lewis Petherick (1854–1939) in 1913. Lewis had been married previously to Sarah Jane Webber (1854–91) in 1872 and they had seven children – Bessie Ellen Petherick 1872, William Webber Petherick 1874, Rosa Mary Petherick 1876, Herbert John Petherick 1878, John Petherick 1880, Lucy Petherick 1883 and Ethel Petherick 1891.
- Henry Sage (1865–1944) was a mason.

Thomas's maternal grandfather, Henry Osmond (c.1835–1872–80), a labourer, married Sarah née Richards (c.1836–1911) in 1858. They were living at West

Manley, Tiverton in 1861 and at Lock Gate, Halberton, Devon by 1871. In addition to Jessie they had six other children:

- Florence Richards Osmond (1859–1920) marriage Robert Milton (1848–1911), a railway plate layer, in 1876. They were living at New Street, Cullompton, Devon in 1901. In 1911 she was living there as a widow. They had nine children – Robert Roland Milton 1878, Netta Milton 1880, William Harry Milton 1882, George Reginald Milton 1884, Lily Milton 1886, Charles Milton 1889, Emily Milton 1890, Bessie Milton 1892 and Florence Milton 1893.
- Elizabeth Thomas Osmond (born 1861) was a sick minder in 1881 and a lace hand trimmer in 1891.
- Henry William Osmond (1864–1939), a basket maker, married Bessie Haskings (1860–1934) in 1884. They had six children – Harry Osmond 1886, Ethel Osmond 1890, Minnie Osmond 1892, Frank Osmond 1894, May Osmond 1896 and Victor Osmond 1902.
- Mary Osmond (1866–1927), a general servant, married Charles Auton (1857–1931), a brewer's labourer, in 1887. They had a daughter, Maud Auton, in 1889 and were living at 14 Sharlands Square, Tiverton in 1911.
- Walter Osmond (1868–75).
- Bessie Richards Osmond (1872–1937) married Joe Ellis (1872–1948), a groom, in 1891. They were living at Periton Lodge, Middlecombe, Minehead, Somerset in 1901. By 1911 he was a coachman domestic and they were living at Willowby Lodge, Yelverton, Devon. They had a son, Clifford Ellis, in 1892.

Sarah Sage married John Broomfield (c.1823–98), a groom, in 1880 at Exeter, Devon. They were living at St Andrew Street, Tiverton in 1881 and had a daughter, Maud Richards Broomfield, the same year.

Thomas was educated at Chilcot's School, Tiverton and was a member of the Church Lads' Brigade. He was employed as a blacksmith by Mr Pethwick in Newport Street and later worked for Messrs Starkey, Knight and Ford's Brewery.

Thomas Sage married Evelyn Maud née Langworthy (1886–1932), a general servant, registered in the 3rd quarter of 1907 at Tiverton. She was living at 9 Bilton Street, West Teignmouth, Devon in 1901. They were living at 9 Hit or Miss Court, Tiverton in 1911. They had five children:

Chilcot School in Tiverton, attended by Thomas Sage, was founded by Robert Chilcot (c.1560–1609), a wool manufacturer from London and nephew of Peter Blundell, founder of nearby Blundells School. The school was built in 1611 and was in use until 1906.

- Beatrice Annie Sage (1907–83) married Samuel Pengelly (1909–) in 1928. They had two children – Eileen BM Pengelly 1931 and Michael T Pengelly 1937.

- Clifford Cecil Sage (1910–81) married May Foss (born 1912) in 1934. They had a daughter, Joan C Sage, in 1946.
- Stanley W Sage (born 1914) married Ivy M Sweet (born 1918) in 1944. They had two children – Patrick J Sage 1946 and Brenda E Sage 1948.
- Irene 'Rene' M Sage (born 1916) married William J Britton (born 1911) in 1940. They had three children – Susan M Britton 1946, Melvyn J Britton 1948 and Amandie I Britton 1955.
- Charles H Sage (born 1921) married Beryl Smith in 1941. They had three children –
Maureen A Sage 1943, Alan C Sage 1947 and Shirley D Sage 1950.

Evelyn Sage's family was living on Radway Street, Bishopsteignton, Devon in 1891.

Evelyn's father, John Henry Langworthy (1860–1929), an agricultural labourer, married Mary née Apps (1854–1920) in 1881. In 1891 they were living at 7 Radway Street, Bishopsteignton, Devon. By 1911 he was working in a forage store and they were living at 9 Seward's Court, Leat Street, Tiverton, Devon. In addition to Evelyn they had eight other children:

- Helena 'Lena' Annie Langworthy (1881–1962), a lace winder, married Charles Frederick Webber (1883–1961) in 1904. They had six sons – Charles Henry Webber 1904, Cecil Frederick Webber 1906, George Herbert Webber 1907, Leslie John Webber 1909, William Clarence Webber 1910 and Sidney Harold Webber 1913.
- Mabel Charlotte Langworthy (twin with Maud) (born and died 1883).
- Maud Annie Langworthy (twin with Mabel) (born and died 1883).
- Charles Henry Langworthy (born and died 1884).
- Louisa Hilda Langworthy (1889–1963) married Sidney Henry Bolt (1888–1934) in 1907. They had six children – Margery Annie Bolt 1908, Gladys L Bolt 1910, Vera M Bolt 1912, Norman J Bolt 1916, Stanley Henry Bolt 1919 and Doreen M Bolt 1923. Stanley served as a private in the Royal Army Medical Corps (7361471) and was killed in action on 18th March 1944 (Beach Head War Cemetery, Anzio, Italy – IV B 4).
- Frederick John Apps Langworthy (1891–1965) enlisted as a boy in the Royal Navy at Devonport on 22nd January 1908 (J171). He signed on for twelve years on 8th July 1909 and was described as an errand boy, 5′ 5½″ tall, with black hair, brown eyes and fresh complexion. He served on various ships/establishments including HMS *Impregnable*, *Cressy*, *Vivid*, *Hannibal*, *Russell*, *Indefatigable*, *Swiftsure*, *Euryalus*, *Minerva*, *Proserpine*, *Egmont*, *Collingwood* and *Colossus*. He

was promoted able seaman 9th May 1911, leading hand 24th January 1914 and petty officer 1st January 1917. He was discharged on 9th June 1922. He married Edith Mary Louisa Webber (1893–1964) in 1919. They had two children – Edna Mary Louisa Langworthy 1920 and Cyril H Langworthy 1922. He rejoined HMS *Drake I* on 3rd November 1939 as a petty officer and was posted to HMS *Lochinvar* on 21st November, a shore training establishment for minesweeping on the Firth of Forth. He was released on 13th August 1945 from HMS *Glendower*, a shore establishment in Caernarfonshire, Wales.

- Cecil Frank A Langworthy (1893–1958) was a porter at an oil store in 1911. He married Mabel Lock (1891–1949) in 1922.
- Charles Herbert 'Bertie' A Langworthy (1895–1919) was a shop assistant in a boot shop in 1911. He was a fitter and turner when he enlisted in the Royal Navy for twelve years (M19324) on 9th March 1916. He was described as 5′ 3″ tall, with black hair, brown eyes and fresh complexion. The ships/establishments he served on included HMS *Vivid I, Dido, Vivid II, Victory and Pembroke*. Charles served as an engine room artificer 4th class. He married Edith Lilian Hinge (1893–1973) in 1917. She was living with her parents at 128 Glencoe Road, Chatham in 1911. Charles and Edith were living at 47 Rochester Terrace, Chatham when he died at RN Hospital Chatham from broncho-pneumonia on 24th March 1919 (Gillingham (Woodlands) Cemetery, Kent – Naval 7 356).

Thomas enlisted on 10th December 1914 and went to France after 31st December 1915. **Awarded the VC for his actions at Tower Hamlets Spur, east of Ypres, Belgium on 4th October 1917, LG 18th December 1917.** He was seriously wounded during the VC action and was treated at Horton (County of London) War Hospital, Epsom, Surrey. His missing eyelid was restored by surgeons and some shrapnel was removed from his thigh, but several pieces remained for the rest of his life. He had recovered sufficiently by 2nd February 1918 to travel to London for the presentation of an illuminated address by the London Tivertonians.

The Royal Navy Depot in Chatham was founded in 1890 aboard three hulks in the Dockyards, *Pembroke, Royal Adelaide* and *Forte*. A permanent shore base was constructed between 1897 and 1902 to accommodate 4,742 officers and men. It was given the title HMS *Pembroke*. In 1957 the barracks and gunnery school closed and reopened in 1959 as the Royal Naval Supply School. As a result of the 1981 Defence Review, the barracks and dockyard closed on 31st March 1984.

Thomas Sage's grave in
Tiverton Cemetery.

Thomas Sage towards the
end of his life.

Horton Hospital, formerly Horton
Asylum, opened for psychiatric patients in
1902. During both world wars the hospital
was commandeered for military use. In
the First World War Horton Asylum was
named Horton (County of London) War
Hospital. The hospital pioneered music
therapy and the treatment of advanced
syphilis and paedophilia. Induced
malaria was used as a cure for a form of
advanced syphilis, but the treatment was
rendered obsolete by 1975 by penicillin.
The hospital closed in 1997, but the
Wolvercote Clinic and a small psychiatric
unit, Horton Haven, remained open. Most
of the buildings were demolished, but a
few were incorporated into a new village
development (*Bourne Hall Museum*).

He was fitted with an artificial eye and on 8th
March returned to Tiverton to a tumultuous
welcome and received £100 in War Bonds and
a case of Treasury notes. He was discharged on
24th May 1918, no longer physically fit for war
service. The VC was presented by the King at
Buckingham Palace on 16th November 1918.

Thomas returned to work at the brewery. On
26th June 1920 he attended the VC Garden Party
at Buckingham Palace and on 9th November
1929 attended the VC Dinner at the Royal Gallery of the House of Lords, London.
Thomas was one of the notable trio of west country VC winners – Veale, Sage and
Onions. His wife died in 1932 and he had to give up work at the brewery due to poor
health in 1933. Later he took a job as caretaker of Tiverton TA Drill Hall.

Thomas Sage died at 44 Council Gardens, Tiverton, Devon on 20th July 1945
and is buried in Tiverton Cemetery (Section XB, Grave XI/36). A headstone was
erected over his grave on 6th December 1986 by the Somerset Light Infantry
Association. At the National Memorial Arboretum, Alrewas, Staffordshire, twenty-
two Berberis shrubs represent the twenty-two members of the Church Lads'
Brigade who were awarded the VC, although none are dedicated to individual VCs.

In addition to the VC he was awarded the British War Medal 1914–20, Victory
Medal 1914–19 and George VI Coronation Medal 1937. The VC is held privately,
but a replica is displayed at the Somerset Military Museum, County Museum, The
Castle, Taunton, Somerset.

LIEUTENANT ROBERT SHANKLAND
43rd Battalion (Cameron Highlanders of Canada), Canadian Expeditionary Force

Robert Shankland was born on 10th October 1887 at 6 Gordon Terrace, Ayr, Ayrshire, Scotland. His father, William Shankland (c.1853–1929), was born at Durisdeer, Dumfriesshire. He was a stonebreaker in 1871 and then worked for the Glasgow & South Western Railway Company for about forty years. He was boarding at 27 Garden Street, St Quivox in 1881. He was a railway pointsman in 1881, a railway porter in 1891 and a railway guard in 1901. He married Jane Russel née McCririck (1853–1928), born at Old Cumnock, Ayrshire, in 1883. She was a housemaid domestic working for Patrick CD Boswell and family, a landed proprietor, at Garrallan, Old Cumnock in 1881. They were living at 6 Gordon Terrace, Ayr in 1891, at 61 Content Street, Ayr in 1901 and by 1916 had moved to 68 Church Street, Ayr. Robert had a sister, Janet Wilson Shankland (1885–1966), who was working as a clerk in a grocer's shop in 1901. She married John McCartney (1883–1937), a railway clerk, in 1921.

Robert's paternal grandfather, Robert Shankland (1821–86), born at Durisdeer, Dumfriesshire, was a railway labourer in 1851 and by 1881 he was a railway platelayer. He married Jane née Marchbank (1824–1907), born at Wamphray, Dumfriesshire, in 1846. In 1851 they were living at Gillhead Cottage, Morton, Dumfriesshire. By 1871 they had moved to Enterkin Bridge Cottages, Durisdeer and to the Railway Cottages, Durisdeer by 1881. In addition to William they had eleven other children:

- James Shankland (born c.1847).
- Mary Shankland (c.1849–80).

Robert's mother was working at Garrallan House in 1881.

Robert's mother and grandparents were from Cumnock, Ayrshire.

- John Shankland (1850–92) was a railway surface man in 1871.
- Margaret Shankland (1852–99) married William McKie (born 1857) in 1877. They had seven children – Jane McKie 1877, Isabella McKie 1879, John McKie 1882, Robert McKie 1886, Elizabeth McKie 1888, Robina M McKie 1890 and William S McKie 1891.

The Shankland family was living on Content Street, Ayr in 1901.

- Robert Shankland (born c.1854) was a stonebreaker in 1871. He married Mary Glencross (born 1869) in 1891. They had five children – Robert Shankland 1893, Janet Shankland 1895, Jeanie Shankland 1898, Maggie Shankland 1900 and John Shankland 1901.
- Elisabeth Shankland (1856–1941) had an illegitimate son, David, in 1877.
- Thomas Shankland (1859–1938) married Jessie Sadler Murray (1861–1936) in 1885. They had six children – Martha Reid Shankland 1887, Jane Marchbank Shankland 1888, Catherine Marchbank Shankland 1890, Catherine Murray Shankland 1895, Bessie Shankland 1900 and Elizabeth Shankland 1900.
- George Shankland (1861–1944).
- Henry Shankland (born 1863).
- Jane Shankland (1865–1940).
- Alexander Giffen Shankland (1867–1940) married Sarah Elizabeth Holloway (1870–1949) in Leicester, England in 1897. He was a clerk in a hardware dealership in 1911 and they were living at 60 Hartington Road, Leicester. They had a son, Hedley M Shankland, in 1898.

His maternal grandfather, John McCririck (c.1815–62), born at Old Cumnock, Ayrshire, married Janet née Wilson (1822–82), a seamstress born at Mauchline, Ayrshire, in 1848. In 1861 they were living at Waterside Row, Cumnock, Ayrshire, by when he was an omnibus coachman. In addition to Jane they had four other children:

- Anne McCririck (born 1849).
- Thomas McCririck (1851–75).
- Margaret McCririck (born 1856), a domestic servant, was living at Miller Road, Ayr when she married Matthew Smith (born c.1856), a tinsmith, in 1882.
- Jessie McCririck (1861–62).

Robert was educated at Smith's Institution and Russell Street School in Ayr and was a member of 2nd Ayr (Parish Church) Company, Boys' Brigade. He was employed as a clerk in the accountant's office of John T Scott, Newmarket Street, Ayr for two years then worked as a clerk at Ayr Railway Station for seven years. Robert was

Russell Street School in Ayr.

Ayr Railway Station, where Robert worked for two years before emigrating to Canada, was opened in January 1886 by the Glasgow and South Western Railway.

Initiated into Ayr St Paul's Freemason Lodge (No.204) on 2nd August 1909. He emigrated to Canada in 1910, where he was an assistant cashier with the Crescent Creamery Co, Winnipeg, Manitoba. He was also secretary-treasurer of the Junior Board of Trade in Winnipeg and at one time managed the Carleton Club. Robert also served in the Militia with 79th Cameron Highlanders of Canada.

On 18th December 1914 he enlisted in A Company, 43rd Battalion CEF (420933) at Minto Street Barracks, Winnipeg. He was described as 5′ 4½″ tall, with sallow complexion, grey eyes, dark brown hair and his religious denomination was Presbyterian. A monthly assignment was taken from his pay and paid to Mrs GJ Ritchie, Crescent Creamery Co, Winnipeg. Robert was rapidly promoted lance corporal, corporal and sergeant. He was appointed regimental orderly room sergeant and sailed with the Battalion on 1st June 1915 on SS *Grampian*, landing in England on 10th June. Promoted to company sergeant major at Shorncliffe, Kent on 14th October. Robert sailed for France on 20th February 1916.

Awarded the DCM for his actions at Sanctuary Wood, near Ypres in

SS *Grampian* (10,187 tons) was built in Glasgow in 1907 for the Allan Line. She operated on the transatlantic route, mainly from Glasgow to Boston, Montreal, St John and Halifax. She was chartered by Canadian Pacific Line in 1912 and was taken over by the company in 1917. In 1921 she was gutted in a fire during a refit at Antwerp and was scrapped in 1925.

Minto Street Barracks, Winnipeg.

June 1916 – he volunteered to lead a party of stretcher-bearers to bring in wounded and partially buried men under heavy shellfire, LG 19th August 1916. He was granted leave 22nd-29th June 1916. Robert was appointed regimental sergeant major and was commissioned as a temporary lieutenant on 27th December 1916. He attended a gas course 3rd-6th January 1917 and was granted leave 19th-29th January. On 1st February he was promoted lieutenant with seniority from 27th December 1916. On 20th June he was appointed temporary captain and was granted leave to England 2nd-12th August.

Awarded the VC for his actions on Bellevue Spur, Passchendaele, Belgium on 26th October 1917, LG 18th December 1917. During the action he was slightly wounded by a gunshot to the back and was treated at No.3 Australian Casualty Clearing Station, returning to duty on 28th October. On 11th November he was wounded in the head, chin and neck and was admitted to 3rd Australian Field Ambulance, No.1 Australian Casualty Clearing Station, No.3 Canadian Casualty Clearing Station and then to 1st British Red Cross Hospital (Duchess of Westminster's) at Le Touquet on 13th November. He was discharged to the Reinforcement Camp, Étaples on 25th November and rejoined the Battalion on 7th December. His leave to UK from 12th to 26th December was extended to allow him to accept the Freedom of the Royal Borough of Ayr on 31st December. During this leave he was with his parents in Ayr when the award of the VC was announced. He was naturally quiet and retiring and had neither written nor spoken of his actions to any of his relatives. His parents were informed of his bravery by the Battalion Chaplain, George Taylor. When he was presented with a gold wristwatch by former members of the Ayr Boys' Brigade, he carefully avoided any mention of his actions except to note that he had learned more about his fight on Bellevue Spur during the civic reception than he knew before.

Robert was appointed adjutant on 28th January 1918 and was promoted captain on 25th February with seniority from 20th June 1917. He was granted leave to UK 21st September–5th October, extended to

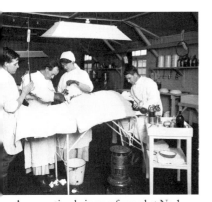

An operation being performed at No.1 Australian Casualty Clearing Station (Australian War Memorial).

1st British Red Cross (Duchess of Westminster's) Hospital at Le Touquet was located at the Casino.

9th October to attend the VC investiture. The VC was presented by the King at York Cottage, Sandringham, Norfolk on 6th October 1918. He was granted leave to Paris 22nd December 1918–1st January 1919. Robert returned to England on 10th February 1919 and sailed for Canada from Liverpool on RMS *Baltic* on 12th March, arriving in Ottawa on 25th March. He was demobilised on 11th April 1919, but remained in the Queen's Own Cameron Highlanders of Canada.

Robert returned to Britain and married Anna Stobo Haining (15th June 1889–22nd January 1952) at St Nicholas Parish Church, Prestwick, Ayrshire on 20th April 1920. She was born at Station Cottage, Elderslie, Renfrewshire and was a clerk at the time of her marriage. They sailed for Canada on 1st May 1920 and settled at St Boniface, Springfield, Manitoba. He was in Britain in 1929 to attend the VC Dinner at the Royal Gallery of the House of Lords, London on 9th November. Robert joined the Canadian Scottish Regiment in Victoria before moving to Vancouver in 1937, where he was appointed secretary of

Robert Shankland flanked by the King and Queen following the VC presentation at Sandringham (Australian War Memorial).

York Cottage, originally known as Bachelor's Cottage, was built as overflow residence for Sandringham House. In 1893 it was given by the future King Edward VII to his son Prince George (later King George V) as a wedding gift. He lived there with his wife, the future Queen Mary, for thirty-three years until the death of Queen Alexandra. York Cottage is now the estate office for Sandringham, holiday accommodation and flats for estate employees.

RMS *Baltic* (23,876 tons) was built in Belfast for the White Star Line in 1903 and for two years was the world's largest ship. She was the third of four ships all over 20,000 tons known as the Big Four (the others were *Celtic*, *Cedric* and *Adriatic*). During her maiden voyage to New York on 29th June 1904 she was commanded by Captain Edward Smith. He was captain of RMS *Titanic* when RMS *Baltic* sent her an ice warning on 14th April 1912, prior to striking the iceberg that resulted in the catastrophic sinking. In August 1914, *Baltic* carried 2,072 passengers fleeing Europe and thereafter was used as a troopship. She survived a U-boat attack undamaged and in 1918 resumed the White Star Line's Liverpool to New York service. In December 1929 *Baltic* rescued the crew of *Northern Lights*, a schooner sinking in a storm off Newfoundland, and a number of crew were awarded medals from The Life Saving Benevolent Association. *Baltic*'s last transatlantic voyage was in September 1932 and she was broken up in Osaka, Japan in 1933.

Hall Securities. Robert was a keen sportsman, playing baseball for his works' team and served as secretary for the provincial soccer champions. He was one of six VCs presented to King George VI and Queen Elizabeth during the Royal Tour of Canada in June 1939 at Vancouver, British Columbia. Anna and Robert had two sons:

- William Stobo McCririck Shankland (10th June 1921–October 2002) married Constance Hilda Bridden (1920–2014) in 1952 at Whatcom County, Washington, USA. He was working for the Federal Government in 1962 and they were living at Apartment 205, 12th Avenue West, Vancouver, British Columbia.
- David Haining Shankland (2nd April 1927–30th April 1989) married and had three children.

Anna's father, David Haining (1861–1930), was the stationmaster at Prestwick, Ayrshire. He married Anne Johnson Hay née Boyd (1860–1931) at 21 Graham Street, Airdrie, Lanarkshire in 1885. They were living at Roseberry Cottage, Prestwick in 1901 and later moved to Broomknoll, Meiklewood Avenue, Prestwick. They were living at Station House, Prestwick during the Great War. In addition to Anna they had two other children:

- Isabella Cleland Haining (1886–1955) never married.
- William Stobo Haining (1894–1917), a clerk, enlisted at Wembley on 16th November 1914 and served with 1st Battery, Motor Machine Gun Service, Royal Horse & Royal Field Artillery (71). He was 5′ 11½″ tall and weighed 122 lbs. He was posted to 15th Battery on 22nd April 1915 and went to France on 29th May, transferring to the Machine Gun Corps on 1st December. He was admitted to Middlesex Hospital, Clacton-on-Sea 3rd–12th April 1916 and Red Cross Hospital, Sudbury 12th–29th April. He was then on leave until 8th May, but was admitted to hospital at Gailes Camp 6th May–19th June with a carbuncle on the back of his neck. On 29th July he applied for a commission while at the Motor Machine Gun Training Centre at Bisley. By then he had grown to 6′ 1″ tall and weighed 136 lbs. From 1st September he trained to be an artillery officer at the Royal Artillery Cadet School, B Reserve Brigade RHA at St John's Wood. However, he suffered from boils, which prevented him from riding and his maths was not good enough for siege artillery work. As a result he transferred to the Machine Gun Corps Officer Cadet Battalion on 1st November and was commissioned into the Machine Gun Corps (Heavy Branch) on 9th December 1916. He embarked at Southampton on 25th June 1917 and disembarked at Le Havre next day to join E Battalion, Tank Corps. He was serving in 14th Company, E Battalion when he was killed in action on 20th November 1917 in the Battle of Cambrai. His tank "Ella" (after his sister) was hit by a shell. He is buried in Ribecourt Road Cemetery, Trescault, France (I B 1).

At the outbreak of the Second World War Robert was recalled to the Queen's Own Cameron Highlanders of Canada in Winnipeg. He was promoted major in January 1940 and was posted to England with the Battalion as OC HQ Company. He was promoted lieutenant colonel and appointed Camp Commandant at Canadian Army HQ in December 1940, serving with the HQ in Aldershot, Hampshire and later at Peper Harow House near Godalming, Surrey. He was discharged in 1946 and returned to his position with Hall Securities in Vancouver.

The Peper Harow estate is mentioned in the Domesday Book and in the 1700s became the home of the Viscounts Midleton. In the Second World War it was HQ of the Canadian Ordnance Corps and much of the planning for the Dieppe Raid and the Normandy invasion took place there. In 1950 it became a school and the main building has since been divided into apartments.

Robert was a life member of the National Building Owners and Managers Association and the Royal Canadian Legion. He also belonged to Fourandex, a war veterans' association in Vancouver. Robert attended the VC Centenary Celebrations at Hyde Park, London on 26th June 1956. He also attended the 4th VC & GC Association Reunion at the Café Royal, London on 16th July 1964. Towards the end of his life he lived at the Terminal City Club in Vancouver.

Robert Shankland died at Shaughnessy Hospital, Vancouver, British Columbia on 20th January 1968. He was cremated at Mountain View Crematorium, Vancouver and his ashes were reportedly scattered in the Garden of Remembrance of Mountain View Cemetery, but the administration have no record of this. An unconfirmed report indicates that some of the ashes were scattered at sea. Robert is commemorated in a number of other places:

Shaughnessy Hospital opened in 1917 as a convalescent home for First World War veterans. By 1919 it had increased its capacity to become a military hospital. In 1941 a new 250 bed hospital building opened, the first such hospital to be built by the Department of Veterans Affairs. Other facilities were added later. In the 1960s and 1970s Shaughnessy began treating increasing numbers of civilian patients. In 1974 it was sold to British Columbia for just $1. It closed in 1993.

• Leo Clarke VC, Frederick Hall VC and Robert Shankland VC all lived on Pine Street, Winnipeg, Manitoba; Clarke at 785, Hall at 778 and Shankland at 733. In honour of them, Pine Street was renamed Valour Road in 1925 through By-Law 11673 and a bronze plaque was mounted on a street lamp at the corner of Portage Avenue and Valour Road by the Women's Canadian Club of Winnipeg. A new site, Valour Road Plaza, at

Valour Road memorial plaza (Nathan Kramer).   Valour Road memorial plaque.

Sargent Avenue and Valour Road was dedicated on 5th November 2005. It features Tyndall Stone monuments supporting steel silhouettes of three soldiers. Bronze plaques to the three VCs were dedicated on 27th May 2012.

- Named on a Victoria Cross obelisk to all Canadian VCs at Military Heritage Park, Barrie, Ontario dedicated by The Princess Royal on 22nd October 2013.
- Named on one of eleven plaques honouring 175 men from overseas awarded the VC for the Great War. The plaques were unveiled by the Senior Minister of State at the Foreign & Commonwealth Office and Minister for Faith and Communities, Baroness Warsi, at a reception at Lancaster House, London on 26th June 2014 attended by The Duke of Kent and relatives of the VC recipients. The Canadian plaque was unveiled outside the British High Commission in Elgin Street, Ottawa on 10th November 2014 by The Princess Royal in the presence of British High Commissioner Howard Drake, Canadian Minister of Veterans Affairs Julian Fantino and Canadian Chief of the Defence Staff General Thomas J Lawson.
- Two 49 cents postage stamps in honour of the 94 Canadian VC winners were issued by Canada Post on 21st October 2004 on the 150th Anniversary of the first Canadian VC's action, Alexander Roberts Dunn VC.

The Canadian Volunteer Service Medal was awarded to military personel who completed eighteen months voluntary active service between 3rd September 1939 and 1st March 1947. A silver clasp with a maple leaf was awarded for sixty days service outside Canada. Eligibility was extended in 2001 to members of the Auxiliary Services, merchant mariners, Corps of Canadian Fire Fighters who served in Britain during the Blitz, Overseas Welfare Workers, Voluntary Aid Detachments, Ferry Command pilots and British Commonwealth Air Training Plan instructors. Members of the Royal Canadian Mounted Police were added in 2003.

- His VC action featured in Issues 795 & 1329 of the Victor Comic dated 15th May 1976 and 9th August 1986 respectively.
- Portrait by AY Jackson at the Canadian War Museum, Ottawa.
- Plaque on a memorial to the ninety-nine Canadian VCs in York Cemetery, Toronto.

In addition to the VC and DCM he was awarded the British War Medal 1914–20, Victory Medal 1914–19, Defence Medal, Canadian Volunteer Service Medal 1939–45 with Maple Leaf clasp, War Medal 1939–45, George VI Coronation Medal 1937 and Elizabeth II Coronation Medal 1953. The medals passed to Robert's son, David, and subsequently to his son. The medals were purchased by the Canadian War Museum at Bonham's, 55 Avenue Road, Toronto, Ontario on 25th May 2009 for CAD$288,000. The group was loaned to the Manitoba Museum on 1st October 2010 to mark the 100th anniversary of the Queen's Own Cameron Highlanders. The VC is held by the Canadian War Museum, Ottawa, Ontario, Canada.

6895 COMPANY SERGEANT MAJOR JOHN KENDRICK SKINNER
1st Battalion, The King's Own Scottish Borderers

John Skinner was born at 76 Henderson Street, Glasgow on 5th February 1883. His father, Walter Cumming Skinner (c.1853–1920), was born in Inver-by-Tain, Ross and Cromarty and was a master tailor and clothier. He was living at 7 Bishop Street, Glasgow on 31st December 1874 when he married Mary née Kendrick (c.1852–89), a book folder, of 6 Clifton Place, Glasgow. They were living at 251 North Woodside Road, Barony, Lanarkshire in 1881, at 5 Leven Street, Govan, Glasgow by 1891, at 165 St Andrew's Road, Glasgow by 1901 and later at 263 Maxwell Road, Pollokshields, Glasgow. In addition to John they had three other children:

- Peter Skinner (1877–1907), a tailor, married Elizabeth Shearer Malcolm (1879–1960) in 1899 at Llangollen, North Wales. By 1901 he was a factor's cutter worker living with his family at Well Road, Moffat, Dumfries-shire. He died at 23 Montgomery Street, Eaglesham, Renfrewshire, usual residence 2 Porter Street, Glasgow. By 1911 Lizzie was living at 2 Holyrood Crescent, Cathcart, Lanarkshire. They had three children:
  - Walter Alexander Skinner (1900–37) was a locomotive inspector living at 2 Holyrood Crescent, Clarkston, Renfrewshire at the time of his marriage to Christina Anne Mackay (c.1902–89), assistant matron of an old people's home at Bearsden, in 1930. On the evening of 10th December 1937 in a whiteout,

the Edinburgh Waverley to Glasgow Queen Street express collided with the late running Dundee Tay Bridge to Glasgow Queen Street service at Castlecary Station. Thirty-five people were killed, seven of whom were train crew, including Walter, who succumbed to a fractured skull. Another 179 people were seriously injured. Walter was living at 5 Templar Avenue, Knightswood, Glasgow at the time.

Wreckage from the Castlecary Station train crash on 10th December 1937 in which John's nephew, Walter, was killed.

- Elizabeth Malcolm Skinner (1902–72) died unmarried.
- Hilda Skinner (born 1905) was a private secretary living at 4 Holyrood Crescent, Clarkston, Renfrewshire when she married Douglas Francis Hugh Gordon (born c.1903), an insurance broker, in 1928.
- Elizabeth Cowan Skinner (1879–91).
- Walter Cumming Skinner (1881–1953) was a brigade fireman living at 33 Ingram Street, Glasgow when he married Olivia Lee, a clerk (1880–1937), in 1905. They were living at 26 Warwick Street, Glasgow in 1911. They had three children – Margaret Mary Skinner 1907, Walter James Skinner 1909 and Ernest Lee Skinner 1912. Walter married Pauline Clark or Cuthbert in 1938.

Mary died of consumption on 21st September 1889 at 3 Marchmont Terrace, Langside, Glasgow. Walter married secondly Barbara Grieve (1860–1952), a domestic servant, on 14th July 1892 at 493 Shields Road, Glasgow. She was born at Peterhouse, Parish of St Andrew's and Deerness, Orkney. They had four children:

- Bessie Skinner (1895–1991) was a typist, living at 283 Maxwell Road, Glasgow, when she married Robert Ireland (born c.1891), a fish merchant, in 1924.
- Annie Eleanor Maud Skinner (1896–2001) died unmarried.
- Alexandra Marion Skinner (1898–1909).
- Allister Skinner (1900–89) was a stockbroker's clerk living at 393 Mosspark Boulevard, Glasgow when he married Doreen Honora Watson (1904–84), a typist, in 1935.

John's paternal grandfather, Peter Skinner (c.1820–70), was a farm labourer and a fisherman. He married Ann née Cumming (born c.1818). In addition to Walter they had five other children – Ann Skinner c.1847, John Skinner c.1849, Janet Skinner c.1853, Isabella Skinner c.1857 and Philip Skinner c.1859.

His maternal grandfather, John Kendrick (born c.1813 in England and died before 1874), was a master tailor. He married Elizabeth née Cowan (c.1817–80) at Perth,

Perthshire. They were living at 43 Irongate Street, Glasgow St Mary in 1851. In addition to Mary they had three other children:

- James Kendrick (born c.1841) was a journeyman tinsmith. He married Isabella McPherson (born c.1843) in 1862.
- Ann Kendrick (born c.1844).
- Elizabeth Kendrick (c.1847–1912) was working in a warehouse and living at 82 George Street, Glasgow when she married James Clark (born c.1841), a journeyman tailor, in 1867. James predeceased his wife.

Queen's Park School in Pollokshields (Scotcities).

John was educated at Queen's Park and Melville Street Schools in Pollokshields and Allan Glen's School in Glasgow. He was employed by GJ Weir, pump and valve makers. He enlisted in the West of Scotland Artillery Militia on 22nd October 1899 aged sixteen, but gave his date of birth as 26th October 1881. On 26th December 1899 he enlisted in the King's Own Scottish Borderers, giving his age as eighteen years and three months and his place of birth as Tain, Ross-shire, believing there was a reluctance to enlist men from Glasgow. While undergoing training he was in hospital at Berwick with an abscess 16th-22nd February 1900.

John was posted to the 1st Battalion on 11th April 1900 and served in the South African War from 30th April. He was awarded fourteen days detention and fined to scale for being drunk in camp at Eerste Fabrieken, Pretoria on 22nd January 1901. He was posted to India on 13th December 1902 and transferred to the 2nd Battalion at Allahabad, India the following day, where he served from 13th January until 29th December 1903, including in Burma 30th November–2nd December. He was appointed lance corporal on 24th January 1903, was awarded Good Conduct Pay from

Allan Glen's School opened in 1853. Allan Glen had been a successful Glasgow tradesman and businessman. The school's emphasis on science and engineering led to it becoming Glasgow's High School of Science. In 1887 it merged with Anderson's College to form the Glasgow and West of Scotland Technical College. In 1912 it became the Royal Technical College, run by Glasgow Corporation. Various moves took place within the city and in 1973 Alan Glen's merged with the City Public School to form a co-educational comprehensive, Allan Glen's Secondary School. It closed in 1989 and the buildings on Cathedral Street became an annex to the nearby Glasgow Central School of Commerce. These buildings were demolished in 2013 to allow construction of new buildings for the City of Glasgow College. Amongst Allan Glen's famous alumni are the actor and writer Sir Dirk Bogarde and the architect, artist and designer, Charles Rennie Mackintosh.

6th March and attained 3rd Class Education on 13th March. He was in hospital with a lymph gland infection 30th March–27th June and was posted to Aden 3rd December 1903–25th December 1906. From 1st February 1904 he was paid as a lance corporal and qualified for promotion to corporal on 11th March.

John extended his service to complete eight years and was awarded Service Pay Class 1 at 6d per day on 1st April 1904. He received a second award of Good Conduct Pay and Service Pay Class 1 at 7d per day from 6th February 1905. He was in hospital under observation 11th–15th February and with syphilis 3rd May–5th June. Having been promoted corporal on 16th November, he qualified for promotion to sergeant on 26th June 1906 and extended his service to complete twelve years on 21st September. On 26th December he returned to Britain and served at various places, including Barry Camp, Glasgow, Berwick on Tweed and Palace Barracks at Holywood, the Curragh and Dublin in Ireland. He was in hospital with

Allahabad in India where John Skinner was based in 1903.

John Skinner served in Aden 1904–06.

gonorrhoea 30th September–18th October 1907. His behaviour, always affected by heavy drinking, deteriorated further. He was severely reprimanded for being drunk in Gairbraid Street, Glasgow on 19th October 1907. From 4th to 9th June 1908 he was in hospital with an inflamed buttock. Having qualified in Mounted Infantry duties on 30th September 1909, he was posted to the Depot on 11th October. He was severely reprimanded for being absent from church parade at Berwick on 26th December and was reduced to lance corporal for improper conduct on parade on 12th January 1910 at Berwick.

John was posted to the 2nd Battalion on 25th January 1910 and was arrested for drunkenness on the line of march at Glasgow on 27th January, for which he was tried by a regimental court martial on 1st February and reduced to the ranks. He was back on the promotion ladder soon after, being appointed unpaid lance corporal on 13th July and paid on 1st August, but it did not last long as he was reduced to private for being drunk on parade at Holywood on 10th October. He was fined 9/6 and confined to barracks for eight days for returning to barracks at Holywood drunk and urinating on the open road on 7th April 1911. Despite his numerous disciplinary infringements, John must have been well thought of as he was allowed to extend his service to complete twenty-one years on 15th September 1911. Two days later he was fined 7/6 for being drunk in camp at the Curragh. On 5th October he was fined 10/6 and confined to barracks for fourteen days for being drunk on the Holywood Road while employed as company storeman and disobeying regimental orders by cycling in service dress. On a more positive note he qualified in chiropody on 10th November.

On 26th January 1912 he was fined 7/6 and confined to barracks for seven days for being drunk and improper conduct by galloping a horse on the Holywood–Belfast road. On 26th August he was fined 5/– and confined to barracks for fourteen days for being drunk and in the company of women in a barrack room at Holywood. He was in hospital at Holywood 14th-19th October 1912 and in Dublin 14th-23rd December 1913. On 28th December 1913 he was confined to barracks for eight days for breaking out of barracks after breakfast roll call, being improperly dressed in Park Gate Street in Dublin, stating a falsehood to the Military Foot Police and being absent from a medical inspection. He was again confined to barracks for seven days at Dublin for neglect of duty when company storeman by allowing the company bedding book to be damaged and (unreadable) to be broken while in his charge on 2nd January 1914.

John went to France with the Battalion on 10th August 1914 and was promoted acting corporal and acting lance sergeant on 4th October. **Awarded the DCM for his actions at Cuinchy on 12th October 1914 – after a heavy engagement he made a reconnaissance in a wood with a patrol under very difficult circumstances, LG 1st April 1915.** He received a gunshot wound to a finger of the left hand on 14th October and was admitted to 13th Field Ambulance before being evacuated to England on 18th October, where he was treated at Edinburgh Royal Infirmary.

From 18th December he served in 3rd (Reserve) Battalion at Portland while recovering. He was in arrest from 26th December awaiting trial for drunkenness. A district court martial on 4th January 1915 reduced him to the ranks. He returned to France as acting corporal, rejoined 2nd Battalion on 16th March and was promoted corporal on 15th April. He was wounded again on 23rd April (gunshot to left foot) on Mauser Ridge, near Ypres and was admitted to 32nd Stationary Hospital, Wimereux (Australian Voluntary Hospital) on 25th April. He was evacuated to England on 28th April and treated at St John's Hospital, Sevenoaks. While there he was on the strength of the Depot until posted to the 3rd Battalion on 28th May. The DCM was presented by the King at Glasgow Green on 18th May. During that investiture, Drummer William Kenny and Private Ross Tollerton received their VCs.

John was appointed acting sergeant on 30th June and went with a draft to the 1st Battalion at Gallipoli, serving there from 3rd July. He was promoted sergeant on 28th July and two days later received a gunshot wound to the right shoulder. He was evacuated to Nasrieh Primary School Hospital, Cairo on 4th August and was on the strength of the Base Depot at Alexandria from 9th October until admitted to the Convalescence Depot at Mustapha on 16th February 1916.

John returned to France with 1st Battalion on 9th March and received a gunshot wound to the right hip/buttock on 1st July on the Somme. He was admitted to

6th Stationary Hospital on 3rd July, evacuated to Britain on 6th July 1916 and taken on strength of the Depot next day. Having been treated at Mile End Military Hospital, London, he was granted leave on 9th August until posted to the 3rd Battalion on 19th August. John embarked at Folkestone and disembarked at Boulogne on 4th October. He joined 21st Infantry Base Depot at Étaples on 5th October and rejoined the Battalion on 17th October. On 28th October he was admitted to 88th Field Ambulance with a foreign body in his eye and to No.38 Casualty Clearing Station next day. An old gunshot wound caused him problems and he was admitted to 18th General Hospital, Camiers on 31st October and No.6 Convalescence Depot from 15th November. He joined 21st Infantry Base Depot again on 25th November and rejoined the Battalion on 5th December.

John Skinner receives his VC from the King outside Buckingham Palace on 26th September 1917.

On 2nd June 1917 John was appointed acting CSM of A Company. **Awarded the VC for his actions at Wijdendrift, Belgium on 16th August 1917, LG 14th September 1917. Awarded the French Croix de Guerre for the same action, LG 17th December 1917.** He was wounded during the VC action and

John Skinner and his wife Annie on their wedding day, 29th September 1917.

treated at 89th and 88th Field Ambulances from 19th August until returning to duty on 23rd August. He was promoted warrant officer class II on 17th September and was granted leave to Britain 25th September–5th October to recover and to receive the VC from the King outside Buckingham Palace on 26th September 1917.

John Skinner married Annie Elizabeth Young née Lee (16th June 1878–4th April 1938) on 29th September 1917 at 2 St John's Road, Glasgow. There were no children. Annie was born at 80 Hutcheson Square, Glasgow, Lanarkshire and was a clerk living at 173 St Andrew's Road, Pollokshields, Glasgow when she married. She was the sister of his brother Walter's first wife. Annie died at 50 St Andrew's Drive, Glasgow, usual residence Rutherglen, Lanarkshire.

Annie's father, James Lee (1845–1902), was a shipbroker's clerk and later a ship's broker. He married Margaret Lyall née Miller (1849–1901), a dressmaker, in 1876. From 1881 to 1901 they were living at 173 St Andrew's Road, Pollockshields, Glasgow. In addition to Annie they had six other children:

- Margaret Lyall Lee (1876–1937) married Thomas King (born c.1873), an engineer's clerk, in 1914.
- Olivia Lee (1880–1937) married Walter Cumming Skinner (VC's brother), a brigade fireman, in 1905. They were living at 26 Warwick Street, Glasgow in 1911. They had three children – Margaret Mary Skinner 1907, Walter James Skinner 1909 and Ernest Lee Skinner 1912. Walter married Pauline Clark or Cuthbert in 1938.
- Alexander Thomas McKenzie Lee (born 1882) was a factor's clerk in 1901.
- John James Richardson Lee (1884–1959) was a mercantile clerk with Lloyd's in 1901. He married Elaine Maggie Brown Hood (born c.1883 and predeceased her husband), a provision saleswoman, in 1911. He was later a tobacco traveller.
- Stewart Young Lee (1886–1942) was a 'Fire Clay M Fos Clerk' in 1901. He married Elizabeth Barbara Wrench (born c.1885 and predeceased her husband), an electrician's clerk, in 1922. By then Stewart was a West African trader and later an engineer's costing clerk.
- Thomas Miller Lee (1888–1942) was a mercantile clerk at the Ministry of Supply. He married Mary Steele (born c.1896) in 1916.

At the end of his investiture leave, John used a return leave warrant to get back to his unit in France although he was on the strength of 3rd (Reserve) Battalion at Duddingston Park, near Edinburgh. He was stopped at Folkestone before reaching the boat and sent to Bevan Military Hospital, Folkestone on 8th October. He was issued a warrant to return to Edinburgh, but proceeded to France instead, rejoining the Battalion on 27th October. The divisional commander saw him on a manoeuvre and expressed his pleasure at having him back, but enquired how he managed it. John replied, *Me for Edinburgh Sir! That was a bit too thick*, and he explained that he had a bet with CQMS Ross, who also had eight wounds, who would be the first to get nine. The General was satisfied. John attended a course at III Corps School from 5th November 1917 to 31st January 1918 and was granted leave to Britain 5th-19th February 1918.

John Skinner won the bet with CQMS Ross. On 16th March 1918 he crawled out into no man's land to recover personal belongings and identification from three bodies, *Their folks will like to hear they got a decent burial.* The following day he went out into no man's land to recover a wounded man who had been lost during a night patrol and was heard calling out in pain. John was shot by a sniper and died instantly. A stretcher-bearer who

The Bevan Military Hospital opened soon after war was declared in an empty convalescent home at Sandgate, Folkestone. It became an annex of Shorncliffe Military Hospital. More than 12,100 patients passed through the hospital during the war and 1,552 operations were performed there.

went out after him was also shot and killed. Others went out later, including CSM Stevenson, to recover John's body. Rather than bury him nearby, the body was carried back to the rest area where he was buried in what is now Vlamertinghe New British Cemetery (XVI H 15).

Accounts disagree on the number of VCs serving in 29th Division who attended the funeral; some state six, while another says nine. At least one of those named, William Grimbaldeston, appears not to have been in Belgium at the time. Another, James Ockendon, was discharged from the Army unfit for further service on 30th April 1918, so it seems unlikely that he could have been injured after 17th March and processed through the medical and discharge systems by the end of the following month, but not impossible. However, Brigadier-General Bernard Freyberg, Captain Robert Gee,

John Skinner's grave in Vlamertinghe New British Cemetery, Belgium.

Sergeants Joseph Lister, John Molyneux, Edward Mott and Charles Spackman and Corporal William Cosgrove were serving with 29th Division at the time and could have attended the funeral. Major Richard Willis may also have been there, but around that time he was posted to the Reinforcement Depot and Officers' Training School at Allouange, Beuvry, France, about forty kilometres away. The funeral took place in pouring rain. The firing party, commanded by CSM Stevenson, fired three volleys over the grave, while the pipes played *Flowers of the Forest*. The ceremony ended with the Last Post.

On 5th September 1918 his personal effects were returned to his wife – photos, cap badge, medal ribbons, a charm, numerals, gold ring, watch and strap, pocket book and case. His wife was awarded a pension of £-/18/9 from 7th October 1918.

The Department for Communities and Local Government decided to provide a commemorative paving stone at the birthplace of every Great War Victoria Cross recipient in the United Kingdom. A commemorative stone for John was dedicated at The Doulton Fountain, People's Palace & Winter Garden, Glasgow Green on 16th August 2017 to mark the centenary of his award.

In addition to the VC and DCM he was awarded the Queen's South Africa Medal 1899–1902 (clasps Cape Colony, Orange Free State & Transvaal), King's South Africa Medal 1901–02 (clasps South Africa 1901 & South Africa 1902), 1914 Star with 'Mons' clasp, British War Medal 1914–20, Victory Medal 1914–19 and French Croix de Guerre 1914–18 with Bronze Palm. His medals were presented to the Regiment by his step-mother and are held by the King's Own Scottish Borderers Museum, Berwick upon Tweed, Northumberland.

15067 PRIVATE THOMAS WHITHAM
1st Battalion, Coldstream Guards

Thomas Whitham was born at Worsthorne, Burnley, Lancashire on 11th May 1888. His father, John Whitham (c.1854–91), was born at Laurencekirk, Kincardineshire. His mother, Catherine née Courtney (c.1853–1905), was born at Glasgow, Lanarkshire. John and Catherine married on 6th November 1874. At the time he was a journeyman mason, living at 4 Buchanan Lane, Calton, Glasgow and she was a cotton mill worker living at Westercraigs, Dennistoun, Glasgow. By 1881 they were living at Embsay cum Eastby, Yorkshire before moving to 18 Gorple Road, Worsthorne, near Burnley, Lancashire. By 1901 Catherine was living at 4 Acre Street, Briercliffe, Burnley. She died on 28th December 1905 at 32 Granville Street, Briercliffe, leaving £148/8/- to her son William. Thomas had seven siblings:

- Jessie Whitham (1875–1934), born at 29 Walkinshaw Street, Glasgow, married Nicholas Pomfret (1878–1935) at St James's Church, Briercliffe, Burnley in 1905. He was a twister (cotton operative) and they were living at 31 Townley Street, Briercliffe in 1911 and at 29 Borrowdale Road, Moreton, Cheshire in 1935. They had a daughter, Ethel Pomfret (1909–24).
- William Courtney Whitham (1876–1930), born at 89 Walkinshaw Street, Glasgow, married Emma Naylor (1877–1967) in 1900 at Burnley. He was a stonemason and they were living at 7 Brockenhurst Street, Burnley in 1911 and at 14 Celia Street in 1930. William served as a sapper in the Royal Engineers during the war. They had two children – John Whitham 1901 and Harry Whitham 1905. Emma married Edward Riley in 1933.

Worsthorne village.

Burnley around the time Thomas lived there.

- John Whitham (1878–1918), a stonemason, was born at 49 Broad Street, Mile End, Camlachie, Glasgow. He married Mary Sutcliffe, a weaver, in 1903 and they were living at 31 Howsie Street, Burnley in 1911. They had twins – Elise and Eveline Whitham in 1907. He served as 19245 Private John Whitham, 3rd Coldstream Guards and died on 17th January 1918 (Level Crossing Cemetery, Fampoux, France – II B 38). Mary lived at 292 Barden Lane, Burnley.

John Whitham's grave in Level Crossing Cemetery, Fampoux, France.

- Henry 'Harry' Whitham (1881–1957), born at Embsay cum Eastby, Yorkshire, was a stonemason. He married Elizabeth Lowcock née Conroy (born 1881) in 1915 and they lived at 136 Berkeley Street, Nelson, Lancashire. Elizabeth had been married previously to Thomas Percival Lowcock (1882–1914) in 1903. They had a daughter, Margaret Annie Lowcock (born 1907), who married Benjamin Leaver (1904–63) in 1928 and had four children – Joan Leaver 1935, Kathleen Leaver 1938, Anne Leaver 1942 and Stuart W Leaver 1947. Harry attested on 9th November 1915 at Preston, Lancashire (160942) and transferred to the Reserve. He was described as 5′ 7½″ tall and weighed 129 lbs. He was called up to No.2 Depot RFA at Preston on 23rd September 1916 and was allocated to 8th Reserve Battery RFA next day, also at Preston. He was posted to 45th Reserve Battery RFA, 3rd Reserve Brigade at Deepcut, Surrey on 28th September. On 20th December he was admitted to hospital at Swanage, Dorset for nine days with bronchitis, probably while at the Central Signalling Depot RFA there. On 14th February 1917 he was confined to barracks for two days for overstaying his leave by a day and went to France on 29th March. He was posted to HQ/310th Brigade RFA from the Base Depot on 27th April and to B Battery, 310th Brigade RFA on 27th October. Harry was gassed on 19th April 1918 and admitted to 6th General Hospital, Rouen. Having been evacuated to Britain, he was treated at a section of 3rd Western General Hospital at Neath, Glamorgan and the Red Cross Hospital, Carmarthen (St John Auxiliary Hospital) until being sent on leave on 8th June. He was at the Royal Artillery Command Depot, Ripon South 18th June–29th September 1918 and was on the strength of 4th Reserve Brigade RFA at Woolwich from 19th June. On 3rd October he was posted to 5C Reserve Brigade RFA, Charlton Park, Woolwich and returned to France on 18th November, where he was posted to D Battery, 186th Brigade RFA from the Base Depot on 1st December. Harry embarked at Boulogne on 3rd July 1919 for Prees Heath Dispersal Camp, near Whitchurch, Shropshire and was demobilised to the Class Z Reserve on 14th July.
- Sarah Ann Whitham, born at Embsay cum Eastby, Yorkshire in 1883.

- Margaret Whitham, born at Burnley, Lancashire in 1886, was a cotton weaver in 1911, living as head of household at 5 Travis Street, Burnley with her brother Harry and sister Jane. Margaret had a daughter, Edna Whitham, in 1907.
- Jane 'Jennie' Whitham (1891–1918) was a cotton weaver in 1911. She married Albert Wood (1890–1977) in 1914 at Angle Street Baptist Church, Burnley and they had a son, John Robert Wood (1916–84). John married Edna Hoyle (1920–78) in 1944 and they had three children – John P Wood 1945 and twins Janet and Philip Wood 1948. Albert married Ethel Schofield in 1920 at Burnley.

Thomas' paternal grandfather, James Whitham (born c.1818), a journeyman mason, born at Ovenden, Yorkshire, married Jessie née McPherson (born c.1819 at Inverness, Scotland). They were living at 12 Rye Hut, Crosby Garrett, Westmorland in 1871.

Crosby Garrett, Westmorland (now part of Cumbria), where Thomas' paternal grandparents were living in 1871.

His maternal grandfather, Henry Courtney (c.1819–73), a canvas weaver, was born in Co Armagh, Ireland. He married Margaret née Chittick (also seen as Chitock/Chattock and other spellings) (c.1828–72) in 1847. She was born in Co Fermanagh, Ireland. They were living at Custom House Lane, Kilpatricks Land, Port Glasgow, Renfrewshire in 1861, at 5 Bowling Green Terrace, Glasgow in 1871 and later at 24 Market Street, Glasgow. In addition to Catherine they had six other children – William Courtney c.1850, Margaret Courtney c.1852, Jane Courtney c.1854, Henry Courtney 1855, Amanda Courtney 1858 and Thomas Courtney c.1864.

Thomas probably began his education at St John's School, Worsthorne as he visited it for tea after a reception in the village following the award of the VC. He also attended Briercliffe County School, Burnley 27th November 1900–16th May 1901 and left to work in a mill. He was employed as a bricklayer and a labourer. On 1st May 1909, Thomas Whitham married Fedora née Bennett (c.1887–1955), a worsted spinner, and they were living at 98 Robinson Street, Burnley in 1911. She is understood to have been born c.1887/88 at Burslem, Staffordshire, but no record has been found. In 1891 she appears as Fedora Dayton aged three, the niece of Stephen and Hannah Bennett, at 49 High Street, Worsborough, Barnsley. Stephen Bennett was Fedora's uncle. However, in the 1939 Register her birth was recorded as 22nd August 1889 and this agrees with her age of sixty-six when she died in September 1955. At the outbreak of war, Thomas and Fedora were living at 111 Barden Lane, Burnley. They had seven children:

- Walter Whitham (1909–16).
- William Henry Whitham (5th May 1911–October 1994) was a civil servant, working for the Ministry of Works. He married Eileen Howarth in 1937 and they

had a daughter, Marilyn Whitham, in 1941. William and Eileen divorced and she married Horace Cockshaw (1916–79) in 1955. William married Marguerite 'Peggy' Stanworth (born 1923) in 1950 and they had two children – Michelle Whitham 1951 and Stuart T Whitham 1952.

- Thomas Whitham, born on 19th July 1912. He married Lilian M Mackenzie (born 1917) in 1936 and they had two children – Maureen L Whitham 1938 and Stephanie I Whitham 1941.
- Jennie Whitham (1914–2004) married Arnold Wade (born 1912) in 1936 and they lived at 48 St John's Road, Burnley. They had twins, Jacqueline and Patricia Wade, in 1938. Jennie married Charles Frederick R Goode (born 1901) in 1952. Charles was previously married to Esther W Potts (born 1915) in 1936. Esther also remarried, to Baden C Compson in 1951.
- Harry Whitham (12th December 1918–1995) was a twin with Jack. He was a heavy textile engineer in 1939 and married Joan Parnell (1921–2012) in 1941.
- Jack Whitham (1918–92) married Ethel Bullen (1920–94) in 1949. Ethel married Arthur Webster in 1940 and while they were separated awaiting divorce she lived with Jack and they had Jack Whitham junior in 1946. They also had Stuart Whitham in 1952. Jack junior played professional football for Sheffield Wednesday, Liverpool, Cardiff and Reading in 111 league games between 1967 and 1976,

scoring forty goals. He made one appearance for England Under-23 against Wales in 1968. He returned to non-League football in 1976 playing for a number of clubs and also managed one of them. Jack ran the 'Wadsley Jack' public house in Sheffield for ten years and then managed the South Yorkshire Police Social Club at Wadsley Bridge. He was a part-time scout for Sunderland 1993–2007 and chief scout for Luton Town. He also joined Wolverhampton Wanderers for a short spell and was appointed head of player recruitment at Sheffield United until June 2010 and was then European Scout for Wolverhampton Wanderers. Jack married Josephine 'Jose' M Wilson in June 1970 and they had two children – Karen Marie Whitham 1972 and Claire Louise Whitham

Thomas' grandson, Jack Whitham, made his debut for Sheffield Wednesday on 6th May 1967, ironically against Burnley, and scored twice in a 7–0 victory. He suffered a number of injury problems, but still scored thirty-one goals in sixty-two appearances, including a hat trick against Manchester United in a 5–4 win on 31st August 1968. He signed for Liverpool in April 1970, but injuries resulted in him playing only fifteen games in four years. Later he played for Cardiff City and Reading before returning to non-League football in 1976. He then ran a pub and a police social club in Sheffield, became a scout for various league clubs and is well known in music clubs in South Yorkshire. Jack is seen here on the right scoring his first goal for Liverpool playing against West Ham on 12th December 1970. Inset – Jack while playing for Sheffield Wednesday.

1975. Jack also became a well-known singer/songwriter in the music clubs in South Yorkshire.
*   Fedora (Dorrie or Dora) Astrap Whitham (3rd October 1920–1998) married Joseph Parkinson (1914–90) in 1942 at Burnley.

Fedora's father, William Henry Bennett (1862–1940), a railway drayman, was born at Camborne, Cornwall. He married Henrietta Rose A née Astrap (1870–1907), but no record has been found. They lived at 48 Ingleby Street, Bradford, Yorkshire and by 1911 had moved to 18 Oxford Street, Brierfield, Lancashire. In addition to Fedora they had eight other children including:

*   Lilly Bennett (born 1891) was a cotton weaver in 1911.
*   Walter Bennett (1894–c.1964) was a cotton weaver in 1911. He emigrated to British Columbia, Canada on 31st March 1921.
*   Elsie Bennett (1895–1967) was a cotton weaver in 1911.
*   Florence Bennett (born 1897) was a cotton weaver in 1911. She married Albert Mayall in 1917 and they had three children – Samuel Mayall 1918, Walter Mayall 1921 and Florrie Mayall 1926.
*   Ethel Bennett (born 1899).
*   Hilda Bennett (born 1902).

Thomas enlisted on 25th January 1915 and served with 5th Battalion. He was absent 1st–7th April 1915 and again on 8th July, for which he was awarded fourteen days Field Punishment No.2. He went to France on 26th October 1915 to join 1st

Thomas and Fedora outside their home with William, Thomas and Jennie.

Thomas shows his VC to Fedora on the left. The lady on the right is understood to be one of his sisters.

Battalion. He was sentenced to fifty-six days Field Punishment No.1 by a field general court martial on 3rd July 1917 for disobeying a lawful command on 26th June. He was still under sentence when he won his VC.

Awarded the VC for his actions north of Pilkem, Belgium on 31st July 1917, LG 6th September 1917. He left France on 6th October and the VC was presented by the King at Buckingham Palace on 20th October. He was also presented with a gold watch and chain and other gifts by the people of Burnley. Thomas served with 5th (Reserve) Battalion at Windsor, England from 29th October 1917 until the end of the war. Appointed unpaid lance corporal on 30th September 1918 and was discharged on 7th March 1919.

Thomas returned to work in the Burnley area as a bricklayer. He was out of work for some time and wrote to Burnley Corporation seeking manual work, but the reply was curt and dismissive. He pawned his VC group in 1921, together with various gifts he had received from his hometown. He found work as a bricklayer on a housing estate at Egremont and his family joined him there until the project ended in 1924. They returned to Burnley and he travelled around on his bicycle

A hero returns to Worsthorne.

Oldham Royal Infirmary where Thomas Whitham died on 24th October 1924.

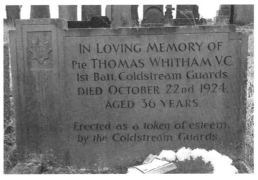

Thomas Whitham's grave in Inghamite Burial Ground, Wheatley Lane, Nelson, Lancashire.

looking for a job. While riding in the Windermere area of Cumberland in May 1924 he suffered severe head trauma and memory loss after crashing into a wall. He was advised by a doctor to rest, but continued and disappeared, ending up in lodgings in Liverpool. He found work in Gatley near Manchester and wrote to his wife before disappearing again, ending up in lodgings at Hollins Green, Middleton,

Lancashire. Fedora had to move in with her father, with two of the children suffering from pneumonia at that time.

Thomas Whitham died of peritonitis and a perforated gastric ulcer at Oldham Royal Infirmary, Lancashire on 24th October 1924. He is buried in Inghamite Burial Ground, Wheatley Lane, Nelson, Lancashire. On 16th March 1952 a headstone was dedicated by members of the Regiment and the North East Lancashire Branch of the Coldstream Guards Association. The headstone and surround were restored by the Regiment in April 1988. Thomas is also commemorated in a number of other places:

No. 15067 PRIVATE THOMAS WHITHAM. VC.
1st Battalion.

31st JULY 1917. Near Boesinghe (Ypres) he, on his own initiative, worked his way from shell-hole to shell-hole through our own barrage, rushed an enemy machine gun which enfiladed the Battalion, and captured it, together with its officer and two men. He thus saved many lives, and enabled our whole line to advance.

The memorial plaque at Inghamite Burial Ground.

- Blue Plaque (Burnley Civic Trust) at Worsthorne, Lancashire.
- Plaque at Inghamite Burial Ground, Wheatley Lane, Wheatley Carr, near Nelson, Lancashire.

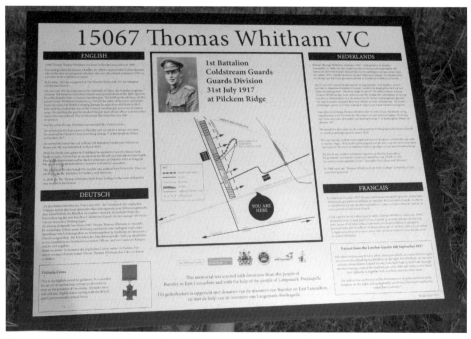

The memorial plaque on the former Ypres–Langemarck railway, near Langemarck, Belgium dedicated on 12th September 2015, close to where Thomas Whitham won his VC.

- Plaque on the former Ypres-Langemarck railway, near Langemarck, Belgium dedicated on 12th September 2015.
- A painting by Ivan Cooke at Towneley Hall, Burnley.
- Thomas Whitham Sixth Form, Barden Lane, Burnley was named on 1st September 2008. It had originally formed in September 2006 as Burnley Schools Sixth Form when the sixth forms of Habergham High School and St Theodore's Roman Catholic High School amalgamated at the site of the former Barden High School in Heald Road.

Thomas Whitham Sixth Form.

Towneley Hall Art Gallery & Museum, Burnley.

In addition to the VC he was awarded the 1914–15 Star, British War Medal 1914–20 and Victory Medal 1914–19. In 1931 Burnley Borough Council learned that his VC and gold watch, held in Fitzpatrick's Pawnbroker Shop on Abel Street for a number of years, were to be offered for sale at public auction. The Council purchased the items for £50 and they were offered to the family provided they paid the £50, agreed to keep the articles within the family and only disposed of the VC by presenting it to the Coldstream Guards. Thomas's son, William, did not receive the offer until sometime later as he had been travelling with his work. By the time he responded, control of Burnley Council had changed and the offer was withdrawn. Towneley Hall Art Gallery & Museum, Burnley holds the VC and Victory Medal and the gold watch. The other medals are assumed to have been lost. William spent forty years trying to have the medals moved to the Guards Museum. The issue was even raised in Parliament in 1994 by Nick Hawkins MP (Blackpool South), but the medals remain in Burnley.

Thomas Whitham's VC and gold watch (Ross Parry).

8387 PRIVATE THOMAS WOODCOCK
2nd Battalion, The Irish Guards

Thomas Woodcock was born at 15 Belvoir Street, Wigan, Lancashire on 19th March 1888. His father, Henry Woodcock (1854–1918), was a colliery worker at Arley Mine. He married Isabella 'Bella' née Twigley (c.1854–1915) on 24th November 1877 at St Patrick's Church, Wigan. She was born in Lanarkshire, Scotland. They were living at 6 Albion Court in 1881, 15 Belvoir Street in 1891, 17 Holland Street in 1901 and 1911 and at 8 Line Street in 1918 (all in Wigan). Henry was suffering from lumbago and was unable to work. He went to bed as normal on 4th July 1918, but was later found to be missing. A jacket and cap were found on the nearby canal lock-gate arm so the canal was dragged and Henry's body was discovered. At the inquest one of his daughters stated that Henry had been troubled by the death of his son Thomas, but seemed to be getting over it. A verdict of 'found drowned' was returned by the Coroner. Thomas had ten siblings:

St Patrick's Church, Hardybutts, Scholes, Wigan was founded in 1848.

• Margaret Woodcock (born 1878) was a cotton ring spinner.
• Isabella Woodcock (born 1883) was also a cotton ring spinner. She is understood to have married William McGuirk (1881–1910) in 1901 and Thomas Green in 1914.
• Ellen Woodcock (born 1885) was a cotton ring spinner.
• Jane Woodcock (born 1886) was a cotton scavenger in 1911.
• Agnes Woodcock (born 1890) was a cotton spinner in 1911.
• Henry Woodcock (born 1893) worked at John Scowcroft Colliery, Hindley Green, Lancashire. He married Mary Bennett in 1912.
• Joseph Woodcock (1896–1980) also worked at John Scowcroft Colliery and in 1911 he was an ostler underground. He married Margaret Ann Simm in 1924 and they had three children – Joseph Woodcock (born and died 1924), Joseph Woodcock 1932 and Margaret Woodcock 1937.
• Alice Woodcock (1899–1926).
• Edward Woodcock (born and died 1900).
• John Woodcock (born 1903) married Edith Prior (born 1902) in 1923. They had three children – Gladys Woodcock 1924, John H Woodcock 1937 and William Woodcock 1938.

Thomas' paternal grandfather, Joseph Woodcock (c.1809–80) was a farm labourer. He married Margaret née Walker (c.1813–63) in 1845. She was married previously to John Molineux in 1837. They lived at Warrington Road, Ince, Wigan. In 1851 Margaret was living at School Common, Wigan with her two sons. In addition to Henry, Joseph and Margaret had two other sons:

- George Woodcock (1846–1934) was a collier. He married Margaret Grimshaw (born c.1845) in 1867. They were living at Hall Green, Upholland in 1871, at 48 High Street, Skelmersdale in 1881 and at 22 Conway Street, Skelmersdale in 1901. They had six children – Mary Woodcock 1863, William Woodcock 1869, Ellen Woodcock 1872, Margaret Woodcock 1875, Jane Woodcock 1880 and Peter Woodcock 1887.
- Thomas Woodcock (1850–54).

Joseph married Martha Parkinson (1840–1913) in 1865. Martha had a son, Henry Parkinson, in 1857. Joseph and Martha had a son, Thomas Woodcock, in 1868 and they were living at Vaughan's House, Scholes, Wigan in 1871, by when he was a furnace man in a coalmine. Martha was lodging as a charwoman at 25 Birkett Bank, Wigan in 1881 and at the Wigan District Union Workhouse in 1901. Thomas' maternal grandparents were John and Jane Twigley.

Thomas was educated at St Patrick's Roman Catholic School, Wigan and was employed as a miner at John Scowcroft Colliery, Hindley Green. Thomas married Mary 'Polly' née Mitchell (1883–1945) at St Patrick's Church, Wigan on 31st July 1909 and they lived at 2 Teck Street, Wigan. They had two children:

- Nora Woodcock (10th April 1911–11th July 1918).
- Mary Woodcock (10th December 1912–8th January 1938) married Robert Collier (born 1910) in 1933. They had two children – Veronica Collier 1934 and Thomas Collier (born and died 1937). Mary died at 6 Dean Street, Wigan, probably due to complications with the birth of her son Thomas.

Thomas' father-in-law, John Mitchell (born c.1861) was a coal miner. He married Honora 'Nora' née McCarthy (c.1854–94) in 1882. They were living at 2 Leaches Yard in 1891 and at 2 Teck Street in 1911. In addition to Mary they had four other children:

- Patrick McCarthy (later Mitchell) (born 1880) was a coal miner in 1911.
- John Mitchell (born 1883), a twin with Mary, was a coal miner in 1911.
- Maria Mitchell (born 1885).
- Thomas Mitchell (born 1892) was a coal miner in 1911. He married Mary Hart (born 1895) in 1916. By 1939 Thomas was a general corporation labourer, living with his wife and children at 2 Teck Street, Wigan. Thomas and Mary had eight

children – Charles Mitchell 1919, Thomas Mitchell 1921, Nora Mitchell 1922, James Mitchell 1924, Kathleen Mitchell 1926, John Mitchell 1927, Charles Mitchell 1930 and Donald Mitchell 1934.

Thomas Woodcock enlisted on 26th May 1915. He was described as 5′ 8″ tall, with a 38″ chest and scars on his second left finger, lower right rib and right shoulder blade. He joined the Depot on 27th May. He embarked at Southampton and landed in France on 22nd December. Having served in 7th (Guards) Entrenching Battalion from 27th December, he joined 2nd Irish Guards on 19th May 1916. He was attached to 174th Tunnelling Company 13th–19th August and was admitted to 9th Field Ambulance with diarrhoea on 21st October. It developed into dysentery and he was moved to No.39 Casualty Clearing Station on 24th October and 4th General Hospital at Camiers on the 27th. He recovered at 6th Convalescence Depot from 11th November and the Guards Division Base Depot from the 16th before returning to the Battalion on 28th November. Thomas attended a Lewis gun course 5–12th February 1917.

Thomas Woodcock's grave in Douchy-les-Ayette British Cemetery.

Awarded the VC for his actions north of the Broenbeek, Belgium on 12th/13th September 1917, LG 17th October 1917. Appointed unpaid lance corporal 6th November 1917. He return to Britain on 27th February 1918. On his homecoming on 3rd March he was presented with a marble clock, an illuminated address and more than £200 in cash. The VC was presented by the King at Buckingham Palace on 9th March 1918. A reception was arranged by the parishioners of St Patrick's Church on the day he left to return to France. During it he said, *I am going back tonight to do a little bit more for the King.*

Thomas returned to France on 17th March 1918 and was killed in action at Bullecourt on 27th March. He is buried in Douchy-les-Ayette British Cemetery (IV F 3). His wife received a parcel of his personal effects, including a bloodstained newspaper and a photograph of him surrounded by his family and civic dignitaries. The photograph was less than a month old. Mary received a widow's pension of £1/5/5 per week for herself and two children from 28th October 1918. In addition to her husband, she also lost her daughter Nora on 11th July 1918. Thomas is commemorated in a number of other places:

The Wigan war memorial outside the parish church of All Saints.

Field Marshal Earl Alexander of Tunis (1891–1969), Colonel of the Irish Guards, received Thomas Woodcock's medals on behalf of the Regiment. He served throughout both world wars with distinction. In the Second World War he oversaw the final stages of the Dunkirk evacuation and held senior commands in Burma, North Africa, Sicily and Italy, culminating in being appointed Supreme Allied Commander Mediterranean and receiving the German surrender in Italy on 29th April 1945. In 1946 he was appointed Governor General of Canada and held the post until 1952, when Churchill made him Minister of Defence. He retired in 1954.

- Woodcock House, Millgate, Wigan.
- St Patrick's Church, Wigan.
- St Patrick's School, Wigan.
- Wigan war memorial outside the parish church of All Saints in Wallgate.
- His VC action featured in Issues 682 and 1229 of the Victor Comic on 16th March 1974 and 8th September 1984, entitled *Open Fire!* and *A True Story of Men at War* respectively.

He was represented at the 1920 VC Garden Party at Buckingham Palace by his son John Henry Woodcock. In addition to the VC he was awarded the 1914–15 Star, British War Medal 1914–20 and Victory Medal 1914–19. On 5th March 1964 his daughter-in-law, Mrs M Hargreaves, loaned the VC to the Irish Guards. The medals were received by the Colonel of the Irish Guards, Field Marshal Earl Alexander of Tunis. The VC is held by the Irish Guards and is in the Guards Museum, Wellington Barracks, Birdcage Walk, London.

Sources

The following institutions, individuals and publications were consulted:

Regimental Museums

British Columbia Regiment Museum, Vancouver, Canada; King's Own Royal Lancaster Regiment Museum, Lancaster; Light Infantry Office (Yorkshire), Pontefract; RHQ The Royal Scots, Edinburgh; Royal Engineers Museum, Chatham; The Royal Gloucestershire, Berkshire and Wiltshire Regiment Museum, Salisbury; Museum of Lincolnshire Life, Lincoln; Museum of the Manchesters, Ashton-under-Lyne; RHQ Worcestershire and Sherwood Foresters, Beeston; Museum of the Northamptonshire Regiment, Northampton; Gordon Highlanders Museum, Aberdeen; RHQ King's Own Scottish Borderers, Berwick-upon-Tweed; Museum of the Royal Leicestershire Regiment, Leicester; Leicestershire County Record Office; The Worcestershire Regiment Museum Trust, Worcester; Regimental Headquarters Coldstream Guards, London; South Wales Borderers and Monmouthshire Regimental Museum, Brecon; RHQ Prince of Wales's Own Regiment of Yorkshire, York; Headquarters The Royal Anglian Regiment (Lincolnshire), Lincoln; Scottish United Services Museum, Edinburgh; Canadian War Museum, Ottawa; Lancashire HQ Royal Regiment of Fusiliers.

Individuals

Doug and Richard Arman, DF Burman, Richard Burman, Dr Michael Carey, J Carmichael, Edward Cooper, Maj John Cotterill, Frank Coyne, David Craven, Mark Davies, Michael Day, Etta Dunlop, MJ Egerton, Christopher Evans, Jim Fallon, Alex J Forsyth, Mike Gomersall, Tony Grant, Hazel Greaves, William & Mary Grimbaldeston, Jean Henderson, Adrian Hilton, Ray Howard, Elizabeth Hunt, Chris & Julie Hutt, Gill James, Joyce Jenkinson, John Jones-Newton, Alan Jordan, Sue Knight, Norman Lawton, Arnold Loosemore, Alasdair Macintyre, Ned Malet de Cartaret, Robert Mansell, M Mayson, Grace McIntosh, Col Gerald Napier, James RA Ockendon, Bryan Perrett, Ifan Rees, Mark Relf, David Fletcher Rogers, Brian Shaw, Dwayne Snow, Vic Tambling, Lord Thomson of Fleet, Anne C Walsh, Ray Walsh, Jack Whitham, Mark Williams, Lt Col Les Wilson MBE.

Record Offices, Libraries and Local Museums

Birmingham Central Library, Leicester County Record Office, London Metropolitan Archives, Nuneaton Library.

Newspapers

Sheffield Star, Leicester Mercury.

Schools and Universities

Eton College, Harrow School; Winchester College.

Divisional Histories

The Guards Division in the Great War. C Headlam. Murray 1929. Two volumes.
The Eighth Division in War 1914–18. Lt Col J H Boraston and Capt C E O Bax. Medici Society 1926.
The History of the 9th (Scottish) Division 1914–19. J Ewing. Murray 1921.
Ireland's Unknown Soldiers – The 16th (Irish) Division in the Great War. Terence Denman. Irish Academic Press 1992.
The 18th Division in the Great War. Capt G H F Nichols. Blackwood 1922.
The History of the 19th Division 1914–18. E Wyrell. Arnold 1932.
A Short History of the 19th (Western) Division 1914–18. Anon. John Murray 1919.
The History of the 20th (Light) Division. Capt V E Inglefield. Nisbet 1921.
The Story of the 29th Division – A Record of Gallant Deeds. Capt S Gillon. Nelson 1925.
The 33rd Division in France and Flanders 1915–19. Lt Col G S Hutchinson. Waterlow 1921.
The Thirty-Fourth Division 1915–19 – The Story of its Career from Ripon to the Rhine. Lt Col J Shakespear. Witherby 1921.
The History of the 51st (Highland) Division 1914–18. Maj F W Bewsher. Blackwood 1921.
The Story of the 55th (West Lancashire) Division. Rev'd J O Coop. Liverpool Daily Post 1919.

Regimental/Unit Histories

History of the Corps of Royal Engineers, Volume V, The Home Front, France, Flanders and Italy in the First World War. Anon. Institute of the Royal Engineers 1952.
The Grenadier Guards in the Great War of 1914–18. Lt Col Sir F Ponsonby. Macmillan 1920. Three volumes.
The Coldstream Guards 1914–18. Lt Col Sir J Ross of Blankenburg. Oxford University Press 1928. Two volumes with a separate volume of maps.
A History of the Coldstream Guards Victoria and George Cross Holders. Sergeant L Pearce. RHQ Coldstream Guards 1995.
The Irish Guards in the Great War. R Kipling. MacMillan 1923.
The Micks, The Story of the Irish Guards. P Verney. Peter Davies 1970.
History of the Welsh Guards, GH Dudley Ward. John Murray 1920.
The Royal Scots 1914–19. Maj J Ewing. Oliver & Boyd 1925. Two volumes.
A Guide to the Queen's Regiment. G Blaxland. Elvy & Gibbs.

History of the Queen's Royal Regiment Volume VII. Col H C Wylly. Gale & Polden 1925.

The King's Own, The Story of a Royal Regiment, Volume III 1914–50. Compiler Col J M Cowper. Gale & Polden 1957.

The Royal Fusiliers in the Great War. H C O'Neill. Heinemann 1922.

History of the Lincolnshire Regiment 1914–18. Editor Maj Gen C R Simpson. Medici Society 1931.

The History of the Suffolk Regiment 1914–27. Lt Col C C R Murphy. Hutchinson 1928.

The West Yorkshire Regiment in the Great War 1914–18. E Wyrell. The Bodley Head 1924–27. Two volumes.

The Green Howards in the Great War 1914–19. Col H C Wylly. Butler & Tanner 1926.

The Green Howards – For Valour 1914–18. Anon. Published 1964.

The History of the Green Howards – 300 Years of Service. G Powell. Arms and Armour 1992.

The History of the Lancashire Fusiliers 1914–18, Volumes I and II. Maj Gen J C Latter. Gale & Polden 1949.

The Lancashire Fusiliers Annual. No 26 – 1916 and No 28 – 1918. Editor Major B Smyth. Sackville Press 1917 and 1919

My Bit, A Lancashire Fusilier at War 1914–18. G Ashcroft, editor R Holmes. Crowood Press 1987.

At Ypres with Best-Dunkley. Thomas Hope Floyd. The Bodley Head 1920.

The History of the Cheshire Regiment in the Great War. A Crookenden. W H Evans 1938.

Ever Glorious, The Story of the 22nd (Cheshire) Regiment Volume I. B Rigby. Evans & Sons 1982.

That Astonishing Infantry, The History of the Royal Welsh Fusiliers 1689–1989. M Glover.

Regimental Records of the Royal Welsh Fusiliers (23rd Foot), Volume III 1914–18 France & Flanders. Compiler Maj C H Dudley Ward. Forster Groon 1928.

The History of the South Wales Borderers 1914–18. C T Atkinson. Medici Society 1931.

The King's Own Scottish Borderers in the Great War. Capt Stair Gillon. Nelson 1930.

The Gloucestershire Regiment in the Great War 1914–18. E Wyrell. Methuen 1931.

The Slasher, A New Short History of the Gloucestershire Regiment 1694–1965. Anon.

The Worcestershire Regiment in the Great War. Capt H Fitzm Stacke. G T Cheshire 1929.

History of the Duke of Wellington's Regiment (West Riding) 1702–1992. J M Brereton and A C S Savoury. Amadeus 1993.

The Royal Hampshire Regiment 1914–1918. CT Atkinson. Reprint N&M Press 2003.

The Northamptonshire Regiment 1914–18. Regimental Historical Committee. Gale & Polden.

History of the King's Own Yorkshire Light Infantry in the Great War, Volume III 1914–18. Lt Col R C Bond. Percy Lund, Humphries 1930.

The King's Own Yorkshire Light Infantry, Register of Officers 1755–1945. CP Deedes.

History of the Manchester Regiment, Volume II 1883–1922. Col H C Wylly. Forster Groom 1925.

Proud Heritage, The Story of the Highland Light Infantry, Volume III 1882–1918. Lt Col L B Oates. House of Grant 1961.

Seaforth Highlanders. Editor Col J Sym. Gale & Polden 1962.

The Life of a Regiment Volume 4, The Gordon Highlanders in the First World War 1914–19. C Falls. University Press 1958.

Neill's Blue Caps, Volume III 1914–22. Col H C Wylly. Gale & Polden 1923.

The History of the Rifle Brigade in the War 1914–18. Volume II, January 1917 – June 1919. W W Seymour. Rifle Brigade Club 1936.

As above. Appendix – List of Officers and Other Ranks of the Rifle Brigade awarded Decorations or MID for services during the Great War. Compiled by Lt Col T R Eastwood and Maj H G Parkyn. Rifle Brigade Club 1936.

Rifle Brigade Chronicles 1915 – 1920. Editor Col W Verner. John Bale 1916 – 1921.

A Rifle Brigade Register 1905–63, Part 1 – A Roll of Officers who have served in the Regiment. Compiled by Col W P S Curtis. Culverlands Press 1964.

Not Least in the Crusade, A Short History of the Royal Army Medical Corps. P Lovegrove. Gale & Polden 1951.

History of the Great War, Medical Services, Volume IV General History. Maj Gen Sir W G MacPherson. HMSO 1924.

Medical Officers in the British Army, Volume II 1898–1960. Lt Gen Sir R Drew. Wellcome Historical Medical Library 1968.

The Royal Army Medical Corps. R Mclaughlin. Leo Cooper 1972.

The Medical Victoria Crosses. Col WEI Forsyth-Jauch. Arrow Press 1984.

The Army Medical Services Magazine.

Official History of Australia in the War of 1914–1918, Volume IV – The Australian Imperial Force in France, 1917. 11th Edition 1941.

They Dared Mightily. Lionel Wigmore, Jeff Williams & Anthony Staunton 1963 & 1986.

Tales of Valour from The Royal New South Wales Regiment. Maj Gen GL Maitland 1992.

The Story of the Fifth Australian Division. Capt AD Ellis MC. Hodder & Stoughton 1920.

The Fortieth: A Record of the 40th Battalion, A.I.F. Captain FC Green. 40th Battalion Association 1922.

Official History of the Canadian Army in the First World War – Canadian Expeditionary Force 1914–19. Col GWL Nicholson 1962.

Canada in Flanders. Sir Max Aitken 1916.

Gallant Canadians; The Story of The Tenth Canadian Infantry battalion 1914–1919. Daniel G Dancocks 1950.

Princess Patricia's Canadian Light Infantry: 1914–1984 Seventy Years Service. Jeffery Williams. Leo Cooper 1972.

Battle Royal: A History of the Royal Regiment of Canada 1862–1962. Major DJ Goodspeed CD. Charters Publishing 1962.

The New Zealand Division 1916–1919. A Popular History Based on Official Records. Col H Stewart CMG DSO MC. Whitcombe & Tombs Ltd, Auckland 1921.

The Wellington Regiment NZEF 1914–1918. WH Cunningham and CAL Treadwell. Wellington: Ferguson & Osborn 1928.

The History of the South African Forces in France. John Buchan. Thomas Nelson & Sons 1920.

General Works

A Bibliography of Regimental Histories of the British Army. Compiler A S White. Society for Army Historical Research 1965.
A Military Atlas of the First World War. A Banks & A Palmer. Purnell 1975.
The Times History of the Great War.
Topography of Armageddon, A British Trench Map Atlas of the Western Front 1914–18. P Chasseaud. Mapbooks 1991.
The Battle Book of Ypres. B Brice. Murray 1927.
Before Endeavours Fade. R E B Coombs. Battle of Britain Prints 1976.
British Regiments 1914–18. Brig E A James. Samson 1978.
Orange, Green and Khaki, The Story of the Irish Regiments in the Great War 1914 – 18. T Johnstone. 1992.
The Ypres Salient, A Guide to the Cemeteries and Memorials of the Salient. M Scott. Gliddon Books 1992.
Norfolk and Suffolk in the Great War. G Gliddon. Gliddon Books 1988.
Leeds in the Great War 1914–1918. Leeds Libraries and Arts Committee 1923.
Battleground Europe – Sanctuary Wood and Hooge. N Cave. Leo Cooper 1993.

Biographical

The Dictionary of National Biography 1901–85. Various volumes. Oxford University Press.
The Cross of Sacrifice, Officers Who Died in the Service of the British, Indian and East African Regiments and Corps 1914–19. S D and D B Jarvis. Roberts Medals 1993.
Australian Dictionary of Biography.
Whitaker's Peerage, Baronetage, Knightage & Companionage 1915.
Our Heroes – Containing Photographs with Biographical Notes of Officers of Irish Regiments and of Irish Officers of British Regiments who have fallen or who have been mentioned for distinguished conduct from August 1914 to July 1916. Printed as supplements to Irish Life from 1914 to 1916.
The Bond of Sacrifice, A Biographical Record of all British Officers Who Fell in the Great War. Volume I Aug – Dec 1915, Volume II Jan – Jun 1915. Editor Col L A Clutterbuck. Pulman 1916 and 1919.
The Roll of Honour Parts 1–5, A Biographical Record of Members of His Majesty's Naval and Military Forces who fell in the Great War 1914–18. Marquis de Ruvigny. Standard Art Book Co 1917–19.
Bloody Red Tabs: General Officer Casualties of the Great War 1914–1918. Frank Davies and Graham Maddocks. Leo Cooper 1995.
The Dictionary of Edwardian Biography – various volumes. Printed 1904–08, reprinted 1985–87 Peter Bell Edinburgh.
Dictionary of Canadian Biography.
Konowal. Lubomyr Y Luciuk & Ron Sorobey. Kashtan Press 1996.

Filip Konowal, VC – The Rebirth of a Canadian Hero. Ron Sorobey. Canadian Military History, Volume 5 of 1996.

I Did All I Could (Arthur Hutt VC). Ian J McClelland.

Charles Harry Coverdale 1888–1955. A short biography of Captain C H Coverdale VC MM West Riding Home Guard, late Manchester Regiment. Roger Colbourne.

For Most Conspicuous Courage. A Biography of Major-General George R Pearkes VC, through Two World Wars. Reginald H Roy. University of British Columbia Press 1977.

Valiant Hearts. Atlantic Canada and the Victoria Cross. John Boileau. Nimbus Publishing, Halifax, Nova Scotia 2005.

Specific Works on the Victoria Cross

The Register of the Victoria Cross. This England 1981 and 1988.

The Story of the Victoria Cross 1856 – 1963. Brig Sir J Smyth. Frederick Muller 1963.

The Evolution of the Victoria Cross, A Study in Administrative History. M J Crook. Midas 1975.

The Victoria Cross and the George Cross. IWM 1970.

The Victoria Cross, The Empire's Roll of Valour. Lt Col R Stewart. Hutchinson 1928.

The Victoria Cross 1856 – 1920. Sir O'Moore Creagh and E M Humphris. Standard Art Book Company, London 1920.

Victoria Cross – Awards to Irish Servicemen. B Clark. Published in The Irish Sword summer 1986.

Heart of a Dragon, VC's of Wales and the Welsh Regiments 1914–82. W Alister Williams. Bridge Books 2006.

Brave Railwaymen. A Stanistreet. Telen Publishing 1989.

The Seven VC's of Stonyhurst College. H L Kirby and R R Walsh. THCL Books 1987.

Devotion to Duty, Tributes to a Region's VCs. J W Bancroft. Aim High 1990.

For Conspicuous Gallantry, A Brief History of the recipients of the VC from Nottinghamshire and Derbyshire. N McCrery. J H Hall 1990.

For Valour, The Victoria Cross, Courage in Action. J Percival. Thames Methuen 1985.

The Four Blackburn VCs. H L Kirby and R R Walsh. THCL 1986.

VC Locator. D Pillinger and A Staunton. Highland Press, Queanbeyan, New South Wales, Australia 1991.

Black Country VCs. B Harry. Black Country Society 1985.

The VC Roll of Honour. J W Bancroft. Aim High 1989.

A Bibliography of the Victoria Cross. W James McDonald. W J Mcdonald, Nova Scotia 1994.

Canon Lummis VC Files held in the National Army Museum, Chelsea.

Recipients of the Victoria Cross in the Care of the Commonwealth War Graves Commission. CWGC 1997.

Hellfire Corner – VCs of Bromsgrove School. Nicholas Lovell.

Victoria Cross Heroes. Michael Ashcroft. Headline Review 2006

Monuments to Courage. David Harvey. 1999.

The Sapper VCs. Gerald Napier. The Stationery Office, London 1998.

Liverpool Heroes – Book 1. Ann Clayton. Noel Chavasse VC Memorial Association.

Beyond the Five Points – Masonic Winners of The Victoria Cross and The George Cross. Phillip May GC, edited by Richard Cowley. Twin Pillars Books, Northamptonshire 2001.

Irish Winners of the Victoria Cross. Richard Doherty & David Truesdale. Four Courts Press, Dublin, Ireland 2000.

The Victoria Crosses and George Crosses of the Honourable East India Company & Indian Army 1856 – 1945. National Army Museum 1962.

Our Bravest and Our Best: The Stories of Canada's Victoria Cross Winners. Arthur Bishop 1995.

A Breed Apart. Richard Leake. Great Northern Publishing 2008.

Beyond Their Duty – Heroes of the Green Howards. Roger Chapman. Green Howards Museum 2001.

VCs of the First World War: Passchendaele 1917. Stephen Snelling 1998.

Other Honours and Awards

Recipients of Bars to the Military Cross 1916–20. J V Webb 1988.

Distinguished Conduct Medal 1914–18, Citations of Recipients. London Stamp Exchange 1983.

Recipients of the Distinguished Conduct Medal 1914–1920. RW Walker.

The Distinguished Service Order 1886–1923 (in 2 volumes). Sir O'Moore Creagh and E M Humphris. J B Hayward 1978 (originally published 1924).

Orders and Medals Society Journal (various articles).

The Old Contemptibles Honours and Awards. First published 1915. Reprinted by J B Hayward & Son 1971.

Burke's Handbook to the Most Excellent Order of the British Empire. A Winton Thorpe (Editor). Burke Publishing Co Ltd, London 1921.

South African War – Honours and Awards 1899–1902.

Honours and Awards of the Indian Army: August 1914 – August 1921. 1931.

The New Zealand Distinguished Service Order. J Bryant Haigh & Alan J Polaschek. 1993.

University and Schools Publications

The OTC Roll – A Roll of Members and Ex-members of the OTC Gazetted to Commissions in the Army August 1914 – March 1915. Tim Donovan 1989.

Harrow Memorials of the Great War Volume 5. Medici Society 1920.

Official Publications and Sources

History of the Great War, Order of Battle of Divisions. Compiler Maj A F Becke. HMSO.

History of the Great War, Military Operations, France and Belgium. Compiler Brig Gen Sir J E Edmonds. HMSO. Published in 14 volumes of text, with 7 map volumes and 2 separate Appendices between 1923 and 1948.

Location of Hospitals and Casualty Clearing Stations, BEF 1914–19. Ministry of Pensions 1923.

London Gazettes
Census returns, particularly for 1881, 1891 and 1901.
Births, Marriages and Deaths records in the Family Records Centre, Islington, London.
Australian service records in the National Archives of Australia.
Service records from the Library and Archives of Canada.
Officers and Soldiers Died in the Great War.

National Archives

Unit War Diaries under WO 95
Military maps under WO 297.
Medal Cards and Medal Rolls under WO 329, 372 and ADM 171.
Royal Navy service records under ADM 11, 29, 196, 240, 336, 337 and 354.
Army service records under WO 25, 76, 97, 339, 363, 365 and 374.
RAF service records under Air 76 and 79.

Official Lists

Navy Lists.
Army Lists – including Graduation Lists and Record of War Service.
Air Force Lists.
Home Guard Lists 1942–44.
Indian Army Lists 1897–1940.
India List 1923–40.

Reference Publications

Who's Who and Who Was Who.
The Times 1914 onwards.
The Daily Telegraph 1914 onwards.
Kelly's Handbook to the Titled, Landed and Official Classes.

Internet Websites

History of the Victoria Cross – www2.prestel.co.uk/stewart – Iain Stewart.
Commonwealth War Graves Commission – www.yard.ccta.gov.uk/cwgc.
Scottish General Registry Office – www.origins.net/GRO.
Noel Chavasse VC – www.chavasse.u-net/chavasse.html
Free Births, Marriages and Deaths – www.freebmd.com
Memorials to Valour – http://www.memorialstovalour.co.uk

Periodicals

This England magazine – various editions.
Coin and Medal News – various editions.
Journal of The Victoria Cross Society.
Gun Fire – A Journal of First World War History. Edited by AJ Peacock, but no longer
    published.

Useful Information

Accommodation – there is a wide variety of accommodation available in France. Search on-line for your requirements. There are also numerous campsites, but many close for the winter from late September.

Clothing and Kit – consider taking:

Waterproofs.
Headwear and gloves.
Walking shoes/boots.
Shades and sunscreen.
Binoculars and camera.
Snacks and drinks.

Customs/Behaviour – local people are generally tolerant of battlefield visitors but please respect their property and address them respectfully. The French are less inclined to switch to English than other Europeans. If you try some basic French it will be appreciated.

Driving – rules of the road are similar to UK, apart from having to drive on the right. If in doubt about priorities, give way to the right, particularly in France. Obey laws and road signs – police impose harsh on-the-spot fines. Penalties for drinking and driving are heavy and the legal limit is lower than UK (50mg rather than 80mg). Most autoroutes in France are toll roads.

Fuel – petrol stations are only open 24 hours on major routes. Some accept credit cards in automatic tellers. The cheapest fuel is at hypermarkets.

Mandatory Requirements – if taking your own car you need:
Full driving licence.
Vehicle registration document.
Comprehensive motor insurance valid in Europe (Green Card).
European breakdown and recovery cover.
Letter of authorisation from the owner if the vehicle is not yours.
Spare set of bulbs, headlight beam adjusters, warning triangle, GB sticker, high visibility vest and breathalyzer.

Emergency – keep details required in an emergency separate from wallet or handbag:
Photocopy passport, insurance documents and EHIC (see Health below).
Mobile phone details.
Credit/debit card numbers and cancellation telephone contacts.
Travel insurance company contact number.

Ferries – the closest ports are Boulogne, Calais and Dunkirk. The Shuttle is quicker, but usually more expensive.

Health

European Health Insurance Card – entitles the holder to medical treatment at local rates. Apply online at www.ehic.org.uk/Internet/startApplication.do. Issued free and valid for five years. You are only covered if you have the EHIC with you when you go for treatment.

Travel Insurance – you are also strongly advised to have travel insurance. If you receive treatment get a statement by the doctor (*feuille de soins*) and a receipt to make a claim on return.

Personal Medical Kit – treating minor ailments saves time and money. Pack sufficient prescription medicine for the trip.

Chemist (*Pharmacie*) – look for the green cross. They provide some treatment and if unable to help will direct you to a doctor. Most open 0900–1900 except Sunday. Out of hours services (*pharmacie de garde*) are advertised in Pharmacie windows.

Doctor and Dentist – hotel receptions have details of local practices. Beware private doctors/hospitals, as extra charges cannot be reclaimed – the French national health service is known as *conventionné*.

Rabies – contact with infected animals is very rare, but if bitten by any animal, get the wound examined professionally immediately.

Money

ATMs – at most banks and post offices with instructions in English. Check your card can be used in France and what charges apply. Some banks limit how much can be withdrawn. Let your bank know you will be away, as some block cards if transactions take place unexpectedly.

Credit/Debit Cards – major cards are usually accepted, but some have different names – Visa is Carte Bleue and Mastercard is Eurocard.

Exchange – beware 0% commission, as the rate may be poor. The Post Office takes back unused currency at the same rate, which may or may not be advantageous. Since the Euro, currency exchange facilities are scarce.

Local Taxes – if you buy high value items you can reclaim tax. Get the forms completed by the shop, have them stamped by Customs, post them to the shop and they will refund about 12%.

Passport – a valid passport is required.

Post – postcard stamps are available from vendors, newsagents and tabacs.

Public Holidays – just about everything closes and banks can close early the day before. Transport may be affected, but tourist attractions in high season are unlikely to be. The following dates/days are public holidays:

1 January
Easter Monday
1 May
8 May
Ascension Day
Whit Monday
14 July
15 August
1 & 11 November
25 December

In France many businesses and restaurants close for the majority of August.

Radio – if you want to pick up the news from home try BBC Radio 4 on 198 kHz long wave. BBC Five Live on 909 kHz medium wave can sometimes be received. There are numerous internet options for keeping up with the news.

Shops – in large towns and tourist areas they tend to open all day. In more remote places they may close for lunch. Some bakers open Sunday a.m. and during the week take later lunch breaks. In general shops do not open on Sundays.

Telephone

To UK – 0044, delete initial 0 then dial the rest of the number.

Local Calls – dial the full number even if within the same zone.

Mobiles – check yours will work in France and the charges. Beware roamer charges and/or disable them before getting on the ferry.

Emergencies – dial 112 for medical, fire and police anywhere in Europe from any landline, pay phone or mobile. Calls are free

British Embassy (Paris) – 01 44 51 31 00.

Time Zone – one hour ahead of UK.

Tipping – a small tip is expected by cloakroom and lavatory attendants and porters. Not required in restaurants, when a service charge is included.

Toilets – the best are in museums and the main tourist attractions. Towns usually have public toilets where markets are held; some are coin operated.

Index

Notes:
1. Not every person or location is included. Most family members named in the Biographies are not.
2. Armed forces units, establishments, etc are grouped under the respective country, except for Britain's, which appear under the three services – British Army, Royal Air Force and Royal Navy. Royal Naval Division units appear under British Army for convenience.
3. Newfoundland appears under Canada although not part of it at the time.
4. Cathedrals, Cemeteries/Crematoria, Churches, Commonwealth War Graves Commission, Hospitals, Schools, Trenches and Universities appear under those group headings.
5. All orders, medals and decorations appear under Orders.
6. Belgium, Britain, France and Germany are not indexed in the accounts of the VC actions as there are too many mentions. Similarly England and Britain are not indexed in the biographies.